Seventh Edition

Criminology TODAY

AN INTEGRATIVE INTRODUCTION

Frank Schmalleger, Ph.D.
Distinguished Professor Emeritus, The University of North Carolina at Pembroke

PEARSON

Boston Columbus Indianapolis New York San Francisco Upper Saddle River
Amsterdam Cape Town Dubai London Madrid Milan Munich Paris Montreal Toronto
Delhi Mexico City São Paulo Sydney Hong Kong Seoul Singapore Taipei Tokyo

For my daughter Nicole,
a next-generation criminologist.

Editorial Director: Vernon R. Anthony
Executive Editor: Gary Bauer
Development Editor: Elisa Rogers, 4development
Editorial Assistant: Kevin Cecil
Director of Marketing: David Gesell
Marketing Manager: Mary Salzman
Senior Marketing Coordinator: Alicia Wozniak
Marketing Assistant: Les Roberts
Team Lead for Project Management: JoEllen Gohr
Senior Project Manager: Steve Robb
Procurement Specialist: Deidra M. Skahill
Creative Director: Andrea Nix
Art Director: Diane Y. Ernsberger
Cover Designer: CFISHDESIGN, Candace Rowley
Cover Images: T, OJO Images Ltd/Alamy; O, Yahya Idiz/Fotolia; D, Rudy Balasko/Shutterstock; A, Lisa F. Young/Fotolia; Y, Thomas Pajot/Fotolia
Media Project Manager: Leslie Brado
Media Coordinator: April Cleland
Full-Service Project Management: Christian Holdener, S4Carlisle Publishing Services
Composition: S4Carlisle Publishing Services
Printer/Binder: Courier/Kendallville
Cover Printer: Lehigh/Phoenix Color Hagerstown
Text Font: Bembo, 10/13

Credits and acknowledgments for content borrowed from other sources and reproduced, with permission, in this textbook appear on the appropriate page within the text.

Library of Congress Cataloging-in-Publication Data
Schmalleger, Frank.
Criminology today : an integrative introduction/Frank Schmalleger.—Seventh edition.
pages cm
Includes index.
ISBN-13: 978-0-13-349553-9
ISBN-10: 0-13-349553-1
1. Criminology. 2. Criminology—United States. I. Title.
HV6025.S346 2015
364—dc23
2013028587

10 9 8 7 6 5 4 3 2 1

Perfect bound ISBN-13: 978-0-13-349553-9
ISBN-10: 0-13-349553-1
Loose leaf ISBN-13: 978-0-13-349573-7
ISBN-10: 0-13-349573-6

Brief Contents

THEORETICAL DEVELOPMENTS

Classical School

Classical Criminology

1764 **Cesare Beccaria** Deterrence through punishment, free will, social contract

1789 **Jeremy Bentham** Hedonistic calculus, utilitarianism

Neoclassical Criminology

1974 **Robert Martinson** Nothing-works doctrine

1975 **James Q. Wilson** Thinking about crime

1979 **Cohen & Felson** Rational choice, routine activities

1988 **Jack Katz** Seductions of crime, emotions and crime

1992 **Clarke & Cornish** Situational choice, situational crime prevention

Biological Theories

Early Positivism

1810 **Franz Joseph Gall** Phrenology, scientific understanding of crime

1830s **Johann Gaspar Spurzheim** Brought phrenology to America

Criminal Anthropology

1863 **Cesare Lombroso** Atavism, born criminals, criminaloids

1913 **Charles Buckman Goring** Challenged Lombroso's theory

1939 **Earnest Hooton** Environment + low-grade human = crime

Criminal Families

1877 **Richard Dugdale** The Juke family

1912 **Henry Goddard** The Kallikak family

1915 **Arthur Estabrook**

Constitutional Theories

1925 **Ernst Kretschmer** Somatotyping

1949 **William Sheldon** Body types, behavioral genetics/twins, heritability, human genome

Twin studies

1968 **Karl Christiansen and Sarnoff Mednick** Genetic determinism

Sociobiology

1975 **Edward O. Wilson** Altruism, territoriality, tribalism, survival of gene pool

Biosocial Criminology

1980 **Darrell J. Steffensmeier**

1997 **Anthony Walsh** Environmental mediation of genetic influences

1990s **Adrian Raine** Brain dysfunction

2003 **Kevin M. Beaver and Anthony Walsh** Biosocial criminology

2010 **Thomas Bernard** Gender-ratio problem

Psychological/ Psychiatric Theories

Modeling Theory

1890 **Gabriel Tarde** Imitation

1973 **Albert Bandura** Aggression is learned, aggression is rewarded, disengagement, social cognition theory, modeling

Psychoanalytic Criminology

1920s–1930s **Sigmund Freud** Psychoanalysis, id, ego, superego, sublimation

1930s **August Aichorn** damaged egos

Personality Disturbances

1941 **Hervey Cleckley** Psychopathology, psychopath, sociopath

1964 **Hans Eysenck** traits, supertraits

1968 **DSM-II** Antisocial personality disorder

Attachment Theory

1950s **John Bowlby** Secure attachment, anxious resistant attachment, anxious avoidance attachment

Behavior Theory

1950s–1970s **B. F. Skinner** Operant conditioning, operant behavior, rewards/punishments, stimulus-response

Frustration–Aggression Theory

1939 **J. Dollard** Displacement, catharsis

Moral Development Theory

1955 **Jean Piaget** stages of human intellectual development

1969 **Lawrence Kohlberg** stages of moral thought

1970 **Stanton Samenow and Samuel Yochelson** the criminal mindset

1971 **S. M. Halleck** Alloplastic adaptation, autoplastic adaptation

1979 **Roger Shank and Robert Abelson** scripts theory

1995 **Linksy, Bachman, Straus** Societal stress, aggression

1998 **Donald Andrews and James Bonta** criminogenic needs, criminogenic domains

IN CRIMINOLOGY

Social Structure Approaches

Social Disorganization

1920 **Thomas & Znaniecki** Displaced immigrants

1920s–1930s **Park & Burgess** Social ecology, social pathology, concentric zones (Chicago School)

1929 **Shaw & McKay** Cultural transmission (Chicago School)

1973 **Oscar Newman** Defensible space

1982 **James Q. Wilson & George L. Kelling** Broken windows, criminology of place

1987 **Rodney Stark** Theory of deviant neighborhoods

Culture Conflict

1927 **Frederic Thrasher** Gangs and gang typologies

1938 **Thorsten Sellin** Conduct norms, primary conflict, secondary conflict

1943 **William F. Whyte** Subcultures

1955 **Albert Cohen** Gangs, reaction formation

1957 **Sykes & Matza** Techniques of neutralization

1958 **Walter B. Miller** Focal concerns

1960s **Cloward & Ohlin** Illegitimate opportunity structure, delinquent subcultures

1967 **Ferracuti & Wolfgang** Violent subcultures

Strain Theory

1938 **Robert Merton** Anomic, conformity, innovation, ritualism, retreatism, rebellion

1982 **Blau & Blau** Relative deprivation, frustration, distributive justice

1992 **Robert Agnew** General strain theory

1994 **Messner & Rosenfeld** American Dream

Social Process & Social Development Theories

Social Learning Theory

1939 **Edwin Sutherland** Differential association

1960 **Daniel Glaser** Differential identification theory

1966 **Burgess & Akers** Differential association-reinforcement

Social Control Theory

1950s **Walter Reckless** Containment theory, inner and outer containment

1969 **Travis Hirschi** Social bond and self control: attachment, commitment, belief, involvement

1970s **Howard Kaplan** Self-degradation

1990 **Hirschi & Gottfredson** Social bonds and self-control, general theory of crime

1995 **Charles Tittle** Control-balance, control surplus, control deficit

1995 **Per-Olof H. Wikström** Situational action theory

Labeling Theory

1938 **Frank Tannenbaum** Tagging, dramatization of evil

1951 **Edwin Lemert** Primary deviance, secondary deviance

1963 **Howard Becker** Outsiders, moral enterprise

1997 **John Braithwaite** Reintegrative shaming, stigmatic shaming

Dramaturgy

1960s **Erving Goffman** Dramaturgy, impression management, discrediting information, total institutions, disculturation

Social Development

1920s **Sheldon & Eleanor Glueck** Family dynamics and delinquent careers

1960s **Marvin Wolfgang** Chronic offending

1980s **David P. Farrington** Delinquent development theory

1987 **Terrence Thornberry** Intereactional theory

1988 **Lawrence E. Cohen and Richard Machalek** Evolutionary ecology

1993 **Robert J. Sampson and John H. Laub** Life course criminology

1993 **Terrie Moffitt** Life course persisters, adolesence-limited offenders

Social Conflict Theories

Conflict Theories

1848 **Karl Marx** The *Communist Manifesto*

1916 **Willem Bonger** Class struggle

1938 **Thorsten Sellin** Culture conflict

Radical Criminology

1958 **George Vold** Political conflict between groups, conflict is normal

1959 **Ralf Dahrendorf** Conflict is normal, destructive change

1969 **Austin Turk** Social order = pattern of conflict, laws serve to control

1970s **William Chambliss** Power gaps, crime reduces surplus labor

1974 **Richard Quinney** Contradictions of capitalism, socialist principles

Left-realist Criminology

1991 **Jock Young & Walter DeKeseredy** The new criminology

Feminist Criminology

1975 **Adler & Simon** Gender socialization

1977 **Carol Smart** Gender bias in criminology

1988 **Daly & Chesney-Lind** Androcentricity, crime may not be normal

1989 **John Hagan** Power-control theory

Peacemaking Criminology

1986 **Pepinsky & Quinney** Restorative justice, participatory justice

1989 **Lozoff & Braswell** New Age principles

Convict Criminology

2001 **John Irwin, Ian Ross, K. C. Carceral, Thomas J. Bernard** Insights from convicted offenders

Contents

PART THREE Crime Causation Revisited

CHAPTER 7 | Social Structure Theories 153

CHAPTER 8 | Theories of Social Process and Social Development 179

CHAPTER 9 | Social Conflict Theories 215

PART FOUR Crime in the Modern World

CHAPTER 10 | Crimes Against Persons 241

CHAPTER 11 | Crimes Against Property 279

CHAPTER 12 | White-Collar and Organized Crime 303

CHAPTER 13 | Drug and Sex Crimes 331

CHAPTER 14 | Technology and Crime 353

CHAPTER 15 | Globalization and Terrorism 375

New to This Edition

The seventh edition of *Criminology Today: An Integrative Introduction* continues to offer students a clear, contemporary, and comprehensive introduction to criminology that encourages critical thinking about the causes of crime and crime-prevention strategies. The text's hallmark thematic approach of social problems versus social responsibility (Is crime a matter of individual responsibility or a symptom of a dysfunctional society?) prompts students to think critically about the causes of crime and helps them see the link between crime theories and crime policies.

New Features in the Seventh Edition

There are many important new features in this seventh edition:

- Visual appeal has been enhanced through the use of new photos and figures.
- The text now includes *two* chapters on biological theories, in recognition of the increasing importance of biosocial perspectives, especially biosocial theories.
- The chapter on psychological theories of crime has been completely revised and expanded.
- Central issues of each major perspective contained in the text are now presented graphically as "Key Elements" for each major theoretical heading, allowing for ease of understanding.
- Most boxed items, including Crime in the News boxes, have been shortened to 600 words or less in order to enhance their focus and promote reader comprehension. Crime in the News boxes are now author written, and derived from multiple sources.
- Professor Speaks boxes have been removed from the book.

New Chapter Content in the Seventh Edition

Chapter 1: What Is Criminology?

A survey of crime statistics is now included in this chapter, having been moved from later parts of the book. A definition of delinquency has been added to complement definitions of crime and deviance. The chapter now includes the story of six Italian geologists who were found guilty of manslaughter for failing to warn of an impending earthquake, and it ends with the story of Adam Lanza, the Connecticut youth who shot to death 20 kindergarten students and six adults in Newtown, Connecticut, in 2012. Discussion of "translational criminology" has been added to the chapter; and the section "What Do Criminologists Do?" has been moved closer to the start of the chapter. The section titled "What Is Criminology?" has been simplified and reduced in length.

Chapter 2: Where Do Theories Come From?

A new story opens the chapter, and threats to the internal and external validity of research designs are now represented in visual form. A new Crime in the News story is included, and the relevance of the Stockholm Prize in Criminology to evidence-based criminology is reiterated. This year's recipient (David Farrington) of the Stockholm Prize is recognized.

Chapter 3: Classical and Neoclassical Thought

The section on capital punishment has been reduced in length and refocused to stress criminological (rather than criminal justice) issues, and a revised Crime in the News box on DNA exonerations is included. Techniques of situational crime control are now represented visually rather than in tabular format.

Chapter 4: Early Biological Perspectives on Criminal Behavior

Whereas the last edition of this text included only one chapter on biological theories, this edition offers two chapters on biological perspectives in recognition of the growing importance of biosocial theories of criminality. Chapter 4 has been revised in detail, and it includes a new opening story along with a new section on traditional biological versus modern biosocial theories. The discussion of the Italian School and criminal anthropology has been revised, and the section on sociobiology has been expanded.

Chapter 5: Biosocial and Other Contemporary Perspectives

This is a completely new chapter, stressing the interplay between biology and the social and physical environments. New biosocial perspectives and supporting research are presented, and President Obama's Brain Activity Map initiative is discussed. A new section on the dysfunctional brain is included, and brain mechanisms involved in aggression are explored. A discussion on the role of lead and heavy metal contamination in crime causation is offered, and the effects of testosterone and serotonin on behavior are included. The *gender ratio problem* in criminology is highlighted, and gender differences in criminality are also explored.

Chapter 6: Psychological and Psychiatric Foundations of Criminal Behavior

This chapter has been extensively revised and opens with a new story about Arizona shooter Jared Loughner. The discussion of personality and trait theories of crime has been greatly enhanced, and an exploration of the Five Factor Model of personality is now included along with a graphic representation of the model. The discussion of moral development theory has been expanded, and a review of script theory has been added. The concept of risk assessment has been fully developed and a discussion of risk-assessment instruments in correctional psychology is now included. Finally, a new section on the criminal mind-set has been added.

Chapter 7: Social Structure Theories

The chapter now includes a Crime in the News box on "broken windows policing," as well as a visual representation of strain theory.

Chapter 8: Theories of Social Process and Social Development

The chapter now begins with a story about Joran van der Sloot, the suspected killer of Natalee Holloway and convicted killer of Stephany Flores. The situational action theory (SAT) of Per-Olof H. Wikström is discussed, and social development theories are given greater clarity. A revised Crime in the News box discusses the question of whether or not there is a "criminal gene," and the discussion of Gottfredson and Hirschi's general theory of crime has been expanded. Coverage of studies exploring the "contextual viability" of the relationship between self-control and offending—in other words, the influence of things like neighborhood variables and economic conditions on self-control—has been added. Results from the Children at Risk study are now discussed, and discussion of Moffitt's dual taxonomic theory has been incorporated into the chapter.

Chapter 9: Social Conflict Theories

The chapter now opens with a discussion of the Occupy Wall Street movement and offers it as an example of social conflict. The distinction between radical and critical criminology has been clarified, and new line art has been added to the chapter to reinforce the concepts that are explored. The idea of "moral time," developed by Donald Black, is provided in an explanation of the multifaceted dynamics involved in a criminal event.

Chapter 10: Crimes Against Persons

This chapter no longer contains detailed discussion of crime-data sources—information on which has been distributed throughout the text—but instead more directly addresses the chapter's main focus: crimes against persons. Data on crimes of violence have been updated throughout the chapter, as has associated line art. Much of the material on gang membership has been removed, especially where it is not directly relevant to crimes of violence. A Crime in the News box on James Holmes—the Colorado movie theater mass shooter—and coverage of other mass shootings have been added. The chapter now includes the redefinition of the crime of rape for statistical reporting purposes set forth by the Federal Bureau of Investigation (FBI), as well as a revised definition of forcible rape from the FBI's Criminal Justice Information Services (CJIS) Division. The discussion of the Prison Rape Elimination Act (PREA) has been updated along with prison rape statistics.

Chapter 11: Crimes Against Property

The chapter begins with a new opening story, and statistics on all property crimes have been updated throughout the chapter. New information about Caroline Giuliani, the daughter of former mayor of New York City Rudolph Giuliani, has been added in the shoplifting section. A Crime in the News box on flash robberies is now included in the chapter, and the discussion of identity theft has been moved here from a later chapter to recognize its status as a theft crime. A photograph of actor Will Smith has been added to the chapter, and it is associated with a discussion of his victimization by an identity thief. A Criminal Profiles box about Colton Harris-Moore, the "barefoot bandit," has been added to the chapter.

Chapter 12: White-Collar and Organized Crime

This chapter has been completely revised, and also shortened. The discussion of the history of white-collar crime has been abbreviated, as has the discussion of traditional organized criminal groups in the United States. Types of financial crimes are now discussed in more detail, and a new graphic presents these various types visually. A discussion of international criminal organizations has been added and includes criminal enterprises in Eurasia, the Balkans, Asia, Africa, and the Middle East. The discussion of transnational organized crime has been updated.

Chapter 13: Drug and Sex Crimes

This chapter has been substantially revised and reduced in length. A tabular presentation of controlled substances replaces the lengthy spreadsheet-like list of such substances in the last edition, and up-to-date information on the costs of drug abuse are now included. Drug-control strategies, including the Office of National Drug Control Policy's new initiatives, are included, as is a discussion of legalization of marijuana (in Colorado and Washington State). The types of prostitutes, discussed later in the chapter, are now represented visually.

Chapter 14: Technology and Crime

A substantial revision has been made to this chapter, and it is now much briefer than the previous version. A global cyberthreat map provides an overview of cybercrimes worldwide, and the profile of computer hackers has been expanded.

Chapter 15: Globalization and Terrorism

As with Chapters 13 and 14, this chapter has been reduced. The focus is now on globalization and its influence on cross-national criminal activity. Human trafficking and smuggling are discussed in greater detail, and the origin countries for both of these illegal activities have been highlighted.

Preface

The opening decade of the twenty-first century was filled with momentous events in the United States, including the destruction of the World Trade Center and an attack on the Pentagon by Islamic terrorists, a fearsome recession, and corporate scandals that cost Americans billions of dollars in lost investments. The second decade saw the advent of a relatively large number of homegrown terrorist efforts to attack American population centers and landmarks, but only the Boston Marathon bombings of 2013 were carried out successfully. The crimes committed by terrorists set a tone for the start of the new century unlike any in living memory. Homeland security became an important buzzword at all levels of American government, while pundits questioned just how much freedom people would be willing to sacrifice to enhance security. Americans felt both physically and economically threatened as stock market losses were traced to the unethical actions of a surprising cadre of corporate executives who had previously been held in high regard in the business world and in the communities where they lived. Soon the media were busily showing a parade of business leaders being led away in handcuffs to face trial on charges of crooked accounting.

Added to the mix by the beginning of 2014 were shocking acts of criminality that emanated from all corners of the world, including mass shootings in the United States, the Boston Marathon bombing, depravities of sex tourism involving human trafficking, sex acts with minors streaming across the Internet in real time, massive copyright-infringement activities like those of New Zealand–based Megaupload, and the theft of hundreds of thousands of personal identities. This last issue constitutes a very intimate crime that can literally cause a person to face the loss of his or her social self in a complex culture that increasingly defines someone's essence in terms of an economic, educational, online, and ever-more-complex social nexus.

Criminologists found themselves wondering what new laws might be enacted to add additional control to handgun sales and ownership; and also focused on the potential misuse of technology by Internet and energy companies, along with emerging computer capabilities and biotechnologies that, while seeming to hold amazing promise to cure disease and reshape humanity's future, threaten the social fabric in a way not seen since the birth of the atomic bomb or the harnessing of electricity. Similarly, climate changes, violent storms such as Superstorm Sandy, Hurricane Katrina, the Gulf oil spill, our nation's desperate need for alternative and additional energy sources, and the instability in the Middle East contribute to a growing awareness that the challenges facing criminologists in the twenty-first century are unlike any they have previously faced.

It was against this backdrop that the need for a comprehensive revision of *Criminology Today* emerged. This new edition addresses the poignant question of how security and freedom interface in an age of increasing globalism. Chapter 15, in particular, provides substantially enlarged coverage of terrorism and cyberterrorism, including an overview of many types of terrorist groups, such as nationalist, religious, state-sponsored, left-wing, right-wing, and anarchist groups. The findings and recommendations of special committees and government bodies that have focused on terrorism in recent years are also discussed, and online links to the full text of their reports are provided. Included here are the reports of the 9/11 Commission, the Gilmore Commission, the three-phased report of the U.S. Commission on National Security in the 21st Century (also known as the Hart-Rudman Commission), the National Commission on Terrorism (also known as the Bremmer Commission), and the report of the Commission on the Prevention of WMD Proliferation and Terrorism.

The seventh edition, which is now available in a variety of print and electronic formats, presents historical and modern criminological approaches with the aid of real-life stories, up-to-date examples and issues, and interactive media. Key features include:

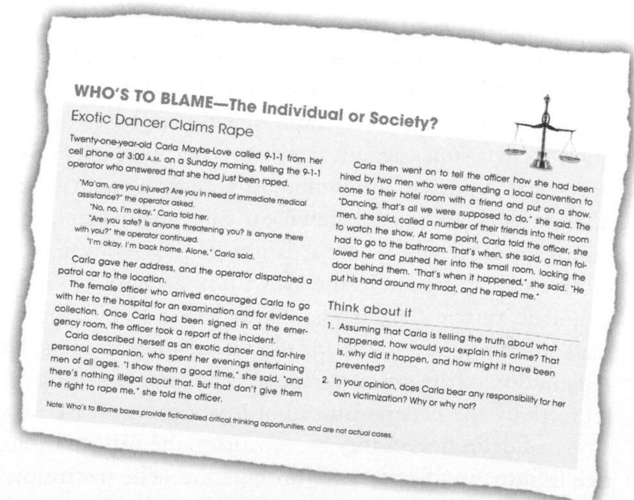

WHO'S TO BLAME—The Individual or Society?

Exotic Dancer Claims Rape

Twenty-one-year-old Carla Maybe-Love called 9-1-1 from her cell phone at 3:00 A.M. on a Sunday morning, telling the 9-1-1 operator who answered that she had just been raped.

"Ma'am, are you injured? Are you in need of immediate medical assistance?" the operator asked.

"No, no, I'm okay," Carla told her.

"Are you safe? Is anyone threatening you? Is anyone there with you?" the operator continued.

"I'm okay. I'm back home. Alone," Carla said.

Carla gave her address, and the operator dispatched a patrol car to the location.

The female officer who arrived encouraged Carla to go with her to the hospital for an examination and for evidence collection. Once Carla had been signed in at the emergency room, the officer took a report of the incident.

Carla described herself as an exotic dancer and for-hire personal companion, who spent her evenings entertaining men of all ages. "I show them a good time," she said, "and there's nothing illegal about that. But that don't give them the right to rape me," she told the officer.

Carla then went on to tell the officer how she had been hired by two men who were attending a local convention to come to their hotel room with a friend and put on a show. "Dancing, that's all we were supposed to do," she said. The men, she said, called a number of their friends into their room to watch the show. At some point, Carla told the officer, she had to go to the bathroom. That's when, she said, a man followed her and pushed her into the small room, locking the door behind them. "That's when it happened," she said. "He put his hand around my throat, and he raped me."

Think about it

1. Assuming that Carla is telling the truth about what happened, how would you explain this crime? That is, why did it happen, and how might it have been prevented?
2. In your opinion, does Carla bear any responsibility for her own victimization? Why or why not?

Note: Who's to Blame boxes provide fictionalized critical thinking opportunities, and are not actual cases.

Who's to Blame boxes in each chapter highlight the book's ever-evolving theme of social problems versus social responsibility, a hallmark feature of this text. In each chapter, Who's to Blame boxes build on this theme by illustrating some of the issues that challenge criminologists and policy makers today. Each box includes a hypothetical case followed by critical thinking questions that ask readers to ponder to what extent the individual or society is responsible for a given crime.

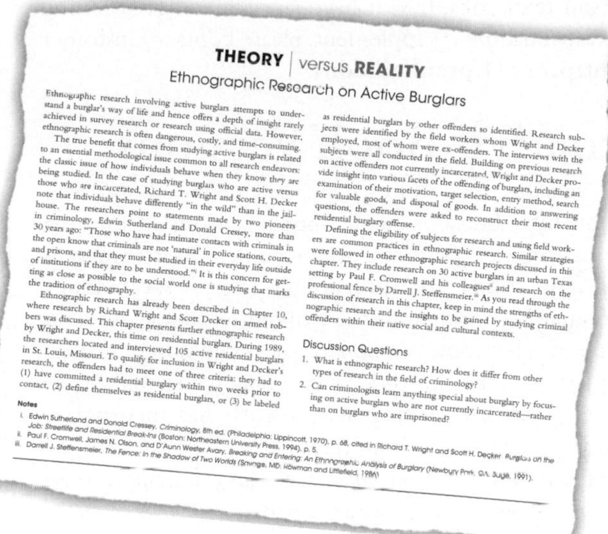

THEORY | versus REALITY
Ethnographic Research on Active Burglars

Ethnographic research involving active burglars attempts to understand a burglar's way of life and hence offers a depth of insight rarely achieved in survey research or research using official data. However, ethnographic research is often dangerous, costly, and time-consuming.

The true benefit that comes from studying active burglars is related to an essential methodological issue common to all research endeavors: the classic issue of how individuals behave when they know they are being studied. In the case of studying burglars who are active versus those who are incarcerated, Richard T. Wright and Scott H. Decker note that individuals behave differently "in the wild" than in the jailhouse. The researchers point to statements made by two pioneers in criminology, Edwin Sutherland and Donald Cressey, more than 30 years ago: "Those who have had intimate contacts with criminals in the open know that criminals are not 'natural' in police stations, courts, and prisons, and that they must be studied in their everyday life outside of institutions if they are to be understood."[i] It is this concern for getting as close as possible to the social world one is studying that marks the tradition of ethnography.

Ethnographic research has already been described in Chapter 10, where research by Richard Wright and Scott Decker on armed robbers was discussed. This chapter presents further ethnographic research by Wright and Decker, this time on residential burglars. During 1989, the researchers located and interviewed 105 active residential burglars in St. Louis, Missouri. To qualify for inclusion in Wright and Decker's research, the offenders had to meet one of three criteria: they had to (1) have committed a residential burglary within two weeks prior to contact, (2) define themselves as residential burglars, or (3) be labeled as residential burglars by other offenders so identified. Research subjects were identified by the field workers whom Wright and Decker employed, most of whom were ex-offenders. The interviews with the subjects were all conducted in the field. Building on previous research on active offenders not currently incarcerated, Wright and Decker provide insight into various facets of the offending of burglars, including an examination of their motivation, target selection, entry method, search for valuable goods, and disposal of goods. In addition to answering questions, the offenders were asked to reconstruct their most recent residential burglary offense.

Defining the eligibility of subjects for research and using field workers are common practices in ethnographic research. Similar strategies were followed in other ethnographic research projects discussed in this chapter. They include research on 30 active burglars in an urban Texas setting by Paul F. Cromwell and his colleagues[ii] and research on the professional fence by Darrell J. Steffensmeier.[iii] As you read through the discussion of research in this chapter, keep in mind the strengths of ethnographic research and the insights to be gained by studying criminal offenders within their native social and cultural contexts.

Discussion Questions

1. What is ethnographic research? How does it differ from other types of research in the field of criminology?
2. Can criminologists learn anything special about burglary by focusing on active burglars who are not currently incarcerated—rather than on burglars who are imprisoned?

Notes

i. Edwin Sutherland and Donald Cressey, *Criminology*, 8th ed. (Philadelphia: Lippincott, 1970), p. 68, cited in Richard T. Wright and Scott H. Decker, *Burglars on the Job: Streetlife and Residential Break-Ins* (Boston: Northeastern University Press, 1994), p. 5.
ii. Paul F. Cromwell, James N. Olson, and D'Aunn Wester Avary, *Breaking and Entering: An Ethnographic Analysis of Burglary* (Newbury Park, CA: Sage, 1991).
iii. Darrell J. Steffensmeier, *The Fence: In the Shadow of Two Worlds* (Savage, MD: Rowman and Littlefield, 1986).

Theory versus Reality boxes throughout the text showcase selected issues and theories in the field of criminology and invite discussion through thought-provoking questions for consideration.

CRIMINAL | PROFILES
Adam Lanza and the Sandy Hook School Shootings

On December 14, 2012, 20-year-old Adam Lanza, a socially awkward young man, went on a shooting rampage at Sandy Hook Elementary School in Newtown, Connecticut. In a matter of minutes, Lanza fired 155 bullets and shot to death 20 kindergarten students, four teachers, a principal, and the school's psychologist.[i] The shooting spree ended when Lanza turned one of his three guns on himself. Before the massacre, Lanza killed his mother at the house they shared only minutes from the school. The horrific shooting was covered by media services for days and reignited an intense national debate about gun control.

Although the Newtown shooting stood out as especially horrific because it ended so many innocent young lives, it is but one of a number of random mass shootings in the United States in recent years. In 2012 alone, there were 12 other random mass killings—including a July attack by a lone gunman in an Aurora, Colorado, movie theater where 12 people were killed and another 58 injured during a midnight showing of the movie *The Dark Knight Rises*.[ii] In that crime, the alleged shooter, 24-year-old James Eagan Holmes, who dressed as the Joker (a nefarious character from the film) during the shooting spree, was arrested outside the theater. He remains jailed as this text goes to press, having entered a plea of not guilty by reason of insanity on June 4, 2013.

Experts tell us that the number of random mass shootings is on the increase. According to the *Wall Street Journal*, there "were 18 random mass shootings in the 1980s, 54 in the 1990s, and 87 in the 2000s."[iii] The *Journal*'s emphasis was on *random* shootings, and it noted that other mass killings—in which victims were in some way known to the shooter—had not significantly increased or decreased in number.

A fair question to ask would be "Why are the number of such random incidents increasing?" Some answers might be found in the personal characteristics of the shooters. Lanza and Holmes shared a number of things in common. Both were middle-class white males in their early twenties who were regarded by their peers as unnervingly intelligent. Holmes had been a former neuroscience graduate student at the University of Colorado's Anschutz Campus, whose academic career unraveled shortly before the movie theater shooting. Lanza, once a prominent member of his high school's technology club and an honors student, was said to have been extraordinarily bright by former teachers. Neither shooter had a previous criminal record.[iv]

What may have contributed to both incidents, however, was one additional feature the two men shared—a disordered personality.[v] According to the American Psychiatric Association, most mentally ill people do not turn to violence, although some forms of mental illness have been associated with aggression and criminal activity, especially when combined with illegal drug use.[vi]

Adam Lanza, the Sandy Hook Elementary School shooter. Why do random mass shootings seem to be so commonplace in the United States today?

Questions about Lanza's mental health were quickly raised following the Sandy Hook shootings by former friends and family members who knew him to be painfully shy, reclusive, and psychologically troubled. Described by personal acquaintances as "very bright" but emotionally disturbed, Lanza may have suffered from a form of Asperger's syndrome and was said to be impervious to physical pain. He had been on numerous medications intended to lower the anxiety that he experienced in everyday social situations, and prior to the Newtown shootings, his mother had repeatedly sought help in controlling her increasingly unresponsive and emotionally withdrawn son. Months after the Sandy Hook shooting, investigators revealed that Lanza had compiled a detailed record to include a timeline of mass shootings across the nation and may have wanted to achieve a "record" of some kind—by killing more than any other attacker ever had.[vii] Holmes, the Colorado shooter, met with at least three mental health professionals prior to the movie theater shooting, and CBS news reports that the fact "adds to the picture of Holmes being clearly on [psychiatrists'] radar in the time period leading up the shooting."[viii]

Notes

i. Michael Isikoff, Tom Winter, and Erin McClam, "Investigators: Adam Lanza Surrounded by Weapons of Mass Attack Took Less Than 5 Minutes," NBC News, March 28, 2013, http://openchannel.nbcnews.com/_news/2013/03/28/17501160-investigators-adam-lanza-surrounded-by-weapons-at-home-attack-took-less-than-5-minutes?lite (accessed March 29, 2013).
ii. "U.S. Mass Shootings in 2012," *The Washington Post*, December 14, 2012, http://www.washingtonpost.com/wp-srv/special/nation/us-mass-shootings-2012 (accessed March 20, 2013).
iii. David Kopel, "Guns, Mental Illness and Newtown," *Wall Street Journal*, December 17, 2012, http://professional.wsj.com/article/SB10001424127887323777204578189391813881534; The same article, however, notes that there has been no long-term increase in mass shootings; only in random mass shootings.
iv. Holly Yan, "Gunman's Family at a Loss to Explain Connecticut Shooting," CNN, December 17, 2012, http://www.cnn.com/2012/12/16/justice/connecticut-shooting-suspect-profile/index.html (accessed March 20, 2013).
v. The Autism Research Institute's Autistic Global Initiative Project notes that autism and Asperger's syndrome are neurodevelopmental issues and does not consider them to be mental health disorders.
vi. American Psychiatric Association, Council on Law and Psychiatry, *Access to Firearms by People with Mental Illness: Resource Document* (Arlington, VA: American Psychiatric Association, 2009).

Criminal Profiles boxes throughout the text offer insights into the lives and criminal motivations of notorious offenders, such as Ted Kaczynski (the "Unabomber").

CRIME | in the NEWS
"Flash Robs" Become a Troublesome Trend

"Flash robs," a crime akin to shoplifting, but on a massive scale, are a form of larceny. Although there were a few flash robs in the news as far back as 2002, these crimes only become a nationwide phenomenon in 2011 and were still being widely reported in 2014. Typically, a large group of teenagers files into a convenience store, takes low-priced candy and sodas, and exits immediately. The whole incident takes as little as one minute.

Flash robs are not technically robberies, because there is no threat of force. Filmed on a store's security video (and then posted later on the Internet), smiling participants form an orderly line and limit themselves to one or two goodies each. They don't brandish any weapons, but store employees are frightened and usually stay out of the way.

This new form of lawbreaking comes at a time when youth crime is relatively low. From 2008 to 2009, juvenile arrests for violent crime fell 10%, according to a 2012 Justice Department report. But the economy is ailing and high percentages of black teenagers don't have jobs. In June 2012, the unemployment rate among blacks ages 16 to 19 was 39.3%—high for African American rates and nearly double the 20.9% rate for whites the same age.

A youthful group dynamic takes hold in a flash rob. "Young people are risk-takers," said Scott Decker, a professor of criminology at Arizona State University. "They do things in groups far more than adults do." He believes they are proud rather than upset when they see themselves in the videos shown on the evening news. They feel protected by the power of numbers, said New York psychologist Jeff Gardere.

The store's security videos help authorities identify perpetrators, but prosecuting them can be frustrating. Many hundreds of dollars' worth of goods may be stolen, but one person's take is just a few bucks, which amounts to nothing more than a Class C misdemeanor. When prosecutors intercept messages on social media from kids planning the event, they can add conspiracy charges, but according to the National Retail Federation, social media is identified in less than half of apprehended cases of flash robs.

To aid prosecution, the Maryland Legislature has been considering a bill that would treat multiple acts of theft in unison as one crime. The measure would automatically define a flash rob as a conspiracy, and charges against each person would depend on the total amount stolen, not on each person's take. The bill failed in 2012, but sponsors plan to reintroduce it soon.

A flash robbery in progress. How do social media facilitate such crimes?

Discussion Questions

1. How do flash robberies differ from other kinds of larceny?
2. What kind of impact might this kind of crime, if it continues to expand, have on retailers?

Sources: Derek Valcourt, "Law Enforcement Frustrated with Growing Number of Flash Mob Crimes in Md.," CBS Baltimore, July 26, 2012, http://baltimore.cbslocal.com/2012/07/26/law-enforcement-frustrated-with-growing-number-of-flash-mob-crimes-in-md/; Ellen Arndt, "Fighting the Rising Tide of Flash Mobs in Retail," *Security*, July 24, 2012, http://www.securitymagazine.com/articles/83326-fighting-the-rising-tide-of-flash-mobs-in-retail; and Tim Dees, "Stay on Top of 'Flash Robs'," PoliceOne.com, June 12, 2012, http://www.policeone.com/police-products/communications/articles/5603418-Stay-on-top-of-flash-robs.

Crime in the News boxes in each chapter present case examples and pose analytical discussion questions about connections between examples and the chapter topics.

THEORY | in PERSPECTIVE
Types of Psychological and Psychiatric Theories

Psychological and psychiatric theories of criminology are derived from the behavioral sciences and focus on the individual as the unit of analysis. This chapter breaks their discussion down into a number of areas as shown in this box.

Personality Theory

This approach envisions a complex set of drives and motives operating from recesses deep within the personality to determine behavior.

Period: 1930s–present
Theorists: Hervey M. Cleckley, Hans J. Eysenck, many others
Concepts: personality, psychopath, sociopath, antisocial personality, personality, traits, Five Factor Model

Cognitive Theory

Cognitive theory, also known as moral development theory, holds that individuals become criminal when they have not successfully completed their intellectual development from child- to adulthood.

Period: 1930s–present
Theorists: Jean Piaget, Lawrence Kohlberg, Roger C. Schank, Robert P. Abelson, Stanton E. Samenow, Samuel Yochelson
Concepts: moral development, cognitive-information processing, scripts, criminal mind-set

Psychoanalytic Criminology

This psychiatric approach, developed by Austrian psychiatrist Sigmund Freud, emphasizes the role of personality in human behavior and sees deviant behavior as the result of dysfunctional personalities or maladaptation to the social environment.

Period: 1920s–present
Theorists: Sigmund Freud, August Aichorn, others
Concepts: Psychiatric criminology, id, ego, superego, sublimation, psychoanalysis, psychotherapy, neurosis, psychosis, sublimation, paranoid schizophrenia

Frustration-Aggression Theory

Frustration is a natural consequence of living and a root cause of crime in this theory, where criminal behavior can be a form of adaptation when it results from stress reduction.

Period: 1940s–present
Theorists: J. Dollard, Albert Bandura, Richard H. Walters
Concepts: Frustration, aggression, displacement

Crime as Adaptation

Criminal behavior can be a form of adaptation when it provides rationalizations for perceived inadequacies.

Period: 1970s–present
Theorists: Seymour L. Halleck, Donald A. Andrews, James Bonta, John Bowlby
Concepts: alloplastic and autoplastic adaptation, criminogenic needs, criminogenic domains, attachment theory

Behavior Theory

A psychological perspective, behavior theory posits that individual behavior that is rewarded will increase in frequency and behavior that is punished will decrease in frequency.

Period: 1940s–present
Theorists: B. F. Skinner, others
Concepts: Operant behavior, operant conditioning, classical conditioning, stimulus–response, reward, punishment

Modeling Theory

This theory states that people learn how to behave by modeling themselves after others whom they have the opportunity to observe.

Period: 1950s–present
Theorists: Gabriel Tarde, Albert Bandura, others
Concepts: Imitation, interpersonal aggression, social cognition theory, modeling, disengagement

Theory in Perspective summary boxes in Parts 2 and 3 outline the main points of various theories for easy reference and study.

In the past few years, crime and criminals have changed in ways that few people had previously imagined would occur, and these changes hold considerable significance for each one of us and for our nation as a whole. It is my hope that this new edition will help today's students both to understand the nature of these changes and to find a meaningful place in the social world that is to come.

FRANK SCHMALLEGER, Ph.D.
Distinguished Professor Emeritus
The University of North Carolina at Pembroke

Supplements

Instructor Supplements

The following supplementary materials are available to support instructors' use of the main text:

- MyCJLab
- Annotated Instructor's Edition
- Instructor's Manual with Test Bank
- PowerPoint presentations
- MyTest computerized test bank
- CourseSmart e-book version of the text

Download Instructor Resources from the Instructor Resource Center

To access supplementary materials online, instructors need to request an instructor access code. Go to **www.pearsonhighered.com/irc** to register for an instructor access code. Within 48 hours of registering, you will receive a confirming e-mail including an instructor access code. Once you have received your code, locate your text in the online catalog and click on the Instructor Resources button on the left side of the catalog product page. Select a supplement, and a log-in page will appear. Once you have logged in, you can access instructor materials for all Pearson textbooks. If you have any difficulties accessing the site or downloading a supplement, please contact Customer Service at **http://247.prenhall.com.**

Alternative Book Versions

Alternative versions to traditional printed textbooks, such as our "Student Value Editions" and e-book versions of the text in the "CourseSmart" platform, are available. CourseSmart is an exciting new choice for students wishing to save money. As an alternative to purchasing the printed textbook, students can purchase an electronic version of the same content. With a CourseSmart eTextbook, students can search the text, make notes online, print out reading assignments that incorporate lecture notes, and bookmark important passages for later review. For more information, or to purchase access to the CourseSmart eTextbook, visit **www.coursesmart.com**

Pearson Online Course Solutions

Criminology Today is supported by online course solutions that include interactive learning modules, a variety of assessment tools, videos, simulations, and current event features. Go to **www.pearsonhighered.com** or contact your local representative for the latest information.

Acknowledgments

A book like *Criminology Today* draws on the talents and resources of many people and is the end result of much previous effort. This text could not have been written without the groundwork laid by previous criminologists, academics, and researchers; hence, a hearty thank-you is due everyone who has contributed to the development of the field of criminology throughout the years, especially to those theorists, authors, and social commentators who are cited in this book. Without their work, the field would be that much poorer. I would like to thank, as well, all the adopters—professors and students alike—of my previous textbooks, for they have given me the encouragement and fostered the steadfastness required to write this new edition of *Criminology Today*.

The Pearson team members, many of whom I have come to know very well and all of whom have worked so professionally with me on this and other projects, deserve special thanks. The team includes Vern Anthony, Gary Bauer, Leslie Brado, Kevin Cecil, April Cleland, Diane Ernsberger, David Gesell, JoEllen Gohr, David Gesell, Leah Jewell, Mike Lackey, Andrea Nix, Les Roberts, Steve Robb, Mary Salzman, Deidra Skahill, and Alicia Wozniak. I would especially like to thank Elisa Rogers at 4development for her commitment and attention to this project. My thanks also to text and cover designer Candace Rowley and to photo researcher Zoe Milgram, whose efforts have helped make *Criminology Today* both attractive and visually appealing. Finally, my sincere thanks to production coordinator Christian Holdener for his very capable handling of numerous details.

My friends and professional colleagues Ellen Cohn at Florida International University, Cassandra Renzi at Keiser University, and Karel Kurst-Swanger at Oswego State University helped in many ways. Dr. Cohn graciously used her deep personal creativity in enhancing the supplements package and creating quality products; she has the exceptional ability of building intuitively on concepts in the text. Thanks also to Bob Winslow at California State University–San Diego for insight and encouragement on a number of important issues and to Jack Humphrey at St. Anselm College and Stephen J. Schoenthaler for their valuable suggestions in the preparation of this new edition.

This book has benefited greatly from the quick availability of information and other resources through online services and in various locations on the Internet's World Wide Web. I am grateful to the many information providers who, although they are too numerous to list, have helped establish such useful resources.

I am thankful as well for the assistance of Prof. Bill Tafoya (retired FBI) and Nancy Carnes of the Federal Bureau of Investigation; E. Ann Carson at the Bureau of Justice Statistics; William Ballweber at the National Institute of Justice; David Beatty, director of public affairs with the National Victim Center; Kris Rose at the National Criminal Justice Reference Service; Marilyn Marbrook and Michael Rand at the Office of Justice Programs; Mark Reading at the Drug Enforcement Administration; and Barbara Maxwell at *USA Today*.

Many manuscript reviewers have contributed to the development of *Criminology Today*. I offer my thanks to the following reviewers for the seventh edition:

Jack Atherton, Northwestern State University
Kevin Beaver, Florida State University
Alison Burke, Southern Oregon University
Ellen Cohn, Florida International University
Amanda Farrell, Old Dominion University
David Forristal, Brown Mackie College
Krista Gehring, University of Houston—Downtown
J. D. Jamieson, Texas State University
David MacDonald, Eastfield College
Christopher McFarlin, Tri-County Technical College
Venezia Michalsen, Montclair State University
Theresa Misiaszek, Cayuga County Community College
Jacqueline Mullany, Triton College
Karen Nardonelemons, Massachusetts Bay Community College
Thomas O'Connor, Austin Peay State University
Bill Shaw, Northwestern State University
Shelly Wagers, University of South Florida
Stewart Weisman, Cazenovia College
Katina Whorton, Delgado Community College–City Park

I also thank the following reviewers for previous editions:

Reed Adams, East Carolina State University
Michael P. Brown, Ball State University
Gregg Buchholz, Keiser University
Bryan D. Byers, Ball State University
Dianne Carmody, Old Dominon University
Steven M. Christiansen, Joliet Junior College
Myrna Cintron, Texas A&M University
Patrick G. Donnelly, University of Dayton
Ronald D. Hunter, State University of West Georgia
Steven Johnson, Eastern Arizona College
Daniel D. Jones, University of Washington
John Kirkpatrick, University of New Hampshire
Joan Luxenburg, University of Central Oklahoma
M. Joan McDermott, Southern Illinois University
William McGovern, Sussex County Community College
Darrell K. Mills, Pima Community College (East Campus)
Robert Mutchnick, Indiana University of Pennsylvania
Michael Pittaro, Lehigh Valley College
Glen E. Sapp, Central Carolina Community College
Jennifer L. Schulenberg, Sam Houston State University
Louis Shepard, West Georgia Technical College
John Siler, Georgia Perimeter College

mson L. Six, Lock Haven University
Dianne Williams, North Carolina A&T State University
Jeffrey Zack, Fayetteville Technical Community College
Anthony W. Zumpetta, West Chester University

Finally, but by no means least, I am indebted to a small but very special group of contemporary criminologists who have laid the foundation for our discipline's presence on the Internet. Among them are Cecil Greek at Florida State University, whose online lecture notes **(www.criminology.fsu.edu/crimtheory)** are massively informative; Tom O'Connor of Austin Peay State University, whose Megalinks in Criminal Justice site **(http://www.drtomocconor.com)** provides an amazingly comprehensive resource; Matthew Robinson at Appalachian State University, whose Crime Theory links **(www.appstate.edu/~robinsnmb/theorylinks.htm)** allow visitors to vote on what they think are the causes of crime; and Bruce Hoffman, whose former Crime Theory site **(http://crimetheory.com)** at the University of Washington offers many great insights into the field. All of these excellent resources are referred to throughout this book—and it is to these modern-day visionaries that *Criminology Today* owes much of its technological depth.

About the Author

Frank Schmalleger, Ph.D., is Professor Emeritus at The University of North Carolina at Pembroke, where he also was recognized as Distinguished Professor. Dr. Schmalleger holds degrees from the University of Notre Dame and The Ohio State University; he earned both a master's (1970) and a doctorate (1974) in sociology, with a special emphasis in criminology, from The Ohio State University. From 1976 to 1994, he taught criminal justice courses at The University of North Carolina at Pembroke, and for the last 16 of those years, he chaired the university's Department of Sociology, Social Work, and Criminal Justice. As an adjunct professor with Webster University in St. Louis, Missouri, Schmalleger helped develop the university's graduate program in security administration and loss prevention and taught courses in that curriculum for more than a decade. Schmalleger has also taught in the New School for Social Research's online graduate program, helping build the world's first electronic classrooms in support of distance learning through computer telecommunications.

Schmalleger is the author of numerous articles as well as many books: *Criminal Justice Today: An Introductory Text for the 21st Century* (Prentice Hall, 2015), now in its 13th edition; *Juvenile Delinquency* (with Clemmens Bartollas; Prentice Hall, 2014); *Criminal Justice: A Brief Introduction*, 10th edition (Prentice Hall, 2014); *Criminal Law Today*, fifth edition (Prentice Hall, 2014); *Corrections in the Twenty-First Century* (with John Smykla; McGraw-Hill, 2015); *Crime and the Justice System in America: An Encyclopedia* (Greenwood Publishing Group, 1997); *Trial of the Century: People of the State of California* vs. *Orenthal James Simpson* (Prentice Hall, 1996); *Career Paths: A Guide to Jobs in Federal Law Enforcement* (Regents/Prentice Hall, 1994); *Computers in Criminal Justice* (Wyndham Hall Press, 1991); *Criminal Justice Ethics* (Greenwood Press, 1991); *Finding Criminal Justice in the Library* (Wyndham Hall Press, 1991); *Ethics in Criminal Justice* (Wyndham Hall Press, 1990); *A History of Corrections* (Foundations Press of Notre Dame, 1983); and *The Social Basis of Criminal Justice* (University Press of America, 1981). He is also founding editor of the journal *Criminal Justice Studies* (formerly *The Justice Professional*).

Schmalleger's philosophy of both teaching and writing can be summed up in these words: "In order to communicate knowledge we must first catch, then hold, a person's interest—be it student, colleague, or policy maker. Our writing, our speaking, and our teaching must be relevant to the problems facing people today, and they must—in some way—help solve those problems."

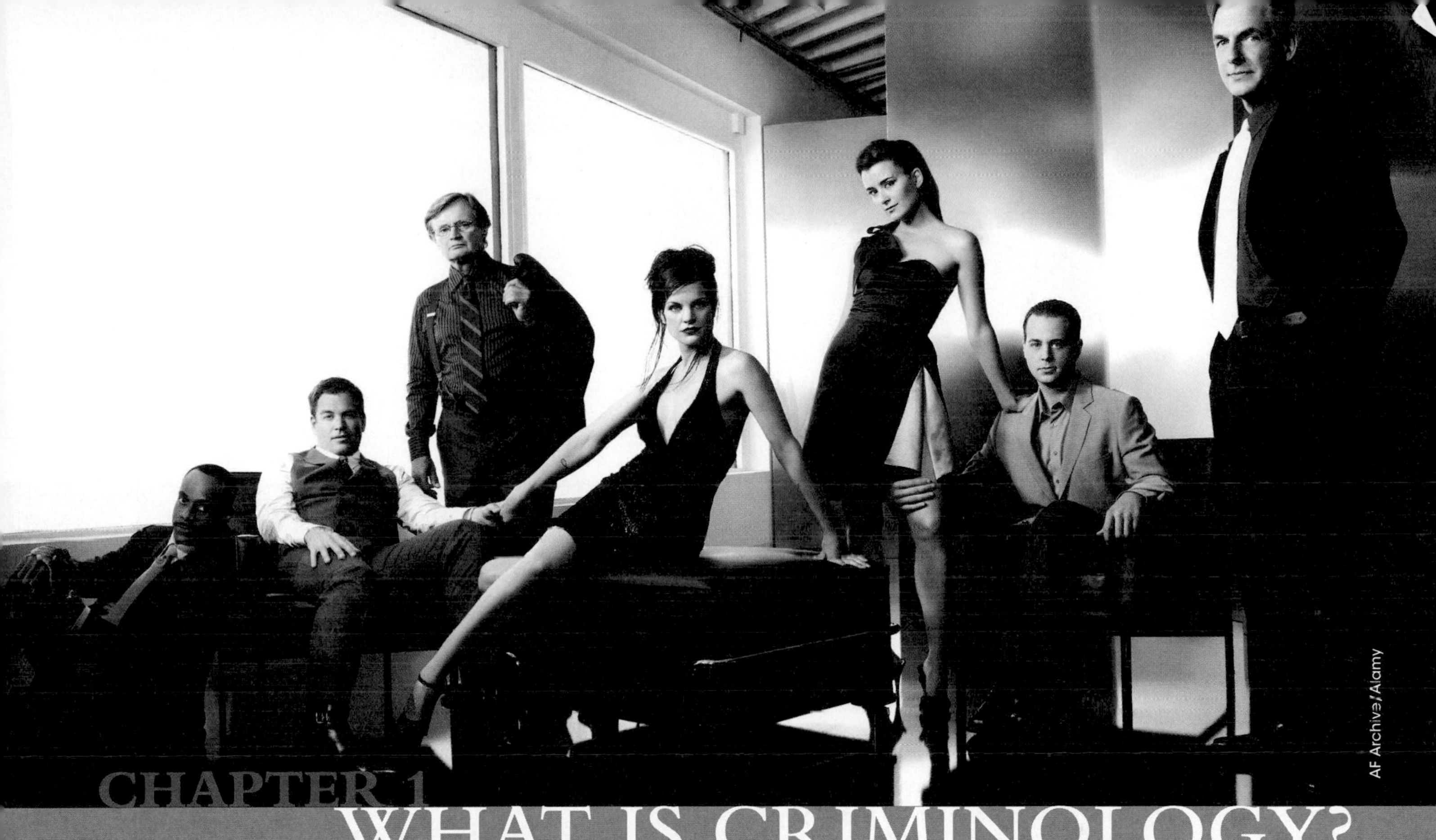
AF Archive/Alamy

CHAPTER 1 WHAT IS CRIMINOLOGY?

LEARNING OUTCOMES

After reading this chapter, you should be able to answer the following questions:

- What is crime? What is the definition of crime that the author of this text has chosen to use?
- What is deviance? How are crime and deviance similar? How do they differ?
- Who decides what should be criminal? How are such decisions made?
- What is the theme of this text? Upon what two contrasting viewpoints does it build?
- What does it mean to say that "criminal activity is diversely created and variously interpreted"?

Introduction

According to social commentators, people are simultaneously attracted to and repulsed by crime—especially gruesome crimes involving extreme personal violence. The popularity of today's TV crime shows, Hollywood-produced crime movies, true-crime books and magazines, and Web sites devoted exclusively to the coverage of crime supports that observation. The CBS TV megahit *CSI: Miami*, for example, which ran for ten seasons until going off the air in 2012, garnered 50 million regular viewers in more than 55 countries. By its eighth season it had become the most popular television show in the world.[1] But *CSI* programming extends well beyond its Miami-based series, and the *CSI* franchise, which includes shows featuring New York City, Las Vegas (now also in reruns), and other locales, is available in both real time and on demand to a global audience of nearly 2 billion viewers in 200 countries around the globe.[2] In 2012, the *CSI* series was named the most watched TV show in the world for the fifth time.[3] Other widely followed TV crime series, both past and present, include shows such as *Awake* (NBC), *Criminal Minds* (CBS), *Blue Bloods* (CBS), *Without a Trace* (CBS), *Magic City* (HBO), *Numb3rs* (CBS), *The Unit* (CBS), *The Unusuals* (ABC), *The Sopranos* (in reruns on HBO), *The Killing* (AMC), *White Collar* (USA), *The District* (CBS), *Boardwalk Empire* (HBO), *The Shield* (FX), *The Wire* (HBO), *Cold Case* (CBS), *NCIS* (CBS), *Prison Break* (Fox), and *Law and Order* (NBC)—along with the *Law and Order* spin-offs, *Law and Order: Criminal Intent* and *Law and Order: Special Victims Unit*. American TV viewers are hungry for crime-related entertainment and have a fascination with criminal motivation and detective work.

Some crimes cry out for explanation. Yet one of the things that fascinates people about crime—especially violent crime—is that it seems to be inexplicable. Some crimes are especially difficult to understand, but our natural tendency is to seek out some reason for the unreasonable. We search for explanations for the seemingly unexplainable. How, for example, can the behavior of child killers be understood, anticipated, and even prevented? Why don't terrorists acknowledge the emotional and personal suffering they inflict? Why do some robbers or rapists kill and even torture, utterly disregarding human life and feelings?

People also wonder about "everyday" crimes such as burglary, drug use, assault, vandalism, and computer intrusion. Why, for example, do people fight? Does it matter to a robber that he may face prison time? How can people sacrifice love, money, careers, and even their lives for access to illegal drugs? What motivates terrorists to give up their own lives to take the lives of others? Why do gifted techno-savvy teens and preteens hack sites on the Internet thought to be secure? While this text may not answer each of these questions, it examines the causative factors in effect when a crime is committed and encourages an appreciation of the challenges of crafting effective crime-control policy.

Sonja Flemming/CBS/Everett Collection

A still image from the highly popular CBS-TV show CSI: Crime Scene Investigation. Cast members appearing in this image from the "Lab Rats" episode are Hodges (Wallace Langham, far left), Archie (Archie Kao, far right), Henry (Jon Wellner), and Mandy (Sheeri Rappaport).Why do many people like to watch TV crime shows like CSI?

What Is Crime?

As the word implies, *criminology* is clearly concerned with *crime*. As we begin our discussion of criminology, let's consider just what the term *crime* means. Like anything else, crime can be defined in several ways, and some scholars have suggested that at least four definitional perspectives can be found in contemporary criminology. These diverse perspectives see crime from (1) legalistic, (2) political, (3) sociological, and (4) psychological viewpoints. How we see any phenomenon is crucial because it determines the assumptions that we make about how that phenomenon should be studied. The perspective that

■ **crime** Human conduct in violation of the criminal laws of the federal government, a state, or a local jurisdiction that has the power to make such laws.

■ **criminalize** To make illegal.

we choose to employ when viewing crime determines the kinds of questions we ask, the nature of the research we conduct, and the type of answers that we expect to receive. Those answers, in turn, influence our conclusions about the kinds of crime-control policies that might be effective.

Without a law that circumscribes a particular form of behavior, there can be no crime. . . .

Seen from a legalistic perspective, **crime** is *human conduct in violation of the criminal laws of a state, the federal government, or a local jurisdiction that has the power to make such laws*. Without a law that circumscribes a particular form of behavior, there can be no crime, no matter how deviant or socially repugnant the behavior in question may be.

The notion of crime as behavior[4] that violates the law derives from earlier work by criminologists like Paul W. Tappan, who defined crime as "an intentional act in violation of the criminal law committed without defense or excuse, and penalized by the state as a felony or misdemeanor."[5] Edwin Sutherland, regarded by many as a founding figure in American criminology, said of crime that its "essential characteristic is that it is behavior which is prohibited by the State as an injury to the State and against which the State may react by punishment."[6]

For purposes of this book, we will employ a legalistic approach because it allows for relative ease of measurement of crimes committed. Official statistics on crime, such as those shown in Figure 1–1, report crime in terms of legislatively established categories, and the number of offenses shown reflect statutory definitions of crime categories.

A serious shortcoming of the legalistic approach to crime, however, is that it yields the moral high ground to powerful individuals who are able to influence the making of laws and the imposition of criminal definitions on lawbreakers. By making their own laws, powerful but immoral individuals can escape the label "criminal." While we have chosen to adopt the legalistic approach to crime in this book, it is important to realize that laws are social products, so crime is socially relative in the sense that it is created by legislative activity. Hence, sociologists are fond of saying that "crime is whatever a society says it is." In Chapter 8, we will explore this issue further and will focus on the process of criminalization, which is the method used to **criminalize** some forms of behavior—or make them illegal—while other forms remain legitimate.

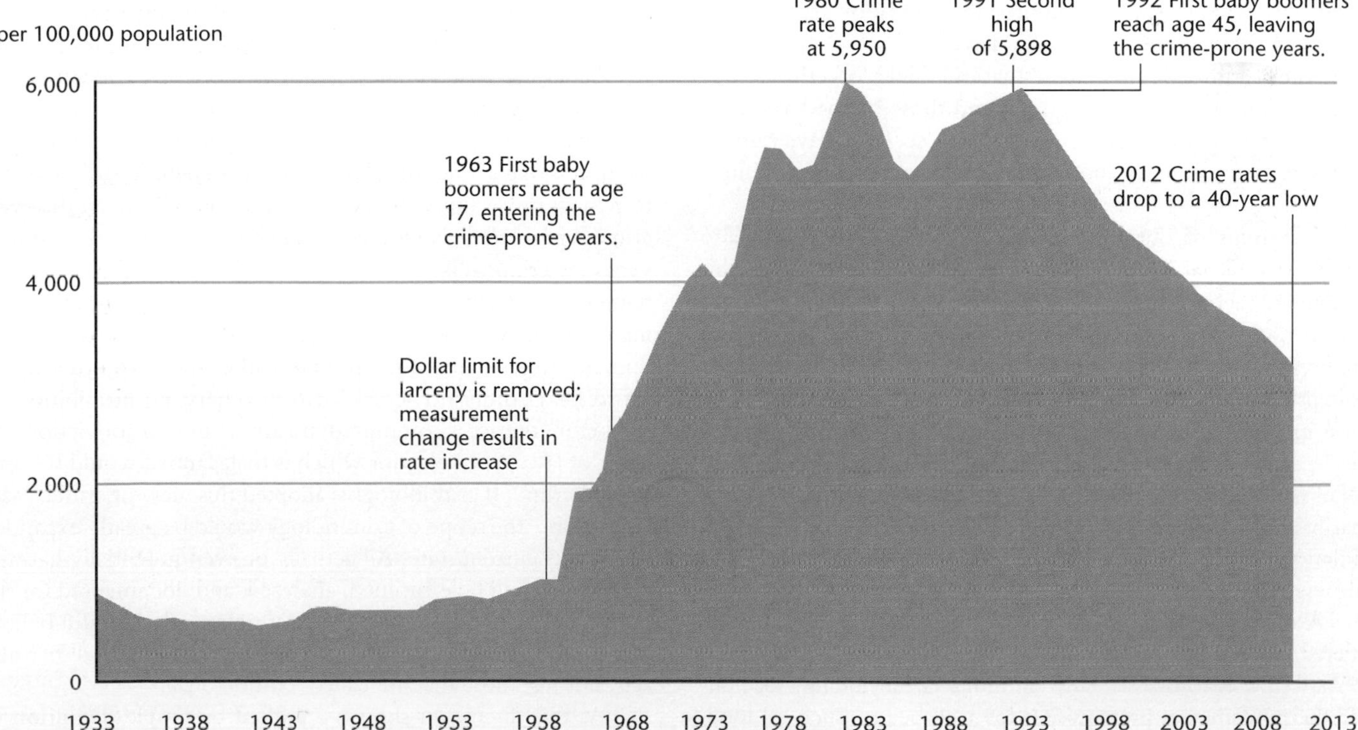

FIGURE 1-1 | **Crime Rates in the United States, 1933–2012**

Source: FBI, Uniform Crime Reports, various years. That's needed because some other crime reports now show crime is rising, and they conflict with the numbers shown here.

A second perspective on crime is the political one, where crime is the result of criteria that have been built into the law by powerful groups and are then used to label selected undesirable forms of behavior as illegal. Those who adhere to this point of view say that crime is a definition of human conduct created by authorized agents in a politically organized society. Seen this way, laws serve the interests of the politically powerful, and crimes are merely forms of behavior that are perceived by those in power as direct or indirect threats to their interests. Thus, the political perspective defines crime in terms of the power structures that exist in society and asserts that criminal laws do not necessarily bear any inherent relationship to popular notions of right and wrong.

Even though political processes that create criminal definitions are sometimes easier to comprehend in totalitarian societies, the political perspective can also be meaningfully applied to American society. John F. Galliher, a contemporary criminologist, summarized the political perspective on crime when he wrote, "One can best understand crime in a class-structured society such as the United States as the end product of a chain of interactions involving powerful groups that use their power to establish criminal laws and sanctions against less powerful persons and groups that may pose a threat to the group in power."[7] Galliher points out that, because legal definitions of criminality are arrived at through a political process, the subject matter of criminality will be artificially limited if we insist on seeing crime solely as a violation of the criminal law.

Some criminologists insist that the field of criminology must include behaviors that go beyond those defined as crimes through the political process; not doing so, they say, restricts rather than encourages inquiry into relevant forms of human behavior.[8]

Adherents of our third perspective, the sociological (also called "sociolegal") viewpoint, would likely agree with this statement, seeing crime as "an antisocial act of such a nature that its repression is necessary or is supposed to be necessary to the preservation of the existing system of society."[9] Some criminologists have gone so far as to claim that any definition of crime must include all forms of antisocial behavior.[10] Ron Claassen, a modern-day champion of restorative justice (discussed in more detail in Chapter 9), suggested, for example, that "crime is primarily an offense against human relationships, and secondarily a violation of a law—since laws are written to protect safety and fairness in human relationships."[11]

A more comprehensive sociological definition of crime was offered by Herman Schwendinger and Julia Schwendinger in 1975: Crime encompasses "any harmful acts," including violations of "the fundamental prerequisites for well-being, [such as] food, shelter, clothing, medical services, challenging work and recreational experiences, as well as security from predatory individuals or repressive and imperialistic elites."[12] The Schwendingers challenged criminologists to be less constrained in what they see as the subject matter of their field, saying that violations of human rights may be more relevant to criminological inquiry than many acts that have been politically or legally defined as crime. "Isn't it time to raise serious questions about the assumptions underlying the definitions of the field of criminology," asked the Schwendingers, "when a man who steals a paltry sum can be called a criminal while agents of the State can, with impunity, legally reward men who destroy food so that price levels can be maintained whilst a sizable portion of the population suffers from malnutrition?"[13]

Jeffrey H. Reiman, another contemporary criminologist, asked similar questions. "The fact is that the label 'crime' is not used in America to name all or the worst of the actions that cause misery and suffering to Americans," said Reiman. "It is primarily reserved for the dangerous actions of the poor." Writing about unhealthy and unsafe workplaces, Reiman asked, "Doesn't a crime by any other name still cause misery and suffering? What's in a name?"[14] While a sociolegal approach to understanding crime is attractive to many, others claim that it suffers from wanting to criminalize activities that cause only indirect harm; that is, it is easier for most people to appreciate the criminality involved in a holdup or a rape than in cost-cutting efforts made by a businessperson.

Doesn't a crime by any other name still cause misery and suffering?

Finally, a psychological (or maladaptive) perspective says that "crime is a form of social maladjustment which can be designated as a more or less pronounced difficulty that the individual has in reacting to the stimuli of his environment in such a way as to remain in harmony with that environment."[15] Seen this way, crime is problem behavior, especially human activity that contravenes the criminal law and results in difficulties in living within a framework of generally acceptable social arrangements. According to Matthew B. Robinson, "[t]he maladaptive view of crime does not require any of the [traditional] elements in order for an act to be a crime: no actual harm to others; no prohibition by law before the act is committed; no arrest; and no conviction in a court of law. Any behavior which is maladaptive would be considered crime. If criminologists adopted this view of crime," said Robinson, "the scope of criminology would be greatly expanded beyond its current state. All actually or even potentially harmful behaviors could be examined, analyzed, and documented for the purpose of gaining knowledge about potentially harmful behaviors and developing strategies to protect people from all harmful acts, not just those that are called 'crime' today."[16]

As this discussion shows, a unified or simple definition of crime is difficult to achieve. The four points of view that we have discussed here form a kind of continuum, bound on one end by strict, legalistic interpretations of crime and on the other by much more fluid, behavioral and moralistic definitions.

■ **deviant behavior** Human activity that violates social norms.

Crime and Deviance

Sociologically speaking, many crimes can be regarded as deviant forms of behavior—that is, as behaviors that are in some way abnormal. Piers Beirne and James Messerschmidt, two contemporary criminologists, defined deviance as "any social behavior or social characteristic that departs from the conventional norms and standards of a community or society and for which the deviant is sanctioned."[17] Their definition does not count as deviant, however, any sanctionable behavior that is not punished or punishable. Hence, we prefer another approach to defining deviance. The definition of **deviant behavior** that we will use in this text is as follows: *Deviant behavior is human activity that violates social norms.*

Abnormality, deviance, and crime are concepts that do not always easily mesh. Some forms of deviance are not violations of the criminal law, and the reverse is equally true (see Figure 1–2). Deviant styles of dress, for example, although perhaps outlandish to the majority, are generally not circumscribed by criminal law unless (perhaps) decency statutes are violated by a lack of clothing. Even in such cases, laws are subject to interpretation and may be modified as social norms change over time.

Some years ago, for example, a judge in Palm Beach County, Florida, held that a city ordinance barring the wearing of baggy pants was unconstitutional.[18] County Judge Laura Johnson ruled that no matter how "tacky or distasteful" baggy pants might be to others, they were merely a fashion statement and that wearing them, especially when no nudity is involved, is a freedom protected under the Fourteenth Amendment to the U.S. Constitution. The ordinance had been overwhelmingly approved by voters only two years earlier. More recently, San Francisco's Board of Supervisors voted to ban total public nudity in their city.[19] The vote came in late 2012 after a series of complaints had been received about men and women strolling through the city's Castro neighborhood without any clothes, and sipping drinks at the city's coffee shops. The local legislation, however, exempted nudity at private beaches and within permitted special events.

Taylor Whitfield holds up a sign protesting the ban by San Francisco's Board of Supervisors on public nudity that was passed in 2012. Who does public nudity hurt? Should it be criminalized?

Some types of behavior, although quite common, are still against the law, even though those who engage in them might not think of them as deviant. Speeding on interstate highways, for example, although probably something that most motorists engage in at least from time to time, is illegal; but most people who engage in such behavior probably don't think of themselves as "deviant" or "criminal." Complicating matters still further is the fact that certain behaviors are illegal in some jurisdictions but not in others. For example, commercialized gambling, especially gambling involving slot machines and games of chance, is against the law in many parts of the United States but has been legitimized in Nevada, on some Indian reservations, on cruise ships operating outside U.S. territorial waters, on some Mississippi riverboats, and in some state-sponsored locales. Even state governments, seeking to enhance revenues, have gotten into the gambling business through state lotteries, which now operate in 45 states,[20] and many states have laws specifically forbidding participation in online gambling, due largely to their interest in protecting their own lottery revenues. Similarly, prostitution, which is almost uniformly illegal in the United States, is an activity that is fully within the law in parts of Nevada as long as it occurs within licensed brothels and as long as those engaged in the activity meet state licensing requirements and abide by state laws that require condom use and weekly medical checkups.

FIGURE 1–2 | The Overlap between Deviance and Crime

Source: Schmalleger, Frank J., *Criminology*. Printed and Electronically reproduced by permission of Pearson Education, Inc., Upper Saddle River, New Jersey.

■ **delinquency** A term often used in conjunction with crime and deviance, it refers to violations of the criminal law and other misbehavior committed by young people.

■ **consensus perspective** A viewpoint that holds that laws should be enacted to criminalize given forms of behavior when members of society generally agree that such laws are necessary.

■ **pluralist perspective** A viewpoint that says that behaviors are typically criminalized through a political process only after debate over the appropriate course of action.

Finally, we should add that **delinquency**, a term often used in conjunction with crime and deviance, refers to violations of the criminal law and other misbehavior committed by young people. The laws of many states proclaim that "youth" ends at a person's eighteenth birthday, although others specify the sixteenth or seventeenth birthday as meeting that requirement. All states, however, specify certain offenses, like running away from home, being ungovernable, and drinking alcohol, as illegal for children, but not for adults.

What Should Be Criminal?

By now, you have probably realized that the question "What is crime?" differs from the question "What should be criminal?" Although most people agree that certain forms of behavior, such as murder, rape, burglary, and theft, should be against the law, there is far less agreement about the appropriate legal status of things like drug use, abortion (including the use of "abortion pills" like RU-486, or Mifeprex), gambling, "deviant" forms of consensual adult sexual behavior, and even the use of salt. In 2012, for example, many people disagreed with the criminal conviction of six Italian geologists and a government official who were found guilty of manslaughter and sentenced to six years in prison for failing to warn the people of a small Italian town of a deadly earthquake. The story, detailed in a News box in this chapter, led some to think that future scientists would refrain from offering expert opinion on a wide variety of issues.

The consensus viewpoint holds that laws should be enacted to criminalize given forms of behavior when members of society generally agree that such laws are necessary.

While the question "What should be criminal?" can be answered in many different ways, the social and intellectual processes by which an answer is reached can be found in two contrasting points of view: (1) the consensus perspective and (2) the pluralist perspective.

The **consensus perspective** holds that laws should be enacted to criminalize given forms of behavior when members of society generally agree that such laws are necessary. The consensus perspective (described in greater detail in Chapter 9) is most applicable to homogeneous societies, or those characterized by shared values, norms, and belief systems. In a multicultural and diverse society like the United States, however, a shared consensus may be difficult to achieve. In such a society, even relatively minor matters may lead to complex debates over the issues involved, and these debates show just how difficult it is to achieve a consensus over even relatively minor matters in a society as complex as our own.

Finally, the question of what should be criminal can be distinguished from issues arising from excessive enforcement of the law. In one surprising case of what many saw as an overreaction by law enforcement officers, a 12-year-old student, Alexa Gonzalez, was arrested in New York City in 2010 for doodling on her junior high school desk with a washable felt-tipped marker.[21] School safety officers took the girl into custody for defacing school property and for creating graffiti—both against the law in New York City. Upon being turned over to New York Police Department (NYPD) officers as required by school policy, Alexa was handcuffed and taken to a police station. After spending hours in confinement, the girl was released into the custody of her mother. Eventually, she was ordered to perform eight hours of community service and assigned to write an essay on what she had learned from the experience. The question in this case was not whether defacing public property is wrong and if there should be a law against it, but how the police should react to such situations.

The second perspective, the **pluralist perspective** of crime (also described in more detail in Chapter 9) recognizes the importance of diversity in societies like ours. It says that behaviors are typically criminalized through a political process only after debate over the appropriate course of action. The political process often takes the form of legislation and may involve appellate court action (by those who don't agree with the legislation). After the horrific shootings that occurred at the Sandy Hook Elementary School in 2012, for example, legislatures at

CRIME | in the NEWS

Scientists Convicted for Failing to Predict Earthquake

In October 2012, six Italian scientists and one government official were convicted of criminal manslaughter and sentenced to six years in prison. Their crime: failing to warn the people of L'Aquila, Italy, of a deadly earthquake that devastated the town in 2009.

Before the tragedy, a number of small tremors were felt in L'Aquila. Fearing this activity would lead to a serious earthquake, authorities appointed the scientists to study the matter and instruct townspeople on what to do. The scientists deliberated and a government official relayed their advice. "The scientific community tells me there is no danger, because there is an ongoing discharge of energy," he stated. "The situation looks favorable."

The quake hit six days later. Striking at night, it killed more than 300 townspeople, injured at least 1,500, and left thousands homeless. The scientists were criminally indicted for giving "inexact, incomplete and contradictory information." Prosecutors insisted the case was not about failing to predict the quake, but about being, in effect, misleadingly reassuring.

As people around the world saw it, however, the Italian scientists were accused of failing to predict an inherently unpredictable event. Although Italy has many earthquakes, the last major quake in L'Aquila occurred in 1703. And while half of large earthquakes start with tremors beforehand, only about 5 percent of tremors presage a large quake. David Rothery, a scientist at the Open University in the United Kingdom, said that before the 2009 earthquake arrived, "the best estimate at the time was that the low-level seismicity was not likely to herald a bigger quake."

Looking back, the scientists might have erred on the side of caution and warned that an earthquake was possible. But they would have been in trouble if there had not been a quake. When an Italian official ordered the evacuation of several towns in 1985 for an earthquake that didn't happen, he was investigated for his error, according to an attorney for the L'Aquila scientists.

The scientists were shocked by the court's decision. "I thought I would have been acquitted," said Enzo Boschi, who was stripped of his position as head of Italy's Institute of Geophysics and Volcanology. "I still don't understand what I was convicted of."

The scientists are appealing the decision. Even though the Italian court's ruling does not affect other countries, scientists around the world fear it will have a chilling effect. The U.S. National Academy of Sciences and the Royal Society in Great Britain issued a joint statement saying the verdict "could lead to a situation in which scientists will be afraid to give expert opinion for fear of prosecution or reprisal."

Discussion Questions

1. Under the laws of the United States, a failure to act can result in criminal liability only where there is a preexisting legal duty to act. Was that likely to have been the case with the scientists in this story?
2. Do you agree with the Italian court that the scientists should have been found guilty of manslaughter? Why or why not?

AFP/Getty Images

Geologist Bernardo de Bernardinis (left) is seen with his lawyer Filippo Dinacci at the start of his trial at L'Aquila, in central Italy on September 20, 2011. De Bernardinis, along with five other Italian scientists and one government official were convicted of criminal manslaughter in 2012 and sentenced to serve six years in prison for failing to warn the townspeople of a coming earthquake. Do you agree with the decision of the Italian criminal court?

Sources: Nicola Nosengo, "L'Aquila Verdict Row Grows," Nature, October 30, 2012, http://www.nature.com/news/l-aquila-verdict-row-grows-1.11683; Alberto Sisto, "Italian Scientists Convicted over Earthquake Warning," Reuters, October 22, 2012, http://articles.chicagotribune.com/2012-10-22/business/sns-rt-us-italy-earthquake-courtbre89l13v-20121022_1_magnitude-earthquake-enzo-boschi-scientists; Alan Johnston, "L'Aquila Quake: Italy Scientists Guilty of Manslaughter," BBC, October 22, 2012, http://www.bbc.co.uk/news/world-europe-20025626.

---

both the state and federal levels began to reexamine gun laws to see if new laws were needed to keep guns out of the hands of potential mass killers. Given the diversity of perspectives that characterize our society, however, agreement was not easy to reach—and gun-control proponents vigorously debated those who sought to retain existing laws supporting gun ownership. For the law's perspective on another issue, see the Who's to Blame box in this chapter. Learn more about both sides of the gun-control debate via **Web Extras 1–1** and **1–2**.

What Is Criminology?

The attempt to understand crime and deviance predates written history. Prehistoric evidence, including skeletal remains showing signs of primitive cranial surgery, seems to indicate that preliterate people explained deviant behavior by reference to spirit possession. Primitive surgery was an attempt to release unwanted spiritual influences. In the thousands of years since, many other theoretical perspectives on crime have been advanced. This text

■ **social policy** A government initiative, program, or plan intended to address problems in society. The war on crime, for example, is a kind of generic (large-scale) social policy—one consisting of many smaller programs.

■ **criminology** An interdisciplinary profession built around the scientific study of crime and criminal behavior, including their forms, causes, legal aspects, and control.

describes various criminological theories and covers some of the more popular ones in detail.

Definition of Terms

Before beginning any earnest discussion, however, it is necessary to define the term *criminology*. As our earlier discussion of the nature of crime and deviance indicates, not only must criminologists deal with a complex subject matter—consisting of a broad range of illegal behaviors committed by frequently unknown or uncooperative individuals—but they also must manage their work under changing conditions mandated by ongoing revisions of the law and fluctuating **social policy**. In addition, as we have already seen, a wide variety of perspectives on the nature of crime abound. All this leads to considerable difficulties in defining the subject matter under study.

There is some evidence that the term *criminology* was coined by a Frenchman, Paul Topinard, in 1889;[22] he used it to differentiate the study of criminal body types within the field of anthropology from other biometric pursuits.[23] While he may have coined the term, Topinard did little to help define it. As with the concept of crime, various definitions of criminology can be found in the literature today. About two decades ago, criminologist Joseph F. Sheley wrote, "There seem to be nearly as many definitions of *contemporary criminology* as there are criminologists."[24]

One straightforward definition can be had from a linguistic analysis of the word *criminology*. As most people know, *-ology* means "the study of something," and the word *crimen* comes from the Latin, meaning "accusation," "charge," or "guilt." Hence, linguistically speaking, the term *criminology* literally means "the study of criminal accusations," that is, "the study of crime." In addition to this fundamental kind of linguistic definition, three other important types of definitions can be found in the literature: (1) disciplinary, (2) causative, and (3) scientific. Each type of definition is distinguished by its focus. Disciplinary definitions are those that, as their name implies, focus on criminology as a discipline. Seen from this viewpoint, criminology is a field of study or a body of knowledge. Some of the earliest criminologists of the past century, including Edwin H. Sutherland, who is often referred to as the "dean of American criminology," offered definitions of their field that emphasized its importance as a discipline of study. Sutherland, for example, wrote in the first edition of his textbook *Criminology* in 1924, "Criminology is the body of knowledge regarding the social problem of crime."[25] Sutherland's text was to set the stage for much of American criminology throughout the rest of the twentieth century. Reprinted in 1934 with the title *Principles of Criminology*,[26] it was to become the most influential textbook ever written in the field of criminology.[27]

Although Sutherland died in 1950, his revered text was revised for many years by Donald R. Cressey and later by David F. Luckenbill. By 1974, Sutherland's classic definition of criminology had been modified by Cressey: "Criminology is the body of knowledge regarding delinquency and crime as a social phenomenon. It includes within its scope the processes of making laws, of breaking laws, and of reacting toward the breaking of laws."[28]

Causative definitions emphasize criminology's role in uncovering the underlying causes of crime. In keeping with such an emphasis, contemporary criminologists Gennaro F. Vito and Ronald M. Holmes stated, "Criminology is the study of the causes of crime."[29]

Finally, some point to the scientific nature of contemporary criminology as its distinguishing characteristic. According to Clemens Bartollas and Simon Dinitz, for example, "[c]riminology is the scientific study of crime."[30] Writing in 1989, Bartollas and Dinitz seemed to be echoing an earlier definition of criminology offered by Marvin E. Wolfgang and Franco Ferracuti, who wrote in 1967, "Criminology is the scientific study of crime, criminals, and criminal behavior."[31]

There is some evidence that the term *criminology* was coined by a Frenchman, Paul Topinard, in 1889. . . .

One of the most comprehensive definitions of the term *criminology* that is available today comes from the European Society of Criminology (ESC), which in its constitution defines *criminology* as "all scholarly, scientific and professional knowledge concerning the explanation, prevention, control and treatment of crime and delinquency, offenders and victims, including the measurement and detection of crime, legislation, and the practice of criminal law, and law enforcement, judicial, and correctional systems."[32] ESC's emphasis is on "knowledge"; even though it mentions the "practice" of what many would call criminal justice (that is, policing, courts, and corrections), it is the study and knowledge of such practice that form the crux of the ESC perspective.

For our purposes, we will use a definition somewhat simpler than that of the ESC but one that brings together the works of previous writers and also recognizes the increasingly professional status of the criminological enterprise. Throughout this book, then, we will say that **criminology** is *an interdisciplinary profession built around the scientific study of crime and criminal behavior, including their forms, causes, legal aspects, and control.* As this definition indicates, criminology includes consideration of possible solutions to the problem of crime. Hence, this text (in later chapters) describes treatment strategies and social policy initiatives that have grown out of the existing array of theoretical explanations for crime.

WHO'S TO BLAME—The Individual or Society?

Should Polygamy Be a Protected Religious Practice?

Taeler Leon, a member of the Fundamentalist Church of Jesus Christ of Latter Day Saints, an ultraconservative offshoot of the Mormon Church, was arrested in a rural area outside Salt Lake City, Utah, and charged with polygamy and the rape of a child. The charges came after the parents of a 13-year-old girl, whom Leon had "married" in a ceremony performed by a church elder, complained to the Utah State Bureau of Investigation (SBI) that Leon was holding their daughter against her will. SBI agents visited Leon's compound and learned that six of Leon's wives and 16 of his children were living at the compound. The compound, which consisted of four houses and a communal building containing a small school, chapel, and dining and meeting areas, was set in a secluded location well off the main road.

A follow-up investigation revealed that the children's births had been officially registered at the county courthouse and that the needed homeschooling papers had been filed with the State Board of Education for each of the school-age children living at the compound—meaning that they were exempt from required attendance at public schools.

Polygamy is a criminal offense in Utah and is banned under the state's constitution. It has been officially repudiated by the mainstream Mormon Church since 1890. After determining that Leon was married concurrently to multiple women, SBI agents took him into custody and interviewed each of his wives. Each told much the same story of how she had been promised by her parents to Leon at an early age, how she had been married in a small ceremony, and how she had borne Leon's children. What surprised investigators, though, was the women's agreement that their way of life, while it might not be common in the wider society, was a matter of choice—and that they should be left alone to practice their faith. "Taeler's committed no crime in the eyes of God," said Adaleen, Leon's first wife, speaking for the others. "We should be free to practice our religion just like others are," she said.

Hendy, another of the wives, pointed out that members of the American Indian Church have been allowed to use peyote in their religious ceremonies, even though it is a banned drug, unavailable to non-Native Americans. "If they can smoke peyote, then why can't we get married and live the way we want to?" she asked. "It's our religion, and it's supposed to be a free country."

Think about it

1. Not all women involved in polygamous unions would agree with Adaleen and Hendy, and those who oppose polygamy argue not only that it is illegal, but that it degrades women, devalues the family, and victimizes young women who are forced into arranged unions. Nonetheless, there are those who would agree with Adaleen and Hendy that the practice should be allowed based on constitutional guarantees of freedom of religion. Which perspective makes more sense to you? Why?
2. Do a bit of historical research and see if you can learn the legal history of the practice of polygamy in the United States. When did it become illegal? Why?
3. What rights, if any, should members of minority faiths have when they advocate or engage in behavior that goes beyond social norms or violates the law? Give some examples.
4. Would the rights you identified above extend to the practice of polygamy? Why or why not?

George Frey/AFP/Newscom

A polygamist family in Utah. Why is the practice of polygamy a violation of the criminal law? Should it be?

Note: Who's to Blame boxes provide fictionalized critical thinking opportunities, and are not actual cases.

■ **criminality** A behavioral predisposition that disproportionately favors criminal activity.

■ **criminal behavior** Human activity, both intentional and negligent, that violates the criminal law. It may include a failure to act when there is a legal obligation to do so.

Our definition is in keeping with the work of Jack P. Gibbs, a notable contemporary criminologist, who writes that the *purpose* of criminology is to offer well-researched and objective answers to four basic questions: (1) "Why do crime rates vary?" (2) "Why do individuals differ as to criminality?" (3) "Why is there variation in reactions to crime?" and (4) "What are the possible means of controlling criminality?"[33] It is important to note that our definition and Gibbs's guiding queries encompass a number of different terms that are sometimes easily confused. Criminology, **criminality**, crime, deviance, and **criminal behavior** are five concepts used in this chapter and throughout this book, and learning the definition of each provides a good start for anyone studying in this field.

As a field of study, criminology in its present form is primarily a social scientific discipline. Contemporary criminologists generally recognize, however, that their field is *interdisciplinary*—that is, it draws upon other disciplines to provide an integrated approach to understanding the problem of crime in contemporary society and to advance solutions to the problems crime creates. Hence, anthropology (especially cultural anthropology or ethnology), biology, sociology, political science, psychology, psychiatry, economics, ethology (the study of character), medicine, law, philosophy, ethics, and numerous other fields all have something to offer the student of criminology, as do the tools provided by statistics, computer science, and other forms of scientific and data analysis (see Figure 1–3).

A criminalist at work. Crime-scene investigators, like the person shown here, can provide crucial clues needed to solve crimes. How does the work of a criminologist differ from that of a criminalist? Would you like either kind of work?

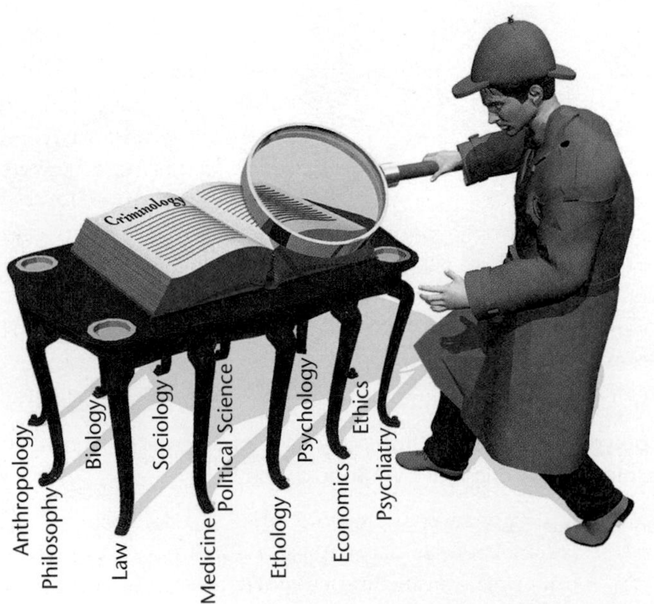

FIGURE 1-3 | **Criminology's Many Roots**

Source: Schmalleger, Frank J., *Criminology*. Printed and Electronically reproduced by permission of Pearson Education, Inc., Upper Saddle River, New Jersey.

The interdisciplinary nature of criminology was well stated by Jim Short, past president of the American Society Criminology (ASC), who said, "The organization of knowledge by traditional disciplines has become increasingly anachronistic, as the generation of knowledge has become more interdisciplinary. From its earliest beginnings, when philosophers grappled with relationships between human nature and behavior and biologists sought to relate human physiology to behavior, criminology's concerns have reached across virtually all disciplines that focus on the human condition. Additionally, much of the impetus for criminology has come from concerns that crime be controlled. Criminology thus cuts across professions as well as disciplines."[34]

It is important to note that, although criminology may be interdisciplinary as well as cross-professional, few existing explanations for criminal behavior have been successfully or fully integrated. Just as physicists today are seeking a unified field theory to explain the wide variety of observable forms of matter and energy, criminologists have yet to develop a generally accepted integrated approach to crime and criminal behavior that can explain the many diverse forms of criminality while also leading to effective social policies in the area of crime control. The attempt to construct criminological theories that are relevant to the problems of today is made all the more difficult because, as discussed earlier, the phenomenon under study—crime—is very wide-ranging and is subject to arbitrary and sometimes unpredictable legalistic and definitional changes.

■ **criminal justice** The scientific study of crime, the criminal law, and components of the criminal justice system, including the police, courts, and corrections.

■ **criminologist** One who is trained in the field of criminology; also, one who studies crime, criminals, and criminal behavior.

■ **criminalist** A specialist in the collection and examination of the physical evidence of crime.

A successfully integrated field of criminology must bring together the contributions of various theoretical perspectives and disciplines, but it must also—if it is to have any relevance—blend the practical requirements of our nation's judicial system with emotional and rational calls for morality and justice. Is the death penalty, for example, justified? If so, on what basis? Is it because it is a type of vengeance and therefore deserved? Can we say that it is unjustified because many sociological studies have shown that it does little to reduce the rate of serious crime such as murder? Just what do we mean by "justice," and what can criminological studies tell us—if anything—about what is just and what is unjust?

The editors of the journal *Theoretical Criminology*,[35] which began publication over a decade ago, wrote in the inaugural issue that "criminology has always been somewhat of a haphazardly-assembled umbrella-like structure which nevertheless usefully shelters a variety of theoretical interests that are espoused and employed by different disciplinary, methodological and political traditions." Such a structure, they said, "has obvious advantages, notably that it facilitates an interdisciplinary and inclusivist formation rather than supposing an exclusive but contentious 'core.' But one of its weaknesses is that its inhabitants, many of whom shuttle backwards and forwards between it and their parent disciplines, tend to communicate honestly and meaningfully only with those who speak the same theoretical language."[36] In other words, while the field of criminology can benefit from the wide variety of ideas available via a multiplicity of perspectives, all of which seek to understand the phenomenon we call "crime," successful cross-disciplinary collaboration can be quite difficult.

As our earlier definition of criminology indicates, however, it is more than a field of study or a collection of theories; it is also a discipline and a profession.[37] More than a decade ago, in his presidential address to the ASC, Charles F. Wellford identified the "primary purposes" of the criminology profession: "Controlling crime through prevention, rehabilitation, and deterrence and ensuring that the criminal justice system reflects the high aspiration we have as a society of 'justice for all' characterize the principal goals that in my judgment motivate the work of our field."[38]

Notably, criminology also contributes to the discipline of **criminal justice**, which emphasizes application of the criminal law and study of the components of the justice system, especially the police, courts, and corrections. As one author stated, "Criminology gives prominence to questions about the *causes of criminality*, while the *control of lawbreaking* is at the heart of criminal justice."[39] Learn more about the interdisciplinary nature of criminology via **Web Extra 1–3**. Read a few articles describing the nature of contemporary criminology at **Library Extras 1–1, 1–2,** and **1–3**.

Peter Casolino/Alamy Images

A police officer speaks to a group of young people. Criminology examines the causes of crime and seeks ways to prevent or control it. Criminal justice examines the criminal justice system, including police, courts, and corrections. How do the two disciplines complement one another?

What Do Criminologists Do?

A typical dictionary definition of a **criminologist** is "one who studies crime, criminals, and criminal behavior."[40] Occasionally, the term *criminologist* is used broadly to describe almost anyone who works in the criminal justice field, regardless of formal training. There is a growing tendency, however, to reserve application of the term *criminologist* to academics, researchers, and policy analysts with advanced degrees who are involved in the study of crime and crime trends and in the analysis of societal reactions to crime. Hence, it is more appropriate today to describe specially skilled investigators, crime-laboratory technicians, fingerprint experts, crime-scene photographers, ballistics experts, and others who work to solve particular crimes as criminalists. A **criminalist** is "a specialist in the collection and examination of the physical evidence of crime."[41] Police officers, corrections professionals, probation and parole officers, judges, district attorneys, criminal defense attorneys, and others who do the day-to-day work of the criminal justice system are best referred to as criminal justice professionals.

Academic criminologists and research criminologists generally hold doctoral degrees (PhDs) in the field of criminology or criminal justice from an accredited university. Some criminologists hold degrees in related fields like sociology and political science but have specialized in the study and control of crime and deviance. Most PhD criminologists teach either criminology or criminology-related subjects in institutions of higher learning, including universities and two- and four-year colleges. Nearly all criminology professors are involved in research or writing projects by which they strive to advance criminological knowledge. Some PhD criminologists are strictly researchers and work for federal agencies like the National Institute of Justice (NIJ), the Bureau of Justice Statistics (BJS), and the National Criminal Justice Reference Service (NCJRS) or for private (albeit often government-funded) organizations with names such as RAND and the Search Group, Inc.

The results of criminological research in the United States are generally published in journals like *Criminology* (the official publication of the American Society of Criminology [ASC]), *Theoretical Criminology*, *Justice Quarterly* (the Academy of Criminal Justice Sciences), *Crime and Delinquency*, the *American Journal of Criminal Justice* (the Southern Criminal Justice Association), the *Journal of Qualitative Criminology*, *Social Problems*, and *Victimology*.[42] International English-language journals are numerous and include the *Canadian Journal of Criminology*, the *Australian and New Zealand Journal of Criminology*, and the *British Journal of Criminology*. Read some of these journals and visit the organizations that sponsor them at **Web Extra 1–4**.

Private security provides another career track for individuals interested in criminology and criminal justice.

People who have earned master's and bachelor's degrees in the field of criminology often find easy entrance into police investigative or support work, probation and parole agencies, court-support activities, and correctional (prison) work. Criminologists also work for government agencies interested in the development of effective social policies intended to deter or combat crime. Many criminologists with master's degrees also teach at two- and four-year colleges and schools.

Private security provides another career track for individuals interested in criminology and criminal justice. The number of personnel employed by private security agencies today is twice that of public law enforcement agencies, and the gap is widening. Many upper- and mid-level private managers working for private security firms hold criminology or criminal justice degrees. The same may soon be true for the majority of law enforcement personnel, especially those in managerial positions.

Anyone trained in criminology has many alternatives (see Table 1–1). Some people with undergraduate degrees in criminology or criminal justice decide to go on to law school. Some teach high school, whereas others become private investigators. Many criminologists provide civic organizations (such as victims' assistance and justice advocacy groups) with much-needed expertise, a few

TABLE 1-1 | What Do Criminologists Do?

The term *criminologist* is usually applied to credentialed individuals, such as those holding advanced degrees in the field, who engage in the study of crime, criminal behavior, and crime trends. The word *criminalist* is used to describe people who specialize in the collection and examination of the physical evidence associated with specific crimes. Others working in the criminal justice system are called *criminal justice professionals*. This table and Figures 1-4 and 1-5 illustrate these differences.

Activities of Criminologists	
Data gathering	Public service
Data analysis	Analysis of crime patterns and trends
Theory construction	Scholarly presentations and publications
Hypothesis testing	Education and training
Social policy creation	Threat assessment and risk analysis
Public advocacy	Service as an expert witness at trial or in other court proceedings
Jobs in the Field of Criminalistics	
Forensics examiner	Crime-scene photographer
Crime-laboratory technician	Polygraph operator
Ballistics expert	Fingerprint examiner
Crime-scene investigator	
Jobs in the Field of Criminal Justice	
Law enforcement officer	Judge
Probation or parole officer	Defense attorney
Correctional officer	Prosecutor
Prison program director	Jailer
Cybercrime investigator	Private security officer
Juvenile justice worker	Victims' advocate

■ **theoretical criminology** A subfield of general criminology, it posits explanations for criminal behavior.
■ **theory** A series of interrelated propositions that attempts to describe, explain, predict, and ultimately control some class of events. A theory gains explanatory power from inherent logical consistency and is tested by how well it describes and predicts reality.
■ **general theory** A theory that attempts to explain all (or at least most) forms of criminal conduct through a single overarching approach.
■ **unicausal** Having one cause. Unicausal theories posit only one source for all that they attempt to explain.
■ **integrated theory** An explanatory perspective that merges (or attempts to merge) concepts drawn from different sources.

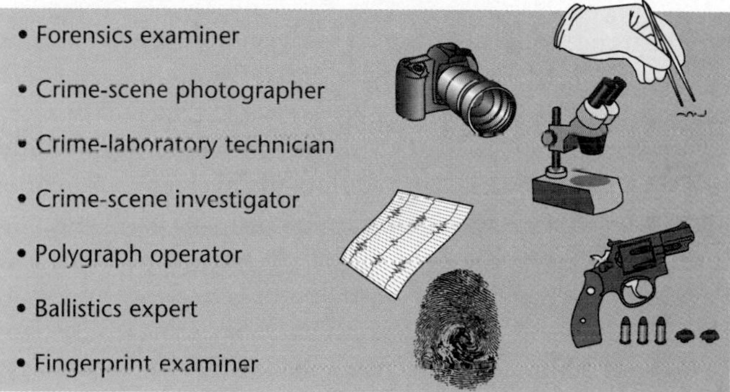

FIGURE 1-4 | **Jobs in the Field of Criminalistics**

Source: Schmalleger, Frank J., *Criminology*. Printed and Electronically reproduced by permission of Pearson Education, Inc., Upper Saddle River, New Jersey.

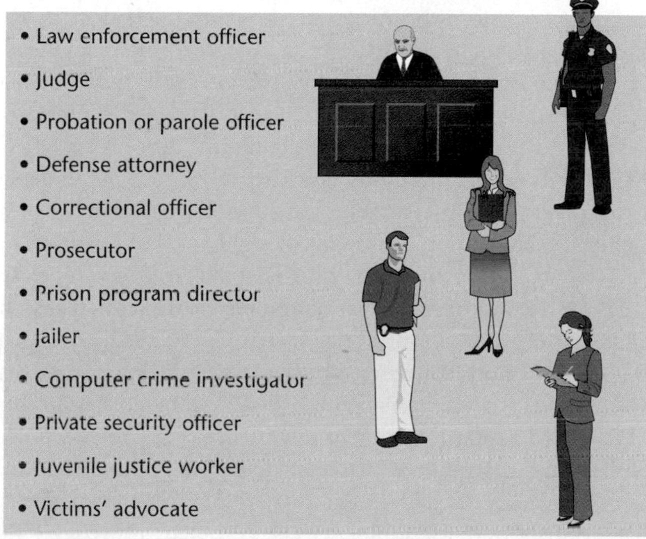

FIGURE 1-5 | **Jobs in the Field of Criminal Justice**

Source: Schmalleger, Frank J., *Criminology*. Printed and Electronically reproduced by permission of Pearson Education, Inc., Upper Saddle River, New Jersey.

work for politicians and legislative bodies, and some appear on talk shows to debate the pros and cons of various kinds of social policies designed to fight crime. Some criminologists even write books like this one! For more thoughts on the role of criminologists in the twenty-first century, read **Library Extra 1–4**.

Theoretical Criminology

Theoretical criminology, a subfield of general criminology, is the type of criminology most often found in colleges and universities. Theoretical criminology, rather than simply describing crime and its occurrence, posits explanations for criminal behavior. As Sutherland stated, "The problem in criminology is to explain the criminality of behavior. However, an explanation of criminal behavior should be a specific part of [a] general theory of behavior and its task should be to differentiate criminal from noncriminal behavior."[43]

To explain and understand crime, criminologists have developed many theories. As we shall see in Chapter 2, a **theory**, at least in its ideal form, is made up of clearly stated propositions that posit relationships, often of a causal sort, between events and things under study. An old Roman theory, for example, proposed that insanity was caused by the influence of the moon and may even follow its cycles—hence the term *lunacy*.

Theories attempt to provide us with explanatory power and help us understand the phenomenon under study. The more applicable a theory is found to be, the more generalizable it is from one specific instance to others—in other words, the more it can be applied to other situations. A **general theory** of crime is one that attempts to explain all (or at least most) forms of criminal conduct through a single overarching approach. Unfortunately, as Don M. Gottfredson, past president of the ASC, observed, "Theories in criminology tend to be unclear and lacking in justifiable generality."[44] When we consider the wide range of behaviors regarded as criminal—from murder to drug use to white-collar crime to cybercrime—it seems difficult to imagine one theory that can explain them all or that might even explain the same type of behavior under varying circumstances. Still, many past theoretical approaches to crime causation were **unicausal** while attempting to be all-inclusive; that is, the approaches posited a single identifiable source for all serious deviant and criminal behavior.

An **integrated theory**, in contrast to a general theory, does not necessarily attempt to explain all criminality but is distinguishable by the fact that it merges (or attempts to merge) concepts drawn from different sources. As noted criminologist Gregg Barak stated, "An integrative criminology seeks to bring together the diverse bodies of knowledge that represent the full array of disciplines that study crime."[45] Hence, integrated theories provide potentially wider explanatory power than narrower formulations. Don C. Gibbons, professor of sociology at Portland State University, noted, "The basic idea of theoretical integration is straightforward; it concerns the combinations of single theories or elements of those theories into a more comprehensive argument. At the same time, it would be well to note that in practice, integration is a matter of degree: some theorists have

■ **translational criminology** A form of criminology whose purpose it is to translate the results of research into workable social policy.

combined or integrated more concepts or theoretical elements than have others."[46]

Both the general applicability and the theoretical integration of criminological theories to a wide variety of law-violating behaviors are intuitively appealing concepts. Even far more limited attempts at criminological theorizing, however, often face daunting challenges. "As we shall see," noted Gibbons, "criminologists have not managed to articulate a large collection of relatively formalized arguments in a general or integrated form."[47] So, although we will use the word *theory* in describing the many explanations for crime covered by this text, it should be recognized that the word will only loosely apply to many of the perspectives on crime causation that we will discuss.

As we shall learn in Chapter 2, many social scientists insist that, to be considered theories, explanations must consist of sets of clearly stated, logically interrelated, and measurable propositions. The fact that only a few of the theories described in this text rise above the level of organized conjecture—and those offer only limited generalizability and have rarely been integrated—is one of the greatest challenges facing criminology today.

Criminology and Social Policy

The ultimate outcome of successful criminological theorizing is a set of meaningful social policies based on scientific evidence that proves the theory's usefulness (see Chapter 2). Translating the results of research in the field of criminology into workable social policy is sometimes referred to as **translational criminology**. The National Institute of Justice (NIJ), an arm of the U.S. Department of Justice, explains it this way: "The idea of translational criminology is simple, yet powerful: If we want to prevent, reduce and manage crime, we must be able to translate scientific discoveries into policy and practice."[48]

It is not always easy to translate research into practice, however, even when solid evidence points to needed changes in policy. Some policy implications, such as those relating to the physical environment, for example, are relatively easy to implement. Not only do most criminologists agree that such changes, such as installing brighter lighting in crime-prone areas, can be effective at preventing crime, but they are also easy to implement.

Other policy innovations, especially those calling for cultural or social changes, can be difficult to implement, even when there is strong evidence for their likely success. In a recent example, an editorial in the highly regarded British magazine, *New Scientist*, asked this question: "Why are we so reluctant to accept that on-screen violence is bad for us?"[49] The article, entitled "In Denial," noted that "by the time the average U.S. schoolchild leaves elementary school, he or she will have witnessed more than 8,000 murders and 100,000 other acts of violence on television." For children who play computer games and watch cable TV, the numbers will be far higher. Scientific studies show the obvious detrimental effects of media violence, according to the article, "yet every time a study claims to have found a link between aggression, violence, educational, or behavioral problems and TV programs or computer games, there are cries of incredulity. . . ."[50]

A number of professional groups—including the American Medical Association, the American Academy of Pediatrics, the American Psychological Association, and the American Academy of Child and Adolescent Psychiatry—agree that violence in television, music, video games, and movies leads to increased levels of violent behavior among children.[51] A joint statement issued by those organizations says that the effects of violence in the media "are measurable and long-lasting." The groups reached the conclusion "based on over 30 years of research . . . that viewing entertainment violence can lead to increases in aggressive attitudes, values and behaviors, particularly in children." Moreover, "prolonged viewing of media violence can lead to emotional desensitization toward violence in real life." Similarly, some years ago the Federal Trade Commission (FTC) issued a report[52] on teenage violence that concluded that "Hollywood aggressively markets violent movies, music and electronic games to children even when they have been labeled as appropriate only for adults."[53] The complete 116-page FTC report *Marketing Violent Entertainment to Children* is available at **Web Extra 1–5**.

Even after such findings, however, policy makers are reluctant to slow the production of violent media. For this reason, violence on TV and in video games is still prominent in the United States. *New Scientist* says media vendors dissuade "any criticism of a multibillion-dollar business" where they would lose profits resulting from any policies aimed at crime reduction.[54]

Anyone interested in the creation of sound social policy must respect the well-researched findings of today's criminologists. In the words of NIJ, "Successful dissemination of the results of criminological research requires that the evidence is implemented correctly. In other words, it is not just about finding evidence that something

■ **social problems perspective** The belief that crime is a manifestation of underlying social problems, such as poverty, discrimination, pervasive family violence, inadequate socialization practices, and the breakdown of traditional social institutions.

■ **social responsibility perspective** The belief that individuals are fundamentally responsible for their own behavior and that they choose crime over other, more law-abiding courses of action.

works; it is figuring out why it works and how to implement the evidence in real-world settings."[55]

Professional criminologists are acutely aware of the need to link sound social policy to the objective findings of well-conducted criminological research. A meeting of the ASC, for example, focused on the need to forge just such a link. At the meeting, ASC president Alfred Blumstein, of Carnegie Mellon University, told criminologists gathered there that "an important mission of the ASC and its members involves the generation of knowledge that is useful in dealing with crime and the operation of the criminal justice system, and then helping public officials to use that knowledge intelligently and effectively."[56] Blumstein added, "So little is known about the causes of crime and about the effects of criminal justice policy on crime that new insights about the criminal justice system can often be extremely revealing and can eventually change the way people think about the crime problem or about the criminal justice system."[57]

FIGURE 1-6 | **The Theme of This Text: Social Problems versus Social Responsibility**

The Theme of This Text

This text builds on a social policy theme both by asking questions about the sources of crime and criminality and by asking what we can do to control crime. Our theme contrasts two perspectives now popular in U.S. society and in much of the rest of the world (see Figure 1–6). One point of view, termed the **social problems perspective**, holds that crime is a manifestation of underlying social problems such as poverty, discrimination, inequality of opportunity, breakdown of traditional social institutions, low level of formal education among some disadvantaged groups, pervasive family violence experienced by some during the formative years, and inadequate socialization practices that leave too many young people without the fundamental values necessary to contribute meaningfully to the society in which they live. Advocates of the social problems perspective, while generally agreeing that crime and violence are serious social problems, advance solutions based on what is, in effect, a public-health model. Adherents of that model say that crime must be addressed in much the same way as public-health concerns like AIDS, herpes, or avian flu.

At the core of today's thinking about crime exists a crucial distinction between those who believe that crime is a *manifestation of underlying social problems* beyond the control of individuals (the social problems perspective) and those who emphasize that crime is a matter of *individual responsibility* (the social responsibility perspective).

Proponents of the social problems perspective typically foresee solutions to the crime problem as coming in the form of large-scale government expenditures in support of social programs designed to address the issues that are perceived to lie at the root of crime. Government-funded initiatives, designed to enhance social, educational, occupational, and other opportunities, are perceived as offering programmatic solutions to ameliorate most causes of crime. The social problems approach to crime is characteristic of what social scientists term a *macro approach* because it portrays instances of individual behavior (crimes) as arising out of widespread and contributory social conditions that enmesh unwitting individuals in a causal nexus of uncontrollable social forces.

A contrasting perspective lays the cause of crime squarely at the feet of individual perpetrators. This point of view holds that individuals are fundamentally responsible for their own behavior and maintains that they choose crime over other, more law-abiding courses of action. Perpetrators may choose crime, advocates of this perspective say, because it is exciting, because it offers illicit pleasures and the companionship of like-minded thrill seekers, or because it is simply personally less demanding than conformity. This viewpoint, which we shall call the **social responsibility perspective**, has a close affiliation with what is known in criminology as rational choice theory (discussed in detail in Chapter 3). It is also closely associated with a strongly held belief in the importance of free will, which is common to Western societies.[58]

Advocates of the social responsibility perspective, with their emphasis on individual choice, tend to believe that social programs do little to solve the problem of crime because, they say, a certain number of crime-prone individuals, for a variety of personal reasons, will always make irresponsible choices. Hence, advocates of the social responsibility approach suggest highly personalized crime-reduction strategies based on firm punishments, imprisonment, individualized rehabilitation, and increased security as well as a wider use of police powers. The social responsibility perspective characteristically emphasizes a *micro approach* that tends to focus on individual offenders and their unique biology, psychology, background, and immediate life experiences.

Over time, the social responsibility perspective has substantially influenced national crime-control policy. Examples of conservatism in our nation's approach to criminals abound. The Violent Crime Control and Law Enforcement Act of 1994, for example (which is discussed in detail later in this text), expanded the number of capital crimes under federal law from a handful of offenses to 52.[59] The law also made billions of dollars available to municipalities to put 100,000 new police officers on the streets and allocated billions for states to build and operate prisons and incarceration alternatives like "boot camps." Prison funding was intended to ensure that additional prison cells would be available to put—and keep—violent offenders behind bars. A subchapter of the 1994 Violent Crime Control and Law Enforcement Act created a federal three-strikes-and-you're-out law that mandated life imprisonment for criminals convicted of three violent federal felonies or drug offenses. Similarly, the law increased or created new penalties for over 70 federal criminal offenses, primarily covering violent crimes, drug trafficking, and gun crimes. Since the 1994 federal legislation was passed, many states have moved to toughen their own laws against violent criminals; violent juveniles and repeat offenders have been especially targeted. The USA PATRIOT Act—enacted in 2001 and renewed with modifications in 2006—targets terrorism and crimes committed in support of terrorist activity. The PATRIOT Act, which was reauthorized again by Congress in 2011, has been criticized by many for going too far in limiting individual freedoms and restricting personal choice, although its supporters argue that its provisions are needed to fight the war on terrorism effectively. The PATRIOT Act and the crime of terrorism are discussed in more detail in Chapter 15.

Advocates of the social responsibility approach suggest crime-reduction strategies based on firm punishments, imprisonment, individualized rehabilitation, and increased security.

A note about wording is in order. Although the social responsibility perspective might also be termed the *individual responsibility perspective* because it stresses individual responsibility above all else, we've chosen to use the term *social responsibility perspective* instead because it holds that individuals must be ultimately responsible to the social group of which they are a part and that they should be held accountable by group standards if they are not. In short, this perspective is characterized by societal demands for the exercise of individual responsibility.

The Social Context of Crime

Crime does not occur in a vacuum. Every crime has a unique set of causes, consequences, and participants. Crime affects some people more than others, having a special impact on those who are direct participants in the act itself—offenders, victims, police officers, witnesses, and so on. Crime, in general, provokes reactions from its victims, from concerned groups of citizens, from the criminal justice system, and sometimes from society as a whole, which manifests its concerns via the creation of new social policy. Reactions to crime, from the everyday to the precedent-setting, may color the course of future criminal events.[60]

In this text, we shall attempt to identify and examine some of the many social, psychological, economic, biological, and other causes of crime while expounding on the many differing perspectives that have been advanced to explain both crime and criminality. Popular conceptions of criminal motivation are typically shaped by media portrayals of offender motivation, which often fail to take into consideration the felt experiences of the law violators. By identifying and studying this diversity of perspectives on criminality, we will discover the characteristic disjuncture among victims, offenders, the justice system, and society about the significance that each assigns to the behavior in question—and often to its motivation. It will not be unusual to find, for example, that sociological or psychological initiatives with which the offenders themselves do not identify are assigned to those offenders by theorists and others.

Making Sense of Crime: The Causes and Consequences of the Criminal Event

This text recognizes that criminal activity is diversely created and variously interpreted. In other words, this text depicts crime not as an isolated individual activity but as a *social event*.[61] Like other

■ **social relativity** The notion that social events are interpreted differently according to the cultural experiences and personal interests of the initiator, the observer, or the recipient of that behavior.

social events, crime is fundamentally a social construction.[62] To say that crime is a social construction is not to lessen the impact of the victimization experiences that all too many people undergo in our society every day, nor does such a statement trivialize the significance of crime-prevention efforts or the activities of members of the criminal justice system. Likewise, it does not underplay the costs of crime to individual victims and to society as a whole. It does recognize, however, that, although a given instance of criminal behavior may have many causes, it also carries with it many different kinds of meanings—at least one for offenders, another (generally quite a different meaning, of course) for victims, and still another for agents of the criminal justice system. Similarly, a wide range of social interest groups, from victims' advocates to prisoner "rights" and gun-control organizations, all interpret the significance of law-breaking behavior from unique points of view, and each arrives at different conclusions about what should be done about the so-called crime problem.

For these reasons, we have chosen to apply the concept of social relativity to the study of criminality.[63] **Social relativity** means that social events are interpreted differently according to the cultural experiences and personal interests of the initiator, the observer, or the recipient of that behavior. Hence, as a social phenomenon, crime means different things to the offender who commits it, to the criminologist who studies it, to the police officer who investigates it, and to the victim who experiences it firsthand.

Figure 1–7 illustrates both the causes and the consequences of crime in rudimentary diagrammatic form. In keeping with the theme of this text, it depicts crime as a social event. The figure consists of a foreground, which describes those features that immediately determine the nature of the criminal event (including responses to the event as it is transpiring), and a background, in which generic contributions to the crime can be seen along with interpretations of the event after it has taken place. We call the background causes of crime *contributions* and use the word *inputs* to signify the more immediate propensities and predispositions of the actors involved in the situation. Inputs also include the physical features of the setting in which a specific crime takes place. Both background contributions and immediate inputs contribute to and shape the criminal event.

The more or less immediate results or consequences of crime are termed *outputs*, whereas the term *interpretations* appears in the diagram to indicate that any crime has a lasting impact both on surviving participants and on society. As Figure 1–7 shows, although the criminal event may occur at a particular point in time and within a given setting, it is ultimately a result of the coming together of inputs provided by (1) the offender, (2) the criminal justice system, (3) the victim, and (4) society.

Crime and the Offender

Offenders bring with them certain background features, such as personal life experiences, a peculiar biology and genetic inventory (insofar as they are unique organisms), a distinct personality, personal values and beliefs, and various kinds of skills and knowledge (some of which may be useful in the commission

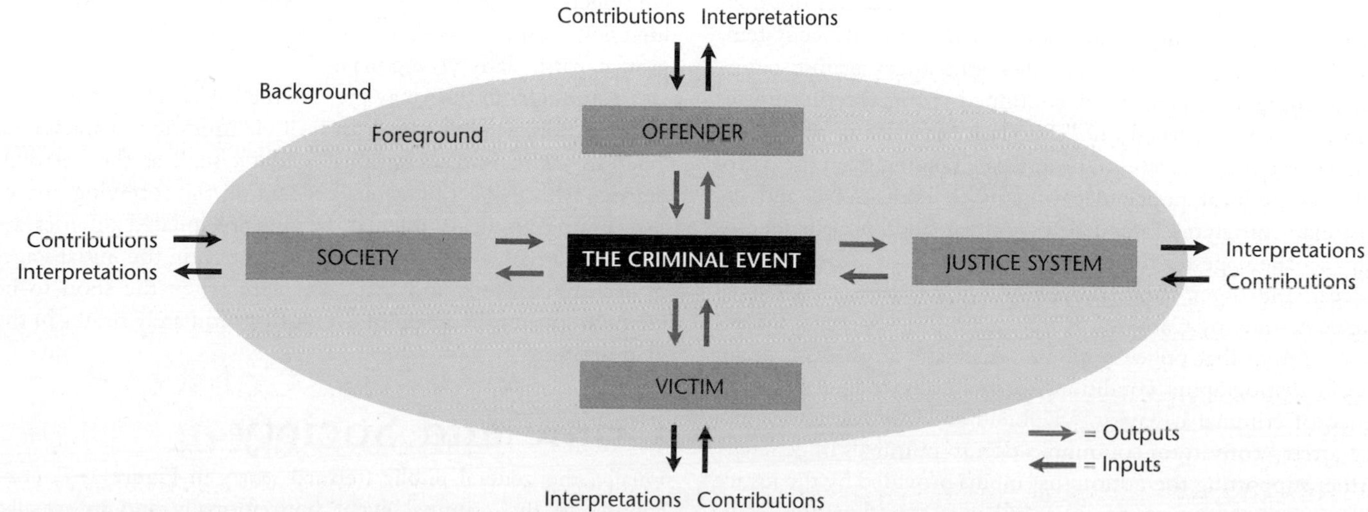

FIGURE 1-7 | **Interpreting the Criminal Event**

■ **criminal justice system** The various agencies of justice, especially the police, courts, and corrections, whose goal is to apprehend, convict, punish, and rehabilitate law violators.

of crime). Background contributions to crime can be vitally important. Research, for example, tends to cement the existence of a link between child-rearing practices and criminality in later life. Joan McCord, reporting on a 30-year study of family relationships and crime, found that self-confident, nonpunitive, and affectionate mothers tend to insulate their male children from delinquency and, consequently, later criminal activity.[64] Difficulties associated with the birthing process have also been linked to crime in adulthood.[65] Negative familial relationships and birth trauma are but two of the literally thousands of kinds of experiences individuals may have. Whether individuals who undergo trauma at birth and are deprived of positive maternal experiences will turn to crime depends on many other things, including their own mixture of other experiences and characteristics, the appearance of a suitable victim, the failure of the justice system to prevent crime, and the evolution of a social environment in which criminal behavior is somehow encouraged or valued.

Each of the parties identified in Figure 1–7 contributes immediate inputs to the criminal event. Foreground contributions by the offender may consist of a particular motivation, a specific intent (in many cases), or a drug-induced state of mind.

Crime and the Criminal Justice System

Like the offender, the **criminal justice system** (meaning the various agencies of justice such as the police, courts, and corrections) also contributes to the criminal event, albeit unwillingly, through its failure to (1) prevent criminal activity, (2) adequately identify and inhibit specific offenders prior to their involvement in crime, and (3) prevent the release of convicted criminals who later become repeat offenders. Such background contributions can be seen in prisons (a central component of the justice system) that serve as "schools for crime," fostering anger against society and building a propensity for continued criminality in inmates who have been "turned out." Similarly, the failure of system-sponsored crime-prevention programs—ranging from the patrol activities of local police departments to educational and diversionary programs intended to redirect budding offenders—helps set the stage for the criminal event.

On the other hand, proper system response may reduce crime. A study by Carol W. Kohfeld and John Sprague, for example, found that police response (especially arrest) can, under certain demographic conditions, dramatically reduce the incidence of criminal behavior.[66] Kohfeld and Sprague also found that arrest "constitutes communication to criminals in general," further supporting the notion that inputs provided by the justice system have the power to either enhance or reduce the likelihood of criminal occurrences. Immediate inputs provided by the justice system typically consist of features of the situation such as the presence or absence of police officers, the ready availability (or lack thereof) of official assistance, the willingness of police officers to intervene in precrime situations, and the response time required for officers to arrive at a crime scene.

Crime and the Victim

Few crimes can occur without a victim. Sometimes the victim is a passive participant in the crime, such as an innocent person killed on the street outside his or her home by random gunfire from a drive-by shooting. In such cases, the victim is simply in the proverbial wrong place at the wrong time. Even then, however, merely by being present the victim contributes his or her person to the event, thereby increasing the severity of the incident (that is, the random shooting that injures no one may still be against the law but is a far less serious crime than a similar incident in which somebody is killed). Sometimes, however, victims more actively contribute to their own victimization by appearing defenseless (having characteristics such as old age, drunkenness, or disability), by failing to take appropriate defensive measures (leaving doors unlocked or forgetting to remove the key from a car's ignition), by unwisely displaying wealth (flashing large-denomination bills in a public place), or simply by making other unwise choices (walking down a dark alley off Times Square at 3 A.M.). In a study of Canadian victimization, Leslie W. Kennedy and David R. Forde found that violent personal victimization "is contingent on the exposure that comes from following certain lifestyles," which was especially true "for certain demographic groups, particularly young males."[67]

> Sometimes victims actively contribute to their own victimization by making unwise choices.

Although lifestyles may provide the background that fosters victimization, a more active form of victimization characterizes "victims" who initiate criminal activity, such as the barroom brawler who picks a fight but ends up on the receiving end of the ensuing physical violence. Victim-precipitated offenses are those that involve active victim participation in the initial stages of a criminal event and that take place when the soon-to-be victim instigates the chain of events that ultimately results in the victimization.

Crime and Society

Finally, the general public (termed *society* in Figure 1–7) contributes to the criminal event both formally and informally. Society's formal contributions sometimes take the form of legislation, whereby crime itself is defined. Hence, as we shall

■ **socialization** The lifelong process of social experience whereby individuals acquire the cultural patterns of their society.

discuss in considerable detail in Chapter 14, society structures the criminal event in a most fundamental way by delineating (through legislation and via statute) which forms of activity are to be thought of as criminal.

Society's less formal contributions to crime arise out of generic social practices and conditions like poverty, poor and informal education, and various forms of discrimination by which pathways to success are blocked as well as **socialization** (the process whereby people acquire the cultural patterns of their society). Socialization has an especially important impact on crime causation because it provides the interpretative foundation used to define and understand the significance of particular situations in which we find ourselves, and it is upon those interpretations that we may (or may not) decide to act. Date rape, for example, can occur when a man concludes that his date "owes" him something for the money he has spent on her. That feeling, however inappropriate from the point of view of the victim and the justice system, probably has its roots in early learned experiences—including values communicated from television, the movies, and popular music—about gender-related roles under such circumstances. In other words, society, through the divergent values and expectations it places on people, property, and behavior under particular conditions, may provide the motivational basis for many offenses.

The contributions society makes to the backgrounds of both offender and victim and to the structure of the justice system and the influences each, in turn, has upon the general social order provide for a kind of "feedback loop" in our vision of crime (even though the loop is not shown in Figure 1–7 for fear of unnecessarily complicating it). Through socialization, for example, individuals learn about the dangers of criminal victimization, but when victimization occurs and is publicized, it reinforces the socialization process, leading to an increased wariness of others and so on. An example can be seen in the fact that children throughout the United States are routinely taught to avoid strangers and to be suspicious of people they do not know. A few decades ago, stranger avoidance was not ordinarily communicated to children; it entered cultural awareness following a number of horrendous and well-publicized crimes involving child victims and is now a shared part of the socialization process experienced by countless children every day throughout the United States.

The contributions made by society to crime are complex and far reaching. Some say that the content of the mass media (Web sites, television, movies, newspapers, popular music, etc.) can lead to crime by exposing young people to inappropriate role models and to the kinds of activity—violence and unbridled sexuality, for example—that encourage criminality.

Society's foreground contributions to crime largely emanate from the distribution of resources and the accessibility of services, which are often the direct result of economic conditions. In a study of the availability of medical resources (especially quality hospital emergency services), William G. Doerner found that serious assaults may "become" homicides when such resources are lacking but that homicides can be prevented through the effective utilization of capable medical technology.[68] Hence, societal decisions leading to the distribution and placement of advanced medical support equipment and personnel can effectively lower homicide rates in selected geographic areas, but homicide rates will be higher in areas where such equipment is not readily available. In Doerner's words, "[t]he causes of homicide transcend the mere social world of the combatants."[69]

The moments that immediately precede any crime are ripe with possibilities. When all the inputs brought to the situation by all those present coalesce into activity that violates the criminal law, a crime occurs. Together, the elements, experiences, and propensities brought to the situation by the offender and the victim, and those that are contributed to the pending event by society and the justice system, precipitate and decide the nature, course, and eventual outcome of the criminal event. As one well-known criminologist explained, "An understanding of crime and criminality as constructed from the immediate interactions of criminals, control agents, victims, and others, and therefore as emerging from a tangled experiential web of situated dangers and situated pleasures, certainly refocuses theories of criminal causality on the criminal moment."[70] While certain circumstances contribute to the criminal event as it unfolds, it is also important to note that some of the inputs brought to the situation may be inhibiting; that is, they may tend to reduce the likelihood or severity of criminal behavior.

The Consequences of Crime

As mentioned earlier, the causes of crime, however well documented, tell only half the criminological story. Each and every crime has consequences. Although the immediate consequences of crime may be relatively obvious for those parties directly involved (for example, the offender and the victim), crime also indirectly affects society and the justice system over the longer term. Figure 1–7 terms the immediate effects of crime *outputs*. As with the causes of crime, however, the real impact of such outputs is mediated by perceptual filters, resulting in what the figure terms *interpretations*. After a crime has taken place, each party to the event must make sense out of what has transpired. Such interpretations consist of cognitive, emotional, and (ultimately) behavioral reactions to the criminal event.

Interpretations are ongoing. They happen before, during, and after the criminal event and are undertaken by all those associated with it. In an interesting and detailed study of the interpretative activity of criminal justice system personnel, James F. Gilsinan documented what happens when callers reach the 9-1-1 operator on police emergency lines.[71] Because many prank calls and calls for information are made to 9-1-1 operators, the operators must judge the seriousness of every call that comes through. What the caller says was found to be only a small part of the informational cues that an operator seeks to interpret before assigning the call to a particular response (or nonresponse) category. Honest calls for help may go unanswered if the operator misinterprets the call. Hence, quite early in the criminal event, the potential exists for a crucial representative of the justice system to misinterpret important cues and to conclude that no crime is taking place.

Other interpretative activities may occur long after the crime has transpired, but they are at least as significant. The justice system, taken as a whole, must decide guilt or innocence and must attempt to deal effectively with convicted offenders. Victims must attempt to make sense of their victimization in a way that allows them to testify in court (if need be) and to pick up the pieces of their crime-shattered lives. Offenders must come to terms with themselves and decide whether to avoid prosecution (if escape, for example, is possible), accept blame, or deny responsibility. Whatever the outcome of these more narrowly focused interpretative activities, society—because of the cumulative impact of individual instances of criminal behavior—will also face tough decisions through its courts and law-making agencies. Society-level decision making may revolve around the implementation of policies designed to stem future instances of criminal behavior, the revision of criminal codes, or the elimination of unpopular laws.

Our perspective takes a three-dimensional integrative view of the social event termed *crime*. We will (1) attempt to identify and understand the multiple causes that give rise to criminal behavior, (2) highlight the processes involved in the criminal event as it unfolds, and (3) analyze the interpretation of the crime phenomenon, including societal responses to it. From this perspective, crime can be viewed along a temporal continuum as an emergent activity that (1) arises out of past complex causes; (2) assumes a course that builds on immediate interrelationships among the victim, offender, and social order that exist at the time of the offense; and (3) elicits a formal response from the justice system, shapes public perceptions, and (possibly) gives rise to changes in social policy after it has occurred.

The advantages of an integrative perspective can be found in the completeness of the picture that it provides. The integrative point of view results in a comprehensive and inclusive view of crime because it emphasizes the personal and social underpinnings as well as the consequences of crime. The chapters that follow employ the integrative perspective advocated here to analyze criminal events and to show how various theoretical approaches can be woven into a consistent perspective on crime. For a different point of view, one that describes crime in terms of the five dimensions of (1) law, (2) offender, (3) target and/or victim, (4) location, and (5) time of the incident, read **Library Extra 1–5**.

Corepics VOF/Shutterstock

A group of young people hanging out. The influence of groups can be strong on their members, explaining why sociological theories of crime causation have long been at the forefront of criminological thinking. What other kinds of explanations might help us understand crime?

The Primacy of Sociology?

This text recognizes the contributions made by numerous disciplines, including biology, economics, psychology, psychiatry, physiology, and political science, to the study of crime and crime causation. It is important to recognize, however, that the primary perspective from which many contemporary criminologists operate is a sociological one. Hence, a large number of today's theoretical explanations of criminal behavior are routinely couched in the language of social science and fall within the framework of sociological theory. The social problems versus social responsibility theme, around which this text is built, is in keeping with such a tradition.

CRIMINAL | PROFILES

Adam Lanza and the Sandy Hook School Shootings

On December 14, 2012, 20-year-old Adam Lanza, a socially awkward young man, went on a shooting rampage at Sandy Hook Elementary School in Newtown, Connecticut. In a matter of minutes, Lanza fired 155 bullets and shot to death 20 kindergarten students, four teachers, a principal, and the school's psychologist.[i] The shooting spree ended when Lanza turned one of his three guns on himself. Before the massacre, Lanza killed his mother at the house they shared only minutes from the school. The horrific shooting was covered by media services for days and reignited an intense national debate about gun control.

Although the Newtown shooting stood out as especially horrific because it ended so many innocent young lives, it is but one of a number of random mass shootings in the United States in recent years. In 2012 alone, there were 12 other random mass killings—including a July attack by a lone gunman in an Aurora, Colorado, movie theater where 12 people were killed and another 58 injured during a midnight showing of the movie *The Dark Knight Rises*.[ii] In that crime, the alleged shooter, 24-year-old James Eagan Holmes, who dressed as the Joker (a nefarious character from the film) during the shooting spree, was arrested outside the theater. He remains jailed as this text goes to press, having entered a plea of not guilty by reason of insanity on June 4, 2013.

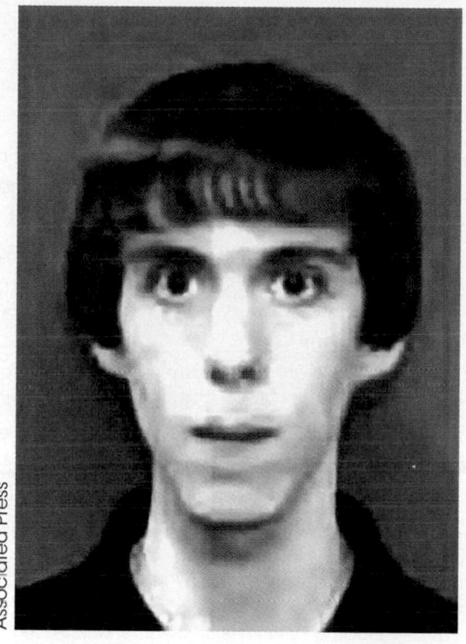

Associated Press

Adam Lanza, the Sandy Hook Elementary School shooter. Why do random mass shootings seem to be so commonplace in the United States today?

Experts tell us that the number of random mass shootings is on the increase. According to the *Wall Street Journal*, there "were 18 random mass shootings in the 1980s, 54 in the 1990s, and 87 in the 2000s."[iii] The *Journal*'s emphasis was on *random* shootings, and it noted that other mass killings—in which victims were in some way known to the shooter—had not significantly increased or decreased in number.

A fair question to ask would be "Why are the number of such random incidents increasing?" Some answers might be found in the personal characteristics of the shooters. Lanza and Holmes shared a number of things in common. Both were middle-class white males in their early twenties who were regarded by their peers as unnervingly intelligent. Holmes had been a former neuroscience graduate student at the University of Colorado's Anschutz Campus, whose academic career unraveled shortly before the movie theater shooting. Lanza, once a prominent member of his high school's technology club and an honors student, was said to have been extraordinarily bright by former teachers. Neither shooter had a previous criminal record.[iv]

What may have contributed to both incidents, however, was one additional feature the two men shared—a disordered personality.[v] According to the American Psychiatric Association, most mentally ill people do not turn to violence, although some forms of mental illness have been associated with aggression and criminal activity, especially when combined with illegal drug use.[vi]

Questions about Lanza's mental health were quickly raised following the Sandy Hook shootings by former friends and family members who knew him to be painfully shy, reclusive, and psychologically troubled. Described by personal acquaintances as "very bright" but emotionally disturbed, Lanza may have suffered from a form of Asperger's syndrome and was said to be impervious to physical pain. He had been on numerous medications intended to lower the anxiety that he experienced in everyday social situations, and prior to the Newtown shootings, his mother had repeatedly sought help in controlling her increasingly unresponsive and emotionally withdrawn son. Months after the Sandy Hook shooting, investigators revealed that Lanza had compiled a detailed record to include a timeline of mass shootings across the nation and may have wanted to achieve a "record" of some kind—by killing more than any other attacker ever had.[vii] Holmes, the Colorado shooter, met with at least three mental health professionals prior to the movie theater shooting, and CBS news reports that the fact "adds to the picture of Holmes being clearly on [psychiatrists'] radar in the time period leading up the shooting."[viii]

Notes

i. Michael Isikoff, Tom Winter, and Erin McClam, "Investigators: Adam Lanza Surrounded by Weapons at Home; Attack Took Less Than 5 Minutes," NBC News, March 28, 2013, http://openchannel.nbcnews.com/_news/2013/03/28/17501282-investigators-adam-lanza-surrounded-by-weapons-at-home-attack-took-less-than-5-minutes?lite (accessed March 29, 2013).

ii. "U.S. Mass Shootings in 2012," *The Washington Post*, December 14, 2012, http://professional.wsj.com/article/SB10001424127887323723104578185271857424036.html?mod=WSJ_hp_mostpop_read&mg=reno64-wsj; http://www.washingtonpost.com/wp-srv/special/nation/us-mass-shootings-2012 (accessed March, 20, 2013). The same article, however, notes that there has been no long-term increase in mass shootings; only in *random* mass shootings.

iii. David Kopel, "Guns, Mental Illness and Newtown," *Wall Street Journal*, December 17, 2012 (accessed March 21, 2013).

iv. Holly Yan, "Gunman's Family at a Loss to Explain Connecticut Shooting," CNN, December 17, 2012, http://www.cnn.com/2012/12/16/justice/connecticut-shooting-suspect-profile/index.html (accessed March 20, 2013).

v. The Autism Research Institute's Autistic Global Initiative Project notes that autism and Asperger's syndrome are neurodevelopmental issues and does not consider them to be mental health disorders.

vi. American Psychiatric Association, Council on Law and Psychiatry, *Access to Firearms by People with Mental Illness: Resource Document* (Arlington, VA: American Psychiatric Association, 2009).

vii. Howard Koplowitz, "Adam Lanza Spreadsheet: Sandy Hook Shooter Compiled Extensive List of Mass Murderers," *International Business Times*, March 18, 2013, http://www.ibtimes.com/adam-lanza-spreadsheet-sandy-hook-shooter-compiled-extensive-list-mass-murderers-1133557# (accessed March 28, 2013).

viii. Rick Sallinger, "James Holmes Saw Three Mental Health Professionals Before Shooting," CBS News, August 21, 2012, http://www.cbsnews.com/8301-201_162-57497820/james-holmes-saw-three-mental-health-professionals-before-shooting/ (accessed March 21, 2013).

Once we understand that guns and certain forms of mental illness can prove to be a dangerous combination, it is important to ask whether something can be done to predict and prevent episodes of random mass violence. Two days after the Newtown shooting, President Obama, for example, told those gathered at a memorial service at the town's high school, "We can't tolerate this anymore,"[ix] and promised to examine federal gun-control options.[x]

Yet the answer may not be as simple as gun control. Lanza and Holmes were known to have serious mental health problems, yet they were able to live freely in society, to arm themselves, and to attack unprotected and innocent people in what should have been safe public places. As this chapter will later explain in some detail, U.S. society is built on a delicate balance between the demand for *personal freedoms* and the need for *public safety*. The tears that appear in the social and legal fabric woven from the attempt to achieve balance between these two contrasting goals is where crimes like random mass shootings can occur.

The case of Adam Lanza raises a number of interesting questions. Among them are the following:

1. What led Lanza to attack an elementary school and take so many lives?
2. What role did biology, society, and his mental state play in contributing to Lanza's crime?
3. Can future random mass shootings be prevented? If so, how?

ix. "Transcript: 'We Have Wept with You'; Obama Says in Newtown Speech," CNN, December 16, 2012, http://politicalticker.blogs.cnn.com/2012/12/16/breaking-we-have-wept-with-you-obama-says-in-newtown-speech (accessed March 20, 1013).

x. Jared A. Favole, "Obama Says All Gun Buyers Should Face Checks," *Wall Street Journal*, December 19, 2012, http://professional.wsj.com/article/SB10001424127887324461604578188680585236550.html?mod=WSJPRO_hps_MIDDLEThirdNews (accessed March 22, 2013).

Many would disagree, however, with those who claim that the sociological perspective should be accorded heightened importance in today's criminological enterprise. Those who argue in favor of the primacy of sociology emphasize the fact that crime, as a subject of study, is a social phenomenon. Central to any study of crime, they say, must be the social context of the criminal event because it is the social context that brings victims and criminals together.[72] Much of contemporary criminology rests on a tradition of social scientific investigation into the nature of crime and criminal behavior that is rooted in European and American sociological traditions that are now well over 200 years old.[73]

One of sociology's problems, however, has been its apparent reluctance to accept the significance of findings from other fields as well as its frequent inability to integrate such findings into existing sociological understandings of crime. Another has been its seeming inability to demonstrate conclusively effective means of controlling violent (as well as other forms of) crime. As Diana Fishbein, professor of criminology at the University of Baltimore, said, "Sociological factors play a role. But they have not been able to explain why one person becomes violent and another doesn't."[74]

The primary significance of crime and of criminal behavior is fundamentally social in nature, and any control over crime must stem from effective social policy.

While sociological theories continue to develop, new and emerging perspectives ask to be recognized. The role of biology in explaining criminal tendencies, for example, appears to be gaining strength as investigations into the mapping of human DNA continue. Charles F. Wellford, past president of the ASC, explained the current state of affairs, saying, "I strongly believe that the future development of causal theory is dependent upon our movement toward integrated theories that involve biological, social, and cultural dimensions. Our failure to achieve much in the way of understanding the causal sequences of crime is in part a reflection of our slowness in moving toward multidisciplinary, integrated theoretical structures. The fact is that for two-thirds of the twentieth century, as criminology developed, we remained committed to a small number of sociological models for which there is extensive proof of their important but limited value. Fortunately in the last 20 years, this has begun to change. Today we see under way substantial research efforts that are based upon models of explanation that far exceed the traditional sociological approaches."[75]

Nonetheless, whatever new insights may develop over the coming years, it is likely that the sociological perspective will continue to dominate the field of criminology for some time to come. Such dominance is rooted in the fact that crime—regardless of all the causative nuances that may be identified in its development—occurs within the context of the social world. As such, the primary significance of crime and of criminal behavior is fundamentally social in nature, and any control over crime must stem from effective social policy.

SUMMARY

- At the start of this chapter, the term *crime* was defined as a violation of the criminal law. Near the end of this chapter, we recognized the complexity of crime, calling it an "emergent phenomenon." In the process, crime was redefined as a lawbreaking event whose significance arises out of an intricate social nexus involving a rather wide variety of participants.
- Deviance, or deviant behavior, refers to a violation of social norms. Some forms of behavior (such as murder, rape, and most serious crimes) are both criminal and deviant. Others may be deviant but not criminal (for example, nudity under certain circumstances), or may be criminal but not regarded as deviant by many members of society (for example, the use of marijuana).
- Decisions about what should be criminal are generally made by legislatures, at both the state and federal levels. Such decisions are made through a political process that involves input from social interest groups, including those in favor of criminalizing certain behaviors and those opposed to criminalizing them.
- *Criminology* is "an interdisciplinary profession built around the scientific study of crime and criminal behavior, including their forms, causes, legal aspects, and control." The term *criminologist* is applied to credentialed individuals who engage in the study of crime, criminal behavior, and crime trends. *Criminalist* is used to describe people who specialize in the collection and examination of the physical evidence associated with specific crimes. *Criminal justice professionals* include law enforcement officers, judges, criminal defense attorneys, prosecutors, cybercrime investigators, victims' advocates, jailers, correctional officers, and so on.
- Criminologists are acutely aware of the need to link sound social policy to the objective findings of well-conducted criminological research. Unfortunately, political considerations and long-standing traditional solutions have formed the basis for much crime-control policy in the past, and the situation is only slowly changing.
- This text builds on a social policy theme by asking what the sources of crime and criminality are and what we can do to control crime. The theme contrasts two perspectives: The *social responsibility perspective* holds that crime is a matter of individual responsibility; the *social problems perspective* holds that crime is a manifestation of underlying social problems beyond the control of individuals.
- This text sees crime as a social event, not an isolated individual activity. A given instance of criminal behavior may have many causes and many different kinds of meanings. Social relativity holds that social events are interpreted differently according to the cultural experiences and personal interests of the initiator, the observer, and the recipient of that behavior.
- The discipline of sociology has had the most impact on theoretical understandings of crime and crime causation, so a large number of today's theoretical explanations of criminal behavior are routinely couched in the language of social science and fall within the framework of sociological theory. Nonetheless, it is important to recognize the contributions made by numerous other disciplines (biology, economics, psychology, psychiatry, physiology, political science), making the study of crime and crime causation interdisciplinary.

KEY TERMS

consensus perspective, 6
crime, 3
criminal behavior, 10
criminalist, 11
criminality, 10
criminalize, 3
criminal justice, 11
criminal justice system, 18
criminologist, 11
criminology, 8
delinquency, 6
deviant behavior, 5
general theory, 13
integrated theory, 13
pluralist perspective, 6
socialization, 19
social policy, 8
social problems perspective, 15
social relativity, 17
social responsibility perspective, 15
theoretical criminology, 13
theory, 13
translational criminology, 14
unicausal, 13

QUESTIONS FOR REVIEW

1. What is crime? What is the definition of *crime* that the author of this text chose to use? How might the notion of crime change over time? What impact does the changing nature of crime have on criminology?
2. What is deviance? How are crime and deviance similar? How do they differ?
3. Who decides what should be criminal? How are such decisions made?
4. What is criminology? What do criminologists do? What are some of the employment opportunities available in the field of criminology?
5. How is social policy in the area of crime control determined? What role does criminological research play in the establishment of such policy?

6. What is the theme of this text? On what two contrasting viewpoints does it build?
7. What does it mean to say that "criminal activity is diversely created and variously interpreted"?
8. What discipline has contributed the most to theoretical understandings of crime causation over the past century?

QUESTIONS FOR REFLECTION

1. This text emphasizes the theme of social problems versus social responsibility. How would you describe both perspectives? How might social policy decisions based on these perspectives differ?
2. Do you think you might want to become a criminologist? Why or why not?
3. Are there any crimes today that you think should be legalized? If so, what are they? Why do you feel this way?
4. Can you think of any advances now occurring in the social or physical sciences that might soon have a significant impact on our understanding of crime and criminality? If so, what would those advances be? How might they affect our understanding of crime and criminal behavior?
5. How would you describe the various participants in a criminal event? How does each contribute to an understanding of the event?
6. In what way is contemporary criminology interdisciplinary? Why is the sociological perspective especially important in studying crime? What other perspectives might be relevant? Why?
7. How does contemporary criminology influence social policy? Do you think that policy makers should address crime as a matter of individual responsibility and accountability, or do you think that crime is truly a symptom of a dysfunctional society? Why?

Cultura Creative/Alamy

CHAPTER 2 WHERE DO THEORIES COME FROM?

LEARNING OUTCOMES

After reading this chapter, you should be able to answer the following questions:

- What is evidence-based criminology? How does the meaning of the word *evidence* in evidence-based criminology differ from the evidence found at a crime scene or the evidence used in criminal trials?
- What four eras have characterized the field of criminology over the past 100 years?
- What is a theory? What purposes do theories serve? What role do research and experimentation play in theory building in criminology?
- What is the role of criminological research in theory building? What is internal validity? External validity? How can threats to internal and external validity be addressed?
- What are the differences between quantitative and qualitative methods in the social sciences? What are the advantages and disadvantages of each method?
- What are some of the ethical considerations involved in conducting criminological research?
- How do criminological research and experimental criminology affect social policy?
- What sections might a typical research report contain?

■ **Follow the author's tweets about the latest crime and justice news at @schmalleger.**

Introduction

In mid-2012, 31-year-old Rudy Eugene was shot to death by Miami police officers on the McArthur Causeway after he attacked a homeless man under an overpass on the six-lane highway and ate the man's face.[1] A bicyclist who observed the frenzied attack alerted police, who intervened and ordered Eugene to the ground, but reports show that he growled at them and continued chewing on his victim. After an initial round into Eugene's torso failed to have any effect, officers shot him four more times, killing him. His victim, 65-year-old Ronald Poppo, who was critically injured, was taken to Miami's Jackson Memorial Hospital where physicians revealed that 80% of his face above his beard had been gnawed away. One of his eyes had been gouged out, and his other eye had been badly damaged, leaving him blind.[2]

Miami Herald/Getty Images

Rudy Eugene, also known as the "Miami Cannibal," was killed by police in 2012 while attempting to eat a homeless man alive. Can criminological theories explain his actions?

Video taken by a surveillance camera on the nearby Miami Herald building captured the entire incident. It showed that Eugene, whom the press later dubbed the Miami Cannibal, had spent about 30 minutes before the attack walking around his car that had broken down. He then left the disabled vehicle, stripping clothing from his body as he walked. The last thing he discarded was a Bible that he'd been clutching. Eugene then came across a prone Poppo lying underneath an overpass and began to beat him. The video showed Eugene pulling off Poppo's pants and hitting and biting him in an attack that lasted for 18 minutes before police arrived.

Although no one knows what drove Eugene to attack Poppo, some experts initially speculated that he had consumed bath salts, designer drugs with an effect similar to amphetamine and cocaine, prior to the attack. Bath salts have been known to raise body temperature to dangerous levels and to cause the brain to overheat, resulting in intense hallucinations. Evidence gathered from Eugene's car, including numerous water bottles that he had apparently consumed before the incident, and his behavior in removing all of his clothing seemed to support the bath salts theory. Toxicology studies of Eugene's remains, however, did not reveal the presence of any exotic drugs in his system, although they showed that he had smoked marijuana.[3]

In an interview given some time after the incident, Eugene's girlfriend suggested that he might have been possessed by the devil or acting under a curse.[4] Eugene, who was from Haiti, apparently believed in voodoo. "That wasn't him," his girlfriend told CBS news reporters. "That was his body but it wasn't his spirit." She said that Eugene had been studying the Bible and texting Bible verses to friends shortly before the attack. "Rudy was battling the devil," she concluded.

The remarks of Rudy Eugene's girlfriend reminded me of the first criminology class that I taught years ago at a small southern college in the heart of what was then referred to as the Bible belt. Many of my students were devoutly religious and thoroughly churched in hallowed concepts such as good and evil, sin, salvation, and redemption. When the three-month course was nearly over and a detailed discussion of biological, psychological, and sociological theories of crime causation had ended, I decided to do some research. I wanted to see which of the theories we had discussed most appealed to the majority of my students. On the last day of class, I took a brief survey. After explaining what I was about to do, I started with the question "How many of you think that most criminal behavior can be explained by the biological theories of crime causation we've studied?" Only one or two students raised their hands. This was a very small number because the class, a popular one, held 131 students and was taught in a small auditorium. "How many of you," I continued, "think psychological theories explain most crime?" Again, only a handful of students responded. "Well, then, how many of you feel sociological theories offer the best explanation for crime?" I asked. A few more hands went up. Still, the majority of students had not voted one way or the other. Fearing that my teaching had been for naught and not knowing what else to ask, I blurted out, "How many of you believe that 'the devil made him do it' is the best explanation for crime that we can offer?" At that, almost all the students raised their hands.

I realized then that an entire semester spent trying to communicate the best thoughts of generations of criminologists had had little impact on most students in the class. They had listened to what I had to say, considered each of the perspectives

■ **evidence based** Built on scientific findings, especially practices and policies founded upon the results of randomized, controlled experiments.

■ **evidence-based criminology** A form of contemporary criminology that uses rigorous social scientific techniques, especially randomized, controlled experiments and the systematic review of research results. Also known as *knowledge-based criminology*.

I presented, and then dismissed all of them out of hand as so much idle conjecture—assigning them the status of ruminations sadly out of touch with the true character of human nature and lacking in appreciation for the true cosmic temper of human activity.

That class held a lesson for me greater than any that the students had learned: It taught me that contemporary criminological theory cannot be fully appreciated until and unless its fundamental assumptions are comprehended. Until students can be brought to see the value of scientific criminology and unless they can be shown why today's criminologists think and reason the way they do, it is impossible to convince them that the criminological enterprise is worthy of serious attention.

Even the best scientific evidence is rarely accorded the significance that it deserves by policy makers.

The lesson I learned that day was given voice by noted criminological researcher Lawrence W. Sherman, who, upon realizing that even the best scientific evidence the field has to offer is rarely accorded the significance that it deserves by policy makers, wrote: "The mythic power of subjective and unstructured wisdom holds back every field and keeps it from systematically discovering and implementing what works best."[5]

Evidence-Based Criminology

This chapter describes how criminologists use contemporary social scientific research methods in the development of criminological theories, policies, and practices that are **evidence based**. It is my way of showing to those embarking upon the study of criminology why the modern-day science of criminology has both validity and purpose—that is, how it is applicable to the problems and realities of today's world. Were it not, the study of criminology would be pointless, and the criminological enterprise would become irrelevant. Because contemporary criminology is built on a social scientific approach to the subject matter of crime, however, criminology—especially **evidence-based criminology** (also called knowledge-based criminology)—has much to offer as we attempt to grapple with the problems of crime and crime control now facing us.

Evidence-based criminology is an increasing popular form of contemporary criminology that is founded upon the experimental method. The method utilizes the techniques of the social sciences (especially randomized, controlled experiments) in theory testing. When used in this context, the word *evidence* refers to scientific findings, *not* to the kind of evidence gathered by the police or used in criminal trials.

Some authors credit David Farrington, Lloyd Ohlin, and James Q. Wilson with helping to popularize the use of randomized experiments in the field of criminology.[6] In the mid-1980s their influential book, *Understanding and Controlling Crime*, recommended the use of such experiments whenever possible to test assumptions in the justice field.[7] Shortly afterward, the National Institute of Justice (NIJ), under then-Director James C. Stewart, funded more than two dozen criminology-related experiments.[8] A decade later, Anthony Petrosino and his colleagues found that 267 criminological experiments had been conducted and published in English.[9]

In 2009, in recognition of the growing significance of evidence-based criminology, the executive board of the American Society of Criminology (ASC) established a new division of experimental criminology; the division's purpose is "the promotion and improvement of experimental evidence and methods in the advancement of criminological theory and evidence-based crime policy."[10]

Today, evidence-based criminology is given voice by the Academy of Experimental Criminology, which is based at the University of Pennsylvania, and by a number of important new journals including the *Journal of Experimental Criminology*, which is the first journal in the field of criminology to focus directly on experimental methods.[11] You can reach the Academy of Experimental Criminology via **Web Extra 2–1**. Another important voice in the area can be found at the University of Cambridge's Institute of Criminology in England. Learn more about the growing body of evidence-based findings in the field of criminology from the institute's experimental criminology Web page at **Web Extra 2–2**.

The Evolving Science of Criminology

In his seminal 2003 presidential address to the ASC, John H. Laub used the framework of life course theory (discussed in Chapter 7) to describe the history of criminological thought.[12] Laub identified three eras that he says have characterized the field of criminology over the past 100 years. The first era, said Laub, covered the years 1900 to 1930 and can "be thought of as the 'Golden Age of Research.'"[13] It was a time when data on crime and criminal behavior were largely gathered and evaluated independent of any particular ideational framework.

The second era, the period from 1930 to 1960, Laub called the "Golden Age of Theory" and described it as a time when intellectual theorizing "dominated the scene." Strangely, said Laub, during this second period, "there was no systematic attempt to link criminological research to theory."[14]

Era three extended from 1960 to 2000 and was "characterized by extensive theory testing of the dominant theories, using largely empirical methods." In other words, the third era identified by Laub was a time of scientific examination of the accuracy of criminological theories that had been advanced previously. Although he didn't address it directly, Laub indicated that the current era (that is, twenty-first-century criminology, or fourth era) is heir to the first three eras and contains "all possible offspring" of what came before.

As Laub's remarks show, criminologists over the past half century have undertaken the task of building a scientific or evidence-based criminology, as distinguished from what had been the "armchair criminology" of earlier times. Armchair criminologists offered their ideas to one another as conjecture—fascinating "theories" that could be debated (and sometimes were) *ad nauseam*. Although the ruminations of armchair criminologists may have achieved a considerable degree of popular acclaim through (1) the involvement of distinguished lecturers, (2) the association of such ideas with celebrated bastions of higher learning, and (3) their publication in prestigious essays, they were rarely founded on anything other than mere speculation.

The ideas of armchair criminologists followed in the intellectual tradition of medieval Christian theologians, who sometimes busied themselves with debates over questions like how many angels could fit on the head of a pin or whether Noah had forgotten to take certain types of insects on board the ark. They were the kinds of things one could probably never know with certainty, no matter how much the ideas were debated, and the ideas being debated were rarely amenable to real-world tests. Under such circumstances, one person's theory was another's fact and still another's wishful thinking.[15]

Although it is easy to dispense with armchair criminology as the relaxed musings of carefree intellectuals undertaken almost as sport, it is far more difficult to agree on the criteria necessary to move any undertaking into the realm of serious scientific endeavor. Present-day criminology is decidedly more scientific, however, than its intellectual predecessor—which means that many of its theories and policy recommendations are amenable to objective scrutiny and systematic testing.

Criminologists over the past century have undertaken the task of building a scientific or evidence-based criminology.

A variety of criteria have been advanced for declaring any endeavor "scientific." Among them are:[16]

- The systematic collection of related facts (as in the building of a database)
- An emphasis on the availability and application of the scientific method
- "The existence of general laws, a field for experiment or observation, and control of academic discourse by practical application"
- "The fact that it has been accepted into the scientific tradition"
- An "emphasis on a worthwhile subject in need of independent study even if adequate techniques of study are not yet available" (as in the investigation of paranormal phenomena)

Probably all the foregoing could be said of today's criminology. For one thing, criminologists do gather facts (Laub's "Golden Age of Research"). However, the mere gathering of facts, although it may lead to a descriptive criminology, falls short of offering satisfactory explanations for crime. Hence, most contemporary criminologists are concerned with identifying relationships among the facts they observe and with attempting to understand the many diverse causes of crime. This emphasis on unveiling causality moves criminology beyond the merely descriptive into the realm of conjecture and theory building. A further emphasis on measurement and objectivity gives contemporary criminology its scientific flavor.

Theory Building

A few years ago, Inspector Andy Parr, of the Sussex Police Department in England, reviewed crime statistics for the town of Brighton and found that violent crime was higher on nights

■ **hypothesis** A tentative explanation accounting for a set of facts that can be tested by further investigation.

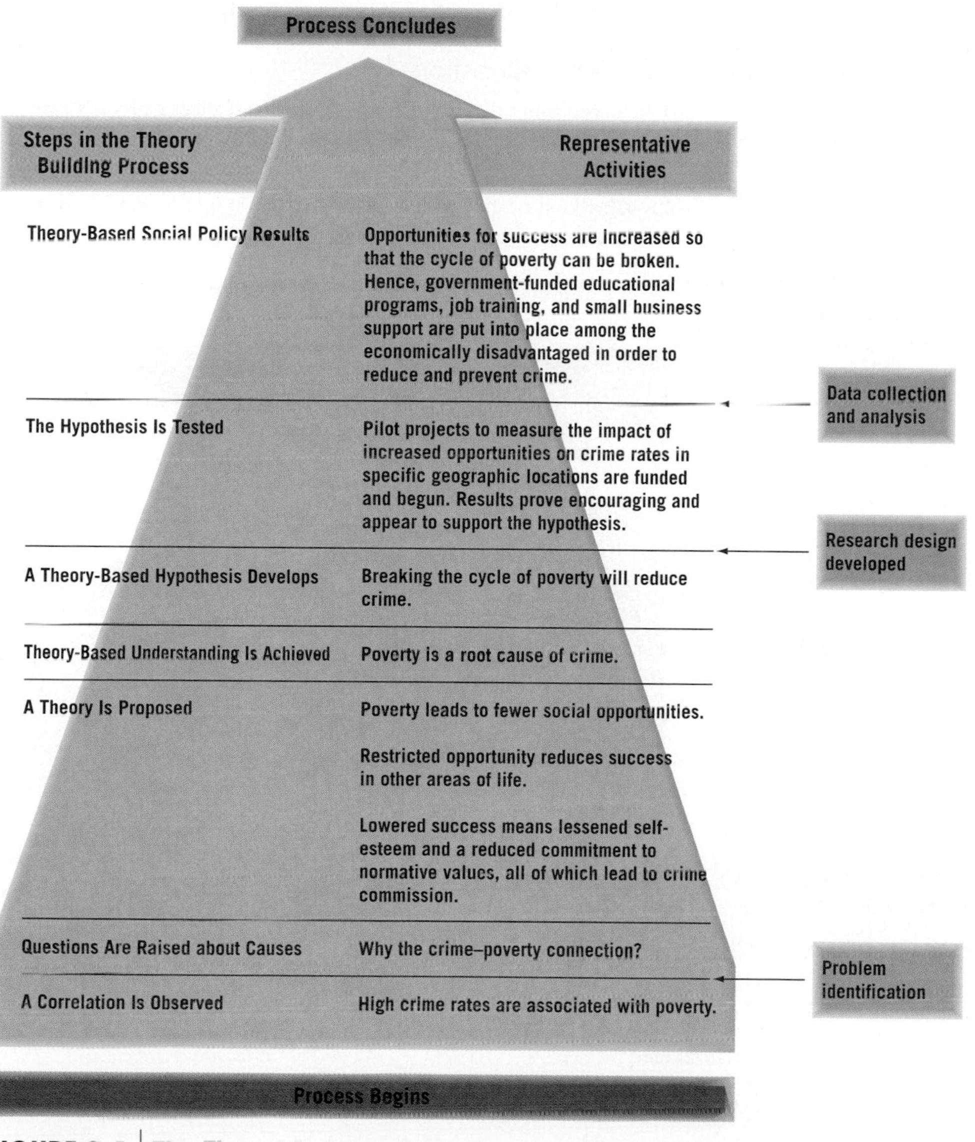

FIGURE 2–1 The Theory Building Process

when the moon was full.[17] "I compared a graph of full moons and a graph of last year's violent crimes and there is a trend," Parr told the United Kingdom's *Telegraph* newspaper. "People tend to be more aggressive" when the moon is full, Parr concluded. His findings were supported, he said, by his patrol experience. "When you try to reason with people on a full moon they become more aggressive and less rational," he told reporters. "When you try to reason with them on a full moon they become more argumentative."

Ultimately, the goal of research in criminology is the construction of theories or models that allow for a better understanding of criminal behavior and that permit the development of strategies intended to address the problem of crime. Simply put, a theory consists of a set of interrelated propositions that provides a relatively complete form of understanding (see Figure 2–1). Hence, even if we find that crime is higher when the moon is full, we must still ask why. Is it because the light from a full moon makes it possible for those who want to commit a crime to see better at night? If so, then we would expect crime to be higher in areas where there is no cloud cover than in areas with clouds. Likewise, lighted cities should show less of a rise in crime during a full moon than rural areas and small towns. In any event, a complete lunar theory of crime causation would contain specific propositions about the causal nature of the phenomena involved. For viewpoints on another issue, the influence of violent video games on adolescents' behavior, see the Crime in the News box.

The word *theory* can be defined in many ways. One cogent definition comes from Don M. Gottfredson, a well-known contemporary criminologist: "Theories consist of postulates [assumptions], theoretical constructs, logically derived hypotheses, and definitions. Theories can be improved steadily through hypothesis testing, examination of evidence from observations, revisions of the theory, and repetitions of the cycle, repeatedly modifying the theory in light of the evidence."[18] (A **hypothesis** is an explanation that accounts for a set of facts and that can be tested by further investigation.) Another well-known methodologist describes theories this way: "A theory is a set of related propositions that suggest why events occur in the manner that

CRIME | in the NEWS

Do Violent Video Games Make Kids Kill?

Mass shooters have been known to play violent video games before their sprees, killing people like so many icons on the screen. The two killers at Columbine High School in 1999 were addicted to Mortal Kombat, and Anders Breivik, the Norwegian gunman who killed 77 people in 2011, said he played Call of Duty to train himself.

But did video games make these people violent? Ninety percent of teenage boys play video games—often violent ones like Mortal Kombat and Grand Theft Auto—and yet the juvenile arrest rate for violent crimes declined sharply from 1994 to 2003 and has remained relatively stable since then.

Even so, video games seem to be getting even more savage, with titles like Super Columbine Massacre, Splatterhouse, and Thrill Kill. Manufacturers have set up a rating system to identify violent video games, but it has no teeth. Stores are expected to withhold violent games from younger kids voluntarily. Almost all violent games are in the Mature category, appropriate for ages 17 and up. The next level is an Adults Only (AO) rating, for ages 18 and over. Manufacturers consider an AO rating a sales killer, and very few violent games ever get it.

Some concerned parents have called for an outright ban on selling violent video games to minors, but that would mean removing free speech protections from video games, which courts refuse to do. In 2011, in what might well be the deathblow for the opposition, the U.S. Supreme Court completely struck down a California law that would have banned sales of violent video games to anyone under age 18. The Court rejected the argument that the interactive nature of video games has a stronger impact on young minds than, say, violent movies, which have free speech protections. Justice Antonin Scalia argued that even literature is interactive, writing: "*Grimm's Fairy Tales*, for example, are grim indeed."

Most Americans, however, did not agree with the ruling. A Rasmussen poll taken afterward found that 67% of the public thought states should have the right to prohibit sales of video games. In addition, several studies have concluded that violent video games cause higher rates of aggression in teenagers. A number of researchers have challenged those conclusions, however, arguing that other causes of aggression were not ruled out.

Meanwhile, two new studies show that multiplayer video games can actually reduce aggressiveness when the players work together. The studies, published in 2012, found that college students who teamed up to play violent video games later showed more cooperative behavior than those who played the games competitively.

Discussion Questions

1. Do you think that violent video games can affect a player's emotions and influence his or her view of the world? Might they also influence his or her real-life behavior? If so, how?
2. What kind of social scientific experiment might be devised to test the assertion that violent video games influence their players' behavior in the real world?

Thomas Frey/Glow Images

A young man plays a game in a video arcade. Some say that violent electronic games can make young people act out their violent fantasies. Other studies, however, seem to show that that is not the case. What do you think?

Sources: Adam Liptick, "Justices Reject Ban on Violent Video Games for Children," *New York Times*, June 27, 2011, http://www.nytimes.com/2011/06/28/us/28scotus.html?pagewanted=all. Shankar Vedantam, "It's a Duel: How Do Violent Video Games Affect Kids?," National Public Radio, July 7, 2011, http://www.npr.org/2011/07/07/137660609/its-a-duel-how-do-violent-video-games-affect-kids. "Violent Video Games Not So Bad When Players Cooperate," *Science Daily*, September 4, 2012, http://www.sciencedaily.com/releases/2012/09/120904170724.htm.

they do. The propositions that make up theories are of the same form as hypotheses: they consist of concepts and the linkages or relationships between them."[19]

These definitions both have something to offer. In fact, the definition of the term theory that we choose to use in this text combines aspects of both. For our purposes, then, a **theory** is a series of interrelated propositions that attempts to describe, explain, predict, and ultimately control some class of events. Theories gain explanatory power from inherent logical consistency and are "tested" by how well they describe and predict reality. In other words, a good theory provides relatively complete understanding, is supported by observations, and stands up to continued scrutiny.

Theories serve a number of purposes. For one thing, they give meaning to observations, explaining what we see in a particular setting by relating it to other things already understood. Hence, a theory of physics can explain the behavior of light by saying that light has properties of both waves and particles. Such a theory is immediately useful because we can easily grasp ideas like waves and particles, even if we have trouble conceptualizing light's essence.

Theories within criminology serve the same purpose as those within the physical sciences, but they are often more difficult to test. For example, few people can intuitively understand the motivation of "lust murderers" (a term developed by the Federal Bureau of Investigation and popularized by the media to refer to men who sexually abuse and kill women, often

■ **theory** A series of interrelated propositions that attempts to describe, explain, predict, and ultimately control some class of events. A theory gains explanatory power from inherent logical consistency and is "tested" by how well it describes and predicts reality.

■ **research** The use of standardized, systematic procedures in the search for knowledge.

■ **applied research** Research based on scientific inquiry that is designed and carried out with practical applications in mind.

■ **pure research** Research undertaken simply for the sake of advancing scientific knowledge.

■ **primary research** Research characterized by original and direct investigation.

■ **secondary research** Research based on new evaluations of existing information that has been collected by other researchers.

sadistically). Some psychiatric theories (discussed in Chapter 5) suggest that lust murderers kill because of a deep seated hatred of women. Hate is something that most minds can grasp, and a vision of lust murder as an extreme example of the age-old battle between the sexes provides an intellectual "handle" that at least some people can comprehend.

Theories provide understanding in a number of ways. Kenneth R. Hoover identified four "uses of theory in social scientific thinking":[20]

1. Theories provide patterns for the interpretation of data. Population density, for example, tends to be associated with high crime rates, and maps showing high population density tend to be closely associated with diagrams that reflect high rates of crime, so some theorists suggest that overcrowding increases aggression and therefore crime. "People," said Hoover, "like to think in terms of images, analogies, and patterns; this helps to simplify complex realities and to lighten the burden of thought."
2. Theories link one study with another. Some years ago, a case study of women's prisons in California found the existence of artificially constructed "families" around which women's lives centered. A similar but later study of a Chinese prison also found that the female inmates had created family-like groups. As a result, some theorists suggested that women feel a need to nurture and be nurtured and that they carry this need with them into prison. The fact that cross-cultural support was found for this suggestion provided a linkage between the two studies, which tended to lend further support to it.
3. Theories supply frameworks within which concepts and variables acquire special significance. The death penalty, for example, although especially significant to individuals condemned to die, acquires special significance when seen as a tool employed by the powerful to keep the powerless under their control.
4. Theories allow us to interpret the larger meaning of our findings for ourselves and for others. Hence, the death penalty has become a moral issue for many Americans today, shrouded as it is in ethical considerations and images of national identity and ultimate justice.

Learn more about the nature of modern social scientific thought and theory construction at **Web Extras 2–3** and **2–4**.

The Role of Research and Experimentation

More important than the claims made by theories and by the theorists who create them are findings of fact that either support those claims or leave them without foundation. Hence, theories, once proposed, need to be tested against the real world via a variety of research strategies, including experimentation and case studies. This is equally true whether the proposed theory is relatively simple or dauntingly complex.

The objective of criminology is the development of a body of general verified principles.

In his 2009 presidential address to the ASC, incoming president Todd Clear told listeners that "if the evidence-based movement means anything, it means that we want to avoid undertaking programs based on stereotypes and cherished pet theories about crime." Clear described the current state of criminology as focused on the "what works model," and said that "the question '[W]hat works?' might be rewritten as 'How effective is a given program or intervention?'"[21]

Reliable determinations of program effectiveness are made through research. **Research** can be defined as the use of standardized, systematic procedures in the search for knowledge.[22] Some researchers distinguish between applied research and nonapplied, or pure, research. **Applied research** "consists of scientific inquiry that is designed and carried out with practical application in mind."[23] In applied research, the researcher is working toward some more or less practical goal. It may be the reduction of crime, the efficient compensation of victims of crime, or an evaluation of the effectiveness of policies implemented to solve some specific aspect of the crime problem. **Pure research**, on the other hand, is undertaken simply for the sake of advancing scientific knowledge and "does not carry the promise or expectation of immediate, direct relevance."[24]

Another type of research, secondary research or secondary analysis, can be distinguished from primary research.[25] **Primary research** "is characterized by original and direct investigation,"[26] whereas **secondary research** consists of new evaluations of existing information that has already been collected by other researchers.

■ **variable** A concept that can undergo measurable changes.
■ **operationalization** The process by which concepts are made measurable.

Scientific research generally proceeds in stages, which can be divided conceptually among (1) problem identification, (2) development of a research design, (3) choice of data-collection techniques, and (4) review of findings (which often includes statistical analysis).

Problem Identification

Problem identification, the first step in any research, consists of naming a problem or choosing an issue to study. Topics may be selected for a variety of reasons. Larry S. Miller and John T. Whitehead, for example, said that "the choice of what criminologists study is influenced by political decisions,"[27] meaning that the availability of government grant monies frequently determines the focus of much contemporary research in the area of crime. It may also be that private foundation monies have become available to support studies in a specific area. Perhaps the researcher has a personal interest in a particular issue and wants to learn more, or maybe a professor or teacher has assigned a research project as part of the requirements for a class. Whatever the reason for beginning research, however, the way in which a research problem is stated and conceptualized will help narrow the research focus and will serve as a guide to the formulation of data-gathering strategies.

Although some criminological research undertaken today is purely descriptive, the bulk of research in criminology is intended to explore issues of causality, especially the claims made by theories purporting to explain criminal behavior. As such, much contemporary research is involved with the testing of hypotheses.

The *American Heritage Dictionary* defines the word *hypothesis* in two ways:[28]

1. "A tentative explanation for an observation, phenomenon, or scientific problem that can be tested by further investigation."
2. "Something that is taken to be true for the purpose of argument or investigation; an assumption."

Within the modern scientific tradition, a hypothesis serves both these purposes. Some criminologists, as mentioned earlier, have observed what appears to be a correlation, or relationship, between the phases of the moon and the rate of crime commission. Such observers may propose the following hypothesis: The moon causes crime. Although this is a useful starting hypothesis, it needs to be further refined before it can be tested. Specifically, the concepts contained within the hypothesis must be translated into measurable variables. A **variable** is simply a concept that can undergo measurable changes.

Scientific precedent holds that only measurable items can be satisfactorily tested. The process of turning a simple hypothesis into one that is testable is called **operationalization**. An operationalized hypothesis is one that is stated in such a way as to facilitate measurement, and it is specific in its terms and in the linkages it proposes. For example, we might move a step further toward both measurability and specificity in our hypothesis about the relationship between the moon and crime by restating it as follows: Rates of murder, rape, robbery, and assault rise when the moon's fullness increases and are highest when the moon is full. Now we have specified what we mean by crime (that is, murder, rape, robbery, and assault), rates of which can be calculated. The degree of the moon's fullness can also be measured. Once we have operationalized a hypothesis and made the concepts it contains measurable, those concepts have, in effect, become variables.

Once the concepts within our hypothesis are measurable, we can test the hypothesis itself; that is, we can observe what happens to crime rates as the moon approaches fullness, as well as what happens when the moon is full, and see whether our observations support our hypothesis. As our dictionary definition tells us, once a hypothesis has been operationalized, it is assumed to be true for purposes of testing. It is accepted, for study

gary718/Shutterstock

The full moon over New York City. It is the job of researchers to determine the validity of claimed relationships—and of theorists to explain why such relationships hold. Are phases of the moon correlated with changes in the rate of occurrence of certain crimes? If so, why?

■ **research design** The logic and structure inherent in an approach to data gathering.

■ **confounding effect** A rival explanation or competing hypothesis that is a threat to the internal or external validity of a research design.

■ **internal validity** The certainty that experimental interventions did indeed cause the changes observed in the study group.

■ **external validity** The ability to generalize research findings to other settings.

purposes, until observation proves it untrue, at which point it is said to be rejected. As two renowned research methodologists have stated, "The task of theory-testing is predominantly one of rejecting inadequate hypotheses."[29]

Development of a Research Design

Research designs structure the research process. They provide a kind of road map to the logic inherent in one's approach to a research problem, and they also serve as guides to the systematic collection of data (see **Library Extra 2–1**).

Research designs consist of the logic and structure inherent in any particular approach to data gathering. A simple study, for example, might be designed to test the assertion that the consumption of refined white sugar promotes aggressive or violent tendencies. One could imagine researchers approaching prison officials with the proposal that inmate diets be altered to exclude all refined white sugar. Under the plan, cafeteria cooks would be instructed to prepare meals without the use of sugar. Noncaloric sweeteners would be substituted for sugar in recipes calling for sugar, and sweetened beverages and carbonated drinks containing sugar would be banned. Likewise, the prison canteen would be prohibited from selling items containing sugar for the duration of the experiment.

The central principle of experimentation is that we must accept the outcome whether or not it is to our liking.

To determine whether the forced reduction in sugar consumption actually affected inmates' behavior, researchers might look at the recorded frequency of aggressive incidents (sometimes called "write-ups" in prison jargon) occurring within the confines of the prison before the experiment was initiated and compare such data with similar information on such incidents following the introduction of dietary changes. A research design employing this kind of logic can be diagrammed as follows:

$$O_1 \times O_2$$

Here O_1 (termed a *pretest*) refers to the information gathered on inmate aggressiveness prior to the introduction of dietary changes (which themselves are shown as X, also called the *experimental intervention*), and O_2 (termed the *posttest*) signifies a second set of observations—those occurring after dietary changes have been implemented. Researchers employing a strategy of this type, which is known as a "one-group pretest-posttest," would likely examine differences between the two sets of observations, one made before introduction of the experimental intervention and the other after. The difference, they may assume, would show changes in behavior resulting from changes in diet—in this case, the exclusion of refined white sugar.

Although this basic research design illustrates the logic behind naïve experiments, it does not provide a good research structure because it does not eliminate other possible explanations of behavioral change. For example, during the time between the first and second observations, inmates may have been exposed to some other influence that reduced their level of aggression. A new minister may have begun preaching effective sermons filled with messages of love and peace to the prison congregation; television cable service to the prison may have been disrupted, lowering the exposure inmates received to violent programming; a new warden may have taken control of the facility, relaxing prison rules and reducing tensions; a transfer or release of especially troublesome inmates, scheduled at some earlier time, may have occurred; a new program of conjugal visitation may have been initiated, creating newfound sexual outlets and reducing inmate tensions; and so on. The possibilities for rival explanations (that is, those that rival the explanatory power of the hypothesis under study) are nearly limitless. Rival explanations like these, called by some researchers "competing hypotheses" and **confounding effects** by others, make the results of any single series of observations uncertain.

Validity in Research Designs

Confounding effects, which may invalidate the results of research, are of two general types: those that limit the certainty that internal interventions caused the changes in research findings, which is called **internal validity**, and those that affect the ability of researchers to generalize the research findings to other settings, which is called **external validity**. Often, when external validity is threatened, researchers do not feel confident that interventions that "worked" under laboratory-like or other special conditions will still be effective when employed in the field. Hence, researchers achieving internal validity may be able to demonstrate that diets low in refined white sugar lower the number of instances of overt displays of aggressiveness in a single prison under study. They may not feel confident (for the reasons shown in Figure 2–2), however, that similar changes in

■ **controlled experiment** An experiment that attempts to hold conditions (other than the intentionally introduced experimental intervention) constant.

■ **quasi-experimental design** An approach to research that, although less powerful than experimental designs, is deemed worthy of use when better designs are not feasible.

diet, if implemented in the general nonprison population, would have a similar effect. Most researchers consider internal validity the most vital component of any planned research because, without it, considerations of external validity become irrelevant.

Factors that routinely threaten the internal validity of a design for research are found in Figure 2–2.[30] Threats to external validity are shown in Figure 2–3.

Experimental and Quasi-Experimental Research Designs

To have confidence that the changes intentionally introduced into a situation are the real cause of observed variations, it is necessary to achieve some degree of control over factors that threaten internal validity. In the physical sciences, controlled experiments often provide the needed guarantees. **Controlled experiments** attempt to hold conditions (other than the intentionally introduced experimental intervention) constant.

> Self-selected subjects may be more interested in participation than others, and they may respond more readily to experimental treatment.

Some researchers have defined the word *experiment* simply as "controlled observation."

Whereas constancy of conditions may be possible to achieve within laboratory settings, it is far more difficult to come by in the social world, which by its very nature is in an ongoing state of flux. Hence, although criminologists sometimes employ true experimental designs in the conduct of their research, they are more likely to find it necessary to use **quasi-experimental designs**, or approaches to research that "are deemed worthy of use where better designs are not feasible."[31] Quasi-experimental designs are especially

Threats to the Internal Validity of a Research Design

History (or Competing Cause)
Specific events that occur between the first and second observations that may affect measurement.

Maturation
Processes occurring within the respondents or subjects that operate as a result of the passage of time. Fatigue along with decreases in response time due to age are examples.

Repeated Testing (or Testing Effects)
Effects of taking a test upon the scores of a later testing. When respondents are measures in some way that requires them to respond, they tend to do better (that is, their scores increase) the next time they are tested. In effect, they have learned how to take the test or how to be measured, even though they may not have acquired more knowledge about the subject matter that the test intends to measure.

Instrumentation (or Instrument Change)
Changes in measuring instruments or in survey takers that occur as a result of time. Batteries wear down, instruments need to be recalibrated, interviewers grow tired or are replaced with others, and so on—all of which can change the nature of the observations made.

Statistical Regression (or Regression Toward the Mean)
Return to more average scores. When respondents have been selected for study on the basis of extreme scores (as may be the case with personality inventories), later testing will tend to show a regression toward the mean because some extreme scores are inevitably more the result of accident or luck than anything else.

Differential Selection
Built-in biases that result when more than one group of subjects are involved in a study and when the groups being tested are initially somehow different. The random assignment of subjects to test groups greatly reduces the chances that such significant differences will exist.

Experimental Mortality (or Differential Attrition)
Differential loss of respondents from comparison groups that may occur when more than one group is being tested. For example, one group loses members at a greater rate than another group, or certain kinds of members are lost from one group but not from another.

Experimenter Bias
Inadvertent and nonconscious effects caused by the experimenters, including favoritism or biased behavior toward selected subjects.

FIGURE 2–2 Threats to the Internal Validity of a Research Design

■ **control group** A group of experimental subjects that, although the subject of measurement and observation, is not exposed to the experimental intervention.
■ **randomization** The process whereby individuals are assigned to study groups without biases or differences resulting from selection.

valuable when aspects of the social setting are beyond the control of the researcher. The crucial defining feature of quasi-experimental designs is that they give researchers control over the "when and to whom" of measurement, even though others decide the "when and to whom" of exposure to the experimental intervention.

Sometimes, for example, legislators enact new laws intended to address some aspect of the crime problem, specifying the kinds of crime-prevention measures to be employed and the segment of the population to receive them. Midnight basketball, intended to keep young people off the streets at night, provides an example of a legislatively sponsored intervention. During debate on the 1994 Violent Crime Control and Law Enforcement Act, midnight basketball became a point of contention, with senators asking whether money spent in support of such an activity would actually reduce the incidence of serious street crime in our nation's inner cities. Unfortunately, no good research data that could answer the question were then available. Now, however, federally funded midnight basketball programs, which have existed for a number of years, could be studied by researchers. Hence, although criminologists were not politically situated to be able to enact midnight basketball legislation, they are able to study the effects of such legislation *after* it has been enacted.[32]

Whether criminologists decide on experimental or quasi-experimental designs to guide their research, they depend on well-considered research strategies to eliminate rival explanations for the effects they observe. One relatively powerful research design that criminologists frequently employ can be diagrammed as follows:

Experimental group $O_1 \times O_2$

Control group $O_3 \times O_4$

The meaning of the notation used here is similar to that of the one-shot case study design discussed earlier. This approach, however, called the "pretest-posttest control group design," gains considerable power from the addition of a second group; it is called a **control group** because it is not exposed to the experimental intervention.

Critical to the success of a research design like this is the use of randomization in the assignment of subjects to both the experimental and the control groups. **Randomization** is the process whereby individuals are assigned to study groups without biases or differences resulting from selection. Self-selection (when some individuals volunteer for membership in either the experimental or the control group) is not permitted, nor are researchers allowed to use personal judgment in assigning subjects to groups.

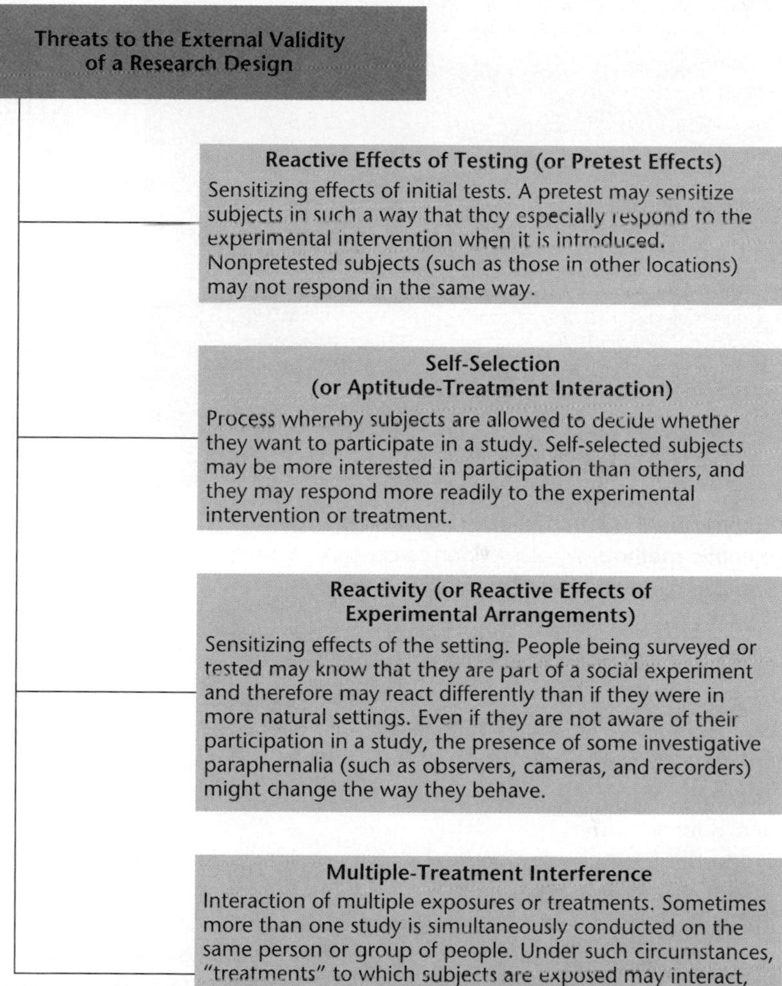

FIGURE 2-3 Threats to the External Validity of a Research Design

Control over potential threats to internal validity is achieved by the introduction of a properly selected control group because it is assumed that both experimental and control groups are essentially the same at the start and that any threats to internal validity will affect both groups equally as the experiment progresses—effectively canceling out when final differences between the two groups are measured. If some particular historical event, for example, affects the experimental group and modifies

■ **survey research** Research using a social science data-gathering technique that involves the use of questionnaires.

Orlin Wagner/AP Wide World Photos

A high school science fair booth pays homage to the scientific method. What is evidence-based criminology? How does it make use of the scientific method?

the measurable characteristics of that group, that event should have the same impact on the control group. Hence, in the previous design, when O_4 is subtracted from O_2, the remaining observable *net effects* are assumed to be attributable to the experimental intervention.

In the prison study discussed earlier, randomization would require that all inmates be systematically but randomly divided into two groups. Random assignments are typically made by using a table of random numbers. In this simple study, however, something as easy as the flip of a coin should suffice. Members of one group (the experimental group) would no longer receive refined white sugar in their diets, while members of the other group (the control group) would continue eating as before. With this one exception in diet, both groups would continue to be exposed to the same environment, so it can be assumed that any other influences on the level of violence within the prison will cancel out when final measurements are taken and that measurable differences in violence between the two groups can be attributed solely to the effects of the experimental variable (in this case, removal of refined white sugar from the diet).

According to Shawn Bushway and David Weisburd at the University of Maryland, criminology is the only field within the social sciences to "show a marked increase in the use of experimental designs over the past 40 years."[33] And the movement has powerful friends. No less an authority than Lawrence W. Sherman, director of the Institute of Criminology at Cambridge University and the former director of research at the Police Foundation, says that the use of experimental design in the field of criminology is the "gold standard" to which evaluations of both theory and practice should be held.[34]

The use of experimental design in the field of criminology sets a "gold standard" for researchers to follow.

Choice of Data-Collection Techniques

The combination of (1) hypothesis building, (2) operationalization, and (3) systematic observation in the service of hypothesis testing has made modern-day criminology scientific and has facilitated scientific theory building within the field. Hence, once a research problem has been identified, concepts have been made measurable, and a research design has been selected, investigators must then decide on the type of data to be gathered and the techniques of data gathering they wish to employ. Ultimately, all research depends on the use of techniques to gather information, or data, for eventual analysis. Like research designs, which structure a researcher's approach to a problem, data-gathering strategies provide approaches to the accumulation of information needed for analysis to occur.

Many first-time researchers select data-gathering techniques on the basis of ease or simplicity, and some choose according to the cost or the amount of time the techniques require. The most important question to consider when beginning to gather information, however, is whether the data-gathering strategy selected will produce information in a usable form. The kind of information needed depends on the questions to be answered. Surveys of public opinion about the desirability of the death penalty, for example, cannot address issues of the punishment's effectiveness as a crime-control strategy.

Five major data-gathering strategies typify research in the field of criminology: surveys, case studies, participant observations, self-reporting, and secondary analysis.

Surveys

Survey research typically involves the use of questionnaires, or surveys. Respondents may be interviewed in person or over the telephone or queried via e-mail or fax. Mail surveys are common, although they tend to have a lower response rate than other types of social surveys. The information produced through the use of questionnaires is referred to as "survey data." Polling companies like Gallup, CNN, and Roper gather data on public opinion, voting preferences, and so forth, and the U.S. Census

■ **participant observation** A strategy in data gathering in which the researcher observes a group by participating, to varying degrees, in the activities of the group.

Bureau data are gathered by trained survey takers. Survey data also inform the National Crime Victimization Survey (NCVS) and result in publications such as *Crime and the Nation's Households, Criminal Victimization*, and other NCVS-related reports produced by the Bureau of Justice Statistics. Surveys have also been used to assess fear of crime, attitudes toward the police, and extent of unreported crime.

Case Studies

Case studies are built around in-depth investigations into individual cases. The study of one (perhaps notorious) offender, the scrutiny of a particular criminal organization, and the analysis of a prison camp may all qualify as case studies. Case studies are useful for what they can tell us to expect about other similar cases. If a study of a street gang, for example, reveals the central role of a few leaders, then we would expect to find a similar organizational style among other gangs of the same kind.

When one individual (a single subject) is the focus of a case study, the investigation may take the form of a subjective life history, which involves gathering as much historical data as possible about a given individual and his or her life experiences. Life histories may also be gathered on groups of individuals, and similarities in life experiences that are thereby discovered may provide researchers with clues to current behavior or with points at which to begin further investigations.

Case studies, although they may suffer from high levels of subjectivity in which feelings cannot be easily separated from fact, provide the opportunity to investigate individual cases—an element lacking in both surveys and participant observations.

Participant Observations

Participant observation "involves a variety of strategies in data gathering in which the researcher observes a group by participating, to varying degrees, in the activities of the group."[35] Some participant researchers operate undercover, whereas others make their identity and purpose known from the outset. As one criminologist stated, participant observation "means that criminologists must venture inside the immediacy of crime."[36]

One of the earliest and best-known participant observers in the field of criminology was William Foote Whyte, who described his 1943 study of criminal subcultures in a slum district that he called "Cornerville" this way:

> My aim was to gain an intimate view of Cornerville life. My first problem, therefore, was to establish myself as a participant in the society so that I would have a position from which to observe. I began by going to live in Cornerville, finding a room with an Italian family. It was not enough simply to make the acquaintance of various groups of people. The sort of information that I sought required that I establish intimate social relations. This active participation gave me something in common with them so that we had other things to talk about besides the weather. It broke down the social barriers and made it possible for me to be taken into the intimate life of the group.[37]

It is possible to distinguish between at least two additional kinds of participant observation: (1) the participant as observer and (2) the observer as complete participant. When researchers make their presence known to those whom they are observing without attempting to influence the outcome of their observations or the activities of the group, they fit the category of participants who are observers. But researchers who make their presence known may inadvertently influence outcomes because people tend to act differently when they know they are being watched.

When they become complete participants in the group they are observing, researchers run the risk of influencing the group's direction. As Whyte explained, "I made it a rule that I should try to avoid influencing the actions of the group. I wanted to observe what the men did under ordinary circumstances; I did not want to lead them into different activities."[38] Another problem facing the participant observer is that of "going native," assuming too close an identification with the subjects or the behavior under study (for example, an undercover police officer who may be tempted to participate in the illegalities he or she is supposed to be monitoring). When that happens, all sense of the research perspective may be lost, and serious ethical problems may arise.

On the other hand, some researchers may feel disgust for the subjects of their research. Data gatherers with a particular dislike of drug abuse, for example, may be hard put to maintain their objectivity when working as participant observers within the drug subculture. Hence, as noted social science researcher Frank Hagan observed, "The researcher must avoid not only over identification with the study group, but also aversion to it."[39]

Self-Reporting

Another subjective data-gathering technique is the self-report that investigates aspects of a problem not otherwise amenable to study. When official records are lacking, research subjects may be asked to record and report rates of otherwise secretive behavior. Self-reports may prove especially valuable in providing checks on official reports consisting of statistical tabulations

■ **intersubjectivity** A scientific principle that requires that independent observers see the same thing under the same circumstances for observations to be regarded as valid.

■ **replicability** A scientific principle that holds that valid observations made at one time can be made again later if all other conditions are the same.

gathered through channels such as police departments, hospitals, and social services agencies.

Self-reports may also be requested of subjects in survey research, so self-reporting is sometimes considered simply another form of survey research. However, many self-reporting techniques require the maintenance of a diary or personal journal and request vigilant and ongoing observations of the study subject's own behavior. Hence, sex researchers may ask subjects to maintain an ongoing record of their frequency of intercourse, the variety of sexual techniques employed, and their preference in partners—items of information that are not easy to come by through other means or that cannot be accurately reconstructed from memory.

Self-reporting enters the realm of the purely subjective when it consists of introspection, or personal reflection. Introspective techniques intended to gather data on secretive feelings and felt motivations are often used by psychologists seeking to assess the mental status of patients. Criminologists have at times used introspective techniques to categorize criminal offenders into types and to initiate the process of developing concepts more amenable to objective study.

Secondary Analysis

Not all data-gathering techniques produce new data. Secondary analysis purposefully culls preexisting information from data that have already been gathered (possibly for another purpose) and examines it in new ways. The secondary analysis of existing data and the use of previously acquired information for new avenues of inquiry are strategies that can save researchers a considerable amount of time and expense.

One important source of data for secondary analysis is the National Archive of Criminal Justice data located in the Institute for Social Research at the University of Michigan. In the words of the U.S. Department of Justice, the archive's sponsoring agency, "The Archive continually processes the most relevant criminal justice data sets for the research community,"[40] maintaining information on victimization, various aspects of the criminal justice system, and juvenile delinquency. Access to archive data is by request, and data sets are available to individual researchers. Visit the archive via **Web Extra 2–5**.

The use of secondary data rarely alerts research subjects to the fact that they (or the data they have provided) are being studied, although they may have been aware of it when the data were first gathered, making secondary analysis "nonreactive." For example, the use of archival records in data analysis constitutes a virtual "goldmine of information waiting to be exploited."[41] Nonetheless, it is important to keep in mind that secondary analysis usually involves the use of information that was collected for a purpose outside the interests of the current researcher.

Problems in Data Collection

Scientific data gathering builds on observations of one sort or another. Observation is not unique to science—individuals continuously make observations and draw a plethora of personal conclusions based on what they see or hear. Scientific observation, however, generally occurs under controlled conditions and must meet the criteria of intersubjectivity and replicability. **Intersubjectivity** means that, for observations to be valid, independent observers must report seeing the same thing under the same circumstances. "Do you see what I see?" is a question that highlights the central role of intersubjectivity in scientific observation. If observers cannot agree on what they saw, then the raw data necessary for scientific analysis have not been acquired. **Replicability** of observations, at least in the field of scientific experimentation, means that, when the same conditions exist, the same results can be expected to follow; hence, valid experiments can be replicated. The same observations made at one time can be made again at a later time if all other conditions are the same.

"Do you see what I see?" is a question that highlights the central role of intersubjectivity in scientific observation.

In the physical sciences, replicability is easy to achieve. Water at sea level, for example, will always boil at 100° Celsius. Anyone can replicate the conditions needed to test such a contention. When replicability cannot be achieved, it casts the validity of the observation into doubt. Some years ago, for example, a few scientists claimed to have achieved nuclear fusion at room temperature. Their supposed accomplishment was dubbed "cold fusion" and was hailed as a major breakthrough

■ **descriptive statistics** Statistics that describe, summarize, or highlight the relationships within data that have been gathered.
■ **inferential statistics** Statistics that specify how likely findings are to be true for other populations or in other locales.

in the production of nuclear energy. However, when scientists elsewhere attempted to replicate the conditions under which cold fusion was said to occur, they could find no evidence that the initial experimenters were correct. Intersubjectivity and replicability are critical to the scientific enterprise, with one researcher stating that "science rests its claim to authority upon its firm basis in observable evidence."[42]

It is important to recognize, however, that some observations—even those that stand up to the tests of intersubjectivity and replicability—can lead to unwarranted conclusions. For example, spirit possession, an explanation for deviance that was apparently widely held in primitive times, must have appeared to be well validated by the positive behavioral changes that became apparent in those who submitted to the surgery called for by the theory, which was a craniotomy intended to release offending spirits from the head of the afflicted person. The actual cause of behavioral reformation may have been brain infections resulting from unsanitary surgical conditions, slips of the stone knife, or the intensity of pain endured by those undergoing the procedure without anesthetics. To the uncritical observer, however, the theory of spirit possession as a cause of deviance and cranial surgery as a treatment technique would probably appear to have been supported by the evidence of induced behavioral change.

Some methodologists noted that "theories are as much involved in the determination of fact as facts are in establishing a theory."[43] Theories are intimately involved in the process of data collection: They determine what kinds of data we choose to gather, what we look for in the data, and how we interpret the information we have gathered. In short, theories determine what we see as well as what we ignore. In the late 1700s, for example, when a meteor shower was reported to the French Academy of Sciences, observers reported that some fragments had struck the ground, causing tremendous explosions. The learned scientists of the academy quickly dismissed these accounts, however, calling them "a superstition unworthy of these enlightened times."[44] Everyone, they said, knows that stones don't fall from the sky.

Mikael Karlsson/Alamy

Social science research within a criminal justice setting. Inmate surveys may increase our knowledge of crime causation. Specifically, what might such surveys tell us?

Review of Findings

Some data, once collected, are simply archived or stored, but most data are subject to some form of analysis. Data analysis generally involves the use of mathematical techniques intended to uncover correlations between or among variables and to assess the likelihood that research findings can be generalized to other settings. These are statistical techniques, and their use in analyzing data is called *statistical analysis*. Some theorists, for example, posit a link between poverty and crime. Hence, we might suspect that low-income areas would be high-crime areas. Once we specify what we mean by "low-income" and "crime" so that they become measurable variables, and we gather data on income levels and the incidence of crime in various locales, we are ready to begin the job of data analysis.

Statistical techniques provide tools for summarizing data and also provide quantitative means for identifying patterns within the data and for determining the degree of correlation that exists between variables. Statistical methods can be divided into two types: descriptive and inferential. **Descriptive statistics** describe, summarize, or highlight the relationships within the data that have been gathered. **Inferential statistics**, on the other hand, attempt to generalize findings by specifying how likely they are to be true for other populations or in other locales.

Descriptive statistics include measures of central tendency, commonly called the mode, median, and mean. *Mode* refers to the most frequently occurring score or value in any series of observations. If, for example, we measure the age of all juvenile offenders held in a state training facility, it may be that they range in age from 12 to 16, with 15 being the most commonly found age; 15, then, would be the modal age for the population under study.

Median defines the midpoint of a data series—half of the scores will be above the mean and the other half will be below. It may be, for example, that in our study of juveniles, we find equal numbers in each age category, so the median age for those offenders would be 14.

WHO'S TO BLAME—The Individual or Society?

Is Criminology Really Just a Form of Academic Excuse Making?

Three teenage boys were arrested in the small town of Hillsboro, Maine, and charged with beating a homeless man to death with a baseball bat in an underground parking garage on a cold January evening. A surveillance camera captured the beating, and the youngsters were identified by residents who watched the video clip on local TV news.

Because the boys were juveniles, a storm of controversy swarmed around a local judge's decision to charge them as adults and to bind them over for trial in criminal court—something that state law allows for serious crimes if the suspected offenders were over 14 years of age at the time of the alleged offense.

Soon opinions were being heard from many quarters, and the news media arranged to interview a criminology professor, Dr. Roy Humbolt, at a local college to see if he might be able to shed some light on the boys' behavior.

The first question came from a reporter holding a digital voice recorder toward Professor Humbolt. "What happened here? How do you explain this kind of senseless killing?"

"Well," Humbolt began, "it's not senseless. Crime is a social event, not just an isolated instance of individual activity. And in much youth crime we see patterns of co-offending."

Humbolt felt as though he was hitting his stride and started lecturing as though he was in the classroom with his undergraduates. "Criminal behavior is often attributable to social failings rather than to individual choice. Consider, for a moment, the backgrounds of these young men. Were they subjected to physical abuse while they were growing up? Was violence what they learned at the hands of older siblings or parents? Were they, in this instance, involved in some adolescent rite of passage, maybe even an initiation into a gang? Did they feel forced to behave this way because of peer pressure? Was it something they saw on television or in video games that they might have played and then decided to reenact?"

"Dr. Humbolt," the reporter asked, bringing the professor back from his reverie, "even if you find that some of those things are true, isn't criminology just an exercise in excuse making for criminals?"

Think about it

1. What do you think of the explanations offered by Professor Humbolt for the boys' behavior? Which of his explanations, if any, makes the most sense? How can we know for sure if those explanations are accurate?
2. What do you think of the reporter's stinging criticism of the professor? Is the reporter right, that criminology is "just an exercise in excuse making for criminals"? Explain your answer.
3. Generally speaking, does understanding absolve responsibility? In other words, if we can understand why someone does something, then should we hold him or her less responsible for doing it? Why or why not?

Note: Who's to Blame boxes provide fictionalized critical thinking opportunities, and are not actual cases.

Mean is the mathematical average of all scores within a given population and is the most commonly used measure of central tendency. It is calculated by simply adding together all the scores (or ages, in our example) and dividing by the total number of observations. Although calculations of the mode, median, and mean will often yield similar results, such will not be the case with populations that are skewed in a particular direction. If our population of juveniles, for example, consisted almost entirely of 16-year-olds, then the mode for that population would inevitably be 16 while other measures of central tendency would yield somewhat lower figures.

Other descriptive statistics provide measures of the standard deviation of a population (that is, the degree of dispersion of scores about the mean) and the degree of **correlation** or interdependence between variables (that is, the extent of variation in one that can be expected to follow from a measured change in another). Although the degree of correlation may vary, the direction of correlation can be described. We say, for example, that if one variable increases whenever another, upon which it is dependent, does the same, a positive correlation (or positive relationship) exists between the two; when one variable decreases in value as another rises, a negative correlation (or inverse relationship) exists.

Another statistical technique, one that provides a measure of the likelihood that a study's findings are the results of chance, is commonly found in criminological literature. **Tests of significance** are designed to provide researchers with confidence that their results are, in fact, true and not the result of sampling error. We may, for example, set out to measure the degree of gun ownership. Let's say that the extent of gun ownership in the area under study is actually 50%. (We have no way of knowing this until our study is complete.) We may decide to use door-to-door surveys of randomly selected households because cost prohibits us from canvassing all households in the study area. Even if we have made our best survey effort, however, some slight probability remains that the households we have chosen to interview may all be populated by gun owners. Although it is very unlikely, we may—by chance—have excluded

■ **correlation** A causal, complementary, or reciprocal relationship between two measurable variables.

■ **test of significance** A statistical technique intended to provide researchers with confidence that their results are, in fact, true and not the result of sampling error.

■ **quantitative method** A research technique that produces measurable results.

those without guns. Assuming that everyone interviewed answers truthfully, we would come away with the mistaken impression that 100% of the population in the study area is armed!

The likelihood of faulty findings increases as sample size decreases. Were we to sample only one or two households, we would have little likelihood of determining the actual incidence of gun ownership. The larger the sample size, however, the greater the confidence we can have in our findings. In other words, a positive correlation exists between sample size and degree of confidence we can have in our results. Even so, in most criminological research, it is not possible to study all members of a given population, so samples must be taken. Statistical tests of significance, expressed as a percentage, assess the likelihood that our study findings are due to chance. Hence, a study that reflects a 95% confidence level can be interpreted as having a 5% likelihood that the results it reports are mere happenstance. To put it another way, for every hundred such studies, five yield misleading results. The problem is that it would be impossible to know (without further research) which five that would be.

Tests of significance are designed to provide researchers with confidence that their results are, in fact, true.

Learn more about statistics and statistical methods from the American Statistical Association and the American Association for the Advancement of Science via **Web Extras 2–6** and **2–7**. Read about statistical tools on the World Wide Web via **Library Extra 2–2**.

Quantitative versus Qualitative Methods

Years ago, during the Clinton administration, then–Attorney General Janet Reno addressed researchers, criminologists, and professors gathered at the annual meeting of the ASC in Miami, Florida. "Let's stop talking about numbers," Reno exhorted the crowd, "and start talking about crime in human terms."[45] With her admonition, Reno placed herself squarely on the side of those who feel that there has been a tendency in American criminology over the past half century to overemphasize **quantitative methods** or techniques, that is, those that produce measurable results that can be analyzed statistically. To be sure, as such critics would be quick to admit, a considerable degree of intellectual comfort must be achieved in feeling that one is able to reduce complex forms of behavior and interaction to something countable (as, say, the frequency of an offense). Intellectual comfort of this sort derives from the notion that anything expressible in numbers must be somehow more meaningful than that which is not.

It is crucial to realize, however, that numerical expression is mostly a result of how researchers structure their approach to the subject matter and is rarely inherent in the subject matter itself. Such is especially true in the social sciences, where attitudes, feelings, behaviors, and perceptions of all sorts are subject to quantification by researchers who impose upon such subjective phenomena artificial techniques for their quantification.

One highly quantitative study, reprinted in the journal *Criminology*, reported on the relationship between personality and crime and found that "greater delinquent participation was associated with a personality configuration characterized by high Negative Emotionality and Weak Constraint."[46] It may seem easy to quantify "delinquent participation" by measuring official arrest statistics (although official statistics may not be a good measure of delinquent behavior because many law violations go undiscovered), but imagine the conceptual nightmares associated with trying to make measurable concepts such as "Negative Emotionality" and "Weak Constraint." In such studies, even those replete with numerical data derived through the use of carefully constructed questionnaires, questions still remain of precisely what it is that has been measured.

Not everyone who engages in social science research labors under the delusion that everything can and must be quantified. Those who do, however, are said to suffer from the "*mystique of quantity*." As some critics have pointed out, "[t]he failure to recognize this instrumentality of measurement makes for a kind of mystique of quantity, which responds to numbers as though they were repositories of occult powers. The mystique of quantity is an exaggerated regard for the significance of measurement, just because it is quantitative, without regard either to what has been measured or to what can subsequently be done with the measure."[47] The "mystique of quantity" treats numbers as having intrinsic scientific value. Unfortunately, this kind of thinking has been popular in the social sciences, where researchers, seeking to make clear their intellectual kinship with physical scientists, have been less than cautious in their enthusiasm for quantification.

Not everyone who engages in social science research labors under the delusion that everything can and must be quantified.

■ **qualitative method** A research technique that produces subjective results, or results that are difficult to quantify.

Qualitative methods, in contrast to those that are quantitative, produce subjective results, or results that are difficult to quantify. Even though their findings are not expressed numerically, qualitative methods provide yet another set of potentially useful criminological research tools. Qualitative methods are important for the insights they provide into the subjective workings of the criminal mind and the processes by which meaning is accorded to human experience. Introspection, life histories, case studies, and participant observations all contain the potential to yield highly qualitative data.[48]

Consider, for example, how the following personal account of homicidal motivation conveys subjective insights into the life of a Los Angeles gang member that would otherwise be difficult to express:

> Wearing my fresh Pendleton shirt, beige khakis, and biscuits [old men's comfort shoes, the first shoe officially dubbed "Crip shoe"], I threw on my black bomber jacket and stepped out into the warm summer night. I walked up Sixty-Ninth Street to Western Avenue and took a car at gunpoint. Still in a state of indecision, I drove toward the hospital.
>
> I intentionally drove through Sixties' hood. Actually, I was hoping to see one of them before I had made it through, and what luck did I have. There was Bank Robber, slippin' [not paying attention, not being vigilant] hard on a side street. I continued past him and turned at the next corner, parked and waited. He would walk right to me.
>
> Sitting in the car alone, waiting to push yet another enemy out of this existence, I reflected deeply about my place in this world, about things that were totally outside the grasp of my comprehension. Thoughts abounded I never knew I could conjure up. In retrospect, I can honestly say that in those moments before Bank Robber got to the car, I felt free. Free, I guess, because I had made a decision about my future.
>
> "Hey," I called out to Robber, leaning over to the passenger side, "got a light?"
>
> "Yeah," he replied, reaching into his pants pocket for a match or lighter. I never found out which.
>
> I guess he felt insecure, because he dipped his head down to window level to see who was asking for a light.
>
> "Say your prayers, muthaf."
>
> Before he could mount a response I blasted him thrice in the chest, started the car, and drove home to watch *Benny Hill.* Bangin' was my life. That was my decision.[49]

The passage was written by Sanyika Shakur, once known as "Monster Kody" to fellow South Central Los Angeles Crips members. Monster, named for his readiness to commit acts of brutality so extreme that they repulsed even other gang members, joined the Crips at age 11. Sent to a maximum-security prison while still in his teens, Monster learned to write, took on the name Sanyika Shakur, and joined the black nationalist New Afrikan Independence Movement. Shakur's prison-inspired autobiography, *Monster*, provides a soul-searching account of the life of a Los Angeles gang member. The purpose of the book, said Shakur, is "to allow my readers the first ever glimpse at South Central from my side of the gun, street, fence, and wall."[50]

Although Shakur's book is a purely personal account and may hold questions of generalizability for researchers, imagine the difficulties inherent in acquiring these kinds of data through the use of survey instruments or other traditional research techniques. Autobiographical accounts, introspection, and many forms of participant observations amount to a kind of

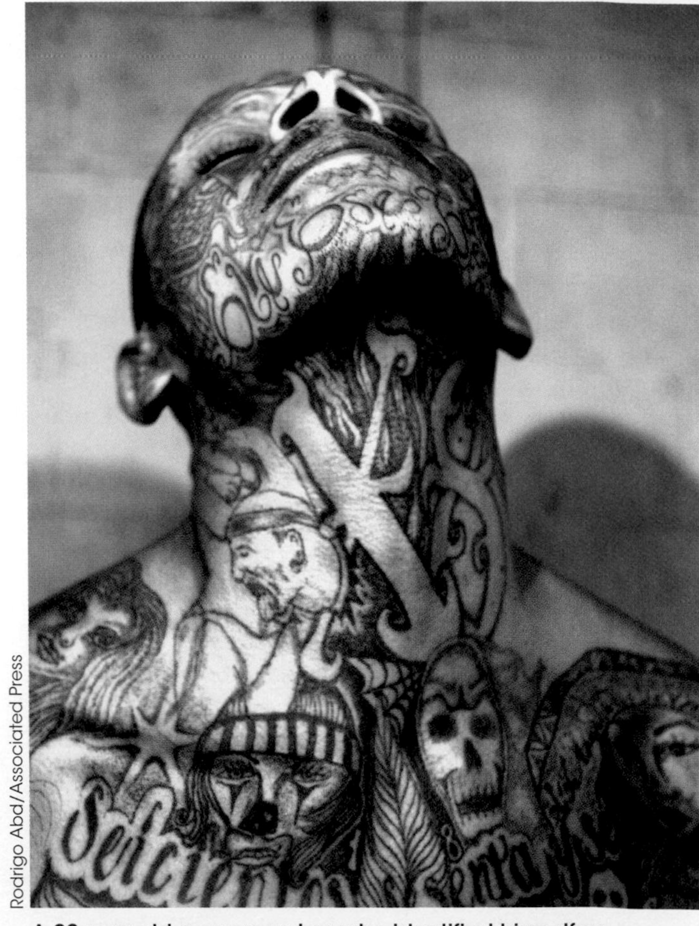

Rodrigo Abd/Associated Press

A 22-year-old gang member who identified himself as "Criminal." Some researchers doubt that quantitative methods can adequately assess the subjective experiences of certain kinds of offenders. What is the nature of such "subjective experiences"?

■ ***verstehen*** The kind of subjective understanding that can be achieved by criminologists who immerse themselves in the everyday world of the criminals they study.

■ **data confidentiality** The ethical requirement of social scientific research to protect the confidentiality of individual research participants while preserving justified research access to the information participants provide.

■ **informed consent** The ethical requirement of social scientific research that research subjects be informed about the nature of the research to be conducted, their anticipated role in it, and the uses to which the data they provide will be put.

phenomenological reporting in which description leads to understanding, and intuition is a better guide to theory building than volumes of quantifiable data.

Jeff Ferrell of Texas Christian University uses the term ***verstehen*** to describe the kind of subjective understanding that can be achieved by criminologists who immerse themselves in the everyday world of the criminals they study. Criminological *verstehen*, a term derived from the early writings of sociologist Max Weber, means, said Ferrell, "a researcher's subjective understandings of crime's situational meanings and emotions—its moments of pleasure and pain, its emergent logic and excitement—within the larger process of research"; Ferrell adds, "It further implies that a researcher, through attentiveness and participation, at least can begin to apprehend and appreciate the specific roles and experiences of criminals, crime victims, crime control agents, and others caught up in the day-to-day reality of crime."[51] Learn more about *verstehen* at "Max Weber's Home Page" via **Web Extra 2–8**. You can learn more about the techniques of social science research at **Library Extra 2–3** and **2–4**.

Values and Ethics in the Conduct of Research

Research, especially research conducted within the social sciences, does not occur in a vacuum. Values enter into all stages of the research process, from the selection of the problem to be studied to the choice of strategies to address it. In short, research is never entirely free from preconceptions and biases, although much can be done to limit their impact.

The most effective way of controlling the effects of biases is to be aware of them at the outset of the research. For example, if researchers know that the project they are working on elicits strong personal feelings but necessitates the use of interviewers, then it would be beneficial to strive to hire interviewers who are relatively free of biases or who can control the expression of their feelings. Data gatherers who are prejudiced against subgroups of potential respondents can represent a threat to the validity of the research results, and they may turn off some respondents, perhaps through racial innuendo, personal style, mannerisms, and so forth.

Of similar importance are ethical issues. Although they may not affect the validity of research results, these issues can have a significant impact on the lives of both researchers and research subjects. The protection of human subjects from harm, the provision of privacy, the need for disclosure of research methods, and **data confidentiality**—which embraces the principle of protecting the confidentiality of individual research participants while preserving justified research access to needed information provided by them—are all critical ethical issues.

To address these and other concerns, the Academy of Criminal Justice Sciences (ACJS) has adopted an official code of ethics. The ACJS Code of Ethics says that researchers "should seek to anticipate potential threats to confidentiality." It goes on to state, "Techniques such as the removal of direct identifiers, the use of randomized responses, and other statistical solutions to problems of privacy should be used where appropriate. Care should be taken to ensure secure storage, maintenance, and/or destruction of sensitive records."[52]

The ACJS code also says, "Confidential information provided by research participants should be treated as such by members of the Academy, even when this information enjoys no legal protection or privilege and legal force is applied. The obligation to respect confidentiality also applies to members of research organizations (interviewers, coders, clerical staff, etc.) who have access to the information. It is the responsibility of administrators and chief investigators to instruct staff members on this point and to make every effort to [ensure] that access to confidential information is restricted."[53]

Informed consent, a strategy used by researchers to overcome many of the ethical issues inherent in criminological research, means that research subjects are informed about the nature of the research to be conducted, their anticipated role in it, and the uses made of the data they provide. Ethics may also require that data derived from personal interviews or the testing of research subjects be anonymous (not associated with the names of individual subjects) and that raw (unanalyzed) data be destroyed after a specified time interval (often at the completion of the research project).

Ethical issues can have a significant impact on the lives of both researchers and research subjects.

Federal regulations require a plan for the protection of human subjects as part of grant proposals submitted to federal agencies. For example, the NIJ, a major source of grant support for researchers in the area of criminology, has this to say:

> All NIJ employees, contractors and award recipients must be cognizant of the importance of protecting the rights and welfare of human subject research participants. All research conducted at NIJ or supported with NIJ funds must comply with all Federal, U.S. Department of Justice (DOJ), Office of Justice Programs and NIJ regulations and policies concerning the protection of human subjects and the DOJ confidentiality requirements.[54]

Learn more about NIJ requirements for confidentiality and the protection of human subjects at **Web Extra 2–9**.

Some universities, research organizations, and government agencies have established institutional review boards with the task of examining research proposals to determine whether expectations of ethical conduct have been met before these proposals are submitted to funding organizations. Institutional review boards often consist of other researchers with special knowledge of the kinds of ethical issues involved in criminological research.

Participant observation sometimes entails an especially thorny ethical issue: Should researchers themselves violate the law if their research participation appears to require it? Those researching gang activities, for example, have sometimes been asked to transmit potentially incriminating information to other gang members, to act as drug couriers, and even to commit crimes of violence to help establish territorial claims important to members of the gang. Researchers who refuse may endanger not only their research but also themselves. Compliance with the expectations of criminal groups evokes other kinds of dangers, including the danger of apprehension and prosecution for violations of the criminal law. As one criminologist explained, "Criminological (and other) field researchers cannot conveniently distance themselves from their subjects of study, or from the legally uncertain situations in which the subjects may reside, in order to construct safe and 'objective' studies. Instead criminological field research unavoidably entangles those who practice it in complex and ambiguous relations to the subjects and situations of study, to issues of personal and social responsibility, and to law and legality."[55]

Although the dilemma of a participant observer, especially one secretly engaged in research, is a difficult one, some of the best advice on the subject is offered by Frank E. Hagan: "In self-mediating the potential conflicting roles of the criminal justice researcher, it is incumbent on the investigator to enter the setting with eyes wide open. A decision must be made beforehand on the level of commitment to the research endeavor and the analyst's ability to negotiate the likely role conflicts. Although there are no hard and fast rules *the researcher's primary role is that of a scientist*."[56]

Hagan also suggested that a code of ethics should guide all professional criminologists in their research undertakings, requiring each researcher to do the following:[57]

- Avoid procedures that may harm respondents.
- Honor commitments to respondents and respect reciprocity.
- Exercise objectivity and professional integrity in performing and reporting research.
- Protect confidentiality and the privacy of respondents.

Hagan's admonition "Exercise objectivity and professional integrity" became especially important in the mid-1990s when supporters of Project D.A.R.E. (Drug Abuse Resistance Education) blocked publication of research results that showed the program to be ineffective.[58] D.A.R.E., a widely popular antidrug program common in the nation's schools, is a favorite of educational administrators because of the funding it provides. The study, a review of most prior D.A.R.E. research, was conducted by the Research Triangle Institute, a respected research firm in North Carolina, and was paid for by the NIJ.[59] When results showed that D.A.R.E. programs did not significantly reduce drug use among student participants, however, NIJ decided not to publish the findings. "We're not trying to hide the study," said NIJ's Ann Voit. "We just do not agree with one of the major findings."[60] In contrast, Research Triangle Institute researcher Susan T. Ennett proposed that results of the study should be used to decide how to spend drug-education money. Other studies have since supported the finding that D.A.R.E. does not have a significant impact on actual drug use, drug-related outcomes, or attitudes toward drugs.[61] Learn more about the D.A.R.E. study via **Library Extra 2–5**.

Scientific research demonstrating that popular—and often widely supported—programs are ineffective will inevitably fuel controversy. Such was the case in 2006, when a group of Italian researchers published findings purporting to show that the 12-step method used by Alcoholics Anonymous (AA) to prevent future problem drinking doesn't work. The researchers concluded that "no experimental studies unequivocally demonstrated the effectiveness of A.A. or professional 12-step theory for reducing alcohol dependence or problems."[62] The research left some people claiming that AA worked for them and others saying that more (and better) studies were needed.

Because criminological research can affect social policy, which often involves the expenditure of public funds, the ethical code of the ASC mandates that criminologists be "committed to enhancing the general well-being of societies and of the individuals and groups within them," further stating that "criminologists have an obligation not to re-create forms of social injustice such as discrimination, oppression, or harassment in their own work."[63]

Learn more about ethics in criminological research directly from the ASC and the ACJS via **Web Extras 2–10** and **2–11**. To read a comprehensive code of ethical standards for general survey research, visit the Council of American Survey Research Organizations via **Web Extra 2–12**. The U.S. Department of Justice's policy on scientific and research integrity is available at **Library Extra 2-6**.

Social Policy and Criminological Research

Ideally, research results in the field of criminology should have both practical implications that can guide daily practice in relevant areas and a significant impact on those who formulate public crime-control policy. Faye S. Taxman of the University of Maryland's Center for Applied Policy Studies explained that "the normative educative model assumes that a rational use of data by policy makers, practitioners, and scientists will be of value to the field."[64] For example, after studies showed that arrests (rather than mere warnings) of domestic violence perpetrators proved effective in reducing the likelihood of reoffending, many police departments across the country began advising their officers to make such arrests, and some state legislators advocated passage of mandatory arrest laws.[65]

Unfortunately, publicly elected officials are often ignorant of current criminological research or do not heed the advice of professional criminologists, seeking instead to create politically expedient policies, which has led some to proclaim the "irrelevance" of criminology. James Austin of George Washington University bemoaned the lack of attention politicians give to the results of research in criminology: "Despite the annual publication of hundreds of peer-reviewed articles and textbooks proudly displayed at our annual conventions, policy makers are paying little if any attention to us. When Congress or state legislatures debate new crime bill legislation or the effectiveness of past actions, their first question is not, 'What do the criminologists think?' I would venture that one would be hard pressed to cite another discipline that has been so ignored for such a long time."[66] Should criminological research influence policy? Read more about the issue at **Library Extra 2–7**.

Three-strikes laws provide an example of the kind of dilemma facing criminologists who hope to influence social policy on the basis of statistical evidence. Three-strikes laws, which became popular with legislatures near the end of the twentieth century, require that felons receive lengthy prison sentences (often life without possibility of parole) following their third felony conviction. Such laws are built on the seemingly commonsense notion that "getting tough" on repeat offenders by putting them in prison for long periods should reduce the crime rate; logic seems to say that lengthy prison sentences for recidivists will reduce crime by removing the most dangerous offenders from society.

Research results in the field of criminology should have a significant impact on those who formulate public crime-control policy.

A study of the three-strikes laws in 22 states concluded, however, that such legislation typically results in clogged court systems and crowded correctional facilities and encourages three-time felons to take dramatic risks to avoid capture.[67] A wider-based study, dubbed "the most comprehensive study ever of crime prevention,"[68] found that "much of the research on prisons was inadequate or flawed, making it impossible to measure how much crime was actually prevented or deterred by locking up more criminals."[69] The central finding of the massive

Zuma Fress, Inc./Alamy

Project D.A.R.E. participants at A. Dorothy Hains Elementary School in Atlanta, Georgia. A decade ago, studies of Project D.A.R.E. questioned its effectiveness, but government officials decided not to publish the results. How can the objectivity of social scientific research be ensured?

■ **meta-analysis** A study that combines the results of other studies about a particular topic of interest. Also a comprehensive and systematic review of other studies.

THEORY | versus REALITY

The Stockholm Prize in Criminology

The 2013 Stockholm Prize in Criminology, presented by Stockholm University and the Stockholm Prize in Criminology Foundation, was awarded to British criminologist David Farrington. Farrington, who is director of Cambridge University's Study in Delinquent Development, has focused on testing evidence in support of early-life crime-prevention programs. "Farrington's work is an excellent example of how good criminological research can help to reduce crime and increase people's quality of life," says Jerzy Sarnecki Professor of Criminology at Stockholm University and one of the two chairs of the prize jury. The prize, which carries a cash award of 1.3 million Swedish kronor (about $140,000), was given in recognition of the importance of Farrington's crime-prevention studies, which identified a number of workable techniques for reducing crime.

Farrington's work is unique because he has combined his own original research with reviews of other research to influence governments around the world. He has focused his recommendations to policy makers on four key findings:

1. Risk and protective factors for crime appear very early in life.
2. Children at high risk can be helped from birth.
3. A wide range of programs for children under 10 are very effective.
4. Investing in early-life programs saves vast sums of taxpayer money.

Farrington has drawn both scholarly and public attention to crucial early opportunities to counteract major risk factors for crime. Effective interventions include prenatal care for mothers at risk, early childhood parental support, preschool programs for at-risk children, parent training for parents of disruptive children, and skills training for the children to teach them to think before they act. Farrington and his colleagues showed that the cost-effectiveness of these programs was often unanticipated; for example, a preschool program saved $11 for every $1 expended because of reduced crime and criminal justice costs up to age 40.

The Stockholm Prize is financed by the Jerry Lee Foundation in the United States, with support from the Japanese Correctional Association, the Hitachi Mirai Foundation, and the Söderberg Foundation of Sweden. Visit **www.criminologyprize.com** for further information about the prize and award recipients and to learn more about the annual Stockholm Criminology Symposium.

Damien Eagers/UPPA/Photoshot/Newscom

David Farrington (left) of Cambridge University, recipient of the 2013 Stockholm Prize in Criminology. What accomplishments does the prize recognize?

study, sponsored by the federal Office of Justice Programs and carried out by researchers at the University of Maryland's Department of Criminology and Criminal Justice, was that current government-sponsored crime-prevention initiatives—totaling over $3 billion annually—are often poorly evaluated, leading to uncertainty over whether funded programs actually work. The study, a **meta-analysis** (that is, a study of other studies), reviewed more than 500 impact evaluations of local crime-prevention programs and practices throughout the nation. Due to largely ineffective evaluation efforts that are often only loosely tied to funded programs, researchers concluded that "the current [government-sponsored research] plan does not provide effective guidance to the nation about what works to prevent crime." Although the three-strikes laws remain popular with the voting public and lawmakers have been quick to seize upon "get tough" crime-prevention policies in the interest of getting votes, solid and consistent research support showing the efficacy of such laws continues to be elusive.

To draw together much of the discussion in this chapter to this point, consider what the internationally known criminologist Lawrence Sherman identified in 2009 as "the 10 principal elements of a viable model for keeping the promise of experimental criminology":[70]

1. Identify key factual questions about policies.
2. Formulate testable hypotheses about competing answers to those questions.
3. Conduct randomized experiments where possible to compare those answers.
4. Conduct quasi-experiments when better designs are not possible.

5. Identify all good evidence on any one question in systematic reviews.
6. Synthesize that evidence, if possible, in single-outcome meta-analyses.
7. Present the research synthesis to committees of practitioners and scientists.
8. Develop succinct operational guidance based on evidence.
9. Communicate or promulgate the guidance.
10. Test and practice methods for obtaining more compliance with that guidance.

One especially important repository of crime- and justice-related literature today can be found at the Campbell Crime and Justice Coordinating Group, a subsidiary project of the Campbell Collaboration, which focuses on what works in the areas of education, social welfare, and criminal justice. The Campbell Collaboration began in 2000 to make systematic reviews of research on the effects of social interventions accessible. You can access the Campbell Collaboration via **Web Extra 2–13**. The Campbell Collaboration Crime and Justice Coordinating Group, which provides a number of the Library Extras referenced throughout this text, can be reached via **Web Extra 2–14**.

The Research Report

Findings from research and analysis of data are typically presented in the form of a report or paper in which suggestions for further study may be made. Policy issues or strategies for addressing the problems identified by the researcher are also frequently discussed. Charts, graphs, and tables may be included in the body of a research report. Most reports are professional-looking documents prepared on a word processor with grammar and spelling checkers and printed on a laser or ink-jet printer. Some are eventually published in professional journals, and a few become staples of the field—frequently cited works that illustrate fundamental criminological or methodological principles.

Most research reports follow a traditional professional format with the following component features:

- **Title page:** The title page contains the names of the report's authors, their institutional or professional affiliations, the date of the report, and its title. Many report titles consist of a main title and a subtitle, which generally gives additional information about the report's subject matter. Some report titles seem all-inclusive: "The Impact of Family Structure and Quality on Delinquency: A Comparative Assessment of Structural and Functional Factors";[71] others are relatively straightforward: "Comparing Criminal Career Models."[72]
- **Acknowledgments:** Often, the author wishes to express appreciation to individuals and organizations that facilitated the study or whose help made the study possible in the first place. Sources of grant support, including funding agencies and foundations, individuals and organizations that either participated in the study or were themselves studied, and people who facilitated various aspects of the study or the production of the report are all frequently acknowledged.
- **Table of contents:** Reports of any length (say, beyond ten pages) often contain a table of contents that helps readers find the needed material quickly and provides structure to the report itself. A table of contents that is helpful for readers lists section headings within the body of the report.
- **Preface (optional):** The purpose of a preface is to allow the author to make observations (often of a personal nature) that might not be appropriate within the body of the report. Reasons for choice of the study's subject, observations about the promise held by the field of study, and wide-ranging statements about the future of criminological research are all frequent topics of prefaces found in research reports.
- **Abstract:** An abstract is a brief (usually one-paragraph) summation of the report's findings, allowing readers to gauge whether the subject matter will be of interest to them without reading the entire report. In this day of electronic information, abstracts serve the additional function of providing a quick synopsis that can be made readily available to those searching large databases containing many research articles.
- **Introduction:** Most authors write an introductory section as part of their research report. The introduction describes the aim and purpose of the study, provides a general statement of the problem studied, and furnishes a general conceptual framework for the remainder of the report. The introduction may also outline issues that are related to the problem under study and could benefit from further investigation.
- **Review of existing literature:** Most research builds on existing knowledge and makes use of previous findings. To cite a few proverbial observations, it is not true that "there is nothing new under the sun" when conducting research, it is also not necessary to "reinvent the wheel." In other words, the relevant works of other researchers should be discussed in any report, and the bearing that previous studies have on the present one should be explained. Sometimes researchers who are engaged in literature reviews discover that the questions they wish to study have already been answered or that someone else

has found a more concise way of stating their concerns. Hence, new investigators can avoid concept development that is merely repetitive and even data gathering that has already been undertaken.

- **Description of existing situation:** Sometimes a description of the existing situation is combined with a report's introduction. If not, then it is appropriate to elaborate on the problem under study by providing details that describe the conditions existing at the beginning of the study.
- **Statement of hypothesis:** Research etiquette in criminology frequently requires the statement of a hypothesis to be tested. Most researchers have an idea of what they expect to find and set out to test a theory or a proposition derived from a theory. For example, researchers may wish to test whether the Brady Law, a federal statute that limits handgun sales, has effectively met its goal of reducing the number of deaths by firearms. A hypothesis should be a clear and concise statement of what the study purports to test. As mentioned previously, hypotheses useful in guiding research are always operationalized, or expressed in terms that are in some way measurable. Descriptive studies, on the other hand, are not designed to prove or disprove assumptions (although they may not be free of them), and such studies may not contain hypotheses.
- **Description of research plan:** The research design, data-gathering strategies, and plans for statistical analysis should all be described. This section, although it may be elaborate and lengthy, simply provides an overview of the methodology employed by the researcher and explains how the problem was investigated and why particular research strategies were chosen.
- **Disclaimers/limitations:** All research is subject to limitations. Shortages of money, time, personnel, and other resources impose limitations on research undertakings, as do shortcomings in statistical techniques and restrictions on the availability of data. Limitations should be honestly appraised and presented in the research report so that readers will be able to assess their impact on the results reported.
- **Findings/results:** Along with an overview of the research as it was actually conducted, the findings provide a statement of research results, and many regard this section as the heart of the report. The manner in which results are presented can be crucial for ease of understanding: Bar charts and pie charts are probably the most commonly employed types of diagrams (although the type of data collected will determine the appropriate format for its presentation). Some researchers choose to employ tables containing raw numbers when pictorial forms of representation like charts and graphs would better facilitate comprehension.
- **Analysis/discussion:** Once findings have been presented, they should be analyzed and discussed. Not all analyses need be of a quantitative sort; however, much of today's criminological literature is replete with statistical analyses, some of them quite sophisticated. Unfortunately, poorly conceptualized research cannot be helped by later analysis, no matter how sophisticated that analysis may be. Therefore, it is crucial to the success of any research endeavor that early planning—including conceptual development, strategies for data collection, and research designs—be undertaken with an eye toward producing data that will lend themselves to meaningful analysis and discussion after data gathering has been completed. The analysis section should also focus on whether the data, as analyzed, support the study's guiding hypothesis.
- **Summary/conclusions:** The summation section encapsulates the study's purpose and findings in a few paragraphs and may also contain suggested improvements or recommended solutions to the problem studied based on the evidence produced by the report. Policy implications are also discussed (if at all) in the conclusion of the report because they are simply broad-based solutions to problems that have been identified.
- **Endnotes/footnotes:** Endnotes or footnotes may be used to reference quoted sources or to refer readers to supporting documents. Sometimes a combination of endnotes and footnotes is employed. Endnotes, as their name implies, appear at the conclusion of a report (often after the summary but before the appendixes), whereas footnotes are found at the bottom of the pages containing the referenced material.
- **Appendixes:** Not all reports contain appendixes. Those that do may place sample questionnaires, accompanying cover letters, concise exhibits from literature reviews, detailed statistical tables, copies of letters of support, detailed interview information, and so forth, near the end of the document. Appendixes should be used only if they serve the purpose of further explicating the report's purpose, methods, or findings. Otherwise, appendixes may appear to pad the report and can discredit the researcher's efforts in the eyes of readers.
- **List of references:** No report is complete without a list of references or a bibliography used in planning the study and in preparing the document. Although all items listed in the bibliography may not be referenced within the body of the report, source material should still be provided if it was reviewed and served some purpose in study development. Literature that is examined, for example, may guide the researcher to other material or may provide useful insights during the study's overall conceptual formation.

Writing for Publication

Criminologists often seek to publish the results of their research to share them with others working in the field. The primary medium for such publication consists of refereed professional journals, those that employ the services of peer reviewers to gauge the quality of the manuscripts submitted to them. Although the review process

The primary medium for research papers consists of refereed professional journals.

■ **Follow the author's tweets about the latest crime and justice news at @schmalleger.**

can be time-consuming, it is believed to result in the publication of manuscripts that make worthwhile contributions to the field of criminology and in the rejection of those of lesser quality.

Perhaps the best-known professional journals in the field of criminology today are *American Journal of Criminal Justice, British Journal of Criminology, Crime and Delinquency, Crime and Social Justice, Criminal Justice and Behavior, Criminal Justice Ethics, Criminal Justice Policy Review, Criminal Justice Review, Criminology, Criminology and Public Policy, Critical Criminology, Journal of Contemporary Criminal Justice, Journal of Crime and Justice, Journal of Criminal Justice Education, Journal of Criminal Law and Criminology, Journal of Quantitative Criminology, Journal of Research in Crime and Delinquency, Justice Quarterly*, and *Theoretical Criminology*.[73] For a comprehensive list of journals in the field of criminology, including many that are Web-based, visit **Web Extra 2–15**.

Each journal has its own requirements for manuscript submission. Some require a single copy of a manuscript, others ask for multiple copies, a few journals request manuscript files on disk along with hard copies, and still others are moving toward electronic submission via the Internet. An increasing number of journals have established submission fees, usually in the $10 to $20 range, to help defray the costs associated with the review process.

Submission etiquette within the field of criminology demands that an article be sent to only one journal at a time. Simultaneous submissions are discouraged and create difficulties for both authors and editors when articles are accepted by more than one publication. Given the complexities of the review and publication processes, it is probably best to write the editor of any journal to which submission is being contemplated to inquire about that journal's particular expectations.

Most journals require that manuscripts be prepared according to a particular style, meaning that citations, capitalization, footnoting, abstracts, notes, headings, and subheadings are all expected to conform to the style of other articles published in the same journal. Two of the most prevalent styles are the American Psychological Association (APA) style and the American Sociological Association (ASA) style.

Most criminological journals, however, utilize a modification of one of these styles. When considering submission of a manuscript for publication review, it is advisable to write to the editor of the journal in question requesting a style sheet or general style guidelines. Style guides are also available from the APA[74] and the ASA, with third-party publishers making style guides available through university and special-purpose bookstores.

If a research report is not intended for publication, other styles may be acceptable. Answers to general questions about report writing and style can be found in publications like William Strunk, Jr., and E. B. White's *The Elements of Style*[75] and Mary-Claire van Leunen's *A Handbook for Scholars*.[76]

SUMMARY

- Criminology is a social science that endeavors to apply the techniques of data collection and hypothesis testing through observation and experimentation. Successful hypothesis testing can lead to theory building and a more complete understanding of the nature of crime and crime causation. Evidence-based criminology offers the promise of building a valuable collection of evidence-based knowledge that can be of service to policy makers and individuals concerned about the fight against crime.
- The three eras that have characterized the field of criminology over the past 100 years are the "Golden Age of Research," the "Golden Age of Theory," and an age characterized by extensive theory testing using empirical methods. The fourth (current) era of evidence-based criminology is heir to the first three eras.
- A theory is a series of interrelated propositions attempting to describe, explain, predict, and ultimately control some class of events. Theories gain explanatory power from inherent logical consistency, are "tested" by how well they describe and predict reality, provide relatively complete understanding, are supported by observations, and stand up to continued scrutiny.
- Research refers to the use of standardized, systematic procedures in the search for knowledge. Determinations of program effectiveness are made through research. Threats to the internal and external validity of research designs refer to confounding effects that might invalidate the results of research.
- Quantitative methods tend to produce results that are easy to measure, whereas qualitative methods produce subjective results that are difficult or impossible to quantify. Quantitative methods are useful in objectively assessing hypotheses and measuring the effects of an experimental intervention; qualitative methods are important for the insights they provide into the subjective workings of the criminal mind and the processes by which meaning is accorded to human experience.

- Values enter into all stages of the research process. Protection of human subjects from harm, need for privacy, disclosure of research methods, and data confidentiality are all critical ethical issues. To address these and other concerns, the Academy of Criminal Justice Sciences (ACJS) has adopted an official code of ethics for research in the field of criminology.
- Ideally, research results in the field of criminology should have a significant impact on public crime-control policy. Unfortunately, publicly elected officials are often ignorant of current criminological research or do not heed the advice of professional criminologists, seeking instead to create politically expedient policies.
- A typical research report might contain the following sections: title page, acknowledgments, table of contents, preface, abstract, introduction, review of existing literature, description of existing situation, statement of hypothesis, description of research plan, disclaimers/limitations, findings/results, analysis/discussion, summary/conclusion, endnotes/footnotes, appendixes, and list of references. Research findings in the field of criminology are published in professional journals.

KEY TERMS

applied research, 31
confounding effect, 33
control group, 35
controlled experiment, 34
correlation, 40
data confidentiality, 43
descriptive statistics, 39
evidence based, 27
evidence-based criminology, 27
external validity, 33
hypothesis, 29
inferential statistics, 39
informed consent, 43
internal validity, 33
intersubjectivity, 38
meta-analysis, 46
operationalization, 32
participant observation, 37
primary research, 31
pure research, 31
qualitative method, 42
quantitative method, 41
quasi-experimental design, 34
randomization, 35
replicability, 38
research, 31
research design, 33
secondary research, 31
survey research, 36
test of significance, 40
theory, 30
variable, 32
***verstehen*, 43**

QUESTIONS FOR REVIEW

1. What is evidence-based criminology? How does the meaning of the word *evidence* in evidence-based criminology differ from the evidence found at a crime scene or the evidence used in criminal trials?
2. What three eras have characterized the field of criminology over the past 100 years? Describe each. What is the most recent, or fourth era?
3. What is a theory? What purposes do theories serve? What role do research and experimentation play in theory building in criminology?
4. What is a hypothesis? How can a hypothesis be tested? What is internal validity? External validity? How can threats to internal and external validity be addressed?
5. What are the differences between quantitative and qualitative methods in the social sciences? What are the advantages and disadvantages of each method?
6. What are some ethical considerations involved in conducting criminological research? How can researchers make sure that such considerations are met?
7. How do criminological research and experimental criminology affect social policy?
8. What sections might a typical research report contain? Where are research findings in criminology published?

QUESTIONS FOR REFLECTION

1. This text emphasizes the theme of social problems versus social responsibility. How might a thorough research agenda allow us to decide which perspective is more fruitful in combating crime?
2. What does it mean to operationalize a hypothesis? Why is operationalization necessary?
3. Why is the task of criminological theory construction so demanding? How do we know if a theory is any good?
4. What is a meta-analysis? For what purposes might a meta-analysis be conducted?
5. What are the various types of data-gathering strategies discussed in this chapter? Describe them. Is any one technique better than another? Why? Under what kinds of conditions might certain types of data-gathering strategies be most appropriate?
6. A few years ago, the Bureau of Justice Statistics announced findings that male military veterans were less than half as likely as male nonveterans of the same age to be in prison (the rates reported were 630 versus 1,390 per 100,000 male prisoners, respectively). Does this mean that we can say with confidence that military service decreases a male's likelihood of committing a criminal offense? What other influences might be operating to lower the likelihood of crime commission by male military veterans? (See the full report at http://www.justicestudies.com/pubs/veterans.pdf.)

CHAPTER 3

CLASSICAL AND NEOCLASSICAL THOUGHT

LEARNING OUTCOMES

After reading this chapter, you should be able to answer the following questions:

- What are the major principles of the Classical School of criminology?
- What were some forerunners of classical thought in criminology?
- Who were some important thinkers of the Classical School of criminology, and what was their legacy?
- What is neoclassical criminology, and how does it differ from the classical perspective? How does it build on it?
- What is the role of punishment in neoclassical criminology?
- What are the policy implications of the Classical School and of neoclassical thought?
- What are the criticisms of classical and neoclassical perspectives on crime?

■ **mores** Behavioral proscriptions covering potentially serious violations of a group's values. Examples include strictures against murder, rape, and robbery.

■ **folkways** Time-honored customs. Although folkways carry the force of tradition, their violation is unlikely to threaten the survival of the group.

■ ***mala in se*** An act that is thought to be wrong in and of itself.

Introduction

A number of crimes are relatively spontaneous unplanned events that occur in the heat of passion or when an unanticipated opportunity presents itself. A wallet left on the seat of an unlocked car whose window is rolled down, for example, is an invitation for anyone walking by to steal the wallet, and some people will be unable to resist the temptation to reach out and grab it. The majority of crimes, however, are likely planned—at least to some degree. Crime planning, which involves rational decision making on the part of the offender, means not only that criminals assess the pros and cons of perpetrating offenses (that is, the benefits versus the likelihood of being caught and punished), but also the means of crime commission. An example of clear thinking in support of criminal activity was recently available on listverse.com, a site that touts itself as "focused on lists that intrigue and educate."[1] One list featured among the site's crime and mystery series is "Top 10 Tips to Commit the Perfect Crime."[2] Among the tips offered are ensuring that anyone contemplating an offense not leave any discoverable DNA at the scene of the crime. Because DNA is ubiquitous, the list author explains that "[t]he best solution . . . is to commit your crime in a place that is likely to have a lot of DNA from strangers." A park, a shopping mall, or "anywhere that a lot of people tend to gather" is recommended as an offense location. The list author opines that "[f]inding your DNA will be like finding a needle in a haystack."[3]

This chapter examines the belief that at least some illegal activity is the result of rational choices made by individuals seeking various kinds of illicit rewards. The perspectives presented in this chapter form the basis for strict policies of social control—those based on punishment as a primary means for curtailing continued criminality. As you read through this chapter, however, you might ask yourself how the theoretical approaches that it describes can effectively counter the rewards of crime that might be imagined by those who are considering violating the law.

Some illegal activity is the result of rational choices made by individuals seeking various kinds of illicit rewards.

Major Principles of the Classical School

This section summarizes the central features of the Classical School of criminological thought, while a later section describes the neoclassical perspective—a modern day offshoot of that early school. The eight key principles of classical and current-day neoclassical criminology are shown in Figure 3–1.

Forerunners of Classical Thought

The notion of crime as a violation of established law did not exist in most primitive societies. Lack of law-making bodies, absence of formal written laws, and loose social bonds precluded the concept of crime as law violation, but all human societies, from the simplest to the most advanced, did evidence their own widely held notions of right and wrong. Sociologists call such fundamental concepts of morality and propriety *mores* and *folkways*. *Mores*, *folkways*, and *law* are terms used by **William Graham Sumner** to describe the three basic forms of behavioral strictures imposed by social groups upon their members.[4] Mores and folkways govern behavior in relatively small primitive societies, whereas in large complex societies, they are reinforced and formalized through written laws.

Mores consist of proscriptions covering potentially serious violations of a group's values (for example, murder, rape, and robbery). **Folkways** are time-honored customs; although they carry the force of tradition, their violation is less likely to threaten the survival of the social group. The fact that American men have traditionally worn little jewelry illustrates a folkway that has given way in recent years to various types of male adornment, including earrings, gold chains, and even makeup. Mores and folkways, although they may be powerful determinants of behavior, are nonetheless informal because only laws have been codified into formal strictures wielded by institutions and created specifically for enforcement purposes.

Another method of categorizing socially proscriptive rules is provided by some criminologists who divide crimes into the dual categories of *mala in se* and *mala prohibita*. Acts that are ***mala in se***

■ ***mala prohibita*** An act that is wrong only because it is prohibited.

Key Principles of Classical and Neoclassical Criminology

- Human beings are fundamentally rational, and most human behavior results from free will coupled with rational choice.
- Pain and pleasure are the two central determining factors of human behavior.
- Punishment serves to deter law violators and serves as an example to others who might contemplate violating the law.
- The principles of right and wrong are inherent in our nature and cannot be denied.
- Society exists to provide benefits to individuals that they would not receive living in isolation.
- When people band together for the protection offered by society, they forfeit some of their personal freedoms in order to enjoy the benefits of living among others cooperatively.
- Certain key rights of the individual are necessary of the enjoyment of life, and governments that restrict and prohibit the exercise of those rights should be disbanded.
- Crime lessens the quality of the contractual bond that exists between individuals and their society. Therefore, criminal acts cannot be tolerated by any members if everyone wants to receive the most benefit from living in a cooperative society.

FIGURE 3-1 | Key Principles of Classical and Neoclassical Criminology

Source: Schmalleger, Frank J., *Criminology*. Printed and Electronically reproduced by permission of Pearson Education, Inc., Upper Saddle River, New Jersey.

AlexandreNunes/Shutterstock

Good and evil are shown attempting to influence a man. Crime and other social evils have always begged for explanation. What would today's criminologists think of the claim that "the devil made him do it"?

are said to be fundamentally wrong, regardless of the time or place in which they occur (for example, forcing someone to have sex against his or her will and the intentional killing of children). Those who argue for the existence of *mala in se* offenses usually point to some fundamental rule, such as religious teachings (the Ten Commandments, the Koran, and so on), to support their belief that some acts are inherently wrong.

Offenses termed ***mala prohibita*** are said to be wrong in areas where they are prohibited (for example, prostitution, gambling, drug use, and premarital sexual behavior). The status of such behaviors as *mala prohibita* is supported by the fact that they are not necessarily crimes in every jurisdiction; prostitution, for example, is legal in parts of Nevada, as is gambling.

The Demonic Era

Since time began, humankind has been preoccupied with what appears to be an ongoing war between good and evil. Evil has often appeared in impersonal guise, as when the great bubonic plague (the "black death") ravaged Europe and Asia in the fourteenth century, leaving as much as three-quarters of the population dead in a span of 20 years. At other times, evil has seemed to wear a human face, as when the Nazi Holocaust claimed millions of Jewish lives during World War II.

Whatever its manifestation, the very presence of evil in the world has begged for interpretation, and sage minds throughout human history have advanced many explanations for the evil conditions that individuals and social groups have at times been

■ **Code of Hammurabi** An early set of laws established by the Babylonian king Hammurabi, who ruled the ancient city of Babylon from 1792 to 1750 B.C.

■ **retribution** The act of taking revenge upon a criminal perpetrator.

■ **Twelve Tables** Early Roman laws written approximately 450 B.C. that regulated family, religious, and economic life.

■ **common law** Law originating from usage and custom rather than from written statutes. The term refers to nonstatutory customs, traditions, and precedents that help guide judicial decision making.

forced to endure. Some forms of evil, like the plague and the Holocaust, appear cosmically based, whereas others—including personal victimization, criminality, and singular instances of deviance—are the undeniable result of individual behavior. Cosmic-level evil has been explained by ideas as diverse as divine punishment, karma, fate, and vengeful activities of offended gods. Early explanations of personal deviance ranged from demonic possession to spiritual influences, to temptation by fallen angels.

Early Sources of Criminal Law

Code of Hammurabi

Modern criminal law is the result of a long evolution of legal principles. The **Code of Hammurabi** is one of the first known bodies of law to survive for study today. King Hammurabi ruled the ancient city of Babylon from 1792 to 1750 B.C. and created a legal code consisting of strictures that were originally intended to establish property and other rights and that were crucial to the continued growth of Babylon as a significant commercial center. Hammurabi's law spoke to issues of theft, property ownership, sexual relationships, and interpersonal violence. Well-known criminologist Marvin Wolfgang observed, "In its day, 1700 B.C., the Hammurabi Code, with its emphasis on retribution, amounted to a brilliant advance in penal philosophy mainly because it represented an attempt to keep cruelty within bounds."[5] Prior to the code, captured offenders often faced barbarous **retribution**, frequently at the hands of revenge-seeking victims, no matter how minor their transgressions had been. Learn more about the Code of Hammurabi at **Web Extra 3–1**.

Early Roman Law

Of considerable significance for our own legal tradition is early Roman law. Roman legions under Emperor Claudius I (10 B.C.–A.D. 54) conquered England in the middle of the first century, and Roman customs, law, and language were forced upon the English population during the succeeding three centuries under the Pax Romana—a peace imposed by the military might of Rome.[6]

Early Roman law derived from the **Twelve Tables**, a collection of basic rules regulating family, religious, and economic life written around 450 B.C. They appear to have been based on common and fair practices generally accepted among early tribes existing prior to the establishment of the Roman Republic; only fragments of the tables survive today.

The best-known legal period in Roman history occurred during the reign of Emperor Justinian I (A.D. 527–565). By the end of the sixth century, the Roman Empire had declined substantially in size and influence and was near the end of its life. Possibly to preserve Roman values and traditions, Justinian undertook the laborious process of distilling Roman laws into a set of writings. This Justinian Code consisted of three lengthy legal documents—the Institutes, the Digest, and the Code itself—and distinguished between two major legal categories: public laws and private laws. Public laws dealt with the organization of the Roman state, its Senate, and governmental offices; private law concerned itself with contracts, personal possessions, legal status of various people (citizens, free people, slaves, freedmen, guardians, husbands, and wives), and injuries to citizens. It contained elements of our modern civil and criminal law, and it influenced Western legal thought up through the Middle Ages. Learn more about early Roman law at **Web Extra 3–2**.

Common Law

Common law refers to a traditional body of unwritten legal precedents that was created through everyday practice in English society, was based on shared traditions and standards, and was supported by court decisions during the Middle Ages. As novel situations arose and were handled by British justices, their declarations became the start for any similar future deliberations.

Common law refers to a traditional body of unwritten legal precedents that was created through everyday practice in English society.

Common law was given considerable legitimacy in the eleventh century with the official declaration that it was the law of the land by King Edward the Confessor (A.D. 1042–1066). The authority of common law was further reinforced by the decision of William the Conqueror to use popular customs as the basis for judicial action following his subjugation of Britain in A.D. 1066.

Eventually, court decisions were recorded and made available to barristers (English trial lawyers) and judges. As criminologist Howard Abadinsky wrote, "Common law involved the transformation of community rules into a national legal system. The controlling element [was] precedent."[7] Today, common law forms the basis for much of our statutory and case law

■ **Enlightenment** A social movement that arose during the eighteenth century and that built upon ideas like empiricism, rationality, free will, humanism, and natural law.

■ **social contract** The Enlightenment-era concept that human beings abandon their natural state of individual freedom to join together and form society. In the process of forming a social contract, individuals surrender some freedoms to society as a whole, and government, once formed, is obligated to assume responsibilities toward its citizens and to provide for their protection and welfare.

and has been called *the* major source of modern criminal law in English-speaking countries around the world. Learn more about common law at **Web Extra 3–3.**

Magna Carta

The Magna Carta (literally, "great charter"), another important source of modern laws and legal procedure, was signed on June 15, 1215, by King John of England at Runnymede, under pressure from British barons who took advantage of his military defeats to demand a pledge to respect their traditional rights and to be bound by law. At the time of its signing, the Magna Carta (63 chapters in length) was little more than a feudal document listing specific royal concessions.[8] Its original purposes were to ensure feudal rights, to guarantee the king would not encroach on landowning barons' privileges, to guarantee the freedom of the church, and to ensure respect for the customs of towns.

Its wording was later interpreted during a judicial revolt in 1613, however, to support individual rights and jury trials. Sir Edward Coke, chief justice under James I, held that the Magna Carta guaranteed basic liberties for all British citizens and ruled that any acts of Parliament that contravened common law would be void, a famous ruling that possibly became the basis for the rise of the U.S. Supreme Court, with its power to nullify laws enacted by Congress.[9] Similarly, a specific provision of the Magna Carta, designed originally to prohibit the king from prosecuting the barons without just cause, was expanded into the concept of due process of law, a fundamental cornerstone of modern legal procedure. Because of these later interpretations, the Magna Carta has been called "the foundation stone of our present liberties."[10]

The Enlightenment

The **Enlightenment** (or the Age of Reason), a highly significant social movement occurring during the seventeenth and eighteenth centuries, was built upon ideas developed by many important thinkers. Because of their indirect contributions to classical criminological thought, it will be worthwhile to spend a few paragraphs discussing the writings of a few of these historical figures. Learn more about the Enlightenment and the intellectual figures who gave it life at **Web Extra 3–4**.

Thomas Hobbes

English philosopher **Thomas Hobbes** (1588–1679) developed what many writers regard as a negative view of human

Chris Maddaloni/CQ Roll Call/Newscom

The Magna Carta, an important source of modern Western laws and legal procedure. What are some other important sources of modern criminal law?

nature and social life, which he described in his momentous work, *Leviathan* (1651). Fear of violent death, he said, forces human beings into a **social contract** with one another to create a state that demands the surrender of certain natural rights and submission to the absolute authority of a sovereign while offering protection and succor to its citizens. The social contract concept significantly influenced many of Hobbes's contemporaries, but much of his writing was condemned for an overly pessimistic view of both human nature and existing governments.

John Locke

In 1690, English philosopher **John Locke** (1632–1704) published his *Essay Concerning Human Understanding*, putting forth the idea that the natural human condition at birth is like a blank slate upon which interpersonal encounters and other experiences indelibly inscribe the traits of personality. In contrast to earlier thinkers, who assumed that people are born with certain innate propensities and rudimentary intellectual concepts and ideas, Locke ascribed the bulk of adult human qualities to life experiences.

In the area of social and political thought, Locke further developed the Hobbesian notion of the social contract and contended that human beings, through a social contract, abandon their natural state of individual freedom and lack of interpersonal responsibility to join together and form society.

■ **natural law** The philosophical perspective that certain immutable laws are fundamental to human nature and can be readily ascertained through reason. Human-made laws, in contrast, are said to derive from human experience and history—both of which are subject to continual change.

■ **natural rights** Rights that, according to natural law theorists, individuals retain in the face of government action and interests.

Although individuals surrender some freedoms to society, government—once formed—is obligated to assume responsibilities toward its citizens, to provide for their protection and welfare, and to guarantee them certain inalienable rights such as the right to life, health, liberty, and possessions. A product of his times (the dictatorial nature of monarchies and the Roman church were being much disparaged), Locke stressed the duties that governments have toward their citizens while paying very little attention to the responsibilities of individuals to the societies of which they are a part, and he argued that political revolutions, under some circumstances, might become an obligation incumbent upon citizens.

Locke also developed the notion of checks and balances between divisions of government, a doctrine elaborated on by French jurist and political philosopher **Charles-Louis de Secondat Montesquieu** (1689–1755). In *The Spirit of Laws* (1748), Montesquieu wove Locke's notions into the concept of a separation of powers between divisions of government. Both ideas later found a place in the U.S. Constitution.

Jean-Jacques Rousseau

Swiss-French philosopher and political theorist **Jean-Jacques Rousseau** (1712–1778) further advanced the notion of the social contract in his treatise of that name (*Social Contract*, 1762), stating that human beings are basically good and fair in their natural state but historically were corrupted by the introduction of shared concepts and joint activities like property, agriculture, science, and commerce. As a result, the social contract emerged when civilized people agreed to establish governments and systems of education to correct the problems and inequalities brought on by the rise of civilization.

Rousseau also contributed to the notion of **natural law**, a concept originally formulated by Saint Thomas Aquinas (1225–1274), Baruch Spinoza (1632–1677), and others to provide an intuitive basis for the defense of ethical principles and morality. Submissive to the authority of the church, secular rulers were pressed to reinforce church doctrine in any laws they decreed. Aquinas wrote in his *Summa Theologica* that any human-made law that contradicts natural law is corrupt in the eyes of God. Hence, natural law was incorporated into English common law throughout the Middle Ages.

Rousseau agreed with earlier writers that certain immutable laws are fundamental to human nature and can be readily ascertained through reason. Human-made law, in contrast, derives from human experience and history, both of which are subject to continual change, so human-made law (or "positive law") changes from time to time and from epoch to epoch. Rousseau expanded the concept of natural law to support emerging democratic principles.

Natural Law and Natural Rights

Thomas Paine (1737–1809), an English-American political theorist and the author of *The Rights of Man* (1791 and 1792), defended the French Revolution, arguing that only democratic institutions could guarantee individuals' **natural rights**. At the Second Continental Congress, Thomas Jefferson (1743–1826) and other congressional representatives (many well versed in the writings of Locke and Rousseau) built the U.S. Constitution around an understanding of natural law as they perceived it. Hence, when Jefferson wrote of inalienable rights to "life, liberty, property," he was following in the footsteps of his intellectual forebears and meant that such rights were the natural due of all men and women because they were inherent in the social contract between citizens and their government.

Natural law and natural rights have a long intellectual history. In a *National Review* article subtitled "If Natural Law Does Not Permit Us to Distinguish between Men and Hogs, What Does?" Harry V. Jaffa, director of the Claremont Institute's Center for the Study of the Natural Law, called an 1854 speech given by Abraham Lincoln "the most moving and compelling exhibition of natural-law reasoning in all political history."[11] In that speech, Lincoln argued in favor of freedom for slaves by succinctly pointing out there is no difference between people, whatever their color: "Equal justice to the South, it is said, requires us to consent to the extending of slavery to new countries. That is to say, inasmuch as you do not object to my taking my hog to Nebraska, therefore I must not object to your taking your slave. Now, I admit this is perfectly logical, if there is no difference between hogs and Negroes."[12] Lincoln's point, of course, was that there is a huge difference between human beings and animals by virtue of their nature and that such a difference cannot be denied by logic.

Other commentators have cited the "crimes against humanity" committed by Nazis during World War II as indicative of natural law principles. The chilling testimony of Rudolf Hess,[13] Hitler's deputy, during the 1945 war crimes trial in Nuremberg, Germany, as he recalled the Fuehrer's order to exterminate millions of Jews, indicates the extent of the planned "final solution": "In the summer of 1941, I was summoned to Berlin to Reichsfuehrer SS Himmler to receive personal orders. He told me something to the effect—I do not remember the exact words—that the Fuehrer had given the order for a final solution of the Jewish question. We, the SS, must carry out that order. If it is not carried out now then the Jews will later on destroy the German people. He had chosen Auschwitz on account of its easy access by rail and also because the extensive site offered space for measures ensuring isolation."[14] Although Hitler's Nazi

■ **Classical School** A criminological perspective of the late 1700s and early 1800s that had its roots in the Enlightenment and that held that humans are rational beings, that crime is the result of the exercise of free will, and that punishment can be effective in reducing the incidence of crime to the degree it negates the pleasure to be derived from crime commission.

Party made the law in Germany at the time, natural law supporters (largely in other countries) argued that Hitler's final solution to the Jewish "question" was inherently wrong and that any laws passed in furtherance of it were immoral and should have been struck down.

Although the concept of natural law has waned somewhat in influence over the past half century, many people today still hold that the basis for various existing criminal laws can be found in immutable moral principles or some other identifiable aspect of the natural order. Modern-day advocates of natural law claim that it comes from outside the social group and that it is knowable through some form of revelation, intuition, or prophecy.

The debate over abortion is an example of the modern-day use of natural law arguments to support both sides in the dispute. Antiabortion forces, frequently called "pro-lifers" or "right-to-lifers," claim that an unborn fetus is a person, that he or she is entitled to all the protection we would give to any other living human being, and that such protection is basic and humane and lies in the natural relationship of one human being to another within the relationship of a society to its children. Abortion (also called "pro-choice") advocates, who are striving for passage of a law or for a reinterpretation of past Supreme Court precedent that would support their position, maintain that abortion is a right of any pregnant woman because she is the only one who should be in control of her body and claim that the legal system must address the abortion question by offering protection for this natural right.

Perhaps the best-known modern instance of a natural law debate occurred during confirmation hearings for U.S. Supreme Court Justice Clarence Thomas. Thomas, who was confirmed in 1991, once wrote an opinion in which he argued from a natural law point of view, but that opinion was later challenged by Senate Judiciary Committee members who felt it reflected an unbending judicial attitude. Learn more about natural law at **Web Extra 3–5**.

Everett Collection Historical/Alamy

Thomas Paine (1737–1809), an important contributor to the concept of natural law. What are the central tenets of natural law?

The Classical School

The Enlightenment fueled the fires of social change, leading eventually to the French and American Revolutions and providing many of the intellectual underpinnings of the U.S. Constitution. It also inspired other social movements and freed innovative thinkers from the chains of convention. As a direct consequence of Enlightenment thinking, superstitious beliefs were discarded and men and women began to be perceived, for the first time, as self-determining entities possessing a fundamental freedom of choice; free will and rational thought came to be recognized as the linchpins of all significant human activity. In effect, the Enlightenment inspired the reexamination of existing doctrines of human behavior from the point of view of rationalism.

Within criminology, the Enlightenment led to the development of the **Classical School** of criminological thought. Crime and deviance, which had previously been explained by reference to mythological influences and spiritual shortcomings, took their place in Enlightenment thought alongside other forms of human activity as products of the exercise of free will. Once people were seen as having control over their own lives, crime came to be explained as a particularly individualized form of evil—that is, as moral wrongdoing fed by personal choice.

Cesare Beccaria

Cesare Beccaria (1738–1794) was born in Milan, Italy, the eldest of four children; he was trained at Catholic schools and had earned a doctor of law degree by the time he was 20. In 1764, Beccaria published his *Essay on Crimes and Punishments*, which consisted of 42 short chapters covering a few major themes to communicate his observations on the laws and justice system of his time. In *Essay*, Beccaria distilled the notion of the social contract into the idea that "laws are the conditions under which independent and isolated men united to form a society."[15] More than anything else, his writings consisted of a philosophy of punishment. Beccaria claimed that the purpose of punishment should be deterrence rather than retribution, and punishment should be imposed to prevent offenders from committing additional crimes. Beccaria saw punishment as a means to an end, not an end in itself, and crime prevention was more important to him than revenge.

Cesare Beccaria claimed that "[t]he more promptly and the more closely punishment follows upon the commission of a crime, the more just and useful will it be."

To help prevent crimes, Beccaria argued, adjudication and punishment should both be swift and, once punishment is decreed, it should be certain: "The more promptly and the more closely punishment follows upon the commission of a crime, the more just and useful it will be." Punishment that is imposed immediately following crime commission, claimed Beccaria, is connected with the wrongfulness of the offense, both in the mind of the offender and in the minds of others who might see the punishment imposed and thereby learn of the consequences of involvement in criminal activity.

Beccaria concluded that punishment should be only severe enough to outweigh the personal benefits to be derived from crime commission and that any additional punishment would be superfluous. "In order," he said, "for punishment not to be, in every instance, an act of violence of one or of many against a private citizen, it must be essentially public, prompt, necessary, the least possible in the given circumstances, proportionate to the crimes, [and] dictated by the laws."

Beccaria distinguished among three types of crimes: those that threaten the security of the state, those that injure citizens or their property, and those that run contrary to the social order. Punishment should fit the crime—theft should be punished through fines, personal injury through corporal punishment, and serious crimes against the state (such as inciting revolution) via application of the death penalty. (Beccaria was opposed to the death penalty in most other circumstances, seeing it as a kind of warfare waged by society against its citizens.)

Beccaria condemned the torture of suspects, a practice still used in the eighteenth century, saying that it was a device that ensured that weak suspects would incriminate themselves, whereas strong ones would be found innocent. Torture was also unjust because it punished individuals before they had been found guilty in a court of law. In Beccaria's words, "No man can be called guilty before a judge has sentenced him, nor can society deprive him of public protection before it has been decided that he has in fact violated the conditions under which such protection was accorded him. What right is it then, if not simply that of might, which empowers a judge to inflict punishment on a citizen while doubt still remains as to his guilt or innocence?"

Beccaria's *Essay* also touched upon a variety of other topics. He distinguished between two types of proof: "perfect proof," where there was no possibility of innocence, and "imperfect proof," where some possibility of innocence remained. Beccaria also believed in the efficacy of a jury of one's peers, recommending that half of any jury panel consist of the victim's peers and the other half of the accused's peers.

Beccaria's ideas were widely recognized as progressive by his contemporaries. His principles were incorporated into the French penal code of 1791 and significantly influenced the justice-related activities of European leaders like Catherine the Great of Russia, Frederick the Great of Prussia, and Emperor Joseph II of Austria. Evidence suggests that Beccaria's *Essay* influenced framers of the U.S. Constitution, and some scholars claim that the first ten amendments to the Constitution, known as the Bill of Rights, might not have existed were it not for Beccaria's emphasis on individuals' rights in the face of state power. Perhaps more than anyone else, Beccaria is responsible for the contemporary beliefs that criminals have control over their behavior, that they choose to commit crimes, and that they can be deterred by the threat of punishment. Learn more about Cesare Beccaria at **Web Extra 3–6** and **Library Extra 3–1**.

Jeremy Bentham

Jeremy Bentham (1748–1832), another founder of the Classical School, wrote in his *Introduction to the Principles of Morals and Legislation* (1789) that "nature has placed mankind under the governance of two sovereign masters, pain and pleasure."[16] To reduce crime or, as Bentham put it, "to prevent the happening of mischief," the pain of crime commission must outweigh the pleasure to be derived from criminal activity. Bentham's claim rested upon his belief, spawned by Enlightenment thought, that human beings are fundamentally rational and that criminals will weigh in their minds the pain of punishment against any

■ **hedonistic calculus** The belief, first proposed by Jeremy Bentham, that behavior holds value to any individual undertaking it according to the amount of pleasure or pain it can be expected to produce for that person.

■ **utilitarianism** Another term for Jeremy Bentham's concept of hedonistic calculus.

■ **Panopticon** A prison designed by Jeremy Bentham that was to be a circular building with cells along the circumference, each clearly visible from a central location staffed by guards.

Jeremy Bentham said "Nature has placed mankind under the governance of two sovereign masters, pain and pleasure."

pleasures thought likely to be derived from crime commission.

Bentham advocated neither extreme nor cruel punishment—only punishment sufficiently distasteful to the offender that the discomfort experienced would outweigh the pleasure to be derived from criminal activity. The more serious the offense is, the more reward it holds for its perpetrator and therefore the more weighty the official response must be. "Pain and pleasure," said Bentham, "are the instruments the legislator has to work with" in controlling antisocial and criminal behavior.

Bentham's approach has been termed **hedonistic calculus** or **utilitarianism** because of its emphasis on the worth any action holds for an individual undertaking it. Bentham stated, "By the principle of utility is meant that principle which approves or disapproves of every action whatsoever, according to the tendency which it appears to have to augment or diminish the happiness of the party whose interest is in question; or, what is the same thing to promote or to oppose that happiness." In other words, Bentham believed that individuals could be expected to weigh the consequences of their behavior before acting to maximize their pleasure and minimize their pain, based on intensity, duration, certainty, and immediacy (or remoteness) in time.

Like Beccaria, Bentham focused on the potential held by punishment to prevent crime and to act as a deterrent for those considering criminal activity. Regarding criminal legislation, he wrote that "the evils of punishment must be made to exceed the advantage of the offence." Bentham distinguished among 11 types of punishment:

1. Capital punishment (death)
2. Afflictive punishment (whipping and starvation)
3. Indelible punishment (branding, amputation, and mutilation)
4. Ignominious punishment (public punishment involving use of stocks or pillory)
5. Penitential punishment (censure by the community)
6. Chronic punishment (banishment, exile, and imprisonment)
7. Restrictive punishment (license revocation and administrative sanction)
8. Compulsive punishment (restitution and appointment with probation officer)
9. Pecuniary punishment (fine)
10. Quasi-pecuniary punishment (denial of services otherwise available)
11. Characteristic punishment (mandates such as wearing prison uniforms)

Utilitarianism is a practical philosophy, and Bentham was quite practical in his suggestions about crime prevention. He recommended the creation of a centralized police force focused on crime prevention and control—a recommendation that resulted in the English Metropolitan Police Act of 1829 establishing London's New Police under the direction of Sir Robert Peel.

Bentham's other major contribution to criminology was his suggestion that prisons be designed along the lines of what he called a "Panopticon House." The **Panopticon** was to be a circular building with cells along the circumference, each clearly visible from a central location staffed by guards, constructed near or within cities so that it might serve as an example to citizens of what would happen to them should they commit crimes. He also wrote that prisons should be managed by contractors who could profit from the labor of prisoners and that each contractor should "be bound to insure the lives and safe custody of those entrusted to him." Although a Panopticon was never built in Bentham's England, French officials funded a modified version of such a prison, which was eventually built at Lyons, and three prisons modeled after the Panopticon concept were constructed in the United States.

Bentham's critics have been quick to point out that punishment often does not seem to work and that even punishment as severe as death appears not to have any effect on the incidence of crimes like murder (discussed in greater detail later in this chapter). Such critics forget Bentham's second tenet: For punishment to be effective, "it must be swift and certain." Learn more about Jeremy Bentham from the Bentham Project via **Web Extra 3–7**.

Neoclassical Criminology

The Classical School was to influence criminological thinking for a long time to come, from the French Revolution and the U.S. Constitution to today's emphasis on deterrence and crime prevention. By the end of the 1800s, however,

■ **positivism** The application of scientific techniques to the study of crime and criminals.

■ **hard determinism** The belief that crime results from forces beyond the control of the individual.

■ **neoclassical criminology** A contemporary version of classical criminology that emphasizes deterrence and retribution, with reduced emphasis on rehabilitation.

■ **nothing-works doctrine** The belief popularized by Robert Martinson in the 1970s that correctional treatment programs have little success in rehabilitating offenders.

Georgios Kollidas/Fotolia

Jeremy Bentham (1748–1832), whose work is closely associated with the Classical School of criminology. What are the key features of the Classical School?

Richard A. Chapman/Associated Press

Stateville Correctional Center in Illinois. The prison, built with cells circling a control area, was based on the Panopticon design proposed by Jeremy Bentham. What did Bentham mean when he said that, for punishment to be effective, "it must be swift and certain"?

Positivism made use of the scientific method in studying criminality.

classical criminology, with its emphasis on free will and individual choice as the root causes of crime, had given way to another approach known as positivism. **Positivism** (discussed in greater detail in Chapter 4) made use of the scientific method in studying criminality and was based on an acceptance of **hard determinism**, the belief that crime results from forces beyond the control of the individual. The original positivists completely rejected the notion of free will and turned their attention to the impact of socialization, genetics, economic conditions, peer group influences, and other factors that might determine criminality. Acceptance of the notion of hard determinism implied that offenders were not entirely (if at all) responsible for their crimes and suggested that crime could be prevented by changing the conditions that produced criminality (see Figure 3–2).

While positivism remains an important component of contemporary criminology, many of its assumptions were undermined in the 1970s by (1) studies that seemed to show that offenders could not be rehabilitated no matter what was tried, (2) a growing and widespread public fear of crime that led to "get tough on crime" policies, and (3) a cultural reaffirmation of the belief that human beings had a rational nature. The resulting resurgence of classical ideals, called **neoclassical criminology**, focused on the importance of character (a kind of middle ground between total free will and hard determinism) and the dynamics of character development, as well as the rational choices that people make when faced with opportunities for crime. The neoclassical movement appears to have started with a number of publications produced in the 1970s, such as **Robert Martinson's** national survey of rehabilitation programs.[17] Martinson found that, when it came to the rehabilitation of offenders, nothing seemed to work because most resumed their criminal careers after release from prison. "Nothing works!" became a rallying cry of conservative policy makers, and the **nothing-works doctrine** received much public attention. Many conservative politicians

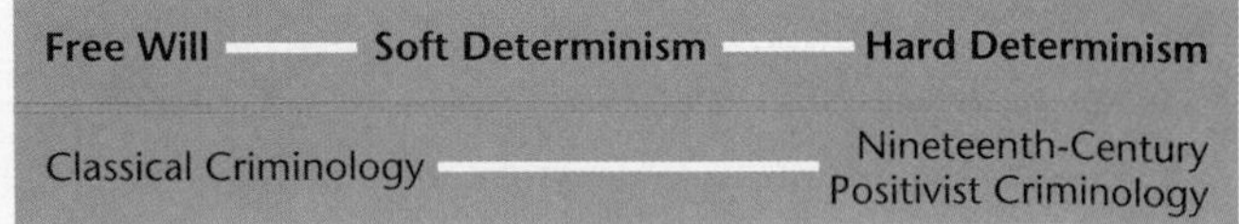

FIGURE 3–2 | **Classical Criminology versus Positivism—The Role of Free Will**

Source: Schmalleger, Frank J., *Criminology*. Printed and Electronically reproduced by permission of Pearson Education, Inc., Upper Saddle River, New Jersey.

■ **justice model** A contemporary model of imprisonment in which the principle of just deserts forms the underlying social philosophy.

■ **three-strikes legislation** A criminal statute that mandates life imprisonment for criminals convicted of three violent felonies or serious drug offenses.

THEORY | versus REALITY

Three-Strikes Legislation

Near the end of the twentieth century, many states jumped on the "get tough on crime" bandwagon and adopted the justice model in their approach to crime-control legislation. In the spring of 1994, for example, California legislators passed the state's now-famous "three strikes and you're out" law. Amid much fanfare, then-Governor Pete Wilson signed the three-strikes legislation into law, calling it "the toughest and most sweeping crime bill in California history." California's law, which is retroactive (in that it counts offenses committed before the date the legislation was signed), requires a 25-year-to-life sentence for three-time felons with convictions for two or more serious or violent prior offenses. Criminal offenders facing a "second strike" can receive up to double the normal sentence for their most recent offense. Under the law, parole consideration is not available until at least 80% of an offender's sentence has been served.

In 2003, in two separate cases, the U.S. Supreme Court upheld the three-strikes California convictions of Gary Ewing and Leandro Andrade.[i] Ewing, who had four prior felony convictions, had received a 25-year-to-life sentence in a California courtroom following his conviction for felony grand theft of three golf clubs. Andrade, who also had a long record, had been sentenced to 50 years in prison for two petty-theft convictions.[ii] In writing for the Court in the *Ewing* case, Justice Sandra Day O'Connor noted that states should be able to decide when repeat offenders "must be isolated from society to protect the public safety," even when nonserious crimes trigger the lengthy sentence. In deciding these two cases, both of which were based on Eighth Amendment claims, the Court found that it is *not* cruel and unusual punishment to impose a possible life term for a nonviolent felony when the defendant has a history of serious or violent convictions.

Practically speaking, California's three-strikes law has had a dramatic impact on the state's criminal justice system. "'Three strikes and you're out' sounds great to a lot of people," says Alan Schuman, president of the American Probation and Parole Association. "But no one will cop a plea when it gets to the third time around. We will have more trials, and this whole country works on plea bargaining and pleading guilty, not jury trials," Schuman said at a meeting of the association. In an early study conducted by RAND, it was estimated that full enforcement of the law could cost as much as $5.5 billion annually—or $300 per California taxpayer per year.

A 2012 review of three-strikes legislation found that 16 states have recently modified such laws in response to difficult economic conditions; this means that the high cost of imprisonment is leading legislatures to rethink long prison terms. Modifications have included giving judges more discretion in sentencing and narrowing the types of crimes that count as a "strike."

In November 2012, California voters overwhelmingly approved a change to their state's three-strikes law.[iii] The changes mean that now only two categories of offenders can be sentenced as three-strikers: (1) those who commit new "serious or violent" felonies as their third offense, and (2) previously released murderers, rapists, or child molesters who are convicted of a new third strike, even if it is not a "serious or violent" felony. Under the new legislation, inmates sentenced under earlier versions of the law are allowed to petition for early release. Estimates are that around 3,000 such inmates may soon be released. Learn more about crime-control policy at the Center for Law and Social Policy via **Web Extra 3–8.**

Discussion Questions

1. Some people suggest that three-strikes sentences should be imposed only on offenders who commit violent crimes, such as murder, rape, armed robbery, and certain types of arson. What do you think?
2. How is three-strikes legislation in keeping with the spirit of the justice model described in this chapter?

Notes

i. *Ewing* v. *California*, 583 U.S. 11 (2003); *Lockyer* v. *Andrade*, 583 U.S. 63 (2003).

ii. Under California law, a person who commits petty theft can be charged with a felony if he or she has prior felony convictions. The charge is known as "petty theft with prior convictions." Andrade's actual sentence was two 25-year prison terms to be served consecutively.

iii. Tracey Kaplan, "Proposition 36: Voters Overwhelmingly Ease Three Strikes Law," *Mercury News*, November 7, 2012.

and some criminologists began calling existing notions of crime prevention and rehabilitation into question amid claims that enhanced job skills, increased opportunities for employment, and lessened punishment did nothing to stem what was a rising tide of crime.

In 1975, Harvard political scientist James Q. Wilson wrote *Thinking about Crime*, suggesting that crime is not a result of poverty or social conditions and cannot be affected by social programs;[18] he argued for the lengthy incarceration of offenders and the elimination of criminal opportunity. Also in 1975, David Fogel published a book called *We Are the Living Proof: The Justice Model of Corrections*.[19] His **justice model**, predicated on the growing belief that prisons do not rehabilitate or cure and that criminal offenders *deserve* punishment because of the choices they make, was proposed to the Illinois state legislature as a model for prison reform. Fogel argued that, for the criminal justice process to work, offenders must be treated "as responsible as well as accountable, that is, volitional."[20] **Three-strikes legislation**, a reflection of the justice model, is discussed in the Theory versus Reality box in this chapter.

■ **rational choice theory** A perspective that holds that criminality is the result of conscious choice and that predicts that individuals choose to commit crime when the benefits outweigh the costs of disobeying the law.

■ **routine activities theory** A brand of rational choice theory posited by Lawrence Cohen and Marcus Felson that suggests that lifestyles contribute significantly to both the volume and the type of crime found in any society. Also known as *lifestyle theory*.

■ **situational choice theory** A brand of rational choice theory that views criminal behavior "as a function of choices and decisions made within a context of situational constraints and opportunities."

■ **capable guardian** One who effectively discourages crime.

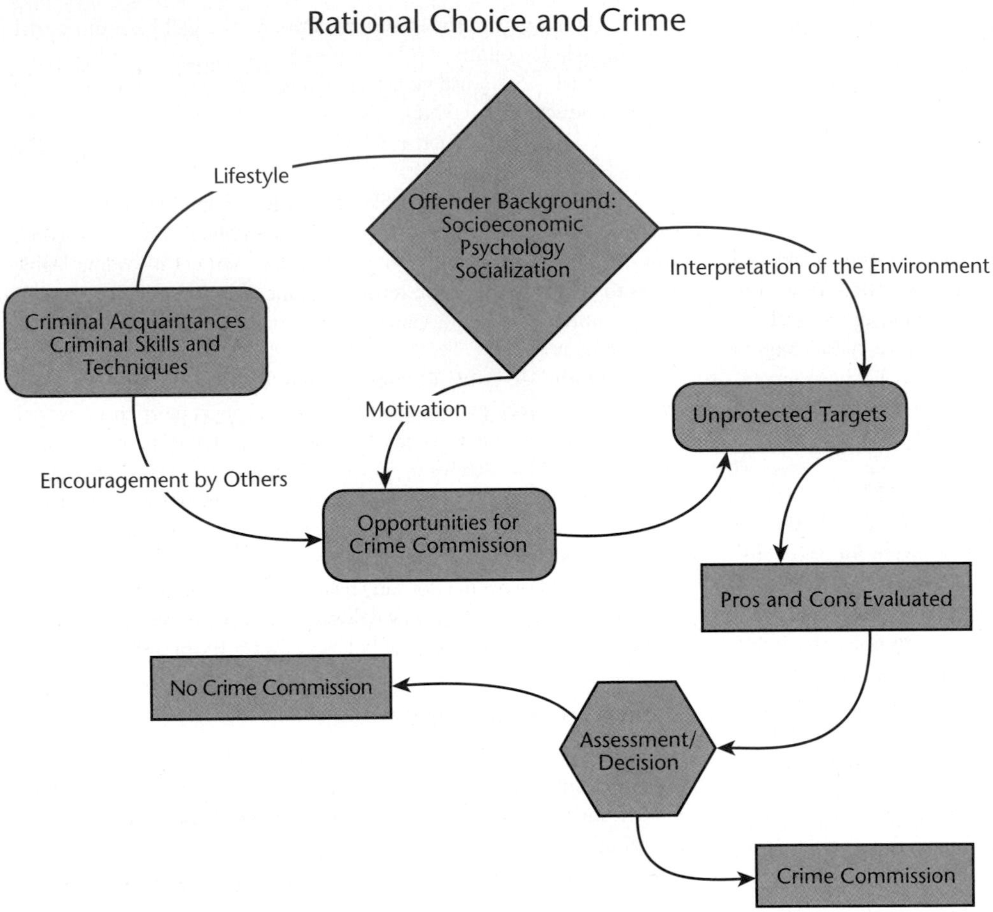

FIGURE 3-3 | **Rational Choice and Crime**

Source: Schmalleger, Frank J., *Criminology*. Printed and Electronically reproduced by permission of Pearson Education, Inc., Upper Saddle River, New Jersey.

Rational Choice Theory (RCT)

Rational choice theory (RCT), a product of the late 1970s and early 1980s, mirrors many of the principles found in classical criminology. The theory rests upon the belief that criminals make a conscious, rational, and at least partially informed choice to commit crime and employs cost–benefit analysis (as in the field of economics), viewing human behavior as the result of personal choices made after weighing both the costs and benefits of available alternatives. "[Rational choice] predicts that individuals choose to commit crime when the benefits outweigh the costs of disobeying the law. Crime will decrease when opportunities are limited, benefits are reduced, and costs are increased."[21] Figure 3–3 diagrams the steps that are likely to be involved in making a choice to commit a crime.

Two varieties of RCT can be identified. One builds on an emerging emphasis on victimization and is called **routine activities theory**; the second, largely an extension of the rational choice perspective, is called **situational choice theory**.

Routine activities theory (also termed *lifestyle theory*) was proposed by **Lawrence Cohen** and **Marcus Felson** in 1979.[22] Cohen and Felson said that lifestyles contribute significantly to both the volume and the type of crime found in any society and suggested that changes in American society during the 1960s and 1970s (increased personal affluence and greater involvement in social activities outside the home) brought about increased rates of household theft and personal victimization by strangers. Central to the routine activities approach is the claim that crime is likely to occur when a motivated offender and a suitable target come together in the absence of a **capable guardian**, one who effectively discourages crime, and that a person who has taken crime-prevention steps is less likely to be victimized. Cohen and Felson stated, "The risk of criminal victimization varies dramatically among the circumstances and locations in which people place themselves and their property."[23] For example, a person who routinely uses an automated teller machine late at night in an isolated location is far more likely to be preyed upon by robbers than someone who stays home after dark. Lifestyles that contribute to criminal opportunities are likely to result in crime because they increase the risk of potential victimization.[24]

■ **soft determinism** The belief that human behavior is the result of choices and decisions made within a context of situational constraints and opportunities.

Central to the routine activities approach is the claim that crime is likely to occur when a motivated offender and a suitable target come together in the absence of a capable guardian.

Although noncriminal lifestyles at a given point in one's lifetime are partly the result of unavoidable social roles and assigned social positions, those who participate in a given lifestyle generally make rational decisions about specific behaviors (such as going to a given automated teller machine at a certain time). The same is true of criminal lifestyles. Hence, the meshing of choices made by both victims and criminals contributes significantly to both the frequency and the type of criminal activity observed in society. Learn more about the routine activities approach, including its implications for crime control, via **Library Extra 3–2**.

In a later work, Felson suggested that a number of "situational insights" might combine to elicit a criminal response from individual actors enmeshed in a highly varied social world, pointing out that "individuals vary greatly in their behavior from one situation to another" and that criminality might flow from temptation, bad company, idleness, or provocation.[25] Convenience stores, for example, create temptations toward theft when they display their merchandise within easy reach of customers. Other authors have defined the term *situation* to mean "the perceptive field of the individual at a given point in time" and have suggested that it can be described "in terms of who is there, what is going on, and where it is taking place."[26]

Situational choice theory provides an example of **soft determinism**, which views criminal behavior "as a function of choices and decisions made within a context of situational constraints and opportunities."[27] The theory holds that "crime is not simply a matter of motivation; it is also a matter of opportunity."[28] Situational choice theory suggests that the probability of criminal activity can be reduced by changing the features of the environment. **Ronald V. Clarke** and **Derek B. Cornish**, collaborators in the development of the situational choice perspective, analyzed the choice-structuring properties of a potentially criminal situation, defining them as "the constellation of opportunities, costs, and benefits attaching to particular kinds of crime."[29] Clarke and Cornish suggested the use of situational strategies to lower the likelihood of criminal victimization in given instances. They also recognized that the rationality of criminal offenders is inevitably bounded or limited, as it is for all of us, by the amount and accuracy of information available to them at the time they are weighing the costs and consequences of future actions.[30]

In brief, rational choice theorists concentrate on "the decision-making process of offenders confronted with specific contexts," and have shifted "the focus of the effort to prevent crime from broad social programs to target hardening, environmental design or any impediment that would [dissuade] a motivated offender from offending."[31] Twenty-five techniques of situational crime control can be identified, and each can be classified according to the five objectives of situational prevention. Figure 3–4 outlines those techniques and provides examples of each. All 25 techniques can be seen in the interactive Web graphic available at http://www.popcenter.org/25techniques. As shown in the figure, the five objectives are as follows:

1. increase the effort involved in committing a crime,
2. increase the risks associated with crime commission,
3. reduce the rewards of crime,
4. reduce the provocations that lead to criminal activity, and
5. remove the excuses that facilitate crime commission.

Earlier approaches focused largely on the balance between pleasure and pain as the primary determinant of criminal behavior, whereas rational choice theory tends to place less emphasis on pleasure and emotionality and more on rationality and cognition. Some rational choice theorists distinguish among the types of choices offenders make as they move toward criminal involvement. One type of choice, known as involvement decisions, has been described as "multistage" and is said to "include the initial decision to engage in criminal activity as well as subsequent decisions to continue one's involvement or to desist."[32] Another type of choice, event decisions, relates to particular instances of criminal opportunity (such as the decision to rob a particular person or let him or her pass); in contrast to involvement decisions, which may take months or even years to reach, these are usually made quickly. Learn more about rational choice theories via **Web Extra 3–9**. You can read about the use of environmental design techniques to reduce crime at

Objective: Increase the effort	Example: Close streets
Objective: Increase the risks	Example: Strengthen surveillance
Objective: Reduce the rewards	Example: Identify property
Objective: Reduce provocations	Example: Reduce emotional arousal
Objective: Remove the excuses	Example: Control drugs/alcohol

FIGURE 3–4 | **Situational Crime Control Techniques with Examples**

Center for Problem-Oriented Policing, www.popcenter.org

Library Extra 3–3. Learn more about crime prevention in general via **Library Extra 3–4**.

The Seductions of Crime

One criminologist who focuses on the relationship between the decision to commit crime and the rewards that such a decision brings is **Jack Katz**, whose book *Seductions of Crime* explains crime as the result of the "often wonderful attractions within the lived experience of criminality."[33] Crime, Katz said, is often pleasurable for those committing it, and pleasure is the major motivation behind crime, even if the kind of pleasure to be derived from crime is not immediately obvious. According to Katz, criminologists have often depicted crime as something to be avoided and have failed to understand just how good crime *feels* to those who commit it:

> The social science literature contains only scattered evidence of what it means, feels, sounds, tastes, or looks like to commit a particular crime. Readers of research on homicide and assault do not hear the slaps and curses, see the pushes and shoves, or feel the humiliation and rage that may build toward the attack, sometimes persisting after the victim's death. How adolescents manage to make the shoplifting or vandalism of cheap and commonplace things a thrilling experience has not been intriguing to many students of delinquency. The description of "cold-blooded, senseless murders" has been left to writers outside the social sciences. Neither academic methods nor academic theories seem to be able to grasp how it makes sense to them to kill when only petty cash is at stake. Sociological and psychological studies of robbery rarely focus on the distinctive attractions of robbery, even though research has now clearly documented that alternative forms of criminality are available and familiar to many career robbers.[34]

For criminal offenders, crime is indeed rewarding, according to Katz. It is exciting and feels good: "The particular seductions and compulsions [which criminals] experience may be unique to crime," he stated, "but the sense of being seduced and compelled is not. To grasp the magic in the criminal's sensuality, we must acknowledge our own."[35] Katz described the almost sexual attraction shoplifting held for one young offender: "The experience was almost orgasmic for me. There was a buildup of tension as I contemplated the danger of a forbidden act, then a rush of excitement at the moment of committing the crime, and finally a delicious sense of release."[36]

Criminologists have often depicted crime as something to be avoided and have failed to understand just how good some crime feels to those who commit it.

Katz's approach stresses the sensual dynamics of criminality, arguing that crime is sensually compelling for many people. As one writer noted, "Jack Katz argues for a redirection of the criminological gaze—from the traditional focus on background factors such as age, gender, and material conditions to foreground or situational factors that directly precipitate criminal acts and reflect crimes' sensuality."[37] Learn more about the seductions of crime at **Web Extra 3–10**.

Andrey Burmakin/Shutterstock

A glittering jewelry store display window. Rational choice theory says that offenders make a conscious, rational choice to commit crimes. Might some crimes also be irrational?

Situational Crime-Control Policy

Building on the work of rational and situational choice theorists, Israeli criminologist David Weisburd described the advantages of a situational approach to crime prevention. "Crime prevention research and policy have traditionally been concerned with offenders or potential offenders. Researchers have looked to define strategies that would deter individuals from involvement in crime or rehabilitate them so they would no longer want to commit criminal acts. In recent years, crime prevention efforts have often focused on the incapacitation of high-rate or dangerous offenders so they are not free to victimize law-abiding citizens. In the public debate over crime prevention policies, these strategies are usually defined as competing approaches."[38] However, Weisburd said that "they have in common a central assumption about crime prevention research and policy: that efforts to understand and control crime must begin with the

■ **situational crime prevention** A social policy approach that looks to develop a greater understanding of crime and more effective crime-prevention strategies through concern with the physical, organizational, and social environments that make crime possible.

■ **target hardening** The reduction in criminal opportunity for a particular location, generally through the use of physical barriers, architectural designs, and enhanced security measures.

offender. In all of these approaches, the focus of crime prevention is on people and their involvement in criminality."

A new approach developed in large part as a response to the failures of traditional theories and programs. "Although this assumption [the focus on people] continues to dominate crime prevention research and policy," said Weisburd, "it has begun to be challenged by a very different approach that seeks to shift the focus of crime prevention efforts." For many scholars and policy makers, this meant having to rethink assumptions about criminality and the ways offenders might be prevented from participating in crime, with some suggesting that a more radical reorientation of crime-prevention efforts was warranted. They argued that the shift must come not in terms of the specific strategies or theories that were used but in terms of the unit of analysis that formed the basis of crime-prevention efforts and called for a focus not on people who commit crime but on the context in which crime occurs.

This approach, which is called **situational crime prevention**, looks to develop greater understanding of crime and more effective crime-prevention strategies through concern with the physical, organizational, and social environments that make crime possible.[39] The situational approach does not ignore offenders; it merely sees them as one part of a broader crime-prevention equation centered on the context of crime. It demands a shift in the approach to crime prevention from one concerned primarily with why people commit crime to one looking primarily at why crime occurs in specific settings. It moves the context of crime into central focus and sees the offender as only one of a number of factors that affect it. Situational crime prevention is closely associated with the idea of a "criminology of place," which is discussed in the Theory versus Reality box in Chapter 9.

Weisburd suggested that a "reorientation of crime prevention research and policy from the causes of criminality to the context of crime provides much promise. At the core of situational prevention is the concept of opportunity."[40] In contrast to offender-based approaches to crime prevention, which usually focus on the dispositions of criminals, situational crime prevention begins with the opportunity structure of the crime situation, meaning the immediate situational and environmental components of the context of crime. This approach to crime prevention tries to reduce the opportunities for crime in specific situations, which involves efforts as simple and straightforward as **target hardening** or access control.

The value of a situational approach lies in the fact that criminologists have found it difficult to identify who is likely to become a serious offender and to predict the timing and types of future offenses that repeat offenders are likely to commit. Weisburd explained that "legal and ethical dilemmas make it difficult to base criminal justice policies on models that still include a substantial degree of statistical error." Weisburd added that "if traditional approaches worked well, of course, there would be little pressure to find new forms of crime prevention. If traditional approaches worked well, few people would possess criminal motivation and fewer still would actually commit crimes."

Situational prevention advocates argue that the context of crime provides a promising alternative to traditional offender-based crime-prevention policies.[41] They assume that situations provide a more stable and predictable focus for crime-prevention efforts than do people, based on commonsense notions of the relationship between opportunities and crime. Shoplifting, for example, is by definition clustered in stores and not residences, and family disputes are unlikely to be a problem outside the home. High-crime places, in contrast to high-crime people, cannot flee to avoid criminal justice intervention, and crime that develops from the specific characteristics of certain places cannot be easily transferred to other contexts.

In short, situational crime control works by removing or reducing criminal opportunity. Felson and Clarke reminded us that "accepting opportunity as a cause of crime also opens up a new vista of crime prevention policies focused upon opportunity-reduction. [Such policies] do not merely complement existing efforts to diminish individual propensities to commit crime through social and community programs or the threat of criminal sanctions. Rather, the newer policies operate on circumstances much closer to the criminal event and thus have a much greater chance to reduce crime immediately."[42]

If we accept that opportunity is a cause of crime equal in importance to the personal and social characteristics that other researchers point to as causes, then, stated Felson and Clarke, we have a "criminology that is not only more complete in its theorizing, but also more relevant to policy and practice."[43] If Felson and Clarke are correct in what they say, then much of the crime prevention work that is already being done by police agencies, private security, and businesses aimed at reducing criminal opportunity directly affects the basic causes of crime.

Learn more about situational crime prevention and target hardening via **Web Extra 3–11**.

Critique of Rational Choice Theory

Rational and situational choice and routine activities theories can be criticized for overemphasizing the importance of individual choice with relative disregard for the role of social factors

THEORY | in PERSPECTIVE

The Classical School and Neoclassical Thinkers

The Classical School is a criminological perspective developed in the late 1700s and early 1800s. It had its roots in the Enlightenment and held that men and women are rational beings and that crime is the result of the exercise of free will and personal choices based on calculations of perceived costs and benefits. Hence, punishment can be effective in reducing the incidence of crime when it negates the rewards to be derived from crime commission.

Classical Criminology

Approach: Application of Classical School principles to problems of crime and justice

Period: 1700s–1880

Theorists: Cesare Beccaria, Jeremy Bentham, others

Concepts: Free will, deterrence through punishment, social contract, natural law, natural rights, due process, Panopticon

Neoclassical Criminology

Approach: Modern-day application of classical principles to problems of crime and crime control in contemporary society, often in the guise of "get tough" social policies

Period: 1970s to the present

Theorists: Lawrence Cohen, Marcus Felson, Ronald V. Clarke, Derek B. Cornish, Jack Katz, many others

Concepts: Rational choice, routine activities theory, capable guardians, situational crime prevention, target hardening, just deserts, determinate sentencing, specific deterrence, general deterrence

Rational choice theory can be criticized for an overemphasis on individual choice and a relative disregard for the role of social factors in crime causation.

in crime causation, such as poverty, poor home environment, and inadequate socialization. One study, for example, found that the routine activities approach explained 28% of property crimes committed in socially disorganized (high-crime) areas of a small Virginia city and explained only 11% of offenses committed in low-crime areas.[44] In the words of the authors, "This research demonstrates more support for routine activities theory in socially disorganized areas than in socially organized areas."[45] Although one could argue that the kinds of routine activities supportive of criminal activity are more likely to occur in socially disorganized areas, it is also true that the presence (or absence) of certain ecological characteristics (that is, the level of social disorganization) may enhance (or reduce) the likelihood of criminal victimization. As the authors state, "Those areas characterized by low socioeconomic status will have higher unemployment rates, thus creating a larger pool of motivated offenders. Family disruption characterized by more divorced or separated families will result in more unguarded living structures, thus making suitable targets more available. Increased residential mobility will result in more non-occupied housing, which creates a lack of guardianship over the property and increases the number of suitable targets."[46]

According to another study, RCT does not adequately consider the impact of emotional states on cognitive ability and the role of psychopharmacological agents in decision making.[47] The study examined the effects of alcohol and anger on aggression and found that "alcohol diminishes individuals' perceptions of the costs associated with aggression and, in some instances, actually increases the perceived benefits." Similarly, high arousal levels, such as those associated with anger and other emotions, appear to impair judgment. So, when acting under the influence of alcohol or when experiencing strong emotions, "the individual's capacity to anticipate gratification and aversion, success and failure, and cost is diminished."[48] The authors note that other studies show that approximately 40% of offenders are under the influence of alcohol when committing the crimes for which they are arrested, and suggest that future research involving the rational choice perspective should include the role of emotions and the potential impact of psychopharmacological agents such as drugs or alcohol on the decisions made by people who commit crimes.

One 2005 study that explored the deterrent effect of punishment offers insight into the potential that rational choice theory holds for social policy. In that study, David Lee and Justin McCrary, both at the University of California–Berkeley, examined how juvenile offenders respond to the likelihood of

■ **displacement** A shift of criminal activity from one location to another.

■ **just deserts model** The notion that criminal offenders deserve the punishment they receive at the hands of the law and that punishments should be appropriate to the type and severity of the crime committed.

significantly higher sanctions associated with criminality when they reach adulthood.[49] They found that a 230% increase in expected sentence length was associated with only a 1.8% reduction in the likelihood of arrest, so they reasoned that even enormous increases in sentence length seem to do little to reduce the probability of repeat offending: "The small behavioral responses that we estimate suggest that potential offenders are extremely impatient, myopic, or both."[50]

A 2009 study conducted by Italian researchers focused on the large number of Italian inmates who were released in 2006 as efforts were made to reduce the prison population in that country.[51] A condition of release was that anyone who reoffended would face new sanctions *and* have to finish the term they were serving at the time of their release. The possibility of added time was found to have a "substantial effect" on the average prisoner, but the most serious offenders (those whose original sentences were 69 months or longer) appeared not to be deterred by the threat of enhanced sentences. The researchers concluded that career offenders were far less likely to be affected by penalty enhancements than offenders who were not as far down the path of criminality.

Rational choice theory assumes that everyone is equally capable of making rational decisions, which is probably not the case. Some individuals are more logical than others by virtue of temperament, personality, or socialization; some are emotional, hotheaded, and unthinking. Empirical studies of RCT have added scant support for the perspective's underlying assumptions, tending to show instead that criminal offenders are often unrealistic in their appraisals of the relative risks and rewards facing them.[52] Similarly, rational and situational choice theories seem to disregard individual psychology and morality, with their emphasis on external situations. Moral individuals, say critics, when faced with easy criminal opportunities, may rein in their desires and turn their backs on temptation.

Finally, the emphasis of rational and situational choice theories on changing aspects of the immediate situation to reduce crime has been criticized for resulting in the **displacement** of crime from one area to another.[53] Target hardening,[54] a key crime-prevention strategy among such theorists, has sometimes caused criminals to find new targets of opportunity in other areas.[55]

Punishment and Neoclassical Thought

Punishment is a central feature of both classical and neoclassical thought. Whereas punishment served the ends of deterrence in classical thought, its role in neoclassical thinking has been expanded to support the ancient concept of retribution, with those advocating retribution seeing the primary utility of punishment as revenge.

> Punishment is a central feature of both classical and neoclassical thought.

Modern neoclassical thinkers argue that, if a person is attracted to crime and chooses to violate the law, then he or she *deserves* to be punished because the consequences of crime were known to the offender before the crime was committed. The criminal *must* be punished so that future criminal behavior can be curtailed.

Notions of revenge and retribution are morally based, built on a sense of indignation at criminal behavior and on the righteousness inherent in Judeo-Christian notions of morality and propriety. Both philosophies of punishment turn a blind eye to the mundane and practical consequences of any particular form of punishment. Hence, advocates of retributive philosophies of punishment easily dismiss critics of the death penalty, who frequently challenge the efficacy of court-ordered capital punishment on the basis that such sentences do little to deter others. Wider issues, including general deterrence, become irrelevant when a person focuses narrowly on the emotions that crime and victimization engender in a given instance. From the neoclassical perspective, some crimes cry out for vengeance while others demand little more than a slap on the wrist or an apology from the offender.

Just Deserts

The old adage "He got what was coming to him" well summarizes the thinking behind the **just deserts model** of criminal sentencing, which refers to the concept that criminal offenders deserve the punishment they receive at the hands of the law and that any punishment imposed should be appropriate to the type and severity of the crime committed. The idea of just deserts has long been part of Western thought, dating back at least to Old Testament times. The Old Testament dictum of "an eye for an eye, and a tooth for a tooth" has been cited by many as divine justification for strict punishments, although some scholars believe that "an eye for an eye" was intended to *reduce* the barbarism of existing penalties, whereby an aggrieved party might exact the severest of punishments for only minor offenses (even petty offenses were often punished by whipping, torture, and sometimes death).

One famous modern-day advocate of the just deserts philosophy was Christian thinker C. S. Lewis. Lewis said that we could ask many questions about punishment, such as whether or

■ **deterrence** The prevention of crime.

■ **specific deterrence** A goal of criminal sentencing that seeks to prevent a particular offender from engaging in repeat criminality.

■ **general deterrence** A goal of criminal sentencing that seeks to prevent others from committing crimes similar to the one for which a particular offender is being sentenced.

■ **recidivism** The repetition of criminal behavior.

■ **recidivism rate** The percentage of convicted offenders who have been released from prison and who are later rearrested for a new crime, generally within five years following release.

not it is an effective deterrent. But, he wrote, the only *important* question is whether it is deserved:

> The concept of desert is the only connecting link between punishment and justice. It is only as deserved or undeserved that a sentence can be just or unjust. . . . Thus when we cease to consider what the criminal deserves and consider only what will cure him or deter others, we have tacitly removed him from the sphere of justice altogether.[56]

According to the neoclassical perspective, doing justice ultimately comes down to an official meting out of what is deserved. Justice for an individual is nothing more or less than what that individual deserves when all the circumstances surrounding that person's situation and behavior are taken into account.

Deterrence

True to its historical roots, **deterrence** is a hallmark of modern neoclassical thought. In contrast to early thinkers, however, today's neoclassical writers distinguish between general and specific deterrence: **Specific deterrence** is a goal of criminal sentencing seeking to prevent a particular offender from engaging in repeat criminality. **General deterrence** works by way of example, seeking to prevent others from committing crimes similar to the one for which a particular offender is being sentenced.

Following their classical counterparts, modern-day advocates of general deterrence frequently stress that, for punishment to be an effective impediment to crime, it must be swift, certain, and severe enough to outweigh the rewards flowing from criminal activity. Unfortunately, those who advocate punishment as a deterrent are often frustrated by the complexity of today's criminal justice system and by the slow and circuitous manner in which cases are handled and punishments are meted out. Punishments today, even when imposed by a court, are rarely swift in their imposition; the wheels of modern criminal justice are relatively slow to grind to a conclusion, given the many delays inherent in judicial proceedings and the numerous opportunities for delay and appeal available to defense counsel. Certainty of punishment is also anything but a reality. Certain punishments are those that cannot be easily avoided, but today even when punishments are ordered, they are frequently not carried out—at least not fully. In contemporary America, offenders sentenced to death, for example, are unlikely to have their sentences finalized; for those who do, an average of nearly 12 years passes between the time a death sentence is imposed and the time it is carried out.[57]

If the neoclassicists are correct, criminal punishments should ideally prevent a repetition of crime, but punishments in the United States rarely accomplish that goal, as high rates of contemporary **recidivism** (repetition of criminal behavior by those already involved in crime) indicate. Recidivism, when used to measure the success of a given approach to the problem of crime, is referred to as a **recidivism rate**, expressed as the percentage of convicted offenders who have been released from prison and who are later rearrested for a new crime, generally within five years following release. Studies show that recidivism rates are high indeed, reaching levels of 80% to 90% in some instances, meaning that eight or nine of every ten criminal offenders released from confinement are rearrested for new law-breaking activity within five years of being set free. Such studies do not measure the numbers of released offenders who return to crime but who are not caught and ignore those who return to crime more than five years after release from prison; if such numbers were available, recidivism rates would likely be even higher.

One reason U.S. criminal justice seems so ineffectual at preventing crime and reducing recidivism may be that punishments that contemporary criminal law provides are rarely applied to the majority of offenders. Statistics show that few lawbreakers are ever arrested and that, of those who are, fewer still are convicted of the crimes with which they have been charged. After a lengthy court process, most offenders processed by the justice system are released, fined, or placed on probation. Relatively few are sent to prison, although short of capital punishment, prison is the most severe form of punishment available to authorities today. To represent this situation, criminal justice experts often use a diagram known as a "crime funnel." See Figure 3–5 for the 2012 crime funnel, which shows that less than 1% of criminal law violators in the United States can be expected to spend time in prison as punishment for their crimes.

Exacerbating the situation is the fact that few people sent to prison ever serve anything close to the sentences that have been imposed on them. Many inmates serve only a small fraction of their sentences due to early release made possible by time off for good behavior, mandated reentry training, and practical considerations necessitated by prison overcrowding.

■ **capital punishment** The legal imposition of a sentence of death upon a convicted offender.

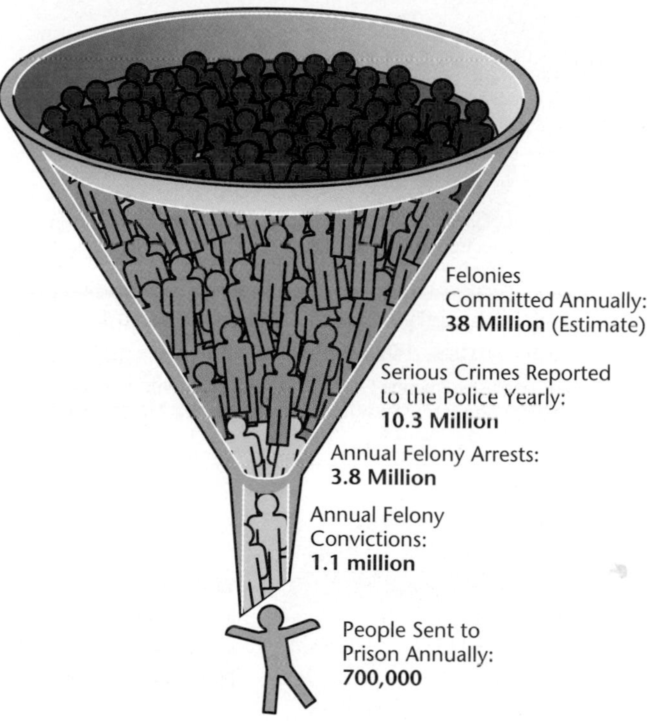

FIGURE 3-5 | **The Crime Funnel**

Note: Includes drug crimes.

Source: Statistics derived from Kathleen Maquire, ed., *Sourcebook of Criminal Justice Statistics*, http://www.albany.edu/sourcebook (accessed May 12, 2013).

Capital Punishment

Notions of deterrence, retribution, and just deserts all come together in **capital punishment**, the legal imposition of a death sentence. The many different understandings of crime and crime control, along with arguments over free will and social determinism, combine with varying philosophies of punishment to produce considerable disagreement over the efficacy of death as a form of criminal sanction.

Opponents of capital punishment make ten claims:

1. Capital punishment does not deter crime.
2. The death penalty has been imposed on innocent people, and no workable system is currently in place to prevent the accidental execution of innocents.
3. Human life, even the life of a murderer, is sacred.
4. State-imposed death lowers society to the same moral (or amoral) level as the murderer.
5. The death penalty has been (and may still be) imposed in haphazard and seemingly random fashion.
6. The death penalty is imposed disproportionately upon ethnic minorities.
7. Capital punishment goes against the most fundamental precepts of almost every organized religion.
8. The death penalty is more expensive than imprisonment.
9. Capital punishment is widely viewed as inhumane and barbaric internationally.
10. There is a better alternative (usually said to be life in prison without possibility of parole). Read more about arguments against the death penalty at **Library Extras 3–5** and **3–6**.

Advocates of capital punishment generally discount each of these claims, countering abolitionist arguments with the proposition that death is *deserved* by those who commit especially heinous acts and that anything short of capital punishment under certain circumstances is an injustice in itself; some people deserve to die for what they have done. Such arguments have evolved from a natural law perspective, are sometimes supported on religious grounds, and are based on the notion of just deserts (discussed earlier).

Strong feelings on both sides of the issue have generated a plethora of studies of the efficacy and fairness of capital punishment as a criminal sanction. The extent to which the death penalty acts as a general deterrent has been widely examined. Some researchers have compared murder rates between states that have eliminated the death penalty and those that retain it, finding little variation in the rate at which murders are committed.[58] Others have looked at variations in murder rates over time in jurisdictions that have eliminated capital punishment, with similar results.[59] A now-classic 1988 Texas study provided a comprehensive review of capital punishment by correlating homicide rates with the rate of executions within the state between 1930 and 1986;[60] the study, which was especially important because Texas has been quite active in the capital punishment arena, failed to find any support for the use of death as a deterrent.

Similarly, in an important study of the deterrent effect of capital punishment published in 2009, Tomislav V. Kovandzic and colleagues found "no empirical support for the argument that the existence or application of the death penalty deters offenders from committing homicide."[61] Kovandzic's study made use of homicide data from all 50 states and the District of Columbia between the years 1977 and 2006, and the study's design allowed researchers both to assess the impact of changes in capital punishment laws and to compare murder rates in death-penalty jurisdictions with those without capital punishment laws.

Regardless of studies to the contrary, many death-penalty advocates remain unconvinced that the sanction cannot be an effective deterrent, saying that a death penalty that is swift and certain is likely to deter others. In 2012, in a succinct summary of studies on the deterrent effect of the death penalty, the Committee on Law and Justice of the National Academies of Sciences released *Deterrence and the Death Penalty*—a publication that included a detailed analysis of previous death penalty research.[62] The committee found that "research to date is not informative about whether capital punishment decreases, increases, or has no effect on homicide rates." It concluded that "claims that research demonstrates that capital punishment decreases or increases the homicide rate or has no effect on it should not influence policy judgments about capital punishment." Read the entire National Academy of Sciences report at **Library Extra 3-7**.

> Punishments that are both swift and certain hold the potential to prevent even the most serious crimes.

Learn more about how capital punishment is seen in contemporary America from the Death Penalty Information Center at **Web Extra 3–12**. Read about the current state of the death penalty at **Library Extra 3–8**. A balanced approach to the subject can be read at **Library Extra 3–9**.

Capital Punishment and Race

According to the Washington-based Death Penalty Information Center, the death penalty has been imposed disproportionately on racial minorities throughout most of U.S. history.[63] Statistics maintained by the center show that "since 1930 nearly 90% of those executed for the crime of rape in this country were African Americans. Currently, about 50% of those on the nation's death rows are from minority populations representing 20% of the country's population." The center, a fervent anti–capital punishment organization, claims that "evidence of racial discrimination in the application of capital punishment continues." Thirty-five percent of those executed since 1976 have been black, even though blacks constitute only 12% of the population. And in almost every death-penalty case, the race of the victim is white. Of the 1,325 executions that have occurred since the death penalty was reinstated [in 1976], the center says, that "only one has involved a white defendant for the murder of a black person." Figures 3–6 and 3–7 show the ethnicity of defendants executed in the United States, as well as the ethnicity of murder victims, over the past 35 years.

On the other hand, capital punishment advocates say that the real question is not whether ethnic differences exist in the rate of imposition of the death penalty but whether the penalty is *fairly* imposed. They argue that if 50% of all capital punishment–eligible crimes were committed by members of a particular (relatively small) ethnic group, then anyone anticipating fairness in imposition of the death penalty would expect to see 50% of death-row populations composed of members of that group (no matter how small the group). In like manner, one would also expect to see the same relative ethnicity among those executed. In short, if fairness is to be a guide, those committing capital crimes should be the ones sentenced to death regardless of race, ethnicity, gender, or other social characteristics.

Although evidence may suggest that African Americans and other minorities in the United States have in the past been unfairly sentenced to die,[64] the present evidence is not so clear. For an accurate appraisal to be made, any claims of disproportionality must go beyond simple comparisons with racial representation in the larger population and must somehow measure both the frequency and the seriousness of capital crimes between and within racial groups. Following that line of reasoning, the Supreme Court, in the 1987 case of *McCleskey* v. *Kemp*,[65] held that a simple showing of racial discrepancies in the application of the death penalty does not amount to a constitutional violation.

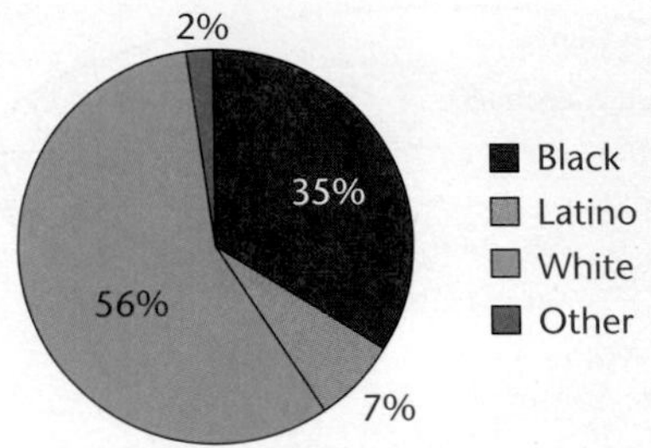

FIGURE 3-6 | Ethnicity of Defendants Executed in the United States, 1976–2013

Source: Death Penalty Information Center, http://www.deathpenaltyinfo.org/race-death-row-inmates-executed-1976 (data current as of March 30, 2013). Reprinted by permission.

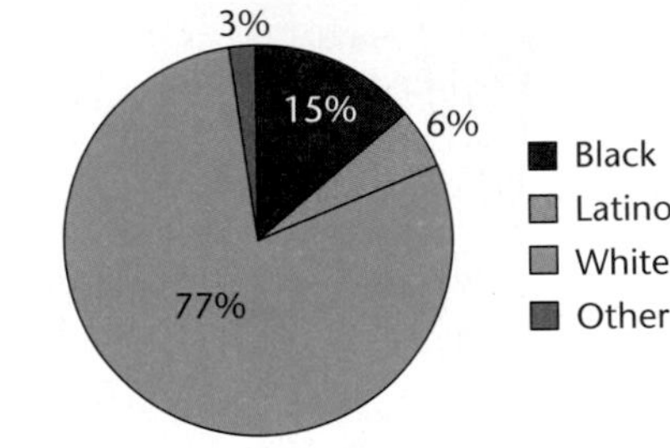

FIGURE 3-7 | Ethnicity of Murder Victims in the United States, 1976–2013

Source: Death Penalty Information Center, http://www.deathpenaltyinfo.org/race-death-row-inmates-executed-1976 (data current as of March 30, 2013). Reprinted by permission.

CRIME | in the NEWS

DNA Exonerations Expose Weaknesses in Judicial System

In October 2012, Damon Thibodeaux became the 300th prisoner in the United States to be exonerated based on DNA evidence, according to the Innocence Project, which successfully pursued his case. It's nice to breathe "free air," said Thibodeaux, who spent 15 years in almost complete isolation on death row. "It's probably the best breath I've ever had."

The Louisiana man had been a suspect in the 1996 rape and murder of his 14-year-old step-cousin. After a nine-hour interrogation, he confessed. "I didn't know that I had done it, but I done it," Thibodeaux said, according to the transcript. The case shows that some people will confess to crimes they never committed.

DNA exonerations of death-row prisoners extend back at least to 1993, when Kirk Bloodsworth was exonerated for the 1984 rape and murder of a 9-year-old girl. Bloodsworth had been linked to the crime by the testimony of five eyewitnesses, but DNA analysis of biological evidence from the crime scene showed that he could not have been the person who committed the crime.

Since Bloodsworth's time, DNA evidence has torn a hole in the U.S. criminal justice system. The 301 prisoners granted DNA exonerations so far served a total of 4,036 years in prison. The Innocence Project says that the leading cause of their wrongful convictions was false eyewitness identification, a factor in 72 percent of cases, followed by improper forensic procedures in 50 percent of cases, false confessions in 27 percent of cases, and false information from informants in 18 percent.

Mladen Antonov/AFP/Getty Images/Newscom

Kirk Noble Bloodsworth (born October 31, 1960) holds a picture of himself as a young man. Bloodsworth is the first American sentenced to death row who was exonerated by DNA evidence. How can innocent people be convicted of such serious crimes?

False eyewitness identifications come up again and again. Witnesses have only fleeting recollections of the crime, which can get blurred when they are asked to pick the perpetrator from many photos at once. David Lee Wiggins was convicted and sentenced to life in prison in 1989 for rape, based on his identification by a rape victim who had just a few glimpses of her assailant. In August 2012, a Texas judge released Wiggins based on DNA evidence.

The Innocence Project reports that it pursues just 1 percent of the 6,000 to 10,000 cases it reviews at any given time. While DNA has freed many prisoners, advocates say thousands more have persuasive evidence of wrongful prosecution but may never be freed due to lack of DNA evidence. Samples were degraded, thrown out, or never collected.

Forty-nine states now allow a prisoner access to DNA testing, but many of them still put up substantial legal barriers to obtaining tests, place time limits on DNA access, and have no consistent guidelines for evidence retention. Only about half the states require automatic preservation of DNA evidence after conviction.

There are signs of progress, though. The National Institute of Justice, the research arm of the Justice Department, is funding the development of guidelines for evidence retention. Eleven states have created commissions to study wrongful convictions and recommend changes in the system. And some states have considered improvements in witness identification, such as requiring investigators to show one photo at a time.

Discussion Questions

1. What are your feelings about capital punishment? Provide reasons to support the way you feel.
2. What do you think are the most significant arguments against the death penalty? What do you consider to be the most convincing arguments in favor of it?
3. How do cases of exoneration, like the ones described in this box, affect public opinion about capital punishment?

Sources: Douglas Blackmon, "Louisiana Death-Row Inmate Damon Thibodeaux Exonerated with DNA Evidence," *Washington Post*, September 28, 2012, http://www.washingtonpost.com/national/louisiana-death-row-inmate-damon-thibodeaux-is-exonerated-with-dna-evidence/2012/09/28/26e30012-0997-11e2-afff-d6c7f20a83bf_story.html; Molly Hennessy-Fiske, "Texan Wrongly Convicted of Rape Freed after 24 Years in Prison," *Los Angeles Times*, August 25, 2012, http://articles.latimes.com/2012/aug/25/nation/la-na-nn-rape-texas-exonerated-20120824; Kevin Johnson, "Storage of DNA Evidence Crucial to Exonerations," *USA Today*, March 28, 2011, http://usatoday30.usatoday.com/news/nation/2011-03-28-crimelab28_ST_N.htm

To reduce the likelihood that capital punishment decisions will be influenced by a defendant's race, the Washington-based Constitution Project[66] recommended that "all jurisdictions that impose the death penalty should create mechanisms to help ensure that the death penalty is not imposed in a racially discriminatory manner."[67] The project said that two approaches are especially appropriate in building such mechanisms: (1) the gathering of statistical data on the role of race in the operation of a jurisdiction's capital punishment system, and (2) the active involvement of members of all races in every level of the capital punishment decision-making process. Read the entire report of the Constitution Project at **Web Extra 3–13**, and view more than 1,000 capital punishment–related Web links at **Web Extra 3–14**.

■ **determinate sentencing** A criminal punishment strategy that mandates a specified and fixed amount of time to be served for every offense category. Under the strategy, for example, all offenders convicted of the same degree of burglary would be sentenced to the same length of time behind bars.

■ **truth in sentencing** A close correspondence between the sentence imposed upon those sent to prison and the time actually served prior to prison release.

■ **incapacitation** The use of imprisonment or other means to reduce the likelihood that an offender will be capable of committing future offenses.

Policy Implications of Classical and Neoclassical Thought

During the past 30 years or so, American justice philosophy has been strongly influenced by the punishment practices of determinate sentencing and truth in sentencing. Because both determinate sentencing and truth in sentencing are rational forms of justice, most criminologists see them as natural consequences of a classical view of crime and punishment.

Determinate sentencing is a strategy that mandates a specified and fixed amount of time to be served for every offense category. Under determinate sentencing schemes, for example, judges might be required to impose seven-year sentences on armed robbers, but only one-year sentences on strong-armed robbers (who use no weapon). Determinate sentencing schemes build on twin notions of classical thought: (1) The pleasure of a given crime can be somewhat accurately assessed, and (2) a fixed amount of punishment necessary for deterrence can be calculated and specified. **Truth in sentencing** requires judges to assess and make public the actual time an offender is likely to serve, once sentenced to prison, and many recently enacted truth-in-sentencing laws require that offenders serve a large portion of their sentence (often 80%) before they can be released.

Truth in sentencing requires judges to assess and make public the actual time an offender is likely to serve, once sentenced to prison.

Because of the widespread implementation of determinate sentencing strategies and the passage of truth-in-sentencing laws during the last quarter century, prison populations today are larger than ever before. By early 2013, the nation's state and federal prison population (excluding jails) stood at 1,571,013 inmates, representing an increase of more than 700% over 1970.[68] Figure 3–8 shows the U.S. prison population growth rate from 1924 to 2012. Today, for the first time in nearly a century, prison populations may have peaked and started to decline as a result of the budgetary crises facing the states.

Imprisonment is one component of a strategy of **incapacitation** (the use of imprisonment or other means to reduce the likelihood that an offender will be capable of committing future offenses). Proponents of modern-day incapacitation often distinguish between the terms *selective incapacitation*, in which crime is controlled via the imprisonment of specific individuals, and *collective incapacitation*, whereby changes in legislation and/or sentencing patterns lead to the removal from society of entire groups of individuals judged to be dangerous. Advocates of selective incapacitation as a crime-control strategy point to studies that show the majority of crimes are perpetrated by a small number of hard-core repeat offenders. The most famous of those studies, conducted by University of Pennsylvania Professor Marvin Wolfgang, focused on 9,000 men born in Philadelphia in 1945.[69] By the time this cohort of men had reached age 18, Wolfgang was able to determine that 627 "chronic recidivists" were responsible for the large majority of all serious violent crimes committed by the group. Other, more recent studies have similarly shown that a small core of criminal perpetrators is probably responsible for most criminal activity in the United States.

Such thinking has led to the development of incapacitation as a modern-day treatment philosophy and to the creation of innovative forms of incapacitation that do not require imprisonment—such as home confinement, use of halfway houses or career training centers for convicted felons, and psychological and/or chemical treatments designed to reduce the likelihood of future crime commission. Similarly, such thinkers argue, the decriminalization of many offenses and the enhancement of social programs designed to combat what they see as the root causes of crime—including poverty, low educational levels, general lack of skills, and inherent or active discrimination—will lead to a much reduced incidence of crime in the future, making high rates of imprisonment unnecessary.

A Critique of Classical Theories

Classical and neoclassical thought represents more a philosophy of justice than it does a theory of crime causation. As Randy

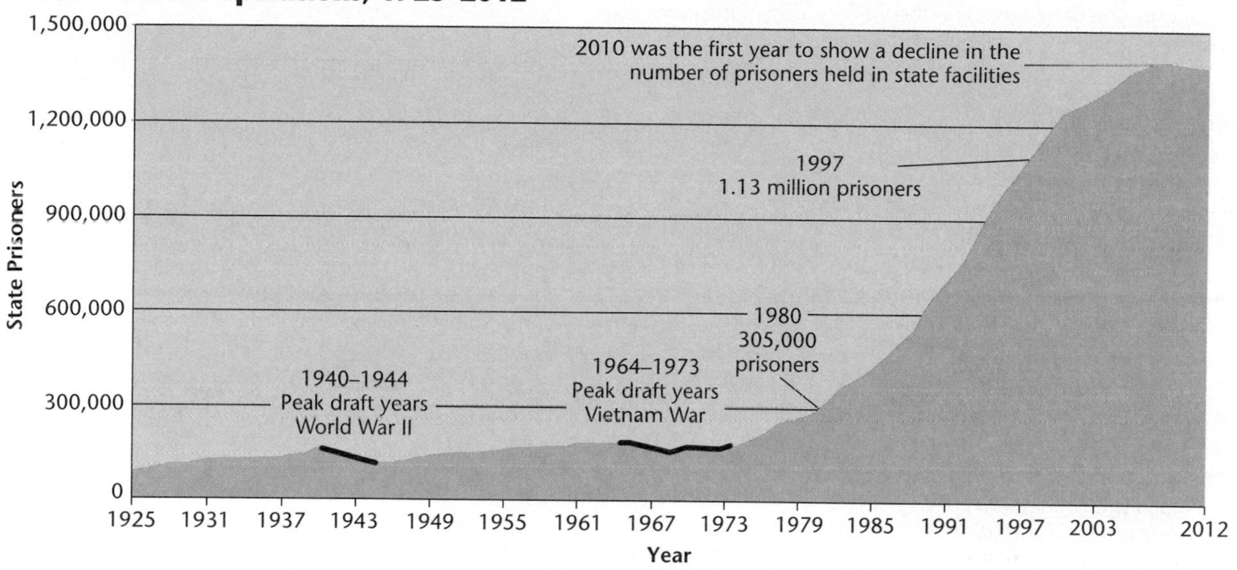

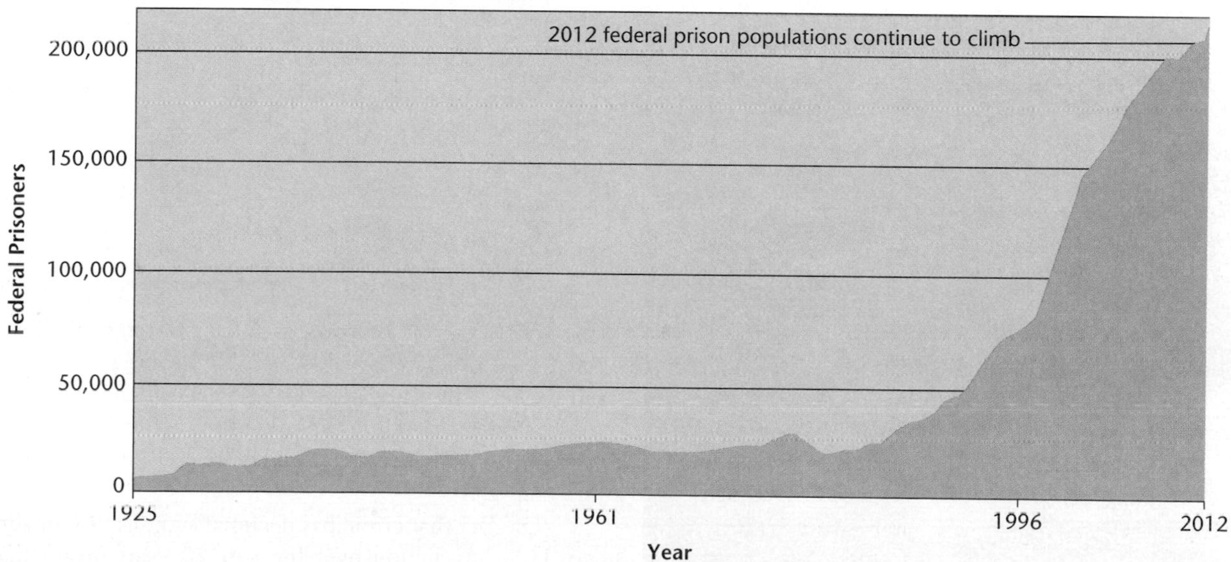

FIGURE 3–8 | **U.S. Prison Populations, 1924–2012**

Sources: Bureau of Justice Statistics, *Crime and Justice Atlas 2000* (Washington, DC: Bureau of Justice Statistics, 2001), pp. 42–43; Bureau of Justice Statistics, *Prisoners in 2012* (Washington, DC: Bureau of Justice Statistics, 2013); and other years.

Martin, Robert J. Mutchnick, and W. Timothy Austin have observed, "The true test of Beccaria's essay can be judged by the influence it has had over time on our justice system."[70] The influence of Beccaria, the Enlightenment, and classical thinkers can be found today in the U.S. Constitution, in "get tough" approaches to crime, and in a continuing emphasis on individual rights. Martin and colleagues concluded that the Classical School "has left behind a legacy that we see in almost every aspect of our present-day justice system."[71]

As we observed in Chapter 2, any perspective gains credence if actions taken on the basis of its assertions appear to bear fruit. Not surprisingly, advocates of today's neoclassical approaches to crime control take much of the credit for the recent drop-off in crime rates. After all, following the implementation

WHO'S TO BLAME—The Individual or Society?

The Excitement of Crime

Following his arrest for the theft of a police car, Moonbeam Kittaro met with one of his friends in the visiting area of the local jail. Here's what he said:

> I stole a cop car and s***, was it exciting!
>
> I mean, the thing was just sitting there running in the parking lot with the keys in it. Who wouldn't take it?
>
> I've never been so high on pure adrenaline. It was an adrenaline rush being behind the wheel of that f***ing car.
>
> It turned my girlfriend on too.
>
> I drove over to her place with the lights and siren on, and as soon as she saw the car she wanted to go for a ride.
>
> We must have hit 140 on the Interstate!
>
> Then we pulled into a rest stop and made love in the back seat.
>
> It was the whole illegal thing that got her so excited.
>
> But that's when we got arrested.
>
> The cops surrounded the car, guns drawn and all that s***.
>
> We didn't even hear them coming.

Think about it

1. Why did Kittaro steal the car? Do you think he knew, before he stole it, that the theft would lead to so much excitement?
2. Can the desire for excitement explain crimes like Kittaro's? Can the same desire explain other kinds of crimes? If so, what might they be?
3. If excitement explains crime commission, then why doesn't everyone commit crime for the excitement it brings?
4. What kinds of crime-prevention programs might be based on the principles illustrated here?

Note: Who's to Blame boxes provide fictionalized critical thinking opportunities, and are not actual cases.

ZUMA Press, Inc./Alamy

Pleasant Valley Prison in Fresno, California. Recent "law and order" approaches have led to dramatically overcrowded prisons. How can prison overcrowding be reduced?

of "get tough on crime" policies like the determinate sentencing schemes called for by the just deserts model, official rates of crime have shown substantial declines. The continuing decrease had led mayors, police chiefs, and politicians throughout the country to declare victory in the battle against crime, and many have taken personal credit for crime's decline. Notable among such politicians have been then–New York City mayor Rudy Giuliani, Los Angeles mayor Antonio Villariagosa, and Los Angeles police chief William J. Bratton.

However, the situation is not so simple. As one journalist recently explained it, taking "responsibility for crime trends depends entirely on whether those trends are good or bad. When . . . crime stats decline, everyone rushes to take credit. The mayor boasts his new initiative is working exactly as he said it would. The police chief proudly declares that the strategy he implemented is a great success. Social service agencies insist their new programs are responsible. And so it goes in city after city. The only thing that varies is the identity of the initiatives, strategies, and programs said to be the cause of the crime drop. . . . Which suggests pretty strongly that all these claims are empty."[72]

The fact that crime has declined significantly in almost every U.S. jurisdiction over the past 20 years means that it has gone down in areas that instituted "get tough" policies, as well as in areas that saw little change in their approach to crime prevention. Realistically, those who take credit for actively reducing crime in their cities and towns must also somehow account for crime's decline in other locations over which they had no control. Recently, for example, after the mayor and police chief in Los Angeles claimed that their crime-fighting policies had been responsible for an 8% drop in homicides throughout the city, one Los Angeles politician looked at murder rates throughout the region and found that while murder *inside* the city was down 8%, a decline of 15% had taken place in surrounding cities. "If [Mayor] Villariagosa were doing things

CRIMINAL | PROFILES

Gary Steven Krist: The Einstein of Crime?

Born in Aberdeen, Washington, in 1945, Gary Steven Krist was raised in the small fishing village of Pelican, Alaska. His father was a poor salmon fisherman, and Krist himself described his mother as "a well-intentioned scatterbrain."[i]

During his parents' absence, Gary and his brother, Gordon, were left in the care of others. As a preteen, Gary showed a propensity for violence, and he once fired a shotgun over his babysitter's and brother's heads because the babysitter made him angry.

He soon became known throughout the tiny Pelican community as a troublemaker. Krist's parents, however, seemed to view this behavior as simply displays of typical youthful exuberance.

As he entered his teens, Krist's delinquency bloomed into full-fledged criminality. At the age of 14, Krist was arrested with a friend for a series of burglaries, various sexual conquests, and much drinking. He later wrote in a memoir that their "crimes arose, I believe, more from an overpowering hungry curiosity coupled with excess physical energy than from any defined hostility or malice toward others."

While on probation for these offenses, Krist stole a car, which got him sent to a reform school in Ogden, Utah. He unsuccessfully tried to escape on two different occasions yet later recalled that he was "happy" in this reform school because he was "accepted."

After being released in 1961, Krist served a series of short jail terms for crimes such as auto theft. In 1965, he married; then he was arrested a year later, again for auto theft. Eight months into a five-year sentence, he engineered an escape during which guards shot his accomplice to death. Since California law permitted capital punishment when an escape led to someone's death, Krist worried that he'd get the gas chamber if he were found, so he moved his young family to Boston and created a new identity as George Deacon, an aspiring scientist.

The undeniably intelligent Krist obtained a job as a lab technician at MIT, which led to his participation in a September 1968 marine science expedition where the still-married Krist began an affair with a female student named Ruth Eisemann Schier. Before the expedition was over Krist confessed his true identity and criminal past to her, and they formed a plan to run off to Australia.

To finance their planned new life together, Krist and Eisemann Schier plotted to kidnap Emory University student Barbara Jane Mackle, the daughter of a prominent Miami family, and bury her in a homemade box, where she would remain until they received a $500,000 ransom.

Krist and Eisemann Schier did abduct and bury Mackle, who ultimately survived 83 hours underground before police, informed by Krist of the burial site, were able to find and release her. The kidnappers were subsequently caught and tried in Decatur, Georgia, in May 1969.

Before his trial, Krist's intellect was evaluated by a psychiatrist as "if not at the genius level, then certainly in the near genius category." Found guilty, the 23-year-old Krist received a life sentence.

Bettmann/Corbis

A bearded Gary Steven Krist is escorted from an elevator by a DeKalb County (Georgia) deputy sheriff en route to jail in 1969. Krist had been found guilty for his part in the kidnapping of Barbara Jane Mackle and was sentenced to life in prison. Paroled after ten years, he entered a new life of crime. Why didn't he reform?

Paroled after ten years, Krist set about lobbying for a complete pardon, which he eventually obtained in 1989. He then enrolled in a medical school in the West Indies and completed his M.D. degree. Several states denied him a medical license before the state of Indiana finally granted him a probationary license in 2001.[ii] That license was revoked two years later when Krist's past criminal record and allegations of sexual assaults on patients surfaced.[iii]

In January 2007, 61-year-old Gary Krist, who once described himself as the "Einstein of crime," was on his way back to prison to serve a five-year five-month sentence. A federal sting operation busted Krist and his 41-year-old stepson in early 2006 for conspiracy to bring cocaine and illegal aliens into the United States.[iv]

The case of Gary Krist raises a number of interesting questions. Among them are the following:

1. Krist had trouble with the law from a young age. What might have been the cause of early law violations?
2. Could Krist's parents have changed the course of his life while he still lived at home? If so, how?
3. Krist was undeniably intelligent. Is there any link between intelligence and crime? If so, what might it be?

Notes

i. Steve Fennessy, "The Talented Dr. Krist." *Atlanta Magazine* Online, http://www.atlantamagazine.com/article.php?id=299, (accessed May 21, 2007).

ii. *Cincinnati Enquirer, The Enquirer*, Online Edition, "Doctor Found to Have Been Imprisoned for Kidnapping," November 16, 2002, http://www.enquirer.com/editions/2002/11/16/loc_In-felondoc16.html (accessed July 10, 2007).

iii. Wishtv.com, "Doctor's License Revoked," August 29, 2003, http://www.wishtv.com/Global/story.asp?S=1423007 (accessed May 21, 2007).

iv. MSNBC, "Georgia Man in 1960s Buried Alive Case Gets 5 Years in Drug Case," http://www.msnbc.msn.com/id/16710294/ (accessed May 21, 2007).

■ **dangerousness** The likelihood that a given individual will later harm society or others. Dangerousness is often measured in terms of recidivism, or the likelihood of new crime commission or rearrest for a new crime within a five-year period following arrest or release from confinement.

THEORY | versus REALITY

Assessing Dangerousness

Dangerousness is a difficult concept to comprehend. Indicators of dangerousness have yet to be well defined in the social scientific literature, and legislators who attempt to codify any assessment of future dangerousness often find themselves frustrated. On the individual level, however, dangerousness might be more easily assessed. What follows is a description of the criteria one judge, Lois G. Forer, used in deciding whether an offender needed to spend a long time away from society.

> I had my own criteria or guidelines—very different from those established by most states and the federal government—for deciding on a punishment. My primary concern was public safety. The most important question I asked myself was whether the offender could be deterred from committing other crimes. No one can predict with certainty who will or will not commit a crime, but there are indicators most sensible people recognize as danger signals:
>
> - First, was this an irrational crime? If an arsonist sets a fire to collect insurance, that is a crime but also a rational act. Such a person can be deterred by being made to pay for the harm done and the costs to the fire department. However, if the arsonist sets fires just because he likes to see them, it is highly unlikely that he can be stopped from setting others, no matter how high the fine. Imprisonment is advisable even though it may be a first offense.
> - Second, was there wanton cruelty? If a robber maims or slashes the victim, there is little likelihood that he can safely be left in the community. If a robber simply displays a gun but does not fire it or harm the victim, then one should consider his life history, provocation, and other circumstances in deciding whether probation is appropriate.
> - Third, is this a hostile person? Was his crime one of hatred, and does he show any genuine remorse? Most rapes are acts of hostility, and the vast majority of rapists have a record of numerous sexual assaults. I remember one man who raped his mother. I gave him the maximum sentence under the law—20 years—but with good behavior, he got out fairly quickly. He immediately raped another elderly woman.
> - Fourth, is this a person who knows he is doing wrong but cannot control himself? Typical of such offenders are pedophiles. One child abuser who appeared before me had already been convicted of abusing his first wife's child. I got him on the second wife's child and sentenced him to the maximum. Still, he'll get out with good behavior, and I shudder to think about the children around him when he does. This is one case in which justice is not tough enough.
> - By contrast, some people who have committed homicide present very little danger of further violence—although many more do. Once a young man came before me because he had taken aim at a person half a block away and then shot him in the back, killing him. Why did he do it? "I wanted to get me a body." He should never get out.

Discussion Questions

1. How are public safety and criminal punishment related?
2. Do you agree that the criteria used by Judge Forer to identify dangerousness are useful? Why?
3. Do you believe that offenders who are identified as dangerous should be treated differently from other offenders? If so, how?
4. What elements of classical or neoclassical thought are apparent in Judge Forer's writing?

Source: Lois G. Forer, "Justice by the Numbers: Mandatory Sentencing Drove Me from the Bench," *Washington Monthly*, April 1992, pp. 12–18. Reprinted with permission from *The Washington Monthly*. Copyright by The Washington Monthly Company, 1611 Connecticut Ave., N.W., Washington, D.C. 20009; 202-462-0128. Web site: www.washingtonmonthly.com.

better than surrounding cities," he asked, "wouldn't the percentage reduction *inside* the city be greater than the reduction *outside* the city?"[73]

Critics also note that the extent of crime's decline might not be as substantial as many people think. Publicized statistical declines may be due at least partially to demographic changes in the American population (i.e., downtown Detroit might have higher rates of reported crime were it not for the movement *out* of the city of many people over the past decade or two) or might be attributed to the changing nature of crime over time (i.e., an increase in virtual or online thefts versus a decline in actual holdups).

Dangerousness (the likelihood that an individual will later harm people or society), is a concept that can be used to decide the value of incarceration in individual cases, but it is not always recognized by "get tough on crime" strategies that seek to make examples of law violators based more on what they have done rather than the likelihood that they will reoffend. Such critics say that it would make more sense to assess the future dangerousness of a convicted offender rather than impose punishment

Critics charge that classical and neoclassical thought lacks comprehensive explanatory power over criminal motivation.

based on the nature of his or her offense. Assessing dangerousness will be discussed in more detail in Chapter 6.

Critics also charge that classical and neoclassical thought lacks comprehensive explanatory power over criminal motivation, other than to advance the relatively simple claim that crime is the result of free will, the personal attractions of crime, and individual choice (see the Criminal Profiles box). Such critics point out that classical theory is largely bereft of meaningful explanations about how a choice for or against criminal activity is made. Similarly, classical theory lacks any appreciation for the deeper fonts of personal motivation, including those represented by aspects of human biology and psychology as well as the social environment. The Classical School, as originally detailed in the writings of Beccaria and Bentham, lacked any scientific basis for the claims it made. Although neoclassical writers have advanced the scientific foundation of classical claims (via studies like those showing the effectiveness of particular forms of deterrence), many still defend their way of thinking by referring to what are purely philosophical ideals, such as just deserts.

SUMMARY

- The Classical School in criminology posits that at least some illegal activity is the result of rational choices made by individuals seeking various kinds of illicit rewards. The classical perspective sees human beings as fundamentally rational, portrays pain and pleasure as the two central determinants of human behavior, and sees punishment as necessary to deter law violators and to serve as an example.
- The Classical School grew out of the Enlightenment. Notions of free will, individual choice, deterrence as a goal of the justice system, and punishment as a natural consequence of crime owe much of their contemporary influence to the Classical School. Influential thinkers of the Enlightenment era include Thomas Hobbes, John Locke, Thomas Paine, Charles-Louis de Secondat Montesquieu, and Jean-Jacques Rousseau.
- Two important thinkers of the Classical School of criminology, Cesare Beccaria and Jeremy Bentham, saw crime as providing pleasure to those who commit it and believed in punishment as the way to prevent it.
- Neoclassical criminology is a contemporary perspective built on classical principles emphasizing the importance of character and character development as well as the choices people make when faced with opportunities for crime. Rational choice theory recognizes the opportunities for crime and the important role that capable guardians play in preventing it.
- In neoclassical criminology, punishment is seen as providing both a deterrent and just deserts. Just deserts implies that criminal offenders deserve the punishment they receive and that any criminal punishment meted out should be appropriate to the type and severity of the crime committed.
- Policy implications of classical and neoclassical thought build on the idea of a rational offender punished by a system working purposefully toward the goals of crime reduction and the prevention of recidivism. Determinate sentencing and truth in sentencing as well as capital punishment are all strategies that flow from Classical School principles.
- Classical perspectives can be criticized for their lack of comprehensive explanatory power over criminal motivation, and they also largely lack both meaningful explanations about how a choice for or against criminal activity is made and any appreciation for the deeper fonts of personal motivation.

KEY TERMS

capable guardian, 62
capital punishment, 69
Classical School, 57
Code of Hammurabi, 54
common law, 54
dangerousness, 76
determinate sentencing, 72
deterrence, 68
displacement, 67
Enlightenment, 55
folkways, 52
general deterrence, 68
hard determinism, 60
hedonistic calculus, 59
incapacitation, 72
just deserts model, 67
justice model, 61
***mala in se*, 52**
***mala prohibita*, 53**
mores, 52
natural law, 56
natural rights, 56
neoclassical criminology, 60
nothing-works doctrine, 60
Panopticon, 59
positivism, 60
rational choice theory, 62
recidivism, 68
recidivism rate, 68
retribution, 54
routine activities theory, 62
situational choice theory, 62
situational crime prevention, 65
social contract, 55
soft determinism, 63
specific deterrence, 68
target hardening, 65
three-strikes legislation, 61
truth in sentencing, 72
Twelve Tables, 54
utilitarianism, 59

KEY NAMES

Cesare Beccaria, 58
Jeremy Bentham, 58
Ronald V. Clarke, 63
Lawrence Cohen, 62
Derek B. Cornish, 63
Marcus Felson, 62
Thomas Hobbes, 55
Jack Katz, 64
John Locke, 55
Robert Martinson, 60
Charles-Louis de Secondat Montesquieu, 56
Thomas Paine, 56
Jean-Jacques Rousseau, 56
William Graham Sumner, 52

QUESTIONS FOR REVIEW

1. What are the major principles of the Classical School of criminology?
2. What were some forerunners of classical thought in criminology?
3. Who were the important thinkers of the Classical School of criminology, and what was their legacy?
4. What is neoclassical criminology, and how does it differ from the classical perspective? How does it build on the classical perspective?
5. What is the role of punishment in neoclassical criminology?
6. What are the policy implications of the Classical School, and what kinds of punishment might work best to prevent crime?
7. What are the shortcomings of the Classical School? Of neoclassical thinking about crime and crime control?

QUESTIONS FOR REFLECTION

1. This text emphasizes a theme of social problems versus social responsibility. Which perspective is more clearly supported by classical and neoclassical thought? Why?
2. How would you define *natural law*? Do you believe that natural law exists? If so, what types of behaviors would be contravened by natural law? If not, why not?
3. What is meant by a social contract? How does the concept of a social contract relate to natural law?
4. What are the central concepts that defined the Classical School of criminological thought? Which of those concepts are still alive? Where do you see evidence for the survival of those concepts?
5. How would you define *recidivism*? What is a recidivism rate? Why are recidivism rates so high today? What can be done to lower them?

CHAPTER 4

EARLY BIOLOGICAL PERSPECTIVES ON CRIMINAL BEHAVIOR

LEARNING OUTCOMES

After reading this chapter, you should be able to answer the following questions:

- What are the differences between historical biological and contemporary biosocial theories of crime?
- What are the basic principles of biological theories of crime?
- How does the positivist school explain criminality?
- How does sociobiology explain crime, and what is the importance of altruism, territoriality, and tribalism in that perspective?
- What are the policy implications of biological theories?
- What are some criticisms of early biological theories of criminal behavior?

Introduction: Diet and Behavior

In 2012, the Dutch Ministry of Justice implemented a program of nutritional supplements in 14 prisons across the Netherlands. Under the program, nearly 500 inmates were provided with healthy diets, devoid of added sugar and supplemented with vitamins and important micronutrients.[1] According to Ap Zaalberg, the project's director, the link between good nutrition and lower levels of antisocial behavior had already been clearly established by studies published in England only a few years earlier, and the Dutch wanted to see if good eating habits could lower levels of violence in their prisons. Zaalberg's interest came from reading an article published in the *British Journal of Psychiatry* in 2002 by Oxford University professor C. Bernard Gesch.[2] Gesch reported on the results of work he had done in recruiting 231 young British prisoners. He assigned half of them to receive carefully selected dietary supplements while the other half received a placebo. Before Gesch's nutritional program was implemented, the placebo and active-treatment groups had been matched according to the number of disciplinary incidents in which each had been involved. There were no significant individual or psychological differences between the two groups in terms of IQ, verbal ability, anger, anxiety, or depression. After Gesch's experimental subjects took specially formulated vitamins, minerals, and essential fatty acids for 142 days, he found that prisoners taking the supplements committed an average of 26.3% fewer offenses compared with the placebo group. He also observed a 35.1% reduction in overall offenses in the group receiving the supplements and a 37% drop in violent incidents. According to Gesch, ". . . evidence is mounting that putting poor fuel into the brain significantly affects social behavior. We need to know more about the composition of the right nutrients. It could be the recipe for peace."[3] Figure 4–1 shows the levels of some of the nutrients in the disadvantaged youths studied by Gesch.

Traditional Biological versus Modern Biosocial Theories

The field of criminology has been slow to give credence to biological theories of deviant behavior.

The field of criminology has been slow to give credence to **biological theories** of deviant behavior. One reason for this, as noted in Chapter 1, is that contemporary criminology's academic roots are

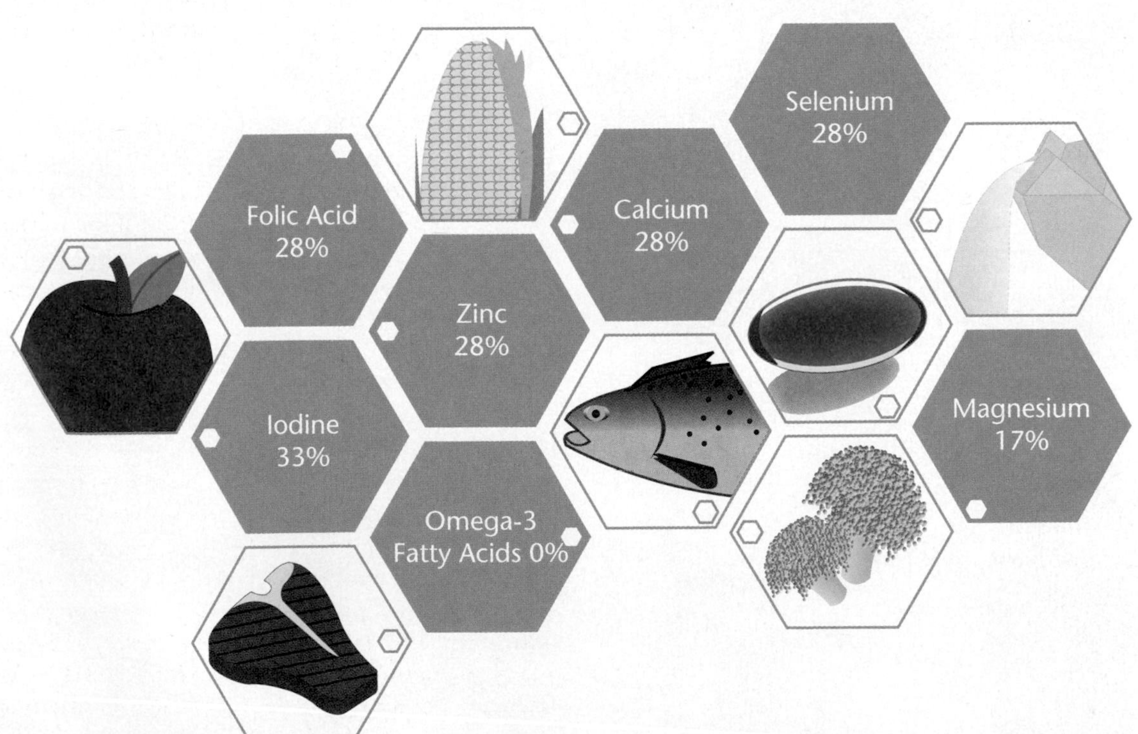

FIGURE 4-1 | **Selected Nutrient Levels in Diets of a Sample of Disadvantaged Youth**

Source: John Bohannon, "The Theory? Diet Causes Violence. The Lab? Prison," *Science*, Vol. 325 (September 25, 2009), p. 1616. Web available at http://www.ifbb.org.uk/files/Science-25-9-09.PDF.

■ **biological theories** Theories that maintain that the basic determinants of human behavior, including criminality, are constitutionally or physiologically based and often inherited.

■ **traits** Notable features or qualities of a biological entity. Traits may be classified as physical, behavioral, or psychological. Traits are passed from generation to the next.

grounded in the social sciences. As well-known biocriminologist **C. Ray Jeffery**, commenting on the historical development of the field, observed, "The term *criminology* was given to a social science approach to crime as developed in sociology. Sutherland's [1924] text *Criminology* was pure sociology without any biology or psychology; beginning with publication of that text, criminology was offered in sociology departments as a part of sociology separate from biology, psychology, psychiatry and law. Many of the academicians who call themselves criminologists are sociologists."[4]

Fortunately for those studying criminology today, the field of criminology is interdisciplinary, recognizing contributions from many different disciplines. This chapter and the next (Chapter 5, "Biosocial and Other Contemporary Perspectives") review both historical and contemporary biological perspectives on crime, including modern-day biosocial theories. Many older biological theories, as we will see in this chapter, were relatively simplistic in their approach to explaining human behavior and crime. Newer biosocial perspectives hold that genes and related biological features are more likely to be facilitators rather than determinants of behavior—an idea that we will explore more fully in the chapter that follows.

J. Carini/The Image Works

A mother reads to her child. The following question forms the essence of the "nature versus nurture" controversy: Are the choices that people make determined more by their biology or by what they have learned?

Principles of Biological Theories

Generally speaking, biological theories focus on the brain as the center of the personality and the major determinant in controlling human behavior. As one biocriminologist explains it, "no matter the source of human behavior, it is necessarily funneled through the brain . . ."[5] Unlike the classical and neoclassical traditions, however, which consider free will and external forces as the cause of behavior, biological theories look to internal sources, including genetic and physical makeup, as they influence mental processes.

Early biological theorists (generally, prior to the 1960s or 1970s) focused primarily on physical features and heredity as the source of criminal behavior. They considered physical **traits** such as facial features, body type, and shape of the skull as significant causes of criminality. Several early theorists proposed that criminality ran in families and could be inherited, or passed down from one generation to another. Such early approaches, while appropriate for the time in which they were developed, appear relatively simplistic when compared with modern biosocial perspectives.

In contrast, contemporary biological theorists (mostly after 1990) have taken a more in-depth look at human biology, leading them to examine a variety of influences on behavior, including genes and chromosomes, diet, hormonal issues, environmental contaminants, and neurophysical conditions. Nonetheless, both early and contemporary biological perspectives share a number of fundamental assumptions, which are shown in Figure 4–2.

One of the major distinguishing features between historical and contemporary biological theories of criminality is the degree of emphasis that each puts on the last item listed in Figure 4–2 (the interplay between biology and the social and physical environments). While most early biological theories of crime ascribed at least some importance to the role of the social environment in producing behavior, that role was relatively minor. In contrast, contemporary biosocial theorists see

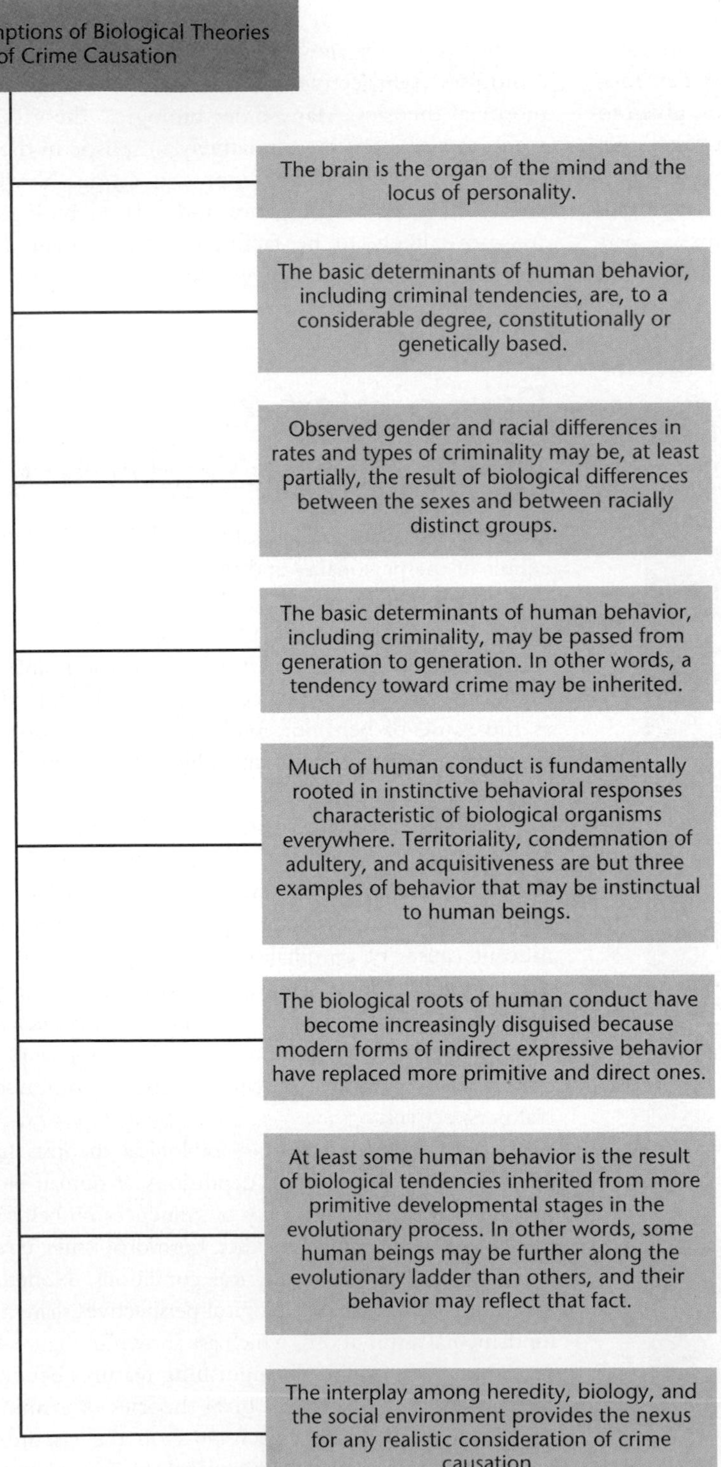

FIGURE 4–2 | Fundamental Assumptions of Biological Theories of Crime Causation

Source: Schmalleger, Frank J., *Criminology*. Printed and Electronically reproduced by permission of Pearson Education, Inc., Upper Saddle River, New Jersey.

the *interaction* between the organism and its environment as the crucial determining factor in almost all behavior.

Early Biological Theories

Early biological theories of crime, while not as sophisticated as their modern counterparts, are especially significant because they built on the scientific tradition of positivism. Positivism, which is both discussed and defined in Chapter 3, is associated with the belief that all valid knowledge is acquired only through observation and not through the mere exercise of reason or blind adherence to belief. As mentioned in that previous chapter, early positivism was built on two important principles: (1) an unflagging acceptance of social determinism, or the belief that human behavior is determined not by the exercise of free choice but by causative factors beyond the control of the individual, and (2) the application of scientific techniques to the study of crime and criminology.

The term *positivism* had its roots in the writings of Auguste Comte (1798–1857), who proposed use of the scientific method in the study of society in his 1851 work *A System of Positive Polity*.[6] Comte, who later became known as the father of sociology, believed that social phenomena could be observed, explained, and measured in objective and quantitative terms. For a strict positivist, reality consists of a world of clearly defined facts that can be scientifically measured and—some would hope—controlled.[7] As a framework for thought and analysis, positivism was a giant leap forward because it established a scientific basis for the burgeoning field of criminology.

Physical Features and Crime

Some of the earliest studies in the field of criminology used data from the fields of biology and anthropology to identify physical abnormalities that early criminologists thought could be used to distinguish criminal offenders from other people. One of the earliest attempts to use bodily features to identify criminals was proposed by European anatomist **Franz Joseph Gall** (1758–1828) in his

■ **phrenology** The study of the shape of the head to determine anatomical correlates of human behavior.

THEORY | in PERSPECTIVE

Early Biological Theories

Biological theories adhere to the principle that many predispositions relating to human behavior, including aggression, risk taking, and criminality, are constitutionally or physiologically influenced and inherited. This chapter discusses early biological approaches to crime.

Early Positivism

Early positivism used data from the fields of biology and anthropology to identify physical abnormalities that early criminologists thought could be used to distinguish criminal offenders from other people.

Period: 1790s–1880s

Theorists: Franz Joseph Gall, Johann Gaspar Spurzheim

Concepts: phrenology

Criminal Anthropology

Criminal anthropology is the scientific study of the relationship between human physical characteristics (in particular, bodily features) and criminality. Today the word is mostly applied to the Italian School of Criminology, whose contributors built on scientific, or positivistic, principles like the use of measurement and observation in applying evolutionary concepts to the study of crime and criminals. Criminal anthropology saw criminals as throwbacks to earlier evolutionary epochs.

Period: 1860s–1930

Theorists: Cesare Lombroso, Enrico Ferri, Raffael Garofalo, Charles Buckman Goring, Earnest A. Hooton

Concepts: Italian School, positivism, criminal anthropology, atavism, born criminals, criminaloids, masculinity hypothesis

Constitutional Theories

These biological theories, sometimes called constitutional theories, explain criminality by reference to offenders' body types, inheritance, genetics, or external observable physical characteristics.

Period: Classical constitutional theories, 1930s–1940s; modern constitutional theories, 1960s to the present

Theorists: Ernst Kretschmer, William H. Sheldon

Concepts: somatotyping, mesomorph, ectomorph, endomorph

Criminal Families

In the late 1800s the focus of criminal anthropology turned to the identification of criminal families, or those family groups that appeared to exhibit criminal tendencies through several generations. The study of criminal families built on developing notions of heredity and genetics.

Period: 1870s–1940s

Theorists: Sir Francis Galton, Richard Louis Dugdale, Arthur H. Estabrook, Henry Herbert Goddard

Concepts: heredity, behavioral genetics, criminal families (Jukes and Kallikaks), genetic determinism, eugenics, eugenic criminology

Sociobiology

This theoretical perspective, developed by Edward O. Wilson, includes the systematic study of the biological basis of all social behavior, which is a branch of evolutionary biology and particularly of modern population biology.

Period: 1975 to the present

Theorist: Edward O. Wilson

Concepts: altruism, tribalism, survival of the gene pool

Twin Studies and Heredity

Genetics and heredity, combined with processes of natural selection, including sexual selection, can produce biologically based differences in behavior. Studies of twins attempted to identify the role that heredity played in criminal behavior, especially among twins who were separated at birth and raised in vastly different environments.

Period: 1920s to the present

Theorists: Karl O. Christiansen, Sarnoff Mednick, and others

Concepts: twin studies (dizygotic and monozygotic twins), genetic determinism

---

theory of **phrenology** (also called craniology). Gall believed that the shape of the human skull was related to personality and could be used to distinguish criminals from normal men and women. Gall's approach built on four themes:

1. The brain is the organ of the mind.
2. Particular aspects of personality are associated with specific locations in the brain.
3. Portions of the brain that are well developed cause personality characteristics associated with them to be more prominent in the individual under study, whereas poorly developed brain areas lead to a lack of associated personality characteristics.
4. The shape of a person's skull corresponds to the shape of the underlying brain and is therefore indicative of the personality.

■ **atavism** A term used by Cesare Lombroso to suggest that criminals are physiological throwbacks to earlier stages of human evolution.

Gall was one of the first Western writers to locate the roots of personality in the brain. Prior to his time, it was thought that aspects of personality resided in various organs throughout the body—a fact reflected in linguistic anachronisms that survive to the present day (for example, when someone is described as being "hard-hearted" or having "a lot of gall"). Greek philosopher Aristotle was said to believe that the brain served no function other than to radiate excess heat from the body, so Gall's perspective, although relatively primitive by today's standards, did much to advance physiological understandings of the mind–body connection in Western thought.

Although Gall's theory depended on physical measurements of the skull and comparisons of such measurements between individuals, it was never tested using today's rigorous methodological standards (including the research designs discussed in Chapter 2). Nonetheless, it was widely accepted by many of his contemporaries because it represented a shift away from the theological perspectives prevalent at the time toward scientific measurement—a trend that was well under way by the time of his writings. Phrenology also provided systematic evaluation of suspected offenders and was intriguing for its ease of use.

One of Gall's students, German physician **Johann Gaspar Spurzheim** (1776–1853), brought phrenological theory to the United States and helped to spread its influence through a series of lectures and publications on the subject. Phrenology's prestige in the United States extended into the twentieth century, finding a place in classification schemes employed to evaluate newly admitted prisoners. Even Arthur Conan Doyle's fictional character Sherlock Holmes was described as using phrenology to solve a number of crimes. It is still popular today among palm readers and fortune-tellers, some of whom offer phrenological "readings"—although a few states have outlawed such activities. Learn more about phrenology at **Web Extra 4–1**.

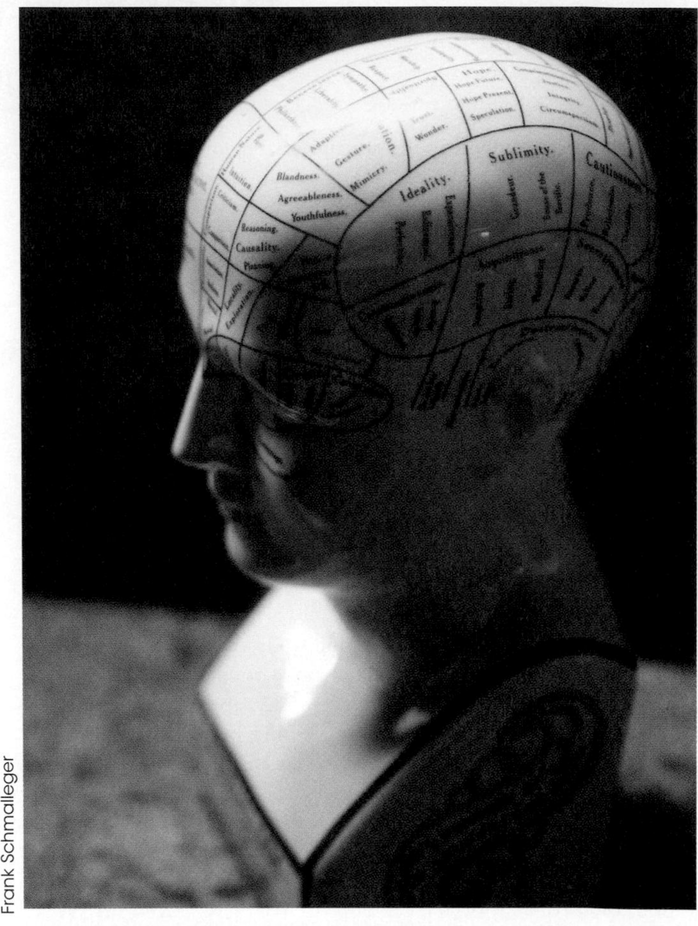

Frank Schmalleger

A phrenological map of the skull. Early criminologists believed that the shape of the skull reflected the brain's ability. Do you think biology plays a significant role in crime?

The Italian School

One of the best-known early scientific biological theorists—nineteenth-century Italian army prison physician **Cesare Lombroso** (1836–1909)—coined the term **atavism** to suggest that criminality was the result of primitive urges that survived the evolutionary process in modern-day human throwbacks. Lombroso, whose work had consisted mostly of postmortem studies of the bodies of executed offenders and deceased criminals, measured the bodies in many different ways.[8] He claimed that, using his system, not only could criminal offenders be separated from the general population, but even specific types of criminals could be identified.

> Cesare Lombroso coined the term *atavism* to suggest that criminality was the result of primitive urges that survived the evolutionary process.

Discussing murderers, for example, Lombroso wrote: "He has a cold concentrated look; sometimes the eye appears injected with blood; the nose is often aquiline or hooked, always large; the ears are long; the jaws powerful; the cheek-bones widely separated; the hair is crisp and abundant; the canine teeth well developed, and the lips thin; often a nervous tic or contraction, upon one side of the face only, uncovers the canine teeth, producing the effect of a threatening look or a sardonic laugh."[9]

Lombroso believed that thieves could be recognized because they have "less cranial capacity" and "a remarkable mobility of countenance, the eye small and restless, the eye-brows thick and meeting, the nose flat, and the forehead always low and retreating."

■ **Italian School of Criminology** A perspective on criminology developed in the late 1800s that held that criminals can be identified by physical features and are throwbacks to earlier stages of human evolution. The Italian School was largely based on studies of criminal anthropology.
■ **criminal anthropology** The scientific study of the relationship between human physical characteristics (in particular anthropometric features, or bodily measurements) and criminality.

■ **born criminal** An individual who is born with a genetic predilection toward criminality.
■ **criminaloid** A term used by Cesare Lombroso to describe the occasional criminal who is enticed into criminality primarily by environmental influences.

Lombroso called physical features that he thought to be indicative of criminality *stigmata of degeneration,* and suggested that they could be used to predict later criminal behavior among individuals who possessed them. He described "the nature of the criminal" as "an atavistic being who reproduces in his person the ferocious instincts of primitive humanity and the inferior animals."[10] Writing around the same time as Lombroso, Italian Raffael Garofalo noted that "[o]ne has but to go into a prison, and by the aid of this description one can distinguish almost at a glance those condemned for theft from those condemned for murder."

Lombroso's ideas gave rise to the **Italian School of Criminology**, also referred to today as criminal anthropology. **Criminal anthropology** is the scientific study of the relationship between human physical characteristics (in particular anthropometric features, or bodily measurements) and criminality. Criminal anthropology probably derives from earlier subjective feelings, prominent for millennia, that unattractiveness, deformity, and disfigurement are somehow associated with evil, spiritual malaise, and general uncleanliness.

Although the earlier works of Gall and others might be subsumed under the umbrella of criminal anthropology, the term is usually reserved in today's criminological literature for the work of Lombroso and other members of the Italian School of Criminology, especially **Enrico Ferri** and **Raffael Garofalo**.

At about the time that Lombroso's ideas were becoming popular, Charles Darwin was making a substantial impact on the scientific world with his theory of biological evolution. Darwin proposed that human beings and other contemporary living organisms were the end products of a long evolutionary process governed by rules such as natural selection and survival of the fittest. Lombroso adapted elements of Darwin's theory to suggest that primitive behavioral traits survived in present-day human populations and led to heightened criminal tendencies among individuals who harbored them. Darwin himself had proposed this idea when he wrote, "With mankind some of the worst dispositions which occasionally without any assignable cause make their appearance in families, may perhaps be reversions to a savage state, from which we are not removed by very many generations."[11]

Lombroso has been called "the father of modern criminology" because he was the first criminologist of note to employ the scientific method—particularly measurement, observation, and generalization—in his work. Other writers have preferred to limit his influence, referring to him simply as the father of

Pictorial Press Ltd./Alamy

Comedian Jay Leno, showing off his strong chin. Cesare Lombroso believed that people with weak chins were especially prone to criminality. How might physical features relate to criminality?

the Italian School of Criminology in recognition of the fact that nineteenth-century positivism began in Italy under his tutelage.

Lombroso's most famous term, *atavism*, implies that criminals are born that way. Lombroso was continuously reassessing his estimates of the proportion, from among all offenders, of **born criminals**. At one point, he asserted that fully 90% of offenders committed crimes because of atavistic influences; he later revised the figure downward to 70%, admitting that normal individuals might be pulled into lives of crime. In addition to the category of born criminal, Lombroso described other categories of offenders, including the insane, "criminaloids," and criminals incited by passion. The insane were said to include mental and moral degenerates, alcoholics, drug addicts, and so forth. **Criminaloids**, also called "occasional criminals," were described as people who were enticed into breaking the law by virtue of environmental influences. Nevertheless, most

■ **masculinity hypothesis** The belief that, over time, men and women will commit crimes that are increasingly similar in nature, seriousness, and frequency. Increasing similarity in crime commission was predicted to result from changes in the social status of women.

■ **constitutional theories** Theories that explain criminality by reference to offenders' body types, inheritance, genetics, or external observable physical characteristics.

criminaloids were seen by Lombroso as exhibiting some degree of atavism and hence were said to "differ from born criminals in degree, not in kind." Those who became criminals by virtue of passion were said to have surrendered to intense emotions, including love, jealousy, hatred, or an injured sense of honor. To read excerpts of a positivist criticizing the classical criminology viewpoint, see the Theory versus Reality box in this chapter.

In 1893, Lombroso published *The Female Offender*.[12] In that book, he expressed his belief that women exhibited far less anatomical variation than do men, but he insisted that criminal behavior among women, as among men, derived from atavistic foundations. Violence among women, although a rarity in the official statistics of the late 1800s, was explained by the **masculinity hypothesis**, or the belief that criminal women exhibited masculine features and mannerisms. Lombroso saw the quintessential female offender, however, as a prostitute, who was "the genuine typical representative of criminality" among women.[13] Prostitutes, he claimed, act out atavistic yearnings and, in doing so, return to a form of behavior characteristic of humankind's primitive past. Learn more about Lombroso and the theory of atavism via **Web Extra 4–2**.

Evaluations of Atavism

Following in Lombroso's positivistic footsteps around the turn of the twentieth century, English physician **Charles Buckman Goring** (1870–1919) conducted a well-controlled statistical study of Lombroso's thesis of atavism. Using newly developed but advanced mathematical techniques to measure the degree of correlation between physiological features and criminal history, Goring examined nearly 3,000 inmates at Turin prison beginning in 1901. Enlisting the aid of London's Biometric Laboratory, he concluded that "the whole fabric of Lombrosian doctrine, judged by the standards of science, is fundamentally unsound."[14] Goring compared the prisoners with students at Oxford and Cambridge Universities, British soldiers, and noncriminal hospital patients and published his findings in 1913 in his lengthy treatise *The English Convict: A Statistical Study*.[15]

A similar study was conducted between 1927 and 1939 by **Earnest A. Hooton**, a professor of anthropology at Harvard University. In 1939, Hooton published *Crime and the Man*,[16] in which he reported having evaluated 13,873 inmates from ten states, comparing them along 107 physiological dimensions with 3,203 nonincarcerated individuals who formed a control group; his sample consisted of 10,953 prison inmates, 2,004 county jail prisoners, 743 criminally insane, 173 "defective delinquents," 1,227 "insane civilians," and 1,976 "sane civilians." Hooton concluded that criminals showed an overall physiological inferiority to the general population and that crime was the result of "the impact of environment upon low grade human organisms."[17] Learn more about the life and work of Earnest Hooton at **Web Extra 4–3**.

Today the ideas of the Italian School, which linked observable physical abnormalities to crime, are largely seen as a dead end in criminological thinking. However, as Nichole Hahn Rafter says, "Because criminal anthropologists' doctrine of the criminal as a physically anomalous human has long been discredited, we tend to ignore their work, at the same time overlooking the legacy of professional that they, as the first criminologists, bequeathed to us."[18]

Even though mainstream criminology is no longer concerned with claims that physical abnormalities may be linked to crime, some contemporary researchers have examined the link between criminality and minor physical abnormalities (MPAs), including neuro-deficits, fetal alcohol syndrome, and hormone deficits. In a study of teenage boys reported in 2000, for example, Canadian researchers L. Arseneault, Richard E. Tremblay, and colleagues conducted hormonal, anthropometric, psychophysiological, neuropsychological, and psychiatric evaluations of 1,037 boys who had attended kindergarten in 1984 in a socially and economically disadvantaged area of Montreal.[19] Using evaluations provided years later by parents, teachers, classmates, and the children themselves, Arseneault and Tremblay concluded that subtle physical abnormalities, including minor abnormalities in the shape of the ears, tongue, and teeth, were associated with an increased risk of behavioral and psychiatric problems in later years. The researchers suggested that such minor physical abnormalities might have resulted from genetic problems or prenatal insults associated with exposure to toxins. They concluded that "both the total count of minor physical anomalies and the total count of minor physical anomalies of the mouth were significantly associated with an increased risk of violent delinquency in adolescence, beyond the effects of childhood physical aggression and family adversity." Arseneault and Tremblay recognized, however, that abnormalities of the type they identified might be associated with neurological deficits and that abnormalities of the mouth could lead to feeding problems in the first months after birth, which might somehow cause problems in development or socialization.

Constitutional Theories

Constitutional theories explain criminality by reference to offenders' body types; genetics; or external, observable physical

■ **somatotyping** The classification of human beings into types according to body build and other physical characteristics.
■ **endomorph** A body type originally described as soft and round or overweight.
■ **mesomorph** A body type described as athletic and muscular.
■ **ectomorph** A body type originally described as thin and fragile, with long, slender, poorly muscled extremities and delicate bones.

THEORY | versus REALITY

Positivism: The Historical Statement

In 1901, Enrico Ferri, one of the founders of positivist criminology, was invited to deliver a series of lectures at the University of Naples. Ferri used the occasion to admonish classical criminologists and to advance the principles of positivism. Following are excerpts from those lectures:

> Let us speak of this new science, which has become known in Italy by the name of the Positive School of Criminology. The 19th century has won a great victory over mortality and infectious diseases by means of the masterful progress of physiology and natural science. But while contagious diseases have gradually diminished, we see on the other hand that moral diseases are growing more numerous. And this makes it very evident that the science which is principally, if not exclusively, engaged in studying these phenomena of social disease should feel the necessity of finding a more exact diagnosis of these moral diseases of society, in order to arrive at some effective and more humane remedy.
>
> The science of positive criminology arose in the last quarter of the 19th century. [T]he positive school of criminology arises out of the very nature of things, the same as every other line of science. It is based on the conditions of our daily life.
>
> The general opinion of classic criminalists and of the people at large is that crime involves a moral guilt, because it is due to the free will of the individual who leaves the path of virtue and chooses the path of crime, and therefore it must be suppressed by meeting it with a proportionate quantity of punishment. And the illusion of a free human will (the only miraculous factor in the eternal ocean of cause and effect) leads to the assumption that one can choose freely between virtue and vice. How can you still believe in the existence of a free will, when modern psychology armed with all the instruments of positive modern research denies that there is any free will and demonstrates that every act of a human being is the result of an interaction between the personality and the environment of man?
>
> And how is it possible to cling to that obsolete idea of moral guilt, according to which every individual is supposed to have the free choice to abandon virtue and give himself up to crime? The positive school of criminology maintains, on the contrary, that it is not the criminal who wills; in order to be a criminal, it is rather necessary that the individual should find himself permanently or transitorily in such personal, physical and moral conditions, and live in such an environment which become for him a chain of cause and effect, externally and internally, that disposes him toward crime. This is our conclusion and it constitutes that vastly different and opposite method, which the positive school of criminology employs as compared to the leading principle of the classic school of criminal science.

Discussion Questions

1. Why did Ferri link control over contagious diseases with the study of crime?
2. If Ferri had been asked to define *positive criminology*, what kind of definition do you think he would offer?
3. How are notions of moral guilt and free will associated in Ferri's line of thought?

Source: Ernest Unterman, trans., *The Positive School of Criminology: Three Lectures Given at the University of Naples, Italy, on April 22, 23, and 24, 1901, by Enrico Ferri* (Chicago: Charles H. Kerr, 1912).

characteristics. A constitutional, or physiological, orientation that found its way into the criminological mainstream during the early and mid-twentieth century was that of **somatotyping** (classifying according to body types), primarily associated with the work of **Ernst Kretschmer** and **William H. Sheldon**. Kretschmer, a professor of psychiatry at the German University of Tubingen, proposed a relationship between body build and personality type and created a rather detailed "biopsychological constitutional typology."

Influenced by Kretschmer, Sheldon utilized measurement techniques to connect body type with personality.[20] Sheldon studied 200 boys between the ages of 15 and 21 at the Hayden Goodwill Institute in Boston and concluded that four basic body types characterized the entire group (Figure 4–3):

1. The **endomorph** is soft and round, with "digestive viscera [that] are massive and highly developed" (the person is overweight and has a large stomach).
2. The **mesomorph** is muscular and athletic, with "somatic structures [that] are in the ascendancy" (the person has larger bones and considerable muscle mass).
3. The **ectomorph** is thin and fragile and has "long, slender, poorly muscled extremities, with delicate, pipestem bones."
4. The balanced type is a person of average build, not overweight, thin, or exceedingly muscular.[21]

Individuals (excluding the balanced type) were ranked along each of the three major dimensions using a 7-point scale. Sheldon

■ **heredity** The passing of traits from parent to child.

■ **behavioral genetics** The study of genetic and environmental contributions to individual variations in human behavior.

■ **Juke family** A well-known "criminal family" studied by Richard L. Dugdale.

■ **Kallikak family** A well-known "criminal family" studied by Henry H. Goddard.

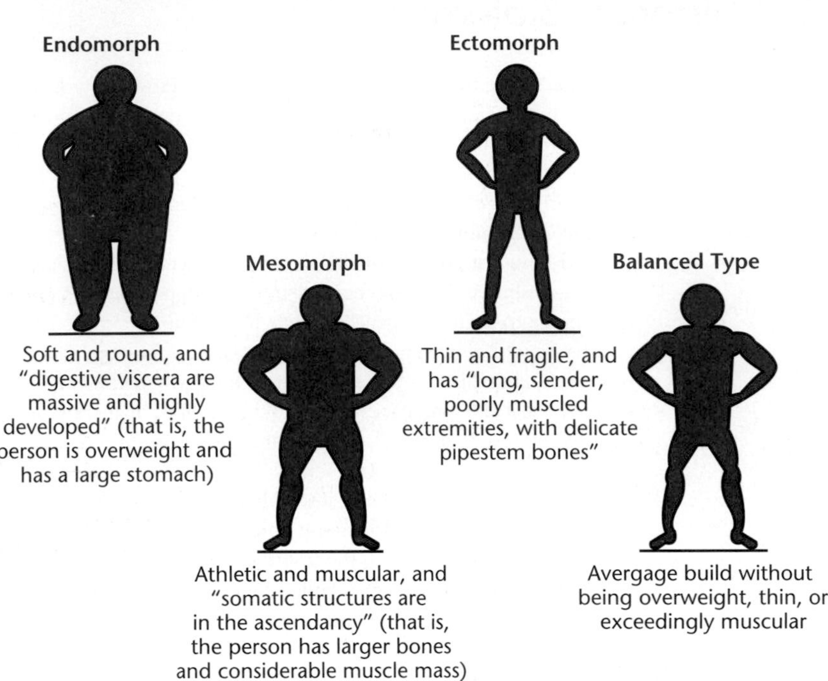

FIGURE 4-3 | **Sheldon's Body Types**

Source: Printed and Electronically reproduced by permission of Pearson Education, Inc., Upper Saddle River, New Jersey.

claimed that varying types of temperaments and personalities were closely associated with each of the body types he identified: Ectomorphs were said to be "cerebrotonic," or restrained, shy, and inhibited; endomorphs were "viscerotonic," or relaxed and sociable. Mesomorphs, or muscular body types, were most likely to be associated with delinquency or "somatotonia," which he described as "a predominance of muscular activity and vigorous bodily assertiveness." Learn more about early theories of body types via **Library Extra 4–1** and **Web Extra 4–4**.

Criminal Families

Sir Francis Galton (1822–1911) was the first Western scientist to systematically study **heredity**, or the passing of traits from parent to child, and its possible influence on human behavior.[22] In 1907, Galton wrote that "the perpetuation of the criminal class by heredity is a question difficult to grapple with on many accounts. It is, however, easy to show that the criminal nature tends to be inherited. . . . The criminal population receives steady accessions from those who, without having strongly marked criminal natures, do nevertheless belong to a type of humanity that is exceedingly ill suited to play a respectable part in our modern civilization, though it is well suited to flourish under half-savage conditions, being naturally both healthy and prolific."[23] Galton's work contributed to the development of the field of **behavioral genetics**, the study of genetic and environmental contributions to individual variations in human behavior. See **Library Extra 4–2** for more about behavioral genetics and crime.

Beginning in the late 1800s, and supported by burgeoning notions of heredity, researchers in the field of criminal anthropology focused on criminal families, or families that appeared to exhibit criminal tendencies across decades. In 1877, American sociologist **Richard Louis Dugdale** (1841–1883) published a study of the **Juke family**, which he described as criminogenic by nature.[24] Dugdale traced the Juke lineage back to a notorious character named Max, a Dutch immigrant who arrived in New York in the early 1700s. Two of Max's sons married into the notorious "Juke family of girls," six sisters, all of whom were said to be illegitimate. Max's male descendants were reputed to be vicious, and one woman named Ada had an especially bad reputation and came to be known as "the mother of criminals." By the time of the study, Dugdale was able to identify approximately 1,200 of Ada's descendants; included among their numbers were seven murderers, 60 habitual thieves, 90 or so other criminals, 50 prostitutes, and 280 paupers. Dugdale compared the crime-prone Jukes with another family, the pure-blooded progeny of Jonathan Edwards, a Puritan preacher and one-time president of Princeton University. Descendants of Edwards included American presidents and vice presidents as well as many successful bankers and businesspeople, and no one was identified among the Edwards lineage who had had a run-in with the law. In 1916, **Arthur H. Estabrook** published a follow-up to Dugdale's work in which he identified an additional 715 Juke descendants, including 378 more prostitutes, 170 additional paupers, and 118 other criminals.[25] **Library Extras 4–3** to **4–5** contain more information about genetics and crime.

Following in the tradition of family tree researchers, **Henry Herbert Goddard** (1866–1957) published a study of the **Kallikak family** in 1912.[26] Goddard attempted to place the study of deviant families within an acceptable scientific framework via the provision of a kind of control group, so

■ **eugenics** The study of hereditary improvement by genetic control.
■ **eugenic criminology** A perspective that holds that the root causes of criminality are passed from generation to generation in the form of "bad genes."

■ **genetic determinism** The belief that genes are the major determining factor in human behavior.
■ **supermale** A male individual displaying the XYY chromosome structure.

for comparison purposes he used two branches of the same family. One branch began as the result of a sexual liaison between Martin Kallikak, a Revolutionary War soldier, and a barmaid whose name is unknown; as a result of this union, an illegitimate son (Martin, Jr.) was born. After the war, Kallikak returned home and married a righteous Quaker girl, and a second line of descent began. The legitimate branch produced only a few minor deviants, but the illegitimate line resulted in 262 feebleminded births and various other epileptic, alcoholic, and criminal descendants. (The term *feebleminded*, which was much in vogue at the time of Goddard's study, was later recast as "mentally retarded," and people exhibiting similar characteristics today might be referred to as "mentally handicapped" or "mentally challenged.") Because feeblemindedness appeared to occur with some predictability in Goddard's study, but criminal activity seemed to be only randomly represented among the descendants of both Kallikak lines, Goddard concluded that a tendency toward feeblemindedness was inherited but that criminality was not.

Like the ideas of the Italian School, constitutional theories and studies of criminal families have largely been discarded today as biosocial researchers develop more sophisticated perspectives on criminology. Early biological theories, because they tended to encourage the **eugenics** movement of the late 1880s and early 1900s, were vigorously opposed by many in the criminological community throughout the latter part of the twentieth century. The eugenics movement proposed selective human breeding as a course to improvement of the species, and **eugenic criminology**, an offshoot of the movement,[27] held that the root causes of criminality were largely passed from generation to generation in the form of "bad genes."

Eugenic criminology, which accepted the idea of **genetic determinism**, or the belief that genes are the major determining factor in human behavior, replaced the idea of the "feebleminded criminal" with the "defective delinquent," and social policies developed during the eugenics movement called for the sterilization of mentally handicapped women to prevent their bearing additional offspring.[28] Those policies were supported by the federal Eugenics Record Office, which funded studies of "cacogenic," or "bad-gened," families and were endorsed by the 1927 U.S. Supreme Court case of ***Buck* v. *Bell*.**[29] In *Buck*, Justice Oliver Wendell Holmes, Jr., writing in support of a Virginia statute permitting sterilization, said, "It is better for all the world, if instead of waiting to execute degenerate offspring for crime, or to let them starve for their imbecility, society can prevent those persons who are manifestly unfit from continuing their kind." The eugenics movement continued in the United Kingdom into the 1960s but was largely discredited in this country by intense condemnation of Nazi genetic research, mass sterilization, and eugenics programs, including those that led to the Holocaust. Learn about the consequences of *Buck* v. *Bell* at **Web Extra 4–5**.

The XYY Supermale

The first well-known study of the modern era to focus on genetic differences as an explanation for criminality was undertaken by **Patricia A. Jacobs**,[30] a British researcher. Jacobs and her colleagues examined 197 Scottish prisoners in 1965 for chromosomal abnormalities through a relatively simple blood test known as karyotyping.[31] Twelve members of the group displayed chromosomes that were unusual, and seven were found to have an XYY chromosome. Normal male individuals possess an XY chromosome structure; normal female individuals are XX. Some other unusual combinations might be XXX, wherein a woman's genetic makeup contains an extra X chromosome, and XXY (also called Klinefelter's syndrome), in which a man might carry an extra X, or female, chromosome. Klinefelter's men often have male genitalia but are frequently sterile and have evidence of breast enlargement and intellectual retardation.[32] The XYY man, however, whose incidence in the prison population was placed at around 3.5% by Jacobs, was quickly identified as potentially violent and was termed a **supermale**.

Following the introduction of the supermale notion into popular consciousness, a number of offenders attempted to offer a chromosome-based defense. In 1969, for example, Lawrence E. Hannell, who was adjudged a supermale, was acquitted of murder in Australia on the grounds of insanity.[33] Such a defense did not work, however, for Richard Speck, who also claimed to be an XYY man but was convicted of killing eight Chicago nursing students in 1966; it was later learned that Speck did not carry the extra Y chromosome. See the Criminal Profiles box for more on Richard Speck.

The supermale phenomenon (also called the XYY syndrome) appears to have been based more on sensationalism than on fact. Today, little evidence exists to suggest that XYY men actually commit crimes of greater violence than do other men, although they may commit somewhat more crimes overall.

■ **dizygotic (DZ) twin** A twin who develops from a separate ovum and who carries the genetic material shared by siblings.

■ **monozygotic (MZ) twin** One of two twins who develop from the same egg and who carry almost identical genetic material.

A 1976 Danish study of 4,000 men born in Copenhagen between 1944 and 1947 may have helped put the issue to rest with its finding that the incidence of XYY men was less than 1% in the general male population.[34] More recent researchers have similarly concluded that "studies done thus far are largely in agreement and demonstrate rather conclusively that males of the XYY type are not predictably aggressive."[35]

Twin Studies and Heredity

More recently, studies of the criminal tendencies of fraternal and identical twins have provided a methodologically sophisticated technique for ferreting out the role of heredity in crime causation. Fraternal twins, or **dizygotic (DZ) twins**, develop from different fertilized eggs and share only the genetic material common among siblings; identical twins, or **monozygotic (MZ) twins**, develop from the same egg and carry virtually the same genetic material. Hence, if human behavior has a substantial heritable component, twins would display similar behavioral characteristics despite variations in their social environment, with any observed relationship being stronger among MZ twins than among DZ twins.

One of the first studies to link MZ twins to criminality was published in the 1920s by German physician Johannes Lange.[36] Examining 13 pairs of MZ twins and 17 pairs of DZ twins, he found that in 10 of the 13 MZ twins, both were criminal, whereas only 2 of the 17 DZ twins exhibited such similarity. Lange's findings drew considerable attention, even though his sample was small and he was unable to separate environmental influences from genetic ones adequately. A much larger twin study was begun in 1968 by European researchers **Karl O. Christiansen** and **Sarnoff Mednick**, who analyzed all twins (3,586 pairs) born on a selected group of Danish islands between 1881 and 1910.[37] Christiansen and Mednick found significant statistical support for the notion that criminal tendencies are inherited: 52% of identical twins and 22% of fraternal siblings displayed the same degree of criminality within the twin pair. Such similarities remained apparent even among twins separated at birth and raised in substantially different environments.

Christiansen and Mednick found significant statistical support for the notion that criminal tendencies are inherited. . . .

Identical twins. The study of twins is used to show the influence of inheritance on human behavior. Does biology determine behavior?

Kenneth Sponsler/Fotolia

The Minnesota Twin Family Study began in 1983.[38] The study's original goal was to establish a registry of all twins born in Minnesota from 1936 to 1955 for psychological research purposes but expanded to include twins born between 1961 and 1964. The Minnesota registry conducted personality and interests tests with more than 8,000 twin pairs and family members (by mail), and its findings seemed to show that MZ twins reared apart are about as similar as MZ twins reared together in personality and temperament, occupational and leisure-time interests, and social attitudes. Study authors warned, however, that "this evidence for the strong heritability of most psychological traits, sensibly construed, does not detract from the value or importance of parenting, education, and other . . . interventions."[39]

The study of twins is still common practice in criminology today, and the area of twin studies provides something of an overlap between this chapter and the next; that is, between early and contemporary biological theories. In 1996, for example, British researchers studying 43 MZ and 38 DZ same-sex twins through the use of self-report questionnaires stated that "common bad behaviors of the sort admitted to by the majority of adolescents have a substantially heritable component. Additive genetic effects account for most of the variation, with no evidence of a contribution from shared environment."[40] The researchers also determined that genetic effects on behavior appear

■ **sociobiology** The systematic study of the biological basis of all social behavior.
■ **paradigm** An example, a model, or a theory.

to increase with age. The British research was supported by the findings of a joint U.S.–Australian examination of 2,682 adult twin pairs; in that study, researchers found "a substantial genetic influence on risk for conduct disorder" (defined to include chronic stealing, lying, bullying, arson, property destruction, weapons use, cruelty to animals or people, fighting, aggression, truancy, and running away from home).[41]

In 2003, researchers examined the behavior of 1,116 pairs of five-year-old twins participating in a longitudinal study and asked mothers, teachers, study examiners, and the children themselves to evaluate the degree of the children's level of antisocial behavior.[42] Findings showed that antisocial children can be identified early in life, that their behavior can be nearly impossible to control by the time they reach kindergarten, and that heredity plays a far greater role in determining such behavior than does home life or parenting. Because of similar behavior among twin pairs, the researchers concluded that genetic influences were extremely powerful determinants of antisocial behavior across diverse social settings, writing that "research and theory on the etiology of childhood antisocial behavior must look beyond the current focus on socioeconomic contexts and parenting processes, to incorporate genetic explanations and develop new theories of nature-nurture interplay."[43] Also in 2003, Florida State University researcher Jeanette Taylor and colleagues studied two separate groups of teenage male twins—142 MZ and 70 DZ twin pairs—and concluded that antisocial traits among study subjects existed prior to adulthood and that they stemmed to a significant degree from genetic factors.[44]

Kane513/Shutterstock

Two male wolves prepare to fight for pack dominance. Sociobiologists tell us that certain traits, such as territoriality, are common to both animals and humans. How might territoriality lead to crime?

Sociobiology

In the introduction to his insightful article summarizing **sociobiology**, Arthur Fisher wrote, "Every so often, in the long course of scientific progress, a new set of ideas appears, illuminating and redefining what has gone before like a flare bursting over a darkened landscape." To some, sociobiology—which burst upon the social science scene in 1975—held the promise of just such a new **paradigm**, or model. The development of this novel paradigm, however, was preceded by the work of ethnologists, including John H. Cook, Sir Julian Huxley, and Austrian Konrad Lorenz, who studied the social behavior of both people and animals and laid the groundwork for later sociobiological perspectives.

The Biological Roots of Human Aggression

In 1966, Austrian animal expert **Konrad Lorenz** published his now-famous work *On Aggression*.[45] In it, Lorenz described how aggression permeates the animal kingdom and asked, "What is the value of all this fighting?" He wrote, "In nature, fighting is such an ever-present process, its behavior mechanisms and weapons are so highly developed and have so obviously arisen under the pressure of a species-preserving function, that it is our duty to ask this question."[46]

Lorenz accepted the evolutionary thesis of nineteenth-century biologist **Charles Darwin** that aggression within a species favored the strongest and best animals in the reproductive process, but he concluded that aggression serves a variety of other purposes as well. Aggression, said Lorenz, ensures an "even distribution of animals of a particular species over an inhabitable area" and provides for a defense of the species from predators.[47] Human aggression, he claimed, meets many of the same purposes but can take on covert forms, and the drive to acquire wealth and power, which was so characteristic of Western men at the time of his writing, is part of the human mating ritual whereby a man might "win" a prized woman through displays of more civilized forms of what could otherwise be understood as intraspecies aggression.

Lorenz's greatest contribution to the study of human behavior may have been his claim that all human behavior is, at least to some degree, "adapted instinctive behavior"; in other words, much of human conduct is fundamentally rooted in instinctive behavioral responses characteristic of biological organisms everywhere and present within each of us in the form of a biological inheritance from more primitive times. Even rational human thought derives its motivation and direction from

■ **altruism** Selfless, helping behavior.
■ **gene pool** The total genetic information of all the individuals in a breeding population.

■ **tribalism** The attitudes and behavior that result from strong feelings of identification with one's own social group.

instinctual aspects of human biology, and the highest human virtues, such as the value placed on human life, "could not have been achieved," said Lorenz, "without an instinctive appreciation of life and death."[48]

Building on the root functions of aggression, Lorenz concluded that much of what we today call "crime" is the result of overcrowded living conditions combined with a lack of legitimate opportunity for the effective expression of aggression. Crowding increases the likelihood of aggression, while contemporary socialization works to inhibit it. In the words of Lorenz, "In one sense we are all psychopaths, for each of us suffers from the necessity of self-imposed control for the good of the community."[49] When people break down, said Lorenz, they become neurotic or delinquent, and crime may be the result of stresses that have been found to typically produce aggression throughout the animal kingdom.

Lorenz's explanations, like many of the biologically based theories, appear to be more applicable to certain forms of crime than to others, but it is important to recognize that modern frustrations and accompanying manifestations of aggression may be symbolically—rather than directly—expressed. Hence, a stockbroker who embezzles a client's money, spurred on by the need to provide material goods for an overly acquisitive family, may be just as criminal as a robber who beats his victim and steals her purse to have money to buy liquor.

The New Synthesis

Evolutionist **Edward O. Wilson** is credited with coining the term *sociobiology*. In his groundbreaking book, *Sociobiology: The New Synthesis*, Edwards defined *sociobiology* as "the systematic study of the biological basis of all social behavior [that is] a branch of evolutionary biology and particularly of modern population biology."[50] Because of the important role of biology in social evolution that Wilson was able to demonstrate, his work brought renewed attention to biological theories throughout the social sciences.

Through studies of primates, Wilson was able to demonstrate that the human brain and mind are the products of natural selection that occurred early in human evolution as developing hominids overcame the limits to sociality posed by weak social ties, which are characteristic of most primates. In so doing, they were able to develop close-knit social groups based on strong social ties. Wilson then showed how the ability to form large-scale societies contributed to the long-term survival of the social group.

Through his entomological study of social insects (especially ants), Wilson provided examples of **altruism** (selfless, helping behavior) in multiple species and, contrary to the beliefs of some evolutionary biologists, he found that helping behavior facilitated the continuity of the **gene pool** among altruistic individuals. The primary determinant of behavior, including human behavior, said Wilson, was the need to ensure the survival and continuity of genetic material from one generation to the next—and altruism played a role in survival.

Territoriality, according to Wilson's writings, explained many of the conflicts, including homicide, warfare, and other forms of aggression, between and among species, especially human beings. In Wilson's words, "Part of man's problem is that his intergroup responses are still crude and primitive, and inadequate for the extended extraterritorial relationships that civilization has thrust upon him." The "unhappy result," as Wilson terms it, may be "**tribalism**," expressed through the contemporary proliferation of street gangs, racial tension, and hardened encampments of survivalist and separatist groups, as well as the resilience of ethnic divides in the Middle East and throughout Europe and Asia.

Sociobiological theory not only tells us that the violence and aggressiveness associated with territoriality are often reserved for strangers but also explains intragroup aggression (violence occurring within groups). Wilson's theory suggested that within the group "a particularly severe form of aggressiveness should be reserved for actual or suspected adultery. In many human societies, where sexual bonding is close and personal knowledge of the behavior of others detailed, adulterers are harshly treated. The sin is regarded to be even worse when offspring are produced."

Hence, territoriality and acquisitiveness extend to location, possessions, and even other people. Human laws, explained Wilson, are designed to protect genetically based relationships that people have with one another, as well as their material possessions and their claimed locations in space; thus, violations of these intuitive relationships result in crime and in official reactions by the legal system.

Wilson's writings propelled social researchers into a flurry of studies intended to test the validity of his assertions. One Canadian study of violence in the homes of adoptive children found that stepchildren run a risk 70 times greater of being killed by their adoptive parents than do children living with their natural parents. Some writers concluded that "murderous behavior, warfare, and even genocide were unavoidable correlates of genetic evolution, controlled by the same genes for territorial behavior that had been selected in primate evolution."[51]

Others have suggested that biological predispositions developed during earlier stages of human evolution color contemporary criminal activity. Male criminals, for example, tend toward robbery and burglary—crimes in which they can continue to enact their "hunter" instincts developed long ago—but the criminality of women often involves shoplifting and simple theft, more typical of "gatherer" instincts.

Human behavioral predilections can be studied in a variety of ways. In the 1989 book *Evolutionary Jurisprudence*, John H. Beckstrom reported on his examination of over 400 legal documents, as well as legal claims and court decisions spanning over 300 years of judicial activity, that showed support for Wilson's contentions that humans tend to act to preserve their territorial claims, their likelihood of successful reproduction, and the continuation of their own particular genetic material.[52] Other theorists have gone so far as to imply that, among humans, there may be a gene-based tendency to experience guilt and to develop a conscience and that notions of right and wrong, whether embodied in laws or in social convention, may flow from such a naturalistic origin. Learn more about sociobiology in general and the sociobiology of sociopathy at **Web Extras 4–6** and **4–7**.

As sociobiology began to receive expanded recognition from U.S. investigators, some social scientists, believing the basic tenets of their profession to be challenged by the movement, began to treat it as "criminology's antidiscipline." By the early 1980s, sociobiology presented such a significant threat to U.S. criminology that it could no longer be ignored. Criticisms were quick and included the following:

- Sociobiology fails to convey the overwhelming significance of culture, social learning, and individual experiences in shaping the behavior of individuals and groups.
- Sociobiology is fundamentally wrong in its depiction of the basic nature of humans; there is no credible evidence of genetically based or determined tendencies to act in certain ways.
- Sociobiology is just another empirically unsupported rationale for the authoritative labeling and stigmatization of despised, threatening, powerless minorities.
- Humans are so thoroughly different from other animal species, even other primates, that there is no rational basis for the application to humans of findings from animal studies.

Many such criticisms were advanced by old-guard academics in an effort to prevent their own discipline's decline in influence in the face of otherwise convincing sociobiological claims. Most criminologists, like most academicians, were wedded to the belief that only social theories could explain nearly all human behavior. The importance of Wilson's work was its recognition that human nature is not so much an inherent quality of our species, but rather the "result of culture workings its ways on a biology that somewhat channeled (but did not fix) the subsequent nature of our species."[53]

Today, many open-minded scholars are beginning to sense the growing need for a new synthesis, a way to integrate the promise of biological theories like sociobiology and insights drawn from studies of twins with other long-accepted perspectives, like sociology and psychology, in explaining human behavior. As a result, the field of criminology appears ripe for a new integrative approach. Some say that this approach can be found in contemporary biosocial explanations of criminal behavior, to which we turn our attention in the next chapter.

Critique of Early Biological Theories of Criminal Behavior

A central concern with all early biological theories of criminal behavior has to do with the fact that they seemed to relegate the role of free will in human behavior to a kind of philosophical dustbin. If a person's behavior is largely determined, for example, by inherent and unchangeable atavistic features, then he or she may be condemned to a life of crime, and efforts at reformation can be expected to have little positive effect on future behavior. Consequently, some people continue to shy away from biological explanations for criminality and disordered behavior because phrases like "genetic determinism," which are often voiced by the popular media, have come to be synonymous with inevitability. People unschooled in criminology or modern biology tend to believe that "biological" equals "hopeless"[54]—after all, the physical makeup of a person is hard to change.

Other concerns stem from aligning the concept of crime with biological variables because crime is itself a social construction and its meaning varies from place to place and from time to time. Years ago, for example, it was illegal to own physical gold for investment purposes in the United States, but today such ownership is permitted. Similarly, Islamic law in Saudi Arabia makes it a crime for a woman to drive a car while unaccompanied by a male relative, but in the United States (and much of the rest of the world) such activity is far from criminal. While it is possible to hypothesize, for example, that a particular biological trait leads to a desire for gold ownership (or for ownership of shiny things of value) or produces the urge to drive a motor vehicle, the fact that such ownership (or driving) may or may not be criminal makes it hard to link specific biological features with potential criminality. It seems unlikely that any biological feature (or a combination of features) could explain the wide variety of criminal offending today—from insider stock trading and white collar crime to violent attacks, rape, and murder.

A more sensible approach might be to work to identify biological influences on characteristics that most criminals share. Such characteristics could include the level of aggression, risk taking, and danger seeking that individuals demonstrate. Possession of these characteristics may be found to increase the likelihood that some people will gravitate toward criminal activity or to related behaviors. Even if that is true, however,

CRIMINAL | PROFILES

Richard Benjamin Speck: "Born to Raise Hell"

In an appalling crime ranked number ten on *Time*'s list of the top 25 crimes of the twentieth century,[i] Richard Speck committed the mass murder of eight nurses from a community hospital in Chicago on the night of July 14, 1966.

Born the seventh of eight children on December 6, 1941, Speck had an early upbringing in Kirkwood, Illinois, that included strict adherence to Baptist religious teachings. When he was just six years old, his father died, and his mother subsequently married a hard-fisted drinker with an arrest record. After the family relocated to Dallas, Texas, Speck performed poorly in school and began sinking into increasingly serious delinquent behavior. His drunken stepfather's response was typically the administration of severe physical punishment for each of Speck's continuing transgressions.[ii] Speck himself became a heavy drinker, an affliction that would haunt him for the remainder of his life.

In spite of incarcerations for various burglaries, thefts, check forgeries, and other low-level crimes, 18-year-old Speck married 15-year-old Shirley Malone in November 1962. Their brief marriage was marked by his repeated absence while imprisoned, punctuated by his physical abuse of both his wife and his mother-in-law whenever he was not in jail. The abuse of his wife included frequent instances of rape at knifepoint.[iii]

Bettmann/Corbis

Mass murderer Richard Speck, killed eight young nurses in 1966, and he admitted during the interview that they would be alive today if one of the women had not spit in his face as he raped her. Speck's case helped popularize the notion of supermales—predators with a distinctive genetic makeup. Do contemporary understandings of biology support the idea of a supermale?

In January 1966, the couple divorced, and Speck left Texas to return by bus to Illinois, ending up in Monmouth, a small town near the Iowa border. Following the rape of a 65-year-old woman in early April and the murder of a barmaid 11 days later, Speck was interrogated. He was let go when he became physically ill, but he promised to return for further questioning. When he failed to show up, investigators who went looking for him found he had fled on a bus headed east, presumably to the Chicago area. Before leaving, he had the phrase *Born to Raise Hell* tattooed on his forearm.

Late on the evening of July 13, 1966, a drunken Speck invaded a townhouse where nursing students from nearby South Chicago Community Hospital resided. Within the first hour, he was able to capture and tie up nine women. After securing all the victims, Speck spent the next three hours systematically taking each student to another room within the townhouse and killing her. Each was violently murdered by strangulation, multiple stab wounds, and/or a cut throat; one was also raped.

Speck lost count of the number of women he had captured, and as a result, one of the women survived by rolling under a bed and hiding there. Speck left the townhouse at approximately 3:30 A.M. The survivor, Corazon Amurao, huddled in terror under the bed until almost 6 A.M. before she finally crawled out a window and began calling for help.[iv]

Speck was soon arrested and tried in Peoria, Illinois. The jury returned a guilty verdict in just 49 minutes, and Speck was sentenced to death.[v]

Speck achieved notoriety in the national press when his lawyers offered the claim that he was an XYY supermale, apparently hoping that the claim could provide a defense to the charges against him. At the time the claim was made, the XYY theory was being debated in academic circles and had become popular with the public. Later tests showed, however, that Speck did not carry the extra Y chromosome.

Speck's death sentence was commuted to 50 to 100 years in prison when the U.S. Supreme Court voided the death penalty in 1972. He died of a heart attack on December 5, 1991.

The case of Richard Speck raises a number of interesting questions. Among them are the following:

1. What caused Richard Speck to go on a murderous crime spree? Do you think it was his background or his biology, or a combination of both?
2. How is the Speck case illustrative of the current debate between advocates of biological theories of crime causation and those who advocate sociological theories?
3. How might a psychologist explain Speck's crimes? A sociologist?

Notes

i. Howard Chua-Eoan, "The Top 25," *Crimes of the Century, Time,* http://www.time.com/time/2007/crimes/9.html (accessed May 22, 2007).
ii. David Lohr, "Richard Speck," *Crime Magazine: An Encyclopedia of Crime,* August 2003, http://crimemagazine.com/03/richardspeck,0820.htm (accessed May 22, 2007).
iii. Connie Fillippelli, "Richard Speck: Born to Raise Hell," Chapter 11, CourtTV Crime Library, 2007, http://www.crimelibrary.com/serial_killers/predators/speck/hell_11.html (accessed May 22, 2007).
iv. Ibid., Chapter 16, http://www.crimelibrary.com/serial_killers/predators/speck/hell_16.html (accessed May 22, 2007).
v. Fillippelli, "Richard Speck," Chapter 16.

■ **Follow the author's tweets about the latest crime and justice news @schmalleger.**

such characteristics might be shared by people who routinely violate the law as well as by those who enforce it. Many on both sides of the law, for example, may be risk takers, danger seekers, and aggressive personalities. Consequently, in some ways criminals and enforcement agents may share any number of characteristics, and even some genes related to behavior propensities, but differ significantly in their orientation toward social life. What separates one from the other might be the nature of the social environment to which people are exposed when growing up.

Given the difficulty in sorting out this kind of complex relationship, it may be impossible to identify any biological features shared solely by criminals. As today's theorists understand, the influence of biology on behavior of any kind is more often the result of an interaction among genetic, hormonal, and other biological features of an individual and his or her social and physical environments. In other words, as the following chapter will show, biological influences are not likely to be the direct cause of crime or conformity but are mediated through a person's surroundings to produce behavior of one sort or another.

SUMMARY

- Early proponents of biological theories argued that at least some human behavior is the result of biological propensities inherited from more primitive developmental stages in the evolutionary process.
- Biological theories of crime causation adhere to the principle that many behavioral predispositions, including aggression and criminality, are constitutionally or physiologically influenced.
- According to some criminologists, human behavior is, to some degree, adapted instinctual behavior, and aggression is a form of biological inheritance from more primitive times. Aggression today may manifest as criminal behavior when environmental conditions conspire to elicit such instinctive responses.
- Some scholars have suggested that a penchant for crime may be inherited and that criminal tendencies are genetically based. Beginning in the late 1800s, researchers in the field of criminal anthropology focused on criminal families. More recently, developments in the field of genetics have led to the study of the role of chromosomes in crime causation. One of the first ideas to make use of chromosomes as an explanation for violent crime was the XYY, or supermale, notion of criminality.
- Sociobiology is a theoretical perspective developed by Edward O. Wilson that can be described as "the systematic study of the biological basis of all social behavior." Wilson believed that the primary determinant of human behavior was the need to ensure the survival and continuity of genetic material from one generation to the next. Sociobiologists often focus on explaining the violence and aggression associated with territoriality. Sociobiology has been employed to explain intergroup and intragroup aggression.
- Twin studies, which began in the 1920s and continue to the present day, show that certain kinds of antisocial traits exist prior to adulthood and likely stem from genetic factors.

KEY TERMS

altruism, 92
atavism, 84
behavioral genetics, 88
biological theories, 80
born criminal, 85
constitutional theories, 86
criminal anthropology, 85
criminaloid, 85
dizygotic (DZ) twins, 90
ectomorph, 87
endomorph, 87
eugenic criminology, 89
eugenics, 89
gene pool, 92
genetic determinism, 89
heredity, 88
Italian School of Criminology, 85
Juke family, 88
Kallikak family, 88
masculinity hypothesis, 86
mesomorph, 87
monozygotic (MZ) twins, 90
paradigm, 91
phrenology, 83
sociobiology, 91
somatotyping, 87
supermale, 89
traits, 81
tribalism, 92

KEY NAMES

Karl O. Christiansen, 90
Charles Darwin, 91
Richard Louis Dugdale, 88
Arthur H. Estabrook, 88
Enrico Ferri, 85
Franz Joseph Gall, 82
Sir Francis Galton, 88
Raffael Garofalo, 85
Henry Herbert Goddard, 88
Charles Buckman Goring, 86
Earnest A. Hooton, 86
Patricia A. Jacobs 89
C. Ray Jeffery, 81
Ernst Kretschmer, 87
Cesare Lombroso, 84
Konrad Lorenz, 91
Sarnoff Mednick, 90
William H. Sheldon, 87
Johann Gaspar Spurzheim, 84
Edward O. Wilson, 92

QUESTIONS FOR REVIEW

1. What's the difference between historical biological and contemporary biosocial theories of crime?
2. What basic principles characterize biological theories of crime causation? How do such theories differ from other perspectives that attempt to explain the same phenomena?
3. What is the positivist school of criminology, and what is the historical importance of positivism?
4. Describe sociobiology; include the role of concepts such as altruism, territoriality, and tribalism.
5. What do twin studies show about the role of biological influences on behavior?
6. What kinds of social policy initiatives might be based on biological theories of crime causation?
7. How can early biological theories of crime be critiqued?

QUESTION FOR REFLECTION

1. This text emphasizes the theme of social problems versus social responsibility. Which perspective is better supported by the early biological theories of crime causation discussed in this chapter? Why?

CHAPTER 5

BIOSOCIAL AND OTHER CONTEMPORARY PERSPECTIVES

LEARNING OUTCOMES

After reading this chapter, you should be able to answer the following questions:

- What was the purpose of the Human Genome Project (HGP), and what is its significance for modern biological theories of crime?
- What role do genetics and heritability play in contemporary explanations for crime?
- How does brain dysfunction relate to criminality?
- How do body chemistry theories—including those involving diet, blood sugar levels, environmental contaminants, and hormones—explain crime?
- What are biosocial theories, and what role does the gender ratio problem play in contemporary criminology?
- What are the policy implications of modern biological theories of crime?

■ **human genome** A complete copy of the entire set of human gene instructions.
■ **genes** Distinct portions of a cell's DNA that carry coded instructions for making everything the body needs.
■ **chromosomes** Bundles of genes

Introduction

In 2013, Connecticut Chief Medical Examiner, H. Wayne Carver, ordered the testing of Newton, Connecticut, school shooter Adam Lanza's DNA in an effort to determine "if he possessed any genetic abnormalities that could have led to his violent behavior."[1] In issuing that order, Carver was relying on new technologies that have recently been developed to map and explore the biological mechanisms that underlie human behavior.

One of the most important recent efforts in understanding human nature is the Human Genome Project (HGP), an international research program designed to construct detailed maps of the **human genome**. The HGP began in the United States in 1990 through a joint effort of the Department of Energy and the National Institutes of Health. It had as its goal the determination of the complete chemical sequence of human DNA. Researchers participating in the project worked together to localize the nearly 100,000 genes within the human genome and to determine the sequences of the 3 billion chemical base pairs that make up human DNA. The HGP was officially declared completed on April 14, 2003[2]—almost exactly 50 years after James Watson and Francis Crick published their historic findings on the double helix, three-dimensional structure of DNA.[3]

The HGP marked the beginning of a new era of research into human biology and recast understandings of human nature, disease, cognition, and behavior. Because the HGP offered radical new insights into fundamental human qualities, we use it as the point of demarcation between earlier biological theories of criminality and those that have been recently developed.

Michael Ventura/Alamy

Dr. Francis Collins, former Director of the Human Genome Project and current Director of the National Institutes of Health. The National Center for Human Genome Research at the National Institutes of Health supported the international Human Genome Project, a research program that determined the complete nucleotide sequence of human DNA. What ethical, legal, and social implications are inherent in such a project?

The Human Genome Project

The human genome refers to a complete copy of the entire set of human gene instructions.[4] **Genes** are made of DNA and carry coded instructions for making everything the body needs. **Chromosomes** are bundles of genes.[5] After completion of the HGP, which resulted in the sequencing of the entire genome sequence of a "reference human genome," the focus of genomics research turned to finding individual differences or variants from that reference sequence.[6] Ongoing research projects include the HapMap Project and the Encyclopedia of DNA Elements (ENCODE), which became operational in 2007. The second phase of ENCODE, the 1,000 Genomes Project, has only recently begun.

The use of genetic knowledge developed by the HGP is likely to have momentous implications for both individuals and society. Many of the questions criminologists have raised about the role of genetics in criminal behavior may be answered by the results of research begun by the HGP.[7] In the area of crime-control policy, HGP-related information is expected to support the development of public policy options related to crime prevention and the treatment of offenders.

Learn more about the federal government's involvement in genetic research from the National Human Genome Research Institute (NHGRI) at **Web Extra 5–1**, and learn more about human DNA research from the international

THEORY | versus REALITY
The Future of Neuroscience

In 2013, President Barack Obama announced a new U.S.-led initiative modeled after the Human Genome Project.[i] Known as the Brain Activity Map, the initiative seeks to learn specific details down to a molecular level about how regions and cells in the brain interconnect and function, and how the brain processes information.[ii] "There's this enormous mystery, waiting to be unlocked," Obama said during remarks at the White House.[iii]

The project, which is anticipated to last decades, will involve federal agencies, private foundations and teams of neuroscientists and nanoscientists working together to advance knowledge of the brain's billions of neurons in an effort to gain greater insights into perception, actions, and consciousness.[iv] Similar projects are currently underway in Europe and elsewhere. Europe's Human Brain Project, an extension of the Blue Brain Project at Switzerland's École Polytechnique Fédérale de Lausanne, started a year ago. According to documents released by the project, "It will bring together everything we know and everything we can learn about the inner workings of the brain's molecules, cells and circuits, collect the knowledge in massive databases and use it to build biologically detailed simulations of the complete human brain."[v]

Susan Walsh/Associated Press

President Obama announcing the Brain Mapping Project in 2013. How might the project be applicable to criminology?

Notes

i. Clive Cookson, "Science: Contours of the Mind," *Financial Times*, February 22, 2013, http://www.ft.com/intl/cms/s/0/06568de8-7cc2-11e2-afb6-00144feabdc0.html#axzz2LmTokbXz (accessed March 3, 2013).

ii. "Obama's Brain Activity Map Could Be the Future of Neuroscience Research," *Huffington Post*, February 23, 2013, http://www.huffingtonpost.com/2013/02/23/obamas-brain-activity-map_n_2747159.html (accessed February 25, 2013).

iii. "Obama's Brain Activity Map Could Be the Future of Neuroscience Research," *Huffington Post*, February 23, 2013, http://www.huffingtonpost.com/2013/02/23/obamas-brain-activity-map_n_2747159.html (accessed February 25, 2013).

iv. David Jackson, "Obama Unveils Brain Mapping Project to Unlock Mysteries," *USA Today*, April 2013, http://www.usatoday.com/story/news/2013/04/02/obama-brain-mapping-project/2045167 (accessed July 4, 2013).

v. Clive Cookson, "Human Brain and Graphene Projects Win Funding," *Financial Times*, January 27, 2013, http://www.ft.com/cms/s/0/0334040a-6706-11e2-8b67-00144feab49a.html#ixzz2LwHLxWpa (accessed March 2, 2013).

HapMap Project at **Web Extra 5–2**. NHGRI also sponsors a YouTube channel, called GenomeTV, at **Web Extra 5–3**.

Genetics and Heritability

In 1993, only three years after the launch of the HGP, Dutch criminologists caught worldwide attention with their claim that they had uncovered a specific gene with links to criminal behavior. Researcher **H. Hilger Ropers**, geneticist **Han Brunner**, and collaborators studied what media sources called "the Netherlands' most dysfunctional family." Although members of the unnamed family displayed IQs in the near-normal range, they seemed unable to control their impulses and often ended up being arrested for violations of the criminal law. The arrests, however, were always of men. Tracing the family back five generations, Brunner found 14 men whom he classified as genetically driven to criminality, but none of the women in the family displayed criminal tendencies, although they were said to have often been victimized by their crime-prone male siblings.

> Some criminologists claim that the evidence is very clear about a genetic factor involved in crime.

According to Ropers and Brunner, because men have only one X chromosome, they are especially vulnerable to any defective gene, whereas women (with two X chromosomes) have a kind of backup system in which one defective gene may be compensated for by another correctly functioning gene carried in the second X chromosome. After a decade of study, Ropers and Brunner announced that they had isolated the specific mutation that caused the family's criminality.[8] This gene, they said, is responsible for the production of an enzyme called monoamine oxidase A (MAOA), which is crucially involved in the process by which signals are transmitted within the brain. MAOA breaks down the chemicals serotonin (a hormone that plays the role of a neurotransmitter, and which

■ **neurotransmitters** Chemical substances that facilitate the flow of electrical impulses from one neuron to the next across nerve synapses.

■ **allele** An alternate form of a gene, or any of several forms of a gene, usually occurring through mutation.

we discuss in more detail later in this chapter) and noradrenaline (another neurotransmitter). **Neurotransmitters** are the chemicals that facilitate the flow of electrical impulses from one neuron to the next across nerve synapses, and the presence or absence of both serotonin and noradrenaline have been linked to aggressive behavior in human beings. Because men with the mutated gene do not produce enough of the enzyme necessary to break down a lot of chemical transmitters, the researchers surmised, their brains are overwhelmed with stimuli, resulting in uncontrollable urges and, ultimately, criminal behavior.

Also in the 1990s, researchers at the University of Texas Health Science Center in San Antonio announced the discovery of a pleasure-seeking gene that, they suspected, plays a role in deviant behavior, addictions, and maybe even murder and violence. The gene, which is a variation (also called an **allele**) of a gene known as "DRD2 A1" is normally involved in controlling the flow of dopamine (a powerful brain chemical that gives people a sense of well-being). When defective, however, the DRD2 A1 allele diminishes dopamine function, which may drive a person to take drugs, drink, or engage in activity that provides a dopamine-like experience. "We think they're seeking out ways of fixing the lack of pleasure," said researcher Kenneth Blum. "You might be a pleasure seeker for alcohol, drugs, sex or maybe you get it from violence or murder."[9]

In 2002, **Avshalom Caspi** and **Terrie E. Moffitt** and their colleagues offered a model of *gene-environment interaction* that recognized that childhood maltreatment appears to be a "universal risk factor for antisocial behavior" in adulthood. Previous research had demonstrated that children who experience abuse—especially those exposed to erratic, coercive, and punitive parenting—frequently develop conduct disorders and display antisocial personality symptoms, and they are known to be at greater risk of becoming violent adult offenders than are children who do not experience such maltreatment.[10] Earlier research had also shown that the younger children are when they experience maltreatment, the more likely they are to display such problems in later life.

Childhood maltreatment appears to be a "universal risk factor for antisocial behavior" in adulthood.

Using data from the Dunedin Multidisciplinary Health and Development Study—a longitudinal study of 1,037 children born in the maternity hospital in Dunedin, New Zealand, between April 1, 1972, and March 31, 1973—Caspi and Moffit noted that not all maltreated children grow up to become criminal,[11] but they hypothesized that the development of antisocial behavior is mediated by an interaction between a gene responsible for the production of the enzyme MAOA and an environment variable (maltreatment). Researchers demonstrated a significant biosocial interaction between MAOA and early child abuse, leading to violence later in life.[12] Their findings showed that maltreatment "has lasting neurochemical correlates in human children" and that deficient MAOA activity may cause "neural hyperreactivity" in children in response to threats. The researchers concluded that "childhood maltreatment predisposes most strongly to adult violence among children whose MAOA is insufficient to constrain maltreatment-induced changes to neurotransmitter systems."[13] Maltreated children with high MAOA activity did not develop antisocial behavior. The finding was supported by two separate Swedish studies published in 2007.[14]

A 2008 analysis of data from the National Longitudinal Study of Adolescent Health (also known as Add Health) by **Kevin M. Beaver** of Florida State University and associates found that low MAOA activity can interact with neuropsychological deficits (defined in this study as poor scores on verbal skills tests) to produce low self-control and delinquency. Hence, according to Beaver, data analysis findings "are supportive of an interdisciplinary scientific approach to the study of crime and delinquency, which views antisocial behavior as a multifactorial phenotype that is the result of genetic factors, neural substrates, and environmental factors working independently and synergistically."[15] In other words, in at least some cases, genetic predispositions plus interaction with the surrounding social and physical environments combine to produce delinquency.

Continued focus on the gene related to MAOA production led to the announced finding of a "warrior gene," and in 2010 National Geographic Television produced a show entitled "Inside the Warrior Gene" that featured men who felt that their lives were controlled by a deep-seated and constant anger that might be ascribed to such a biological condition.[16] Variants of the gene were found in boys more likely to engage in violence, to use weapons, and to join gangs.

In 2007, researchers at the University of Texas Southwestern Medical Center discovered that mice carrying certain mutations in what is called the clock gene exhibited manic behaviors, such as recklessness and hyperactivity, and also displayed a preference for addictive substances, such as

■ **heritability** A statistical construct that estimates the amount of variation in the traits of a population that is attributable to genetic factors.

■ **epigenetics** The study of the chemical reactions that occur within a genome, and which switch parts of the genome on or off at strategic times and locations.

■ **gene expression** The process by which the coded information that is stored within a gene is used to create a biological product, usually a protein. Also, the manifestation of a trait in an individual carrying the gene or genes that determine that trait.

cocaine, but that treatment with the antipsychotic medicine lithium caused them to behave normally. Somewhat later, Francis McMahon of the National Institute of Mental Health in Bethesda, Maryland, reported finding a number of specific genes that act by influencing how the brain responds to neurotransmitters such as dopamine and that might be associated with bipolar disorder.[17]

In 2008, researchers with the National Institute on Drug Abuse announced that "as much as half of an individual's risk of becoming addicted to nicotine, alcohol, or other drugs depends on his or her genes."[18] The researchers stated, "Pinning down the biological basis for this risk is an important avenue of research for scientists trying to solve the problem of drug abuse."

In 2011, making a genetic argument for at least some forms of callous-unemotional behavior, **Nathalie Fontaine** of Indiana University and colleagues, reported that **heritability** (which is a statistical construct that estimates the amount of variation in the traits of a population that is attributable to genetic factors) leads to persistently high levels of such behavior among twin boys.[19] The data on which Fontaine reported were derived from the United Kingdom's ongoing Twin Early Development Study (TEDS), which uses information gathered from over 15,000 families to explore how people change through childhood and adolescence.[20] A similar study, conducted at about the same time, examined differences in self-control between male and female twins. The study authors concluded that "there are genetic differences in self-control that are operating across the sexes in adolescence and adulthood."[21] The results of the study showed that "the same genetic factors influence levels of self-control in males and females," meaning that the "genetic influences on self-control are not gender-specific."

Some of the studies discussed here may appear to point to criminal genes that, once inherited, inevitably produce antisocial behavior. Such a conclusion, however, is not warranted. As we shall see later in this chapter, genes may simply influence the way in which people respond to their surroundings. As one researcher puts it, "genes and environments operating in tandem [are] required to produce significant antisocial behavior."[22] Hence, so-called criminal genes may be nothing more than genetic predispositions to respond in certain ways to a criminogenic environment.

The study of the chemical reactions that occur within a genome, and which switch parts of the genome on or off at strategic times and locations, is referred to as **epigenetics**. Epigenetics is informed by the principle that "the genome dynamically responds to the environment. Stress, diet, behavior, toxins and other factors activate chemical switches that regulate **gene expression**."[23] A video explaining epigenetics can be found at **Web Exta 5-4**.

Future Directions in the Study of Genes and Crime

The HGP, the Brain Activity Mapping project, and studies like those cited here notwithstanding, behavioral geneticists examining the crime problem face some daunting issues: coming up with a generally acceptable definition of criminality, determining how best to measure criminality once it has been defined, separating the influences of the social and physical environments from genetic influences on behavior, and distinguishing among the multiple and potentially interrelated influences of many genes. In the final analysis, the explanatory power of heritability appears to be limited by the fact that it may apply only to specific environments that existed at the time of a given study. For example, red roses grown under optimal conditions will likely all be similar in size, shape, and color, but grow the same roses in a desert or put food coloring in their water, and their appearance is likely to change substantially. As one noted geneticist says, "If the population or the environment changes, the heritability most likely will change as well. Most important, heritability statements provide no basis for predictions about the expression of the trait in question in any given individual."[24] In other words, even red roses watered with blue food coloring are unlikely to end up being red.

New understandings about how genes operate also seem to call into question previous notions that genes are strong determinants of human behavior. Researchers in the field of neurobiology, for example, have found 17 genes, known as CREB genes, that are switched on and off in response to environmental influences. The CREB genes lay down neural pathways in the brain and form the basis of memory; the act of learning turns the CREB genes on and is made possible by them.[25] Hence, the CREB genes respond to human experience rather than determine it. One writer explains it this way: "These genes are at the mercy of our behavior, not the other way around."[26] The FOXP2 gene on chromosome 7 allows the development of language skills in human beings. The CREB and FOXP2 genes have taught researchers that genes are not just carriers of heredity; they are active during life and respond to the environment.

■ **frontal brain hypothesis** A perspective that references physical changes in certain parts of the brain to explain criminality.

The interaction of genes and the behavioral possibilities that they represent, with features of the social and physical environments produce meaningful human activity.

In sum, it is important to recognize that genes are both the cause and the consequence of our actions—and that they do not so much *determine* human action as *enable* it. Nonetheless, as one researcher puts it, "Single genes can have quite large effects, though, when they are paired with criminogenic environments."[27]

Learn more about the HGP by visiting the National Human Genome Research Institute via **Web Extra 5–5**; you might also want to visit the U.S. Department of Energy's Human Genome Program site at **Web Extra 5–6**. You can read about how DNA and genetics might influence human behavior at **Library Extras 5–1**, **5–2**, and **5–3**.

The Dysfunctional Brain

A number of contemporary researchers have explored brain dysfunction as it relates to criminality. For example, studies using positron emission tomography (PET) of the prefrontal cortex of subjects' brains have shown interesting results. Among other things, PET technology can measure the uptake of glucose by the brain. In a 1994 study conducted by University of Pennsylvania professor **Adrian Raine** and his colleagues, PET scans of the brains of 22 murderers (including some who had only attempted murder) revealed that the study subjects showed much lower levels of glucose uptake in the prefrontal cortex than did members of a control group.[28] "The differences that Raine observed were not related to age, gender, handedness, ethnicity, motivation, history of head injury, or presence of schizophrenia. In addition, no subjects were taking psychoactive drugs at the time of the test."[29] Raine observed that their data strongly suggested that "deficits localized to the prefrontal cortex may be related to violence" in some offenders (Figure 5–1). He also noted that "frontal damage is associated with impulsivity, loss of self-control, immaturity, lack of tact, inability to modify and inhibit behavior appropriately, and poor social judgment."[30]

PET scans of the brains of murderers showed much lower levels of glucose uptake in the prefrontal cortex than did the controls.

Raine and other researchers who were involved in the study explained that prefrontal cortex dysfunction must be evaluated in terms of how individuals who exhibit the condition interact with features of the environment, including social and psychological influences. Because prefrontal cortex dysfunction may result in failure in school, inability to hold a job, problems in relationships, and so forth, it may not be a direct cause of crime but might predispose someone afflicted with the condition to "a criminal and violent way of life."[31] Raine later replicated the study using 41 murderers who had claimed to be not guilty by reason of insanity (NGRI), and who were matched with 41 "normal" controls. Similar results were obtained, leading Raine to conclude "that murderers pleading NGRI are characterized by . . . reduced glucose metabolism in (the) bilateral prefrontal cortex."[32] Still later, Raine and his colleagues used PET studies to show that differences exist between the brains of people prone to impulsive violence and those who preplan violent crimes.[33]

Seventeen years later, in a 2011 presentation made to the American Association for the Advancement of Science, Raine identified an 18% reduction of the volume of the portion of the brain called the amygdala in psychopaths when compared to nonpsychopaths, along with reductions in the size of the prefrontal cortex.[34] Raine claimed that, by examining the brains of children as young as three years, criminologists could already see signs indicating the potential for troubled behavior in the future.[35]

Other researchers, using less sophisticated techniques, have been able to show that "violent psychopathology in youth is associated with structural and functional damage" to the brain's orbital cortex.[36] The orbital cortex is that part of the brain that is directly over the orbits of the eyes. Some researchers have termed the neuroanatomical findings from studies like these the **frontal brain hypothesis**.[37]

In 2010, researchers from Columbia University's Medical Center were able to show how a gene defect that leads to a communications breakdown in the brain predisposes people with the defect to schizophrenia.[38] Maria Karayiorgou, Chief of the Division of Medical Genetics in the Department of Psychiatry at Columbia University, first noticed the relationship between the genetic variant and schizophrenia more than ten years earlier and was able to identify a definite pathophysiological mechanism of how the risk of schizophrenia is

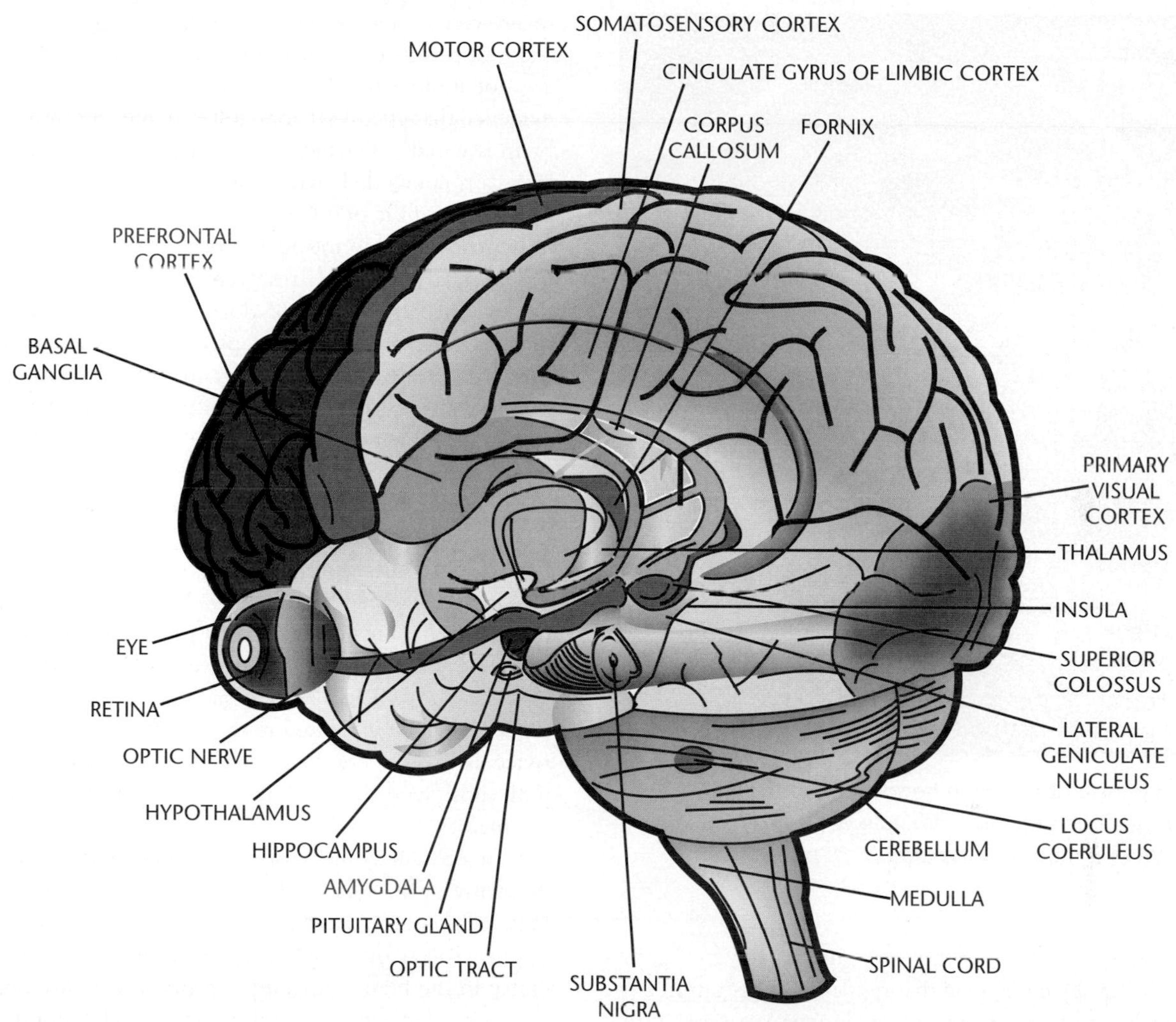

FIGURE 5-1 | **The Human Brain Showing the Prefrontal Cortex and the Amygdala**

Source: Schmalleger, Frank J., *Criminology*. Printed and Electronically reproduced by permission of Pearson Education, Inc., Upper Saddle River, New Jersey.

enhanced by a small deletion of genetic material on a specific chromosome shared by all human beings. She found that 30% of people with the missing genetic material go on to develop schizophrenia, making it one of the biggest genetic risk factors for the disease.

Other brain mechanisms may also be involved in aggression. Allergic reactions to common foods, for example, have been reported as the cause of violence and homicide by a number of investigators.[39] Some foods—including milk, citrus fruit, chocolate, corn, wheat, and eggs—are thought to produce allergic reactions in sensitive individuals, leading to a swelling of the brain and the brain stem. Such swelling is thought to impede the higher faculties, reducing people's sense of morality and creating conditions that support impulsive behavior. Involvement of the central nervous system in such allergies may reduce the amount of learning that occurs during childhood and may contribute to delinquency as well as to adult criminal behavior.

Physical injuries, emotional trauma, disease, and even long-term exposure to stress can also lead to changes in the brain. One 2010 study found that the brains of monkeys whose mothers had the flu while they were pregnant exhibited physical changes similar to those in people with schizophrenia.[40] Researchers noted that their findings supported the suggestion that flu in human mothers-to-be can affect brain development.

Similarly, in 2010, Princeton University's Douglas S. Massey discovered a link between stressors in the social environment and brain structure. Massey, who studied the impact of social stratification on thought processes among residentially segregated minorities, found that "people who are exposed to high levels of stress over a prolonged period of time are at risk of having their

■ **neuroplasticity** The ability of the brain to alter its structure and function in response to experience.

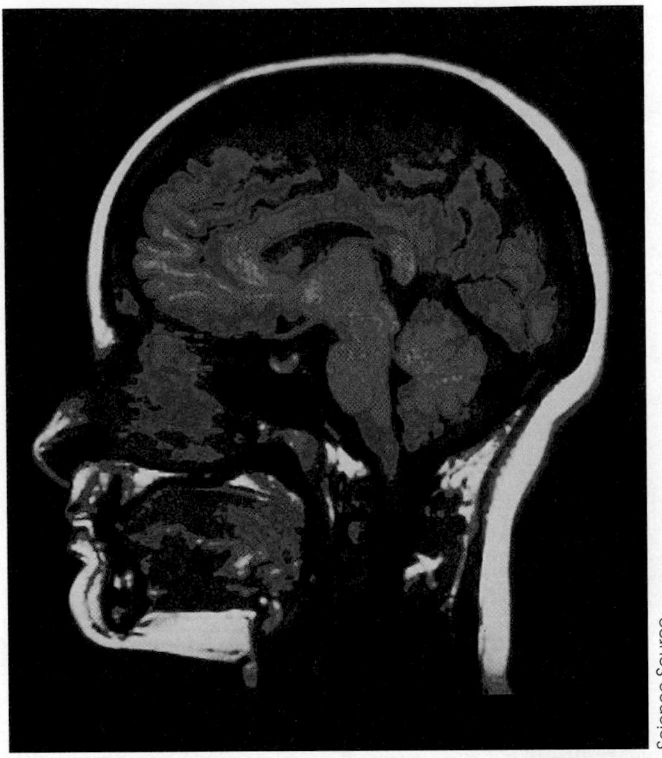
Science Source

An infrared image of a human head showing the brain. How might changes in the physical structure of the brain affect behavior? What is meant by the term *brain plasticity*?

brains re-wired in a way that leaves them with fewer cognitive resources."[41] Massey concluded that residential segregation based on race produces life-long stressors, including exposure to violence, social disorder, and poverty, that result in high-risk behavior, including criminality, among deprived minorities.

Recently, some scientists have advanced the term **neuroplasticity** (sometimes called *brain plasticity* or *cortical plasticity*) to mean that the brain can alter its structure and function in response to experience or injury, and to explain why some people experience significant changes in personality when undergoing powerful new experiences. It is well known, for example, that when portions of the brain are physically damaged through trauma, stroke, or other types of injury, adjacent parts of the brain can assume some of the psychological or motor functions that would have otherwise been lost.

In 2003, Harvard University Medical School researchers discovered that the normally thick cable of nerve cells (the *corpus callosum*) connecting the right and left hemispheres in the brain is generally smaller in children who have been abused than in children who were free from abuse.[42] Brain scans show that neglect also reduces the size of the connector, as does constant and severe verbal abuse. According to Martin Teicher, associate professor of psychiatry at Harvard Medical School, "These changes are not limited to physical and sexual abuse; there's growing evidence that even verbal assault can alter the way a developing brain is wired." Teicher and other psychiatrists who conducted the scans concluded that "a smaller *corpus callosum* leads to less integration of the two halves of the brain, and that this can result in dramatic shifts in mood and personality."[43]

Similarly, in 2011, researchers at University College London scanned the brains of dozens of children and found that those who had experienced physical violence at the hands of caregivers showed extra activity in the amygdala and the anterior insula—regions of the brain involved in threat perception and the anticipation of pain. The changes were the same, the researchers said, as those found in soldiers exposed to combat. Eamon McCrory, one of the researchers explained, "Maltreated kids and active soldiers are adapting to survive in a threatening or dangerous environment."[44]

In 2013, researchers in New Mexico reported on scanning the brains of 96 male prisoners just prior to their release to assess impulsivity and inhibitory control.[45] They found that prisoners who showed less activity in the anterior cingulate cortex (ACC)—which is located in the front of the brain—were about twice as likely to reoffend over the next four years compared with those who showed more activity in that specific region of the brain.

In a recent symposium, researchers with the U.S. National Academy of Sciences and the Canadian Institute for Advanced Research reported advances in research on biological *embedding*, or the process by which social experiences change neural circuitry in the brain.[46] Changes in brain structure brought about by embedded stressful and traumatic childhood experiences were found to influence a child's development and to persist throughout life. In the words of the researchers, "experiences of childhood adversity affect cellular pathways and translate into the molecular and genetic changes that result in biological effects on development and health."[47]

Researchers have also found positive changes: Neural circuitry in the brains of practiced meditators changes—apparently in response to thousands of hours spent meditating—as evidenced by the fact that the brain waves of meditators were significantly different from those of nonmeditators.[48] Scientists who study neuroplasticity now believe not only that the brain changes in response to external stimuli or physical trauma but also that it is malleable in response to internal stimuli (thoughts). If true, simple self-improvement techniques—such as positive thinking and silently repeated self-affirmations—may foster positive alterations in personality and produce an increased likelihood of socially approved behaviors. A few years ago, for example, UCLA psychiatrist Jeffrey M. Schwartz demonstrated that patients

THEORY | in PERSPECTIVE

Modern Biological Theories

Modern biological theories of criminality stress the interaction between biological influences and the surrounding social and physical environments. Unlike earlier biological theories, modern biosocial perspectives recognize the role of the environment in shaping both biological processes and behavioral propensities that are related to those processes.

Genetics and Heritability

Genetic characteristics and variations in human chromosomes are thought to play a role in aggression and crime causation. Although contemporary criminologists do not believe that there is one single and identifiable "criminal gene," they do believe that individuals who are genetically predisposed to certain types of behavior may become aggressive or criminal through interaction with the surrounding physical and social environments. Sex-linked chromosomes have special explanatory power by virtue of the fact that the majority of violent offenders are male.

Period: 1965 to the present

Theorists: Patricia A. Jacobs, Nathalie Fontaine, H. Hilger Ropers, Han Brunner, Adrian Raine, Darrell J. Steffensmeier, Thomas Bernard

Concepts: genes, genome, chromosomes, XYY supermale, heritability, gender ratio problem, sexual selection

Brain Dysfunction

Organic problems with the brain may lead to behavioral anomalies, including crime and deviance.

Period: 1990s to the present

Theorists: Adrian Raine and others

Concepts: frontal brain hypothesis, neuroplasticity, embedding

Body Chemistry Theories

Violent or disruptive behavior can sometimes be linked to nutrition, vitamin deficiencies, and other conditions that affect the body. Studies of eating habits, endocrinology, and environmental contaminants have all contributed to advances in understanding such behavior.

Period: 1940s to the present

Theorists: Adrian Raine, Stephen Schoenthaler, Alexander G. Schauss, David Fergusson

Concepts: hypoglycemia, frontal brain hypothesis, environmental pollution, toxic metals, vitamins, food allergies, environmental pollution, prenatal exposure to toxins

Hormones and Criminality

These biological theories explain violent or disruptive and criminal behavior by identifying hormonal influences on human cognition and action.

Period: 1940s to the present

Theorists: Alan Booth, D. Wayne Osgood, Paul C. Bernhardt, Kevin Beaver, Anthony Walsh, Lee Ellis

Concepts: testosterone, evolutionary perspective, evolutionary neuroandrogenic theory, serotonin, premenstrual syndrome (PMS), hormones (testosterone, cortisol, norepinephrine), neurotransmitters (dopamine), monoamine oxidase inhibitors (MAOIs)

Biosocial Criminology

This theoretical perspective sees the interaction between biology and the physical and social environments as key to understanding human behavior, including criminality.

Period: 1987 to the present

Theorists: James Q. Wilson, Richard J. Herrnstein, Hans J. Eysenck, Anthony Walsh, Avshalom Caspi, Terrie E. Moffitt, Kevin M. Beaver,

Concepts: Biosocial perspectives incorporate many of the concepts previously listed in this box, including genetics, heritability, hormones, brain dysfunction, body chemistry, the gender ratio problem, natural and sexual selection. Neuroplasticity and epigenetics are additional associated concepts. The most important contribution from this perspective, however, comes in recognizing the influence of biological factors as they are mediated through the physical and social environments in producing criminal behavior.

> Biological theories are theories of criminality, not crime.

suffering from obsessive-compulsive disorder (OCD) are capable of consciously rechanneling compulsive urges into more socially acceptable activities and that by doing so, they could actually alter their brains' neuronal circuitry.[49] Hence, physical changes to the brain in response to experiences that were once thought possible only in the very young can also characterize adults in some situations. One writer explained that "the brain physically 'captures' the environment as it wires itself in response to environmental experience."[50] The same writer noted, however, that "the brain has many assumptions built into it over eons of evolutionary time; it is no *tabula rasa*."[51] With these considerations in mind, some suggest that the interplay among heredity, biology, and the social and physical environments may be much more complicated than once thought and may provide the key nexus in any consideration of crime causation.

Body Chemistry and Criminality

Today's biological theorists have made significant studies in linking violent or disruptive behavior to body chemistry. Body chemistry is influenced by factors such as eating

■ **hypoglycemia** A medical condition characterized by low blood sugar.

"You are what you eat" may contain more than a grain of truth.

habits, vitamin deficiencies, environmental contaminants, and the endocrine system. We now turn to those issues.

Ingested Substances and Nutrition

One of the first studies to focus on chemical imbalances in the body as a cause of crime was reported in the British medical journal *Lancet* in 1943.[52] The authors of the study linked murder to **hypoglycemia**, or low blood sugar. Low blood sugar, produced by too much insulin in the blood or by near-starvation diets, was said to reduce the mind's capacity to reason effectively or to judge the long-term consequences of behavior. More recent studies have linked excess consumption of refined white sugar to hyperactivity, aggressiveness, excitability, and impairment of the ability to make reasoned decisions, and popular books like *Sugar Blues* provide guides for individuals seeking to free themselves from the negative effects of excess sugar consumption.[53]

Even the courts have accepted the notion that excess sugar consumption resulting in hyperglycemia may be linked to crime. In the early 1980s, for example, Dan White, a former San Francisco police officer, was given a reduced sentence after his lawyers used what came to be known as the "Twinkie Defense."[54] They argued that White's nightlong binge on large amounts of Coca-Cola and Twinkies before he murdered San Francisco Mayor George Moscone and City Councilman Harvey Milk was evidence of White's unbalanced mental state; the consumption of junk food was presented as evidence of depression because White was normally very health conscious.

More than ten years later, however, a well-conducted 1994 study reported in the *New England Journal of Medicine* seemed to contradict the notion that sugar may lead to hyperactivity;[55] neither sugar nor artificial sweeteners were shown to have any link to an increase in learning disabilities. In the study, researchers at Vanderbilt University and the University of Iowa varied the diets of supposedly sugar-sensitive youngsters from a diet that was high in sugar to a diet that was low in sugar but that contained the artificial sweetener aspartame, and a third experimental diet contained very little sugar but had added saccharin. After surveying parents, teachers, and babysitters and testing the study group for changes in memory, concentration, and math skills, the researchers concluded, "We couldn't find any difference in terms of their behavior or their learning on any of the three diets."[56] Hence, to date, the evidence concerning sugar's impact on behavior is unclear.

Some studies have implicated food additives, such as the flavor enhancer monosodium glutamate, dyes, and artificial flavorings, in producing criminal violence.[57] Other research has found that coffee and sugar may trigger antisocial behavior;[58] researchers were led to these conclusions through finding that inmates consumed considerably greater amounts of coffee, sugar, and processed foods than others.[59] It is unclear, however, whether inmates drink more coffee because of boredom or whether "excitable" personalities feel a need for the kind of stimulation available through coffee consumption. On the other hand, habitual coffee drinkers in nonprison populations have not been linked to crime, and other studies, like the one conducted by Mortimer Gross of the University of Illinois, showed no link between the amount of sugar consumed by inmates and hyperactivity.[60] Nonetheless, some prison programs have been designed to limit intake of dietary stimulants through nutritional management and substitution of artificial sweeteners for refined sugar.

Other studies appear to show that diets deficient in various vitamins and other nutrients can increase aggressiveness and agitation, and can open the door to crime. In recent years, for example, **Stephen Schoenthaler**, a researcher at the California State University in Stanislaus, has demonstrated significant declines in bad behavior in incarcerated adults and in schoolchildren receiving specifically designed vitamin-mineral supplementation.[61] In one of Schoenthaler's studies, for example, schoolchildren receiving vitamin supplements showed a 47% lower rate of antisocial behavior than children who received placebos.[62] More important, the drop in disciplinary infractions among children taking the supplements was due mostly to a decrease in infractions by those who had been identified as habitual offenders before entering the study.

Other nutrients have been studied to assess their possible behavioral impact. In 2003, for example, Ingrid Bergliot Helland reported that maternal diet during pregnancy can strongly affect IQ and early infant behavior, and concluded that it might also determine the risk of delinquency and criminality in later life.[63] Helland and her colleagues supplemented the diets of pregnant and lactating women with either omega-3 (DHA) or omega-6 fatty acids and followed the development of their offspring for years after the supplementation program had ended. They found that children receiving dietary omega-3 supplementation had significantly higher IQ levels by age four and performed better on problem-solving tests than those receiving omega-6 fatty acids.

A year later, a study of the relationship between omega-3 intake levels and chronic hostility among 3,600 urban young adults concluded that higher consumption of omega-3 fatty acids was related to significantly lower levels of hostility, with researchers stating that "high dietary intake of DHA and consumption

prenatal substance exposure Fetal exposure to maternal drug and alcohol use. Prenatal substance exposure can significantly increase a child's risk for developmental and neurological disorders.

High dietary intake of DHA and consumption of fish rich in omega-3 fatty acids may be related to less hostility in young adulthood.

of fish rich in omega-3 fatty acids may be related to lower likelihood of high hostility in young adulthood."[64] A 2007 study conducted in the United Kingdom found that antisocial behavior could be reduced in children through dietary supplementation with polyunsaturated fatty acids.[65]

Finally, a 2013 study reported in *Pediatrics*, a journal of the American Medical Association, revealed a clear link between the length of time a child is breast fed and later intelligence; with longer breast-feeding times being correlated with higher intelligence in the developing child.[66] The study controlled for environmental factors, including the mothers' intelligence and diet, and seemed to indicate that nutrients which are found only in breast milk, including fatty acids linked to brain development, are responsible for the observed increase in intelligence. Read more about diet and its possible contribution to criminal behavior at **Library Extra 5–4**.

Environmental Pollution

Various substances found in our environment have been shown to be linked to criminal behavior. In 1997, British researchers Roger D. Masters, Brian Hone, and Anil Doshi published a study purporting to show that industrial and other forms of environmental pollution cause people to commit violent crimes.[67] The study used statistics from the FBI's Uniform Crime Reporting Program and data from the U.S. Environmental Protection Agency's Toxic Release Inventory. A comparison between the two data sets showed a significant correlation between juvenile crime and high environmental levels of both lead and manganese. Masters and his colleagues suggested an explanation based on a *neurotoxicity hypothesis*. Another author stated, "According to this approach, toxic pollutants—specifically the toxic metals lead and manganese—cause learning disabilities, an increase in aggressive behavior, and—most importantly—loss of control over impulsive behavior. These traits combine with poverty, social stress, alcohol and drug abuse, individual character, and other social and psychological factors to produce individuals who commit violent crimes."[68] See the Crime in the News box for more information on lead exposure and its effects.

The largest study of lead contamination and its effects on behavior was an examination of 1,000 black children in Philadelphia. It showed that the level of exposure to lead was a reliable predictor of the number of juvenile offenses among the exposed male population, the seriousness of juvenile offenses, and the number of adult offenses. More recent studies, including many that Masters was unaware of, seem to support his thesis.[69]

The researchers reasoned that toxic metals affect individuals in complex ways. Because lead diminishes a person's normal ability to detoxify poisons, it may heighten the effects of alcohol and drugs. Industrial pollution, automobile emissions, lead-based paints, and aging water-delivery systems are all possible sources of lead contamination. In a recent interview, Roger D. Masters, Research Professor at Dartmouth College, noted, "The presence of pollution is as big a factor [in crime causation] as poverty. It's the breakdown of the inhibition mechanism that's the key to violent behavior."[70] When brain chemistry is altered by exposure to heavy metals and other toxins, people lose the natural restraint that holds their violent tendencies in check.

More recent studies have focused on **prenatal substance exposure** to substances like marijuana, tobacco smoke, and alcohol. In 2000, for example, L. Goldschmidt and colleagues reported the results of a ten-year study that monitored the development of children of more than 600 low-income women. The study, which began during the women's pregnancies, found that prenatal marijuana use was significantly related to increased hyperactivity, impulsivity, inattention, increased delinquency, and externalizing problems;[71] the findings remained significant even when researchers controlled for other lifestyle features.

In 1998, **David Fergusson** and colleagues, in a study of 1,022 New Zealand children who had been followed for 18 years, found that "children whose mothers smoked one pack of cigarettes or more per day during their pregnancy had mean rates of conduct disorder symptoms that were twice as high as those found among children born to mothers who did not smoke during their pregnancy."[72] The observed relationship was twice as strong among male teens as among females. Similar relationships between prenatal smoking and both aggression and hyperactivity in later life have been reported by Dutch researchers.[73] A similar 2006 meta-analysis by researchers at Washington State University found that smoking by pregnant mothers contributed slightly to their children's subsequent antisocial behavior.[74]

Prenatal alcohol exposure also seems to be linked to delinquency and psychiatric problems later in life. A 1999 study of 32 children by Tresa M. Roebuck and colleagues found that

CRIME | in the NEWS

Exposure to Lead, Other Substances Linked to Crime Rate

focusemotions/Shutterstock

A leaky water pipe in an older home. Pipes like these sometimes contain lead, which can contaminate the water they carry. What role might childhood lead consumption play in the development of delinquency and antisocial behavior?

A set of environmental laws that Congress passed in the late 1970s and 1980s may have done more to reduce the U.S. crime rate than any advance in crime detection. These laws removed lead from paint, gasoline and plumbing in response to growing evidence that lead harms the body in a wide variety of ways—including leading people into crime.

It has long been established that lead is a potent neurotoxin, and that lead poisoning causes increased aggression, especially among young children, whose small, growing bodies are sensitive to even tiny amounts of lead. Lead interferes with normal brain development in children by destroying the myelin sheaths that surround brain cells, which in turn interferes with neurotransmission.

In 2012, a study published in *Environment International* measured the impact of lead poisoning on crime rates over more than two decades, as affected children grew up and became criminals. In the study, researchers examined the amounts of lead released in six cities from 1950 to 1985. They correlated these rates with levels of aggravated assaults 22 years later, after the exposed children had grown up. The study found that for each 1 percent increase in the amount of environmental lead, aggravated assaults rose 0.46 percent. "Up to 90 percent of the variation in aggravated assault across the cities is explained by the amount of lead dust released 22 years earlier," researchers wrote.

The study seemed to confirm a prediction that Mark A. R. Kleiman, a professor of public policy at the University of California, Los Angeles, made in 2007: "It's quite plausible that the removal of lead from gasoline in the 1980s had more to do with the crime collapse of the late 1990s than any other single factor."

About the same time, Rick Nevin, of the National Center for Health Housing, reported results from more recent international studies. He found that "the relationship between lead exposure, arrest, and crime trends . . . is evident across many crime categories and across nations with divergent preschool blood lead and crime rate trends." The Nevin study, shows what appears to be a strong correlation between childhood lead exposure and index crime rates, albeit with a 19-year lag between the two.

Researchers have also connected manganese—used in gasoline, aluminum products, and disposable batteries—to heightened aggression and crime. For example, a study in Australia found that the incidence of severe crime was highest near the country's largest manganese mine. Unlike lead, however, manganese cannot be banned because it is an essential part of the human body. Low doses are harmless, but excessive amounts may be found at work sites, where the U.S. government has set standards on acceptable levels.

Mercury and copper have been linked to aggressiveness, but many other substances have not been tested yet for their effect on the brain. Researchers writing in the British medical journal *Lancet* in 2006 reported that more than 1,000 industrial chemicals show evidence of neurotoxicity in animal tests and need more study about their effect on humans. "Of the thousands of chemicals used in commerce, fewer than half have been subjected to even token laboratory testing for toxicity," the researchers wrote.

Discussion Questions

1. What does this feature say is the likely link between childhood lead exposure and later criminality?
2. What steps can be taken to reduce childhood exposure to environmental lead? What steps have already been taken?

Sources: Rick Nevin, "Understanding International Crime Trends: The Legacy of Preschool Lead Exposure," *Environmental Research*, February 2007, Vol. 104, pp. 315–336; Whet Moser, "Youth Violence: The Lead Cause?," *Chicago Reader*, October 20, 2009, http://www.chicagoreader.com/Bleader/archives/2009/10/20/youth-violence-the-lead-cause.; Noah Schultz-Byard, "Study Links Lead Exposure to Violent Crimes," ABC Broken Hill, April 12, 2012, http://www.abc.net.au/local/stories/2012/04/12/3475505.htm.; Jim Haner, "Studies Suggest Link between Lead, Violence," *Baltimore Sun*, May 9, 2000, http://www.baltimoresun.com/news/maryland/bal-te.lead09may09,0,584142.story.

■ **hormone** A chemical substance produced by the body that regulates and controls the activity of certain cells or organs.

■ **testosterone** The primary male sex hormone. It is produced in the testes, and its function is to control secondary sex characteristics and sexual drive.

alcohol-exposed children exhibited greater delinquency and less intelligence than a control group of children who had not suffered from alcohol exposure while in the womb. The researchers concluded that their findings, which are consistent with the work of other researchers,[75] showed that "alcohol-exposed children, although less impaired intellectually, are more likely than children with mental retardation to exhibit antisocial behaviors, lack of consideration for the rights and feelings of others, and resistance to limits and requests of authority figures."[76] Learn more about the role of environmental contaminants, fetal alcohol exposure, and other factors and their contributions to criminality at **Web Extra 5–7**. Read about pollution's possible link to crime and toxic threats to child development at **Library Extras 5–5** and **5–6**.

Hormones and Criminality

A **hormone** is a chemical substance produced by the body that regulates and controls the activity of certain cells or organs. Hormones have come under scrutiny as potential behavioral determinants. The male sex hormone **testosterone**, for example, has been linked to aggression and appears to play an important role in increasing the propensity toward violence and aggression among men. Testosterone is a steroid hormone from the androgen group that is primarily secreted by the testes. Although females produce some testosterone, it is normally present in far higher quantities in the blood and tissues of males.

A few authors have suggested that testosterone is the agent *primarily* responsible for male criminality and that its relative lack in women leads them to commit fewer crimes. A growing body of evidence supports just such a hypothesis. Studies have shown, for example, that female fetuses exposed to elevated testosterone levels during gestation develop masculine characteristics, including a muscular build and a demonstrably greater tendency toward aggression later in life.[77] Other studies show that testosterone continues to influence behavior strongly and that it creates what some have called "sexually dismorphic brains."[78]

Most studies on the subject have consistently shown a relationship between high blood testosterone levels and increased aggressiveness in men, and focused studies have unveiled a direct relationship between the amount of the chemical present and the degree of violence demonstrated by sex offenders.[79] Other researchers have linked anabolic steroid abuse among bodybuilders to destructive urges and psychosis.[80] Anabolic steroids are human-made drugs that have similar effects to testosterone in the body.

Some contemporary investigations have demonstrated a link between testosterone levels and aggression in teenagers,[81] and others have shown that adolescent problem behavior and teenage violence rise in proportion to the amount of testosterone in the blood of young men.[82] In 1987, for example, a Swedish researcher, Dan Olweus, reported that boys ages 15 to 17 showed levels of both verbal and physical aggression that correlated with the level of testosterone present in their blood. He stated that boys with higher levels of testosterone "tended to be habitually more impatient and irritable than boys with lower testosterone levels."[83] He concluded that high levels of the hormone led to increased frustration and habitual impatience and irritability.

SI1 WENN Photos/Newscom

A photo of professional wrestler Ryback Where, participating in the 2013 WWE Revenge Tour in Dublin, Ireland. Sex hormones, such as testosterone, have been linked to aggressive behavior; testosterone also enhances secondary sexual characteristics like body hair and muscle mass in males. What kinds of crimes might be hormonally influenced?

■ **serotonin** A neurotransmitter that is commonly found in the pineal gland, the digestive tract, the central nervous system, and blood platelets.

In what may be the definitive work to date on the subject, **Alan Booth** and **D. Wayne Osgood** concluded that there is a "moderately strong relationship between testosterone and adult deviance" but suggested that the relationship "is largely mediated by the influence of testosterone on social integration and on prior involvement in juvenile delinquency."[84] In other words, measurably high levels of testosterone in the blood of young men may have some effect on behavior, but that effect is likely to be moderated by the social environment.

Similar conclusions were reached in 1998 by Swedish researchers who evaluated 61 men undergoing forensic psychiatric examinations for blood levels of free testosterone, total testosterone, and sex hormone–binding globulin (SHBG).[85] SHBG is known to determine the level of testosterone concentration in the blood and in body tissue. The Swedish researchers found that blood levels of total testosterone and SHBG were closely related to the extent of antisocial personality, alcoholism, and criminality exhibited by the subjects under study.

A 2007 study by University of Michigan researchers showed a relationship between testosterone, vigilance, and facial expressions of anger (considered to be signals of an impending dominance challenge). People with higher levels of testosterone were more prone to respond aggressively to displays of anger in others. According to the researchers, higher levels of testosterone "may generally decrease aversion to threatening stimuli, and/or may specifically facilitate approach towards signals of dominance challenge . . . [and that] a signal of an impending dominance challenge could be rewarding to individuals [who] have a history of success in such encounters."[86] The researchers concluded that the "relationship between testosterone and dominance appears to be reciprocal: winners of dominance challenges show increases in [testosterone], and in turn, higher [testosterone] leads to a greater likelihood to aggress and/or to pursue further dominance challenges, in nonhuman animals and potentially also in humans."[87] See the Who's to Blame box for a hypothetical example of the possible influence of testosterone on crime causation.

A few limited studies have attempted to measure the effects of testosterone on women. Although women's bodies manufacture roughly one-tenth the amount of the hormone secreted by men, subtle changes in testosterone levels in women have been linked to changes in personality and sexual behavior.[88] One such study showed that relatively high blood levels of testosterone in female inmates were associated with "aggressively dominant behavior" in prison.[89]

Another study whose results were reported in 2003 attempted to measure the impact of high levels of androgens (male hormones, including testosterone) on both males and females.[90] The study examined the "externalizing behavior" of 87 fourteen-year-olds (51 females and 36 males); other data on externalizing behavior, including aggression, were available from information gathered when the children were 8, 11, and 14 years old. Findings showed that boys with the highest blood plasma levels of androgens exhibited the most persistent aggression, but no association was found between aggression and androgen levels in females.

Fluctuations in the level of female hormones may also bear some relationship to law violation. In 1980, a British court exonerated Christine English of charges that she murdered her live-in lover after English admittedly ran him over with her car following an argument; English's defense rested on the fact that she was suffering from PMS at the time of the homicide. An expert witness, Dr. Katharina Dalton, testified at the trial that PMS had caused English to be "irritable, aggressive, and confused, with loss of self-control."[91]

Serotonin

A 1997 study by **Paul C. Bernhardt** found that testosterone might not act alone in promoting aggression.[92] Bernhardt discovered that aggressive behavior in men may be influenced by high testosterone levels combined with low brain levels of the neurotransmitter **serotonin**. Serotonin, a neurotransmitter, is a hormone that is commonly found in the pineal gland, the digestive tract, the central nervous system, and blood platelets. Serotonin plays an important role in the regulation of learning, mood, and sleep, and in the constriction of blood vessels. Most of the body's serotonin is in the intestines, where it regulates intestinal movements. The rest is found in the neurons of the central nervous system.

> Aggressive behavior in men may be influenced by high testosterone levels combined with low brain levels of the neurotransmitter serotonin.

Bernhardt postulated that testosterone's true role is to produce dominance-seeking behavior but not necessarily overt aggression. According to Bernhardt, when individuals are frustrated by their inability to achieve dominance, serotonin acts to reduce the negative psychological impact of frustration, producing calmer responses. Men whose brains are lacking in serotonin, however, feel the effects of frustration more acutely and therefore tend to respond to frustrating circumstances more aggressively, especially when testosterone levels are high.

WHO'S TO BLAME—The Individual or Society?

Hormones and Criminal Behavior

Lamont Ridgeway, 22, was arrested and charged with rape after 21-year-old Nicole Bachman called police to her Minneapolis home at 2:00 A.M. Ridgeway and Bachman had met in an evening art class at the local community college, and Bachman invited Ridgeway to her apartment for a glass of wine after the class was over. Officers couldn't help but notice that Bachman was an unusually attractive young woman whose clothes were in disarray and that she was visibly intoxicated and slurred her words as she spoke; Ridgeway was passed out on her couch, apparently after having had far too much to drink.

"He raped me!" Bachman told the two officers who responded to her call for help. "I told him to stop, and he wouldn't," she said.

Ridgeway was roused from sleep, arrested, searched, handcuffed, and taken to jail, where he was booked and charged with rape. After being advised of his rights not to speak and to have a lawyer represent him, he decided to tell the officers who were questioning him that it wasn't really rape. "She came on to me," he said. "She took her blouse off, then her pants. And she gave me a lot to drink. Yeah, she said 'No,' but by then we were already there. I couldn't stop. Why would she want to, anyway?"

When Ridgeway's lawyer arrived, he advised Ridgeway not to say anything more. The lawyer, hired by Ridgeway's wealthy parents, read the statement that he had given to the police and then hired a neurophysiologist to help in building a defense that might stand up in court.

When the case went to trial two months later, the neurophysiologist testified as an expert witness for the defense. He told the jury that blood tests showed that Ridgeway had abnormally large amounts of testosterone naturally occurring in his blood, that testosterone was the chemical messenger responsible for the male sex drive (which, he said, differed substantially from that of women), and that Ridgeway had consequently been unable to control his behavior on the night of the alleged rape. "The young man was simply doing what his hormones made him do," the neurophysiologist testified. "It's my professional opinion," he concluded, "that with that amount of testosterone affecting his judgment, he really didn't have much choice in his behavioral responses once he was offered alcohol and was then visually stimulated by the young woman's removal of her clothes. If this was my patient," the neurophysiologist added, "I'd treat him with the testosterone antagonist Depo-Provera, and we would see the strength of his sex drive substantially diminished. You could be sure that this kind of thing wouldn't happen again."

In response, the prosecution called their own expert, a noted biochemist who, citing various studies, said that there was no clearly established link between blood levels of testosterone and aggressive sexual behavior in human beings. "Even if there were," he said, "people are not mindless animals. We have free choice. We are not so driven by our blood chemistry that we cannot decide what we are going to do in any given situation."

Think about it

1. With which expert witness do you agree more—the neurophysiologist or the biochemist? Why?
2. Do you believe that blood chemistry can ever be an explanation for behavior? For crime?
3. If you answered yes to the previous question, do you think that blood chemistry can ever be an effective excuse for criminality? If you answered no to the previous question, why is blood chemistry not an explanation for behavior?
4. How do our understandings of criminal motivation and crime causality influence our policies on the treatment, punishment, and reformation of those who violate the law?

Note: Who's to Blame boxes provide fictionalized critical thinking opportunities, and are not actual cases.

In 1999, researchers set out to test the hypothesis that enhancing brain levels of serotonin might reduce aggression and impulsivity in aggressive male criminals.[93] In the volunteer-only study, ten young male offenders were given daily injections of d,l-fenfluramine, a drug that makes serotonin more available to brain cells. Findings showed that "the drug produced a significant, dose-dependent decrease in aggressive responding 2 to 4.5 hours after dosing . . . [and that] all ten subjects decreased their aggressive responding following the highest 0.8 mg/kg dose."[94] Subjects exhibiting the highest rates of aggression showed the greatest decreases in aggression levels after being treated with d,l-fenfluramine; impulsivity similarly decreased.

Serotonin has been called a "behavior-regulating chemical," and animal studies have demonstrated a link between low levels of serotonin in the brain and aggressive behavior. For example, monkeys with low serotonin levels in their brains have been found to be more likely to bite, slap, and chase others of their kind. Studies at the National Institute on Alcohol Abuse and Alcoholism have linked low serotonin levels in humans to impulsive crimes. Men convicted of premeditated murder, for example, have been found to have normal serotonin levels, whereas those convicted of crimes of passion had lower levels.[95]

Other studies have found that the presence of excess manganese lowers brain levels of serotonin and dopamine, both of which are associated with impulse control and planning.[96] Roger D. Masters, whose work was discussed previously in this chapter, also claimed that children raised from birth on infant formula rather than breast milk absorb five times as much manganese as breast-fed infants; calcium deficiency is known to increase the absorption of manganese, and "a combination of manganese toxicity and calcium deficiency adds up to 'reverse' Prozac."[97]

One 1998 study of 781 men and women age 21 found a clear relationship between elevated *blood* levels of serotonin (which correspond to lower *brain* levels of the chemical) and violence in men.[98] The study controlled for a host of possible intervening factors, including gender, diet, psychiatric medications, illicit drug use, season of the year (during which the blood test was done), plasma levels of tryptophan (dietary precursor of serotonin), alcohol and tobacco use, psychiatric diagnoses, platelet count, body mass, socioeconomic status, IQ, and history of suicide attempts. The relationship held true when both court records and self-reports of violence were assessed. No relationship between serotonin levels and aggression was seen in female subjects. According to the study's authors, "This is the first study to demonstrate that a possible index of serotonergic function is related to violence in the general population. The epidemiological serotonin effect was not small [but rather] indicated a moderate effect size in the population."[99]

Similar research by Swedish neuropsychiatrists in 2003 found that a "dysregulation of serotonin" in the brain and central nervous system could lead to increased impulsivity, irresponsibility, aggression, and need for stimulation.[100] The researchers examined the cerebrospinal fluid (CSF) of 28 violent and sexual offenders and noted that an imbalance between levels of serotonin and dopamine was highly associated with psychopathic traits.

Hormones, such as testosterone and the thyroid hormone T_3, along with the neurotransmitter dopamine and the stress hormones cortisol and norepinephrine have all been implicated in delinquency and poor impulse control.[101] In 2000, for example, Keith McBurnett and colleagues reported the results of a study that evaluated 38 boys between the ages of seven and 12 who had been referred to a clinic for the management of behavioral problems.[102] The children were studied for four years, using various medical and psychological assessment tools. McBurnett and fellow researchers found that the "meanest" boys had the lowest levels of the hormone cortisol in their saliva: "Low cortisol levels were associated with persistence and early onset of aggression. Boys with lower cortisol concentrations exhibited triple the number of aggressive symptoms and were named as most aggressive by peers three times as often as boys who had higher cortisol concentrations." Although the researchers did not explain why low cortisol levels might be linked to aggression, they suggested that "children with persistent conduct disorder may have genes that predispose them to produce certain hormones differently, or their hormone production may have been altered before or soon after birth."[103]

Low cortisol levels were associated with early onset of aggression.

A few years ago, two separate Swedish studies found evidence suggesting that elevated levels of the thyroid hormone T_3 were related to alcoholism, psychopathy, and criminality.[104] Blood serum levels of the thyroid hormone T_4 (thyroxine), on the other hand, were negatively related to antisocial behavior. The researchers concluded that the results of their studies indicate an intimate relationship between T_3 and T_4 and abuse and antisocial behavior. They emphasize the importance of further studies on T_3 as a biological marker for abuse, social deviance, and repeated violent behavior.

Not all hormones produce aggression or are linked to violence, of course. A 2012 study of what has been billed as the trust molecule showed that increased levels of a chemical messenger known as oxytocin helps to explain why some people are routinely giving and altruistic, while others are seen as cold-hearted and stingy.[105] In the brain oxytocin appears to be the chemical that creates bonds of trust in all types of human relationships. Although oxytocin is primarily a female reproductive hormone that controls contractions during labor, it is also responsible for the bond that forms between mothers and their babies. It is even thought to be responsible for the warm feelings that people feel during lovemaking, or when giving and sharing hugs. The 2012 study found that when oxytocin levels rise in the blood, people respond generously and caringly, even to strangers.

As Georgia State University criminologist Leah E. Daigle points out, however, "changes in hormone levels alone do not account for aggressive behavior. Instead, these hormonal changes may affect a third, unspecified variable (such as self-control or social bonds) that lead to aggressive responses."[106] In other words, says Daigle, "rather than directly affecting behavior, hormones may instead interact with social factors to produce criminal behavior."

Climate, Weather, and Crime

In early January 2013, as temperatures hovered around 11 degrees Fahrenheit, New York City went without a single murder for more than nine days. Newscasters opined that "the cold, perhaps, pacified a city accustomed, on average, to more than a murder a day."[107] Research on crime and weather has looked at everything from sunshine and humidity to wind speed, barometric pressure, and rainfall. After reviewing both published and unpublished research in this area, **James Rotton** and **Ellen G. Cohn** of Florida International University concluded that temperature is the only weather variable that is consistently and reliably related to criminal behavior[108] (see Figure 5–2). In general, field research has found a definite positive correlation between temperature and violent crime—more violent crime is reported to the police on warm days than on cold days. However, the relationship between temperature and criminal behavior is more complex than it first appears. Rotton and Cohn's research incorporated not only temperature but also a variety of time-based variables, such as time of the day and day of the week. Their findings suggested that relationships between temperature and various types of criminal behavior are affected, or moderated, by time of day, day of the week, and season of the year.

In a study of assaults in Minneapolis, Cohn and Rotton found that relationships between temperature and assaults were strongest during evening and early hours of the night.[109] A replication conducted in Dallas also found that temperature's correlation with assaults was strongest during evening hours, which are usually the coolest time of day.[110] Other studies conducted in Minneapolis found that temperature was significantly correlated with certain property crimes (burglary, larceny, and robbery),[111] with domestic violence,[112] and with disorderly conduct.[113]

Cohn and Rotton's findings are consistent with predictions that might be derived from routine activities theory (discussed in Chapter 3). They suggested that uncomfortably hot and cold temperatures keep people apart, resulting in less opportunity for victims and motivated offenders to come in contact with one another. Temporal variables, such as time of day and day of the week, moderate the relationship between temperature and crime by also affecting opportunity; offenders and victims are more likely to come in contact with each other during evening and weekend hours than during the day, when many people are busy at work or school or are engaged in other routine activities.

Other researchers have found an apparent link between barometric pressure and violent criminal offending. Using data on suicides and violent crimes during 1999 in the Louisville, Kentucky, area, Thomas J. Schory and colleagues discovered that "the total number of acts of violence and emergency psychiatry visits are significantly associated with low barometric pressure";[114] low pressure appears to be associated with changes in cerebral blood flow and may lead to increased impulsivity.

Finally, in 2013, University of California Berkeley researchers analyzed data on ancient wars, road rage, and other forms of aggressive behavior and found an historical correlation between high temperatures, extreme rainfall patterns, and violence. Extrapolating their findings into the future, they concluded that the incidence of war and civil unrest may increase by up to 56% between now and 2050 due to global warming and the changes in weather patterns that are expected to accompany it.[115]

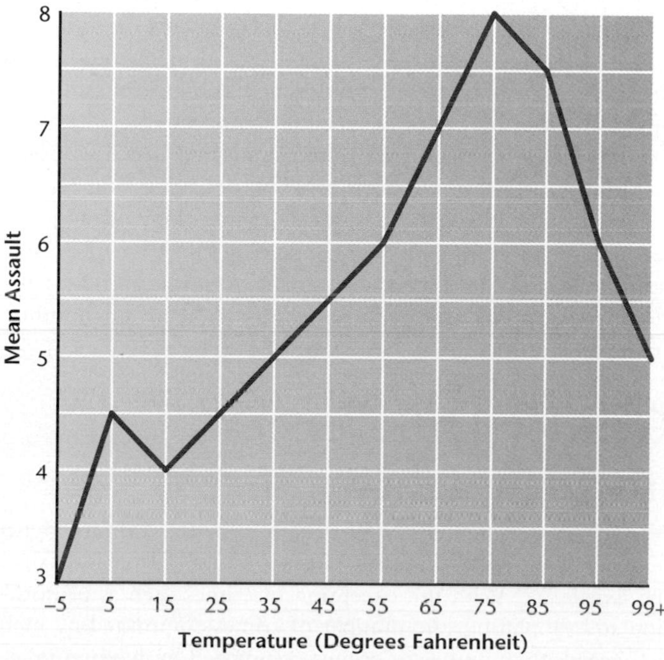

FIGURE 5-2 | **Assault as a Function of Temperature**

Source: E. G. Cohn and J. Rotton, "Assault as a Function of Time and Temperature: A Moderator-Variable Time-Series Analysis," *Journal of Personality and Social Psychology*, Vol. 72 (1997), pp. 1322-1334. Data used with permission.

Biosocial Criminology

In the mid-1980s, criminologist **James Q. Wilson** and psychologist **Richard J. Herrnstein** teamed up to write *Crime and Human Nature*, a book-length treatise that restated and refined many of the arguments proposed by biological criminologists over the preceding century.[116] Part of their purpose was to reopen discussion of biological causes of crime. "We want to show," Herrnstein said, "that the pendulum is beginning to swing away from a totally sociological explanation of crime."[117] Their avowed goal was "not to state a case just for genetic factors, but to state a comprehensive theory of crime that draws together all the different factors that cause criminal behavior."[118]

Wilson and Herrnstein cited several constitutional factors that they believed made important and undeniable contributions to criminal behavior:[119]

- **Gender.** "Crime has been predominantly male behavior."
- **Age.** "In general, the tendency to break the law declines throughout life."
- **Body type.** "A disproportionate number of criminals have a mesomorphic build."

■ **biosocial criminology** A theoretical perspective that sees the interaction between biology and the physical and social environments as key to understanding human behavior, including criminality.

- **Intelligence.** Criminality is said to be clearly and consistently associated with low intelligence.
- **Personality.** Criminals are typically aggressive, impulsive, and cruel.

Although personality, behavioral problems, and intelligence may be related to and at least partially determined by environment, the authors said that "each involves some genetic inheritance." Wilson and Herrnstein recognized social factors in the development of personality but suggested that constitutional factors predispose a person to specific types of behavior and that societal *reactions* to such predispositions may determine, to a large degree, the form of continued behavior.

In the 1990s, **Anthony Walsh** of Boise State University, who is one of today's best known proponents of **biosocial criminology**, continued the movement toward recognizing biology's contributions to understanding criminal behavior. Walsh emphasized the importance of the *interaction* between biology and the environment in the formation of behavioral responses to given situations. "Biological factors do not operate in an environmental vacuum," said Walsh, "nor do environmental factors operate in a biological vacuum, and we must cease formulating our theories as if they do."[120]

Biological factors do not operate in an environmental vacuum, nor do environmental factors operate in a biological vacuum.

Walsh became one of the founders of contemporary biosocial criminology—a scientific endeavor that attempts to take all that is known about the biological underpinnings of human behavior and to use that knowledge to assess how human biology interacts with the surrounding physical, cultural, and social environments in producing a criminal event. Biosocial criminology is not so much a theory about crime as it is a perspective on criminality that recognizes the importance of the interaction between biology and the surrounding physical and social environments.

Walsh observes that biosocial perspectives are theories of criminality, not crime.[121] He goes on to explain that crime is a "legal label" that is placed on specific behaviors that violate the criminal law. Criminality, on the other hand, says Walsh, "is a property of individuals, a continuous trait that is itself an amalgam of other continuous traits, and thus belongs to a more inclusive kind of criminology."[122] According to Walsh, criminality can be seen as the willingness to violate individual rights and social norms, whether or not such behavior is against the law. Criminality, says Walsh, consists of "a relative lack of empathy, conscience, self-control, and fear, as well as self-centeredness, and a penchant for risky behavior."[123] Seen this way, biosocial explanations of criminality are more likely to be couched in terms of a propensity for violence, aggression, deceit, recklessness, fearlessness, and so on, and features of the surrounding environment determine how such propensities are expressed.

Behavioral science expert Diana Fishbein of the Research Triangle Institute (RTI) puts it this way: "[N]umerous behavioral science subdisciplines, including molecular and behavioral genetics, neurobiology, physiology, psychology, cognitive neuroscience, endocrinology, and forensic psychiatry, provide substantial evidence" that certain traits possessed by individuals lead to increased risk for antisocial behavior.[124]

Fishbein notes that "the vast range of studies from these disciplines on vulnerability to antisocial personality disorder, violence, and drug abuse . . . reveal a pattern that may characterize vulnerable individuals." These patterns, which include individual biological differences in heart rate, hormone levels, and EEG recordings, demonstrate that "vulnerability to antisocial behavior is partially a function of genetic and biological makeup" that is expressed, says Fishbein, "during childhood as particular behavioral, cognitive, and psychological traits, such as impulsivity, attention deficits, aggressiveness, and conduct disorder."

Echoing Walsh, Fishbein notes that "biological differences do not function in a vacuum to increase risk." Instead, she writes that biological factors interact dynamically with many social and environmental conditions "to contribute to or protect from social dysfunction." It is this emphasis on *interaction* between biology and the environment—especially culture and the social environment—that differentiates biosocial criminology from other biological perspectives on crime.

Researchers are beginning to understand just how complex the relationship between biology, behavior, and the social environment can be. Biosocial criminology attempts to recognize this complexity by embracing the role of a multitude of factors leading to criminality (Figure 5–3) and including the interaction of those factors with the surrounding environment.

Gender Differences in Criminality

A number of contemporary writers propose that criminologists must recognize that "the male is much more criminalistic than the female."[125] With the exception of crimes such as prostitution and shoplifting, the number of crimes committed by men far exceeds the number of crimes committed by women in almost all categories, and when women commit crimes, they are far more likely to assume the role of followers than leaders.[126] Leading biosocial researcher Kevin Beaver explains it this way: "In virtually every study ever conducted, males are much more

■ **gender ratio problem** The need for an explanation of the fact that the number of crimes committed by men far exceeds the number of crimes committed by women in almost all categories.

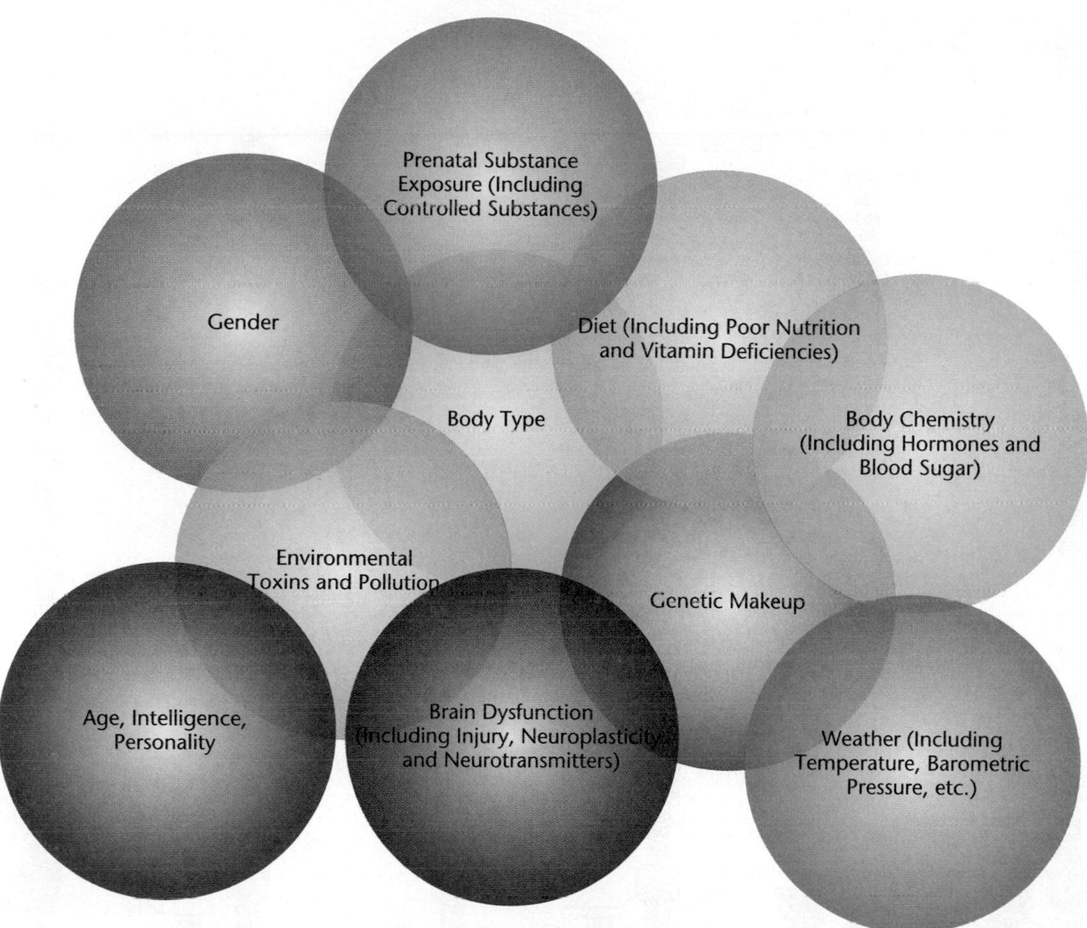

FIGURE 5–3 | **Selected Biological Factors Recognized by Biosocial Theory**

likely than females to engage in violence, aggression, and serious crimes. As the seriousness of the offense/behavior increases, the gender gap also tends to increase, such that the most violent criminal acts are almost exclusively a male phenomenon." Beaver calls the differences between female and male rates of offending the *gender gap*. He and other writers also refer to it as the **gender ratio problem** and call for its explanation.[127]

The data on the extent of male–female criminality in the United States show surprising regularity over time: The proportion of homicides committed by men versus women has remained more or less constant for decades (Figure 5–4). Similarly, the proportion of men murdered by men versus the proportion of women murdered by women has been consistent, indicating a much greater propensity for men to murder one another.

If culture exercises the major role in determining criminality, as many social scientists today believe, then we would expect to see recognizable increases in the degree and nature of female criminality over time, especially as changes in socialization practices, cultural roles, and other ethnographic patterns increase the opportunity for women to commit what had previously been regarded as traditionally male offenses. With the exception of a few crimes, such as embezzlement, drug abuse, and liquor-law violations, such has not been the case. Although women comprise 51% of the population of the United States, they are arrested for less than 20% of all violent crimes and almost 38% of property crimes[128]—a proportion that has remained surprisingly constant since the FBI began gathering crime data nearly a century ago—in spite of all the cultural changes creating new possibilities for women to commit crimes. These gender differences can also be seen in cross-cultural studies.

Such findings contrast with the suggestions of authors like **Freda Adler**, who, in her classic 1975 book *Sisters in Crime*, proposed that as women entered nontraditional occupations and roles, there "would be a movement toward parity with men in the commission of crime in terms of both incidence and type."[129] **Darrell J. Steffensmeier**, who studied changes in women's criminality

■ **sexual selection** A form of natural selection that influences an individual's ability to find or choose a mate.

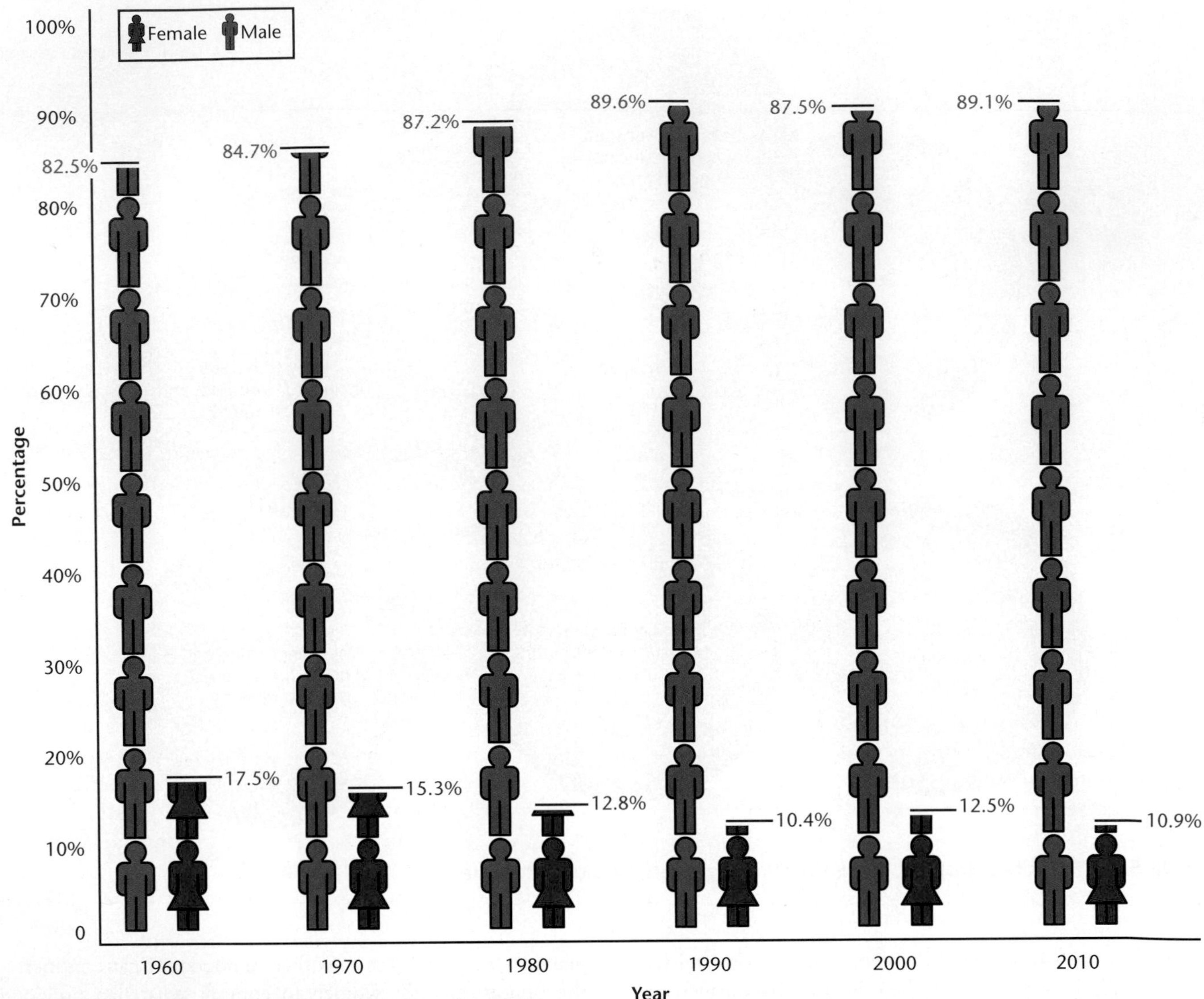

FIGURE 5-4 | **Male and Female Murder Perpetrators as a Percentage of All Arrests for Homicide, 1960–2010**

Source: Schmalleger, Frank J., *Criminology*. Printed and Electronically reproduced by permission of Pearson Education, Inc., Upper Saddle River, New Jersey.

following publication of Adler's book, found almost no evidence to support the belief that a new female criminal is emerging or that female criminality is undergoing the kind of increase Adler expected.[130] The lack of contemporary validation for Adler's thesis suggests that something else is occurring, that some element other than cultural inhibition or equality of opportunity is preventing women from taking their place alongside men as equals in crime.

Penn State criminologist **Thomas Bernard** and colleagues Jeffrey Snipes and Alexander Gerould have advanced the proposition that "the issue of why always and everywhere males commit more criminal acts than females is the 'single most important fact that criminology theories must be able to explain.'"[131] Biosocial criminologists suggest that the organic correlates of gender provide the needed explanation. Walsh, for example, says that the gender ratio problem is only a problem "if we are constrained to operate under sociology's strict environmentalist paradigm, which is suspicious of psychological or biological factors that differentiate among individuals and categories of individuals. . ."[132] If we admit, Walsh writes, that "there is something about gender per se" that is responsible for the observed differences, the problem is resolved.[133]

One of the primary contemporary paradigms useful in understanding gender differences in criminality is the concept of **sexual selection**. Sexual selection, which is a form of natural selection that influences an individual's ability to find or choose a mate, derives from Charles Darwin's theory of evolution.[134] While Darwin was most concerned with explaining how the

■ **evolutionary perspective** A theoretical approach that (1) seeks to explain behavior with reference to human evolutionary history and (2) recognizes the influence that genes have over human traits.

AFP Photo/Jack Guez/GettyImages

Women's boxing champion, Chungneijang Mary Kom Hmangte of India, after winning a quarter-finals match in the 2012 Olympic Games. Women's boxing, a relatively new sport, reflects women's changing social roles. Male-female differences in criminality, however, seem to display considerable regularity over time. Does this mean that men and women have inherently different behavioral tendencies?

process of natural selection (survival of the fittest) determines trait differences between species, the concept of sexual selection seeks to explain male/female differences within species. Contemporary writers, for example, claim that the important roles of child bearing, child protection, and child rearing created evolutionary pressures for females to become sensitive to immediate environmental stimuli—or what is happening in their immediate vicinity. Such awareness, they claim, provided the ability to identify threats and to shield their offspring from danger. Consequently, because of evolutionary forces, females today may be more sensitive than men to many environmental stimuli, are more easily aroused, are quicker to respond to what is going on around them, and tend to avoid dangerous or threatening situations. Some researchers have found support for such an argument in discoveries that the reticular activating system (RAS), which accounts for sensitivity and response, is more finely tuned in women than in men.[135] To compensate for lower levels of arousal, men tend to be more sensation-seeking than women, these researcher say, and their desire for increased arousal and environmental stimulation are closely linked to risk-taking and crime.[136]

Genetically based behavioral differences between men and women are moderated by aspects of the social environment.

None of this, of course, denies the fact that genetically based behavioral differences between men and women are moderated by aspects of the social environment, including socialization, the learning of culturally prescribed roles, and the expectations of others. Still, as Walsh puts it, criminological theories that continue to deny the important role of biology and gender differences in criminality are akin to the "drunk who knew he hadn't lost his keys under the lamppost, but perversely continued looking there anyway because that's where the light is." In sum, Walsh concludes, "we must realize that gender socialization rests on the solid bedrock of sex-differentiated biology forged by countless thousands of years of contrasting sexual selection pressures."[137]

Evolutionary Theory

In 2010, Kevin M. Beaver, John P. Wright, and Anthony Walsh discovered that the number of sexual partners that men have is associated with criminal involvement.[138] In other words, the greater the number of partners, the higher the likelihood of criminal behavior. The researchers noted, however, that "the question . . . is why there is a high degree of covariation between criminal involvement and the number of sexual partners."

Utilizing an **evolutionary perspective**—or one that (1) seeks to explain behavior with reference to human evolutionary history[139] and (2) recognizes the influence that genes have over human traits—they came to the conclusion that behavioral traits are "manifestations of multiple genes working independently and synergistically" in response to the environment. They proposed that some of the same genes must be involved in both reproductive activity and criminality. Through an analysis of data from the National Longitudinal Study of Adolescent Health (Add Health), they concluded that differing versions of the dopamine transporter gene known as DAT1 were "related to both a greater number of sexual partners and to increased involvement in antisocial behavior for adult males."

Different versions of the same gene are referred to as *polymorphism*, and the word *allele* (used earlier in this chapter) is used to describe an alternative form of a gene that is located at a given position on a specific chromosome. Men who possessed what is known as the 10R allele were determined to be more likely to have multiple sex partners and to demonstrate greater criminal involvement. Hence, the 10R allele was described as the "risk allele for a number of maladaptive outcomes."

■ **evolutionary neuroandrogenic (ENA) theory**
A perspective that holds that (1) the propensity for crime commission evolved among humans beings as part of the male reproductive strategy, and (2) a particular neurochemistry, which is characteristic of males, increases the probability of criminality among males relative to females.

In 2005, Minot State University professor **Lee Ellis**, added his **evolutionary neuroandrogenic (ENA) theory** to the growing body of biosocial perspectives.[140] Ellis's theory consists of two propositions: (1) the propensity for crime commission evolved among human beings as part of the male reproductive strategy and (2) a particular neurochemistry, which is characteristic of males, "increases the probability of criminality among males relative to females." Ellis believes that reproductive strategies have guided human evolution, with human males seeking to produce multiple offspring in order to ensure the survival of their genetic material, while human females developed a much different strategy to achieve the same goal—that is, finding a reproductive partner who could ensure the resources necessary over time for the survival of her and her offspring. Ellis argues that early men learned to engage in what he terms "competitive/victimizing behavior" (or CVB), including that aggression thought necessary to win over a mate, or to forcibly mate with her. CVB, argues Ellis, is largely fueled by the male sex hormones, or androgens (including testosterone and androsterone). "Androgens," says Ellis, "have the ability to affect the brain in ways that increase the probability of" CVB. In primitive societies, Ellis says, CVB probably took the form of direct physical intimidation and victimization. As society became more sophisticated, however, expressions of CVB took sophisticated "commercial" form.

Policy Implications of Biological Theories

In 1992 the term *standard social science model* (SSSM) was introduced to the general public by Jerome H. Barkow and his colleagues in the edited volume *The Adapted Mind*.[141] The SSSM—which assumes that human beings come into this world like blank slates and acquire almost all of their values, behavioral patterns, and modes of thought through socialization into their surrounding cultures—was identified as the perspective that had characterized much social scientific thought during the twentieth century. According to Barkow, the SSSM provided the underpinnings for the work of many famous sociologists, social psychologists, and social anthropologists of the 1900s, including anthropologists Margaret Mead and Leslie White and sociologist Ellsworth Faris.

Only in the last decade or two has the SSSM largely given way to broader perspectives that include an examination of the role of biology and genetic influences on human behavior. In a more recent book, *The Blank Slate: The Modern Denial of Human Nature*,[142] MIT cognitive scientist Steven Pinker told readers that today's social scientists still continue to ignore unjustly the biological basis of human behavior, replacing it instead with three myths: (1) the blank slate, (2) the Noble Savage, and (3) the Ghost in the Machine. The blank slate myth (mentioned above) holds that the human mind has no innate traits and that the human personality is fully malleable by society. The Noble Savage myth says that human nature is essentially good; and the Ghost in the Machine myth holds that each person has an individual soul-like quality that allows him or her to make choices that can be completely independent of any biological predispositions. These three myths, according to Pinker, comprise the SSSM of the modern era and have led to misguided social and political policies, but it is only when the impact of biology on human behavior is fully recognized that effective social policies—including those aimed at controlling crime—can be developed.

In 1997, in an attempt to bring biological theorizing into the criminological mainstream, Lee Ellis and Anthony Walsh expanded on the theme of genetic predispositions, noting that "in the case of behavior, nearly all of the effects of genes are quite indirect because they are mediated through complex chains of events occurring in the brain. This means that there are almost certainly no genes for something as complex as criminal behavior. Nevertheless, many genes may affect brain functioning in ways that either increase or reduce the chances of individuals learning various complex behavior patterns, including behavior patterns that happen to be so offensive to others that criminal sanctions have been instituted to minimize their recurrence."[143] More than a decade later, Terrie Moffitt, through a meta-analysis of more than 100 studies of genetic influences on antisocial behavior, was able to conclude that "genes influence 40% to 50% of population variation in antisocial behavior."[144]

Critiques of Biological and Biosocial Theories

This chapter discusses a variety of biological and biosocial approaches to explaining crime, including those related to genetics, brain dysfunction, body chemistry, and contemporary understandings of evolutionary theory. Many such perspectives have been criticized because they fail to predict criminality accurately while purporting to understand its causes. For example, if a particular defect in the brain is associated with a greater tendency toward law violation, then why would such theories fail to predict which individuals with those deficits

CRIMINAL | PROFILES

Jodi Arias

How could a petite, soft-spoken woman who had no record of past violence shoot her former lover in the face, slit his throat from ear to ear, and stab him 27 times?

Jodi Arias first denied any role in the 2008 killing and then confessed, claiming she did it in self-defense. At the end of a four-month trial, however, a jury found her guilty of first-degree murder, deciding the killing was so brutal that it could merit the death penalty.

The victim, Travis Alexander, was a leader of the Mormon Church in the Phoenix area who hid his steamy sexual relationship with Arias even from friends. Arias's trial was attended by many and was punctuated with photos of the couple engaging in several different sex acts; a 30-minute tape of phone sex between them; and photos of them both naked, apparently just moments before the murder was committed.[i]

The prosecution portrayed Arias as an obsessed stalker who went out of control when Alexander wanted to date other women. Before the murder, witnesses said she slashed his tires, looked into his windows, and hacked into his Facebook account.[ii]

However, an examination of Arias's past revealed little evidence of the sex-crazed stalker that seemed to emerge after she met Alexander. She claimed her parents had beaten her, but she had no problems with previous boyfriends, at work, or with friends. She had no arrests, convictions, or other legal issues.

Arias grew up in the small town of Yreka, California. "She was a sweet girl, you know, the kind of girl that you just always wanted to be around," her best friend told the Headline News Network. She "definitely wasn't" promiscuous, she added.[iii]

The obsessive, on-again, off-again relationship between Arias and Alexander ended up in murder. They met in Las Vegas in September 2006 at a conference for Prepaid Legal Services, a nationwide company where they both worked. They were both single and about the same age. In addition to being a company salesperson, Alexander worked as a motivational speaker. Arias had recently discovered the Mormon faith. Two months later, Alexander baptized her into the faith and they had sex afterward.[iv]

Alexander's image as a devout Mormon virgin, which he projected to friends, clashed with the erotic adventures he had with Arias. A friend who lived with Alexander testified he did not know he was having sex, saying it could have led to excommunication from the church. Arias's defense attorney said Arias was "his dirty little secret."[v] The prosecution speculated that Arias took pictures of Alexander in sex acts to blackmail him if he tried to leave her.

The couple carried on a long-distance romance between her home in California and his in Mesa, Arizona. They broke up in June 2007 but continued to see each other for sex. Arias moved to Mesa that summer, waiting tables and cleaning Alexander's home for income, then moved back to California in the spring of 2008.

AP Photo/The Arizona Republic, Rob Schumacher, Pool

Jodi Arias, convicted in 2013 of the brutal murder of her boyfriend, Travis Alexander. Why did the televised trial draw such large media audiences?

"I want you to understand how evil I think you are," Alexander wrote her in an e-mail a week before he died.[vi] He had invited another woman to go to Cancun, Mexico, with him. In early June, Arias drove to Mesa, arriving at Alexander's home at 4 A.M., and killed him later that day.

Friends found Alexander's mangled body slouched in his shower. Arias's palm print was found in blood at the scene, along with nude photos of them from the day of the killing. When she was later arrested, Arias denied any involvement and blamed it on masked intruders. It was two years later that she first admitted to killing Alexander, saying he became violent after she dropped his new camera, which she was using to take pictures of their sex play.

At the trial, Arias showed little emotion when asked about the killing. The jurors didn't accept Arias's plea of self-defense and wrote to her: "After all the lies you have told, why should we believe you now?"

The case of Jodi Arias raises some interesting questions. Among them are the following:

1. How could a woman who had no record of past violence commit such a gruesome murder?
2. What aspects of Arias and Alexander's relationship led to the killing?

Notes

i. Tamara Holder, "Four Reasons Why Jodi Arias Should Be Found Guilty of Murder," FoxNews, April 2, 2013, http://www.foxnews.com/opinion/2013/04/02/four-reasons-why-jodi-arias-should-be-found-guilty-murder/.

ii. Dale Archer, "Is Jodi Arias a Sociopath?" *Psychology Today*, March 11, 2013, http://www.psychologytoday.com/blog/reading-between-the-headlines/201303/is-jodi-arias-sociopath.

iii. Kat McCullough and Beth Carey, "Arias' Childhood Best Friend: 'She was a sweet girl,'" HLN, April 17, 2013, http://www.hlntv.com/article/2013/04/17/jodi-arias-childhood-best-friend-she-was-sweet-girl.

iv. "Timeline of Events in Jodi Arias Murder Case," ABC News, May 15, 2013, http://abcnews.go.com/US/wireStory/timeline-events-jodi-arias-murder-case-19185819#.UZPcUXCCMUU.

v. Ryan Owens, "Jodi Arias: Who Is the Admitted Arizona Killer?," ABC News, January 8, 2013, http://abcnews.go.com/US/jodi-arias-admitted-arizona-killer/story?id=18159181#.UZPvN3CCMUU.

vi. Brian Skoloff, "Prosecutor Calls Jodi Arias a Manipulative Liar," Associated Press, May 2, 2013, http://news.yahoo.com/prosecutor-calls-jodi-arias-manipulative-liar-195750776.html.

■ **Follow the author's tweets about the latest crime and justice news @schmalleger.**

will offend and which will obey the law? The same questions could be asked about genetic attributes and differences in body chemistry. Many of the critiques identified in regard to chemical precursors can be applied to perspectives involving hormones and criminal behavior. Hormones, after all, are chemicals that are made by the body (or are sometimes injected into the bloodstream). As is the case with chemical precursors, hormones apparently don't affect everyone the same way. Not all men with high testosterone levels, for example, are violent or aggressive.

Biosocial theories, for their part, can be criticized in a number of ways.[145] Some critics claim, for example, that biosocial research is fraught with methodological problems because studies in the area have often been based on small, nonrepresentative samples.[146] Also, most research in the area of biosocial theory has been done on offenders who have been placed in clinical treatment settings, making it impossible to tell if study findings are relevant only to convicted criminals in correctional facilities or to the criminal population as a whole. Findings from such studies are difficult to generalize to other settings, and it may be difficult to draw definitive conclusions from small samples that have been studied under unique conditions.

Other critics note that biosocial theories fail to explain regional and temporal variations in crime rates. Biosocial theories, for example, do not seem to explain adequately why one country has higher rates of violent crime than others, or why one region of a city has different rates of property crime. Similarly, biosocial theories cannot totally account for changes in crime rates over time or among different age groups within the same population.

Biological theories that focus on environmental and chemical precursors to crime cannot explain why certain kinds of crime are more likely to occur in certain parts of the country, in particular types of communities, and among members of specific subcultures rather than in others. Such differences imply that much more is at work than chemicals themselves and suggest that cultural differences play a significant role in criminality.

Critics also claim that theories involving chemical precursors cannot account for changes in crime rates over time. Crime rates have trended substantially downward over the past two or three decades, during the same time period that exposure to chemical substances of all types throughout the general population has expanded.

Some biosocial criminologists have been accused of racial and class bias for failing to explain why a disproportionate number of certain kinds of crime are committed by poor people and by racial and ethnic minorities.[147] Critics say that it would be more useful to focus on social settings rather than on biological variables to explain such differences and that characteristics of the social environment—including racism, oppression, discrimination, and economic strain—are more effective at explaining differences in criminality between racial and ethnic groups and social classes. These critics also note that some people may try to use biosocial perspectives to support their own biases and to justify continued social inequality.

SUMMARY

- This chapter began with a discussion of the Human Genome Project (HGP), which was completed in 2003, and recognizes it as corresponding to the start of a new era of biosocial theories in criminology.
- Genetic characteristics and variations in human chromosomes are thought to play an important role in aggression and crime causation. The contemporary study of human genetics builds on a model of gene–environment interaction and employs the concept of heritability to help explain law-breaking behavior. Although contemporary criminologists do not believe that there is one single and identifiable "criminal gene," they do believe that individuals who are genetically predisposed to certain types of behavior may become aggressive or criminal through interaction with the surrounding physical and social environments.
- Some criminologists have explored brain dysfunction and developed the frontal brain hypothesis, which references physical changes in certain parts of the brain to explain criminality. Neuroplasticity, or the ability of the brain to alter its structure and function in response to experience or injury, may be useful in explaining changes in personality and behavior.
- Body chemistry theories say that violent or disruptive behavior can sometimes be linked to poor nutrition, vitamin deficiencies, and other conditions that affect the body. Studies of eating habits, endocrinology, and environmental contaminants have all contributed to advances in understanding such behavior.
- Criminologists have studied hormone levels in the blood to explain violent or disruptive behavior by identifying hormonal influences on human cognition and action. Specific hormones studied include neurotransmitters.
- Biosocial criminology sees the interaction between biology and the physical and social environments as key to understanding human behavior, including criminality. It holds that genetic predispositions and their interaction with the surrounding social and physical environments may combine to produce criminality. Neuroplasticity, a concept that is central to some biosocial perspectives, may influence and facilitate much of human behavior.
- In the past, biology was often seen as deterministic. The eugenics movement, Nazi extermination programs, and enforced sterilization all resulted from an inaccurate assessment of the power of genes or other physical factors to determine behavior. At the same time, the once widely held belief that the human organism was a blank slate at birth appears now to be a fallacy. A contemporary crime-prevention program needs to be based on modern understandings of the link between biology and crime. A medical perspective could replace the current legalistic interpretation of criminality, leading to the right to treatment for criminal offenders.
- Establishing a workable definition of criminality has been a problem. Few biological studies adequately conceptualize criminality, methodological problems have been found in many studies attempting to evaluate the role of genetics in crime, and results obtained outside the United States may not be applicable within this country. Many criminologists continue to believe that biology provides a context for human behavior, but biological predispositions are overshadowed by the role of volition, mechanisms of human thought, and undeniable influences of socialization and acculturation.

KEY TERMS

allele, 100
biosocial criminology, 114
chromosomes, 98
epigenetics, 101
evolutionary neuroandrogenic (ENA) theory, 118
evolutionary perspective, 117
frontal brain hypothesis, 102
gender ratio problem, 115
gene expression, 101
genes, 98
heritability, 101
hormone, 109
human genome, 98
hypoglycemia, 106
neuroplasticity, 104
neurotransmitters, 100
prenatal substance exposure, 107
serotonin, 110
sexual selection, 116
testosterone, 109

KEY NAMES

Freda Adler, 115
Kevin M. Beaver, 100
Thomas Bernard, 116
Paul C. Bernhardt, 110
Alan Booth, 110
Han Brunner, 99
Avshalom Caspi, 100
Ellen G. Cohn, 112
Lee Ellis, 118
David Fergusson, 107
Nathalie Fontaine, 101
Richard J. Herrnstein, 113
Terrie E. Moffitt, 100
D. Wayne Osgood, 110
Adrian Raine, 102
H. Hilger Ropers, 99
James Rotton, 112
Stephen Schoenthaler, 106
Darrell J. Steffensmeier, 115
Anthony Walsh, 114
James Q. Wilson, 113

QUESTIONS FOR REVIEW

1. How strong are research findings linking genetics and crime? What have research studies in the field of genetics had to say about possible causes of crime?
2. What is the gender ratio problem in criminology? What traditional explanations had been offered for the problem? Why is the gender ratio problem not a problem from the point of view of biosocial criminology?
3. What is sociobiology? What contributions has sociobiology made to the study of criminality?
4. What is biosocial criminology? How is criminality explained from a biosocial perspective?
5. What are the social policy implications of biological and biosocial theories of crime? What modern-day social policies reflect the biological and biosocial approaches to crime causation?
6. What are the shortcomings of biological theories of criminal behavior? Why have biological approaches to crime causation encountered stiff criticism?

QUESTIONS FOR REFLECTION

1. This text emphasizes the theme of social problems versus social responsibility. Which perspective is better supported by biosocial theories of crime causation? Why?
2. Past president of the American Society of Criminology C. Ray Jeffery once said: "Open inquiry requires objective consideration of all points of view and an unbiased examination of each for its ability to shed light on the subject under study"? Do you agree or disagree with this assertion? Why is it especially relevant to biosocial theorizing in criminology?

Albert Foster Mirrorpix/Newscom

CHAPTER 6 PSYCHOLOGICAL AND PSYCHIATRIC FOUNDATIONS OF CRIMINAL BEHAVIOR

LEARNING OUTCOMES

After reading this chapter, you should be able to answer the following questions:

- What are the major principles of psychological perspectives on criminal behavior?
- What two major ideas characterized early psychological theories, and what was the difference between them?
- How does personality explain criminality?
- What is psychopathology, and how does it explain crime? How does it relate to antisocial personality disorder?
- What are cognitive theories, and what two types of cognitive theories does this chapter discuss?
- What insights into criminal behavior does the psychoanalytic perspective offer?
- What role does frustration play in influencing aggression, according to psychological theories?
- How can criminality be seen as a form of adaptive behavior?
- What are criminogenic needs?
- How does attachment theory explain behavior, and what are the three forms of attachment?
- How does behavior theory explain the role of rewards and punishments in shaping behavior?
- How does social cognition explain how aggressive patterns of behavior, once acquired, can be activated?
- What are the treatment implications of psychological understandings of criminality?
- What are some assumptions underlying the practice of criminal psychological profiling?
- How does the legal concept of insanity differ from behavioral definitions of the same concept?

■ **forensic psychology** The application of the science and profession of psychology to questions and issues relating to law and the legal system; also called *criminal psychology*.
■ **criminal psychology** The application of the science and profession of psychology to questions and issues relating to law and the legal system; also called *forensic psychology*.
■ **forensic psychiatry** A branch of psychiatry having to do with the study of crime and criminality.

Introduction

On January 8, 2012, survivors of a Tucson, Arizona, shooting that seriously injured U.S. Democratic Representative Gabrielle Giffords and killed six other people, including a nine-year-old girl and an Arizona district court chief judge, gathered to support one another.[1] One year earlier, a total of 19 people were shot in the parking lot of a Safeway store when 22-year-old Tucson resident Jared Lee Loughner shot Giffords in the head and then fired indiscriminately into the crowd that had gathered to hear her speak. After emptying the first clip in his 9mm semiautomatic pistol, Loughner stopped to reload, but fumbled and dropped a second clip to the ground, providing an opportunity for members of the crowd to overpower him and hold him until police arrived. Dozens of people witnessed the shooting, and it was captured by video surveillance cameras.

On May 25, 2011, while being held at the Federal Correctional Institution in Phoenix, Loughner appeared before a federal judge, who found Loughner incompetent to stand trial on the basis of two medical evaluations that had been performed while he was in custody. On August 7, 2012, however, after being forcibly medicated with antipsychotic drugs for more than a year in a Missouri prison medical facility, Loughner was ruled legally competent. He entered a plea of guilty to killing 6 people and wounding 13 others. Loughner's plea spared him the death penalty, but he was sentenced to seven life sentences in federal prison without the possibility of parole.[2]

Mug Shot/Alamy

Jared Loughner, sentenced to life in prison without parole after pleading guilty to 19 charges of murder and attempted murder in an attack on people gathered to hear U.S. Representative Gabrielle Giffords speak in Tucson, Arizona in 2011. What role did Loughner's personality play in the shootings?

Principles of Psychological and Psychiatric Theories

Anyone who saw early courtroom recordings of Jared Loughner knew that he was psychologically damaged. Courtroom images showed Loughner, with his hair dyed bright orange, sitting in front of a judge who read the charges against him and asked if he understood those charges. Loughner grimaced and squirmed, and seemed to want to fall asleep repeatedly, but then jerked his eyes wide open. An earlier photo taken by the Pima County Sheriff's Office following Loughner's arrest showed an intense-looking young man with a vacant expression—whom some likened to a person without a soul. The *Washington Post* described the picture as "smirking and creepy, with hollow eyes ablaze."[3] Was Loughner insane at the time of the shootings? Even if his behavior and state of mind did not meet the judicial standards for insanity (discussed later in this chapter), can we identify features of his personality that led to crime commission? If so, might he have been stopped? Questions like these concern all criminologists, but they are especially relevant from a psychological perspective.

Psychological determinants of deviant or criminal behavior are couched in various terms, such as *exploitative personality characteristics*, *poor impulse control*, *emotional arousal*, *an immature personality*, and so forth. Before beginning a discussion of psychological theories, however, it is necessary to provide a brief overview of the terminology used to describe the psychological study of crime and criminality. **Forensic psychology**, one of the fastest-growing subfields of psychology, is the application of the science and profession of psychology to questions and issues relating to law and the legal system.[4] Forensic psychology is sometimes referred to as **criminal psychology**, and forensic psychologists are also called criminal psychologists, correctional psychologists, and police psychologists. Unlike

■ **personality** The characteristic patterns of thoughts, feelings, and behaviors that make a person unique, and that tend to remain stable over time. Personality influences an individual's thoughts, behavior, and emotions.
■ **behaviorism** A psychological perspective that stresses observable behavior and disregards unobservable events that occur in the mind.
■ **conditioning** A psychological principle that holds that the frequency of any behavior can be increased or decreased through reward, punishment, or association with other stimuli.
■ **psychoanalytic theory** A perspective developed by psychiatrist Sigmund Freud in the early 1900s that explains the structure of personality and behavior in terms of both conscious and unconscious components and the conflicts between them.
■ **psychopathy** A personality disorder characterized by antisocial behavior and lack of affect.
■ **schizophrenia** A serious mental illness that distorts the way a person thinks, feels, and behaves. Primary features of schizophrenia include the inability to distinguish between real and imagined experiences and the inability to think logically.

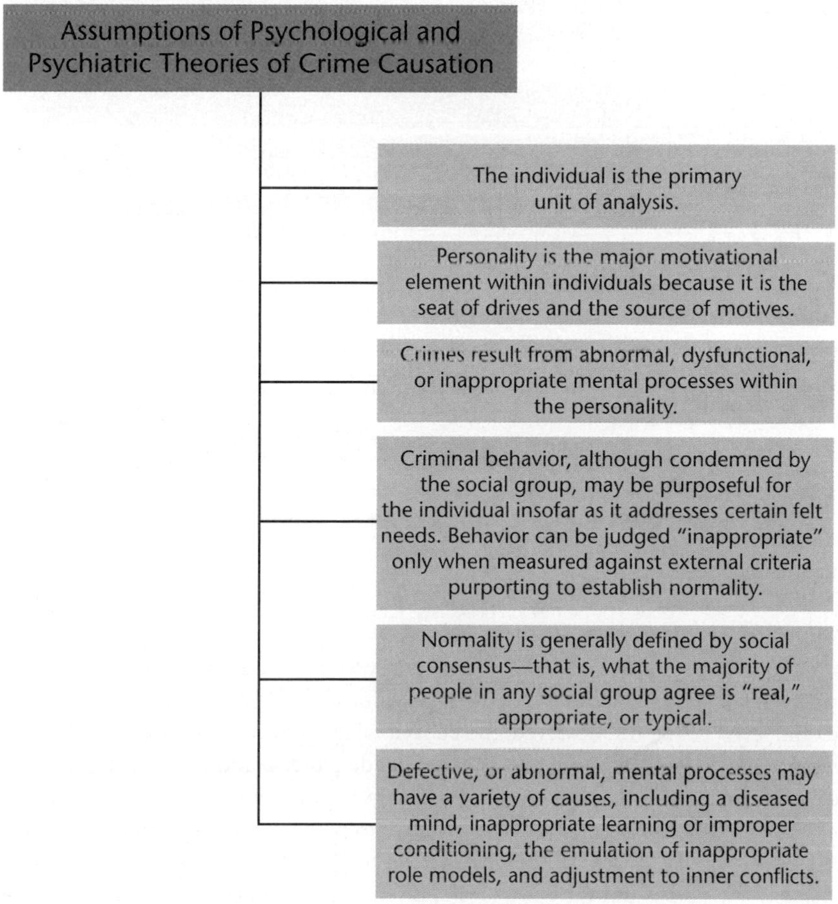

Assumptions of Psychological and Psychiatric Theories of Crime Causation

- The individual is the primary unit of analysis.
- Personality is the major motivational element within individuals because it is the seat of drives and the source of motives.
- Crimes result from abnormal, dysfunctional, or inappropriate mental processes within the personality.
- Criminal behavior, although condemned by the social group, may be purposeful for the individual insofar as it addresses certain felt needs. Behavior can be judged "inappropriate" only when measured against external criteria purporting to establish normality.
- Normality is generally defined by social consensus—that is, what the majority of people in any social group agree is "real," appropriate, or typical.
- Defective, or abnormal, mental processes may have a variety of causes, including a diseased mind, inappropriate learning or improper conditioning, the emulation of inappropriate role models, and adjustment to inner conflicts.

FIGURE 6–1 | **Assumptions of Psychological and Psychiatric Theories of Crime Causation**

Source: Schmalleger, Frank J., *Criminology*. Printed and Electronically reproduced by permission of Pearson Education, Inc., Upper Saddle River, New Jersey.

Forensic psychiatry is a branch of psychiatry having to do with the study of crime and criminality.

forensic psychologists (who generally hold PhDs), forensic psychiatrists are medical doctors, and **forensic psychiatry** is a medical subspecialty that applies psychiatry to the needs of crime prevention and solution, criminal rehabilitation, and issues of criminal law.[5] The assumptions that characterize psychological and psychiatric theories of crime causation are shown in Figure 6–1.

History of Psychological Theories

Two major ideas characterized early psychological theories: **personality** and **behaviorism**. Personality theory built on the burgeoning area of cognitive science, including personality disturbances, the process of moral development, and diseases of the mind, whereas behaviorism (also known as *behavior theory*) examined social learning with an emphasis on behavioral **conditioning**. Together, these two areas formed the early foundation of psychological criminology. This chapter discusses theories of cognitive science and behaviorism as they relate to criminality. A separate discussion of **psychoanalytic theory**, an outgrowth of personality theory, rounds out this chapter.

Personality Disturbances

Psychologists working in the first half of the twentieth century adapted the disease model—a paradigm that had worked so well in the field of medicine—in an effort to cure mental and emotional problems. Consequently, early cognitive perspectives in psychology were couched in terms of mental disease, personality disorder, and **psychopathy**.

Psychologists and psychiatrists today distinguish between the terms *psychopathy* and *psychopathology*. In the psychological literature, psychopathology "refers to any sort of psychological disorder that causes distress either for the individual or for those in the individual's life."[6] Today, depression, **schizophrenia**, attention deficit hyperactivity disorder, alcoholism, and bulimia are all considered forms of psychopathology, or mental disease.

■ **psychopath** An individual who has a personality disorder, especially one manifested in aggressively antisocial behavior, and who is lacking in empathy; also called *sociopath*.

■ **sociopath** An individual who has a personality disorder, especially one manifested in aggressively antisocial behavior, and who is lacking in empathy; also called *psychopath*.

One of the most serious of mental diseases is psychopathy, "a very specific and distinctive type of psychopathology."[7]

The Psychopath

Psychopathy is a personality disorder characterized by antisocial behavior and by a lack of sympathy, empathy, and embarrassment. Psychopaths, many of whom are known as effective manipulators, and who clearly understand the motivations of others, are said to especially lack empathy or sensitivity toward others.

The concept of psychopathy, called "one of the most durable, resilient and influential of all criminological ideas,"[8] may have evolved from the work of French physician Philippe Pinel (1745–1826), who described a form of "insanity without delirium." The concept is summarized in the words of Nolan D. C. Lewis, who wrote that "the criminal, like other people, has lived a life of instinctive drives, of desires, of wishes, of feelings, but one in which his intellect has apparently functioned less effectually as a brake upon certain trends. His constitutional makeup deviates toward the abnormal, leading him into conflicts with the laws of society and its cultural patterns."[9]

The term *psychopathy* comes from the Greek words *psyche* (meaning "soul" or "mind") and *pathos* (meaning "suffering" or "illness"). The word, which appears to have been coined by German neurologist Richard von Krafft-Ebing (1840–1902),[10] made its way into English psychiatric literature through the writings of Polish-born American psychiatrist Bernard H. Glueck (1884–1972)[11] and British psychiatrist William Healy (1869–1963).[12]

The **psychopath** has been historically viewed as perversely cruel, often without thought or feeling for his or her victims.[13] By the Second World War, the role of the psychopathic personality in crime causation had become central to psychological theorizing. The concept of a psychopathic personality, which by its very definition is antisocial, was fully developed by neuropsychiatrist **Hervey M. Cleckley** in his 1941 book *The Mask of Sanity*[14]—a work that had considerable impact on the field of psychology. Cleckley described the psychopath as a "moral idiot," or as one who does not feel empathy for others, even though that person may be fully aware of what is happening around him or her. The central defining characteristic of a psychopath is described as a "poverty of affect," or the inability to accurately imagine how others think and feel. Therefore, it becomes possible for a psychopath to inflict pain and engage in cruelty without appreciation for the victim's suffering. Charles Manson, for example, whom some regard as a psychopath, once told a television reporter, "I could take this book and beat you to death with it, and I wouldn't feel a thing. It'd be just like walking to the drugstore."[15]

In *The Mask of Sanity*, Cleckley describes numerous characteristics of the psychopathic personality, some of which are shown in Figure 6–2. For Cleckley, "psychopathy was defined by a

Selected Characteristics of the Psychopathic Personality
Superficial charm and "good intelligence"
Absence of delusions, hallucinations, or other signs of psychosis
Absence of nervousness or psychoneurotic manifestations
Inability to feel guilt or shame
Unreliability
Chronic lying
Ongoing antisocial behavior
Poor judgment and inability to learn from experience
An impersonal, trivial, and poorly integrated sex life
Unresponsiveness in general interpersonal relations
Failure to follow any life plan
Self-centeredness and incapacity to love

FIGURE 6–2 | Selected Characteristics of the Psychopathic Personality

Source: Schmalleger, Frank J., *Criminology*. Printed and Electronically reproduced by permission of Pearson Education, Inc., Upper Saddle River, New Jersey.

constellation of dysfunctional psychological processes as opposed to specific behavioral manifestations."[16] Cleckley noted that in cases he had observed, the behavioral manifestations of psychopathy varied with the person's age, gender, and socioeconomic status.

Even though psychopaths have a seriously flawed personality, they can easily fool others into trusting them—hence the title of Cleckley's book. According to Cleckley, indicators of psychopathy appear early in life, often in the teenage years. They include lying, fighting, stealing, and vandalizing. Even earlier signs may be found, according to some authors, in bed-wetting, cruelty to animals, sleepwalking, and fire setting.[17] Others have described psychopaths as "individuals who display impulsiveness, callousness, insincerity, pathological lying and deception, egocentricity, poor judgment, an impersonal sex life, and an unstable life plan."[18]

Cleckley believed that there were two kinds of psychopaths: primary and secondary. In later work, psychologist David Lykken refined those terms, saying that *primary psychopaths* are somehow neurologically different from other people, and that makes them behave the way they do.[19] Hence, primary psychopaths are born with psychopathic personalities, whereas *secondary psychopaths* (sometimes called **sociopaths**) are born with a "normal" personality, but personal experiences (frequently physical and emotional abuse) when they are young cause them to develop psychopathic characteristics.

Other types of psychopaths have also been identified, including the *charismatic psychopath* and the *distempered psychopath*. Charismatic psychopaths are charming and attractive, but also habitual liars. They manipulate others to achieve their personal goals, without considering others' feelings. Distempered psychopaths are easily offended and fly into rages even at slight provocations. They have been characterized as having strong urges, including sexual drives, that often lead to addiction.

A definitive modern measure of psychopathy can be found in the Psychopathy Checklist (PCL), developed by Robert Hare (sometimes called the Hare Psychopathy Checklist).[20] The checklist, when used by qualified experts employing information from subject interviews and official records, produces a series of ratings assessing degree of psychopathy. The checklist uses two kinds of indicators: affective and interpersonal traits (glibness, emotional detachment, egocentricity, superficial charm, shallow affect) and traits associated with a chronic unstable and antisocial lifestyle (irresponsibility, impulsivity, criminality, proneness to boredom).[21] Hence, psychopathy has both emotional and behavioral components.

A recent study of eight Canadian maximum-security male prisoners classified as psychopaths according to the PCL found that the men were not only impaired emotionally but also unable to efficiently process abstract words, perform abstract categorization tasks, understand metaphors, and process emotionally weighted words and speech.[22] During a test on abstract concepts, the men's brains were scanned using functional magnetic resonance imaging (fMRI), and scans showed that a section of each of their brains did not activate as it should have. The researchers concluded that their findings "support the hypothesis that there is an abnormality in the function of the right anterior superior temporal gyrus in psychopathy."[23] Other studies in neurobiology have linked this part of the brain with abstract problem solving and insight.[24] Deficiencies in this part of the brain may also be associated with autism and the development of childhood schizophrenia.[25]

Some have questioned whether psychopaths merely lack empathy or really don't know the difference between right and wrong. Recent research seems to show that the ability to tell right from wrong is something that human beings are born with, that the human brain is hard-wired to make moral distinctions, and that the same distinctions tend to be made across cultures.[26] You can test your own sense of right and wrong by taking the Moral Sense Test (MST) online. The MST, which researchers are using to detail the nature of moral psychology, is accessible through Harvard University's Cognitive Evolution Laboratory online at **Web Extra 6–1**.

Traditionally, psychopathology has been regarded as difficult or impossible to treat. But a recent study of adolescent psychopaths found that "youth with psychopathic features who received intensive treatment" in sanction-based programs that held youth accountable for their actions "had significantly lower rates of violent recidivism and a longer time to rearrest for violent behavior" than those who received treatment in a typical juvenile correctional facility.[27] In 2007, the United Kingdom launched an unprecedented treatment and research program focused on "Dangerous People with Severe Personality Disorder" (DPSPD).[28] Although not everyone placed in the program had been diagnosed as a psychopath, in order to be eligible for the program participants had to be diagnosed with a severe personality disorder, and there had to be a demonstrable link between that disorder and the risk of violent offending. Some stated that the program "holds the best chance yet of showing whether violent psychopaths can be reformed." Learn more about the concept of the psychopath as a clinical construct by visiting the Society for Research in Psychopathology via **Web Extra 6–2**. Read about the issues involved in identifying criminal psychopaths via **Library Extras 6–1** and **6–2**.

Brooke Palmer/Associated Press

Mads Mikkelsen as Dr. Hannibal Lecter in the NBC-TV series *Hannibal*. What motivates the fictional Lecter to commit crime?

Antisocial Personality Disorder

In recent years, the terms *sociopath* and *psychopath* have fallen into disfavor. In an attempt to identify sociopathic individuals, some psychologists have come to place greater emphasis on the type of behavior exhibited rather than on identifiable personality traits. By 1968, the American Psychiatric Association's (APA's) *Diagnostic and Statistical Manual of Mental Disorders* had completely discontinued use of the words *sociopath* and *psychopath*,

■ **antisocial personality** An individual who is unsocialized and whose behavior pattern brings him or her into repeated conflict with society.

■ **antisocial personality disorder (ASPD)** A psychological condition exhibited by individuals who are basically unsocialized and whose behavior pattern brings them repeatedly into conflict with society.

■ **electroencephalogram (EEG)** The electrical measurement of brain wave activity.

■ **traits (psychological)** Stable personality patterns that tend to endure throughout the life course and across social and cultural contexts.

replacing them with the terms *antisocial personality* and *asocial personality*.[29] In that year, the APA manual changed its description of **antisocial personality** types to "individuals who are basically unsocialized and whose behavior pattern brings them repeatedly into conflicts with society. They are incapable of significant loyalty to individuals, groups, or social values. They are grossly selfish, callous, irresponsible, impulsive, and unable to feel guilt or to learn from experience and punishment. Frustration tolerance is low. They tend to blame others or offer plausible rationalization for their behavior."[30] In most cases, individuals exhibiting an antisocial personality through their behavioral patterns are said to be suffering from **antisocial personality disorder** (sometimes referred to in clinical circles as APD, ASPD, or ANPD).

Individuals exhibiting an antisocial personality are said to be suffering from antisocial personality disorder.

The causes of ASPD are unclear. Somatogenic causes (those based on physiological features) are said to include a malfunctioning of the central nervous system, which is characterized by a low state of arousal driving the sufferer to seek excitement, and brain abnormalities, which may have been present since birth. Some studies show that an **electroencephalogram (EEG)** taken of an individual diagnosed as having ASPD is frequently abnormal, reflecting "a malfunction of some inhibitory mechanisms" that makes it unlikely that someone characterized by ASPD will "learn to inhibit behavior that is likely to lead to punishment."[31] It is difficult, however, to diagnose ASPD through physiological measurements because similar EEG patterns show up in patients with other types of disorders. Psychogenic causes (those rooted in early interpersonal experiences) include inability to form attachments to parents or other caregivers early in life, sudden separation from the mother during the first six months of life, and other forms of insecurity during the first few years of life. In short, a lack of love or the sensed inability to unconditionally depend upon one central loving figure (typically the mother in most psychological literature) immediately following birth is often posited as a major psychogenic factor contributing to the development of ASPD.

Most studies of ASPD have involved male subjects. Only rarely have researchers focused on women with antisocial personalities, and it is believed that only a small proportion of those afflicted with ASPD are women.[32] What little research there is suggests that females with ASPD possess many of the same definitive characteristics as their male counterparts, and that they assume their antisocial roles at similarly early ages.[33] The lifestyles of antisocial females, however, appear to include sexual misconduct and abnormally high levels of sexual activity, but such research can be misleading because the cultural expectations of female sexual behavior inherent in early studies may not always have been in keeping with reality—that is, early researchers may have had so little accurate information about female sexual activity that the behavior of women judged to possess antisocial personalities may have actually been far closer to the norm than originally believed.

Trait Theory

In 1964, **Hans J. Eysenck**, a British psychologist, published *Crime and Personality*, a book in which he explained crime as the result of fundamental personality characteristics, or **traits**, which he believed are largely inherited.[34] Psychological traits are stable personality patterns that tend to endure throughout the life course and across social and cultural contexts. They include behavioral, cognitive, and affective predispositions to respond to given a situation in a particular way. According to trait theory, as an individual grows older or moves from one place to another, his or her personality remains largely intact—defined by the traits that comprise it. Trait theory links personality (and associated traits) to behavior, and holds that it is an individual's personality, combined with his or her intelligence and natural abilities,[35] that determines his or her behavior in a given situation.[36]

Eysenck believed that the degree to which just three universal supertraits are present in an individual accounts for his or her unique personality. He termed these supertraits (1) introversion/extraversion, (2) neuroticism/emotional stability, and (3) psychoticism. Eysenck, like many other psychologists, accepted the fact that personality holds steady throughout much of life, but stressed that it is largely determined by genetics. He argued that what we call *personality* is a reflection of variations in

■ **Five Factor Model** A psychological perspective that builds on the Big Five core traits of personality.

the component operating systems of the major behavioral pathways of the brain.

In support of his idea of the genetic basis of personality, Eysenck pointed to twin studies showing that identical twins display strikingly similar behavioral tendencies, whereas fraternal twins demonstrate far less likelihood of similar behaviors. Eysenck also argued that psychological conditioning occurs more rapidly in some people than in others because of biological differences, and that antisocial individuals are difficult to condition (or to socialize) because of underlying genetic characteristics. He believed that up to two-thirds of all "behavioral variance" could be strongly attributed to genetics.[37]

Of Eysenck's three personality dimensions, one in particular—psychoticism—was thought to be closely correlated with criminality at all stages.[38] According to Eysenck, psychoticism is defined by such characteristics as lack of empathy, creativeness, tough-mindedness, and antisociability. Extroverts, Eysenck's second personality group that was associated with criminality, are described as carefree, dominant, and venturesome, operating with high levels of energy. "The typical extrovert," Eysenck wrote, "is sociable, likes parties, has many friends, needs to have people to talk to, and does not like reading or studying by himself."[39] Neuroticism, the third of the personality characteristics Eysenck described, is said to be typical of people who are irrational, shy, moody, and emotional.

According to Eysenck, psychotics are the most likely to be criminal because they combine high degrees of emotionalism with similarly high levels of extroversion; individuals with such characteristics are especially difficult to socialize and to train and do not respond well to the external environment. Eysenck cited many studies in which children and others who harbored characteristics of psychoticism performed poorly on conditioning tests designed to measure how quickly they would respond appropriately to external stimuli. Because conscience is fundamentally a conditioned reflex, Eysenck said, an individual who does not take well to conditioning will not fully develop a conscience and will continue to exhibit the asocial behavioral traits of a very young child. In essence, criminality can be seen as a personality type characterized by self-centeredness, indifference to the suffering and needs of others, impulsiveness, and low self-control—which, taken together, lead to law-violating behavior.

Today, trait theories of personality have expanded beyond Eysneck's basic three-trait model to encompass five basic traits: (1) openness to experience, (2) extraversion, (3) conscientiousness,

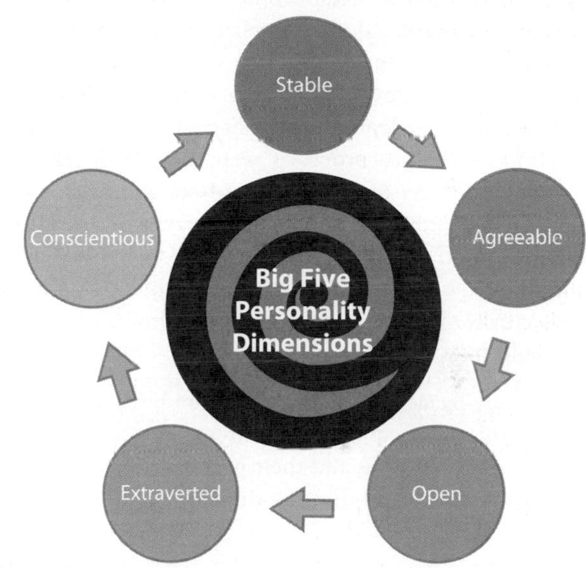

FIGURE 6-3 | The Big Five Personality Dimensions

(4) neuroticism, and (5) agreeableness. People are said to possess more or less of any one trait, and the combination of traits and the degree to which they are characteristic of an individual define that person's personality. Psychologists call these traits the *Big Five*, and they form the basis of the **Five Factor Model** of psychology (see Figure 6–3). According to many psychologists, "the Big Five are strongly genetically influenced, and the genetic factor structure of the Big Five appears to be invariant across European, North American, and East Asian samples,"[40] which suggests that personality traits, to a greater or lesser degree, are universally shared by all peoples. Conscientiousness, for example, is related to self-control, and is unlikely to be associated with criminality.

Cognitive Theories

Theories of cognition form a third area of personality theory. Cognitive approaches are learning theories that examine thought processes, and seek to explain how people: (1) learn to solve problems, including those that involve questions of value and morality, and (2) perceive and interpret the social environment. Cognitive theory has a number of branches, including one that focuses on moral and intellectual development, and another that examines how people process information.

■ **moral development theory** A perspective on crime causation holding that individuals become criminal when they have not successfully completed their intellectual development from child- to adulthood.

Moral Development Theory

The first branch of cognitive theory, **moral development theory**, holds that individuals become criminal when they have not successfully completed their intellectual development from child- to adulthood. One of the first comprehensive maps of human psychological development was created by Swiss developmental psychologist **Jean Piaget**. Piaget believed that human thinking and intellectual processes went through a number of biopsychological stages of development—something that Piaget saw as a natural extension of evolutionary adaptation. Just as a species adapts to its environment, Piaget believed, individual human beings respond to their environment by developing intellectually. He posited four stages of human intellectual development:[41]

1. The *sensory-motor stage*, which lasts from birth to age two. During this stage, children are extremely egocentric (or focused on themselves and their personal experiences), and learn about the world through the physical senses and the movement of their bodies.
2. The *preoperational stage*, which lasts from ages two to seven. During this stage, children are not able to reason well or to use logical thinking, but egocentrism begins to weaken, and motor skills are acquired. Piaget said that this stage was dominated by magical thinking, explaining why beliefs in Santa Claus, the Easter Bunny, and similar mythical characters are typical among younger children.
3. The *concrete operational stage*, which runs from ages 7 to 11. In this stage, children start to develop the ability to reason and to think logically, although they are very concrete in their thinking, and often require practical aids such as buttons or coins to aid in counting and arithmetic. By the time children reach the end of this stage they are no longer egocentric, and are able to appreciate the needs and feelings of others.
4. The *formal operational stage*, which lasts from ages 11 to 16 and continues into adulthood. During this stage, the developing adolescent acquires abstract reasoning skills, and learns how to think and reason without the need for external aids.

Central to Piaget's perspective on moral development is the idea that as children grow and learn, they become able to reflect on their own actions—acquiring a sense of the unspoken rules that govern human interaction. According to Piaget, children apply their burgeoning ability to reflect and use it to examine themselves; in the process, they learn right from wrong. In his words, "the child is someone who constructs his own moral world view, who forms ideas about right and wrong, and fair and unfair, that are not the direct product of adult teaching and that are often maintained in the face of adult wishes to the contrary."[42]

Once a child has moved through the four developmental stages, said Piaget, he or she would have moved from moral absolutism (in which the child unquestioningly accepts the dictates of his or her parents or caregivers) to moral relativism (where actions are seen as right or wrong depending on the circumstances in which they are undertaken).

Following Piaget, **Lawrence Kohlberg** offered an expanded cognitive structural theory of morality in a six-stage typology (Figure 6–4).[43] In Kohlberg's first stage, people only obey the law because they are afraid of being punished if they

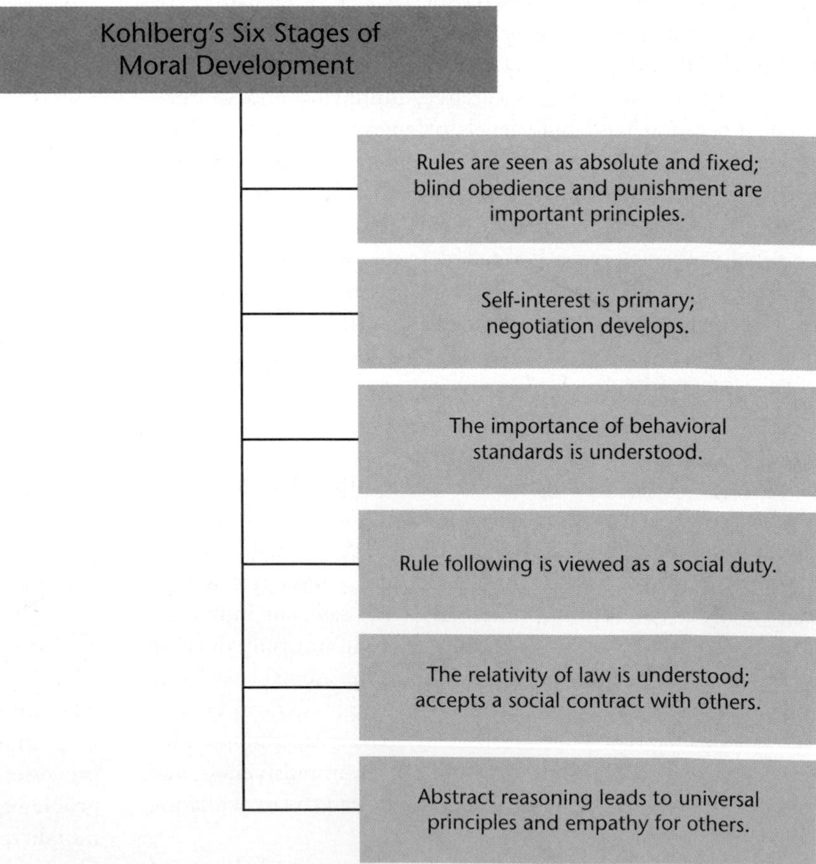

FIGURE 6–4 | Kohlberg's Six Stages of Moral Development

■ **cognitive information-processing theory (CIP)** A psychological perspective that involves the study of human perceptions, information processing, and decision making.

■ **scripts** Generalized knowledge about specific types of situations that is stored in the mind.

don't. By the final, or sixth, stage, however, obedience to the law becomes an obligation that is willingly assumed, and people chose not to violate the law because they value the principle of fairness and believe in interpersonal justice. Those who have evolved to higher stages of moral reasoning are unlikely to commit crimes because they appreciate not only their own needs, but the needs and interests of others as well.

Kohlberg argued that a preference for higher levels of moral thinking must be universal in human beings, although not necessarily inborn. He believed that people who have successfully moved through all stages of moral development have developed the ability to objectively evaluate opinions and either accept them or reject them without irrationally clinging to their own beliefs. Kohlberg posited that people may turn to crime if they are unsuccessful at making the normal transition between developmental stages of moral reasoning.

Research based on Kohlberg's work has demonstrated that offenders have less ability in making moral judgments than do noncriminals, even when they have similar backgrounds and experiences.[44]

epa european press photo agency b.v./Alamy

Anders Behring Breivik clenches his fist as he arrives in the courtroom for the first day of his trial in Oslo, Norway, April 16, 2012. Breivik, a militant anti-Islamic extremist, was convicted of killing 77 people in Norway and was given a 21-year prison sentence by an Oslo court. Breivik claimed that he acted in self-defense and said that his victims were traitors for embracing multiculturalism. How might moral development theory apply to Breivik?

Cognitive Information-Processing Theory

A second major area of cognitive theory applicable to criminology is **cognitive information-processing theory (CIP)**. CIP involves the study of human perceptions, information processing, and decision making. Psychological research suggests that people make decisions by engaging in a series of complex thought processes, or steps. In the first step, they encode and interpret the information they are presented with or the experiences they have. In the next stage, they search for an appropriate response; in the third stage they act on their decision.[45]

Some information-processing theorists believe that violent individuals may be using information incorrectly when making decisions. Violence-prone individuals, for example, may see people as more aggressive or threatening than they actually are. Such a view may result in violence even at the slightest provocation. Supportive research suggests that some people engage in violent attacks on others because they believe that they are actually defending themselves, even in the face of misperceived threat.[46] Because of the way that some people process information, they are unable to recognize the harm they are doing to others.[47]

Script Theory

In the late 1970s, **Roger C. Schank** and **Robert P. Abelson** of Yale University developed script theory in order to explain the understanding process that occurs during a situation or event.[48] **Scripts** refer to generalized knowledge about specific types of situations that is stored in the mind. More formally, Schank and Abelson described a script as "a predetermined, stereotyped sequence of actions that define a well-known situation."

People use ready-made scripts in everyday life to anticipate an appropriate sequence of events in a given context. We build scripts in our minds to allow for a number of different roles for those actors (others than ourselves) whose presence is anticipated to play out in the script, and we allow for possible variations in the physical scene and in the progression of events. In this sense, scripts are like stories that we use to structure our expectations of and reactions to circumstances that we expect to typically encounter. Take, for example, the internal script that we might use for restaurant dining. We know that when we arrive at a restaurant we should check with the host or hostess to see if a table is available. We expect that he or she will take us to our table and that a server will arrive soon after we are seated to present us with a menu and to take our drink order. We have similar expectations as to what will occur as our dinner progresses, including the eventual arrival of the check or bill, and the amount or percentage of a tip to be left at the completion of the evening. Because most events play out according to the scripts that we have in mind, things typically go smoothly. Sometimes, however, we can be surprised and find ourselves forced to innovate. In our restaurant example, we might unexpectedly be served the wrong meal, or (worse) the server might trip and spill food onto us. Unless we are surprised, however, things generally go according to plan and events fit with previous experiences we have had involving the same kind of activity.

According to Helen Gavin and David Hockey, two British criminologists writing in 2010, "scripts are used to guide behavior because the script provides the holder with a set of expectations about what will happen during the unfolding of an event, thus offering a way of predicting the outcome and aid[ing] the individual to act accordingly."[49] Gavin and Hockey recognize that people develop scripts based on the learning opportunities and experiences that are presented to them within their social environment. The idea is similar to that involved in role-playing, whereby children engage in role play as a kind of practice for the adult roles they will assume later in life.

The applicability of scripts to criminal behavior can be seen in the fact that career offenders routinely develop scripts to guide them through criminal activity. Gavin and Hockey say that these particular kinds of scripts "consist of a goal aim, a criminal belief system, a criminally motivated perception, and a self-serving set of distorted cognitions that protect the individual's low self-esteem." Criminals use scripts in their approach to crime commission, much of which becomes routine over time. Consequently, criminal motivations and drives underpin criminal scripts.

In their 2010 study of criminal scripts, Gavin and Hockey detailed the scripts of career offenders and found that they could "be acquired through. . . . various relevant psychological processes,"[50] along with other more conservative scripts that most people use in their daily lives. Moreover, they concluded that criminal scripts help to form a criminal identity once they have been internalized.

The Criminal Mind-set

In 1970 **Stanton E. Samenow**, a young clinical psychologist, began working with psychiatrist **Samuel Yochelson** in the Program for the Investigation of Criminal Behavior at St. Elizabeth's Hospital, a large federal psychiatric facility in Washington, D.C. Yochelson had abandoned a lucrative psychiatric practice in New York and moved to Washington to direct the criminal behavior research project, which studied and treated serious criminal offenders. After Samenow joined the program, he and Yochelson began to realize that many of the patients they were seeing "were in conflict with society [and] not suffering from internal psychological conflicts."[51] The two came to believe that criminals make entirely different assumptions about living and behaving than noncriminals do because of ingrained and pervasive errors of thinking.

After more than six years of working together, Yochelson and Samenow published a three-volume series, *The Criminal Personality*, in which they wrote that many offenders share an identifiable mind-set that is largely immune to environmental influences and that, for the most part, develops independently of social experience.[52]

In 1984 Samenow published the book *Inside the Criminal Mind*, which was republished 20 years later in a revised edition. The criminal personality, Samenow claims, develops early in childhood and consists of ways of thinking that are characteristic of many types of criminals, but are not shared by noncriminals. In the theoretical model that Samenow developed, he focuses largely on the criminal mind-set, and notes that criminals think differently than do noncriminals. Characteristics of the criminal mind-set include anger as a way of life, a focus on excitement without any real consideration of the cost to others, a lack of any feelings of obligation to others, lack of empathy, and prejudgment with which offenders approach most situations. The mind-set of a criminal is not "caused" by poverty, mental illness, or social conditions, Samenow argued, but rather by the need for excitement. It manifests, Samenow said, through personal choices made by offenders.

Although offenders come from a diversity of backgrounds, and although they engage in many different patterns of criminal behavior, Samenow argued that almost all criminal offenders are alike in the way they think. "A gun-toting, uneducated criminal off the streets of Southeast Washington, D.C., and a crooked Georgetown business executive are extremely similar in their view of themselves and the world," he wrote. The difference between a person with a criminal worldview and one with a conformist worldview is so different, said Samenow, that "it's as though the criminal were a different breed."

Samenow wrote that "the criminal chooses crime; he chooses to reject society long before society rejects him." Seen this way, crime resides within the person, Samenow said, and is "caused" by the way the individual thinks, not by his or her environment.[53] Criminal offenders are driven by excitement and self-interest, Samenow believed, and he suggested that if certain forms of criminal behavior were legalized they would lose their excitement, causing people committed to a life of law violations to engage in some other form of forbidden behavior. "No matter how many victims he has and how much damage he does," Samenow argues, "the criminal has little, if any, remorse and continues to regard himself as a good person."

Samenow believed that "behavior follows in the wake of thought,"[54] so the only way to rehabilitate an offender, he said, is to force the individual to see him- or herself realistically and develop responsible patterns of thought. Changed thoughts will lead to a reassessment of the criminal worldview and, hopefully, to positive behavioral change.

■ **psychiatric criminology** A theory that is derived from the medical sciences (including neurology) and that, like other psychological theories, focuses on the individual as the unit of analysis. Psychiatric theories form the basis of psychiatric criminology.
■ **psychoanalysis** The theory of human psychology founded by Sigmund Freud on the concepts of the unconscious, resistance, repression, sexuality, and the Oedipus complex.
■ **neurosis** A functional disorder of the mind or of the emotions involving anxiety, phobias, or other abnormal behavior.
■ **psychosis** A form of mental illness in which sufferers are said to be out of touch with reality.
■ **sublimation** The psychological process whereby one aspect of consciousness comes to be symbolically substituted for another.
■ **psychotherapy** A form of psychiatric treatment based on psychoanalytical principles and techniques.
■ **id** The aspect of the personality from which drives, wishes, urges, and desires emanate. More formally, this division of the psyche is associated with instinctual impulses and demands for immediate satisfaction of primitive needs.
■ **ego** The reality-testing part of the personality; also called the *reality principle*. More formally, this personality component is conscious, most immediately controls behavior, and is most in touch with external reality.

The Psychoanalytic Perspective—Criminal Behavior as Maladaptation

Psychiatric criminology (also called *forensic psychiatry*) envisions a complex set of drives and motives operating from hidden recesses deep within the personality to determine behavior. Perhaps the best-known psychiatrist of all time is **Sigmund Freud** (1856–1939). Freud coined the term **psychoanalysis** in 1896 and based an entire theory of human behavior on it.

> Psychiatric criminology envisions a complex set of drives and motives operating from hidden recesses deep within the personality to determine behavior.

Freud said nothing about criminal behavior, and it wasn't until later that other psychoanalysts began to apply concepts that Freud had developed to the study of criminal behavior. From the point of view of psychoanalysis, criminal behavior is maladaptive, or the product of inadequacies in the offender's personality. Significant inadequacies may result in full-blown mental illness, which can be a direct cause of crime. The psychoanalytic perspective encompasses diverse notions such as personality, **neurosis**, and **psychosis**, and more specific concepts such as transference, **sublimation**, and repression. **Psychotherapy**, referred to in its early days as the "talking cure" because it relied on patient–therapist communication, is the attempt to relieve patients of their mental disorders through the application of psychoanalytic principles and techniques.

> Sublimation is the psychological process whereby one item of consciousness is symbolically substituted for another.

Mary Evans Picture Library/Alamy

Sigmund Freud (1856–1939) in the office of his Vienna home, circa 1930. How have Freud's theories influenced contemporary criminology?

According to Freud, the personality is made up of three components—the id, the ego, and the superego—as shown in Figure 6–5. The **id** is the fundamental aspect of the personality from which drives, wishes, urges, and desires emanate. Freud focused primarily on love, aggression, and sex as fundamental drives in any personality. The id operates according to the pleasure principle, seeking full and immediate gratification of its needs. Individuals, however, according to Freud, are rarely fully aware of the urges that manifest (occasionally into awareness) from the id because it is a largely unconscious region of the mind. Nonetheless, from the Freudian perspective, each of us carries within our id the prerequisite motivation for criminal behavior. We are, each one of us, potential murderers, sexual aggressors, and thieves—our drives and urges kept in check only by other controlling aspects of our personalities.

The **ego** is primarily charged with reality testing. Freud's use of the word *ego* should not be confused with popular usage, whereby a person might talk about an "inflated ego" or an "egotistical person." For Freud, the ego was primarily concerned with how objectives might be best accomplished. The ego tends to effect strategies for the individual that maximize pleasure and minimize pain. It lays out the various paths of action that can

■ **superego** The moral aspect of the personality, much like the conscience. More formally, this division of the psyche develops by the incorporation of the perceived moral standards of the community, is mainly unconscious, and includes the conscience.

■ **repression** The psychological process through which a person rejects his or her own desires and impulses toward pleasurable instincts by excluding them from consciousness, thereby removing them from awareness and rendering them unconscious.

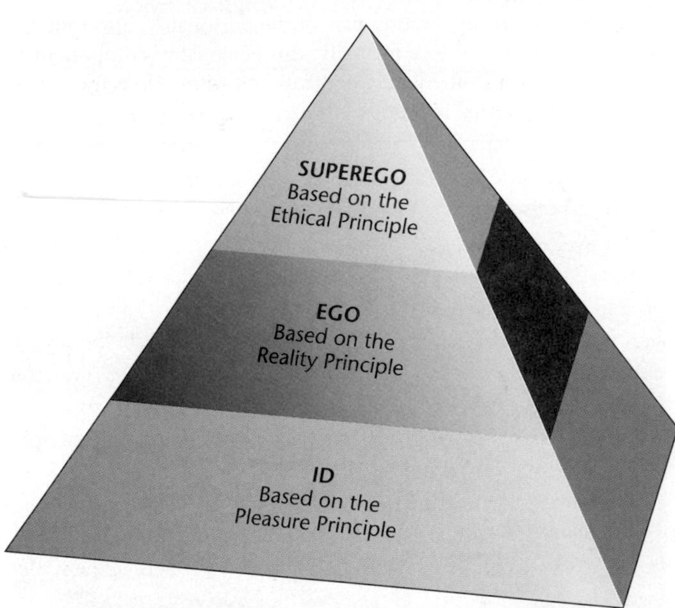

FIGURE 6-5 | **The Psychoanalytic Structure of Personality**

Source: Schmalleger, Frank J., *Criminology*. Printed and Electronically reproduced by permission of Pearson Education, Inc., Upper Saddle River, New Jersey.

lead to wish fulfillment. The ego inherently recognizes that it may be necessary to delay gratification to achieve a more fulfilling long-term goal.

The **superego** is much like a moral guide to right and wrong. If properly developed, it evaluates the ego's plans, dismissing some as morally inappropriate while accepting others as ethically viable. The id of a potential rapist, for example, might be filled with lustful drives, and his ego may develop a variety of alternative plans whereby those drives might be fulfilled, some legal and some illegal. His superego will, if the individual's personality is relatively well integrated and the superego is properly developed, turn the individual away from law-violating behavior based on his sensual desires and guide the ego to select a path of action that is in keeping with social convention. When the dictates of the superego are not followed, feelings of guilt may result. The superego is one of the most misunderstood of Freudian concepts. In addition to elements of conscience, the superego also contains what Freud called the "ego-ideal," which is a symbolic representation of what society values. The ego-ideal differs from the conscience in that it is less forceful in controlling behavior in the absence of the likelihood of discovery.

Although, as previously mentioned, Freud did not directly address crime, he did spend much of his time examining abnormal behaviors, many of which might lead to violations of the criminal law. One way in which a person might be led into crime, according to the perspective of psychoanalysis, is as the result of a poorly developed superego. In the individual without a fully functional superego, the mind is left to fall back on the ego's reality-testing ability. To put it simply, the ego, operating without a moral guide, may select a path of action that, although expedient at the time, violates the law. Consequently, without a fully functioning superego, offenders come to be characterized by id-dominated personalities, and the id's need for instant gratification determines their behavior. Individuals suffering from poor superego development are unlikely to give thought to the long-term consequences of the choices they make.

Although Freud actually wrote very little about criminality, **August Aichorn**, another psychoanalyst, did. Aichorn saw the behavior of violent criminals as dominated by the id, leaving them unable to control their impulsive and pleasure-seeking drives stemming from the id.[55] Aichorn believed that as a result of negative life experiences, especially at an early age, violence-prone individuals suffer from damaged egos that are too weak to be able to deal with stressful circumstances and urges that well up from the id.

Another path to criminality from a psychiatric viewpoint is through repressed needs. The psychoanalytical concept of **repression** holds that a person may seek to reject his or her own desires and impulses toward pleasurable instincts by excluding them from his or her own consciousness, thereby removing them from awareness and rendering them unconscious.

One secret need of many criminals, according to some psychologists, is the need to be punished, which arises, according to psychiatric theory, from a sense of guilt. Psychiatrists who suggest that the need to be punished is a motivating factor in criminal behavior are quick to point out that this need may be a closely guarded secret, unknown even to the offender. Hence, from the psychiatric point of view, many drives, motives, and wishes are unconscious or even repressed by people who harbor them. The concept of repression holds that the human mind may choose to keep certain aspects of itself out of consciousness, possibly because of shame, self-loathing, or a simple lack of adequate introspection.

The need to be punished is a motivating factor in some criminal behavior.

Freudian theory was very popular during the middle part of the twentieth century, but by the 1980s, the notions of ego and id were considered antiquated by most psychiatrists. Attention shifted to the study of chemical imbalances in the brain, and psychopharmacology supplemented—if not replaced—the earlier

■ **paranoid schizophrenic** A schizophrenic individual who suffers from delusions and hallucinations.

■ **risk assessment** The practice of using a structured instrument that combines information about individuals in order to classify them as being low, moderate, or high risk for violent behavior, reoffending, or continued criminal activity.

ideas of Freud and his followers. Marti Olsen Laney, a neuroscience researcher in Portland, Oregon, found that the brains of introverted children functioned somewhat differently from those of extroverts. Brain scans of introverted kids found much more overall activity—especially in the brain's frontal lobes, which are areas associated with problem solving, introspection, complex thinking, and planning.[56]

The field of psychiatry has seen a rekindling of interest in Freudian psychology, however, because psychopharmacology (the use of drugs to treat psychiatric symptoms and disorders) has been unable to provide an alternative grand theory of personality, emotion, and motivation.[57] Moreover, today's neuroscientists are busily creating a chemical map of the mind that seems to validate the general sketch that Freud provided decades ago, and soon a new unified perspective that reconciles the work of neurologists and psychiatrists may emerge. The recognition of just such a possibility prompted Eric R. Kandel of Columbia University, the 2000 Nobel laureate in physiology and medicine, to say that psychoanalysis is "still the most coherent and intellectually satisfying view of the mind."[58]

The Psychotic Offender

Some seemingly inexplicable forms of criminality may be the result of psychosis. People with psychotic disorders are out of touch with reality in some fundamental way, possibly suffering from hallucinations, delusions, or other breaks with reality. Psychoses may be either organic (resulting from physical damage to or abnormalities in the brain) or functional (having no known physical cause). Canadian criminologist Gwynn Nettler said, "Thought disorder is the hallmark of psychosis. People are called crazy when, at some extremity, they cannot 'think straight.'"[59] She identified three characteristics of psychotic individuals: "(1) a grossly distorted conception of reality, (2) moods, and swings of mood, that seem inappropriate to circumstance, and (3) marked inefficiency in getting along with others and caring for oneself."[60]

Psychiatrists today recognize at least nine different types of psychotic disorders, and one important category is schizophrenia. Schizophrenics (mentioned earlier) are characterized by disordered or disjointed thinking, in which the types of logical associations they make are atypical of other people. **Paranoid schizophrenics**, one of the four major subgroups of schizophrenics, also suffer from delusions and hallucinations. Schizophrenia is a disorganization of the personality, and in its most extreme form, it may manifest itself in seemingly irrational behavior as well as hallucinations and delusions.

A recent study of male schizophrenics found that 37% started a criminal career, and 13% had committed their first violent crime, before any contact with the psychiatric hospital system. Study authors concluded that "the criminality committed [by schizophrenics] before first contact to the psychiatric hospital system is substantial, especially among males with schizophrenia."[61] Many studies confirm the association between violence and schizophrenia, but recent evidence from a study conducted in the U.K. suggests that the proportion of violent crime directly attributable to schizophrenia is below 10%.[62] When substance abuse is added to the mix, however, the amount of violence associated with schizophrenia increases considerably. Consequently, a 2009 article in the *Journal of the American Medical Association* (JAMA) found that schizophrenics are four to six times as likely as members of the general population to commit a violent crime, and noted that current medical guidelines "recommend that violence **risk assessment** should be conducted for all patients with schizophrenia."[63]

Not all people who are psychotic commit crimes, and many remain law abiding throughout their entire lives. Psychoses, however, may lead to crime in a number of ways. Following the Vietnam War, for example, several American soldiers suffering from a kind of battlefield psychosis killed friends and family members, thinking they were Vietcong soldiers (the enemy). These men, who had been traumatized by battlefield experiences in Southeast Asia, relived their past on American streets. In other crimes committed by psychotics, thought disorders may be less obvious or may exist only temporarily.

Frustration–Aggression Theory

In his early writings, Freud suggested that aggressive behavior is a natural response to frustration and limitations imposed upon a person. This *frustration–aggression thesis* was later developed more fully in the writings of **J. Dollard**, **Albert Bandura**, **Richard H. Walters**, and others. Dollard's frustration–aggression theory held that although frustration can lead to various forms of behavior—including regression, sublimation, and aggressive fantasy—direct aggression toward others is its most likely consequence.[64] Because everyone suffers frustration at times in life (beginning with weaning and toilet training), aggression is a natural consequence of living, but that aggression can be manifested in socially acceptable ways (contact sports, military or law enforcement careers, simple verbal attacks) and/or engaged in vicariously by observing others who are acting violently (in movies, on television, in fiction).

■ **alloplastic adaptation** A form of adjustment that results from changes in the environment surrounding an individual.

■ **autoplastic adaptation** A form of adjustment that results from changes within an individual.

Dollard applied the psychoanalytical term *displacement* to the type of violence that is vented on something or someone who is not the source of the original frustration and suggested that satisfying one's aggressive urges via observation was a form of "catharsis."

Some psychologists have tried to identify what it is that causes some individuals to displace aggression or to experience it vicariously, whereas others respond violently and directly toward the immediate source of their frustrations. Andrew F. Henry and James F. Short, Jr., for example, suggested that child-rearing practices are a major determining factor in such a causal nexus.[65] Restrictive parents who both punish and love their children, said Henry and Short, will engender in their children the ability to suppress outward expressions of aggression, but when one parent punishes and the other loves, or when both punish but neither shows love, children can be expected to show anger directly and perhaps even immediately because they will not be threatened with the loss of love. Physical punishment rarely threatens the loss of love, and children so punished cannot be expected to refrain from direct displays of anger.

In 1960, Stewart Palmer studied murderers and their siblings to determine the degree of frustration to which they had been exposed as children.[66] He found that male murderers had experienced much more frustration than their brothers and that more than twice as many frustrating experiences—ranging from difficult births to serious illnesses, childhood beatings, severe toilet training, and negative school experiences—were reported by the murderers than by their law-abiding siblings.

Crime as Adaptation

Some psychiatrists see crime as an adaptation to life's stresses. According to **Seymour L. Halleck**, a psychiatrist and adjunct professor of law at the University of North Carolina at Chapel Hill, turning to crime can provide otherwise disenfranchised individuals with a sense of power and purpose.[67] Halleck says that crime can also provide "excellent rationalizations" for perceived inadequacies—especially for those whose lives have been failures when judged against the benchmarks of the wider society. "The criminal is able to say . . ., 'I could have been successful if I had not turned to crime. All my troubles have come to me because I have been bad.'" Thus, crime, according to Halleck, provides "a convenient resource for denying, forgetting or ignoring . . . other inadequacies."[68]

Insofar as the choice of crime reduces stresses the individual faces by producing changes in the environment (empowerment), it is referred to as **alloplastic adaptation**. When crime leads to stress reduction as a result of internal changes in beliefs, value systems, and so forth, it is called **autoplastic adaptation**. The offender who is able to deny responsibility for other failures by turning to crime is said to be seeking autoplastic adaptation. Because other forms of behavior also may meet many of the same needs as crime, Halleck points out, an individual may select crime over various other behavioral alternatives only when no reasonable alternatives are available or when criminal behavior has inherent advantages—as might be the case under instances of economic or social oppression. (That is, individuals who are actively discriminated against may find personal and political significance in violating the laws of the oppressing society.)

From Halleck's point of view, crime "has many advantages even when considered independently of the criminal's conscious or unconscious needs for gratification."[69] Even though crime can be immediately rewarding or intensely pleasing, such a reward is more like a "fringe benefit"; its central significance is that it "is an action which helps one survive with dignity."[70] Halleck explained that "we cannot understand the criminal unless we appreciate that his actions are much more than an effort to find a specific gratification."[71]

In another approach to stress as a causative agent in crime commission, Arnold S. Linsky, Ronet Bachman, and Murray A. Straus suggested that stress may lead to aggression toward others and toward oneself (self-destructive behavior like suicide, smoking, and abuse of alcohol).[72] Linsky and his colleagues measured stress at the societal level, arguing that although the relationship between stress and aggression has been studied at the individual level, "the neglect of social stress as an explanation for society-to-society differences in aggression may be partially due to a lack of an objective means of comparing the stressfulness of life in different societies."[73] Concluding that societal stress levels heighten levels of aggression, the authors suggested that social policies should be created to reduce the impact of such stressful events as having to stop work, foreclosing on a mortgage, and dropping out of school.

Finally, we should recognize that perceptions vary and that although criminal behavior may appear to be a valid choice for some individuals who are seeking viable responses to perceived stresses and oppression, their perceptions may not be wholly accurate.

■ **criminogenic needs** Dynamic attributes (also known as dynamic risk factors) of offenders and their circumstances that are associated with rates of recidivism.

■ **attachment theory** A social-psychological perspective on delinquent and criminal behavior holding that the successful development of secure attachment between a child and his or her primary caregiver provides the basic foundation for all future psychological development.

Criminogenic Needs

In 1998, **Donald A. Andrews** and **James Bonta** identified major risk factors associated with criminal conduct that they termed **criminogenic needs**.[74] Criminogenic needs, which Andrews and Bonta referred to in later writings as "criminogenic domains,"[75] can be described as dynamic attributes of offenders and their circumstances that are associated with rates of recidivism.[76] Among the "needs" or risk factors that Andrews and Bonta listed are (1) antisocial attitudes, values, and beliefs; (2) antisocial personality, including low self-control; (3) antisocial associates and friends; (4) low levels of social achievement, including a lack of educational, vocational, or financial achievement; (5) family factors, including marital instability, a criminal family, and poor parenting skills; (6) substance abuse; and (7) a lack of prosocial pursuits. Criminogenic needs, because they are dynamic or amenable to change, can be targeted by treatment strategies intended to reduce criminality and recidivism.

In their writings, Andrews and Bonta developed the term "criminogenic domain" to refer to major risk factors for continuing criminality. They identified criminal history as a major criminogenic domain, and noted that together in combination with antisocial attitudes, criminal associates, and antisocial personality, these represent the "big four" risk factors. Andrews and Bonta were careful, however, not to include criminal history as a criminogenic need because it is a static element unamenable to change.[77]

Later writers have developed an enriched concept of criminogenic needs, suggesting that they are not positive desires that individuals seek to fulfill. Rather, according to Australian criminologists Tony Ward and Claire Stewart, "they can be seen as internal and external obstacles . . . linked to basic need distortion." Unlike our general understanding of needs, Ward and Stewart suggest that criminogenic needs arise in "the absence of the internal and external conditions necessary for a person to lead a fulfilling life."[78] Seen this way, criminogenic needs are not actually needs in themselves, but are psychopathological symptoms or indicators of maladaptive functioning. Hence, offenders see "criminal acts as advantageous (because they are) causally related to socioemotional deficits . . ."[79] Hence, the fulfillment of criminogenic needs provides a proxy for meeting an individual's otherwise valid needs. So, for example, the need for social achievement can be fulfilled through criminal activity even though the offender does not have the education or skills needed for gainful employment.

Ward and Stewart criticize Andrews and Bonta's description of criminogenic needs, saying that "their theory is essentially a framework and does not provide clear descriptions of the relevant causal mechanisms that generate criminogenic needs."[80] From the point of view of Ward and Stewart, "criminogenic needs arise from frustrated basic human needs and involve the acquisition of proxy goals and their accompanying dysfunctional beliefs and behavioral strategies." Moreover, Ward and Stewart add, criminogenic needs "can be viewed as means to the commission of a crime" because "they represent the social and psychological conditions necessary for a crime to occur."[81]

Attachment Theory

Another psychological approach to explaining crime and delinquency is **attachment theory**, first proposed by English child psychiatrist **John Bowlby** (1907–1990), who observed children during his tenure at the London Child Guidance Clinic after World War II.[82] Bowlby was especially interested in the maladjusted behavior of children who lacked a solid relationship with a mother figure, and he concluded that for healthy personality development to occur, "the infant and young child should experience a warm, intimate, and continuous relationship with his mother (or permanent mother substitute) in which both find satisfaction and enjoyment."[83]

Bowlby identified three forms of attachment: secure attachment, anxious-avoidant attachment, and anxious-resistant attachment.[84] Only the first is healthy, and it develops early in life when a child is confident that the mother figure will be responsible and available when needed. The successful development of secure attachment between children and their primary caregivers, Bowlby said, provides the basic foundation for all their future psychological development, with children developing a secure psychological base when they are "nourished physically and emotionally, comforted if distressed [and] reassured if frightened."[85]

> The successful development of secure attachment provides the basic foundation for future psychological development.

According to attachment theory, delinquent behavior arises when nonsecure attachments are created. Anxious-avoidant attachment develops when children feel rejection and lack confidence concerning parental support and care. Anxious-resistant attachment develops from similar experiences and results in feelings of uncertainty, causing the child (and later, the adult) to feel anxious, to be fearful of his or her environment, and to cling to potential caregivers or partners. Bowlby called delinquents "affectionless," meaning they did not form intimate attachments as

THEORY | in PERSPECTIVE

Types of Psychological and Psychiatric Theories

Psychological and psychiatric theories of criminology are derived from the behavioral sciences and focus on the individual as the unit of analysis. This chapter breaks their discussion down into a number of areas as shown in this box.

Personality Theory

This approach envisions a complex set of drives and motives operating from recesses deep within the personality to determine behavior.

Period: 1930s–present

Theorists: Hervey M. Cleckley, Hans J. Eysenck, many others

Concepts: personality, psychopath, sociopath, antisocial personality, personality, traits, Five Factor Model

Cognitive Theory

Cognitive theory, also known as moral development theory, holds that individuals become criminal when they have not successfully completed their intellectual development from child- to adulthood.

Period: 1930s–present

Theorists: Jean Piaget, Lawrence Kohlberg, Roger C. Schank, Robert P. Abelson, Stanton E. Samenow, Samuel Yochelson

Concepts: moral development, cognitive-information processing, scripts, criminal mind-set

Psychoanalytic Criminology

This psychiatric approach, developed by Austrian psychiatrist Sigmund Freud, emphasizes the role of personality in human behavior and sees deviant behavior as the result of dysfunctional personalities or maladaptation to the social environment.

Period: 1920s–present

Theorists: Sigmund Freud, August Aichorn, others

Concepts: Psychiatric criminology, id, ego, superego, sublimation, psychoanalysis, psychotherapy, neurosis, psychosis, sublimation, paranoid schizophrenia

Frustration-Aggression Theory

Frustration is a natural consequence of living and a root cause of crime in this theory, where criminal behavior can be a form of adaptation when it results from stress reduction.

Period: 1940s–present

Theorists: J. Dollard, Albert Bandura, Richard H. Walters

Concepts: Frustration, aggression, displacement

Crime as Adaptation

Criminal behavior can be a form of adaptation when it provides rationalizations for perceived inadequacies.

Period: 1970s-present

Theorists: Seymour L. Halleck, Donald A. Andrews, James Bonta, John Bowlby

Concepts: alloplastic and autoplastic adaptation, criminogenic needs, criminogenic domains, attachment theory

Behavior Theory

A psychological perspective, behavior theory posits that individual behavior that is rewarded will increase in frequency and behavior that is punished will decrease in frequency.

Period: 1940s–present

Theorists: B. F. Skinner, others

Concepts: Operant behavior, operant conditioning, classical conditioning, stimulus–response, reward, punishment

Modeling Theory

This theory states that people learn how to behave by modeling themselves after others whom they have the opportunity to observe.

Period: 1950s–present

Theorists: Gabriel Tarde, Albert Bandura, others

Concepts: Imitation, interpersonal aggression, social cognition theory, modeling, disengagement

children and cannot form such attachments later in life. Attachment theory predicts that the most problematic individuals will be those who were abandoned at an early age, who experienced multiple placements (in foster homes and so on), who had to deal with the early absence of one or both parents, and who faced traumatic conditions (physical, sexual, or other abuse) in early childhood.

Tests of attachment theory seem to confirm that difficulties in childhood (especially before the age of eight) produce criminality later in life.[86] Studies have shown that children who were raised in insecure environments are likely to engage in violent behavior as adults and that childhood insecurity leads to a relative lack of empathy.[87] Some attachment theorists believe that the development of empathy is the single most important factor leading to

■ **behavior theory** A psychological perspective positing that behavior that is rewarded will increase in frequency and behavior that is punished will decrease in frequency.
■ **operant behavior** Behavior that affects the environment so as to produce responses or further behavioral cues.
■ **reward** A desirable behavioral consequence likely to increase the frequency of occurrence of that behavior.
■ **punishment** An undesirable behavioral consequence likely to decrease the frequency of occurrence of that behavior.

conformity. When children do not receive empathy from those around them, they appear to also be unable to see others as deserving of empathy and become more likely to inflict injury on others. Learn more about attachment theory by visiting the Attachment Research Center via **Web Extra 6–3**, and read about the development of attachment theory at **Library Extra 6–3**.

Behavior Theory

Behavior theory, the second main thrust of early psychological theorizing, built upon the concept of conditioned behavior. The idea that behavior could be "conditioned" or *shaped*, was popularized through the work of Russian physiologist Ivan Pavlov (1849–1936), whose work with dogs won the Nobel Prize in Physiology or Medicine in 1904. The dogs, which salivated when food was presented to them, were always fed in the presence of a ringing bell. Soon, Pavlov found, the dogs would salivate as if in preparation for eating when the bell alone was rung, even when no food was present. Hence, salivation, an automatic response to the presence of food, could be conditioned to occur in response to some other stimulus, demonstrating that animal behavior could be predictably altered via association with external changes arising from the environment surrounding the organism. The kind of conditioning that Pavlov demonstrated, which is the association of a particular response to a conditioned stimulus, is referred to today as *classical conditioning*.

The concept of conditioned behavior was popularized through the work of Russian physiologist Ivan Pavlov.

Behavioral Conditioning

Behavior theory has sometimes been called the "stimulus–response theory of human behavior." When an individual's behavior results in rewards or feedback that the individual regards as pleasurable and desirable, then that the behavior will likely become more frequent. Under such circumstances, the behavior in question is reinforced, and the rewards themselves are referred to as *reinforcements*. Conversely, when punishment follows behavior, chances are that the frequency of that type of behavior will decrease. The individual's responses are termed **operant behavior** because a person's behavioral choices effectively operate on the surrounding environment to produce consequences for the individual.

Behavior theory is often used by parents seeking to control children through a series of **rewards** and **punishments**. Young children may be punished, for example, by being spanked, by having a favored toy taken away, and by the television being turned off. Older children are often told what rules they are expected to obey and what rewards they can anticipate if they adhere to those rules. They also know that punishments will follow if they do not obey the rules.

Rewards and punishments have been further divided into four conceptual categories: (1) positive reinforcements, which increase the frequency of approved behavior by adding something desirable to the situation—as when a "good" child is given a toy; (2) negative reinforcements, which increase the frequency of approved behavior by removing something distressful from the situation—as when a "good" child is permitted to skip the morning's chores; (3) positive punishments, which decrease the frequency of unwanted behavior by adding something undesirable to the situation—as when a "bad" child is spanked; and (4) negative punishments, which decrease the frequency of unwanted behavior by removing something desirable from the situation—as when a "bad" child's candy is taken away. According to behavior theory, it is through the application of rewards and punishments that behavior is shaped.

Behavior theory differs from other psychological theories in that the major determinants of behavior are envisioned as existing in the environment surrounding the individual rather than within the individual. Perhaps the best-known proponent of behavior theory is **B. F. Skinner** (1904–1990), who created the term *operant conditioning*. Skinner, a former Harvard professor, rejected unobservable psychological constructs, focusing instead on patterns of responses to external rewards and stimuli. Skinner did extensive animal research involving behavioral concepts and created the notion of programmed instruction, which allows students to work at their own pace and provides immediate rewards for learning accomplishments.

Behavior theory is important in the study of criminology because much human behavior is the result of conditioning, and people can be conditioned to respond to situations with either prosocial or antisocial conduct. It's important, too, because it is the foundation on which social cognition theory (which

■ **social cognition theory** The perspective that people learn how to act by observing others.

■ **modeling** A form of learning where individuals imitate actions or performances by observing other people in order to add those actions to their own behavioral repertoire.

is discussed in the following section) is built. In fact, teachers and parents often use punishments and rewards in an effort to condition their students and children, respectively, to engage in appropriate or desired behavior. Consequently, from the perspective of behavior theory, crime can be explained as the result of inappropriate behavioral conditioning.

Social Cognition and the Role of Modeling

One of the earliest attempts to explain crime and deviance as learned behavior can be found in the work of **Gabriel Tarde** (1843–1904), a French social theorist of the late 1800s. Tarde discounted the biological theories of Lombroso and others. The basis of any society, Tarde believed, was imitation, the tendency of people to pattern their behavior after the behavior of others. Tarde developed a theory of human behavior that built upon three laws of imitation and suggestion.[88] Tarde's first law held that individuals in close intimate contact with one another tend to imitate each other's behavior. His second law stated that imitation moves from the top down. This means that poor people tend to imitate wealthy people, youngsters tend to emulate those who are older, lower-class people tend to imitate members of the upper class, and so forth. The third law of imitation is the law of insertion, which says that new acts and behaviors tend to either reinforce or replace old ones. Hence, the music of each generation replaces the music of the one that preceded it, the politics of young people eventually become the politics of the nation, faddish drugs are substituted for traditional ones, and new forms of crime tend to take the place of older ones (for example, when computer criminals become a more serious threat to financial institutions than bank robbers).

More recently, Albert Bandura developed a comprehensive **social cognition theory** of aggression that depends for its explanatory power on cognitive processes. Bandura believed that reinforcement theory could not account for all types of learning. Although everyone is capable of aggression, Bandura said, "people are not born with . . . repertories of aggressive behavior. They must learn them."[89] Bandura, a psychology professor at Stanford University and past president of the American Psychological Society, is often referred to as the creator of *social learning theory* in the field of psychology (a parallel tradition of social learning theories in sociology will be discussed in later chapters). Because of the central role of cognition in Bandura's learning theory, however, he preferred to call his approach *social cognition theory*. Central to Bandura's theory are the ideas of observation, imitation, and modeling.

The concept of **modeling** acknowledges the fact that people learn how to act through their life experiences, and especially by observing others. Bandura wrote that "Most human behavior is learned observationally through modeling: from observing others, one forms an idea of how new behaviors are performed, and on later occasions this coded information serves as a guide for action."[90] In some of his early work, Bandura experimented with children who observed adult role models striking inflatable cartoon characters. When the children were observed after their encounter with adult behavior, they, too, exhibited similarly aggressive behavior. Bandura also studied violence on television and concluded that "television is an effective tutor. Both laboratory and controlled field studies in which young children and adolescents are repeatedly shown either violent or nonviolent fare, disclose that exposure to film violence shapes the form of aggression and typically increases interpersonal aggressiveness in everyday life."[91] A later study by other researchers showed that even after ten years, the level of violence that young adults engaged in was directly related to the degree of violent television they had been exposed to as children.[92]

Aggression can be provoked, Bandura suggests, through physical assaults and verbal threats and insults, as well as by thwarting a person's hopes or obstructing his or her goal-seeking behavior. Deprivation and "adverse reductions in the conditions of life" (a lowered standard of living, the onset of disease, a spouse leaving or caught cheating, for example) are other potential triggers of aggression. Bandura adds, however, that a human being's ability to foresee the future consequences of present behavior adds another dimension to the activation of learned patterns of aggression. That is, aggressive behavior can be perceived as holding future benefits for individuals exhibiting it. In short, it can be seen as a means to a desired end.

Bandura also says that individuals sometimes become aggressive because they are rewarded for doing so. The early-twentieth-century American concept of a "macho"—virile and masculine—male figure, for example, was often associated with the expectation of substantial reward. Whether this perception was accurate, a significant proportion of American men subscribed to it nonetheless, and for many decades, it served as a guide to daily behavior.

Another form of reward can flow from aggression. Bandura called it the "reduction of aversive treatment." By this, he meant that simply standing up for oneself can improve the way one is treated by others. For example, standing up to a bully may be the most effective way of dealing with the harassment one might otherwise face. Bandura recognized that everyone has self-regulatory mechanisms that can inhibit the tendency toward aggression. People reward or punish themselves, Bandura said, according to internal standards they have for judging their own behavior. Thus, aggression may be inhibited

WHO'S TO BLAME—The Individual or Society?

The Video Game Killer

In early 2013, 17-year-old Jason Sutter was pulled over in a small midwestern town for various traffic offenses, including going 70 mph in a 35-mph zone, running a red light, failing to yield for a blue light and siren, and driving recklessly. When officers discovered that he didn't have a driver's license, Sutter was handcuffed, briefly searched, placed in the back of a patrol car, and driven to the local police station for booking.

After he was photographed and fingerprinted, detective Joe Lockman sat down with him in a small interrogation room. Lockman, a 25-year veteran of the force, was working late and was in the station at 2:00 a.m. when Sutter arrived. The building was nearly empty, so Lockman decided to remove Sutter's handcuffs for what he hoped would be an informal chat. Sutter, who stood only 5 feet 4 inches tall and weighed 135 pounds, reminded Lockman of his son, and the detective hoped that he could teach the boy something about right and wrong.

As Lockman leaned forward to unshackle Sutter, a number of unfortunate events came together with deadly results. Sutter was a high school dropout and video game fanatic who spent most of his waking hours playing violence-themed games—including three in which the "heroes" killed pursuing police officers. Sutter had been improperly handcuffed with his hands in front, giving him easy access to Lockman's service revolver. Lockman carried an older model .38-caliber revolver (instead of a 9mm semiautomatic pistol), which was loaded with deadly hollow-point ammunition and did not have a safety. When Sutter grabbed the weapon, he was able to immediately pull the trigger and fire two shots into Lockman's chest, killing him instantly.

Sutter fled out the front door of the police station past the surprised desk sergeant. The sergeant, realizing what had happened, pursued Sutter through the front door, and the two exchanged shots. Sutter was wounded in the exchange and captured; he was taken to an area hospital where he underwent surgery and recovered. He was charged with the murder of Detective Lockman, and the district attorney said that he would seek to have Sutter put away for the rest of his life.

Sutter's parents hired an attorney to defend their son. The lawyer held a press conference during which he announced his defense strategy—that Sutter had been brainwashed by video games and that at the time of the shooting he had been unable to distinguish reality from fantasy. "Jason was confused by all that happened. He thought that he was playing a game," the attorney said. "He didn't realize that someone might really get hurt." He also announced that he was filing a lawsuit against the two media companies that had made the games Sutter played.

Think about it

1. Who is primarily responsible for the murder of Detective Lockman, Sutter or the video game manufacturers? Do both bear at least some responsibility?
2. What role, if any, did society play in Detective Lockman's death? Should government regulations control the content of video games?
3. What role did free will and individual choice play in Sutter's quick decision to take Lockman's gun and shoot him? How much control did Sutter have over his own behavior, and how much of his behavior was merely a response to experiences he had in the past?

Note: Who's to Blame boxes provide fictionalized critical thinking opportunities, and are not actual cases.

in people who, for example, value religious, ethical, or moral standards of conduct such as compassion, thoughtfulness, and courtesy. Bandura concluded that people who devalue aggression may still engage in it via a process he called *disengagement*. Disengagement may result from (1) "attributing blame to one's victims"; (2) dehumanization through bureaucratization, automation, urbanization, and high social mobility; (3) vindication of aggressive practices by legitimate authorities; and (4) desensitization resulting from repeated exposure to aggression in any of a variety of forms.

■ **correctional psychology** The branch of forensic psychology concerned with the diagnosis and classification of offenders, the treatment of correctional populations, and the rehabilitation of inmates and other law violators.

Policy and Treatment Implications of Psychological and Psychiatric Approaches

No discussion of social policy as it relates to the insights of criminal psychology would be complete without mention of correctional psychology. **Correctional psychology** is concerned with the diagnosis and classification of offenders, the treatment of correctional populations, and the rehabilitation of inmates and other law violators.

Various forms of psychological and psychiatric treatments for criminal offenders have been developed based on the theories discussed in this chapter. In 2006, John C. Norcross and colleagues used a panel of 101 experts to generally assess the effectiveness of differing psychological assessments and treatments.[93] Fifty-nine treatments and 30 assessment techniques were evaluated, with the experts scoring each on a scale of 1 (not at all discredited) to 5 (totally discredited). Discredited assessment measures included the Luscher Color Test, the Szondi Test, and the Lowenfeld Mosaic Test for personality assessment, along with handwriting analysis (graphology). Similarly, voice stress analysis for lie detection received a failing grade from the experts. Although it is beyond the scope of this chapter to discuss these and most other techniques in detail, the panel of experts found that the Myers-Briggs Type Indicator and the Rorschach inkblot test, along with some others, were useful assessment techniques.

The most successful techniques for psychological treatment were identified as behavior therapy for sex offenders, cognitive behavioral interventions (discussed later in this chapter), psychodrama, and laughter or humor therapy (for treatment of depression). The least successful treatment techniques included "fringe" methods, such as the use of pyramids for energy restoration, orgone therapy (use of an orgone energy accumulator), crystal healing, rebirthing, and past lives therapy.

Although there are many different psychological and psychiatric treatments available today, including psychotherapy, guide group interaction, behavioral modification, parent training, peer programs, and individual counseling, some of the most successful have aimed to change impulsivity and other offender personality characteristics. One of the most effective correctional techniques, as the Norcross study (mentioned previously) showed, is *cognitive behavioral intervention (CBI)*. CBI is based on the belief that offenders need to acquire better social skills in order to become more prosocial. Cognitive skill-building enables offenders to modify their cognitive processes to control themselves and interact positively with others. According to one source, "the goal of cognitive skills is to teach offenders to manage their own behavior by engaging in processes that develop self-control, making them responsible for and in charge of their actions no matter how stressful the situation. These specific skills include problem solving, social skills training (learned behaviors that enable one to interact with others in ways that elicit positive responses), anger management, and empathy training."[94]

CBI programs not only target the offender's environment, behavioral responses, and skill development, they also seek to increase the offender's reasoning skills and problem-solving abilities, and expand the offender's empathy toward others.

CBI is based, in part, on the work of Stanton Samenow (discussed earlier in this chapter) and was first outlined in a six-part video series entitled *Commitment to Change* that Samenow created. The first three parts of the series emphasize the value of looking at one's own thinking and help to define and identify thinking errors. The next video addresses specific thinking errors that are crucial in problem solving, and the last part outlines various methods useful in overcoming thinking errors.

Finally, it should be noted that psychopathology has been regarded as notoriously resistant to treatment of any kind. One of the first comprehensive studies of treatments intended for psychopaths, conducted by the NATO Advanced Study Institute, concluded that "no demonstrably effective treatment has been found." However, a more recent survey by Frederich Losel, a psychology professor at the University of Nurnberg (Germany) found that only a small proportion of 500 English psychiatrists shared that viewpoint.[95] Losel concluded that effective treatment with psychopaths should involve behavior modification techniques, educational measures, involvement in therapeutic communities, and pharmacological agents.

Assessing Dangerousness

In 2011, the U.S. Supreme Court rejected the significance of the argument that violence in the media can lead to criminal behavior via imitation, saying that any such concerns were trumped by the free speech rights of video game manufacturers guaranteed under the First Amendment to the U.S. Constitution.[96] In the words of the Court, "This country has no tradition of specially restricting children's access to depictions of violence. And California's claim that 'interactive' video games present special problems, in that the player participates in the violent action on screen and determines its outcome, is unpersuasive."

If, as the Court says, violent media content is protected by the Constitution, the same is not true of violent behavior. Consequently, those who violate the law can be apprehended

■ **selective incapacitation** A social policy that seeks to protect society by incarcerating those individuals deemed to be the most dangerous.

and punished, and those who persist in law violation can be effectively removed from society. **Selective incapacitation**, although it is not a crime-prevention policy developed by psychologists, is based on the notion of career criminality and predicated upon the use of psychological techniques to effectively identify likely future offenders and those who are likely to reoffend.[97] Career criminals, also called "habitual offenders," are people who repeatedly violate the criminal law. Research has shown that only a small percentage of all offenders account for most of the crimes reported to the police. Some studies have found that as few as 8% of all offenders commit as many as 60% serious crimes each year.[98]

A recent Wisconsin study found that imprisonment of individuals determined to be career offenders saved the state approximately $14,000 per year per offender when the cost of imprisonment was compared with the estimated cost of new crimes.[99] Researchers in the Wisconsin study concluded that "prison pays" and suggested that the state continue pursuing a policy of aggressive imprisonment of career offenders, even in the face of escalating costs and vastly overcrowded prisons. The strategy of selective incapacitation, however, depends on accurately identifying potentially dangerous offenders in existing criminal populations. Consequently, in recent years, a central focus of correctional psychologists has been on the development of a number of empirically based risk assessment and classification tools. Such tools have gone through four generations of development, as follows:[100]

- First generation: For most of the twentieth century, professional judgment or intuition was the most common method used to predict criminal behavior. Clinical professionals and correctional psychologists were guided by their own training and experiences, and the lessons they learned were often anecdotal.
- Second generation: Beginning in the 1970s, the assessment of risk began to depend more upon actuarial, evidence-based science and less on professional judgment and intuition. Second-generation risk assessments are often referred to as actuarial risk assessments, and consider individual indicators (e.g., a history of substance abuse) that have been demonstrated to increase the risk of reoffending and assign these items quantitative scores.
- Third generation: In the early 1980s, risk-assessment instruments began to take into consideration dynamic risk factors and are commonly referred to as risk-need assessments. Third-generation instruments combine the static predictor variables of the second-generation instruments with measured changes in an offender's circumstances.
- Fourth generation: Beginning in the early 2000s, fourth-generation risk-assessment instruments began to assess a broader range of risk factors along with what are referred to as "responsivity factors," which many regard as important to treatment. Responsivity factors include reading and cognitive abilities, race, gender, and motivation to change, as well as external factors such as treatment setting and counselor characteristics.

Two of the most commonly used classification instruments in correctional facilities today are the Level of Service Inventory-Revised (LSI-R) and Correctional Offender Management Profiling for Alternative Sanctions (COMPAS). The LSI-R scores offenders as low, moderate, or high risk based on 54 items about the offender that are categorized into ten sublevels: criminal history, education/employment, financial situation, family/marital relationships, accommodation, leisure and recreation, companions, alcohol or drug use, emotional/mental health, and attitudes and orientation.[101] A 2007 study of Iowa offenders showed "that the total LSI-R score is significantly related to the prediction of future criminal behavior."[102] The higher the total risk score, the study showed, the more likely that the client would reoffend.

COMPAS is a risk-assessment tool that was created to measure risks in adult correctional populations in order to provide information to aid in decision making with regard to placement of offenders in the community.[103] COMPAS provides an Overall Risk Potential, which is a composite score of individual risk estimates for violence, recidivism, failure to appear, and community failure as measured by the instrument. Evaluation studies of both LSI-R and COMPAS vary, and have produced mixed results—especially with nonwhite or female populations.[104] Studies, however, reveal support for previous empirical evidence that criminal history is strongly related to future offending.

Two other important risk-assessment models used in corrections are the risk-need-responsivity (RNR) model and the Good Lives Model (GLM).[105] The RNR model works to match the intensity of treatment interventions to assessed risk levels, and "specifically target(s) criminogenic needs" while tailoring "treatment to the personal and interpersonal needs and capacities of participants."[106] The risk principle of the RNR model holds that the intensity of correctional interventions must match the level of risk represented by the offender. The needs aspect asks that treatment programs target an offender's problems that lead the individual into crime. The responsivity principle requires treatment providers to examine offender idiosyncrasies in designing interventions and treatment plans, and says that treatment must be presented in a style and mode that is responsive to the offender's learning style and abilities.[107]

Critics of the RNR model say that it focuses mostly on the negative features of an offender, and that it does not motivate offenders to participate in their own treatment. Advocates of the alternative GLM model claim that, in contrast, it regards offenders as "whole beings in need of focus in many principal life areas" (including family, employment, leisure, community, and personal well-being).[108] Under the GLM model, offenders "are regarded as active, goal-seeking beings who seek to acquire fundamental primary human goods" (actions, experiences, and activities) "that are intrinsically beneficial to their individual well-being."[109] Consequently, GLM advocates say that the model is focused on "positive, strength-based" features in an offender's life and personality.[110]

Of course past criminal records may also provide a guide to future criminal offending, at least in some cases. For that reason, the federal 1984 Comprehensive Crime Control Act,[111] which established the U.S. Sentencing Commission, targeted career offenders. Guidelines created by the commission contain, as a central feature, a "criminal history" dimension, which substantially increases the amount of punishment an offender faces based on his or her history of law violations. The sentencing guidelines originally classified a defendant as a career offender if "(1) the defendant was at least 18 years old at the time of the . . . offense, (2) the . . . offense is a crime of violence or trafficking in a controlled substance, and (3) the defendant has at least two prior felony convictions of either a crime of violence or a controlled substance offense."[112] The definition, however, later came under fire for casting individuals with a history of minor drug trafficking into the same category as serial killers and the like.

> Dangerousness is not an objective quality like obesity or brown eyes; rather, it is an ascribed quality like trustworthiness.

Definitions of dangerousness are fraught with difficulty because, as some have pointed out, "dangerousness is not an objective quality like obesity or brown eyes, rather it is an ascribed quality like trustworthiness."[113] Dangerousness is not necessarily a personality trait that is stable or easily identifiable. Even if it were, some studies of criminal careers seem to show that involvement in crime decreases with age.[114]

Nonetheless, *assessing dangerousness* is a central issue in criminology, and is especially true of psychological approaches to criminality.[115] Consequently, those who score high on dimensions meant to measure dangerousness are often committed to mental or forensic hospitals or other controlled facilities, even in the absence of overt criminal behavior.

One decade-long study of violence risk factors among people with mental disorder is the MacArthur Violence Risk Assessment Study.[116] The MacArthur study examined psychiatric patients who had been released from hospitals, and evaluated 134 risk factors that study authors had previously identified as possible indicators of later violence. Although a total of 70 factors were found to have a relationship to later violence, a few stood out as especially important during the first 20 weeks following hospitalization. They included:

- **Psychopathy.** Psychopathy, as measured by the Hare Psychopathy Checklist, was more strongly associated with violence than any other risk factor studied.
- **Prior violence.** All measures of prior violence—self-report, arrest records, and hospital records—were strongly related to future violence.
- **Violent thoughts.** Thinking or daydreaming about harming others was associated with later violence, particularly if the thoughts or daydreams were persistent.
- **Anger.** The higher a patient scored on a proprietary anger scale in the hospital, the more likely he or she was to be violent later in the community.
- **Childhood experiences.** The seriousness and frequency of having been physically abused as a child predicted subsequent violent behavior, as did having a parent—particularly a father—who was a substance abuser or a criminal.
- **Diagnosis.** A diagnosis of a major mental disorder—especially a diagnosis of a personality or adjustment disorder—was strongly predictive of violence if it co-occurred with a diagnosis of substance abuse.
- **Suspiciousness:** A generally "suspicious" attitude toward others was found to be related to later violence.

Risk factors that bore no special relationship to later violence included:

- **Delusions.** The presence of delusions—or the type of delusions or the content of delusions—was not associated with violence.
- **Hallucinations.** Hallucinations in general did not elevate the risk of violence. If voices specifically commanded a violent act, however, the likelihood of violence was increased.
- **Diagnosis of schizophrenia.** A diagnosis of schizophrenia was associated with a lower rate of violence than a diagnosis of a personality disorder.

Similarly, the MacArthur study found little relationship between neighborhood, race, or gender and violent behavior following release.

Predicting Criminality

In terms of assessment, it is one thing to be able to identify offenders after they have already violated the law; but it is another to predict beforehand which individuals are likely to offend so that they can be prevented from harming others. One recent study found a strong relationship between childhood behavioral difficulties and later problem behavior.[117] According to the authors of the study, "Early antisocial behavior is the best predictor of later antisocial behavior. It appears that this rule holds even when the antisocial behavior is measured as early as the preschool period." Prediction, however, requires more than generalities. It is one thing to say, for example, that generally speaking, 70% of children who evidence aggressive behavior will show violent tendencies later in life and quite another to be able to predict which individuals will engage in future violations of the criminal law.

A few years ago, psychologists were able to demonstrate a clear relationship between a constellation of personality factors termed "hyperactivity-impulsivity-attention-deficit" (HIA) and offending. Studies found that the future delinquency of children who were characterized by HIA disorder at ages eight through ten could reliably be predicted.[118]

Critique of Psychological and Psychiatric Theories of Crime

Critics say that by focusing on the individual, psychological and psychiatric theories of criminality do not sufficiently take into account social or environmental conditions that produce crime. In fact, if social conditions are the primary cause of crime, as some claim, then individual change brought about by psychological or psychiatric interventions will not necessarily reduce levels of criminal offenses or lower rates of crime.

Similarly, psychological and psychiatric theories place the locus of control within the individual by positing a sense of moral reasoning. However, effective social control may actually stem from within social and physical arrangements that comprise the environment in which the individual functions. In other words, physical and social barriers to crime (such as the presence of a police officer) may be more effective at preventing crime than the sense of right or wrong that psychological theories find so important.

Freudian theory, discussed earlier, has been criticized on several levels. The first and most fundamental criticism of this perspective is its lack of scientific support. Critics point out that Freud's theories are not based on research and that there is no substantial support for his concepts. As such, Freudian theory has been seen as less of a scientific explanation for human behavior based on sound methodology and more of a belief system, valuable as a tool for literary and philosophical interpretation.[119]

Moreover, some claim that psychiatric theories, as distinguished from psychological ones, are appropriate only for explanations of abnormal cognition and do not apply well to otherwise normal people who turn to crime. In fact, some criminologists point to the fact that criminological predicators such as offense history are more accurate in forecasting future offenses than are psychological assessments and diagnosis, even among individuals characterized as mentally disordered.[120]

Freudian theory was very popular during the middle part of the twentieth century. By the 1980s, however, the notions of ego and id were considered antiquated by most psychiatrists. Attention shifted to the study of chemical imbalances in the brain, and psychopharmacology, or the use of drugs to treat psychiatric symptoms and disorders, has supplemented—if not replaced—the earlier ideas of Freud and his followers. Recently, however, the field of psychiatry has seen a rekindling of interest in Freudian psychology. The reason, according to some contemporary thinkers, is that psychopharmacology has been unable to provide an alternative grand theory of personality, emotion, and motivation.[121] Moreover, today's neuroscientists are busily creating a chemical map of the mind that seems to validate the general sketch that Freud provided decades ago. As noted earlier, it is possible that soon a new and unified perspective that reconciles the work of neurologists and psychiatrists may emerge.

Behavior theory has been criticized for ignoring the role that cognition plays in human behavior. Martyrs, for example, persist in what may be defined by the wider society as undesirable behavior, even in the face of severe punishment—including the loss of their own lives. Rewards and punishments as controls over human behavior seem to lose any explanatory power because even the most severe punishment is unlikely to deter a martyr who answers to some higher call. Similarly, criminals who are punished for official law violations may find that their immediate social group interprets criminal punishment as status-enhancing—meaning that punishment actually becomes a reward.

Modeling theory, a more sophisticated form of cognitive theory, has been criticized for lacking comprehensive explanatory power. How, for example, can striking differences in sibling behavior, when early childhood experiences were likely much the same, be explained? Similarly, why do apparent differences exist between the sexes with regard to degree and type of criminality, irrespective of social background and early learning experiences?

Modeling theory, a form of social learning theory, asserts that people learn how to act by observing others.

More recent versions of modeling theory, sometimes called "cognitive social learning theory,"[122] attempt to account for such differences by hypothesizing that reflection and cognition

■ **psychological profiling** The attempt to categorize, understand, and predict the behavior of certain types of offenders based on behavioral clues they provide; also called *criminal profiling* and *behavioral profiling*.

play a significant role in interpreting what one observes and in determining responses. Hence, few people are likely to behave precisely as others do because they will have their own ideas about what observed behavior means and about the consequences of imitation.

Criminal Psychological Profiling

During World War II, the U.S. War Department recruited psychologists and psychiatrists in an attempt to predict the future moves that enemy forces might make. In addition, psychological and psychoanalytic techniques were applied to the study of German leader Adolf Hitler, Italian leader Benito Mussolini, Japanese general and prime minister Hideki Tojo, and other Axis leaders. Such psychological profiling of enemy leaders may have given the Allies the edge in battlefield strategy.

After the war ended, little work was done in the field until the 1970s when Federal Bureau of Investigation (FBI) special agent Howard Teten and others began to apply psychological profiling techniques to violent criminal behavior. In July, 1984, the Bureau opened the National Center for the Analysis of Violent Crime (NCAVC) on the grounds of the FBI National Academy in Quantico, Virginia. One division within the NCAVC, the Behavioral Sciences Unit (later renamed the Behavioral Analysis Unit), began to look for unique psychological patterns in the behavior of serial rapists and killers and launched the practice of routinely profiling high-interest criminal offenders.

Today, **psychological profiling** (also called *criminal profiling* and *behavioral profiling*) is used to assist police investigators seeking to better understand individuals wanted for serious offenses. Psychological profiling is built on the idea that behavioral clues left behind at a crime scene may reflect the personality of the offender.

During an interview, famed profiler John Douglas, the retired FBI special agent who became the model for the Scott Glenn character in Thomas Harris's *Silence of the Lambs*, described criminal profiling: "It is a behavioral composite put together of the unknown subject after analyzing the crime scene materials, to include the autopsy protocol, autopsy and crime scene photographs, as well as the preliminary police reports. It is also a detailed analysis of the victim and putting that information together. To me, it's very much like an internist in medicine who now attempts to put a diagnosis, say, on an illness; I'm trying to put a diagnosis on this particular case that's relative to motive, as well as the type of person(s) who would perpetrate that type of crime."[123]

Profilers develop a list of typical offender characteristics and other useful principles by analyzing crime-scene and autopsy data, in conjunction with interviews and studies of past offenders, in the belief that almost any form of conscious behavior (including behavior the offender engaged in during a criminal episode) is symptomatic of the individual's personality. The way a kidnapper approaches victims, the type of attack used by a killer, and the specific sexual activities of a rapist—all of these might help paint a picture of the offender's motivations, personal characteristics, and likely future behavior. Sometimes psychological profiles can provide clues as to what an offender might do following an attack: Some offenders have been arrested after returning to the crime scene, a behavior typically predicted by specific behavioral clues left behind, and a remorseful type can be expected to visit the victiM's grave, permitting fruitful stakeouts of a cemetery.

Although criminal profiling may not be useful in every case, it can help narrow the search for an offender in repetitive crimes involving one offender, such as serial rape or murder. Knowledge gleaned from profiling can also help in the interrogation of suspects and can be used to identify and protect possible victims before the offender has a chance to strike again.

Criminal profiling techniques have also been used in hostage negotiation, where law enforcement officers need to know as much as possible about the hostage taker, and in the analysis of anonymous communications—especially when those communications contain threats of violence. To analyze such communications, profilers have developed a "threat dictionary," in which words contained in the message are weighted and compared to standard speech patterns.[124] An analysis of the communications may indicate the educational level, gender, financial standing, and the social group to which the writer belongs. Similarly, "signature" words or phrases that appear unique to the writer may help to identify him or her.

Profilers have also contributed significantly to the criminological literature. In a well-known study of lust murderers (men who kill and often mutilate victims during or following a forced sexual episode), FBI Special Agents Robert R. Hazelwood and John E. Douglas distinguished between the organized nonsocial and the disorganized asocial types.[125] The organized nonsocial lust murderer exhibits complete indifference to the interests of society and is completely self-centered, methodical, cunning, and "fully cognizant of the criminality of his act and its impact on society."[126] The disorganized asocial lust murderer was described this way: "[He] exhibits primary characteristics of societal aversion. This individual prefers his own company to that of others and would be typified as a loner. He experiences difficulty in negotiating interpersonal relationships and consequently feels rejected and lonely. He lacks the cunning of the nonsocial type and commits the crime in a more frenzied and less methodical

■ **insanity (legal)** A legally established inability to understand right from wrong or to conform one's behavior to the requirements of the law.

Photo by Orion Pictures Corporation/ZUMA Press. © Copyright 1991 by Orion Pictures Corporation

Scott Glenn, starring as Jack Crawford in the crime thriller *Silence of the Lambs*, which publicized the practice of criminal profiling. How can psychological profiling assist criminal investigations?

manner. The crime is likely to be committed in close proximity to his residence or place of employment, where he feels secure and more at ease."[127]

Critics of psychological profiling say that it is still more art than science. In a recent article published on the American Psychological Association's website, for example, psychologist Lea Winerman says that psychological profiling "is still a relatively new field with few set boundaries or definitions. Its practitioners don't always agree on methodology or even terminology."[128] Moreover, many early FBI profilers were not psychologists, and the techniques they developed were not necessarily based on accepted psychological perspectives or accepted methodology.

Terms like *offender profiling* and *crime-action profiling* are used today to describe the work of profilers. Today's profilers tend to analyze crime-scene data and offender interviews, searching for commonalities that can be used to distinguish between types of offenders. Another term commonly used today is *investigative psychology*, which can be defined as "the scientific discipline of applying, analyzing, or developing psychological principles, theories or empirical findings to aid investigations and the legal process."[129]

Some contemporary psychologists discount the value of profiling. In 2007, a metaanalysis of profiling studies found that "trained profilers did only slightly better than non-profilers at estimating the overall characteristics of offenders from information about their crimes."[130] The studies compared the ability of profilers with nonprofilers to gauge an offender's physical characteristics, thinking processes (including motives), and personal habits.[131] Nonetheless, profiling remains highly visible in today's media and continues to be popular with the public. Visit the Center for Investigative Psychology at the University of Liverpool at **Web Extra 6–4**, and learn more about the FBI's Behavioral Science Unit via **Web Extra 6–5.**

Insanity and the Law

Unfortunately for criminologists, psychological conceptions of mental illness, antisocial personality, and even psychopathy are not readily applicable to the criminal justice system, which relies instead on the legal concept of insanity.[132] **Insanity**, for purposes of the criminal law, is strictly a legal, not a clinical, determination. Seen this way, insanity is a term that refers to a type of defense allowable in criminal courts. Although the legal concept of insanity is based upon claims of mental illness, it has no precise counterpart in the jargon of contemporary psychologists or psychiatrists, who speak instead in terms of mental status or, at most, psychosis and personality disorder. As a consequence, legal and psychiatric understandings of mental impairment rarely coincide.

The legal concept of insanity has no precise counterpart in the jargon of psychologists.

One of the first instances within the Western legal tradition where insanity was accepted as a defense to criminal liability can be found in the case of Daniel M'Naughten (also spelled "McNaughton" and "M'Naghton"). M'Naughten was accused

■ **M'Naughten rule** A standard for judging legal insanity that requires that offenders did not know what they were doing, or if they did, that they did not know it was wrong.

■ **irresistible-impulse test** A standard for judging legal insanity that holds that a defendant is not guilty of a criminal offense if the person, by virtue of his or her mental state or psychological condition, was not able to resist committing the crime.

■ **guilty but mentally ill (GBMI)** A finding that offenders are guilty of the criminal offense with which they are charged, but because of their prevailing mental condition, they are generally sent to psychiatric hospitals for treatment rather than to prison. Once they have been declared cured, such offenders can be transferred to correctional facilities to serve out their sentences.

of the 1843 killing of Edward Drummond, the secretary of British prime minister Sir Robert Peel. By all accounts, M'Naughten had intended to kill Peel, but because M'Naughten was suffering from mental disorganization, he shot Drummond instead, mistaking him for Peel. At his trial, the defense presented information to show that M'Naughten was suffering from delusions, including the belief that Peel's political party was persecuting him. The court accepted his lawyer's claims, and the defense of insanity was established in Western law. Other jurisdictions were quick to adopt the M'Naughten rule, as the judge's decision in the case came to be called. The **M'Naughten rule** holds that individuals cannot be held criminally responsible for their actions if at the time of the offense (1) they did not know what they were doing or (2) they did not know that what they were doing was wrong.

Today, the M'Naughten rule is still followed by many states when insanity is at issue in criminal cases. Critics of the M'Naughten rule say that although the notion of intent inherent within it appeals greatly to lawyers, "it is . . . so alien to current concepts of human behavior that it has been vigorously attacked by psychiatrists. An obvious difficulty with the M'Naughten rule is that practically everyone, regardless of the degree of his [mental] disturbance, knows the nature and quality and rightness or wrongness of what he is doing."[133]

The M'Naughten ruling opened the floodgates for other types of insanity claims offered as defenses to charges of criminal activity. One interesting claim is that of irresistible impulse. The **irresistible-impulse test**—employed by 18 states, some of which also follow the dictates of the M'Naughten rule—holds that a defendant is not guilty of a criminal offense if the person, by virtue of his or her mental state or psychological condition, was not able to resist committing the action in question.

Jeffrey Markowitz/Sygma/Corbis

Insanity can be used as a defense against criminal charges. Lorena Bobbitt sobs on the witness stand before acquittal on charges she severed her husband's penis with a kitchen knife; Bobbitt claimed a kind of irresistible impulse. Should she have been acquitted?

Guilty But Mentally Ill (GBMI)

A verdict of **guilty but mentally ill (GBMI)** means that a person can be held responsible for a specific criminal act, even though a degree of mental incompetence may be present. In most GBMI jurisdictions, a jury must return a finding of "guilty but mentally ill" if (1) every statutory element necessary for a conviction has been proved beyond a reasonable doubt, (2) the defendant is found to have been mentally ill at the time the crime was committed, and (3) the defendant was not found to have been legally insane at the time the crime was committed. The difference between mental illness and legal insanity is crucial because a defendant can be mentally ill by standards of the medical profession but sane for purposes of the law.

Upon return of a GBMI verdict, a judge may impose any sentence possible under the law for the crime in question.

Several states permit findings of guilty but mentally ill (GBMI).

Offenders who are declared GBMI are, in effect, found guilty of the criminal offense with which they are charged but, because of their mental condition, are generally sent to psychiatric hospitals for treatment rather than to prison. Once they have been declared "cured," however, such offenders can be transferred to correctional facilities to serve out their sentences.

CRIMINAL | PROFILES

Andrea Yates

David J. Phillip/AP Wide World Photos

Andrea Yates (center), who admitted drowning her five children in a bathtub at the family home, leaving the Harris County (Texas) Criminal Justice Center with her attorney, Yates was sent to a maximum-security mental hospital where she will be held until she is cured. What do you think should have been done with Yates?

Few crimes have shocked American society as deeply as the drowning of five young children by their mother, Andrea Pia (Kennedy) Yates, in a bathtub in their suburban Houston, Texas, home on June 20, 2001. Her subsequent trial, conviction, life sentence, successful appeal, and second trial brought under intense scrutiny the insanity defense based on a claim of postpartum psychosis.

Yates's early life showed promise for future success. High school valedictorian and swim team captain, she went on to earn an undergraduate degree in nursing from the University of Texas. After obtaining a job as a registered nurse, she met Rusty Yates. Their shared deep Christian faith was a significant factor in their attraction to each other.

When Andrea and Rusty finally married, they planned on having as many children as God intended. The birth of their first child, Noah, a year after their marriage, however, brought unexpected difficulties.

Unaware of the extent of mental illness that had plagued her own family, the new mother was tormented when she began to have violent visions of stabbings and came to believe that Satan was speaking directly to her. Yates hid these frightening experiences from everyone, including her husband. The Yates's had two more children, after which Andrea miscarried. She then had their fourth child, but the birth was followed by pronounced depressive manifestations—including chewed fingers, uncontrollable shaking, hallucinations, voices in her head, suicidal and homicidal thoughts, and two suicide attempts. Soon she entered into a series of psychiatric counseling sessions with various doctors. A wide variety of drug therapies were tried, many of which Andrea rejected by flushing the prescriptions down the toilet.

Despite extensive hospitalizations and medication for her ongoing depression and emerging psychosis—and against the advice of her psychiatrist—Yates became pregnant again, delivering her fifth child, Mary, in November 2000. The pregnancy had resulted from the urging of her husband, who also ignored the strong medical opposition to the birth of another child.[i]

When Yates's father died just four and a half months after her fifth child was born, her mental health declined dramatically.[ii] Both a hospitalization at the end of March and her medication, however, were terminated by her psychiatrist, Dr. Mohammed Saeed, because, he claimed, she did not seem psychotic. Yates returned to the hospital again for ten days in May. Upon her release, she was advised to think positive thoughts and to see a psychologist.

Two days later, she systematically drowned each of her five children.

Following a sensational trial, Yates was convicted and sentenced to life in prison. That conviction was subsequently overturned. In July 2006, Yates was retried, but this time she was acquitted of capital murder charges and found not guilty by reason of insanity. She was immediately ordered to be committed to a mental hospital, where she will remain until she is no longer considered a threat to herself or others.[iii] Today, Yates is held at the Kerrville State Hospital, located 70 miles south of San Antonio. She has been diagnosed with bipolar disorder, and is medicated by daily injection.[iv]

The case of Andrea Yates raises a number of interesting questions. Among them are the following:

1. Could Yates be considered a psychopath? Why or why not?
2. How could Yates's mental issues be seen in light of the theories presented in this chapter?
3. Could the irresistible-impulse test be applicable to Yates's case? The M'Naughten rule? Which seems to fit best?

Notes

i. Charles Montaldo, "Profile of Andrea Yates," About.com: Crime/Punishment, 2007, http://crime.about.com/od/current/p/andreayates.htm (accessed June 16, 2010).
ii. Ibid.
iii. "Jury: Yates Not Guilty by Reason of Insanity," July 26, 2006, MSNBC/Associated Press, http://www.msnbc.msn.com/id/14024728 (accessed June 16, 2007).
iv. Andrew Cohen, "How Andrea Yates Lives, and Lives with Herself, A Decade Later," *The Atlantic*, March 12, 2012, http://www.theatlantic.com/national/archive/2012/03/how-andrea-yates-lives-and-lives-with-herself-a-decade-later/254302 (accessed July 3, 2013).

Problems with the Insanity Defense

Although insanity defenses are popular in courtroom fiction, they are rarely used in the real world. When they are raised, they must be brought before the court and proven by the defense. Studies show that fewer than 1% of all criminal defendants adopt an insanity defense.[134] Even when employed, the defense rarely works, and 75% of those who claim insanity are convicted anyway.[135] And if a defendant is found "not guilty by reason of insanity," he or she is likely to spend a long time in court-ordered institutional psychiatric treatment. Only 15% are immediately set free.[136]

Finally, some critics ask whether the idea of mental illness, or the legal concept of insanity, is even useful in the study of criminology. Confusion, they charge, arises when considering whether mental illness should be seen as a cause, an explanation, or an excuse for criminal behavior.[137]

SUMMARY

- Psychological and psychiatric theories of criminal behavior emphasize individual propensities and characteristics in explaining criminality. Whether the emphasis is on conditioned behavior, human cognition, or the psychoanalytic structure of the human personality, these approaches see the wellsprings of human motivation, desire, and behavioral choice as being firmly rooted in the individual.
- Two major ideas characterized early psychological theories: personality and behaviorism. Personality theory built on the burgeoning area of cognitive science, including personality disturbances and diseases of the mind; behaviorism examined social learning with an emphasis on behavioral conditioning.
- Some early psychologists adapted the disease model, which had worked so well in the field of medicine, in an effort to cure mental and emotional problems. Hence, early psychological perspectives were couched in terms of mental disease, personality disorder, and psychopathy.
- The psychopathic personality, one that is cunning and self-serving but without empathy, offers an explanation for personality found in the unrestrained desires of offenders. The antisocial personality, in contrast, is essentially unsocialized and generally in conflict with society.
- Cognitive theories are learning theories that examine thought processes, and seek to explain how people learn to solve problems and how they perceive and interpret their social environment. Cognitive theory has a number of branches, including one that focuses on moral and intellectual development, and another that examines how people process information.
- Psychiatric criminology, or forensic psychiatry, sees crime as caused by biological and subconscious psychological urges mediated through consciousness. From the point of view of psychoanalysis, criminal behavior is maladaptive, the product of inadequacies in the offender's personality. The psychoanalytic perspective, advanced by Sigmund Freud in the early 1900s, encompasses diverse notions such as personality, neurosis, and psychosis as well as transference, sublimation, and repression.
- Frustration–aggression theory holds that frustration can lead to various forms of behavior—including regression, sublimation, and aggressive fantasy—but that direct aggression toward others is its most likely consequence. Because everyone suffers frustration at times in life, aggression is a natural consequence of living. Aggression, however, can be manifested in socially acceptable ways and/or engaged in vicariously by observing others who are acting violently; but it can also manifest as criminality.
- Some psychiatric perspectives see criminality as a form of adaptive behavior to stresses, holding that law violation represents an individual's most satisfactory method of adjustment to inner conflicts that he or she cannot otherwise express.
- Criminogenic needs are dynamic attributes of offenders and their circumstances that are associated with rates of recidivism. Criminogenic needs can be targeted by treatment strategies intended to reduce criminality and recidivism.
- Attachment theory says that the successful development of secure attachment between a child and his or her primary caregiver, believed to form early in childhood, provides the basic foundation for all future psychological development and that delinquent behavior arises whenever non-secure attachments are created. Three forms of attachment are secure attachment, anxious-avoidant attachment, and anxious-resistant attachment.
- Behavior theory (or the stimulus–response approach to human behavior) holds that behavior is directly determined by the environmental consequences it produces for the individual exhibiting the behavior. When an individual's behavior results in rewards or positive feedback, that behavior will increase in frequency; when punishment follows behavior, that behavior will decrease.

- Social cognition theory says that aggressive patterns of behavior are acquired through the learning process and that, once acquired, can be activated when a person's hopes and desires are blocked.
- Some theorists now consider that psychological criminology can be used for the development of consistent and dependable social policy in the prediction of dangerousness, the treatment and rehabilitation of offenders, and selective incapacitation as a workable policy to prevent future criminality.
- Psychological profiling of criminal offenders, based on the belief that almost any form of conscious behavior is symptomatic of the individual's personality, is a serious crime-fighting undertaking that may change the nature of localized crime-prevention strategies.
- Psychological and psychiatric conceptions of mental illness, antisocial personality, and even psychopathy are not readily applicable to the criminal justice system, which relies instead on the legal concept of insanity. Although the legal concept of insanity is based upon claims of mental illness, it has no precise counterpart in the jargon of contemporary psychologists or psychiatrists.

KEY TERMS

alloplastic adaptation, 136
antisocial personality, 128
antisocial personality disorder (ASPD), 128
attachment theory, 137
autoplastic adaptation, 136
behavior theory, 139
behaviorism, 125
cognitive information-processing theory (CIP), 131
conditioning, 125
correctional psychology, 142
criminal psychology, 124
criminogenic needs, 137
ego, 133
electroencephalogram (EEG), 128
Five Factor Model, 129
forensic psychiatry, 125
forensic psychology, 124
guilty but mentally ill (GBMI), 148
id, 133
insanity (legal), 147
irresistible-impulse test, 148
M'Naughten rule, 148
modeling, 140
moral development theory, 130
neurosis, 133
operant behavior, 139
paranoid schizophrenic, 135
personality, 125
psychiatric criminology, 133
psychoanalysis, 133
psychoanalytic theory, 125
psychological profiling, 146
psychopath, 126
psychopathy, 125
psychosis, 133
psychotherapy, 133
punishment, 139
repression, 134
reward, 139
risk assessment, 135
schizophrenia, 125
scripts, 131
selective incapacitation, 143
social cognition theory, 140
sociopath, 126
sublimation, 133
superego, 134
traits, 128

KEY NAMES

Robert P. Abelson, 131
August Aichorn, 134
Donald A. Andrews, 137
Albert Bandura, 135
James Bonta, 137
John Bowlby, 137
Hervey M. Cleckley, 126
J. Dollard, 135
Hans J. Eysenck, 128
Sigmund Freud, 133
Seymour L. Halleck, 136
Lawrence Kohlberg, 130
Jean Piaget, 130
Stanton E. Samenow, 132
Roger C. Schank, 131
B. F. Skinner, 139
Gabriel Tarde, 140
Richard H. Walters, 135
Samuel Yochelson, 132

QUESTIONS FOR REVIEW

1. What are the major principles of psychological perspectives on criminal behavior?
2. What were some early psychological and psychiatric theories offered to explain criminality?
3. How does personality explain criminality?
4. What is moral development theory, and how does it explain crime?
5. What insights into criminal behavior does the psychoanalytic perspective offer?
6. What role does frustration play in influencing aggression, according to psychological theories?
7. How can criminality be seen as a form of adaptive behavior?
8. How does attachment theory explain behavior, and what are the three forms of attachment?
9. How does behavior theory explain the role of rewards and punishments in shaping behavior?
10. How does social cognition theory explain how aggressive patterns of behavior, once acquired, can be activated?
11. What types of crime-control policies might be based on psychological understandings of criminality?

QUESTIONS FOR REFLECTION

1. This book emphasizes the theme of social problems versus social responsibility. Which perspective is better supported by psychological theories of crime causation? Why?
2. How do psychological theories of criminal behavior differ from other types of theories presented in this book? How do the various psychological and psychiatric approaches presented in this chapter differ from one another?
3. How would the perspectives discussed in this chapter suggest that offenders might be prevented from committing additional offenses? How might they be rehabilitated?
4. How can crime be a form of adaptation to one's environment? Why would an individual choose such a form of adaptation over others that might be available?
5. Which of the various standards for judging legal insanity discussed in this chapter do you find the most useful? Why?

P.J Image Group/Alamy

CHAPTER 7
SOCIAL STRUCTURE THEORIES

LEARNING OUTCOMES

After reading this chapter, you should be able to answer the following questions:

- What is the nature of sociological theorizing, and what are the assumptions upon which sociological perspectives on crime causation rest?
- What do sociologists mean by the term *social structure*, and how might the organization and structure of a society contribute to criminality?
- What three key sociological explanations for crime are discussed in this chapter, and what are the characteristics of each?
- What are the policy implications of the theories discussed in this chapter?
- What are the shortcomings of the social structure approaches to understanding and preventing crime?

■ **Follow the author's tweets about the latest crime and justice news @schmalleger.**

■ **sociological theory** A perspective that focuses on the nature of the power relationships that exist between social groups and on the influences that various social phenomena bring to bear on the types of behaviors that tend to characterize groups of people.

■ **social structure** The pattern of social organization and the interrelationships among institutions characteristic of a society.

Introduction

There's an old saying, something to the effect that you can take the criminal out of a bad environment, but you can't take the bad environment out of the criminal. Although we don't necessarily believe this to be true, some suggest that the negative influences of the social environment—especially things like poverty, lack of education, broken families, disorganized neighborhoods, episodes of discrimination, and socialization into unproductive values—predispose certain people to lives of crime and that such negative influences may remain active even when people's circumstances change. Central to this perspective is the idea that crime is a social phenomenon, and central to any understanding of crime is the role that society, social institutions, and social processes play in its development and control.

Cutting California's dropout rate in half would prevent 30,000 juvenile crimes and save $900 million yearly in enforcement costs.

A homeless man asks for assistance. Ecological theories suggest that crime shows an unequal geographic distribution. Why might certain geographic areas be associated with identifiable patterns of crime?

Major Principles of Sociological Theories

Theories that explain crime by reference to social structure are only one of three major sociological approaches to crime causation. The other two are social process theories and social conflict approaches (which we describe in Chapters 8 and 9). Although sociological perspectives on crime causation are diverse, most build upon the principles shown in Figure 7–1.

Sociological theories examine both institutional arrangements within a **social structure** (i.e., interrelationships among

Major Principles of Sociological Theories of Crime

- Social groups, social institutions, the arrangements of society, and social roles all provide the proper focus for criminological study.
- Group dynamics, group organization, and subgroup relationships form the causal nexus out of which crimes develop.
- The structure of society and its relative degree of organization or disorganization are important factors contributing to criminal behavior.
- Although it may be impossible to predict the specific behavior of a given individual, statistical estimates of group characteristics are possible. Hence, the probability that members of a certain group will engage in a specific type of crime can be estimated.

FIGURE 7–1 | **Major Principles of Sociological Theories of Crime**

Source: Schmalleger, Frank J., *Criminology*. Printed and Electronically reproduced by permission of Pearson Education, Inc., Upper Saddle River, New Jersey.

■ **social process** The interaction between and among social institutions, groups, and individuals.
■ **social life** The ongoing (typically) structured interaction—including socialization and social behavior in general—that occurs between persons in a society.
■ **social structure theory** A theory that explains crime by reference to the economic and social arrangements in society. This type of theory emphasizes relationships among social institutions and describes the types of behavior that tend to characterize groups of people rather than individuals.

society's institutions) and **social processes** (i.e., interactions between and among different social institutions, groups, and individuals) as they affect socialization and have an impact on **social life** (i.e., social interaction). In contrast to more individualized psychological theories, which have what is called a "micro" focus, sociological approaches utilize a "macro" perspective, stressing the type of behavior likely to be exhibited by group members rather than attempting to predict the behavior of specific individuals. As noted in Chapter 1, sociological thought has influenced criminological theory construction more significantly than any other perspective during the past half century, due (at least in part) to a widespread concern with social problems including civil rights, the women's movement, issues of poverty, and the decline in influence experienced by many traditional social institutions, such as the family, government, organized religion, and educational systems.

Although all sociological perspectives on crime share some characteristics, particular theories give greater or lesser weight to selected components of social life. We can identify three key sociological explanations for crime:

1. **Crime is the result of an individual's location within the structure of society.** This approach focuses on the social and economic conditions of life, including poverty, alienation, social disorganization, weak social control, personal frustration, relative deprivation, differential opportunities, alternative means to success, and deviant subcultures and subcultural values that conflict with conventional values. (These are the primary features of *social structure theories*, which are discussed in this chapter and in Chapter 10 in the section "Structural Explanations for Homicide.")
2. **Crime is the end product of various social processes.** This approach stresses inappropriate socialization and social learning as well as interpersonal relationships, strength of the social bond, lack of self-control, and personal and group consequences of societal reactions to deviance as they contribute to crime. (These are the primary characteristics of *social process theories* and *social development theories*, which are discussed in Chapter 8, and in Chapter 10 where the subculture of violence thesis is described.)
3. **Crime is the product of class struggle.** This perspective emphasizes existing power relationships between social groups, distribution of wealth within society, ownership of the means of production, and economic and social structures of society as they relate to social class and social control. (These are the primary features of *social conflict theories*, which are discussed in Chapter 9.)

Social Structure Theories

Social structure theories explain crime by reference to the economic and social arrangements (or structure) of society. They see the various formal and informal arrangements between social groups (that is, the structure of society) as the root causes of crime and deviance. Structural theories predict that negative aspects of societal structure, such as disorganization within the family, poverty or income inequality within the economic arrangements of society, and disadvantages due to lack of success in the educational process, produce criminal behavior.

Although different kinds of social structure theories have been advanced to explain crime, they all have one thing in common: They highlight those arrangements within society that contribute to the low socioeconomic status of identifiable groups as significant causes of crime. Social structure theorists view members of socially and economically disadvantaged groups as being more likely to commit crime, and they see economic and social disenfranchisement as fundamental causes of crime. Poverty, lack of education, absence of salable skills, and subcultural values conducive to crime are all thought to be predicated on the social conditions surrounding early life experiences, and they provide the causal underpinnings of social structure theories. Environmental influences, socialization, and traditional and accepted patterns of behavior are all used by social structuralists to portray the criminal as a product of his or her social environment, and the immediate social environment is viewed as a consequence of the structure of the society to which the offender belongs. Although criminality is recognized as a form of acquired behavior, it is depicted as the end result of social inequality, racism, and feelings of disenfranchisement to which existing societal arrangements give rise. Similarly, social structure, insofar as it is unfair and relatively unchangeable, is believed to perpetuate the fundamental conditions that cause crime. Consequently, viewed from a social

■ **social disorganization theory** A perspective on crime and deviance that sees society as a kind of organism and crime and deviance as a kind of disease, or social pathology. This type of theory is often associated with the perspective of social ecology and with the Chicago School of criminology, which developed during the 1920s and 1930s.

THEORY | in PERSPECTIVE

Types of Social Structure Theories

Social structure theories emphasize poverty, lack of education, absence of marketable skills, and deviant subcultural values as fundamental causes of crime. These theories, which portray crime as the result of an individual's location within the structure of society and focus on the social and economic conditions of life, are divided into three types.

Social Disorganization

Depicts social change, social conflict, and the lack of social consensus as the root causes of crime and deviance; an offshoot, social ecology, sees society as a kind of organism and crime and deviance as a disease or social pathology.

Period: 1920s–1930s

Theorists: Robert Park, Ernest Burgess, W. I. Thomas, Florian Znaniecki, Clifford Shaw, Henry McKay

Concepts: Social ecology, ecological theories, social pathology, social disorganization, Chicago School, Chicago Area Project, demographics, concentric zones, delinquency areas, cultural transmission (Criminology of place, environmental criminology, defensible space, and the broken windows theory represent, at least in part, a contemporary reinterpretation of early ecological notions.)

Strain Theory

Points to a lack of fit between socially approved success goals and the availability of socially approved means to achieve those goals. As a consequence, according to the perspective of strain theory, individuals who are unable to succeed through legitimate means turn to other avenues (crime) that promise economic and social recognition.

Period: 1930s–present

Theorists: Robert K. Merton, Steven F. Messner, Richard Rosenfeld, Peter Blau and Judith Blau, Robert Agnew

Concepts: Anomie, goals, means, innovation, retreatism, ritualism, rebellion, differential opportunity, relative deprivation, distributive justice, general strain theory (GST)

Culture Conflict

Sees the root cause of crime in a clash of values between variously socialized groups over what is acceptable or proper behavior.

Period: 1920s–present

Theorists: Thorsten Sellin, Frederic M. Thrasher, William F. Whyte, Walter B. Miller, Gresham Sykes, David Matza, Franco Ferracuti, Marvin Wolfgang, Richard A. Cloward, Lloyd E. Ohlin, Albert Cohen, many others

Concepts: Subculture, violent subcultures, socialization, focal concerns, delinquency and drift, techniques of neutralization, illegitimate opportunity structures, reaction formation, conduct norms

structure perspective, crime is seen largely as a lower-class phenomenon, while the criminality of the middle and upper classes is generally discounted as less serious, less frequent, and less dangerous.

Types of Social Structure Theories

This chapter describes three major types of social structure theories: (1) social disorganization theory (also called the *ecological approach*), (2) strain theory, and (3) culture conflict theory (also called *cultural deviance theory*). All have a number of elements in common, and the classification of a theory into a subcategory is often a matter of which aspects a writer chooses to emphasize rather than any clear-cut definitional elements inherent in that theory (see the Theory in Perspective box in this chapter).

Social Disorganization Theory

Social disorganization theory (which depicts social change, social conflict, and lack of social consensus as the

■ **human ecology** The interrelationship between human beings and the physical and cultural environments in which they live.

■ **social disorganization** A condition said to exist when a group is faced with social change, uneven development of culture, maladaptiveness, disharmony, conflict, and lack of consensus.

■ **social ecology** An approach to criminological theorizing that attempts to link the structure and organization of a human community to interactions with its localized environment.

■ **social pathology** A concept that compares society to a physical organism and that sees criminality as an illness.

root causes of crime and deviance) is closely associated with the ecological school of criminology. Much early criminology in the United States was rooted in the study of urban settlements and communities[1] as well as the human ecology movement of the early twentieth century. *Ecology* is a term borrowed from biology that describes the interrelationships between living organisms and their environment, and social scientists use the term **human ecology** to describe the interrelationship between human beings and the physical and cultural environments in which they live.[2] Pioneers in the human ecology movement saw cities as "superorganisms" that incorporated areas adapted to specific groups, including ethnic groups (e.g., "Little Italy," "Chinatown"), which were functional enclaves within a larger organized whole that possessed its own dynamics.

The idea of the community as a functional whole that directly determines the quality of life for its members was developed and explored around the beginning of the twentieth century by sociologists such as Emile Durkheim (1858–1917),[3] Ferdinand Toennies (1855–1936),[4] and Georg Simmel (1858–1918).[5] Durkheim believed that crime was a normal part of all societies and that law was a symbol of social solidarity, so an act was "criminal when it offends strong and defined states of the collective conscience."[6]

Some of the earliest sociologists to study American communities were **W. I. Thomas** and **Florian Znaniecki**. In *The Polish Peasant in Europe and America*, Thomas and Znaniecki described the problems Polish immigrants faced in the early 1900s when they left their homeland and moved to American cities.[7] The authors noted that crime rates rose among displaced people and hypothesized that the cause was the **social disorganization** that resulted from immigrants' inability to successfully transplant guiding norms and values from their home cultures into the new one (see **Library Extra 7–1**). Learn more about early social disorganization perspectives via **Web Extra 7–1;** read more about classical sociological theory at **Web Extra 7–2**.

The Chicago School

Some of the earliest sociological theories to receive widespread recognition can be found in the writings of **Robert Park** and **Ernest Burgess**. In the 1920s and 1930s at the University of Chicago, they developed what became known as **social ecology**, or the ecological school of criminology.[8] The social ecology movement, influenced by the work of biologists on the interactions of organisms with their environments, concerned itself with how the structure of society adapts to the quality of natural resources and to the existence of other human groups.[9] One writer stated that social ecology is "the attempt to link the structure and organization of any human community to interactions with its localized environment."[10] Because ecological models build on an organic analogy, it is easy to portray social disorganization as a disease or pathology.[11] Hence, social ecologists who studied crime developed a disease model built around the concept of **social pathology**, defined as "those human actions which run contrary to the ideals of residential stability, property ownership, sobriety, thrift, habituation to work, small business enterprise, sexual discretion, family solidarity, neighborliness, and discipline of will."[12] Over time, the concept of social pathology changed and came to represent the idea that some aspects of society are pathological, or "sick," and produce deviant behavior among groups and individuals who are exposed to such social conditions.

> Some of the earliest sociological theories to receive widespread recognition were found in the Chicago School and focused on what became known as social ecology.

Social disorganization and social pathology may arise when a group is faced with "social change, uneven development of culture, maladaptiveness, disharmony, conflict, and lack of consensus."[13] Due to the rapid influx of immigrant populations at the beginning of the twentieth century, American cities were caught up in swift social change, and Park and Burgess saw in them an ideal focus for the study of social disorganization. They viewed cities as having five concentric zones, much like the circles on a target, each with unique characteristics and populations (see Figure 7–2): Zone I, or the "loop," contained retail businesses and light manufacturing; Zone II, surrounding the city center, was in transition from residential to business uses, was home to recent immigrant groups, and was characterized by deteriorating houses and factories and abandoned buildings; Zone III contained mostly working-class tenements; Zone IV was occupied by middle-class citizens with single-family homes; and Zone V, the suburbs, was called the "commuter zone." Park and Burgess noticed that residents of the inner zones

■ **cultural transmission** The idea that delinquency is transmitted through successive generations of people living in an area through the same process of social communication by which languages, social roles, and attitudes are transmitted.

■ **ecological theory** A type of sociological approach that emphasizes demographics (the characteristics of population groups) and geographics (the mapped location of such groups relative to one another) and that sees the social disorganization that characterizes delinquency areas as a major cause of criminality and victimization.

■ **Chicago School of criminology** An ecological approach to explaining crime that examines how social disorganization contributes to social pathology.

■ **criminology of place** A perspective that emphasizes the importance of geographic location and architectural features as they are associated with the prevalence of criminal victimization; also called *environmental criminology*.

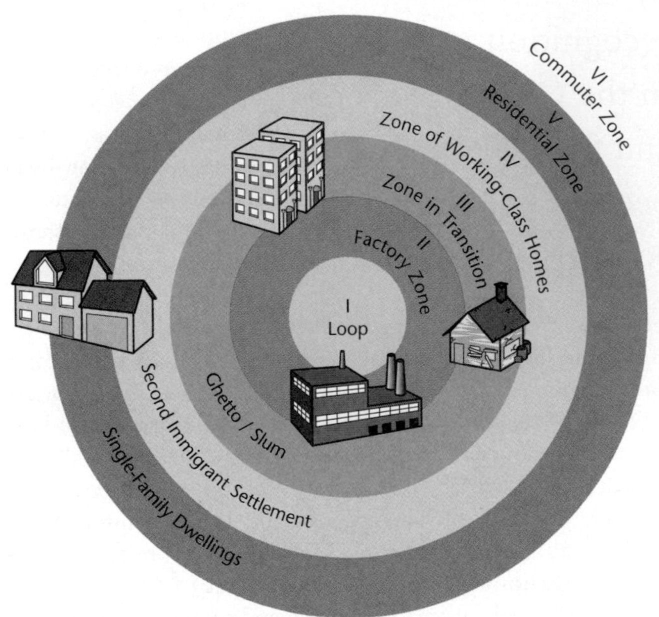

FIGURE 7-2 | **Chicago's Concentric Zones**

Source: Robert E. Park, Ernest W. Burgess, and R. D. McKenzie, *The City* (Chicago: University of Chicago Press, 1925), p. 55. Copyright © 1925 University of Chicago Press. Reprinted by permission.

tended to migrate to outer zones as their economic positions improved.

Clifford Shaw and **Henry McKay**, other early advocates of the ecological approach, applied the concentric zones to the study of juvenile delinquency, conducting empirical studies of Chicago juveniles' arrest rates in 1900–1906, 1917–1923, and 1927–1933 (years associated with high rates of neighborhood transition). Shaw and McKay found that rates of offending remained relatively constant over time within zones of transition and concluded that delinquency was caused by the nature of the environment in which immigrants lived rather than by characteristics of the immigrant groups themselves.[14] Shaw and McKay saw social disorganization as the inability of local communities to solve common problems and believed that the degree of disorganization in a community was largely predicated upon the extent of residential mobility and racial heterogeneity present in that community. As a result of their studies, they developed the idea of **cultural transmission**: Traditions of delinquency were transmitted to successive generations in the same zone in the same way that languages, roles, and attitudes were communicated.

> Cultural transmission theory says that delinquency is transmitted to new generations in the same way that languages, roles, and attitudes are.

Because early **ecological theories** focused on selected geographic areas, their methodology came to be known as "area studies." Because 1920s Chicago served as the model for most such studies, they became collectively referred to as the **Chicago School of criminology**. Although the applicability of these early studies to other cities or other time periods was questionable, the Chicago School had demonstrated the tendency for criminal activity to be associated with urban transitional zones, which were typified by social disorganization, turmoil, lower property values, poverty, and lack of privacy.

The greatest contribution the ecological school made to criminological literature can be found in its claim that society wields a major influence on human behavior.[15] Ecological theorists of the Chicago School used two sources of information: (1) population statistics and official crime and (2) ethnographic data. Population statistics (demographics), when combined with crime information, provided empirical material that gave scientific weight to ecological investigations; ethnographic information, gathered in the form of life stories (ethnographies), described the lives of city inhabitants. By comparing one set of data with the other—demographics with ethnographies—ecological investigators were able to show that life experiences varied from one location to another and that personal involvement in crime was strongly associated with place of residence. Learn more about the Chicago School of criminology at **Web Extra 7–3**.

The Criminology of Place

Ecological approaches to crime causation have found a modern rebirth in the **criminology of place** (also called

■ **environmental criminology** A perspective that emphasizes the importance of geographic location and architectural features as they are associated with the prevalence of criminal victimization; also called *criminology of place*.

■ **broken windows theory** A perspective on crime causation that holds that physical deterioration in an area leads to increased concerns for personal safety among area residents and to higher crime rates in that area.

■ **defensible space** The range of mechanisms that combine to bring an environment under the control of its residents.

environmental criminology), which builds on the contributions of routine activities theory and situational crime prevention (both of which were discussed in Chapter 3). It emphasizes the importance of geographic location and architectural features in terms of prevalence of victimization. Such "hot spots" of crime, including neighborhoods, specific streets, and even individual houses and businesses, have been identified by recent writers. Lawrence W. Sherman, for example, and colleagues tells of a study that revealed that 3% of places (addresses and intersections) in Minneapolis produced 50% of all calls to the police. Crime, noted Sherman, although relatively rare in Minneapolis and similar urban areas, is geographically concentrated.[16]

Policing hot spots, also known variously as *place-based policing* and *place-based crime prevention*, is a concept that was popularized by George Mason University's David Weisburd, University of Maryland's John Eck, Harvard University professor Anthony Braga, and others.[17]

Place-based crime prevention has been shown to be a potentially effective crime-reduction technique. In a 2004 report, the National Research Council Committee to Review Research on Police Policy and Practices concluded that "[t]here has been increasing interest over the past two decades in police practices that target very specific types of crimes, criminals, and crime places. In particular, policing crime hot spots has become a common police strategy for reducing crime and disorder problems. . . . [A] strong body of evidence suggests that taking a focused geographic approach to crime problems can increase the effectiveness of policing."[18]

Reflecting the questions first addressed by Shaw and McKay, researcher **Rodney Stark** asked, "How is it that neighborhoods can remain the site of high crime and deviance rates despite a complete turnover in their populations? There must be something about places as such that sustains crime."[19] Stark developed a *theory of deviant neighborhoods* consisting of 30 propositions, including the following:[20]

- To the extent that neighborhoods are dense and poor, homes will be crowded.
- Where homes are more crowded, there will be a greater tendency to congregate outside the home in places and circumstances that raise levels of temptation and offer opportunity to deviate.
- Where homes are more crowded, there will be lower levels of supervision of children.
- Reduced levels of child supervision will result in poor school achievement, with a consequent reduction in stakes in conformity and an increase in deviant behavior.
- Poor, dense neighborhoods tend to be mixed-use neighborhoods.
- Mixed use increases familiarity with and easy access to places offering the opportunity for deviance.

Central to the criminology of place is the **broken windows theory**, which holds that physical deterioration such as increases in unrepaired buildings leads to greater concerns for personal safety among area residents.[21] These concerns lead to further decreases in maintenance and repair; to increased delinquency, vandalism, and crime; and to even further deterioration in safety and the physical environment—all resulting in offenders from other neighborhoods being increasingly attracted by the area's perceived vulnerability. Physical disorder, left unchecked, leads to crime by driving residents indoors and sending a message to would-be offenders that a neighborhood is out of control.[22]

The broken windows theory says that neighborhood physical deterioration leads to increased delinquency, vandalism, and crime.

The broken windows perspective, first advanced in a 1982 article by James Q. Wilson and George L. Kelling titled "Broken Windows: The Police and Neighborhood Safety,"[23] led to an increase in the use of "order maintenance policing" and a crackdown on quality-of-life offenses, such as panhandling, graffiti, littering, and prostitution, in some of our nation's cities. In 2000 in New York City, (then) Mayor Rudolph Giuliani announced a new police campaign using computer mapping to track crime and to target offenses such as jaywalking, public urination, panhandling, graffiti, public drinking, and prostitution.

Even within high-crime neighborhoods and neighborhoods characterized by urban decay, crimes tend to be concentrated at specific locations, such as street blocks or multiple-family dwellings, and some units within specific apartment buildings are more likely to be the site of criminal occurrences. The criminology of place employs the concept of **defensible space** (evolving from a 1994 conference at Washington University in St. Louis, Missouri[24]), meaning "the range of mechanisms—real and symbolic barriers, strongly defined areas of influence, and

■ **strain theory** A sociological approach that posits a disjuncture between socially and subculturally sanctioned means and goals as the cause of criminal behavior.
■ **anomie** A social condition in which norms are uncertain or lacking.

improved opportunities for surveillance—that combine to bring an environment under the control of its residents."[25] The St. Louis conference brought criminologists, police officers, and architects face to face and focused on crime problems characteristic of public-housing areas. Conference findings demonstrated that specific architectural changes that enhanced barriers, defined boundaries, and removed criminal opportunity could do much to reduce the risk of crime—even in the middle of high-crime neighborhoods.

The criminology of place holds that location can be as predictive of criminal activity as the lifestyles of victimized individuals or the social features of victimized households. (*Place* has been defined by researchers as "a fixed physical environment that can be seen completely and simultaneously, at least on its surface, by one's naked eyes."[26]) Places can be criminogenic because they have certain routine activities associated with them or because they provide the characteristics that facilitate crime commission.

Recognizing the importance of criminology of place, New York City police developed a program called Operation Padlock designed to close businesses with repeated crime problems; it appeared to be successful in reducing the incidence of certain kinds of crime. Author Sherman pointed out that "neither capital punishment of places (as in arson of crack houses) nor incapacitation of the routine activities of criminal hot spots (as in revocation of liquor licenses) seems likely to eliminate crime. But since the routine activities of places may be regulated far more easily than the routine activities of persons, a criminology of place would seem to offer substantial promise for public policy as well as theory."[27]

Sometimes it is the public or city governments that take the initiative in crime prevention using environmental design. In 2012, for example, the Washington, D.C., Metropolitan Police Department was asked to appoint environmental design experts to a planning committee being created by the city to develop two new projects—the Anacostia River front and the Wharf.[28] City officials believed that embedding crime-prevention architects with developers in the planning team would help in the construction of safety-oriented developments.

Some crime-prevention programs are combining ideas derived from the criminology of place with spatial-mapping techniques to fight crime (the Theory versus Reality box provides information about crime-mapping techniques). Visit the National Institute of Justice's MAPS program via **Web Extra 7–4** to learn more about crime mapping, and read more about the broken windows theory at **Library Extra 7–2**.

More recent studies of the broken windows concept have cast doubt on the assertion, made by Wilson and Kelling, that police intervention into the process that links disorder and crime can be effective in reducing crime.[29] It may be that disorder and crime have common roots and that one is more associated with the other than produced by it.[30] Hence, efforts to target quality-of-life offenses in urban areas experiencing high levels of social disorganization may not have the desired effect of reducing crime. David Thacher, professor of public policy and urban planning at the University of Michigan, explained that "these challenges to the broken windows theory have not yet discredited order maintenance policing with policymakers or the public. But among criminologists, order maintenance is clearly under siege."[31] See the Crime in the News box in this chapter for more on broken windows theory.

Strain Theory

The second type of social structure theory discussed in this chapter is strain theory. *Strain* can be defined as the pressure that individuals feel to reach socially determined goals.[32] The classic statement of **strain theory**—which depicts delinquency as a form of adaptive problem-solving behavior committed in response to problems involving frustrating and undesirable social environments—was offered in 1938 by **Robert K. Merton**, who also refined the concept of **anomie** (a French word meaning "normlessness").

> Robert K. Merton popularized the term *anomie*, a French word meaning "normlessness."

Anomie was popularized by Emile Durkheim in his 1897 book *Suicide*, in which he used the term to explain how a breakdown of predictable social conditions can lead to feelings of personal loss, dissolution, and lack of a sense of belonging.[33] Merton's use of the term *anomie* was somewhat different and meant a disjunction between socially approved means to success and legitimate goals.[34] Merton maintained that legitimate goals, such as wealth, status, and personal happiness, are generally portrayed as desirable for everyone, but the widely acceptable means to these goals, such as education, hard work, and financial savings, are not equally available. As a consequence, crime and deviance tend to arise as alternative means to success when individuals feel the strain of being pressed to succeed in socially approved ways but find that the tools necessary for such success are not available to them, and that strain increases as the

THEORY | versus REALITY

The Criminology of Place, Routine Activities, and Crime Mapping

Today's law enforcement agencies are using the criminology of place and routine activities theories (discussed in Chapter 3) to develop situational crime-prevention techniques that combine technology with crime mapping. One implementation of this approach is the Mapping and Analysis Program (MAPS) of the National Institute of Justice. Crime mapping, used in conjunction with geographic information systems (GISs), makes effective use of law enforcement resources by helping police administrators direct patrols to places where they are most needed.

In the routine activities interpretation, crimes are seen as needing three ingredients: a likely offender, a suitable target, and the absence of a guardian capable of preventing the criminal act. Then comes the term *density paradox*: On the one hand, high population densities create a high potential for crime because people and property are crowded in small spaces, resulting in many likely offenders and suitable targets; on the other hand, surveillance is plentiful, so criminal acts in public spaces are likely to be observed by others (guardians). Crime can be reduced or prevented by making people less likely to offend (by increasing guilt and fostering development of the "inner policeman" who tames criminal impulses), by making targets less available (also called *situational crime prevention*), and by making guardians more numerous or effective. Putting the routine activities approach and situational crime prevention into a geographic context involves asking how each element is distributed in geographic space. Where are the likely offenders? (What is the geography of the youthful male population?) Where are the suitable targets? (What is the geography of convenience stores, malls, ATMs, poorly illuminated pedestrian areas?) Where are the guardians? (What is the potential for surveillance, both formal and informal, of targets or areas that may contain targets?)

The perspective that focuses on criminal spatial behavior develops a scenario in which the motivated (potential) criminal uses cues, or environmental signals, to assess victims or targets. Clusters and sequences of cues relating to the social and physical aspects of the environment are seen as a *template*, which the offender uses to evaluate victims or targets; tied to this process is the concept of *activity space*, the area where the offender customarily moves about that is familiar to him or her.

Activity spaces vary with demographics. Historically, younger persons tended to have more constricted activity spaces, not having resources to travel far, and women had more geographically limited activity areas than men because men worked farther from home and their jobs gave them greater mobility; both are less true today.

Analysts considering crime patterns from a theoretical perspective might ask some "filter" questions: How important is geography in explaining a pattern? Is the pattern random or not? If not, why not? Can routine activities theory or criminal spatial behavior theory help explain this pattern? Is this pattern normal or unusual for this area? If the pattern is an anomaly, why is this? What resources can be used to better understand the social and other environmental dynamics of the area of interest?

For a list of Web sites displaying active crime maps, see **Web Extra 7–5**.

Discussion Questions

1. How does routine activities theory support the concepts involved in the spatial analysis of crime?
2. What is the density paradox? What implications does it have for crime prevention?
3. What "filter" questions are discussed in this box? Can you think of any others that might be asked?

Source: National Institute of Justice, "Mapping and Analysis for Public Safety (MAPS)," http://www.ojp.gov/nij/maps (accessed May 28, 2007); and Keith Harries, *Mapping Crime: Principles and Practice* (Washington, DC: National Institute of Justice, 1999), http://www.ojp.usdoj.gov/cmrc (accessed December 15, 2005).

gulf between the goals and the means available to achieve them widens. Merton's emphasis on the felt strain resulting from a lack of fit between goals and means led to his approach being called *strain theory*.

Complicating the picture further, Merton maintained that not everyone accepts the legitimacy of socially approved goals. Merton diagrammed possible combinations of goals and means as shown in Table 7–1. The first row, labeled *conformity*, signifies acceptance of the goals that society holds as legitimate for everyone, with ready availability of the means approved for achieving those goals; the mode of adaptation associated with this combination of goals and means typifies most middle- and upper-class individuals.

TABLE 7–1 | **Goals and Means Disjuncture**

	GOALS	MEANS
Conformity	+	+
Innovation	+	−
Ritualism	−	+
Retreatism	−	−
Rebellion	±	±

Source: Adapted from Robert K. Merton, "Social Structure and Anomie," *American Sociological Review*, Vol. 3, No. 5 (October 1938), pp. 672–682.

Innovation arises when an emphasis on approved goal achievement combines with a lack of opportunity to participate fully in socially acceptable means to success, which is experienced by many lower-class individuals who have been socialized to desire traditional success symbols (expensive cars, large homes, big bank accounts) but do not have ready access to approved means of acquiring them (educational opportunity); innovative behavioral responses, including crime, can be expected to develop when individuals find themselves deprived. Merton said that "poverty as such, and consequent limitation of opportunity, are not sufficient to induce a conspicuously high rate of criminal behavior. Even the often mentioned 'poverty in

CRIME | in the NEWS

"Broken Windows" Policing Helps Restore Communities

JAMES Q. WILSON, who died on March 2, 2012, is credited with co-authoring one of the most influential policing theories of all time. His "broken windows" theory posits that crime develops from small things, such as shattered windows, spray-painted gang signs, and panhandling. These outward signs tell criminals that a community is ripe for the picking.

When the theory was first published in 1982, it broke with the orthodoxy of the time, which focused on giving would-be criminals economic incentives to become law-abiding citizens. Wilson, who viewed himself as politically independent, was heralded as a new conservative voice. Republican Mayor Rudy Giuliani of New York City endorsed Wilson's theory when he entered office in 1993.

Rather than just focusing on major crimes, New York City police started going after small crimes in a big way. Misdemeanor arrests increased 70% during the rest of the decade, and Giuliani faced complaints of police harassment. But New York City's crime rate dropped dramatically, much more than a corresponding drop in the nationwide rate. Violent crime in the city declined by more than 56%, compared with a 28% U.S. drop, and property crimes fell by about 65%, compared with 26% nationally.

Los Angeles, Chicago, and Boston also successfully adopted aspects of broken windows, and the theory has led to hot-spot policing, which focuses patrols on areas with high crime. This technique is currently used in several U.S. cities, from Oakland, California, to St. Louis, Missouri.

Broken windows has become so embedded in law enforcement that it is rarely noted anymore. A new police program piloted in a Detroit neighborhood in 2012, however, specifically referenced the theory. The city partnered with the Manhattan Institute, a conservative think-tank that brought in George L. Kelling, Wilson's co-author on the original 1982 broken windows paper and an executive at the institute.

In the Detroit project, police officers spent extra time interacting with the community, and community members were encouraged to report suspicious activity. At the end of the 120-day pilot in August 2012, the community noted 32% fewer home invasions in the area compared to the same time last year. Detroit police plan to extend the program to other Detroit neighborhoods.

Mary Evans Picture Library/Alamy

An abandoned house in a run-down neighborhood. What does broken windows theory say about places like this?

The Michigan Youth Violence Prevention Center is also taking a page from broken windows as it builds social and institutional relationships on the streets of Flint, Michigan. "Our Community Policing initiative is largely grounded in Wilson's work, aiming to promote problem-solving and facilitate cooperation between police officers and community residents," wrote Sophie Aiyer, a postdoctoral fellow at the center.

Discussion Questions

1. How would you describe the broken windows theory of policing?
2. What implications does the broken windows theory hold for crime-prevention policy? Do you know of any communities in which you'd like to see it applied?

Sources: Brian Dickerson, "Broken Windows Theory of Community Policing Will Get Major Test in Detroit," *Detroit Free Press*, May 24, 2012, http://www.freep.com/apps/pbcs.dll/article?AID=2012205240458; Joan Petersilia, "Remembering James Q. Wilson," *The Crime Report*, March 18, 2012, http://www.thecrimereport.org/news/inside-criminal-justice/2012-03-remembering-james-q-wilson; and Sophie Aiyer, "James Q. Wilson, Who Developed Broken Windows Theory, Dies at 80," Michigan Youth Violence Prevention Center, March 6, 2012, http://yvpc.sph.umich.edu/2012/03/06/james-q-wilson-developed-broken-windows-theory-dies-80/.

the midst of plenty' will not necessarily lead to this result."[35] It is when those who find themselves in poverty are pressured to achieve material success and acquire other associated symbols of status that innovation results.

The third row, *ritualism*, refers to the type of behavior arising when members of society participate in socially desirable means but show little interest in goal achievement. A ritualist may get a good education, work every day in an acceptable occupation, and appear to be leading a solid middle-class lifestyle, yet care little for the symbols of success, choosing to live an otherwise independent lifestyle.

Retreatism describes the behavior of those who reject both the socially approved goals and the means. They may become dropouts, drug abusers, or homeless persons or participate in alternative lifestyles, such as communal living; they are often socially and psychologically quite separate from the larger society around them.

Merton's last category, *rebellion*, describes the actions of a person who wishes to replace socially approved goals and means with some other system; political radicals, revolutionaries, and antiestablishment agitators fit into this category. Merton believed that conformity is the most common mode of adaptation prevalent in society and that retreatism is the least common.

■ **relative deprivation** A sense of social or economic inequality experienced by those who are unable, for whatever reason, to achieve legitimate success within the surrounding society.

■ **distributive justice** The rightful, equitable, and just distribution of rewards within a society.

Oli Scarff/Getty Images, Inc.

London's Metropolitan Police officers view displays from closed circuit television (CCTV) cameras around London in the Special Operations Room of their Central Communications Command. Defensible space can be defined in terms of barriers to crime commission and preventive surveillance opportunities. How might such features be enhanced in high-crime areas?

A 2006 study by sociologists Thomas M. Arvanites and Robert H. Defina at Villanova University tested a prediction based on Merton's theory: that negative economic conditions and declining business cycles can increase social strain, resulting in heightened rates for certain kinds of crimes, especially property crimes. By comparing society's economic conditions over time with rates for such crimes, the researchers concluded that "an improving economy has a negative and statistically significant effect on all four index property crimes and robbery." Because financial gain is the primary purpose of robbery, they noted that "a finding that robbery is the only violent crime to be influenced by the business cycle was not surprising."[36]

Relative Deprivation

Another version of Merton's anomie theory has been proposed by Steven F. Messner and Richard Rosenfeld, who suggested that inconsistencies in the American Dream are to be blamed for most criminal activity: "Our thesis is that the American Dream itself exerts pressures toward crime by encouraging an anomic cultural environment, an environment in which people are encouraged to adopt an 'anything goes' mentality in the pursuit of personal goals."[37]

It is often said that Americans are the richest people on earth and that even the poorest Americans are far richer than the average citizen of many Third World nations, but even if such an assertion is true, it means little to someone who is living in the United States and is poor when judged in terms of U.S. standards. Deprivation has an important psychological component and cannot be accurately assessed in absolute terms.

Relative deprivation refers to the economic and social gaps that exist between rich and poor who live in close proximity to one another. According to sociologists Judith Blau and Peter Blau, two proponents of the relative deprivation concept, people assess their position in life by way of comparison with things and people they already know.[38] According to the Blaus, relative deprivation creates feelings of anger, frustration, hostility, and social injustice on the part of those who experience it. According to **distributive justice**, which refers to people's perceptions of their rightful place in the reward structure of society, even wealthy and socially privileged individuals may feel slighted or shortchanged if they feel inadequately rewarded for their behavior or accomplishments. But the perception of the rightful distribution of rewards appears to be highly dependent upon cultural expectations; for example, even successful Americans sometimes feel they deserve more, whereas studies show that Japanese society has been able to accommodate rapid socioeconomic growth without generating a felt sense of economic injustice, even among its least successful members, and without experiencing a substantial increase in crime.[39]

Surveys provide evidence for distinguishing between two types of relative deprivation: personal and group.[40] Personal relative deprivation is characteristic of individuals who feel deprived compared with other people; group relative deprivation is a communal sense of injustice that is shared by members of the same group. People who experience personal deprivation are likely to feel socially isolated and personally stressed, and those who believe their entire social group is deprived relative to other groups are more prone to participate in social movements and may actively attempt to change the social system, making group relative deprivation a powerful force for social change.

■ **general strain theory (GST)** A perspective that suggests that law-breaking behavior is a coping mechanism that enables those who engage in it to deal with the socioemotional problems generated by negative social relations.

■ **negative affective state** An adverse emotion such as anger, fear, depression, or disappointment that derives from the experience of strain.

General Strain Theory

In 1992, strain theory was reformulated by **Robert Agnew** and others who molded it into a comprehensive perspective called **general strain theory (GST)**.[41] GST sees law-breaking behavior as a coping mechanism enabling those who engage in it to deal with the socioemotional problems generated by negative social relations (Figure 7–3). In 2006, Agnew restated the six central propositions of GST, as shown in Figure 7–4.[42]

GST sees law-breaking as a coping mechanism for dealing with socio-emotional problems.

Agnew explained that the strains most likely to cause crime in Western societies include child abuse and neglect; negative secondary school experiences; abusive peer relations; chronic unemployment; marital problems; parental rejection; erratic, excessive, and or/harsh supervision or discipline; criminal victimization; homelessness; racial, ethnic, or gender discrimination; and failure to achieve selected goals. Factors that increase the likelihood of criminal coping include poor conventional coping skills and resources; availability of criminal skills and resources; low levels of conventional social support; routine association with criminal others; personal beliefs and values favorable to crime; frequent exposure to situations where the costs of crime are low; low levels of social control, including weak bonds to conventional others; and lack of investment in conventional institutions. Agnew's strategies for reducing exposure to strains include eliminating strains conducive to crime, altering strains to make them less conducive to crime, removing individuals from exposure to strain, and equipping individuals with the traits and skills needed to avoid strains conducive to crime.

GST expands on traditional strain theory in several ways. First, it significantly widens the focus of strain theory to include all types of negative relations between an individual and others; second, GST maintains that strain is likely to have a cumulative effect on delinquency after reaching a certain threshold; third, general strain theory provides a more comprehensive account of the cognitive, behavioral, and emotional adaptations to strain than traditional strain approaches; and finally, GST more fully describes the wide variety of factors affecting the choice of delinquent adaptations to strain.

Agnew saw the crime-producing effects of strain as cumulative and concluded that whatever form it takes, "strain creates a predisposition for delinquency in those cases in which it is chronic or repetitive."[43] Predispositions may be manifested in the form of **negative affective states**, meaning emotions such as anger, fear, depression, and disappointment.

An analysis by Agnew of other strain theories found that all such theories share at least two central explanatory features.[44] Agnew said that strain theories focus (1) "explicitly on negative relationships with others, relationships in which the individual is not treated as he or she wants to be treated," and he argued that (2) "adolescents are pressured into delinquency by the negative affective states—most notably anger and related emotions—that often result from negative relationships."[45]

In 1994, Raymond Paternoster and Paul Mazerolle tested some of the assumptions underlying GST through an analysis of data from the National Youth Survey.[46] They found partial support for GST and discovered that negative relations with adults, feelings of dissatisfaction with friends and school life, and experiences of stressful events were positively related to delinquency, as was living in an unpleasant neighborhood (with social problems and physical deterioration). When conceived of more broadly as exposure to negative stimuli, general strain was found to be significantly related to delinquency.

Contrary to Agnew's hypothesis, however, Paternoster and Mazerolle found no evidence that the effects of strain were enhanced when they were experienced for longer periods of time or that they were diminished when adolescents classified the area of their life in which they experienced strain as "unimportant." Consistent with earlier findings,[47] Paternoster and Mazerolle found that feelings of general strain were positively related to later delinquency—regardless of the number of delinquent peers, moral beliefs, self-efficacy, and level of conventional social support—and that general strain leads to delinquency by weakening the conventional social bond and strengthening the unconventional bond with delinquent peers.

In a more recent test of GST, Lisa M. Broidy of the University of New Mexico examined the intervening role of negative emotions and legitimate coping strategies as they impact the relationship between strain and crime and found that strain can produce anger and other negative emotions and that different sources of strain tend to produce different emotions.[48] "Hence, although evidence of a relationship exists between strain and negative emotions, the nature of this relationship depends on the specific type of strain and negative emotions considered."[49] Strain-induced anger was more likely to lead to criminal outcomes among men than among women, even though members of both genders experienced anger equally under certain specific types of strained circumstances. Broidy also discovered that "negative emotional responses to strain other than anger are associated with a significant increase in legitimate coping and significant decrease in illegitimate/criminal outcomes."[50]

FIGURE 7–3 | **A Visual Representation of Strain Theory**

Source: Schmalleger, Frank J., *Criminology*. Printed and Electronically reproduced by permission of Pearson Education, Inc., Upper Saddle River, New Jersey.

A 2002 study by Robert Agnew and associates further refined GST by explaining why some individuals are more likely than others to react to strain with delinquency.[51] They found that juveniles who measured high in negative emotionality and low in constraint were more likely to react to strain with delinquency and noted that the "incorporation of such traits into GST represents an integration between strain theory and the rapidly growing research on behavioral genetics and crime."[52] Hence, it may be that certain biological factors make some individuals particularly susceptible to the effects of strain in their lives.

Finally, in 2010, Joan R. Hipp at the University of California, Irvine, reporting on a study of crime rates in 352 American metropolitan areas over a 30-year period, reinforced the notion of strain as a cause of crime.[53] Hipp, whose study focused on the effect of economic resources and racial/ethnic composition on the change in crime rates, found that economic inequality increases the amount of crime in cities, but

■ **culture conflict theory** A sociological perspective on crime that suggests that the root cause of criminality can be found in a clash of values between variously socialized groups over what is acceptable or proper behavior; also called *cultural deviance theory*.

■ **conduct norms** Shared expectations of a social group relative to personal conduct.

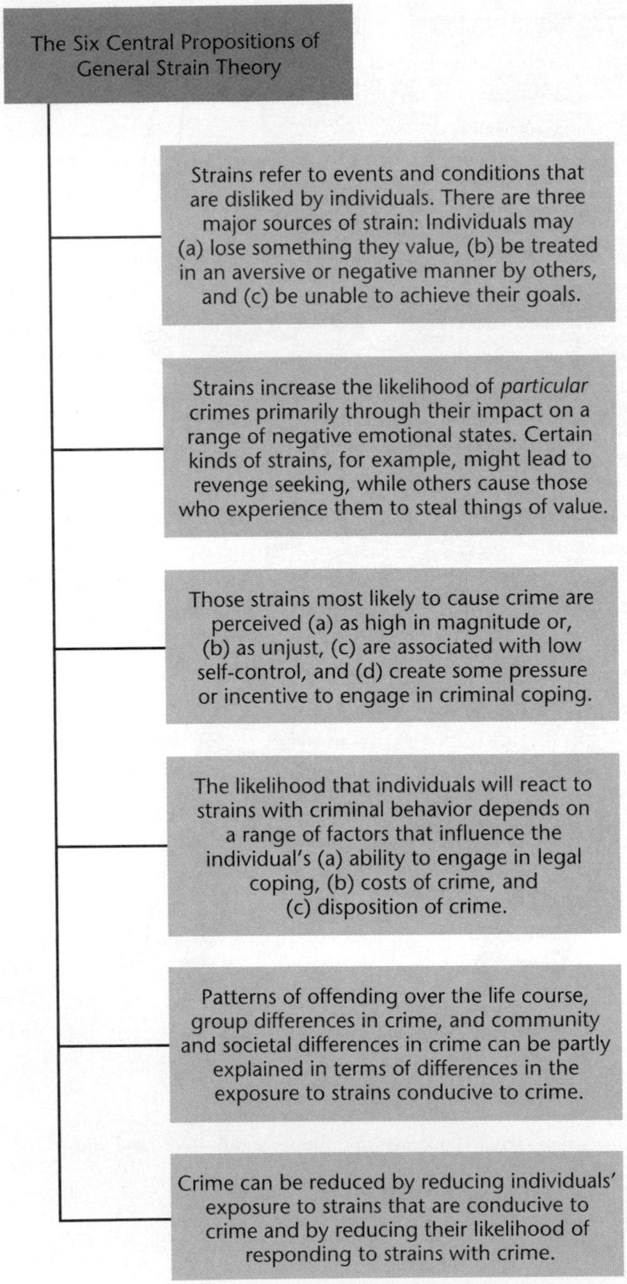

The Six Central Propositions of General Strain Theory

- Strains refer to events and conditions that are disliked by individuals. There are three major sources of strain: Individuals may (a) lose something they value, (b) be treated in an aversive or negative manner by others, and (c) be unable to achieve their goals.
- Strains increase the likelihood of *particular* crimes primarily through their impact on a range of negative emotional states. Certain kinds of strains, for example, might lead to revenge seeking, while others cause those who experience them to steal things of value.
- Those strains most likely to cause crime are perceived (a) as high in magnitude or, (b) as unjust, (c) are associated with low self-control, and (d) create some pressure or incentive to engage in criminal coping.
- The likelihood that individuals will react to strains with criminal behavior depends on a range of factors that influence the individual's (a) ability to engage in legal coping, (b) costs of crime, and (c) disposition of crime.
- Patterns of offending over the life course, group differences in crime, and community and societal differences in crime can be partly explained in terms of differences in the exposure to strains conducive to crime.
- Crime can be reduced by reducing individuals' exposure to strains that are conducive to crime and by reducing their likelihood of responding to strains with crime.

FIGURE 7–4 | **The Six Central Propositions of General Strain Theory**

Source: The Six Central Propositions of General Strain Theory by Robert Agnew from *Pressured Into Crime: An Overview of General Strain Theory*. Published by Schmalleger, Frank.

that the distribution of inequality across the census tracts of a city has important interaction effects. In cities with high levels of inequality, Hipp discovered, higher levels of economic segregation actually lead to much higher levels of the the types of crime that she studied (including aggravated assaults, robberies, burglaries, and motor vehicle thefts). In contrast, Hipp found, in cities with low levels of inequality, it is mixing of households in neighborhoods with varying levels of income that leads to higher levels of crime. Learn more about strain theory via **Web Extra 7–6**.

Culture Conflict Theory

The third type of social structure theory discussed in this chapter is **culture conflict theory** (also called *cultural deviance theory*), which suggests that the root cause of criminality can be found in a clash of values between differently socialized groups over what is acceptable or proper behavior. The culture conflict concept is inherent in ecological criminology (discussed earlier in this chapter) and its belief that zones of transition tend to be in flux and harbor groups of people whose values are often at odds with those of the larger society.

The culture conflict perspective found its clearest expression in the writings of **Thorsten Sellin** in his 1938 book *Culture Conflict and Crime*, where he stated that the root cause of crime could be found in different values for what is acceptable or proper behavior.[54] According to Sellin, **conduct norms**, which provide the valuative basis for human behavior, are acquired early in life through childhood socialization, and it is the clash of norms between variously socialized groups that results in crime. Because crime is a violation of laws established by legislative decree, the criminal event itself is nothing other than a disagreement over what should be acceptable behavior.

Conduct norms are acquired early in life through childhood socialization.

Sellin described two types of culture conflict. *Primary conflict* arises when a fundamental clash of cultures occurs, as when an immigrant father kills his daughter's lover following an Old World tradition that demands a family's honor be kept intact.[55] *Secondary conflict* occurs, according to Sellin, when smaller cultures within the primary one clash, as when middle-class values (on which most criminal laws are based) find fault with inner-city or lower-class norms, resulting in the social phenomenon we call *crime*.

■ **subculture** A collection of values and preferences that is communicated to subcultural participants through a process of socialization.
■ **subcultural theory** A sociological perspective that emphasizes the contribution made by variously socialized cultural groups to the phenomenon of crime.

■ **focal concerns** The key values of any culture, especially a delinquent subculture.

Subcultural Theory

Fundamental to the notion of culture conflict is the idea of a **subculture**, a collection of values and preferences that is communicated to subcultural participants through a process of socialization. Subcultures differ from the larger culture in that they claim the allegiance of smaller groups of people. For example, the wider American culture may proclaim that hard work and individuality are valuable, but a particular subculture may espouse the virtues of deer hunting, male bonding, and recreational alcohol consumption. Countercultures, which tend to reject and invert the values of the surrounding culture, and criminal subcultures, which actively espouse deviant activity, represent extremes. **Subcultural theory** is a sociological perspective that emphasizes the contributions made by variously socialized cultural groups to the phenomenon of crime.

Early writings on subcultures include *The Gang* by **Frederic M. Thrasher**.[56] Thrasher studied 1,313 gangs in Chicago in 1927, and his descriptive work led to a typology in which he described different types of gangs. In 1943, **William F. Whyte**, drawing on Thrasher's work, published *Street Corner Society*.[57] Whyte, in describing his three-year study of the Italian slum he called "Cornerville," further developed the subcultural thesis, showing that lower-class residents of a typical slum could achieve success through the opportunities afforded by slum culture, including racketeering and bookmaking. Read more on culture in conflict at **Library Extra 7–3**.

Focal Concerns

In 1958, **Walter B. Miller** attempted to detail the values that drive members of lower-class subcultures into delinquent pursuits, describing lower-class culture as "a long established, distinctively patterned tradition with an integrity of its own."[58] According to that article, titled "Lower Class Culture as a Generating Milieu of Gang Delinquency," a large body of systematically interrelated attitudes, practices, behaviors, and values characteristic of lower-class culture are designed to support and maintain the basic features of the lower-class way of life. In areas where these differ from features of middle-class culture, action oriented to the achievement and maintenance of the lower-class system may violate norms of the middle class and be perceived as deliberately nonconforming. "This does not mean, however, that violation of the middle-class norm is the dominant component of motivation; it is a by-product of action primarily oriented to the lower-class system."

Miller also outlined what he termed the **focal concerns** (key values) of delinquent subcultures: trouble, toughness, smartness, excitement, fate, and autonomy. Miller concluded that subcultural crime and deviance are not the direct consequences of poverty and lack of opportunity but emanate from specific values characteristic of such subcultures. According to Miller, *trouble* is a dominant feature of lower-class culture. Getting into trouble, staying out of trouble, and dealing with trouble when it arises become focal points in the lives of many members of lower-class culture. Miller recognized that getting into trouble is not necessarily valued in and of itself but is seen as a necessary means to valued ends.

Like many theorists of the time, Miller was primarily concerned with the criminality of men. The lower-class masculine concern with *toughness* may have been due to many men in the groups he examined being raised in female-headed families and may have reflected an almost obsessive concern with masculinity as a reaction to the perceived threat of overidentification with female role models.

Miller described *smartness* as the "capacity to outsmart, outfox, outwit, dupe, take, [or] con another or others and the concomitant capacity to avoid being outwitted, taken or duped oneself. In its essence, smartness involves the capacity to achieve a valued entity—material goods, personal status—through a maximum use of mental agility and a minimum of physical effort." *Excitement* was seen as a search for thrills—often necessary to overcome the boredom inherent in lower-class lifestyles. Fighting, gambling, picking up women, and making the rounds were all described as derivative aspects of the lower-class concern with excitement. *Fate* is related to the quest for excitement and to the concept of luck. As Miller stated, "Many lower-class persons feel that their lives are subject to a set of forces over which they have relatively little control. These are not supernatural forces or organized religion but relate more to a concept of 'destiny' or man as a pawn. This often implicit worldview is associated with a conception of the ultimate futility of directed effort toward a goal."

Autonomy, manifested in statements like "I can take care of myself" and "No one's going to push me around," produces behavioral problems from the perspective of middle-class expectations when it surfaces in work environments, public schools, or other social institutions built on expectations of conformity.

Miller's work on subcultures and their focal concerns is derived almost entirely from his study of black inner-city delinquents in the Boston area in the 1950s and may have less relevance to members of lower-class subcultures in other places or at other times.

■ **techniques of neutralization** Culturally available justifications that can provide criminal offenders with the means to disavow responsibility for their behavior.

Delinquency and Drift

Members of delinquent subcultures are, to varying degrees, participants in the larger culture that surrounds them. Why do subcultural participants choose behavioral alternatives that seemingly negate the norms and values of the larger society? How can a person give allegiance to two seemingly different sets of values—those of the larger culture and those of a subculture—at the same time? **Gresham Sykes** and **David Matza** provided an answer to this question in their 1957 article "Techniques of Neutralization."[59] Sykes and Matza suggested that offenders and delinquents are aware of conventional values, understand that their offending is wrong, but engage in neutralizing self-talk before offending to mitigate the anticipated shame and guilt associated with violating societal norms.[60] Offenders can overcome feelings of responsibility when involved in crime commission by using five types of justification:

1. **Denying responsibility.** They point to their background of poverty, abuse, and lack of opportunity: "The trouble I get into is not my fault."
2. **Denying injury.** They explain that everyone does it or that individuals or companies can afford it: "They're so rich, they'll never miss it." (See Figure 7–5.)
3. **Denying the victim.** They justify the harm done by claiming that the victim deserved the victimization: "I only beat up drunks."
4. **Condemning the condemners.** They assert that authorities are corrupt or are responsible for their own victimization and that society has made them what they are and must now suffer the consequences: "They're worse than I am. They're all on the take."
5. **Appealing to higher loyalties.** They use defense of their family honor, gang, girlfriend, or neighborhood: "I have to protect myself."

In the words of Sykes and Matza, "It is our argument that much delinquency is based on what is essentially an unrecognized extension of defenses to crimes, in the form of justifications for deviance that are seen as valid by the delinquent but not by the legal system or society at large."[61]

A few years later, Matza went on to suggest that delinquents tend to drift into crime when available **techniques of neutralization** combine with weak or ineffective values espoused by the controlling elements in society, stating that the delinquent "drifts between criminal and conventional action,"[62] choosing whichever is more expedient at the time. By employing techniques of neutralization, delinquents need not be fully alienated from the larger society because these techniques provide an effective way of overcoming their feelings of guilt so that they can commit crimes. Matza used the phrase "soft determinism" to describe drift, saying that delinquents are neither forced to make choices because of fateful experiences early in life nor entirely free to make choices unencumbered by the realities of their situation.

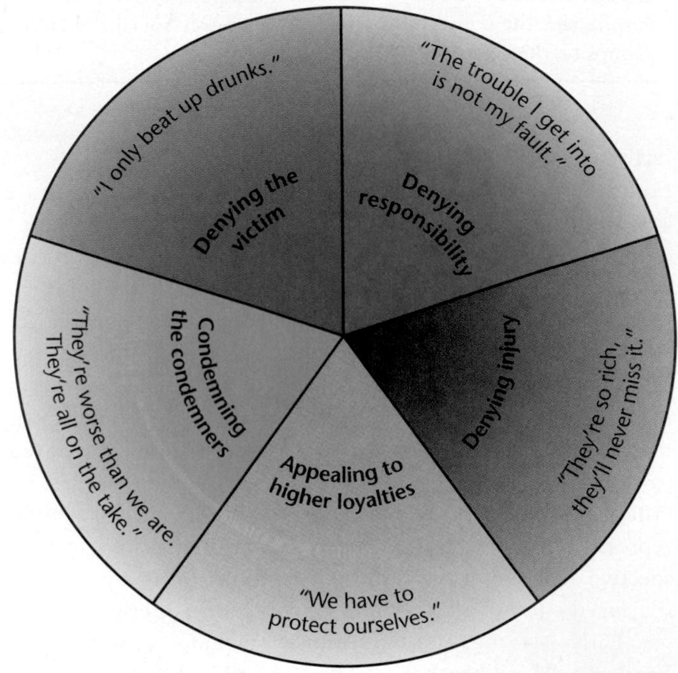

FIGURE 7-5 | **Techniques of Neutralization**

Source: Schmalleger, Frank J., *Criminology*. Printed and Electronically reproduced by permission of Pearson Education, Inc., Upper Saddle River, New Jersey.

More recent studies have found that whereas "only a small percentage of adolescents generally approve of violence or express indifference to violence, [a] large percentage of adolescents accept neutralizations justifying the use of violence in particular situations."[63] Studies have found that young people who disapprove of violence but associate with delinquent peers often use neutralization techniques as justifications for violence in which they personally engage.[64]

Hard-core, active, noninstitutionalized drug dealers, street robbers, and carjackers have also used neutralization techniques.[65] Sociologist Ken Levi found that professional contract killers, or hit men, tend to begin adapting to the role of professional killer by learning to view killing as "just a job" or as "just business," which allows them to deny responsibility for contracted killings and to view themselves as "hired guns," and their victims as "targets" rather than people.[66]

A 2003 study by sociologist Lois Presser of the University of Tennessee on remorse and neutralization among violent male offenders, based on interviews with 27 men who had committed serious violent crimes, found that the men excused or justified their violent actions through five rationalizations: (1) Victims were to blame for harms that resulted from provoking the offender, (2) victims were themselves offenders or deserving of harm,

(3) harm to a victim that was not premeditated or intended carried no blame, (4) the legal sanctioning of an offender negated any harm, and (5) harms to the offender and his or her family stemming from the crime negated any harms caused by the offender.[67]

In innovative research published in 2008, Orly Turgeman-Goldschmidt of Israel's Bar-Ilan University conducted 54 unstructured, in-depth, face-to-face interviews with malicious Israeli computer vandals (hackers) in order to determine what kinds of neutralization techniques they employ and found that the hackers used neutralization techniques common to other offenders, although their language reflected the cyber-realm.[68] Some hackers were found to be similar to political criminals, assuming responsibility by means of internal justifications (by attacking al-Qaeda Web sites or bringing down computers of the Arab news network Al-Jazeera and seeing the activity as a positive contribution to their sociopolitical environment); these "hacktivists" defined themselves as hackers with political consciences.[69] Other hackers justified illegal hacking as simply being fun, rewarding, or self-fulfilling and argued that anyone or anything affected (financial institutions) could afford it and that no one was physically hurt.

Violent Subcultures

Some subcultures are decidedly violent and built around themes and values supporting violent activities. In 1967, **Franco Ferracuti** and **Marvin Wolfgang** published their seminal work *The Subculture of Violence: Toward an Integrated Theory of Criminology*,[70] which drew together many of the sociological perspectives previously advanced to explain delinquency and crime. Ferracuti and Wolfgang's main thesis was that violence is a learned form of adaptation to certain problematic life circumstances and that learning to be violent takes place within the context of a subcultural milieu emphasizing the advantages of violence over other forms of adaptation. These subcultures of violence both expect violence from their members and legitimize it when it occurs: "The use of violence is not necessarily viewed as illicit conduct, and the users do not have to deal with feelings of guilt about their aggression."[71]

Ferracuti and Wolfgang based their conclusions on an analysis of data that showed substantial differences in the rates of homicides between racial groups in the Philadelphia area—nonwhite men had a homicide rate of 41.7 per 100,000 versus a homicide rate of only 3.4 for white men, and nonwhite women showed a homicide rate of 9.3 versus 0.4 for white women. Explaining these findings, Ferracuti and Wolfgang stated, "Homicide is most prevalent, or the highest rates of homicide occur, among a relatively homogeneous subcultural group in any large urban community. The value system of this group . . . constitutes a subculture of violence. From a psychological viewpoint, we might hypothesize that the greater the degree of integration of the individual into this subculture, the higher the probability that his behavior will be violent in a variety of situations."[72]

Ferracuti and Wolfgang extended their theory of subcultural violence with the following "corollary propositions":[73]

- No subculture can be totally different from or totally in conflict with the society of which it is a part.
- To establish the existence of a subculture of violence does not require that the actors sharing in these basic value elements should express violence in all situations.
- The potential resort or willingness to resort to violence in a variety of situations emphasizes the penetrating and diffusive character of this culture theme.
- The subcultural ethos of violence may be shared by all ages in a subsociety, but this ethos is most prominent in a limited age group, ranging from late adolescence to middle age.
- The counternorm is nonviolence.
- The development of favorable attitudes toward violence and its use in a subculture usually involves learned behavior and a process of differential learning, association, or identification.
- The use of violence in a subculture is not necessarily viewed as illicit conduct, and the users therefore do not have to deal with feelings of guilt about their aggression.

Other writers have commented on geographic distinctions among violent subcultures in different parts of the United States. For example, there are claims that certain forms of criminal violence are more acceptable in the southern United States than in northern portions of the country.[74] Some writers referred to variability in the degree to which interpersonal violence has been accepted in the South over time, whereas others suggested that violence in the South might be a traditional tool in the service of social order.[75]

In 1998, James W. Clarke, a political science professor at the University of Arizona, posited that the high rate of black underclass homicide in the United States flows from a black subculture of violence created by generations of white-on-black violence that first emerged with the "generation of black males that came of age after emancipation."[76] According to Clarke, many black males learned from earlier generations to seek status through their ability to "harm, intimidate, and dominate others."[77]

The wider culture often recognizes a violent subculture's internal rules, so when one member of such a subculture kills another, the wider society may take the killing less seriously than if someone outside the subculture had been killed. Franklin Zimring and his associates described what they called "wholesale" and "retail" costs for homicide: Killings that are perceived

■ **illegitimate opportunity structure** A subcultural pathway to success that the wider society disapproves of.

to occur within a subculture of violence (when both the victim and the perpetrator are seen as members of a violent subculture) generally result in a less harsh punishment than do killings that occur outside that subculture.[78] Punishments relate to the perceived seriousness of the offense; if members of the subculture in which a crime occurs accept the offense as part of the landscape, so will members of the wider culture.

Differential Opportunity Theory

In 1960, **Richard A. Cloward** and **Lloyd E. Ohlin** published *Delinquency and Opportunity*.[79] Their book, a report on the nature and activities of juvenile gangs, blends the subcultural thesis with ideas derived from strain theory, and identifies two types of socially structured opportunities for success: legitimate and illegitimate. Legitimate opportunities are generally available to individuals born into middle-class culture, but participants in lower-class subcultures are often denied access to them, so illegitimate opportunities for success are often seen as quite acceptable by participants in so-called illegitimate subcultures.

Cloward and Ohlin used the term **illegitimate opportunity structure** to describe preexisting subcultural paths to success not approved of by the wider culture. Where illegitimate paths to success are not already in place, alienated individuals may undertake a process of ideational evolution through which "a collective delinquent solution" or a "delinquent means of achieving success" may be decided upon by members of a gang. Because the two paths to success—legitimate and illegitimate—differ in their availability to members of society, Cloward and Ohlin's perspective has been called "differential opportunity."

Illegitimate opportunity structures are preexisting subcultural paths to success not approved of by the wider culture.

According to Cloward and Ohlin, delinquent behavior may result from the ready availability of illegitimate opportunities and the effective replacement of the norms of the wider culture with expedient and "legitimate" subcultural rules. "A delinquent subculture is one in which certain forms of delinquent activity are essential requirements for the performance of the dominant roles supported by the subculture."[80] Its most critical elements are the "prescriptions, norms, or rules of conduct that define the activities required of a full-fledged member."[81] They continued, "A person attributes legitimacy to a system of rules and corresponding models of behavior when he accepts them as binding on his conduct."[82] They concluded, "Delinquents have withdrawn their support from established norms and invested officially forbidden forms of conduct with a claim to legitimacy."[83]

Cloward and Ohlin noted that there are two necessary parts to a delinquent act—"It is behavior that violates basic norms of the society, and, when officially known, it evokes a judgment by agents of criminal justice that such norms have been violated."[84] For Cloward and Ohlin, however, crime and deviance are just as normal as any other form of behavior supported by group socialization: "Deviance and conformity generally result from the same kinds of social conditions, [and] deviance ordinarily represents a search for solutions to problems of adjustment." In their view, deviance is just as much an effort to conform (albeit to subcultural norms and expectations) as conformity to the norms of the wider society. "[I]t has been our experience that most persons who participate in delinquent subcultures, if not lone offenders, are fully aware of the difference between right and wrong, between conventional behavior and rule-violating behavior. They may not care about the difference, or they may enjoy flouting the rules of the game, or they may have decided that illegitimate practices get them what they want more efficiently than legitimate practices."[85]

Cloward and Ohlin described three types of delinquent subcultures: (1) criminal subcultures, in which criminal role models are readily available for adoption by those being socialized into the subculture; (2) conflict subcultures, in which participants seek status through violence; and (3) retreatist subcultures, in which drug use and withdrawal from the wider society predominate. These delinquent subcultures have at least three identifiable features: "acts of delinquency that reflect subcultural support are likely to recur with great frequency, access to a successful adult criminal career sometimes results from participation in a delinquent subculture, and the delinquent subculture imparts to the conduct of its members a high degree of stability and resistance to control or change."[86]

Cloward and Ohlin divided lower-class youths into four types based on degree of commitment to middle-class values and material achievement: Type I youths desire entry to the middle class via improvement in their economic position, Type II youths desire entry to the middle class but not improvement in their economic position, Type III youths desire wealth but not entry to the middle class and are seen as the most crime-prone, and Type IV youths are dropouts who retreat from the cultural mainstream through drug and alcohol use (see the creative example in the Who's to Blame box in this chapter).

Reaction Formation

Another criminologist whose work is often associated with both strain theory and the subcultural perspective is **Albert Cohen**,

reaction formation The process by which a person openly rejects that which he or she wants or aspires to but cannot obtain or achieve.

WHO'S TO BLAME—The Individual or Society?

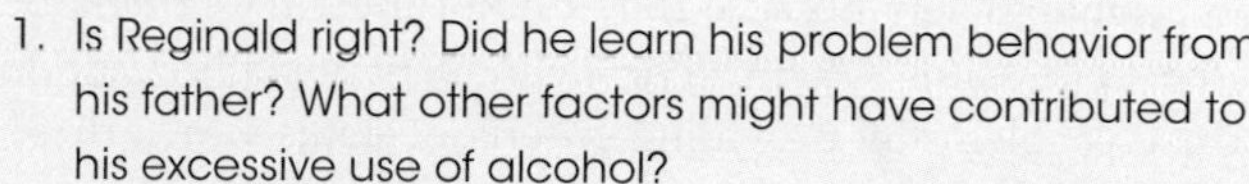

Like Father, Like Son

Reginald Barfield, age 22, was arrested for driving under the influence (DUI) of alcohol and taken to jail. A judge set bail at $500, and his mother came to the jail to post bond for her son. She didn't have much money, so she used the services of a bondsman, who charged her a $70 fee and arranged for Reginald's release. As she drove her son home, she began yelling at him, telling him that he had turned out just like his father, who had had a long-standing problem with alcohol.

"You're just like your father, and if you don't change, you'll end up just like him—dead."

Reginald became angry and blurted out that he drank because that was all he had known as a child. "What do you mean?" his mother asked.

"Whenever Dad had a problem or when you two fought," Reginald said, "Dad broke open a bottle and killed the pain. It worked for him. It works for me. So you're right. I'm just like him. But it's not my fault. I learned it from him. You didn't stop him. And you didn't stop me."

Think about it

1. Is Reginald right? Did he learn his problem behavior from his father? What other factors might have contributed to his excessive use of alcohol?
2. Might the concept of reaction formation help explain Reginald's behavior? If so, how?
3. If you were Reginald's mother, to what degree would you hold your son responsible for his problem drinking? To what degree would you hold him responsible if you were a judge hearing his case in court?
4. Are questions about responsibility merely exercises in blame shifting? Is blame shifting ever appropriate when assessing criminal responsibility?

Note: Who's to Blame boxes provide fictionalized critical thinking opportunities, and are not actual cases.

who focused primarily on the gang behavior of delinquent youths: "When we speak of a delinquent subculture, we speak of a way of life that has somehow become traditional among certain groups in American society. These groups are the boys' gangs that flourish most conspicuously in the 'delinquency neighborhoods' of our larger American cities. The members of these gangs grow up, some to become law-abiding citizens and others to graduate to more professional and adult forms of criminality, but the delinquent tradition is kept alive by the age-groups that succeed them."[87] Cohen argued that youths from all backgrounds are generally held accountable to the norms of the wider society through a "middle-class measuring rod" of expectations related to school performance, language proficiency, cleanliness, punctuality, neatness, nonviolent behavior, and allegiance to other similar standards, but noted that not everyone is prepared, by birth circumstances and subsequent socialization, to effectively meet such expectations.

In an examination of vandalism, Cohen found that "non-utilitarian" delinquency, in which things of value are destroyed rather than stolen or otherwise used for financial gain, is the result of middle-class values turned upside down.[88] Delinquent youths, often alienated from middle-class values and lifestyles through deprivation and limited opportunities, can achieve status among their subcultural peers via vandalism and other forms of delinquent behavior.

Children from deprived backgrounds turn to delinquency because they experience status frustration when judged by adults and others according to middle-class standards and goals that they are unable to achieve, Cohen claimed. Because it is nearly impossible for them to succeed in middle-class terms, they also may overcome anxiety through the process of **reaction formation**, in which hostility toward middle-class values develops. (Cohen adapted

Reaction formation means the process in which a person openly rejects that which he or she wants, or aspires to, but cannot obtain or achieve.

reaction formation from psychiatric perspectives and used it to mean "the process in which a person openly rejects that which he wants, or aspires to, but cannot obtain or achieve."[89])

Cohen discovered the roots of delinquent subcultures in what he termed the "collective solution to the problem of status."[90] When youths who experience the same kind of alienation from middle-class ideals band together, they achieve a collective and independent solution and create a delinquent subculture. "The delinquent subculture, we suggest, is a way of dealing with the problems of adjustment. These problems are chiefly status problems: certain children are denied status in the respectable society because they cannot meet the criteria of the respectable status system. The delinquent subculture deals with these problems by providing criteria of status which these children can meet."[91]

Cohen's approach is effectively summarized in a theoretical scenario offered by Donald J. Shoemaker, who said that lower-class youths undergo a working-class socialization combining lower-class values and habits with middle-class success values.[92] Lower-class youths experience failure in school because they cannot live up to the middle-class norms operative in American educational institutions, suffer a consequent loss of self-esteem and increased feelings of rejection, drop out of school and associate with delinquent peers, and experience hostility and resentment toward middle-class standards through reaction formation. Such alienated youths achieve status and a sense of improved self-worth through participation in a gang of like-minded peers; delinquency and crime are the result.

The Code of the Street

Work by Elijah Anderson, who studied African American neighborhoods along Philadelphia's Germantown Avenue and published the results in his book titled *The Code of the Street*, offered a subcultural ethnography of the social mores operating in some American inner cities today.[93] In *The Code*, Anderson detailed aspects of street code that stress a hyperinflated notion of manhood resting squarely on the idea of respect: "At the heart of the code is the issue of respect, loosely defined as being treated 'right' or being granted one's 'props' (or proper due) or the deference one deserves." In street culture, a man's sense of worth is determined by the respect he commands when in public.

A crucial distinction between both families and individuals in inner-city neighborhoods like Germantown is expressed by what residents call the "decent family" and the "street family," marking people as either trying to uphold positive values or being oriented toward the street. Street life, Anderson explained, involves displays of physical strength and intellectual prowess meant to demonstrate that "I can take care of myself" and "I can take care of my own." Those who wholeheartedly embrace the street code are proud to live the "thug life," they identify with role models like Tupac Shakur and Young Jeezy, and they see people and situations as obstacles to be subdued or overcome, learning to outsmart or hustle others while avoiding being hustled themselves. See the Criminal Profiles box on gang member Sanyika Shakur, aka Monster Kody Scott.

Gangs Today

Gangs have become a major source of concern in contemporary American society. Although the writings of investigators like Cohen, Thrasher, and Cloward and Ohlin focused on the illicit activities of juvenile gangs in the nation's inner cities, most gang-related crimes involved vandalism, petty theft, and battles over turf. Today the ethnic distinctions that gave rise to gang culture in the 1920s through the 1950s are largely forgotten, and Italian, Hungarian, Polish, and Jewish immigrants, whose children made up many of the early gangs, have been successfully integrated into modern America.

Gangs have become a major source of concern in contemporary American society.

Today's gangs are quite different from the gangs of the first half of the twentieth century. More than one-third of jurisdictions covered by the 2010 National Youth Gang Survey (NYGS) conducted by the National Gang Center (NGC) reported experiencing gang problems in 2010, the highest annual estimate since before 1999.[94] Overall, an estimated 3,500 jurisdictions served by city and county law enforcement agencies reported gang problems. Survey results also indicated that an estimated 756,000 gang members and 29,400 gangs were active in the United States during 2010.

The 2010 NYGS confirmed previous findings that gang members are often involved in a variety of serious and violent crimes. Almost half of the law enforcement agencies reporting gang problems are involved in collaborative efforts with other law enforcement and criminal justice agencies to combat youth gangs and the serious and violent crimes they commit.

In addition to conducting surveys, the NGC provides a compilation of gang-related legislation, maintains a repository of gang-related literature, analyzes gang-related data and statistics, and coordinates the activities of the Youth Gang Consortium; you can visit the NGC via **Web Extra 7–7**. Another group of special interest to anyone wanting to know more about gangs is the National Alliance of Gang Investigators Associations; see **Web Extra 7–8**.

Although its data are older than data available through the NYGS, the National Gang Crime Research Center's Project

CRIMINAL | PROFILES

Sanyika Shakur—aka Monster Kody Scott

It is tempting to rely on Sanyika Shakur's compelling autobiography, *Monster: The Autobiography of an L.A. Gang Member*, as the primary reference for this box. But although much of the material is drawn from his memoir—Shakur is undeniably the world's expert on his alter ego Monster Kody Scott—there is more to this story than can be gleaned from his own writings.

Shakur repeatedly justifies brutal assaults he has committed as being the only reasonable solution "[w]hen the police and other government agencies don't seem to care about what is going on in our communities, those of us who live in them must take responsibility for their protection and maintenance."[i] Yet he also chillingly recounts other assaults, and even murders, as being a form of self-administered therapy to relieve his tensions from such terrible pressures as his mother telling him she disapproved of his lawless lifestyle and use of drugs.

For example, his need "to shoot somebody, eager to vent my anger," after being scolded by his mother for his criminality and marijuana use compelled him (at age 16) to go on the prowl on a bicycle, looking for suitable victims. Upon encountering "three cats who looked about my age leaning against a van, talking and drinking beer," he circled past them and opened fire with a .45-caliber pistol, leaving one victim "motionless in the street." Shakur said he went home, "put the bike in the garage, went to my room [and] fell asleep. I slept very well."[ii]

Susan Ragan/Associated Press

Sanyika Shakur (born Kody Scott), aka Monster Kody Scott, photographed at Pelican Bay prison in June 1993 through Plexiglas. The gangster thug of the literary set was sent back to prison in 2008 for beating a man and stealing his car while out on parole. Is Shakur a villain or a hero?

Born in the tumultuous 1960s (1963), 11-year-old Kody Scott (he adopted the name Sanyika Shakur in prison years later) earned initiation into the infamous Crips street gang with eight blasts from a shotgun aimed at a group of the notorious Bloods, a rival gang. His teen years were an odyssey of violent crime, interspersed with repeated stays in various juvenile detention centers and, ultimately, the California State Penitentiary.

His "Monster" moniker came from one such crime. After being robbed and beaten, the victim had the audacity to strike Shakur in the face, so Shakur "beat him, and stomped him and disfigured him," leaving the young man in a coma.[iii] The severity of the damage caused one investigating police officer to use the word *monster* to refer to the perpetrator, and Shakur decided to adopt the name. "[I]t was just power," he says, proudly. "And I felt it. And I just took that name."[iv]

Feared even by his fellow Crips, Shakur rose through the gang's leadership ranks until he eventually became one of its top leaders and achieved status as an Original Gangster (O.G.), the highest "honor" a gang member can receive.

Shakur calls his behavior inevitable, asserting there are no other options available to him and those like him to achieve success legitimately, portraying himself as the "inevitable product of a hellish environment."[v]

Shakur has been dubbed an "iconic figure" of the hip-hop culture by independent filmmaker Billy Wright, stating that Shakur's "real life encapsulates what hip hop imagery is all about."[vi] Wright's current project, titled *Can't Stop, Won't Stop*, tells Shakur's life story.

In December 2006, out on parole from yet another term in the California State Penitentiary, Shakur broke into a man's home and beat him in order to steal his car. In May 2008, as a result of those charges, he was sentenced to six years in prison. He had faced a possible life sentence without the possibility of parole as a persistent felon under California's three-strikes law.[vii]

The case of Sanyika Shakur raises a number of interesting questions. Among them are the following:

1. What approach to crime offered in this chapter might best explain Shakur's criminality?
2. How might differential association explain Shakur's criminality? Strain theory?
3. Shakur refers to his criminal behavior as "inevitable." Why would he say that? What does he mean?

Notes

i. Sanyika Shakur, *Monster: The Autobiography of an L.A. Gang Member* (reprint, New York: Grove Press, 2004), p. 379.
ii. Ibid., pp. 173–174.
iii. Mandalit Del Barco, "Gang Member Turned Author Arrested in L.A.," *Morning Edition*, National Public Radio, March 9, 2007, http://www.npr.org/templates/story/story.php?storyId=7793148 (accessed July 14, 2007).
iv. Ibid.
v. Mark Horowitz, "In Search of a Monster," *Atlantic Monthly*, December 1993, http://www.theatlantic.com/doc/199312/monster (accessed July 14, 2009).
vi. "America's O.G. Gangster—Monster Kody (aka Sanyika Shakur)," http://www.rapindustry.com/monster_cody.htm (accessed September 14, 2009).
vii. Del Barco, "Gang Member Turned Author Arrested in L.A."

David Grossman/Alamy

Three young men in the Sunset Park section of Brooklyn, New York, showing off gang signs. What would ecological theories say about gangs?

Gangfact provided a profile of gangs and gang members nationwide, based on data collected by 28 researchers in 17 states:[95]

- The average age for joining a gang nationally is 12.8 years of age.
- Over half who joined gangs have tried to quit.
- More than two-thirds of gangs have written rules for members to follow.
- Over half of all gangs hold regular weekly meetings.
- Nearly 30% of gangs require their members to pay dues.
- Approximately 55% of gang members were recruited by other gang members; the remainder sought out gang membership.
- Most gang members (79%) say they would leave the gang if given a second chance at life.
- Four-fifths of gang members report that their gangs sold crack cocaine.
- Most gangs (70%) are not racially exclusive and consist of members drawn from a variety of ethnic groups.
- One-third of gang members report that they have been able to conceal their gang membership from their parents.
- Most gangs (83%) report having female members, but few allow female members to assume leadership roles.
- Many gang members (40%) report knowing male members of their gangs who had raped females.

Gangs can also be big business. In addition to traditional criminal activities like burglary, extortion, vandalism, and protection rackets, drug dealing has become a mainstay of many inner-city gangs. Los Angeles police estimate that at least four city gangs earn over $1 million each per week through cocaine sales.[96] The potential for huge drug-based profits appears to have changed the nature of the gangs, making them more prone to violence and cutthroat tactics; gang killings, including the now-infamous drive-by shootings, have become commonplace in our nation's cities.

Rodney Dailey, a self-avowed former Boston-area drug dealer and gun-wielding gang member who is now the founder of Gang Peace, an outreach group that tries to reduce gang-related violence, said of today's gang world that "shoot before you get shot is the rule" and that today "things that normally people would have had fistfights about can get you shot or stabbed."[97]

Contemporary researchers are drawing some new distinctions between gangs and violence. G. David Curry and Irving A. Spergel, in a study of Chicago communities, distinguished between juvenile delinquency and gang-related homicide.[98] They found that communities characterized by high rates of delinquency do not necessarily experience exceptionally high rates of crime or of gang-related homicides, and they concluded that although gang activity may be associated with homicide, "gang homicide rates and delinquency rates are ecologically distinct community problems." Gang-related homicide seems to be well explained by classical theories of social disorganization and is especially prevalent in city areas characterized by in-migration and the "settlement of new immigrant groups." In their study, high rates of juvenile delinquency seemed to correlate more with poverty, which they defined as "social adaptation to chronic deprivation." According to Curry and Spergel, "Social disorganization and poverty rather than criminal organization and conspiracy may better explain the recent growth and spread of youth gangs to many parts of the country. Moreover, community organization and social opportunity in conjunction with suppression, rather than simply suppression and incapacitation, may be more effective policies in dealing with the social problem."[99] In proposing a national gang strategy, Finn-Aage Esbensen reminded policy makers that many gang members are delinquent before they become associated with gangs.[100] Esbensen stated that "concerns with gang suppression should not supplant efforts to implement effective delinquency intervention and prevention strategies."[101]

The term *co-offending* refers to the fact that youthful offenders tend to commit crimes in the company of their peers and is especially prevalent in the lives of gang members—about 40% of juvenile offenders commit most of their crimes with others. Co-offenders are also more likely to be recidivists; when young co-offenders were compared with young solo offenders, the co-offenders had high recidivism rates and committed high numbers of violent crimes. In a 2005 study of co-offending made

■ **Chicago Area Project** A program originating at the University of Chicago during the 1930s that focused on urban ecology and that attempted to reduce delinquency, crime, and social disorganization in transitional neighborhoods.

---

with grant support from the National Institute of Justice, Temple University Professor Joan McCord and fellow researchers found that violence appears to be learned in the company of others: "Co-offending actually may increase the likelihood that offenders will commit violent crimes. When young offenders affiliate with offenders who have previously used violence, the result appears to be an increase in the likelihood that they will subsequently commit a violent crime?[Y]oung offenders pick up attitudes and values from their companions."[102] Learn more about gangs from Professor Mike Carlie's online book *Into the Abyss* via **Library Extra 7–4**, and read a report on co-offending at **Library Extra 7–5**.

Policy Implications of Social Structure Theories

Theoretical approaches that fault social structure as the root cause of crime point in the direction of social action as a panacea. In the 1930s, for example, Clifford Shaw, in an effort to put his theories into practice and to reduce delinquency in transitional neighborhoods, established the **Chicago Area Project**. Shaw analyzed oral histories gathered from neighborhood citizens to determine that delinquents were essentially normal youngsters who entered into illegal activities at early ages, often through street play, so he worked to increase opportunities for young people to embark on successful work careers.

The Chicago Area Project attempted to reduce social disorganization in slum neighborhoods through the creation of community committees staffed with local residents rather than professional social workers. The project had three broad objectives: (1) improving the physical appearance of poor neighborhoods, (2) providing recreational opportunities for youths, and (3) involving project members directly in the lives of troubled youths through school and courtroom mediation. Although no effective assessment programs were established to evaluate the Chicago Area Project during the program's tenure, in 1984 RAND Corporation published a 50-year review of the program, declaring it "effective in reducing rates of juvenile delinquency."[103]

> The Chicago Area Project attempted to reduce social disorganization in slum neighborhoods through the creation of community committees.

Mobilization for Youth (a programmatic outgrowth of Cloward and Ohlin's theory of differential opportunity) provides a bold example of the treatment implications of social structure theories, seeking not only to provide new opportunities but also through direct social action to change the fundamental arrangements of society and thereby address the root causes of crime and deviance. Leaders of Mobilization for Youth decided that "what was needed to overcome formidable barriers to opportunity was not community organization but community action" that attacked entrenched political interests, so the program promoted "boycotts against schools, protests against welfare policies, rent strikes against 'slum landlords,' lawsuits to ensure poor people's rights, and voter registration."[104] A truly unusual government-sponsored program for its time, Mobilization for Youth was eventually disbanded amid protests that "the mandate of the President's Committee was to reduce delinquency, not to reform urban society or to try out sociological theories on American youths."[105]

The War on Poverty declared by the Kennedy and Johnson administrations during the 1960s and subsequent federal and state-run welfare programs that provided supplemental income assistance have been cited[106] as examples of programs that at least held the potential to reduce crime rates by redistributing wealth in American society.[107] Such programs, however, came under fire for perpetuating injustices and for financially penalizing responsible citizens who had to fund the programs. The federal Welfare Reform Reconciliation Act of 1996[108] reduced or eliminated long-term benefits that had previously been available through avenues like the federal Aid to Families with Dependent Children (AFDC) program and established stricter work requirements for welfare recipients through a new Welfare-to-Work program under the Personal Responsibility and Work Opportunity Reconciliation Act of 1996.[109]

Critique of Social Structure Theories

The fundamental assumption of social structure approaches is that social inequality, racism, and poverty are the root causes of crime. Hence, the social structure perspective is intimately associated with the first part of this text's theme, the social problems approach (described in Chapter 1). If the assumptions that inform social structure theories are true, they largely negate the claims of those who advocate our theme's other part, the social responsibility perspective.

> The fundamental assumption of social structure approaches is that social inequality, racism, and poverty are the root causes of crime.

Social structural explanations for criminality received an enormous boost during the 1960s with the report of President Lyndon B. Johnson's Commission on Law Enforcement and Administration of Justice, a widely disseminated and highly influential document that portrayed social inequality and stifled opportunity as fundamental causes of crime. Later, a number of social commentators began to question the nature of the relationship among poverty, apparent social inequities, and crime.[110] Some argued the inverse of the root causes argument: Poverty and social inequality are produced by crime rather than the other way around; disorder, fear, and crime undermine positive social and economic institutions; and families, schools, churches, businesses, and other institutions cannot function properly in social settings where crime is a taken-for-granted part of the social landscape. If this proposed inverse relationship is even partially true, then addressing poverty and social inequality as the root causes of crime is not only an ineffective crime-prevention strategy but also an unnecessarily costly one.

This chapter has identified three types of social structure theory, and each can be critiqued. Some authors have suggested that ecological theories give too much credence to the notion that spatial location determines crime and delinquency because the nature of any given location changes over time, and evolutions in land-use patterns (such as movement away from homeownership and toward rental or low-income housing) may seriously affect the nature of a neighborhood and the concomitant quality of its social organization. Rates of neighborhood crime and delinquency may be "an artifact of police decision-making practices" and may bear little objective relationship to the actual law violations in an area.[111] If police bias (focus on low-income inner-city areas) exists, it may seriously mislead researchers into categorizing certain areas as high in crime when enforcement decisions made by police administrators merely make them appear that way.

Another critique of the ecological school can be found in its seeming inability to differentiate between the condition of social disorganization and the things it is said to cause. What is the difference between social disorganization and high rates of delinquency? Isn't delinquency a form of the very thing said to cause it? Stephen J. Pfohl observed that early ecological writers sometimes used the incidence of delinquency as "both an example of disorganization and something caused by disorganization,"[112] making it difficult to gauge the efficacy of their explanatory approach.

Similarly, those who criticize the ecological approach note that many crimes occur outside of geographic areas said to be characterized by social disorganization. Murder, rape, burglary, drug use, and assault all occur in affluent, well-established neighborhoods; white-collar crime, cybercrime, and environmental crime may actually occur *more often* in well-established neighborhoods. Hence, the ecological approach is clearly not an adequate explanation for all crime or for all types of crime.

From a social responsibility perspective, those who criticize strain theory noted that Merton's strain theory is probably less applicable to American society today than it was in the 1930s because in the ensuing decades considerable effort has been made toward improving success opportunities for all Americans, regardless of ethnicity, race, or gender. Travis Hirschi criticized contemporary strain theory for its inability "to locate people suffering from discrepancy" and noted that human beings are naturally optimistic—a fact that "overrides [the] aspiration-expectation disjunction," concluding that "expectations appear to affect delinquency, but they do so regardless of aspirations, and strain notions are neither consistent with nor required by the data."[113] More recent studies have found that "delinquents do not report being more distressed than other youth."[114] Delinquent youths who are not afforded the opportunities for success available to others appear to be well shielded from sources of stress and despair through their participation in delinquency, so "although strain theorists often have portrayed the lives of delinquents in grim terms, this depiction does not square well with the lived world of delinquency."[115]

Subcultural approaches (the last of the three types of social structure explanations for crime discussed in this chapter) have been questioned by some criminologists who see them as lacking explanatory power. Canadian criminologist Gwynn Nettler called the notion of violent subcultures tautological, or circular, arguing that saying that people "are murderous because they live violently" does little to explain their behavior and that attributing fighting to "other spheres of violence" may be true but that it is fundamentally "uninformative."[116]

The subcultural approach has also been criticized for being racist because many so-called violent subcultures are said to be populated primarily by minorities. Margaret Anderson stated that "the problem with this explanation is that it turns attention away from the relationship of black communities to the larger society and it re-creates dominant stereotypes about blacks as violent, aggressive, and fearful. Although it may be true that rates of violence are higher in black communities, this observation does not explain the fact."[117] In sociological jargon, an observed correlation between race and violence does not necessarily provide a workable explanation for the relationship.

There are other problems with social structure theories that routinely link low levels of socioeconomic status to high levels of delinquency. Empirical studies have consistently found weak or nonexistent correlations between an individual's economic standing and his or her self-reported delinquency.[118] Although low socioeconomic status may promote delinquency by increasing social alienation and financial strain and by decreasing educational opportunity and occupational aspiration, high socioeconomic status may also promote delinquency by increasing a person's willingness to take risks and by decreasing the influence of conventional values. Parental monitoring (knowing where the child is and what he or she is doing) and parental discipline are far more effective predictors of the degree of delinquent involvement.[119]

According to Nettler, social structure theories suffer from another shortcoming that generally affects most other sociological perspectives on crime causation: "The conceptual bias of social scientists emphasizes environments—cultures and structures—as the powerful causes of differential conduct. This bias places an intellectual taboo on looking elsewhere for possible causes as, for example, in physiologies. This taboo is strongly applied against the possibility that ethnic groups may have genetically transmitted differential physiologies that have relevance for social behavior."[120] In other words, social scientists unnecessarily downplay the causative role of nonsociological factors. Many outside of sociology believe that such factors are important, but because sociological theorizing has captured the lion's share of academic attention over the past few decades, the role of other causative factors in the etiology of criminal behavior is in danger of being shortchanged.

Some also see the inability of social structure theories to predict which individuals—or what proportion of a given population—will turn to crime as a crucial failure of such perspectives. Although the large majority of people growing up in poverty-ridden inner-city areas probably experience an inequitable opportunity structure firsthand, only a relatively small number of them become criminal. Even if substantially more people living under such conditions become criminal compared to those living in other types of social environments, a large proportion of people being raised in deviant subcultures and experiencing strain still embrace noncriminal lifestyles. In his book *The Moral Sense*, James Q. Wilson suggested that most people—regardless of socialization experiences and structural aspects of their social circumstances—may still carry within them an inherent sense of fairness and interpersonal morality.[121] If what Wilson suggested is even partially true, then the explanatory power of social structure theories will inevitably be limited by human nature itself. Read a PBS interview with Wilson at **Library Extra 7–6**.

SUMMARY

- Sociological theories explore relationships among groups and institutions and envision crime as the result of social processes, as the natural consequence of aspects of social structure, or as the result of economic and class struggle. Sociological theories examine institutional arrangements within society and interactions among individuals, groups, and social institutions that affect socialization and have an impact on social behavior.
- Although different kinds of social structure theories have been advanced to explain crime, they all have one thing in common: They highlight those arrangements within society that contribute to the low socioeconomic status of identifiable groups—poverty, lack of education, absence of marketable skills, and subcultural values—as significant causes of crime and view members of socially and economically disadvantaged groups as being more likely to commit crime.
- Three subtypes of social structure theories can be identified: social disorganization theory, strain theory, and culture conflict theory. Social disorganization theory encompasses social pathology, seeing society as a kind of organism and crime and deviance as a kind of disease (or social pathology), and is often associated with social ecology and the Chicago School of criminology. Strain theory points to a lack of fit between socially approved success goals and the availability of socially approved means to achieve those goals, so individuals unable to succeed through legitimate means turn to other avenues (crime) that promise economic and social recognition. Culture conflict theory suggests that the root cause of criminality can be found in a clash of values between differently socialized groups over what is acceptable or proper behavior.
- Because theories of social structure look to the organization of society for their explanatory power, intervention strategies based on them typically seek to alleviate the social conditions thought to produce crime through social programs that increase socially acceptable opportunities for success and availability of meaningful employment.
- Social structure theories are open to criticisms. Social structure approaches assume that social inequality, racism, and poverty are the root causes of crime, but some argue the inverse: Poverty and social injustices are produced by crime rather than the other way around. If this proposed inverse relationship is even partially true, then addressing poverty and social inequality as the root causes of crime is not only an ineffective crime-prevention strategy but also an unnecessarily costly one.

KEY TERMS

anomie, 160
broken windows theory, 159
Chicago Area Project, 175
Chicago School of criminology, 158
conduct norm, 166
criminology of place, 158
cultural transmission, 158
culture conflict theory, 166
defensible space, 159
distributive justice, 163
ecological theory, 158
environmental criminology, 159
focal concern, 167
general strain theory (GST), 164
human ecology, 157
illegitimate opportunity structure, 170
negative affective state, 164
reaction formation, 171
relative deprivation, 163
social disorganization, 157
social disorganization theory, 156
social ecology, 157
social life, 155
social pathology, 157
social process, 155
social structure, 154
social structure theory, 155
sociological theory, 154
strain theory, 160
subcultural theory, 167
subculture, 167
technique of neutralization, 168

KEY NAMES

Robert Agnew, 164
Ernest Burgess, 157
Richard A. Cloward, 170
Albert Cohen, 170
Franco Ferracuti, 169
David Matza, 168
Henry McKay, 158
Robert K. Merton, 160
Walter B. Miller, 167
Lloyd E. Ohlin, 170
Robert Park, 157
Thorsten Sellin, 166
Clifford Shaw, 158
Rodney Stark, 159
Gresham Sykes, 168
W. I. Thomas, 157
Frederic M. Thrasher, 167
William F. Whyte, 167
Marvin Wolfgang, 169
Florian Znaniecki, 157

QUESTIONS FOR REVIEW

1. What is the nature of sociological theorizing? What are the assumptions on which sociological perspectives on crime causation rest?
2. What do sociologists mean by the term *social structure*? How might the organization and structure of a society contribute to criminality?
3. What are the three types of social structure theories that this chapter describes? What are the major differences among them?
4. What are the policy implications of the theories discussed in this chapter? What kinds of changes in society and in government policy might be based on the theories discussed here? Would they be likely to bring about a reduction in crime?
5. What are the shortcomings of the social structure approaches to understanding and preventing crime? Can these shortcomings be overcome?

QUESTIONS FOR REFLECTION

1. This text emphasizes the theme of social problems versus social responsibility. Which of the theoretical perspectives discussed in this chapter best support the social problems approach? Which support the social responsibility approach? Why?
2. What do we mean by the term *ecological*? Do you believe that ecological approaches have a valid place in contemporary criminological thinking? Why or why not?
3. How does the notion of a criminology of place differ from more traditional ecological theories? Do you see the approach of criminology of place as capable of offering anything new over traditional approaches? If so, what?
4. What is a violent subculture? Why do some subcultures seem to stress violence? How might participants in a subculture of violence be turned toward less aggressive ways?

Gina Sanders/Fotolia

CHAPTER 8
THEORIES OF SOCIAL PROCESS AND SOCIAL DEVELOPMENT

LEARNING OUTCOMES

After reading this chapter, you should be able to answer the following questions:

- How does the process of social interaction contribute to criminal behavior?
- What are the various social process perspectives discussed in this chapter?
- What kinds of social policy initiatives might be based on social process theories of crime causation?
- What are the shortcomings of the social process perspective?
- What are the various social development perspectives discussed in this chapter?
- What are the central concepts of social development theories?
- What kinds of social policy initiatives might be suggested by social development perspectives?
- What are the shortcomings of social development perspectives on criminality?

■ **social process theory** A theory that asserts that criminal behavior is learned in interaction with others and that socialization processes that occur as the result of group membership are the primary route through which learning occurs; also called interactionist theory.

■ **social development theory** An integrated perspective on human development that simultaneously examines many different levels of development—psychological, biological, familial, interpersonal, cultural, societal, and ecological.

Introduction: Labeling a Killer

In 2012, 24-year-old Joran van der Sloot stood before a Peruvian judge and pled guilty to the 2010 murder of 21-year-old Stephany Flores in a Lima, Peru, hotel room. "Yes, I want to plead guilty. I wanted from the first moment to confess sincerely," he told the judge. "I truly am sorry for this act. I feel very bad."[1] Van der Sloot, who gained notoriety as the prime suspect in the 2005 disappearance of 18-year-old Alabama cheerleader Natalee Holloway while she was vacationing on the island of Aruba, fled to Chile after the murder, but was extradited to face prosecution in Peru. Prior to sentencing, attorneys for Van der Sloot asked the judge for leniency, saying that their client killed Flores as a result of "extreme psychological trauma" that he had suffered as a result of the intense negative publicity he had received in the international news media following Holloway's disappearance. Rejecting his pleas, the judge imposed a sentence of 28 years in prison and ordered him to pay the Flores family $75,000 in reparations. He will be eligible for parole in 2026.[2]

Social process theories draw their explanatory power from the process of interaction between individuals and society.

Paolo Aguilar/EPA/Newscom

Joran van der Sloot in a Peruvian courtroom. Van der Sloot, who plead guilty to the murder of a 21-year-old Peruvian woman, remains the main suspect in the disappearance of Alabama cheerleader Natalee Holloway. How would social process theories explain his behavior?

The Perspective of Social Interaction

The theories discussed in the first part of this chapter are called **social process theories**, or interactionist perspectives, because they depend on the process of interaction between individuals and society for their explanatory power. The various types of social process theories include social learning theory, social control theory, and labeling theory. The second part of this chapter focuses on **social development theories**, which tend to offer an integrated perspective and place a greater emphasis on changes in offending over time. Figure 8–1 details the principles of social process and social development theories.

Social process theories of crime causation assume that everyone has the potential to violate the law and that criminality is not an innate human characteristic; instead, criminal behavior is learned in interaction with others, and the socialization process occurring as the result of group membership is seen as the primary route through which learning occurs. Among the most important groups contributing to the process of socialization are the family, peers, work groups, and reference groups with which one identifies because they instill values and norms in their members and communicate their acceptable worldviews and patterns of behavior.

Social process perspectives hold that the process through which criminality is acquired, deviant self-concepts are established, and criminal behavior results is active, open-ended, and ongoing throughout a person's life. They suggest that individuals who have weak stakes in conformity are more likely to be influenced by the social processes and contingent experiences that lead to crime, and that criminal choices tend to persist because they are reinforced by the reaction of society to those whom it has identified as deviant.

Types of Social Process Approaches

A number of theories can be classified under the social process umbrella: social learning theory, social control theory, labeling theory, reintegrative shaming, and dramaturgical perspective.

■ **Follow the author's tweets about the latest crime and justice news @schmalleger.**

■ **social learning theory** A perspective that places primary emphasis on the role of communication and socialization in the acquisition of learned patterns of criminal behavior and the values that support that behavior; also called learning theory.

■ **social control theory** A perspective that predicts that when social constraints on antisocial behavior are weakened or absent, delinquent behavior emerges. Rather than stressing causative factors in criminal behavior, social control theory asks why people actually obey rules instead of breaking them.

■ **differential association** The sociological thesis that criminality, like any other form of behavior, is learned through a process of association with others who communicate criminal values.

Principles of Social Process and Social Development Theories

- Social process theories of crime causation assume that everyone has the potential to violate the law and that criminality is not an innate human characteristic.
- Criminal behavior is learned through interaction with others, and the socialization process that occurs as the result of group membership is seen as the primary route through which learning occurs.
- Among the most important groups contributing to the process of socialization are family, peers, work groups, and reference groups with which one identifies.
- This is the process through which criminality is acquired; deviant self-concepts are established; and criminal behavior results are active, open-minded, and ongoing throughout a person's life.
- Individuals who have low stakes in conformity are more likely to be influenced by the social processes and contingent experiences that lead to crime. Criminal choices, once made, tend to persist because they are reinforced by the reaction of society to those whom it has identified as deviant.
- The social development perspective understands that development begins at birth (and perhaps even earlier) and occurs primarily within a social context.
- Human development occurs on many levels simultaneously, including psychological, biological, familial, interpersonal, cultural, societal, and ecological. Hence, social development theories tend to be integrated theories, or theories that combine various points of view on the process of development.
- Social development theories focus more on individual rates of offending and seek to understand both increases and decreases in rates of offending over the individual's lifetime. Social development theories generally use longitudinal (over time) measurements of delinquency and offending, and they pay special attention to the transitions that people face as they move through the life cycle.
- Most theories of social development recognize that a critical transitional period occurs as a person moves from childhood to adulthood.

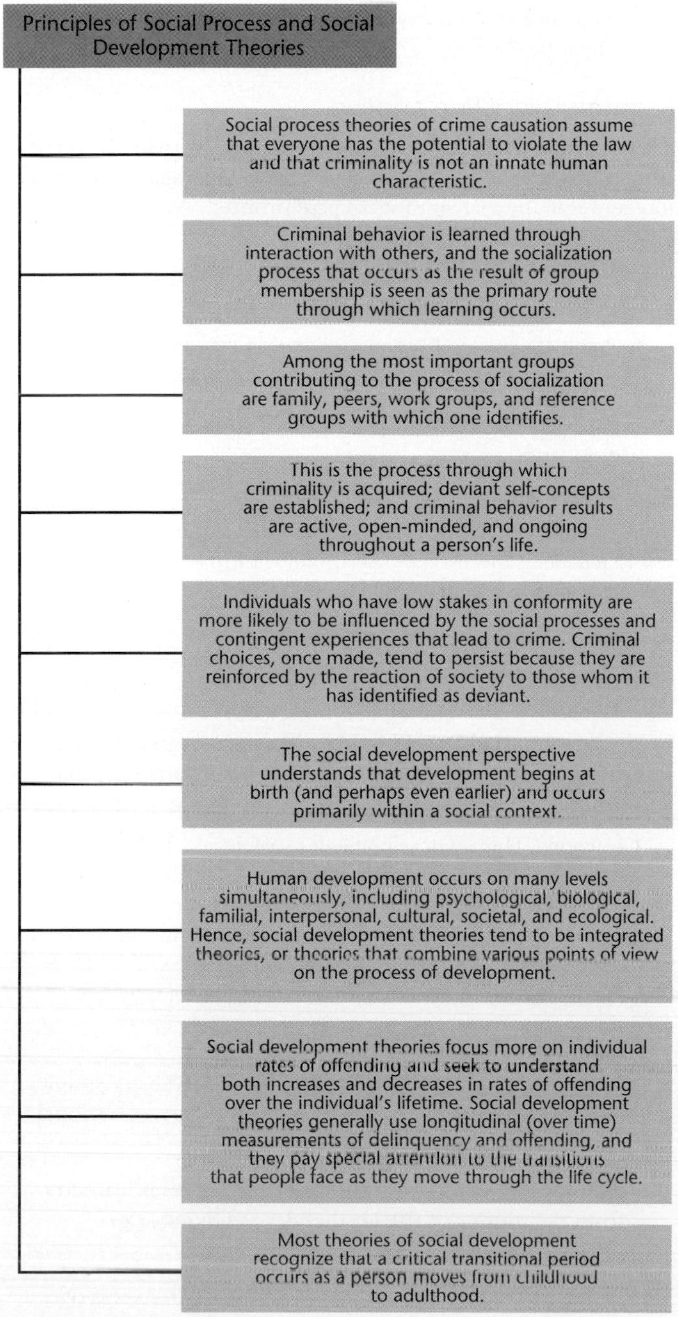

FIGURE 8-1 | Principles of Social Process and Social Development Theories

Source: Schmalleger, Frank J., *Criminology*. Printed and Electronically reproduced by permission of Pearson Education, Inc., Upper Saddle River, New Jersey.

Social learning theory places primary emphasis on the role of communication and socialization in the acquisition of learned patterns of criminal behavior and the values supporting that behavior, whereas **social control theory** focuses on the strength of the bond people share with individuals and institutions around them, especially as those relationships shape their behavior. Labeling theory points to the special significance of society's response to the criminal and sees the process through which a person comes to be defined as a criminal, along with society's imposition of the label "criminal," as a significant contributory factor in future criminality. Reintegrative shaming, a contemporary offshoot of labeling theory, emphasizes possible positive outcomes of the labeling process; the dramaturgical perspective focuses on how people can effectively manage the impressions they make on others. It is to different social learning theories that we now turn our attention.

Social Learning Theory

Social learning theory (also called learning theory) says that all behavior is learned in much the same way and that such learning includes the acquisition of norms, values, and patterns of behaviors conducive to crime, meaning that crime is also learned and that people learn to commit crime from others. Criminal behavior is a product of the social environment, not an innate characteristic of particular people.

Differential Association

One of the earliest and most influential forms of social learning theory was advanced by **Edwin Sutherland** in 1939, who stated that criminality is learned through a process of **differential association** with others who communicate criminal values and who advocate the commission of crimes.[3] He emphasized the role of social learning as an explanation for crime because he believed that many concepts popular in the field of criminology at the time—including social pathology, genetic inheritance, biological characteristics, and personality flaws—were inadequate to explain the process by which an otherwise normal individual turns to crime. Sutherland was the first well-known criminologist to suggest that all significant human behavior is learned and that crime is not substantively different from any other form of behavior.

Although Sutherland died in 1950, the tenth edition of his famous book, *Criminology*, was published in 1978 under the authorship of Donald R. Cressey, a professor at the University

THEORY | in PERSPECTIVE

Types of Social Process Theories

Social process theories (also called interactionist theories) depend on the process of interaction between individuals and society for their explanatory power. They assume that everyone has the potential to violate the law and that criminality is not an innate human characteristic; instead, criminal behavior is learned in interaction with others, and the socialization process that occurs as the result of group membership is seen as the primary route through which learning occurs.

Social Learning Theory

Social learning theory (also called learning theory) says that all behavior is learned in much the same way and that crime is also learned. It places primary emphasis on the roles of communication and socialization in the acquisition of learned patterns of criminal behavior and the values supporting that behavior.

Period: 1930s–present

Theorists: Edwin Sutherland, Robert Burgess, Ronald L. Akers, Daniel Glaser

Concepts: Differential association, differential association–reinforcement (including operant conditioning), differential identification

Social Control Theory

Social control theory focuses on the strength of the bond people share with the individuals and institutions around them, especially as those relationships shape their behavior, and seeks to identify those features of the personality and of the environment that keep people from committing crimes.

Period: 1950s–present

Theorists: Walter C. Reckless, Howard B. Kaplan, Travis Hirschi, Michael Gottfredson, Charles R. Tittle, Per-Olof H. Wikström, and others

Concepts: Inner and outer containment, self-derogation, social bond, control–balance, general theory of crime (GTC), situational action theory (SAT)

Labeling Theory

Labeling theory (also called social reaction theory) points to the special significance of society's response to the criminal and sees continued crime as a consequence of limited opportunities for acceptable behavior that follow from the negative responses of society to those defined as offenders.

Period: 1938–1940, 1960s–1980s, 1990s

Theorists: Frank Tannenbaum, Edwin M. Lemert, Howard Becker, John Braithwaite, others

Concepts: Tagging, labeling, outsiders, moral enterprise, primary and secondary deviance, reintegrative shaming, stigmatic shaming

Dramaturgical Perspective

The dramaturgical perspective depicts human behavior as centered around the purposeful management of impressions and seeks explanatory power in the analysis of social performances.

Period: 1960s–present

Theorists: Erving Goffman, others

Concepts: Total institutions, impression management, back and front regions, performances, discrediting information, stigma, spoiled identity

The Social Development Perspective

The social development perspective provides an integrated view of human development that examines multiple levels of maturity simultaneously, including the psychological, biological, familial, interpersonal, cultural, societal, and ecological levels.

Period: 1980s-present

Theorists: Sheldon and Eleanor Glueck, Terrie E. Moffitt, Robert J. Sampson, John H. Laub, Glen H. Elder, Jr., David P. Farrington and Donald J. West, Marvin Wolfgang, Lawrence E. Cohen and Richard Machalek, Terrence Thornberry, and others

Concepts: Human development, social development perspective, life course criminology, career criminal, life course, human agency, turning points, social capital, life course–persistent offenders, adolescence-limited offenders, persistence, desistance, evolutionary ecology

---

of California at Santa Barbara. The 1978 edition of *Criminology* contained the finalized principles of differential association (which, for all practical purposes, were complete as early as 1947). Nine in number, the principles read as follows:[4]

1. Criminal behavior is learned.
2. Criminal behavior is learned in interaction with others in a process of communication.
3. The principal part of the learning of criminal behavior occurs within intimate personal groups.
4. When criminal behavior is learned, the learning includes (a) techniques of committing the crime, which are sometimes very complicated and sometimes very simple, and (b) the specific direction of motives, drives, rationalizations, and attitudes.
5. The specific direction of motives and drives is learned from definitions of the legal codes as favorable or unfavorable.
6. A person becomes delinquent because of an excess of definitions favorable to law violation over definitions unfavorable to law violation.
7. Differential associations may vary in frequency, duration, priority, and intensity.

8. The process of learning criminal behavior by association with criminal and anticriminal patterns involves all mechanisms involved in any other learning.
9. Although criminal behavior is an expression of general needs and values, it is not explained by those general needs and values because noncriminal behavior is also an expression of the same needs and values.

Differential association found considerable acceptance among mid-twentieth-century theorists because it combined then-prevalent psychological and sociological principles into a coherent perspective on criminality. Crime as a form of learned behavior became the catchword, and biological and other perspectives were largely abandoned by those involved in the process of theory testing.

Differential Association–Reinforcement Theory

In 1966, **Robert Burgess** and **Ronald L. Akers** published an article titled "A Differential Association–Reinforcement Theory of Criminal Behavior."[5] The perspective, often termed differential reinforcement theory or sociological learning theory, expands on Sutherland's original idea of differential association by adding the idea of reinforcement, the concept of the power of punishments and rewards to shape behavior (see the heading "Behavior Theory" in Chapter 5). In developing their perspective, Burgess and Akers integrated psychological principles of operant conditioning with sociological notions of differential association, and they reorganized Sutherland's nine principles into seven, the first of which stated, "Criminal behavior is learned according to the principles of operant conditioning."[6] Fundamental to this perspective is the belief that human beings learn to define behaviors that are rewarded as positive and that an individual's criminal behavior is rewarded at least sometimes by individuals and groups that value such activity.

Although the 1966 Burgess–Akers article only alluded to the term *social learning*, Akers began to apply that term to differential association–reinforcement theory with the 1973 publication of his book *Deviant Behavior: A Social Learning Approach*.[7] According to Akers, "The basic assumption in social learning theory is that the same learning process, operating in a context of social structure, interaction, and situation, produces both conforming and deviant behavior."[8] Akers identified two primary learning mechanisms: differential reinforcement (also called instrumental conditioning), in which behavior is a function of the frequency, amount, and probability of experienced and perceived contingent rewards and punishments, and imitation, in which the behavior of others and its consequences are observed and modeled. These learning mechanisms, said Akers, operate in a process of differential association involving direct and indirect verbal and nonverbal communication, interaction, and identification with others. As with Sutherland's theory of differential association, the relative frequency, intensity, duration, and priority of associations remain important because they determine the amount, frequency, and probability of reinforcement of behavior that is either conforming or deviant. Interpersonal association also plays an important role because it can expose individuals to deviant or conforming norms and role models.

Differential association theory says that criminality is learned through a process of association with criminal others.

Akers continued to develop learning theory and in 1998 published the book *Social Learning and Social Structure*, in which he explained crime rates as a function of social learning that occurs within a social structure.[9] He called this explanation of the model of crime the social structure–social learning model (SSSL) and summarized it in seven concise propositions:[10]

1. Deviant behavior is learned according to the principles of operant conditioning.
2. Deviant behavior is learned both in nonsocial situations that are reinforcing or discriminating and through social interaction in which the behavior of others is reinforcing or discriminating for such behavior.
3. The principal part of the learning of deviant behavior occurs in those groups that comprise or control the individual's major source of reinforcements.
4. The learning of deviant behavior, including specific techniques, attitudes, and avoidance procedures, is a function of the effective and available reinforcers and the existing reinforcement contingencies.
5. The specific class of behavior learned and its frequency of occurrence are a function of the effective and available reinforcers and the deviant or nondeviant direction of the norms, rules, and definitions that in the past have accompanied the reinforcement.
6. The probability that a person will commit deviant behavior is increased in the presence of normative statements, definitions, and verbalizations that, in the process of

■ **differential identification theory** An explanation for crime and deviance that holds that people pursue criminal or deviant behavior to the extent that they identify themselves with real or imaginary people from whose perspective their criminal or deviant behavior seems acceptable.

differential reinforcement of such behavior over conforming behavior, have acquired discriminative value.

7. The strength of deviant behavior is a direct function of the amount, frequency, and probability of its reinforcement. The modalities of association with deviant patterns are important insofar as they affect the source, amount, and scheduling of reinforcement.

Akers's SSSL theory says that social learning is the social-psychological mediating process through which social structural aspects of the environment work to cause crime and that it integrates two levels of explanation—social structure and social learning—by specifying the links between the larger social context and the individual relationships that lead to criminal behavior.[11] Hence, a person's location in the social structure—defined by age, gender, ethnicity, place of residence, and so on—is seen as a major determinant of how that person is socialized and what he or she will learn.

Differential Identification Theory

Like Akers, **Daniel Glaser** built on Sutherland's notion of differential association, and Glaser offered a **differential identification theory**.[12] The central tenet of Glaser's differential identification theory is that "a person pursues criminal behavior to the extent that he identifies himself with real or imaginary persons from whose perspective his criminal behavior seems acceptable."[13] Glaser proposed that the process of differential association leads to an intimate personal identification with lawbreakers, resulting in criminal or delinquent acts. Glaser recognized that people will identify with various people and that some of these identifications will be relatively strong and others weaker—hence the term *differential identification*. According to Glaser, it is not the frequency or intensity of association that determines behavior (as Sutherland believed) but the symbolic process of identification. Identification with a person or with an abstract understanding of what that person might be like can be more important than actual associations with real people. Role models can consist of abstract ideas as well as actual people, so an individual might identify with a serial killer or a terrorist bomber even though he or she has never met that person. Glaser also recognized the role of economic conditions, frustrations with one's place in the social structure, learned moral creeds, and group participation in producing differential identifications. Alternatively, identification with noncriminals offers the possibility of rehabilitation.

Identification with noncriminals offers the possibility of rehabilitation.

A recent meta-analysis of 133 empirical studies of social learning theory that had been published in leading criminology journals between 1974 and 2003 found strong support for concepts such as differential association and "definitions favorable to law violations," but less support for ideas like differential reinforcement and modeling/imitation.[14] The authors concluded that "the empirical support for social learning theory stacks up well relative to the criminological other perspectives that have been subjected to metaanalysis." Learn more about social learning and adolescent development via **Library Extras 8–1** and **8–2**.

James King-Holmes/Science Photo Library/Photo Researchers, Inc.

A child watching his mother smoke a cigarette. Social learning theory says that social behavior is learned. Will this child grow up to be a smoker?

Social Control Theories

We mentioned earlier that theories of social control focus primarily on the strength of the bond that people share with the individuals and institutions around them, especially as those relationships shape their behavior. According to **Charles R. Tittle**, a prominent sociologist at Washington State University with a specialty in crime and deviance, social control theory emphasizes "the inhibiting effect of social and psychological integration with others whose potential negative response, surveillance, and expectations regulate or constrain criminal impulses."[15] In other words, social control theorists seek to identify those features

■ **containment theory** A form of control theory that suggests that a series of both internal and external factors contributes to law-abiding behavior.

of the personality (see Chapter 6) and the environment (see Chapter 7) that keep people from committing crimes. According to Tittle, social control theorists take a step beyond static aspects of the personality and physical features of the environment in order to focus on the process through which social integration develops. The extent of a person's integration with positive social institutions and with significant others determines that person's resistance to criminal temptations, and social control theorists focus on the process through which such integration develops. Rather than stressing causative factors in criminal behavior, social control theories tend to ask why people actually obey rules instead of breaking them.[16]

Containment Theory

In the 1950s, a student of the Chicago School of criminology, **Walter C. Reckless**, wrote *The Crime Problem*.[17] He tackled head-on the realization that most sociological theories, although conceptually enlightening, offered less-than-perfect predictability, being unable to predict which individuals (even those exposed to various "causes" of crime) would become criminal. Reckless thought that prevalent sociological perspectives offered only half of a comprehensive theoretical framework, writing that crime was the consequence of both social pressures to become involved in violations of the law and failures to resist such pressures. Reckless called his approach **containment theory** and compared it with a biological immune response, saying that only some people exposed to a disease actually come down with it and that both sickness and crime result from the failure of control mechanisms, some internal and others external.

In the case of crime, Reckless wrote that external containment consists of "the holding power of the group."[18] Under most circumstances, Reckless said that "the society, the state, the tribe, the village, the family, and other nuclear groups are able to hold the individual within the bounds of the accepted norms and expectations."[19] In addition to setting limits, he saw society as providing individuals with meaningful roles and activities, also important factors of external containment.

Reckless stated that inner containment "represents the ability of the person to follow the expected norms, to direct himself."[20] For Reckless, this ability is enhanced by a positive self-image, a focus on socially approved goals, personal aspirations in line with reality, a tolerance for frustration, and a general adherence to society's norms and values.

In Figure 8–2 (a diagram of containment theory), "Pushes toward Crime" represents those factors in an individual's background that might propel him or her into criminal behavior, including a criminogenic background or upbringing involving participation in a delinquent subculture, deprivation, biological propensities toward deviant behavior, and psychological maladjustment. "Pulls toward Crime" signifies all the perceived

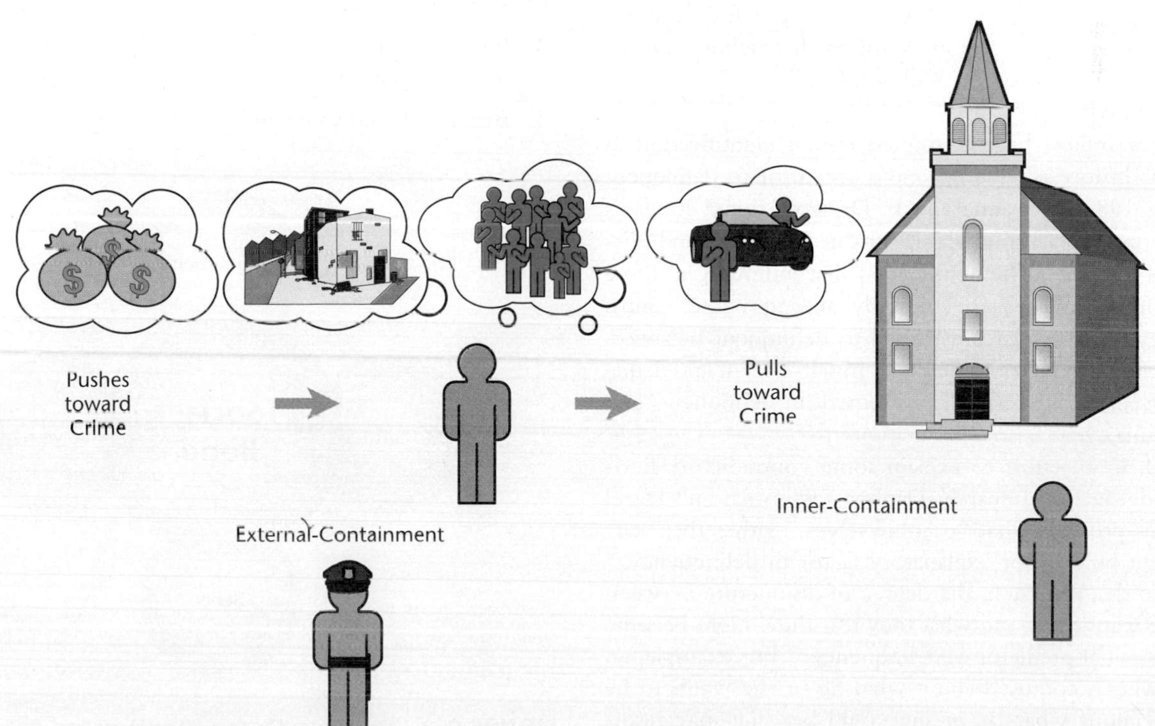

FIGURE 8–2 | A Diagrammatic Representation of Containment Theory

■ **containment** An aspect of the social bond that acts as a stabilizing force to prevent individuals from committing crimes and that keeps them from engaging in deviance.

■ **social bond** The link, created through socialization, between individuals and the society of which they are a part.

rewards, including financial gain, sexual satisfaction, and higher status, that crime may offer. **Containment** is a stabilizing force that blocks such pushes and pulls from leading the individual into crime.

Reckless believed that inner containment was far more effective than external containment in preventing law violations. "As social relations become more impersonal, as society becomes more diverse and alienated, as people participate more and more for longer periods of time away from a home base, the self becomes more and more important as a controlling agent."[21]

Delinquency and Self-Esteem

Social control theory predicts that when social constraints on antisocial behavior are weakened or absent, delinquent behavior will emerge. An innovative perspective on social control was offered by **Howard B. Kaplan** in the mid-1970s, when he proposed that people who are ridiculed by their peers suffer a loss of self-esteem, assess themselves poorly, and abandon the motivation to conform.[22] This approach has come to be known as the *self-derogation theory of delinquency*.

Numerous studies appear to support the idea that low self-esteem fosters delinquent behavior.[23] However, it appears that delinquency can also enhance self-esteem, at least for some delinquents;[24] for example, one study found that delinquent behavior enhances self-esteem in adolescents whose self-esteem is already very low.[25]

Some researchers have examined ethnic identification as both a factor in low self-esteem and a precursor to delinquent behavior. In 1986, K. Leung and F. Drasgow tested Kaplan's self-derogation theory using white, African American, and Hispanic youth groups.[26] They concluded that although all three groups reported low self-esteem, only among white youths were low levels of self-esteem related to delinquent behavior. Other researchers found no differences in self-esteem and delinquency between white and African American delinquents and nondelinquents.[27]

In 1990, in an effort to explain some contradictory findings of self-derogation research, Daphna Oyserman and Hazel Rose Markus proposed that "possible selves," rather than self-esteem, might be a major explanatory factor in delinquency.[28] According to this approach, the degree of disjuncture between what people want to be and what they fear they might become is a good potential predictor of delinquency.[29] For example, an adolescent who is confused about what he or she wants to be or is fearful about what he or she could become may resort to delinquency in order to resolve the conflict. Oyserman and Markus suggested that the highest levels of delinquency can be found among youths who lack balance between their expected selves and their feared selves.

Social Bond Theory

An important form of social control theory was popularized by **Travis Hirschi** in his 1969 book *Causes of Delinquency*.[30] Hirschi's approach was well received by criminologists and "epitomized social control theorizing for nearly three decades."[31] Hirschi argued that through successful socialization, a bond forms between individuals and the social group, but when that bond is weakened or broken, deviance and crime may result. Hirschi described four components of the **social bond** (Figure 8–3):

> A social bond forms between individuals and society; when that bond is weakened or broken, deviance and crime may result.

1. Attachment (a person's shared interests with others)
2. Commitment (the amount of energy and effort put into activities with others)
3. Involvement (the amount of time spent with others in shared activities)
4. Belief (a shared value and moral system)

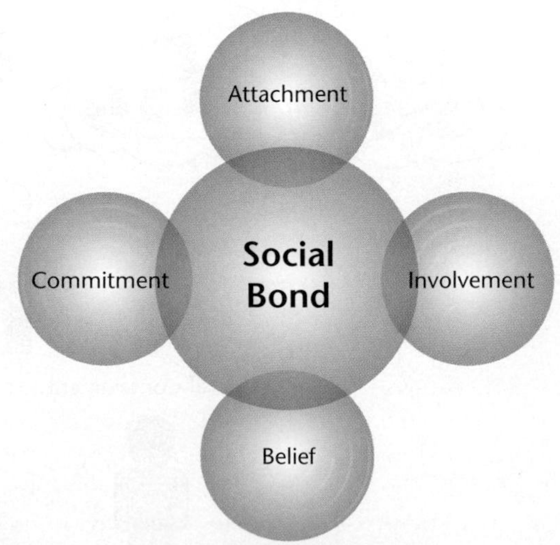

FIGURE 8–3 | **The Four Components of the Social Bond**

Source: Schmalleger, Frank J., *Criminology*. Printed and Electronically reproduced by permission of Pearson Education, Inc., Upper Saddle River, New Jersey.

CRIME | in the NEWS

Is There a Crime Gene?

After Dale Vincent Bogle, a lifelong criminal, died in 1998, researchers counted 28 members of his immediate family—including brothers, sons, daughters, and grandchildren—who served prison time. "Rooster," as he was called, shepherded his sons into crime, teaching them to shoplift at an early age. But according to scientific research, genes might also explain why so many Bogle family members took up crime.

A study released in 2012 found that genetic influences were even more significant than environmental factors in producing lifelong criminals. Surveying identical twins, fraternal twins, nontwin siblings, half-siblings, and first cousins, University of Texas at Dallas criminologist J. C. Barnes and colleagues found that genetic factors explained 56% to 70% of the variance for lifelong criminals.

The role of genes in criminality still makes some researchers nervous. It harkens back to eugenics, a theory that viewed criminals as hereditary degenerates. Harvard criminologist Earnest A. Hooton, who died in 1954, linked physical features such as sloping foreheads to criminal traits, and he advocated sterilization for those who had these traits.

Today, criminologists exploring genetics have a very different attitude. Barnes and others do not examine physical characteristics and believe genes cannot fully predetermine crime. Rather, they think genetic predispositions have to be triggered by several environmental factors, such as a chaotic home life and reprobate friends. "Criminals are not born, but the odds at the moment of birth of becoming one are not even," said Irving Gottesman, a psychologist at the University of Virginia.

Researchers like Barnes do not believe there is a specific "crime gene." "There are likely to be hundreds, if not thousands, of genes that will incrementally increase your likelihood of being involved in a crime, even if it only ratchets that probability by 1 percent," Barnes said. This theory may not help us predict crime, but it does help explain why so many members of Rooster Bogle's extended family gravitated to crime.

Barnes's stipulation that people can defy the genetic odds is also readily apparent. When James "Whitey" Bulger, a Boston gang leader, was arrested in 2011, after a 16-year manhunt, his life of crime was contrasted with the life of his younger brother, William "Billy" Bulger, who served as president of the Massachusetts Senate for 18 years. While a young Whitey Bulger was serving time in Alcatraz, Billy was going to law school.

Discussion Questions

1. This article seems to say that crime runs in families. Is that assertion likely to be true? If so, why?
2. What kinds of social policies might be built on the ideas expressed in this article?

Sources: Patricia Cohen, "Genetic Basis for Crime: A New Look," *New York Times*, June 19, 2011, http://www.nytimes.com/2011/06/20/arts/genetics-and-crime-at-institute-of-justice-conference.html?pagewanted=all&_r=0; Fox Butterfield, "Father Steals Best: Crime in an American Family," *New York Times*, August 21, 2002, http://www.nytimes.com/2002/08/21/us/father-steals-best-crime-in-an-american-family.html?pagewanted=all&src=pm; and Rick Klein, "Tale of Two Brothers: Whitey and Billy Bulger's Rise to Power in Crime and Politics," ABC News, January 23, 2011, http://abcnews.go.com/Politics/james-whitey-bulger-billy-bulger-powerful-brothers-powerful/story?id=13915585#.UKPMkBzhO_F.

The first component, attachment, refers to a person's shared interests with others. In his writings, Hirschi cites the psychopath as an example of the kind of person whose attachment to society is nearly nonexistent.[32] Other relatively normal individuals may find their attachment to society loosened through "the process of becoming alienated from others [which] often involves or is based on active interpersonal conflict," says Hirschi. "Such conflict could easily supply a reservoir of socially derived hostility sufficient to account for the aggressiveness of those whose attachments to others have been weakened."[33]

The second component of the social bond—commitment—reflects a person's investment of time and energies into conforming behavior and the potential loss of the rewards that he or she has already gained from that behavior. In Hirschi's words, "The idea, then, is that the person invests time, energy, himself, in a certain line of activity—say, getting an education, building up a business, acquiring a reputation for virtue. Whenever he considers deviant behavior, he must consider the costs of this deviant behavior, the risk he runs of losing the investment he has made in conventional behavior."[34] For such a traditionally successful person, committing petty theft is stupid because the potential loss far exceeds the possible gains. Recognizing that his approach applies primarily to individuals who have been successfully socialized into conventional society, Hirschi added, "The concept of commitment assumes that the organization of society is such that the interests of most persons would be endangered if they were to engage in criminal acts."[35]

Involvement, the third aspect, means "engrossment in conventional activities"[36] and is similar to Reckless's concept of meaningful roles. In explaining the importance of involvement in determining conformity, Hirschi cited the colloquial saying that "idle hands are the devil's workshop"—time and energy are limited, so if a person is busy with legitimate pursuits, he or she will have little opportunity for crime and deviance.

Belief (the last of his four aspects of the social bond) sets Hirschi's control theory apart from subcultural approaches because "control theory assumes the existence of a common value system within the society or group whose norms are being

■ **general theory of crime (GTC)** The assertion that the operation of a single mechanism, low self-control, accounts for "all crime, at all times," including acts ranging from vandalism to homicide, from rape to white-collar crime.

GTC holds that crime is a natural consequence of unrestrained human tendencies to seek pleasure and avoid pain.

violated. We not only assume the deviant has believed the rules [but also] assume he believes the rules even as he violates them."[37] How can a person simultaneously believe it is wrong to commit a crime and still commit it? Hirschi's answer would be that "many persons do not have an attitude of respect toward the rules of society."[38] Although they know the rules exist, they basically do not care and invest little of their sense of self in moral standards.

The General Theory of Crime

In 1990, **Michael Gottfredson**, in collaboration with Hirschi, proposed a **general theory of crime (GTC)** based on the concepts advanced earlier in control theory.[39] "Gottfredson and Hirschi's general theory of crime claims to be general, in part, due to its assertion that the operation of a single mechanism, low self-control, accounts for 'all crime, at all times'; acts ranging from vandalism to homicide, from rape to white-collar-crime."[40] Gottfredson and Hirschi defined self-control as the degree to which a person is vulnerable to temptations of the moment.[41] They proposed that self-control is acquired early in life and that low self-control is the premier individual-level cause of crime. It develops by the end of childhood and is fostered through parental emotional investment in the child, monitoring the child's behavior, recognizing deviance when it occurs, and punishing the child.

Gottfredson and Hirschi thought that it was important to ask, "What is crime?" Because nearly all crimes are mundane, simple, trivial, easy acts aimed at satisfying desires of the moment, their general theory is built on a classical or rational choice perspective—the belief that crime is a natural consequence of unrestrained human tendencies to seek pleasure and avoid pain. They concluded that crime is little more than a subset of general deviant behavior and bears little resemblance to the explanations offered in the media, by law enforcement officials, or by most academic thinkers on the subject.

According to Gottfredson and Hirschi, the offender is neither the diabolical genius of fiction nor the ambitious seeker of the American Dream often portrayed by other social scientists. Offenders appear to have little control over their own desires,

Steve Rubin/The Image Works

An example of a social bond forming early in life. What might this child be learning?

so when personal desires conflict with long-term interests, those who lack self-control often opt for the desires of the moment, thus contravening legal restrictions and becoming involved in crime.[42]

Central to Gottfredson and Hirschi's thesis is the belief that a well-developed social bond will result in the creation of effective mechanisms of self-control. "For Gottfredson and Hirschi, self-control is the key concept in the explanation of all forms of crime as well as other types of behavior. Indeed, they believe that all current differences in rates of crime between groups and categories may be explained by differences in the management of self-control."[43]

One recent Canadian study found that the effect of good parenting on the development of positive self-control was very strong, but that the role of factors such as household size and family structure also could make an important difference.[44] Families in which children lived with both biological parents seemed to be best at developing self-control in their children, whereas lower levels of self-control were found in single-parent families and in reconstituted families in which the parents had been divorced and remarried. The researchers concluded that "overall, regardless of family structure, it is evident that a nurturing, accepting family environment is positively associated with self-control."[45]

■ **situational action theory (SAT)** A perspective on crime holding that criminal behavior is the result of human decision making based on personal morality when viewed within the context of the existing situation. SAT stresses the importance of moral interpretations over a person's ability to exercise self-control.

Some researchers have called the argument that self-control develops early in childhood and persists over time the *stability thesis*. In research reported in 2006, Florida State University criminologists Carter Hay and Walter Forrest conducted a test of the stability thesis, finding moderately strong support for it:[46] Levels of self-control that developed early in childhood tended to persist, but not as strongly as the general theory of crime would suggest; 16% of the study population showed changes in levels of self-control over time, and those individuals demonstrating the greatest stability in self-control started at the highest levels.

More recent research appears to show that low self-control tends to lead to peer rejection and isolation—especially among juveniles.[47] Consequently, young people with low self-control tend to associate with their deviant peers, meaning that those with low levels of self-control are essentially self-selected into groups of people who share their characteristics. Constance L. Chapple of the University of Nebraska explained that "the delinquent peer group may provide increased opportunities for crime or exert situational pushes towards delinquency" because of the lack of self-control that characterizes its members.[48]

Gottfredson and Hirschi rejected the notion that some people have an enduring propensity to commit crime or that any such propensity compels people to do so.[49] Crimes require "no special capabilities, needs, or motivation; they are, in this sense, available to everyone."[50] However, some people have a tendency to ignore the long-term consequences of their behavior; they tend to be impulsive, reckless, and self-centered, and they often end up committing crime because of such tendencies.[51]

A meta-analysis (a summary analysis of other research) of 21 studies of self-control theory conducted by Travis Pratt and Francis Cullen in 2000 found considerable support for the thesis that lack of self-control plays a central role in crime and deviance.[52] Looking at various studies that explored self-control as a delinquency preventative—including those on self-reported juvenile delinquency, self-reported and projected crime and deviance among college students, adult criminal behavior, and official delinquency—Pratt and Cullen concluded that low self-control is "one of the strongest known correlates of crime."

Carter Hay of Washington State University studied the role that parenting plays in the development of self-control and concluded that effective parenting can contribute to the development of self-control in children.[53] He pointed out that although Gottfredson and Hirschi recognized the importance of parenting in the development of self-control, they failed to adequately consider the nature of effective parenting, which must involve fair and nonphysical forms of discipline; harsh or unfair discipline did not appear to contribute to the development of children's self-control. Hay stated, "The sort of discipline that teaches children to control their behavior is not simply that which consistently occurs in the wake of deviance; other factors may be consequential as well, including the extent to which discipline is perceived as fair and is not reliant on physical force."[54]

In 2002, Karen L. Hayslett-McCall and Thomas J. Bernard of Pennsylvania State University proposed a new theory of disproportionate male offending that combined elements of Gottfredson and Hirschi's theory of low self-control with ideas from attachment theory.[55] Hayslett-McCall and Bernard examined the strong relationship between gender and criminality (men are more likely than women to offend in almost all offense categories) and concluded that gender-based differences in offending are caused by disruptions in attachments to primary caregivers early in childhood and that such disruptions are more likely to occur in the lives of boys than girls because of cultural differences in the way boys are treated. Boys are held less, comforted less when they cry, and spoken to less than girls in their early years because of child rearing patterns that are thoroughly ingrained in our culture—"boys disproportionately experience disruptions of early attachment and these disruptions are causally related to elements of what is often described as the masculine gender role." Low self-control among males, concluded Hayslett-McCall and Bernard, is the final result of gendered differences in attachment disruptions.

In 2006, **Per-Olof H. Wikström** at the University of Cambridge proposed that self-control could best be analyzed as a situational concept (i.e., a factor in the process of choice), rather than as an individual trait.[56] Wikström's **situational action theory (SAT)** proposes that an individual's ability to exercise self-control is an outcome of the interaction between his or her personal traits and the situation in which he or she takes part. SAT highlights the *situation* as the core unit of analysis, and places emphasis on a person's sense of morality—which expresses itself when an individual is faced with a particular set of circumstances. In other words, Wikström proposes that acts of violence are essentially moral actions, and that all such acts can be explained by a theory of moral action that takes into account both personal characteristics and the social setting.

SAT argues that there is no fundamental difference between people who follow or break moral rules in general, and those who follow or break rules defined by the law as criminal. The basic causal processes that operate in both cases are the same, it says—but the decision-making process is one in which moral interpretations are more important than degree of self-control.[57]

SAT says that explaining human moral action, such as acts of violence, has to do ultimately with understanding the interplay between common moral rules of conduct, an individual actor's personal moral rules, and the actor's interpretation of how his or her moral rules apply to the situation at hand.[58] The theory suggests that the particulars of a given situation, in combination with an actor's understanding of moral rules, determines what is right or wrong for that individual and, consequently, what that person will do.

■ **control ratio** The amount of control to which a person is subject versus the amount of control that person exerts over others.

Deterrence is seen as the "main causal mechanism through which formal and informal social controls influence a person's moral actions." Deterrence is defined by Wikström as "the felt worry about or fear of consequences when considering breaking a moral rule or committing an act of crime." Motivation and frictions are other important concepts in SAT. Motivation is defined as goal-directed attention, in which people are tempted to fill desires and commitments, and will seek out opportunities for fulfillment. Provocations, another important concept in SAT, can result from frictions, or unwanted interferences (i.e., verbal insults, physical interference), that arise in situation-specific circumstances.

For most people and in most circumstances, Wikström says that the decision as to whether or not to engage in acts of crime or deviance is not so much a question of a person's ability to exercise self-control, but rather a question of his or her morality. He argues that the ability to exercise self-control is only a relevant factor in crime causation in those situations where an individual actually deliberates about whether or not to engage in a criminal act. In his 2011 Presidential Address to the American Society of Criminology, Steven F. Messner applauded SAT, saying that it provided the "glimmer of a moral awakening in criminology."[59]

Although the general theory of crime is well accepted today as an explanation for many forms of criminality, some writers note that the most powerful predictors of crime can be found when individuals with low self-control encounter criminal opportunities. They point out that the context of self-control is an important determining factor. In 2010, for example, two German researchers found support for the belief that the interaction between self-control and criminal opportunities is more effective at explaining criminal behavior than self-control alone.[60] Other contextual variables have also been explored. In 2008, for example, a group of researchers reported finding that "diminished language skills" are predictive of low self-control, and that the link between language and self-control had both a genetic and environmental basis.[61]

Finally, in 2012, Gregory M. Zimmerman and colleagues explored the "contextual viability" of the relationship between self-control and offending—in other words, the influence of things like neighborhood variables and economic conditions on self-control.[62] They expected to find that the relationship between self-control and crime would "be amplified in disadvantaged neighborhoods where, due to low social control, opportunities for crime are presumed to be in abundance." In order to test that idea, the researchers looked at data from 1,431 respondents across 41 neighborhoods in two Eastern European cities: one in Russia and the other in the Ukraine. Their findings showed that the morality of a neighborhood was more important than things like socioeconomic status (SES) and neighborhood opportunities for crime. Neighborhood morality was measured by examining the firmness of moral convictions within the community, using a set of questions that assessed the extent to which various acts would be morally acceptable to people living there. They found that the amount of crime in both rich and poor communities was primarily influenced by the strength of moral rules that characterized the community. The researchers explained their findings by noting that "the effects of neighborhood economic conditions are mediated, at least in part, by community social processes." The importance of their findings is to show that the relationship between self-control and crime may vary depending on the social context in which people find themselves.

Control–Balance Theory

Traditional control theories posit that deviance and crime result from either weak social bonds or low levels of self-control, but a novel form of control theory can be found in the control–balance theory of Charles R. Tittle.[63] Tittle's control–balance approach resulted from blending the social bond and containment perspectives, and he argued that too much control can be just as dangerous as too little. The crucial concept in Tittle's approach is what he called the **control ratio**—the amount of control to which a person is subject versus the amount of control that person exerts over others—which predicts not only the probability that a person will engage in deviance but also the specific form that deviance will take (Figure 8–4).

High levels of control (or overcontrol) are termed *control surplus*; low levels are called *control deficit*. Individuals with

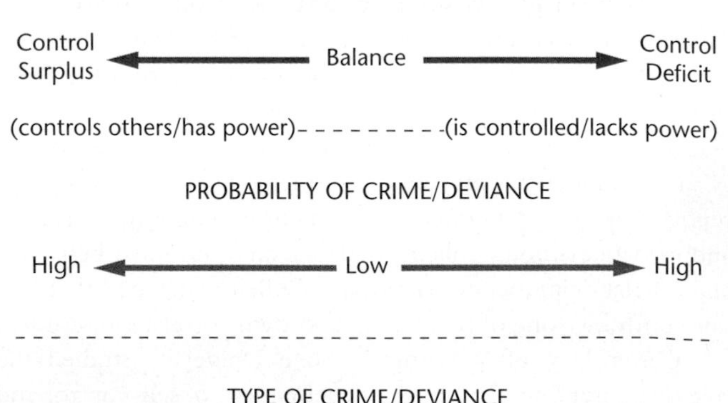

FIGURE 8-4 | Control-Balance Theory

Source: Schmalleger, Frank J., *Criminology*. Printed and Electronically reproduced by permission of Pearson Education, Inc., Upper Saddle River, New Jersey.

■ **tagging** The process whereby an individual is negatively defined by agencies of justice.

■ **primary deviance** The initial deviance often undertaken to deal with transient problems in living.

■ **secondary deviance** The deviant behavior that results from official labeling and from association with others who have been so labeled.

control surpluses are able to exercise a great deal of control over others and will work to extend their degree of control even further. Their efforts lead to deviant actions involving exploitation, plunder, and decadence—frequently seen in cases of white-collar crime and political corruption.[64] Tittle explained that control surpluses build on "the fundamental drive toward autonomy," which involves "a desire to extend control as far as possible" and results in forms of deviance that he called "autonomous."[65]

A control deficit exists for people unable to exercise much control over others (and who are hence overly controlled) and results in deviance as an attempt to escape repressive controls. Deviance engendered by control deficit takes the form of predation (physical violence, theft, sexual assault, robbery), defiance (challenges to conventional norms, including vandalism, curfew violations, and sullenness), or submission ("passive, unthinking, slavish obedience to the expectations, commands, or anticipated desires of others"[66]). According to Tittle, control imbalance only sets the stage for deviance: Deviance ultimately occurs once a person realizes, at some level, that acts of deviance can reset the control ratio in a favorable way. Opportunity also plays a significant role in Tittle's theory. "No matter how favorable the motivational and constraint configuration," said Tittle, "the actual likelihood of deviance occurring depends on there being an opportunity for it to happen."[67]

Labeling Theory

In the early 1990s, James Hamm, a convicted murderer who had served 18 years for shooting a man in the head over a drug deal gone bad, found himself at the center of a vicious controversy. While in prison, Hamm had earned a bachelor's degree in sociology and had been active in Middle Ground Prison Reform, Inc., a prisoners' rights group. He was paroled after Arizona's parole board had judged him "rehabilitated" and was about to enter Arizona State University School of Law. Students at the university challenged his access to law school, saying that a convicted murderer did not deserve to be admitted. Mark Killian, (then) Arizona Republican house speaker, said, "There are a lot of hard-working young people out there who could not get into law school because he did."[68] Members of the Arizona Board of Regents, which runs the state's public universities, called for a review of policies admitting ex-convicts to the schools. Nonetheless, Hamm, who scored in the top 5% of all applicants taking the law school admissions test nationwide, was eventually admitted to law school and graduated in 1997. Following graduation, he passed the bar exam and applied to be allowed to practice law in Arizona, but the state's parole board refused to terminate his parole, leaving him ineligible to work as an attorney, so he went to work as a paralegal in the areas of criminal defense, civil rights, and appellate law.[69]

The case of James Hamm provides an example of how society's continued reaction to criminal behavior can change the course of an offender's life—even after he or she has paid his dues. Although there are plenty of ex-cons, there is no such thing as an "ex-ex-con" ("once a con, always a con"). Society seems to never forget. Society's response to known or suspected offenders is important not only because it determines the future of those who are labeled as criminals but also because it may contribute to a heightened incidence of criminality by reducing the behavioral options available to labeled offenders.

Tagging

An early description of societal reaction to deviance can be found in the work of **Frank Tannenbaum**, whose 1938 book *Crime and the Community* popularized the term **tagging** to explain what happens to offenders following arrest, conviction, and sentencing. Tannenbaum told his readers that crime is essentially the result of two opposing views—those of the delinquent and those of the community at large. "This conflict over the situation is one that arises out of a divergence of values. As the problem develops, the situation gradually becomes redefined. The attitude of the community hardens definitely into a demand for suppression. There is a gradual shift from the definition of the specific acts as evil to a definition of the individual as evil, so that all his acts come to be looked upon with suspicion. From the community's point of view, the individual who used to do bad and mischievous things has now become a bad and unredeemable human being. . . . There is a persistent demand for consistency in character. The community cannot deal with people whom it cannot define."[70]

After the process whereby an offender comes to be seen as ultimately and irrevocably bad has been completed, Tannenbaum said, the offender "now lives in a different world. He has been tagged. The process of making the criminal, therefore, is a process of tagging."[71] Once the offender has been defined as bad, he or she finds that few legitimate opportunities remain open and that only other people who have been similarly defined by society as bad are available to associate with him or her, and this continued association with negatively defined others leads to continued crime.

Primary and Secondary Deviance

Using terminology developed by **Edwin M. Lemert**, it became fashionable to call an offender's initial acts of deviance **primary deviance** and his or her continued acts of deviance (especially those resulting from forced association with other offenders) **secondary deviance**. Primary deviance may be

■ **labeling theory** An interactionist perspective that sees continued crime as a consequence of limited opportunities for acceptable behavior that follow from the negative responses of society to those defined as offenders; also called social reaction theory.

■ **moral enterprise** The efforts made by an interest group to have its sense of moral or ethical propriety enacted into law.

undertaken to solve some immediate problem or to meet the expectations of one's subcultural group. For example, the robbery of a convenience store by a college student temporarily desperate for tuition money may be the first serious criminal offense he or she has ever committed, and he or she may well intend for it to be the last, but if arrest ensues and the student is tagged with the status of a criminal, then secondary deviance may occur as a means of adjustment to the negative status. In Lemert's words, "When a person begins to employ his deviant behavior or a role based upon it as a means of defense, attack, or adjustment to the overt and covert problems created by the consequent societal reaction to him, his deviation is secondary."[72]

Secondary deviance is especially important due to the forceful role it plays in causing tagged individuals both to internalize the negative labels applied to them and to assume the role of the deviant. According to Lemert, "Objective evidences of this change will be found in the symbolic appurtenances of the new role, in clothes, speech, posture, and mannerisms, which in some cases heighten social visibility, and which in some cases serve as symbolic cues to professionalization."[73]

Labeling

The person most often associated with labeling theory is **Howard Becker**, who published *Outsiders: Studies in the Sociology of Deviance*, the work in which the perspective of **labeling theory** (the idea that society's response to the criminal and the process through which a person comes to be defined as a criminal and labeled "criminal" are significant contributory factors in future criminality) found its fullest development.[74] In *Outsiders*, Becker described the deviant subculture in which jazz musicians live and the process by which an individual becomes a marijuana user, but his primary focus was explaining how a person becomes labeled as an outsider, as "a special kind of person, one who cannot be trusted to live by the rules agreed on by the group."[75] The central fact is that society creates both deviance and the deviant person by responding to circumscribed behaviors. In Becker's words, "Social groups create deviance by making the rules whose infraction constitutes deviance, and by applying those rules to particular people and labeling them as outsiders. From this point of view, deviance is not a quality of the act the person commits, but rather a consequence of the application by others of rules and sanctions. The deviant is one to whom that label has been successfully applied."[76] For Becker and other labeling theorists, no act is intrinsically deviant or criminal but must be defined as such by others; becoming deviant involves a sequence of steps that eventually leads to commitment to a deviant identity and participation in a deviant career.

Becker said that society creates both deviance and the deviant person by responding negatively to circumscribed behaviors.

In developing labeling theory, Becker attempted to explain how some rules carry the force of law whereas others have less weight or apply only within the context of marginal subcultures. His explanation centered on the concept of **moral enterprise**, meaning all the efforts a particular interest group makes to have its sense of propriety embodied in law. "Rules are the products of someone's initiative, and we can think of the people who exhibit such enterprise as moral entrepreneurs."[77]

An early example of moral enterprise can be found in the Women's Christian Temperance Union (WCTU), a group devoted to the prohibition of alcohol. From 1881 to 1919, the WCTU was highly visible in its nationwide fight against alcohol—holding marches and demonstrations, closing drinking establishments, and lobbying legislators. Press coverage of the WCTU's activities swayed many politicians into believing that the lawful prohibition of alcoholic beverages was inevitable, and an amendment to the U.S. Constitution soon followed, ushering in the age of prohibition.

A more contemporary example of moral enterprise is NORML—the National Organization for the Reform of Marijuana Laws. NORML says that its mission is "to move public opinion sufficiently to achieve the repeal of marijuana prohibition so that the responsible use of cannabis by adults is no longer subject to penalty."[78] Other recent examples of moral entrepreneurs can be found in those individuals and organizations that lobbied for the creation of Amber Alert systems and the passage of Megan's Laws (which authorize local law enforcement agencies to notify the public about convicted sex offenders living or working nearby) following the abduction and murder of young girls.

Moral enterprise is used, Becker claimed, by groups seeking to support their own interests with the weight of law. Often the group that is successful at moral enterprise does not represent a popular point of view. The group is simply more effective than others at maneuvering through the formal bureaucracy that accompanies legislation.

Becker was especially interested in describing deviant careers and the processes by which individuals become members of deviant subcultures and take on the attributes associated with the deviant role. Becker argued that most deviance is likely to be transitory but that transitory deviance can be effectively stabilized in a person's behavioral repertoire through the labeling process. Once a person is labeled deviant, opportunities for conforming behavior are seriously reduced and behavioral opportunities that remain open are primarily deviant ones; the budding deviant increasingly exhibits deviant behavior because his or her choices are restricted by society. Successful deviants must acquire the techniques and resources necessary to undertake the deviant act (drug use, bank robbery) and develop the mind-set characteristic of others like them. Near the end of a deviant career, the person labeled a deviant has internalized society's negative label, has assumed a deviant self-concept, and is likely a member of a deviant subgroup. "A drug addict once told me that the moment she felt she was really 'hooked' was when she realized she no longer had any friends who were not drug addicts."[79] In this way, explained Becker, deviance becomes a self-fulfilling prophecy, so labeling is a cause of crime insofar as the actions of society in defining the rule breaker as deviant push the person further in the direction of continued deviance.

Contributions of Labeling Theory

Labeling theory contributed a number of unique ideas to criminological literature:

- Deviance is the result of social processes involving the imposition of definitions rather than the consequence of any quality inherent in human activity itself.
- Deviant individuals achieve their status by virtue of social definition rather than inborn traits.
- The reaction of society to deviant behavior and to those who engage in such behavior is the major element in determining the criminality of the behavior and the person in question.
- Negative self-images follow processing by the formal criminal justice system rather than precede delinquency.
- Labeling by society and handling by the justice system tend to perpetuate crime and delinquency rather than reduce them.

Becker's typology of delinquents—the pure deviant, the falsely accused deviant, and the secret deviant—helped explain the labeling approach (Figure 8–5). The pure deviant is one who commits norm-breaking behavior and is accurately appraised by society, who is tried and convicted, and who gets what he or she deserves. The falsely accused individual is one who is not guilty but is labeled deviant nonetheless, who experiences the impact of conviction and of the experiences that attend prison life, and who is left with a negative self-concept and with group associations practically indistinguishable from those of a true deviant. This person demonstrates the power of social definition—the life of the falsely accused is changed just as thoroughly as the life of the pure deviant by the process of labeling. The secret deviant violates social norms, but his or her behavior is not noticed, so negative societal reactions do not follow; a secret deviant again demonstrates the power of societal reaction, but in this case by the lack of consequences.

Although labeling theory fell into disregard during the late 1970s and early 1980s due to accusations that it was vague and ambiguous, some criminologists have recast the approach as a developmental theory of structural disadvantage.[80] The theory is now seen as one that points out the cumulative effects over time of official intervention on future life chances and opportunities for approved success. Robert J. Sampson and John H. Laub observed that labeling theory is "truly developmental in nature because of its explicit emphasis on processes over time."[81] Contemporary proponents of the labeling perspective generally see labeling as only one factor contributing to cumulative disadvantages in life chances. In 2003, Jon Gunnar Bernburg and Marvin D. Krohn studied the impact of negative official interventions on young men in Rochester, New York, from the time they were about 13.5 years old until they reached the age of 22. In keeping with what labeling theory would predict, Bernburg and Krohn found that official intervention during adolescence led to increased criminality in early adulthood because it reduced life chances for educational achievement and successful employment, and that poor people were more negatively impacted by

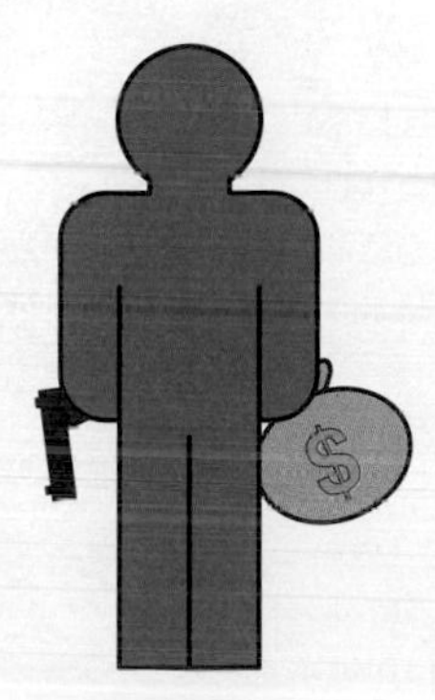
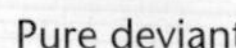

FIGURE 8-5 | **Becker's Types of Delinquents**

Source: Schmalleger, Frank J., *Criminology*. Printed and Electronically reproduced by permission of Pearson Education, Inc., Upper Saddle River, New Jersey.

■ **reintegrative shaming** A form of shaming, imposed as a sanction by the criminal justice system, that is thought to strengthen the moral bond between the offender and the community.

■ **stigmatic shaming** A form of shaming, imposed as a sanction by the criminal justice system, that is thought to destroy the moral bond between the offender and the community.

official processing, probably because they were already disadvantaged along other important social dimensions.[82]

Negative labels can carry significant visible liabilities as well as hidden ones. A 2004 study by the Legal Action Center, a crime and justice policy group, found that all 50 states have laws that hamper the ability of former offenders to reenter society.[83] Four states—Colorado, Georgia, South Carolina, and Virginia—were rated as places where ex-offenders have the least chance to become productive citizens. According to the center, many states prohibit ex-offenders from obtaining professional licenses to work in businesses as diverse as real estate, medicine, and law; 27 states, in keeping with a requirement imposed by Congress on states seeking federal highway funds, revoke or refuse to issue driver's licenses to former drug felons, effectively prohibiting access to many job sites.

Mike S. Adams proposed a general sociological learning theory of crime and deviance that incorporated components of labeling theory and differential association.[84] Adams contended that "labeling effects are mediated by associations with delinquent peers," concluding that labeling is not a direct cause of delinquency and crime but "appears to cause delinquency indirectly via the effects of associations with delinquent peer groups" and that "the causal chain linking primary to secondary deviance must incorporate links that account for the effects of associations with delinquent [peers]."[85]

Finally, in 2013, Emily Restivo and her colleague Mark M. Lanier reported the results of a three-year study in which they randomly examined 677 juveniles selected from the Children at Risk study. They found that official intervention by the criminal justice system in the lives of those juveniles led to "an increased delinquent self-identity, decreased pro-social expectations, and an increased association with delinquent peers."[86] Further, those features were found to contribute to an increased likelihood of future offending. Learn more about labeling theory at **Web Extra 8–1**, and read about the post-prison consequences of a criminal label at **Library Extra 8–3**.

Reintegrative Shaming

In a more contemporary offshoot of labeling theory, **John Braithwaite** and colleagues at the Australian National University (ANU) reported initial results of studies in 1997 on **reintegrative shaming**, which describes processes by which a deviant is labeled and sanctioned but then is brought back into a community of conformity through words, gestures, or rituals.[87]

Called RISE (for Reintegrative Shaming Experiments), the project assessed the efficacy of each approach using several criteria: (1) prevalence and frequency of repeat offending, (2) victim satisfaction with the process, (3) estimated cost savings within the justice process, (4) changes in drinking or drug use among offenders, and (5) perceptions of procedural justice, fairness, and protection of rights.[88]

At the core of the study was Braithwaite's belief that two different kinds of shame exist. **Stigmatic shaming** is thought to destroy the moral bond between the offender and the community, whereas reintegrative shaming is thought to strengthen the moral bond between the offender and the community. According to Braithwaite and co-author Heather Strang, "Stigmatic shaming is what American judges employ when they make an offender post a sign on his property saying 'a violent felon lives here,' or a bumper sticker on his car saying 'I am a drunk driver.' Stigmatic shaming sets the offender apart as an outcast—often for the rest of the offender's life. By labeling him or her as someone who cannot be trusted to obey the law, stigmatic shaming says the offender is expected to commit more crimes."[89]

Their alternative to stigmatic humiliation is "to condemn the crime, not the criminal."[90] Through carefully monitored diversionary conferences, Braithwaite and Strang hoped to give offenders the opportunity to rejoin the community as law-abiding citizens, but to earn the right to a fresh start, offenders must express remorse for their past conduct, apologize to any victims, and repair the harm caused by the crime.

Preliminary results from the RISE studies supported the claimed value of reintegrative shaming, but most of these results have been measured using interviews with offenders following diversionary conferences and consist primarily of anecdotal

ZUMA Press/Newscom

Minor offenders in Hillsborough County, Florida, performing court-ordered duties in public view. Some people believe that shaming can be an effective rehabilitative tool. What different kinds of shaming can you identify?

■ **dramaturgical perspective** A theoretical point of view that depicts human behavior as centered around the purposeful management of interpersonal impressions.

■ **impression management** The intentional enactment of practiced behavior that is intended to convey to others one's desirable personal characteristics and social qualities.

■ **discrediting information** Any information that is inconsistent with the managed impressions being communicated in a given situation.

■ **total institution** A facility from which individuals can rarely come and go and in which communal life is intense and circumscribed. Individuals in total institutions tend to eat, sleep, play, learn, and worship together.

Reintegrative shaming is thought to strengthen the moral bond between the offender and the community.

evidence based on the reported feelings of respondents. These findings showed that offenders are far more likely to feel ashamed of their crimes if they are handled through conferences rather than through formal court processing, and that both offenders and victims find conferences fairer than official court proceedings. Learn more about reintegrative shaming experiments at **Web Extra 8–2** and **Library Extras 8–4** and **8–5**.

Dramaturgical Perspective

Another social process approach to the study of criminology can be found in the work of **Erving Goffman** in his 1959 book *The Presentation of Self in Everyday Life*, which introduced students of criminology to dramaturgy.[91] The **dramaturgical perspective** says that individuals play a variety of nearly simultaneous social roles—such as mother, teacher, daughter, wife, and part-time real estate agent—and that such roles must be sustained in interactions with others. Goffman argued that social actors present themselves more or less effectively when acting out a particular role and that role performances basically consist of managed impressions. Criminals, through a similar process of managed impressions and by the fear engendered in their victims, may likewise achieve cooperation.

Impression management, according to Goffman, is a complex process involving a never-ending give-and-take of information. When it has been successful, said Goffman, dramatic realization has occurred: "Together, the participants contribute to a single overall definition of the situation which involves not so much a real agreement as to what exists but rather a real agreement as to whose claims concerning what issues will be temporarily honored."[92]

Deviant behavior finds its place in the dramaturgical perspective through the concept of discreditable disclosure. Some actors, said Goffman, may find themselves targeted by the introduction of **discrediting information**, information they have sought to hide that is inconsistent with managed impressions. The flow of interaction is then disrupted, and the nature of the performance may be altered substantially.

Goffman's work takes on considerable relevance for criminology in his later writings, especially his book *Stigma: Notes on the Management of Spoiled Identity*, in which he advanced the notion that discredited or stigmatized individuals differ significantly from "normals" in the way that society responds to them.[93] By definition, he said that "we believe that a person with a stigma is not quite human. On this assumption, we exercise varieties of discrimination, through which we effectively, if often unthinkingly, reduce his life chances. We construct a stigma-theory, an ideology to explain his inferiority and account for the danger he represents. We tend to impute a wide range of imperfections on the basis of the original one."[94] A stigma may be physical (birthmarks), behavioral (theft), or ideational (low rank in the pecking order).

In *Stigma*, Goffman was primarily concerned with how "normals" and stigmatized individuals interact. At times, discredited individuals are known to others before they come in contact with them, and when that happens, normal people approach the stigmatized ones with expectations of encountering further stigmatizing behavior. When discrediting information does not precede interpersonal encounters, the stigmatized individuals may attempt to pass as normal by using various techniques of concealment, including aliases and misrepresentation.

According to Goffman, societal reactions, although they may forcibly create social identities, are also instrumental in the formation of group identities. When similarly discredited individuals come together in like-minded groups, they may align themselves against the larger society; in so reacting, they may justify their own deviant or criminal behavior. At the conclusion of *Stigma*, Goffman reminded us, "The normal and the stigmatized are not persons, but rather perspectives. These are generated in social situations during mixed contacts by virtue of the unrealized norms that are likely to play upon the encounter."[95]

In his book titled *Asylums*, Goffman described **total institutions**—facilities from which individuals can rarely come and go and in which communal life is intense and circumscribed.[96] Individuals in total institutions tend to eat, sleep, play, learn, and worship together; military camps, seminaries, convents, prisons, rest homes, and mental hospitals are all types of total institutions. Goffman believed that residents of total

■ **prosocial bond** A bond between the individual and the social group that strengthens the likelihood of conformity. Prosocial bonds are characterized by attachment to conventional social institutions, values, and beliefs.

institutions bring "presenting cultures" with them to their respective facilities, so some inmates would carry street culture into correctional facilities. However, residents undergo a period of "disculturation," during which they drop aspects of their native culture that are not consistent with existing institutional culture—a culture that they must acquire. Read about jails as total institutions at **Library Extra 8–6**.

Policy Implications of Social Process Theories

Social process theories suggest that crime-prevention programs should work to enhance self-control and to build **prosocial bonds** (bonds that strengthen conformity). One program that seeks to build strong prosocial bonds while attempting to teach positive values to young people is the Juvenile Mentoring Program (JUMP) of the Office of Juvenile Justice and Delinquency Prevention (OJJDP), funded by Congress in 1992 under an amendment to the Juvenile Justice and Delinquency Prevention Act of 1974.[97] JUMP programs, commencing in 1996, place at-risk youths (those at risk of delinquency, gang involvement, educational failure, or dropping out of school) in a one-on-one relationship with favorable adult role models.

The most recent data showed that 9,200 youths (average age just under 12) enrolled in more than 200 JUMP programs nationwide. Based on evaluation data, both youths and mentors were very positive when rating various aspects of their mentoring experiences.[98] Learn more about JUMP at **Library Extra 8–7**.

Another social control–based program is Preparing for the Drug Free Years (PDFY), designed to increase effective parenting as part of the Strengthening America's Families Project.[99] PDFY works with parents of children in grades four to eight in an effort to reduce drug abuse and behavioral problems in adolescents, seeks to teach effective parenting skills as a way to decrease the risks that juveniles face, and incorporates both behavioral skills training and communication-centered approaches into parent training. Through a series of ten one-hour sessions, parents learn to (1) increase their children's opportunities for family involvement, (2) teach needed family participation and social skills, and (3) provide reinforcement for positive behavior and appropriate consequences for misbehavior. Early studies showed that program participation (session attendance) tends to be high and that the program is effective at improving general child-management skills among parents.[100] Learn more about PDFY at **Web Extra 8–3.**

A program emphasizing the development of self-control is the Montreal Preventive Treatment Program, which addresses early-childhood risk factors for gang involvement by targeting boys from poor socioeconomic backgrounds who display disruptive behavior while in kindergarten.[101] The program offers training sessions for parents designed to teach family crisis management, disciplining techniques, and other parenting skills while the boys participate in training sessions emphasizing the development of prosocial skills and self-control. At least one evaluation of the program showed that it was effective at keeping boys from joining gangs.[102]

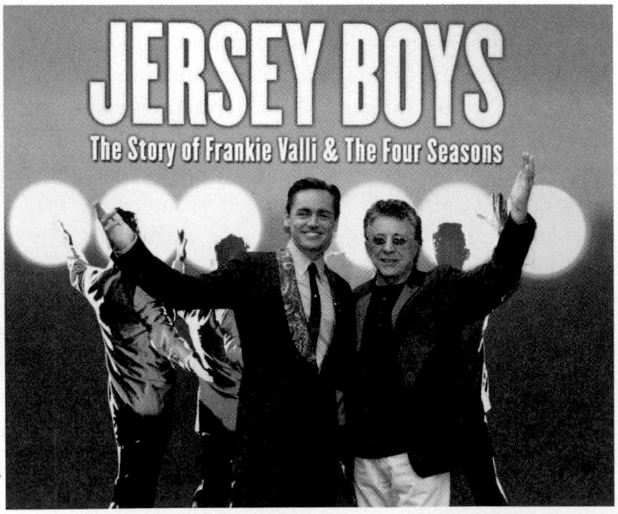

Daily Mail/Rex/Alamy

A scene from the musical *Jersey Boys*. Some criminologists suggest that people, like actors on a stage, intentionally present themselves to others in ways calculated to produce predictable social responses. How might criminals manipulate impressions?

Critique of Social Process Theories

Criticisms of social process theories are many and varied. Perhaps the most potent criticism of association theory is the claim that Sutherland's initial formulation of differential association is not applicable at the individual level because even people who experience an excess of definitions favorable to law violation may still not become criminal and those who rarely associate with recognized deviants may still turn to crime. Also, the theory is untestable because most people experience a multitude of definitions—both favorable and unfavorable to law violation—and it is up to them to interpret what those experiences mean, so classifying experiences as either favorable or unfavorable to crime commission is difficult at best.

Other critics suggest that differential association alone is not a sufficient explanation for crime. In effect, association theory

■ **human development** The relationship between the maturing individual and his or her changing environment, as well as the social processes that the relationship entails.

■ **social development perspective** An integrated view of human development that examines multiple maturational levels, including psychological, biological, familial, interpersonal, cultural, societal, and ecological, simultaneously.

chrcmatika/Fotolia

A baby holds on to a spoon. What concepts are key to the social development approach?

The labeling approach does little to explain the origin of crime and deviance.

does not seem to provide for free choice in individual circumstances, nor does it explain why some individuals, even when surrounded by associates committed to lives of crime, are still able to hold on to noncriminal values. Finally, association theory fails to account for the emergence of criminal values, addressing only the communication of those values.

Although the labeling approach successfully points to the labeling process as a reason for continued deviance and as a cause of stabilization in deviant identities, it does little to explain the origin of crime and deviance, and few studies seem to support the basic tenets of the theory. Critics of labeling have pointed to its "lack of firm empirical support for the notion of secondary deviance, [and] many studies have not found that delinquents or criminals have a delinquent or criminal self-image."[103] There is also a lack of empirical support for the claim that contact with the justice system is fundamentally detrimental to the personal lives of criminal perpetrators, but even if that were true, one must ask whether it would ultimately be better if offenders were not caught and forced to undergo the rigors of processing by the justice system. Although labeling theory hints that official processing makes a significant contribution to continued criminality, it seems unreasonable to expect that offenders untouched by the system would forgo the rewards of future criminality. Finally, labeling theory has little to say about secret deviants (people who engage in criminality but are never caught). Can they be expected to continue in lives of deviance if never caught?

Goffman's work has been criticized as providing a set of "linked concepts" rather than a consistent theoretical framework.[104] Other critics have faulted Goffman for failing to offer suggestions for institutional change or for not proposing treatment modalities based on his assumptions. Goffman's greatest failing may be taking the analogy of the theater too far and convincing readers that real life is but a form of playacting; according to George Psathas, "Performing and being are not identical."[105]

The Social Development Perspective

Over the past 25 years, an appreciation for the process of **human development** (the relationship between the maturing individual and his or her changing environment and the social processes that relationship entails) has played an increasingly important role in understanding criminality.[106] Students of human development recognize that the process of development occurs through reciprocal dynamic interactions that take place between individuals and various aspects of their environment, and the social development perspective posits that development, which begins at birth (and perhaps even earlier), occurs primarily within a social context. Unlike social learning theory (discussed earlier in this chapter), social development sees socialization as only one feature of that context. If socialization were the primary determinant of criminality, then we might expect that all problem children would become criminals as adults, but because that doesn't happen, there must be other aspects to the developmental process that social learning theories don't fully cover.

According to the **social development perspective**, human development simultaneously occurs on many levels—psychological, biological, familial, interpersonal, cultural, societal, and ecological—so social development theories tend to be integrated theories combining various points of view. The rest of this chapter describes life course criminology, the major social development perspective; various ideas contributing to the life course perspective, along with other perspectives on social development, are also described. You can learn more about such perspectives at **Web Extra 8–4**.

Concepts in Social Development Theories

Most sociological explanations for crime involve the study of groups and the identification of differences among groups of offenders, but social development theories focus more on individual rates of offending and seek to understand both increases and decreases in rates of offending over the individual's lifetime. Social development theories generally employ longitudinal (over time) measurements of delinquency and offending, and they pay special attention to the transitions that people face as they move through the life cycle.

Most theories of social development recognize that a critical transitional period occurs as a person moves from childhood to adulthood, and life course theorists have identified at least seven developmental tasks that American adolescents must confront: (1) establishing identity, (2) cultivating symbiotic relationships, (3) defining physical attractiveness, (4) investing in a value system, (5) obtaining an education, (6) separating from family and achieving independence, and (7) obtaining and maintaining gainful employment.[107] Youths are confronted with many obstacles or risks in their attempts to resolve these issues as they work to make a successful transition to adulthood. Figure 8–6 provides a conceptual model of the developmental processes that a maturing youth experiences during adolescence. Learn more about the transitional process leading to adulthood at **Web Extra 8–5**.

The Life Course Perspective

Traditional explanations for crime and delinquency often lack a developmental perspective because they generally ignore developmental changes throughout the life course and

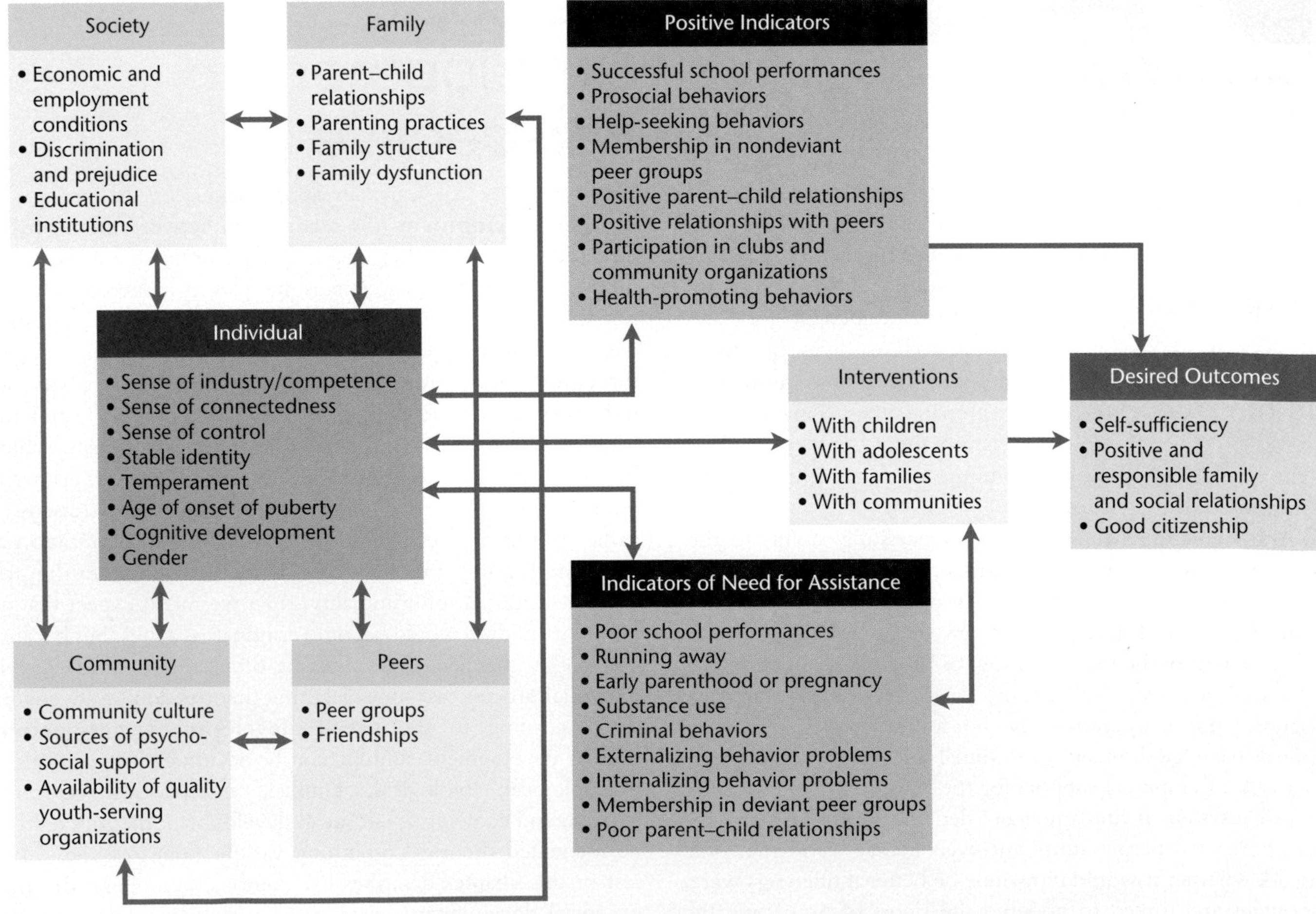

FIGURE 8–6 | **A Conceptual Model of Adolescent Development**

Source: Family and Youth Services Bureau, *Understanding Youth Development: Promoting Positive Pathways of Growth* (Washington, DC: U.S. Department of Health and Human Services, 2000).

■ **life course perspective** A perspective that draws attention to the fact that criminal behavior tends to follow a distinct pattern across the life cycle; also called life course criminology.

■ **criminal career** The longitudinal sequence of crimes committed by an individual offender.

■ **life course** The different pathways through the age-differentiated life span; the course of a person's life over time.

Developmental theories draw attention to the fact that criminal behavior tends to follow a distinct pattern across the life cycle.

frequently fail to distinguish between different phases of criminal careers.[108] In contrast, developmental theories draw attention to the fact that criminal behavior tends to follow a distinct pattern across the life cycle: Criminality is relatively uncommon during childhood, tends to begin as sporadic instances of delinquency during late adolescence and early adulthood, and then diminishes and sometimes completely disappears from a person's behavioral repertoire by age 30 or 40. Of course, some people never commit crimes or do so only rarely, whereas others become career criminals and persist in lives of crime.

The **life course perspective** (also called *life course criminology*) shifted the traditional focus away from the reasons why people begin offending to questions about what the dimensions of criminal offending are over the entire life course.[109] It has its roots in a 1986 National Academy of Sciences (NAS) panel report prepared by Alfred Blumstein, Jacqueline Cohen, Jeffrey Roth, and Christy Visher that emphasized the importance of the study of criminal careers and of crime over the life course.[110] The NAS panel defined a **criminal career** as "the longitudinal sequence of crimes committed by an individual offender."[111] The report was especially important for its analysis of "offending development," a concept that underlies the life course perspective (see the Theory in Perspective box).

The panel noted (Figure 8–7) that criminal careers can be described in terms of four dimensions: participation, frequency, duration, and seriousness. *Participation*, which refers to the fraction of a population that is criminally active, depends on the scope of criminal acts considered and the length of the observation period.[112] *Frequency* refers to the number of crimes committed by an individual offender per unit of time. Hence, a burglar who commits one burglary a year has a much lower frequency than one who is active monthly or weekly. Frequency is generally not constant and varies over the life course—even for habitual offenders. *Duration* refers to the length of the criminal career. A criminal career can be very short, consisting of only one offense, or it can be quite long, as in the case of habitual or chronic criminals. *Seriousness* is relatively self-explanatory, although it is worthwhile to note that some offenders with long criminal careers commit only petty crimes, whereas others are serious habitual offenders, and still others commit offenses with a mixed degree of seriousness.

Life course criminology was given its name in a seminal book written by **Robert J. Sampson** and **John H. Laub** in 1993, entitled *Crime in the Making*.[113] Earlier, the concept of **life course** had been defined as "pathways through the life span involving a sequence of culturally defined, age-graded roles and social transitions enacted over time."[114] Life course theories, which build on social learning and social control principles, recognize that criminal careers may develop as the result of various criminogenic influences that affect individuals over the course of their lives.

Researchers who focus on the life course as it leads to delinquency, crime, and criminal identities are interested both in evaluating the prevalence, frequency, and onset of offending and in identifying different developmental pathways to delinquency. Life course researchers ask a variety of questions: How do early-childhood characteristics (for example, antisocial behavior) lead to adult behavioral processes and outcomes? How do life transitions (for example, shifts in relationships from parents to peers, transitions from same-sex peers to opposite-sex peers, moves from school to work, marriage, divorce) influence behavior and behavioral choices? How do offending and victimization interact over the life cycle?[115]

Life course researchers examine "trajectories and transitions through the age-differentiated life span."[116] According to Sampson and Laub, "Trajectories refer to longer-term patterns and sequences of behavior, whereas transitions are marked by specific life events (for example, first job or the onset of crime) that are embedded in trajectories and evolve over shorter time spans."[117] The concept of age differentiation (or age grading) recognizes the fact that certain forms of behavior and some experiences are more appropriate (in terms of their social consequences) in certain parts of the life cycle than in others. Life course theorists search for evidence of continuity between childhood or adolescent experiences and adult outcomes or lifestyles.

FIGURE 8–7 | **Aspects of Criminal Careers**

Source: Schmalleger, Frank J., *Criminology*. Printed and Electronically reproduced by permission of Pearson Education, Inc., Upper Saddle River, New Jersey.

THEORY | in PERSPECTIVE

Social Development Theories

Social development theories are integrated theories of human development that simultaneously examine many different levels of development—psychological, biological, familial, interpersonal, cultural, societal, and ecological.

Life Course Perspective

The life course perspective highlights the development of criminal careers, which are seen as the result of various criminogenic influences that affect individuals throughout the course of their lives.

Period: 1980s–present

Theorists: Alfred Blumstein, John H. Laub, Robert J. Sampson, David P. Farrington, Donald J. West, Lawrence E. Cohen, Richard Machalek, Terence Thornberry

Concepts: Criminal career, life course, trajectory, turning points, age grading, social capital, human agency, developmental pathways, life course persisters, persistence, desistance, resilience, cohort, cohort analysis, longitudinal research, evolutionary ecology

---

Three sets of dynamic concepts are important to the life course perspective: (1) activation, (2) aggravation, and (3) desistance.[118] *Activation*, the way that delinquent behaviors are stimulated and the processes by which the continuity, frequency, and diversity of delinquency are shaped, comes in three types: (1) acceleration (increased frequency of offending over time), (2) stabilization (increased continuity over time), and (3) diversification (propensity of individuals to become involved in more diverse delinquent activities). *Aggravation*, the second dynamic process, refers to the existence of a developmental sequence of activities that escalates or increases in seriousness over time. *Desistance*, the third process, which is discussed in greater detail later in this chapter, describes a slowing down in the frequency of offending (deceleration), a reduction in its variety (specialization), or a reduction in its seriousness (de-escalation).[119]

The life course perspective highlights the development of criminal careers.

Another central organizing principle of life course theories is linked lives, a concept meaning that human lives "are typically embedded in social relationships with kin and friends across the life span";[120] these relationships exercise considerable influence on the life course of most people.

Glen H. Elder, Jr., has identified four important life course principles (Figure 8–8) that provide a concise summary of life course theory:[121]

1. The principle of historical time and place. The life course of individuals is embedded in and shaped by the historical times and places they experience over their lifetime. Hence, children born in the United States during the Great Depression or in Nazi Germany during World War II were no doubt strongly influenced by the conditions around them. Similarly, surviving children whose parents were lost in the Holocaust experienced trajectories in their life course that probably would have been far different had they been born in a different place or at a different time.
2. The principle of timing in lives. The developmental impact of a succession of life transitions or events is contingent on when they occur in a person's life. Early marriage, for example, or childbearing at an early age can significantly influence the course of people's lives through the long-term consequences of such events. People who start families early may find themselves excluded from further schooling by the demands of parenthood, and those who

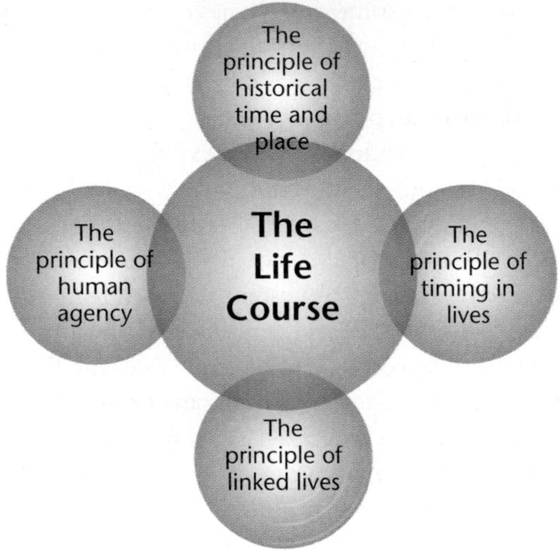

FIGURE 8–8 | Four Important Life Course Principles

Source: Schmalleger, Frank J., *Criminology*. Printed and Electronically reproduced by permission of Pearson Education, Inc., Upper Saddle River, New Jersey.

■ **human agency** The active role that people take in their lives; the fact that people are not merely subject to social and structural constraints but actively make choices and decisions based on the alternatives they see before them.

leave home and marry at an early age may find that parental financial support is not as readily available to them as it might have been if they had continued to live at home.

3. The principle of linked lives. Lives are lived interdependently, and social and historical influences are expressed through a network of shared relationships. If a child or a spouse develops a serious illness, for example, the lives of other family members are likely to be affected. Caring for an ill family member is emotionally and financially costly, and it takes time. Because of such costs, opportunities that might have been otherwise available are likely to be lost.
4. The principle of **human agency**. Human agency refers to the fact that individuals construct their own life course through the choices they make and the actions they take within the opportunities and constraints of history and social circumstances. The example that Elder gives is of hard-pressed Depression-era parents who "moved their residence to cheaper quarters and sought alternative forms of income." In making such choices, they were involved in the process of building a new life course.

Life course theories are supported by research dating back over three-quarters of a century. During the 1920s and 1930s, **Sheldon Glueck** and **Eleanor Glueck** studied the life cycles and careers of 500 nondelinquent and 500 known delinquent boys and another 500 girls in an effort to identify the causes of delinquency.[122] Study group participants were matched on age, intelligence, ethnicity, and neighborhood residence. Data were collected through psychiatric interviews with subjects, parent and teacher reports, and official records obtained from police, court, and correctional files, and surviving subjects were interviewed again between 1949 and 1965.

Significantly, the Gluecks investigated possible contributions to crime causation on four levels: sociocultural (socioeconomic), somatic (physical), intellectual, and emotional-temperamental and concluded that family dynamics played an especially significant role in the development of criminality—"the deeper the roots of childhood maladjustment, the smaller the chance of adult adjustment."[123] Delinquent careers, said the Gluecks, tend to carry over into adulthood and frequently lead to criminal careers.

In 2012, in an interesting test of life course theory and turning points, David S. Kirk at the University of Texas at Austin showed that former prisoners returning home to New Orleans were far less likely to continue lives of crimes if they moved to new neighborhoods. Kirk found that the displacement produced by Hurricane Katrina generally led to lower rates of recidivism among those former prisoners because it resulted in a reduction of criminal opportunities and a loss of association with former criminal peers.[124]

Read more about the life course perspective at **Library Extra 8–8**, and review a paper comparing the life course perspective to other theories discussed in this book at **Library Extra 8–9**.

Laub and Sampson's Age-Graded Theory

John H. Laub and Robert J. Sampson dusted off 60 cartons of nearly forgotten data that had been collected by the Gluecks and stored in the basement of the Harvard Law School.[125] Upon reanalysis of the data, Laub and Sampson found that children who turned to delinquency were frequently those who had trouble at school and at home and who had friends who were already involved in delinquency. They also discovered that two events in the life course—marriage and job stability—seemed to be especially important in reducing the frequency of offending in later life.

Using a sophisticated cyberanalysis of the Gluecks' original data, Laub and Sampson developed an "age-graded theory of informal social control."[126] Like Hirschi (discussed earlier), Laub and Sampson suggested that delinquency is more likely to occur when an individual's bond to society is weak or broken, but they also recognized that "social ties embedded in adult transitions (for example, marital attachment, job stability) explain variations in crime unaccounted for by childhood deviance."[127] Hence, although it incorporated the concept of social bonds, Laub and Sampson's perspective also emphasized the significance of continuity and change over the life course.

Central to Laub and Sampson's approach is the idea of turning points in a criminal career—"the interlocking nature of trajectories and transitions may generate turning points or a change in the life course."[128] Turning points were first identified by G. B. Trasler in 1980 when he wrote, "As they grow older, most young men gain access to other sources of achievement and social satisfaction—a job, a girlfriend, a wife, a home and eventually children—and in doing so become gradually less dependent upon peer-group support."[129] Given the importance of turning points—which may turn a person toward or away from criminality and delinquency—a clear-cut relationship between early delinquency and criminality later in life cannot be assumed. Sampson and Laub also identified two significant turning points: employment and marriage. Other important turning points can

Delinquency is more likely to occur when an individual's bond to society is weak or broken.

CRIMINAL | PROFILES

Seung-Hui Cho—An Angry Young Man

Seung-Hui Cho was born January 18, 1984. He rarely talked and possessed a disassociated manner, displaying little reaction to what was occurring around him. Cho came to America from the Republic of Korea when he was just eight years old, a sullen, withdrawn, brooding child, but he is remembered today as the campus shooter who took the lives of 27 students and five professors at Virginia Tech University in 2007.

Interviewed after the tragic events at Virginia Tech, Cho's 84-year-old great-aunt Yang-Soon Kim said: "When I told his mother that he was a good boy, quiet but well behaved, she said she would rather have him respond to her when talked to than be good and meek."[i]

After coming to America and moving to the tight-knit Korean community in Centreville, Virginia, the family maintained an "uncommonly private" existence.[ii] Cho's progression through elementary school was unremarkable; at nearby Westfield High School, Cho was teased and bullied, especially about his poor English and deep-throated voice;[iii] he remained a quiet and aloof loner who acted, a neighbor observed, "like he had a broken heart."[iv]

Whereas others (including his own sister, Sun-Kyung) in the success-oriented community were heralded in the community newspaper for making the selection lists at some of the most elite Ivy League universities, Cho's less-than-stellar grades kept him off such lists, so he went to Virginia Tech in the Blue Ridge Mountains.

Cho's freshman, sophomore, and junior years as an English major at Virginia Tech were noteworthy for the palpable anger of his writings, and the disturbingly violent nature of his papers caused the chairwoman of the English Department to remove him from a creative writing class. She attempted to teach him one on one and then sought assistance from the university's counseling department and other university officials.[v]

The anger within Cho was also of concern to his fellow students, who openly discussed whether he could become a school shooter.[vi] *New York Times* columnist Benedict Carey eloquently explained afterward that "the tragedy illustrates how human social groups, whether in classrooms, boardrooms or dormitories, are in fact exquisitely sensitive to a threat in their midst."[vii]

The attacks on the Virginia Tech campus were planned and executed with near-military precision. Weeks before the shooting, Cho acquired two handguns, extra magazines, ammunition, and lengths of chain to secure the doors of classroom buildings so that potential victims would be unable to escape. Days before the killings, he videotaped a raging manifesto-like diatribe/suicide note blaming society for making him into what he'd become.[viii]

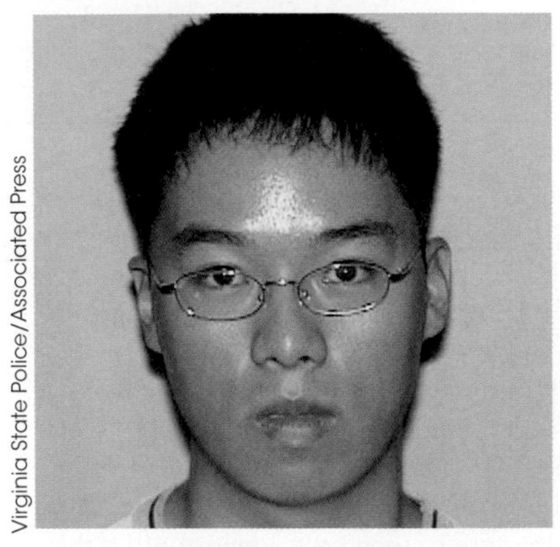

Virginia State Police/Associated Press

Seung-Hui Cho, age 23, of South Korea, identified by police as the shooter in a massacre that left 33 people dead at Virginia Tech in Blacksburg, Virginia, on April 16, 2007. The shooting is said to be the deadliest killing by a single gunman in modern U.S. history. How can crimes like Seung-Hui's be understood?

Shortly after 7 A.M. on April 16, 2007, Cho killed his first two victims, which police mistakenly believed was the result of a lovers' quarrel. Their error gave Cho the time he needed to make his last preparations for another attack.[ix]

Entering Norris Hall around 9:30 A.M., Cho secured the interior door handles with chains and then systematically slaughtered everyone he encountered. During the next 15 minutes, he fired more than 175 rounds of ammunition from two weapons, leaving 30 people dead.[x] When Cho heard police blast through the entrance doors to gain access to the building, he turned the gun on himself. His rampage is the worst of its kind in U.S. history, leaving a total of 32 victims.

The case of Seung-Hui Cho raises a number of interesting questions. Among them are the following:

1. Why was Cho so angry? Could his lack of social bonds be partially to blame?
2. How might Cho's bonds with those around him have been strengthened, perhaps avoiding the tragedy at Virginia Tech?
3. What did Cho mean when he blamed society for making him what he'd become?

Notes

i. N. R. Kleinfield, "Before Deadly Rage, a Life Consumed by Troubling Silence," *New York Times*, April 22, 2007, http://www.nytimes.com/2007/04/22/us/22vatech.html?_r=1&n=Top%2fReference%2fTimes%20Topics%2fPeople%2fC%2fCho%2c%20Seung%2dHui&oref=slogin (accessed July 1, 2007).

ii. Ibid.

iii. "High School Classmates Say Gunman Was Bullied," MSNBC, April 19, 2007, http://www.msnbc.msn.com/id/18169776/ (accessed July 1, 2007).

iv. Kleinfield, "Before Deadly Rage."

v. "Professor: Shooter's Writing Dripped with Anger," Cable News Network, April 18, 2007, http://www.cnn.com/2007/US/04/17/vtech.shooting/index.html (accessed July 1, 2007).

vi. Kleinfield, "Before Deadly Rage."

vii. Benedict Carey, "When the Group Is Wise," *New York Times*, April 22, 2007, http://www.nytimes.com/2007/04/22/weekinreview/22carey.html?_r=1&ref=weekinreview&oref=slogin (accessed July 1, 2007).

viii. Ned Potter et al., "Killer's Note: You Caused Me to Do This," ABC News, April 28, 2007, http://abcnews.go.com/US/Story?id=3048108&page=1 (accessed July 1, 2007).

ix. Ibid.

x. Aamer Madhani, E. A. Torriero, and Rex W. Huppke, "Danger Signs Festered below Aloof Surface," *Chicago Tribune*, April 17, 2007, http://www.chicagotribune.com/news/nationworld/chi-070417vtech-shootings,0,1137509.story?page=1&coll=chi-homepagepromo440-fea (accessed July 1, 2007).

■ **social capital** The degree of positive relationships with others and with social institutions that individuals build up over the course of their lives.

■ **life course–persistent offender** An individual who displays more or less constant patterns of misbehavior throughout life.

occur in association with leaving home, having children, getting divorced, graduating from school, and receiving a financial windfall. According to Laub and Sampson, even chronic offenders can be reformed when they experience the requisite turning points, whereas individuals with histories of conventionality can begin offending in response to events and circumstances that undermine previously restraining social bonds.[130]

Because transitions in the life course are typically associated with age and because transitional events either enhance or weaken the social bond, Sampson and Laub contended that "age-graded changes in social bonds explain changes in crime"; because these events are not the result of "purposeful efforts to control," they are dubbed "informal social controls."[131]

In 2001, an examination of data from the Dunedin Study (referred to in Chapter 5) suggested the idea of life course interdependence, in which "the effects of social ties on crime vary as a function of criminal propensity."[132] In other words, prosocial ties that deter crime (education, marriage, steady employment) are more likely to discourage criminality among those who are already predisposed to avoid it than among those who are not; researchers dubbed this the "social-protection effect." Conversely, a "social-amplification effect" could be identified in antisocial ties (delinquent friends) that promote crime among individuals predisposed to criminality. The researchers concluded that certain features of the social environment could serve as positive turning points in the lives of antisocial individuals, but the social-amplification effect could produce negative turning points in the lives of the same people.

Another important concept in Laub and Sampson's theory is **social capital**, which refers to the degree of positive relationships with other people and with social institutions that individuals build up over the course of their lives.[133] Social capital directly impacts life course trajectories: The greater a person's social capital, the less chance there is of criminal activity.[134]

A study of how two primary constituents of social capital—marriage and full-time employment—impact life course trajectories was reported by Matthew G. Yeager in 2003. He examined the lives of 773 adult male prisoners released from the Canadian federal prison system between 1983 and 1984, following them for a period of three years.[135] He found that being married reduced the likelihood of return to prison, but an even stronger indicator of postprison success was full-time employment, which Yeager described as having "a strong suppression effect on general criminal recidivism." Because employment is something for which prisoners can be prepared and because it can be offered by the state or federal government, Yeager suggested that it provides a rare opportunity for successful intervention in the lives of released prisoners.

In 2006, Sampson and Laub reported on the application of sophisticated data-analysis techniques to subjects from the Gluecks' original study group who were reinterviewed at age 70. The 2006 study supported the conclusion that "being married is associated with an average reduction of approximately 35 percent in the odds of crime compared to nonmarried status for the same man."[136]

An interesting evaluation of social capital—commitment to a romantic partner, strong job attachment, and nature of close friends among adult subjects—was reported by a group of criminologists in 2002.[137] They found that adolescent delinquency tended to result in involvement with an antisocial romantic partner for both males and females and that such a relationship tended to influence the nature of adult relationships and to increase the likelihood of later criminality. Conventional romantic partners and friends, along with strong job attachment, were found to be especially likely to reduce the chance of criminality among young adult women, but only conventional adult friends had the same effect among males.

Finally, in 2006, Lisa M. Broidy and Elizabeth E. Cauffman reexamined the Glueck's early data on girls in order to determine how social capital contributed to desistance from crime among women.[138] Using data on 500 female offenders originally collected by the Gluecks, the researchers found that social capital in the form of marriage, motherhood, and positive work experiences led to desistance from crime "in a manner that transcends both gender and historical content." Because much of the data gathered by the Gluecks came from the 1920s, Broidy and Cauffman concluded that marriage, because it was regarded as a universal goal for women during that period of time and because it signified a commitment to conventional norms, represented a significant turning point in the life of young women that marked the start of the desistance process. Learn more about the concept of social capital via **Library Extra 8–10**.

Moffitt's Dual Taxonomic Theory

Criminologists have long noted that although adult criminality is usually preceded by antisocial behavior during adolescence, most antisocial children do not become adult criminals. Psychologist **Terrie E. Moffitt** developed a two-path (dual taxonomic) theory of criminality that helps to explain this observation.[139] Moffit's theory contends that as a result of neuropsychological deficits (specifically, early brain damage or chemical imbalances) combined with poverty and family dysfunction, some people come to display more or less constant patterns of misbehavior throughout life.[140] These people are called **life course–persistent offenders** or *life course persisters*. Life course persisters tend to fail in school and become involved in delinquency at an

■ **adolescence-limited offender** An individual who goes through limited periods where they exhibit high probabilities of offending.

■ **persistence** A person's continuity in crime or continual involvement in offending.

■ **desistance** A person's cessation of criminal activity or termination of a period of involvement in offending behavior.

early age. As a consequence, their opportunities for legitimate success become increasingly limited with the passage of time.

Other teenagers, says Moffitt, go through limited periods where they exhibit high probabilities of offending. Probabilities of offending are generally highest for these people, says Moffitt, during the mid-teen years. This second group, called **adolescence-limited offenders**, is led to offending primarily by structural disadvantages, according to two-path theory. The most significant of these disadvantages is the status anxiety of teenagers that stems from modern society's inadequacy at easing the transition from adolescence to adulthood for significant numbers of young people. Moffitt hypothesizes that a significant source of adolescent strain arises from the fact that biological maturity occurs at a relatively early age (perhaps as early as 12) and brings with it the desire for sexual and emotional relationships as well as personal autonomy.[141] Society, however, does not permit the assumption of autonomous adult roles until far later (around age 18). As adolescents begin to want autonomy, they are prevented from achieving it because of preexisting societal expectations and societally limited opportunities, resulting in what Moffitt calls a "maturity gap." They might be told, "You're too young for that," or "Wait until you grow up." Lacking the resources to achieve autonomy on their own, they are drawn into delinquent roles by lifelong deviants who have already achieved autonomy and serve as role models for others seeking early independence. At least an appearance of autonomy is achievable for adolescence-limited offenders by engaging in actions that mimic those routinely undertaken by life course–persistent offenders. Once adolescence-limited offenders realize the substantial costs of continuing misbehavior, however, they abandon such social mimicry and the participation in delinquent acts that characterizes it. As they mature, they begin to aspire toward achieving legitimate autonomy. Those who fail to make the transition successfully add to the ranks of the life course–persistent population.

Moffitt notes that adolescence-limited offenders display inconsistencies in antisocial behavior from one place to another. They might, for example, participate in illicit drug use with friends or shoplift in stores. They might also experiment sexually. Still, their school behavior is likely to remain within socially acceptable bounds, and they will probably act with respect toward teachers, employers, and adults. Life course–persistent offenders, on the other hand, consistently engage in antisocial behavior across a wide spectrum of social situations.

Research findings indicate that positive developmental pathways are fostered when adolescents are able to develop (1) a sense of industry and competency, (2) a feeling of connectedness to others and to society, (3) a belief in their ability to control their future, and (4) a stable identity.[142] Adolescents who develop these characteristics appear more likely than others to engage in prosocial behaviors, exhibit positive school performances, and be members of nondeviant peer groups. Competency, connectedness, control, and identity are outcomes of the developmental process. They develop through a person's interactions with his or her community, family, school, and peers. The following kinds of interactions appear to promote development of these characteristics:

- Interactions in which children engage in productive activities and win recognition for their productivity
- Interactions in which parents and other adults control and monitor adolescents' behaviors in a consistent and caring manner while allowing them a substantial degree of psychological and emotional independence
- Interactions in which parents and other adults provide emotional support, encouragement, and practical advice to adolescents
- Interactions in which adolescents are accepted as individuals with unique experiences based on their temperament; gender; biosocial development; and family, cultural, and societal factors

Farrington's Delinquent Development Theory

Life course theorists use the term **persistence** to describe continuity in crime or continual involvement in offending; **desistance** refers to the cessation of criminal activity or the termination of a period of involvement in offending behavior. Desistance (mentioned briefly earlier in this chapter) can be unaided or aided: Unaided desistance refers to desistance that occurs without the formal intervention or assistance of criminal justice agencies like probation or parole agencies, the courts, or prison or jail, and aided desistance, involving agencies of the justice system, is generally referred to as rehabilitation. Delinquents often mature successfully and grow out of offending; even older persistent offenders may tire of justice system interventions, lose the personal energy required for continued offending, and "burn out."

A number of early criminologists noted the desistance phenomenon. Marvin Wolfgang described the process as one of "spontaneous remission,"[143] although it was recognized far earlier—in 1833, Adolphe Quetelet argued that the penchant for crime diminished with age "due to the enfeeblement of physical vitality and the passions."[144] The Glueck later developed the

■ **Cambridge Study in Delinquent Development** A longitudinal (life course) study of crime and delinquency tracking a cohort of 411 boys born in London in 1953.

■ **resilience** The psychological ability to successfully cope with severe stress and negative events.

■ **cohort analysis** A social scientific technique that studies a population with common characteristics over time. Cohort analysis usually begins at birth and traces the development of cohort members until they reach a certain age.

concept of maturational reform to explain the phenomenon and suggested that the "sheer passage of time" caused delinquents to "grow out" of this transitory phase and to "burn out" physiologically, concluding, "Ageing is the only factor which emerges as significant in the reformative process."[145]

In 1985, Walter R. Grove proposed a maturational theory of biopsychosocial desistance that sees the desistance phenomenon as a natural or normal consequence of the aging process.[146] "As persons move through the life cycle, (1) they will shift from self-absorption to concern for others; (2) they will increasingly accept societal values and behave in socially appropriate ways; (3) they will become more comfortable with social relations; (4) their activities will increasingly reflect a concern for others in their community; and (5) they will become increasingly concerned with the issue of the meaning of life."[147] Some criminologists argued, however, that the claim that aging causes desistance is meaningless because it doesn't explain the actual mechanisms involved.

Longitudinal studies of crime over the life course conducted by **David P. Farrington** and **Donald J. West** have shown far greater diversity in the ages of desistance than in the ages of onset of criminal behavior.[148] In 1982, in an effort to explain the considerable heterogeneity of developmental pathways, Farrington and West began tracking a cohort of 411 boys born in London in 1953 in an ongoing study known as the **Cambridge Study in Delinquent Development**, which uses self-reports of delinquency as well as psychological tests and in-depth interviews. To date, participants have been interviewed eight times, with the earliest interviews being conducted at age eight.

The Cambridge study reveals that life course patterns found in the United States are also characteristic of English delinquents. Farrington found that the study's persistent offenders suffered from "hyperactivity, poor concentration, low achievement, an antisocial father, large family size, low family income, a broken family, poor parental supervision, and parental disharmony."[149] Other risk factors for delinquency included harsh discipline, negative peer influences, and parents with offense histories of their own. Chronic offenders were found to have friends and peers who were also offenders, and offending was found to begin with early antisocial behavior, including aggressiveness, dishonesty, problems in school, truancy, hyperactivity, impulsiveness, and restlessness. Consistent with other desistance studies, Farrington found that offending tends to peak around the age of 17 or 18 and then declines. By age 35, many subjects were found to have conforming lifestyles, although they were often separated or divorced and had poor employment records and patterns of residential instability. Many former offenders were also substance abusers and consequently served as very poor role models for their children.

Although studies of desistance are becoming increasingly common, one of the main methodological problems for researchers is determining when desistance has occurred. Some theorists conceptualize desistance as the complete or absolute stopping of criminal behavior of any kind, whereas others see it as the gradual cessation of criminal involvement.[150] In 1990, Rolf Loeber and Marc LeBlanc identified four components of desistance:[151] (1) deceleration—a slowing down in the frequency of offending, (2) specialization—a reduction in the variety of offenses, (3) de-escalation—a reduction in the seriousness of offending, and (4) reaching a ceiling—remaining at a certain level of offending and not committing more serious offenses.

Resilience, another important concept in life course research, refers to the psychological ability to successfully cope with severe stress and negative events and has important implications for the development of delinquency and criminal offending.[152] One recent study of resilience among teenage girls exposed to a number of risk factors associated with delinquency development (physical and sexual assault, neglect, poverty, unemployed parents, female-headed households) found a number of protective factors that could enhance resilience among girls. Included were things like religiosity, school connectedness and success, and presence of a caring adult; the latter offered the most protection against delinquency. "The most consistent protective effect . . . was the extent to which a girl felt she had caring adults in her life."[153]

Resilience is the psychological ability to successfully cope with severe stress and negative events and has important implications for the development of delinquency and criminal offending.

Evolutionary Ecology

Because life course theory uses a developmental perspective in the study of criminal careers, life course researchers typically use longitudinal research designs involving **cohort analysis**, which usually begins at birth and traces the development of a population whose members share common characteristics until they reach a certain age. One well known analysis of a birth cohort,

■ **evolutionary ecology** An approach to understanding crime that draws attention to the ways people develop over the course of their lives.

■ **interactional theory** A theoretical approach to exploring crime and delinquency that blends social control and social learning perspectives.

undertaken by **Marvin Wolfgang** during the 1960s, found that a small nucleus of chronic juvenile offenders accounted for a disproportionately large share of all juvenile arrests.[154] Wolfgang studied male individuals born in Philadelphia in 1945 until they reached age 18 and concluded that a small number of violent offenders were responsible for most of the crimes committed by the cohort—6% of cohort members accounted for 52% of all arrests (Figure 8–9). A follow-up study found that the seriousness of the offenses among the cohort increased in adulthood but that the actual number of offenses decreased as the cohort aged.[155] Wolfgang's analysis has since been criticized for its lack of a second cohort, or control group, against which the experiences of the cohort under study could be compared.[156]

The ecological perspective on crime control, pioneered by **Lawrence E. Cohen** and **Richard Machalek**, provides a more contemporary example of a life course approach.[157] **Evolutionary ecology** builds on the approach of social ecology while emphasizing developmental pathways encountered early in life. Criminologist Bryan Vila stated that "the evolutionary ecological approach draws attention to the ways people develop over the course of their lives. Experiences and environment early in life, especially those that affect child development and the transmission of biological traits and family management practices across generations, seem particularly important."[158] According to Vila, evolutionary ecology "attempts to explain how people acquire criminality—a predisposition that disproportionately favors criminal behavior—when and why they express it as crime, how individuals and groups respond to those crimes, and how all these phenomena interact as a dynamic self-reinforcing system that evolves over time."[159]

Thornberry's Interactional Theory

Terence Thornberry proposed what he calls an **interactional theory** regarding crime, which integrates social control and social learning explanations of delinquency.[160] In constructing his approach, Thornberry was attentive to the impact of social structure on behavior and noted how delinquency and crime seem to develop within the context of reciprocal social arrangements. Reciprocity was especially important to Thornberry because he believed that too many other theories were overly simplistic in their dependence on simple unidirectional causal relationships (see the Theory versus Reality box).

The fundamental cause of delinquency according to interactional theory is a weakening of a person's bond to conventional society.[161] Thornberry pointed out that adolescents who are strongly attached to their parents and family and who strive to achieve within the context of approved social arrangements, such as education, rarely turn to serious delinquency. It takes more than weak conventional bonds, however, for delinquency to develop; it requires the presence of an environment in which delinquency can be learned and in which rule-violating behavior can be positively rewarded. Delinquent peers are especially important in providing the kind of environment necessary for criminal behavior to develop, and gang membership can play a highly significant role in the development and continuation of such behavior. Associating with delinquent peers, said Thornberry, leads to delinquent acts but also involves a causal loop such that those who commit delinquent acts are likely to continue associating with others like themselves—creating a mechanism of social reinforcement and resulting in ever-escalating levels of criminal behavior. Thornberry also predicted that delinquents will seek out association with ever-more delinquent groups if their delinquency continues to be rewarded, so delinquency is seen as a process that unfolds over the life course.

In a test of interactional theory, Thornberry used data drawn from the Rochester Youth Development Study, a multiwave panel study designed to examine drug use and delinquent behavior among adolescents in the Rochester, New York, area.[162] Study findings (discussed in more detail later) supported the loop-type aspects of interactional theory and showed that delinquency is part of a dynamic social process,

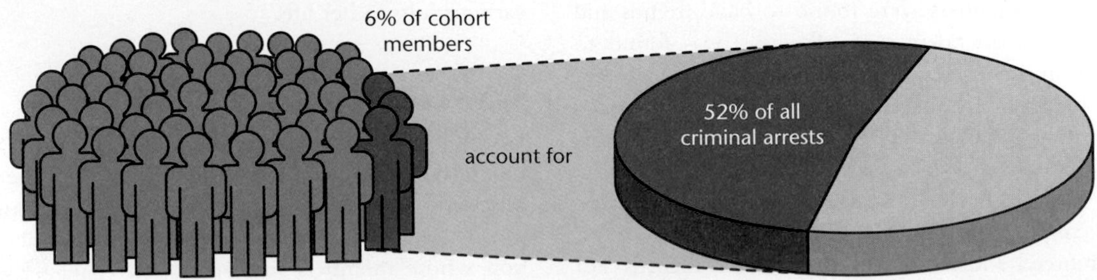

FIGURE 8-9 | **The Nucleus of Chronic Offenders**

Source: Schmalleger, Frank J., *Criminology*. Printed and Electronically reproduced by permission of Pearson Education, Inc., Upper Saddle River, New Jersey.

THEORY | versus REALITY

Social Influences on Developmental Pathways

A report by the Family and Youth Services Bureau (an agency of the U.S. Department of Health and Human Services) identified five "aspects of the social context" that can either promote or block the development of prosocial behavior among adolescents:

1. Biophysical aspects of the individual. Biophysical characteristics found to influence developmental pathways during adolescence include temperament, gender, cognitive development, and age of onset of puberty. The influence of these factors on development depends to a large extent on how others in the social context react to them. Individuals bring these aspects of self to the interactions in which they are engaged, and the reaction of the social context to these aspects determines the quality and nature of the interactions.
2. Aspects of the society. Society may be understood as the economic and institutional structures, values, and mores that constitute a national identity. Some of the aspects of society that influence the development of a sense of competency, connectedness, control, and identity are current economic and employment conditions, discrimination and prejudice, and educational institutions. Societal factors influence adolescent development directly and indirectly through their effects on communities and families. The societal factors of prejudice and discrimination often present barriers to positive developmental pathways for minority and economically disadvantaged youths, so for these youths, community and family contexts are particularly important for moderating the potentially negative influences of societal factors.
3. Aspects of the community. The community context (neighborhood or town) incorporates where individuals spend their time and with whom they spend it. The aspects of the community context that have been studied with respect to their effects on adolescent development include community culture, availability of sources of support to parents and youths, and availability of quality community institutional or organizational resources for children and youths. As with societal factors, community factors have both direct and indirect influences on developmental pathways during adolescence. Formal and informal broad-based community institutions and organizations, in particular, influence adolescent development directly by teaching and encouraging prosocial behaviors and indirectly by supporting parents in their parenting efforts.
4. Aspects of the family. The following aspects of the family context have received considerable research attention with respect to their influences on developmental pathways: quality of the parent–child relationship, parenting styles or practices, family structure, and family dysfunction. In general, family practices that serve to monitor and control adolescents' behaviors in a caring and consistent manner, provide support and encouragement to adolescents, and allow them psychological and emotional independence appear to be most effective in fostering the development of a sense of competency, connectedness, control over one's fate in life, and identity.
5. Aspects of peer relationships. Research findings do not support the popular notion that adolescent problem behaviors are the result of peer pressure; instead, it has been shown that peers do not direct adolescents to new behaviors as much as they reinforce existing dispositions that helped direct the adolescent to a particular peer group in the first place. Close friendships with peers during adolescence have been found to promote positive growth because they foster the development of conceptions of fairness, mutual respect, empathy, and intimacy, through which youths are able to develop a sense of connectedness to others and a stable sense of identity.

The information in the Family and Youth Services Bureau report suggested that interventions designed to assist youths in making successful transitions to adulthood will need to provide adolescents, either directly or through parents and community resources, with opportunities to engage in interactions that foster the development of a sense of competency, connectedness, control, and identity and that interventions must address children, families, and communities as a unit if they are to be effective for large numbers of children and their families.

Discussion Questions

1. How would you rank the five aspects of the social context identified in this box as impacting the development of prosocial behavior among adolescents in order of relative importance? Why would you choose such a ranking?
2. How might the five aspects of the social context interact?
3. Are there other important aspects of the social context that can be identified? If so, what might they be?

Source: Family and Youth Services Bureau, *Understanding Youth Development: Promoting Positive Pathways of Growth* (Washington, DC: U.S. Department of Health and Human Services, January 1997).

not merely the end result of static conditions. The study also found that the development of beliefs supportive of delinquent behavior tends to follow that behavior in time. In other words, commitment to delinquent values may be more a product of delinquent behavior that is rewarded than an initial cause of such behavior.

Thornberry also found that childhood maltreatment (based on official records) could be an important element of the developmental process leading to delinquency and that the degree of maltreatment experienced in childhood bore some relationship to the extent of delinquent involvement later in life.[163] While maltreatment appears to weaken the bond to conventionality, it also weakens the family bond. Suman Kaker of Florida International University, in an extension of interactional theory, noted that delinquency also puts stress on the family, resulting in a further weakening of the familial bond.[164]

Developmental Pathways

Researchers have found that manifestations of disruptive behaviors in childhood and adolescence are often age dependent, reflecting a developing capability to display different behaviors with age.[165]

Childhood maltreatment is an important element of the developmental process leading to delinquency.

Budding behavioral problems can often be detected at an early age. In 1994, Rolf Loeber and Dale F. Hay described the emergence of opposition to parents and aggression toward siblings and peers as a natural developmental occurrence during the first two years of life.[166] As toddlers develop the ability to speak, they become increasingly likely to use words to resolve conflicts, with oppositional behaviors declining between ages three and six as children acquire greater verbal skills for expressing their needs and for dealing with conflict, but children who are unable to develop adequate verbal coping skills commit acts of intense aggression, initiate hostile conflict, and are characterized by parents as having a difficult temperament.[167] Figure 8–10 shows the order in which disruptive and antisocial childhood behaviors tend to manifest between birth and late adolescence, and Figure 8–11 shows the order of development of skills and attitudes deemed necessary for successful prosocial development during childhood and adolescence.

One of the most comprehensive studies to date attempting to detail life pathways leading to criminality, which began in 1986, is the Program of Research on the Causes and Correlates of Delinquency, sponsored by the U.S. Department of Justice's Office of Juvenile Justice and Delinquency Prevention. The program, a longitudinal study producing ongoing results, aims to better understand serious delinquency, violence, and drug use by examining how youths develop within the context of family, school, peers, and community.[168] It has compiled data on 4,500 youths from three distinct but coordinated projects: the Denver Youth Survey, conducted by the University of Colorado; the Pittsburgh Youth Study, undertaken by University of Pittsburgh researchers; and the Rochester Youth Development Study, fielded by professors at the State University of New York at Albany.

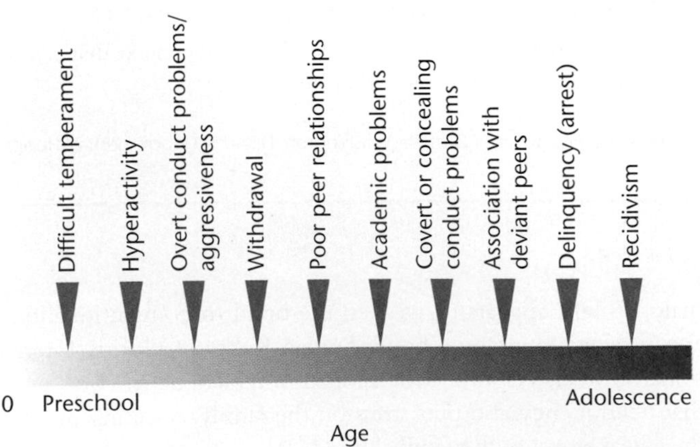

FIGURE 8–10 | Manifestations of Disruptive and Antisocial Behaviors in Childhood and Adolescence

Source: Barbara Tatem Kelley et al., *Developmental Pathways in Boys' Disruptive and Delinquent Behavior* (Washington, DC: Office of Juvenile Justice and Delinquency Prevention, December 1997).

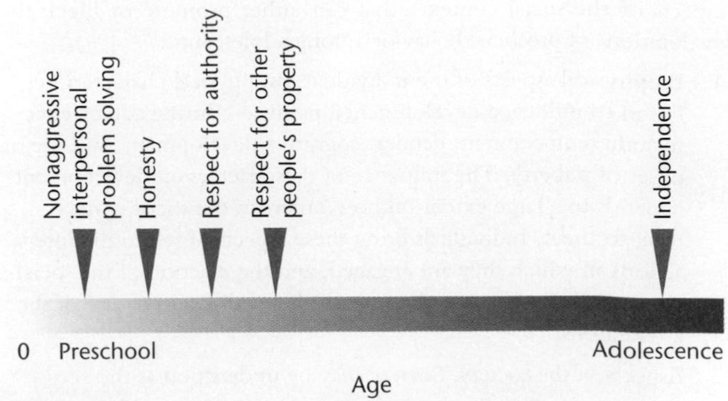

FIGURE 8–11 | The Order of Development of Skills and Attitudes Necessary for Successful Prosocial Development

Source: Barbara Tatem Kelley et al., *Developmental Pathways in Boys' Disruptive and Delinquent Behavior* (Washington, DC: Office of Juvenile Justice and Delinquency Prevention, December 1997).

The Causes and Correlates projects, using a similar research design, are longitudinal investigations involving repeated contacts with youths during a substantial portion of their developmental years. Researchers conduct individual face-to-face interviews with inner-city youths considered to be at high risk for involvement in delinquency and drug abuse. Multiple perspectives on each child's development and behavior were obtained through interviews with the child's primary caretakers and with teachers. In addition to interview data, the studies collect extensive information from official agencies, including police, courts, schools, and social services.[169] Following are some program results:

1. Delinquency is related to individual risk factors such as impulsivity.
2. The more seriously involved in drugs a youth is, the more seriously that juvenile will be involved in delinquency.
3. Children who are more attached to and involved with their parents are less involved in delinquency.
4. Greater risks exist for violent offending when a child is physically abused or neglected early in life.
5. Students who are not highly committed to school have higher rates of delinquency, and delinquency involvement reduces commitment to school.
6. Poor family life, especially poor parental supervision, exacerbates delinquency and drug use.

7. Affiliation with street gangs and illegal gun ownership are both predictive of delinquency.
8. Living in a bad neighborhood doubles the risk for delinquency.
9. A family being on public assistance (welfare) is associated with the highest risk of delinquency (followed by a family having low socioeconomic status).[170]

Results showed that "peers who were delinquent or used drugs had a great impact on [other] youth" and that "the best predictors of success were having conventional friends, having a stable family and good parental monitoring, having positive expectations for the future, and not having delinquent peers."[171]

Research findings indicated that positive developmental pathways are fostered when adolescents are able to develop (1) a sense of industry and competency, (2) a feeling of connectedness to others and to society, (3) a belief in their ability to control their future, and (4) a stable identity.[172] Competency, connectedness, control, and identity develop through youths' interactions with their community, family, school, and peers. Adolescents who develop these characteristics appear more likely than others to engage in prosocial behaviors, exhibit positive school performance, and be members of nondeviant peer groups. The following interactions appear to promote these characteristics:

- Children engage in productive activities and win recognition for their productivity.
- Parents and other adults control and monitor adolescents' behaviors in a consistent and caring manner while allowing them a substantial degree of psychological and emotional independence.
- Parents and other adults provide emotional support, encouragement, and practical advice to adolescents.
- Adolescents are accepted as individuals with unique experiences based on their temperament, gender, and biosocial development as well as family, cultural, and societal factors.

Perhaps the most significant result of the Causes and Correlates study is the finding that three separate developmental pathways to delinquency (shown in Figure 8–12) exist:[173]

1. Authority conflict pathway. Subjects appear to begin quite young (three or four years of age) on the authority conflict pathway. "The first step," said the study authors, "was stubborn behavior, followed by defiance around age 11, and authority avoidance—truancy, staying out late at night, or running away."
2. Covert pathway. "Minor covert acts such as frequent lying and shoplifting usually [start] around age 10." Delinquents following the covert pathway quickly progress "to acts of property damage, such as fire starting or vandalism, around age 11 or 12, followed by moderate and serious forms of delinquency."

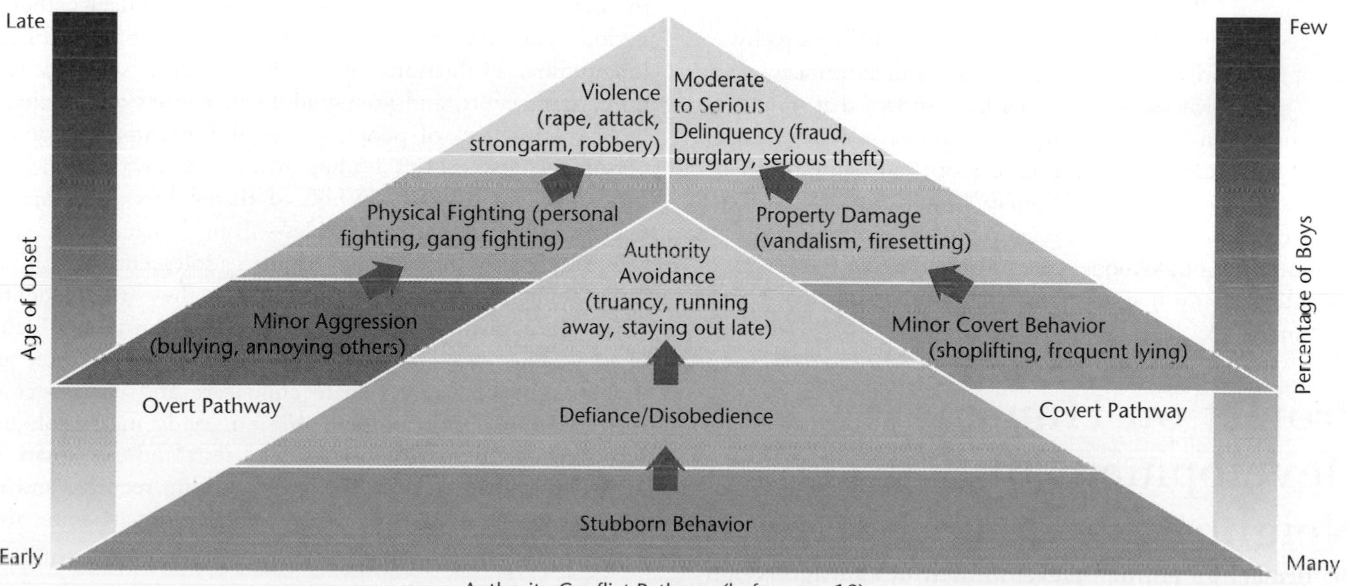

FIGURE 8–12 | **Three Pathways to Disruptive Behavior and Delinquency**

Source: Barbara Tatem Kelley et al., *Developmental Pathways in Boys' Disruptive and Delinquent Behavior* (Washington, DC: Office of Juvenile Justice and Delinquency Prevention, December 1997).

■ **Project on Human Development in Chicago Neighborhoods (PHDCN)** An intensive study of Chicago neighborhoods employing longitudinal evaluations to examine the changing circumstances of people's lives in an effort to identify personal characteristics leading toward or away from antisocial behavior.

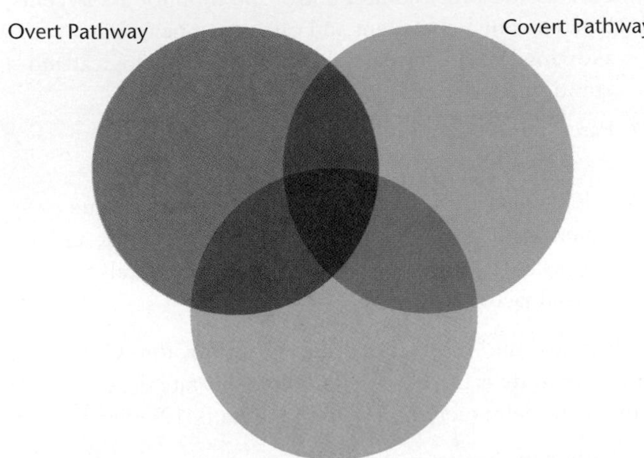

FIGURE 8–13 | **Single or Multiple Disruptive Pathways**

Source: Barbara Tatem Kelley et al., *Developmental Pathways in Boys' Disruptive and Delinquent Behavior* (Washington, DC: Office of Juvenile Justice and Delinquency Prevention, December 1997).

3. Overt pathway. The first step on the overt pathway is minor aggression such as "annoying others and bullying—around age 11 or 12." Bullying was found to escalate into "physical fighting and violence as the juvenile progressed along this pathway." The overt pathway eventually leads to violent crimes like rape, robbery, and assault.

Researchers have found that these three different pathways are not necessarily mutually exclusive and can at times converge (see Figure 8–13). Self-report data have shown that simultaneous progression along two or more pathways leads to higher rates of delinquency.[174] Learn more about the Causes and Correlates study and view results from each study site at **Web Extra 8–6**. Read more about the Program of Research on the Causes and Correlates of Delinquency at **Library Extra 8–11**, and review literature on developmental pathways at **Library Extras 8–12** and **8–13**.

Project on Human Development in Chicago Neighborhoods (PHDCN)

The **Project on Human Development in Chicago Neighborhoods (PHDCN)**, begun in 1990, is jointly sponsored by the National Institute of Justice and the John D. and Catherine T. MacArthur Foundation.[175] The PHDCN is directed by physician Felton J. Earls, professor of human behavior and development at Harvard University's School of Public Health; also involved are Robert Sampson, professor of sociology at the University of Chicago, and Stephen Raudenbush, professor of education at Michigan State University. Earls and Albert J. Reiss described the ongoing research as "the major criminologic investigation of this century."[176]

> The Project on Human Development in Chicago Neighborhoods (PHDCN) has been called "the major criminologic investigation of the century."

The PHDCN, which consists of a longitudinal analysis of how individuals, families, institutions, and communities evolve together, is now "tracing how criminal behavior develops from birth to age 32."[177] It involves experts from a wide range of disciplines, including psychiatry, developmental and clinical psychology, sociology, criminology, public health and medicine, education, human behavior, and statistics.

The project is actually two studies combined into a single comprehensive design: One is an intensive study of Chicago's neighborhoods that evaluates the social, economic, organizational, political, and cultural components of each neighborhood and seeks to identify changes that have taken place in the neighborhoods over the study's eight-year data-gathering period. The second study consists of a series of coordinated longitudinal evaluations of 7,000 randomly selected children, adolescents, and young adults that looks at the changing circumstances of people's lives and attempts to identify personal characteristics leading toward or away from antisocial behavior (see the Who's to Blame box). Researchers explore a wide range of variables—from prenatal drug exposure, lead poisoning, and nutrition to adolescent growth patterns, temperament, and self-image—as they try to identify which individuals might be most at risk for crime and delinquency. They also study children's exposure to violence and its consequences and evaluate child care and its impact on early childhood development. Various study methodologies, including self-reports, individualized tests and examinations, direct observations, examination of existing records, and reports by informants, are being used. Following are some areas and questions being explored:[178]

- **Communities.** Why do some communities experience high rates of antisocial behavior whereas apparently similar communities are relatively safe?

WHO'S TO BLAME—The Individual or Society?

Sexual Abuser Claims Victim Status

Mortimer Rataway was arrested after authorities received a report of a man struggling with a boy in a Short Stop food and beverage store. A police officer on nearby patrol arrived at the scene within minutes and observed Rataway forcing the boy, nine-year-old Justin, into an old sedan outside the convenience store. When the officer asked Rataway what was going on, the boy blurted out that he had been kidnapped.

The officer had heard reports on his radio describing the kidnapping of a nine-year-old boy from a school bus stop in an adjacent city two days earlier, and he quickly took Rataway into custody on suspicion of kidnapping.

Justin was taken to a special area reserved for juveniles in the local police station, where he told detectives that he was the boy who had been kidnapped. Although he was physically okay, he told police that Rataway had forced him to engage in repeated masturbation and that Rataway had taken many photographs of him naked.

A search of Rataway's apartment uncovered a number of digital cameras and a computer Web server hosting a child pornography site. The camera and computer contained photos of many other young boys; some of the photos had probably been purchased over the Internet, but Rataway later admitted taking others.

"I never hurt anybody," Rataway told investigators. "Most of the boys agreed to serve as models after I paid them. But I got carried away and grabbed Justin because I thought he'd make one of my best models.

"Yeah, I'm gay," Rataway told the police in a recorded statement. "And sure, I like boys. But it isn't my fault. When I was growing up as a young Catholic I was taught to enjoy my body and to like other men by the parish priest. Now I know that most priests are good men and that the crisis in the Church has been way overblown by the media. But if that hadn't happened to me, I know I would have been straight, and I'm sure I would have gotten married and had kids of my own. Because of what happened to me when I was a kid, I'm as much a victim as anybody. It doesn't matter how much you punish me, I'm never going to change my sexual orientation."

Think about it

1. Do you see Rataway as a criminal or a victim (as he claims)? Might he be both?
2. Some people describe child molesters as "sick." Is Rataway "sick"? If so, how can he be cured?
3. Will sending Rataway to prison rehabilitate him? Why or why not? How can you ensure that he won't pose a future threat if he is released back into society someday?
4. How does this case illustrate the way our understandings of criminal motivation and crime causality influence our notions of fairness and justice in the treatment of offenders?

Note: Who's to Blame boxes provide fictionalized critical thinking opportunities, and are not actual cases.

- **Schools.** Some children have achievement problems early in school, and others have behavioral or truancy problems; some exhibit both kinds of problems, and others neither kind. Why do these differences exist? What are their causes and effects?
- **Peers.** Delinquent youths tend to associate with delinquent peers and usually act in groups. Does this association lead to delinquency, or is it simply a case of "like finding like"? Are the influences of peers equally important for girls and for boys, or are their developmental pathways entirely different?
- **Families.** Poor parenting practices are strongly associated with substance abuse and delinquency, but are they the cause of such behaviors? If so, then social programs in parenting skills could make a difference. But what if there are underlying factors, such as temperamental characteristics or social isolation, that cause problems in both parents and children?
- **Individual differences.** What health-related, cognitive, intellectual, and emotional factors in children promote positive social development? What factors put them at risk of developing antisocial behaviors?

PHDCN study results have led to targeted interventions intended to lower rates of offending. According to Sampson, "Instead of external actions (for example, a police crackdown), we stress in this study the effectiveness of 'informal' mechanisms by which residents themselves achieve public order. In particular, we believe that collective expectations for intervening on behalf of neighborhood children [are] a crucial dimension of the public life of neighborhoods."[179] Life course perspectives, like the one informing the PHDCN, often point to the need for early intervention with nurturant strategies that build self-control through positive socialization. As Vila pointed out, "There are two main types of nurturant strategies: those that improve early life experiences to forestall the development of strategic styles based on criminality, and those

■ **Comprehensive Strategy for Serious, Violent, and Chronic Juvenile Offenders program** A National Institute of Justice initiative that provides participating communities with a framework for preventing delinquency, intervening in early delinquent behavior, and responding to serious, violent, and chronic offending.

Danita Delimont/Alamy

A tug-of-war in Chicago during the annual Youth Fest. The Project on Human Development in Chicago Neighborhoods (PHDCN) is a multidisciplinary project, consisting of a longitudinal analysis of how individuals, families, institutions, and communities evolve together, is jointly sponsored by the National Institute of Justice and the John D. and Catherine T. MacArthur Foundation. What results has the study produced?

that channel child and adolescent development in an effort to improve the match between individuals and their environment."[180] Nurturant crime-control strategies are discussed in more detail in Chapter 14. Learn more about the PHDCN at **Web Extra 8–7**. **Library Extra 8–14** discusses cultural mechanisms involved in neighborhood violence.

Policy Implications of Social Development Theories

Social development strategies have been widely applied to juvenile justice and human services settings. The OJJDP adopted the social development model as the foundation for its **Comprehensive Strategy for Serious, Violent, and Chronic Juvenile Offenders program**, which provides participating communities with a framework for preventing delinquency, intervening in early delinquent behavior, and responding to serious, violent, and chronic offending. It assists communities in establishing or modifying a juvenile justice continuum of care through risk-focused prevention, risk and needs assessment, structured decision making, and graduated sanctions training and technical assistance. The OJJDP's Comprehensive Strategy program centers around the following six components:

1. Strengthening families in their role of providing guidance and discipline and instilling sound values as the first and primary teacher of children
2. Supporting core social institutions, including schools, churches, and other community organizations, so that they can reduce risk factors and help children develop their full potential
3. Promoting prevention strategies that enhance protective factors and reduce the impact of negative risk factors affecting the lives of young people at risk for high delinquency
4. Intervening immediately and constructively when delinquent behavior first occurs
5. Identifying and controlling a small segment of violent and chronic juvenile offenders
6. Establishing a broad spectrum of sanctions that ensure accountability and a continuum of services

A few years ago, the OJJDP began a national evaluation of the Comprehensive Strategy Program. Learn more about the program via **Web Extra 8–8**, where you can keep abreast of the ongoing evaluation.

Another contemporary example of social intervention efforts tied to a developmental model is Targeted Outreach, a program operated by Boys and Girls Clubs of America.[181] The program has its origins in the 1972 implementation of a youth development strategy based on studies undertaken at the University of Colorado, which showed that at-risk youths could be effectively diverted from the juvenile justice system through the provision of positive alternatives. Using a wide referral network made up of local schools, police departments, and various youth services agencies, club officials work to end what they call the "inappropriate detention of juveniles."[182]

THE OJJDP adopted the social development model as the foundation for its Comprehensive Strategy for Serious, Violent, and Chronic Juvenile Offenders program.

The program's primary goal is to provide a positive and productive alternative to gangs for the youths who are most vulnerable to their influences or are already entrenched in gang activity. It recruits at-risk youngsters (as young as seven years old) and diverts them into activities intended to promote a sense of belonging, competence, usefulness, and self-control: A sense of belonging is fostered through clubs that provide familiar settings where each child is accepted; competence and usefulness are developed through opportunities for meaningful activities, which young people in the club program can successfully undertake; and self-control is developed as youthful participants have a chance to be heard and to influence decisions affecting their future. To date, Targeted Outreach has served more than 10,000 at-risk youths and hopes to eventually involve more than 1.5 million youngsters between the ages of seven and 17. Mobilization for Youth and Targeted Outreach are the kinds of programs that theorists who focus on the social structure typically seek to implement.

Critique of Social Development Theories

Social development theories have been criticized for definitional issues. What, for example, do life course concepts like turning point, pathway, risk factor, persistence, desistance, and criminal career really mean? Precise definitions of such concepts are necessary if hypotheses derived from life course theories are to be tested. Some writers have identified "associated problems of how to develop risk/needs assessment devices and how to use these both in fundamental research (to maximize the yield of serious offenders while still making it possible to draw conclusions about the general population) and in applied research (to decide which populations should be targeted by interventions)."[183]

Like the social structural approaches discussed in Chapter 6, social development theories are intimately associated with the first prong of this text theme—the social problems approach (described in Chapter 1). For policy makers, important questions include: What role (if any) does individual choice play in human development? Do people actively select components of the life course? Do they influence their own trajectories? Because so many important life course determinants are set in motion in early childhood and during adolescence, should those who make wrong choices be held accountable?

SUMMARY

- According to social process theories, criminal behavior is learned in interaction with others. The socialization process occurring as the result of group membership—in families, peer groups, work groups, and reference groups—is seen as the primary route through which learning occurs. Social process theories suggest that individuals who have weak stakes in conformity are more likely to be influenced by the social processes and contingent experiences that lead to crime, and that criminal choices tend to persist because they are reinforced by the reaction of society to those whom it has identified as deviant.
- A number of theories can be classified under the social process umbrella: social learning theory, social control theory, labeling theory, reintegrative shaming, and dramaturgical perspective.
- Social process theories suggest that crime-prevention programs should enhance self-control and build prosocial bonds. Preparing for the Drug Free Years (PDFY) is designed to increase effective parenting and is part of the Strengthening America's Families Project.
- Criticisms of social process theories are many and varied. Differential association theory is not applicable at the individual level; in addition, the theory is untestable. The labeling approach does little to explain the origin of crime and deviance. Dramaturgical perspective's greatest failing may be in taking the analogy of the theater too far and convincing readers that real life is but a form of playacting.
- The life course perspective is the major social development perspective discussed in this chapter and emphasizes turning points in a criminal career. Age-graded theory incorporates the element of social bonds and also stresses the idea of turning points in a criminal career. The delinquent development approach places an emphasis on desistance and persistence over the life course, and interactional theory points to a weakening of a person's bond to conventional society as the fundamental cause of delinquency.
- The central concepts of social development theories include: criminal careers, the life course, trajectory, turning points, age grading, social capital, human agency, developmental pathways, life course persisters, persistence, desistance, resilience, cohort, cohort analysis, longitudinal research, and evolutionary ecology.
- Social development strategies have been widely applied to juvenile justice and human services settings. The OJJDP has adopted the social development model as the

foundation for its Comprehensive Strategy for Serious, Violent, and Chronic Juvenile Offenders program, which provides participating communities with a framework for preventing delinquency, intervening in early delinquent behavior, and responding to serious, violent, and chronic offending.

- Social development theories have been criticized for definitional issues. What do life course concepts like turning point, pathway, risk factor, persistence, desistance, and criminal career really mean? Precise definitions of such concepts are necessary if hypotheses derived from life course theories are to be tested.

KEY TERMS

adolescence-limited offenders, 204
Cambridge Study in Delinquent Development, 205
cohort analysis, 205
Comprehensive Strategy for Serious, Violent, and Chronic Juvenile Offenders program, 212
containment, 186
containment theory, 185
control ratio, 190
criminal career, 199
desistance, 204
differential association, 181
differential identification theory, 184
discrediting information, 195
dramaturgical perspective, 195
evolutionary ecology, 206
general theory of crime (GTC), 188
human agency, 201
human development, 197
impression management, 195
interactional theory, 206
labeling theory, 192
life course, 199
life course–persistent offenders, 203
life course perspective, 199
moral enterprise, 192
persistence, 204
primary deviance, 191
Project on Human Development in Chicago Neighborhoods (PHDCN), 210
prosocial bond, 196
reintegrative shaming, 194
resilience, 205
secondary deviance, 191
situational action theory (SAT), 189
social bond, 186
social capital, 203
social control theory, 181
social development perspective, 197
social development theory, 180
social learning theory, 181
social process theory, 180
stigmatic shaming, 194
tagging, 191
total institution, 195

KEY NAMES

Ronald L. Akers, 183
Howard Becker, 192
John Braithwaite, 194
Robert Burgess, 183
Lawrence E. Cohen, 206
David P. Farrington, 205
Daniel Glaser, 184
Eleanor Glueck, 201
Sheldon Glueck, 201
Erving Goffman, 195
Michael Gottfredson, 188
Travis Hirschi, 186
Howard B. Kaplan, 186
John H. Laub, 199
Edwin M. Lemert, 191
Richard Machalek, 206
Terrie E. Moffitt, 203
Walter C. Reckless, 185
Robert J. Sampson, 199
Edwin Sutherland, 181
Frank Tannenbaum, 191
Terence Thornberry, 206
Charles R. Tittle, 184
Donald J. West, 205
Per-Olof H. Wikström, 189
Marvin Wolfgang, 206

QUESTIONS FOR REVIEW

1. How does the process of social interaction contribute to criminal behavior?
2. What are the various social process perspectives discussed in this chapter? Describe each.
3. What kinds of social policy initiatives might be based on social process theories of crime causation?
4. What are the shortcomings of the social process perspective?
5. What are the various social development perspectives discussed in this chapter? Describe each.
6. What are the central concepts of social development theories? Explain each.
7. What kinds of social policy initiatives might be suggested by social development perspectives?
8. What are the shortcomings of social development perspectives on criminality?

QUESTIONS FOR REFLECTION

1. This chapter describes both social process and social development perspectives. What are the significant differences between these two perspectives? What kinds of theories characterize each?
2. This text emphasizes the theme of social problems versus social responsibility. Which of the perspectives discussed in this chapter (if any) best support the social problems approach? Which (if any) support the social responsibility approach? Why?
3. This chapter contains a discussion of the labeling process. What are a few examples of the everyday imposition of positive (rather than negative) labels? Why is it so difficult to impose positive labels on individuals who were previously labeled negatively?
4. Do you believe that Erving Goffman's dramaturgical perspective, which sees the world as a stage and individuals as actors on that stage, provides any valuable insights into crime and criminality? If so, what are they?
5. Examine your personal life course. What turning points did you experience that led to where you are today?

CHAPTER 9

SOCIAL CONFLICT THEORIES

LEARNING OUTCOMES

After reading this chapter, you should be able to answer the following questions:

- What three analytical perspectives on law and social order are described in this chapter?
- What are the central tenets of radical criminology?
- What five emerging conflict perspectives discussed in this chapter purport to explain crime and criminality?
- What are the crime-control implications of social conflict theories?

■ **consensus perspective** An analytical perspective on social organization that holds that most members of society agree about what is right and wrong and that the various elements of society work together toward a common vision of the greater good.

Introduction

In 2012, a series of protests swept through New York City's financial district. Known as the Occupy Wall Street movement, the movement's organizers wanted protestors to fight back against the corrosive power that they said major banks and multinational corporations held over the democratic process. They said that they were also protesting the "role of Wall Street in creating an economic collapse that has caused the greatest recession in generations."[1] One of the slogans adopted by the movement was "We are the 99 percent," referring to the widespread belief that the wealthiest 1% of Americans control the economic and political system of the United States. One of movement's Web sites, with the URL *wearethe99percent.com,* welcomed visitors with these words:

> America has been in the grip of accelerating inequality for decades. Politicians have been supporting policies that benefit the few at the expense of everyone else. No matter what you call it—trickle down economics, free market fundamentalism, crony capitalism—it is all rooted in the idea that if you take care of the people at the very top, everyone benefits. That is a lie and we reject it.

Learn more about the Occupy Wall Street movement from the organizer's Web site at **Library Extra 9–1**.

Occupy Wall Street Protests in 2012. How did American economic conditions influence these protestors?

Law and Social Order Perspectives

Views like those of the members the Occupy Wall Street movement, which saw government working in league with big business at the expense of the working man and woman, existed throughout parts of Europe during the middle to late 1800s. Among the most important thinkers of that period were **Karl Marx** (discussed in more detail later) and Friedrich Engels. In 1848, in *The Communist Manifesto*, Marx and Engels advanced the idea that communism would inevitably replace capitalism as the result of a natural historical process, or dialectic. Their egalitarian ideals fed the communist ideology that led to the Marxist-inspired Bolshevik Revolution of 1917, the fall of the Romanov dynasty in Russia, the coming to power of Vladimir Lenin and (later) Joseph Stalin in Russia, and the rise of the Soviet Union. But communism soon came to denote a repressive totalitarian system in which a single political party controlled the government, which owned the means of production and supposedly distributed wealth with the professed aim of establishing a classless society.[2]

Communism came to denote a repressive totalitarian system in which a single political party controlled the government.

The decline of European monarchies during the first half of the twentieth century, the rise of socialist ideals, and the advent of Marxist-inspired revolutions all conspired to change laws and create new kinds of criminal activity. An understanding of the interplay between law and social order is critical to any study of social change and of theories of criminology that emphasize the role of social conflict as it underlies criminality. Three analytical perspectives shed some light on this subject: the consensus perspective, the pluralist perspective, and the conflict perspective.

The Consensus Perspective

The **consensus perspective** of social organization (described briefly in Chapter 1) posits that most members of society agree on what is right and wrong and that the various elements of society—including institutions such as churches, schools, government agencies, and businesses—work together toward a shared vision of the greater good. According to **Raymond J. Michalowski**, whose work is used to describe each of the three major approaches discussed in this section, the consensus perspective is characterized by four principles:[3]

1. **Most members of a society believe in the existence of core values.** The consensus perspective holds that

THEORY | versus REALITY

The Unabomber and Domestic Terrorism

In April 1996, 52-year-old Harvard-educated Theodore Kaczynski, a Lincoln (Montana) recluse, was arrested and charged with the infamous Unabomber terrorist bombings. Kaczynski admitted responsibility for the bombings in early 1998 and was sentenced to life in prison without parole. The Unabomber's 18-year-long mail-bomb campaign had targeted universities, airlines, and researchers, killing three people and injuring 23 others in 16 separate bombing incidents. Prior to Kaczynski's arrest, a 56-page "manifesto" was mailed to the offices of the *New York Times*, the *Washington Post*, and *Penthouse* magazine. Titled "Industrial Society and Its Future," the Unabomber manifesto was a rambling thesis condemning American social institutions and high technology, blaming many of the world's existing problems on the Industrial Revolution, forecasting an Orwellian future in which helpless humans would be controlled by computers, and calling for a new social order based on a return to simpler times. Excerpts from the manifesto were widely published and helped lead to Kaczynski's capture. This box contains the introductory paragraphs of the Unabomber's manifesto. Read the Unabomber's entire manifesto online at **Web Extra 9–1**. A Criminal Profiles box later in this chapter provides more details about Kaczynski's life and crimes.

> The Industrial Revolution and its consequences have been a disaster for the human race. They have greatly increased the life-expectancy of those of us who live in "advanced" countries, but they have destabilized society, have made life unfulfilling, have subjected human beings to indignities, have led to widespread psychological suffering (in the Third World to physical suffering as well) and have inflicted severe damage on the natural world. The continued development of technology will worsen the situation. . . .
>
> The industrial-technological system may survive or it may break down. If it survives, it MAY eventually achieve a low level of physical and psychological suffering, but only after passing through a long and very painful period of adjustment and only at the cost of permanently reducing human beings and many other living organisms to engineered products and mere cogs in the social machine. . . .
>
> If the system breaks down the consequences will still be very painful. But the bigger the system grows the more disastrous the results of its breakdown will be, so if it is to break down it had best break down sooner rather than later.
>
> We therefore advocate a revolution against the industrial system. This revolution may or may not make use of violence; it may be sudden or it may be a relatively gradual process spanning a few decades. We can't predict any of that. But we do outline in a very general way the measures that those who hate the industrial system should take in order to prepare the way for a revolution against that form of society.

Discussion Questions

1. What motivated the Unabomber? Why did he advocate "a revolution against the industrial system"?
2. Do you think the Unabomber really believed his bombings would create a better world? If so, how did he think they would bring about such change?

---

shared notions of right and wrong characterize the majority of society's members.

2. **Laws reflect the collective will of the people.** Law is seen as the result of a consensus, achieved through legislative action, and represents a kind of social conscience.
3. **Law serves all people equally.** From the consensus point of view, the law not only embodies a shared view of justice but also is perceived to be just in its application.
4. **Law violators represent a unique subgroup with distinguishing features.** The consensus approach holds that law violators must somehow be improperly socialized or psychologically defective or must suffer from some other lapse that leaves them unable to participate in what is otherwise widespread agreement on values and behavior.

The consensus perspective was operative in American politics and characterized social scientific thought in this country throughout much of the early 1900s and found its greatest champion in **Roscoe Pound**, former dean of Harvard School of Law and one of the greatest legal scholars of modern times. Pound developed the notion that the law is a tool for engineering society, meets the needs of men and women living together in society, and can be used to fashion society's characteristics and major features. Pound distilled his ideas into a set of jural postulates explaining the existence and form of all laws insofar as laws reflect shared needs:[4]

- In civilized society, men and women must be able to assume that others will commit no intentional aggressions upon them.[5]
- In civilized society men and women must be able to assume that they may control for beneficial purposes what

■ **pluralist perspective** An analytical approach to social organization that holds that a multiplicity of values and beliefs exists in any complex society but that most social actors agree on the usefulness of law as a formal means of dispute resolution.

■ **conflict perspective** An analytical perspective on social organization that holds that conflict is a fundamental aspect of social life and can never be fully resolved.

they have discovered and appropriated to their own use, what they have created by their own labor, and what they have acquired under the existing social and economic order.

- In civilized society men and women must be able to assume that those with whom they deal in the general intercourse of society will act in good faith. . . .
- In civilized society men and women must be able to assume that those who are engaged in some course of conduct will act with due care not to cause an unreasonable risk of injury upon others.
- In civilized society men and women must be able to assume that those who maintain things likely to get out of hand or to escape and do damage will restrain them or keep them within their proper bounds.

The Pluralist Perspective

Contrary to the assumptions made by consensus thinkers, it has become quite plain to most observers of the contemporary social scene that not everyone agrees on what the law should say and that society is rife with examples of conflicting values and ideals—consensus is hard to find. Modern debates center on issues such as abortion, euthanasia, the death penalty, purposes of criminal justice agencies in a diverse society, social justice, rights and responsibilities of minorities and other underrepresented groups, women's issues, the proper role of education, economic policy, social welfare, functions of the military in a changing world, environmental concerns, and appropriate uses of high technology. There exists within America today a great diversity of social groups, each with its own point of view regarding right and wrong, each with its own agenda. Add to that the plethora of self-proclaimed individual experts busily touting their own points of view, and anything but a consensus of values seems characteristic of society today.

Such a situation is described by some writers as "pluralist." A **pluralistic perspective** (described briefly in Chapter 1) mirrors the thought that a multiplicity of values and beliefs exists in any complex society and that each different social group will have its own set of beliefs, interests, and values. A crucial element of this perspective is the assumption that although different viewpoints exist, most individuals agree on the usefulness of law as a formal means of dispute resolution, so from a pluralist perspective, the law exists as a peacekeeping tool that allows officials and agencies within the government to effectively settle disputes between individuals and among groups. It also assumes that whatever settlement is reached will be acceptable to all parties because of their agreement on the fundamental role of law in dispute settlement. Following are five basic principles of the pluralist perspective:[6]

1. Society consists of many diverse social groups. Differences in age, gender, sexual preference, ethnicity, and the like often provide the basis for much naturally occurring diversity.
2. Each group has its own set of values, beliefs, and interests. Variety in gender, sexual orientation, economic status, and ethnicity, as well as other forms of diversity, produces interests that may unite like-minded individuals but may also place them in natural opposition to other social groups.
3. A general agreement exists on the usefulness of formalized laws as a mechanism for dispute resolution. People and groups accept the role of law in the settlement of disputes and accord decisions reached within the legal framework at least a modicum of respect.
4. The legal system is value neutral, that is, free of petty disputes and above the level of general contentiousness that may characterize relationships among groups.
5. The legal system is concerned with the best interests of society. Legislators, judges, prosecutors, attorneys, police officers, and correctional officials are assumed to perform idealized functions beyond the reach of the everyday interests of self-serving groups, so official functionaries can be trusted to act in accordance with the greater good, to remain unbiased, and to maintain a value-free system for the enforcement of laws.

According to the pluralist perspective, conflict is essentially resolved through the peacekeeping activities of unbiased government officials exercising objective legal authority.

The Conflict Perspective

A third point of view, the **conflict perspective**, maintains that conflict is a fundamental aspect of social life that can never be fully resolved. Formal agencies of social control merely coerce the unempowered and disenfranchised to comply with the rules established by those in power. Laws are a tool of the powerful, useful in keeping

> The conflict perspective maintains that conflict is a fundamental aspect of social life and can never be fully resolved.

■ **bourgeoisie** The "haves," or the class of people who own the means of production, in Marxist theory.
■ **proletariat** The "have-nots," or the working class, in Marxist theory.

others from wresting control over important social institutions. Rather than being the result of any consensus or process of dispute resolution, social order rests on the exercise of power through law. Those in power must work ceaselessly to remain there, although the structures they impose on society—including the patterns of wealth building that they define as acceptable and the circumstances under which they authorize the exercise of legal power and military might—give them all the advantages they are likely to need. Figure 9–1 lists the key elements of the conflict perspective, which is also known as the *social conflict perspective*. See the Criminal Profiles box on the Unabomber, someone who fits the conflict perspective. **Library Extra 9–2** provides related information.

One of the best-known writers on social conflict was Karl Marx, whose writings on the conflicts inherent in capitalism led to the formulation of communist ideals and the rise of communist societies in the twentieth century. According to Marx, two fundamental social classes exist in any capitalist society: the haves or the **bourgeoisie**, who are capitalists and wealthy owners of the means of production (factories, businesses, land, natural resources), and the have-nots or the **proletariat**, who are relatively uneducated workers without power.

According to Marx, members of the proletariat, possessing neither capital nor means of production, must earn their living by selling their labor, and the powerful bourgeoisie oppose the proletariat in an ongoing class struggle. Marx saw such a struggle between classes as inevitable in the evolution of any capitalist society and believed that the natural outcome of such a struggle would be the overthrow of the capitalist social order and the birth of a truly classless, or communist, society. Learn more about the life and writings of Karl Marx at **Web Extras 9–2** and **9–3**.

Marx saw a struggle between classes as inevitable in the evolution of any capitalist society.

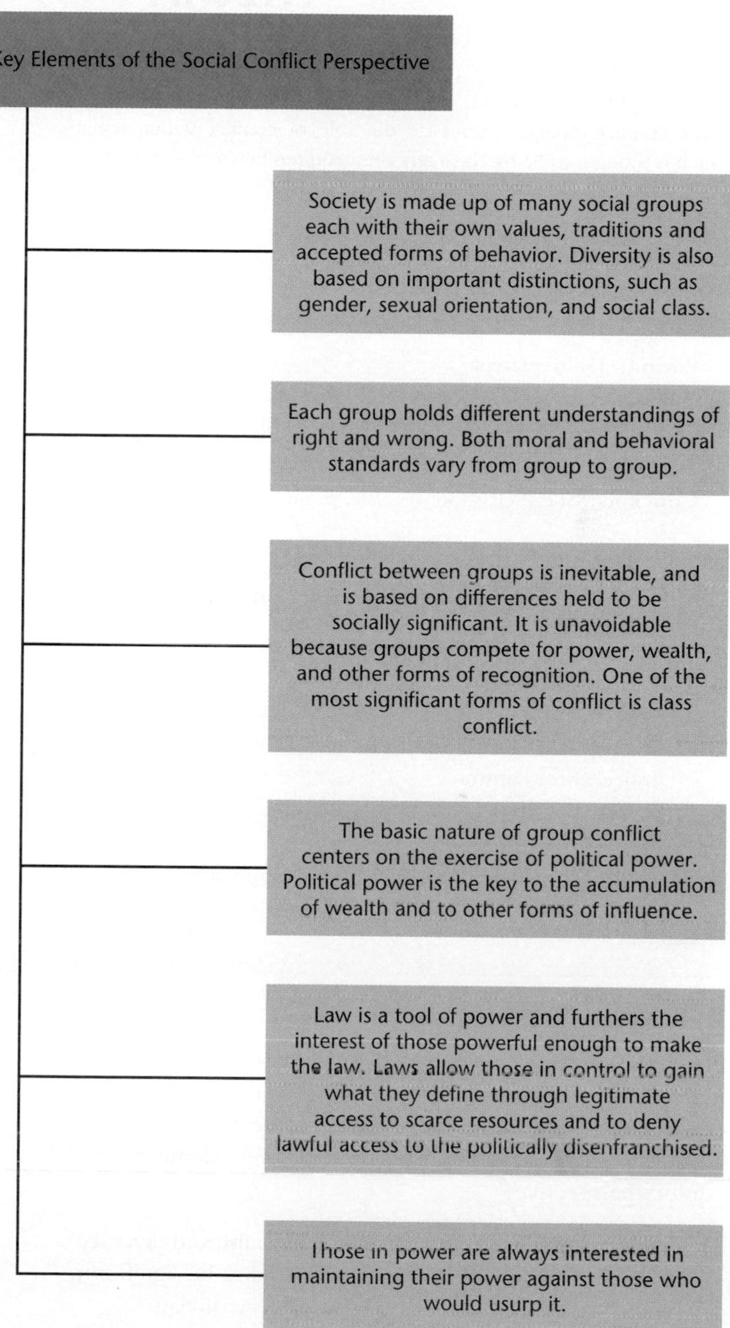

FIGURE 9-1 | **Key Elements of the Social Conflict Perspective**

Conflict theory in the social sciences has a long history. In 1905, the writings of **Willem Bonger** echoed Marxist principles by describing the ongoing struggle between the haves and the have-nots as a natural consequence of capitalist society;[7] he advanced the notion that in such societies only those who lack power are routinely subject to the criminal law. Georg Simmel's 1908 text *Conflict and the Web of Group Affiliations* highlighted the role of social conflict in two- and three person groups, which Simmel called diads and triads.[8] Thorsten Sellin's notion of culture conflict (discussed

■ **social class** A distinction made between individuals based on important social characteristics.

THEORY | in PERSPECTIVE
Social Conflict Theories

Social conflict theories emphasize the role of conflict within society, which is thought to be based largely on inequities between social classes.

Radical Criminology

Radical criminology holds that the causes of crime are rooted in social conditions empowering the wealthy and the politically well organized but disenfranchising those who are less successful.

Period: 1960s–present

Theorists: Karl Marx, Ralf Dahrendorf, George B. Vold, Richard Quinney, William J. Chambliss, Raymond J. Michalowski, Austin Turk

Concepts: Social class, bourgeoisie, proletariat

Left-Realist Criminology

This branch of radical criminology posits that crime is a real social problem experienced by the lower classes.

Period: 1980s–present

Theorists: Walter DeKeseredy, Jock Young

Concepts: Radical realism, critical realism, street crime, social justice, crime control

Feminist Criminology

This radical criminological approach to the explanation of crime sees the conflict and inequality present in society as being based primarily on gender.

Period: 1970s–present

Theorists: Freda Adler, Rita J. Simon, Kathleen Daly, Meda Chesney-Lind, John Hagan

Concepts: Power-control issues, gender socialization, empowerment

Peacemaking Criminology

Peacemaking criminology holds that crime-control agencies and citizens must work together to alleviate social problems, including crime.

Period: 1980s–present

Theorists: Harold E. Pepinsky, Richard Quinney

Concepts: Compassionate criminology, restorative justice

Convict Criminology

Convict criminology consists of writings and musings on criminology by convicted felons and ex-inmates who have acquired academic credentials or are associated with credentialed others.

Period: 2001–present

Theorists: Ian Ross, Stephen Richards

Concepts: Issues-based writings, personal experience as valid information, critical of system

---

in Chapter 6) also incorporated the notion of social conflict. Since Sellin's day, many other thinkers have contributed to the development of conflict theory, but before discussing specific ideas, it is important to understand six key elements of the conflict perspective:[9]

1. Society is made up of diverse social groups, and diversity is based on distinctions that people hold to be significant, such as gender, sexual orientation, and social class.
2. Each group holds to differing definitions of right and wrong, so moralistic conceptions and behavioral standards vary from group to group.
3. Conflict between groups is both socially significant and unavoidable because groups defined by characteristics such as ethnicity, gender, and social class compete for power, wealth, and other forms of recognition.
4. The fundamental nature of group conflict centers on the exercise of political power, which is the key to the accumulation of wealth and other forms of power.
5. Law is a tool of power and furthers the interests of those powerful enough to make it. Laws allow those in control to gain what they define as legitimate access to scarce resources and to deny such access to the politically disenfranchised.
6. Those in power are inevitably interested in maintaining their power against those who would usurp it.

Central to the conflict perspective is the notion of **social class** (distinctions made between individuals based on characteristics such as race, religion, education, profession, income, wealth, family background, housing, artistic tastes, aspirations, cultural pursuits, child-rearing habits, speech, and accent).

Some authors maintain that "class is nothing but an abbreviation to describe a way of living, thinking, and feeling."[10] Individuals are assigned to classes by others and by themselves on the basis of characteristics that are both ascribed and achieved: Ascribed characteristics are those a person is born with, such as race or gender; achieved characteristics are acquired through personal effort or chance over the course of a person's life and include level of education, income, place of residence, and profession.

Although Marx concerned himself with only two social classes, most social scientists today talk in terms of at least three groups—the upper, middle, and lower classes. Some, such as Vance Packard, have distinguished among five hierarchically arranged classes (the real-upper, semiupper, limited-success, working, and real-lower classes) and further subdivided classes horizontally according to ascribed characteristics such as race and religion.[11]

In his 1958 book *Theoretical Criminology*, **George B. Vold** described crime as the product of political conflict between groups, an ongoing struggle for power, control, and material well-being.[12] Conflict is "a universal form of interaction," and groups are naturally in conflict because their interests and purposes "overlap, encroach on one another and [tend to] be competitive."[13] Vold's most succinct observation of the role conflict plays in contributing to crime stated: "The whole political process of law making, law breaking, and law enforcement becomes a direct reflection of deep-seated and fundamental conflicts between interest groups. Those who produce legislative majorities win control over the power and dominate the policies that decide who is likely to be involved in violation of the law."[14]

Kamira/Shutterstock

The tomb of Karl Marx in Highgate Cemetery, London. Marxist thought underpins the writings of many radical criminologists. How did Marxism influence criminology?

From Vold's point of view, the body of laws that characterizes any society is a political statement, and crime is a political definition imposed on those whose interests lie outside those that the powerful, through the law, define as acceptable.

Conflict theorists of the early and mid-1900s saw in the concept of social class the rudimentary ingredients of other important concepts like authority, power, and conflict. **Ralf Dahrendorf** wrote that "classes are social conflict groups the determinant of which can be found in the participation in or exclusion from the exercise of authority."[15] For Dahrendorf, conflict was ubiquitous, fundamental, and coextensive: "Not the presence but the absence of conflict is surprising and abnormal, and we have good reason to be suspicious if we find a society or social organization that displays no evidence of conflict."[16]

From Dahrendorf's perspective, power and authority were most at issue between groups and the cause of class conflicts. It is out of conflict that change—either destructive or constructive—arises. Destructive change brings a lessening of social order, whereas constructive change increases cohesiveness within society.

Another mid-twentieth-century conflict theorist, **Austin Turk**, said that in the search for an explanation of criminality, "one is led to investigate the tendency of laws to penalize persons whose behavior is more characteristic of the less powerful than of the more powerful and the extent to which some persons and groups can and do use legal processes and agencies to maintain and enhance their power position vis-à-vis other persons and groups."[17] In his 1969 seminal work, *Criminality and Legal Order*, Turk wrote that in any attempt to explain criminality, "it is more useful to view the social order as mainly a pattern of conflict" rather than to offer explanations for crime based on behavioral or psychological approaches.[18] Turk, like most other conflict criminologists, saw the law as a powerful tool of prominent social groups seeking continued control over others and crime as the natural consequence of such intergroup struggles, resulting from definitions imposed by the laws of the powerful on the disapproved strivings of the unempowered.

■ **radical criminology** A perspective that holds that the causes of crime are rooted in social conditions empowering the wealthy and the politically well organized, but disenfranchising the less fortunate.

■ **Marxist criminology** A perspective on crime and crime causation based on the writings of Karl Marx.

Radical Criminology

The conflict perspective is today thoroughly entrenched in **radical criminology**, which holds that the causes of crime are rooted in social conditions empowering the wealthy and the politically well organized but disenfranchising those less fortunate; it is also called *new criminology* and *critical criminology* as well as **Marxist criminology** (when based on Marx's writings). Radical criminology is the intellectual child of three important historical circumstances: (1) the ruminations of nineteenth-century social utopian thinkers, including Karl Marx, Friedrich Engels, Georg Wilhelm Friedrich Hegel, Georg Simmel, Willem Bonger, and Max Weber; (2) the rise of conflict theory in the social sciences; and (3) the dramatic radicalization of American academia in the 1960s and 1970s. **William J. Chambliss**, a well-known spokesperson for radical thinkers, succinctly summarized the modern perspective: "What makes the behavior of some criminal is the coercive power of the state to enforce the will of the ruling class."[19]

Radical criminology holds that the causes of crime are rooted in social conditions empowering the wealthy.

In 1971, Chambliss, along with Robert T. Seidman, published a critically acclaimed volume titled *Law, Order, and Power*, which represented a bridge between earlier conflict theorists and the more radical approach of the Marxists. Through its emphasis on social class, class interests, and class conflict, *Law, Order, and Power* presented a Marxist perspective stripped of any overt references to capitalism as the root cause of crime. "The more economically stratified a society becomes, the more it becomes necessary for the dominant groups in the society to enforce through coercion the norms of conduct which guarantee their supremacy."[20] Chambliss and Seidman outlined their position in four propositions:[21]

1. The conditions of one's life affect one's values and norms.
2. Complex societies are comprised of groups with widely different life conditions and highly disparate and conflicting sets of norms.
3. The probability of a given group having its particular normative system embodied in law is not distributed equally but is closely related to the political and economic position of that group.
4. The higher a group's political or economic position is, the greater the probability that its views will be reflected in laws.

Chambliss also believed that middle- and upper-class criminals are more apt to escape apprehension and punishment, not because they are any smarter or more capable of hiding their crimes than lower-class offenders but because of a "very rational choice on the part of the legal system to pursue those violators that the community will reward them for pursuing and to ignore those violators who have the capability for causing trouble for the agencies."[22]

By the 1970s, Chambliss's writings assumed a much more Marxist flavor. In a 1975 article, Chambliss once again recognized the huge power gap separating the haves from the have-nots, saying that crime is created by the ruling class, who define as criminal any undertakings and activities contravening their interests yet sometimes violate the criminal law with impunity because it is their own creation.[23]

Crime is created by members of the ruling class, who define as criminal any undertakings and activities contravening their interests, yet sometimes violate the criminal law with impunity because it is their own creation.

art_zzz/Fotolia

A deteriorating factory in Russia. Radical criminology has its origins in the writings of Karl Marx, whose thinking was strongly influenced by the social conditions of the industrial era. How did the downfall of the Soviet Union impact radical thought in criminology?

■ **instrumental Marxism** A perspective that holds that those in power intentionally create laws and social institutions that serve their own interests and keep others from becoming powerful.

■ **structural Marxism** A perspective that holds that the structural institutions of society influence the behavior of individuals and groups by virtue of the type of relationships created.

Soon the Marxist flavor of Chambliss's writing became undeniable: "As capitalist societies industrialize and the gap between the bourgeoisie and the proletariat widens, penal law will expand in an effort to coerce the proletariat into submission."[24] For Chambliss, the economic consequences of crime within a capitalist society were partially what perpetuated it. Socialist societies, he wrote, should reflect much lower crime rates than capitalist societies because a "less intense class struggle should reduce the forces leading to and the functions of crime."[25] Learn more about the writings of William J. Chambliss at **Web Extra 9–4**.

Although Chambliss provided much of the intellectual bedrock of contemporary radical criminology, that school of thought found its most eloquent expression in the writings of **Richard Quinney**, who attempted to challenge and change American social life for the better by setting forth in 1974 his six Marxist propositions for an understanding of crime:[26]

1. American society is based on an advanced capitalist economy.
2. The state is organized to serve the interests of the dominant economic class—that is, the capitalist ruling class.
3. Criminal law is an instrument of the state and ruling class used to maintain and perpetuate the existing social and economic order.
4. Crime control in a capitalist society is accomplished through a variety of institutions and agencies established and administered by a governmental elite, representing ruling-class interests, for the purpose of establishing domestic order.
5. The contradictions of advanced capitalism—the disjunction between existence and essence—require that the subordinate classes remain oppressed by whatever means necessary, especially through the coercion and violence of the legal system.
6. Only with the collapse of the capitalist society and the creation of a new society, based on socialist principles, will there be a solution to the crime problem.

Later, Quinney published *Class, State, and Crime*, in which he argued that almost all crimes committed by members of the lower classes are necessary for the survival of individual members of those classes and are actually an attempt by the socially disenfranchised "to exist in a society where *survival* is not assured by other, collective means."[27] He concluded, "Crime is inevitable under capitalist conditions [because crime is] a response to the material conditions of life. Permanent unemployment—and the acceptance of that condition—can result in a form of life where criminality is an appropriate and consistent response."[28] The solution offered by Quinney to the problem of crime is the development of a socialist society: "The *ultimate meaning* of crime in the development of capitalism is the need for a socialist society."[29]

Contemporary radical criminology attributes much existing propensity toward criminality to differences in social class, especially those societal arrangements that maintain class differences. Quinney explained, "Classes are an expression of the underlying forces of the capitalist mode of production."[30]

Today's radical criminologies can be divided into two schools: structuralist and instrumentalist. **Structural Marxism** sees capitalism as a self-maintaining system in which the law and the justice system work to perpetuate the existing system of power relationships. Even the rich are subject to certain laws designed to prevent them from engaging in forms of behavior that might undermine the system of which they are a part, and laws regulating trade practices and monopolies regulate the behavior of the powerful and ensure survival of the capitalist system. **Instrumental Marxism** sees the criminal law and the justice system as tools that the powerful use to control the poor and to keep them disenfranchised. The legal system serves not only to perpetuate the power relationships that exist within society but also to keep control in the hands of those who are already powerful. A popular book by **Jeffrey H. Reiman** titled *The Rich Get Richer and the Poor Get Prison* is built on this premise, contending that the criminal justice system is biased against the poor from start to finish and that well-to-do members of society control the criminal justice system from the definition of crime through the process of arrest, trial, and sentencing.[31]

Reiman also claimed that many actions undertaken by well-off people, such as refusal to make workplaces safe, refusal to curtail deadly industrial pollution, promotion of unnecessary surgery, and prescription of unnecessary drugs, should be defined as criminal but aren't. This kind of self-serving behavior creates occupational and environmental hazards for the poor and those less well-off and produces as much death, destruction, and financial loss as the so-called crimes of the poor. Learn more about radical criminology at **Web Extra 9–5**.

■ **critical criminology** A perspective that holds that crime is the natural product of a capitalist system.

WHO'S TO BLAME—The Individual or Society?

Human Trafficking, Illegal Aliens, and the American Dream

Jose Gonzales, a naturalized U.S. citizen who worked for a Houston-based trucking company, was driving a tractor trailer through a U.S. Customs checkpoint on the Mexican border near San Diego when his truck was searched and found to contain 45 illegal immigrants concealed in Brazilian-made caskets that were being shipped to Los Angeles. Each of the immigrants had been supplied with plastic bottles containing water, and a few even had portable radios to keep them entertained on what had been planned as an hours-long trip.

The illegal immigrants were interrogated and fingerprinted and then taken back across the border to the Mexican border town of Tijuana in a U.S. Customs and Border Protection van. They were released into the custody of a Mexican Federal Investigative Agency official at a local police station, with instructions not to attempt an illegal return into the United States.

Gonzales's fate was quite different. Arrested and charged under the federal Immigration and Nationality Act with attempting to bring unauthorized aliens into the United States, he was held in a federal jail in southern California, where he met with his court-appointed lawyer. The lawyer, Felix Alverez, told Gonzales that agents had him cold, and that he might as well confess in return for a plea bargain that might get him only a brief stint in a federal correctional facility. "Why confess?" Gonzales replied. "I was only trying to help those people have better lives. Many of them were my friends. I didn't even take money for what I was doing."

"Why you were doing what you were doing doesn't matter," Alverez said. "You broke the law, and they are going to punish you."

"No," Gonzales replied. "I am a citizen. I want a trial. You can show them that I was only trying to help unfortunate people live the American Dream. Most of the people who live here and are going to be on a jury have immigrant ancestors. A lot of them were illegal. They won't dare find me guilty." **Library Extras 9-3 and 9-4** relate to this box.

Think about it

1. Why did Gonzales attempt to smuggle illegal immigrants into the United States? Do you think it was primarily for money or for altruistic motives?
2. How likely would Gonzales have been to commit this offense if he had a different ancestry—say, African American or European?
3. What do you think of Gonzales's claim that a jury won't find him guilty? Should he be held responsible for violating the law? Why or why not?

Note: Who's to Blame boxes provide fictionalized critical thinking opportunities, and are not actual cases.

Critical Criminology

Many writers use the phrase *radical-critical criminology* to refer to all theoretical perspectives on crime that build on significant differences in economic, social, and political power between distinct social groups. This chapter follows that convention. Some theorists, however, distinguish between *critical criminology* and *radical criminology*. Those who do say that the former is simply a way of critiquing social relationships that lead to crime, whereas the latter constitutes a proactive call for radical change in the social conditions that lead to crime. That is, critical criminology provides a focused critique of current social and economic arrangements as they are related to crime, whereas radical criminology issues a call to action and asks for changes in political and economic systems that are responsible for fostering criminality.

Gresham M. Sykes further explained **critical criminology** this way: "It forces an inquiry into precisely how the normative content of the criminal law is internalized in different segments of society, and how norm-holding is actually related to behavior."[32] Sykes's use of the word *inquiry* reveals the central role of critical inquiry in critical criminology. See the Who's to Blame box for a present-day issue regarding whether something should be "criminal."

A cogent example of the critical perspective in contemporary criminology can be seen in the work of Elliott Currie, who claimed that "'market societies'—those in which the pursuit of

■ **Follow the author's tweets about the latest crime and justice news @schmalleger.**

private gain becomes the dominant organizing principle of social and economic life—are especially likely to breed high levels of violent crime."[33] Market societies are characterized by more than free enterprise and a free market economy; they are societies in which striving after personal economic gain runs rampant and becomes the hallmark of social life, and this striving leads to high crime rates because it undercuts and overwhelms more traditional principles that "have historically sustained individuals, families, and communities." The United States is the world's premier market society, and its culture provides "a particularly fertile breeding ground for serious violent crime." According to Currie, seven "profoundly criminogenic and closely intertwined mechanisms" operate in a market society to produce crime:

1. "The progressive destruction of livelihood," which results from the long-term absence of opportunities for stable and rewarding work and is a consequence of the fact that market societies view labor "simply as a cost to be reduced" rather than as an asset with intrinsic value
2. "The growth of extremes of economic inequality and material deprivation," which causes many children to spend their developmental years in poverty
3. "The withdrawal of public services and supports, especially for families and children," which results from the fact that "it is a basic operating principle of market society to keep the public sector small"
4. "The erosion of informal and communal networks of mutual support, supervision, and care," which is brought about by the high mobility of the workforce characteristic of market societies
5. "The spread of a materialistic, neglectful, and 'hard' culture," which exalts brutal forms of individualized competition
6. "The unregulated marketing of the technology of violence," which includes ready availability of guns, emphasis on advancing technologies of destruction (such as the military), and mass-marketed violence on television and in other media
7. "The weakening of social and political alternatives," which leaves people unable to cope effectively with the forces of the market society, undermines their communities, and destroys valuable interpersonal relationships

Currie suggested that as more nations emulate the "market society" culture of the United States, crime rates throughout the world will rise, and that an increasing emphasis on punishment and the growth of huge prison systems will consequently characterize most of the world's nations in the twenty-first century.

Radical-Critical Criminology and Policy Issues

According to more contemporary writers on radical criminology, "Marxist criminology was once dismissed as a utopian perspective with no relevant policy implication except revolution. At best, revolution was considered an impractical approach to the problems at hand. Recently, however, many radicals have attempted to address the issues of what can be done under our current system."[34] Most radical-critical criminologists today have come to terms with the collapse of the Soviet Union, a society representing utopian Marxism in practice, and have recognized that a sudden and total reversal of existing political arrangements within the United States is highly unlikely. Such theorists have begun to focus instead on promoting a gradual transition to socialism and to socialized forms of government activity, including "equal justice in the bail system, the abolition of mandatory sentences, prosecution of corporate crimes, increased employment opportunities, and promoting community alternatives to imprisonment."[35] Programs to reduce prison overcrowding, efforts to highlight injustices in the current system, elimination of racism and other forms of inequality in handling both victims and offenders, and increased equality in criminal justice system employment are all frequently mentioned as midrange strategies for bringing about a justice system that is more fair and closer to the radical ideal (Figure 9–2).

Michalowski summarized well the policy directions envisioned by today's radical-critical criminologists: "We cannot be free from the crimes of the poor until there are no more poor; we cannot be free from domination of the powerful until we reduce the inequalities that make domination possible; and we cannot live in harmony with others until we begin to limit the competition for material advantage over others that alienates us from one another."[36] Even so, few radical-critical criminologists seem to expect to see dramatic changes in the near future. Michael J. Lynch and W. Byron Groves explained, "In the end, the criminal justice system has failed as an agent of social change because its efforts are directed at an individual as opposed to social remedies. For these reasons, radicals suggest that we put our efforts into the creation of economic equality or employment opportunities to combat crime."[37]

Critique of Radical-Critical Criminology

Radical-critical criminology has been criticized for its nearly exclusive emphasis on methods of social change at the expense of well-developed theory. William V. Pelfrey stated, "It is in

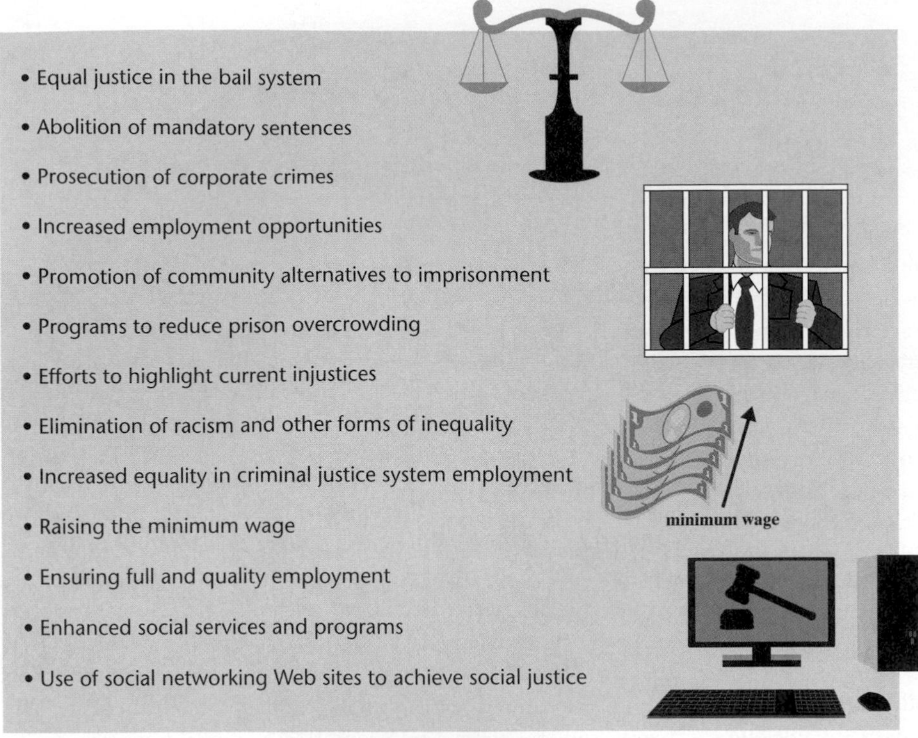

FIGURE 9-2 | **Conflict Criminology's Mid-Level Approaches to Crime Reduction**

Source: Schmalleger, Frank J., *Criminology*. Printed and Electronically reproduced by permission of Pearson Education, Inc., Upper Saddle River, New Jersey.

the Radical School of Criminology that theory is almost totally disregarded, except as something to criticize, and radical methods are seen as optimum."[38] Radical-critical criminology can also be criticized for failing to recognize what appears to be a fair degree of public consensus about the nature of crime—that crime is undesirable and that criminal activity should be controlled. If criminal activity was a true expression of the sentiments of the politically and economically disenfranchised, as some radical criminologists claim, then public opinion might be expected to offer support for at least certain forms of crime, but even the sale of illicit drugs (a type of crime that may provide an alternative path to riches for the otherwise disenfranchised) is frequently condemned by residents of working-class communities.[39]

An effective criticism of Marxist criminology centers on the fact that Marxist thinkers appear to confuse issues of personal politics with social reality, allowing personal values and political leanings to enter the criminological arena and sacrificing their objectivity. Jackson Toby claimed that Marxist and radical thinkers are simply building on an "old tradition of sentimentality toward those who break social rules."[40] Such sentimentality can be easily discounted when we realize that "color television sets and automobiles are stolen more often than food and blankets."[41] The Marxist perspective also fails to recognize that personal success in any society often comes as the result of hard work and preparation and is not merely the result of luck, so wording characterizing social failures as less "fortunate" than others does not take into account the efforts made by those who have succeeded and seems to blame them for the failures of others who have not expended equal effort.

Marxist criminology has also been refuted by contemporary thinkers who find that it falls short in appreciating the multiplicity of problems that contribute to the problem of crime. Astute criminologist Hermann Mannheim critiqued Marxian assumptions by showing how "subsequent developments" have shown that "Marx was wrong in [his] thinking" in several areas: (1) "that there could be only two classes in a capitalist society," (2) that "class struggle was entirely concerned with the question of private property in the means of production," (3) "that the only way in which fundamental social changes could be effected was by violent social revolution," and (4) "that all conflicts were class conflicts and all social change could be explained in terms of class conflicts."[42] Mannheim also pointed out that the development of a semiskilled workforce along with the advent of highly skilled and well-educated workers has led to the creation of a multiplicity of classes within contemporary capitalist societies and that their growth effectively spreads the available wealth in those societies where such workers are employed and reduces the likelihood of revolution.

A now-classic critique of radical criminology was offered in 1979 by Carl Klockars.[43] Klockars charged that Marxists are unable to explain low crime rates in some capitalist countries, such as Japan, and seem equally unwilling to acknowledge or address the problems of communist countries, which often have terrible human rights records. Writing more than 20 years ago, Klockars claimed that Marxist criminologists behaved more like "true believers" in a "new religion" who were unwilling to objectively evaluate their beliefs.[44]

Marxist criminologists are unable to explain low crime rates in some capitalist countries.

Marxist criminology has suffered a considerable loss of prestige among many would-be followers in the wake of the collapse of the former Soviet Union and its client states in Eastern Europe and other parts of the world and seems to have lost some of its impetus. Many would argue that the work of writers like Quinney and Chambliss presaged the decline of Soviet influence and had already moved Marxist and radical criminology into new areas. The work of Currie and others has since led in a post-Marxist direction while retaining a critical emphasis on the principles out of which radical criminology was fashioned. Today's radical criminologists have largely rescinded calls for revolutionary change and escalated their demands for the eradication of gender, racial, and other inequalities in the criminal justice system; the elimination of prisons; the abolition of capital punishment; and an end to police misconduct.

■ **left-realist criminology** An approach to criminology based on ideas inherent in the perspective of left realism.

■ **left realism** A conflict perspective that insists on a pragmatic assessment of crime and its associated problems; also called *radical realism* or *critical realism.*

Emerging Conflict Theories

The radical ideas associated with mid-twentieth-century Marxist criminology contributed to the formation of new and innovative approaches to crime and criminology, such as left-realist criminology, feminist criminology, postmodern criminology, peacemaking criminology, and convict criminology. It is to these perspectives that we now turn our attention.

Left-Realist Criminology

Left-realist criminology, a natural outgrowth of concerns with street crime, the fear of crime, and everyday victimization, approaches criminology based on the ideas of **left realism**, which uses a pragmatic assessment of crime and its problems. Left-realist criminology faults radical-critical criminologists for romanticizing street crime and the criminals who commit it. It does not reject the conflict perspective inherent in radical-critical criminology but shifts the focus to the assessment of crime and the needs of crime victims, seeking to portray crime in terms understandable to those most affected by it—victims and their families, offenders, and criminal justice personnel. The test insisted on by left-realist criminology is not whether a particular perspective on crime control or an explanation of crime causation complies with rigorous academic criteria but whether it speaks meaningfully to those faced with crime on a routine basis. "For realists crime is no less harmful to its victims because of its socially constructed origins."[45]

Left-realist criminology is generally considered synonymous with left realism (also called *radical realism* or *critical realism*) but tends to distance itself from some of the more visionary claims of early radical and Marxist theory.[46] Daniel J. Curran and Claire M. Renzetti portrayed left realism as a natural consequence of increasingly conservative attitudes toward crime and criminals in both Europe and North America: "Though not successful in converting many radicals to the right, this new conservatism did lead a number of radical criminologists to temper their views a bit and to take what some might call a less romanticized look at street crime."[47]

Some authors credit **Walter DeKeseredy**[48] with popularizing left-realist notions in North America, and **Jock Young**[49] is identified as a major source of left-realist writings in England. Prior to the writings of DeKeseredy and Young, radical criminology, with its emphasis on the crime-inducing consequences of existing power structures, tended to portray the ruling class as the "real criminals" and saw street criminals as social rebels who were acting out of felt deprivation; DeKeseredy and Young were successful in refocusing leftist theories on the serious consequences of street crime and on the crimes of the lower classes. Left realists argued that victims of crime are often the poor and disenfranchised who fall prey to criminals with similar backgrounds and saw the criminal justice system and its agents not as pawns of the powerful but as institutions that could offer useful services if modifications were made to reduce their use of force and to increase their sensitivity toward the public.

A central tenet of left realism is that radical ideas must be translated into realistic social policies if contemporary criminology is to have any practical relevance. Concrete suggestions with respect to community policing models are indicative of the direction left realists are headed. Instead of seeing the police as oppressors working on behalf of the state, left realists recommend that the police work with, and answer to, the communities they serve.[50] The major goal of left realism is to achieve a just and orderly society through a practical emphasis on social justice.[51]

Critique of Left-Realist Criminology

Left-realist criminology has been convincingly criticized for being more of an ideological emphasis than a theory. As Don C. Gibbons explained, "Left realism can best be described as a general perspective centered on injunctions to 'take crime seriously' and to 'take crime control seriously' rather than as a well-developed criminological perspective."[52] Realist criminologists appear to build on preexisting theoretical frameworks but rarely offer new testable propositions or hypotheses, but they do suggest crime-control approaches in keeping with the needs of the victimized. Policies promulgated by left realists understandably include an emphasis on community policing, neighborhood justice centers, and dispute-resolution mechanisms, whereas right realists are more punitive in their policy suggestions. Piers Beirne and James W. Messerschmidt summarized the situation this way: "What left realists have essentially accomplished is an attempt to theorize about conventional crime realistically while simultaneously developing a 'radical law and order' program for curbing such behavior."[53]

Left-realist criminology has been criticized for being more of an ideology than a theory.

Read some original writings in the area of critical criminology via **Library Extras 9–5, 9–6**, and **9–7**.

■ **feminist criminology** A corrective model intended to redirect the thinking of mainstream criminologists to include gender awareness.

■ **liberal feminism** A feminist perspective in criminology that sees gender-role socialization as the primary source of women's oppression.

■ **radical feminism** A perspective that sees patriarchy as the cause of women's oppression.

■ **Marxist feminism** A perspective in feminist criminology that sees the oppression of women as caused by their subordinate class status within capitalist societies.

■ **socialist feminism** A perspective in modern criminology that sees gender oppression as a consequence of the interaction between the economic structure of society and gender-based roles.

■ **postmodern feminism** A perspective in modern criminology that questions the social construction of concepts typically used in discussions of crime and justice.

Feminist Criminology

As some have observed, "Women have been virtually invisible in criminological analysis until recently and much theorizing has proceeded as though criminality is restricted to men."[54] Others put it this way: "Criminological theory assumes a woman is like a man."[55] But beginning in the 1970s, advances in feminist theory were applied to criminology, resulting in what has been called a **feminist criminology** (a model redirecting criminologists' thinking to include gender awareness).

Feminism is a way of seeing the world, not a sexual orientation. To be a feminist is to "combine a female mental perspective with a sensitivity for those social issues that influence primarily women."[56] Central to understanding feminist thought is the realization that feminism views gender in terms of power relationships. According to feminist approaches, men have traditionally held much more power in the patriarchal structure of Western society than women and have excluded women from much decision making in socially significant areas, and sexist attitudes—deeply ingrained notions of male superiority—have perpetuated inequality between the sexes. The consequences of sexism and the unequal gender-based distribution of power have been far-reaching, affecting fundamental aspects of social roles and personal expectations at all levels.

Five strands of feminist thought inform feminist criminology today: liberal feminism, radical feminism, Marxist feminism, socialist feminism, and postmodern feminism. Each of these perspectives argues that conflict in society is based on inequalities focused around issues of gender. Learn more at **Library Extra 9–8**.

Liberal Feminism

Liberal feminism sees gender-role socialization as the primary source of women's oppression.[57] Liberal feminists describe a power-based and traditional domination of women's bodies and minds by men throughout history and blame present inequalities on the development within culture and society of "separate and distinct spheres of influence and traditional attitudes about the appropriate role of men and women."[58] Liberal feminists call for elimination of traditional divisions of power and labor between the sexes as a way of eliminating inequality and promoting social harmony.

Radical Feminism

Radical feminism sees patriarchy, or male dominance, as the cause of women's oppression, depicting men as being fundamentally brutish, aggressive, and violent and controlling women through sexuality by taking advantage of both women's biological dependence during childbearing years and their lack of physical strength relative to men. The exploitation of women by men triggers women's deviant behavior, because young women who are sexually or physically exploited may run away or abuse substances and become criminalized, so the elimination of male domination should reduce crime rates for women and "even precipitate a decrease in male violence against women."[59]

Marxist Feminism

The oppression of women caused by their subordinate working-class status in capitalist societies is the main tenet of **Marxist feminism**. Within capitalist society, women may be drawn into crime commission in an effort to support themselves and their children; men commit violent street crimes more often, whereas women commit property and vice crimes.[60]

Social Feminism

Socialist feminism, a fourth perspective, sees gender oppression as a consequence of the interaction between the economic structure of society and gender-based roles. Egalitarian societies would be built around socialist or Marxist principles with the aim of creating a society that is free of gender and class divisions.

Postmodern Feminism

The social construction of concepts typically used in any discussion of criminology—including concepts like justice and crime—are questioned by **postmodern feminism**. According to criminologist Amanda Burgess-Proctor, postmodern feminism departs from the other feminist perspectives by questioning the existence of any one "truth," including "women's oppression," and that "postmodern feminists reject fixed categories and universal concepts in favor of multiple truths and as such examine the effects of discourse and symbolic representation on claims about knowledge."[61]

■ **patriarchy** The tradition of male dominance.
■ **androcentricity** A male-dominated perspective, as in the case of criminologists who study only the criminality of males.

■ **power-control theory** A perspective that holds that power relationships existing in the wider society are reflected in domestic settings and in everyday relationships among men, women, and children in the context of family life.

Proponents of Feminist Criminology

Feminist criminology points out the inequities inherent in patriarchal forms of thought. According to James W. Messerschmidt, **patriarchy** (male dominance) is a "set of social relations of power in which the male gender appropriates the labor power of women and controls their sexuality."[62]

Early works in the field of feminist criminology include *Sisters in Crime* by **Freda Adler**[63] and *Women and Crime* by **Rita J. Simon**,[64] both published in 1975. In these books, the authors attempted to explain existing divergences in crime rates between men and women as being due primarily to socialization rather than biology. Women were taught to believe in personal limitations, faced reduced socioeconomic opportunities, and suffered from lowered aspirations. As gender equality increased, they said, it could be expected that male and female criminality would take on similar characteristics, but such has not been the case, and the approach of Adler and Simon has not been validated by observations surrounding increased gender equality over the past few decades. One exception, however, comes from Mexico, where the number of women incarcerated for federal crimes grew 400% between 2007 and 2012.[65] Most of the crimes for which women are serving time in Mexican federal prisons are drug-related, and it may be that that country's crackdown on drug crime over the past several years has had more of an impact on the number of imprisoned women than actual changes in the rate of crime committed by Mexican women.

Another early work, *Women, Crime and Criminology*, was published in 1977 by British sociologist Carol Smart;[66] it sensitized criminologists to sexist traditions within the field and led to recognition of women's issues. Smart pointed out that men and women experience and perceive the world in different ways, and she showed how important it is for women to have a voice in interpreting the behavior of other women as opposed to having women's behavior interpreted from a man's standpoint.

Early feminist theorizing may not have borne the fruit that some researchers anticipated, but it has led to a heightened awareness of gender issues within criminology. Two of the most insightful contemporary proponents of the need to apply feminist thinking to criminological analysis are **Kathleen Daly** and **Meda Chesney-Lind**, who are concerned about the existence of an **androcentricity** (male-dominated) perspective in criminology and point out that "gender differences in crime suggest that crime may not be so normal after all."[67] Traditional understandings of what is typical about crime are derived from the study of men, especially that small group of men who commit most crimes. The relative lack of criminality exhibited by women is rarely acknowledged as having criminological significance, which calls into question many traditional assumptions about crime—especially the assumption that crime is somehow a "normal" part of social life. Daly and Chesney-Lind have identified the following five elements of feminist thought that set it apart from other types of social and political thought:[68]

Gender differences in crime suggest that crime may not be so normal after all.

1. Gender is not a natural fact but a complex social, historical, and cultural product that is related to, not simply derived from, biological sex differences and reproductive capacities.
2. Gender and gender relations order social life and social institutions in fundamental ways.
3. Gender relations and constructs of masculinity and femininity are not symmetrical but are based on an organizing principle of men's superiority and their social, political, and economic dominance over women.
4. Systems of knowledge reflect men's views of the natural and social world; the production of knowledge is gendered.
5. Women should be at the center, not the periphery, of intellectual inquiry; they should not be invisible or treated as appendages to men.

In a more recent analysis of feminist criminology, Susan Caulfield and Nancy Wonders described "five major contributions that have been made by feminist scholarship and practice" to criminological thinking: (1) a focus on gender as a central organizing principle of contemporary life, (2) an awareness of the importance of power in shaping social relationships, (3) a heightened sensitivity to the way in which social context helps shape human relationships, (4) the recognition that social reality must be understood as a process and that the development of research methods should take this into account, and (5) a commitment to social change as a crucial part of feminist scholarship and practice.[69]

John Hagan built on defining features of power relationships in his book *Structural Criminology*, in which he explained that power relationships existing in the wider society are effectively "brought home" to domestic settings and are reflected in everyday relationships among men, women, and children within the context of family life.[70] Hagan's approach, termed **power-control theory**, suggested that "family class structure shapes the social reproduction of gender relations, and in turn the social distribution of delinquency."[71]

In a cogent analysis encompassing much of contemporary feminist theory, Daly and Chesney-Lind suggested that feminist thought is more important for the way it informs and challenges existing criminology than for the new theories it offers. Theories of crime causation and prevention must include women, and more research on gender-related issues in the field is badly needed. Daly and Chesney-Lind explained that "criminologists should begin to appreciate that their discipline and its questions are a product of white, economically privileged men's experiences" and that rates of female criminality, which are lower than those of males (Figure 9–3), may highlight the fact that criminal behavior is not as "normal" as once thought.[72] Because modern-day criminological perspectives were mostly developed by white middle-class men, the perspectives failed to take into consideration women's "ways of knowing."[73] Feminist criminologists Daly and Chesney-Lind asked: Given the current situation in theory development, do existing theories of crime causation apply as well to women as they do to men, or "do theories of men's crime apply to women?"[74]

Other feminists have analyzed the process by which laws are created and legislation passed and have concluded that modern-day statutes frequently represent characteristically masculine modes of thought and that existing criminal laws are overly rational and hierarchically structured, reflecting traditionally male ways of organizing the social world.[75] Until recently, many jurisdictions viewed assault victims differently based on the gendered relationships involved in the offense. *Assault* (or *battery*) is defined as an attack by one person on another, but until the last few decades of the twentieth century, domestic violence statutes tended to downplay the seriousness of the attacks involved, giving the impression that because they occurred within the home

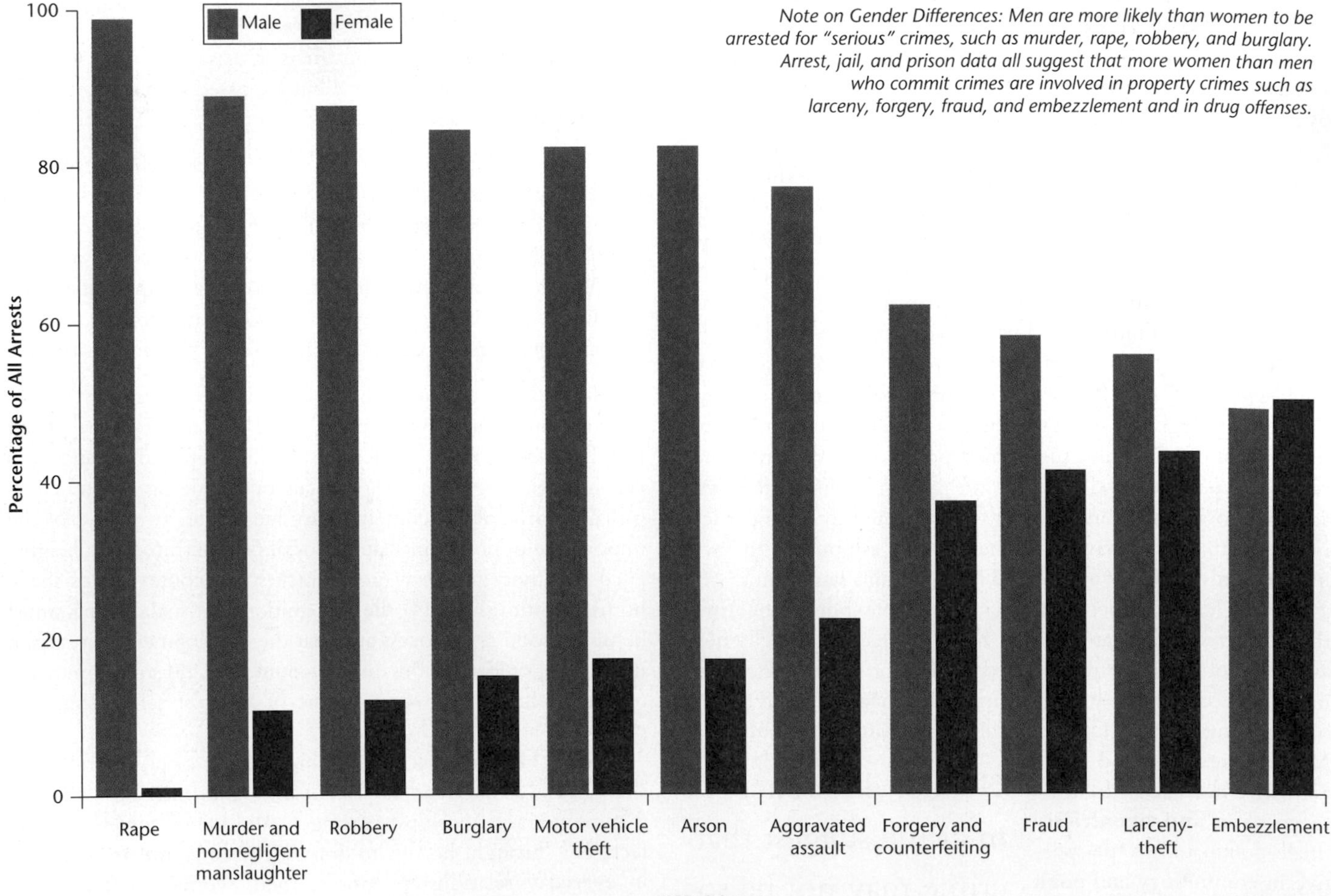

FIGURE 9-3 | **Male and Female Involvement in Crime: Offense Patterns, 2012**

Source: Federal Bureau of Investigation, *Crime in the United States, 2012* (Washington, DC: U.S. Department of Justice, 2013).

■ **gender gap** The observed differences between male and female rates of criminal offending in a given society.

■ **postmodern criminology** A brand of criminology that builds on the tenets inherent in postmodern social thought.

Art Directors & TRIP/Alamy

Female jail inmates participate in a drug treatment seminar in Santa Ana, California. Some say that the criminality of women is beginning to rival that of men, at least in some areas. Might these women serve as an example of just such a trend? Why or why not?

and the victims were typically women, they weren't as important to the justice system as other forms of assault. Some analysts have suggested that existing laws need to be replaced by "a system of justice based upon the specifically feminine principles of care, connection and community."[76]

In the area of social policy, feminist thinkers have pointed to the need for increased controls over men's violence toward women, the creation of alternatives (to supplement the home and traditional family structures) for women facing abuse, and the protection of children. They also questioned the role of government, culture, and the mass media in promulgating pornography, prostitution, and rape and portrayed ongoing crimes against women as characteristic of continuing traditions in which women are undervalued and controlled. Many radical feminists have suggested the replacement of men with women in positions of power, especially within justice system and government organizations, but others noted that replacement still would not address needed changes in the structure of the system itself, which is gender biased due to years of male domination. Centrists, on the other hand, have offered a more balanced approach, believing that individuals of both genders have much to contribute to a workable justice system.[77] Learn more about feminist criminology at **Web Extras 9–6** and **9–7**.

Critique of Feminist Criminology

Some would argue that feminist criminology has yet to live up to its promise because few comprehensive feminist theories of crime were proposed; feminist criminology focused instead on descriptive studies of female involvement in crime.[78] Male violence against women was seen as adding support to the central tenet of feminist criminology (that the relationship between the sexes is primarily characterized by the exercise of power), but that did not make for broad theory building. As one writer explained, "Feminist theory is a theory in formation."[79]

Some would argue that feminist criminology has yet to live up to its promise.

Feminist criminology has faced criticism from many other directions. Predicted increases in female crime rates have failed to materialize as social opportunities available to both genders have become more balanced, and the **gender gap** in crime—with males accounting for much more law violation than females—continues to exist. Criminologist Karen Heimer noted that the gender gap is "virtually a truism in criminology. The relationship holds, regardless of whether the data analyzed are arrest rates, victimization incidence reports on characteristics of offenders, or self-reports of criminal behavior. . . . [A]s far as we can tell, males have always been more criminal than females, and gender differences emerge in every society that has been studied systematically."[80] Other critics have pointed to fundamental flaws in feminist thought, asking such questions as "If men have more power than women, then why are so many more men arrested?"[81]

Some critics have even argued that a feminist criminology is impossible. Daly and Chesney-Lind agreed that although feminist thought may inform criminology, "a feminist criminology cannot exist because neither feminism nor criminology is a unified set of principles and practices."[82] A criminology built solely on feminist principles is unlikely because neither feminist thought nor criminology meets the strict requirements of formal theory building. Read more about feminist perspectives on crime and criminology at **Library Extras 9–9, 9–10**, and **9–11**.

Postmodern Criminology

Some significant new approaches now emerging within criminology are largely the result of postmodern social thought and can be lumped together under the rubric **postmodern criminology**, which applies understandings of social change inherent in postmodern philosophy to criminological theorizing and to issues of crime control.

Postmodern thought, which developed primarily in Europe after World War II, represents "a rejection of the enlightenment belief in scientific rationality as the main vehicle

■ **deconstructionist theory** A postmodern perspective that challenges existing criminological theories in order to debunk them and that works toward replacing traditional ideas with concepts seen as more appropriate to the postmodern era.

■ **peacemaking criminology** A perspective that holds that crime-control agencies and the citizens they serve should work together to alleviate social problems and human suffering and thus reduce crime; also called *compassionate criminology*.

to knowledge and progress."[83] One of its important aspects can be found in its efforts to demonstrate the systematic intrusion of sexist, racist, capitalist, colonialist, and professional interests into the very content of science. Contemporary feminist scholar Joycelyn M. Pollock put it this way: "Post-modernism questions whether we can ever 'know' something objectively; so-called neutral science is considered a sham and criminology's search for causes is bankrupt because even the question is framed by androcentric, sexist, classist, and racist definitions of crime, criminals, and cause."[84]

All postmodern criminologies build on the feeling that past criminological approaches have failed to realistically assess the true causes of crime and have failed to offer workable solutions for crime control. Hence, much postmodern criminology is deconstructionist, and its theories are sometimes called **deconstructionist theories**, meaning approaches that challenge existing criminological perspectives to debunk them and to work toward replacing them with approaches more relevant to the postmodern era.

Two notable authors in the field of postmodern criminology are **Stuart Henry** and **Dragan Milovanovic**,[85] whose constitutive criminology, rooted in phenomenology, claimed that crime and crime control are not "object-like entities" but are constructions produced through a social process in which offender, victim, and society are all involved.[86] A central feature of their constitutive criminology is its assertion that individuals shape their world while also being shaped by it.

Semiotics, or the study of signs and symbols, is another important concept in constitutive criminology. Semiotics can be applied to the notion of crime, itself a socially constructed category or sign. In the words of Henry and Milovanovic, crime "is a categorization of the diversity of human conflicts and transgressions into a single category 'crime,' as though these were somehow all the same. It is a melting of differences reflecting the multitude of variously motivated acts of personal injury into a single entity."[87] Crime should be understood as an integral part of society, not as something separate from it.

From this perspective, a kind of false consciousness, or lack of awareness, gives rise to criminal activity. According to Werner Einstadter and Stuart Henry, crime is seen to be the culmination of certain processes that allow persons to believe they are somehow not connected to other humans and society, that place others in categories or stereotypes, and that make them different or alien, denying their humanity; this results in the denial of responsibility for other people and to other people.[88] Learn more about postmodern criminology at **Web Extra 9–8**, and read an interesting paper by Dragan Milovanovic at **Library Extra 9–12**.

Critique of Postmodern Criminology

Ian Taylor is a British sociologist who lent focus to radical-critical criminology in the 1970s with the publication of two well-received books.[89] He criticized postmodern approaches to crime and deviance for their "increasing incoherence."[90] In other words, postmodern criminologists employ vaguely defined terminology. Taylor also explained that the "battle with orthodox criminology" has led postmodern approaches to increasingly obfuscate their most basic claims, so a second result of the postmodern influence on criminology "has been the development of a social account of crime that entirely lacks a value or ethical foundation."[91] Deconstructionism may challenge traditional theories, but unless it offers viable alternatives for crime control and prevention, it does little good.

Peacemaking Criminology

Throughout much of history, formal agencies of social control—the police, officials of the courts, and corrections personnel—have been seen as pitted against criminal perpetrators and would-be wrongdoers, and crime control has been depicted as an epic struggle in which diametrically opposed antagonists continuously engage one another but in which only one side can emerge victorious. Another point of view has come to the fore: **Peacemaking criminology** (also called *compassionate criminology*), a form of postmodern criminology with roots in Christian and Eastern philosophies, advances the notion that social control agencies and the citizens they serve should work together to alleviate social problems and human suffering and thus reduce crime.[92] Peacemaking criminology includes the notion of service and suggests that "compassion, wisdom, and love are essential for understanding the suffering of which we are all a part and for practicing a criminology of nonviolence."[93]

Peacemaking criminology is popularized by the works of **Harold E. Pepinsky**[94] and Richard Quinney.[95] Both Pepinsky and Quinney restated the problem of crime control from one of how to stop crime to one of how to make peace within

■ **peace model** An approach to crime control that focuses on effective ways for developing a shared consensus on critical issues that can seriously affect the quality of life.

■ **participatory justice** An informal type of criminal justice case processing that makes use of local community resources rather than requiring traditional forms of official intervention.

society and between citizens and criminal justice agencies (see Figure 9–4). Peacemaking criminology draws attention to many issues: (1) perpetuation of violence through continuation of social policies based on dominant forms of criminological theory, (2) role of education in peacemaking, (3) commonsense theories of crime, (4) crime control as human rights enforcement, and (5) conflict resolution within community settings.[96]

Richard Quinney and John Wildeman summarized the underpinnings of peacemaking criminology by stating that "a criminology of peacemaking—a nonviolent criminology of compassion and service—seeks to end suffering and thereby eliminate crime."[97]

Other contributors to the peacemaking movement include Bo Lozoff, Michael Braswell, and Clemens Bartollas. In *Inner Corrections*, Lozoff and Braswell claimed that "we are fully aware by now that the criminal justice system in this country is founded on violence. It is a system which assumes that violence can be overcome by violence, evil by evil. Criminal justice at home and warfare abroad are of the same principle of violence. This principle sadly dominates much of our criminology."[98] *Inner Corrections* provides meditative techniques and prayers for those seeking to become more compassionate and includes a number of letters from convicts who demonstrate the book's philosophy.

In a work titled "Correctional Treatment, Peacemaking, and the New Age Movement," Bartollas and Braswell applied New Age principles to correctional treatment:[99] "Most offenders suffered abusive and deprived childhoods. Treatment that focuses on the inner child and such qualities as forgiveness and self-esteem could benefit offenders."[100] In a fundamental sense, peacemaking criminologists exhort their colleagues to transcend personal dichotomies to end the political and ideological divisiveness that separates people.

Participatory and Restorative Justice

Peacemaking criminology suggests that effective crime control can best be achieved by the adoption of a **peace model** of crime control based on cooperation rather than retribution and focused on effective ways of developing a shared consensus on critical issues that could seriously affect people's quality of life. Major issues include crimes like murder and rape but also extend to property rights, rights to the use of new technologies, and ownership of information; minor issues, including sexual preference, nonviolent sexual deviance, gambling, drug use, noise, child-custody claims, and publicly offensive behavior, can be dealt with in ways that require few resources beyond those immediately available in the community.

Alternative dispute resolution plays an important role in peacemaking perspectives.[101] Mediation programs, such as dispute-resolution centers and neighborhood justice centers, are characterized by cooperative efforts to reach dispute resolution rather than the adversarial proceedings now characteristic of most American courts. Dispute-resolution programs, now operating in over 200 areas throughout the country, are based on **participatory justice**—all parties to a dispute accept a kind of binding arbitration by neutral parties, often utilize administrative

FIGURE 9–4 | **The Differences between Peacemaking and Traditional Punishment**

Source: Schmalleger, Frank J., *Criminology*. Printed and Electronically reproduced by permission of Pearson Education, Inc., Upper Saddle River, New Jersey

■ **restorative justice** A postmodern perspective that stresses solutions and restoration rather than imprisonment, punishment, and neglect of victims; also called *reparative justice*.

■ **balanced and restorative justice (BARJ) model** A form of restorative justice which holds that the community, victim, and offender should receive balanced attention and all three should gain tangible benefits from their interactions with the justice system.

hearings and ombudsmen, and are staffed by volunteers who work to resolve disputes without assigning blame.

Miami's drug court, a local judicial initiative begun in 1989, provides an example of dispute-resolution programs. It diverts nonviolent drug users from the traditional path of streets to court to jail. Officially called the Dade County Diversion and Treatment Program, the drug court "channels almost all nonviolent defendants arrested on drug possession charges into an innovative court-operated rehabilitation program as an alternative to prosecution."[102] Drug-court processing appears to be successful at reducing the incidence of repeat offenses, does not result in a criminal record for those completing the program, and offers drug-dependent offenders a second chance at gaining control over substance-abuse problems.

Alternative dispute resolution is not without its critics, who charge that this type of program is often staffed by poorly qualified individuals who are ill-prepared to mediate disputes effectively. But as case-processing expenses continue to rise and minor cases continue to flood justice system agencies, we can expect that an emphasis on alternative dispute resolution will continue.

Many dispute-resolution strategies are really a form of **restorative justice** (also called *reparative justice*), "a new system based on remedies and restoration rather than on prison, punishment and victim neglect."[103] It is "a system rooted in the concept of a caring community," and adherents hope it leads to social and economic justice and increased concern and respect for both victims and victimizers.[104]

Restorative justice is a modern social movement that stresses healing rather than retribution.

But restorative justice is more than a system—it is a modern social movement to reform the criminal justice system that stresses healing rather than retribution.[105]

Restoration (repairing the harm done by crime and rebuilding relationships in the community) is the primary goal of restorative justice, and its effectiveness is measured by how many relationships are healed rather than by how much punishment is inflicted on the offender. Table 9–1 highlights some of the significant differences between traditional retributive justice and restorative justice.

The Balanced and Restorative Justice (BARJ) Model

One form of restorative justice is the **Balanced and Restorative Justice (BARJ) Model**. (See Figure 9–5.) Under this model, the community, victim, and offender should receive balanced attention and all three should gain tangible benefits from their interactions with the justice system. Its three components may be described as follows:[106]

- **Accountability.** When an offense occurs, an obligation to the victim results. Victims and communities should have

TABLE 9–1 Differences between Retributive and Restorative Justice

RETRIBUTIVE JUSTICE	*RESTORATIVE JUSTICE*
Crime is an act against the state, a violation of a law, an abstract idea.	Crime is an act against another person or the community.
The criminal justice system controls crime.	Crime control lies primarily with the community.
Offender accountability is defined as taking punishment.	Offender accountability is defined as assuming responsibility and taking action to repair harm.
Crime is an individual act with individual responsibility.	Crime has both individual and social dimensions of responsibility.
Victims are peripheral to the process of resolving a crime.	Victims are central to the process of resolving a crime.
The offender is defined by deficits.	The offender is defined by the capacity to make reparation.
The emphasis is on adversarial relationships.	The emphasis is on dialogue and negotiation.
Pain is imposed to punish, deter, and prevent.	Restitution is a means of restoring both parties; the goal is reconciliation.
The community is on the sidelines, represented abstractly.	The community is the facilitator in the restorative process by the state.
The response is focused on the offender's past behavior.	The response is focused on harmful consequences of the offender's behavior; the emphasis is on the future and on reparation.
There is dependence on proxy professionals.	There is direct involvement by both the offender and the victim.

Source: Adapted from Gordon Bazemore and Mark S. Umbreit, *Balanced and Restorative Justice: Program Summary* (Washington, DC: Office of Juvenile Justice and Delinquency Prevention, 1994), p. 7.

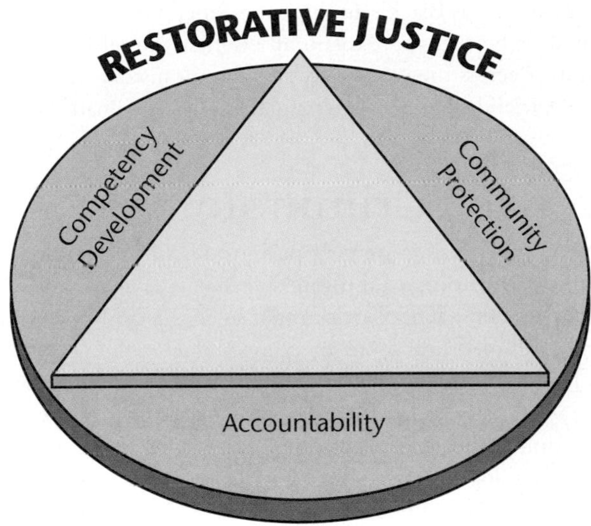

FIGURE 9-5 | **The Balanced and Restorative Justice (BARJ) Model**

Source: Office of Juvenile Justice and Delinquency Prevention, *Balanced and Restorative Justice: Program Summary* (Washington, DC: OJJDP, no date), p. 1.

their losses restored by the actions of offenders making reparation, and victims should be empowered as active participants in the justice process.

- **Community protection.** The public has a right to a safe and secure community and must be protected during the time the offender is under supervision. The justice system must provide a range of intervention alternatives geared to the varying risks presented by the offenders.
- **Competency development.** Offenders who come within the jurisdiction of the court should leave the system capable of being productive and responsible in the community. Rather than simply receiving treatment and services aimed at suppressing problem behavior, offenders should make measurable improvements in their ability to function as productive, responsible citizens.

Restorative justice programs make use of a number of techniques, but central to all of them is restorative conferencing, also called "community conferencing," in which victim, offender, and affected community members meet face-to-face in a safe setting with an impartial facilitator to discuss the facts and the impact of a particular offense.[107] The victim can ask questions and express directly to the offender how the crime has affected his or her life. Conferencing provides the victim with greater access to the criminal justice process and a strong voice in the process.[108] Conferencing also humanizes the incident for the offender so that he or she may better understand the real human consequences of his or her wrongdoing. The offender can propose steps that he or she can take to help restore the harm caused to the victim and the community. Participation in conferences is voluntary for victims and offenders. In some cases, a victim unwilling to participate in a face-to-face meeting may make a written statement to be used in the conference, or a surrogate victim may take his or her place. Learn more about restorative justice at **Web Extra 9–9**, and read a paper on restorative justice at **Library Extra 9–13**.

Critique of Peacemaking Criminology

Peacemaking criminology has been criticized as being naïve and utopian and for failing to recognize the realities of crime control and law enforcement because few victims would expect to gain much from attempting to make peace with their victimizers (although such strategies do occasionally work). Such criticisms may be improperly directed at a level of analysis that peacemaking criminologists have not assumed. Although it involves work with individual offenders, peacemaking criminology envisions positive change on the societal and institutional levels and does not suggest to victims that they attempt to effect personal changes in offenders.

Moral Time

A very different approach to conflict is offered by Donald Black in his book *Moral Time*.[109] Black uses the concept of social time to refer to specific events that alter relationships within what he refers to as *social space*. Black notes that crime is dynamic, and that it is an event, not a thing, or a condition. Although it may be people who commit crime, it is an event in social time that is the direct cause of crime. An event, in Black's terms, is a change in the attributes of our relationships towards one another. His use of the word "time" is meant to encompass change.

According to Black, conflict is everywhere. Black says that conflict "is inevitable and inescapable," and suggests that it is the result of a clash between what people view as right or wrong and the ability to apply that sense to events in social time. "The fundamental cause of conflict" says Black, "is the movement of social time." Social time, as Black conceives of it, "includes the fluctuations of every dimension of social space," and has three dimensions: relational time, vertical time, and cultural time. Relational time is an increase or decrease in intimacy; vertical time is an increase or decrease of inequality; and cultural time is an increase or decrease of diversity. Seen this way, social events, and the personal experiences derived from them, are movements of social time. Black says that rape, divorce, achievement, loss,

■ **convict criminology** A radical paradigm consisting of writings on criminology by convicted felons and ex-inmates who have acquired academic credentials or who are associated with credentialed others; also called *alternative criminology*.

contact with a foreigner, or the creation of something new is a movement in social time. As Black sees it:

> Social time moves when someone increases or decreases intimacy with someone else, achieves more or less than someone else, or accepts or rejects an idea of someone else. It moves when someone allows a relationship to weaken, disobeys an authority, or converts to another religion. It moves when strangers become acquaintances, when a marriage begins or ends, when a business hires or fires an employee, and when a nation rises or falls. It moves when someone gains or loses wealth, gives birth or dies, commits a crime or punishes a criminal. . . .

According to Black, conflict is produced by increases or decreases in the amount of intimacy, inequality, or diversity. Rapid change along any of these dimensions produces conflict. This movement in social space is what Black refers to as *social time*. The greater the speed and intensity of social time, the greater the conflict. Social norms and a group's sense of morality, however, seek to prevent social change. As Black sees it, morality "forbids the movement of social time." He adds, however, that "morality does not forbid every movement of social time, but everything morality forbids is a movement of social time."

Black emphasizes the idea that conflict is a social event, and notes that social time causes conflict in human relationships. Every movement of social time that causes conflict, says Black, is an increase or decrease in social closeness. Seen this way, conflict is a direct function of closeness, and a change in closeness can result in overcloseness or undercloseness. Although crime results from a movement of social time, says Black, the seriousness of an offense varies with intimacy. For example, he says, the rape of a stranger is a greater offense than the rape of a spouse because strangers were not intimate before the encounter took place—resulting in a greater movement of social time than that produced by the rape of an intimate. Greater movements in social time, says Black, attract greater social control.

Static conditions cannot cause crime, says Black—only changes in intimacy, or movements in social time. Black uses the example of the loss of a job, which might lead to violence because of the loss of social status that it confers upon an individual, or the loss of intimacy that occurs when a woman leaves her husband, which might also result in a violent offense. When social time does not lead to crime, Black says, then the ripples in the fabric of society that it creates must be resolved in some other way—such as though mediation, the use of civil courts, or personal changes.

Black's ideas should be testable. One idea that he proposes, for example, is that it's not the *condition* of poverty that is criminogenic, but rather the process of becoming poor—that is, a person's downward movement in social space.

Moral Time is Black's attempt at a general theory of conflict, and with it he seeks to explain all conflicts, in all human relationships, "across the world and throughout history . . . between relatives, friends, colleagues, strangers, groups, or nations."

Convict Criminology

A new radical paradigm emerging in the field of criminology is **convict criminology** (also called *alternative criminology*), which is not so much a school of thought as it is a body of writings and musings on criminology by convicted felons and ex-inmates who have acquired academic credentials or who are associated with credentialed others. It was formalized in 2001 with the publication of the article "Introducing the New School of Convict Criminology" by Stephen C. Richards in the journal *Social Justice*.[110] With the publication of "Convict Criminology" by Ian Ross and Stephen Richards in 2002,[111] the writings of convict criminologists went mainstream and began garnering attention from those in the discipline as well as the media. Today convict criminology (sometimes referred to as the New School of Convict Criminology) offers a blend of writings by credentialed ex-inmates and critical criminologists who have joined forces in distrust of mainstream criminology.[112] Convict criminology is largely issues based and personal; it has an agenda and tends to assume a critical perspective with regard to the justice system—especially corrections. The language of convict criminologists is different from that of academic criminologists who do not share their convict background (the latter use words like *convicts* instead of *offenders* and *inmates* instead of *prisoners*). The distinction is an important one, because the terminology used by academic criminologists is "managerial," consistent with the language of controlling agents in the justice system such as police officers, correctional officers, probation and parole officers, and court officials. By using the language of convict insiders, convict criminologists signify their allegiance to an insider's perspective and refer to traditional criminology as *managerial criminology*.[113]

> Convict criminology is largely issues based and personal.

The method used by convict criminologists is based in ethnography, a branch of anthropology that studies other cultures (in this case, inmate society). Ethnographers (discussed in Chapter 2) depend on lived experiences and oral communications about them (interviews, stories, conversations of study subjects). The advantage of convict criminologists is that they are their own subjects, so the long hours needed to gather

roman023/Fotolia

A homeless man in New York City. Peacemaking criminology holds that the alleviation of social problems and the reduction of human suffering will lead to a truly just world and thus reduce crime. What do you think?

experiences have already been spent—usually in prison or in personal interactions with the justice system.

The prototype convict criminologist is John Irwin, who spent five years in California's Soledad Prison in the 1950s for armed robbery. While imprisoned, Irwin earned college credits and after release went on to attend San Francisco State College and then UCLA. "The point is, I made my transition from the life of a thief, drug addict, and convict to one of a 'respectable' professional." Irwin went on to write *The Felon*, an academic work that shared the career criminal's point of view with interested readers.[114]

More recent works in convict criminology result from the collaboration between traditional criminologists and ex-convicts: *Behind Convict's Eyes*[115] and *Prison, Inc.: A Convict Exposes Life inside a Private Prison*,[116] both by the author team of K. C. Carceral (a convict serving life in prison who holds an associate's degree in paralegal studies), Thomas J. Bernard (a criminologist at Penn State University), and others.

Convict criminology is the source of a number of recommendations for improving the justice system that stem not from traditional forms of social scientific research but from "personal research" based on the lived experiences of the convict criminologists:[117]

1. Prisons hold far too many people, do not effectively reduce crime, and hold far too many people who have committed minor crimes.
2. Prison expansion has disproportionately and unfairly impacted the nation's poor—especially young men of color—who have made bad decisions in their lives and committed relatively harmless and bothersome crimes.
3. A substantial reduction in the number of federal and state prisoners is needed. Many of today's prisoners are nonviolent drug offenders who committed property crimes in support of drug habits or who were caught with drugs in their possession for either personal use or resale; diversion and treatment are viable alternatives to incarceration. The nation's "war on drugs"—seen as having a negative impact on all society—should be terminated.
4. Corrections today can benefit significantly from the use of smaller prisons instead of large institutions that now characterize many state facilities because they are less dangerous than large ones and tend to result in heightened rates of rehabilitation.
5. Treatment should be given precedence over security because most inmates will eventually return to society, and treatment offers the best hope for desistance from crime. Institutional priorities should be reversed—treatment programs need to receive top-level funding.

Critique of Convict Criminology

Not everyone agrees that convict criminology offers an edge over traditional criminology. Critics say that having been in prison might actually distort a criminologist's view of the field rather than enhance it and that personal experience rarely gives anyone the entire picture needed to understand a phenomenon. Focusing on the injustices of prison life might keep someone from appreciating the reformative effects of punishment. Read more about convict criminology at **Library Extra 9–14**.

Policy Implications of Social Conflict Theories

The policy implications of social conflict theory are fairly clear: Bring about social change and redistribute the wealth in society, and crime rates will fall. At one extreme, radical-Marxist criminologists argue that the only effective way of reducing conflict is through a total dismantling of the existing capitalist system in the United States and its replacement by a socialist economic structure. At the other extreme are the calls of peacemaking criminologists for a practical application of the principles of conflict resolution. Between these two extremes lie left realism and feminist criminology, although the solutions they offer vary from the reduction of paternalism in all its forms to a practical recognition of the consequences of crime to victims.

CRIMINAL | PROFILES

Theodore John "Ted" Kaczynski—the Unabomber

Born in Chicago on May 22, 1942, Kaczynski recalled his childhood as "uneventful." (Interestingly, he claimed to have been the victim of verbal and emotional abuse—but those claims never surfaced until he was in his 20s.) An introspective child and youth, Ted Kaczynski did not socialize easily or well and periodically underwent episodes of intense brooding and withdrawal. As he grew older, the episodes were increasingly accompanied by a seething rage.[i] Consumed with obsessions and emotionally crippled, the reclusive Kaczynski would eventually resolve his contempt for society's technological advances by mounting a bombing campaign that killed three people and injured 29 others.

His academic abilities enabled him to skip both the 6th and 11th grades, start undergraduate studies at Harvard at age 16, and earn his doctoral degree at the age of 25, but the promise of his remarkable early academic achievements foundered quickly.[ii] Upon completing his PhD, Kaczynski accepted an assistant professorship in mathematics at the University of California–Berkeley in 1967, but in June 1969, declaring there was "no relevance" to what he was doing, he quit his teaching post and then worked only sporadically out of financial necessity, living off the land in a hermit's existence of self-exile in a ramshackle cabin in the remote Montana wilderness for almost 25 years.[iii]

Kaczynski also experienced lifelong difficulties with sexual relationships. He struggled with his own sexuality, came to believe he should undergo a sex-change operation, and initiated the process, but when finally seen by a doctor, he claimed to be there for an entirely different reason and then left in a rage; subsequently, he described the experience as shameful and humiliating.[iv] In the ensuing years, he attempted to establish meaningful relationships with women but was never able to do so.

As he retreated deeper into his isolationist lifestyle, Kaczynski handwrote a lengthy manifesto railing against contemporary life, stating "The Industrial Revolution and its consequences have been a disaster for the human race."[v]

Between May 25, 1978, and April 24, 1995, Kaczynski left or sent a total of 16 homemade pipe bombs to various targets, primarily associated with universities and airlines. (The Federal Bureau of Investigation's designation of the investigation as the "Unabomb" case derives from these early university targets.) The first ten bombs caused serious injuries to numerous people; the 11th resulted in the first death.[vi]

Kaczynski's intermittent attacks were anonymous, a trait inexplicably broken when he began sending letters to a newspaper threatening to bomb an airplane. He also stated that he would stop the bombings if his 35,000-word manifesto was published in the *Washington Post*,[vii] and its subsequent publication eventually led to his capture.

Associated Press

Former University of California–Berkeley math professor Theodore John Kaczynski —aka the Unabomber—being led to an interview at the Federal Administrative Maximum Prison in Florence, Colorado, in 1999. What motivated Kaczynski?

Upon reading the manifesto, David Kaczynski (Ted's younger brother) immediately realized that "the tone of the language . . . almost had the feeling for me of one of Ted's angry letters over the years."[viii] The content and wording of the manifesto led David Kaczynski to contact the Federal Bureau of Investigation (FBI). The FBI went to Kaczynski's cabin in the isolated Montana wilderness and found overwhelming evidence that he was the Unabomber: a live bomb, meticulous notes of past bombings, bomb-making materials, and the original copy of his infamous manifesto.

On January 22, 1998, after reaching a plea agreement, Kaczynski pleaded guilty to four bombings that occurred in 1985, 1993, and 1995. Kaczynski also admitted to the three deaths his bombings had caused, and all other charges against him were resolved; he was sentenced to a life term without parole.[ix] Kaczynski remains imprisoned at the maximum-security federal prison in Florence, Colorado. Nine years after he entered prison, Kaczynski, filed suit against the federal government and a group of his victims, seeking to prevent the sale of more than 40,000 pages of his original writings and correspondence.[x]

Notes

i. Paul Ferguson, "A Loner from Youth," CNN Interactive, http://www.cnn.com/SPECIALS/1997/unabomb/accused/early (accessed May 28, 2007).
ii. Ted Ottley, "Ted Kaczynski: The Unabomber," CourtTV Crime Library, http://www.crimelibrary.com/terrorists_spies/terrorists/kaczynski/1.html (accessed May 28, 2007).
iii. CNN and Time Interactive, "The Unabomb Case," Cable News Network, http://www.cnn.com/SPECIALS/1997/unabomb/index.html (accessed May 28, 2007).
iv. Ottley, "Ted Kaczynski."
v. "The Unabomber's Manifesto: Industrial Society and Its Future," *Sacramento Bee*, http://www.unabombertrial.com/manifesto/index.html (accessed May 28, 2007).
vi. CNN and Time Interactive, "The Unabomb Case."
vii. Paul Ferguson, "Tracking the Unabomber: More Luck Than Computer Analysis," CNN Interactive, http://www.cnn.com/SPECIALS/1997/unabomb/investigation/puzzle/index.html (accessed May 28, 2007).
viii. "When Your Brother Is the Unabomber," MSNBC, December 29, 2006, http://www.msnbc.msn.com/id/16304477 (accessed May 28, 2007).
ix. "Kaczynski Admits He Is Unabomber, Sentenced to Life without Parole," CNN Interactive, January 22, 1998, http://www.cnn.com/US/9801/22/unabomb.plea (accessed June 16, 2007).
x. Serge F. Kovaleski, "Unabomber Wages Legal Battle to Halt Sale of Papers," *New York Times*, January 22, 2007, http://www.nytimes.com/2007/01/22/us/22unabomber.html?ex=1327122000&en=3fda08d949905a96&ei=5088&partner=rssnyt&emc=rss (accessed May 28, 2007).

The case of Ted Kaczynski raises a number of interesting questions. Among them are the following:

1. Although Kaczynski is not a criminologist, it is likely that he would agree with some of the principles of the social conflict perspective. With which of those principles do you think he would be most comfortable? Why?
2. How does Kaczynski being a loner fit with the crimes he committed? Might it indicate that he was in conflict with the wider society? Explain.
3. How might Kaczynski's difficulties with gender relationships provide further evidence of his difficulties with social life in general?
4. What similarities do you see between Kaczynski's writings and those of Karl Marx? (Learn more about Marx at http://www.philosophypages.com/ph/marx.htm.)

SUMMARY

- Three analytical perspectives on law and social order are discussed in this chapter: the consensus perspective, the pluralist perspective, and the conflict perspective. The consensus perspective is built around the notion that most members of society agree on what is right and wrong and that various elements of society work together toward a shared vision of the greater good. The pluralistic perspective holds that a multiplicity of values and beliefs exists in any complex society and that each different social group will have its own set of beliefs, interests, and values. The conflict perspective maintains that conflict is a fundamental aspect of social life itself that can never be fully resolved.
- Radical criminology holds that the root causes of crime are found in social conditions empowering the wealthy and the politically well organized but disenfranchising the less successful and that law is a tool of the powerful, who use it to control the less fortunate.
- Five perspectives offer explanations of crime and criminality: left-realist criminology, feminist criminology, postmodern criminology, peacemaking criminology, and convict criminology. Left-realist criminology is concerned with street crime, fear of crime, and everyday victimization and embraces radical and Marxist criminology. Feminist criminology believes that sexism and an unequal gender-based distribution of power in our patriarchal society affect both crime and its understanding in the field of criminology. Postmodernist criminologists doubt that an objective study of crime is possible and believe that criminology's search for the causes of crime is doomed because its questions are framed by sexist, class-specific, and racist assumptions. Peacemaking criminology restates the problem of crime control from how to stop crime to how to make peace within society and between citizens and criminal justice agencies. Convict criminology is a body of writings on criminology by convicted felons and ex-inmates who have acquired academic credentials or who are associated with credentialed others.
- Conflict theories hold that social conflict and its manifestations are the root causes of crime; the crime-control implications involve redressing injustices to end the marginalization of the politically and economically disadvantaged.

KEY TERMS

androcentricity, 229
balanced and restorative justice (BARJ) model, 234
bourgeoisie, 219
conflict perspective, 218
consensus perspective, 216
convict criminology, 236
critical criminology, 224
deconstructionist theory, 232
feminist criminology, 228
gender gap, 231
instrumental Marxism, 223
left realism, 227
left-realist criminology, 227
liberal feminism, 228
Marxist criminology, 222
Marxist feminism, 228
participatory justice, 233
patriarchy, 229
peace model, 233
peacemaking criminology, 232
pluralistic perspective, 218
postmodern criminology, 231
postmodern feminism, 228
power-control theory, 229
proletariat, 219
radical criminology, 222
radical feminism, 228
restorative justice, 234
social class, 220
socialist feminism, 228
structural Marxism, 223

KEY NAMES

Freda Adler, 229
Willem Bonger, 219
William J. Chambliss, 222
Meda Chesney-Lind, 229
Ralf Dahrendorf, 221
Kathleen Daly, 229
Walter DeKeseredy, 227
John Hagan, 229
Stuart Henry, 232
Karl Marx, 216
Raymond J. Michalowski, 216
Dragan Milovanovic, 232
Harold E. Pepinsky, 232
Roscoe Pound, 217
Richard Quinney, 223
Jeffrey H. Reiman, 223
Rita J. Simon, 229
Austin Turk, 221
George B. Vold, 221
Jock Young, 227

QUESTIONS FOR REVIEW

1. What three analytical perspectives on law and social order are described in this chapter?
2. What are the central tenets of radical criminology? What are its shortcomings?
3. What five emerging conflict perspectives discussed in this chapter purport to explain crime and criminality?
4. What are the crime-control implications of social conflict theories?

QUESTIONS FOR REFLECTION

1. This text emphasizes the theme of social problems versus social responsibility. Which of the theoretical perspectives discussed in this chapter (if any) support the social problems approach? Which (if any) support the social responsibility approach? Why?
2. What are the differences among the consensus, pluralist, and conflict perspectives? Which comes closest to your way of understanding society? Why?
3. What is Marxist criminology? How (if at all) does it differ from radical criminology? From critical criminology?
4. Does the Marxist perspective hold any significance for contemporary American society? Why?
5. What are the fundamental propositions of feminist criminology? How would feminists change the study of crime?
6. What does it mean to say that traditional theories of crime need to be "deconstructed"? What role does deconstructionist thinking play in postmodern criminology?

Jeff Morgan 13/Alamy

CHAPTER 10 CRIMES AGAINST PERSONS

LEARNING OUTCOMES

After reading this chapter, you should be able to answer the following questions:

- What is criminal homicide, and what are the key issues involved in explaining patterns of homicide?
- How is the crime of rape defined, and what are the key issues involved in understanding the crime of rape?
- What does the term *child sexual abuse* encompass? What are the various types of child sex abusers?
- How is the crime of robbery defined, and what are the different kinds of robbery?
- How is the crime of assault defined, and what are the various kinds of assault?
- What three additional forms of interpersonal violence does this chapter discuss?

■ **Follow the author's tweets about the latest crime and justice news @schmalleger.**

■ **National Crime Victimization Survey (NCVS)** A survey conducted annually by the Bureau of Justice Statistics that provides data on surveyed households reporting that they were affected by crime.

■ **Uniform Crime Reporting (UCR) Program** A Federal Bureau of Investigation data-gathering initiative that provides an annual tally of statistics consisting primarily of information on crimes reported to the police and on arrests.

■ **National Incident-Based Reporting System (NIBRS)** An enhanced statistical reporting system to collect data on each incident and arrest within 22 crime categories.

■ **murder** An unlawful homicide; also called *criminal homicide*.

■ **homicide** The killing of one human being by another.

Introduction

In October 2012, as the Detroit Tigers prepared to play the Oakland Athletics in a baseball game, members of the Detroit Police Officer Association (DPOA) stood outside the Tigers' Comerica Park stadium holding signs warning tourists to "Enter at Your Own Risk."[1] DPOA spokesperson Donato Iorio told onlookers that "Detroit is America's most violent city, its homicide rate is the highest in the country and yet the Detroit Police Department is grossly understaffed." It turns out that Iorio was mistaken. According to the Federal Bureau of Investigation (FBI), Detroit has the *second* highest rate of violent crime in the country—just behind that of Flint, Michigan, only 66 miles away. According to the FBI, Flint's violent crime rate in 2012 was 2,729 per every 100,000 residents; while Detroit's was "only" 2,123 per 100,000.[2]

Before 1930, Detroit officials would not have known how their city ranked in terms of violent crime rates. That's because the government-sponsored gathering of crime data for the nation as a whole began in 1930 in the United States. Before then, the gathering of statistics was random at best, and most accounts were anecdotal and either spread by word of mouth or printed in local newspapers (or both). Today's official U.S. crime statistics come from the Bureau of Justice Statistics (BJS), which conducts the annual **National Crime Victimization Survey (NCVS)**, and from the FBI, which publishes yearly data under its summary-based **Uniform Crime Reporting (UCR) Program** and its more detailed **National Incident-Based Reporting System (NIBRS)**; the latter provides a more complete picture of crimes reported and committed.

NCVS data appear in a number of annual reports, the most important of which is *Criminal Victimization in the United States*, and FBI data take the form of the annual publication *Crime in the United States*. Numerous other surveys and reports are made available through the BJS and cover not only the incidence of crime and criminal activity in the United States but also many other aspects of the criminal justice profession, including justice system expenditures, prisons and correctional data, probation and parole populations, jail inmate information, law enforcement agencies and personnel data, and information on state and federal courts. These and other reports are generally made available free of charge to interested parties through the National Criminal Justice Reference Service (NCJRS).[3] The largest collection of facts about all aspects of U.S. crime and criminal justice is the *Sourcebook of Criminal Justice Statistics*, using data compiled yearly by the BJS and made available through the auspices of the State University of New York at Albany on the Web at **Library Extra 10-1**.

The UCR/NIBRS and the NCVS both use their own specialized definitions in deciding which events should be scored as crimes. Sometimes the definitions vary considerably between programs, and none of the definitions used by the reporting agencies is strictly based on federal or state statutory crime classifications. For the most part the definitions and statistics that we will present in this chapter and the next are consistent with those used by the FBI and its annual publication, *Crime in the United States*. This chapter discussed violent crimes, including murder, rape, robbery, and aggravated assault (Figure 10–1).

Murder

The terms *homicide* and **murder** are often used interchangeably, although they are not the same. Homicide is the willful killing of one human being by another, whereas murder is an unlawful homicide. Some homicides, such as those committed in defense of oneself or one's family, may be justifiable and therefore legal. The term used by most courts and law enforcement agencies to describe murder is **homicide**. In legal parlance, *criminal homicide*

Peter Lovino/Showtime/Everett Collection

A still image from the Showtime TV series *Dexter*. Dexter, a fictional serial killer who strives to eliminate evil, works as a blood-spatter expert in a police department. What kinds of criminal offenses are likely to be self-reported? Which ones are unlikely to be self-reported? Why?

■ **first-degree murder** The premeditated unlawful killing of a human being.

■ **second-degree murder** The unlawful intentional killing of a human being without premeditation.

■ **negligent homicide** The unlawful killing of a human being that occurs as a result of an unlawful or negligent action.

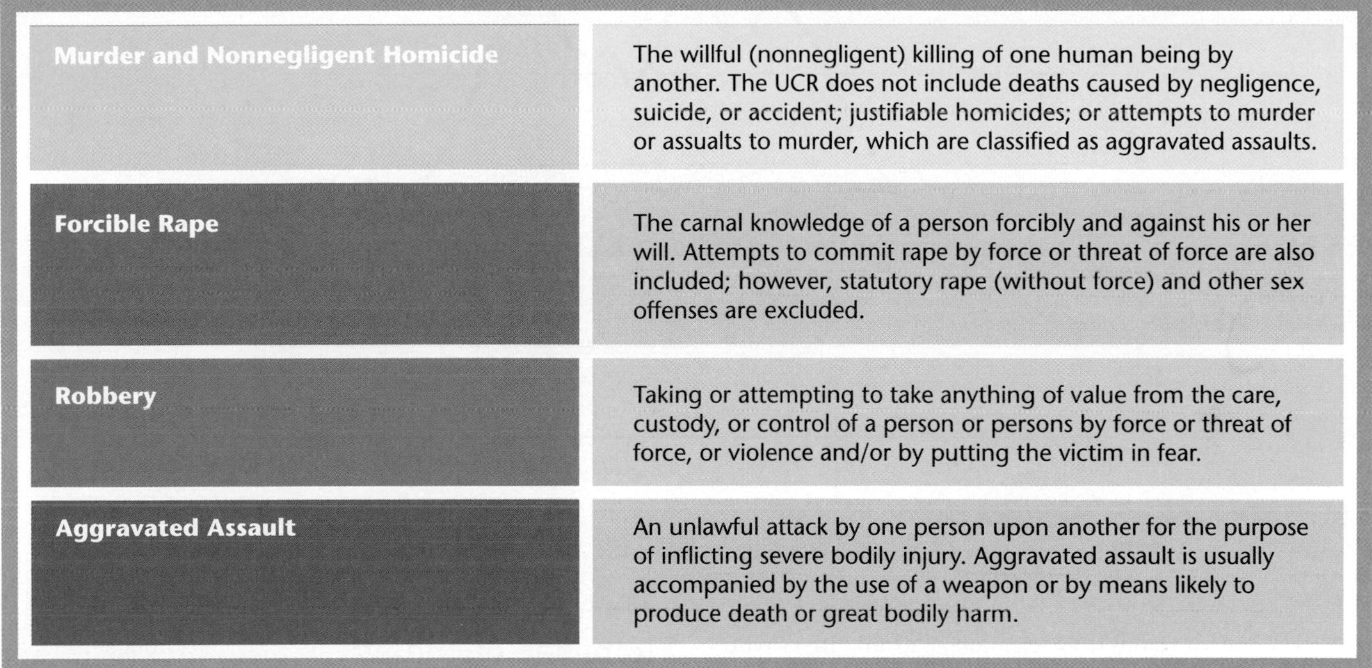

Murder and Nonnegligent Homicide	The willful (nonnegligent) killing of one human being by another. The UCR does not include deaths caused by negligence, suicide, or accident; justifiable homicides; or attempts to murder or assaults to murder, which are classified as aggravated assaults.
Forcible Rape	The carnal knowledge of a person forcibly and against his or her will. Attempts to commit rape by force or threat of force are also included; however, statutory rape (without force) and other sex offenses are excluded.
Robbery	Taking or attempting to take anything of value from the care, custody, or control of a person or persons by force or threat of force, or violence and/or by putting the victim in fear.
Aggravated Assault	An unlawful attack by one person upon another for the purpose of inflicting severe bodily injury. Aggravated assault is usually accompanied by the use of a weapon or by means likely to produce death or great bodily harm.

FIGURE 10-1 | **Violent Crimes and Their Definitions**
Source: FBI, Uniform Crime Reporting Program.

means "the causing of the death of another person without legal justification or excuse."

According to the Uniform Crime Reports/National Incident Based Reporting System (UCR/NIBRS), 14,827 murders were committed throughout the United States in 2012.[4] The 2012 rate of criminal homicide was 4.7 people murdered for every 100,000 individuals in the U.S. population. As is the case with other major crimes, rates of criminal homicide in the United States increased between 1960 and the early 1990s, but then began decreasing until they reached levels not seen since the 1960s (Figure 10–2). General features of criminal homicide in the United States today are shown in Figure 10–3.

Jurisdictions generally distinguish among various types of murder. Among the distinctions made are **first-degree murder**, also called "premeditated murder"; **second-degree murder**; and third-degree murder, or **negligent homicide**. First-degree murder differs from the other two types of murder in that it is planned. It involves what some statutes call "malice aforethought," which may become evident by someone "lying in wait" for the victim, but can also be proved by a murderer's simple action of going into an adjacent room to find a weapon and returning with it to kill. In effect, any activity in preparation to kill that demonstrates the passage of time, however brief, between formation of the intent to kill and the act of killing itself is technically sufficient to establish the legal requirements needed for a first-degree murder prosecution.

Second-degree murder, on the other hand, is a true crime of passion. It is an unlawful killing in which the intent to kill and the killing itself happen almost simultaneously. Hence, a person who kills in a fit of anger is likely to be charged with second-degree murder, as is one who is provoked into killing by insults, physical abuse, and the like. For a murder to be second-degree, however, the killing must follow immediately upon the abuse. Time that elapses between abuse or insults and the murder itself allows the opportunity for thought to occur and hence for premeditation.

Both first- and second-degree murderers intend to kill. Third-degree murder, although it varies in meaning between jurisdictions, most often refers to homicides that are the result of some action that is unlawful or negligent. Hence, it is frequently called "negligent homicide," "negligent manslaughter," "manslaughter," or "involuntary manslaughter." Under

■ **felony murder** An unlawful homicide that occurs during the commission or attempted commission of a felony, or certain felonies specified by law.

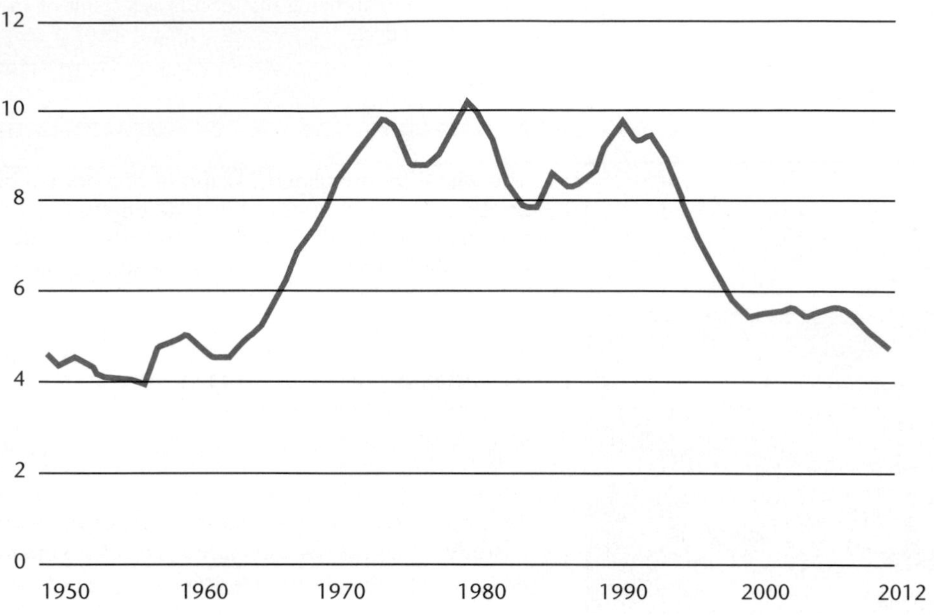

FIGURE 10-2 | **Murder Rates, 1950–2012**

Source: Alexis Cooper and Erica L. Smith, *Homicide Trends in the United States, 1980–2008: With Annual Rates for 2009 and 2010* (Washington, DC: Bureau of Justice Statistics, November 2011), p. 2; and FBI, *Crime in the United States, 2012* (Washington, DC: U.S. Department of Justice, 2013).

negligent homicide statutes, for example, a drunk driver who causes a fatal accident may be charged with third-degree murder even though that person had not the slightest intent to kill.

Some jurisdictions have created a special category of **felony murder**, whereby an offender who commits a crime during which someone dies can be found guilty of first-degree murder even though the person committing the crime had no intention of killing anyone. Bank robberies in which one of the robbers is shot to death by police, for example, or in which a bank patron succumbs to a fear-induced heart attack may leave a surviving robber subject to the death penalty under the felony murder rule. Hence, felony murder is a special class of criminal homicide whereby an offender may be charged with first-degree murder when that person's criminal activity results in another person's death.

Significant contributions to the understanding of the crime of homicide are being made today by the Homicide Research Working Group (HRWG). The HRWG brings together researchers, academicians, and investigators working in the area of interpersonal violence from numerous disciplines. Prior to the creation of the HRWG, work in lethal violence had been scattered among numerous disciplines and was largely uncoordinated. To address this lack of coordination, homicide experts from various disciplines, including criminology, public health, demography, medicine, sociology, criminal justice, and other fields, joined together to create the HRWG.

Homicide offending is very much patterned in terms of sociodemographics.

Although homicide offenders include men and women, young and old, rich and poor, homicide offending is very much patterned in terms of sociodemographics, with members of some groups being disproportionately represented as offenders. Distinctive patterns of homicide can be identified by such factors as individual characteristics, cultural norms, community characteristics, geographic region, availability of weapons and weapons used, gang activity and affiliation, and the victim–offender relationship. All of these sociodemographic features have been used to further our understanding of homicide patterns and to create typologies surrounding homicide.

The Subculture of Violence Thesis

What causes some cities to have high rates of violence while others don't? High rates of unemployment, poverty, and low educational attainment are frequently associated with violence, although they might not necessarily be its cause. In Flint, Michigan, for example, the poverty rate in 2012 was 40.6%, the percent of adults with a high school degree was only 82.9, and the median household income was just $23,380 — the second-lowest of all

■ **subculture of violence thesis** The belief that certain groups or subcultures in society have values and attitudes that are conducive to crime and violence.

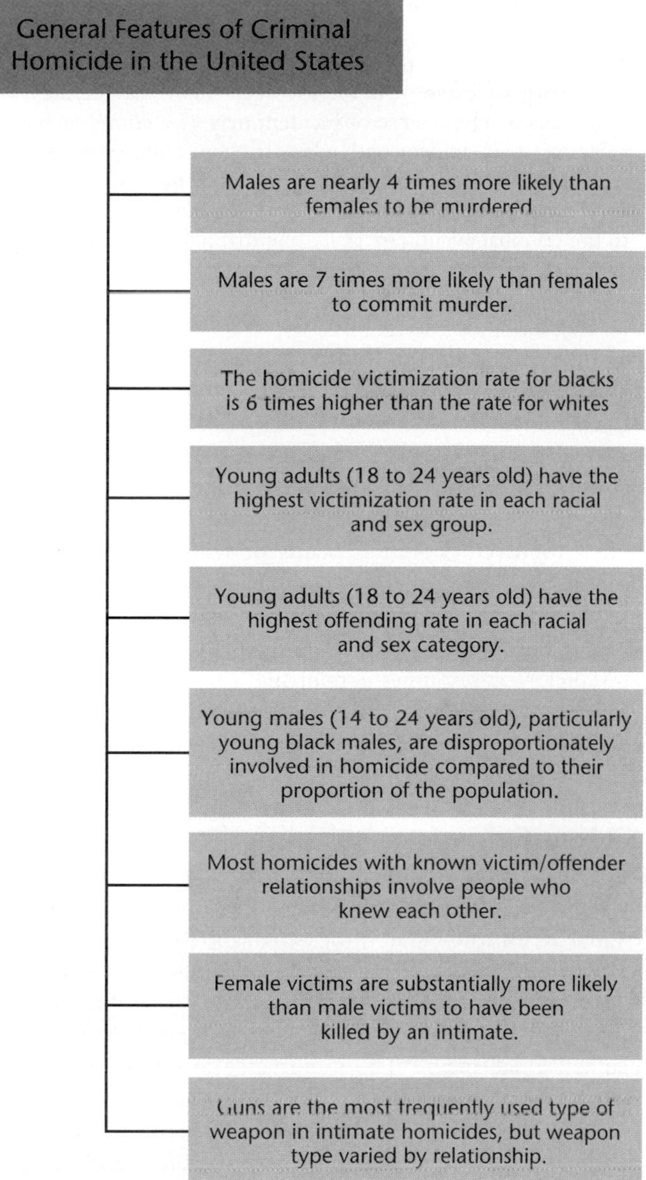

FIGURE 10-3 | General Features of Criminal Homicide in the United States

Source: Alexis Cooper and Erica L. Smith, *Homicide Trends in the United States, 1980–2008: With Annual Rates for 2009 and 2010* (Washington, DC: Bureau of Justice Statistics, November 2011).

555 cities in the United States measured by the U.S. Census Bureau.[5] Association is not the same thing as causation, however, and some say that although "it is very clear that poverty in particular is associated with higher crime rates," it's "very difficult to say whether crime makes places poorer, or poverty causes more crime."[6]

An alternative perspective is the subculture of violence thesis that was originally formulated by Marvin Wolfgang and Franco Ferracuti,[7] and which was discussed in Chapter 7. These authors stressed that certain groups share norms and values in lifestyles of violence. Ethnic and racial differences in criminal activity rely on interaction with others, including a shared sense of history, language, values, and beliefs. A subculture requires a sufficient number of people who share not only values and beliefs, but also a social forum that expresses membership. Such a forum may be something as elusive as a street corner. It is primarily the nature of this situation that makes it difficult to test empirically. The subculture of violence thesis has been the primary theoretical perspective used to explain the similarity between homicide victims and offenders. First, homicide statistics reveal that victims and offenders share similar sociodemographic characteristics such as age, gender, and race. African Americans are disproportionately represented in the homicide statistics as both victims and offenders.[8] Second, victims and offenders who know each other well are disproportionately represented in homicide statistics. An analysis of supplemental homicide reports shows that approximately 60% of victims and offenders have some prior relationship.[9]

> The subculture of violence thesis holds that certain groups share norms and values that contribute to lifestyles involving violence.

The **subculture of violence thesis** has also been explored at the community level, where the emphasis is on the importance of "critical masses" as support for the existence of subcultures.[10] Early research argued that the disproportionate rate at which African Americans commit homicide is associated with the presence of a large African American population, the "critical mass" necessary for the "transmission of violence-related models" and subcultural behavior patterns.[11] However, most of the research that found higher homicide rates to be associated with higher percentages of African Americans in the population did not take into consideration socioeconomic status, level of education, and so forth.[12] Research by Robert Sampson, using more sophisticated measures and stronger research designs, revealed that the racial composition of an area alone did not have a significant effect on the homicide rates for either whites or African Americans.[13]

Homicide: A Closer Look

Marvin Wolfgang's now-famous 1958 study of homicides in Philadelphia revealed that approximately 25% of all homicides were between family members and that women were far more likely than men to be both offenders and victims within this category than within any other.[14] Males are more likely to be killed by

■ **primary homicide** A murder involving a family member, friend, or acquaintance.
■ **expressive crime** A criminal offense that results from acts of interpersonal hostility, such as jealousy, revenge, romantic triangles, and quarrels.
■ **nonprimary homicide** A murder that involves a victim and an offender who have no prior relationship and that usually occurs during the course of another crime, such as robbery.
■ **instrumental crime** A goal-directed offense that involves some degree of planning by the offender and little or no precipitation by the victim.
■ **exposure-reduction theory** A theory of intimate homicide that claims that a decline in domesticity, accompanied by an improvement in the economic status of women and a growth in domestic violence resources, explains observed decreases in intimate-partner homicide.
■ **sibling offense** An offense or incident that culminates in homicide. The offense or incident may be a crime, such as robbery, or an incident with a less stringent criminal definition, such as a lovers' quarrel involving assault or battery.
■ **victim precipitation** A contribution made by the victim to the criminal event, especially one that led to its initiation.

friends and strangers than by their family members, and very few women (relative to men) are murderers. However, when a male is killed by a female, the offender is most likely to be his spouse.[15] Other researchers have emphasized qualitative differences in the pattern of homicide within the victim–offender relationship. Figure 10–4 shows the relationship between killers and their victims.

The Victim–Offender Relationship

The work of **Robert Nash Parker** and Dwayne Smith represented the first systematic research that focused on differentiating homicide according to the victim–offender relationship.[16] Their work used two classifications of homicide: primary and nonprimary. **Primary homicides** are the most frequent and involve family members, friends, and acquaintances, and they are usually characterized as **expressive crimes** because they often result from interpersonal hostility, based on jealousy, revenge, romantic triangles, and minor disagreements.[17]

Nonprimary homicides involve victims and offenders who have no prior relationship and usually occur in the course of another crime such as robbery; these are referred to as **instrumental crimes** because they involve some degree of premeditation by the offender and are less likely to be precipitated by the victim. The difference between expressive and instrumental motives for homicide continues to be important in criminological research, and we will return to this shortly.

Further attention to the heterogeneous nature of homicide is found in the work of K. R. Williams and R. L. Flewelling, who disaggregated homicide rates according to two criteria: (1) the nature of the circumstances surrounding the homicide, which included whether there was some indicator of a fight or argument precipitating the homicide, and (2) the victim–offender relationship, distinguishing between victims and offenders who were family members, acquaintances, or strangers.[18] By comparing how factors like poverty and population size have different effects on different types of homicide, Williams and Flewelling found that some factors are more important in explaining certain forms of homicide. Poverty is a stronger predictor of family homicide, population size is more important in explaining stranger homicide, and both the victim–offender relationship and the context of the homicide (for example, the end result of a robbery) are crucial factors in explaining patterns of homicide.

Beginning in the 1980s, the intimate-partner homicide rate began to decline, a decline that has continued to the present day. Using homicide data from a sample of 29 large cities in the United States from 1976 to 1992, Laura Dugan, Daniel S. Nagin, and Richard Rosenfeld offered an **exposure-reduction theory** of intimate-partner homicide.[19] These researchers examined the ability of the "decline in domesticity, improved economic status of women, and growth in domestic violence resources" to explain decreases in intimate-partner homicide in urban areas.[20] Analysis of the data did support the major hypotheses offered by Dugan, Nagin, and Rosenfeld—as resources supporting a nonviolent exit from a violent relationship increase, rates of intimate-partner homicide decrease. Read more about intimate-partner violence at **Library Extra 10–2**.

Sibling Offenses

Not all homicide offenders intend to kill their victims. This may be the case when the incident begins as a robbery motivated by instrumental ends, such as getting money. An argument may also precede a homicide, but this circumstance is expressive rather than instrumental because "the dominant motivation is the violence itself," even if lethal violence is not planned in advance.[21] The importance of instigating incidents is explored in research by Carolyn Rebecca Block and Richard Block.[22] The Blocks use the term **sibling offense** to refer to the incident that begins the homicide. A sibling offense may be a crime, such as robbery, or another incident, such as a lover's quarrel. It is crucial to take these sibling offenses into account because they help explain why some robberies end in murder and others do not. The Blocks developed an elaborate typology of homicide to illustrate how an understanding of the patterns of nonlethal violence can assist in the prevention of lethal violence. For example, there are a great many incidents of street gang violence, most of which do not end in death, and understanding those nonlethal incidents can assist in preventing homicides.[23]

Victim Precipitation

The concept of **victim precipitation** focuses on the characteristics of victims that may have precipitated their

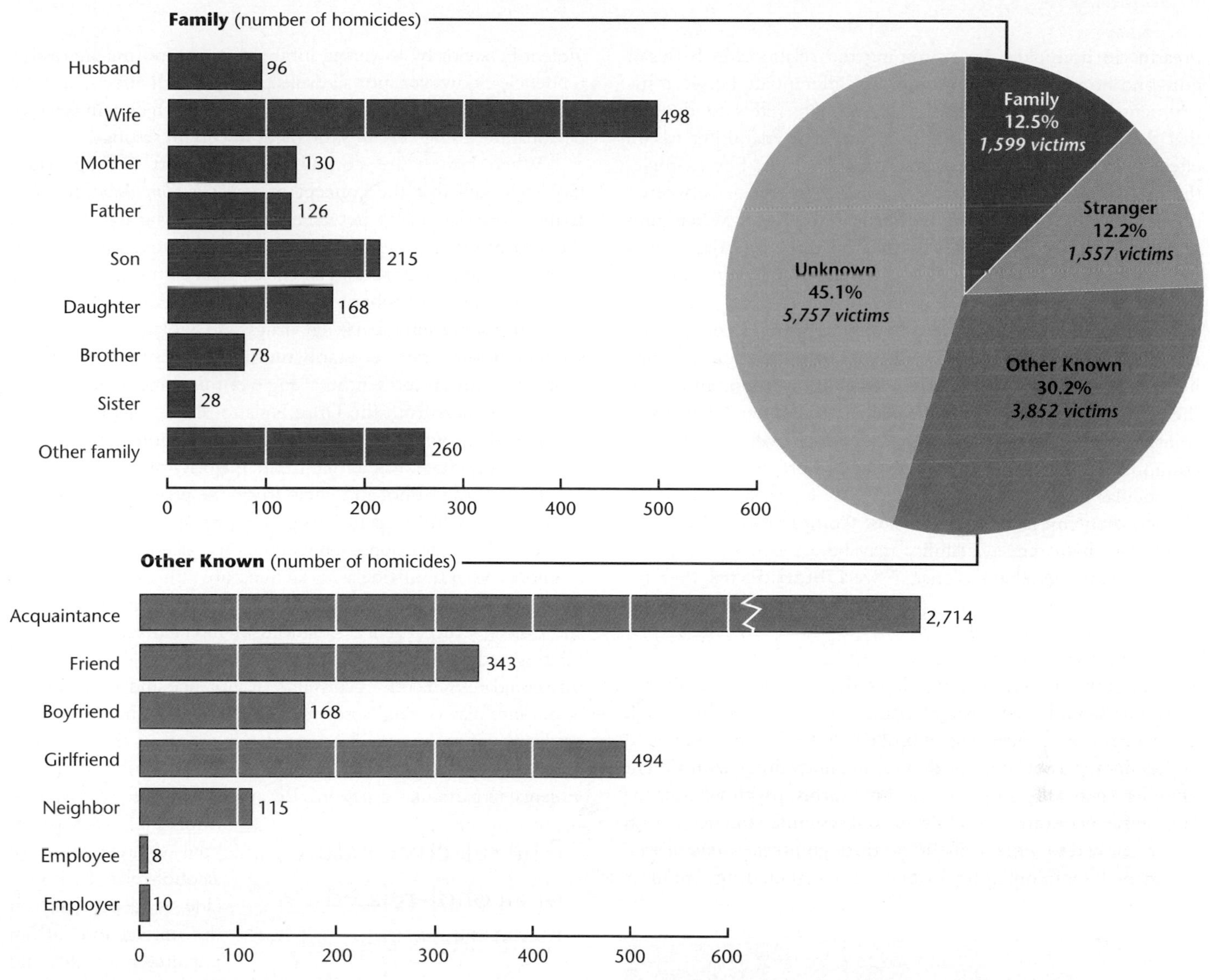

FIGURE 10–4 | **Murder by Relationship of Victim or Offender, 2012**

Source: Federal Bureau of Investigation, *Crime in the United States, 2012* (Washington, DC: FBI, 2013).

victimization. Victim precipitation seems to blame the victim, which makes it quite controversial. From a scholarly point of view, however, the thrust of the concept of victim precipitation is not to blame the victim for the event, but to examine both individual and situational factors that may have contributed to and initiated the crime. This is especially important in studying patterns of homicide because quite often a homicide begins as a fight or an argument between people who know each other. The circumstances of the particular encounter determine whether the event will end as some type of assault or as a homicide.

Wolfgang also identified alcohol use as a factor in homicide cases where the "victim is a direct, positive precipitator in the crime."[24] He concluded that the positive and significant association between alcohol and victim-precipitated homicides may be explained by the fact that the victim was the "first to slap, punch, stab, or in some other manner commit an assault" and that if the victim had not been drinking, he or she would have been less violent.[25] Wolfgang's research on homicide revealed that most victims of spousal homicide had been drinking at the time of the incident, a situation that did not apply to homicide offenders.[26]

Weapon Use

There are different perspectives on the role that weapons play in crime, with most of the discussion centering on the role of

■ **selective disinhibition** A loss of self-control due either to the social setting or to drugs or alcohol, or a combination of both.

firearms in homicide. In examining the relationship between guns and homicide, it is important to differentiate between instrumentality and availability. *Instrumentality* refers to the fact that the type of weapon used in a particular encounter has an effect on whether the encounter ends in death. For example, the involvement of a gun may mean the difference between a criminal event ending as an assault or a homicide. When guns are used in robberies, the fatality rate is "three times as high as for robberies with knives and 10 times as high as for robberies with other weapons."[27]

Availability refers to issues surrounding how access to guns may increase their presence in all types of interactions, including criminal ones.[28] The ease of availability is important, given the relative spontaneity of some violent encounters. The availability of guns is important at the individual level as well as the community level because the greater the presence of guns in a particular neighborhood, the easier the access for individuals beyond their immediate households. Compared to gun instrumentality, then, gun availability may be a much stronger factor in explaining lethal violence.[29] See **Library Extra 10–3** for more information.

Alcohol and Drug Use

An important conceptual typology detailing the relationship between alcohol or drugs and crime was developed by Paul J. Goldstein in an article first published in 1985.[30] According to Goldstein, the association of alcohol and illicit drugs with violent offending generally takes one of three forms: psychopharmacological use, economic compulsion, and systemic violence. Drugs may be linked to violent offending through *psychopharmacological use*, whereby infrequent or chronic use of certain drugs produces violent behavior by lowering inhibitions or elevating aggressive tendencies; however, not all drugs produce such effects, and the relationship appears to hold only for people with certain types of personalities using certain substances in certain settings.

Elizabeth Robertson/The Inquirer/Newscom

A purse snatcher (green jacket) running off with his loot. Why do victimologists suggest that some people contribute to their own victimization?

When crimes are committed to support a drug habit, Goldstein said that the concept of *economic compulsion* best describes the relationship between crime and drug use. He used the idea of *systemic violence* to describe the connection between drugs and trafficking, and it can take several forms, ranging from rival drug wars to robberies of drug dealers. Although distinct types of relationships between drugs and violence can be described, these are not necessarily mutually exclusive, with one or more relationships present in a single criminal incident.

Researchers from the Drug Relationships in Murder Project (DREIM), which analyzed incarcerated homicide offenders in New York State, found that in the majority of homicide cases involving both alcohol and illicit drugs, the primary basis for the connection with the crime was psychopharmacological.[31]

One theoretical approach focused on explaining the role that alcohol plays in homicide as social in nature rather than biochemical is **selective disinhibition**, advanced by Robert Nash Parker and others.[32] In particular situations or interactions, the "disinhibiting" effect of alcohol may operate to suspend certain factors that could restrain the occurrence of violence and may operate to put into play certain factors that could increase the occurrence or degree of violence. This perspective relies on the existence of norms operating both to prohibit and to proscribe the use of violence in particular situations. Because alcohol can reduce both forms of constraint, "the selective nature of alcohol-related homicide is dependent on the interaction of an impaired rationality and the nature of the social situation."[33] Parker and his colleagues tested this model by analyzing data on homicides in several cities in 1980, in several cities between 1960 and 1980, and in several states from 1976 to 1983. One key finding from this research was the ability of alcohol to significantly predict primary homicide. In relationships between individuals who are known to each other, alcohol may operate to disinhibit restraints against violence, but the norms that operate to govern interactions between strangers are more rigid in terms of the type of conduct that is proscribed. The use of violence against those known to us is treated with greater tolerance—tolerance that can be increased even more in the presence of alcohol.[34]

The selective nature of alcohol-related homicide is dependent on the interaction of an impaired rationality and the nature of the social situation.

■ **serial murder** A type of criminal homicide that involves the killing of several victims in three or more separate events.
■ **visionary serial killers** Serial killers motivated by auditory or visual hallucinations.
■ **comfort serial killers** Serial killers motivated by financial or material gain.
■ **hedonistic serial killers** Serial killers who derive pleasure from killing.
■ **power seekers** Serial killers who relish having power over another human being.

In his research using state-level data, Parker tested several hypotheses derived from competing theoretical perspectives about the effect of alcohol on homicide.[35] Based on the victim-offender relationship, five types of homicides were identified: "robbery, other felony, family intimate, family other, and primary nonintimate."[36] Poverty had a stronger effect on both robbery and other felony homicides in states with "above average rates of alcohol consumption";[37] alcohol consumption had direct effects on two of the three types of primary homicide.

Serial murder is a criminal homicide that "involves the killing of several victims in three or more separate events."[38] Criminologists **James Alan Fox** and **Jack Levin** have written extensively on both serial killing and mass murder.

Contrary to some commonly held beliefs, the vast majority of serial killers are not legally insane or medically psychotic. "They are more cruel than crazy," according to Fox and Levin. "Their crimes may be sickening but their minds are not necessarily sick."[39] Many serial killers are diagnosed as sociopaths, a term for those with antisocial personalities. Because they lack a conscience, sociopaths do not consider the needs or basic humanity of others in their decision making or their view of the world. They do not see themselves as being bound by conventional rules or by the expectations of others. Sociopaths view other people as "tools to be manipulated for the purpose of maximizing their personal pleasure."[40] However, many sociopaths are neither serial killers nor involved in violent crime, even though "they may lie, cheat, or steal."[41]

Although not an exclusive characteristic of serial killers, sexual sadism is a strong pattern. In many of the typologies developed by researchers, this characteristic forms the basis for a type of serial killer. Typologies of serial killers are organized around different, but generally related, themes. Some criminologists identify four different types of serial killers: **Visionary serial killers** hear voices and have visions that are the basis for a compulsion to murder; **comfort serial killers** are motivated by financial or material gain; **hedonistic serial killers** murder because they find it enjoyable and derive psychological pleasure from killing; and **power seekers** operate from some position of authority over others, and their killings usually involve a period where the killer plays a kind of cat-and-mouse game with the victim.[42] Fox and Levin offer a three-part typology. They classify serial murderers as thrill-motivated, mission-oriented, or expedience-directed killers. *Thrill-motivated killers*, the most common type of serial killer, may be of two types: the sexual sadist and the dominance killer. *Mission-oriented killers* are not as common and generally have either a reformist or visionary orientation. Reformists want to rid the world of evil, and visionaries hear voices commanding them to do certain activities. Visionary killers are quite rare and tend to be genuinely psychotic. *Expedience-directed serial killers* are driven by either profit or protection. Profit-driven killers may kill for financial or material gain, and protection-oriented killers commit murder to mask other crimes, such as robbery.[43]

Female Serial Killers

Although the vast majority of serial killers are male, there have been female serial killers, and the patterns of their activities are sometimes distinct from those of male serialists.[44] Female serial killers typically select their victims from among people they know, unlike male serial killers, who tend to target strangers.[45] A type of serial killer found primarily among women is the *disciple killer*, who murders as the result of the influence of a charismatic personality. The women who killed at the behest of Charles Manson were of this type. Male serial killers often commit their crimes some distance from their homes, generally without regard to type of neighborhood. However, geographic stability characterizes almost all of the known female serial killers.[46]

Elaine Thompson/AP Wide World Photos

Gary L. Ridgway, age 54, the self-confessed Green River strangler. Ridgway, reputed to be the nation's worst captured serial killer, admitted to killing 48 women over a 20-year period in the Pacific Northwest. He is now serving life in prison without possibility of parole. Why did it take so long to stop Ridgway?

■ **Violent Criminal Apprehension Program (VICAP)** The program of the Federal Bureau of Investigation focusing on serial murder investigation and the apprehension of serial killers.

■ **mass murder** The illegal killing of three or more victims at one location within one event.

Michael D. Kelleher and C. L. Kelleher researched female serial killers from a historical perspective and developed a typology based on motivation. Arguing that there are two broad categories of female serial killers—those who act alone and those who work in partnership with others—Kelleher and Kelleher present a typology based on distinct motivation, selection of victim, and method of killing.[47] The categories include the *black widow*, who generally kills spouses and usually for economic profit, and the *angel of death*, who generally kills "those in her care or who rely on her for some form of medical attention or similar support."[48] The typical career of a female serial killer is longer than that of her male counterpart. Other than women who commit their crimes with others, usually men, female serial killers tend to approach their crimes in a systematic fashion—a characteristic that may explain their longer careers.[49]

Apprehending Serial Killers

Fox and Levin contended that it is extremely difficult to identify and apprehend serial killers because of the cautiousness and skill with which they operate—the very factors that allow them to kill often enough to be labeled *serial killers*. The FBI established the **Violent Criminal Apprehension Program (VICAP)** in 1985 to increase the efficiency and effectiveness of serial killer apprehension. Although Fox and Levin called VICAP an "excellent concept in theory," they noted several practical problems with the program.[50] First, the data complexity and the associated record keeping have limited reporting compliance by law enforcement officials, seriously affecting VICAP's potential usefulness; second, the recognition of patterns among serial killers, even with the assistance of powerful computers, is not easily achieved; and third, VICAP functions more as a detection tool than an apprehension tool.

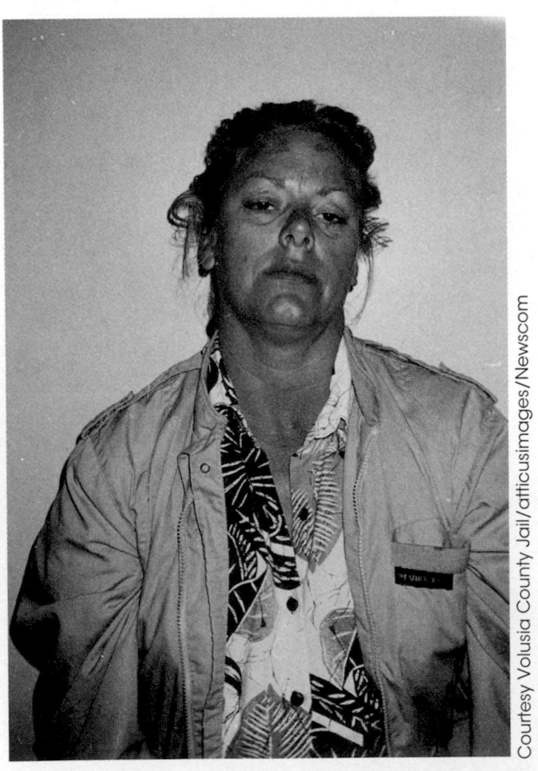

Courtesy Volusia County Jail/atticusimages/Newscom

Serial killer Aileen Wuornos, who was executed by the state of Florida in 2002 after refusing further appeals. Although some women are moving into areas of traditional male criminality, the number of women committing violent crimes is still far smaller than the number of men. How does the criminality of women appear to differ from that of men?

In addition to VICAP, the FBI employs crime analysts who assist local law enforcement. Employing a classification system based on two prongs, FBI analysts distinguish between organized social killers and disorganized asocial killers. Organized social killers have a higher level of intelligence, better social skills, and a greater ability to function in all areas of life than do disorganized killers. These two types also differ in their method of killing—although variation exists among them, the "organized/disorganized continuum is used as an overall guideline for drawing inferences from the crime scene to the behavioral characteristics of the killer."[51] More recent attempts to identify serial killers rely on geomapping techniques to approximate the killer's probable location.[52] Learn more about serial killers from the FBI's Behavioral Analysis Unit via **Web Extra 10–1.**

Mass murder is the illegal killing of three or more individuals at a single time.[53] Mass murder can follow the political motivations of the offenders, as was the case with the 1995 Oklahoma City bombing, in which 168 individuals, including children, were killed. The most notable politically motivated mass murder was the September 11, 2001, destruction of the World Trade Center towers in New York City, in which 2,753 people died.

Other mass murderers kill for more personal reasons. The mass killing of 32 people at the Virginia Polytechnic Institute and State University (Virginia Tech) campus in Blacksburg, Virginia, in 2007 by student gunman Seung-Hui Cho (described in Chapter 6) appears to have been at least partially motivated by a seething anger against those whom Cho perceived as being more successful than he, and the bombings carried out by two Chechen brothers at the 2013 Boston Marathon, in which three people died, was likely politically motivated.[54]

Mass murderers tend to surprise their victims because they often attack in everyday locales that are considered safe and because they erupt spontaneously. In 2012, for example, as described in the Crime in the News box, shooter James E. Holmes opened fire in a crowded movie theater at a midnight showing of the movie *The Dark Knight Rises* in Aurora, Colorado, killing 12 people and injuring 58.[55] Although mass murders do not occur with great frequency, they cause great concern because

CRIME | in the NEWS

Why Mass Shootings Won't Go Away

James Holmes was a 24-year-old graduate student in neuroscience. He had no criminal record, and even though he was a loner, fellow students did not take him as a threat. But after getting a bad grade on a major exam, he dropped out of school, dyed his hair orange, and bought two Glock pistols, a shotgun, and an AR-15—a semiautomatic assault rifle that can fire up to 100 rounds of bullets before reloading.

In Aurora, Colorado, in July 2012, Holmes went to a midnight screening of *The Dark Knight Rises*, the newest Batman movie. He got up on stage and started firing at the audience, killing 12 and injuring 58 more. When apprehended, he told authorities he had been portraying the Joker, Batman's sworn enemy.

A few months later, 20-year-old Adam Lanza, a mentally troubled young man, killed 25 people at an elementary school in Newtown, Connecticut—20 of them children.

Mass shootings show no signs of declining, despite a drop in the U.S. homicide rate. "The frequency of gun violence does not fluctuate much year to year," said James Alan Fox, a criminology professor at Northeastern University. Looking back 35 years, Fox counted 19 such shootings in 1976 and 18 in 2010, with a range of 7 in 1985 to 30 in 2003.

Past incidents reveal a portrait of the mass shooter. He tends to be a young man without friends and recently encountered some humiliation. He's aiming for a high body count. Sometimes he copies another mass shooter or a figure from the movies, as Holmes did. Although many mass shooters are depressed, they rarely suffer psychosis, according to James L. Knoll, a psychiatrist at SUNY Upstate Medical Center.

Little in this portrait, however, can help predict future mass shootings. Mass shooters rarely talk about their exploits in advance. But many of them do undergo a personality change just before their crimes, such as evidenced by Holmes dyeing his hair orange. Larry Burton, a professor at Bryn Mawr College in Pennsylvania, thinks people should notice these changes and report them to authorities.

Other ways to address mass shootings might be to ban assault rifles, which could reduce the carnage, and the imposition of stricter background checks for gun purchases. But a mass shooter, like Holmes, without a criminal record might not be identified and prevented from buying weapons. Fox argues that preventing these calamities is pretty much impossible. "We're not going to turn our country into one big fortress," he said. "People hate it when I say this, but it's true. This kind of tragedy is one of the unfortunate prices we pay for our freedoms."

Discussion Questions

1. Why have random mass shootings become relatively commonplace in American society?
2. What can be done to prevent future incidents of random mass shootings?

Seth K. Hughes/Alamy

The Aurora, Colorado, movie theater where James Holmes killed 12 people and injured 58 others in 2012. How can mass killings be prevented?

Sources: Seth Cline, "Are Mass Shootings a Fact of Life in America?" *US News & World Report*, August 28, 2012, http://www.usnews.com/news/articles/2012/08/28/are-mass-shootings-a-fact-of-life-in-america; Joel Achenbach, "Colorado Shootings Add Chapter to Long, Unpredictable Story of U.S. Mass Murder," *Washington Post*, July 24, 2012, http://www.washingtonpost.com/national/health-science/colorado-shootings-add-chapter-to-long-unpredictable-story-of-us-mass-murder/2012/07/24/gJQAK6Xe7W_story.html; and Nigel Barber, "What We Have Learned about Rampage Killings," *Psychology Today*, July 23, 2012, http://www.psychologytoday.com/blog/the-human-beast/201207/what-we-have-learned-about-rampage-killings.

---

they shatter the sense of safety that characterizes everyday life. Given the number of mass shootings that have occurred over the past few years, however, many schools, hospitals, and businesses across the nation are taking steps to deal with such events.[56]

Fox and Levin offer a four-part typology of mass murder that differentiates these crimes by motive:[57]

- *Revenge* murderers represent the largest category of such killers. They are motivated by *revenge* against either particular individuals or groups of individuals. Other revenge-motivated murderers may be less specific in the selection of a target, as in the case of George Hennard, who hated "all of the residents of the county in which he lived." In 1991, Hennard drove his truck through the front window of Luby's Cafeteria in Killeen, Texas, and then "indiscriminately opened fire on customers as they ate their lunch, killing 23."[58]
- Mass murderers motivated by *love* have a sense of love that is distorted and obsessive. They often commit suicide after they murder, and in the case of a spouse killing, they may also kill their children.
- Mass murderers who kill for *profit* are usually trying to eliminate witnesses in an effort to cover up a major crime.

■ **rape** The penetration, no matter how slight, of the vagina or anus with any body part or object, or oral penetration by a sex organ of another person, without the consent of the victim.

■ **forcible rape** The carnal knowledge of a person forcibly and against his or her will.

- Some mass murderers are motivated by *terror*, such as the individuals who participated in the Charles Manson killings. These people want to send a message to society.

Although most mass murders strike the public as senseless acts of a crazy person, Levin and Fox contend that "most massacres are not madmen."[59] Yet why would a person such as James Huberty, a former security guard, walk calmly into a fast-food restaurant in 1984 and fatally shoot 21 victims at random, most of whom were children? Why would Patrick Edward Purdy shoot and kill 5 children and wound 30 others at Cleveland Elementary School in Stockton, California, in 1989?[60] And what of the motivation of 20-year-old Adam Lanza, who shot and killed 20 children and 6 adults at the Sandy Hook Elementary School in Newton, Connecticut, in 2013? Levin and Fox argue that factors such as frustration, isolation, blame, loss, failure, and other external and internal motivations and situational elements contribute to the activities of mass murderers. They delineate three types of contributing factors: *predisposers*, "long-term and stable preconditions that become incorporated into the personality of the killer," which are nearly always present in his or her biography; *precipitants*, "short-term and acute triggers," that is, catalysts; and *facilitators*, conditions, usually situational, that "increase the likelihood of a violent outburst but are not necessary to produce that response."[61] Using this typology to explain why, for example, most mass murderers are middle-aged, Levin and Fox contend that it takes a long time to accumulate the kind of rage and frustration that sets off some mass murderers. Mass murderers often select targets that have some significance for them, such as workers at a site of former employment. As Fox and Levin state, "A majority of mass killers target victims who are specially chosen, not just in the wrong place at the wrong time. The indiscriminate slaughter of strangers by a 'crazed' killer is the exception to the rule."[62] Unlike serial murderers, mass murderers are relatively easy to apprehend because they rarely leave the scene of the crime, either because they commit suicide after the killing or because they stay long enough to be detected and apprehended.

Rape

In early 2012, Attorney General Eric Holder announced a significant change in the FBI's definition of the word **rape**. The previous definition, which had been used for statistical data-gathering purposes under the Uniform Crime Reporting (UCR) Program for the past 80 years, was not part of any federal statute. It defined rape as "the carnal knowledge of a female forcibly and against her will." Critics charged, however, that the definition was biased in at least three ways because it did not (1) allow for the rape of male victims, (2) count nonvaginal sexual assault as rape, and (3) count rapes that omitted direct physical force. Moreover, the term *carnal knowledge* in the old definition left unclear just what actions were prohibited, although established precedent had generally interpreted the term to mean vaginal penile intrusion.

The new gender-neutral definition, which Holder announced, was approved by FBI Director Robert Mueller and the agency's Criminal Justice Information Services (CJIS) Division's Advisory Policy Board. It reads: "The penetration, no matter how slight, of the vagina or anus with any body part or object, or oral penetration by a sex organ of another person, without the consent of the victim."[63] In keeping with the revised terminology, the CJIS Division of the FBI revised its definition of forcible rape, also making it gender-neutral. Under the FBI's UCR program, the term **forcible rape** now means "the carnal knowledge of a person forcibly and against their will."[64]

UCR/NIBRS statistics on rape, as currently reported, include cases of both rape and attempted rape. Statutory rape (sexual relations between an underage female minor and an adult male) and other sex offenses are excluded from the count of rape crimes. In 2012, 84,376 rapes were reported nationwide under the UCR Program, a slight increase over the previous year. The rate of reported forcible rape was officially put at 53.8 rapes per 100,000 women. As Figure 10–5 shows, the risk of sexual assault victimization for

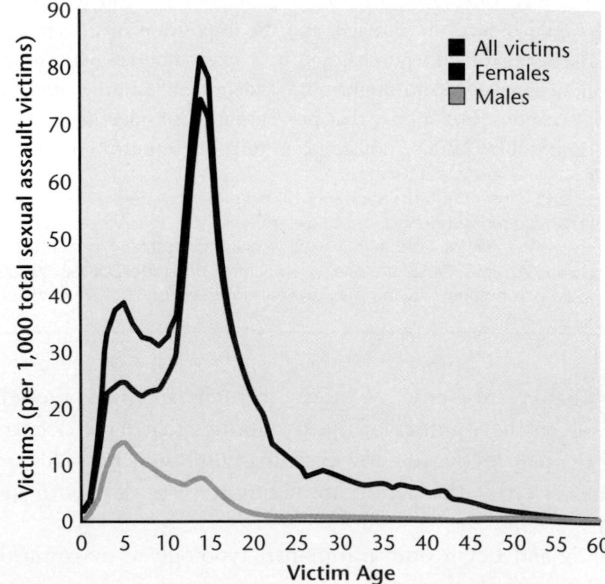

FIGURE 10–5 | Sexual Assault Victimization Rates by Age and Sex

Source: Office of Juvenile Justice and Delinquency Prevention, *Juvenile Offenders and Victims: 2006 National Report* (Washington, DC: OJJDP, 2006), p. 31.

CRIMINAL | PROFILES

Karla Homolka—A Woman Rapist?

On October 17, 1987, then-17-year-old Karla Homolka met then-23-year-old Paul Bernardo in an Ontario hotel restaurant.[i] Their physical attraction was immediate and intense, and two hours later the couple had sex in one of the hotel's rooms.

Unbeknownst to Homolka, the handsome boy-next-door Paul Bernardo had already embarked on a clandestine career as a serial rapist. In May of 1987, Bernardo raped a young woman in Scarborough, a small suburban town northeast of Toronto on the shores of Lake Ontario. Hers was to be the first of at least 14 rapes that the man dubbed the "Scarborough Rapist" would admit to committing during the next five years. Additionally, he was convicted of murdering two of his rape victims.[ii]

As the relationship between Bernardo and Homolka evolved, Bernardo began to assert increasingly outrageous sexual demands with which Homolka willingly complied. Eventually, he expressed his annoyance that she had not been a virgin when he first met her. To resolve the problem, Homolka arranged to present Bernardo her own virgin younger sister, Tammy, as a Christmas gift. On December 23, 1990, then-15-year-old Tammy was fed alcohol laced with the sedative Halcion. When Tammy passed out, Bernardo raped and sodomized her while Homolka kept a drug-laced rag over Tammy's face to maintain her unconscious state. Both Bernardo and Homolka videotaped the rape as it was occurring, including Tammy's death at the end of the incident.[iii]

When Bernardo later complained to Homolka that she had cost him future sexual opportunities with Tammy by allowing her to die, Homolka found a replacement virgin whom she offered to Bernardo as a prewedding gift. Homolka invited a 15-year-old family acquaintance to dinner at the house she had rented with Bernardo. As with Tammy, the girl was fed Halcion until she became unconscious. Bernardo then videotaped Homolka performing sexual acts on the sleeping girl, then raped and brutally sodomized the girl as Homolka videotaped his acts.[iv]

On June 14, 1991, Bernardo abducted 14-year-old Leslie Mahaffy and brought her back to the house he shared with Homolka. After stripping and blindfolding the terrified girl, Bernardo woke his future wife and proceeded to act as a movie director while videotaping Homolka performing lesbian sexual acts on Mahaffy. Homolka then took over the camera while Bernardo initiated a violent assault on the young girl, including brutal anal rape. Bernardo's violence continued to escalate until Mahaffy finally died. The two then dismembered her body and dumped the parts into Lake Ontario.[v]

Bernardo and Homolka married on June 29, 1991, and Bernardo continued his campaign of rape, often with Homolka's encouragement and assistance. At least one victim recalled seeing a woman videotaping her rape.

On April 16, 1992, the married rapists/killers abducted 16-year-old Kristen French from the parking lot outside of French's church. They then raped, tortured, and murdered the pretty young girl and left her nude body in a roadside ditch.

A courtroom sketch of notorious Canadian sex criminal Karla Homolka as she appeared in court in Joliette, Quebec, on June 3, 2005. She was set free after having served 12 years in prison for helping her former husband rape and murder three teenage girls, including her younger sister. Homolka remarried following release and is the mother of a baby boy; she lives under the name Leanne Teale. Why are female sex killers so rare?

DNA evidence finally led to Bernardo's arrest on February 17, 1993. Homolka agreed to testify against him in exchange for a sentence of just 12 years for her role as an accomplice.

In July 1993, Homolka pleaded guilty and her sentence, as agreed to in the plea bargain, was pronounced. Controversy exploded, however, when the numerous videotapes of the rapes and murders surfaced in September 1994, and the public became aware of the full extent of Homolka's willing participation in the atrocities.[vi]

Bernardo was convicted of the two murders on September 15, 1995, and was sentenced to life in prison without possibility of parole. Public ire again boiled over following Homolka's release from prison on parole on July 4, 2005, when it became known that Homolka was complaining about the postrelease restrictions to which she was subjected. In February 2007, the Canadian media reported that Homolka, with a new husband and a new name—Leanne Teale—had given birth to a baby boy.[vii]

The case of Karla Homolka raises a number of interesting questions. Among them are the following:

1. Which of the theories discussed in previous chapters might best explain Homolka's behavior? Would any of them have helped authorities identify Homolka before she could kill again?
2. What motivated Homolka? Did she share the same motivation as her husband, killer Paul Bernardo?

Notes

i. Posted by Her Karma on Vancouver Forum, The Discover Vancouver Bulletin Board, July 3, 2005, http://www.discovervancouver.com/forum/topic.asp?TOPIC_ID521791&whichpage52 (accessed May 28, 2011).
ii. Marilyn Bardsley, "Paul Bernardo and Karla Homolka," CourtTV Crime Library, http://www.crimelibrary.com/serial_killers/notorious/bernardo/index_1.html (accessed May 28, 2007).
iii. Anne M. Griffy, "The Evil Within: The Twisted Minds of Paul Bernardo and Karla Homolka," Justice Junction, http://www.justicejunction.com/judicial_injustice_the_evil within.htm (accessed May 27, 2010).
iv. Ibid.
v. Ibid.
vi. Linda Diebel, "Professor Alan Young on Karla Homolka's Deal," *Toronto Star*, May 28, 2005, http://osgoode.yorku.ca/media2.nsf/83303ffe5af03ed585256ae6005379c9/47f95c9ce0cae5438525701007096ca!OpenDocument (accessed May 28, 2007).
vii. "Victims' Families 'Distressed' over Homolka Baby: Lawyer," CBC News, February 13, 2007, http://www.cbc.ca/canada/montreal/story/2007/02/13/homolka-baby.html (accessed May 28, 2010).

both females and males varies greatly by age. Figure 10–6 details the age at the time of first rape victimization among females.

Reports to the police of the crime of rape rarely reveal its true incidence. In 2011, the National Center for Injury Prevention and Control (a part of the federal Centers for Disease Control and Prevention) released its *National Intimate Partner and Sexual Violence Survey*. Using data from a 2010 survey, the report showed that nearly 1 in 5 women (18.3%) and 1 in 71 men (1.4%) in the United States have been raped at some time in their lives, including completed forced penetration, attempted forced penetration, and alcohol- or drug-facilitated completed penetration. The survey also found that 51.1% of female victims of rape reported being raped by an intimate partner and 40.8% by an acquaintance.[65]

Theoretical Perspectives on Rape

Several theoretical perspectives have been offered to explain what the individual motivations for rape are, why rape is more prevalent in particular contexts, and how certain cultural values may reinforce rape. Many of these perspectives attempt to explain how rape is patterned according to the context, the victim–offender relationship, and the motivations of the rapist.

Feminist Perspectives

There is no single feminist perspective on rape, but some common elements run through the various feminist perspectives (also discussed in Chapter 9). Feminists view gender as a social construct rather than a biological given and regard as problematic the way in which gender is used to structure social relations and institutions. The patriarchal relations and structures within our society contributing to the privileged status of men are inseparable from rape itself because rape serves as a social control mechanism. Rape is viewed as an act of power or domination in which the "tool" used to subordinate is sexual—rape is a crime of violence that is sexual in nature, but this aspect is considered secondary to the power dynamics that occur in rapes.[66]

Socialization patterns, cultural practices, structural arrangements, media images, sexuality norms, and women's status in society all combine to create a rape culture in which both men and women come to view male aggression as normal, even in sexual relations.[67] Within this culture, women are blamed for their own rapes by virtue of the fact that males are naturally incapable of controlling their sexual desire. For feminists like **Catherine MacKinnon**[68] and **Andrea Dworkin**,[69] rape and sex are not easily distinguishable under patriarchy because the male dominance that characterizes patriarchy is inherent in both the act of rape and the social construction of sex. Who women are and what women choose for themselves become problematic in the perspectives of these feminists because heterosexuality is "compulsory" under patriarchy. The views of feminists like MacKinnon and Dworkin are often met with resistance by others and are misunderstood as "male bashing." MacKinnon and Dworkin did not focus on individual males as somehow being either "good" or "bad" but on the construction of gender and all that flows from it under patriarchy. The work of Dworkin, MacKinnon, and others also stressed the existence of a rape culture that has the effect of equating sex with violence and objectifying women to the point that they lack an identity separate from that which is defined by men.

Pornography is often thought to contribute to the manner in which women are objectified because violence and sex are combined in a manner that makes the association normative. In an essay first published in 1974, Robin Morgan asserted that "pornography is the theory, and rape the practice."[70] Susan Brownmiller also discussed both pornography and prostitution as institutions that encourage and support social patterns and responses to rape.[71] Although not everyone shares the same view of the role of pornography in supporting the inequality of women and justifying violence against women, pornography is frequently associated with rape in the writings and research of many prominent feminists.

Pornography and prostitution are institutions that support social patterns and responses to rape.

James W. Messerschmidt acknowledged the positive contributions of feminist thought but critiqued these perspectives for their often one-dimensional view of masculinity.[72] Ngaire Naffine also shared Messerschmidt's positive evaluation of this body of work, saying that "Dworkin is trying to shatter our complacency about everyday life for women, to get us to see the daily criminal violence and injustice done to women that has been rendered utterly ordinary and so invisible."[73] Messerschmidt also contended that the response of the state to violence against women is not monolithic; although there are limits to how the state will respond on behalf of women, the state is viable as a site for positive change in terms of women and feminist ideals, and the emergence of rape crisis centers and changes in institutional protocol regarding rape victims illustrate that a state that is basically patriarchal in nature can be pushed to respond to women in ways that are positive and that increase women's autonomy.

Psychopathological Perspective

The psychopathological perspective on rape is based on two assumptions: (1) Rape is the "result of idiosyncratic mental disease," and (2) "it often includes an uncontrollable sexual

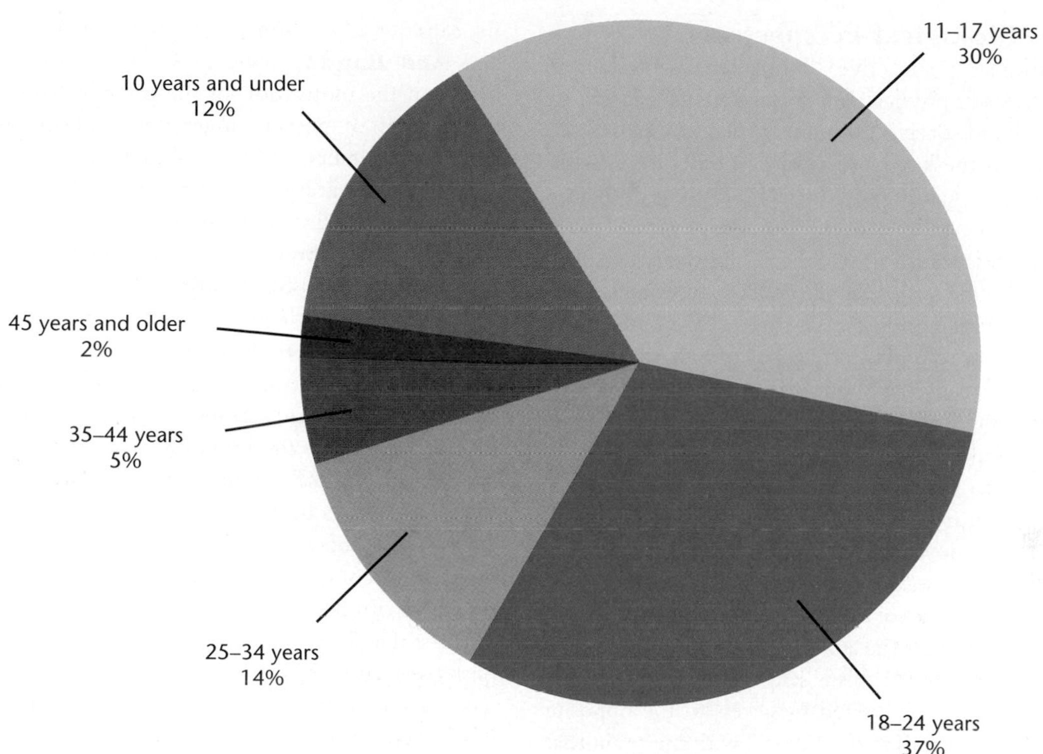

FIGURE 10-6 | **Age at Time of First Completed Rape Victimization among Female Victims**

Source: Centers for Disease Control, National Center for Injury Prevention and Control, *National Intimate Partner and Sexual Violence Survey Factsheet* (Atlanta, GA: Centers for Disease Control and Prevention, National Center for Injury Prevention and Control, November 2011).

impulse."[74] Acknowledgment that rape is connected to issues like power and anger is found in the frequently cited work of **Nicholas Groth**[75] (other works also contained elements of this psychopathological perspective).[76] Some researchers claimed that Groth's model does not appear to successfully characterize the majority of men who rape, yet this model has been applied as if that were the case.[77] However, Russell did find elements of Groth's model to be useful in developing her own typology for men who rape within marriage.[78] Several of the factors that Groth identifies as important to understanding the motivation and pattern of rapes are found in other typologies of rapists.

Integrated Theory of Rape

Larry Baron and **Murray A. Straus** offered what they termed an "integrated theory of rape."[79] They combined elements from other theoretical explanations of rape into one model positing that (1) support for legitimate violence, (2) higher levels of gender inequality, and (3) social disorganization combine to produce higher rates of rape at the state level. The phrase "support for legitimate violence" refers to norms and institutional arrangements that serve to justify the expression of violence in certain contexts as normative.

"Higher levels of gender inequality" are related to rates of rape because as women's status in society improves, rape is challenged as a mechanism of social control over women. This occurs as socialization patterns change and as women attain positions of power within society. The connection between gender inequality and rape is supported in cross-cultural and anthropological research.[80]

The wording "social disorganization" refers to the inability of communities to sustain viable social institutions—institutions that serve as a buffer to all sorts of social ills, including criminal activity. Poverty alone is not enough to directly produce crime, but in the absence of other factors that strengthen institutional structures within communities, poverty is linked to crime by virtue of its association with other factors.

In a test of their theory at the state level, Baron and Straus found support for the direct effect of gender inequality on rape rates: The higher the level of gender inequality—a combination of several measures relating to economic indicators—the higher was a state's rape rate. They examined the direct effect of pornography and found that higher rates of pornography were associated with higher rates of rape within the state; high levels of social disorganization, measured by such things as residential mobility, percentage of female-headed households, and divorce rates, were also tied to increased rates of rape.[81]

Evolutionary/Biological Perspectives

Within the evolutionary perspective, "humanity is a product of evolution in which both physical and social traits conducive to survival are selected and survive through a process of natural selection. Propagation is the key to survival of a trait, as a genetic predisposition can be passed on only through offspring."[82] Natural selection favors those traits that are most adaptive, and over several generations these traits survive. An evolutionary perspective does not identify rape as an adaptation but focuses on certain motives and ends that are conducive to rape. The environment is also thought to play a role because "genes cannot make traits without environmental causes acting in concert."[83] According to **Randy Thornhill** and **Craig T. Palmer**, "Selection favored different traits in females and males, especially when the traits were directly related to mating. Although some of these differences could have arisen from what Darwin called natural selection, most of them are now believed to have evolved through sexual selection."[84] *Sexual selection* refers to the observation that some traits appear to survive not because they are related to survival, but because they further the attainment of mates or defense against competition over mates; this is said to apply primarily to males because "male fitness is limited by access to the opposite sex much more directly than is female fitness, with the result that females compete for mates much less than do males."[85]

The specialized jargon and knowledge that inform evolutionary perspectives make it difficult to understand how they apply to social behaviors like rape, and these perspectives have been severely criticized for justifying rape as "natural." Proponents of the usefulness of evolutionary perspectives on rape contend that evolutionary perspectives can explain why rape is so prevalent and why it takes the forms that it does, arguing that "biology provides understanding, not justification, of human behavior."[86] Evolutionary perspectives contend that the feminist position on rape that equates it primarily with expressions of violence diminishes the fact that there is a biologically based sexual motivation and that ignoring this eliminates one avenue by which rape may be understood and prevented. Rather than being counter to the agenda of feminists, evolutionary psychologists offer their perspective as another avenue through which rape can be approached, understood, and thereby prevented.

Evolutionary perspectives have been criticized for justifying rape as "natural."

Typologies of Rapists

Several researchers have attempted to develop typologies of rapists. Nicholas Groth's work represented one of the first systematic attempts to do this based on empirical evidence, gathered in his capacity as a prison psychologist. **Robert R. Hazelwood** and **Ann Burgess** developed a four-part typology of rapists based on the motivation of the offender and revolving around the themes of power, anger, and sadism:[87] power–assertive, power–reassurance, anger–retaliatory, and anger–excitation.

Based on interviews with 61 serial rapists (all incarcerated in a South Carolina maximum-security prison for the crime of rape), Dennis J. Stevens offered a typology of his own based on motivations. Using Groth's "Protocol for the Clinical Assessment of the Offender's Sexual Behaviors" to structure the interview, Stevens explored the areas of premeditation, victim selection, style of attack, degree of violence associated with the rape, accompanying fantasies, and role of aggression. One of his major findings was the role of lust as a primary motive among a large proportion of the rapists (42%). Although acknowledging that "lust is not a new idea concerning predatory rape," Stevens believes it to be a primary rather than a secondary motive for rapists.[88] A constant theme emerging throughout Stevens's interviews with the rapists was that, for most of them, the amount of force that accompanied the rape was just enough to accomplish the victim's submission, but in cases in which extreme violence accompanied all stages of the rape, the violence would have been present regardless of the level of victim resistance. Therefore, one of the conclusions reached by Stevens is that advocating the idea that women should not resist their attackers is ill-advised.

Another way to approach a typology of men who rape is represented in the work of **Diana Scully**, a professor at Virginia Commonwealth University.[89] Scully's research involved intensive interviews with 114 convicted rapists in seven prisons, all of whom volunteered to be interviewed. Scully rejected the psychopathological perspective on rape and instead employed a feminist sociocultural perspective premised on several assumptions. First, rape is "socially learned behavior," involving "not only behavioral techniques, but also a host of values and beliefs, like rape myths, that are compatible with sexual aggression against women."[90] This premise is based on the assumption that both positive and negative forms of social behavior are learned "socially through direct association with others as well as indirectly through cultural context."[91] Second, Scully viewed rape not as a reflection of pathology but as a reflection of a continuum of normality in which it is important to understand "how sexual violence is made possible in a society [and] what men who rape gain from their sexually violent behavior."[92] Scully thus approached these interviews with convicted rapists from the feminist perspective of wanting to understand the explanations given by the rapists and their sociocultural beliefs about women and sexual violence. Scully identified several patterns in the rationalizations used by men who rape, and she organized these according to two broad types of rapists: admitters and deniers.

■ **acquaintance rape** A rape characterized by a prior social, although not necessarily intimate or familial, relationship between the victim and the perpetrator.

WHO'S TO BLAME—The Individual or Society?

Exotic Dancer Claims Rape

Twenty-one-year-old Carla Maybe-Love called 9-1-1 from her cell phone at 3:00 A.M. on a Sunday morning, telling the 9-1-1 operator who answered that she had just been raped.

"Ma'am, are you injured? Are you in need of immediate medical assistance?" the operator asked.

"No, no, I'm okay," Carla told her.

"Are you safe? Is anyone threatening you? Is anyone there with you?" the operator continued.

"I'm okay. I'm back home. Alone," Carla said.

Carla gave her address, and the operator dispatched a patrol car to the location.

The female officer who arrived encouraged Carla to go with her to the hospital for an examination and for evidence collection. Once Carla had been signed in at the emergency room, the officer took a report of the incident.

Carla described herself as an exotic dancer and for-hire personal companion, who spent her evenings entertaining men of all ages. "I show them a good time," she said, "and there's nothing illegal about that. But that don't give them the right to rape me," she told the officer.

Carla then went on to tell the officer how she had been hired by two men who were attending a local convention to come to their hotel room with a friend and put on a show. "Dancing, that's all we were supposed to do," she said. The men, she said, called a number of their friends into their room to watch the show. At some point, Carla told the officer, she had to go to the bathroom. That's when, she said, a man followed her and pushed her into the small room, locking the door behind them. "That's when it happened," she said. "He put his hand around my throat, and he raped me."

Think about it

1. Assuming that Carla is telling the truth about what happened, how would you explain this crime? That is, why did it happen, and how might it have been prevented?
2. In your opinion, does Carla bear any responsibility for her own victimization? Why or why not?

Note: Who's to Blame boxes provide fictionalized critical thinking opportunities, and are not actual cases.

In the interviews, Scully explored how these two groups could operate from an understanding of reality that justified their behavior and tended to normalize it as well as what they gained from such behavior. Although some of the rapists in the admitter group relied on rape myth ideology, this was a more prevalent pattern among the deniers. The rape myths' definition of a very narrow group of individuals as legitimate rape victims was a common theme in the interviews given by these rapists. Although variations existed, the majority of rapists in both groups expressed little guilt or empathy for their victims. Read more about the violent criminal victimization of women in America via **Library Extras 10–4 and 10–5**.

Rape: A Closer Look

Although rape can occur in almost any social context, certain social situations are characterized by a higher prevalence of rape and by a difference in the offender's motivation.

Acquaintance Rape

The vast majority of rapes occur when the victim and the offender have some prior relationship—although not necessarily an intimate or familial one. Some researchers and activists who work with rape victims have stated that **acquaintance rape** is the most common scenario for rapes. Among adults, acquaintance rape usually occurs within the context of a dating relationship and is sometimes referred to as *date rape*.

Researchers have identified college campuses as places that typically have a high incidence of rape. Societal awareness and concern for rape on college campuses did not emerge until the 1980s. Helping to publicize the problem have been a number of high profile rape cases on college campuses in which the victims not only went public with their experiences, but also grabbed headlines and the covers of major publications such as *Time*, *Newsweek*, and *People*.[93] Media publicity has emphasized the reality of the college setting as a site of rape, and in 1992, the Campus Sexual Assault Victims' Bill of Rights Act became law.[94] It requires campus authorities to "conduct appropriate disciplinary hearings, treat sexual assault victims and defendants with respect, making their rights and legal options clear, and cooperate with them in fully exercising those rights."[95]

A great deal of the research on rape in college settings has focused on identifying the unique factors of campus life that

■ **spousal rape** A rape of one spouse by the other. The term usually refers to the rape of a woman by her husband.

may be conducive to rape. Some researchers contend that college fraternities "create a sociocultural context in which the use of coercion in sexual relations with women is normative and in which the mechanisms to keep this pattern of behavior in check are minimal at best and absent at worst."[96] The increased awareness of campus rape has led to the development of services and programs that assist victims of sexual violence and present information that challenges rape myths.

Spousal Rape

Until the 1970s, under common law, a legally married husband could not be charged with raping his wife. Rape, as research indicates, happens to many women within marriage as part of a practice of *spousal abuse* that may involve beatings and other violence. Until 1976, **spousal rape** could not be prosecuted in any state. Today, it is illegal in every state in the United States.

The first researcher to systematically examine spousal rape was **Diana E. H. Russell**. Based on an analysis of interview data, Russell developed a four-part typology of men who rape their wives:

- Husbands who prefer raping their wives to having consensual sex with them
- Husbands who are able to enjoy both rape and consensual sex with their wives or who are indifferent to which it is
- Husbands who would prefer consensual sex with their wives but are willing to rape them when their sexual advances are refused
- Husbands who might like to rape their wives but do not act out these desires

Thus, rather than being one-dimensional, rape within marriage has several forms that reflect various motivational nuances on the part of offenders.

Rape in Prison

Prison rape, which is generally considered to involve physical assault, represents a special category of sexual victimization behind bars. In 2003, Congress mandated the collection of statistics on prison rape as part of the Prison Rape Elimination Act (PREA).[97] The purposes of the PREA are to[98]

- Establish a zero-tolerance standard for prison rape.
- Make prison rape prevention a top priority in correctional facilities and systems.
- Develop and implement national standards for the detection, prevention, reduction, and punishment of prison rape.
- Increase the availability of information on the incidence and prevalence of prison rape.
- Increase the accountability of corrections officials with regard to the issue of sexual violence in U.S. prisons.

The PREA requires the Bureau of Justice Statistics (BJS) to collect data in federal and state prisons, county and city jails, and juvenile institutions, with the U.S. Census Bureau acting as the official repository for collected data.

In 2013, the BJS published the results of its third annual national inmate survey (NIS).[99] The survey was conducted in 233 state and federal prisons, 358 local jails, and 15 special confinement facilities operated by Immigration and Customs Enforcement (ICE). A total of 92,449 inmates participated. The survey was also administered to 527 juveniles ages 16 to 17 held in state prisons and 1,211 juveniles of the same age held in local jails. Among the findings:

- An estimated 4.0% of state and federal prison inmates and 3.2% of jail inmates reported experiencing one or more incidents of sexual victimization by another inmate or facility staff in the past 12 months.
- Among state and federal prison inmates, 2.0% (or an estimated 29,300 prisoners) reported an incident involving another inmate, 2.4% (34,100) reported an incident involving facility staff, and 0.4% (5,500) reported both an incident by another inmate and staff.
- About 1.6% of jail inmates (11,900) reported an incident with another inmate, 1.8% (13,200) reported an incident with staff, and 0.2% (2,400) reported both an incident by another inmate and staff.
- An estimated 1.8% of juveniles ages 16 to 17 held in adult prisons and jails reported being victimized by another inmate, compared to 2.0% of adults in prisons and 1.6% of adults in jails; an estimated 3.2% of juveniles ages 16 to 17 held in adult prisons and jails reported experiencing staff sexual misconduct.
- Inmates who reported their sexual orientation as gay, lesbian, bisexual, or other were among those with the highest rates of sexual victimization. Among non-heterosexual inmates, 12.2% of prisoners and 8.5% of jail inmates reported being sexually victimized by another inmate; 5.4% of prisoners and 4.3% of jail inmates reported being victimized by staff.

PREA surveys are only a first step in understanding and eliminating prison rape. As the BJS notes, "Due to fear of reprisal from perpetrators, a code of silence among inmates, personal embarrassment, and lack of trust in staff, victims are often reluctant to report incidents to correctional authorities."[100]

Lee H. Bowker, a criminologist who specializes in studying life inside prisons, summarizes studies of sexual violence in prison with the following observations:[101]

- Most sexual aggressors do not consider themselves homosexuals.
- Sexual release is not the primary motivation for sexual attack.

■ **child sexual abuse (CSA)** A term encompassing a variety of criminal and civil offenses in which an adult engages in sexual activity with a minor, exploits a minor for purposes of sexual gratification, or exploits a minor sexually for purposes of profit.

- Many aggressors must continue to participate in gang rapes to avoid becoming victims themselves.
- The aggressors have themselves suffered much damage to their masculinity in the past.

As in cases of heterosexual rape, sexual assaults in prison are likely to leave psychological scars on the victim long after the physical event is over.[102] Victims of prison rape live in fear, may feel constantly threatened, and can turn to self-destructive activities.[103] Many victims question their masculinity and undergo a personal devaluation.

Child Sexual Abuse

Child sexual abuse (CSA) is a term encompassing a variety of criminal and civil offenses in which an adult engages in sexual activity with a minor, exploits a minor for purposes of sexual gratification, or exploits a minor sexually for purposes of profit. The term includes a variety of activities and motivations, including child molestation, child sexual exploitation (CSE), and the commercial sexual exploitation of children (CSEC).

The National Institute of Justice (NIJ) observes that "few criminal offenses are more despised than the sexual abuse of children, and few are so little understood in terms of incidence (the number of offenses committed), prevalence (the proportion of the population who commit offenses), and reoffense risk."[104]

The NIJ also notes that sexual offenses are more likely than other types of criminal conduct to elude the attention of the criminal justice system. Self-reports from both sex offenders and sexually abused children reveal far more abuse than officially reported.[105] The Child Molestation Research and Prevention Institute, based in Atlanta, Georgia, estimates that at least two out of every ten girls and one out of every ten boys have been sexually abused by the time they turn 14.[106]

Self-reports from both sex offenders and sexually abused children reveal far more abuse than officially reported.

One of the most informative offender self-report studies on the adult sexual victimization of children comes from research conducted slightly more than two decades ago.[107] In that study, investigators recruited 561 adult subjects who engaged in what the researchers described as "child-focused sexual behavior." The subjects, who were guaranteed anonymity, were recruited through health care workers, media advertising, presentations at

U.S. Department of Justice–Office of Justice Programs

The home page of the U.S. Department of Justice's National Sex Offender Public Registry at www.nsopr.gov. Community notification laws frequently result in the posting of online offender databases. How do such databases help victims?

meetings, and in other ways. All were free from confinement at the time of the interviews. The 561 adults interviewed reported a total of 291,737 "paraphiliac acts" over the course of their adult lives committed against 195,407 victims under the age of 18. The results of this study make it clear that in cases of CSA, a relatively small number of offenders can commit a large number of crimes.

Types of Child Sex Abusers

Almost all pedophiles are male, with one study of more than 4,400 offenders finding fewer than 0.5% of convicted child sex offenses committed by females.[108] Other than that, little can be said about similarities among child sexual abusers. As individuals, they tend to be highly dissimilar from one another in terms of personal characteristics, life experiences, and criminal histories. No single "molester profile" exists.[109] Child molesters appear to arrive at deviancy via multiple pathways and engage in many different sexual and nonsexual "acting-out" behaviors. Figure 10–7 shows the number of registered predatory child sex offenders by state.

In 1983, Nicholas Groth and his associates proposed a simple two-part distinction among pedophiles whereby offenders were classified as either "regressed" or "fixated."[110] Regressed offenders, said Groth, are attracted sexually primarily to members of their own age groups but are passively aroused by minors. Generally speaking, the use of alcohol, drugs, or other inhibition-lowering substances, combined with social circumstances

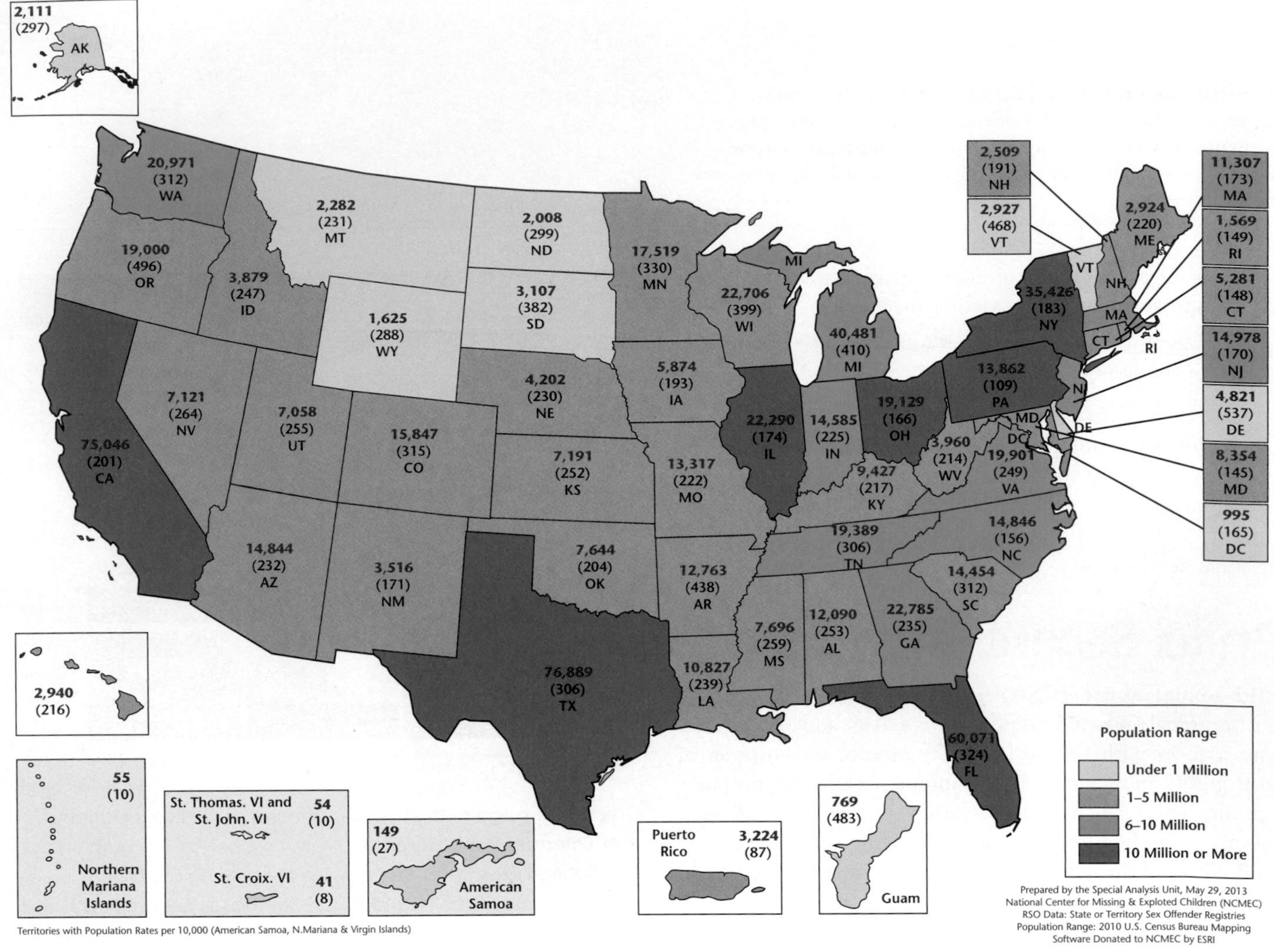

FIGURE 10-7 | **Registered Sex Offenders by State**

Source: National Center for Missing & Exploited Children, http://www.missingkids.com. Reprinted with permission.

providing opportunity, can cause the regressed offender to act out his or her interest in having sexual encounters with children. Fixated offenders, said Groth, are adult pedophiles who engage in planned sexual acts with children and whose behavior is not necessarily influenced by drugs or alcohol.

A U.S. Department of Justice publication representing a compilation of studies produced by the NIJ shows that most victims of childhood sexual abuse do not go on to become child molesters.[111] However, the NIJ points out that sexual victimization as a child, if accompanied by other factors—such as the co-occurrence of physical and verbal abuse—may contribute to the child-victim's development as a perpetrator of CSA later in life. Similarly, says the NIJ, social competence deficits are significant in child molestation, but an individual's inadequate social and interpersonal skills do not, by themselves, make his or her sexual abuse of children inevitable.

Some evidence exists to suggest that child molestation may be related to an offender's restaging of his or her own childhood sexual victimization.[112] Tests of the restaging theory on a sample of 131 rapists and child molesters revealed that child molesters who committed their first assault when they were 14 or younger were sexually victimized at a younger age than offenders who committed their first assault in adulthood; they also experienced more severe sexual abuse than offenders with adult onset of sexual aggression.[113]

Some evidence exists to suggest that child molestation may be related to an offender's restaging of his or her own childhood sexual victimization.

Nonetheless, sexual victimization alone is unable to fully explain child molestation. Studies show that most victims of childhood sexual abuse do not go on to become perpetrators.[114] As is true for other kinds of maltreatment, childhood sexual victimization may be one critical element in the presence or absence of a variety of other factors (for example, co-occurrence of other types of abuse, availability of supportive caregivers, ego strength of child-victim at the time of abuse, and availability of treatment), all of which appear to moderate the likelihood of becoming a child molester.

Not all adults involved in the sexual abuse of children pursue personal sexual gratification. Some have a profit motive, as is the case in instances of *commercial sexual exploitation of children*, or CSEC. CSEC refers to all offenses in

■ **child pornography** A visual representation of any kind that depicts a minor engaging in sexually explicit conduct that is obscene and that lacks serious literary, artistic, political, or scientific value.

which an adult victimizes a child sexually for profit, including the prostituting of a child and creating or trafficking in child pornography.

Awareness of **child pornography** exploded onto the American scene in the 1990s, as the advent of rapid transmission of high-quality images and video became possible through the growth of the Internet. Child pornography can be defined as a visual representation of any kind that depicts a minor engaging in sexually explicit conduct that is obscene and that lacks serious literary, artistic, political, or scientific value.

The Internet created special problems in enforcement of the laws designed to control pedophiles and child pornographers. Because it is an international medium, the Internet is hard to police, and activities through which information on the Internet is transmitted may be illegal in one jurisdiction and not so in another. Similarly, the relative anonymity of buyers and sellers of child pornography over the Internet provides both a sense of security and impersonality to those involved in such transactions.

According to the United Nations Children's Fund (UNICEF), tens of thousands of children in the United States and tens of millions of children worldwide are involved in CSEC.[115] UNICEF says the number of sexually exploited children worldwide may exceed 100 million, not all of whom are located in "poor" or "developing" countries.

Read a comprehensive report on the commercial sexual exploitation of children in the United States, Canada, and Mexico via **Library Extra 10–6**.

Robbery

In 2010, 31-year-old Indiana resident Brian Kendrick was convicted of shooting a pregnant Indianapolis bank teller named Katherine Shuffield in the abdomen during a robbery that took place in 2008.[116] The shooting, which critically injured Shuffield, resulted in the deaths of twin girls that she was carrying. Kendrick was convicted of attempted murder, robbery, feticide, and illegal possession

TABLE 10-1 Hypothetical Profiles of Child Sex Predators

	INTERPERSONAL	NARCISSISTIC	EXPLOITATIVE	MUTED SADISTIC	NONSADISTIC AGGRESSIVE	SADISTIC
Amount of Contact with Children	High	High	Low	Low	Low	Low
Sexual Acts	Fondling, caressing, frottage (nonphallic sex)	Phallic nonsadistic sex	Phallic nonsadistic sex	Sodomy, "sham" sadism[a]	Phallic nonsadistic sex	Sadism
Relationship of Offender to Victim	Known	Known or stranger	Stranger	Stranger	Stranger	Stranger
Amount of Physical Injury to Victim	Low	Low	Instrumental[b]	Instrumental	High	High
Amount of Planning in Offenses	High[c]	Moderate	Low	Moderate	Low	High

[a]"Sham" sadism implies behaviors or reported fantasies that reflect sadism without the high victim injury present in the sadistic type.

[b]Instrumental aggression implies only enough force to gain victim compliance.

[c]Interpersonal types know their victims and may spend a considerable amount of time "grooming" them (setting them up), but the offenses often appear to be unplanned or spontaneous.

Source: Adapted from Robert A. Prentky, Raymond A. Knight, and Austin F. S. Lee, *Child Sexual Molestation: Research Issues* (Washington, DC: National Institute of Justice, 1997).

■ **personal robbery** A robbery that occurs on a highway or a street or in a public place (also called a *mugging*) or a robbery that occurs in a residence.

■ **institutional robbery** A robbery that occurs in a commercial setting, such as a convenience store, gas station, or bank.

of a handgun and was sentenced to 53 years in prison. At sentencing, Shuffield told the court about the sorrow she felt at the loss of her daughters-to-be: "We will never hear them laugh," she said, "or speak their first words or take their first steps." Kendrick could have received a sentence of up to 87 years in prison.

Robbery is classified as a violent crime because it involves the threat or use of force, but it also involves a property component because its express purpose is to take the property of another.[117] Robberies can occur in different locations and are quite often categorized in this manner by both law enforcement agencies and social science researchers. Robberies that occur on the highway or street are often referred to as highway robberies or muggings; muggings and robberies that occur in residences are types of **personal robbery**. Although residential robberies are certainly deterred by the presence of security precautions, the effectiveness of deterrents depends on the type of neighborhood in which the residence is located. Terance D. Miethe and David McDowall found that security precautions that tend to be effective in neighborhoods characterized by a viable social control structure are ineffective in socially disorganized neighborhoods.[118] Security precautions, such as not leaving the home unoccupied, are not enough in socially disorganized neighborhoods to compensate for the strong effect that neighborhood context has on increasing the likelihood of robbery. Homes and persons do not exist as potential targets for motivated offenders in a vacuum but appear as more or less attractive targets based on their perceived vulnerability and the social context of the surrounding neighborhood in which they are found. The FBI reported that an estimated 354,520 robberies occurred in 2012.

Robbery is classified as a violent crime because it involves the threat or use of force.

Robberies that occur in commercial settings (Figure 10–8), such as convenience stores, gas stations, and banks, are **institutional robberies**.[119] Several research studies have found that institutional robberies may be prevented through environmental and policy changes. Scott A. Hendricks and his colleagues found in a study of convenience store robberies that "the robber chooses a target based on various situational crime prevention factors";[120] these factors include staffing, hours of

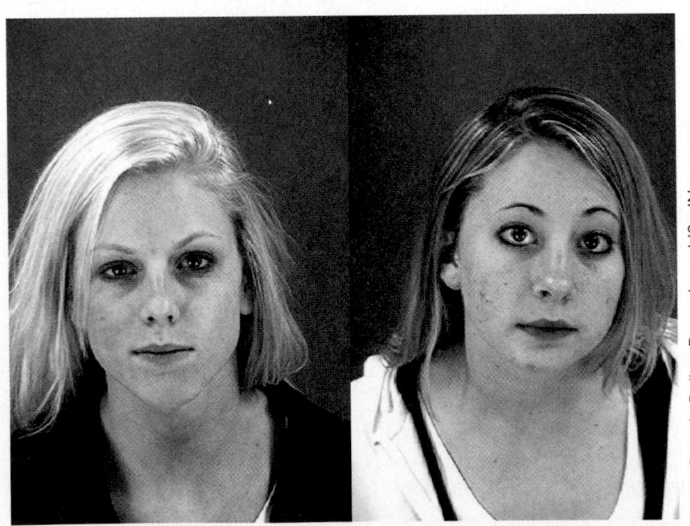

Cobb County Police Department/Sp/Newscom

Mug shots showing Ashley Nicole Miller (left) and Heather Lyn Johnston (right), both 19-years-old. The pair robbed a bank located in a grocery store in Acworth, Georgia, in 2007. Cameras caught the fashionably dressed unarmed teenagers smiling and giggling as they produced a holdup note and were handed money. Some news outlets were quick to christen the pair the "Barbie Bandits." It was later discovered that the robbery was an inside job aided by Benny Herman Allen, a 22-year-old bank employee. Why are female bank robbers the exception rather than the rule?

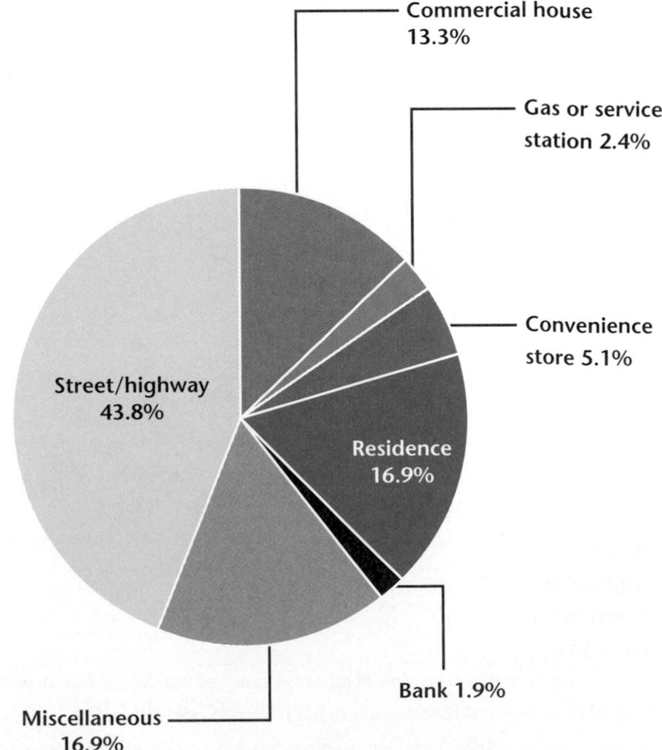

FIGURE 10–8 Robbery Locations

Source: Federal Bureau of Investigation, *Crime in the United States, 2012* (Washington, DC: FBI, 2013).

operation, cash-handling policies, and characteristics of the surrounding neighborhood. Many of the precautions that lower the risk of robbery are costly, so not all businesses can afford them. As Richard T. Wright and Scott H. Decker noted, "This puts businesses located in high-crime neighborhoods in a no-win situation because their clientele frequently are too poor to bear increased prices to support crime prevention measures."[121] Additionally, if the business fails as a result of robberies, the community loses again because the exodus of businesses that are forced to relocate makes the community less viable. Most of the robbers interviewed by Wright and Decker in their ethnographic study of robbers who selected commercial targets generally selected liquor stores, taverns, and pawnshops, because of the large amount of cash available, and targeted businesses with low levels of customer activity, because they viewed customers as an unpredictable risk factor. The robbers interviewed as part of Floyd Feeney's research in California during the 1970s reported very little planning overall, but those who engaged in commercial robbery were much more likely to report planning than those who engaged in personal robberies (60% compared with 30%).[122]

The Lethal Potential of Robbery

Robbery carries the threat of injury—often lethal injury—for the victim. Reported injuries were found among one in every three robbery victims whose data were entered into the NIBRS.[123] Robbery provides the context for 6% of all homicides annually. Approximately 15% of all homicides occur during the commission of another felony, and among these cases, robbery is the most likely felony to result in homicide, accounting for almost one-half (42%) of all felony murders.[124] The weapon most often used in robbery homicides is a firearm, accounting for 42% of all cases; the type of firearm used in the vast majority of these cases (85%) is a handgun.[125] See **Library Extra 10–7**.

Criminal Careers of Robbers

Are robbers specialists (specialize in only robbery) or generalists (vary the types of crimes they commit)? The majority of robbery offenders are generalists who have fairly lengthy but varied criminal careers.[126] Research on a sample of inmates in California prisons found that less than 10% of convicted robbers could be labeled specialists who engaged solely in robbery to the exclusion of other offenses;[127] in a survey of inmates sponsored by RAND Corporation, approximately 18% of offenders were primarily involved in only one type of offense.[128] Diversity in offense type appears to be the norm for the vast majority of offenders, based on both ethnographic and survey data.

The majority of robbers are generalists who have fairly lengthy but varied criminal careers.

Robbery and Public Transportation

One setting in which crime-prevention strategies can be quite effective is public transportation. According to Martha J. Smith and Ronald V. Clarke, "Robbery on mass transit is a rare event, even in systems with relatively high numbers of incidents such as New York City."[129] Viewing instances of robbery on public transportation as reflecting a "lack of supervision," Smith and Clarke contended that the majority of these robberies follow one of three scenarios: (1) Offenders purposefully select their victims from among passengers in isolated areas of large subway stations, especially when the station is not crowded, meaning that security measures (such as using closed-circuit television and closing off unused parts of the station) may serve to effectively deter these offenders;[130] (2) offenders select their victims outside the station at particular locales and times that are relatively isolated; and (3) offenders act on opportunity and often lie in wait for passengers leaving public transportation.[131] Prevention strategies to deter these types of robberies include a variety of surveillance techniques. In addition to targeting public transportation customers, robbers also target the staff in order to steal the fare money; Smith and Clarke stated that policies such as exact fare and other similar changes "led to a dramatic fall in the number of bus robberies in New York City."[132]

According to Smith and Clarke, "Transit workers with perhaps the greatest risk of robbery are taxicab drivers, who carry cash, travel by themselves around cities with strangers, and do not choose their destinations."[133] Derek Cornish offered several strategies, ranging from having a weapon to screening passengers for potential threats, that taxicab drivers can use to prevent robberies.[134] Although "drivers can use informal passenger screening practices such as refusing to pick up fares at certain locations," such screening practices "can discriminate against those who live in poorer areas or are from certain racial or age groups, making it difficult for them to use the service."[135] These very practices have recently been the subject of debate because of claims of discrimination.

Other strategies, such as the installation of protection partitions between the driver and passenger, can be quite effective in deterring crime. Under the New York City Police Department's special Taxi-Livery Task Force, created in 1992, police in unmarked cars stop taxis in particular neighborhoods, often according to some strategy such as every fifth taxi. A similar strategy was also adopted in Boston, again as a response to the substantial number of violent crimes (especially robberies) experienced by cab drivers. Whereas the Boston statute withstood court review, the New York Court of Appeals ruled in December 1999 that the policy of the police department "gave officers too much discretion to stop taxis carrying passengers when they had no reason to suspect any crime was afoot."[136] The U.S. Supreme Court was asked to review both rulings and declined, allowing the rulings of the lower courts to stand. Policies like those in New York and Boston clearly illustrate the tension involved in policing a democratic society; measures that might prevent certain forms of crime must be weighed against the potential violation of individual liberties.

The Motivation of Robbers

Research tends to support the idea that most robberies, of both people and places, involve very little planning on the part of the offender. Floyd Feeney's research in California during the early 1970s found little evidence that the majority of bank robbers had even been in the bank before the robbery.[137] Most of the robbers Feeney studied did very little planning, no matter what the target, and the planning that did occur was minor and "generally took place the same day as the robbery and frequently within a few hours of it."[138] The motivation and decision making of street robbers were evaluated in a series of research studies conducted by Bruce A. Jacobs, Richard Wright, and others at the University of Missouri at St. Louis involving 86 active robbers in St. Louis. Jacobs and Wright found that the decision to offend occurs as part of ongoing social action that is "mediated by prevailing situations and subcultural conditions."[139] Fast cash was the direct need that robbery satisfied, but this need can be properly understood only against the backdrop of street culture. Jacobs and Wright hypothesized that street culture was the intervening force that connected background factors (such as low self-esteem, deviant peer relations, and weak social bonds) to the motivation to offend, and they found that the majority of robbers gave little thought to planning robberies until they found themselves needing money. For less than half the robbers, the financial need was for basic necessities; mostly, it was connected to a fairly hedonistic lifestyle.

Jacobs and Wright considered three alternatives that these individuals could have employed for money: (1) performing legitimate work, (2) borrowing, and (3) committing other crimes. Legitimate employment was not a viable option for these individuals for several reasons. Most of the robbers had neither the skills nor the education to obtain decent-wage jobs, and even if they did have such resources, their perceived need for cash was too immediate for legitimate work to satisfy; additionally, legitimate work was viewed as an impediment to their lifestyle of "every night is a Saturday night." Borrowing money was not a viable route because many had no one to turn to for a loan, and for those who did, borrowing was not part of the self-sufficient code of the streets. Robbery was preferable to committing other crimes because it was perceived to be safer than burglary and quicker than fencing stolen goods. Other research has found that some robberies do begin as another crime, such as burglary, and become robberies more by accident than design.[140] Jacobs and Wright concluded that the economic motivation behind robbery should not be interpreted as "genuine financial hardship" but as an ongoing crisis situation experienced as a result of the logic of the street context of robbers' daily lives.[141] For the individuals whom Jacobs and Wright interviewed, "being a

Ed Bailey/Associated Press

A possible robbery victim. Some robbers seem to give little thought to planning their crimes until they need fast cash. Why might this person be an attractive target for such robbers?

street robber . . . is a way of behaving, a way of thinking, an approach to life."[142] Such individuals are unlikely to be easily deterred by legal sanctions, and the rationality of their decision making is unlikely to be adequately explained outside the context of their street culture.

> Being a street robber is a way of behaving, a way of thinking, an approach to life.

In 2006, Trevor Bennett and Fiona Brookman interviewed 120 English robbery offenders in a study funded by Britain's Economic and Social Research Council (ESRC).[143] Bennett and Brookman found that financial gain was only one of many motivations reported by robbers. Others included having a "sheer desire to fight," desiring to set right a perceived injustice, enhancing one's street credibility, and doing it "just for kicks." Some offenders participating in the study had been arrested as many as 50 times and reported that they were addicted to robbery. One told the researchers, "I was more addicted to robbing than I was to drugs" (drug connections were mentioned in 60% of all robberies studied).

Drug Robberies

In their ethnographic research on armed robbers, Richard T. Wright and Scott H. Decker found that "six out of every ten offenders who specialized in street robbery—forty-three of seventy-three—said that they usually preyed on individuals who themselves were involved in lawbreaking."[144] These are generally not reflected in official statistics on crime because the victims do not report their victimization to the police due to their own illegal behavior, so they can be victimized with relative impunity. Because the overriding motivation behind the robberies for many offenders in Wright and Decker's research was to get high, it follows that drug dealers would be an obvious target. Among offenders who stated that they selected victims involved in crime, the vast majority targeted drug dealers, although rarely major drug dealers. "Almost all of these offenders targeted young, street-level dealers who sold quantities of crack cocaine directly to consumers."[145] According to one robber, the attraction of robbing drug dealers was twofold: "It satisfies two things for me; my thirst for drugs and the financial aspect."[146] The neighborhoods in which these robbers lived and conducted their routine activities were generally characterized by an abundance of drug dealers, which increased their suitability as targets. Because they were also unlikely to report their victimization to the police, drug customers were perceived as ideal targets. Additionally, offenders were well aware that the police did not take drug robberies seriously. However, these factors do not consider the one element that makes robbing drug dealers very risky: "There always is a possibility of violent retaliation."[147]

Further analysis of the ethnographic research on the armed robbers in St. Louis by Bruce A. Jacobs, Volkan Topalli, and Richard Wright explored the issue of retaliation by asking, "Why should offenders elect to reduce their chances of getting arrested at the cost of increasing their odds of being killed?"[148] To answer this, the researchers looked at the findings from 25 in-depth interviews with active drug robbers conducted as part of the larger study of robbers in St. Louis. The researchers conceptualized retaliation as an informal sanction "capable of deterrence in its own right; to be sure, it may be the sole sanction offenders face."[149] Drug dealers who are victimized are cut off from one avenue of redress, the formal sanctions provided by police, and "have a strong incentive to retaliate."[150]

The drug robbers interviewed in the St. Louis study were completely aware of the risk involved in targeting drug dealers and sought to minimize it by selecting one of three strategies: intimidation, anonymity, or hypervigilance. Drug robbers primarily targeted dealers "whose retributive potential was weak."[151] Some of the offenders stated that "some street corner dealers simply dismissed robberies as an occupational hazard and accepted their losses with equanimity."[152]

The second strategy used by robbers who targeted drug dealers, anonymity, involved robbing only those dealers with whom they were totally unfamiliar so that "retaliation becomes moot" because the victim does not know the robber.[153] Hypervigilance, the third strategy, refers to how offenders consciously "devoted a significant portion of their day-to-day cognitive resources to minimizing the prospect of postoffense victim contact."[154] For offenders engaged in a substantial volume of robberies, the chances of running into a victim were increased even if the victim was initially unknown to them, so offenders avoided the sites of previous robberies until they could be fairly sure that the threat of recognition or retaliation had subsided, and the nomadic lifestyle of drug robbers allowed them to easily do this.

Circumstances and situations bring offenders and victims together in unexpected ways—"the more members of a network there are, and the denser that network is, the more likely run-ins become. Bus stops, mini-malls, grocery stores, bars, theaters, and fast-food restaurants emerge as contexts fraught with potential risk."[155] This not only hinders the offender's ability to manage the risk of retaliation but also increases the potential for violence within the entire community itself, based on the extent of drug robberies. Jacobs and his colleagues concluded that this community effect represents the "contagion-like processes through which violence is contracted and contained," and if "street justice" is stronger than the formal justice represented by law enforcement, the community becomes increasingly unstable.[156] They explained, "The more entrenched informal justice becomes, and the more likely formal authorities will 'look the other way,'" the more the community becomes disorganized

■ **aggravated assault** The unlawful, intentional inflicting, or attempted or threatened inflicting, of serious injury upon the person of another.

and violence spreads beyond robbers and their victims.[157] This becomes one set of dynamics that creates and sustains the "tangled web of violence we see in so many high-crime urban locales across the country."[158]

The Gendered Nature of Robbery

According to researcher **Jody Miller**, "With the exception of forcible rape, robbery is perhaps the most gender differentiated serious crime in the United States."[159] Women represent robbery offenders in approximately 11% of all incidents.[160] Miller's research goal was to assess the extent to which gender impacts robbery offending, so she analyzed a subset of the interviews with active robbers from the research data used by Jacobs and Wright consisting of 37 robbers, 14 women and 23 men. The two groups were matched on current age and age at first robbery. In her examination of motivations for robbery, Miller found that economic incentives were the primary motivation for both men and women but that there were significant differences in the way in which men and women carried out street robberies. Men exhibited a fairly uniform pattern. Their robberies were characterized by "using physical violence and/or a gun placed on or at close proximity to the victim in a confrontational manner";[161] the presence of a gun was almost a constant in robberies conducted by men. While perceiving women to be easier targets, male robbers tended to rob other men rather than women because of another perception—that men tended to carry more money. The majority of males targeted as victims were those involved in "street life."

With the exception of forcible rape, robbery is the most gender differentiated serious crime in the United States.

Female robbers tended to fall into one of three patterns. The robbery of other women in a "physically confrontational manner" was the most prevalent way in which female robbers worked, but they also used their sexuality to attract male victims and acted as accomplices to male robbers in offenses against other men.[162] Except when they were robbing men, female robbers generally did not use guns. Although similar cultural and structural forces can drive men and women to offend in the same way, gender continues to exert an influence on shaping the nature of robbery incidents. Learn more about the crime of robbery at **Web Extra 10–2.**

Aggravated Assault

On Christmas Eve, 2011, Jacquetta Simmons, 26, a Batavia, New York, resident was arrested after she punched a Walmart female greeter in the face and knocked her down, resulting in fractures to her facial bones.[163] The greeter had asked Simmons to see receipts for items she was carrying before she hit the greeter and ran out of the store. Employees and customers gave chase and held Simmons until police arrived. A state police spokesperson later told reporters that Simmons, who was charged with two counts of assault, had store receipts for everything in her possession.

There are two types of assault: simple and aggravated. **Aggravated assault**, which the FBI defines as "the unlawful attack by one person upon another wherein the offender uses a weapon or displays it in a threatening manner, or the victim suffers obvious or severe bodily injury,"[164] is the more serious type of assault and the one that concerns us here. According to the FBI, 760,739 aggravated assaults were reported to police agencies across the nation in 2012, producing an aggravated assault rate of 242.3 for every 100,000 people in the country.

The profile of a typical offender in aggravated assault mirrors that of homicide, with disproportionate involvement of males, African Americans, 15- to 34-year-olds, those of lower socioeconomic status, those with prior arrest records, and offenders demonstrating little evidence of offense specialization.[165] Also consistent with most homicides, aggravated assaults are "spontaneous, triggered by a trivial altercation or argument that quickly escalates in the heat of passion."[166]

Based on statistics from the National Crime Victimization Survey (NCVS), which tallies simple as well as aggravated assault, the majority of assaults reported by victims to NCVS interviewers are simple rather than aggravated assault. According to the NCVS, the overall decline in the nation's crime rate between 1993 and 2012 was mostly due to decreases in the rate of simple assault.

Aggravated assaults are distinguished according to those involving injury and those not involving injury. The victims and offenders in aggravated assault are, for the most part, equally likely to be strangers or nonstrangers to each other. When you look at the gender of the victim, a pattern emerges. A slight majority of male victims are assaulted by a stranger, whereas slightly more than one-third (39%) of female victims are assaulted by a stranger in aggravated assaults. Simple assaults, by contrast, are more likely to involve nonstrangers (58%).

Almost one-half (47%) of male victims are assaulted by nonstrangers, whereas 71% of female victims are assaulted by nonstrangers in these cases. Whether it is an aggravated or simple assault, the largest category of nonstranger offenders of female victims is represented by friends and acquaintances followed by intimate partners. Weapons are present in less than one-fourth (23%) of all assaults, and when a weapon is present, it is most likely to be something other than a gun or a knife.[167]

Stranger Assault

The possibility of stranger violence elicits a great deal of fear and concern among most members of the population. But based on research using victimization data in both the United States and Great Britain, "the probability of suffering a serious personal crime by strangers is very low,"[168] with this likelihood varying by demographic characteristics such as gender, age, marital status, and lifestyle. For example, individuals who have an active social life away from home and in the evening are far more likely to be victimized by strangers, but this effect depends very much on the community context in which the individuals engage in their leisure pursuits.

Assault within Families

As the statistics from several sources reveal, the majority of assaults involve victims and offenders who are known to each other, quite often in a familial or an intimate relationship. In the sections that follow, the familial context of assault is examined, with a special emphasis on how key variables like weapons and alcohol help us understand the patterns of these crimes.

Family Privacy

Although statistics on homicide have long supported the violent potential of families, criminologists were not the pioneers in studies centered on the violent aspects of our society's most basic institution. Richard J. Gelles, a leading family-violence researcher, correctly asserted in the 1970s that violence within the family concerned criminologists only when someone was killed.[169] Criminology as a discipline began to give more attention to violent behavior within the family just as societal attention turned to viewing the halo of privacy that has long surrounded the family with a bit more scrutiny. Empirical research concerning the phenomenon of family violence encounters several problems. The family as a social institution is intensely private, and the discussion of physical, emotional, and sexual violence among family members violates this privacy; these types of abuse also represent extremely sensitive parts of a person's experience, which an individual may be reluctant to discuss. Michael Hindelang conducted research on crime-reporting behavior and found that two of the most common reasons for not reporting crimes to the police were that it was a private matter and that there might be reprisal from the offender.[170] Current research has shown that such rationales supporting nonreporting continue to characterize incidents involving violence among family members.

Early Studies of Family Violence

The initial research on violence within the family came from small clinical studies and official records, the latter consistently revealing that women were much more likely than men to become victims of domestic violence. Based on an examination of emergency room victims in the late 1970s, Evan Stark and colleagues found that approximately 25% of all women who had been injured had been the victim of a spousal attack.[171] Murray Straus and colleagues at the University of New Hampshire were the first to develop a survey methodology for the study of family violence nationally and conducted the first National Survey on Family Violence (NSFV) in 1975 with a representative sample of 2,146 families; the second NSFV was conducted in 1985 with a sample of 4,032 households.[172] In both surveys, the key tool developed for measuring family violence was the Conflict Tactics Scale, containing a series of 18 items that range from calm discussion to the use of a potentially lethal weapon. By the time a respondent reaches the questions concerning spousal behavior, Straus reasoned that familiarity with the questions would diminish the respondent's uneasiness about answering whether he or she had ever hit a spouse.[173] The rate of violence between spouses in the 1985 NSFV was 161 per 1,000 couples.[174] Although this rate was lower than that reported in 1975, it still remained higher than estimates produced from other studies not specifically directed at family violence, such as the NCVS.

Current Survey Information on Family Violence

In the years since survey research was first used to estimate violence against family members, other surveys have emerged to assess this phenomenon, and existing data sources have improved. A few years ago the FBI released specialized reports on family violence based on available NIBRS data. Using a measure of violent crime that includes murder, rape, robbery, and assault, NIBRS data revealed that 51% of violent crimes involved victims and offenders who were related. Among all offenses involving family members that came to the attention of the police, the overwhelming majority (94%) were assaults, a percentage that is "4 points higher than the frequency of assault offenses in overall crimes of violence."[175] Thus, although assault is the most frequently occurring violent crime both among

■ **intimate-partner assault** A gender-neutral term used to characterize assaultive behavior that takes place between individuals involved in an intimate relationship.

■ **separation assault** A type of violence inflicted by a partner on a significant other who attempts to leave an intimate relationship.

the general population and within the family, the percentage is even higher within the family. Whereas aggravated assault accounted for 18% of all violent offenses, the percentage of all family violence offenses involving aggravated assaults is slightly smaller, at 15%.[176]

Compared with aggravated assaults, firearms are less likely to be used in family assaults; fists, hands, and knives are more common, and a slight majority of aggravated assaults involve some type of injury both in the general population (57.5%) and within the family (60.8%). Women are more likely to be the victims of both aggravated assaults and simple assaults within the family than in the general population (60% versus 41% and 72% versus 60%, respectively).[177] Learn more about family violence and the crimes it engenders via **Web Extra 10–3**.

Intimate-Partner Assault

Intimate-partner assault is a term used to characterize assaultive behavior that takes place between individuals involved in an intimate relationship. Based on research using various data sources, the overwhelming majority of victims of marital violence within heterosexual relationships are women. This does not deny that men can be the victims of violence at the hands of their wives but merely states that based on official records, self-reports, emergency room records, and small clinical samples, it is women who emerge as victims. In line with this empirical reality, Neil Websdale titled his ethnographic exploration of violence in rural areas of Kentucky *Rural Woman Battering and the Justice System*.[178] However, the terms *woman battering* and *wife assault* are biased in terms of heterosexual relationships, so some researchers now use the term *intimate-partner assault* to avoid this bias. We will also use this term in our discussion because it now frequently appears in the literature on assault among intimates and because it reflects the changing nature of most sexual assault laws and mandatory arrest laws, which are becoming gender neutral and moving away from the legal relationship as the criterion that defines an intimate relationship.

Intimate-partner assault refers to assaultive behavior that takes place between individuals involved in an intimate relationship.

For many individuals, the notion of assault between intimate partners gives rise to the response "If I was hit, I would leave," but this places the burden on the victim to justify why she stays and takes the burden off the offending partner. More crucially, this type of response ignores the reality that when most women do leave violent relationships, that behavior may trigger a particularly violent response by the male partner, labeled **separation assault** by Martha R. Mahoney.[179] A woman who attempts to leave a violent relationship is seen as violating the right of her husband to control her, and even if she does manage to leave, many times the husband will follow her and attempt to take her back.

Violent relationships between intimate partners are characterized by a cycle of violence in which numerous forms of social control may be used. Men in Websdale's research disconnected telephone lines, disabled cars, and threatened women at their place of work, actions that narrowed the abused partner's options to leave, especially in the case of women in rural settings where powerful notions of family loyalty and gender roles work against leaving as an option. As Websdale noted in his research, many women who are battered by their husbands must face the fact that if they leave their husbands, they will be leaving their communities. Physical assaults often involve other tactics of abuse, such as emotional abuse and attacks or threats against children—most women who have reported abuse by intimate partners also had dependent children.[180]

In analyzing the cases of women in two counties in Massachusetts who applied for restraining orders during 1992 and 1993, as well as observations in the courtroom, **James Ptacek** developed a typology of the strategies men used to control women in violent relationships.[181] He analyzed both the types of abuse that women reported in their petitions for restraining orders and the rationales that women provided in their affidavits that "gave some indication of the objectives behind the men's violence and abuse."[182] In 18% of the cases, the woman reported that her male partner had used violence to prevent her from leaving, and in 22% of the cases, the woman reported that violence was used to get back at her for leaving. Ptacek argued that women are assaulted in the process of leaving their abusers, and some of the incidents of separation assault had occurred more than a year following legal separation or divorce. Men also used "punishment, coercion, and retaliation against women's actions concerning children," which could take several forms.[183] Some men attacked their wives during pregnancy, other men attacked women who challenged their parental authority over the children, and still others attacked partners who had requested child support through the courts. In about 12% of the cases, the affidavits of women revealed that men used violence in response to other types of legal action. Ptacek labeled this "retaliation or coercion against women's pursuit of court or police remedies," in which the men responded with violence to actions that women were thought to have taken, whether those actions were real or imaginary. The final motivation for the violence of males was "retaliation for other perceived challenges to authority." These challenges included comments that the woman made concerning her male partner's behavior, ranging from drinking behavior to financial matters. As with the other motivational categories, the challenge to male authority was viewed as actionable, and violence was considered a justified course of action.[184] Ethnographic research like that of Websdale and Ptacek is an important avenue for increasing our knowledge of intimate-partner violence.

Another source of information is survey research such as the NVAW Survey (mentioned earlier), which had the goal of estimating both the extent and the nature of physical abuse among intimate partners. At some point during their lifetime, 22% of women and slightly more than 7% of men reported having been physically assaulted by an intimate partner, and during the study year, slightly more than 1% of women and less than 1% of men reported physical assault by an intimate partner. The vast majority of behaviors considered to be physical assault were acts like grabbing and shoving rather than acts using a gun or knife. In both same-sex and opposite-sex relationships, males more often perpetrate intimate-partner violence (Figure 10–9).

On the extent of injury in intimate-partner assaults, the NVAW Survey revealed that women are more likely than men to report injuries and that most of the injuries received are minor in nature. More findings from the NVAW Survey are presented in the section of this chapter examining stalking. Learn more about intimate-partner violence via **Web Extra 10–4**.

Other Forms of Interpersonal Violence

This chapter concludes with an overview of three special forms of interpersonal violence: workplace violence, hate crimes, and stalking. We begin our discussion with the topic of workplace violence.

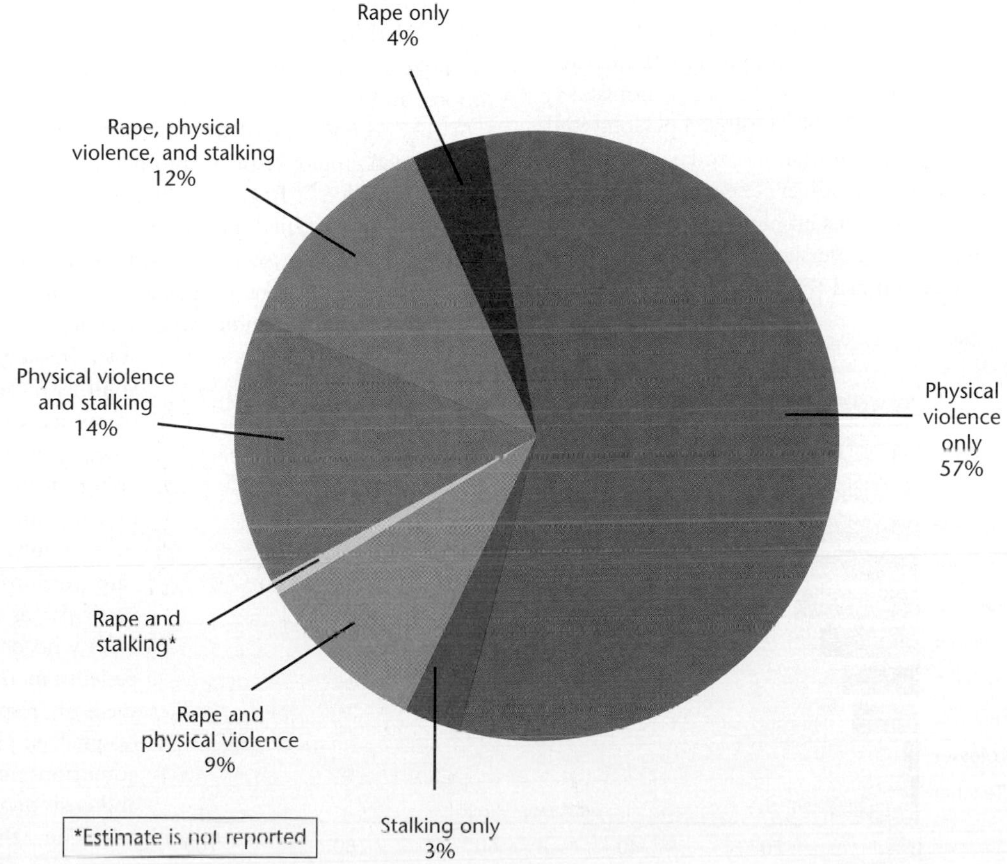

FIGURE 10–9 | Overlap of Lifetime Intimate Partner Rape, Stalking, and Physical Victimization

Source: Centers for Disease Control and Prevention, National Center for Injury Prevention and Control, *The National Intimate Partner and Sexual Violence Survey: Factsheet 2010* (Atlanta, GA: Centers for Disease Control and Prevention, National Center for Injury Prevention and Control), p. 2.

■ **workplace violence** Nonfatal violence (rape/sexual assault, robbery, and aggravated and simple assault) against employed persons age 16 or older.

Workplace Violence

Workplace violence (murder, rape, robbery, and assault committed against persons who are at work or on duty) is a significant problem in America today. The FBI says that "workplace violence is now recognized as a specific category of violent crime that calls for distinct responses from employers, law enforcement, and the community."[185] In a given year, approximately 570,000 nonfatal violent crimes (rape/sexual assault, robbery, and aggravated and simple assault) occur against persons age 16 or older while they are at work or on duty, based on findings from the National Crime Victimization Survey (NCVS).[186] This accounts for about 24% of nonfatal violence against employed persons age 16 or older. Nonfatal workplace violence is about 15% of all nonfatal violent crime against persons age 16 or older.

Workplace violence is a significant problem in America today.

Today an estimated 4 violent crimes per 1,000 employed persons age 16 or older are committed while victims are at work or on duty, compared to 6 violent crimes per 1,000 employed persons age 16 or older in 2002. In 1993, the rate of nonfatal violence was 16 violent crimes per 1,000 employed persons while at work, a rate that was 75% higher than it is today.

As might be expected, police officers experience workplace violence at rates higher than persons employed in any other occupation, whereas college or university professors are among persons least likely to be victimized (Figure 10–10).

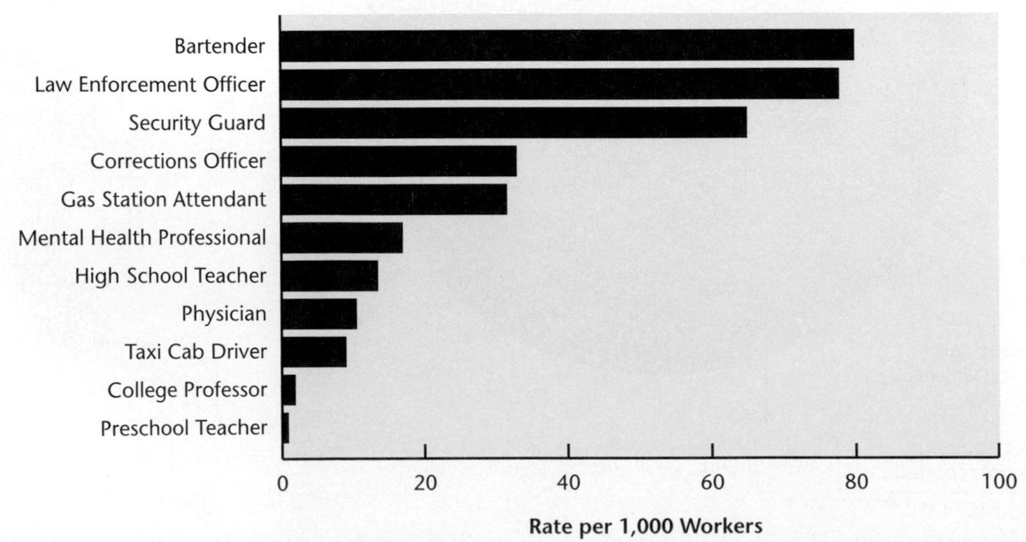

FIGURE 10–10 | Rate of Violent Workplace Victimization by Occupation

Source: Erika Harrell, *Workplace Violence, 1993–2009* (Washington, DC: Bureau of Justice Statistics, 2011), p. 4.

Workplace violence falls into four broad categories:

1. Violent acts by criminals who have no other connection with the workplace but who enter to commit robbery, acts of terrorism, or another crime
2. Violence directed at employees by customers, clients, patients, students, inmates, or any others for whom an organization provides services
3. Violence against coworkers, supervisors, or managers by a present or former employee
4. Violence committed in the workplace by someone who doesn't work there but who has a personal relationship with an employee, such as an abusive spouse or domestic partner

Violence committed by criminals otherwise unconnected to the workplace accounts for nearly 80% of all workplace homicides.[187] In such incidents, the motive is usually theft, and in a great many cases, the criminal is carrying a gun or other weapon, increasing the likelihood that the victim(s) will be killed or seriously wounded. This type of violence falls heavily on particular occupational groups whose jobs make them vulnerable: taxi drivers, late-night retail or gas station clerks and others on duty at night, workers in isolated locations or dangerous neighborhoods, and workers with cash or access to it.

The second type of workplace violence typically involves assaults on an employee by a customer, patient, or someone else receiving a service.[188] In general, the violent acts occur as workers are performing their daily tasks. In some occupations (police officers, correctional officers, security guards, and mental health workers), dealing with dangerous people is a part of the job. In other occupations, violent reactions by a customer or client are unpredictable, possibly triggered by an argument, anger at the quality of service or denial of service, a delay, or some other precipitating event. Employees experiencing the largest number of these assaults are those in health care occupations—nurses, in particular, as well as doctors and aides who deal with psychiatric patients; members of emergency medical response teams; and hospital employees working in admissions, emergency rooms, and crisis or acute care units.

The third and fourth types of violence—incidents of violence by past or present employees and acts committed by domestic abusers and

■ **hate crime** A criminal offense in which the motive is hatred, bias, or prejudice based on the actual or perceived race, color, religion, national origin, ethnicity, gender, or sexual orientation of another individual or group of individuals.

other personal relational issues that follow an employee into the workplace—are often the kind of workplace violence reported in the media. Violence in these categories is no less damaging than any other violent act, but when the violence comes from an employee or someone close to an employee, there is a much greater chance that some warning sign will have reached the employer prior to the violent act.

A BJS study revealed the following facts about workplace violence:[189]

- Private-sector and federal government employees are victimized at similar rates.
- More than 80% of all workplace homicides are committed with a firearm.
- Rape and sexual assault, robbery, and homicide account for a small percentage (6%) of all workplace violent crime; the majority of workplace violent incidents (almost 19 of every 20) are aggravated or simple assaults.
- Males experience more workplace violence (except for rape and sexual assault) than females, with about two-thirds of all robberies, aggravated assaults, and simple assaults in the workplace being committed against males.
- People ages 20–34 experience workplace violence at a rate higher than any other age group.
- The workplace violent crime rate for whites (13 per 1,000 in the workforce) is 25% higher than the rate for blacks (10 per 1,000) and 59% higher than the rate for other races (8 per 1,000); whites experience more than four-fifths of all rapes and sexual assaults (88%), robberies (81%), aggravated assaults (86%), and simple assaults (89%) occurring in the workplace, but blacks have the highest rates of overall violent crime (including both workplace and nonworkplace violence).
- Most workplace victimizations are intraracial—about six in ten white and black victims of workplace crime perceive their assailant to be of the same race.
- Almost four of every ten robberies occurring while the victim is at work or on duty are committed against someone in retail sales or transportation.
- About 12% of all workplace violence victims sustain injuries from the incident; of those injuries, about 10 out of 11 are minor injuries.

The National Institute for Occupational Safety and Health (NIOSH)[190] recommends a number of prevention strategies to lower the incidence of workplace violence, including environmental design factors that physically separate workers from customers: bullet-resistant barriers or enclosures, high counters to prevent customer access to workers and goods, and limited avenues of access and egress.[191] Also recommended are enhanced

ZUMA Press/Newscom

University of Alabama-Huntsville (UAH) shooter Amy Bishop conferring with her lawyer in Madison Circuit Court (Alabama). In 2012, Bishop, age 47, plead guilty to killing three fellow UAH biology faculty members and wounding three others during a shooting rampage at a faculty meeting on campus on February 12, 2010. She received a life sentence. Can anything be done to reduce the number of incidents of workplace violence?

administrative controls such as staffing plans and work practices that include the prescreening of patients or customers and the training and education of employees in conflict-resolution strategies.

Visit NIOSH's Occupational Violence Center to learn more about workplace violence and techniques to prevent it at **Web Extra 10–5**. Read two articles about workplace violence at **Library Extras 10–8** and **10–9**, and learn about recommendations for curtailing workplace violence from the FBI at **Library Extra 10–10**; a Canadian perspective on workplace violence is available at **Library Extra 10–11**.

Hate Crimes

At 12:49 P.M. on June 10, 2009, the U.S. Holocaust Memorial Museum in Washington, D.C., became the scene of a violent **hate crime** (a crime whose motive is hatred, bias, or prejudice). James von Brunn, an 88-year old Maryland resident who

■ **stalking** A course of conduct directed at a specific person that involves repeated visual or physical proximity; nonconsensual communication; verbal, written, or implied threats; or a combination thereof that would cause a reasonable person fear.

had served five years in a federal prison for a 1981 attempted armed kidnapping, entered the museum with a .22-caliber rifle and opened fire.[192] One security officer was killed before von Brunn, a known white supremacist and gun rights activist, was shot and seriously wounded by two other officers.

The collection of hate-crime statistics was mandated by the U.S. Congress with passage of the Hate Crime Statistics Act of 1990.[193] Under the law, the FBI is required to serve as a repository for data collected on crimes motivated by religious, sexual orientation, ethnic, or racial prejudice. The Violent Crime Control and Law Enforcement Act of 1994 mandated the addition to the category of hate crimes any crimes motivated by biases against people with disabilities, and the UCR Program began reporting such crimes in 1997.[194]

> The collection of hate-crime statistics was mandated by the U.S. Congress in 1990.

According to the BJS, hate crimes (also called *bias crimes*) are characterized by "manifest evidence of prejudice based on race, religion, sexual orientation, or ethnicity, including where appropriate the crimes of murder, non-negligent manslaughter, forcible rape, aggravated assault, simple assault, intimidation, arson, and destruction, damage, or vandalism of property."[195] In 2009, President Barack Obama signed into law a bill that enhances the federal protection of gays by specifically adding acts of violence against gay, lesbian, bisexual, and transgender people to the list of federal hate crimes.[196]

Olivier Douliery/AbacaPress/MCT/Newscomm

Glass doors damaged by gunfire being examined at the U.S. Holocaust Memorial Museum in Washington, D.C. On June 10, 2009, James van Brunn, an anti-Semitic 88-year-old, opened fire on security officers inside the museum; he killed one officer before he was injured and detained. What are hate crimes?

Based on FBI statistics on hate crimes, 6,222 hate-crime incidents were reported in 2011. These incidents involved 7,254 victims, with approximately 70% of the incidents involving a single victim.[197] (Because a single incident may involve multiple offenses, it is important to state also that the 6,222 reported incidents accounted for a total of 7,254 chargeable offenses.) Of all the incidents reported 46.9% were motivated by racial bias, 20.8% were motivated by a sexual-orientation bias, 19.8% were motivated by religious bias, and 11.6% were motivated by an ethnicity/national origin bias. Bias against a disability accounted for less than one percent of single-bias incidents. Of the 4,623 hate crime offenses classified as crimes against persons in 2011, intimidation accounted for 45.6%, simple assaults for 34.5%, and aggravated assaults for 19.4%. Four murders and seven forcible rapes were reported as hate crimes.

In addition to violent crimes, 2,611 hate crime property offenses occurred in 2011. The majority of these (81.4%) were acts of vandalism. Robbery, burglary, larceny-theft, motor vehicle theft, arson, and other offenses accounted for the remaining 18.6% of crimes against property. Fifty-nine percent of the 5,731 known offenders were white; 20.9% were black. The race was unknown for 10.8%, and other races accounted for the remaining known offenders.

Role of Hate Groups

Hate groups like the Ku Klux Klan (KKK), the Aryan Nations, the National Alliance, and the Identity church movement have existed for many years and have long been associated with acts of violence. It is easy to classify groups in the hate-group category when their fundamental purpose is grounded in prejudice, but in the case of some other organizations, classification is not as easy. Are all militia groups hate groups? Given its anti-Semitic position, does the Nation of Islam, led by Louis Farrakhan, qualify as a hate group?

Are hate groups a necessary feature of hate crimes? Citing a wide array of research studies, James B. Jacobs and Kimberly A. Potter found that "the vast majority of reported hate crimes are not committed by organized hate groups and their members, but by teenagers, primarily white males, acting alone or in a group."[198] Visit the NCJRS Hate Crime Resources page via **Web Extra 10–6** and the Anti-Defamation League's Combating Hate page at **Web Extra 10–7**, and read **Library Extras 10–12** and **10–13** to learn more about hate crimes. View the latest FBI statistics on hate crimes via **Library Extra 10–14**.

Stalking

Although **stalking**—conduct directed at a specific person involving repeated visual or physical proximity, nonconsensual communication, and threats—is not new, making this behavior worthy of societal concern and undesirable enough to be criminalized is relatively new. Several high-profile cases have illustrated the dangerous potential of stalking behavior. John Hinkley was obsessed with actress Jodie Foster and thought he could capture her attention and admiration by shooting President Ronald Reagan in 1981. Mark David Chapman, the man who shot John Lennon in 1980, considered himself to be one of Lennon's biggest fans. Talk-show host David Letterman was stalked from 1988 to 1993 by a woman who professed her love for him by breaking into his house repeatedly, trespassing on his property, and stealing his car. Michael David Barrett, a 47-year-old divorced Chicago-area man, pleaded guilty in 2009 to interstate stalking for filming ESPN reporter Erin Andrews through a peephole while she undressed in her neighboring hotel room.[199] That same year, Michael Lawrence Kozelka of Townsend, Maryland, was arrested on charges of stalking singer-songwriter Jewel at her Texas ranch; at the time of his arrest, Kozelka, age 50, told authorities that he had been on a mission from God.[200] Although these high-profile cases may capture media attention because they involve celebrities, stalking often involves average individuals as they go about their lives.

The first antistalking statute was passed in 1990 in California;[201] now all states and the federal government have antistalking laws. Rather than being an offense that occurs once, stalking is conceptualized as a pattern of behavior that causes victims to fear for their personal safety. The definition used in the Model Antistalking Code for States, developed by the NIJ, is "a course of conduct directed at a specific person that involves repeated visual or physical proximity, nonconsensual communication, or verbal, written or implied threats, or a combination thereof, that would cause a reasonable person fear"[202] (*repeated* is defined to mean at least two occasions).

Statutory definitions of *stalking* encompass a number of diverse but interrelated behaviors: making phone calls, following the victim, sending letters, making threats in some manner, vandalizing property, and watching the victim. Rather than viewing these behaviors in isolation from one another, antistalking laws take into account the totality of the circumstances so that seemingly benign behaviors are seen in light of how they are connected to other behaviors. For example, sending unwanted letters might be seen as innocuous behavior, but when this activity is combined with following the victim and standing outside his or her place of work or residence, the behavior takes on a more threatening tone and may be the precursor for more serious offenses like assault, rape, and murder.[203]

Extent of Stalking

Recent data on stalking come from the BJS report *Stalking Victimization in the United States*, which shows that during a recent 12-month period, an estimated 3.4 million persons age 18 or older were victims of stalking.[204] The BJS report, derived from data accumulated under the NCVS, identified seven types of harassing or unwanted behaviors consistent with conduct experienced by stalking victims: (1) receiving unwanted phone calls; (2) receiving unsolicited or unwanted letters or e-mails; (3) being followed or spied upon; (4) having the stalker show up at places without a legitimate reason; (5) having the stalker wait at places for the victim; (6) receiving unwanted items, presents, or flowers; and (7) having the stalker post information or spread rumors about the victim on the Internet, in a public place, or by word of mouth. The BJS noted that these acts, taken individually, may not be criminal, but "collectively and repetitively these behaviors may cause a victim to fear for his or her safety or the safety of a family member."

The BJS report found the following during the 12-month data-gathering period:[205]

- An estimated 14 in every 1,000 persons age 18 or older were victims of stalking.
- About half (46%) of stalking victims experienced at least one unwanted contact per week, and 11% of victims said they had been stalked for five years or more.
- The risk of stalking victimization was highest for individuals who were divorced or separated—34 per 1,000 individuals.
- Women were at greater risk than men for stalking victimization; however, women and men were equally likely to experience harassment.
- A pattern of decreasing risk for stalking victimization existed for persons residing in households with higher incomes.
- Male (37%) and female (41%) stalking victimizations were equally likely to be reported to the police.
- Approximately one in four stalking victims reported some form of cyberstalking, such as through e-mail (83%) or instant messaging (35%).
- About 46% of stalking victims felt fear of not knowing what would happen next.
- Nearly three in four stalking victims knew their offender in some capacity.
- More than half of stalking victims lost five or more days from work as a result of experiencing stalking.

The most common reasons victims perceived as the cause of stalking behavior were retaliation, anger, spite (37%), or desire to control the victim (33%). About one in six victims believed the stalking started to keep him or her in the relationship with the offender, and one in ten reported that the stalking began while living with the offender. About a tenth of victims did not know why the stalking began.

For stalking victims, the most common fear cited was not knowing what would happen next; 9% of stalking victims reported their worst fear was death, 29% feared the behavior would never stop, and more than 50% feared bodily harm to themselves, their children, or another family member. More than seven in ten victims felt angry or annoyed at the beginning of the unwanted contacts or as they progressed. Stalking victims were about twice as likely as harassment victims to feel anxious or concerned at the beginning of the unwanted contacts (52.7% versus 25.4%), and as the unwanted contacts progressed, about 15% of stalking victims felt depressed or sick, and 1% reported feeling suicidal.

About 139,000 stalking victims were attacked with a weapon, with stalkers equally likely to use a knife, blunt instrument, or other object; 23% used handguns. Of the 279,000 victims who were injured in an attack, nearly all (99%) sustained minor bruises and other injuries, and about 20% sustained serious injuries, including gunshot or knife wounds, internal injuries, or broken bones.

Examining the behaviors that stalkers engage in, Patricia Tjaden and Nancy Thoennes (principal investigators for the NVAW Survey) concluded that antistalking laws requiring that an overt threat be made against the victim before action can be taken against the stalker are ill-advised and that laws should be strengthened to allow for early action by the justice system to prevent later harm to stalking victims.[206]

Types of Stalkers

A psychiatric study of 145 Canadian stalkers who had been referred to a forensic psychiatry center for treatment found that most were men (79%) and that many were unemployed (39%).[207] Perhaps not surprisingly, most (52%) had never had an intimate relationship. Five types of stalkers were identified (Figure 10–11):

1. **Rejected stalkers.** Rejected stalkers pursue their victims in order to reverse, correct, or avenge a felt rejection (for example, divorce, separation, termination).
2. **Intimacy-seeking stalkers.** Wanting to establish an intimate, loving relationship with the victim, intimacy-seeking stalkers may see the victim as a soul mate, someone whom they are fated to be with.
3. **Incompetent suitors.** Incompetent suitors have a romantic or sexual interest in the victim despite having poor social or courting skills.
4. **Resentful vendetta-motivated stalkers.** Vendetta-motivated stalkers act out revenge based on a perceived wrong or a grievance against the victim, and their intent is generally to frighten and distress the victim.
5. **Predatory stalkers.** Predatory stalkers spy on the victim in preparation for an attack, which is usually sexual in nature.

FIGURE 10-11 | A Psychiatric Typology of Stalker Types

Source: Derived from Paul E. Mullen et al., "Study of Stalkers," *American Journal of Psychiatry*, Vol. 156 (August 1999), pp. 1244–1249. Reprinted with permission from the *American Journal of Psychiatry* (Copyright 1999).

Delusional disorders were found to be common among the stalkers treated, and 30% were determined to suffer consistently from delusions about those they stalked. Stalking behavior among those studied lasted anywhere from four weeks to 20 years, with an average of 12 months. Rejected and intimacy-seeking stalkers tended to persist the longest in stalking behavior. About 63% of stalkers made threats toward their victims, and 36% were assaultive. The researchers concluded, "Stalkers have a range of motivations, from reasserting power over a partner who rejected them to the quest for a loving relationship."[208] Read more about the types of stalkers identified in the social scientific literature and their motivations at **Library Extra 10–15**.

Victim–Offender Relationships in Stalking

The majority of stalking victims identified in the NVAW Survey are women (78%, or four out of every five victims), and the majority of individuals who stalk are men (94% of women and 60% of men identify a male as the stalker). The majority of stalking victims are young, with 52% between the ages of 18 and 29 and 22% between the ages of 30 and 39. Results from the NVAW Survey confirmed previous research showing that the majority of victims know their stalkers—a stranger was identified as the stalker in only 23% of the cases where a woman was stalked and 36% of the cases where a man was stalked. For women who are stalked, the majority (59%) are more likely to be stalked by an intimate partner than by a stranger, an acquaintance, or a relative other than the spouse, but the majority of men are stalked by strangers or acquaintances (70%), usually a male in both cases (90%). Tjaden and Thoennes stated that although there is no

■ **cyberstalking** An array of high-technology options, including e-mail and the Internet, that an offender uses to harass or "follow" another individual.

clear explanation for this finding, it may be related to a greater risk of stalking among homosexual as opposed to heterosexual men because the survey found that stalking was more often experienced by male respondents who indicated that they had lived as a couple with another male. The belief that stalkers suffer from mental illness or personality disorder was not confirmed by the survey findings, as only 7% of the victims stated that they were stalked by offenders who were "mentally ill or abusing drugs or alcohol."[209] Learn more at **Library Extra 10–16**.

Stalking in Intimate-Partner Relationships

Almost one-fourth (21%) of female respondents in the NVAW Survey who had been stalked by an intimate partner stated that they were stalked before the end of the relationship, 43% indicated that the stalking occurred after the relationship had ended, and slightly over one-third (36%) reported that they were stalked both before and after the end of the relationship with their partner.[210] The survey found that other forms of violence often accompany stalking. For women stalked by an intimate partner, 81% were also physically assaulted, and about 33% were sexually assaulted by the stalker; the percentage of women experiencing assault of either kind by a current or former intimate partner who stalked them was higher than the percentage experiencing some form of assault but no stalking (20% of women who had ever married or lived with a male partner had experienced physical assault by that partner and 5% had experienced sexual assault).[211] Men who stalked their former wives were "significantly more likely than ex-husbands who did not stalk to engage in emotionally abusive and controlling behavior toward their wife."[212]

Consequences of Stalking

Respondents in the NVAW Survey reported a number of consequences of stalking that negatively affected their lives, with women who had been stalked reporting a significantly higher level of concern for their personal safety than those who had not been stalked. Almost one-third reported seeking counseling, and slightly more than one-fourth lost time from work. Women took a variety of extra self-protective measures as a response to the stalking: 17% stated they had bought a gun, 11% stated they had changed residences, and 11% stated they had moved out of state. Women who had been stalked were more likely than men to have obtained a protective order against the stalker (23% versus 10%, respectively).[213]

Women who had been stalked reported a significantly higher level of concern for their personal safety than those who had not been stalked.

Because the definition used in the NVAW Survey to assess stalking required high levels of fear on the part of victims, it is worthwhile to note the data on whether the victims reported stalking to the police—a higher percentage of women than men reported the stalking to police (55% versus 48%, respectively). When asked their reasons for not reporting stalking to the police, victims consistently gave fairly general reasons: 20% defined it as not a police matter, 17% did not believe the police could do anything, 16% were afraid of reprisal from the stalker, 12% said they resolved it on their own, and smaller percentages reported that the police would not believe them or that it was a private matter.[214] Responses to questions on satisfaction with law enforcement's handling of the case indicated that about half of respondents approved of police procedure, but in cases where an arrest was made in the stalking, three-fourths of the victims were satisfied with the police handling of the case.[215] Learn more about the crime of stalking at the federal Stalking Resource Center at **Web Extra 10–8**.

Cyberstalking

Cyberstalking—the use of electronic communication like e-mail or the Internet to harass individuals—has received attention as efforts progress to better understand the consequences of our increased reliance on electronic communication and the Internet.[216] One federal government report made the following recommendations to help control cyberstalking:[217]

- A review of all stalking laws at the state level is needed to ensure that provisions for cyberstalking are included.
- An amendment to federal law is needed to make transmission of communication in specified forms of commerce actionable if the intent involves threatening behavior or causes the recipient fear.
- Training on cyberstalking should be offered at all levels of law enforcement.
- A Web site with information on cyberstalking should be created and made available to the public.

Learn more about the crime of cyberstalking from the Stalking Resource Center run by the National Center for Victims of Crime at **Web Extra 10–9**, and read an article describing the growing use of technology and other menacing stalking behaviors at **Library Extra 10–17**. Find out more about the activities of cyberstalkers and how to combat the crime of cyberstalking at **Library Extra 10–18**.

CRIMINAL | PROFILES

Dennis Rader—The BTK Killer

He "hid for more than 30 years in plain sight."[i] That's how a leading news service described Wichita, Kansas, serial killer Dennis Rader's evasion of capture for more than three decades. Rader, the self-proclaimed BTK killer ("BTK" being a nickname he gave himself to denote his propensity to "bind, torture, and kill" his victims), lived a normal, rather mundane existence with his wife and two children, all the while concealing his second persona: a murderous predator. His "front" included his ordinance enforcement officer job in the Wichita suburb of Park City, service as a Cub Scout troop leader, and active participation in his Lutheran church.[ii]

Rader was born March 9, 1945, the eldest of four brothers. After high school, he did a four-year stint in the U.S. Air Force before returning to Park City, where he completed an undergraduate degree in administration of justice at Wichita State University in 1979. Beginning in 1974, Rader worked in a variety of positions at ADT Security Services over the next 14 years.[iii] It was also in 1974 that Rader committed the first of what eventually became ten grisly murders.

His initial murderous foray occurred mid-morning on January 15, 1974, when Rader killed four members of the Otero family: dad Joseph, mom Julie, 11-year-old Josephine, and 9-year-old Joseph II. Each victim was subjected to various acts of torture before ultimately being strangled. The bodies were discovered when 15-year-old Charlie Otero returned from school later that afternoon.[iv]

The shocking murders were only the start of a long criminal career. Kathryn Bright, 20, was stabbed to death just three months later, on April 4, 1974. Amazingly, her 19-year-old brother, Kevin, survived the attack despite being shot twice in the head.

Almost three years elapsed before BTK struck again on March 17, 1977, by strangling 26-year-old Shirley Vian. Uncharacteristically, BTK locked the three young Vian children in the closet and allowed them to survive. Just nine months later, on December 8, 1977, police found Nancy Jo Fox, 25, dead in her bedroom, strangled with a nylon stocking. BTK's final three killings occurred on April 27, 1985 (Marine Hedge), September 16, 1986 (Vicki Wegerle), and January 18, 1991 (Dolores Davis); all were strangled.[v]

A strange component of the BTK murders was the way the killer periodically wrote taunting letters to the local police and newspapers.[vi] The frequency of the BTK letters decreased by the end of the 1980s, as he apparently became dormant. In 1991, Rader became a Park City Compliance Officer,[vii] where he developed a reputation as a by-the-book "bureaucratic bully."[viii]

In March 2004, new BTK letters began surfacing. Over the course of the next year, a total of 11 communications were received. One, a computer floppy disk, was forensically identified as having been used by Rader's church and containing residue that included the name "Dennis." That disk directly led to Rader's arrest on February 25, 2005. At his arraignment on May 3, Rader stood mute, and a trial date of June 27 was set.

Rader subsequently surprised everyone when, on June 27, he confessed in open court to the murders of ten people. In response to direct questioning from the judge, Rader recounted in chillingly graphic and dispassionate detail exactly how he had killed each of the ten victims.

Travis Heying/Associated Press

Convicted BTK killer Dennis Rader listening during a court proceeding on October 12, 2005, at the El Dorado Correctional Facility in El Dorado, Kansas. A judge recommended that Rader receive treatment as a sexual offender and have restrictions placed on what he can receive or do in prison while he serves the rest of his life behind bars. Rader, a 60-year-old former church congregation president and Cub Scout leader, pleaded guilty in 2005 to ten murders that haunted Wichita over three decades. Why wasn't he caught sooner?

At a sentencing hearing on August 17 and 18, 2005, Rader received the harshest possible sentence under Kansas law when Judge Gregory Waller gave him ten life sentences to be served consecutively. The consecutive service provision means that Rader must serve a minimum of 175 years before becoming eligible for parole consideration.[ix]

The case of Dennis Rader raises a number of interesting questions. Among them are the following:

1. Which of the theories discussed in previous chapters might best explain Rader's behavior? Would any of them have helped authorities identify Rader before he could kill again?
2. Why did Rader write taunting letters to the media? What purpose did those letters serve?
3. Do you think that Rader could ever be "rehabilitated"? If he could, would you be willing to set him free if you had the power to make such a decision? Why or why not?

Notes

i. "Neighbors Paint Mixed Picture of BTK Suspect," MSNBC, February 27, 2005, http://www.msnbc.msn.com/id/7036219 (accessed June 16, 2007).

ii. Ibid.

iii. Ibid.

iv. Marilyn Bardsley, Rachael Bell, and David Lohr, "BTK—Birth of a Serial Killer," CourtTV Crime Library, http://www.crimelibrary.com/serial_killers/unsolved/btk/index_1.html (accessed June 16, 2007).

v. Ibid.

vi. "Neighbors Paint Mixed Picture of BTK Suspect," MSNBC.

vii. "Report: Daughter of BTK Suspect Alerted Police," Cable News Network, April 19, 2005.

viii. Bardsley.

ix. *State of Kansas* v. *Dennis Rader*, Office of the Sedgwick County, Kansas, District Attorney Web site, February 1, 2006, http://www.sedgwickcounty.org/da (accessed June 16, 2010).

SUMMARY

- Criminal homicide, the illegal killing of one human being by another, ranges from serial killing and mass murder to murder in intimate settings. Patterns of murder vary along subcultural and social structural dimensions such as economic inequality and community social disorganization.
- The FBI defines rape as "The penetration, no matter how slight, of the vagina or anus with any body part or object, or oral penetration by a sex organ of another person, without the consent of the victim." Forcible rape is defined as "The carnal knowledge of a person forcibly and against their will."
- The term *child sexual abuse* encompasses a variety of criminal and civil offenses in which an adult engages in sexual activity with a minor, exploits a minor for purposes of sexual gratification, or exploits a minor sexually for purposes of profit. The term includes a variety of activities and motivations, including child molestation, child sexual exploitation (CSE), and the commercial sexual exploitation of children (CSEC).
- The FBI defines robbery as the taking of or attempting to take anything of value from the care, custody, or control of someone by using force or threat of force or violence or by putting the victim in fear. Muggings and robberies in residences are personal robbery, and robberies in commercial settings are institutional robberies. The majority of robbery offenders are generalists with a fairly lengthy but varied criminal career who put very little planning into their robberies.
- Assaults are either simple or aggravated (violent unlawful attacks for the purpose of inflicting severe or aggravated bodily injury). Intimate-partner violence characterizes assaultive behavior between individuals involved in an intimate relationship.
- Workplace violence is a widespread significant problem today and includes murder, rape, robbery, and assault committed against persons who are at work or on duty. Hate crimes are criminal offenses motivated by hatred, bias, or prejudice based on the race, religion, national origin, ethnicity, gender, or sexual orientation of another person. Stalking is repeated visual or physical proximity, nonconsensual communication, and/or threats that would cause someone to be fearful; cyberstalking is a special type of stalking that uses high technology to harass someone.

KEY TERMS

acquaintance rape, 257
aggravated assault, 266
child pornography, 261
child sexual abuse (CSA), 259
comfort serial killers, 249
cyberstalking, 275
exposure-reduction theory, 246
expressive crime, 246
felony murder, 244
first-degree murder, 243
forcible rape, 252
hate crime, 271
hedonistic serial killers, 249
homicide, 242
institutional robbery, 262
instrumental crime, 246
intimate-partner assault, 268
mass murder, 250
murder, 242
National Crime Victimization Survey (NCVS), 242
National Incident-Based Reporting System (NIBRS), 242
negligent homicide, 243
nonprimary homicide, 246
personal robbery, 262
power seekers, 249
primary homicide, 246
rape, 252
second-degree murder, 243
selective disinhibition, 248
separation assault, 268
serial murder, 249
sibling offense, 246
spousal rape, 258
stalking, 272
subculture of violence thesis, 245
Uniform Crime Reporting (UCR) Program, 242
victim precipitation, 246
Violent Criminal Apprehension Program (VICAP), 250
visionary serial killers, 249
workplace violence, 270

KEY NAMES

Larry Baron, 255
Ann Burgess, 256
Andrea Dworkin, 254
James Alan Fox, 249
Nicholas Groth, 255
Robert R. Hazelwood, 256
Jack Levin, 249
Catherine MacKinnon, 254
Jody Miller, 266
Craig T. Palmer, 256
Robert Nash Parker, 246
James Ptacek, 268
Diana E. H. Russell, 258
Diana Scully, 256
Murray A. Straus, 255
Randy Thornhill, 256

QUESTIONS FOR REVIEW

1. What is criminal homicide, and what are the key issues involved in explaining patterns of homicide?
2. How is the crime of rape defined, and what are the key issues involved in explaining the crime of rape?
3. What does the term "child sexual abuse" encompass, and what are the various types of child sex abusers that this chapter identifies?
4. How is the crime of robbery defined, and what are the different kinds of robbery?
5. How is the crime of assault defined, and what are the various kinds of assault?
6. What three additional forms of interpersonal violence does this chapter discuss?

QUESTIONS FOR REFLECTION

1. Are violent crimes primarily rational activities?
2. Why was reform of rape laws necessary? What have been the beneficial aspects of reform for rape victims?
3. Is robbery primarily a rational activity? Why or why not?

An Guangxi/Xinhua/Photoshot/Newscom

CRIMES AGAINST PROPERTY

LEARNING OUTCOMES

After reading this chapter, you should be able to answer the following questions:

- What are the major forms of property crime discussed in this chapter?
- What constitutes the crime of burglary? What are some of its characteristics?
- What constitutes the crime of larceny-theft? What forms does it take?
- What is motor vehicle theft? How prevalent is it?
- What constitutes the crime of arson?
- What are some characteristics of persistent and professional thieves?
- What are the typical activities of receivers of stolen property, and how are stolen goods distributed?

■ **property crime** According to the FBI's Uniform Crime Reporting program, a crime category that includes burglary, larceny, motor vehicle theft, and arson.

■ **burglary** The unlawful entry of a structure to commit a felony or a theft.

Introduction

In 2012, Pedro Antonio Marcuello Guzman, 46, and Maria Martha Elisa Ornelas Lazo, 50, were arrested and charged with possession of stolen goods when they tried to sell a painting created in 1925 by the French Impressionist Matisse.[1] The painting, titled *Odalisque a la culotte rouge,* depicts a bare-chested woman sitting cross-legged on the floor wearing a pair of scarlet trousers. It is estimated to be worth over $3 million, and had been stolen from the Caracas Museum of Contemporary Art in Venezuela a decade earlier. Guzman and Lazo, who admitted knowing that the painting was stolen, had offered to sell it for $740,000 to undercover agents of the Federal Bureau of Investigation (FBI) posing as art collectors.

Art theft can be a lucrative business. In May 2010, a lone thief stole five paintings from the Paris Museum of Modern Art, including works by Picasso and Matisse.[2] Estimates put the value of the art stolen at hundreds of millions of dollars. Two years prior to the Paris incident, armed robbers stole four paintings from a private museum in Zurich, Switzerland, with an estimated value of $163 million. The art included works by van Gogh and Monet, some of which were recovered. Similarly, in 2007, three paintings by Pablo Picasso were stolen in two separate incidents—one in Brazil and the other in Paris, France. The latter involved a night-time burglary at the home of one of Picasso's granddaughters. Art thefts are relatively common, and occur with great regularity.

The largest art theft in U.S. history took place at the Isabella Stewart Gardner Museum in Boston in 1990, when thieves made off with several paintings worth more than $300 million. In that case, two people disguised as Boston police officers entered the museum, incapacitated security guards, and made off with the paintings as well as surveillance tapes.[3] The Boston art theft was atypical for several reasons. According to Lynne Chafinch, an expert in art theft with the FBI, the vast majority of "stolen art is lower value" and hence represents works that will not be easily recognized.[4] Even though the FBI maintains a listing of stolen art and cultural property in its National Stolen Art File, the bureau investigates such thefts only if they occur in a "museum as defined by federal statute, [and then] a stolen artwork has to be either more than 100 years old and worth more than $5,000 or less than 100 years old and worth more than $100,000."[5] According to Don Hrycyk, who leads the art theft unit of the Los Angeles Police Department, one of the few of its kind nationally, many people involved in art theft are common burglars who steal art along with any other goods available. Other art thieves do not fit a conventional criminal profile and instead come from the ranks of college professors, gallery owners, and individuals involved in insurance fraud.[6] In more than a decade of such investigation, Hrycyk noted that about the only type of crook that he hasn't come across is the sophisticated, debonair thief portrayed in movies like *Entrapment* and *The Thomas Crown Affair.*[7] Learn more about art theft at **Web Extra 11–1**.

SuperStock/Glow Images

Henri Matisse's painting, "Pastoral" (1905), stolen from the National Museum of Modern Art in Paris in 2010. The painting remains unrecovered. Do you think that most art thieves know the value of the art that they steal?

Types of Property Crime

Both the Uniform Crime Reporting (UCR) Program and the National Crime Victimization Survey (NCVS) report data on property crimes. According to the FBI, the major **property crimes** are burglary, larceny, motor vehicle theft, and arson. Definitions used by the FBI for statistical data-gathering purposes are shown in Figure 11–1.

Burglary

Burglary is a common crime. The FBI defines **burglary** as the unlawful entry into a structure for the purpose of felony commission, generally a theft. The structure may be a business, a residence, or some other type of building. Force is not a necessary ingredient of burglary, but the FBI distinguishes between

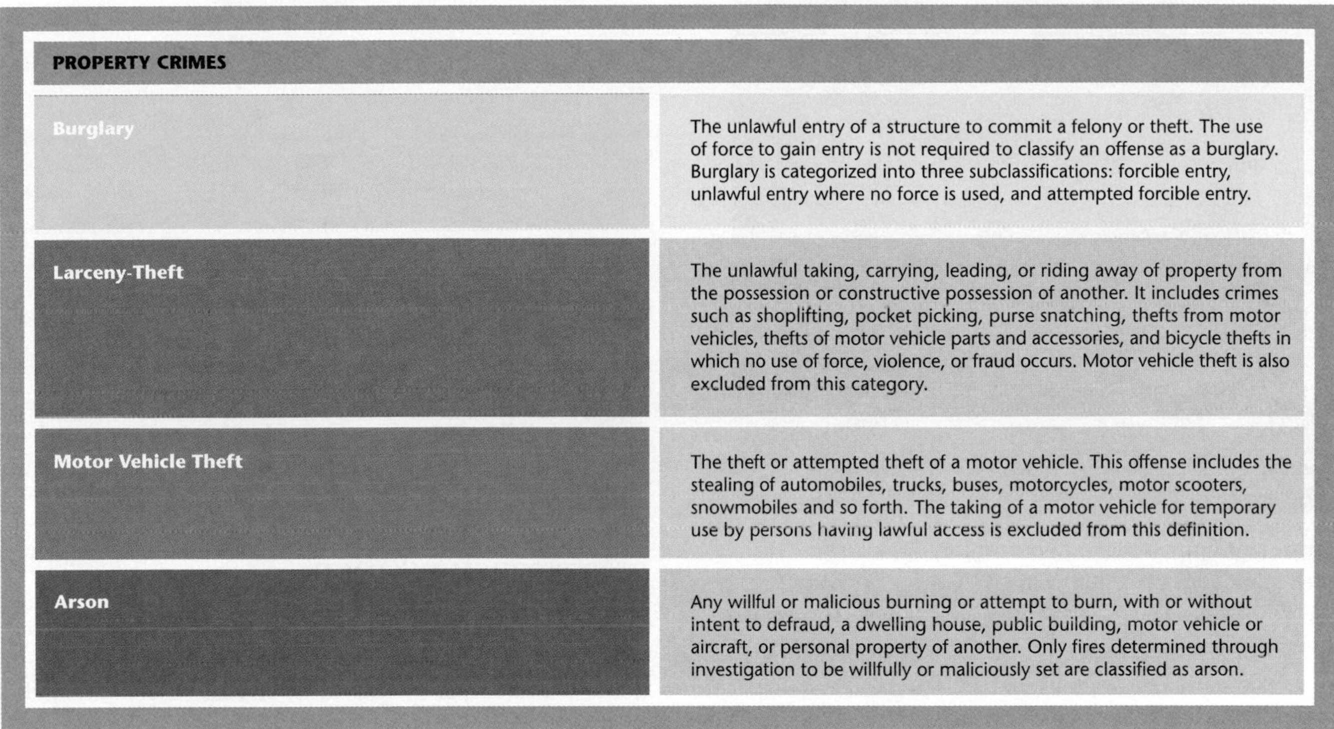

PROPERTY CRIMES	
Burglary	The unlawful entry of a structure to commit a felony or theft. The use of force to gain entry is not required to classify an offense as a burglary. Burglary is categorized into three subclassifications: forcible entry, unlawful entry where no force is used, and attempted forcible entry.
Larceny-Theft	The unlawful taking, carrying, leading, or riding away of property from the possession or constructive possession of another. It includes crimes such as shoplifting, pocket picking, purse snatching, thefts from motor vehicles, thefts of motor vehicle parts and accessories, and bicycle thefts in which no use of force, violence, or fraud occurs. Motor vehicle theft is also excluded from this category.
Motor Vehicle Theft	The theft or attempted theft of a motor vehicle. This offense includes the stealing of automobiles, trucks, buses, motorcycles, motor scooters, snowmobiles and so forth. The taking of a motor vehicle for temporary use by persons having lawful access is excluded from this definition.
Arson	Any willful or malicious burning or attempt to burn, with or without intent to defraud, a dwelling house, public building, motor vehicle or aircraft, or personal property of another. Only fires determined through investigation to be willfully or maliciously set are classified as arson.

FIGURE 11-1 | **Property Crimes and Their Definitions**
Source: FBI, Uniform Crime Reporting Program.

burglaries involving forcible entry, unlawful entry, and attempted forcible entry.[8] Based on a recent examination of victimization data, 72% of households within the United States are burglarized at least once.[9] In contrast to lifetime risk, however, the risk of burglary occurring within any given year is much lower. Even so, burglary is feared because the offense invades the sanctity of the home and threatens the existence of businesses.

In 2012, according to the FBI, there were an estimated 2,103,787 burglaries throughout the country. In that year, burglary accounted for 23.4% of the total number of property crimes committed. In 2012, burglary offenses cost victims an estimated $4.7 billion in lost property, and the average dollar loss per burglary offense was $2,230. Burglary of residential properties accounted for 74.5% of all burglary offenses, and 36% of residential burglaries occurred during the daytime, whereas 56.4% of nonresidential burglaries occurred during nighttime hours. Only about 15% of burglaries were cleared by arrest or other means in 2012.

In contrast to UCR/NIBRS reports, NCVS statistics on burglary paint quite a different picture. The NCVS reported 3,764,540 household burglaries and attempted burglaries in 2012—nearly 90% more than UCR/NIBRS estimates.[10] Rates of burglary were generally higher for African American households than for white households, regardless of family income levels, although wealthy African American families had far lower burglary rates than did low-income white families.

According to UCR/NIBRS data for 2012, most burglaries involve forcible entry, followed in prevalence by unlawful entry and then by attempted forcible entry. Most residential burglaries are likely to occur during the day.[11] Most residential burglars commit their offenses at a time when residents are unlikely to be home. This is an important factor in their choice of target.

The consequences of both residential and commercial burglary can be profound for the victim. Residential burglaries, by definition, do not involve direct confrontation between the victims and the perpetrators, although the invasion of one's home produces a level of fear and apprehension beyond the dollar loss of the property taken. In cases of commercial burglary, because the targets are likely to be smaller, less stable businesses, the loss from burglaries can seriously affect the business's viability.[12]

The Social Ecology of Burglary

Rates of property crimes vary across cities, communities, and states, with higher burglary rates in large metropolitan areas

Mediacolor's/Alamy

A ransacked home following a burglary. Burglary is a property crime that can turn violent if victims encounter the perpetrator. What are the characteristics of a professional burglar?

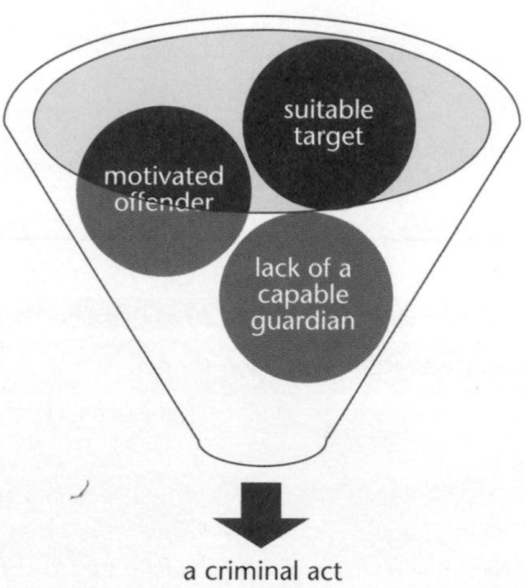

FIGURE 11-2 | The Social Ecology of Burglary

Source: Schmalleger, Frank J., *Criminology*. Printed and Electronically reproduced by permission of Pearson Education, Inc., Upper Saddle River, New Jersey.

and in particular regions, such as the South. Much research on variations in property crime at the aggregate level has examined how economics influences rates of crime. Lifestyle theory[13] and routine activities theory[14] (described in Chapter 3) have had a significant impact on explanations of how the nature and level of property crime have changed in response to alterations in the structures and routine activities of daily living. Both of these theoretical perspectives emphasize how criminal opportunity is affected by the everyday activities and environments experienced by victims and offenders. For a criminal act to occur, three ingredients are necessary: (1) someone who wants something (a *motivated offender*) coming in direct contact with (2) someone who has that thing (a *suitable target*) and (3) the lack of anything or anyone to inhibit the crime (a *capable guardian*). See Figure 11–2. The basic contention of both lifestyle theory and routine activities theory is that what people do, where they do it, how often they do it, and with whom they do it all influence the risk of criminal victimization, and the theories explore not why people commit crimes but rather "how the structure of social life makes it easy or difficult for people to carry out these inclinations," which are taken as a given.[15]

In a study of residential burglary, Lawrence E. Cohen and David Cantor set out to test Michael Hindelang's hypothesis that household wealth was a more important factor in selection of burglary targets than was ease of access to the household because they wanted to resolve often contradictory findings of previous research on the relationship between the impact of income and race on burglary victimization.[16] Cohen and Cantor found that,

Both the highest- and the lowest-income households have the greatest victimization risk.

independent of race, the highest-income households and the lowest-income households in areas both within and outside the central city had the greatest victimization risk, which meant that high-income households (with items of special value) and low-income households (with ease of access) were both targeted.

Using data from the British Crime Survey, Robert J. Sampson and John D. Wooldredge estimated the risk for crimes like burglary and personal theft.[17] Given the specific implications of two components of opportunity theory for victimization risk—the proximity of suitable targets and motivated offenders and the spatial structure of community organization—these researchers were concerned with the impact of community context on lifestyle. Sampson and Wooldredge's research revealed that the highest victimization risks for burglary were found in single-adult households, in households with younger adults as heads, and in households left unguarded. Of the seven community-level variables, all but one had moderate to strong effects: The highest victimization risks were for residents in areas characterized by high unemployment, high building density, primary individual households, and single-parent households with children. Even controlling for individual factors of single-person households, the community measure of percentage of single-adult households continues to have a significant effect on increasing the risk of burglary victimization.

Sampson and Wooldredge found that victimization risk for personal theft was less for those who were married, older, and male and higher for individuals with more education and for women.[18] The community factors of (1) the percentage of single adults with children, (2) social cohesion, and (3) street activity were significantly related to victimization risk—areas characterized by a high degree of family disruption, low social cohesion, and a large amount of street activity had higher victimization risks for personal theft. You can learn

THEORY | versus REALITY

Ethnographic Research on Active Burglars

Ethnographic research involving active burglars attempts to understand a burglar's way of life and hence offers a depth of insight rarely achieved in survey research or research using official data. However, ethnographic research is often dangerous, costly, and time-consuming.

The true benefit that comes from studying active burglars is related to an essential methodological issue common to all research endeavors: the classic issue of how individuals behave when they know they are being studied. In the case of studying burglars who are active versus those who are incarcerated, Richard T. Wright and Scott H. Decker note that individuals behave differently "in the wild" than in the jailhouse. The researchers point to statements made by two pioneers in criminology, Edwin Sutherland and Donald Cressey, more than 30 years ago: "Those who have had intimate contacts with criminals in the open know that criminals are not 'natural' in police stations, courts, and prisons, and that they must be studied in their everyday life outside of institutions if they are to be understood."[i] It is this concern for getting as close as possible to the social world one is studying that marks the tradition of ethnography.

Ethnographic research has already been described in Chapter 10, where research by Richard Wright and Scott Decker on armed robbers was discussed. This chapter presents further ethnographic research by Wright and Decker, this time on residential burglars. During 1989, the researchers located and interviewed 105 active residential burglars in St. Louis, Missouri. To qualify for inclusion in Wright and Decker's research, the offenders had to meet one of three criteria: they had to (1) have committed a residential burglary within two weeks prior to contact, (2) define themselves as residential burglars, or (3) be labeled as residential burglars by other offenders so identified. Research subjects were identified by the field workers whom Wright and Decker employed, most of whom were ex-offenders. The interviews with the subjects were all conducted in the field. Building on previous research on active offenders not currently incarcerated, Wright and Decker provide insight into various facets of the offending of burglars, including an examination of their motivation, target selection, entry method, search for valuable goods, and disposal of goods. In addition to answering questions, the offenders were asked to reconstruct their most recent residential burglary offense.

Defining the eligibility of subjects for research and using field workers are common practices in ethnographic research. Similar strategies were followed in other ethnographic research projects discussed in this chapter. They include research on 30 active burglars in an urban Texas setting by Paul F. Cromwell and his colleagues[ii] and research on the professional fence by Darrell J. Steffensmeier.[iii] As you read through the discussion of research in this chapter, keep in mind the strengths of ethnographic research and the insights to be gained by studying criminal offenders within their native social and cultural contexts.

Discussion Questions

1. What is ethnographic research? How does it differ from other types of research in the field of criminology?
2. Can criminologists learn anything special about burglary by focusing on active burglars who are not currently incarcerated—rather than on burglars who are imprisoned?

Notes

i. Edwin Sutherland and Donald Cressey, *Criminology*, 8th ed. (Philadelphia: Lippincott, 1970), p. 68, cited in Richard T. Wright and Scott H. Decker, *Burglars on the Job: Streetlife and Residential Break-Ins* (Boston: Northeastern University Press, 1994), p. 5.
ii. Paul F. Cromwell, James N. Olson, and D'Aunn Wester Avary, *Breaking and Entering: An Ethnographic Analysis of Burglary* (Newbury Park, CA: Sage, 1991).
iii. Darrell J. Steffensmeier, *The Fence: In the Shadow of Two Worlds* (Savage, MD: Rowman and Littlefield, 1986).

more about burglary trends by reading a special 2013 Bureau of Justice Statistics (BJS) report on household burglary via **Web Extra 11–2** and read about the most common targets of burglars at **Library Extra 11–1**. See the Theory versus Reality box for ethnographic research on active burglars.

A Typology of Burglars

A three-part typology of burglary types was offered by **Mike Maguire**: low-level, middle-range, and high-level burglars (Figure 11–3).[19] **Neil Shover** determined how the social organization of burglary varied based on Maguire's three types. *Low-level burglars* (primarily juveniles) often commit their crimes "on the spur of the moment," usually work with others, and are easily dissuaded from a particular target by sound locks, alarms, and/or other such security devices, and the rewards are generally not significant, so many desist from burglary as they get older and feel "the pull of conventional relationships and fear of more severe adult sanctions."[20] Members of this group never develop connections that allow them to move large volumes of stolen goods.

Middle-range burglars are a bit older (although they may have begun their offending as juveniles) and go back and forth between legitimate pursuits and involvement in crime, and the use of alcohol and other drugs is more common. These offenders select targets that take into account both the potential payoff and the risk involved; however, they are not as easily dissuaded

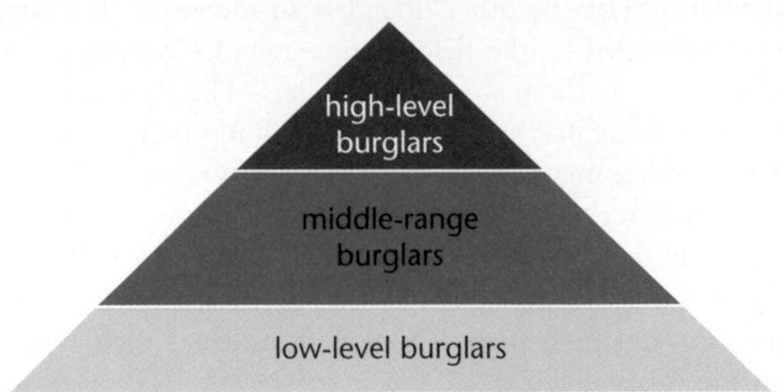

FIGURE 11-3 | **Types of Burglars**

Source: Schmalleger, Frank J., *Criminology*. Printed and Electronically reproduced by permission of Pearson Education, Inc., Upper Saddle River, New Jersey.

by security devices as the low-level burglars. Although their take from their crimes may be substantial at times, they lack the type of connections that would permit dealing in stolen goods on a large scale.

High-level burglars are professionals who work in organized crews and "are connected with reliable sources of information about targets."[21] Members of this group earn a good living from the proceeds of their crimes, which have carefully planned targets based on the assistance of outside sources (like the art theft described at the beginning of this chapter).

The Locales and Times of Burglary

Burglars may target residences and/or commercial buildings. Although most research has focused on residential burglary, many findings on offender patterns apply to both types. Police reports generally detail the time of the burglary, with nighttime residential burglary and daytime commercial burglary being considered the most serious. Evening hours are the time burglars are most likely to face homeowners, and daytime hours present the greatest risk of confrontation between offenders and customers or workers.[22] According to NCVS data, slightly more residential burglaries take place during the daytime than during the evening hours, but one-third of burglary reports do not contain information on when the burglary occurred, so those incidents could significantly change the temporal pattern of occurrence.[23]

Burglary is known as a "cold" crime because there is usually little physical evidence to link the offender to the offense. By the time the victim realizes there has been a burglary and calls the police, the burglar is long gone. However, commercial buildings are more likely to have alarms or other security devices.

The Motivation of Burglars

Rational choice perspectives (discussed in Chapter 3), which have guided a great deal of research on decision making among property offenders, contend that the decision-making process is not defined by only one objective or shared view of rationality but is guided by the logic and perspective of an individual offender. The way offenders justify their decisions may not make sense objectively, but their decisions have their own logic based on the offenders' social world and reflect the fact that many of them are "limited information processors with various simplifying strategies for resolving decisions."[24]

The most prevalent rationale behind residential burglary is economic: a need for fast cash.[25] Based on ethnographic research conducted in Texas[26] and in St. Louis,[27] active burglars do not have a conventional lifestyle, and most of their everyday concerns revolve around maintaining their street status and supporting a lifestyle of self-indulgence and often gratuitous consumption of drugs. Wright and Decker contended that the need to maintain a party lifestyle, to "keep up appearances," and to provide basic necessities for themselves and their families are all key factors that drive offenders' decisions to commit a burglary.[28]

The most common rationale behind residential burglary is a need for fast cash.

As in the ethnographic research on the lifestyle of armed robbers (discussed in Chapter 10), Wright and Decker found that the vast majority of residential burglars they interviewed were committed to a lifestyle of "every night is a Saturday night," so when offenders discussed their offending as a means of survival, it had to be interpreted against the backdrop of this lifestyle, for it was only in this context that an understanding of what they meant by "survival" emerged. The vast majority of offenders were committed to street culture, and almost three-fourths of the money they obtained from burglary pursuits went to support their party lifestyle, which included illicit drugs, alcohol, and sexual pursuits. Keeping up appearances resulted in the need to buy things that assisted in maintaining street status (the right clothes, the right car). Although some offenders interviewed by Wright and Decker did use the proceeds from their burglaries to pay their bills, the researchers noted that "the bills were badly delinquent because the offenders avoided paying them for as long as possible—even when they had the cash—in favor of buying, most typically, drugs."[29] The lifestyle of these offenders all but guaranteed that "the crimes they commit will be economically motivated," but it is not an economic motivation that results from a desire to satisfy needs as opposed to wants.[30]

Burglaries of commercial establishments are generally thought to be even more associated with instrumental ends—usually economic gain—than residential burglaries. The same is true of professional burglars, who invest more planning and strategy into their offenses, calculating and carefully weighing risks and benefits.

What causes offenders to focus on burglary as their crime of choice? Some offenders selected burglary quite simply because "they regarded burglary as their 'main line.'"[31] Because most of the offenders interviewed by Wright and Decker regarded themselves as hustlers, "people who were always looking to get over by making some fast cash," they would commit offenses other than burglary if an opportunity presented itself; otherwise, they stayed with burglary.[32] For many, burglary was not as risky as selling drugs, which has carried increasingly stiffer penalties that offenders fear. Robbery was perceived as too risky because it involved direct confrontation with the victim and hence a higher likelihood of being injured, and some offenders stated they did not own guns. Because guns can be easily translated into cash in the street economy, "offenders who are in need of immediate cash often are tempted to sell their weapon instead of resorting to a difficult or risky crime."[33]

A small number of offenders in Wright and Decker's research in St. Louis indicated that "they did not typically commit burglaries as much for the money as for the psychic rewards."[34] This is consistent with Katz's concept of sneaky thrills: "If we looked more closely at how [offenders] define material needs, we might get a different image of these 'serious thieves.'"[35] Based on his ethnographic research with property offenders, **Kenneth D. Tunnell** concluded that "excitement was present but only as a latent benefit—a by-product of the criminal act."[36]

Target Selection for Burglary

The sites for commercial burglaries are usually selected on the basis of suitability. Retail establishments are four times as likely to be burglarized as other types of establishments, such as wholesale or service businesses.

How do residential burglars select their targets? According to Wright and Decker, most residential burglars already have potential targets in mind before committing their offenses. Generally, burglars select a target by drawing on their knowledge of the occupants, "through receiving a tip," or "through observing a potential target."[37]

Whereas a prior relationship between offenders and victims has long characterized many violent crimes, property crimes generally do not involve known victims, and the pattern of the victim–offender relationship in property crimes does not mirror that of violent crimes; however, there are some interesting dynamics. The residential burglars interviewed by Wright and Decker rarely selected residences of close friends or relatives as targets, but they did quite often purposefully select as targets residences of individuals otherwise known to them.[38] An offender may also target known drug offenders because they can be victimized with relative impunity. A job provides offenders with the opportunity to get to know the occupants of a household and their daily routine as well as to determine their target suitability. When offenders did target residences of friends and loved ones, it was generally in two scenarios: One occurred when an argument or some type of wrongdoing on the victim's part had occurred, and the burglary was as much for revenge as for economic gain; the other involved the offender having such a desperate need for money that anyone was fair game. Although many offenders expressed remorse over having burglarized the homes of close family members, this was not universally the case, and burglars' expressions of remorse must be interpreted with the knowledge that "their allegiances seemed forever to be shifting to suit their own ends."[39]

Burglars may also select a target based on information from tipsters, who "regularly pass on intelligence about good burglary opportunities for a fee or a cut of the take."[40] Those who use tipsters do so in a variety of ways, including using individuals who work in service capacities in households and businesses and acting in collusion with insurance agents or other middle-class people who feed the offender information in exchange for money or for some stolen merchandise.

Approximately one-fourth of burglaries do not involve any type of forced entry, "the world affords abundant poorly protected opportunities for burglars."[41] Although offenders may not go out actively searching for potential targets, they are "continually 'half looking' for targets."[42]

Target selection is also influenced by other key elements such as signs of occupancy because "most offenders are reluctant to burglarize occupied dwellings," according to Wright and Decker.[43] Burglars have reported that they avoid occupied homes because they want to avoid injury to their victims and to themselves. For some offenders, the fear of their own injury was greater than the fear of apprehension: "I'd rather for the police to catch me versus a person catching me breaking in their house because the person will kill you."[44] To ensure that a residence was unoccupied, offenders would knock on the door (ready to offer some excuse if someone actually answered), phone the residence, or even phone the householder at work.

Most residential burglars also avoid residences with complex security devices because they generally lack the expertise to bypass such systems. Dogs also will deter an offender from a potential target because they make noise and could injure the offender. Offenders tended to stay in the same area, sometimes within walking distance, because of lack of a car. As one offender in Wright and Decker's research noted, "It's hard as hell getting on a bus carrying a big picture or a vase."[45]

The Costs of Burglary

According to the NCVS, well over three-fourths (86%) of all household burglaries involve some type of economic loss. Approximately 20% of household burglaries involve losses exceeding $1,000, 21% involve losses between $250 and $1,000, 24% involve losses between $50 and $249, and slightly more than 14% involve losses under $50.[46] What do offenders steal from homes? According to self-reports of victims of household burglary, 29% of items stolen from homes are personal in nature, with the largest categories being jewelry and clothing; household furnishings represent 11% of all stolen items, followed by tools (6%) and cash (6%). Another type of crime cost can be gauged by looking at whether victims lose time from work as a result of their victimization: Among all victims of household burglaries, approximately 7% lose some time from work, with 33% of those losing less than one day, slightly over 50% losing from one to five days, and 7% losing six days or more.[47]

Using NCVS data to test the relationship between criminal victimization and a household's decision to move, researcher **Laura Dugan** revealed that property crimes like burglary have a greater effect on the decision to move than violent crimes.[48] Dugan had hypothesized that experiencing a violent crime would have a greater effect on the decision to move—a hypothesis not supported by the data. Instead, she found that a household's likelihood of moving increased after experiencing a criminal victimization near the home, an effect that was significant and strong for property crime but not for violent crime. Communities are also affected because the more affluent households are the ones most likely to relocate after experiencing victimization.

The Burglary–Drug Connection

During the 1980s, the parallel rates of robbery and burglary began to diverge, with robbery increasing and burglary decreasing. Using city-level data from 1984 to 1992, research by Eric Baumer and colleagues linked these changes to the effects of an increased demand for crack cocaine on altering structures of offending.[49] As a stimulant, crack use is characterized by short highs that are "followed by an intense desire for more crack."[50] If users are funding their drug habit through criminal pursuits, they need to rely on offenses that complement the demands of their drug of choice—offenses like robbery—that can net cash quickly, directly, anytime; burglary is more likely to net stolen goods than cash. As the illicit market for crack drove down the street value of stolen property, "dramatically enhancing the attractiveness of cash," burglary became an offense with diminishing rewards.[51] Ethnographic research on active burglars supported the claim that in areas with a strong crack cocaine trade, there was also a "preference for cash-intensive crimes like robbery and a corresponding reduced preference for burglary."[52] This is consistent with research that emphasized that most property offenders are generalists rather than strictly committed to one type of property offense.

The Sexualized Context of Burglary

Although economic gain is the primary motive for the vast majority of burglaries, some criminologists say that there is a category of burglaries with "hidden sexual forces lying at their root."[53] According to Louis B. Schlesinger and Eugene Revitch, the sexual dynamics associated with burglaries may be of two general interrelated types: One type of offender craves fetishes, stealing particular items as an outlet for sexual gratification rather than for their material value. A voyeuristic burglar has a more subtle sexual dynamic in which the goal may be just to "look around, to inspect the drawers," but not to actually take anything.[54] Schlesinger and Revitch analyzed the clinical records of 52 sexual murderers and found that the majority of these offenders had a history of burglaries, so burglary may serve as a precursor to more serious offenses and may constitute part of a pattern of sexual offending. A certain number of sexually motivated homicides begin as other offenses, such as burglary, and the ability to link the two early in the investigation is important for effective forensic assessment, so details of a burglary should be more purposefully evaluated because they could be related to a progression of events that could culminate in homicide.

Some sexually motivated homicides begin as other offenses, such as burglary.

Mark Warr investigated the connection of sexual offenses with property crimes from a different perspective.[55] Not only can sexual motives underlie property crimes, Warr argued, but the theoretical perspective of opportunity theory (discussed in Chapter 6) can explain patterns of rape and burglary. Warr said that "residential rape and burglary can be viewed as crimes of stealth that involve the unlawful entry of a structure [and] have very similar opportunity structures."[56] Using city arrest data, Warr found support for his contention that both the type of residence and the type of people victimized are similar enough

■ **larceny-theft** The unlawful taking, carrying, leading, or riding away of property (other than a motor vehicle) from the possession or constructive possession of another (attempts are included), according to the UCR/NIBRS.

in certain rape and burglary incidents to call into question the idea that rape shares a criminal etiology exclusively with violent offending.

For a certain category of rape termed *home-intrusion rape*, "the traditional distinction between violent crime and property crime may not apply," and such incidents represent a "hybrid offense"; they are "a violent crime with the opportunity structure of a property crime."[57] According to Warr, the correspondence in the opportunity structures of rape and burglary warrants consideration if research and investigative procedures are to identify the "proximate causes of rape."[58]

Larceny-Theft

Larceny-theft is defined by the UCR Program as "the unlawful taking, carrying, leading, or riding away of property from the possession, or constructive possession, of another."[59] Just about anything can be stolen. In California during November 2000, for example, thieves stole "more than 1,200 young orange trees during nightly raids at the San Joaquin Valley, heartland of the state's citrus crop."[60]

The FBI reports that during 2012, there were an estimated 6.2 million larceny-thefts nationwide and larceny-thefts accounted for an estimated 68.5% of all property crimes. The rate of larceny-theft is 1,959 per every 100,000 people living in the United States. On average, larceny-theft offenses cost victims an estimated $6.1 billion in lost property annually.

Larceny is the most frequently occurring property offense according to official data compiled by the FBI and data from the NCVS. Within the offenses subsumed under the category of larceny in UCR/NIBRS data, the largest category is theft from motor vehicles, followed by shoplifting and theft from buildings (Figure 11–4).[61] Offenses such as pocket picking and purse snatching constitute a small percentage of all larcenies, less than 1% each. Just as rates of different offenses within the category of larceny differ, so, too, do estimated losses to victims.

As a form of theft, larceny (as opposed to burglary) does not involve the use of force or other means of illegal entry. For this reason, among others, larceny is a crime "less frightening than burglary because to a large, perhaps even to a preponderant extent, it is a crime of opportunity, a matter of making off with whatever happens to be lying around loose: Christmas presents in an unlocked car, merchandise on a store counter, a bicycle in a front yard."[62]

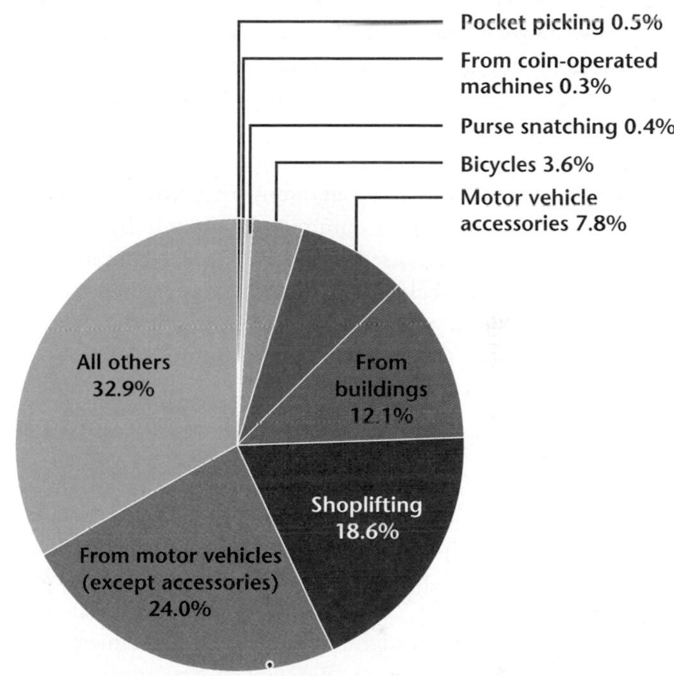

FIGURE 11–4 | **Larceny-Theft Distribution, 2012**

Source: Federal Bureau of Investigation, *Crime in the United States, 2012* (Washington, DC: FBI, 2013).

Shoplifting and Employee Theft

Thefts cost U.S. retailers a staggering $33.6 billion in an average year.[63] Some retail theft is shoplifting, but other theft is committed by store employees. "The theft of merchandise by employees can range from the simple act of walking out the door with stolen goods to complex schemes requiring the manipulation of documents and/or involving several employees."[64] Most of the employees engaging in theft of either cash or merchandise are short-term workers. They are typically found in retail establishments with higher-than-average sales and a significant degree of turnover in management. Many retailers believe the issue of internal theft to be more serious than the economic loss caused by customer shoplifting.

Nonetheless, retailers must consider that efforts to combat shoplifting might impact sales. This concern was reflected by a marketing director who commented, "You don't want to hinder sales by intimidating the shopper. We used to think just about stopping shoplifting. We didn't think enough about selling more merchandise."[65]

Technology represents one of the best ways to address both shoplifting and employee theft. The use of computerized inventory counts to track merchandise is useful in quickly identifying thefts by employees. As will be discussed shortly, the widespread prevalence of shoplifting among youths who are fast and often operate together in small gangs means that increased security personnel in stores are less successful at detection than are electronic and other devices.

Shoplifting continues to be an offense that crosses class lines, although it is not an offense committed primarily by women. The dominant motivation used today to explain shoplifting does not rely on medical labels. Even though "respectable" people continue to be found among those who commit this offense, there is no evidence that these individuals constitute a significant segment of offenders.

Who Shoplifts?

On August 4, 2010, Caroline Giuliani, the 20-year-old daughter of former New York City Mayor Rudolph Giuliani, was arrested and placed in handcuffs after she stuffed makeup worth about $100 into her jacket pockets at a Sephora store in New York's Upper East Side.[66] The younger Giuliani, a Harvard University student, was caught on store security cameras and charged with larceny. Many people viewed the arrest as ironic because her father, a former presidential candidate, became famous as a strong law-and-order mayor. One month later, in a plea deal arranged in Manhattan Criminal Court, Giuliani was ordered to serve one day of community service working for the city's Sanitation Department.[67]

Giuliani is not the first well-known person to be charged with shoplifting. In another case, on December 6, 2002, actress Winona Ryder was sentenced to three years of probation and required to perform 480 hours of community service for shoplifting more than $5,500 in merchandise from a Beverly Hills, California, Saks Fifth Avenue store a year earlier; and in 2011, Lindsay Lohan was charged with felony grand theft for allegedly stealing a $2,500 necklace from a Venice, California, jewelry store.[68]

Neither the Ryder, Lohan, nor the Giuliani case, however, is that of a typical shoplifter. In self-reports of offending, official arrest data, and store records, juveniles are overrepresented as shoplifters. Variation exists in the frequency of offending among adolescents, but most offending patterns are fairly sporadic and are characterized by a greater prevalence among younger adolescents. The sporadic nature of shoplifting among adolescents is typical across all social classes even though the most serious and chronic forms are found among the economically disadvantaged. Although females represent the majority of offenders in some shoplifting data sources, this finding has been seriously challenged in research since the 1970s.[69]

Research by **Lloyd W. Klemke**, which used self-report techniques to assess juvenile shoplifting, revealed that almost two-thirds of the sample had shoplifted at some point in their lifetime.[70] Although previous research by **Mary Owen Cameron**, using department store records, had revealed that females were more likely than males to be apprehended for shoplifting,[71] Klemke found the reverse to be true. The difference in these findings may be attributed to the fact that Klemke's research included only adolescents, whereas Cameron's research also included adults.

Youths from lower-income households are more likely to shoplift than are their higher-income counterparts. However, this relationship is a moderate one at best, and the fact remains that shoplifting is reported by a solid majority of youths in several self-report studies. The relationship between social class and likelihood of shoplifting is stronger among adults.

Among Klemke's other findings was a "maturing out" pattern, whereby "shoplifting activity peaked in the under ten age category" and decreased considerably as the youths entered adolescence.[72] These findings are contrary to other research that supports escalation during late adolescence.

Flash Mobs and Larceny

Over the past few years, a new term has entered the popular lexicon—flash mobs. Flash mobs are purposeful crowds of people brought together on a moment's notice through the use of social media Web sites such as Twitter and Facebook. Sometimes the gatherings are peaceful and fun—as was the case in 2011 when a McDonald's restaurant in Chicago asked people to dress in beach

Lisa S./Shutterstock

A young shoplifter in action. As the text points out, shoplifting is a common offense. Who shoplifts and why?

CRIME | in the NEWS

"Flash Robs" Become a Troublesome Trend

"Flash robs," a crime akin to shoplifting, but on a massive scale, are a form of larceny. Although there were a few flash robs in the news as far back as 2002, these crimes only become a nationwide phenomenon in 2011 and were still being widely reported in 2014. Typically, a large group of teenagers files into a convenience store, takes low-priced candy and sodas, and exits immediately. The whole incident takes as little as one minute.

Flash robs are not technically robberies, because there is no threat of force. Filmed on a store's security video (and then posted later on the Internet), smiling participants form an orderly line and limit themselves to one or two goodies each. They don't brandish any weapons, but store employees are frightened and usually stay out of the way.

This new form of lawbreaking comes at a time when youth crime is relatively low. From 2008 to 2009, juvenile arrests for violent crime fell 10%, according to a 2012 Justice Department report. But the economy is ailing and high percentages of black teenagers don't have jobs. In June 2012, the unemployment rate among blacks ages 16 to 19 was 39.3%—high for African American rates and nearly double the 20.9% rate for whites the same age.

A youthful group dynamic takes hold in a flash rob. "Young people are risk-takers," said Scott Decker, a professor of criminology at Arizona State University. "They do things in groups far more than adults do." He believes they are proud rather than upset when they see themselves in the videos shown on the evening news. They feel protected by the power of numbers, said New York psychologist Jeff Gardere.

The store's security videos help authorities identify perpetrators, but prosecuting them can be frustrating. Many hundreds of dollars' worth of goods may be stolen, but one person's take is just a few bucks, which amounts to nothing more than a Class C misdemeanor. When prosecutors intercept messages on social media from kids planning the event, they can add conspiracy charges, but according to the National Retail Federation, social media is identified in less than half of apprehended cases of flash robs.

To aid prosecution, the Maryland Legislature has been considering a bill that would treat multiple acts of theft in unison as one crime. The measure would automatically define a flash rob as a conspiracy, and charges against each person would depend on the total amount stolen, not on each person's take. The bill failed in 2012, but sponsors plan to reintroduce it soon.

DailyMail/Rex/Alamy

A flash robbery in progress. How do social media facilitate such crimes?

Discussion Questions

1. How do flash robberies differ from other kinds of larceny?
2. What kind of impact might this kind of crime, if it continues to expand, have on retailers?

Sources: Derek Valcourt, "Law Enforcement Frustrated with Growing Number of Flash Mob Crimes in Md.," CBS Baltimore, July 26, 2012, http://baltimore.cbslocal.com/2012/07/26/law-enforcement-frustrated-with-growing-number-of-flash-mob-crimes-in-md/; Ellen Arndt, "Fighting the Rising Tide of Flash Mobs in Retail," *Security*, July 24, 2012, http://www.securitymagazine.com/articles/83326-fighting-the-rising-tide-of-flash-mobs-in-retail; and Tim Dees, "Stay on Top of 'Flash Robs'," PoliceOne.com, June 12, 2012, http://www.policeone.com/police-products/communications/articles/5603418-Stay-on-top-of-flash-robs.

attire and to converge on its location.[73] Other flash mobs, however, can have more insidious purposes and even involve organized criminal activity. In April 2011, for example, scores of teenagers organized through Tweets descended on a high-end men's clothing retailer in Washington, D.C., and stole about $20,000 worth of merchandise. Frantic employees tried to grab the apparel back as it was taken from shelves, but the crowd was too large.

Loss-prevention specialists refer to larcenies committed by flash mobs as multiple-offender crimes, and statistics show that 10% of retail establishments report being victimized by multiple offenders who formed flash mobs during a recent 12-month period.[74] In 2012, in recognition of the problem, the National Retail Federation issued a report outlining steps that stores could take to combat criminal flash mobs.[75] Those steps include

■ **identity-theft** The unauthorized use of another individual's personal identity to fraudulently obtain money, goods, or services; to avoid the payment of debt; or to avoid criminal prosecution.

■ **Identity Theft and Assumption Deterrence Act** The first federal law to make identity theft a crime. The 1998 statute makes it a crime whenever anyone "knowingly transfers or uses, without lawful authority, a means of identification of another person with the intent to commit, or to aid or abet, any unlawful activity that constitutes a violation of federal law, or that constitutes a felony under any applicable state or local law."

■ **Identity Theft Penalty Enhancement Act** A 2004 federal law that added two years to federal prison sentences for criminals convicted of using stolen credit card numbers and other personal data to commit crimes.

documenting the larceny, especially through the use of video recordings and store security cameras, and quickly reporting the events to law enforcement agencies. Some states have even considered criminalizing flash mobs in an effort to prevent the kinds of crimes to which they can lead.

Identity Theft

Identity theft—the misuse of another individual's personal information to commit fraud[76]—is a relatively new form of larceny that appears to be growing rapidly. Identity theft involves obtaining credit, merchandise, or services by fraudulent personal representation. Usually, individuals learn that they have become identity theft victims only after being denied credit or employment or when a debt collector seeks payment for a debt the victim did not incur. The most threatening aspects of identity theft are its potential relationship to international terrorism. Even where terrorism is not involved, identity theft can be used broadly by transnational crime rings.

The misuse of stolen personal information can be classified into two broad categories. *Existing account fraud* occurs when thieves obtain account information involving credit, brokerage, banking, or utility accounts that are already open. Existing account fraud is typically less costly, but more prevalent. A stolen credit card may lead to thousands of dollars in fraudulent charges, for example, but the card generally will not provide a thief with enough information to establish a false identity. Moreover, most credit card companies do not hold consumers liable for fraudulent charges, and federal law caps liability of victims of credit card theft at $50.

The second and more serious category is *new account fraud*. In new account fraud, identity thieves use personal information such as Social Security numbers, birth dates, and home addresses to open new accounts in the victim's name, make charges indiscriminately, and then disappear. Although this type of identity theft is less likely to occur, it imposes much greater costs and hardships on victims. In addition, identity thieves sometimes use stolen personal information to obtain government, medical, or other benefits to which the criminals are not legally entitled.

In addition to the losses that result when identity thieves fraudulently open accounts or misuse existing accounts, monetary costs of identity theft include indirect costs to businesses for fraud prevention and mitigation of the harm once it has occurred (for example, for mailing notices to consumers and upgrading systems). Similarly, individual victims often suffer indirect financial costs, including the costs incurred in dealing with civil litigation initiated by creditors and in overcoming the many obstacles they face in obtaining or retaining credit. Victims of nonfinancial identity theft, for example, including health-related or criminal record fraud, face other types of harm and frustration.

Consumers' fears of becoming identity theft victims can also harm the digital economy. In a recent online survey conducted by the Business Software Alliance and Harris Interactive, nearly 30% of adults interviewed said that security fears caused them to shop online less or not at all.[77] Identity theft became a federal crime in 1998 with the passage of the **Identity Theft and Assumption Deterrence Act**.[78] The law makes it a crime whenever anyone "knowingly transfers or uses, without lawful authority, a means of identification of another person with the intent to commit, or to aid or abet, any unlawful activity that constitutes a violation of federal law, or that constitutes a felony under any applicable state or local law."

The 2004 **Identity Theft Penalty Enhancement Act**[79] added two years to federal prison sentences for criminals convicted of using stolen credit card numbers and other personal data to commit crimes. It also prescribed prison sentences for those who use identity theft to commit other crimes, including terrorism, and it increased penalties for defendants who exceed or abuse the authority of their position in unlawfully obtaining or misusing means of personal identification.

The Incidence of Identity Theft

In 2011, the Bureau of Justice Statistics (BJS) provided information on the incidence of identity theft derived from the National Crime Victimization Survey (NCVS).[80] For statistical reporting purposes, the BJS defines *identity theft* to include the following three behaviors: (1) the unauthorized use or attempted use of existing credit cards, (2) the unauthorized use or attempted use of other existing accounts such as checking accounts, and (3) the misuse of personal information to obtain new accounts or loans or to commit other crimes.

BJS surveyors found that at least one member of 7% of all households, or about 8.6 million households, had been the victim of identity theft during the previous year. The most

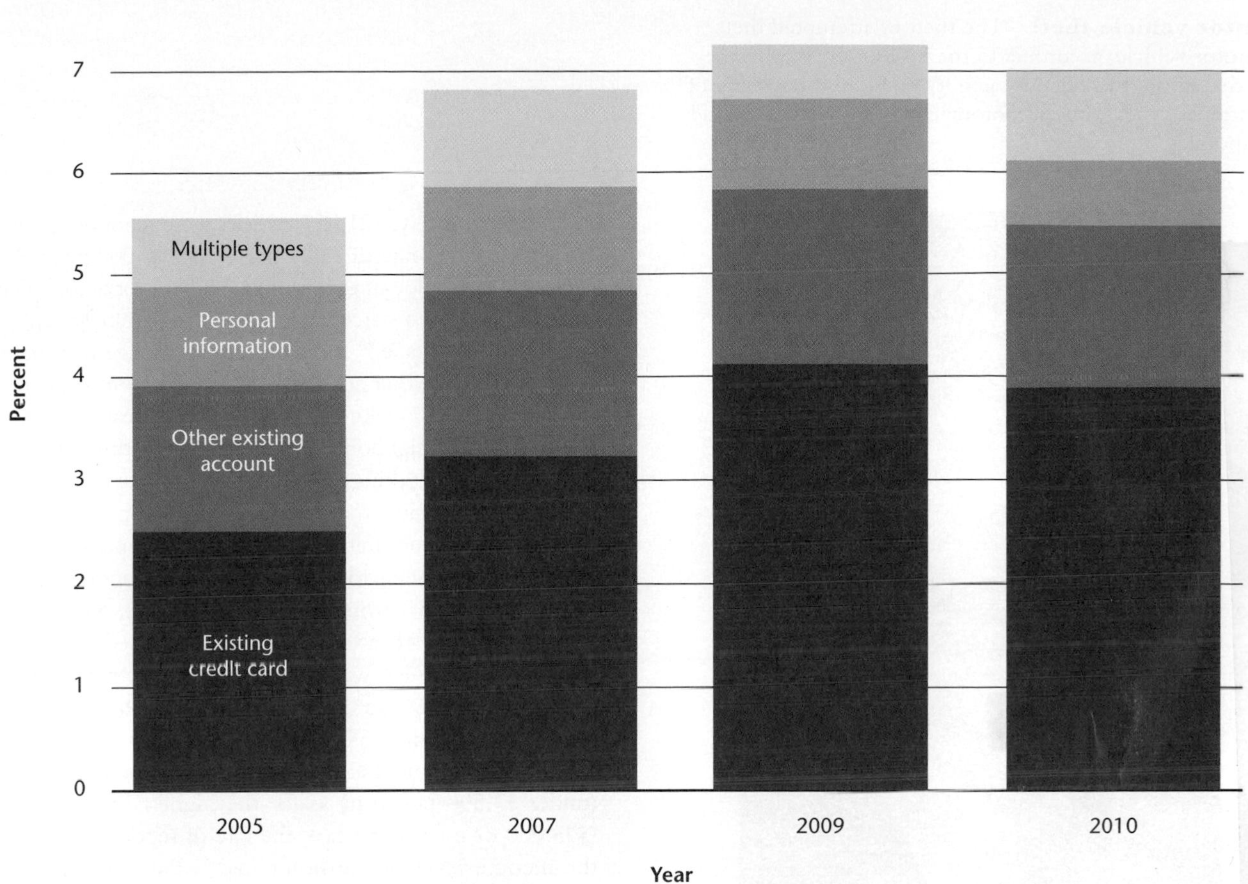

FIGURE 11-5 | **Percent of Households that Experienced Identity Theft, by Type of Theft, 2005-2010**
Source: Lynn Langton, *Identity Theft Reported by Households, 2005-2010* (Washington, DC: Bureau of Justice Statistics, 2011), p. 1.

common type of identity theft uncovered was the unauthorized use of credit cards, experienced by 5.5 million households in the 12-month period covered by the survey (Figure 11–5). About 3 million households reported being victimized by the theft of an existing account other than a credit card account, such as the use or attempted use of a cell phone account, bank account, or debit card/checking account without permission.

The BJS survey also revealed that about one in six victimized households had to pay higher interest rates as the result of identity theft and that one in nine households was denied phone or utility service as a consequence of being victimized.[81] About 7% of victimized households were turned down for insurance or had to pay higher rates, 5% became the subject of a civil suit or judgment, 4% became the subject of a criminal investigation, and about 20% reported other kinds of problems.

Identity Thieves: Who They Are

Unlike some groups of criminals, identity thieves cannot be readily classified.[82] According to a survey of identity theft by the Federal Trade Commission (FTC), about 14% of victims claim to know the perpetrator, who may be a family member, a friend, or an in-home employee. Identity thieves can act alone or as part of a criminal enterprise. Each poses unique threats to the public.

Identity thieves often have no prior criminal background and sometimes have preexisting relationships with the victims. They have been known to prey on people they know, including coworkers, senior citizens for whom they may be serving as caretakers, and even family members. Some identity thieves use minimal sophistication, such as stealing mail from homeowners' mailboxes or trash containing financial documents. In some jurisdictions, identity theft by illegal immigrants has resulted in passport, employment, and Social Security fraud. Occasionally, loosely knit groups of individuals with no significant criminal records work together to obtain personal information and even to create false or fraudulent documents.[83]

Law enforcement agencies also have seen increased involvement of foreign organized criminal groups in computer- or Internet-related identity theft schemes. In Asia and Eastern Europe, for example, organized groups are increasingly sophisticated both in the techniques they use and in the complexity of their tools. According to law enforcement agencies, such groups also are demonstrating increasing levels of sophistication and specialization in their online crime, even selling goods and

■ **motor vehicle theft** The theft or attempted theft of a motor vehicle, according to the UCR/NIBRS. In the FBI's definition, this offense category includes the stealing of automobiles, trucks, buses, motorcycles, motor scooters, and snowmobiles.

Presselect/Alamy

Actor Will Smith. Smith became the victim of identity theft in 2009 when Carlos Lomax, 45, used Smith's legal name, "Willard C. Smith," along with other personal information about the actor to open 14 bogus credit accounts in the Pittsburgh area. Could *your* identity be stolen?

services—such as software templates for making counterfeit identification cards and payment card magnetic strip encoders—that make the stolen data even more valuable to those who have it.

Motor Vehicle Theft

The UCR Program defines **motor vehicle theft** as "the theft or attempted theft of a motor vehicle," where the term *motor vehicle* refers to various means of transportation, including automobiles, buses, motorcycles, and snowmobiles.[84] Automobiles are the type of vehicle most often stolen. Cars represent more than merely a possession; for many Americans, they are an extension of their identity. The type of car a person drives reflects social status and personal identity.

The theft of a car, then, violates the victim in a way that goes beyond financial loss. Auto theft also makes it difficult for many people to get to work and sometimes requires them to take time away from work to take care of the incident.[85]

Approximately, 721,053 vehicles were reported stolen in 2012 (for an auto theft rate of 229.7 per every 100,000 people), with an estimated total value in excess of $4.3 billion (or $6,019 per vehicle stolen). The largest percentage of thefts was vehicles stolen from a parking lot or garage.[86] A significant percentage of motor vehicle theft took place either at or quite near the victim's residence, with approximately 17% taking place on a street near the home.[87] Depending on the neighborhood in which the victim resides, *near home* can mean different things, and the same distance from the residence in urban communities may be more of a risk for motor vehicle theft than in other communities. Marcus Felson contends that the risks posed by where one parks are related to population density.

Based on data from NCVS, on average, 81% of all motor vehicle thefts, both attempted and completed, are reported to the police. As is seen with other offenses, the reporting percentage is higher (90%) for completed motor vehicle thefts than for attempted incidents (54%).[88] Although the rate of motor vehicle victimization is the same for the lowest-income households (under $7,500 per year) as for the highest-income households ($75,000 or more per year), the rate of reporting increases with the income level of the household.[89] Based on available data, approximately 62% of stolen cars are recovered.[90] Both law enforcement agencies and insurance companies keep records of recovered vehicles, but each uses its own definition of *recovery*, and some "recovered" cars may actually have been totally destroyed.

Theft of Car Parts

Cars are stolen for a variety of reasons, including joyriding, temporary transportation needs, use in a crime, and stripping. Each of these rationales is representative of a fairly distinctive offender profile. Given the wide variety of rationales supporting automobile theft, almost any type of car is a target. However, thieves tend to prefer certain cars. According to Robert Bryant, chief executive officer of the National Insurance Crime Bureau, "Vehicle thieves follow market trends and target the most popular vehicles because they provide the best market for stolen vehicle parts and illegal export to other countries."[91]

Approximately one-third of stolen vehicles that are scored as "recovered" are completely stripped at chop shops, and another third are stripped of easy-to-sell accessories like radios, air bags, and seats.[92] The theft of car parts is variously motivated. Some car parts are worth a significant sum on the illegal market and can be sold easily by even the most inexperienced thieves. Novice thieves usually do not have access to the type of network required to sell "hot cars." Also, stolen car parts are more difficult to identify than entire cars.[93]

In the United States, the Motor Vehicle Theft Law Enforcement Act,[94] passed by Congress in 1984, "called for the marking of the major sheet metal parts of high-theft automobiles

CRIMINAL | PROFILES

Frank W. Abagnale, Jr.—"Catch Me If You Can"

High school dropout Frank Abagnale never met a credential he couldn't cheerfully ignore. He simply assumed any role that needed a credential and let you assume that he had it—or helped you assume he had it by showing you convincing forgeries of qualifying documents. Airline pilot, attorney, pediatrician, college professor, stockbroker, and FBI agent were all roles that Abagnale convincingly assumed at one point or other in his criminal career.[i]

Born April 17, 1948, Abagnale started a life of crime by conning his father out of $2,500 just after the younger Abagnale's sixteenth birthday. Allowed to use his father's gas credit card, Abagnale schemed for spending money by using the card to buy tires from a gas station, then selling them back to the station owner at half price for cash.[ii] The scam was discovered at the same time that Abagnale's parents were divorcing, which gave him an excuse to run off to New York.

He was a 16-year-old runaway when he made his first big score—$40,000—by printing up a bunch of bank deposit slips with his own account number (obtained, of course, under a false name) printed on them in magnetic ink. He then placed them at the service desk in the bank's lobby in place of the generic deposit slips provided by the bank for customer use. Other customers used the slips to make deposits, thinking that the deposit would be credited to their own account. In reality, the automated processing equipment would read Abagnale's account number magnetically encoded on the slip and credit his account for the amount of the deposit. When the account balance reached $40,000, he simply withdrew the funds and closed the account.

After five years of tricking people around the world, Abagnale was arrested while pretending to be a licensed commercial airline pilot when an Air France flight attendant recognized him from a wanted poster on the bulletin board in the employee lounge. Abagnale subsequently served time in prisons in France (six months) and Sweden (six months) before he was finally extradited to the United States. Convicted of federal forgery charges, he received a 12 year sentence to federal prison.[iii]

Abagnale's exploits during that infamous five-year period of non-stop cons were the subject of Steven Spielberg's highly successful film *Catch Me If You Can*, released in 2002.

After Abagnale had served four years of his sentence, he received an offer from the U.S. government that changed his life. Wanting to learn how to prevent future Abagnale-like scams, the U.S. government asked Abagnale to teach them how he carried out the frauds, and how to prevent others from doing them in the future. Specifically, they wanted to explore his ability to manipulate official documents so as to virtually eliminate any chance of detection. In exchange, the government offered him immediate release from prison.[iv]

And that is how Frank Abagnale, the most successful con man of the twentieth century, morphed into a world-renowned expert on forgery, embezzlement, and document security. Today, he heads Abagnale and Associates, a highly respected secure document consultancy. Abagnale has become an extraordinarily successful author and lecturer whose speeches, according to multiple-Oscar–winner Tom Hanks, "may be the best one-man show you will ever see."[v]

Lucy Nicholson/Associated Press

Frank Abagnale, Jr., posing for a photo at the Four Seasons Hotel in Beverly Hills, California. Abagnale, portrayed by actor Leonardo DiCaprio in the film *Catch Me If You Can* is the real-life subject of a book he wrote about his time as a successful con artist. How does Abagnale differ from most other property offenders?

The case of Frank Abagnale raises a number of questions. Among them are the following:

1. Abagnale pretended to be someone he wasn't. But is the phrase *identity theft* applicable to Abagnale, or should his crimes be described in other ways?
2. What might life course theory say about Abagnale's early deviance? How did his behavior differ from others who commit property crimes?
3. Why did Abagnale persist in criminal behavior even though he knew he'd probably get caught?
4. Today Abagnale runs a fraud-prevention business. How do you think his criminal experience aided his new professional career?

Notes

i. Bernie Alexander, "Frank Abagnale: From Fraud to FBI," AskMen.com, http://www.askmen.com/toys/special_feature/36_special_feature.html (accessed July 10, 2007).

ii. Norman Swan, "Frank Abagnale–New Life," *Life Matters*, March 17, 2000, http://www.abc.net.au/rn/talks/lm/stories/s111098.htm (accessed July 10, 2007).

iii. Rachael Bell, "Skywayman: The Story of Frank W. Abagnale Jr.," CourtTV Crime Library, http://www.crimelibrary.com/criminal_mind/scams/frank_abagnale/index.html (accessed July 10, 2007).

iv. Ibid.

v. Keppler Speakers home page, http://www.kepplerspeakers.com/speakers/speakers.asp?1+FV+1175 (accessed May 21, 2007).

■ **joyriding** An opportunistic car theft, often committed by a teenager, for fun or thrills.

WHO'S TO BLAME—The Individual or Society?

Body Parts for Sale

On March 20, 2013, Dr. Paul Sutter, a Palm Beach, Florida, plastic surgeon, was arrested and charged with a federal crime after he allegedly purchased facial bones that he knew had been illegally removed from a cadaver, and implanted them into a wealthy female patient undergoing elective facial reconstructive surgery following a car accident. The doctor and a mortician, who sold him the bones, were both charged with violating the National Organ Transplant Act of 1984, which expressly prohibits interstate trafficking in human tissue for profit.

In an interview the doctor gave after posting bail, Sutter told reporters, "I understand that there's a law against what I did. But it's not my fault that the materials I need to work with are frequently so hard to acquire. There needs to be a better system in place for the distribution of bones and other tissues that are so desperately needed by patients like the woman whose face I reconstructed in this case."

Think about it

1. Why did Sutter violate the law? What do you think was his primary motivation for what he did?
2. Do you think it would have mattered to Sutter's patient had she known that the bones used in her surgery had been acquired illegally?
3. Can body parts be considered items of property, like a person's other possessions? If so, should he or she have the right to sell them—perhaps to the highest bidder?

Learn more about the illegal trade in body parts at **Library Extra 11-2**.

Note: Who's to Blame boxes provide fictionalized critical thinking opportunities, and are not actual cases.

with Vehicle Identification Numbers (VINs). The point of the law was to enable detection of persons engaged in the presumably widespread sale of stolen parts to the auto body repair industry."[95] Although data are scarce on how many car thefts are carried out for stripping, some research has been conducted in this regard both in the United States and elsewhere.

Joyriders: Car Theft for Fun

Some car thefts are opportunistic in nature, committed by teenagers, usually in groups, for the purpose of fun or thrills. These offenses are referred to as **joyriding**. Because these thefts involve the temporary use of a vehicle primarily to satisfy needs ranging from excitement to personal autonomy, joyriding is often characterized as an "expressive act with little or no extrinsic value."[96] This motivation for auto theft is not characterized by planning and quite often involves an unlocked car left in a public place, frequently with the keys in the ignition.[97]

Most vehicles stolen for purposes of joyriding are recovered, usually found abandoned, often after they have been crashed. Although adolescents may select a vehicle for joyriding that belongs to strangers, they are more likely to select the car of a known owner.[98]

Research offers no definite answer as to whether there is a distinctive social class profile of the joyriding offender. Some research indicates that higher social class can be associated with greater involvement in auto theft because of greater access to cars and an earlier association of cars as status symbols. On the other hand, the "disadvantaged-group hypothesis" contends that youths from lower socioeconomic classes are more likely to be involved in car thefts because conventional means of acquiring status symbols such as cars are blocked, and they are left with only the avenue of illegitimate acquisition.[99] Although some support has been found for each of these perspectives, other research has failed to find a link between social class and involvement in auto theft among adolescents.[100]

Although representing the most costly and most serious form of auto theft, professional thefts are not as common as thefts for other uses, such as joyriding. Like joyriders, professional auto thieves operate in groups, but their groups are characterized by a great deal more planning and calculation in target selection. The cars targeted by professional thieves are luxury cars that may be driven across national borders or shipped overseas. Professional thefts have the lowest recovery rates. Still, professionals are only a small part of the vehicle theft problem.

■ **arson** The willful or malicious burning (or attempt to burn), with or without intent to defraud, of a house, public building, motor vehicle or aircraft, or personal property of another.

Arson

The FBI defines **arson** as "any willful or malicious burning or attempt to burn, with or without intent to defraud, a dwelling house, public building, motor vehicle or aircraft, personal property of another, etc."[101] It is only after a fire has been investigated and officially classified as arson by the proper investigative authorities that the FBI records the incident as an arson. Fires that are suspicious or of unknown origin are not included in the FBI's arson statistics.[102]

In 2012, the FBI received reports of 52,766 arsons that occurred throughout the country, for an arson rate of 18.7 offenses for every 100,000 inhabitants. Arsons involving structures (for example, residential, storage, and public) accounted for 47% of the total number of arson offenses. Mobile property was involved in 23.1% of arsons, and other types of property, such as crops, timber, and fences, accounted for 30.1% of reported arsons. The average dollar loss due to arson was $12,796 per offense, whereas arson involving industrial/manufacturing structures resulted in the highest average dollar losses (an average of $212,388 per arson). In 2012, arson offenses decreased slightly when compared with arson data reported in 2011. Nationally, the clearance rate for arson was only 20.4% in 2012. Of all arson arrests, 37% involve juveniles—a higher percentage than for any other major crime. In addition, 76% of arson arrestees are white and 83% are male.

Several diverse motives may underlie arson, from profit to thrill seeking. On August 1, 2003, for example, a 206-unit San Diego condominium complex burned down while under construction. A 12-foot banner found at the scene declared, "If you build it, we will burn it." The banner was signed with the letters *ELF*, which stand for the Earth Liberation Front. Less than a month later, ELF arsonists attacked a number of car dealerships in Los Angeles, targeting those that sold gas-guzzling SUVs such as Hummers. Although one person was arrested, he was soon released.

The ELF, described as an ecoterrorist group by law enforcement officials, may have begun in California as the Environmental Life Force in 1977. The present day ELF targets what it deems to be threats to the environment—including residential and commercial construction in environmentally sensitive areas, certain types of animal research facilities, and sometimes Starbucks restaurants.

Fire Setters

Whatever the motive, the vast majority of those involved in arson are juveniles. According to UCR/NIBRS data, juveniles represent the offenders in arson incidents at a much higher rate than is found in any other index offense; 49% of all arsons that are cleared are found to have involved a juvenile offender. Juveniles are a bit more likely to be involved in arsons in cities than in suburbs or rural areas. Overall, among the arson types, "juveniles account for 21 percent of the clearances for arsons of mobile property, 40 percent of structural arson clearances and 41 percent of clearances for arsons of all other property."[103] According to Jay K. Bradish, editor of *Firehouse* magazine, "Arson is the third leading cause of residential fires and the second-leading cause of residential fire deaths nationwide. Arson is the leading cause of deaths and injuries and accounts for the highest dollar loss in commercial fires."[104] In both residential and commercial arson, juveniles are involved more often than adults.

Three general groups of juvenile fire setters can be identified.[105] The first consists of children younger than seven who generally start fires by accident or out of curiosity. The second group is children between the ages of 8 and 12 who may start fires out of curiosity, but "a greater proportion of their fire setting represents underlying psychosocial conflicts."[106] The final group, youths between the ages of 13 and 18, has had a history of fire setting, usually undetected. It is believed that many of the fires started by juveniles go undetected by law enforcement officials because they are started on school property, perhaps even accidentally, and are discovered early by janitors or other school staff who do not report the incidents. In response to a growing awareness of the problem created by juvenile fire setters, several agencies and organizations, including the U.S. Fire Administration, have developed model programs to mobilize community agencies across the nation to deal more effectively with juvenile fire setters.

For more information on the problem of fire setting among juveniles, as well as the prevalence of and issues surrounding arson in the United States, visit the National Fire Data Center online via **Web Extra 11–3**. Learn more about the crime of arson from **Library Extras 11–3** and **11–4**.

Understanding Property Crimes

Criminologists have identified various types of property criminals and examined the motivation behind property crimes. In the final section of this chapter, we will explore some of these dimensions.

■ **professional criminal** A criminal offender who makes a living from criminal pursuits, is recognized by other offenders as professional, and engages in offending that is planned and calculated.

■ **persistent thief** One who continues in common law property crimes despite no better than an ordinary level of success.

■ **offense specialization** A preference for engaging in a certain type of offense to the exclusion of others.

■ **occasional offender** A criminal offender whose offending patterns are guided primarily by opportunity.

Persistent and Professional Thieves

Although legal distinctions separate the offenses of larceny and burglary, both are basically property crimes of theft, and those who commit such offenses are thieves. Willie Sutton, a famous bank robber, saw himself as a professional and defined a professional thief quite simply as "a man who wakes up every morning thinking about committing a crime, the same way another man gets up and goes to his job."[107] In a classic study of the professional thief, Edwin H. Sutherland defined this offender as one who "makes a regular business of stealing," plans carefully, possesses "technical skills and methods which are different from those of other professional criminals," and moves from locale to locale in offending pursuits.[108] Neil Shover defined **professional criminals** as those "who commit crime with some degree of skill, earn reasonably well from their crimes, and despite stealing over long periods of time, spend rather little time incarcerated."[109] This is certainly not the profile of most offenders, who continue to commit crimes but never exhibit signs of a professional approach to lawbreaking; instead of being viewed as professional, they are best understood as persistent.

Professional criminals commit crime with some degree of skill, earn reasonably well from their crimes, and spend little time incarcerated.

Persistent thieves are those who continue in "common-law property crimes despite their, at best, ordinary level of success."[110] Rather than specializing to any significant degree, the vast majority of persistent thieves alternate between a variety of crimes like burglary, robbery, car theft, and confidence games. Even though they exhibit a generalist approach to offending, persistent thieves may have "crime preferences" that take the form of characteristics such as "whether to avoid or to confront their victim(s)."[111]

Similarly, **offense specialization**, a preference for a certain type of offense, is quite limited among property offenders and does not allow the classification of most offenders as professionals or specialists. Significant numbers of property offenders are fully immersed in a street culture and lifestyle characterized by a hedonistic approach to life and a disregard for conventional pursuits, and their everyday lives are filled with a wide array of petty crimes, including confidence games, gambling, and minor thefts.[112]

Malcolm W. Klein used the term *cafeteria-style offending* in his research to refer to the heterogeneous and unplanned nature of offending among gang members.[113] In analyzing offending among gang members for possible patterns, he likened it to "a cafeteria display with [several] choices of food. Imagine the gang member walking along the display, choosing to try a little petty theft, then a group assault, then some truancy, then two varieties of malicious mischief, and so on."[114] Research using data sources ranging from official crime statistics to offenders' self-reports to ethnographies confirms that a minimal level of specialization exists among property offenders.[115] Shover, who has studied burglary and professional thieves for more than two decades, suggested that terms like *burglar* have little utility if conceived of in a strict sense of exclusive offending within that crime type. Many offenders engaged in burglary prefer this type of offending to offenses like robbery because burglary does not involve direct contact with victims.[116]

Because of the short-term, sporadic nature of their offending, property offenders are also known as **occasional offenders**[117]

Mark Stahl/Associated Press

Warren (Ohio) Police Detective Jeff Hoolihan (left) and Canfield (Ohio) Police Detective Sergeant Andy Bodzar standing in front of items seized from members of a theft-to-order burglary ring that operated in and around Youngstown, Ohio. What's the difference between larceny and burglary?

(the label "occasional" refers not to the frequency of offending but to the nature and character of offending), whom **John R. Hepburn** defined as those whose crimes "occur on those occasions in which there is an opportunity or situational inducement to commit the crime."[118] This observation (which fits well with rational choice theory discussed in Chapter 3) has been confirmed in subsequent research, such as the work of Richard T. Wright and Scott H. Decker, who stated that the burglars they interviewed are not a "continually motivated group of criminals; the motivation for them to offend is closely tied to their assessment of current circumstances and prospects."[119] This does not mean that offenders plan their crimes carefully or accurately assess a situation; it means only that they are seeking to achieve some personal benefit through criminal activity. Often offenders don't succeed because they rarely have all the information they need, they do not devote enough time to planning their actions, they take risks, and they make mistakes. This is how we all behave in everyday decision making and is what theorists call *limited* or *bounded rationality*.[120] So although some degree of rationality characterizes the criminal activity of most property offenders, it is only a limited or bounded rationality.

The Criminal Careers of Property Offenders

Criminologists have long studied the criminal careers of offenders, both violent offenders and property offenders. Neil Alan Weiner defined a criminal career as "criminal behavior [that] is an integrated, dynamic structure of sequential unlawful acts that advances within a wider context of causal and correlative influences, including among others, those of biological, psychological, and informal social and formal criminal justice origins."[121]

According to Alfred Blumstein and colleagues, a criminal career in property offending consisted of three distinct phases.[122] The first phase is the "break-in" period, which characterizes the early years of an offender's career, a time when young offenders become increasingly committed to criminal careers and explore various kinds of criminality; this initial phase generally lasts for the first 10 to 12 years. The second phase, the "stable" period, is the time of highest commitment, the period in an offender's career when he or she identifies most closely with a criminal lifestyle and probably also the period when rehabilitation efforts are most likely to fail. The final phase of a criminal career, the "burnout" period, begins around age 40 and is characterized by increasing dropout rates and a lowered commitment to criminal lifestyles.

In a study of violent offending, D. S. Elliott and fellow researchers examined data from the National Youth Survey and found that the careers of violent offenders were typically quite short—averaging just 1.58 years.[123] Only about 4% of subjects studied by Elliott and others had a violent criminal career of five years or more. However, they defined *career length* as the maximum number of consecutive years the individual was classified as a serious violent offender during the study period.

It was long assumed that offending becomes more serious and more frequent over time, but that assumption was strongly challenged by Michael R. Gottfredson and Travis Hirschi.[124] They posited that although the idea of deviance and crime as an orderly process similar to the rationality of conventional activities may be appealing for social policy purposes, evidence on offense specialization and the trajectories associated with chronic offending offers more support for crime as a fragmented pursuit than as a "career." Other researchers have found that although there is a certain logic to offenders' lifestyles, it is not one that easily complies with "a concept appropriate in a distinctly different culture (lawful society)."[125]

Based on ethnographic research on street criminals in urban settings, **Mark S. Fleisher** argued that the "social maturation" of the street life cycle "allows hustlers at any age to speak and act like adolescents and never acquire responsibilities similar to those marking social maturation in lawful society. In the sociocultural world of hustlers, youth is marked by gang membership, 'kids' crimes,' the onset of drug and alcohol addictions, and juvenile detention."[126] From the cradle to the grave, the lifestyle of street criminals is "created less by design than by default."[127] Fleisher explained that street criminals do not have careers, so thinking of their offenses or the pattern of their lives as following a series of life events similar to those outside this sociocultural environment will do little to increase understanding of the patterns of property offending because there is not enough planning in how the street criminal approaches life and crime to constitute a career. The type of offense specialization existing among property offenders is a loosely based preference for certain types of offending but not necessarily for a particular offense.

The lifestyle of street criminals is created less by design than by default.

Property Offenders and Rational Choice

Property crimes are often investigated from the perspective of rational choice theories (discussed in Chapter 3). One definition of *rationality* offered by Dermot Walsh was "activities identified by their impersonal, methodical, efficient, and logical components";[128] however, the rationality of the typical

■ **fence** An individual or a group involved in the buying, selling, and distributing of stolen goods.

criminal offender is not the same as "the rationality used by the civil engineer."[129] Thomas Bennett and Richard Wright researched the rationality surrounding decision making by burglars.[130] Walsh's conclusions agreed with theirs—that offenders employ a "limited, temporal rationality. . . . Not all these men are highly intelligent, and few are equipped to calculate Bentham-style, even supposing the information were available. Yet it is very common for rationality to be used. Of course it is partial and limited rather than total, but at the time, the actor feels he has planned enough and weighed enough data."[131] Although some offenders (especially those closer to the end of the continuum marked professional) use a higher degree of rationality and others may exhibit totally senseless behavior, most expressions of rationality are not dramatically clear. As Neil Shover and David Honaker explained, "Rationality is not a dichotomous variable," so given the extent to which it is shaped by the social context of offenders' lives, researchers must "learn more about the daily worlds that comprise the immediate contexts of criminal decision making behavior."[132] The extent to which property crimes are rational pursuits for either expressive or instrumental gains is a question that can be addressed by examining a wide variety of research on typologies of property crimes. Learn more about trends in property crimes from **Library Extra 11–5**.

Receivers of Stolen Property

Darrell J. Steffensmeier posited that "the 1827 English statute—'a person receiving stolen property knowing the same to be stolen is deemed guilty of a felony'—is the prototype of subsequent American law. The exact wording may vary from one state to another, but the basic elements of the crime—'buying and receiving,' 'stolen property,' and 'knowing it to be stolen'—have remained essentially intact."[133] Only small numbers of thieves steal for their own consumption, steal mostly cash, and have no need to translate the goods into cash. In other cases, it is necessary for stolen goods to be translated into cash, and "there are many paths that stolen property may take from thieves to eventual customers."[134] Receiving stolen property is engaged in for profit by individuals and groups with varying skill levels. Some burglars commit their offenses specifically to get something they know someone wants and sell their merchandise directly to a waiting customer.[135] Burglars may sell to people they know or may take stolen goods to places like flea markets or auctions. Other options for disposing of stolen goods "involve the thief and dabbling 'middlemen' who buy and sell stolen property under the cover of a bar, a luncheonette, or an auto service station with the encouragement, if not the active participation, of the proprietor."[136] Some burglars also sell their merchandise to merchants by representing it as legal goods. The most complicated path from the thief to customers is through a **fence** (someone involved in buying, selling, and/or distributing stolen goods); the use of a fence is the least common method of disposing of stolen goods for the majority of thieves but the most common method used by professional burglars.

Steffensmeier linked the rise of fences to industrialization and the availability of mass-produced goods, which made fencing profitable for significant numbers of people.[137] Steffensmeier used case studies to research the fence, as did **Carl Klockars** in his classic work.[138] Klockars detailed the career of Vincent Swaggi, a successful fence for more than 20 years; Steffensmeier profiled Sam Goodman, a 60-year-old white male whom he began interviewing in early 1980.[139] Building on Klockars's definition, Steffensmeier defined a *fence* as one who "purchases stolen goods both on a regular basis, and for resale."[140] The defining characteristics of the professional fence are that he or she "[has] direct contact with thieves, . . . buys and resells stolen goods regularly and persistently, . . . [and is a] public dealer—recognized as a fence by thieves, the police, and others acquainted with the criminal community."[141] Other variations and distinguishing characteristics exist for those who are part of the puzzle of how stolen goods move from the original owner to the open market.

The Role of Criminal Receivers

In their ethnographic research on residential burglars, **Paul F. Cromwell** and his colleagues offered a three-part typology of criminal receivers: professional receivers, avocational receivers, and amateur receivers.[142] *Professional receivers* fit the definition of *fences* provided by Steffensmeier: those who purchase stolen goods on a regular basis for resale. The use of a professional fence to dispose of stolen goods is uncommon for most residential burglars, who lack "sophisticated underworld connections."[143] Such connections often distinguish "high-level burglars" from the more typical and prevalent residential burglars.[144] Burglars and other thieves who develop access to fences have cited a number of advantages to disposing of stolen goods this way. First, the professional fence offers a safe and quick means of disposing of goods, especially for burglars who commit

The professional fence offers a safe and quick means of disposing of goods.

■ **Follow the author's tweets about the latest crime and justice news @schmalleger.**

National Geographic Image Collection/Alamy

A Las Vegas pawnshop owner displays goods acquired from clients. Could this shop serve as a front for a fencing operation?

high-visibility crimes and have easily recognizable goods. In Wright and Decker's ethnographic research on residential burglars, one burglar who had stolen from a local celebrity's house stated, "We couldn't just sell [the jewelry] on the street, it was like too hot to handle."[145] Second, fences are the best outlet for a large volume of stolen goods. Some professional fences are "generalists" who deal in a wide variety of stolen goods, and others are "specialists" who deal only in certain types of goods. Goodman (the professional fence described in Steffensmeier's research) started as a specialist but evolved into a generalist as a "function of greater capital and a growing knowledge of varied merchandise."[146] The vast majority of professional fences are involved in a legitimate business that serves as a cover for their criminal activity and facilitates it. For example, Goodman operated a secondhand store whose inventory partially matched the stolen goods he received, a characteristic that made him quasi-legitimate, a "partly covered fence." Fences who are "fully covered" do not deal in stolen goods that are outside their inventory in the legitimate business, and "noncovered" fences are those whose "illicit lines of goods are distinct from the legitimate commerce."[147] The more a fence is able to cover illicit activities by incorporating them into legitimate enterprises, the safer the fence is from criminal detection and prosecution.

There is a great deal of variety in the businesses that fences use as a front for their criminal activity, ranging from those viewed by the "community-at-large as strictly clean," like restaurants, to businesses that "are perceived as clean but somewhat suspect," like auto parts shops and antique shops, to businesses that are viewed as "quasi-legitimate or marginal," like pawnshops.[148] Some of the residential burglars interviewed by Wright and Decker stated that they avoided marginal businesses like pawnshops when disposing of stolen goods because, given the increasingly strict regulations of pawnshops, owners must often demand identification and take photos of those selling to them, and they have "hot sheets" of recently stolen goods. In addition, pawnshops generally do not provide the greatest return on the merchandise. Given the fact that many residential burglars commit their offenses for fast cash, "pawnshops almost always [have] the upper hand in negotiations."[149] The residential burglars who did regularly use pawnshops reported having an established relationship with the owner that enabled them "to pawn stolen property 'off camera'" because they had made transactions with the owner previously that had not resulted in "bringing additional police pressure to bear on his business."[150]

A second type of fence is *avocational receivers*, who buy stolen property as a part-time endeavor "secondary to, but usually associated with, their primary business activity."[151] This is a fairly diverse group that can include individuals involved in respectable occupations, such as lawyers or bail bondsmen who "provide legitimate professional services to property offenders who cannot pay for these services with anything but stolen property."[152] Others involved in illegitimate occupations, such as drug dealers, may also accept stolen goods.

Amateur receivers are those "otherwise honest citizens who buy stolen property on a relatively small scale, primarily, but not exclusively, for personal consumption. Crime is peripheral rather than central to their lives."[153] These individuals are quite sporadic in their involvement in activities that generate stolen goods. Cromwell and colleagues cited as an example a "public-school teacher who began her part-time fencing when she was approached by a student who offered her a 'really good deal' on certain items."[154] Although these individuals do not engage in receiving stolen property at the same level as professional or avocational fences, "they represent a large market for stolen goods" because they "compensate for lack of volume with their sheer numbers."[155] Stuart Henry's study of property crime among ordinary people, which he termed "hidden-economy crime," described the involvement of ordinary citizens in a wide variety of property offenses, including receiving stolen property.[156] Learn more about how fences operate at **Web Extra 11–4**.

CRIMINAL | PROFILES

Colton Harris-Moore—the Barefoot Bandit

On January 27, 2012, Colton Harris-Moore, 21, was sentenced to six and one-half years in federal prison for dozens of crimes he had committed in three different countries. Harris-Moore, who gained celebrity for his widely publicized attempts to evade arrest, came to be known as the "Barefoot Bandit" because he reportedly committed some of his crimes while barefoot.[i]

Harris-Moore began living a survivalist lifestyle in his home state of Washington at age seven and would break into homes and businesses to steal food, blankets, and other supplies. At 12, he was convicted of possessing stolen property, and he quickly built a record of continued juvenile offenses. Diagnosed with attention deficit disorder and depression, he was ordered to community service or brief stays in a detention facility following each offense. By 2008, then-17-year-old Harris-Moore was stealing ever-more-expensive items and was sentenced to spend three years in a halfway house. He fled soon after arriving at the home.[ii]

His criminal career eventually expanded to include more than 100 larcenies, involving thefts of cars, bicycles, boats, and airplanes. Eventually, Harris-Moore went on the run, leaving a trail of thefts and stolen vehicles from the state of Washington to Indiana. He became a sensation on Facebook when a fan page was created to follow his exploits. On July 4, 2010, he stole a Cessna single-engine airplane from the Bloomington, Indiana, airport and, using skills he had learned from flight simulation software and airplane manuals, flew it to Great Abaco Island in the Bahamas, where he crash-landed in water. After drinking beer in a local bar, Harris-Moore stole a 44-foot power boat from a marina on Great Abaco and used it to travel to nearby Eleuthera Island. Spotted by authorities, he attempted to flee, but officers shot out the engine and captured him.

On December 16, 2011, Harris-Moore was sentenced in Island County, Washington, to more than seven years in prison on charges ranging from identity theft and theft of a firearm to residential burglary. His lawyers had argued that he was abused as a child, suffered from prenatal alcohol exposure, and was raised by a drunken mother. In a statement provided to the judge, Harris-Moore said that his childhood was one he wouldn't wish on his "darkest enemies." Judge Vickie Churchill apparently agreed, saying, "This case is a tragedy in many ways, but it's a triumph of the human spirit in other ways." Describing Harris-Moore's childhood as a "mind numbing absence of hope," she stated that the 20-year-old was genuinely remorseful for his crimes.[iii]

In an e-mail a few days after his sentencing in state court, Harris-Moore wrote to his supporters, saying, "When all the acting and spreading of high propaganda on the part of the state was over and my lawyers argued the true facts, the judge gave me a much-appreciated recognition and validation, calling my story a 'triumph of the human spirit.' She wasn't having none of the weak argument the prosecution tried to peddle, and ended up handing down a sentence that was the lowest possible within the range. . . . Once again, I made it through a situation I shouldn't have."[iv]

RHB WENN Photos/Newscom

Colton Harris-Moore, the "Barefoot Bandit," under arrest. Harris-Moore committed dozens of crimes in three different countries and became something of a folk hero before his arrest. Why did Harris-Moore turn to crime?

Harris-Moore has said that he plans to study in preparation for applying to college to earn a degree in aeronautical engineering. Fox bought the movie rights in a deal that could be worth $1.3 million, and Dustin Lance Black, who won an Academy Award for writing *Milk*, a movie about the gay rights activist Harvey Milk, is working on the screenplay.

The case of the Barefoot Bandit raises a number of interesting questions. Among them are the following:

1. What led Harris-Moore to embark on a crime spree?
2. What role did his mother and father (or his mother's boyfriends) play in contributing to Harris-Moore's criminal lifestyle?
3. Would Harris-Moore have turned to crime had he been raised under different circumstances? Explain.

Notes

i. Laura L. Myers, " 'Barefoot Bandit' Gets 6.5 Years of Federal Time," *Chicago Tribune* via Reuters, January 27, 2012, http://www.chicagotribune.com/news/sns-rt-us-barefoot-bandit-sentencingtre80q1tm-20120127,0,4418476.story (accessed March 1, 2012).

ii. Manual Valdes, "'Barefoot Bandit' Sentenced to 6½ Years," Pantagraph.com via AP, January 31, 2012, http://www.pantagraph.com/news/weird-news/barefoot-bandit-sentenced-to-years/article_e671e808-4c28-11e1-81c6-0019bb2963f4.html (accessed May 2, 2012).

iii. Charles Montaldo, "'Barefoot Bandit' Gets 6½ Federal Years," About.com/Crime and Punishment, January 28, 2012, http://crime.about.com/b/2012/01/28/barefoot-bandit-gets-7-federal-years.htm (accessed March 2, 2012).

iv. Gene Johnson, "'Barefoot Bandit' Emails Ridicule Law Enforcement," Associated Press, January 25, 2012, http://abcnews.go.com/US/wireStory/barefoot-bandit-emails-ridicule-law-enforcement-15432245#.Tyln_mNSRak (accessed May 1, 2012).

SUMMARY

- Professional thieves commit thefts with some degree of skill, earn reasonably good money from their crimes, and spend relatively little time incarcerated. Persistent thieves continue in property crimes despite their ordinary level of success; professional thieves are characterized by greater planning and financial reward. Strict specialization is rarely found among property offenders.
- The major forms of property crime discussed in this chapter are larceny-theft, motor vehicle theft, burglary, and arson.
- Larceny-theft is the unlawful taking or attempted taking, carrying, leading, or riding away of property from the possession or constructive possession of another (motor vehicles are excluded). The largest category is theft from motor vehicles, followed by shoplifting and theft from buildings; pocket picking and purse snatching are much less common.
- Motor vehicle theft is the theft of a motor vehicle and does not include farm equipment, bulldozers, airplanes, construction equipment, or motorboats; almost 1 million motor vehicles are stolen in the United States each year.
- Burglary is the unlawful entry of a structure (residential or commercial) with intent to commit a felony or a theft. Burglars often cross the line to more serious violent crimes like homicide, rape, and robbery, but even in the absence of violent crime, the social costs of burglary to victims and to society are numerous.
- Property crimes usually involve stolen goods that need to be turned into cash. Those who receive stolen goods range from the amateur receiver, who is occasionally involved in fencing, to the professional fence, who buys and sells stolen goods in volume and offers a safe, quick means of disposing of goods, especially for burglars who have committed high-visibility crimes and have easily recognizable goods. Most professional fences are also involved in legitimate businesses that serve as a cover for their criminal activity and facilitate it.
- Arson, the burning or attempted burning of property with or without intent to defraud, has the potential to result in both great economic loss and loss of life. Although arson for profit and for protest certainly occurs, most arsons involve adolescents with various motives for fire setting.

KEY TERMS

arson, 295

burglary, 280

fence, 298

identity theft, 290

Identity Theft and Assumption Deterrence Act, 290

Identity Theft Penalty Enhancement Act, 290

joyriding, 294

larceny-theft, 287

motor vehicle theft, 292

occasional offender, 296

offense specialization, 296

persistent thief, 296

professional criminal, 296

property crime, 280

KEY NAMES

Mary Owen Cameron, 288

Paul F. Cromwell, 298

Laura Dugan, 286

Mark S. Fleisher, 297

John R. Hepburn, 297

Malcolm W. Klein, 296

Lloyd W. Klemke, 288

Carl Klockars, 298

Mike Maguire, 283

Neil Shover, 283

Darrell J. Steffensmeier, 298

Kenneth D. Tunnell, 285

QUESTIONS FOR REVIEW

1. What are the major forms of property crime discussed in this chapter?
2. What constitutes the crime of burglary? What are some of its characteristics?
3. What constitutes the crime of larceny-theft? What forms does it take?
4. What is motor vehicle theft? How prevalent is it?
5. What constitutes the crime of arson?
6. What are some characteristics of persistent and professional thieves?
7. What are the typical activities of receivers of stolen property, and how are stolen goods distributed?

QUESTIONS FOR REFLECTION

1. To what extent is thrill seeking a motivation behind certain types of property offenses? How might it contribute to the crime of shoplifting?
2. Why is so much attention given to shoplifting among adolescents? Should it be? Why or why not?
3. How are "honest" citizens and professional criminal receivers connected?
4. To what extent are property offenders rational actors? Use examples from larceny, burglary, and receipt of stolen property to illustrate your answer.
5. What does the phrase "sexualized context of burglary" mean? How can burglary have a sexual component or motivation?
6. How are drugs involved in the offending patterns of some burglars? Might effective drug-treatment programs reduce the number of burglaries committed? Why or why not?Mark Stahl/Associated Press

CHAPTER 12

WHITE-COLLAR AND ORGANIZED CRIME

LEARNING OUTCOMES

After reading this chapter, you should be able to answer the following questions:

- What is the history of white-collar crime in this country?
- What is white-collar crime? What are the various kinds of white-collar crimes?
- What is corporate crime? How does it differ from more traditional forms of white-collar crime? Can businesses be charged with corporate crime?
- What are the causes of white-collar crime? How do the motivations of white-collar criminals differ from those of other criminals?
- How can white-collar and corporate crime be controlled?
- What is the history of organized crime in this country?
- What is transnational organized crime, and what are some of the most infamous transnational criminal groups operating today?
- How can organized crime be controlled? What is the RICO statute?

■ **Follow the author's tweets about the latest crime and justice news @schmalleger.**

Introduction

In 2011, Attorney General Eric Holder announced the results of a nationwide takedown that involved Medicare Fraud Strike Force operations in Houston, Baton Rouge, Brooklyn, Chicago, Dallas, Detroit, Los Angeles, and Miami.[1] As a result of the operation, a total of 91 individuals were arrested and charged with various Medicare-fraud-related offenses, including fraudulent billings of approximately $295 million to the U.S. government. Included among those charged were:

- 45 individuals in Miami—including a doctor and a nurse—who were charged for their participation in various fraud schemes involving a total of $159 million in fraudulent Medicare billings in the areas of home health care, mental health services, occupational and physical therapy, durable medical equipment, and HIV infusion
- 6 people in Los Angeles—including one doctor—who were charged for their roles in schemes to defraud Medicare of more than $10.7 million
- 3 defendants in Brooklyn—including two doctors—who were charged in a fraud scheme involving more than $3.4 million in false claims for medically unnecessary physical therapy.
- 18 people in Detroit—including doctors, nurses, clinic operators, and other health-care professionals—who were charged for schemes involving an additional $28 million in false billing.

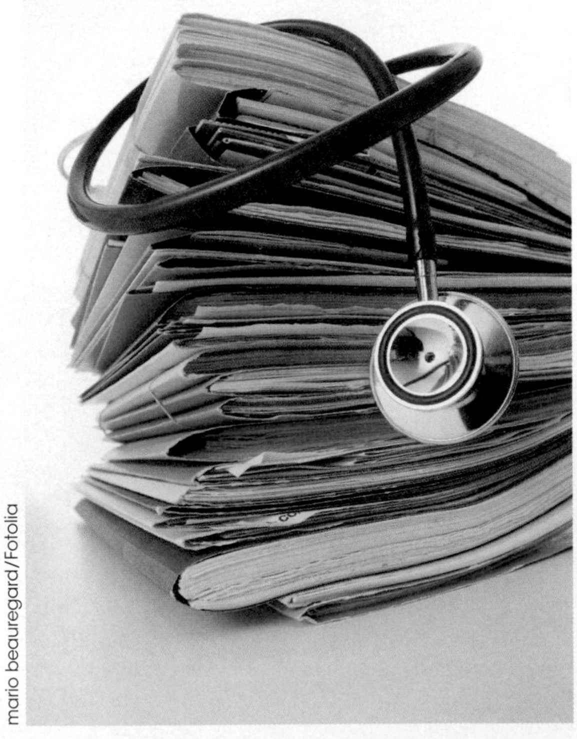

mario beauregard/Fotolia

Medical records. Medicare fraud is a major area of criminal activity in the United States. What kinds of fraudulent activities would be included?

The Medicare Fraud Strike Force, coordinated jointly by the Department of Justice (DOJ) and the Department of Health and Human Services (HHS), is a multiagency team of federal, state, and local investigators that combats Medicare fraud by analyzing Medicare claims and payout data.

A Brief History of White-Collar Crime

White-collar crime is not unique to the twenty-first century. Financial scandals have a long and ubiquitous history in the United States, sometimes even involving government regulators. In 1929, the Teapot Dome scandal, which embroiled the administration of President Warren Harding, began in 1921 when Secretary of the Interior Albert B. Fall secretly leased naval oil reserves at Teapot Dome, Wyoming, and Elk Hills, California, to developers without asking for competitive bids. A Senate investigation later revealed that large sums of federal money had been loaned to developers without interest. Fall was eventually fined and sent to prison, and a 1927 U.S. Supreme Court decision ordered the fields restored to the U.S. government.

The insider-trading scam of stock market tycoon Ivan Boesky and the securities fraud conviction of junk-bond king Michael Milken in the 1980s demonstrated again how fortunes could be amassed through white-collar law violations. Boesky was estimated to have netted a profit of $250 million for himself and a few close friends; Milken paid a $600 million fine—far less than the amount he is estimated to have reaped from illegal bond trading.

Today, it's easier to steal money with a computer than it is with a gun.

The nationwide savings and loan (S&L) disaster of the 1980s, which some have called the "biggest white-collar crime in history," serves as another example of white-collar crime. The S&L fiasco was the result of years of intentional mismanagement and personal appropriation of depositors' funds by institutional executives. Although the actual amount of money lost or stolen during the scandal may never be known, it has been estimated to run into the hundreds of billions of dollars. The collapse of just one such institution, Charles Keating's California-based Lincoln Savings and Loan Association, cost taxpayers—who were left to redeem the insolvent institution—approximately $2.5 billion, and the collapse of Neil Bush's Silverado Banking Savings and Loan in Denver cost nearly $1 billion.

Another type of white-collar crime sprang from the low interest rates characteristic of the early and mid-1990s.

■ **securities fraud** The theft of money resulting from intentional manipulation of the value of equities, including stocks and bonds. Securities fraud also includes theft from securities accounts and wire fraud.

■ **insider trading** A type of equity trading based on confidential information about important events that may affect the price of the issue being traded.

■ **bank fraud** Any fraud or embezzlement that occurs within or against financial institutions that are insured or regulated by the U.S. government. Fraud of financial institutions includes commercial-loan fraud, check fraud, counterfeit negotiable instruments, mortgage fraud, and false credit applications.

Sham banking operations flourished by offering high interest rates and double-digit rates of return on investments, but such "phantom banks" evaporated as quickly as they were formed, leaving investors stunned and sometimes penniless.

The past two decades have seen a number of infamous white-collar crime prosecutions, including those involving executives at the former energy-trading giant Enron Corporation, which had used complex off-balance-sheet partnerships to hide losses and inflate revenues. The company's collapse in 2001 set the stage both for massive reforms in the business and financial world and for federal and state investigations into the accounting practices and business dealings of all publicly traded companies in the United States. Share prices for Enron's stock grew quickly during 2000 as the company positioned itself as a major player in what appeared to be a lucrative energy-trading business. The business, which did not require that Enron own or produce any of the energy it traded, began to unravel in early 2001 when bankrupt California utility Pacific Gas and Electric Co. was unable to pay $570 million for energy that it had purchased, and Enron was subsequently unsuccessful in bids to extend its credit lines. In November 2001, Enron executives surprised stockholders when they revised the company's financial statements for the prior five years in order to account for hundreds of millions of dollars in losses that they had previously hidden, and a month later, Enron filed for Chapter 11 bankruptcy protection and laid off more than 4,000 workers. The bankruptcy wiped out at least $24 billion in retirement plans, stock accounts, and mutual funds as the company's stock plummeted.

Enron's bankruptcy was followed by congressional hearings into the collapse of the company as well as by a U.S. Department of Justice investigation seeking to find out how five of the company's former officers had made over $300 million in profits from sales of company stock prior to bankruptcy while ordinary investors had lost everything. The company's former chairman, Kenneth Lay, was convicted in 2006 on numerous counts of securities and wire fraud along with other charges. Lay died of a heart attack before sentencing, and his convictions were later abated (a form of legal nullification) following federal precedent.

On July 21, 2002—less than a year after the collapse of Enron—WorldCom, Inc., a huge telecommunications company, filed for what was then the largest-ever U.S. bankruptcy. At least $11 billion of the company's money had been lost in an accounting fraud intended to save the failing company.

One month later, a federal grand jury indicted former WorldCom top executives Buford Yates and Scott Sullivan on charges of conspiracy, **securities fraud**, and false filings with the Securities and Exchange Commission (SEC).

Yates pleaded guilty and helped federal prosecutors build cases against others at the company; he was sentenced in 2005 to a year and a day in prison. Sullivan became the government's star witness at the criminal trial of former WorldCom CEO Bernard Ebbers. Sullivan received a five-year sentence, but Ebbers was found guilty of nine counts of conspiracy, securities fraud, and false regulatory filings and was sent to prison for 25 years. For a list of *Time* magazine's "Top 10 Crooked CEOs" of recent years, visit **Web Extra 12–1**.

Allegations of criminal wrongdoing spread to other companies. In 2002, officials at cable television provider Adelphia Communications were charged with failing to adequately disclose loans and loan guarantees of $3.1 billion to the company's founder, John J. Rigas, and members of his family. About the same time, executives at a number of corporations—CMS Energy; Computer Associates International; Dynegy; Global Crossing; Halliburton; Kmart; Lucent Technologies; Network Associates; Qwest Communications International, Inc.; Reliant Resources; Trump Hotels and Casinos; Waste Management; and Xerox—were accused by the SEC, stockholders, and independent prosecutors of intentionally misstating revenues or hiding losses.

> In 2002 insider trading threatened the home-decorating empire of Martha Stewart.

Also in 2002, ImClone founder Dr. Sam Waksal pleaded guilty to six federal charges of bank fraud and conspiracy involving **insider trading** (equity trading based on confidential information that could affect stocks being traded) that threatened the home-decorating empire of Martha Stewart. Prosecutors alleged that Waksal had tipped off family members and friends, including Stewart and her stockbroker, that the Food and Drug Administration (FDA) would not approve his company's experimental cancer drug, Erbitux.

Waksal, who admitted to **bank fraud** for forging the name of ImClone's chief attorney to a document securing a line of credit, was sentenced to seven years in prison, and Martha Stewart was ordered to spend five months behind bars.

Securities firms were pulled into the fray when Salomon Smith Barney (the investment arm of Citigroup, Inc.); Goldman Sachs Group, Inc.; Merrill Lynch & Co.; Deutsche Bank AG; and U.S. Bancorp's Piper Jaffray unit came under investigation by federal regulators on suspicion that they had created conflicts of interest in handing out shares in initial public offerings of companies that they supported financially to select stock-research analysts.

Regulators also charged the firms with providing biased research to mislead investors into buying stock in companies in which the firms had vested interests. Although some felt that criminal charges of securities fraud would be brought, an agreement between the SEC and the Wall Street firms in December 2002 ended the possibility of criminal prosecution and required the companies to pay $1.4 billion in fines. Table 12–1 describes the terminology of white-collar crime.

CRIME | in the NEWS

U.S. Authorities Grapple with the Rise of Transnational Gangs

IN JANUARY 2010, the National Intelligence Council completed the first comprehensive U.S. government assessment of transnational organized crime since 1995. The report concluded that criminal activities had expanded dramatically in size, scope, and influence, and had begun to pose a significant threat to U.S. and international security.

Following up on the assessment, President Obama in 2011 issued an executive order creating a new threat category, transnational criminal organizations (TCOs). It named four TCOs and directed the Treasury Department to freeze their U.S. assets. The acronym "TCO" is patterned after that for FTOs, the U.S. government's designation for foreign terrorist organizations. After the September 11, 2001, attacks, President George W. Bush used the same executive powers to block assets of persons aiding terrorists.

The four TCOs Obama named are the Brothers' Circle in the former Soviet Union, the Camorra in Italy, the Yakuza in Japan, and the Los Zetas drug cartel in Mexico. His order authorized the Treasury Department to add more TCOs to the list, and in 2012 the Treasury added MS-13, originally a Los Angeles street gang founded by immigrants from El Salvador. "These organizations facilitate and aggravate violent civil conflicts and increasingly facilitate the activities of other dangerous persons," the president said. "They are increasingly entrenched in the operations of foreign governments and the international financial system."

The National Strategy to Combat Transnational Organized Crime, a background document released along with the executive order, acknowledged that international criminal organizations had been around for years, but they were "largely regional in scope, hierarchically structured and had only occasional links to terrorism. Today's criminal networks are fluid, striking new alliances with other networks around the world and engaging in a wide range of illicit activities, including cybercrime, and providing support for terrorism."

MS-13, for example, evolved from an LA street gang into an organized crime network, overseeing a broad range of illegal activities across borders—from prostitution in the Washington, D.C., area to close affiliation with the Los Zetas drug cartel in Mexico. The Treasury Department said MS-13 now operates in 40 U.S. states. Once known for their distinctive tattoos all over their bodies, MS-13 members now often try to look like average Americans, holding down regular jobs.

Similarly, the Treasury Department reported that Italy's Camorra is involved in money laundering, extortion, alien smuggling, robbery, blackmail, kidnapping, political corruption, and counterfeiting around the world. By freezing its assets, the U.S. government aims "to squeeze the Camorra out of the global financial system and protect the U.S. financial system from laundering of its criminal proceeds," the department stated.

Discussion Questions

1. What are TCOs? How do they differ from traditional criminal organizations?
2. What kinds of international cooperation are needed to combat TCOs?

Saul Loeb/AFP/Getty Images/Newscom

President Barack Obama speaks to members of the press in the Rose Garden of the White House. How will the president's executive order discussed in this box fight transnational organized crime?

Sources: Howard LaFranchi, "MS-13 Gang Labeled Transnational Criminal Group, a First for US Street Gang," *Christian Science Monitor*, October 12, 2012, http://www.csmonitor.com/USA/Foreign-Policy/2012/1012/MS-13-gang-labeled-transnational-criminal-group-a-first-for-US-street-gang; Adam R. Pearlman, "Sanctions, Transnational Organized Crime," The Federalist Society, October 3, 2011, http://www.fed-soc.org/publications/detail/sanctions-transnational-organized-crime; and Robert Chesney, "Material Support to . . . Transnational Criminal Organizations?" Lawfare Blog, July 25, 2011, http://www.lawfareblog.com/2011/07/material-support-to-transnational-criminal-organizations/.

TABLE 12-1 The Terminology of White-Collar Crime
Antitrust violation: Any activity that illegally inhibits competition between companies within an industry, such as price fixing and monopolies in restraint of trade. Antitrust violations are infractions of the Sherman Act (15 U.S.C. Sections 1–7) and the Clayton Act (15 U.S.C. Sections 12–27).
Bank fraud (also financial fraud or financial institution fraud): Fraud or embezzlement that occurs within or against financial institutions that are insured or regulated by the U.S. government. Financial institution fraud includes commercial loan fraud, check fraud, counterfeit negotiable instruments, mortgage fraud, and false credit applications.
Bankruptcy fraud: The misleading of creditors through the concealment and misstatement of assets. Bankruptcy fraud also involves illegal pressure on bankruptcy petitioners.
Economic espionage/trade secret theft: The theft or misappropriation of proprietary economic information (that is, trade secrets) from an individual, a business, or an industry.
Embezzlement: The unlawful misappropriation for personal use of money, property, or other thing of value entrusted to the offender's care, custody, or control.
Environmental law violation: Any business activity in violation of federal and state environmental laws, including the discharge of toxic substances into the air, water, or soil, especially when those substances pose a significant threat of harm to people, property, or the environment.
Government fraud: Fraud against the government, especially in connection with federal government contracting and fraud in connection with federal and/or federally funded programs. Such programs include public housing, agricultural programs, defense procurement, and government-funded educational programs. Fraudulent activities involving government contracting include bribery in contracts or procurement, collusion among contractors, false or double billing, false certification of the quality of parts or of test results, and substitution of bogus or otherwise inferior parts.
Health-care fraud: Fraudulent billing practices by health-care providers, including hospitals, home health care, ambulance services, doctors, chiropractors, psychiatric hospitals, laboratories, pharmacies, and nursing homes, that affect health-care consumers, insurance providers, and government-funded payment providers such as Medicare and Medicaid. Fraudulent activities include receiving kickbacks, billing for services not rendered, billing for unnecessary equipment, and billing for services performed by a less qualified person.
Insider trading: Equity trading based on confidential information about important events that may affect the price of the issue being traded. Because confidential information confers advantages on those who possess it, federal law prohibits them from using that knowledge to reap profits or to avoid losses in the stock market.
Insurance fraud: Fraudulent activity committed by insurance applicants, policyholders, third-party claimants, or professionals who provide insurance services to claimants. Such fraudulent activities include inflating, or "padding," actual claims and fraudulent inducements to issue policies and/or establish a lower premium rate.
Kickbacks: The return of a certain amount of money from seller to buyer as a result of a collusive agreement.
Mail fraud: The use of the U.S. mail in furtherance of criminal activity.
Money laundering: The process of converting illegally earned assets, originating as cash, to one or more alternative forms to conceal such incriminating factors as illegal origin and true ownership.
Securities fraud: The theft of money resulting from intentional manipulation of the value of equities, including stocks and bonds. Securities fraud also includes theft from securities accounts and wire fraud.
Tax evasion: Fraud committed by filing false tax returns or not filing tax returns at all.
Wire fraud: The use of an electric or electronic communications facility to intentionally transmit a false and/or deceptive message in furtherance of a fraudulent activity.
Sources: Cynthia Barnett, *The Measurement of White-Collar Crime Using Uniform Crime Reporting Data*, Federal Bureau of Investigation, Criminal Justice Information Services Division, http://www.fbi.gov/ucr/whitecollarforweb.pdf (accessed June 18, 2009); Clifford Karchmer and Douglas Ruch, "State and Local Money Laundering Control Strategies," *NIJ Research in Brief* (Washington, DC: National Institute of Justice, 1992); and Legal Information Institute, "White-Collar Crime: An Overview," http://www.law.cornell.edu/topics/white_collar.html (accessed July 1, 2011).

■ **white-collar crime** A violation of the criminal law committed by a person of respectability and high social status in the course of his or her occupation.

■ **occupational crime** An act punishable by law that is committed through opportunity created in the course of a legal occupation.

Understanding White-Collar Crime

In 1939, **Edwin H. Sutherland** defined **white-collar crime** as violations of the criminal law "committed by a person of respectability and high social status in the course of his occupation."[2] Many criminologists do not properly understand crime, Sutherland claimed, because they fail to recognize that the secretive violations of public and corporate trust by those in positions of authority are just as criminal as predatory acts committed by people of lower social standing.

According to Sutherland, the criminality of upper-class persons has been demonstrated again and again.

Sutherland also noted that white-collar criminals are far less likely to be investigated, arrested, or prosecuted than are other types of offenders. In Sutherland's day, when they were convicted, white-collar offenders were much less likely to receive active prison terms than were "common criminals." The deference shown to white-collar criminals, said Sutherland, is due primarily to their social standing. Many white-collar criminals have been well respected in their communities, and many have taken part in national affairs.

Given these kinds of sentiments, criminologists felt compelled for years to address the question "Is white-collar crime really crime?" As recently as 1987, writers on the subject were still asking, "Do persons of high standing commit crimes?"[3] Although most criminologists today would answer the question with a resounding *yes*, members of the public were slower to accept the notion that violations of the criminal law by businesspeople share conceptual similarities with street crime. Attitudes, however, have quickly changed during the past few years as headline-making charges have been filed against a number of corporate scam artists and financial managers who duped investors out of billions of dollars.

Definitional Evolution of White-Collar Crime

Between the early and later definitions of *white-collar crime*, many investigators refined its conceptual boundaries. **Herbert Edelhertz** defined *white-collar crime* as any "illegal act or series of illegal acts committed by nonphysical means and by concealment or guile, to obtain money or property, to avoid the payment or loss of money or property, or to obtain business or personal advantages."

Gilbert Geis grappled with the notion of "upperworld crime," which he called "a label designed to call attention to the violation of a variety of criminal statutes by persons who at the moment are generally not considered, in connection with such violations, to be the 'usual' kind of underworld and/or psychologically aberrant offenders."

Many writers were quick to realize that "upperworld," or white-collar, crime might have its counterpart in certain forms of blue-collar crime committed by members of less prestigious occupational groups, so the term *blue-collar crime* emerged as a way of classifying the law-violating behavior of people involved in appliance and automobile repair, yard maintenance, house cleaning, and general installation services. See the Theory versus Reality box for more on definitions of white-collar crime.

In an effort to bring closure to the concept of work-related crime, the term **occupational crime**—"any act punishable by law that is committed through opportunity created in the course of an occupation which is legal"—emerged as a kind of catchall category that included the job-related law violations of both white- and blue-collar workers. An excellent four-part typology of occupational crime is offered by **Gary S. Green** in his book *Occupational Crime*:

1. **Organizational occupational crime.** An organizational occupational crime is committed for the benefit of an employer or organization, but only the employer or organization—not individual employees—benefits.
2. **State authority occupational crime.** A state authority occupational crime is committed by people exercising their state-based authority, is occupation specific, and can be committed only by officials in public office or those working for them.
3. **Professional occupational crime.** A professional occupational crime is committed by professionals while in their occupational capacity (such as physicians, attorneys, and psychologists).
4. **Individual occupational crime.** An individual occupational crime, committed by an individual acting alone, is a kind of catchall category that includes personal-income-tax evasion, theft of goods and services by employees, and filing of false expense reports.

The idea of occupational crime became a kind of catchall category.

For an interesting presentation of white-collar and occupational crime typologies, visit the National Check Fraud

■ **corporate crime** A violation of a criminal statute either by a corporate entity or by its executives, employees, or agents acting on behalf of and for the benefit of the corporation, partnership, or other form of business entity.

Center and Cornell Law School's white-collar crime page via **Web Extras 12–2** and **12–3**. Learn more about white-collar crime and its measurement from **Library Extra 12–1**.

White-Collar Crime Today

The chief criterion for a crime to be "white collar" is that "it occurs as a part of, or a deviation from, the violator's occupational role."[4] This focus on the violator, rather than on the offense, in deciding whether to classify a crime as white collar was accepted by the 1967 Presidential Commission on Law Enforcement and Administration of Justice. In its classic report *The Challenge of Crime in a Free Society*, members of the commission wrote, "The 'white-collar' criminal is the broker who distributes fraudulent securities, the builder who deliberately uses defective material, the corporation executive who conspires to fix prices, the legislator who peddles his influence and votes for private gain, or the banker who misappropriates funds in his keeping."[5]

Over the past few decades, the concept of white-collar crime has undergone considerable refinement.[6] The reason, according to the U.S. DOJ, is that "the focus has shifted to the nature of the crime instead of the persons or occupations involved."[7] The methods used to commit white-collar crime, such as the use of a computer and the Internet, and the special skills and knowledge necessary for attempted law violation have resulted in a contemporary understanding of white-collar crime that emphasizes the type of offense being committed rather than the social standing or occupational role of the person committing it. Some reasons for this shift are changes in the work environment and in the business world itself. Other reasons are pragmatic. In the words of the Justice Department, "The categorization of 'white-collar crime' as crime having a particular modus operandi [committed in a manner that utilizes deception and special knowledge of business practices and committed in a particular kind of economic environment] is of use in coordinating the resources of the appropriate agencies for purposes of investigation and prosecution."[8]

Visit the National White Collar Crime Center and the Internet Crime Complaint Center (ICC3) at **Web Extras 12–4** and **12–5**. Both report on white-collar crimes committed via the Internet. Figure 12–1 shows the top ten Internet crime complaint categories recorded by the IC3 for 2010.

Corporate Crime

Corporate malfeasance, which is essentially another form of white-collar crime, has been dubbed "corporate crime." **Corporate crime** can be defined as "a violation of a criminal statute either by a corporate entity or by its executives, employees, or agents acting on behalf of and for the benefit of the corporation, partnership, or other form of business entity."[9] Corporate

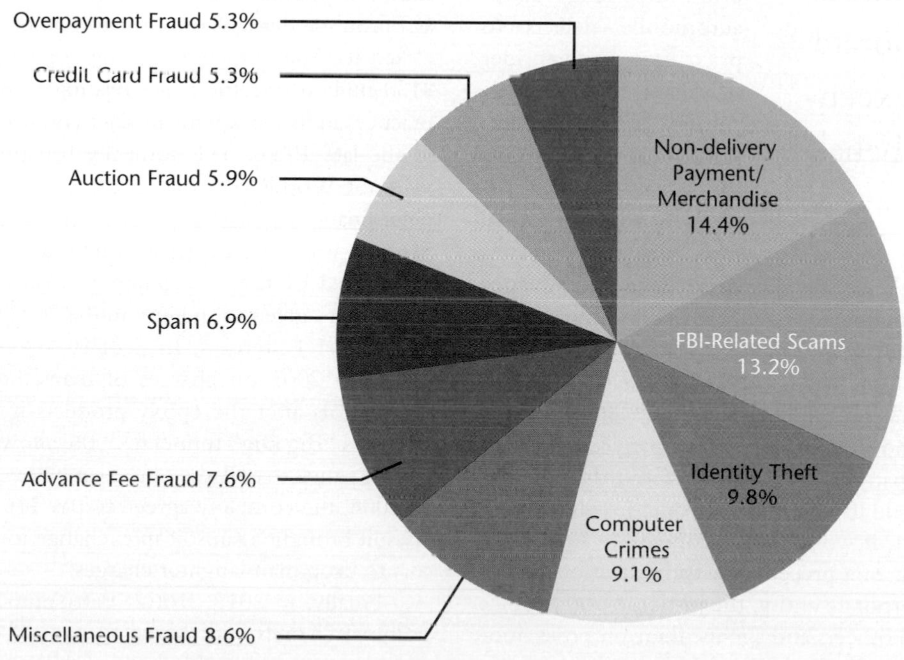

FIGURE 12–1 | **Top Ten Internet Crime Complaint Categories**

Source: National White Collar Crime Center, *Annual Report, 2010*, p. 10, http://www.ic3.gov/media/annualreport/2010_ic3report.pdf (accessed March 11, 2012). Used with permission. ©2011. NW3C, Inc. d/b/a the National White Collar Crime Center. All rights reserved.

THEORY | versus REALITY

White-Collar Crime: The Initial Statement

At least one eminent criminologist has called the concept of white-collar crime "the most significant development in criminology, especially since World War II."[i] The roots of the concept go back to 1939, when Edwin Sutherland first coined the term *white-collar crime* in his presidential address to the American Sociological Society. Details of that address are discussed elsewhere in this chapter. His speech concluded with the following five points:

1. White-collar criminality is real criminality, being in all cases in violation of the criminal law.
2. White-collar criminality differs from lower-class criminality principally in implementation of the criminal law, which segregates white-collar criminals administratively from other criminals.
3. The theories of the criminologists that crime is due to poverty or to psychopathic and sociopathic conditions statistically associated with poverty are invalid because, first, they are derived from samples that are grossly biased with respect to socioeconomic status; second, they do not apply to the white-collar criminals; and third, they do not even explain the criminality of the lower class, as the factors are not related to a general process characteristic of all criminality.
4. A theory of criminal behavior that will explain both white-collar criminality and lower-class criminality is needed.
5. A hypothesis of this nature is suggested in terms of differential association and social disorganization.

Discussion Questions

1. Why is white-collar crime possibly the most significant development in criminology since World War II?
2. Why did Sutherland have to remind people that "white-collar criminality is real criminality"? Why might some have thought otherwise?

Note

i. Donald J. Newman, "White-Collar Crime: An Overview and Analysis," *Law and Contemporary Problems*, Vol. 23, No. 4 (autumn 1958).

Source: Edwin Sutherland, "White-Collar Criminality," *American Sociological Review*, Vol. 5 (February 1940), pp. 1–12.

Corporate crime is a violation of a criminal statute by a corporate entity or by its executives, acting on behalf of the corporation.

crimes come in many forms, ranging from prior knowledge about automobile defects to price fixing and insider securities trading. Culpability, which often results in civil suits against the corporation along with possible criminal prosecutions, is greatest where company officials can be shown to have had advance knowledge about product defects, dangerous conditions, or illegal behavior on the part of employees.

In 1909, in the case of *New York Central and Hudson River Railroad Co.* v. *United States*,[10] the U.S. Supreme Court reasoned that the criminal acts and intentions of a company's employees can extend to the company itself. The Court said that because corporations could be held liable for civil wrongs involving their employees' bad conduct, it would be appropriate to hold them criminally liable as well. In a precedent-setting decision assigning legal liability to a corporate entity, the justices wrote, "Since a corporation acts by its officers and agents, their purposes, motives, and intent are just as much those of the corporation as are the things done."

In 2002, in an example of how corporations can be held criminally responsible for the acts of their officials, the accounting firm of Arthur Andersen was convicted of obstruction of justice after its employees destroyed documents related to Enron Corporation audits. Arthur Andersen, which had served as Enron's auditor, was forced to relinquish its U.S. licenses and closed its American offices. The company also paid more than $130 million to settle issues relating to questionable accounting practices in its work with another company, Waste Management, in the late 1990s. The company had provided accounting services for WorldCom, Inc., prior to the arrest of that company's chief financial officer and other executives.[11] In 2005, however, the firm was at least partially vindicated when its conviction was overturned by the U.S. Supreme Court, which found that the instructions given to the jury in the 2002 trial had been flawed.[12]

Power Fasterners, Inc., of Brewster, New York, was indicted in 2007 on charges of manslaughter by Massachusetts prosecutors after the epoxy products it manufactured failed in Boston's "Big Dig" tunnel in 2006, allowing 20 tons of concrete ceiling panels to collapse onto a car below, killing the passenger.[13] In 2008, the company agreed to pay $16 million to settle a civil lawsuit brought against it in exchange for a promise by prosecutors to drop manslaughter charges.[14]

Finally, in 2012, British Petroleum (BP) pleaded guilty to criminal charges and agreed to pay a $4.5 billion in fines—in addition to the tens of billions of dollars it had already agreed to pay for cleanup and to reimburse victims whose livelihood had been affected by the oil spill from the company's Deepwater Horizon oil rig in 2010 in the Gulf of Mexico.[15]

■ **corporate fraud** A type of organizational fraud, such as accounting schemes, self-dealing by corporate executives, obstruction of justice, insider trading, kickbacks, and misuse of corporate property for personal use.

■ **securities and commodities fraud** A crime involving investments, such as stock-market manipulation, high-yield-investment fraud (Ponzi schemes, pyramid schemes, and prime bank schemes), advance fee fraud, hedge fund fraud, commodities fraud, foreign exchange fraud, and broker embezzlement.

■ **Ponzi scheme** A form of high-yield-investment fraud that uses money collected from new investors, rather than profits from the purported underlying business venture, to pay high rates of return promised to earlier investors.

It should be noted that corporate criminal liability is what some have called a unique form of "American exceptionalism," as few other countries hold corporations criminally accountable.[16]

Financial Crime

Most white-collar crimes are financial crimes, meaning illegal activities generally committed for monetary profit by businesses and those who run them. The FBI classifies the following types of activities as financial crimes: corporate fraud, securities and commodities fraud, health-care fraud, mortgage fraud, insurance fraud, mass-marketing fraud, and money laundering (Figure 12–2).[17] We will discuss each in the pages that follow.

Corporate Fraud

The term **corporate fraud** refers to accounting schemes, self-dealing by corporate executives, and obstruction of justice as well as insider trading, kickbacks, and misuse of corporate property for personal gain. The majority of these cases pursued at the federal level are built on accounting schemes intended to deceive investors, auditors, and analysts about the financial health of a corporation; in addition to significant financial losses to investors, corporate fraud has the potential to cause damage to both investor confidence and the U.S. economy.

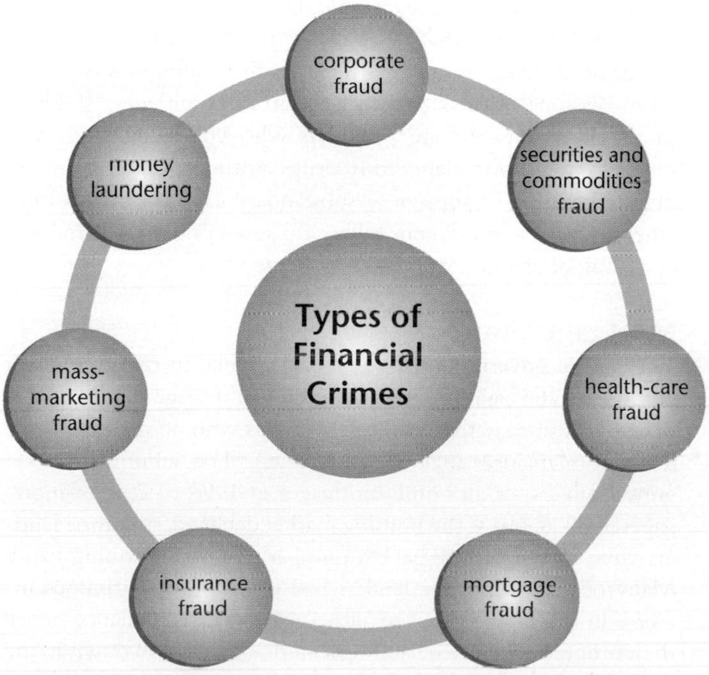

Corporate fraud sometimes involves the backdating of executive stock options under which the date of options is set to a time in the past when the price of the stock was lower than on the date the options were actually issued. Backdating stock options inflates the value of the options to the holder at the expense of regular shareholders.

Obstruction of justice occurs when activities are undertaken that are designed to conceal any of the types of criminal conduct noted here, particularly when the obstruction impedes the inquiries of the SEC, other regulatory agencies, and/or law enforcement agencies.

corporate fraud
securities and commodities fraud
health-care fraud
mortgage fraud
insurance fraud
mass-marketing fraud
money laundering
Types of Financial Crimes

FIGURE 12-2 | Types of Financial Crime

Source: Derived from Federal Bureau of Investigation, *Financial Crimes Report to the Public, Fiscal Year 2007*, http://www.fbi.gov/publications/financial/fcs_report2007/financial_crime_2007.htm#financial (accessed May 10, 2010).

Securities and Commodities Fraud

Securities and commodities fraud includes crimes such as stock market manipulation, high-yield-investment fraud (Ponzi schemes, pyramid schemes, and prime bank schemes), advance fee fraud, hedge fund fraud, commodities fraud, foreign exchange fraud, and broker embezzlement.

Securities and commodities fraud includes crimes such as stock market manipulation and investment fraud.

Stock market manipulation schemes (commonly referred to as "pump and dumps") create artificial buying pressure for a targeted security, generally a low-volume stock in the over-the-counter securities market, that is largely controlled by the fraud perpetrators. This artificially increased trading volume unfairly increases the price of the targeted security (the "pump"), which is rapidly sold off into the inflated market created for the security by the fraud perpetrators (the "dump"), resulting in illicit gains for the perpetrators and losses for innocent third-party investors.

High-yield investment fraud takes various forms, all of which are characterized by offers of low- or no-risk investments that guarantee unusually high rates of return. **Ponzi schemes** use money collected from new investors, rather than business profits, to pay high rates of return

Ponzi schemes use money collected from new investors to pay off earlier investors.

promised to earlier investors, giving them the impression that this is a legitimate money-making enterprise when, in reality, investors' money is the only source of funding. The term *pyramid scheme* refers to money collected from newer victims of the fraud to pay earlier victims to provide a veneer of legitimacy; the victims themselves are induced to recruit more victims through the payment of recruitment commissions. *Prime bank schemes* (another form of high-yield-investment fraud) induce victims to invest in financial instruments, allegedly issued by well-known institutions, offering risk-free opportunities for high rates of return. The benefits are supposedly the result of access to a secret worldwide exchange ordinarily open only to the world's largest financial institutions, but such networks don't exist or the perpetrators don't have access to them, and the perpetrators keep the money with which they've been entrusted.

Advance fee fraud encompasses a broad variety of schemes designed to induce victims into remitting upfront payments in exchange for the promise of goods, services, and/or prizes; victims are informed that to participate in this promising investment opportunity, they must first pay various taxes and/or fees—which go directly to the perpetrators.

Hedge fund fraud uses private investment partnerships that have generally experienced a relative lack of regulatory scrutiny, and the fraud perpetrated by fund managers can involve the overstatement or misappropriation of fund assets overcharges for fund management fees, insider trading, market timing, and late trading.

Commodities fraud typically involves the deceptive or fraudulent sale of commodities investments (for example, gold, silver, oil, copper, and natural gas); false or deceptive sales practices are used to solicit victim funds for commodities transactions that either never occur or are inconsistent with the original sales promises. Commodities market participants may also attempt to illegally manipulate the market for a commodity by fraudulently reporting price information or cornering the market to artificially increase the price of the targeted commodity.

Foreign exchange fraud uses false or deceptive sales practices alleging high rates of return for minimal risk to induce victims to invest in the foreign currency exchange market. The transactions never occur or are executed for the sole purpose of generating excessive trading commission—in breach of the trader's responsibilities to the client. Alternatively, individual currency traders employed by large financial institutions may illegally attempt to manipulate foreign currency exchange prices to generate illicit trading profits for their own enrichment.

Schemes using *broker embezzlement* involve illicit, unauthorized actions by brokers to steal directly from their clients; these may be facilitated by the forging of client documents, the doctoring of account statements, or unauthorized trading and fund transfers in violation of the broker's legal obligations to the client.

According to the FBI, the losses associated with these types of fraud range from the macroeconomic (erosion of investor confidence in capital markets) to the corporate (reduction in the economic health of corporations/industries due to decreased market capitalization) to the intensely personal (devastation of retirement and investment portfolios).[18] Victims of these kinds of fraud include government entities, corporations, financial institutions, pension funds, and individual investors.

Health-Care Fraud

All health-care programs are subject to fraud, with Medicare and Medicaid being most victimized. Estimates of fraudulent billings to health-care programs (public and private) are said to be between 3% and 10% of all health-care expenditures. According to the FBI, health-care fraud is not limited to any particular geographic area, targets large health-care programs (public and private) as well as beneficiaries, has become more sophisticated and complex over time, and is even being perpetrated by a number of organized crime groups.

Estimates of fraudulent billings to health-care programs (public and private) are said to be between 3% and 10% of all health-care expenditures.

The FBI stated that "one of the most significant trends in recent health-care fraud cases includes the willingness of medical professionals to risk patient harm in their schemes."[19] These cases involve health-care providers who conduct unnecessary surgeries, prescribe dangerous drugs without medical necessity, and engage in abusive or substandard care practices. Other schemes involve fraudulent billing for services not rendered and upcoding of charges for services provided.[20]

Mortgage Fraud

The federal government has reported a spike in the number of corporate fraud cases involving subprime-mortgage-lending companies[21] (businesses that lend to borrowers who do not qualify for loans from mainstream loan companies). The subprime market grew from 2% of all home mortgages in 1998 to 20% of mortgages in 2006, but as the housing market declined, subprime lenders were forced to buy back a number of nonperforming loans. Many of these subprime lenders had relied on a continuous increase in real estate values to allow borrowers to refinance or sell their properties before defaulting, but due to the slowdown in the housing market, loan defaults increased.

As subprime lenders suffered financial difficulties due to rising defaults, analyses of company financials by regulators identified instances of false accounting entries and fraudulently inflated assets and revenues. Federal investigations then determined that many now-bankrupt subprime lenders manipulated their reported loan portfolio risks and used various accounting schemes to inflate and falsify their financial reports; in addition, before the value of these subprime lenders' stocks rapidly declined, some executives with insider information sold their equity positions and made illegal profits.

Mortgage fraud, which is not confined to the subprime market, involves material misstatements, misrepresentations, and/or omissions relating to the property or potential mortgage relied on by an underwriter or lender to fund, purchase, or insure a loan. As initial mortgage products are repackaged and sold on secondary markets, the process can conceal or distort the original fraud so that it is not reported, leading the FBI to explain that "the true level of mortgage fraud is largely unknown."[22]

Current mortgage fraud, according to the FBI, includes equity skimming, property flipping, and mortgage debt elimination. *Equity skimming* uses corporate shell companies, corporate identity theft, and bankruptcy/foreclosure (or the threat of it) to dupe homeowners and investors. *Property flipping* involves purchasing properties and artificially inflating their value through false appraisals; the overvalued properties are then repurchased several times for a higher price by associates of the "flipper." After three or four sham sales, the properties are foreclosed on by victim lenders. Often flipped properties are ultimately repurchased for 50% to 100% of their original value. *Mortgage debt elimination* uses e-mail or Web-based ads to promote the elimination of mortgage loans, credit card debt, and other debt for an up-front fee to prepare documents to satisfy the debt, but these documents (typically referred to as Declaration of Voidance, Bond for Discharge of Debt, Bill of Exchange, Due Bill, or Redemption Certificate) do not achieve debt-elimination goals; they only gain profit for the scammers.

> *Flipping* involves purchasing properties and inflating their value through false appraisals; overvalued properties are repurchased several times for higher prices by associates of the "flipper."

Insurance Fraud

The U.S. insurance industry consists of thousands of companies and collects nearly $1 trillion in premiums each year, so its size makes it a prime target for criminal activity.[23] The Coalition Against Insurance Fraud (CAIF) estimated that the cost of fraud in the industry is as high as $80 billion each year, a cost passed on to consumers in the form of higher premiums. The National Insurance Crime Bureau (NICB) calculated that insurance fraud raises the yearly cost of premiums by $300 for the average household.

Insurance fraud involving arson is also related to the mortgage crisis. Some distressed homeowners, property flippers, and other real estate investors have resorted to committing arson to avoid real estate foreclosure; the insurance policyholders for these properties receive otherwise-unobtainable proceeds/profits through the filing of false insurance claims.

With the downturn in the American and worldwide economies that started in the first decade of this century, workers' compensation fraud has soared. Workers' compensation insurance accounts for as much as 46% of small-business owners' operating expenses, so small-business owners have an incentive to shop for workers' compensation insurance on a regular basis. This has created an illicit opportunity for entities purporting to provide workers' compensation insurance to enter the marketplace, offer reduced premiums, and misappropriate funds without providing insurance, leaving injured and deceased victims without workers' compensation coverage to pay medical bills.

Mass-Marketing Fraud

Mass-marketing fraud is a general term for any fraud connected with communications media such as telemarketing, mass mailings, and the Internet. Mass-marketing fraud takes a variety of forms that share a common theme: use of false and/or deceptive representations to induce potential victims to make advance-fee-type payments to fraud perpetrators. Although there are no comprehensive statistics on the subject, it is estimated that mass-marketing frauds victimize millions of Americans each year and generate losses in the hundreds of millions of dollars. Following is a brief description of three key concepts and schemes associated with mass-marketing fraud:

1. **Nigerian letter fraud.** Victims of Nigerian letter fraud are contacted regarding substantial sums of money held in foreign accounts that they are told is owed to them, and they are requested to pay various fees to secure the transfer of these monies to the United States; these fees are kept by the perpetrators. Victims also may be asked to act as U.S. agents in securing the release of such funds and are provided with counterfeit instruments to be cashed to pay any required fees, only to discover that they must reimburse their financial institutions for cashing counterfeit instruments.
2. **Foreign lottery/sweepstakes fraud.** Victims are informed that they have won a substantial prize in a foreign lottery or sweepstakes but must remit payment for various taxes/fees to receive their winnings; the taxes/fees are paid to the perpetrators. Victims may be given financial documents, supposedly representing a portion of the winnings, to be cashed to pay the required fees, only to discover that they must reimburse their financial institutions for cashing counterfeit instruments.

■ **money laundering** The process of converting illegally earned assets from cash to one or more alternative forms to conceal factors such as illegal origin and true ownership.

■ **environmental crime** A violation of the criminal law committed by businesses, business officials, organizational entities, and/or individuals that damages some protected or otherwise significant aspect of the natural environment.

3. **Overpayment fraud.** Victims who have advertised some item for sale are contacted by buyers who remit counterfeit instruments in excess of the purchase price for payment; the victims are told to cash the instruments, deduct any expenses, and return or forward the excess funds to an individual identified by the buyer, only to discover that they must reimburse their financial institution for cashing counterfeit instruments.

Money Laundering

Money laundering is the process by which illegal gains are disguised as legal income. A more formal definition is offered by the National Institute of Justice for *money laundering*: "the process of converting illegally earned assets, originating as cash, to one or more alternative forms to conceal such incriminating factors as illegal origin and true ownership."[24] In 2010, Wachovia Corporation (now part of Wells Fargo & Company) agreed to pay $160 million to settle federal charges that it failed to establish an adequate program to prevent money laundering through its facilities.[25] The plea resulted from transactions involving Wachovia and Mexican money exchanges between 2004 and 2007 that facilitated money transfers between the United States and Mexico; a federal investigation found that drug dealers routinely used them to move funds between the two countries.

In money laundering, illegal gains are disguised as legal income.

Title 18, Section 1956, of the U.S. Criminal Code specifically prohibited what it called the "laundering of monetary instruments" and defined *money laundering* as "[efforts] to conceal or disguise the nature, the location, the source, the ownership, or the control of the proceeds of specified unlawful activity."[26] To assist in the identification of money launderers, a provision of the 1986 federal Money Laundering Control Act required that banks report to the government all currency transactions in excess of $10,000. The Bank Secrecy Act (BSA), formally known as the Currency and Foreign Transactions Reporting Act, required financial institutions to assist government agencies in detecting and preventing activities related to money laundering, to report cash transactions exceeding an aggregate amount of $10,000 daily per account, and to report suspicious financial activity. However, high-end money launderers know these requirements and routinely evade them by dealing in commodities such as gold, using foreign banks, or making a series of smaller deposits and transfers, often involving numerous financial institutions. Reliable official estimates of the amount of money laundered in the United States are hard to establish. However, the Drug Enforcement Administration reported that estimates provided by the International Monetary Fund pegged worldwide money-laundering activities at between 2% and 5% of the world's gross domestic product, or about $600 billion annually.[27]

The problem of money laundering may be getting worse: A 2010 report by the Senate Permanent Subcommittee on Investigations found that billions of dollars are leaving the United States every year to be put into the flow of commerce and returned to this country as laundered capital.[28] The report also identified a number of individuals and organizations suspected of bringing millions of dollars from illegal activities into the country by funneling it through offshore accounts.

Environmental Crimes and Green Criminology

Crimes against the environment constitute a relatively new area of corporate and white-collar criminality.

A relatively new area of corporate and white-collar criminality, which is defined solely in terms of violations of the criminal law, is that of crimes against the environment.[29] **Environmental crimes** are violations of the criminal law that, although typically committed by businesses or business officials, may also be committed by other individuals or organizational

Mark & Audrey Gibson Stock Connection Worldwide/Newscom

Cleanup workers at an illegal dump site clean up at the end of their shift. Environmental crimes have recently become an area of special concern to criminologists. Why have such offenses only recently been recognized as crimes?

■ **green criminology** The study of environmental harm, crime, law, regulation, victimization, and justice.

entities and that damage some protected or otherwise significant aspect of the natural environment.

Whaling in violation of international conventions, for example, constitutes a form of environmental crime. So, too, does intentional pollution, especially when state or federal law contravenes the practice. Sometimes negligence contributes to environmental criminality, as in the case of the 1,000-foot *Valdez* supertanker owned by Exxon Corporation, which ran aground off the coast of Alaska in 1989, spilling 11 million gallons of crude oil over 1,700 miles of pristine coastline. In September 1994, an Alaskan jury ordered Exxon to pay $5 billion in punitive damages to 14,000 people affected by the 1989 spill and another $287 million in actual damages to commercial fishermen in the region. Exxon also agreed to pay $100 million in criminal fines.

British Petroleum Products North America, Inc. (BPPNA), pleaded guilty in 2007 to one felony count of violating the federal Clean Air Act; it was ordered to pay $50 million in fines and was placed on three years of federal probation. The conviction stemmed from an explosion at the BPPNA Texas City refinery on March 23, 2005, that caused the death of 15 employees. The company admitted that several procedures required under the Clean Air Act for ensuring the integrity of safety equipment either had not been established or were being ignored. The British Petroleum subsidiary BP Exploration Alaska (BPXA) pleaded guilty to one count of violating the federal Clean Water Act as a result of a 2006 oil spill of 267,000 gallons at its facility on Alaska's North Slope.[30] Authorities charged that the spill occurred because company officials had conspired to save money by acting to conceal corrosion in a pipeline used to transfer oil and falsifying financial reports detailing money spent to fix the corrosion. The company agreed to pay a $20 million fine and was placed on three years' probation.[31]

As mentioned earlier, British Petroleum (BP) has agreed to pay billions of dollars in compensation stemming from the Gulf oil spill that began on April 20, 2010, when the company's deepwater drilling platform Deepwater Horizon suffered an explosion and fire and sank, releasing 206 million gallons of oil into the Gulf of Mexico from a wellhead 5,000 feet below the surface.[32]

The devastating fires set in oil fields throughout Kuwait by retreating Iraqi Army troops during the Gulf War in 1991 provide an example of arson that resulted in global pollution while negatively affecting fossil fuel reserves throughout much of the Middle East. These intentional fires, although properly classified as environmental criminality, also serve as an example of ecological terrorism because they were set for the purpose of political intimidation.

Green criminology is the study of environmental harm, crime, law, regulation, victimization, and justice. The term was recently introduced by Michael J. Lynch at the University of South Florida and Paul B. Stretesky at the University of Colorado, Denver. According to Lynch and Stretesky, green criminology has increasing relevance to contemporary problems at local, national, and international levels.

Learn more about environmental crimes from the Duke Environmental Law and Policy Forum and the FBI at **Web Extras 12–6** and **12–7**; read about the conviction and sentencing of some defendants in environmental-crime prosecutions at **Library Extra 12–2**.

Terrorism and White-Collar Crime

Terrorist activity frequently involves some form of white-collar crime because terrorists need money for daily living expenses and for weapons, travel, and communications. Terrorist groups also frequently send a portion of the money acquired from illegal activities back to their home country or pass it along to those higher up in the chain of command. Involvement in white-collar crime allows terrorist groups to maintain a significantly lower profile than if they raised funds through other crimes such as bank robberies and illegal drug sales.

Involvement in white-collar crime allows terrorist groups to maintain a low profile.

John Kane and April Wall, in a report prepared for the White Collar Crime Center, pointed out that "curtailing terrorist activity may be achieved through the combined efforts of nations, through legislation that criminalizes the financing of terrorism, modifications to regulations that govern non-profit or charity-based corporations, international cooperation, and a willingness of the international banking community to adhere to reporting rules designed to detect money laundering and suspicious activity" and that shell companies have been used by terrorist groups to receive and distribute money.[33] The term *shell companies* refers to entities engaged in legitimate activities to establish a good reputation in the business community and provide a veneer of legitimacy; they can launder funds by creating invoices for nonexistent products or services that then appear to be paid by another company to provide a channel for profits from illegal activities (such as insurance fraud and identity theft) so that the money enters the legitimate flow of cash disguised as revenue from legitimate activities. In 2001, for example, an American telecommunications company was indicted on charges of aiding members of al-Qaeda in preparation for the 9/11 terrorist attacks by handling more than $500,000 in monthly money transfers. Table 12-2 provides examples of the kinds of white collar crimes associated with terrorism in recent years, along with information on federal criminal statutes that these kinds of activities violate.

TABLE 12-2 White-Collar Crimes Associated with Terrorism Cases

TYPE OF OFFENSE	DESCRIPTION OF OFFENSE	STATUTE
Identification Document Fraud	Fraud in connection with identification documents	18 USC 1028
	Forgery or false use of passports	18 USC 1543
	Misuse of passports	18 USC 1544
	Fraud and misuse of visas, permits, and other documents	18 USC 1546
	Social Security fraud	42 USC 408
Financial Fraud	Bribery of public officials and witnesses	18 USC 201
	Counterfeited or forged securities of states and private entities	18 USC 513
	False statements on credit application	18 USC 1014
	Bank fraud	18 USC 1344
	Money laundering	18 USC 1956
	Unlicensed money-transmitting business	18 USC 1960
	Racketeering	18 USC 1962
	Transactions structured to evade reporting requirements	31 USC 5324
Mail and Wire Fraud	Mail fraud	18 USC 1341
	Fraud by wire, radio, or television	18 USC 1343
Credit Card Fraud	Fraud in connection with access devices	18 USC 1029
Tax Fraud	Materially false income tax returns	26 USC 7206
	Corrupt endeavors to impede IRS laws	26 USC 7212
Immigration Fraud	Deportable alien	8 USC 1227
	Alien failing to report address change	8 USC 1305
	Alien smuggling	8 USC 1324
	Evasion of immigration laws	8 USC 1325
	False representations as U.S. citizen	18 USC 911
	Illegal alien	18 USC 922
	False statements regarding naturalization, citizenship, or alien registry	18 USC 1015
	Unlawful procurement of citizenship or naturalization	18 USC 1425
Other Related Charges	Aiding and abetting	18 USC 2
	Conspiracy to commit offenses against or defraud the U.S.	18 USC 371
	Materially false statements	18 USC 1001
	Perjury	18 USC 1621
	Provision of material support to terrorists	18 USC 2339
	Conspiracy to give or receive funds, goods, or services for designated terrorist	50 USC 595

Causes of White-Collar Crime

When Edwin H. Sutherland first coined the term *white-collar crime*, he wrote, "A hypothesis is needed that will explain both white-collar criminality and lower-class criminality."[34] The answer Sutherland gave to his own challenge was that "white-collar criminality, just as other systematic criminality, is learned."[35] He went on to apply elements of his famous theory of differential association (discussed in Chapter 7) to white-collar crime, saying that "it is learned in direct or indirect association with those who already practice the behavior."[36]

Edwin Sutherland said that white-collar criminality is learned, just like other forms of criminal activity.

Other authors have since offered similar integrative perspectives. **Travis Hirschi** and **Michael Gottfredson**, for example, in an issue of the journal *Criminology* published half a century after Sutherland's initial work, write, "In this paper we outline a general theory of crime capable of organizing the facts about white-collar crime at the same time it is capable of organizing the facts about all forms of crime."[37] Their analysis of white-collar crime focuses squarely on the development of the concept itself. Hirschi and Gottfredson suggest that if we were not aware of the fact that the concept of white-collar crime arose "as a reaction to the idea that crime is concentrated in the lower class, there would be nothing to distinguish it from other" forms of crime.[38] "It may be, then," they write, "that the discovery of white-collar criminals is important only in a context in which their existence is denied by theory or policy."[39] In other words, nothing is unusual about the idea of white-collar crime other than the fact that many people are loath to admit that high-status individuals commit crimes just as people of lower status do.

In fact, say Hirschi and Gottfredson, white-collar criminals are motivated by the same forces that drive other criminals: self-interest, the pursuit of pleasure, and the avoidance of pain. White-collar crimes certainly have special characteristics. They are not as dangerous as other "common" forms of crime, they provide relatively large rewards, the rewards they produce may follow quickly from their commission, sanctions associated with them may be vague or only rarely imposed, and they may require only minimal effort from those with the requisite skills to engage in them.

Hirschi and Gottfredson conclude, however, that criminologists err in assuming that white-collar criminality is common or that it is as common as the forms of criminality found among the lower classes. They reason that the personal characteristics of most white-collar workers are precisely those we would expect to produce conformity in behavior. High educational levels, a commitment to the status quo, personal motivation to succeed, deference to others, attention to conventional appearance, and other inherent aspects of social conformity—all of which tend to characterize those who operate at the white-collar level—are not the kinds of personal characteristics associated with crime commission. "In other words," say Hirschi and Gottfredson, "selection processes inherent to the high end of the occupational structure tend to recruit people with relatively low propensity to crime."[40]

One other reason most criminologists are mistaken about the assumed high rate of white-collar criminality is because "white-collar researchers often take organizations as the unit of analysis" and confuse the crimes committed by organizational entities with those of individuals within those organizations.[41] Similarly, rates of white-collar offending tend to lump together the crimes of corporations with crimes committed by individual representatives of those organizations when making comparisons with the rate of criminal activity among blue-collar and other groups.

A complementary perspective by Australian criminologist **John Braithwaite** says that white-collar criminals are frequently motivated by a disparity between corporate goals and the limited opportunities available to businesspeople through conventional business practices.[42] When pressured to achieve goals that may be unattainable within the existing framework of laws and regulations surrounding their business's area of endeavor, innovative corporate officers may turn to crime to meet organizational demands.[43]

Braithwaite believes that a general theory covering both white-collar and other forms of crime can be developed by focusing on inequality as the central explanatory variable in all criminal activity.[44] Although alienation from legitimate paths to success may lead lower-class offenders to criminal activity in an effort to acquire the material possessions necessary for survival, greed can similarly motivate relatively successful individuals to violate the law to acquire even more power and more wealth.[45] New types of criminal opportunities and new paths to immunity from accountability arise from inequitable concentrations of wealth and power. Inequality thus worsens crimes of poverty motivated by the need to survive as well as crimes of wealth motivated by greed.

Braithwaite also suggests that corporate culture socializes budding executives into clandestine and frequently illegal behavioral modalities, making it easier for them to violate the law when pressures to perform mount. The hostile relationship that frequently exists between businesses and the government agencies that regulate them may further spur corporate officers to evade the law. Braithwaite emphasizes his belief that the potential for shame associated with discovery—whether by enforcement agencies, the public, or internal corporate regulators—can

■ **Sarbanes-Oxley Act** Officially known as the Public Company Accounting Reform and Investor Protection Act, requires chief executive officers and chief financial officers to personally vouch for the truth and fairness of their companies' financial disclosures and establishes an independent oversight board to regulate the accounting profession. The law also gives the federal Securities and Exchange Commission the authority to bar dishonest corporate directors and officers from ever again serving in positions of corporate responsibility, and increases the maximum federal prison term for common types of corporate fraud from 5 to 20 years.

have a powerful deterrent effect on most corporate executives because they are fundamentally conservative individuals who are otherwise seeking success through legitimate means.[46]

Braithwaite also recommends implementation of an "accountability model," which would hold all those responsible for corporate crimes accountable.[47] Rather than merely punishing corporations through fines, personal punishment meted out to corporate lawbreakers, says Braithwaite, should have the potential to substantially reduce white-collar offending.[48]

In sum, Braithwaite contends that an integrated theory of organizational crime would include insights garnered from (1) strain theories, as to the distribution of legitimate and illegitimate opportunities; (2) subcultural theory, as applied to business subcultures; (3) labeling theory, or the way stigmatization can foster criminal subculture formation; and (4) control theory, as to how potential white-collar offenders can be made accountable.[49]

Curtailing White-Collar and Corporate Crime

It is far easier to convict street criminals than white-collar criminals, and it may even be difficult for prosecutors to show that a white-collar crime has occurred. "When someone breaks into a house and takes the TV and VCR," says Harvard University criminal law professor William Stuntz, "it's a matter of proving who did it. With white-collar crime it's usually not even clear what happened."[50]

White-collar crimes are often difficult to investigate and prosecute for a number of other reasons. For one thing, white-collar criminals are generally better educated compared to other offenders and are therefore better able to conceal their activities.[51] Similarly, cases against white-collar offenders must often be built on evidence of a continuing series of offenses, not a single crime, such as a bank robbery. Often the evidence involved is only understandable to financial or legal experts and can be difficult to explain to jurors. Finally, business executives, because they often have the financial resources of an entire corporation at their disposal and because they sometimes earn salaries and bonuses in the millions of dollars, are able to hire excellent defense attorneys and can tie up the courts with motions and appeals that might not be as readily available to defendants with fewer resources.

Events such as the 2001 collapse of Enron Corporation left investors around the world leery of American stock markets and forced federal legislators to enact sweeping financial reform. At the same time, the Securities and Exchange Commission (SEC) renewed efforts to enforce existing regulations and mandated new rules for investment bankers. By the start of 2001, the atmosphere of distrust that had been created by corporate criminals had become so severe that President George W. Bush believed it was necessary to make significant efforts to help restore investor confidence and to bring order to American financial markets. Consequently, the president created a federal Corporate Fraud Task Force within the U.S. DOJ, and on July 30, 2002, he signed the **Sarbanes-Oxley Act** (officially known as the Public Company Accounting Reform and Investor Protection Act), which set stiff penalties for corporate wrongdoers.[52]

In 2007, the U.S. DOJ announced that activities of the task force had resulted in 1,236 fraud convictions, including those of 214 chief executive officers and 53 chief financial officers, since 2002.[53] In announcing the convictions, then-Attorney General Alberto Gonzales noted that "perhaps the most important accomplishment is the criminal conduct that never occurred because of the widespread deterrent effect" of the task force.[54]

In 2009, President Barack Obama replaced President Bush's Corporate Fraud Task Force with an interagency task force targeting financial crimes. Called the Financial Fraud Enforcement Task Force, the organization consists of senior-level officials from more than 20 federal departments, agencies, and offices.[55] The new task force, which was given a wider mandate than its predecessor, was charged with combating mortgage fraud, securities fraud, Recovery Act fraud, and discrimination by financial institutions in the making of loans and in other financial activities. The task force also aimed to fully enforce the Fraud Enforcement and Recovery Act of 2009,[56] which targeted the recovery of federal funds spent on fraudulent claims made under the American Recovery and Reinvestment Act of 2009 (also known as the Financial Stimulus Act),[57] fraudulent claims under the Troubled Assets Relief Program (TARP),[58] and financial fraud related to any "other form of Federal assistance."

In his 2012 State of the Union Address to Congress, President Obama announced the creation of two more enforcement initiatives—one of which will be charged with targeting financial crimes; the other, with fighting unfair trade practices. The first, the Residential Mortgage-Backed Securities Working Group, will operate under the previously created Financial Fraud Enforcement Task Force; the second, which will investigate unfair trade practices in countries such as China, will likely be run from the White House under the Deputy National Security Advisor for International Affairs.[59]

■ **organized crime** The unlawful activity of members of a highly organized association engaged in supplying illegal goods and services, including gambling, prostitution, loan-sharking, narcotics, and racketeering.

■ **Mafia** A criminal organization of Sicilian origin; also called *La Cosa Nostra*.

■ **La Cosa Nostra** A criminal organization of Sicilian origin; also call *the Mafia*. The term literally means "our thing."

The Sarbanes-Oxley Act, referred to earlier, has been called the most far-reaching reform of U.S. business practices since the time of Franklin Delano Roosevelt. The law authorizes funding for investigators and for the development of new technologies at the SEC targeted at uncovering corporate wrongdoing. Under the Sarbanes-Oxley Act, the SEC has the authority to bar dishonest corporate directors and officers from ever again serving in positions of corporate responsibility. Similarly, penalties for obstructing justice and shredding documents are greatly increased, corporate officers who profit illegally can be forced to return their gains to investors, and the maximum federal prison term for common types of corporate fraud has been increased from 5 to 20 years.

The Sarbanes-Oxley Act also requires chief executive officers and chief financial officers to personally vouch for the truth and fairness of their companies' financial disclosures and establishes an independent oversight board to regulate the accounting profession. The board is required to set clear standards to uphold the integrity of public audits and has the authority to investigate abuses and discipline offenders. Similarly, the Sarbanes-Oxley Act prohibits auditing firms from providing consulting services that create conflicts of interest. Finally, under the law, officials in public corporations are barred from buying or selling stock during periods when employees are prevented from making stock transactions in their retirement or 401(k) accounts.

The Sarbanes-Oxley Act was the latest in a long line of federal legislation relating to the conduct of U.S. business that extends back more than 100 years. Some of the earliest such legislation can be found in the federal Sherman Act,[60] which became law in 1890. The Sherman Act was passed to eliminate restraints on trade and competition and specifically to prevent the development of trusts and monopolies in restraint of trade. The Clayton Act,[61] passed in 1914, prohibits mergers and acquisitions in which the effect "may be substantially to lessen competition, or to tend to create a monopoly."

The Securities Act of 1933[62] and the Securities Exchange Act of 1934[63] were enacted by federal legislators reeling from the effects of the Great Depression, which began with the stock market crash of 1929. Often referred to as the "truth-in-securities" law, the Securities Act of 1933 has two basic objectives: (1) to require that investors receive financial and other significant information concerning securities being offered for public sale and (2) to prohibit deceit, misrepresentations, and other fraud in the sale of securities.

The Securities Exchange Act of 1934 gave birth to the SEC and conferred upon the SEC broad authority over all aspects of the securities industry. This includes the power to register, regulate, and oversee brokerage firms, transfer agents, and clearing agencies as well as the nation's stock exchanges. The act also identified and prohibited certain types of conduct in the markets and provides the SEC with disciplinary powers over regulated entities and people associated with them. Finally, the act empowered the SEC to require periodic reporting of information by companies with publicly traded securities.

Certain forms of occupational crime may be easier to address than others. Individual occupational crimes especially may be reduced by concerted enforcement and protective efforts, including enhanced IRS auditing programs, theft-deterrent systems, and good internal financial procedures. Consumer information services can help eliminate fraudulent business practices, and increases in both victim awareness and reporting can help target businesses and individuals responsible for various forms of white-collar or occupational crime.

Learn more about corporate responsibility and ethical business practices from the Interfaith Center on Corporate Responsibility and the Center for Business Ethics and Social Responsibility at **Web Extras 12–8** and **12–9**; similar resources, including many government links, the American Institute of Certified Public Accountants' Antifraud and Corporate Responsibility Center, and the Carnegie Mellon Center for International Corporate Responsibility, can be found at **Web Extras 12–10** and **12–11**. Links to various corporate codes of ethics can be found online at **Web Extra 12–12**. A discussion about deterring white-collar crime can be found at **Library Extra 12–3**.

Organized Crime

Organized crime specifically refers to unlawful activities of the members of a highly organized, disciplined association engaged in supplying illegal goods and services, including prostitution, gambling, loan-sharking, narcotics, and labor racketeering. In 1967, the President's Commission on Law Enforcement and Administration of Justice investigated organized crime in the United States and found that—at the time—many organized crime families were of Italian descent. The Commission depicted the structure of a typical Italian American organized crime family as shown in Figure 12–3.

Much of what most Americans traditionally think of today as organized crime—sometimes called the **Mafia** or **La Cosa Nostra**—has roots that predate the establishment of the United States. For hundreds of years, secret societies have flourished in Italy.[64] Italian criminal organizations that came to the United States with the wave of European immigrants during the late nineteenth and early twentieth centuries included the Mafia and the Black Hand. The Black Hand (in Italian, *La Mano Negro*)

ethnic succession The continuing process whereby one immigrant or ethnic group succeeds another by assuming its position in society.

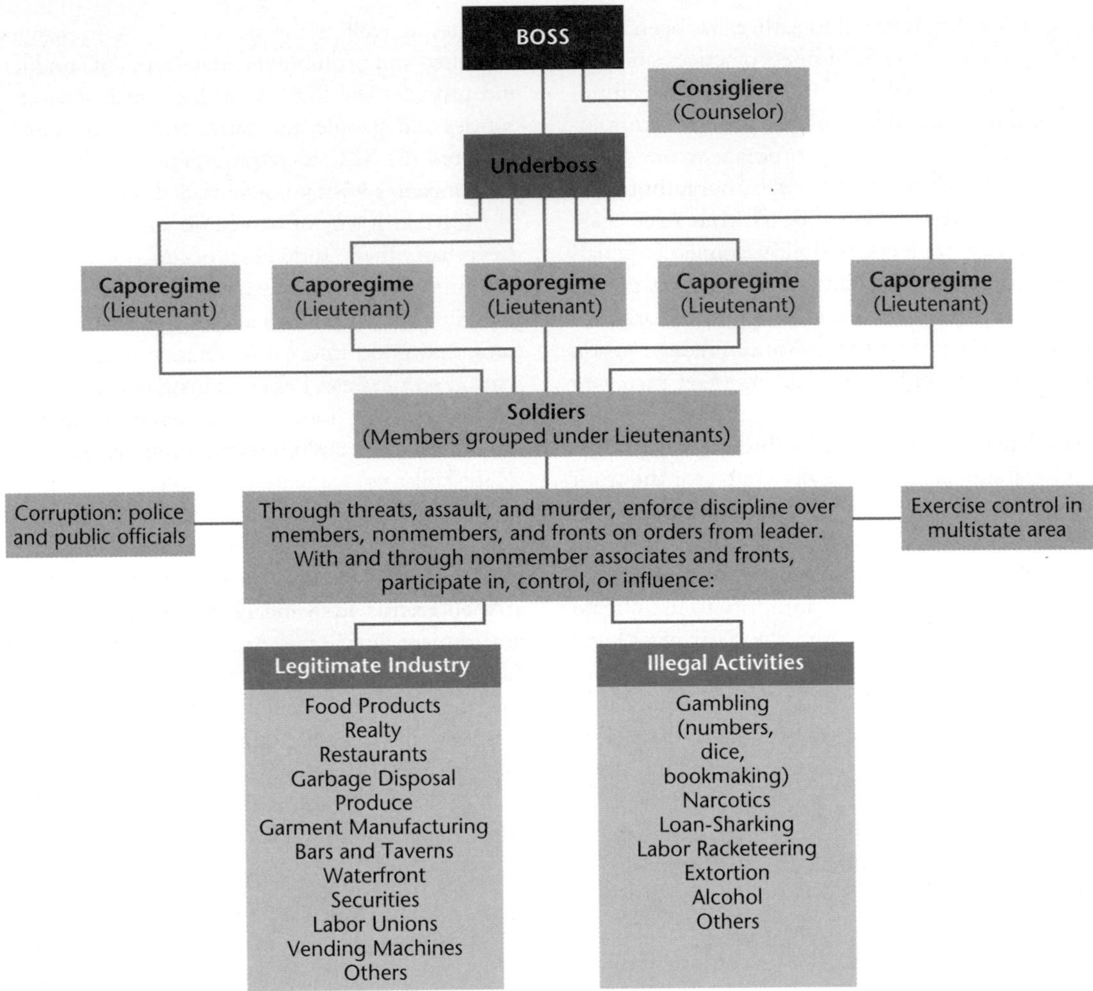

FIGURE 12-3 | **A Typical Italian American Organized Crime Family**

Source: Adapted from the President's Commission on Law Enforcement and Administration of Justice, *The Challenge of Crime in a Free Society* (Washington, DC: U.S. Government Printing Office, 1967), p. 47.

"specialized in the intimidation of Italian immigrants,"[65] typically extorting protection money and valuables.

The Mafia worked to become a quasi-police organization in the Italian ghetto areas of the burgeoning American cities of the industrial era—often enforcing its own set of laws and codes. Secret societies in Italy were all but expunged during the 1930s and early 1940s under Fascist dictator Benito Mussolini. Surviving Mafia members became vehemently anti-Fascist, sentiments that endeared them to American and Allied intelligence services during World War II. Following the war, *mafioso* leaders resumed their traditional positions of power within Italian society, and links grew between American criminal organizations and those in Italy.

Other organized criminal groups, including Jewish and Irish gangs, flourished in New York City prior to the arrival of large numbers of Italian immigrants in the late 1800s. Ethnic succession has been as much a reality in organized crime as in most other aspects of American life. **Ethnic succession** refers to the continuing process whereby one immigrant or ethnic group succeeds another through assumption of a particular position in society.

Throughout the late nineteenth and early twentieth centuries, for example, Jewish gangsters such as Meyer Lansky, Benjamin "Bugsy" Siegel, "Dutch" Schultz, and Lepke Buchalter ran many of the "rackets" in New York City, only to have Italian immigrants who arrived a few years later take their places.

■ **criminal enterprise** A group of individuals with an identified hierarchy who are engaged in significant criminal activities.

Around the middle of the twentieth century, organized criminal activity in the United States became the domain of Italian American immigrants and their descendants, especially those of Sicilian descent. Keep in mind that most Sicilians who immigrated to this country did not have ties or experience with Mafia organizations in the old country. Many Sicilian Americans immigrated to the United States to escape Mafia despotism at home, and most became productive members of their adopted society. The few who did involve themselves in organized crime created an organization known variously as the Mafia, the Outfit, the Mob, La Cosa Nostra ("our thing"), the syndicate, or simply the organization. Because *Mafia* is used most often, we will use it to describe Sicilian American organized criminal groups.

Prohibition and Official Corruption

In many ways, the advent of Prohibition was a godsend for Mafia leaders. Prior to Prohibition, Mafia operations in American cities were concerned mostly with gambling, protection rackets, and loan-sharking. Many *mafiosi*, however, were well versed in the manufacture of low-cost, high-proof, untaxed alcohol,[66] an expertise they had brought from their native country. In addition, the existing infrastructure of organized crime permitted easy and efficient entry into the running and sale of contraband liquor. The huge profits to be had from bootlegging led to the wholesale bribery of government officials and to the quick corruption of many law enforcement officers throughout the country. Nowhere was corruption more complete than in Chicago, where runners working for organized crime distributed illegal alcohol under police protection[67] and corrupt city government officials received regular payoffs from criminal cartels.

Activities of Organized Crime

The 1976 federal Task Force on Organized Crime identified five types of activity that may qualify as organized crime: racketeering, vice operations, theft/fence rings, gangs, and terrorism. Throughout the past half century, Sicilian American criminal cartels have continued to be involved in (1) the establishment and control of both legalized and illicit forms of gambling, including lotteries, bookmaking, horse race wagering, and bets on athletic contests; (2) loan-sharking, which involves the lending of money at rates far higher than legally prescribed limits; (3) large-scale drug trafficking; (4) the fencing of stolen goods, including securities; (5) infiltration of legitimate businesses, including labor unions and corporations that can be used as quasi-legitimate fronts for money laundering and other activities; and (6) labor union racketeering through which legitimate businesses are intimidated by threats of strikes, walkouts, and sabotage.

Organized crime is involved in many kinds of rackets, including gambling and the illegal copying and distribution of copyrighted software, music, and other forms of recorded media. The provision of elaborately staged recorded pornographic productions, including "snuff movies" (in which a sex "star" is actually killed in front of the camera), and elements of child pornography can also be traced to organized criminal activity.

Other Organized Criminal Groups

The FBI defines a **criminal enterprise** as "a group of individuals with an identifiable hierarchy, and extensive supporting networks, engaged in significant criminal activity."[68] According to **Howard Abadinsky**, the hallmark of true criminal organizations is that they function independently of any of their members, including their leaders, and have continuity over time as personnel within them change.[69] Abadinsky mentioned the James Gang, which dissolved with the death of its leader, Jesse James. In contrast, says Abadinsky, "When Al Capone was imprisoned fifty years later, the 'Capone Organization' continued, and in its more modern form (the 'Outfit') it continues to operate in Chicago."[70]

The terms *organized crime* and *criminal enterprise* are closely related and are often used interchangeably, but various federal criminal statutes have specifically defined the elements of a criminal enterprise that need to be proven to convict individuals or groups of individuals under those statutes. The federal Continuing Criminal Enterprise statute defines a *criminal enterprise* as any group of six

The terms *organized crime* and *criminal enterprise* are often used interchangeably.

or more people—with one of the six occupying an organizing, supervisory, or management position—that generates substantial income or resources and is engaged in a continuing series of violations of Subchapters I and II of Chapter 13 of Title 21 of the U.S. Code (Chapter 13 is that portion of federal law concerned with drug-abuse prevention and control).[71]

State laws defining criminal enterprise are generally more inclusive than federal statutes. The laws of New York, for example, stated that "the concept of criminal enterprise should not be limited to traditional criminal syndicates or crime families, and may include persons who join together in a criminal enterprise . . . for the purpose of corrupting . . . legitimate enterprises or infiltrating and illicitly influencing industries."[72] New York criminal statutes have defined *criminal enterprise* as "a group of persons sharing a common purpose of engaging in criminal conduct, associated in an ascertainable structure distinct from a pattern of criminal activity, and with a continuity of existence, structure and criminal purpose beyond the scope of individual criminal incidents."[73]

When people think of criminal enterprises, they often picture the Italian and Sicilian *mafioso* of popular television shows and movies, but the face of organized crime in the United States has changed, and its threat is broader and more complex than ever, with criminal enterprises of different origins. Some especially noteworthy groups include the following:

- Russian mobsters who fled to the United States in the wake of the Soviet Union's collapse
- Groups from African countries such as Nigeria that engage in drug trafficking and financial scams
- Chinese tongs, Japanese *Boryokudan*, and other Asian crime rings
- Enterprises based in Eastern European nations such as Hungary and Romania

Many organized crime groups of different nationalities currently operate in the United States.

Many organized crime groups of different nationalities—including Eurasian, Balkan, Asian, African, and Middle Eastern—currently operate in the United States or are targeting U.S. citizens from afar using the Internet and other technologies; we will describe each of these.

Eurasian Criminal Enterprises

The term *Eurasian organized crime* refers to organized crime groups comprising criminals born in or with family ties to the former Soviet Union or Central or Eastern Europe.[74] Eurasian organized crime in the United States is rooted in the *Vory V Zakone* (meaning "thieves in law"), career criminals who banded together for support and profit in the Soviet prison system; their leaders operated outside the official Soviet system and were illegally paid to acquire scarce consumer goods and to divert raw materials and finished goods from production lines for the benefit of *Nomenklatura* (the educated elite) and criminals.

With the collapse of the Soviet Union in 1991, members of the *Vory V Zakone* joined with corrupt public officials to acquire control of industries and resources that were being privatized, which gave the criminal syndicate a one-time infusion of wealth and supplied the infrastructure with continuing cash flows and opportunities to launder criminal proceeds. In February 1993, Boris Yeltsin, the first elected president of the Federation of Russian States, said, "Organized crime has become the No. 1 threat to Russia's strategic interests and to national security. . . . Corrupted structures on the highest level have no interest in reform."

Organized crime members first emerged in the West in the 1970s when so-called Soviet *Refuseniks* were allowed to immigrate to Europe, Israel, and the United States. Secreted among the *Refuseniks* were criminals who sought to exploit their newfound freedoms and helped major criminal groups expand to the West; when the Soviet Union collapsed, the people of the region were able to move about freely, many coming to join their criminal colleagues already in the United States and Western Europe.

In the United States, Eurasian criminal organizations are heavily involved in health-care fraud, auto insurance fraud, securities and investment fraud, money laundering, drug trafficking, extortion, auto theft, and interstate transportation of stolen property as well as human smuggling and prostitution.

Balkan Criminal Enterprises

The term *Balkan organized crime* applies to criminal enterprises originating from or operating in Albania, Bosnia-Herzegovina, Bulgaria, Croatia, Greece, Kosovo, the former Yugoslav Republic of Macedonia, Romania, and Serbia and Montenegro and is an emerging threat in the United States today. The FBI noted that although several of these groups are active in various cities across the country, "they do not yet exhibit the established criminal sophistication of traditional Eurasian or La Cosa Nostra (LCN) organizations."

Organized crime in the rural areas of the Balkans sprang from traditional clan structures, which had large familial ties for protection and mutual assistance. Starting in the fifteenth century, clan relationships operated under the *kanun* (code), which

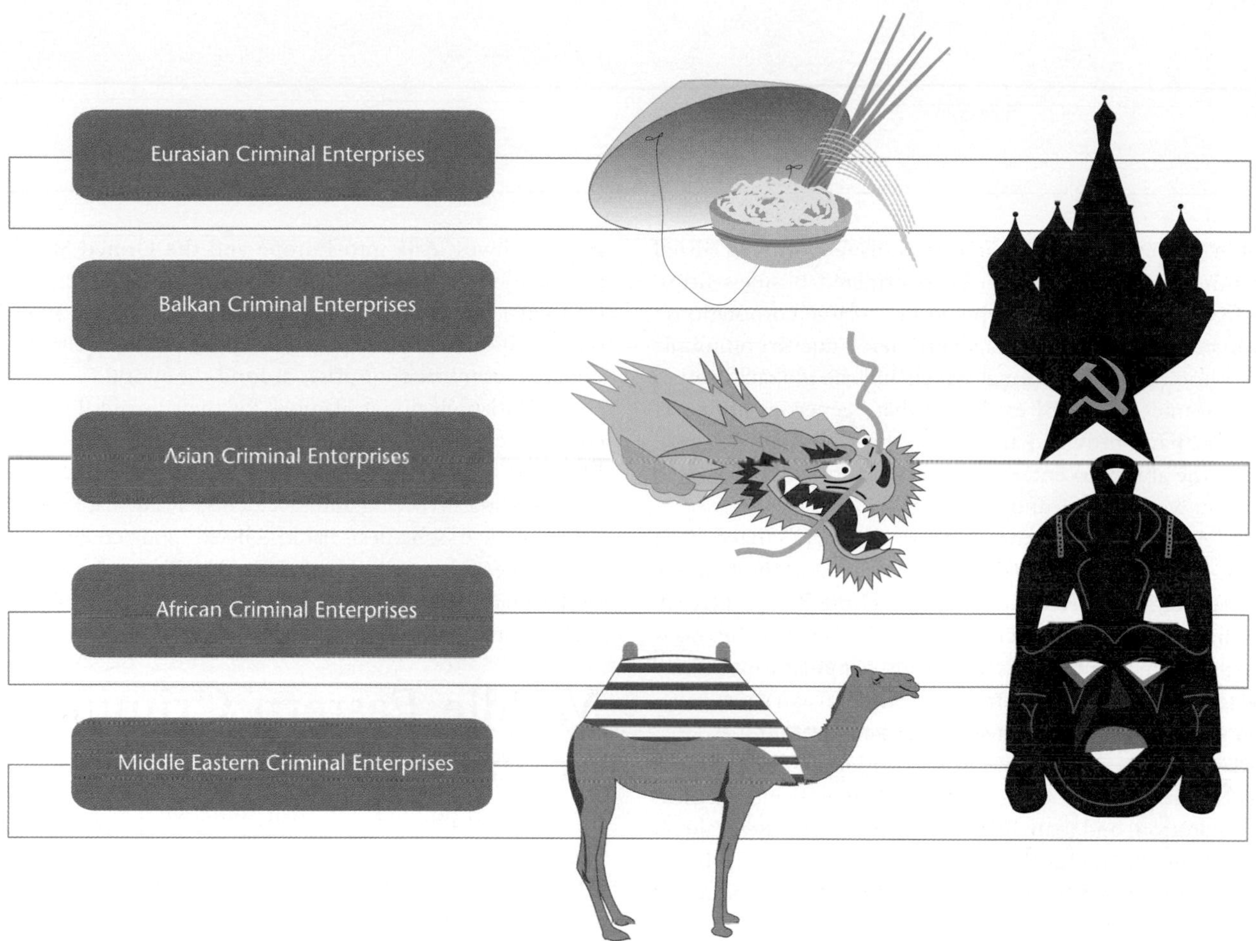

FIGURE 12-4 | **International Organized Criminal Groups Whose Activities Impact the United States**

Source: Schmalleger, Frank J., *Criminology*. Printed and Electronically reproduced by permission of Pearson Education, Inc., Upper Saddle River, New Jersey.

values loyalty and *besa*, or secrecy. Each clan established itself in specific territories and controlled the criminal activities and illicit interests there; the protection of these interests often led to violence between clans.

Years of communist rule led to black market activities in the Balkans, but the impact of those activities was mostly limited to the region. However, when Soviet-style communism collapsed in the late 1980s and early 1990s, Balkan organized crime activities expanded. Within the Balkans, organized crime groups infiltrated newly established democratic institutions, further expanding opportunities for criminal profits. Criminal markets once closed to Balkan groups suddenly opened, which led to the creation of an international criminal network.

Balkan criminal organizations have been active in the United States since the mid-1980s.[75] Initially, they were involved in low-level crimes, such as bank robberies, ATM burglaries, and home invasions. Later, ethnic Albanians affiliated themselves with established Mafia families in New York and acted as low-level participants; as their communities and presence became more established, they expanded their own organizations.

Balkan organized crime is not structured like the traditional Sicilian Mafia. The members brought their clanlike structure to the United States, meaning they are not clearly defined or organized, but instead are grouped around central leaders who maintain ties with the Balkan region while establishing close-knit communities in many cities across the nation. According to the FBI, "Albanian organized crime activities in the United States include gambling, money laundering, drug trafficking, human smuggling, extortion, violent witness intimidation, robbery, attempted murder, and murder" and are said to "have recently expanded into more sophisticated crimes including real estate fraud."[76]

Asian Criminal Enterprises

Asian criminal enterprises have been active in the United States since the early 1900s.[77] The first of these groups evolved from Chinese tongs—social organizations formed by early Chinese American immigrants. A century later, the criminalized tongs continue to thrive and have been joined by similar organizations with ties to East and Southeast Asia. The FBI has stated that "members of the most dominant Asian criminal enterprises affecting the United States have ties—either directly or culturally—to China, Korea, Japan, Thailand, the Philippines, Cambodia, Laos, and Vietnam."[78] Groups from the South Pacific island nations are also emerging as a threat.

Asian organized criminal groups rely on extensive networks of national and international criminal associates that are fluid and mobile, easily adapt to changes, have multilingual abilities, are sophisticated in their criminal operations, and have extensive financial capabilities. Some enterprises have commercialized their criminal activities and can be considered business firms, ranging from small family-run operations to large corporations.

Asian criminal enterprises have prospered due to communications technology, international travel, and the globalization of world economies. The FBI explained that "generous immigration policies have provided many members of Asian criminal enterprises the ability to enter and live on every populated continent in the world today undetected."[79]

Two categories of Asian criminal enterprises have been identified. Traditional criminal enterprises include the Chinese triads (or underground societies) based in Hong Kong, Taiwan, and Macau, as well as the Japanese *Yakuza* or *Boryokudan*; nontraditional criminal enterprises comprise criminally influenced Chinese tongs, triad affiliates, and other ethnic Asian street gangs found in several countries with sizable Asian communities.

Today's Asian criminal enterprises conduct traditional racketeering activities: extortion, murder, kidnapping, illegal gambling, prostitution, and loan-sharking. They also smuggle aliens, traffic in heroin and methamphetamine, commit financial fraud, steal automobiles and computer chips, produce counterfeit computer and clothing products, and launder money.

In this country, Asian criminal enterprises have been identified in more than 50 metropolitan areas but are more prevalent in Boston; Chicago; Honolulu; Las Vegas; Los Angeles; Newark; New Orleans; New York; Philadelphia; Portland; San Francisco; Seattle; and Washington, D.C.

African Criminal Enterprises

African criminal enterprises have developed quickly since the 1980s due to advances in communications technology and the globalization of the world's economies.[80] Easier international travel, expanded world trade, and transnational financial transactions have enabled these groups to target international victims and to develop criminal networks within prosperous countries and regions. The political, social, and economic conditions in African countries such as Ghana, Liberia, and Nigeria also have helped some enterprises expand globally.

African criminal enterprises actively operate in several major metropolitan areas in the United States but are most prevalent in Atlanta; Baltimore; Chicago; Dallas; Houston; Milwaukee; Newark; New York; and Washington, D.C. Nigerian criminal enterprises are the most significant group and operate in more than 80 countries around the world. The FBI stated that "they are among the most aggressive and expansionist international criminal groups and are primarily engaged in drug trafficking and financial frauds."[81]

The most profitable activity for Nigerian groups is drug trafficking, primarily the delivery of cocaine from South America into Europe and South Africa and heroin from Southeast and Southwest Asia into Europe and the United States. (Large populations of ethnic Nigerians in India, Pakistan, and Thailand have given them direct access to 90% of the world's heroin production.) Money laundering has also helped establish Nigerian criminal enterprises around the world.

Nigerian groups are famous for their financial frauds, which cost U.S. citizens, businesses, and government offices an estimated $1 billion to $2 billion each year. Their schemes are diverse: "insurance fraud involving auto accidents; health-care billing scams; life insurance schemes; bank, check, and credit card fraud; advance-fee schemes known as 4-1-9 letters; and document fraud to develop false identities." The Internet and e-mail have made such crimes even more profitable and prevalent.

Middle Eastern Criminal Enterprises

The FBI has pointed out "that some Middle Eastern criminal groups have no nexus to terror. Instead, these groups have the same goals as any traditional organized crime ring—to make

Associated Press

Kansas City pharmacist Robert R. Courtney, age 48, who pleaded guilty in 2002 to 20 felony counts charging him with the fraudulent distribution of diluted intravenous chemotherapy drugs to at least 34 patients. Other charges included tampering with consumer products, adulteration of drugs, and misbranding of drugs. Courtney, who is estimated to have made hundreds of thousands of dollars in the scheme, was caught when a drug salesman noticed that he was billing doctors for more medication than he was buying. His ten-year prison sentence was upheld in 2004 by the U.S. Court of Appeals for the Eighth Circuit. How does Sutherland's definition of *white-collar crime* apply in a case like this?

■ **transnational organized crime** An unlawful activity undertaken and supported by organized criminal groups operating across national boundaries.

money through illegal activities."[82] Middle Eastern criminal enterprises originate from Afghanistan, Algeria, Bahrain, Egypt, India, Iran, Iraq, Israel, Jordan, Kuwait, Lebanon, Libya, Morocco, Oman, Pakistan, Qatar, Saudi Arabia, Syria, Tunisia, Turkey, United Arab Emirates, and Yemen.

Middle Eastern criminal groups have been active in the United States since the 1970s, tending to operate in areas with significant Middle Eastern or Southwest Asian populations; according to the FBI, they are most active in Illinois, Ohio, New Jersey, and New York.

The FBI explains that these enterprises engage in "automobile theft, financial fraud, money laundering, interstate transportation of stolen property, smuggling, drug trafficking, document fraud, health-care fraud, identity fraud, cigarette smuggling, and the theft and redistribution of infant formula."[83] They rely on extensive networks of international criminal associates and can be highly sophisticated in their criminal operations; internationally, they thrive in Afghanistan, Canada, Iran, Pakistan, Turkey, and the United Arab Emirates.

Suzanne Plunkett/Associated Press

Georgiy Gleyzer being escorted from the federal building in New York City. Gleyzer was arrested in connection with Russian mob activities and charged with terrorizing citizens of Russian communities in New York. What is the likely future of Russian organized crime in the United States?

Transnational Organized Crime

Transnational organized crime, which refers to unlawful activity undertaken and supported by organized criminal groups operating across national boundaries, is emerging as one of the most pressing challenges of the early twenty-first century.[84]

Russian organized crime is of special interest because it has grown quickly following the collapse of the Soviet Union and because it has taken root in the United States and other countries outside the former Soviet sphere of influence.

With the dissolution of Soviet-style controls between 1992 and 1994, the Russian Mafia quickly seized control of the country's banking system through the investment of ill-gotten gains, money laundering, intimidation, fraud, murder, and the outright purchase of financial institutions. Ninety-five Russian bankers were murdered by *Mafiya* operatives between 1995 and 2000, and hundreds of reform-minded business leaders and investigative journalists have been assassinated or kidnapped.[85] In September 2006, Russian Central Bank deputy chairman Andrei Kozlov was fatally shot as he left a soccer stadium in Moscow. Kozlov had been a crusader against money laundering and had suspended or withdrawn the licenses of dozens of banks. After Kozlov's death, President Vladimir Putin created a task force to combat financial crime.

The Analytical Center for Social and Economic Policies, a Russian think tank, estimates that four out of every five Russian businesses pay protection money to the mob.[86] In response to the wave of organized crime that Russia is currently experiencing, more than 25,000 private security firms have sprung up throughout the country. Analysts say, however, that few of these firms are legitimate, with many being fronts for Russian gangsters.[87]

Russian organized criminals differ from their counterparts in the United States because their ranks consist largely of ex-KGB officers, veterans of the 1979–1989 war in Afghanistan, underpaid military officers, and former Communist Party operatives who formed powerful economic alliances with traditional gangsters and black marketers years ago. As some observers note, Russian organized crime seems to be a natural outgrowth of the corrupt practices of officials who operated in the days of strict Soviet control, combined with a huge underground criminal black market that had already developed a complex organizational structure long before the Soviet Union fell apart.[88]

While Russian organized crime profits from American-style activities such as narcotics, prostitution, racketeering, and illicit gambling, it is also heavily involved in human trafficking, product diversion and counterfeiting of popular Western goods (including software, video, and music duplication), and illicit arms sales and smuggling on a massive scale.

■ **Racketeer Influenced and Corrupt Organizations (RICO) Act** A statute that is part of the federal Organized Crime Control Act of 1970 whose goal is to combat criminal conspiracies.

■ **asset forfeiture** The authorized seizure of money, negotiable instruments, securities, or other things of value. In federal antidrug laws, it is the authorization of judicial representatives to seize all monies, negotiable instruments, securities, and other things of value furnished or intended to be furnished by any person in exchange for a controlled substance, as well as all proceeds traceable to such an exchange.

Over the past decade or two, hundreds of thousands of Russian citizens have immigrated to the United States. As U.S. officials have now discovered, many of these people were former black market profiteers and hard-core offenders who had been released by the KGB from the Soviet gulag.[89]

Russian organized criminal groups today operate out of 17 American cities in 14 states. According to one source, "The FBI believes there are 15 separate organized crime groups and 4,000 hard-core Mafia criminals from the former Soviet Union at work in the United States They are engaged in money laundering, automobile theft, smuggling, contract murder, loan-sharking, medical insurance fraud, narcotics, and credit card and telecommunications fraud. The theft of electronic serial numbers from cellular phones and the duplication (cloning) of these PIN numbers have grown into a multimillion-dollar industry."[90]

The globalization of crime has necessitated the enhanced coordination of law enforcement efforts in different parts of the world and the expansion of American law enforcement activities beyond national borders. U.S. police agencies routinely send agents to assist law enforcement officers in other countries who are involved in transnational investigations.

The globalization of crime has necessitated the enhanced coordination of law enforcement efforts in different parts of the world.

Organized Crime and the Law

For many years, American law enforcement agencies had few special weapons in the fight against organized crime. Instead, they prosecuted organized criminal operatives under statutes directed at solitary offenders, using laws such as those against theft, robbery, assault, gambling, prostitution, drug abuse, and murder. Innovative prosecutors at times drew upon other statutory resources in the drive to indict leaders of organized crime. On October 17, 1931, for example, Al Capone was convicted on various charges of income tax evasion after federal investigators were able to show that he had paid no taxes on an income in excess of $1 million. Laws regulating the sale of alcohol and drugs and statutes circumscribing acts of prostitution have also been used against organized criminals, although with varying degrees of success.

The first federal legislation aimed specifically at curtailing the activities of organized crime was the Hobbs Act, which encompassed a series of statutes that were passed beginning in 1946. In essence, the Hobbs Act made it a violation of federal law to engage in any form of criminal behavior that interferes with interstate commerce. It also criminalized interstate or foreign travel in furtherance of criminal activity and made it a crime to use the highways, telephone, or mail in support of activities such as gambling, drug trafficking, loan-sharking, and other forms of racketeering.

The single most important piece of federal legislation ever passed that specifically targets the activities of organized crime is the **Racketeer Influenced and Corrupt Organizations (RICO) Act**, which was part of the federal Organized Crime Control Act of 1970. The Organized Crime Control Act defines *organized crime* as "the unlawful activities of the members of a highly organized, disciplined association engaged in supplying illegal goods and services, including but not limited to gambling, prostitution, loansharking, narcotics, labor racketeering, and other unlawful activities of members of such organizations."[91] The RICO portion of the act brought under one single piece of legislation the many and diverse activities of American organized crime and made each punishable in a variety of new ways. RICO did not make racketeering itself illegal but, rather, focused on the ill-gotten gains derived from such activity, specifying that it will be unlawful for anyone involved in a pattern of racketeering to derive any income or proceeds from that activity.

Punishments provided for under RICO include **asset forfeiture**, which makes it possible for federal officials to seize the proceeds of those involved in racketeering. In the words of the statute, "Whoever violates any provision of this chapter shall be fined or imprisoned not more than 20 years (or for life if the violation is based on a racketeering activity for which the maximum penalty includes life imprisonment), or both, and shall forfeit to the United States, irrespective of any provision of State law any property derived from any proceeds that the person obtained, directly or indirectly, from racketeering activity or unlawful debt collection."[92] Hence, as a result of RICO, federal agents are empowered to seize the financial and other tangible fruits of organized criminal activity, including businesses, real estate, money, equities, gold and other commodities, vehicles (including airplanes and boats), and just about anything else that can be shown to have been acquired through a pattern of racketeering activity.

Policy Issues: The Control of Organized Crime

In a cogent analysis of organized crime, **Gary W. Potter** tells us that "the question of what we [should] do about organized crime is largely predicated on how we conceptualize [of] organized crime."[93] To understand organized crime and to deal effectively with it, according to Potter, we must study the social context in which it occurs. Such study reveals "that organized crime is simply an integral part of the social, political, and economic system,"[94] says Potter. Any effective attack on organized crime, therefore, would involve either meeting or eliminating the demands of the consumers of organized crime's products and services. Potter suggests that this can be accomplished by punishing the consumers more effectively and/or by educating them about the perils of their own behavior.

Fighting corruption in politics and among law enforcement personnel and administrators is another track Potter suggests in the battle against organized crime. If organized crime has been successful at least partially because it has been able to corrupt local politicians and enforcement agents, then, Potter asks, why not work to reduce corruption at the local level?

Howard Abadinsky recommends four approaches to the control of organized crime, each involving changes at the policy-making level:[95]

- Increase the risk of involvement in organized crime by increasing the resources available to law enforcement agencies that are useful in fighting organized crime.
- Increase law enforcement authority so as to increase the risks of involvement in organized crime. Money-laundering statutes that expand the scope of law enforcement authority, racketeering laws, and forfeiture statutes may be helpful in this regard.[96]
- Reduce the economic lure of involvement in organized crime by making legitimate opportunities more readily available. Educational programs, scholarships, job-training initiatives, and so on, might play a role in such a strategy.
- Decrease organized criminal opportunity through decriminalization or legalization. This last strategy is perhaps the most controversial. It would decriminalize or legalize many of the activities from which organized crime now draws income, such as through state-run gambling and the ready and legitimate availability of narcotics.

STR NEW/Reuters

Salvatore "Sammy the Bull" Gravano, shown in court. He admitted to 19 murders and has been called the "most significant witness in the history of organized crime." How has La Cosa Nostra been impacted by witnesses like Gravano?

Strict enforcement of existing laws is another option. This strategy has been used with considerable success by a number of federal and state law enforcement operations that have targeted organized crime. One of the most spectacular mob trials was that of John "Dapper Don" Gotti, who took over control of New York's Gambino crime family after orchestrating the murder of "Big Paul" Castellano in 1985. Over the years, Gotti had been arrested on many occasions and had been prosecuted at least five times for various offenses. His ability to escape conviction earned him the title "Teflon Don." That changed on April 2, 1992, when Gotti was convicted on 13 federal charges, including murder and racketeering, and was sentenced to life in prison without the possibility of parole. Gotti's major mistake was personally participating in several executions, including that of Castellano. After Gotti went to prison, his son, John, Jr., took over control of the family, but in 1999, he pleaded guilty to charges of bribery, extortion, gambling, fraud, tax evasion, and loan-sharking and was sentenced to six and a half years in prison.[97] After being released from prison, John, Jr., was tried on a number of racketeering charges, resulting in three hung juries, and following his last trial, he vowed to leave New York, saying he might move his family to the Midwest or to Florida; his father died of cancer at a federal prison hospital in 2002 at the age of 61.

The senior Gotti's downfall came at the hands of Salvatore "Sammy the Bull" Gravano, a former underboss in the Gambino crime family. Gravano, who admitted to 19 murders, shared family secrets with federal investigators in return for leniency and succor through the federal witness protection program. Gravano spent days on the witness stand testifying against his former boss,

CRIMINAL | PROFILES

Bernie Madoff

On July 24, 2009, convicted Ponzi schemer and formerly wealthy investment counselor Bernard (Bernie) Madoff arrived by prison bus at the federal correctional institution in Butner, North Carolina, to begin serving a 150-year sentence.[i] The 71-year-old Madoff had been convicted only days earlier of multiple fraud and securities violations stemming from a scheme in which he exploited thousands of clients who had entrusted him with their money for over 20 years. Among his victims were very wealthy people from places as diverse as New York City and Palm Beach, Florida.[ii]

Some estimates put losses to investors as high as $65 billion dollars—money that seemed to evaporate into thin air and that investigators struggled to recover. By the time Madoff went to prison, only about $1.2 billion had been found and insurance payments of around $500,000 had been made to investors.[iii] Madoff's scheme has been called "the largest investor fraud ever committed by a single person."[iv]

In fact, Madoff may not have invested any of his clients' money, instead paying off redemptions from his fund with money from new clients. The false account statements that Madoff issued to "investors" showed their accounts rapidly growing in value—outpacing the investment results of even the most savvy investment managers. The stock market downturn of 2008, however, led to a record number of redemption requests—and when Madoff was unable to meet them, the game was up.

Born Bernard Lawrence Madoff on April 29, 1938, in Queens, New York, Madoff began his adult life as a plumber; he also worked as a lifeguard and a landscaper. He soon went to college, graduating from New York's Hofstra University in 1960 with a degree in political science. A year later, he dropped out of Brooklyn Law School to become a stockbroker, eventually rising through the financial ranks to serve as a chairman of the NASDAQ stock exchange. In 1960, Madoff founded his own firm, Bernard L. Madoff Investment Securities, LLC. He served as chairman of that company until his arrest on December 11, 2008.

Doubts about Madoff preceded his arrest by at least ten years, as his firm had faced a number of investigations by the SEC, some of which had apparently been dropped by the SEC for lack of money. At the time of this writing, only one other person—Madoff's longtime accountant, David Friehling—has been charged in connection with the fraud, although authorities suspect that others must have been involved. Madoff refused to cooperate in the investigation, claiming that he was the only person with knowledge of the scam. Federal prosecutors reached a settlement with Madoff's wife under which she abandoned claims to $85 million in assets that the couple had owned, leaving her with $2.5 million in cash. The couple's sons, Mark and Andrew, both of whom had worked with their father, denied any claims of any wrongdoing. On the second anniversary of the day his father was arrested in the worst investment fraud in American history, Mark Madoff, 46, was found dead in the living room of his SoHo loft. He was hanging from a black dog leash while his 2-year-old son slept nearby.

During the sentencing stage of the proceedings against him, the elder Madoff apologized to his victims, saying, "I have left a legacy of shame . . . to my family and my grandchildren. This is something I will live with for the rest of my life. I'm sorry."[v]

Everett Collection Inc/Alamy

Disgraced financier Bernard Madoff leaving the federal court in Manhattan after appearing at a bail hearing on January 5, 2009, in New York City. Madoff was convicted of operating a Ponzi scheme that bilked investors out of $50 billion. He is currently serving a 150-year sentence at the medium-security Federal Correctional Institution in Butner, North Carolina. Some people thought that his sentence was too harsh; others that it was too lenient. What do you think?

The case of Bernie Madoff raises a number of interesting questions. Among them are the following:

1. Do you think that Madoff originally set out to build a Ponzi scheme? If not, how might the scheme have evolved?
2. How do the crimes of Madoff differ from the criminal activities of other offenders discussed in criminal profile boxes throughout this book? In what way might they be the same?
3. Do the theories of criminal behavior that this book discusses seem as applicable to white-collar criminals, like Bernie Madoff, as they do to other offenders who commit crimes of violence? If so, what theoretical approach might explain Madoff's behavior?
4. How would you compare Madoff to other white-collar criminals? What do they have in common?

Notes

i. Zachery Kouwe, "Madoff Arrives at Federal Prison in North Carolina," *New York Times*, July 14, 2009, http://www.nytimes.com/2009/07/15/business/15madoff.html (accessed July 21, 2009).
ii. Michael Moore, "Bernie Madoff," The 2009 TIME 100, http://www.time.com/time/specials/packages/article/0,28804,1894410_1893837_1894189,00.html (accessed July 20, 2009).
iii. "The Ticker," *Washington Post*, July 14, 2009; and Elizabeth Dwoskin, "Bernie Madoff's Accountant Charged, Pleads Not Guilty," *The Village Voice*, July 17, 2009, http://blogs.villagevoice.com/runninscared/archives/2009/07/bernie_madoffs.php (accessed July 21, 2009).
iv. "Topic: Bernard Madoff," *New York Post* (various dates), http://www.nypost.com/topics/topic.php?t=Bernard_Madoff (accessed August 12, 2009).
During the sentencing stage of the proceedings against him, the elder Madoff apologized to his victims, saying, "I have left a legacy of shame . . . to my family and my grandchildren. This is something I will live with for the rest of my life. I'm sorry."[v]
v. "Transcript of Madoff's Sentencing Statement," *New York Post*, June 29, 2009, http://www.nypost.com/seven/06292009/news/regionalnews/partial_transcript_of_madoffs_sentencing_176718.htm (accessed August 12, 2009).

and federal prosecutor Zachary Carter later called Gravano "the most significant witness in the history of organized crime."[98]

In 1997, Gravano again assumed center stage when he testified in federal district court in Brooklyn as the star prosecution witness in the murder and racketeering trial of Vincent Gigante, reputed head of the powerful Genovese crime family. Gravano was assailed by defense lawyers for being a notorious liar and for leading "a life of lies," facts he largely admitted in his best-selling book *Underboss*.[99] Although Gravano was sent to Phoenix, Arizona, under the witness protection program, he found it hard to lead a straight life. In 2000, he was arrested on three separate occasions on drug-running and money-laundering charges and was indicted by a New York federal grand jury and charged with financing and running a major Ecstasy drug ring in conjunction with an Israeli organized crime syndicate.[100]

Finally, in 2013, in a sign that traditional American organized crime remains active, Stephen Rakes, a 59-year-old South Boston man who had waited decades for the opportunity to testify against crime boss James "Whitey" Bulger, was found dead prior to being put on the witness stand.[101] Later that same year, Bulger was convicted of racketeering and conspiracy by a Boston jury that found he was involved in 11 murders and numerous other crimes.[102] Bulger had been on the run for 16 years, and had apparently lived quietly in California before his capture.

SUMMARY

- White-collar crime is not unique to the twenty-first century. Financial scandals have a long and ubiquitous history in the United States, sometimes even involving government regulators. The insider-trading scam of stock market tycoon Ivan Boesky and the securities fraud conviction of junk-bond king Michael Milken in the 1980s demonstrated again how fortunes could be amassed through white-collar law violations. The past two decades have seen a number of infamous white-collar crime prosecutions, including those involving executives at the former energy-trading giant Enron Corporation, which had used complex off-balance-sheet partnerships to hide losses and inflate revenues.
- This chapter distinguishes between white-collar, occupational, corporate, and organized crime. White-collar crimes can be further broken down into antitrust violations, bank fraud, bankruptcy fraud, economic espionage, embezzlement, environmental law violations, government fraud, health-care fraud, insider trading, insurance fraud, kickbacks, mail fraud, securities fraud, tax evasion, and wire fraud.
- Corporate crimes, or corporate malfeasance, come in many forms, ranging from prior knowledge about dangerous automobile defects to price fixing and insider securities trading. Businesses may be charged with corporate crimes for the acts of their corporate officers, as can individuals for legal wrongs committed in their corporate capacity.
- White-collar criminals have many of the same motivations as do other criminals, and criminologists generally agree that white-collar crime, like other crime, is learned. Although white-collar criminals may not be directly dangerous to the health and physical well-being of their victims, they are motivated by the same forces that drive other criminals: self-interest, the pursuit of pleasure, and the avoidance of pain. Other authors have held that white-collar criminals are motivated by a disparity between corporate goals and the limited opportunities available to businesspeople through conventional business practices.
- White-collar and organized crimes are often difficult to investigate and prosecute. Nonetheless, the U.S. SEC has recently renewed efforts to enforce existing regulations and has mandated new rules for investment bankers. The now-defunct U.S. DOJ's Corporate Fraud Task Force, the Obama administration's Financial Fraud Enforcement Task Force, the 2002 Sarbanes-Oxley Act, and RICO statutes all provided law enforcers with new tools to fight white-collar and organized crime.
- Much of what most Americans traditionally think of today as organized crime—sometimes called the Mafia or La Cosa Nostra—has roots that predate the establishment of the United States and extend to secret societies that have flourished in Italy for hundreds of years. Other organized criminal groups, including Jewish and Irish gangs, flourished in New York City prior to the arrival of large numbers of Italian immigrants in the late 1800s, and ethnic succession has been as much a reality in organized crime as it has in most other aspects of American life. The huge profits to be had from bootlegging under Prohibition in the United States led to the wholesale bribery of government officials and to the quick corruption of many law enforcement officers throughout the country. The

activities of organized crime include the establishment and control of both legalized and illicit forms of gambling; loan-sharking; large-scale drug trafficking; the fencing of stolen goods (including securities); the infiltration of legitimate businesses, including labor unions and corporations; labor union racketeering; and other crimes.

- A criminal enterprise is a group of individuals with an identifiable hierarchy, and extensive supporting networks, engaged in significant criminal activity. Some of the most important criminal gangs operating in the United States today are Eurasian criminal enterprises such as the *Vory V Zakone*, Balkan organized criminal groups, Asian criminal enterprises such as the *Yakuza*, African criminal groups, and Middle Eastern criminal enterprises.
- Transnational organized crime refers to unlawful activity undertaken and supported by organized criminal groups operating across national boundaries. Transnational organized crime is emerging as one of the most pressing challenges of the twenty-first century.
- The first federal legislation aimed specifically at curtailing the activities of organized crime was the Hobbs Act, which encompassed a series of statutes that were passed beginning in 1946. The single most important piece of federal legislation ever passed that specifically targets the activities of organized crime, however, is the Racketeer Influenced and Corrupt Organizations (RICO) Act, which was part of the federal Organized Crime Control Act of 1970.
- Organized crime is an integral part of the social, political, and economic systems in our society. As such, any effective attack on organized crime would involve meeting or eliminating the demands of the consumers of organized crime's products and services.

KEY TERMS

asset forfeiture, 326
bank fraud, 305
corporate crime, 309
corporate fraud, 311
criminal enterprise, 321
environmental crimes, 314
ethnic succession, 320
green criminology, 315
insider trading, 305
La Cosa Nostra, 319
Mafia, 319
money laundering, 314
occupational crime, 308
organized crime, 319
Ponzi scheme, 311
Racketeer Influenced and Corrupt Organizations (RICO) Act, 326
Sarbanes-Oxley Act, 318
securities and commodities fraud, 311
securities fraud, 305
transnational organized crime, 325
white-collar crime, 308

KEY NAMES

Howard Abadinsky, 321
John Braithwaite, 317
Herbert Edelhertz, 308
Gilbert Geis, 308
Michael Gottfredson, 317
Gary S. Green, 308
Travis Hirschi, 317
Gary W. Potter, 327
Edwin H. Sutherland, 308

QUESTIONS FOR REVIEW

1. What are some examples of white-collar crime in American history?
2. What is white-collar crime? How did the idea of white-collar crime develop in the criminological literature?
3. What is corporate crime? How does corporate crime differ from white-collar crime, if at all?
4. What are some of the causes of white-collar crime? How do white-collar criminals differ from other offenders?
5. How can white-collar and corporate crime be controlled? What are four areas of reform through which white-collar crime might be effectively addressed?
6. What is organized crime? How does it differ from white-collar crime?
7. What are of the organized criminal groups that this chapter discusses? What kinds of activities do they engage in?
8. What transnational organized criminal groups does this chapter identify? How do their activities differ from those of traditional organized crime families?
9. Identify federal statutes and other initiatives that target organized crime.
10. What strategies does this chapter discuss for combating the activities of organized crime?

QUESTIONS FOR REFLECTION

1. What linkages, if any, might exist between white-collar and organized crime?
2. What types of white-collar crime has this chapter identified? Is corporate crime a form of white-collar crime? Is occupational crime a form of white-collar crime?
3. How would you describe a typical "traditional" organized crime family, as outlined in this chapter? Why does a crime family contain so many different "levels"?
4. What is money laundering? How might money laundering be reduced or prevented? Can you think of any strategies this chapter does not discuss for the reduction of money-laundering activities in the United States? If so, what are they?

Mediablitz images Limited/Alamy

CHAPTER 13 DRUG AND SEX CRIMES

LEARNING OUTCOMES

After reading this chapter, you should be able to answer the following questions:

- What can be said about the history of drugs, drug abuse, and drug-control legislation in the United States?
- What are the various categories of controlled substances described by federal law, and what is a dangerous drug?
- How can drug addiction be understood, and how can it be treated?
- What is drug trafficking, and what efforts are being made to curtail it?
- What government strategies have been used to reduce the incidence of drug use in the United States?
- What is prostitution, and what are the various types of prostitutes identified in this chapter?

■ **Follow the author's tweets about the latest crime and justice news @schmalleger.**

■ **psychoactive substance** A substance that affects the mind, mental processes, or emotions.

Introduction

In January 2012, 14 cadets at the U.S. Coast Guard Academy in New London, Connecticut, were dismissed for using Spice—a smokable herbal marijuana substitute.[1] Marijuana substitutes, known by names such as K2, Genie, Blaze, Red X Dawn, Spice Gold, Zoha, and herbal incense, mimic the effects of marijuana but are difficult to control because they don't contain the chemical tetrahydrocannabinol (THC), which is the active ingredient in marijuana. As a result, they don't fall under the purview of long-standing antidrug laws. As of this writing, however, 40 states have banned synthetic marijuana, and the U.S. Drug Enforcement Administration (DEA) used its emergency scheduling authority to make the substance illegal under federal law. Nonetheless, those who produce the drugs continue to alter their herbal formulations in an effort to skirt official restrictions. Links to news and research articles about synthetic marijuana can be found on at **Web Extra 13–1**.

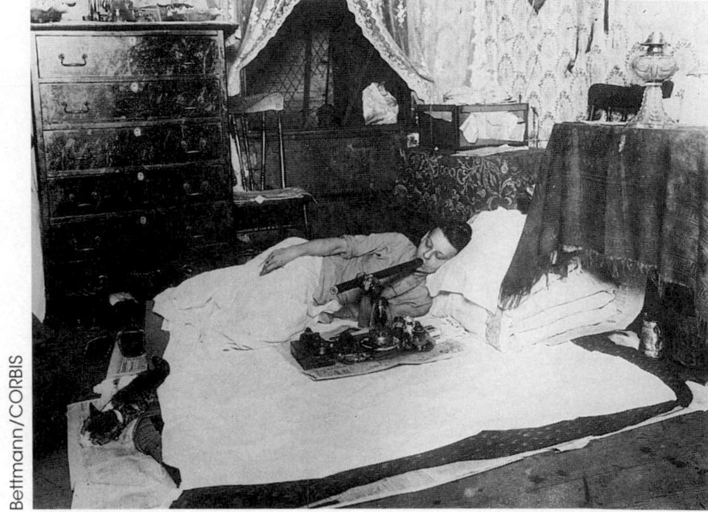
Bettmann/CORBIS

A smoker in an opium den in Chinatown, San Francisco, circa 1925. How have American attitudes toward drugs changed over time?

History of Drug Abuse in the United States

The rampant, widespread use and abuse of mind- and mood-altering drugs, so commonplace in the United States today, is of relatively recent origin. Throughout the 1800s and early 1900s, the use of illegal drugs in America was mostly associated with artistic individuals and fringe groups and was almost exclusively confined to small groups of musicians, painters, poets, and other highly imaginative individuals seeking to enhance their creativity. One significant exception existed in the form of opium dens, which flourished in West Coast cities and eventually made their way across the country as a result of increased Asian immigration; some Chinese immigrants had brought opium products with them and introduced other segments of the American population to opium smoking.

ZUMA Archive/ZUMAPRESS/Newscom

The herbal marijuana substitute Spice, or K2. Why are illegal drugs so pervasive in American society?

Psychoactive substances (substances affecting mental processes and emotions) gained widespread acceptance during the hippie movement during the late 1960s and early 1970s, which was characterized by slogans like "If it feels good, do it" and "Tune in, turn on, drop out," promoting free love, personal freedom, experimentation with subjective states of consciousness, and "mind expansion."

One influential figure in the drug-inspired movement of the times was Harvard professor Timothy Leary, who formed the League of Spiritual Discovery in the mid-1960s, "an orthodox, psychedelic religion that permits the use of LSD and marijuana as sacraments by League members."[2] With the advent of the hippie era, marijuana, lysergic acid diethylamide (LSD), hashish, psilocybin, and peyote burst on the national scene as an ever-growing number of individuals began to view drugs as recreational substances and as more and more young people identified with the tenor of the period.

■ **National Survey on Drug Use and Health (NSDUH)** A national survey of illicit drug use among people 12 years of age and older that is conducted annually by the Substance Abuse and Mental Health Services Administration.

Extent of Drug Abuse

Data on drug abuse in the United States are available through a variety of sources, such as the *Monitoring the Future* (MTF) study, conducted by the University of Michigan's Institute for Social Research with funding from the National Institute on Drug Abuse at the National Institutes of Health; the **National Survey on Drug Use and Health (NSDUH)**, conducted annually by the Substance Abuse and Mental Health Services Administration (SAMHSA); the National Narcotics Intelligence Consumers Committee *NNICC Report*, published in conjunction with the Drug Enforcement Administration (DEA); the National Institute of Justice (NIJ) quarterly Arrestee Drug Abuse Monitoring Program report; the Office of National Drug Control Policy (ONDCP) *Pulse Check: National Trends in Drug Abuse*, which reports at least once a year on drug-use trends; and annual reports published by SAMHSA's Drug Abuse Warning Network.

The annual National Survey on Drug Use and Health is conducted by the Substance Abuse and Mental Health Services Administration.

According to NSDUH data released in 2012, an estimated 22.5 million Americans ages 12 and older were current users of illicit drugs in 2011, meaning they used an illicit drug at least once during the 30 days prior to being interviewed (Figure 13–1).[3] This estimate represents 8.7% of the population aged 12 or older. Illicit drugs include marijuana/hashish, cocaine (including crack), heroin, hallucinogens, inhalants, or prescription-type psychotherapeutics used nonmedically. The report describes the number and percentage of persons aged 12 or older who were current users of specific drugs in 2011 as follows:[4]

- Marijuana was the most commonly used illicit drug, with 18.1 million current users (or 8.7% of the American population aged 12 or older). It was used by 80.5% of current illicit drug users and was the only drug used by 64.3% of them.
- Between 2007 and 2011, the rate of marijuana use increased from 5.8 to 7.0%, and the number of users increased from 14.4 million to 18.1 million.
- 6.1 million persons (2.4% of the population) were nonmedical users of prescription-type psychotherapeutic drugs, including 5.1 million users of pain relievers, 2.2 million users of tranquilizers, 1.1 million users of stimulants, and 374,000 users of sedatives.
- 439,000 (0.1%) were methamphetamine users.
- 1.4 million (0.5%) were current users of cocaine.

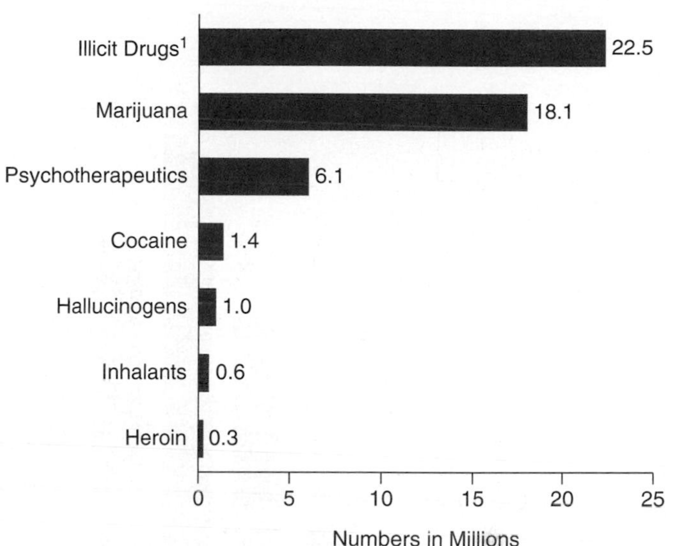

FIGURE 13-1 | **Past-Month Use of Selected Illicit Drugs among Persons Ages 12 and Older by Type of Drug, 2011**

Source: Substance Abuse and Mental Health Services Administration, *National Survey on Drug Use and Health, 2011* (Washington, DC: U.S. Government Printing Office, 2012).

- Hallucinogens were used in the past month by 972,000 persons (0.4%) aged 12 or older, including 695,000 (0.3%) who had used Ecstasy.
- The overall rate of current illicit drug use among persons aged 12 or older in 2011 (8.7%) was similar to the rate in 2010, but it was higher than the rates in 2002 through 2008.
- In 2011, the rate of illicit drug use was highest among young adults aged 18 to 25 (21.4%). As Figure 13–2 shows, rates of use generally declined in each successively older age group, with only 6.3% of people ages 55 to 59 and 1.0% of those ages 65 and older reporting current illicit use.

Other findings show that:

- Most illicit drug users were employed. Of the 20.2 million current illicit drug users aged 18 or older in 2011, 13.1 million (65.7%) were employed either full or part time.
- Among unemployed adults aged 18 or older in 2011, 17.2% were current illicit drug users, which was higher than the 8.0% of those employed full time and 11.6% of those employed part time.
- In 2011, 9.4 million persons aged 12 or older reported driving under the influence of illicit drugs during the past

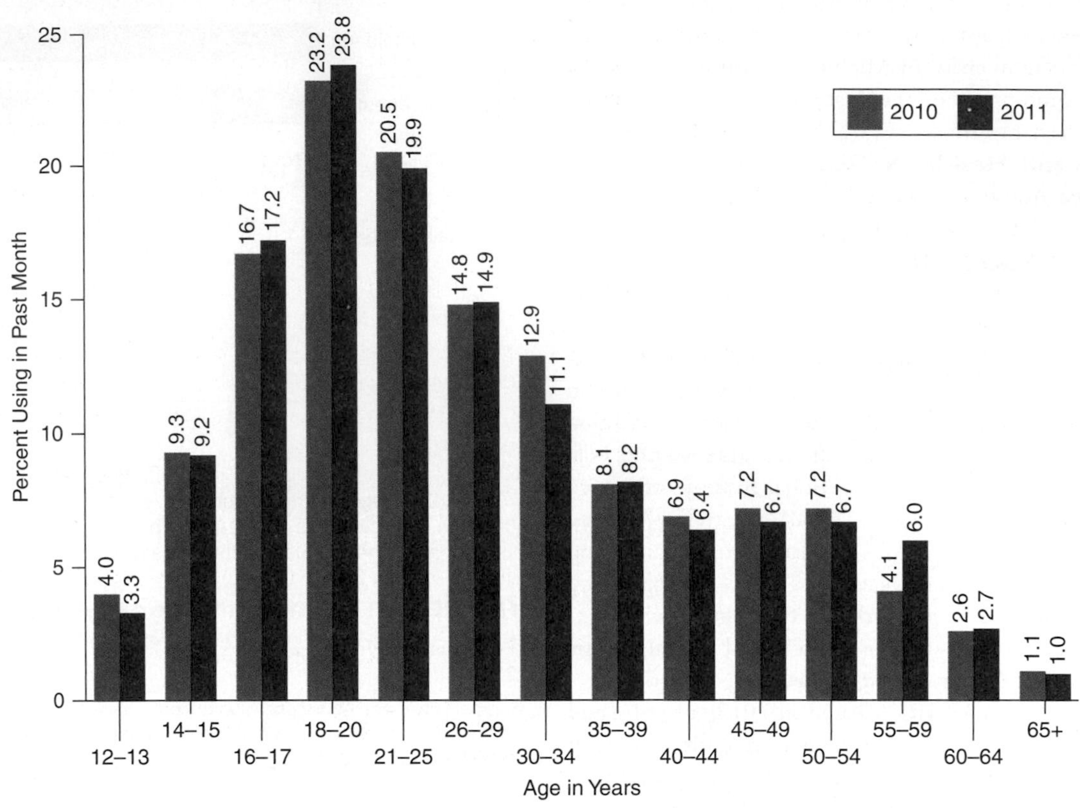

FIGURE 13-2 | **Past-Month Illicit Drug Use among Persons Ages 12 and Older, by Age, 2010 and 2011**

Source: Substance Abuse and Mental Health Services Administration, *National Survey on Drug Use and Health, 2011* (Washington, DC: U.S. Government Printing Office, 2012).

year. This corresponds to 3.7% of the population aged 12 or older, which was lower than the rate in 2002 (4.7%).

The NSDUH found that rates of illicit drug use for major racial and ethnic groups in 2011 were 8.2% for whites, 8.7% for Hispanics, and 7.2% for blacks. The rates were highest among the American Indian/Alaska Native population (16.8%) and among people reporting multiple races (9.0%), and Asians had the lowest rate (3.3%).

The rate of illicit drug use in metropolitan areas was higher than in nonmetropolitan areas: 8.4% in large metropolitan areas, 8.2% in small metropolitan areas, and 6.3% in nonmetropolitan areas. Rural counties had a 4.6% rate of illicit drug use. The NSDUH and the MTF study showed a leveling or declining national trend in illicit drug use, marijuana use, and cigarette use among adolescents since 1997, following a period of significant increases in the early 1990s.

As in previous NSDUH data, the 2011 survey found that substance-abuse rates remained highly correlated with educational status: Among young adults 18 years and older, those who had not completed high school had the highest rate of abuse (11.1%), whereas college graduates had the lowest rate of abuse (5.4%), despite the fact that adults who had completed four years of college were more likely to have tried illicit drugs in their lifetime than adults who had not completed high school (51.8% versus 39.7%). Hence, it appears that the more education a person receives, the more likely he or she is to discontinue using drugs with age.

If NSDUH results are accurate, they would seem to indicate that drug abuse is now somewhat less of a problem than it was two decades ago. In 1979, the number of current illicit drug users was at its highest level, when estimates of current users reached 25 million; the largest ever annual estimate of marijuana use put routine users at 22.5 million in 1979, and the greatest cocaine use was estimated at 5.3 million in 1985—figures that are notably greater than those of today. Growth of the American population over time gives the estimated decline even greater weight.

There are some methodological problems associated with any nationwide survey, and in recognition of these problems,

NSDUH authors wrote, "Sample size, coverage, and validity problems are likely to be more pronounced for NSDUH estimates of heavy users than for other measures generated by the survey. Therefore, estimates of heavy use are considered conservative, and changes over time are generally not statistically significant. . . . Clearly there is considerable uncertainty about the size of the heavy drug-using population."[5] Read the latest NSDUH report at **Library Extra 13–1**.

Whereas the use of illicit drugs provides one measure of the drug problem facing our country, the ready availability of such drugs provides another. Data from the National Crime Victimization Survey (NCVS) showed that two of three students ages 12 to 19 reported ready availability of illegal drugs at their school.[6] Students in public schools reported a wider availability of drugs than those in private schools, and students in higher grades (9 through 12) reported more drugs available to them than those in the lower grades. Similar rates of availability were reported by white students (69% of whom said drugs were available to them at school), black students (67%), and students living in cities (66%), suburban areas (67%), and rural areas (71%).

Dr. Timothy Leary, guru of the 1960s psychedelic movement. Leary died in 1996, and his ashes were shot into space a year later. What was Leary's message?

Young People and Drugs

While NSDUH data provided a picture of drug abuse among all those 12 years of age and older, the National Institute on Drug Abuse's MTF study supplied data on drug abuse among junior high school and high school students, tracking 12th-graders' illicit drug use, their perceived availability of drugs, and their attitudes toward drugs since 1975; in 1991, 8th- and 10th-graders were added to the survey. The 2012 survey gathered responses from about 45,000 students in close to 400 schools across the nation about lifetime use, past-year use, past-month use, and daily use of drugs, alcohol, cigarettes, and smokeless tobacco. For access to the full 2012 MTF data describing the use of many other drugs, including inhalants, view **Library Extra 13–2**. See the Theory versus Reality box for information on some college students' drinking patterns. **Library Extra 13–3** provides still more information.

MTF researchers noted that in the late twentieth century, illicit drug use among young Americans had reached very high levels. In 1975, when the MTF survey began, the majority of young people (55%) reported having used an illicit drug by the time they left high school, and this figure rose to two-thirds (66%) by 1981 before a long and gradual decline to 41% by 1992, the low point. After 1992, the proportion rose again, reaching a high of 55% in 1999, and stood at 49% in 2012.[7]

In the late twentieth century, drug use among young Americans reached very high levels.

Because marijuana use is much more common than that of any other illicit drug, trends in marijuana use significantly influence the index of "any illicit drug use" reported by the survey. In 1975, over one-third (36%) of 12th-graders had tried some illicit drug other than marijuana, a figure that rose to 43% by 1981 and then declined for a long period to a low of 25% in 1992. Some increases followed in the 1990s as the use of a number of drugs rose steadily, reaching 30% by 1997; then the rate fell to 24% in 2012.

Marijuana has been the most widely used illicit drug throughout all the years of this study. Annual marijuana use peaked at 51% among 12th-graders in 1979, following a rise that began during the 1960s, and then steadily declined for the next 13 years, bottoming out at 22% in 1992—a decline of more than half. The 1990s saw a resurgence in marijuana use. After a considerable increase, annual prevalence rates peaked in 1996 at the 8th-grade level and in 1997 at 10th- and 12th-grade levels. Following the peak, there was a gradual decline among 8th-graders, but the decline appeared to halt in 2005, with an annual prevalence rate in 2010 about equal to that of 2004; in the upper grades, only a very modest decline occurred between 1997 and 2002, followed by a continuing gradual decline since

■ **Office of National Drug Control Policy (ONDCP)** A national office charged by Congress with establishing policies, priorities, and objectives for the nation's drug-control program. The ONDCP is responsible for annually developing and disseminating the *National Drug-Control Strategy*.

Since the MTF survey began in 1975, between 83% and 90% of the members of every senior class have said they could get marijuana "fairly easily" or "very easily" if they wanted some, so marijuana has remained a highly accessible drug. Since 1991, when data became available for 8th- and 10th-graders, marijuana has become considerably less accessible to younger adolescents; however, in 2012 two-fifths of 8th-graders (37%) and almost three-quarters of all 10th-graders (69%) reported it as being accessible, compared to 82% of seniors.

Costs of Drug Abuse

The **Office of National Drug Control Policy (ONDCP)** estimates that Americans annually spend around $63 billion to purchase illegal drugs. (See Figure 13–3.) The true costs of drug abuse, however, are difficult to measure, but a 2011 report by the National Drug Intelligence Center (NDIC) placed the total annual cost of illicit drug abuse in the United States at $193 billion.[8] As Figures 13–4, 13–5, and 13–6 show, the NDIC breaks down that amount into direct and indirect costs, including direct justice system costs ($109,498,643,000), indirect health0care costs ($11,416,232,000), and indirect costs of lost productivity due to drug abuse ($72,182,055,000).

Although the NDIC report is comprehensive, it still might not include all of the social costs associated with drug abuse.

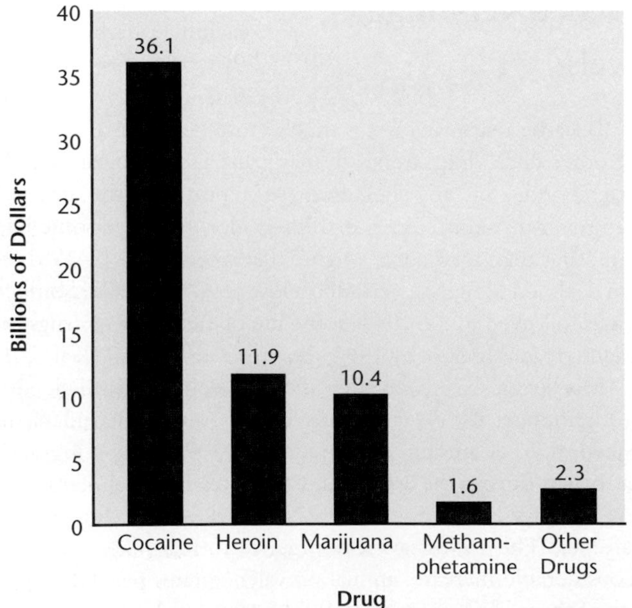

FIGURE 13-3 | **The Annual Amount Spent on Illegal Drugs in the United States**

Source: Office of National Drug Control Policy, *Drug Data Summary* (Washington, DC: ONDCP, 2003).

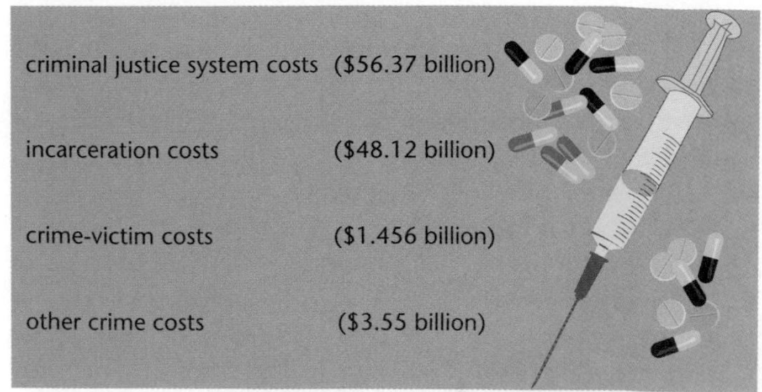

FIGURE 13-4 | **Annual Direct Costs of Illegal Drug Use in the United States: Justice System and Victimization**

Note: Annual criminal justice system amounts due to drug abuse total $109,498,643,000. They include the costs associated with investigation, arrest, adjudication, and parole and probation, plus the costs of incarceration, which are shown separately.

Source: National Drug Intelligence Center, *The Economic Impact of Illicit Drug Use on American Society* (Washington, DC: U.S. Department of Justice, 2011).

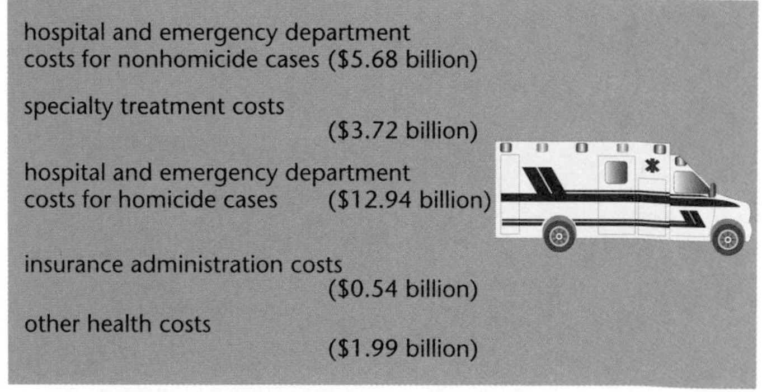

FIGURE 13-5 | **Annual Indirect Costs of Illegal Drug Use in the United States: Health Care**

Note: Annual health-care costs due to drug abuse total $11,416,232,000.

Source: National Drug Intelligence Center, *The Economic Impact of Illicit Drug Use on American Society* (Washington, DC: U.S. Department of Justice, 2011).

Many cases of acquired immunodeficiency syndrome (AIDS), for example, can be traced to intravenous drug use, and AIDS/HIV has proved to be a costly disease in social terms. Researchers at the Centers for Disease Control and Prevention (CDC) say that AIDS/HIV is the leading cause of death of black and Hispanic men aged 25 to 44. AIDS/HIV, says the CDC, has become the second leading cause of death among black women aged 25 to 44. The CDC says that 47% of HIV infection among minority women is traceable to intravenous drug use, whereas 37% appears to be due to heterosexual intercourse. Still, the hidden impact of sexual intercourse with intravenous drug users is not entirely clear. In the words of the CDC:

■ **controlled substances** Chemical substances or drugs as defined under the 1970 federal controlled substances act.

■ **dangerous drug** A controlled substance other than cocaine, opiates, and cannabis products. Amphetamines, LSD, methamphetamines, methcathinone, and phencyclidine (PCP), as well as designer drugs, are all considered dangerous drugs.

■ **addiction** A chronic brain disease characterized by compulsive drug seeking and use despite harmful consequences.

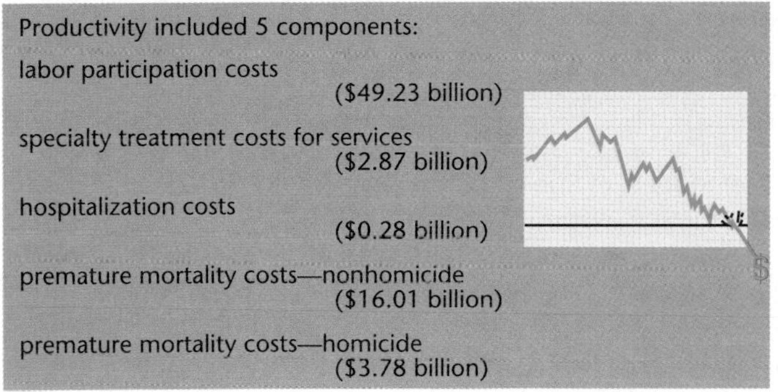

FIGURE 13-6 | **Annual Indirect Costs of Illegal Drug Use in the United States: Lost Productivity**

Note: Annual costs of lost productivity due to drug abuse total $72,182,055,000.
Source: National Drug Intelligence Center, *The Economic Impact of Illicit Drug Use on American Society* (Washington, DC: U.S. Department of Justice, 2011).

"Sharing syringes and other equipment for drug injection is a well known route of HIV transmission, yet injection drug use contributes to the epidemic's spread far beyond the circle of those who inject. People who have sex with an injection drug user (IDU) also are at risk for infection through the sexual transmission of HIV. Children born to mothers who contracted HIV through sharing needles or having sex with an IDU may become infected as well."[9]

The proportion of HIV infection among minority women traceable to intravenous drug use is 47%.

Types of Illegal Drugs

Controlled substances are grouped into five schedules under the 1970 Controlled Substances Act (CSA). Table 13-1 shows those schedules, the criteria for inclusion of a drug under each schedule, a list of drugs in each schedule, and street names for drugs.

Federal law also allows for the control of other **dangerous drugs**, a term used by the DEA to refer to "broad categories or classes of controlled substances other than cocaine, opiates, and cannabis products."[10] The availability of precursor chemicals, such as the popular decongestant pseudoephedrine used in the manufacture of methamphetamine, is also limited under the Combat Methamphetamine Epidemic Act of 2005.

Controlled substances are generally grouped into seven categories: stimulants, depressants, cannabis, narcotics, hallucinogens, anabolic steroids, and inhalants.

One category of drugs that deserves special mention is inhalants. Nitrous oxide, carbon tetrachloride, amyl nitrite, butyl nitrite, chloroform, Freon, acetate, and toluene, as well as other volatile solvents, are all in the inhalant category. Inhalants are found in fast-drying glues, nail polish remover, room and car deodorizers, lighter fluid, paint thinner, kerosene, cleaning fluids, household sealants, and gasoline. Although some of these substances (for example, ether, nitrous oxide, amyl nitrate, and chloroform) have legitimate medical uses, others are employed only to produce a sense of light-headedness often described in colloquial terms as a "rush." Inhalants are generally sniffed, inhaled, huffed, or snorted. It has been estimated that there are over 1,000 substances that are abused. The use of inhalants "can disturb vision, impair judgment, and reduce muscle and reflex control."[11]

Drug Addiction

The term *drug addiction* is widely used but often not well understood. The National Institute on Drug Abuse (NIDA), a part of the National Institutes of Health, defines **addiction** as "a chronic, relapsing brain disease that is characterized by compulsive drug seeking and use, despite harmful consequences."[12] NIDA notes that people often underestimate the complexity of drug addiction, which leads to physical changes in the brain, resulting in modified structure and functioning of this crucial organ. NIDA researchers explained that brain imaging studies of drug-addicted individuals showed changes in areas of the brain that are critical to judgment, decision making, learning and memory, and behavior control.[13] Because it is a disease that impacts the brain, said NIDA, "stopping drug abuse is not simply a matter of willpower." Whether a person becomes addicted to drugs depends on a number of factors: the age at first use; the frequency of initial use, with genetic and environmental factors interacting with critical developmental stages; gender, ethnicity,

■ **drug trafficking** The manufacturing, distributing, dispensing, importing, and/or exporting of a controlled substance or a counterfeit substance.

TABLE 13-1 Controlled Substances under the Federal Controlled Substances Act

SCHEDULE	DESCRIPTION OF SCHEDULE	DRUGS IN SCHEDULE	STREET NAMES
I	• high potential for abuse • no currently accepted medical use in the United States • lacks accepted safety standards for use under medical supervision	marijuana, heroin, opioids, hallucinogenic substances, peyote, mescaline, gamma-hydroxybutyric acid (GHB), and others	pot, weed, grass, reefer, joint, angel dust, horse
II	• high potential for abuse • currently accepted for medical use • may lead to severe psychological or physical dependence	cocaine, opium, oxycodone, methadone, morphine, Seconal, methamphetamine, and other amphetamines	snow, crack, coke, meth, speed, uppers
III	• potential for abuse less than the drugs or other substances in Schedules I and II • currently accepted for medical use • may lead to moderate or low physical dependence or high psychological dependence	anabolic steroids, ketamine, hydrocodone, and a number of barbiturates and sedatives	downers, goof balls, yellow jackets
IV	• lower potential for abuse relative to the drugs or other substances in Schedule III • currently accepted for medical use • may lead to limited physical dependence or psychological dependence relative to the drugs or other substances in Schedule III	some antidiarrheal drugs; some partial opioid analgesics; some sleeping pills such as Zolpidem; long-acting barbiturates; and benzodiazepines such as Xanax, Librium, and Valium	blues, peaches, bars, zombie pills, no-go-pills, A-minus
V	• low potential for abuse relative to the drugs or other substances in Schedule IV • currently accepted for medical use • may lead to limited physical dependence or psychological dependence relative to the drugs or other substances in Schedule IV	some cough suppressants, anticonvulsants, and selected perscription pain pills	

and preexisting mental disorders; and social influences in the environment, such as peer pressure, physical and sexual abuse, stress, and parental involvement.[14] See the first Who's to Blame box in this chapter for a creative example of how drugs can affect two brothers differently.

Drug Trafficking

The term *drug trafficking* has a variety of meanings. On one hand, it refers to the illegal shipment of controlled substances across state and national boundaries. On the other hand, it means the sale of controlled substances. Hence, in colloquial usage, a person who "traffics" in drugs may simply sell them. Technically speaking, **drug trafficking** includes manufacturing, distributing, dispensing, importing, and exporting (or possessing with intent to do the same) a controlled or counterfeit substance.[15] Federal law enforcement agencies, in their effort to reduce trafficking, focus largely on the prevention of smuggling and on the apprehension of smugglers.

Drugs such as cocaine, heroin, and LSD are especially easy to smuggle because relatively small quantities of these drugs can

■ **Heroin Signature Program (HSP)** A Drug Enforcement Administration program that identifies the geographic source of a heroin sample through the detection of specific chemical characteristics in the sample peculiar to the source area.

WHO'S TO BLAME—The Individual or Society?

His Brother's Keeper

In March 2013, Nicole Smithfield received a letter from her former boyfriend, Derek Little. The letter came from the state's maximum-security prison where Derek was serving life without possibility of parole for the murder of his older brother, Hamilton. The brothers had grown up together and attended school in the same small town where Nicole lived. Derek began dealing drugs at age 13, bringing in a few dollars selling marijuana to some friends at school. By the time he was 24, Derek was operating one of the largest drug distribution networks in the county and bringing in thousands of dollars a week. He drove an expensive car, had the best clothes and high-tech gadgets, and carried a lot of cash with him wherever he went. People who knew him said that he also carried a nine-shot semiautomatic pistol strapped to his waist.

Hamilton took a different path and joined the army. He went to Afghanistan and then to Iraq for two tours of duty. One night, when he was home on leave, Hamilton stopped by his brother's house and an argument ensued. Hamilton wanted Derek to get out of the drug business and to turn his life around. "It's only a matter of time before you get arrested," Hamilton told his brother. "Do you want to spend the rest of your life in prison?"

"I'm too smart for that," Derek responded. "I've got too many layers [of dealers] protecting me. They'll never get anything on me."

"Yeah—but what about all the lives you're affecting? What about all the kids from our neighborhood who are getting strung out on drugs because of you? You're preying on society," Hamilton said, angry now. "And if you don't quit, I'll make you."

"What do you mean by that?" Derek asked, jumping out of his chair.

"I just think you need to stop, and if I have to, then I'll find a way to make you," Hamilton said, and left, beginning the walk home to his mother's mobile home less than a mile away.

According to evidence presented at his trial, that's when Derek got into his pickup truck and started down the road, accelerating to 80 mph before swerving onto the shoulder and hitting his brother. Hamilton's body flew 40 feet through the air before hitting the ground and then tumbled another 30 feet through the brush.

Prosecutors tried to present additional evidence showing that Derek was likely responsible for the deaths of three other people who had threatened him during the past two years, or who had said that they would turn him in to authorities—but the judge would not allow the jury to hear those claims. When the trial concluded, Derek was found guilty of killing his brother and sentenced to life in prison without the possibility of parole.

Think about it

1. How is it that two brothers raised in the same environment might choose such different paths? What might explain their choices?
2. How would you explain the attraction that the drug trade seems to have for so many people in this country?
3. If you were able to set crime-control policies for the nation, how would you address the drug problem? Would you consider the decriminalization of any substances? If so, which ones and why? (See **Library Extra 13-4**.)

Note: Who's to Blame boxes provide fictionalized critical thinking opportunities, and are not actual cases.

be adulterated with other substances to provide large amounts of illicit commodities for sale on the street. Figure 13–7 and Figure 13–8 provide maps of major cocaine and heroin trafficking routes (sometimes called "pipelines"), respectively, worldwide. Most cocaine that enters the United States originates in the Western Hemisphere, especially in the South American nations of Colombia, Peru, and Bolivia. Transportation routes into the United States include (1) shipment overland from South America through Central America, (2) direct shipments to U.S. ports while concealed in containers or packed with legitimate products, (3) flights into the United States via commercial airplanes or in private aircraft, and (4) airdrops to vessels waiting offshore for smuggling into the United States.

The DEA follows heroin trafficking through its **Heroin Signature Program (HSP)**, which identifies the geographic source area of a heroin sample through the laboratory detection of specific chemical characteristics in the sample that are peculiar to that area. The HSP employs special chemical analyses to

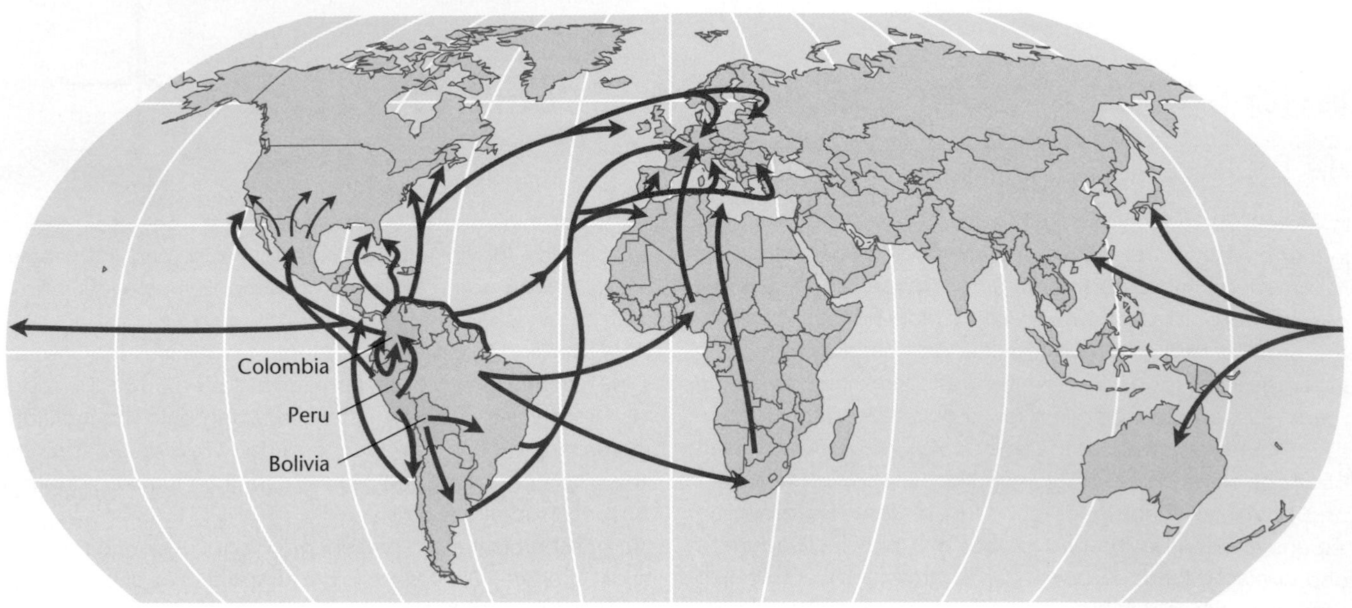

FIGURE 13-7 | **Global Cocaine Trafficking: Source Countries and Pipelines**

Source: Adapted from the Office of National Drug Control Policy, *The National Drug Control Strategy: 2000 Annual Report* (Washington, DC: U.S. Government Printing Office, 2000), p. 78.

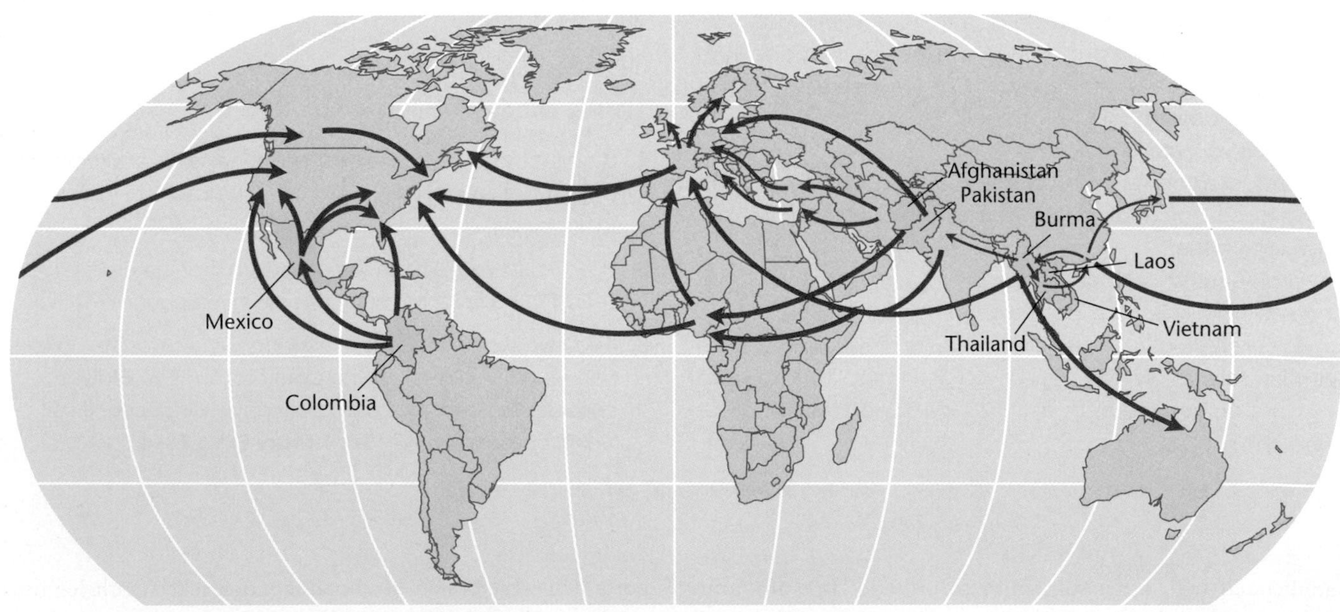

FIGURE 13-8 | **Global Heroin Trafficking: Source Countries and Pipelines**

Source: Adapted from Office of National Drug Control Policy, *The National Drug Control Strategy: 2000 Annual Report* (Washington, DC: U.S. Government Printing Office, 2000), p. 81.

identify and measure chemical constituents of a sample of seized heroin. Results of the HSP show that 62% of heroin in the United States originates in South America, 17% in Southeast Asia, 16% in Southwest Asia, and 5% in Mexico. According to the DEA, most heroin originating in Southeast Asia is produced in the Golden Triangle area, which encompasses Burma, Laos, and Thailand. Shipments are "controlled by ethnic Chinese criminal groups . . . while U.S.-based ethnic Chinese traffickers

■ **pharmaceutical diversion** The process by which legitimately manufactured controlled substances are diverted for illicit use by illegal prescribing (physicians) and/or illegal dispensing (pharmacists).
■ **designer drug** A new substance designed by slightly altering the chemical makeup of other illegal or tightly controlled drugs.
■ **drug-defined crime** A violation of the laws prohibiting or regulating the possession, use, or distribution of illegal drugs.
■ **drug-related crime** A crime in which drugs contribute to the offense (excluding violations of drug laws).
■ **narcoterrorism** The distribution of a controlled substance in order to provide something of pecuniary value to a person or group that has engaged or is engaging in terrorist activity.

with links to these international criminal groups [are] the most prolific importers and distributors of Southeast Asian heroin" within the United States.[16] HSP data were based on examination of over 800 random samples, including some obtained through undercover purchases, domestic seizures, and seizures made at U.S. ports of entry.

Pharmaceutical Diversion and Designer Drugs

The pharmaceutical diversion and subsequent abuse of legitimately manufactured controlled substances are a major source of drug-related addiction or dependence, medical emergencies, and death. **Pharmaceutical diversion** occurs through illegal prescribing by physicians and illegal dispensing by pharmacists. "Doctor shopping," the process of finding a physician who is liberal in prescribing types and amounts of certain drugs, and visits to numerous physicians for the purpose of collecting large quantities of prescribed medicines exacerbate the problem. Depressants, including sedatives, tranquilizers, and antianxiety drugs (especially Xanax and Valium), along with stimulants and anabolic steroids, constitute the types of drugs most often diverted.

A number of drugs, especially those that fall into the "designer" category, are manufactured in drug facilities that are sometimes called "basement laboratories" because they are operated by individuals out of their homes. **Designer drugs** are so named because "they are new substances designed by slightly altering the chemical makeup of other illegal or tightly controlled drugs."[17] Designer drugs such as Nexus, a new reputed aphrodisiac, usually fall under the rubric "synthetic narcotic" or "synthetic hallucinogen."

Drugs and Crime

While the manufacture, sale, transportation, and use of controlled substances are themselves criminal, drugs and crime are also linked in other ways. The addict who is so habituated to the use of illegal drugs that he or she steals to support a "habit," the drug importer who kills a rival dealer, and the offender who commits a criminal act due to the stimulation provided by drugs are examples of how drug abuse may be linked to other forms of criminal activity.

Recognizing these differences, the Bureau of Justice Statistics (BJS) distinguishes between drug-defined and drug-related crimes. **Drug-defined crimes** are "violations of laws prohibiting or regulating the possession, use, or distribution of illegal drugs."[18] The costs of all drug-defined crime, says the BJS, are directly attributable to illegal drug use. **Drug-related crimes**, on the other hand, "are not violations of drug laws but are crimes in which drugs contribute to the offense."[19] Illegal drug use, says the BJS, "is related to offenses against people and property in three major ways: (1) pharmacologically drugs can induce violent behavior, (2) the cost of drugs induces some users to commit crimes to support their drug habits, [and] (3) violence often characterizes relations among participants in the drug distribution system."[20]

According to the U.S. Department of Justice (DOJ), "There is extensive evidence of the strong relationship between drug use and crime." This relationship can be summarized in the following three points, each of which, the department says, is supported "by a review of the evidence":[21]

Extensive evidence shows the strong relationship between drug use and crime.

- Drug users report greater involvement in crime and are more likely than nonusers to have criminal records.
- People with criminal records are much more likely than others to report being drug users.
- Crimes rise in number as drug use increases.

Narcoterrorism

In 2012, a U.S. Circuit Court of Appeals upheld the 2008 conviction of Khan Mohammed, 38, a member of an Afghan Taliban terrorism cell, on **narcoterrorism** charges. Following conviction, Mohammed had been ordered by U.S. District Judge Colleen Kollar-Kotelly to serve two life sentences as well as 60 months of supervised release.[22] His conviction followed a seven-day jury trial on one count of distribution of heroin knowing and intending that it be imported into the United States, and one count of narcoterrorism. During the trial, Judge Kollar-Kotelly told the jury that narcoterrorism consisted of "the distribution of a controlled substance . . . in order to provide something of pecuniary value to

AP Photo/Associated Press

A Taliban militant holding an AK-47 automatic weapon (right) as farmers collect resin from poppies in an opium poppy field in Helmand province, southwest Afghanistan. Helmand province is one of the world's top opium-producing regions. How does this photo illustrate the link between illegal drugs and terrorism?

a person or group that has engaged or is engaging in terrorist activity." The conviction represented the first time a defendant had been convicted in federal court of narcoterrorism charges since the enactment of a narcoterrorism statute in March 2006.[23] At Mohammed's trial, DEA agents testified that the Taliban has played a central role in every stage of opium/heroin production and transportation, relying on it as a principal source of funding for its activities. One agent testified that more than 50% of current DEA cases have a definitive Taliban component.

Social Policy and Drug Abuse

Prior to 1907, any and all drugs could be bought and sold in the United States without restriction. Manufacturers were not required to disclose the contents of their products. Patent medicines of the time were trade secrets. This came to an end with the federal Pure Food and Drug Act of 1906, which required manufacturers to list their ingredients and specifically targeted mood-changing chemicals.

The Harrison Act, passed by Congress in 1914, was the first major piece of federal antidrug legislation. It required anyone dealing in opium, morphine, heroin, cocaine, or their derivatives to register with the federal government and to pay a tax of $1 per year. The act, however, only authorized the registration of physicians, pharmacists, and other medical professionals, effectively outlawing street use of these drugs. However, by 1920, court rulings severely curtailed the use of heroin for medical purposes, claiming that it only caused addiction.

In 1919, the Eighteenth Amendment to the U.S. Constitution, which prohibited the manufacture, sale, and transportation of alcoholic beverages, was ratified. Support for Prohibition began to wane not long after the amendment was enacted. Objections to Prohibition included the claims that it gave the government too much power over people's personal lives, was impossible to enforce, corrupted agents of enforcement, and made many bootleggers wealthy. The coming of the Great Depression, which began in 1929, magnified the effect of lost alcohol tax revenues on the federal government, and in 1933, Congress proposed and the states ratified the Twenty-first Amendment, which repealed Prohibition.

In 1937, passage of the Marijuana Tax Act effectively outlawed marijuana, a federal stance that was reinforced by the Boggs Act of 1951. The Boggs Act also mandated deletion of heroin from the list of medically useful substances and required its complete removal from all medicines.

In 1991, steroids were added to the list of Schedule III controlled substances by congressional action, and in 1996, the Drug-Induced Rape Prevention Act[24] increased penalties for trafficking in the drug Rohypnol, which is known as the "date rape drug" because of its use by "young men [who] put doses of the drug in women's drinks without their consent in order to lower their inhibitions."[25] The drug is variously known as "roples," "roche," "ruffles," "roofies," and "rophies" on the street.

Another date rape drug, gamma hydroxybutyrate (GHB), has effects similar to those of Rohypnol, but was once sold in health food stores as a supplement to enhance body building. In 1990, the FDA banned the use of GHB except under the supervision of a physician.

Recent Legislation

On the federal level, recent drug control legislation includes the Comprehensive Methamphetamine Control Act (CMCA) of 1996 and relevant portions of the Violent Crime Control and Law Enforcement Act of 1994. The CMCA, which contains provisions for the seizure of chemicals used in the manufacture of methamphetamine, regulated the use of iodine (used in meth labs); created new reporting requirements for distributors of combination products containing ephedrine, pseudoephedrine (a common decongestant), and phenylpropanolamine; and

■ **interdiction** An international drug-control policy whose goal is to stop drugs from entering the country illegally.

■ **forfeiture** A legal procedure that authorizes judicial representatives to seize "all moneys, negotiable instruments, securities, or other things of value furnished or intended to be furnished by any person in exchange for a controlled substance and all proceeds traceable to such an exchange."

increased penalties for the manufacture and possession of equipment used to make controlled substances.

The far-reaching Violent Crime Control and Law Enforcement Act of 1994 included a number of drug-related provisions. Specifically, the act allocated other drug-treatment moneys for the creation of state and federal programs to treat drug-addicted prisoners and provided $1 billion for drug court programs for nonviolent offenders with substance abuse problems. The law also expanded the federal death penalty to include large-scale drug trafficking and mandated life imprisonment for criminals convicted of three drug-related felonies.

Some states, however, are moving to legalize the personal use of marijuana, or to allow the use of marijuana for medical purposes. Medical marijuana, or the use of physician-prescribed marijuana to alleviate pain and nausea associated with various physical ailments, is legal in 17 states.[26] In 2012, voters in Colorado and Washington State approved ballot initiatives that legalized the possession and use of small amounts of marijuana for recreational use in private; and on April 20–21 the nation's first Cannabis Cup held in Denver, Colorado, drew more than 50,000 people—many of whom openly smoked marijuana in violation of that state's privacy requirement.[27]

John Moore/Getty Images

The 2013 Denver Cannabis Cup celebration. Why have some states moved to legalize small amounts of marijuana for private recreational or medical use? Why does the drug remain illegal elsewhere?

In response to state action, in 2013 the U.S. Department of Justice issued a memorandum to all federal prosecutors providing guidance on enforcement of the Controlled Substances Act in those jurisdictions. The memorandum took a "hands-off" approach and established federal enforcement priorities with regard to marijuana distribution and use in states that legalized the drug. Those priorities include preventing the distribution of marijuana to minors and preventing marijuana sales revenue from going to criminal enterprises and cartels.[28]

Drug-Control Strategies

Major policy initiatives in the battle against illicit drugs have included antidrug legislation and strict enforcement, interdiction, crop control, forfeiture, and antidrug education and drug treatment.[29] Much legislative emphasis in recent years has shifted from targeting users to arresting, prosecuting, and incarcerating the distributors of controlled substances. Similar shifts have occurred among employers requiring routine drug testing as a condition of employment and retention.

Interdiction is an international drug control policy designed to stop drugs from entering the country illegally. Another antidrug strategy, crop control, has both international and domestic aspects. During 2010, for example, the DEA's Domestic Cannabis Eradication and Suppression Program was responsible for the eradication of 9,866,766 cultivated outdoor marijuana plants and 462,419 indoor marijuana plants in the United States. In addition, the same program was responsible for 9,687 arrests, and agents seized 5,081 weapons and $34,311,819 in assets.[30]

Forfeiture, or asset forfeiture, is another strategy in the battle against illegal drugs. **Forfeiture** is a legal procedure that authorizes judicial representatives to seize "all moneys, negotiable instruments, securities, or other things of value furnished or intended to be furnished by any person in exchange for a controlled substance . . . [and] all proceeds traceable to such an exchange."[31]

THEORY | versus REALITY

The Harvard Alcohol Study

In 1993, the Harvard School of Public Health conducted its first College Alcohol Study (CAS). The study surveyed a random sample of students at 140 colleges in 39 states and the District of Columbia. The study was the first national examination of the drinking patterns of college students.

The original CAS identified a style of drinking that study authors called "binge drinking." *Binge drinking* was defined as the consumption of five or more drinks in a row for men and four or more for women at least once in the two weeks preceding the survey. The CAS, with its emphasis on binge drinking, focused media attention on alcohol-related college deaths, including deaths from acute alcohol poisoning, falls, drownings, automobile accidents, fires, and hypothermia resulting from exposure to the elements. The study also led to passage of a congressional resolution to address binge drinking as a national problem and to the appointment of a National Institute on Alcoholism and Alcohol Abuse special task force on college drinking.

The CAS was repeated in 1997, 1999, and 2001. The study reported on the drinking behavior of four categories of students: (1) frequent binge drinkers—defined as those students who had binged three or more times in the past two weeks; (2) occasional binge drinkers—those students who had binged one or two times in the same period; (3) nonbinge drinkers—those students who had consumed alcohol in the past year but who had not binged in the previous two weeks; and (4) abstainers—those students who had not consumed alcohol in the past year.

The 2001 CAS surveyed students at 119 four-year colleges that also participated in the 1993, 1997, and 1999 studies. Responses in the four survey years were compared to determine trends in heavy alcohol use, alcohol-related problems, and encounters with college and community prevention efforts. In 2001, approximately two in five college students reported binge drinking, a rate almost identical to rates in the previous three surveys. Very little change in overall college binge drinking was observed in the surveys over time, although a sharp rise in frequent binge drinking was noted among students attending all-women's colleges. The most significant finding, however, was an observed 18% increase in the college student population that reported driving under the influence of alcohol in the previous year (Figure 13–9).

The study also found that about 19% of surveyed students were abstainers and 23% were frequent binge drinkers. As in earlier studies, binge drinkers, and particularly frequent binge drinkers, were more likely than other students to experience alcohol-related problems. At colleges with high binge-drinking rates, students who did not binge drink were at high risk of experiencing the secondhand effects of others' heavy drinking. These secondhand effects included having study patterns interrupted, being kept awake at night, being insulted or humiliated, being subjected to unwanted sexual advances, and having to take care of drunken fellow students.

For a summary of research findings based on CAS data, visit the Harvard School of Public Health's College Alcohol Study information page at **Web Extra 13–2**. Additional information on binge drinking is available from the National Survey of Drug Use and Health (Figure 13–10).

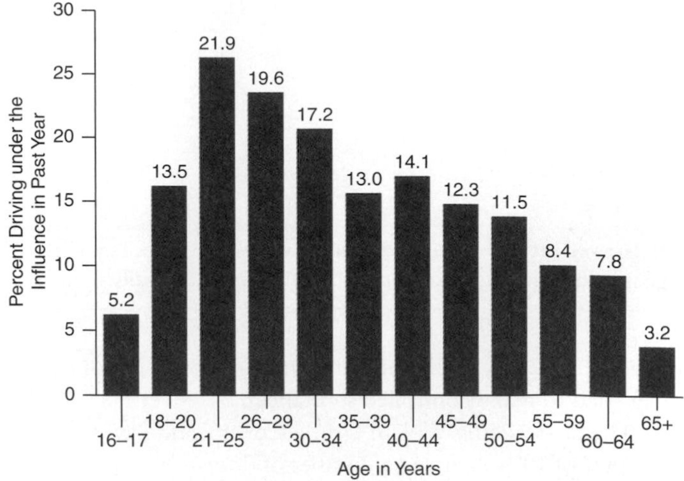

FIGURE 13-9 | Driving under the Influence of Alcohol in the Past Year among Persons Ages 16 and Older, by Age, 2011

Source: Office of Applied Studies, Substance Abuse and Mental Health Services Administration, *National Survey on Drug Use and Health, 2011* (Washington, DC: U.S. Government Printing Office, 2013).

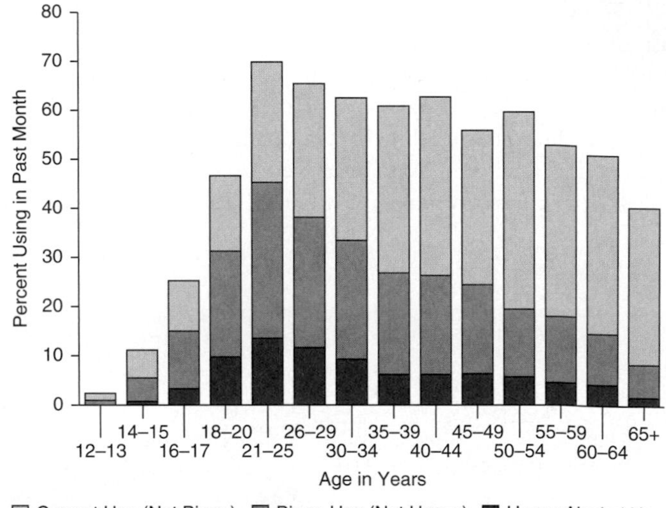

FIGURE 13-10 | Current, Binge, and Heavy Alcohol Use among Persons Ages 12 and Older, by Age, 2011

Source: Office of Applied Studies, Substance Abuse and Mental Health Services Administration, *National Survey on Drug Use and Health, 2011* (Washington, DC: U.S. Government Printing Office, 2013).

Discussion Questions

1. Do you know students who consume alcohol on or off campus? If so, do you think that the College Alcohol Study categories provide a useful way of classifying the different kinds of drinking patterns among members of the student body?
2. What percentage of the student body at your school would you assign to each of the CAS categories?
3. Why might such categories be useful to policymakers?

Sources: Henry Weschler et al., "Trends in College Binge Drinking during a Period of Increased Prevention Efforts: Findings from 4 Harvard School of Public Health College Alcohol Study Surveys: 1993–2001," http://www.hsph.harvard.edu/cas/Documents/trends/Trends.pdf (accessed July 10, 2007); Ralph Hingson et al., "Magnitude of Alcohol-Related Mortality and Morbidity among U.S. College Students Ages 18–24: Changes from 1998 to 2001," *Annual Review of Public Health*, Vol. 26 (2005), pp. 259–279; and Henry Weschler et al., "College Binge Drinking in the 1990s: A Continuing Problem: Results of the Harvard School of Public Health 1999 College Alcohol Study," http://www.hsph.harvard.edu/cas/rpt2000/CAS2000rpt.shtml (accessed January 15, 2011).

■ **prostitution** The act of engaging in sexual activity for money or its equivalent.

WHO'S TO BLAME—The Individual or Society?

Gangs, Teenagers, and Peer Pressure

Fourteen-year-old Lakisha Jackson found herself in trouble with the law at her junior high school prom when her 18-year-old boyfriend, Jamal Carter, was caught smoking pot behind the curtain covering the school's stage. Jamal told off-duty police officers working the dance that the marijuana wasn't his, but that Lakisha had given it to him.

Jamal was known to the officers as a member of the Top 6 gang and bore a number of tattoos indicating his gang affiliation. Officers from the police department's juvenile division were called to the school, and both Lakisha and Jamal were taken to the police station for questioning. No additional drugs were found on either youth.

What bothered officers, however, was Lakisha's hostile attitude. While they expected that Jamal would refuse to say more than he already had about the source of the marijuana, they had hoped that Lakisha would either refute Jamal's story or tell them where she had gotten the substance. Lakisha, however, refused to say anything about the incident, calling the officers "pigs" and telling them to mind their own business. "I don't rat on nobody," was all she would volunteer.

A police psychologist who was present during the interviews later explained the youth's behavior in terms of gang and subcultural loyalties. "Even if this case involved a serious crime like a murder—maybe even especially then—you wouldn't get any cooperation from these kids," he said. "You can be sure that if they knew who committed a crime they wouldn't talk. It's not only part and parcel of their gang loyalties, but pretty much a value inherent in the subculture in which they've been raised. Maybe in another neighborhood things would be different—but not here."

Think about it

1. Do you agree with the police psychologist? Is his explanation for why these youngsters won't talk to the police a plausible one, or is there likely to be some other explanation?
2. If the psychologist is correct in his assessment of the situation, then do you think that Lakisha and Jamal should "know better" than to let subcultural values influence them? Why or why not?
3. Are the police likely to get any more information from Lakisha or her boyfriend? Why or why not?

Note: Who's to Blame boxes provide fictionalized critical thinking opportunities, and are not actual cases.

> Those who favor educational attacks on the problem of drug abuse claim that other techniques have not been effective.

Another strategy, antidrug education and drug treatment, has gained significant popularity over the past decade. Those favoring educational attacks on the problem of drug abuse are quick to claim that other measures have not been effective in reducing the incidence of abuse. Antidrug education programs often reach targeted individuals through schools, corporations, and media campaigns.

Prostitution

In late-2012, the small town of Kennebunk, Maine, was shaken by a prostitution scandal that involved a Zumba fitness instructor who was charged with running a sex-for-hire business out of her downtown studio.[32] Twenty-nine-year-old fitness instructor Alexis Wright was arrested after her landlord called police, complaining of strange sounds coming from her office. Following Wright's arrest, a judge ordered the release of 21 names of an estimated 150 johns found on a list of customers that she had maintained. The list included the names of prominent Maine businessmen and professionals, along with men from Massachusetts and New Hampshire. Wright also faced charges of invasion of privacy for allegedly creating secret video recordings of her sexual encounters. Prosecutors announced that they would charge not only Wright, but the men to whom she sold sexual services, who were charged with soliciting a prostitute—a misdemeanor under Maine law. In May 2013, Wright pled guilty to 20 misdemeanor counts, although the original indictment against her had charged her with 106 counts of prostitution, tax evasion, and other things.[33]

Prostitution can be defined as the act of engaging in sexual activity for money. In heterosexual prostitution involving men as clients (or "johns") and women as sexual "service providers," the men can also be charged with and found guilty of the offense of prostitution. Same-sex prostitution, which generally involves male prostitutes serving male clients, is also illegal when

Robert F. Bukaty/Associated Press

Zumba instructor Alexis Wright, arrested in 2012 in the town of Kennebunk, Maine, on charges of prostitution. Why is prostitution illegal in most parts of the United States? Why is it legal in other parts?

the exchange of money or other valuables is involved. Except for in parts of Nevada, all forms of prostitution are criminal acts in the United States and are generally classified as misdemeanors.

In the United States, over 92,000 men, women, and juveniles are arrested yearly for the crime of prostitution.[34] The number of juveniles engaging in prostitution is estimated to be between 100,000 and 300,000 annually.

Morals Legislation

Laws against prostitution have a long and varied history in the United States, and have largely focused on traditional forms of prostitution, which involve women servicing men; and that is the form of prostitution that this chapter focuses on. Underlying statutes forbidding prostitution are fundamental questions about legislating morality. Whether and to what extent the criminal law should reflect and enforce the morality of the society it represents is one of the classic debates in criminal law literature. Most people agree that actions that harm others, as in the case of child prostitution, should be controlled, but not everyone sees prostitution, especially when willingly undertaken, as harmful (see **Library Extra 13–5**).

Some people argue that every organized society is permitted—even obligated—to enforce morality by means of criminal and other legal sanctions. Arguments in favor of criminalizing street prostitution can be seen in Table 13-2.

The classic statement that the law should not unnecessarily criminalize what are personal moral decisions that harm no one (other than possibly the person making them) was offered by the nineteenth-century English philosopher John Stuart Mill, who argued that society should interfere with an individual's freedom of action only "to prevent harm to others. His own good, either physical or moral, is not a sufficient warrant" for interference.[35]

A Typology of Prostitutes

There are many different venues where sexual services are sold: so-called red-light districts, commercial houses of prostitution, massage parlors, studios for nude photography, strip clubs, stag parties, and theaters for erotic dance.[36] Using location as the basis for a typology of prostitutes produces the categories of streetwalkers, bar/hotel prostitutes, call girls, and hotel/brothel prostitutes; others don't clearly fit any of these categories (Figure 13–11).

Streetwalkers are generally seen as the lowest class of prostitute because they solicit customers in public—often on foot and

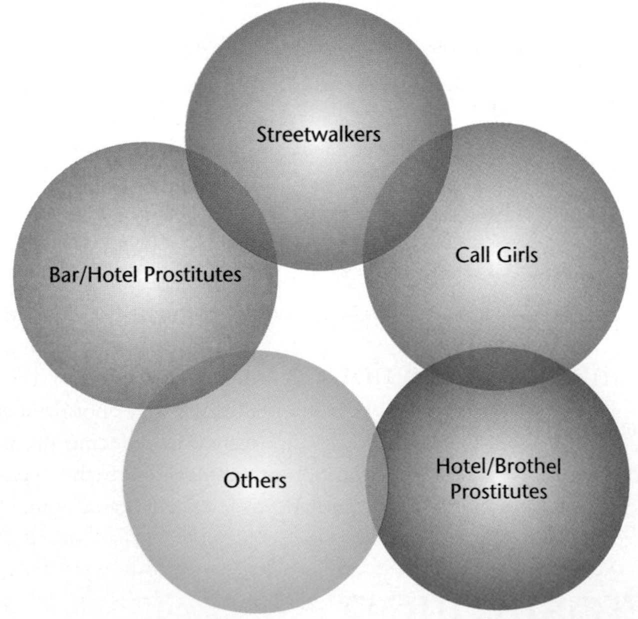

FIGURE 13-11 | **Types of Prostitutes**

TABLE 13-2 | **Harms Caused by Street Prostitution**

Moral and Nuisance Concerns • Prostitution offends some citizens' moral standards. • Prostitution is a nuisance to passersby and nearby residents and businesses. • Prostitutes and clients offend uninvolved people when they solicit them. • Juveniles who are less capable of making informed choices may become prostitutes. **Public Health Concerns** • Prostitutes and clients may spread sexually transmitted diseases such as syphilis, herpes, and AIDS. • Used condoms, syringes, and other paraphernalia left on the ground are unsightly and potentially hazardous. • Prostitutes without access to proper facilities may relieve themselves or bathe in public. **Personal Safety Concerns** • Clients may harm prostitutes. • Clients or prostitutes may be defrauded, robbed, or assaulted. • Pimps may financially and physically exploit prostitutes and clients.	**Spillover-Effect Concerns** • Street prostitution and drug markets are often linked. • Prostitution may provide a seedbed for organized crime. • Prostitutes create parking and traffic problems where they congregate. • Prostitution attracts strangers and criminals to a neighborhood. **Economic Concerns** • Legitimate businesses may lose customers who avoid the area because of prostitution. • Prostitutes' presence may negatively affect the area's economy, reducing property values and limiting property use. **Civil Rights Concerns** • Prostitutes have rights that need to be protected. **Police-Integrity Concerns** • Policing prostitution creates special opportunities for police officers to engage in unethical conduct, such as taking payments in exchange for nonenforcement, because prostitutes, pimps, and clients are in weak positions to complain about police misconduct.

Source: Adapted from Michael S. Scott and Kelly Dedel, *Street Prostitution*, 2nd ed. (Washington, DC: Office of Community Oriented Policing Services, U.S. Department of Justice, 2006).

from curbside. They tend to be highly visible, and their dress is revealing, both of which advertise their services and entice customers. Streetwalkers, who perform their services in customers' cars, alleyways, nearby hotels, and darkened doorways, command the lowest prices and have little bargaining power over things like condom use and choice of sexual practices; they face the highest risk of harm from customers or others and run the highest risk of arrest.

Bar/hotel prostitutes work in bars, clubs, and hotels and may have a standing relationship with managers, bartenders, and security personnel, with whom they share their profits or for whom they provide "free" services. They tend to "work" conventions, sporting events, and business meetings. Desk clerks, valets, and even discreet concierges sometimes refer clients to prostitutes, whose services are typically provided in the establishment, perhaps in a dark corner, a back room, or a hotel room rented by the customer or prostitute; the prices charged by bar/hotel prostitutes vary considerably according to the prestige of the establishment with which they are associated. A prostitute's risk of harm and arrest is low to moderate as long as the collaborative relationship with the establishment is maintained.

Call girls work for escort services—which advertise in flyers, in newspapers, in the yellow pages, on TV, and via the Internet (sometimes referred to as "cyberprostitution")—on an "outcall" basis and are not restricted to specific locales. Most call girls see relatively well-to-do clients who prefer the anonymity of a referral service, and many customers are regulars who maintain a standing relationship with the service. Prostitutes are typically assigned by the agency to customers who may select them from pictures printed in brochures or posted on the Internet. Fees are often charged to credit cards by the customer before the girl is dispatched; on site, prostitutes may negotiate with the customer for specific services. Through this arrangement, the escort service tends to insulate itself from legal action, claiming that it simply arranged for companionship. Call girls depend on the agency to screen customers, which can be done by referrals from other agencies or by established clients

Most call girls see well-to-do clients who prefer the anonymity of a referral service.

CRIME | in the NEWS

International Sex Traffickers Turn Girls into Slaves

Prostitution is not necessarily voluntary. According to wide-ranging estimates from the United Nations (UN) and the FBI, hundreds of thousands of girls around the world are in bondage to sex traffickers, and the numbers are rising. The victims are typically aged 8 to 18, and some are as young as 4 or 5.

In poor countries like Cambodia, families reportedly sell a young daughter to sex traffickers for the equivalent of $10. Some of these girls are later rescued and sent to shelters. Then-Secretary of State Hillary Clinton visited one such shelter in Cambodia in 2010. "I met with dozens of girls, most of them very young, who had been sexually exploited and abused," she recalled. "They had been given refuge at the shelter and they were learning valuable skills to help them reenter society."

Sex traffickers are most active within their own countries, but many of them cross borders and even enter the United States. In some cases, they lure their victims with promises of a legitimate job, and then keep them in bondage until they pay off excessively high debts for their transportation. The Department of Justice reported 1,220 sex trafficking incidents in the United States from January 2007 to September 2008.

These girls are often afraid to contact authorities for fear of being identified as illegal immigrants, the State Department reports. They have justification, the department explained in a 2012 report. When they are found out, they are often arrested, incarcerated, and deported, rather than given shelter.

To address this rising international crime, Congress in 2000 passed the Trafficking Victims Protection Act, which also addresses indentured laborers. On the international level, the law authorizes the State Department to create public awareness programs, assess trafficking in each foreign country, and develop sanctions against countries that fail to take action.

Within the United States, the law steps up prosecution of traffickers based on new federal crimes and heightened penalties. The U.S. Immigration and Customs Enforcement unit oversees prosecution, and victims are protected from deportation through a new T visa. Although no more than 5,000 T visas are allowed per year, less than half that amount is granted, but the number is growing.

In a related action in 2003, the FBI launched the U.S. Innocence Lost National Initiative, in conjunction with other federal agencies. In June 2012, the FBI reported that the initiative had rescued almost 900 children and helped secure the convictions of more than 500 sex traffickers.

Discussion Questions

1. How might transnational criminal organizations be involved in prostitution?
2. What is the goal of the Trafficking Victims Protection Act? How can it be used to combat the types of crime described in this box?

Dan Vincent/Alamy

Child prostitutes in Bangladesh. What special issues face children who have been rescued from prostitution?

Sources: Amanda Walker-Rodriguez and Rodney Hill, "Human Sex Trafficking," *Law Enforcement Bulletin*, March 2011, http://www.fbi.gov/stats-services/publications/law-enforcement-bulletin/march_2011/human_sex_trafficking; "Trafficking in Persons Report," Department of State, June 2012, http://www.state.gov/documents/organization/192587.pdf; and Hillary Clinton, "Remarks on the Release of the 2011 Trafficking in Persons Report," Department of State, June 27, 2011, http://www.state.gov/secretary/rm/2011/06/167156.htm.

---

with connections to the agency. Prices in this market segment reach the highest levels, and escorts have considerable bargaining power over such things as use of condoms and kinds of sexual services provided; call girls face the lowest risk of harm or arrest.

House or brothel prostitutes ply their trade in legal environments, which are limited to a few venues in the United States. Legalized prostitution, however, is common in a number of other countries, including Australia (where laws vary by state), New Zealand, the Netherlands (which outlaws pimping and trafficking of human beings), and Germany (where advertising sex services remains illegal). In countries where prostitution is legal, it is still subject to health and locality controls as well as age and other restrictions. In such locales, prostitutes are generally licensed sex workers who pay taxes, belong to unions, and are eligible for government benefits such as unemployment wages and medical services. Some countries tolerate prostitution but restrict activities associated with it, such as pimping, operating brothels, and advertising services; others technically permit prostitution but have other kinds of restrictions making its practice difficult. In this latter category are countries like Brazil, Canada, Costa Rica, and Scotland. In Denmark, prostitution is legal, but profiting from it is not, and Sweden allows the selling of sexual services but criminalizes pimping and the purchasing of sex services (on the theory that such activity demeans women). In Japan, vaginal prostitution is illegal, but fellatio for money is not considered prostitution.

In the United States, brothel prostitution is an option in some rural counties in Nevada. Nevada's house prostitutes operate with posted fees and generally earn 40% to 60% of the revenue they generate. State law requires that they be fingerprinted, undergo regular health examinations, and keep financial records for tax purposes. All forms of prostitution are illegal in Nevada's

Clark County (which contains Las Vegas). See the Criminal Profiles box on Heidi Fleiss, who ran a prostitution business in Hollywood and Los Angeles.

Clients of Prostitutes

About ten years ago, the NIJ undertook sponsorship of an extensive study conducted by Martin A. Monto of prostitutes' clients—commonly known as "johns"—that explored the sex-related behavior characteristic of men who solicited prostitutes.[37] The study, whose results were published in 2000, examined the effects of the First Offender Prostitution Program (FOPP) in San Francisco and similar programs in other cities.[38] These programs offered johns an opportunity to pay a fine and attend a daylong seminar rather than go to jail, and participants were advised that no further legal action would be taken against them if they successfully avoided rearrest for a year, but if there was a subsequent offense, they would be prosecuted for the new offense and the original charge would be reinstated.

Monto surveyed 1,291 men arrested for soliciting street prostitutes before they participated in FOPP or similar programs in Las Vegas, Nevada; Portland, Oregon; and Santa Clara, California. He collected data on their reasons for use of prostitutes, their attitudes regarding violence against women, and the consequences of their views of sex as a commodity. Monto found that 72% of the men, who ranged in age from 18 to 84 years (median age of 37), had attended some college and were less likely to be married than other men. Although their motives for seeking sex with a prostitute differed, there were similarities among certain groups: Married clients and college graduates more often wanted a different kind of sex than they had with their regular partners; unmarried clients and those without college degrees felt shy and awkward when trying to meet women but did not feel intimidated by prostitutes.

Researcher Monto also explored men's attitudes toward rape myths (discussed in Chapter 9). Less than 0.5% of the men surveyed indicated acceptance of the majority of rape myths, but 20% demonstrated acceptance of four or more of them. Although the evidence wasn't clear, researchers believed that it was this latter group that may be responsible for perpetrating violent acts against women for hire.

The greater a man's belief that women and sex were commercial products, the more frequently he would visit prostitutes.

Concerning the degree to which clients regarded sexuality as a commercial commodity, Monto found that the greater a client's belief that women and sex were commercial products, the more frequently he would visit prostitutes. This mind-set was also a strong predictor of the acceptance of rape myths, less frequent condom use with prostitutes, and a disinclination to view prostitution as a demeaning profession for women.

Monto and his colleagues also studied the recidivism of those clients who participated in the San Francisco and Portland FOPPs. Although both programs had a recidivism rate of about 2%, researchers acknowledged that conclusions about the programs' efficacy in reducing recidivism were hampered by a lack of available baseline data for comparative purposes. Read Monto's entire 80-page report on street prostitution at **Library Extra 13–6**.

Feminist Perspectives on Prostitution

Prostitution represents a significant issue in today's feminist thought. Some feminist thinkers argue that prostitution exploits and demeans women and subjects them to the dangers of violence and disease. Andrea Dworkin, an ex-prostitute and anti-pornography crusader, wrote that commercial sex is a form of rape perpetrated by poverty and frequent overt violence (often by pimps).[39]

Others take a different approach, saying that selling sex need not be inherently exploitative and might actually be liberating because it fulfills a woman's rights to control her body and her sexuality; they see prostitution as legitimate sex work and argue for the legalization of prostitution (with added protections for those who choose sex work as a trade). The redefinition of prostitution as sex work has been accompanied by the development of an activist movement comprising organizations such Call Off Your Old Tired Ethics (COYOTE). COYOTE, founded in 1973, advocates for the repeal of prostitution laws and an end to the stigma associated with sex work.

Feminists who believe that prostitution is inherently exploitative reject the idea that prostitution can be reformed. The assumptions that women exist for men's sexual enjoyment, that all men need sex, and that women's bodily integrity and sexual pleasure are irrelevant underlie the whole idea of prostitution, making it an inherently exploitative sexist practice. One feminist argument against Dworkin's position is that prostitution is exploiting men more than it exploits women.

In an interesting critique of what he calls "extreme radical feminist theory," as represented by the writings of Dworkin and others, sociologist Ronald Weitzer of George Washington University listed four core claims characterizing this body of literature:[40]

1. Prostitution involves male domination and exploitation of women regardless of historical time period, societal context, or legal status.

CRIMINAL | PROFILES

Heidi Lynne Fleiss—Madame to the Stars

Heidi Fleiss's notorious high-priced prostitution ring was the stuff of Hollywood lore, but no more so than her arrest, trial, incarceration, and postrelease emergence as an unrepentant sex entrepreneur.[i] Fleiss was initially arrested in June 1993 on state charges that included five counts of pandering and one count of narcotics possession. On July 28, 1994, during her California trial, she was indicted by a federal grand jury on charges of income tax evasion, money laundering, and conspiracy.

Fleiss was convicted in federal court of income tax evasion, money laundering, and eight counts of conspiracy in August 1995. She also pled guilty in state court to the pandering charges. The combined sentences resulted in her serving three years in prison.

Born in Los Angeles on December 30, 1965, Heidi Fleiss showed a precocious flair for business as early as age 12. A popular and responsible babysitter, she soon found herself with more job offers than she could handle herself, so she established a babysitting service by hiring her friends from school to handle some of the jobs. She, of course, got a cut of all the fees.[ii]

Her school performance, however, did not keep pace with her business enterprise. Low grades in junior high and high school ultimately led to her dropping out in the tenth grade. For the next few years, she held a variety of low-wage jobs. Fleiss's aspirations never wavered, however, and she was constantly on the lookout for the right opportunity.

That opportunity came when she and a friend attended a party at 61-year-old millionaire financier Bernie Cornfeld's estate. Impressed with Fleiss, Cornfeld hired her as his personal secretary, an arrangement that, in short order, evolved into a personal relationship. Fleiss sought to deepen the relationship to a live-in level, which she hoped would result in her enjoying a financially secure life of privilege and hedonistic pursuits. Cornfeld, however, had a well-known appetite for classical beauties, which he enthusiastically indulged. His continued dalliances signaled an unwillingness to remain in a monogamous relationship, and the couple eventually broke up.

Still, Fleiss walked away with newly acquired business skills learned from associating with Cornfeld and his friends. A chance meeting with the reigning queen madam of the Los Angeles area, Madam Alex, gave Fleiss entrée to the sex industry.

Madam Alex was, at that time, looking for a replacement to take over her business operations so that she could live a privileged retirement. Fleiss's business acumen fit the bill so well that she increased Madam Alex's profits by more than 400%. But when Madam Alex proved to be less than generous in sharing her largess, Fleiss went off on her own.

And the rest is sex industry history. Ultimately, Fleiss's client base included top producers, directors, and movie stars from the Hollywood scene, as well as some of the world's most famous (and wealthiest) men. Business tycoons, Middle Eastern sheiks, members of royalty, and various heads of state are counted among those to whom she provided women for sexual services.[iii]

Since her release from prison, Fleiss has parlayed her notoriety into a series of successful business ventures, including a men's apparel store in Los Angeles called "Heidi's Wear." A book (*Pandering*), a DVD (*Sex Tips*), a Web site, and repeated appearances on late-night talk shows kept her in the public eye for years. Ever the sensationalist, Fleiss's current project, which she describes as a "stud farm,"[iv] involves converting a brothel in southern Nevada into a resort staffed by male prostitutes to service Fleiss's hoped-for female customers.[v]

Regis Martin/Getty Images

Renowned Hollywood Madame Heidi Fleiss at the Melbourne, Australia, Stock Exchange for the start of trading of "The Daily Planet" bordello—the first brothel in the world to be listed on a national stock exchange. For years, Fleiss's prostitution business had catered to the rich and famous in Hollywood and Los Angeles, but she spent 20 months in prison after being convicted in 1995 on federal charges of conspiracy, tax evasion, and money laundering. Should Fleiss have received a longer sentence?

The case of Heidi Fleiss raises a number of interesting questions. Among them are the following:

1. Did the crimes that Fleiss committed hurt anyone? If so, what kind of damage did they cause?
2. How did Fleiss get involved in prostitution? What makes her different from other women who might not have taken advantage of the criminal opportunities that presented themselves to her?
3. Will Fleiss ever get out of the sex business? If so, what kind of work might she pursue?

Notes

i. "Then & Now: Heidi Fleiss," CNN, June 19, 2005, http://www.cnn.com/2005/US/02/28/cnn25.tan.fleiss (accessed June 1, 2010).
ii. Rachael Bell, "Heidi Fleiss: The Million Dollar Madam," CourtTV Crime Library, http://www.crimelibrary.com/notorious_murders/celebrity/heidi_fleiss/index.html (accessed June 1, 2010).
iii. Ibid.
iv. "Fleiss Plans Makeover for Nevada Brothel," *USA Today*, November 16, 2005, http://www.usatoday.com/life/people/2005-11-16-fleiss_x.htm (accessed June 1, 2007).
v. Steve Friess, "Betting on the Studs," *Newsweek*, December 12, 2005, http://www.msnbc.msn.com/id/10313009/site/newsweek (accessed June 1, 2007).

■ **legalization** The elimination of laws and criminal penalties associated with certain behaviors—usually the production, sale, distribution, and possession of a controlled substance.

■ **decriminalization** The redefinition of certain previously criminal behaviors as regulated activities that become "ticketable" instead of "arrestable."

2. Violence is omnipresent in prostitution.
3. Female prostitutes lack agency (they cannot actively make choices about whether or not to stay in prostitution).
4. Legalization or decriminalization would only make the situation worse.

Weitzer saw these claims as counterproductive because they tend to stifle debate over prostitution and effectively divert research programs through what he calls "considerable ideological contamination of our understanding of prostitution."[41] Extreme feminists have contributed to a growing moral panic over prostitution by tying it to sex trafficking and the trafficking of children for sex. Many of the radicals' claims, explained Weitzer, are simply false; violence is not inevitably associated with prostitution, some prostitutes (especially those engaged in legal prostitution) see themselves positively, and prostitution can be lawfully organized in ways that protect the prostitutes' health, rights, and freedoms.

Legalization and Decriminalization of Prostitution

Numerous arguments have been made in favor of legalizing or decriminalizing prostitution. Under **legalization**, women beyond a specified age would be able to offer paid sexual services with few restrictions (as in parts of Nevada). **Decriminalization** would significantly reduce the criminal penalties associated with prostitution but would still regulate the practice and might require counseling and alternative employment programs for women in that line of work in an effort to curtail the practice (see **Library Extra 13–7**).

Legalization of prostitution would free up law enforcement resources to be used in the investigation of more serious types of crime.

Those who argue in favor of legalization say that keeping prostitution illegal tends to force prostitution out of areas where it might naturally be found (certain hotels, massage parlors) and onto the streets and into other parts of the community and that prostitutes will continue to be viewed as easy targets for pimps, sex offenders, and violent predators. Legalization of prostitution would free up law enforcement resources to be used in the prevention and investigation of more serious types of crime.

Those who argue for keeping prostitution illegal point out that it is regarded as morally and ethically wrong, that it is often not a line of work that is freely chosen, and that it is dangerous for sex workers as well as for their clients because of the disease and violence often associated with it.[42]

SUMMARY

- Drug abuse has a long and varied history in American society, from the use of illegal drugs by artistic individuals seeking to enhance their creativity to citizens using medicinal elixirs containing cocaine, alcohol, and opium. Policy responses to drug abuse have been equally diverse.
- Controlled substances are grouped into seven categories: stimulants, depressants, cannabis, narcotics, hallucinogens, anabolic steroids, and inhalants. A separate eighth category, dangerous drugs, provides a kind of legal and definitional catchall. The Controlled Substances Act established five schedules of federally controlled substances based on the effects of a drug and its potential for abuse.
- The National Institute on Drug Abuse (NIDA), a part of the National Institutes of Health, defines addiction as "a chronic, relapsing brain disease that is characterized by compulsive drug seeking and use, despite harmful consequences." Brain-imaging studies of drug-addicted individuals showed changes in areas of the brain that are critical to judgment, decision making, learning and memory, and behavior control. Whether a person becomes addicted to drugs depends on a number of factors: the age at first use; the frequency of initial use, with genetic and environmental factors interacting with critical developmental stages; gender, ethnicity, and preexisting mental disorders; and social influences in the environment, such as peer pressure, physical and sexual abuse, stress, and parental involvement.

- Drug trafficking includes manufacturing, distributing, dispensing, importing, and exporting (or possessing with intent to do the same) a controlled substance or a counterfeit substance. Federal law enforcement agencies focus on the prevention of smuggling and the apprehension of smugglers.
- Strategies to reduce the flow of illegal drugs into this country are supplemented with programs of education and treatment to reduce the demand for controlled substances. Major policy initiatives have included (1) antidrug legislation and strict enforcement, (2) interdiction, (3) crop control, (4) forfeiture, and (5) antidrug education and drug treatment.
- Prostitution is a morals offense. Using location as the basis for a typology of prostitutes results in the categories of streetwalkers, bar/hotel prostitutes, call girls, and hotel/brothel prostitutes, as well as others who don't fit any of these categories.

KEY TERMS

addiction, 337
controlled substances, 337
dangerous drug, 337
decriminalization, 351
designer drug, 341
drug-defined crime, 341
drug-related crime, 341
drug trafficking, 338
forfeiture, 343
Heroin Signature Program (HSP), 339
interdiction, 343
legalization, 351
narcoterrorism, 341
National Survey on Drug Use and Health (NSDUH), 333
Office of National Drug Control Policy (ONDCP), 336
pharmaceutical diversion, 341
prostitution, 345
psychoactive substance, 332

QUESTIONS FOR REVIEW

1. What can be said about the history of drugs, drug abuse, and drug-control legislation in the United States?
2. What are the various categories of controlled substances described by federal law? What is a dangerous drug?
3. What is drug trafficking, and what efforts are being made to curtail it?
4. What is the relationship among drug trafficking, drug abuse, and other forms of crime?
5. What government strategies have been used to reduce the incidence of drug use in the United States?
6. What is prostitution? What are the various types of prostitutes identified in this chapter?

QUESTIONS FOR REFLECTION

1. This book emphasizes the theme of social problems versus social responsibility. Which of the social policy approaches to controlling drug abuse discussed in this chapter (if any) appear to be predicated on a social problems approach? Which (if any) are predicated on a social responsibility approach? Explain the nature of the relationship.
2. What are some of the costs of illicit drug use in the United States today? Which costs can be more easily reduced than others? How would you reduce the costs of illegal drug use?
3. What is the difference between decriminalization and legalization? Should drug use remain illegal? What do you think of the arguments in favor of legalization? Those against?
4. What is asset forfeiture? How has asset forfeiture been used in the fight against illegal drugs? How have U.S. Supreme Court decisions limited federal asset seizures? Do you agree that such limitations were necessary? Why or why not?
5. How is prostitution like other crimes? How does it differ?
6. Do you think that prostitution should be legalized? Why or why not?

Rex Features via AP Images

CHAPTER 14

TECHNOLOGY AND CRIME

LEARNING OUTCOMES

After reading this chapter, you should be able to answer the following questions:

- How does advancing technology produce new forms of crime?
- How does high technology provide new criminal opportunities?
- What is the extent of cybercrime today?
- What different types of cybercriminals does this chapter describe?
- What new technologies are being used in today's fight against crime?
- What is being done to combat cybercrime and to secure the Internet today?
- What are some of the personal freedoms that are threatened by today's need for advanced security?

Introduction

On January 20, 2012, New Zealand police broke into the mega-mansion of ex-German national Kim Dotcom.[1] Dotcom, 38, whose given name is Kim Schmitz, is founder of the Internet piracy Web site Megaupload.com—a site that U.S. officials estimate cost legal copyright holders in this country at least $500 million in lost revenues. Megaupload, which is registered in Hong Kong, was reported to have 150 million registered users and 50 million daily visitors. The site, which accounted for 4% of all daily traffic on the Web,[2] illegally made music, videos, PDFs, and other copyrighted files available to anyone willing to pay a small fee. Those fees, however, along with money spent on advertisements posted to the site, added up, and authorities estimate that Dotcom earned hundreds of millions of dollars from his illegal operations, including $42 million in 2010 alone.

When police arrived at his $30 million mansion, one of the largest private homes in New Zealand, the 6-foot, 7-inch 300-pound Dotcom locked them out using high-tech electronic security devices and fled to a safe room stocked with weapons. More than 100 officers, many with special equipment, were needed to extract him and to place him under arrest.

EPA/Alamy

The New Zealand home of Mega-upload founder Kim Dotcom.
What were Dotcom's crimes?

The Advance of Technology

Technology and crime have always been closely linked.

Technology and crime have always been closely linked. The con artist who uses a telephone in a financial scam, the robber who uses a firearm and drives a getaway car, even the murderer who wields a knife—all employ at least rudimentary forms of technology in the crimes they commit. Technology can be employed by both crime fighters and lawbreakers. Early forms of technology, including the telegraph, telephone, and automobile, were embraced by agents of law enforcement as soon as they became available. Evidence derived from fingerprint and ballistics analysis is routinely employed by prosecutors; and emerging technologies promise to keep criminologists and law enforcement agents in step with high-tech offenders.

As technology advances, it facilitates new forms of behavior, so we can be certain that tomorrow's crimes will differ from those of today. Personal crimes of violence and traditional property crimes will continue to occur, but advancing technology will create new and as-yet-unimaginable opportunities for criminals and other international actors positioned to take advantage of it and of the power it will afford.

A frightening preview of such possibilities was seen during the collapse of the Soviet Union when the resulting social disorganization made the acquisition of fissionable materials, stolen from Soviet stockpiles, simple for even relatively small outlaw organizations. In what is a nightmare for authorities throughout the world, Middle Eastern terrorist groups are making forceful efforts to acquire former Soviet nuclear weapons and the raw materials necessary to manufacture their own bombs, and some evidence suggests that nuclear weapons parts may have already been sold to wealthy international drug cartels and organized criminal groups, who could hoard them to use as bargaining chips against possible government prosecution.

More recently, in 2012 and 2013, the Obama administration identified the Chinese military as the source of cyberintrusions into public and private Web sites throughout the United States, and the 2013 Verizon Data Breach Investigations Report found that "state-affiliated actors tied to China are the biggest mover in 2012. Their efforts to steal IP" addresses, the report said, "comprise about one-fifth of all breaches" covered by the report.[3] About the same time, U.S. defense officials announced that hackers linked to China's government broke into an American computer system used to send commands to nuclear weapons.[4] In response, the Obama administration began efforts in 2013 to combat the persistent Chinese cyberespionage campaign.[5]

■ **hacker** A person who uses computers for exploration and exploitation.

■ **cybercrime** Any crime that involves the use of computers or the manipulation of digital data as well as any violation of a federal or state cybercrime statute.

The New York Times building in New York City. In 2013, the *Times* alleged that Chinese military hackers had infiltrated several of its computers. What is cybercrime?

High Technology and Criminal Opportunity

The twenty-first century has been termed the postindustrial information age. Information is vital to the success of any endeavor, and certain forms of information hold nearly incalculable value for those who possess it. Patents on new products, pharmaceutical formulations, corporate strategies, and the financial resources of corporations all represent competitive and corporate trade secrets. Government databases, if infiltrated, can offer terrorists easy paths to destruction and mayhem.

Some criminal perpetrators intend simply to destroy or alter data without otherwise accessing or copying the information. Disgruntled employees, mischievous computer **hackers**, business competitors, and others may have varied degrees of interest in destroying the records or computer capabilities of others.

High-tech criminals seeking illegitimate access to computerized information take a number of routes. One is the path of direct access, wherein office workers or corporate spies, planted as seemingly innocuous employees, use otherwise legitimate work-related entry to a company's computer resources to acquire wanted information.

Another path of illegal access, called *computer trespass*, involves remote access to targeted machines. Anyone equipped with a computer and Internet access has potential access to numerous computer systems. Many such systems have few, if any, security procedures in place. Similarly, electromagnetic field (EMF) decoders can scan radio frequency emanations generated by all types of computers. Keystroke activity, internal chip-processed computations, and disk reads, for example, can be detected and interpreted at a distance by such sophisticated devices. Computers secured against such passively invasive practices are rarely found in the commercial marketplace, although the military had adopted them for many applications. Within the last decade, wireless networking has heightened fears of data theft, and cell phones, handheld devices, and other forms of radio communication offer opportunities for data interception.

The realities of today's digital world have led to a relatively new form of crime, called cybercrime, and to new laws intended to combat it. Simply put, **cybercrime**, or *computer crime*, is any violation of a federal or state computer-crime statute. Many argue that only those crimes that use computer technology as central to their commission may properly be called "cybercrimes." However, a number of other kinds of offenses can also be described as cybercrimes.[6] A Federal Bureau of Investigation (FBI) typology distinguishes between five types of cybercrimes: (1) internal cybercrimes, such as viruses; (2) Internet and telecommunications crimes, including illegal hacking; (3) support of criminal enterprises, such as databases supporting drug distribution; (4) computer-manipulation crimes, such as embezzlement; and (5) hardware, software, and information theft.[7] Table 14–1 lists these five categories, with additional examples of each. Learn more about cybercrime typologies by reading **Library Extra 14–1**.

The person most likely to invade your computer is currently on your payroll.

When discussing cybercrime, it is important to realize that a huge number of today's financial transactions are computerized. Although most people probably think of money as bills and coins, money today is really just information—information stored in a computer network, possibly located within the physical confines of a bank, but more likely existing as bits and bytes of data on service providers' machines. Typical financial customers give little thought to the fact that very little "real" money is held by their bank, brokerage house, mutual fund, or commodities dealer. Nor do they often consider the threats to their financial well-being by activities such as electronic theft or the sabotage of existing accounts. Unfortunately, however, the threat is very

■ **software piracy** The unauthorized and illegal copying of software programs.

TABLE 14-1 Categories of Cybercrime
Internal Cybercrimes (Malware)
Trojan horses
Logic bombs
Trap doors
Viruses
Internet and Telecommunications Crimes
Phone phreaking
Hacking
Denial of service attacks
Illegal websites
Dissemination of illegal material (for example, child pornography)
Misuse of telecommunications systems
Theft of telecommunications services
Illegal eavesdropping
Illegal Internet-based gambling
Support of Criminal Enterprises
Databases to support drug distribution
Databases to support loan-sharking
Databases to support illegal gambling
Databases to keep records of illegal client transactions
Electronic money laundering
Communications in furtherance of criminal conspiracies
Computer-Manipulation Crimes
Embezzlement
Electronic fund transfer fraud
Other fraud/phishing
Extortion threats/electronic terrorism
Hardware, Software, and Information Theft
Software piracy (warez)
Thefts of computers
Thefts of microprocessor chips
Thefts of trade secrets and proprietary information
Identity theft

real. Computer criminals equipped with enough information (or able to find the data they need) can quickly and easily locate, steal, and send vast amounts of money anywhere in the world.

No reliable estimates exist as to the losses suffered in such transactions due to the activities of technologically adept criminal perpetrators. Accurate estimates are lacking largely because sophisticated high-tech thieves are so effective at eluding apprehension.

The Extent of Cybercrime

A recent estimate by the U.S. Secret Service in conjunction with the CERT Cybersecurity Center puts the annual cost of cybercrime in the United States at around $666 million.[8] The 2011 CSO (Chief Security Officer) Cyber Security Watch Survey, a cooperative effort between the U.S. Secret Service, Deloitte & Touche, Carnegie Mellon's Software Engineering Institute (CERT), and *CSO* magazine, found that a sophisticated cybercrime-fueled underground economy exists in America and that its members continue to develop a sophisticated arsenal of damaging software tools with which most companies cannot keep pace while remaining focused on their core businesses. At about the same time, a white paper entitled *Cyber Crime: A Clear and Present Danger* was released by Deloitte & Touche's Center for Security & Privacy Solutions. The paper pointed out the following facts:

- Cybercrime is now serious, widespread, aggressive, growing, and increasingly sophisticated, and it poses major implications for national and economic security.
- Many industries and institutions and public- and private-sector organizations (particularly those within the critical infrastructure) are at significant risk.
- Relatively few organizations have recognized organized cybercriminal networks (instead of hackers) as their greatest potential cybersecurity threat; even fewer are prepared to address this threat.
- Cyberattacks and security breaches are increasing in frequency and sophistication, with discovery usually occurring only after the fact, if at all.
- Current perimeter-intrusion detection, signature-based malware, and antivirus solutions are providing little defense and are rapidly becoming obsolete.
- Effective deterrents to cybercrime are not known, available, or accessible to many practitioners, many of whom underestimate the scope and severity of the problem.
- There is a likely nexus between cybercrime and a variety of other threats, including terrorism, industrial espionage, and foreign intelligence services.[9]

Another industry group, the Computer Security Institute (CSI), surveyed 351 business organizations and found that computer crime cost most companies an average of less than $100,000 in 2010; although two companies lost much more than that—$20 million in one case and more than $25 million in another.[10] **Software piracy**, or the unauthorized and illegal copying of software, is rampant. According to the Business Software Alliance, global losses from pirated software (known as *warez* in the computer underground) totaled $59 billion in 2010.[11] The Alliance found that 42% of all personal computer (PC) software installed in 2010 was pirated. The problem is worse in certain countries. In the European country of Georgia, for example, it is estimated that 93% of all software used there has been illegally copied.

■ **phishing** An Internet-based scam to steal valuable information such as credit card numbers, Social Security numbers, user IDs, and passwords.

William S. Speer/Bloomberg News

Dr. Ali-Reza Ghasemi and his wife, Shahla Ghasemi, of Tampa (Florida). They lost $400,000 to an advance fee scheme on the Internet. Advance fee schemes (often called Nigerian e-mail fraud because many of the messages appear to come from Nigeria) promise victims a lot of money in return for advancing fees to cover legal services and transfer of funds. How can you tell when an e-mail message is likely to be a fraud?

Phishing (pronounced "fishing") is a relatively new scam that uses official-looking e-mail to steal valuable information such as credit card numbers, Social Security numbers, user IDs, and passwords from victims. The e-mails appear to come from a user's bank, credit card company, retail store, or Internet service provider (ISP) and generally inform the recipients that some vital information in their account urgently needs to be updated. Those who respond are provided with an official-looking Web form on which they can enter their private financial information. Once the information is submitted, it enters the phisher's database.

The Anti-Phishing Working Group (APWG), a coalition of banks and ISPs, says that a typical phishing scheme reaches up to 1 million e-mail in-boxes. The watchdog group had identified more than 38,000 different phishing websites that were still in operation as of March 2011.[12] Figure 14–1 shows the number of unique phishing sites the APWG detected during the first part of 2013. Although servers that run those sites can be anywhere in the world, the APGW found that more than 50% of them are located in the United States.

Phishing sites often attempt to hijack brand names, and some phishers are capable of sending e-mails that are difficult to distinguish from legitimate ones. When that happens and customers respond to those e-mails in significant numbers, a brand (such as the name of a bank or credit card company) is said to have been hijacked. Figure 14–2 shows the number of hijacked brands by month during the first half of 2013. Some observers have noted that in addition to losses suffered by individuals and institutions, phishing has the potential to threaten the viability of e-commerce and to call into question the safety of all Web-based financial transactions.[13]

Phishing has the potential to threaten the viability of e-commerce and to call into question the safety of all Web-based financial transactions.

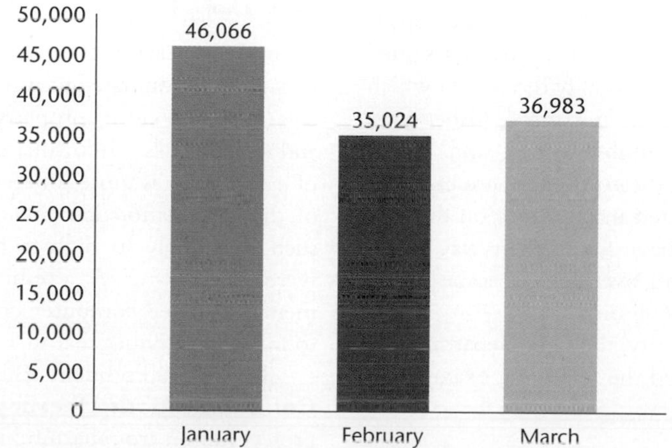

FIGURE 14–1 | **Unique Phishing Web Sites by Month, January–March 2013**

Source: Unique Phishing Websites by Month from The Anti-Phishing Working Group, *Phishing Activity Trends Report. 1st Half.* Copyright © 2011 by APWG. Used by permission of APWG..

■ **computer virus** A set of computer instructions that propagates copies or versions of itself into computer programs or data when it is executed.

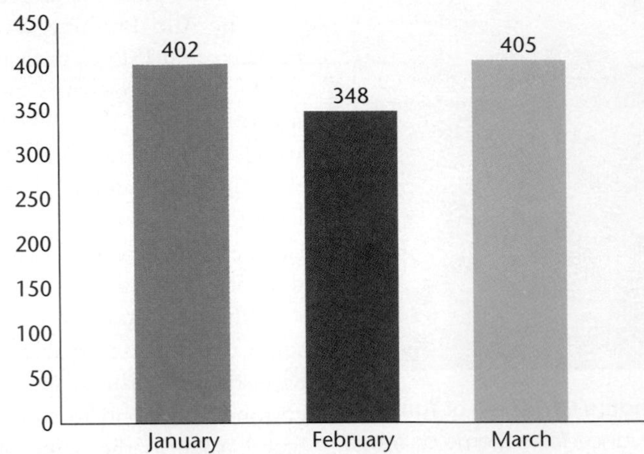

FIGURE 14–2 | **Hijacked Brands by Month, January–March, 2013**

Source: Hijacked Brands by Month from The Anti-Phishing Working Group, *Phishing Activity Trends Report: 1st Half.* Copyright © 2011 by APWG. Used by permission of APWG.

Not all cybercrime is committed for financial gain. Some types of computer crime, including the creation and transmission of destructive computer viruses, "worms," spyware, and other malicious forms of programming code (often called *malware*), might better be classified as "criminal mischief." Perhaps not surprisingly, these types of activities are typically associated with young, technologically sophisticated male miscreants seeking a kind of clandestine recognition from their computer-savvy peers. Computer crimes committed by youthful and idealistic offenders may represent a novel form of juvenile delinquency—one aimed at expressing dissatisfaction with the status quo.

Computer viruses have shown signs of becoming effective terrorist-like tools in the hands of young, disaffected "technonerds" intent on attacking or destroying existing social institutions. A **computer virus** is a computer program that is designed to secretly invade computer systems to modify the way in which they operate or to alter the information they store.[14] Other types of destructive programs are logic bombs, worms, and Trojan horse routines. Distinctions among these programs are based on the way in which they infect targeted machines or on the way in which they behave once they have found their way into a computer. Figure 14–3 provides an overview of some of the most damaging computer viruses of all time.

In a recent report on cybersecurity, the U.S. Department of Homeland Security (DHS) provided the following examples of damage caused by malware:[15]

- Symantec Corporation, maker of computer security software, reports that more than 15,000 new types of malware are entering networks worldwide every day.
- *Consumer Reports* estimates that U.S. consumers lost $8.5 billion and replaced 2.1 million computers because of viruses, spyware, and other forms of malware between 2006 and 2008.

Significant government cybersecurity reports (all of which can be accessed at http://www.cyber.st.dhs.gov) are shown in Figure 14–4. Learn more about botnets, computer viruses, and malware at **Web Extra 14–1**.

Cybercrime and the Law

In the early years of computer-based information systems, most U.S. jurisdictions tried to prosecute unauthorized computer access under preexisting property crime statutes, including burglary and larceny laws. Unfortunately, because the actual carrying off of a computer is quite different from copying or altering some of the information it contains, juries were confused by how such laws apply to high-tech crimes and computer criminals were often let free. As a result, all states and the federal government developed computer-crime statutes specifically applicable to invasive activities that illegally access stored information.

In 1996, President Bill Clinton signed into law the **Communications Decency Act (CDA)**,[16] which sought to protect minors from harmful material on the Internet. A portion of the CDA criminalized the knowing transmission of obscene or indecent messages to any recipient under 18 years of age. Another section prohibited the knowing sending or displaying to

■ **Communications Decency Act (CDA)** A federal statute labeled Title 5 of the federal Telecommunications Act of 1996 (Public Law 104–104, 110 Stat. 56) that seeks to protect minors from harmful material on the Internet and that criminalizes the knowing transmission of obscene or indecent messages to any recipient under 18 years of age. In 1997, in *Reno* v. *ACLU* (521 U.S. 844), the U.S. Supreme Court found the bulk of the CDA to be unconstitutional, ruling that it contravenes First Amendment free speech guarantees.

■ **No Electronic Theft Act (NETA)** A 1997 federal law (Public Law 105–147) that criminalizes the willful infringement of copyrighted works, including by electronic means, even when the infringing party derives no direct financial benefit from the infringement (such as when pirated software is freely distributed online).

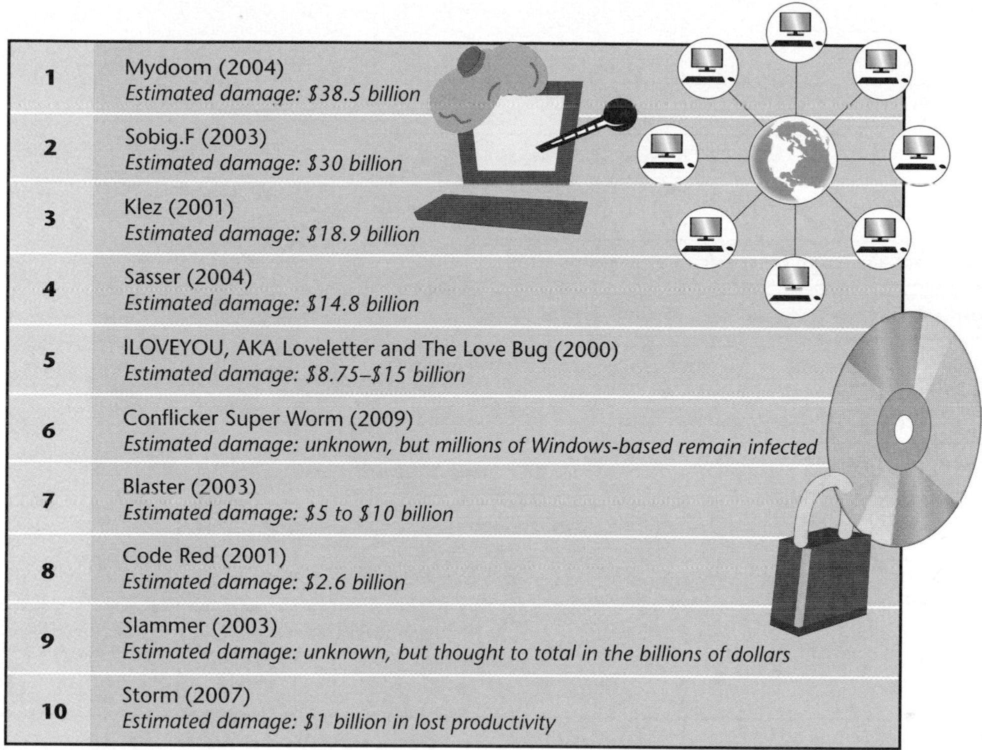

FIGURE 14-3 | **The Ten Most Damaging Computer Viruses and Worms of All Time**

Sources: *Smithsonian Magazine*, "Top Ten Most-Destructive Computer Viruses," http://www.smithsonianmag.com/science-nature/Top-Ten-Most-Destructive-Computer-Viruses.html#ixzz2SNIYZ0Tz (accessed May 10, 2013); PC Security World, "Most Notorious Computer Virus, Worms of All Time," http://forum.pcsecurityworld.com/showthread.php?tid=233 (accessed February 8, 2013); Buzzle.com, "The Most Damage Causing Computer Viruses Revealed," http://www.buzzle.com/articles/the-most-damage-causing-computer-viruses-revealed.html (accessed October 22, 2013); Christopher Null, "The Worst Computer Viruses of All Time," Yahoo! Tech, http://tech.yahoo.com/blogs/null (accessed October 22, 2011); and George Jones, "The 10 Most Destructive PC Viruses of All Time," Tech Web, July 5, 2006, http://www.techweb.com/tech/160200005 (accessed June 26, 2012).

a person under 18 any message "that, in context, depicts or describes, in terms patently offensive as measured by contemporary community standards, sexual or excretory activities or organs." Shortly after the law was passed, however, the American Civil Liberties Union (ACLU) and a number of other plaintiffs filed suit against the federal government, challenging the constitutionality of the law's two provisions relating to the transmission of obscene materials to minors.

In 1996, a three-judge federal district court entered a preliminary injunction against enforcement of both challenged provisions, ruling that they contravened First Amendment guarantees of free speech. The government then appealed to the U.S. Supreme Court. The Court's 1997 decision *Reno* v. *ACLU*[17] upheld the lower court's ruling and found that the CDA's "indecent transmission" and "patently offensive display" provisions abridge "the freedom of speech" protected by the First Amendment. Most other federal legislation aimed at keeping online pornography away from the eyes of children has not fared any better when reviewed by the Court. Although the Children's Internet Protection Act (CIPA), which requires public and school libraries receiving certain kinds of federal funding to install pornography filters on their Internet-linked computers, was approved by the justices, most observers acknowledge that the Court has placed the Internet in the same category as newspapers and other print media, where almost no regulation is permitted.

Enacted in 1997, the **No Electronic Theft Act (NETA, or NET Act)** criminalizes the willful infringement of copyrighted works, including by electronic means, even when the infringing party derives no direct financial benefit from the infringement (such as when pirated software is freely distributed

■ **Digital Theft Deterrence and Copyright Damages Improvement Act** A 1999 federal law (Public Law 106–160) that amends Section 504(c) of the Copyright Act by increasing the amount of damages that could be awarded in cases of copyright infringement.

■ **Cyber Security Enhancement Act (CSEA)** A federal law found in the Homeland Security Act of 2002 that directs the U.S. Sentencing Commission to take specific factors into account in creating new sentencing guidelines for cybercriminals.

■ **computer-related crime** An illegal act using computer technology in its perpetration, investigation, or prosecution.

■ **computer abuse** An unlawful incident associated with computer technology in which a victim suffers loss or a perpetrator reaps benefit.

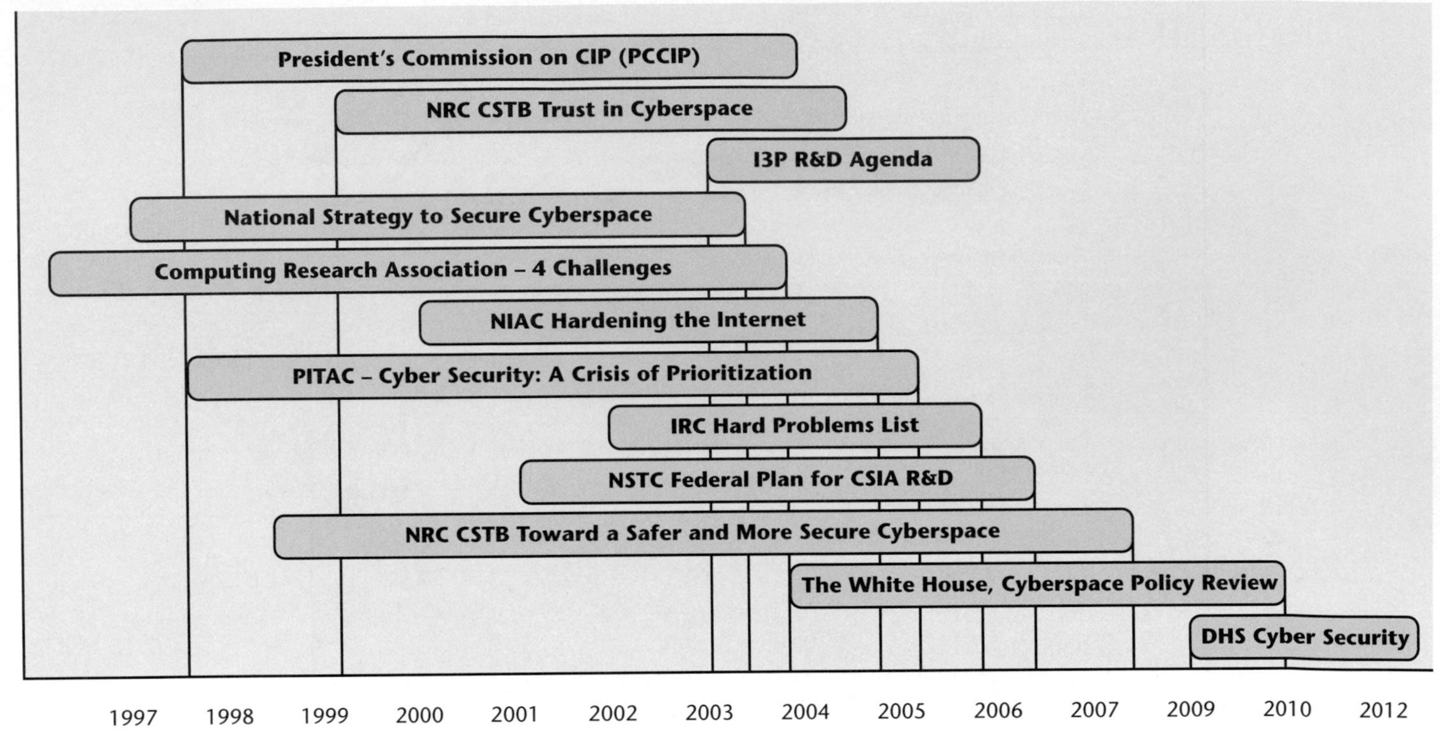

FIGURE 14-4 | Timeline of Federal Research Reports on Cybercrime

Source: Adapted from Kevin Thompson, *Cyber Security* (Washington, DC: U.S. Department of Homeland Security—Command, Control and Interoperability Division, June 24, 2009), p. 23; and Department of Homeland Security, Cyber Security Research and Development Center, "Recent News," http://www.cyber.st.dhs.gov (accessed March 12, 2013).

online). In keeping with requirements of the NETA, the U.S. Sentencing Commission enacted amendments to its guidelines to increase penalties associated with electronic theft. The **Digital Theft Deterrence and Copyright Damages Improvement Act** of 1999 increased the amount of damages that could be awarded in cases of copyright infringement—a crime that is intimately associated with software piracy. The **Cyber Security Enhancement Act (CSEA)** of 2002,[18] which is part of the Homeland Security Act of 2002, directed the U.S. Sentencing Commission to take several factors into account in creating new sentencing guidelines for computer criminals. The law told the commission to consider not only what financial loss was caused by computer crime, but also what level of planning was involved in the offense, whether the crime was committed for commercial or private advantage, and whether malicious intent existed on the part of the perpetrator. Under the law, computer criminals can face life in prison if they put human lives in jeopardy. Certain future illegitimate activities using computer equipment may not be adequately covered by existing law. On the other hand, some crimes committed with the use of a computer may be more appropriately prosecuted under "traditional" laws. For that reason, some experts distinguish between computer crime, computer-related crime, and computer abuse. **Computer-related crime** is "any illegal act for which knowledge of computer

Money today is really only information stored in a computer network as bits and bytes of data.

■ **phone phreak** A person who uses switched, dialed-access telephone services for exploration and exploitation.

technology is involved for its investigation, perpetration, or prosecution," whereas **computer abuse** is said to be "any incident without color of right associated with computer technology in which a victim suffered or could have suffered loss and/or a perpetrator by intention made or could have made gain."[19]

The History and Nature of Hacking

Some authors suggest that computer hacking began with the creation of the interstate phone system and direct distance dialing implemented by AT&T in the late 1950s.[20] Early switching devices used audible tones that were easily duplicated by electronics hobbyists, and "blue boxes" capable of emulating such tones quickly entered the illicit marketplace. **Phone phreaks** used special telecommunications access codes and other restricted technical information to avoid paying long-distance charges. Some were able to place calls from pay phones, and others fooled telephone equipment into billing other callers.

A modern form of phone phreaking involves the electronic theft of cellular telephone numbers and access codes. Thieves armed with simple mail-order scanners and low-end computers can "literally grab a caller's phone number and identification number out of the air."[21] Say experts, "Those numbers are [then] used to program computer chips, which are placed inside other cellular phones—or 'clones'—so the long-distance calls appear on the victim's bill."[22] Such high-profile figures as former New York Mayor Rudolph Giuliani and his police commissioner have been among the victims of cellular phone piracy.

Another form of illegal telephone access that has recently become popular is voice-mail hacking. Private voice-mail boxes have become the targets of corporate raiders and young vandals alike. In a recent case, two New York City teenage brothers caused an estimated $2.4 million in lost business by gaining illegal access to the New Hampshire–based International Data Group's voice-mail system. Security experts at the company, who first thought the mailboxes were malfunctioning, were alerted to the intentional disruptions by obscene outgoing messages planted by the brothers that greeted unsuspecting callers.[23]

Voice-mail fraud, another form of telephone crime, involves schemes in which mailbox access codes are shared in such a way that callers to toll-free numbers can leave messages for one another in voice-mail boxes, thereby avoiding personal long-distance charges.[24] Companies that provide access to voice-mail systems through toll-free numbers often learn of the need for access-code security only after they have been victimized by such schemes. See **Library Extra 14–2** for a discussion of self-defense in cyberspace.

A Profile of Cybercriminals

In November 2012, a federal grand jury in New Hampshire returned an indictment charging Anil Kheda, 24, of the Netherlands, with conspiring to hack into and disable computer servers belonging to Rampid Interactive, a New Hampshire–based company that publishes and hosts a multiplayer online role-playing game called "Outwar."[25] Kheda was charged with the federal crimes of conspiring to commit computer intrusion and one count of interstate extortion.

The indictment alleges that from November 2007 to August 2008, Kheda and other members of the conspiracy, all of whom were avid "Outwar" players, accessed Rampid's computer servers without authorization and rendered "Outwar" unplayable for days at a time. According to the indictment, Kheda and his alleged co-conspirators also used their unauthorized access to Rampid's servers to alter user accounts—causing the restoration of suspended player accounts and the accrual of unearned game points—and to obtain a copy of all or portions of the "Outwar" computer source code, which they used to help create a competitor online game, "Outcraft." The indictment also alleges that Kheda and his alleged co-conspirators sent Rampid interstate e-mail communications threatening to continue to hack into Rampid's computer systems unless Rampid agreed to pay them money.

The indictment says that, as a result of the defendants' hacking activities, Rampid was unable to operate "Outwar" for a total of approximately two weeks over a nine-month period and incurred over $100,000 in lost revenues, wages, hosting costs, long-term loss of business, as well as the loss of exclusive use of their proprietary source code, which it had invested approximately $1.5 million in creating.

According to court documents, Kheda earned approximately $10,000 in profits from operating "Outcraft," which has approximately 10,000 players worldwide. If convicted, Kheda faces a maximum sentence of five years in prison on the conspiracy charge and two years in prison on the interstate threats charge.

The indictment of Anil Kheda illustrates both the potential for high-technology offenders to thwart government efforts at prosecution by operating internationally as well as the transnational nature of hacker subculture. It is from hacker subculture

■ **cyberspace** The computer-created matrix of virtual possibilities, including online services, in which human beings interact with one another and with the technology itself.

CRIME | in the NEWS

Cyberbanging

In 2010 a new term, *cyberbanging*—referring to the use of the Internet and social networking Web sites by street gangs to tout their exploits, recruit new members, post threats, and socialize—entered the law enforcement lexicon. Videos and lyrics glorifying gang activities can be found on Facebook, MySpace, and Twitter, and some gangs have their own home pages and even run their own servers. "Gangs are going to use any form of communication they can," stated George W. Knox, director of the National Gang Crime Research Center, "including Twitter, including Facebook." Law enforcement experts have said that gangs sometimes use social networking sites to circumvent court injunctions forbidding members from meeting face-to-face.

A 2013 study of Internet gang activity, however, found that gangs are not using the Web to recruit new members or to commit cybercrimes. Instead, they "are doing online what they are doing on the street," the study found. That means that they are using sites like Facebook, Twitter, and YouTube for self-promotion, bragging, and making territorial claims. According to study authors, the virtual world is viewed by gang members as another territory, or turf, on which to post electronic graffiti, gang signs, and images. The study was based on interviews with 585 young adult gang members from five cities.

Police agencies and criminal prosecutors have begun scouring social networking sites looking for evidence they can use to disrupt gang activities or to prosecute gang members for crimes they've committed. "Five years ago we would find evidence in a gang case on the Internet and say, 'Wow!'" Bruce Riordan, director of antigang operations for the Los Angeles City Attorney's office commented. "Well, there's no more 'Wow' anymore. It's much more routine."

Discussion Questions

1. What is cyberbanging? What purpose does it serve?
2. Can you imagine any new and innovative ways in which gangs might make use of the Internet and social media?

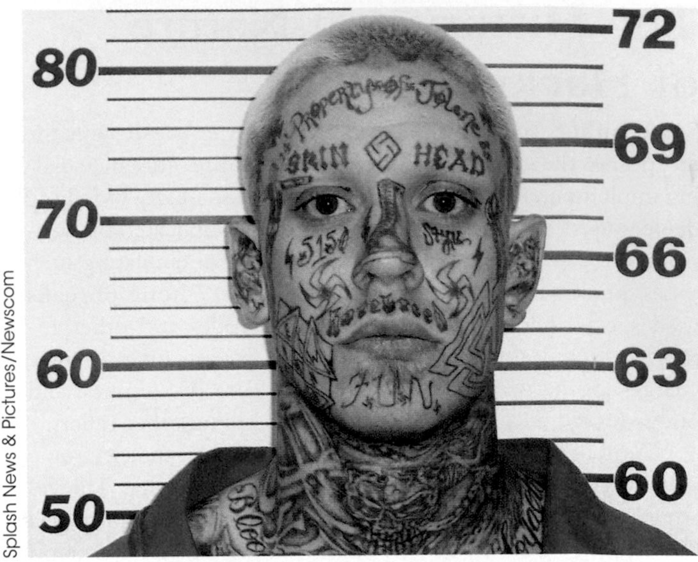

Splash News & Pictures/Newscom

A prisoner charged with murdering a corrections officer who took him to a hospital appointment in Utah. Curtis Allgier, a neo-Nazi affiliated with the Aryan Brotherhood, is alleged to have wrestled the guard's gun from him and shot him; he then carjacked a vehicle and led police on a chase before being apprehended. Why are street gangs turning to the Internet?

Sources: Tony Castro, "Valley Gangs Leave Trail on Web," *Los Angeles Daily News*, December 5, 2009, http://www.dailynews.com/news/ci_13931149 (accessed May 12, 2012); "Study Explores Gang Activity on the Internet," Science Codex, March 26, 2013, http://www.sciencecodex.com/study_explores_gang_activity_on_the_internet-109243 (accessed May 22, 2013); and David C. Pyrooz, Scott H. Decker, and Richard K. Moule, "Criminal and Routine Activities in Online Settings: Gangs, Offenders, and the Internet," *Justice Quarterly*, Spring 2013.

that cybercriminals tend to come because hackers and hacker identities are the products of **cyberspace**, a realm that exists only within electronic networks where computer technology and human psychology meet. For many hackers, cyberspace provides the opportunity for impersonal interpersonal contact, technological challenges, and game playing. Fantasy role-playing games are popular among hackers and may engross many "wave riders," who appear to prefer what is called "virtual reality" to the external physical and social worlds around them: "Cyberspace is hacker heaven."[26]

No one knows the actual identity of many of these people, but computer-security experts have come up with a rough profile of the average hacker.[27] He is a male between the ages of 16 and 25 who lives in the United States, is a computer user but not a programmer, and hacks with software written by others; his primary motivation is to gain access to Web sites and computer networks, not to profit financially (see the Who's to Blame box).

Hackers can be distinguished both by their purpose and by their method of operation, but such categorization is descriptive; distinctions can also be made on the basis of personality

WHO'S TO BLAME—The Individual or Society?

Criminal Activity or Mischievous Gaming?

Late in 2012, Kelvin Mutchnak was arrested and charged under federal law with interfering with the operation of computers owned by the federal government. The computers, mostly Apple iMacs, ran Apple's latest operating system, popularly referred to as Mac OS X Mountain Lion, and were located in Veterans Administration (VA) hospitals across the country.

Mutchnak was especially taken with the long-standing popular impression that Apple's operating system was secure and impenetrable—a myth that computer hackers had long known was untrue, but that Apple corporate officials had done little to dispel. The feeling of those who worked for Apple, Mutchnak concluded, was that the popular myth could help sell computers. Nonetheless, most hackers continued to focus their efforts on Microsoft's Windows operating system because of its greater popularity, and because it was easier to hack. After the advent of Windows Vista in 2006, however, and with the introduction of Macintosh computers able to dual-boot both Vista and OS X, and able to run both simultaneously, attention in the hacker community had increasingly turned to identifying backdoors into the Apple operating system.

Soon Mutchnak was devoting all of his spare time to dispelling Apple's myth of invincibility, and to writing malware—malicious software code—that could successfully invade almost any of Apple's higher-end computers that were connected to the Internet.

After writing a malicious script that he could insert into a tiny QuickTime video, Mutchnak sent the video as an e-mail attachment to VA hospital computers, making the e-mail look as though it contained administrative data that would be of significance to people in charge of the facilities. Although the e-mail had to be opened and the video file clicked on, and although the person reading the e-mail had to be logged in under an administrative account (most, he found, were), Mutchnak's plan was very successful, and soon most Apple computers in federally run hospitals across the country were infected. Unfortunately for Mutchnak, however, federal anticyberterrorism officials had been running a drill responding to a mock cyberterrorism attack when his e-mail made its way onto the Net. Within minutes of its release, Mutchnak's malicious e-mail had been traced to the IP address assigned to his home by his ISP.

A warrant for his arrest was drawn up, and Mutchnak was arrested by federal agents who charged him with violating various federal computer crime laws, including one meant to deter terrorists.

Think about it

1. Do you believe that Mutchnak saw his activity as criminal? As terrorist activity? If not, how did he perceive it?
2. Was Mutchnak, as he claimed, doing a service by showing weaknesses in parts of the nation's computer infrastructure?
3. Might there have been other ways for Mutchnak to make his point? Would those ways have been as effective as the computer mischief in which he engaged? Why or why not?

Note: Who's to Blame boxes provide fictionalized critical thinking opportunities, and are not actual cases.

and lifestyle. Some experts have suggested that hackers can be grouped according to psychological characteristics:[28]

- **Pioneers.** Individuals who are fascinated by the evolving technology of telecommunications and explore it without knowing exactly what they are going to find are called pioneers; few hard-core criminals are found among this group.
- **Scamps.** Hackers with a sense of fun, with no intention to harm, are referred to as scamps.
- **Explorers.** Explorers are hackers motivated by their delight in discoveries associated with breaking into new computer systems—the farther away geographically such systems are from the hackers' physical locations or the more secure such systems are, the greater the excitement associated with breaking into them.
- **Game players.** Game players enjoy defeating software or system copy protection and may seek to illegally access computer systems with games to play. Hacking itself becomes a game for this sort of hacker.
- **Vandals.** Malicious hackers who deliberately cause damage with no apparent gain for themselves are called vandals. The original 414 Gang in Milwaukee, which broke into the Sloan-Kettering Cancer Institute's computers and wiped out patient records, is an example of this type of hacker.

- **Addicts.** Classic computer nerds who are addicted to hacking and to computer technology are addicts. They may also be addicted to illicit drugs (some hacker bulletin board systems post information on drugs as well as on modems, passwords, and vulnerable systems).

Psychologist Percy Black argued for the existence of an underlying theme in all cases of hacking, calling it "the search for a feeling of power, possibly stemming from a deep-seated sense of powerlessness."[29] Hacking may serve as compensation for feelings of personal inferiority; by challenging the machine and by winning against machine culture, hackers go through a kind of rite of passage into adulthood, whereby they prove themselves capable of success.

Because most hackers are young adolescent males, it is important to realize that "their other favorite risky business is the time-honored adolescent sport of trespassing. They insist on going where they don't belong. But then teen-age boys have been proceeding uninvited since the dawn of human puberty. It seems hard-wired. The only innovation is in the new form of the forbidden zone and the means of getting in it."[30]

Unfortunately, not all computer hackers are simply kids trying their hand at beating technological challenges. Many are "high-tech computer operators using computers to engage in unlawful conduct."[31] Learn more about hackers and information security at the CERT Coordination Center, which can be reached via **Web Extra 14–2**.

Cybercrime as a Form of White-Collar Crime

Numerous analysts have suggested that cybercrime is merely a new form of white-collar crime or maybe its ultimate expression (white-collar crime is discussed in detail in Chapter 12). Donn B. Parker, author of the National Institute of Justice (NIJ) *Computer Crime: Criminal Justice Research Manual*, compared white-collar criminals with computer criminals, stating that both share certain "common criminal behavior-related issues":[32]

- Both types of acts are often committed through nonviolent means, although certain industrial, consumer, and environment-related crimes have life-threatening consequences.
- Access to computers or computer storage media, through employment-related knowledge or technical skills, is often needed.
- These acts generally involve information manipulations that either directly or indirectly create profits or losses.
- These crimes can be committed by an individual, by several individuals working in collusion, or by organizations, with the victims in the last case ranging from individual clients to customers to employees in other organizations.

See the Criminal Profiles box for the story of a convicted hacker who became an author.

According to Parker, cybercrime and white-collar crime also share the following similarities:

- These crimes are difficult to detect, with discovery often started by accident or by customer complaint rather than as the result of direct investigation.
- The general public views many of these acts as less serious than crimes involving physical violence.
- These crimes cost individuals, organizations, and society large amounts of money and other resources.
- Prevention of these crimes requires a combination of legal, technical, managerial, security, and audit-monitoring controls.

Technology in the Fight Against Crime

Technology is a double-edged sword: It arms evildoers with potent new weapons of crime commission, yet it provides police agencies and criminal justice personnel with powerful tools useful in the battle against crime. Criminally useful or evasive technologies and law enforcement capabilities commonly leapfrog one another. Consider traffic radar, which has gone from early always-on units through trigger-operated radar devices to today's sophisticated laser-based speed-measuring apparatus—each change being an attempt by enforcement agencies to keep a step ahead of increasingly sophisticated radar-detection devices marketed to drivers. Radar-jamming devices and laser jammers are also now used by people apparently intent on breaking speed-limit laws. Not to be outdone, suppliers to law enforcement agencies have created radar-detector detectors, which are used by authorities in states where radar detectors have been outlawed.[33]

> Criminal technologies and law enforcement capabilities leapfrog one another.

Other potent technologies in law enforcement today are computer databases of known offenders (including public access to sex-offender databases), machine-based expert systems, cellular communications, video surveillance (often combined with face-recognition technology), electronic eavesdropping, deoxyribonucleic acid (DNA) analysis, and less-lethal weapons. Transponder-based automated vehicle location (AVL) systems now use patrol car–based transmitters in tandem with orbiting global positioning system (GPS) satellites to pinpoint locations of police vehicles to within 50 feet so that dispatchers can better allocate available resources on a given shift and be able to

CRIMINAL | PROFILES

Kevin Mitnick—Hacker Turned Security Expert

At the time of his arrest in February 1995, Kevin Mitnick was the most-wanted computer criminal in U.S. history. His crimes included wire fraud, computer fraud, and wire communication interception, and the cost to his victims included millions of dollars in lost licensing fees, marketing delays, lost research and development, and the costs of repairing compromised computer systems.[i]

Cloned cellular telephones, hacker software programs, "sniffer" devices, and so-called social engineering were the tools Mitnick used to conduct the computer crime spree that launched a lengthy investigation beginning in 1992. The evidence amassed by the FBI during its three-year probe was sufficient to force Mitnick to accept a plea bargain rather than risk more severe penalties by going to trial.[ii] His corporate victims included a number of Fortune 500 companies, and he used University of Southern California computer systems to hide software code and obscure his identity.

Born August 6, 1963, and a product of a blue-collar upbringing in California's San Fernando Valley, Mitnick's 1981 juvenile arrest for stealing computer manuals led to his being placed on probation. The experience had little deterrent effect, however, as evidenced by his subsequent arrests in 1989 (for possession of unauthorized access devices) and in 1992 (for allegedly hacking into California Department of Motor Vehicles computers).[iii]

An intriguing element of Mitnick's case was the manner in which he was finally caught. Computer expert Tsutomu Shimomura, infuriated after Mitnick hacked into and stole information from his home computer, employed a dramatic cybersleuthing effort to track Mitnick down, resulting in Mitnick's arrest by the FBI in a Raleigh, North Carolina, apartment complex.

As a result of his 1995 arrest, Mitnick spent more than five years in prison, with more than eight months of it in solitary confinement. Now, at 50-years-old a significantly matured Mitnick has done a 180-degree turnaround in his approach to computer security. On March 1, 2000, he testified before the U.S. Senate's Governmental Affairs Committee, during which he suggested that the millions of dollars corporations spend on firewalls and secure access devices are negated by the "the weakest link in the security chain: the people who use, administer and operate computer systems."[v] Mitnick regaled the committee with tales of his use of "social engineering" (what he defines as "using manipulation, influence, and deception to get a trusted insider to release information and to perform some sort of action item") that enables a hacker to successfully attack the insider's own computer system.

Mitnick now heads up a highly successful computer consulting firm that specializes in advising on computer security issues. He suggests that it is easier to hack today than it was years ago, citing social engineering as still an extraordinarily effective technique for computer exploit. Mitnick's message is clear: Notwithstanding tremendous advances in both hardware and software security measures, the weak link is still the human element.[vi]

Joe Cavaretta/AP Wide World Photos

Hacker-turned-author Kevin Mitnick posing for a portrait in 2002 in Las Vegas. Barred by the terms of his probation from using computers, ex-convict Mitnick turned to writing about them, baring the tricks of his former trade of hacking in a book titled *The Art of Deception*. Mitnick was granted an exemption to use a computer to write his book. What is he doing today?

The case of Kevin Mitnick raises a number of interesting questions. Among them are the following:

1. What theoretical perspectives might explain Mitnick's involvement in crime?
2. What was Mitnick's motivation to become involved in cybercrime?
3. What does Mitnick mean by "social engineering"? Does the concept of social engineering apply to other types of crimes?

Notes

i. "Kevin Mitnick Sentenced to Nearly Four Years in Prison," U.S. Department of Justice Press Release, August 9, 1999; and "Computer Hacker Ordered to Pay Restitution to Victim Companies Whose Systems Were Compromised," U.S. Attorney's Office, Central District of California, August 9, 1999, http://www.cybercrime.gov/mitnick.htm (accessed June 2, 2010).

ii. Ibid.

iii. John Christensen, "The Trials of Kevin Mitnick," CNN, March 18, 1999, http://www.cnn.com/SPECIALS/1999/mitnick.background (accessed June 2, 2010). It is said that Mitnick served as the inspiration for the 1983 film *War Games* by breaking into the U.S. Department of Defense's North American Defense Command (NORAD) computers in 1982.[iv]

iv. Ibid.

v. Elizabeth Wasserman, "Mitnick Schools Feds on Hacking 101," CNN, March 3, 2000, http://archives.cnn.com/2000/TECH/computing/03/03/mitnick.the.prof/mitnick.the.prof.html (accessed June 2, 2007).

vi. "A Convicted Hacker Debunks Some Myths," CNN, October 13, 2005, http://www.cnn.com/2005/TECH/internet/10/07/kevin.mitnick.cnna (accessed June 2, 2010).

■ **DNA profiling** The use of biological residue found at a crime scene for genetic comparisons in aiding the identification of criminal suspects.

substantially reduce police response times in crisis situations. (Chip-based transponders are also installed in private vehicles to deter thieves and to help trace stolen automobiles.)

In jurisdictions with computer-aided dispatch (CAD) systems, police dispatchers are prompted by computers for important information that allows them to distinguish a location (such as a particular McDonald's). CAD systems also quickly provide information about how often officers have been called to a given site and can tell responding officers what they might expect to find based on past calls from that location.

More innovative crime-fighting technologies are becoming available. The "Spiderman snare," being tested for its usefulness in incapacitating fleeing suspects, is a 16-foot-wide net that is compressed into a small shotgun-like shell. The net has small weights at its circumference and wraps itself around its target after being fired. The snare's impact is harmless, and test subjects report being able to watch with open eyes as the net wraps around them. Another example is a special-frequency disco-like strobe light which quickly disorients human targets by causing intense dizziness, leaving subjects unable to resist cuffing and arrest (operators wear special glasses designed to counter the influence of the light). Because high-speed chases pose a substantial danger to the public, scientists have developed an electromagnetic pulsing device that can be used to temporarily disable a vehicle's electrical system, causing the engine to stall. The prototype is said to be safe enough to use on vehicles driven by those wearing pacemakers.

As new technologies are developed, their potential usefulness in law enforcement activities is evaluated by the FBI, the NIJ, and other agencies. The NIJ's Technology Assessment Program (TAP) focuses on four areas of advancing technology: protective equipment, such as bulletproof vests and other body armor; forensic sciences, including advances in DNA technology; transportation and weapons, such as electronic stun guns and other less-lethal weapons; and communications and electronics, including computer security and electronic eavesdropping.

Recently, the U.S. Department of Justice's National Law Enforcement and Corrections Technology Center (NLECTC) began testing a high-power compact microwave source designed for vehicle immobilization.[34] The microwave beam emitted by the device can interfere with an automobile's computer circuitry, effectively shutting down a car's engine from up to 35 feet away. As the technology is improved, the device will likely become operable over longer distances, and it may soon become a routine tool in police work.

Other groups, such as the National Computer Security Association, the American Cryptography Association, and the American Society for Industrial Security, bring more specialized high-tech expertise to the private-security and public law enforcement professions.

DNA Technology

On January 16, 2001, Christopher Ochoa, age 34, was released from a Texas prison after serving 13 years for a murder he did not commit.[35] Ochoa had confessed to the rape and murder of 20-year-old Nancy DePriest at a Pizza Hut in Austin in 1988; although Ochoa later said he had been coerced by homicide detectives into confessing, no one believed him. A decade after he began serving a life sentence, law students at the Wisconsin Innocence Project at the University of Wisconsin–Madison took an interest in his case, studied surviving information, and concluded that DNA evidence conclusively proved that someone else had killed DePriest. The students and their law professor took the evidence to District Judge Bob Perkins, who called the case "a fundamental miscarriage of justice" and ordered Ochoa set free. According to authorities, evidence of DePriest's murder now points to Texas inmate Achim Joseph Marino, who confessed to her murder in 1996 following a religious conversion. Marino, currently serving three life sentences for other crimes, has provided investigators with the gun and handcuffs used to commit the crime.

The law students involved in the case used **DNA profiling**, matching DNA samples taken from mouth swabs of Marino with the DNA found in semen taken from the victim's body. Without DNA profiling, Ochoa would still be in prison, and DePriest's real killer would be unknown.

A person's genetic code is contained in his or her DNA, whose composition is unique to each individual (except in the case of identical twins). DNA samples can be taken from blood, hair, semen, saliva, or even small flakes of skin left at the scene of a crime. After processing, DNA profiles appear like bar codes on film negatives, codes that can exonerate a suspect or provide nearly irrefutable evidence of guilt.

DNA evidence is long lasting—fossilized DNA is now being used to reconstruct genetic maps of long-extinct plant and animal species. Although DNA analysis is theoretically possible using only a single cell, most reputable DNA laboratories require a considerably greater quantity of material to conduct an effective analysis, but that could change. Using a Nobel Prize–winning technique called "polymerase chain-reaction technology," minute strands of DNA can be effectively amplified so that even the identity of a person taking a single puff from a cigarette can be accurately established from the trace DNA left on the cigarette. Although the cost and complexity are prohibitive, these technological advances are expected to be available to a range of forensic analysts.

The National Research Council called DNA profiling "a highly reliable forensic tool" but admits that it is not infallible.[36] Obvious differences in scrutinized DNA samples can easily eliminate a suspect, but testing provides less certainty with positive

■ ***Daubert* standard** A test of scientific acceptability applicable to the gathering of evidence in criminal cases.

identification, with human error in conducting the tests being perhaps the greatest threat to reliable results. At least 20 states and the federal government generally accept DNA evidence in criminal trials. Other jurisdictions, including California, are less clear in their recognition of DNA testing, and trial judges in those states may offhandedly exclude the use of such evidence when experts disagree as to its validity.

In 1993, the U.S. Supreme Court, in the civil case of *Daubert* v. *Merrell Dow Pharmaceuticals, Inc.*, revised the criteria for the admissibility of scientific evidence;[37] the ruling rejected the previous admissibility standard established in the 1923 case of *Frye* v. *United States*.[38] The *Daubert* Court ruled that the older *Frye* standard, requiring "general acceptance" of a test or procedure by the relevant scientific community, "is not a necessary precondition to the admissibility of scientific evidence," which is established by Rule 402 of the *Federal Rules of Evidence*, published after *Frye* and superseding it. Rule 402 says that "all relevant evidence is admissible [in a trial], except as otherwise provided by the Constitution of the United States, by Act of Congress, by these Rules, or by other rules prescribed by the Supreme Court pursuant to statutory authority."[39] The Court said that although "the *Frye* test was displaced by the Rules of Evidence, [it] does not mean that the Rules themselves place no limits on the admissibility of purportedly scientific evidence. Nor is the trial judge disabled from screening such evidence. To the contrary, under the Rules the trial judge must ensure that any and all scientific testimony or evidence admitted is not only relevant, but reliable." The real test for the admissibility of scientific expert testimony is for the trial judge to decide "at the outset whether the expert is proposing to testify to (1) scientific knowledge that (2) will assist the trier of fact to understand or determine a fact in issue." The Court concluded that the trial judge's task is one of "ensuring that an expert's testimony both rests on a reliable foundation and is relevant to the task at hand. Pertinent evidence based on scientifically valid principles will satisfy those demands."

The plaintiffs in *Daubert* were not arguing the merits of DNA testing but were claiming that the drug Bendectin caused birth defects, but the ***Daubert* standard** eased the criteria for the introduction of scientific evidence at both civil and criminal trials—and effectively cleared the way for the use of DNA evidence in the courtroom.[40] The *Daubert* Court found that the following factors may be used to determine whether a form of scientific evidence is reliable:

- It has been subjected to testing.
- It has been subjected to peer review.
- It has known or potential rates of error.
- It has standards controlling application of the techniques involved.

One observer, discussing the quality of DNA identification methods, noted, "The challenges today are no longer technical; instead they lie in taking the technology and building a meaningful legal infrastructure around it."[41] As DNA evidence is accepted throughout jurisdictions nationwide and worldwide, digitized forensic DNA databases (similar to widely used fingerprint archives) are useful at the state and national levels, and most of the states and the federal government (through the FBI laboratory) already have them. In 1998 the FBI announced that its National DNA Index System (NDIS)—which enables U.S. forensic laboratories to exchange and compare DNA profiles electronically, thereby linking unsolved serial violent crimes to each other and to known offenders—had begun operation.[42] Shortly thereafter, all 50 states had passed legislation requiring convicted offenders to provide samples for DNA databases, and all states have been invited to participate in NDIS. The federal DNA Identification Act of 1994 authorized the FBI to establish DNA indexes for (1) offenders convicted of crimes, (2) samples recovered from crime scenes, and (3) samples recovered from unidentified human remains.[43] There is the potential for coordination between the federally funded multibillion-dollar Human Genome Project and forensic DNA programs, which could lead to explosive growth in the use of DNA in criminal case processing.

In 1995 the British police, operating under a new nationwide crime bill, became the first national police force in the world to begin routine collection of DNA samples from anyone involved in a "recordable" offense (a serious crime).[44] It appears that genetic profiling will become one of the most significant crime-fighting technologies of the twenty-first century. "Genetic profiling—the use of biotechnology to identify the unique characteristics of an individual's DNA—is about to become as prevalent as the Breathalyzer and more important than the fingerprint."[45]

Genetic profiling will become one of the most significant crime-fighting technologies of the twenty-first century.

In 1996, the NIJ released a comprehensive report, titled *Convicted by Juries, Exonerated by Science*, on the applicability of DNA testing to criminal case processing, calling DNA testing "the most important technological breakthrough of twentieth-century forensic science" and providing a detailed review of 28 cases in which postconviction DNA evidence exonerated defendants who had been sentenced to lengthy prison terms.[46] The 28 cases were selected on the basis of a detailed examination of records that indicated the convicted defendants might have actually

■ **expert system** A system of computer hardware and software that attempts to duplicate the decision-making processes used by skilled investigators in the analysis of evidence and in the recognition of patterns that such evidence might represent.
■ **data encryption** The process by which information is encoded, making it unreadable to all but its intended recipients.
■ **threat analysis** A complete and thorough assessment of the kinds of perils facing an organization.

been innocent. The men in the study had served, on average, seven years in prison, and most had been tried and sentenced prior to the widespread availability of reliable DNA testing. "Momentum is growing, spurred in part by the public's education from the Simpson trial, for DNA testing in criminal cases. Juries may begin to question cases where the prosecutor does not offer 'conclusive' DNA test results if the evidence is available for testing. More defense attorneys in court-appointed cases may file motions for DNA testing and request the State to pay for the tests."[47]

Finally, it is important to note that a growing number of jurisdictions are requiring the gathering of DNA information from arrestees; and in 2013 the U.S. Supreme Court held, in the case of *Maryland* v. *King*, that "When officers make an arrest supported by probable cause . . . and bring the suspect to the station to be detained in custody, taking and analyzing a cheek swab of the arrestee's DNA is, like fingerprinting and photographing, a legitimate police booking procedure that is reasonable under the Fourth Amendment."[48]

Learn more about the science behind forensic DNA testing and how it has been used to convict as well as exonerate criminal defendants at **Library Extra 14–3**. An assessment of its likely future is available as **Library Extra 14–4**.

Computers as Crime-Fighting Tools

Computers are used to keep records of every imaginable sort—from point-of-sale contacts to inventory maintenance and production schedules. Computers assist in the design of new technologies and aid in the assignment of resources to problem areas.

Computers also connect people. The Internet contains a large number of law-oriented and law enforcement–oriented newsgroups and provides access to the United Nations and worldwide crime data through its link to the United Nations Criminal Justice Information Network. Other computer services provide access to security information and to software useful in law enforcement administration. Innovative computer technologies facilitate the work of enforcement agents. Among them are automated fingerprint identification systems, or AFISs (often with interstate and even international links); computerized crime-scene simulations and reenactments; expert systems; and online clearinghouses containing data on criminal activity and offenders. AFISs allow investigators to complete in a matter of minutes what would otherwise consume weeks or months of work manually matching a suspect's fingerprints against stored records. AFIS computers are able to compare and eliminate from consideration many thousands of fingerprints per second, sometimes leading to the identification of a suspect in a short time. Once crime-related information or profiles of criminal offenders have been generated, they are typically stored in a database and often made accessible to law enforcement agencies at other sites. Other specialized database programs now track inner-city gang activity and gang membership, contain information on known sexual predators, and describe missing children.

Forensic expert systems deploy machine-based artificial intelligence to draw conclusions and to make recommendations to investigators and others interested in solving problems related to crime and its commission. **Expert systems**, developed by professional "knowledge engineers" who work with "knowledge bases" and computer software called "inference engines," attempt to duplicate the decision-making processes used by skilled investigators in the analysis of evidence and in the recognition of patterns that such evidence might represent. One such system is currently being perfected by the FBI's National Center for the Analysis of Violent Crime (NCAVC). The NCAVC expert system attempts to profile serial killers by matching clues left at a crime scene with individual personality characteristics.

Finally, a number of specialized software programs, such as ImAger, which is produced by Face Software, Inc., and Compu-Sketch, a product of Visatex Corporation, can assist police artists in rendering composite images of suspects and missing victims.

Combating Cybercrime

In 1982, sales of information security software products to private companies and government agencies totaled only $51 million; by 1997, expenditures exceeded $425 million; and by 2003, they had grown to $1.17 billion.[49] Research conducted by Infonetics Research indicated that worldwide network security appliance and software sales reached more than $4.5 billion in 2006 and surpassed $5 billion in 2007.[50] Among the products in use are **data encryption**, key log detectors, and Web servers supporting major security protocols. Data encryption is the process by which information is encoded, making it unreadable to all but its intended recipients.

Software alone, however, is not enough. Any effective program intended to secure a company or business operation against the threat of high-tech crime must be built on a realistic threat analysis. **Threat analysis**, sometimes called "risk analysis," involves a complete and thorough assessment of the potential disasters facing an organization. Some risks, such as floods,

■ **audit trail** A sequential record of system activities that enables auditors to reconstruct, review, and examine the sequence of states and activities surrounding each event in one or more related transactions from inception to output of final results back to inception.

■ **DCS–3000** An FBI-developed network diagnostic tool that is capable of assisting in criminal investigations by monitoring and capturing large amounts of Internet traffic. It was originally called *Carnivore*.

tornadoes, hurricanes, and earthquakes, arise from natural events and are often unpredictable. Others, including fire, electrical outages, and disruptions in public services, may be of human origin—but equally difficult to predict. Theft, employee sabotage, and terrorist attacks constitute yet another category of risk. Responses to unpredictable threats can nonetheless be planned, and strategies for dealing with almost any kind of risk can be implemented.

Any program intended to secure a company against high-tech crime must be built on a realistic threat analysis.

Once specific threats are identified, strategies tailored to dealing with them can be introduced. For example, one powerful tool useful to identify instances of computer crime when they occur is the audit trail. Formally defined, an **audit trail** is "a sequential record of system activities that enables auditors to reconstruct, review, and examine the sequence of states and activities surrounding each event in one or more related transactions from inception to output of final results back to inception."[51] In other words, audit trails, which (once implemented) are recorded in some form of computer memory, trace and record the activities of computer operators and facilitate the apprehension of computer criminals.

Police Investigation of Computer Crime

Many state and local police departments do not have personnel skilled in the investigation of computer crimes. Most officers know little about tracing the activities of computer criminals, and some police investigators find it difficult to understand how a crime can actually have occurred when nothing at the scene appears to be missing or damaged. Horror stories of botched police investigations are plentiful. They include tales of officers standing by while high-tech offenders perform seemingly innocuous activities that destroy evidence, of seized magnetic or optical media allowed to bake in the sun on the dashboards of police vehicles, and of the loss of evidence stored on magnetic media due to exposure to police clipboards and evidence lockers containing magnets.

Police departments also may intentionally avoid computer-crime investigations because they are complex and demanding. The amount of time and money spent on computer-crime investigations, it is often believed, could better be spent elsewhere. In addition, investigators who spend a great deal of time on crimes involving computers tend not to be promoted as readily as their more glamorous counterparts in the homicide and property crime divisions, and personnel who are skilled in computer applications are apt to take jobs with private industries, where pay scales are far higher than in police work. As a consequence of these considerations and others, many police departments and their investigators make cybercrime a low priority.

Police departments sometimes intentionally avoid cybercrime investigations because they can be complex and demanding.

But the situation has been changing due to federal intervention. In 1992, the FBI formed a National Computer Crime Squad (NCCS)[52] to investigate violations of the federal Computer Fraud and Abuse Act of 1984[53] and other federal computer-crime laws. Prior to the creation of the Department of Homeland Security (DHS), the FBI's Washington Field Office housed the agency's Infrastructure Protection and Computer Intrusion Squad (IPCIS). The squad, whose duties have been transferred to the DHS, investigated the illegal interception of signals (especially cable and satellite signal theft) and the infringement of copyright laws related to software. Visit the IPCIS via **Web Extra 14-3**.

Automated monitoring of network traffic is an area of considerable interest to law enforcement officials. One network "sniffer" created by the FBI called DCS–1000 (previously known as "Carnivore") was a diagnostic tool intended to assist in criminal investigations by monitoring and capturing large amounts of Internet traffic. DCS–1000 was to be installed by FBI agents in ISP data centers as necessary to monitor the electronic communications of individuals suspected of federal crimes such as terrorism. The Carnivore/DCS–1000 initiative was later retitled **DCS–3000**, and its focus was changed to intercepting suspect personal communications delivered via wireless services.[54]

Although goods and materials will always need to be created, transported, and distributed, information is what forms the lifeblood of the new cyberworld. Nations that can effectively manage valuable information and make it accessible to their citizens will receive enhanced productivity and greater wealth as a reward. Moving information safely and securely is also important; today, a large part of that responsibility falls to the Internet. The Internet provides amazing and constantly

■ **Internet** The world's largest computer network for moving data and making information accessible.

growing capabilities. Unfortunately, as the Internet has grown, it has been targeted by hackers and computer criminals, some of whom have introduced rogue computer programs into the network's machines.

Cybercrime and Internet Security

America is a service-oriented, information-rich society. John Naisbitt, author of *Megatrends*, explained it this way: "The transition from an industrial to an information society does not mean manufacturing will cease to exist or become unimportant. Did farming end with the industrial era? Ninety percent of us produced 100 percent of the food in the agricultural era; now 3 percent of us produce 100 percent. In the information age, the focus of manufacturing will shift from the physical to more intellectual functions on which the physical depends."[55]

Although goods and materials will always need to be created, transported, and distributed, it is information that forms the lifeblood of the new world order and is a very valuable resource, comparable to (or exceeding) natural resources like oil, gas, coal, and gold. According to Naisbitt, "Information is an economic entity because it costs something to produce and because people are willing to pay for it."[56] Nations that are able to effectively manage valuable information and make it accessible to their citizens experience enhanced productivity and greater wealth. Moving information safely and securely is important, and today a large part of that is done on the **Internet**, the world's largest computer network. It began with the linkage of military and scientific computer facilities already existing on the Arpanet and Milnet and today consists of a vast resource of tens of thousands of computers around the world all linked together as a way of moving data quickly and making information accessible to masses of citizens.

The Internet provides some amazing and constantly growing capabilities: Web sites, e-mail, mailing lists, newsgroups, and file-transfer capability. Internet access was originally restricted to commercial users, researchers, and university personnel, but access to the Internet is now routinely available through ISPs that furnish Internet access to anyone able to pay the monthly fee. Web browsers combine with search engines like Google to make it easy to search the tremendous amount of information on the Web and to interact with other Internet users.

As the Internet has grown, it has been targeted by hackers and cybercriminals, some of whom have introduced rogue computer programs into the network's machines. In 1988, the infamous Internet "worm" written by Cornell University graduate student Robert T. Morris, Jr., circulated through computers connected to the Internet, effectively disabling many of them. Morris was later arrested, sentenced to 400 hours of community service and three years of probation, and was fined $10,000. Since then, many other hackers have exploited loopholes in the software and hardware supporting the Internet.

In response to the growing threat to the nation's information systems, President Clinton created the Commission on Critical Infrastructure Protection, which was charged with assessing threats to the nation's computer networks and recommending policies to protect them.[57] Security issues related to information systems that control the nation's telecommunications, electric power, oil and gas, banking and finance, transportation, water supply, emergency services, and government operations were studied by the commission. Its October 1997 report proposed (1) establishing an Information Analysis and Warning Center to collect information on computer security breaches in industry and government; (2) creating legislation to permit private companies to conduct special background checks when hiring computer experts for sensitive positions; (3) creating a White House office to coordinate the information security roles of government, including the departments of Commerce, Defense, Energy, Justice, Treasury, and Transportation; and (4) quadrupling research on cyberspace security to $1 billion by the year 2004.[58]

The National Infrastructure Protection Center (NIPC), created in 1998 and located at the FBI's headquarters in Washington, D.C., served as the federal government's center for threat assessment, warnings, investigation, and response for threats or attacks against the nation's critical infrastructures. Its successor, the Office of Infrastructure Protection (IP Office), operates today within the DHS. Visit the IP Office via **Web Extra 14–4**.

In February 2000, the President's Working Group on Unlawful Conduct on the Internet released a report titled *The Electronic Frontier: The Challenge of Unlawful Conduct Involving the Use of the Internet*.[59] The group reported that "similar to the technologies that have preceded it, the Internet provides a new tool for wrongdoers to commit crimes, such as fraud, the sale or distribution of child pornography, the sale of guns or drugs or other regulated substances without regulatory protections, or the unlawful distribution of computer software or other creative material protected by intellectual property rights."

The group said that "although the precise extent of unlawful conduct involving the use of computers is unclear, the rapid growth of the Internet and e-commerce has made such unlawful conduct a critical priority for legislators, policymakers, industry,

■ **First and Fourth Amendments to the U.S. Constitution** The amendments that guarantee each person freedom of speech and security in his or her "persons, houses, papers, and effects, against unreasonable searches and seizures."

and law enforcement agencies." Because of the Internet's potential to reach vast audiences easily, the potential scale of unlawful conduct is equally wide.

Cybercriminals are no longer hampered by the existence of national or international boundaries because information and property can be easily transmitted through communications and data networks. A computer server running a Web page designed to defraud senior citizens might be located in Thailand, but victims of the scam could be scattered throughout the world. Evidence of a crime can be stored at a remote location, either for concealment of the crime from law enforcement or due to the design of the network. "A cyberstalker in Brooklyn, New York, may send a threatening e-mail to a person in Manhattan. If the stalker routes his communication through Argentina, France, and Norway before reaching his victim, the New York Police Department may have to get assistance from the Office of International Affairs at the Department of Justice in Washington, D.C., which, in turn, may have to get assistance from law enforcement in (say) Buenos Aires, Paris, and Oslo just to learn that the suspect is in New York." In this example, the working group points out, the perpetrator needs no passport and passes through no checkpoints as he commits his crime, while law enforcement agencies are burdened with cumbersome mechanisms for international cooperation—mechanisms that often derail or slow investigations. Because the gathering of information in other jurisdictions and internationally is crucial to investigating and prosecuting cybercrimes, the President's Working Group concluded that "all levels of government will need to develop concrete and reliable mechanisms for cooperating with each other." Read the entire text of *The Electronic Frontier* via **Web Extra 14–5**.

In September 2003, the U.S. government established the United States Computer Emergency Readiness Team (US–CERT), a partnership between the DHS and public and private sectors to protect the nation's Internet infrastructure and to coordinate defenses against cyberattacks across the nation. US–CERT is in charge of the National Cyber Alert System: "America's first cohesive national cyber security system for identifying, analyzing, and prioritizing emerging vulnerabilities and threats."[60] The Cyber Alert System relays computer security updates and warning information to anyone who subscribes to its bulletins and provides all citizens—from computer security professionals to home-computer users with basic skills—with free, timely, actionable information to better secure their computer systems. Visit US–CERT at **Web Extra 14–6**.

After taking office, President Barack Obama identified cybersecurity as one of the most serious economic and national-security challenges facing the United States and noted that the country was not adequately prepared to counter cybersecurity threats. In May 2009, the president decided to implement recommendations from the Comprehensive National Cybersecurity Initiative (CNCI), which had been launched by President George W. Bush in January 2008.[61] In December 2009, President Obama announced the appointment of Howard A. Schmidt as White House Cybersecurity Coordinator.[62] Schmidt, who served as chief security officer for Microsoft and eBay, was charged with coordinating cybersecurity activities across the federal government. Learn more about the CNCI at **Library Extra 14–5**, and read about new legislation to address the problem of cybercrime at **Library Extra 14–6**. The White House's recently drafted *Cyberspace Policy Review* is available at **Library Extra 14–7**.

Policy Issues: Personal Freedoms in the Information Age

The continued development of telecommunications resources has led not only to concerns about security and data integrity, but also to an expanding interest in privacy, free speech, and personal freedoms. Although the **First and Fourth Amendments to the U.S. Constitution** guarantee each person freedom of speech and security in his or her "persons, houses, papers, and effects, against unreasonable searches and seizures," the Constitution is understandably silent on the subject of electronic documents and advanced forms of communication facilitated by technologies that did not exist at the time of the Constitutional Convention.

Within the context of contemporary society we are left to ask these questions: What is speech? What are papers? Do electronic communications qualify for protection under the First Amendment, as does the spoken word? In an era when most houses are wired for telephones and many support data links that extend well beyond voice capabilities, it becomes necessary to ask what constitutes one's "speech" or one's "home." Does e-mail qualify as speech? Where does the concept of a home begin and end for purposes of constitutional guarantees? Do activities within the home that can be accessed from without (as when a computer Web site is run out of a home) fall under the same constitutional guarantees as a private conversation held within the physical confines of a house?

Complicating matters still further are today's "supersnoop" technologies, which provide investigators with the ability to literally hear through walls (using vibration detectors), listen to conversations over great distances (with parabolic audio receivers), record voices in distant rooms (via laser readings of windowpane vibrations), and even look through walls

■ **Electronic Frontier Foundation (EFF)** A nonprofit organization formed in July 1990 to help ensure that the principles embodied in the Constitution and the Bill of Rights are protected as new communications technologies emerge.

using forward-looking infrared (FLIR) devices, which can detect temperature differences of as little as two-tenths of a degree.

In 1990, concerned individuals banded together to form the **Electronic Frontier Foundation (EFF)**, a citizens' group funded by private contributions that set for itself the task of actively assisting in refining notions of privacy and legality as they relate to telecommunications and other computer-based media. In the foundation's own words, "The Electronic Frontier Foundation (EFF) was founded in July of 1990 to ensure that the principles embodied in the Constitution and the Bill of Rights are protected as new communications technologies emerge. From the beginning, EFF has worked to shape our nation's communications infrastructure and the policies that govern it in order to maintain and enhance First Amendment, privacy and other democratic values. We believe that our overriding public goal must be the creation of Electronic Democracy."[63]

The EFF, which also supports litigation in the public interest, has been an active supporter of the public advocacy group Computer Professionals for Social Responsibility (CPSR). The CPSR maintains a Computing and Civil Liberties Project in keeping with the EFF's purpose. The EFF also supported challenges to the CDA that resulted in the 1997 Supreme Court ruling in *Reno* v. *ACLU*, which found key provisions of the act unconstitutional. Visit the EFF on the Web via **Web Extra 14–7**.

SUMMARY

Technology and criminology have always been closely linked—as technology advances, it facilitates new forms of criminal behavior.

- High-technology offenses can dramatically change our understanding of crime. Some forms of high-tech crime, committed without regard for national borders or even the need for physical travel, hold dangers never before imagined.
- High technology provides new criminal opportunities by making available to perpetrators new tools and advanced techniques useful in the commission of crime, and by contributing to the development of items of value, such as computer codes, that did not previously exist.
- Cybercrime is serious, widespread, aggressive, growing, and increasingly sophisticated, and it poses major implications for national and economic security.
- Hackers can be pioneers (those fascinated by the evolving technology of telecommunications and its exploration), scamps (those with a sense of fun and no intent to harm), explorers (those motivated by personal delight in discoveries associated with breaking into new systems), game players (those whose joy is in defeating software or copyright protection), vandals (those with the goal of intentional damage without personal apparent gain), and/or addicts (those computer nerds addicted to hacking and computer technology).
- Technology in law enforcement today involves computer databases of known offenders, expert systems, cellular communications, video surveillance and face-recognition technology, electronic eavesdropping, DNA analysis, and less-lethal weapons.
- Any effective program to combat cybercrime and secure an organization against the threat of high-tech crime must use threat analysis. Once specific threats are identified, strategies tailored to dealing with them can be implemented.
- Efforts to control high-tech crime through criminal investigation and prosecution impact issues of individual rights, from free speech to technological privacy in the context of digital interconnectedness. There will need to be an acceptable balance between constitutional guarantees of continued freedom of access to legitimate high-tech activities and effective enforcement initiatives for the massive threat high-tech crimes represent.

KEY TERMS

audit trail, 369

Communications Decency Act (CDA), 358

computer abuse, 361

computer-related crime, 360

computer virus, 358

cybercrime, 355

Cyber Security Enhancement Act (CSEA), 360

cyberspace, 362

data encryption, 368

***Daubert* standard, 367**

DCS–3000, 369

Digital Theft Deterrence and Copyright Damages Improvement Act, 360

DNA profiling, 366

Electronic Frontier Foundation (EFF), 372

expert system, 368

First and Fourth Amendments to the U.S. Constitution, 371

hacker, 355

Internet, 370

No Electronic Theft Act (NETA), 359

phishing, 357

phone phreak, 361

software piracy, 356

threat analysis, 368

QUESTIONS FOR REVIEW

1. How does advancing technology produce new forms of crime?
2. How does high technology provide new criminal opportunities?
3. What different types of cybercriminals does this chapter describe?
4. What is identity theft, and how can identities be stolen?
5. What new technologies are being used in today's fight against crime?
6. What currently is being done to combat cybercrime and to secure the Internet?
7. What are some personal freedoms that are threatened by today's need for advanced security?

QUESTIONS FOR REFLECTION

1. This book emphasizes the theme of social problems versus social responsibility. Which perspective better explains the involvement of capable individuals in criminal activity necessitating high-tech skills? What is the best way to deal with such criminals?
2. What is the difference between high-tech crime and traditional forms of criminal activity? Will the high-tech crimes of today continue to be the high-tech crimes of tomorrow? Why or why not?
3. What forms of high-tech crime can you imagine that this chapter has not discussed? Describe each briefly.
4. Do you believe that high-tech crimes will eventually surpass the abilities of enforcement agents to prevent or solve them? Why or why not?
5. What different kinds of high-tech offenders can you imagine? What is the best way to deal with each type of offender? Give reasons for your answers.

CHAPTER 15
GLOBALIZATION AND TERRORISM

LEARNING OUTCOMES

After reading this chapter, you should be able to answer the following questions:

- What is comparative criminology, and what are the advantages of a comparative approach to the study of crime and criminals?
- What role does globalization play in understanding criminal activities today?
- What are the differences between human smuggling and human trafficking?
- What is terrorism, and what are the various types of terrorism that this chapter discusses?
- How is the War on Terrorism being fought, and what are some of its most important tools?

■ **comparative criminology** The cross-national study of crime.
■ **comparative criminologist** A criminologist involved in the cross-national study of crime.

■ **globalization** A process of social homogenization by which the experiences of everyday life, marked by the diffusion of commodities and ideas, can foster a standardization of cultural expressions around the world.
■ **Follow the author's tweets about the latest crime and justice news @schmalleger.**

Introduction

In January 2012, federal prosecutors indicted ten suspected La Mara Salvatrucha (MS-13) gang members for crimes ranging from conspiracy to commit murder and attempted murder to racketeering and smuggling. Those gang members had nicknames that sounded like cartoon characters, including Doofy, Casper, Sonic, and Lobo.[1]

Federal prosecutors said that the men had committed numerous crimes of violence on the streets of Flushing, a part of Queens, in New York City. Their alleged crimes included extortion rackets in which the men were said to have participated in stabbings, a beating using a baseball bat, and at least one machete attack.

Prosecutors also charged the men with conspiring with other MS-13 gang members around the country and in El Salvador to wire money overseas in an effort to smuggle gang members into the United States. MS-13 is a well-known transnational criminal enterprise whose membership is comprised primarily of immigrants from Central America. It has branches throughout North America, and the Federal Bureau of Investigation (FBI) puts its estimated membership at more than 10,000 in the United States alone.[2]

Jan Sochor/Alamy

An imprisoned MS-13 gang member shows off a hand sign signifying the "Devil's head". How do gangs, like MS-13, contribute to transnational crime?

Comparative Criminology

Comparative criminology is the study of crime on a cross-national level. When crime patterns in one country are compared with those in another, theories and policies that have been taken for granted in one place can be reevaluated in the light of world experience. As some noted **comparative criminologists** have observed, "The challenge for comparative criminologists is to develop theories with increased specificity while managing to construct them in such a way that they can be applied across more than one culture or nation-state. This eventually must demand that theories be developed to conceptualize societies as totalities and that theories that manage to provide a world context in which total societies behave be further constructed."[3]

An important force in the modern world is **globalization**, which can be defined as a process of social homogenization by which the experiences of everyday life, marked by the diffusion of commodities and ideas, can foster a standardization of cultural expressions around the world.[4] The increasing integration of previously isolated events and their impact is an important aspect of globalization, and the idea of globalization encompasses the increasingly interconnectedness of people, ideas, and things on a worldwide scale.

> The term *globalization of knowledge* describes the increase in understanding that results from a sharing of information between cultures.

Some have used the term *globalization of knowledge* to describe the increase in understanding that results from a sharing of information between cultures. The globalization of knowledge is beginning to play a significant role in both the process of theory formation within criminology and the development of American crime control policies. According to some, "Globalization will make it increasingly difficult for nation-states to ignore the criminal justice information of other countries." A few years ago, as recipient of the prestigious Vollmer Award in Criminology, Franklin E. Zimring, of the University of California, Berkeley, addressed the American Society of Criminology, complaining about the fact that American criminology had been self-obsessed and "particularly inattentive to the value and necessity of transnational comparisons." Zimring sees comparative efforts as providing a context for evaluating knowledge and reviewing observations. Using this perspective, Zimring demonstrated that the crime decline in the United States during the 1990s was not unique to America—and that the same decline occurred in Canada at the same time.

■ **ethnocentrism** The phenomenon of "culture-centeredness" by which one uses one's own culture as a benchmark against which to judge all other patterns of behavior.

Ethnocentrism

One important issue facing comparative criminologists is **ethnocentrism**. Ethnocentrism, or culture-centeredness, can interfere with the work of comparative criminologists in a number of ways, including the ways in which crime statistics are gathered, analyzed, and presented.

Only in recent years have American specialists in criminology begun to closely examine crime in other cultures. Not all societies are equally open, and it is not always easy to explore them. In some societies, even the *study* of crime is taboo. As a result, data-gathering strategies taken for granted in Western culture may not be well received elsewhere. One author, for example, has observed that in China, "the seeking of criminal justice information through face-to-face questioning takes on a different meaning than it does generally in the Western world. While we accept this method of inquiry because we prize thinking on our feet and quick answers, it is offensive in China because it shows lack of respect and appreciation for the information given through the preferred means of prepared questions and formal briefings."[5] Most of the information available about Chinese crime rates comes by way of officialdom, and routine Western social science practices such as door-to-door interviews, participant observation, and random surveys might not produce results in China.

Similar difficulties arise in the comparison of crime rates from one country to another. The crime rates of different nations are difficult to compare because of (1) differences in the way a given crime is defined; (2) diverse crime-reporting practices; and (3) political, social, economic, and other influences on the reporting of statistics to international agencies.[6]

Definitional differences create the biggest problem in reporting crime.

Definitional differences create what may be the biggest problem in reporting crime (see the Theory versus Reality box). For cross-national comparisons of crime data to be meaningful, it is essential that the reported data share conceptual similarities, but that is often not the case because nations report offenses according to the legal criteria by which their arrests are made and under which their prosecution can occur. Switzerland includes bicycle thefts in its reported data on what we call "auto theft" because Swiss data gathering focuses more on the concept of personal transportation than on the type of stolen vehicle; the Netherlands has no crime category for robberies, counting them as thefts; Japan classifies an assault resulting in death as an assault or an aggravated assault, not as a homicide; Greek rape statistics include crimes of sodomy, lewdness, seduction of a child, incest, and prostitution, and China reports only robberies and thefts that involve citizens' property, using crimes against state-owned property as a separate category.

Reporting practices vary substantially among nations. The International Criminal Police Organization (INTERPOL) and the United Nations (UN) are the only international organizations that regularly collect crime statistics from a large number of countries, and both can only request data and have no way of checking on the accuracy of those data. Many countries do not disclose the requested information, and those that do sometimes make only partial reports; in general, small countries are more likely to report than large ones, and nonsocialist countries are more likely to report than are socialist nations.

International comparisons are also difficult because complete up-to-date data are not easy to acquire, as the information made available to agencies like INTERPOL and the UN is reported at different times and according to schedules varying from nation to nation. In addition, official UN crime surveys are conducted infrequently at the international level (as of 2013, only ten such surveys have been undertaken).[7]

Economic differences among countries compound these difficulties. Auto-theft statistics between countries like the United States and Bangladesh need, for example, to be placed into an economic as well as a demographic context. Whereas the United States has two automobiles for every 3 people, Bangladesh has only one car per every 2,600 of its citizens.[8] For the auto theft rate in Bangladesh to equal that of the United States, every automobile in the country would have to be stolen over 100 times each year!

Crime statistics also reflect social and political contexts, with some nations not accurately reporting the frequency of certain kinds of culturally reprehensible crimes. Communist countries appear loathe to report crimes like theft, burglary, and robbery because the very existence of such offenses might appear to demonstrate felt inequities within the communist system, and the social norms in some societies may make it almost impossible for women to report cases of rape or sexual abuse, whereas in others, women are encouraged to come forward.

With all these caveats in mind, it can still be instructive to look at crime rates in other countries and attempt comparisons with U.S. crime rates. A useful tool for international crime rate comparisons is *The Eleventh United Nations Survey on Crime Trends and the Operations of Criminal Justice System,* which covers the years 2007–2008. To some, U.S. violent crime rates seem high compared with violent crime rates of other developed countries, but American crime rates are far from the highest in the world, and UN surveys typically place U.S. crime rates well below world

TABLE 15-1 | **World Homicide Rates for Selected Countries, 2011**

COUNTRY	NUMBER OF MURDERS	RATE PER 100,000
Denmark	44	0.8
England & Wales	540	1.0
Canada	529	1.5
United States	*14,612*	*4.7*
Russia Federation	13,826	9.7
Nicaragua	738	12.6
Mexico	27,199	23.7
Belize	124	39.0
El Salvador	4,371	70.2

Source: United Nations Office on Drugs and Crime, *International Homicide, Count and Rate per 100,000 Population (1995–2011)*, http://www.unodc.org/documents/data-and-analysis/statistics/crime/Homicide_statistics2013.xls (accessed September 16, 2013).

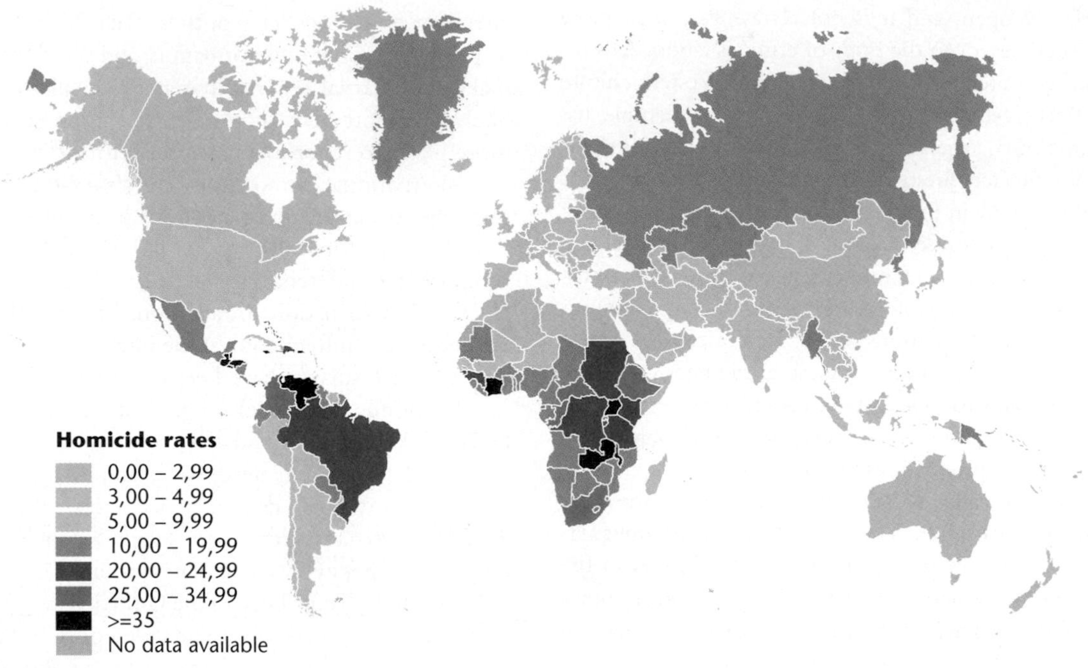

FIGURE 15-1 | **Homicide Rates by Country**

Source: United Nations Office on Drugs and Crime (UNDOC), *2011 Global Study on Homicide: Trends, Contexts, Data* (Vienna: UNODC, 2011), p. 9, http://www.unodc.org/documents/data-and-analysis/statistics/Homicide/Globa_study_on_homicide_2011_web.pdf.

highs (see Table 15–1 for comparative murder rates). Figure 15–1 shows worldwide homicide rates by country. As this text goes to press, a 12th UN crime survey is under way, gathering comprehensive data for 2012.[9]

Lawless areas without strong central governments and countries experiencing strong social upheaval might be expected to have high violent crime rates, but some other parts of the world do as well. Murder rates in Colombia and South Africa are more than 12 times that of the United States, Russia has a murder rate that is almost four times the U.S. rate, and homicide rates in Mexico are more than twice that of those in the United States. The rate of reported rape in South Africa is four times that of the United States, whereas Canada and Australia have rape rates more than double the U.S. figure. Spain has a robbery rate many times higher than that of the United States, and many countries have rates of assault that are greater than that reported in the United States.

See more international crime statistics at **Web Extra 15–1**, and visit the National Institute of Justice (NIJ) International Center at **Web Extra 15–2**. The comprehensive Global Criminology Web site run by Professor Robert W. Winslow at San Diego State University can be found at **Web Extra 15–3**. Read an intriguing paper on comparative criminology at **Library Extra 15–1**; the *Eleventh United Nations Survey on Crime Trends*, covering 64 countries, is available at **Library Extra 15–2**; and the *European Sourcebook of Crime and Criminal Justice Statistics* can be accessed via **Library Extra 15–3**.

THEORY | versus REALITY
UN Offense Definitions

The UN Office on Drugs and Crime regularly conducts a survey of international crime trends. The latest such survey, the eleventh, covers the years 2007–2008. In an effort to standardize reporting practices, the UN provides the following crime definitions to guide survey participants:

> *Intentional homicide* may be understood to mean death deliberately inflicted on a person by another person, including infanticide.
>
> *Non-intentional homicide* may be understood to mean death not deliberately inflicted on a person by another person. That includes the crime of manslaughter but excludes traffic accidents that result in the death of persons.
>
> *Assault* may be understood to mean physical attack against the body of another person, including battery but excluding indecent assault. Some criminal or penal codes distinguish between aggravated assault and simple assault, depending on the degree of resulting injury. If such a distinction is made in your country, please provide the relevant data for aggravated assault under the category "Major assault." Under the category "Total assault" should be included data on both aggravated assault (i.e., major assault) and simple assault. Please provide the main criterion for distinguishing between aggravated assault and simple assault if such a distinction is made in your country.
>
> *Rape* may be understood to mean sexual intercourse without valid consent. Please indicate whether statutory rape is included in the data provided. If, in your country, a distinction is made between sexual assault and actual penetration, please provide relevant information.
>
> *Robbery* may be understood to mean the theft of property from a person, overcoming resistance by force or threat of force.
>
> *Theft* may be understood to mean the removal of property without the property owner's consent. "Theft" excludes burglary and housebreaking as well as theft of a motor vehicle. Some criminal and penal codes distinguish between grand and petty theft, depending on the value of the goods and property taken from their rightful owner. If such a distinction is made in your country, please provide the relevant data for grand theft under the category "Major theft." The category "Total theft" should include data on both grand theft (i.e., major theft) and petty theft. Please provide the main criterion for distinguishing between grand theft and petty theft if such a distinction is made in your country.
>
> *Automobile theft* may be understood to mean the removal of a motor vehicle without the consent of the owner of the vehicle.
>
> *Burglary* may be understood to mean unlawful entry into someone else's premises with the intention to commit a crime. . . .
>
> *Embezzlement* may be understood to mean the wrongful appropriation of another person's property that is already in the possession of the person doing the appropriating.
>
> *Drug-related crimes* may be understood to mean intentional acts that involve the cultivation, production, manufacture, extraction, preparation, offering for sale, distribution, purchase, sale, delivery on any terms whatsoever, brokerage, dispatch, dispatch in transit, transport, importation, exportation and possession of internationally controlled drugs.
>
> *Recorded crimes* may be understood to mean the number of penal code offences or their equivalent (i.e., various special law offences), but excluding minor road traffic offences and other petty offences, brought to the attention of the police or other law enforcement agencies and recorded by one of those agencies.
>
> If the categories above are not fully compatible with the legal code in your country, please try to adjust the data as far as possible. Alternatively, you may indicate what kinds of crime are included in your statistics that might be comparable to the categories suggested or how the comparable types of crime are defined in your country.

View the entire *United Nations Survey on Crime Trends* questionnaire online at http://www.justicestudies.com/pubs/unsurvey.pdf. The UN *Criminal Justice Assessment Toolkit* is available at http://justicestudies.com/pubs/untoolkit.pdf.

Source: United Nations Office on Drugs and Crime, *Questionnaire for the Tenth United Nations Survey on Crime Trends and the Operations of Criminal Justice Systems* (New York: UN, 2005). Reprinted by permission.

Transnational Crimes

Globalization is making it impossible to ignore criminal activity in other parts of the world, especially where that crime is perpetrated by transnational criminal and terrorist organizations. Transnational crime, which is also discussed in Chapter 10, has emerged as one of the most pressing challenges of the early twenty-first century. The growing globalization of crime has required the coordination of law enforcement efforts in different parts of the world and the expansion of U.S. law enforcement activities internationally. Transnational crimes range from relatively simple fraudulent e-mail and phishing schemes to the more dangerous and threatening illegal trafficking in human beings, human organs, and illicit drugs. It includes the activities of multinational drug cartels, the support of terrorist groups by criminal organizations seeking armed

No one is immune to the economic effects of transnational crime.

■ **human smuggling** A type of illegal immigration in which an agent is paid to help a person cross a border clandestinely.

■ **trafficking in persons (TIP)** The exploitation of unwilling or unwitting people through force, coercion, threat, or deception.

Abdul Khaliq/Associated Press

Afghans collecting resin from a poppy field in Lashkar Gah, south of Kabul, Afghanistan, in 2007. Afghanistan is one of the top producers of opium in the world, where its growth is largely controlled by Taliban militia who either befriend or intimidate local poppy growers. Much of the heroin manufactured from opium produced in Afghanistan is sold in the United States, completing an international cycle that forms one aspect of globalization and serves as a source of funds for the ongoing Taliban resistance in Afghanistan. How can the cycle be broken?

protection, and well-funded and sophisticated efforts by organized criminal groups looking to overthrow the ruling regime in regions with others sympathetic to their operations.

Human Smuggling and Trafficking

Comparative criminologists compare crime patterns in one country with those in another.

According to the United Nations,[10] trafficking in persons and human smuggling are some of the fastest-growing areas of international criminal activity today. There are important distinctions between the two. The U.S. State Department defines **human smuggling** as "the facilitation, transportation, attempted transportation or illegal entry of a person(s) across an international border, in violation of one or more country's laws, either clandestinely or through deception, such as the use of fraudulent documents."[11] In other words, human smuggling refers to illegal immigration in which an agent is involved for payment to help a person cross a border clandestinely.[12] Human smuggling may be conducted to obtain financial or other benefits for the smuggler, although sometimes people smuggle others to reunite their families. Human smuggling generally occurs with the consent of the people being smuggled, who often pay for the services. Once in the country they've paid to enter, they usually are no longer in contact with the smuggler. The State Department notes that the vast majority of people who are assisted in illegally entering the United States annually are smuggled rather than trafficked.

Although smuggling might not involve active coercion, it can be deadly. In January 2007, for example, truck driver Tyrone Williams, 36, a Jamaican citizen living in Schenectady, New York, was sentenced to life in prison for causing the deaths of 19 illegal immigrants in the nation's deadliest known human smuggling attempt.[13]

The Intelligence Reform and Terrorism Prevention Act of 2004[14] established the Human Smuggling and Trafficking Center (HSTC) within the Department of Homeland Security (DHS). U.S. Immigration and Customs Enforcement (ICE), the largest investigative agency within the DHS, has primary responsibility for enforcing laws related to human smuggling and trafficking. As a result, ICE plays a leading role in the fight against human smuggling and trafficking.

In contrast to smuggling, **trafficking in persons (TIP)** can be compared to a modern-day form of slavery. Trafficking involves the exploitation of unwilling people through force, coercion, threat, or deception and includes human rights abuses such as debt bondage, deprivation of liberty, or lack of control over freedom and labor. Trafficking is often undertaken for purposes of sexual exploitation or labor exploitation. The Global Fast Fund, a nonprofit international charity that tracks TIP incidents, says that "the primary countries of destination for victims of trafficking are the United States, Italy, Japan, Canada, Australia, and other 'advanced nations.'"[15] The map from Global Fast in Figure 15–2 shows countries of both origin and destination for victims of trafficking. Figure 15–3 shows where victims of trafficking into the United States end up.

A 2011 report by the United Nations Office on Drugs and Crime says that "The term trafficking in persons can be misleading [because] it places emphasis on the transaction aspects of a crime that is more accurately described as enslavement. Exploitation of people, day after day. For years on end."[16]

Practically speaking, it is sometimes difficult to distinguish between a smuggling case and a trafficking case because trafficking often includes an element of smuggling (that is, the illegal crossing of a national border.) Some trafficking victims may believe they are being smuggled when they are really being trafficked, but are unaware of their eventual fate. This happens, for example, when women trafficked for sexual exploitation

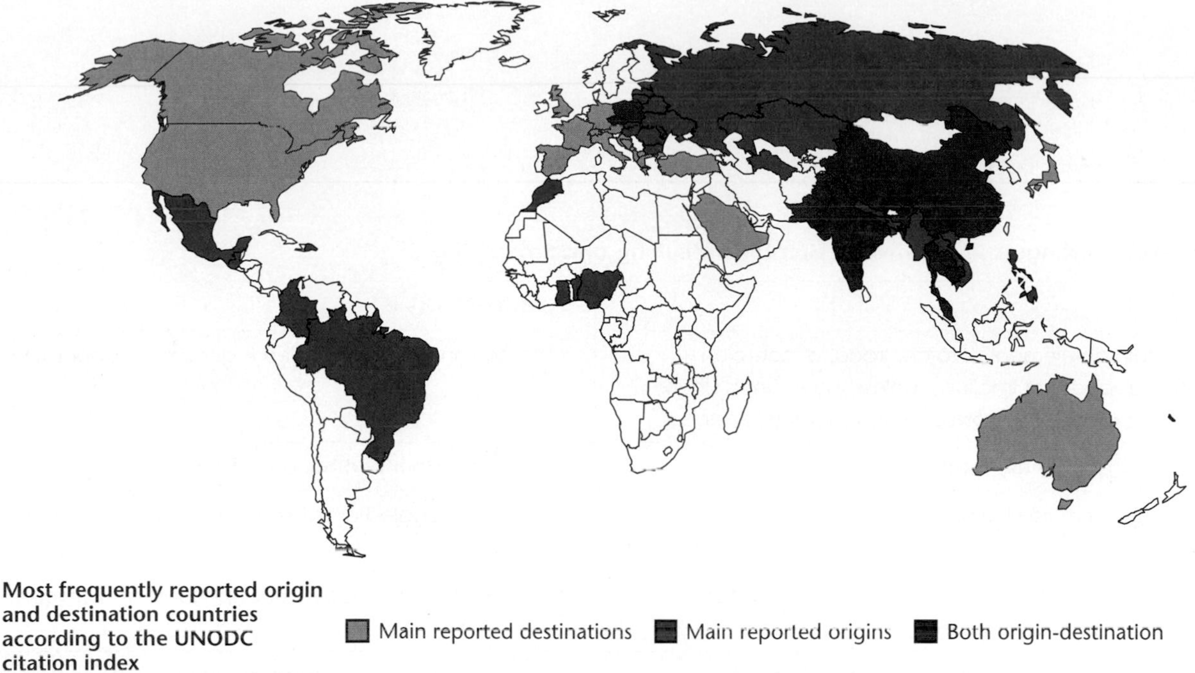

FIGURE 15-2 | **Human Trafficking—Countries of Origin and Destination**

Source: United Nations Office on Drugs and Crime (UNODC), "Trafficking in Persons: Global Patterns," April 2006, p. 17, http://www.unodc.org/documents/human-trafficking/HT-globalpatterns-en.pdf.

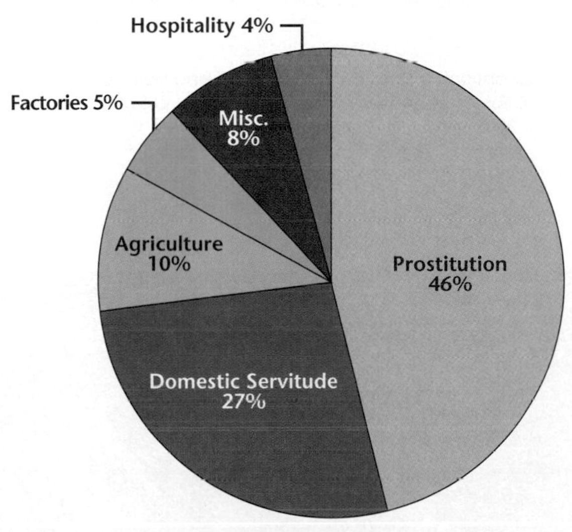

FIGURE 15-3 | **Human Trafficking into the United States—Endpoint Sectors**

Source: Human Trafficking into the United States—Endpoint Sectors from Hidden Slaves, Forced Labor in the United States. Copyright © 2004 by Human Rights Center. Used by permission of Human Rights Center.

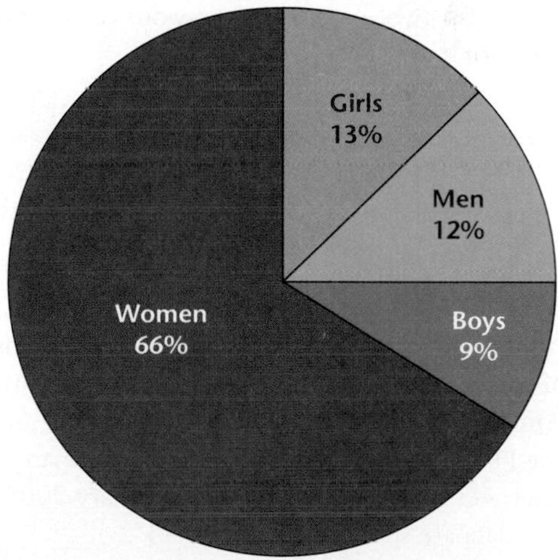

FIGURE 15-4 | **Profile of Worldwide Trafficking Victims**

Source: United Nations Office on Drugs and Crime (UNDOC), *Global Report on Trafficking in Persons* (New York: United Nations, 2009), p. 11. Used by permission of United Nations Office on Drugs and Crime.

may have thought they were agreeing to work in legitimate industries for decent wages—part of which they may have agreed to pay to the trafficker who smuggled them. They didn't know that upon arrival, the traffickers would keep them in bondage, subject them to physical force or sexual violence, force them to work in the sex trade, and take most or all of their income. Table 15–2 draws some important distinctions between human trafficking and smuggling.

Human Trafficking

U.S. government officials estimate that 800,000 to 900,000 victims are trafficked globally each year and that 17,500 to 18,500 are trafficked into the United States. Women and children comprise the largest group of victims, and they are often physically and emotionally abused (see Figure 15–4). Although TIP is often an international crime that involves the crossing of borders, it is important to note that TIP victims can be trafficked within their own country and community. Traffickers can move victims between locations within the same country and often sell them to other trafficking organizations.

TABLE 15-2 | **Distinguishing between Human Trafficking and Smuggling**

TRAFFICKING	SMUGGLING
Must contain an element of force, fraud, or coercion (actual, perceived, or implied), unless the victim is under 18 years of age and is involved in commercial sex acts.	The person being smuggled is generally cooperating.
Forced labor and/or exploitation.	No forced labor or other exploitation.
Persons trafficked are victims.	Persons smuggled are violating the law. They are not victims.
Enslaved, subjected to limited movement or isolation, or had documents confiscated.	Persons are free to leave, change jobs, and so forth.
Need not involve the actual movement of the victim.	Facilitates the illegal entry of person(s) from one country into another.
No requirement to cross an international border.	Smuggling always crosses an international border.
Person must be involved in labor/services or commercial sex acts (that is, must be "working").	Person must only be in the country or attempting entry illegally.

Note: This table is meant to be conceptual and is not intended to provide precise legal distinctions between smuggling and trafficking.
Source: Adapted from U.S. Department of State, Bureau for International Narcotics and Law Enforcement Affairs, Human Smuggling and Trafficking Center, *Distinctions between Human Smuggling and Human Trafficking* (Washington, DC: January 1, 2005).

A few years ago, the Department of Justice funded the creation of the Human Trafficking Reporting System (HTRS) to report on human trafficking within the United States. The most recent HTRS report provides data on human trafficking incidents that were investigated between January 2008 and June 2010. Those data are shown in Table 15–3.

Seen globally, the International Labour Organization (ILO), the United Nations agency charged with addressing labor standards, employment, and social protection issues, estimates that 12.3 million people are in forced labor, bonded labor, forced child labor, and sexual servitude throughout the world today.[17] Other estimates range as high as 27 million.

Stefanos Kouratzis/AFP Photo/Newscom

Russian father Nikolai Rantchev holding up a portrait of his dead daughter, Oxana, at a hotel in Nicosia on November 20, 2008, during a conference on human trafficking. Only days after Oxana left Russia for the Mediterranean island of Cyprus, duped into thinking she would work as a translator, her body was found slumped at the foot of a building. Her father, a former Soviet army officer, believes she was killed by human traffickers who wanted to turn her into a sex slave. What different forms does human trafficking take?

Federal Immigration and Trafficking Legislation

The United States had open national borders until the 1880s, when limited federal controls on immigration began.

The United States had open national borders until the 1880s, when limited federal controls on immigration began. One of the nation's first immigration laws was the Chinese Exclusion Act,

TABLE 15-3 | Number of Alleged Human Trafficking Incidents in the United States, January 2008 to June 2010

TYPE OF HUMAN TRAFFICKING INCIDENT	TOTAL INCIDENTS NUMBER	PERCENT
All incidents*	**2,515**	**100.0**
Sex trafficking	2,065	82.1
Adult prostitution	1,218	48.4
Child sex trafficking	1,016	40.4
Sexualized labor	142	5.6
Other sex trafficking	61	2.4
Labor trafficking	350	13.9
Commercial industry labor	132	5.2
Unregulated industry labor	230	9.1
Other	26	1.0
Other suspected trafficking	65	2.6
Unknown	172	6.8

*One trafficking incident may involve many victims.

Source: Duren Banks and Tracey Kyckelhahn, *Characteristics of Suspected Human Trafficking Incidents, 2008–2010* (Washington, DC: Bureau of Justice Statistics, 2011), p. 3.

which became law in 1882 and was enforced for ten years; it was enacted in response to large numbers of Chinese male laborers who had immigrated to the western United States in the mid-1800s looking for work and often took jobs on railroads and in the mining industry.

A more comprehensive piece of federal immigration legislation was the 1924 Immigration Act limiting the number of immigrants who could be admitted from any one country to 2% of the number of people from that country who were already living here (calculated using the Census of 1890). The law also barred immigration from specific parts of the Asia-Pacific Triangle, including Cambodia, China, Japan, Korea, Laos, the Philippines, and Thailand. The Immigration and Nationality Act (INA) of 1952, establishing the Immigration and Naturalization Service (INS) while continuing numerical ethnic quotas, provided criminal penalties for anyone bringing or attempting to bring unauthorized aliens into the United States,[18] years later, the INA amendments of 1965 abolished quotas based on ethnicity.[19] The Homeland Security Act of 2002 (HSA) dissolved the INS and transferred most of its functions to three branches of the DHS: Citizenship and Immigration Services (CIS), Customs and Border Protection (CBP), and ICE.

Recognizing that human smuggling and TIP were serious social issues, Congress passed the Trafficking Victims Protection Act of 2000 (TVPA), which addressed the significant problem of TIP for the purposes of having people commit commercial sex acts (termed *sex trafficking*) and of subjecting them to involuntary servitude, peonage, or debt bondage and increased the protections afforded victims of trafficking.[20] The TVPA specified severe forms of trafficking: "a.) sex trafficking in which a commercial sex act is induced by force, fraud, or coercion, or in which the person induced to perform such an act has not attained 18 years of age; or b.) the recruitment, harboring, transportation, provision, or obtaining of a person for labor or services, through the use of force, fraud, or coercion for the purpose of subjection to involuntary servitude, peonage, debt bondage, or slavery."[21]

Under the TVPA, human trafficking does not require the crossing of an international border or even the transportation of victims from one locale to another because victims of certain forms of trafficking are not just illegal aliens, but also U.S. citizens, legal residents, or visitors. Victims do not have to be women or children; they may also be adult males.

The Trafficking Victims Protection Reauthorization Act (TVPRA) of 2003 added a new initiative to the original law to collect foreign data on trafficking investigations, prosecutions, convictions, and sentences. Its 2006 data showed that reporting jurisdictions prosecuted 5,808 people for trafficking-related offenses and secured 3,160 convictions, the lowest number of reported foreign prosecutions since reporting began in 2003.[22] TVPA was again reauthorized in 2005 and 2008. As this text goes to press, a 2013 congressional reauthorization is pending. The 2012 reauthorization would improve the original legislation by, among other things, authorizing the TIP Office to negotiate child protection compacts with designated focus countries to increase resources to eradicate child trafficking.

Section 7202 of the Intelligence Reform and Terrorism Prevention Act of 2004 established the HSTC within the U.S. State Department, and the secretary of state, the secretary of the

■ **terrorism** An act of premeditated, politically motivated violence perpetrated against a noncombatant target by a subnational group or clandestine agent.

■ **domestic terrorism** The unlawful use of force or violence by an individual or group based and operating entirely within the United States and its territories, without foreign influence, directed at the U.S. government, the civilian population, or any segment thereof for political or social objectives.

DHS, the attorney general, and members of the National Intelligence Community oversee it. The center was created to achieve greater integration and overall effectiveness in the U.S. government's enforcement of issues related to human smuggling, TIP, and criminal support of clandestine terrorist travel.

Terrorism

The U.S. Department of State defines **terrorism** as "premeditated, politically motivated violence perpetrated against noncombatant targets by subnational groups or clandestine agents, usually intended to influence an audience."[23] Europol says that "[t]errorism is not an ideology or movement, but a tactic or a method for attaining political goals."[24] Paul Pillar, former deputy chief of the Counterterrorist Center of the Central Intelligence Agency (CIA), has identified four key features of terrorism that distinguish it from other forms of violence.[25] Those features are shown in Table 15–4.

Terrorist acts are inherently criminal because they violate the law, involve criminal activity, and produce criminal results.

Terrorist acts are criminal because they violate the criminal law, because they involve criminal activity, and because they produce criminal results. The primary distinction between violent criminal acts and acts of terrorism, however, has to do with the political motivation or social ideology of the offender.[26]

Terrorist organizations vary in their goals and can be categorized as follows:

1. **Nationalist terrorists** seek to change the entire political, social, and economic system to an extreme right, or ultraconservative, model.
2. **Religious terrorists** use violence to bring about social and cultural changes that are in keeping with their religious views.
3. **State-sponsored terrorists** are deliberately employed by radical nations as foreign policy tools.

TABLE 15-4 Characteristics of Terrorism

TERRORISM USUALLY IS	TERRORISM USUALLY IS NOT
Premeditated or planned	Impulsive or an act of rage
Politically motivated (that is, intended to change the existing political order)	Perpetrated for criminal gain (that is, illicit personal or financial benefit)
Aimed at civilians	Aimed at military targets or combat-ready troops
Carried out by subnational groups	Perpetrated by the army of a country

4. **Left-wing terrorists** seek to replace economies based on free enterprise with socialist or communist economic systems.
5. **Right-wing terrorists** are motivated by fascist ideals and work toward the dissolution of democratic governments.
6. **Anarchist terrorists** are revolutionary, anticapitalist, and antiauthoritarian. Although these groups are often motivated by domestic politics, they also are usually part of wider international campaigns and may fight against free-trade agreements, what they see as ecologically damaging practices, and so forth.

Figure 15–5 lists examples of contemporary terrorist groups according to the categories listed here.

Terrorist acts are criminal because they violate the criminal law, because they involve criminal activity, and because they produce criminal results.

The United States has to deal with two types of terrorism: domestic and international.

The United States is faced today with two major types of terrorism: domestic and international. **Domestic terrorism** is unlawful force or violence by a group or an individual who is based and operates entirely within the

■ **international terrorism** The unlawful use of force or violence by an individual or group with a connection to a foreign power or whose activities transcend national boundaries against people or property to intimidate or coerce a government, the civilian population, or any segment thereof for political or social objectives.

FIGURE 15-5 | Types of Terrorist Groups

Source: Derived from information provided by the Council on Foreign Relations and the Markle Foundation, "Types of Terrorism," http://www.terrorismanswers.com/terrorism/types.html (accessed January 10, 2010) and http://www.cfr.org/issue/135/ (accessed July 10, 2012).

United States and its territories without foreign direction and whose acts are directed at elements of the U.S. government or population.[27] **International terrorism** is unlawful force or violence by a group or an individual who has a connection to a foreign power or whose activities transcend national boundaries against persons or property to intimidate or coerce a government, the civilian population, or any segment thereof, in furtherance of political or social objectives.[28] International terrorism is sometimes incorrectly called *foreign terrorism*, a term that, strictly speaking, refers only to acts of terrorism that occur outside the United States.

Domestic Terrorism

Twenty years ago, the 1995 terrorist bombing of the Alfred P. Murrah Federal Building in downtown Oklahoma City, Oklahoma, which killed 168 people and wounded hundreds more, showed just how vulnerable the United States is to domestic terrorist attacks. The nine-story building was devastated by a homemade bomb. The fertilizer and diesel fuel device used in the attack was left in a parked rental truck beside the building, and the blast left a crater 30 feet wide and 8 feet deep and spread debris over a ten-block area.

In June 1997, a federal jury found 29-year-old Timothy McVeigh guilty of 11 counts ranging from conspiracy to first-degree murder in the bombing. Jurors concluded that McVeigh had conspired with Terry Nichols, a friend he had met while both were in the army, and with unknown others to use a truck bomb to destroy the Murrah building.

Today, the activities of numerous groups in the United States fall under the heading of domestic terrorism. One of the largest and fastest growing is the sovereign citizen movement, a group of loosely affiliated individuals who argue that they are not subject to local, state, or federal laws. Many do not recognize the authority of the justice system, including the courts and police. Recently, the DHS and the National Counterterrorism Center (NCTC) listed the sovereign citizen movement as a major threat, placing it alongside white supremacists and homegrown Islamic terrorists.[29] The FBI classifies the organization as an "extremist antigovernment group." According to Mark Potok, a senior fellow at the Southern Poverty Law Center, more that 100,000 Americans "have aligned themselves" with the sovereign citizens movement.[30]

International Terrorism

According to the NCTC, 11,500 terrorist attacks against noncombatants occurred in 72 countries during 2010, resulting in over 50,000 deaths, injuries, and kidnappings.[31] In that year, the

CRIME | in the NEWS

"Lone-Wolf" Terrorists Remain Difficult to Track Down

"Lone-wolf" terrorists defy the traditional definition of terrorism. Terrorism tends to be a collective enterprise—replete with recruiters, cells of fighters, and its own hierarchy—whereas lone wolves choose their own path, standing outside organizations. But like any terrorists, these solitary fighters are totally dedicated to their cause and can be extremely violent.

The Internet would seem to be a boon for lone wolves, because it makes it easier to communicate extremist messages and learn terrorist skills without having to join a group. But there has been no significant increase in lone-wolf activities in the past two decades, according to an international study by the Institute for Security and Crisis Management in the Netherlands.

That study, limited to a dozen European countries plus Australia, Canada, and the United States, found that that lone-wolf attacks represented just over 1 percent of all terrorist incidents in these countries. But in the United States alone, the study found that lone wolves made up almost 42 percent of the total. Moreover, 80 percent of U.S. lone wolves were involved in domestic issues, rather than international issues like Muslim fundamentalism.

U.S. lone wolves' objectives vary widely. Theodore Kaczynski, the Unabomber, protested advances in technology by mailing package bombs that killed three people and injured 23 between 1978 and 1995. In 2009, Nidal Malik Hassan, a military psychiatrist at Fort Hood, Texas, killed 13 soldiers and wounded 43 more in the name of Islam. Wade Michael Page, who in August 2012 killed six and injured three at a Sikh temple in Oak Creek, Wisconsin, advocated white power. And finally, the Tsarnaev brothers, Dzhokhar, age 19, and Tamerlan, age 26, who fit into the lone-wolf category even though they were two people because they acted without supervision by a unified group, killed three and injured hundreds at the finish line of the Boston Marathon in 2013.

White supremacist writers have championed lone-wolf tactics. Louis Beam, a former Ku Klux Klan and Aryan Nations member, advocated "leaderless resistance" in the 1980s. A decade later, Tom Metzger encouraged fellow extremists to commit violent acts on their own, so that they could not easily be detected. It is very difficult for authorities to track down terrorists who don't communicate with anybody, which explains why the Unabomber could wreak havoc for 17 years.

In 2009, President Obama announced the Lone Wolf Initiative, citing a rise in hate speech and gun sales. Working within the FBI, the initiative involves studying past lone-wolf attacks and developing new tactics. One tactic others have identified is reaching out to communities of disgruntled Americans that might inspire lone wolves and delegitimizing the lone wolf's extreme approach.

When the initiative was launched, Michael Heimbach, the FBI's assistant director for counterterrorism, said lone-wolf terrorism "will only be prevented by good intelligence, the seamless exchange of information among law enforcement at every level and vigilant citizens reporting suspicious activity."

Discussion Questions

1. What are lone-wolf terrorists? Why are they of concern to criminologists?
2. How can lone-wolf terrorists be identified before they strike?

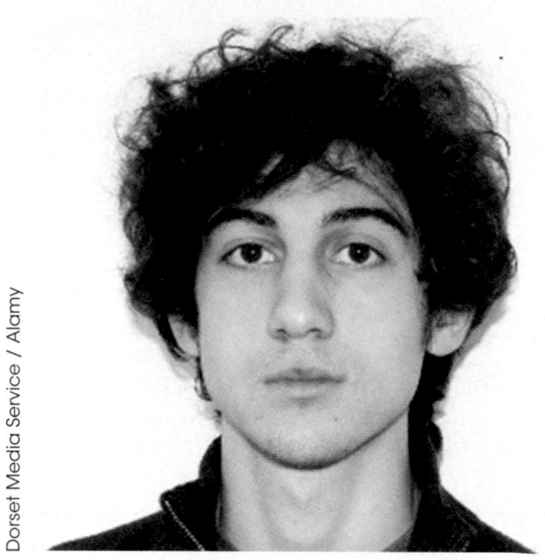

Dorset Media Service / Alamy

Nineteen-year-old Dzhokar Tsarnaev, the surviving 2013 Boston marathon bomber. What motivated Tsarnaev? Could he be considered a "lone wolf" terrorist?

Sources: Randall Law, "Lone Wolf Terrorism: Understanding the Motives behind Mass Shootings," *The Hill*, September 5, 2012, http://thehill.com/blogs/congress-blog/homeland-security/247633-lone-wolf-terrorism-understanding-the-motives-behind-mass-shootings; George Michael, "What's to Stop a 'Lone Wolf' Terrorist?" *The Chronicle of Higher Education*, September 5, 2012, http://chronicle.com/blogs/conversation/2012/09/05/whats-to-stop-a-lone-wolf-terrorist/; and Kevin Johnson, "Feds Try to Detect 'Lone Offenders,'" *USA Today*, August 12, 2009, http://usatoday30.usatoday.com/news/nation/2009-08-11-lone-offenders_N.htm.

---

largest number of terrorist attacks took place in the Middle East and South Asia. These two regions were the locations for 75% of the world's terrorist attacks as well as terrorism-related deaths in 2010. (See Figure 15–6.) The NCTC reports the following for 2010:[32]

- The Near East and South Asia in 2010 suffered a combined total of 8,960 attacks that caused 9,960 deaths.
- Attacks in Afghanistan and Iraq rose in 2010. Almost a quarter of worldwide attacks occurred in Iraq, a slight increase from 2009, although deaths fell for the fourth consecutive year.
- The number of deaths in Africa fell by more than 30 percent, from 3,239 in 2009 to 2,131 in 2010, although attacks rose slightly, from 853 in 2009 to 878 in 2010.
- The number of Lord's Resistance Army attacks in the Democratic Republic of Congo declined sharply, but in June, Algeria saw its first suicide-vehicle-borne improvised explosive device (VBIED) since September 2008.
- The number of attacks and deaths in Europe and Eurasia declined slightly in 2010, with the vast majority again

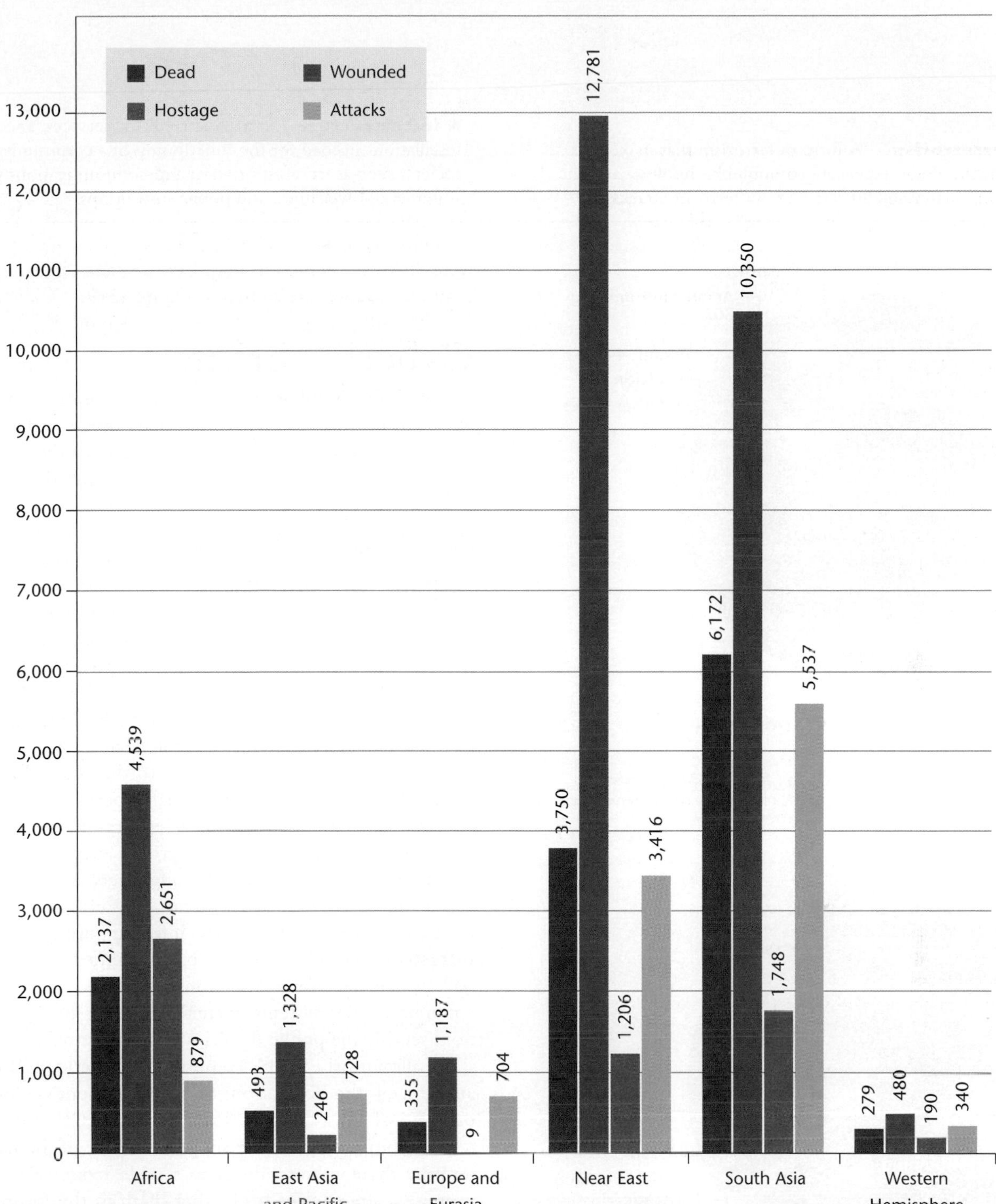

FIGURE 15–6 | **Terrorist Attacks and Victims by Region of the World, 2010**
Source: National Counterterrorism Center (NCC), *2010 Report on Terrorism* (Washington, DC: NCC, April 2011), p. 11, http://www.nctc.gov/witsbanner/docs/2010_report_on_terrorism.pdf.

occurring in Russia. Attacks fell from 737 in 2009 to 706 in 2010, and deaths fell from 367 in 2009 to 355 in 2010.

- The fewest incidents in 2010 were reported in the Western Hemisphere, where both attacks and deaths declined by roughly 25 percent. In the Western Hemisphere, attacks fell from 444 in 2009 to 340 in 2010 and deaths fell from 377 in 2009 to 279 in 2010.

Most attacks in 2010 were perpetrated by terrorist organizations using conventional methods of terrorism, such as armed attacks, bombings, and kidnappings. (See Figures 15–7 and 15–8.) Terrorists continued the practice of coordinated attacks that included secondary attacks on first responders at attack sites, and they continued to reconfigure weapons and other materials to create improvised explosive devices.

■ **cyberterrorism** A form of terrorism that makes use of high technology, especially computer technology and the Internet, in planning and carrying out terrorist attacks.

■ **infrastructure** The basic facilities, services, and installations needed for the functioning of a community or society, such as its transportation and communications systems, water and power lines, and public institutions.

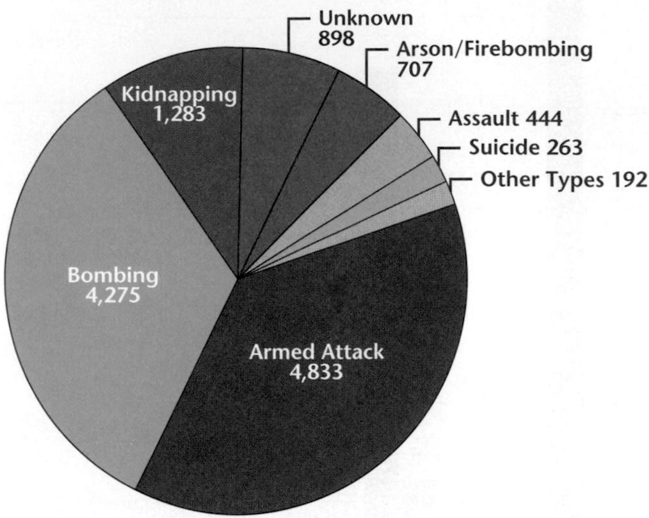

FIGURE 15-7 | Worldwide Terrorism Attacks by Method, 2010

Source: National Counterterrorism Center, *2010 Report on Terrorism* (Washington, DC: NCC, April 2011), p. 13, http://www.nctc.gov/witsbanner/docs/2010_report_on_terrorism.pdf.

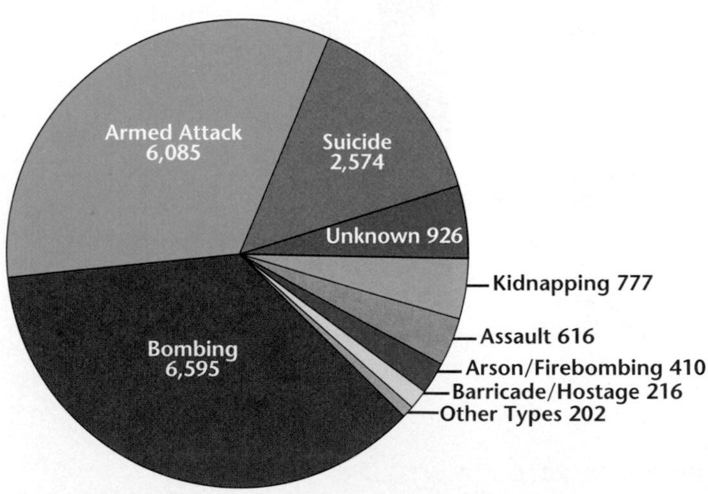

FIGURE 15-8 | Worldwide Deaths from Terrorist Attacks by Method of Attack, 2010

Source: National Counterterrorism Center, *2010 Report on Terrorism* (Washington, DC: NCC, April 2011), p. 14, http://www.nctc.gov/witsbanner/docs/2010_report_on_terrorism.pdf.

As has been the case since 2005, substantial numbers of victims of terrorist attacks in 2010 were Muslim. In fact, well over 50% of victims worldwide were Muslims, and most of those were victims of attacks in Iraq, Pakistan, and Afghanistan. Total deaths by country are shown in Figure 15–9.

Cyberterrorism

There is a new kind of threat called **cyberterrorism**, a form of terrorism that makes use of high technology, especially computers, the Internet, and the World Wide Web, for planning and carrying out terrorist attacks. Most common forms of terrorism target people and things—the physical world; cyberterrorism targets software, information, and communications—the virtual world. The term *cyberterrorism* was coined in the 1980s by Barry Collin, a senior research fellow at the Institute for Security and Intelligence in California, who used it to refer to the convergence of cyberspace and terrorism.[33] It was later popularized by a 1996 RAND report that warned of an emerging "new terrorism" being implemented by terrorist groups organizing and using technology; it warned of a coming "netwar," or "infowar," consisting of coordinated cyberattacks on our nation's economic, business, and military infrastructures.[34] A country's **infrastructure** consists of the basic facilities, services, and installations needed for its functioning, such as transportation and communications systems, water and power lines, and institutions serving the public (banks, schools, post offices, prisons).[35]

> Cyberterrorism makes use of high technology in planning and carrying out terrorist attacks.

Following the RAND report, (then) President Bill Clinton announced the formation of the President's Commission on Critical Infrastructure Protection (PCCIP) to study the critical components of the support systems of the nation, determine their vulnerabilities to a wide range of threats, and propose a strategy for protecting them in the future.[36] Eight critical infrastructure components were identified: telecommunications, banking and finance, electrical power, oil and gas distribution and storage, water supply, transportation, emergency services, and government services.[37] The PCCIP was the first national effort to address the vulnerabilities created by the information age.[38]

Earlier in 1998, the federal National Infrastructure Protection Center (NIPC) was created to serve as a focal point within the U.S. government for threat assessment, warning, investigation, and response to threats or attacks against the nation's critical infrastructure. NIPC functions have since been assumed by various groups within the DHS Information Analysis and Infrastructure Protection (IAIP) Directorate.

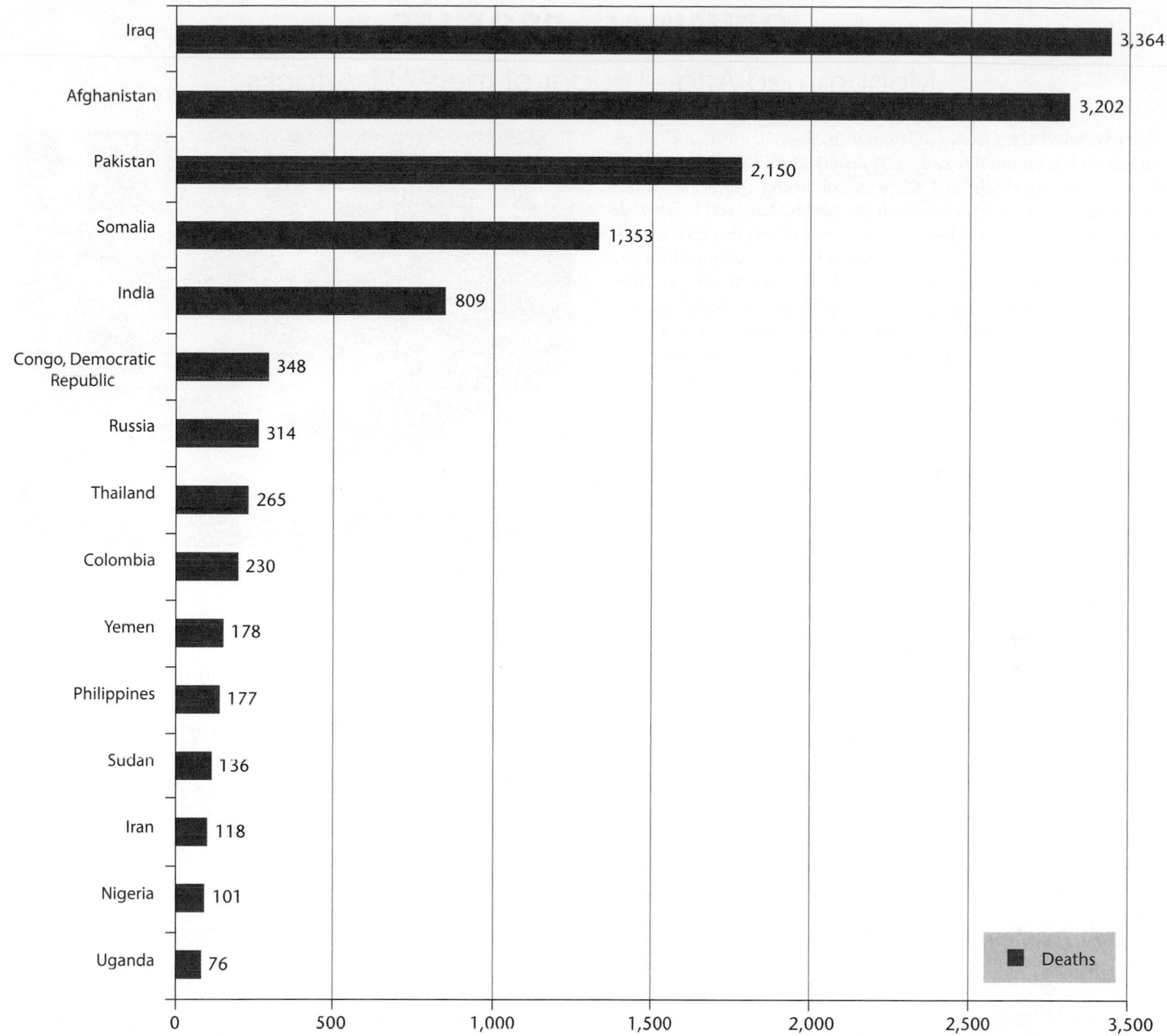

FIGURE 15-9 | **International Terrorism Death Totals by Country, 2010**

Source: National Counterterrorism Center, *2010 Report on Terrorism* (Washington, DC: NCC, April 2011), p. 17, http://www.nctc.gov/witsbanner/docs/2010_report_on_terrorism.pdf.

The Critical Infrastructure Assurance Office (CIAO) was created by a Presidential Decision Directive in May 1998 to coordinate the federal government's initiatives on critical infrastructure protection, and its responsibilities expanded in 2001 when (then) President George W. Bush signed an executive order establishing the President's Critical Infrastructure Protection Board (PCIPB).[39] In September 2002, the board released a study called *The National Strategy to Secure Cyberspace*, which stated that "for the United States, the Information Technology Revolution quietly changed the way business and government operate. Without a great deal of thought about security, the nation shifted the control of essential processes in manufacturing, utilities, banking, and communications to networked computers. As a result, the cost of doing business dropped and productivity skyrocketed."[40] The board found that "our economy and national security are fully dependent upon information technology and the information infrastructure. A network of networks directly supports the operation of all sectors of our economy—energy (electric power, oil and gas), transportation (rail, air, merchant marine), finance and banking, information and telecommunications, public health, emergency services, water, chemical, defense industrial base, food, agriculture, and postal and shipping. The reach of these computer networks exceeds the bounds of cyberspace. They also control physical objects such as electrical transformers, trains, pipeline pumps, chemical vats, radars, and stock markets."[41] In 2003, the functions of the CIAO were

CRIMINAL | PROFILES

Mohammed Atta—Leader of the 9/11 Attacks

This profile box is somewhat different from those in previous chapters. Background information regarding Mohammed Atta, the subject of this box, is sparse, unreliable, and rife with conflicting claims. Given that Atta trained as a terrorist, came from the Middle East, and likely made efforts to live a life "under the radar," it is unsurprising that extensive research into Atta's pre-9/11 life yields little information about which one can feel confident. Although some facts about Atta's life are verifiable, many of the available sources appear to be speculative or outright rumor.

We know, for example, that Atta was born in Kafr El Sheikh in Egypt's Nile Delta, grew up in Cairo, and received an undergraduate degree in architecture from Cairo University. He is known to have resided in Germany from 1993 to 1999, where he pursued an urban planning degree at the University of Hamburg. Reliable records also show that he was a licensed pilot who moved to Venice, Florida, in 2000 to pursue additional flight training at Huffman Aviation International. Records and witness information tell us that he was a committed fundamentalist Muslim.[i] We can conclude that he was intensely motivated by personal ideals and zealous spiritual beliefs, most of which were acquired through his life experiences.

Other claims, however, cannot be as readily confirmed. For example, England's *Telegraph* online daily newspaper reported on December 13, 2003, that documents it had obtained showed that during the summer of 2001 Atta underwent an intensive three-day "work programme" in Baghdad under the tutelage of notorious Palestinian terrorist Abu Nidal. The handwritten, top secret memo the *Telegraph* had acquired was, ostensibly, prepared by the former head of Iraq's Intelligence Service and submitted to then-president Saddam Hussein. The memo purportedly lauds Atta's "extraordinary effort" in preparing to lead the team that would be "responsible for attacking the targets that we have agreed to destroy."[ii] Numerous subsequent investigations, however—including the U.S. government's own 9/11 Commission—have failed to confirm a direct link between Hussein's Iraqi government and the al-Qaeda terrorist group of which Atta was a member and that later claimed responsibility for the 2001 World Trade Center attacks.[iii]

In Atta's case, extensive scrutiny of existing information sources reveals a confusing and often conflicting profile of a man whose movements and activities during the period immediately preceding the World Trade Center attacks cannot be reliably confirmed. Available news reports starkly conflict with official documents. Some government agency documents conflict with the documentary evidence provided by other government agencies. "Highly reliable" information reported by reputable news sources in the period immediately following the attacks has subsequently proven to be almost completely inaccurate. It is the nature of the terrorists' nether world. Secrecy, disinformation, obfuscation, and orchestrated confusion are tools of the trade in such an environment.

Portland Police Department/Associated Press

September 11 hijacker Mohammed Atta. Why do we know so little about him?

The life experiences and complex motivations of terrorists do not fit the motivational patterns of the (for lack of a better word) *ordinary* criminals described in previous chapters. Those seeking to understand terrorist behavior would probably be best served by examining the cultural, educational, ideological, and religious influences that shape the terrorists' worldviews, as those same views also serve to justify in the terrorist's mind even the most horrendous behavior in their pursuit of "correcting" perceived wrongs.

The case of Mohammed Atta raises a number of interesting questions. Among them are the following:

1. Is terrorism a crime so different in form that it requires a separate explanation than other crimes? If not, how can it be explained within the theoretical frameworks offered by this text?
2. Does conflict theory offer an adequate explanation for most acts of terrorism?
3. How can future acts of terrorism be prevented? Would prevention measures involve primarily security measures, or social initiatives designed to reduce the attraction that radical political ideas hold for some people?

Notes:

i. John Hooper, "The Shy, Caring, Deadly Fanatic," *The Observer* (Hamburg), September 23, 2001, http://observer.guardian.co.uk/waronterrorism/story/0,,556630,00.html (accessed June 3, 2007).

ii. Con Coughlin, "Terrorist behind September 11 Strike Was Trained by Saddam," *Telegraph* (United Kingdom), December 13, 2003, http://www.telegraph.co.uk/news/main.jhtml?xml=/news/2003/12/14/wterr14.xml&sSheet=/portal/2003/12/14/ixportaltop.html (accessed June 3, 2007).

iii. Walter Pincus and Dana Milbank, "Al-Qaeda-Hussein Link Is Dismissed," *Washington Post*, June 17, 2004, http://www.washingtonpost.com/wp-dyn/articles/A47812-2004Jun16.html (accessed June 3, 2007).

WHO'S TO BLAME—The Individual or Society?

The Making of a Suicide Bomber

Khaled Al-Rasheed was born in New York City to Egyptian parents and repeatedly visited the Middle East with his father. His last trip was in 2008 when Khaled spent part of the summer with his grandparents near the world-famous Aswan dam. Although his American passport didn't show it, Khaled, a Muslim, had traveled extensively throughout the Arab world while he was growing up, sometimes in the company of his father, and sometimes with his grandfather.

He had seen firsthand the damage done by the first Gulf War in 1991, much of which hadn't been repaired by the time he first visited the region. He had also experienced the resentment festering among the huge non-Arab populations in Saudi Arabia and Kuwait, where oil money paid for the extravagant lifestyles of the royal families but didn't find its way into the hands of the working class.

By the time he was 15, he had befriended a group of radical young Islamists living in Jordan, who blamed the problems in the Middle East on the Great Satan—their name for America. "Americans are stealing our region's wealth," he was told, "and polluting the holy land with their vice and nonbelief."

Returning to the United States in the fall of 2008, Khaled had become radicalized and was ready to strike a blow in what he saw as a worldwide holy war against nonbelievers. As a U.S. citizen, he could travel easily in and out of the country, and on one of his trips he was able to smuggle in the equipment necessary to manufacture a new kind of explosive—one that could be packed into condoms and swallowed like the heroin and cocaine that often crossed the country's southern borders. Equipped with a small blasting-cap whose thin wire ran up the esophagus and into his mouth, the last charge to be swallowed could be set off by simply biting down on a tiny switch clenched between Khaled's molars. The device, which used very little metal, was virtually undetectable.

One day, Khaled swallowed six explosive-filled condoms, passed through security, and boarded a plane at New York's John F. Kennedy airport. Once the plane, bound for Los Angeles, was airborne, Khaled bit down on the detonator. To his surprise, nothing happened. An hour into the flight, however, one of the swallowed condoms ruptured, and Khaled became violently ill as its contents entered his digestive system. Taken off the plane when it landed in Los Angeles, he was taken to a hospital where the explosives were discovered. An operation saved his life, and he recovered in the medical wing of the Los Angeles County Men's Central Jail.

Think about it

1. What does it mean to say, as this scenario does, that "Khaled had become radicalized"? Might the term be applied to other kinds of offenders? If so, which ones?
2. How could someone like Khaled, born in America, be so taken with a foreign ideology?
3. If you were in charge of policy making for America's "War on Terror," what would you want to see happen to Khaled?
4. If you were a judge in charge of sentencing Khaled for his attempted terrorist attack, what kind of sentence would you give him? Is there any chance that he might be rehabilitated? What does "rehabilitation" mean in this context?

Note: Who's to Blame boxes provide fictionalized critical thinking opportunities, and are not actual cases.

transferred to the National Cyber Security Division (NCSD) of the newly created DHS; the creation of NCSD improved protection of critical cyberassets by "maximizing and leveraging the resources" of previously separate offices; and in 2009 President Obama created the position of Cybersecurity Czar in his cabinet to address national issues of cybersecurity (see Chapter 14).[42]

Scenarios describing cyberterrorism possibilities are imaginative and diverse, ranging from a successful cyberterrorist attack on the nation's air traffic control system, causing multiple airplanes to collide in midair, to an attack on food and cereal processing plants, drastically altering the levels of certain nutritional supplements to sicken or kill a large proportion of our nation's young children. Other terrorist attacks could cause the country's power grid to collapse or could muddle the records and transactions of banks and stock exchanges. The possibilities are almost endless.

In an effort to protect its vital interests from future acts of terrorism, the U.S. government planned to build a whole new Internet of its own. Dubbed "GovNet" (govnet.net), the service was planned to be a voice and data network based on the Internet Protocol (IP) that had very limited connectivity with commercial or public networks and was to be physically and electronically separate from existing Internet routers and gateways. The idea was to create a network that could performs its functions with very minimal risk of penetration or disruption from users on other networks.[43] The idea for GovNet was first offered by Richard Clarke, President Bush's cybersecurity adviser, in late 2001: "We'll be working to secure our cyberspace from a range of possible threats, from hackers to criminals to terrorist groups, to foreign nations, which might use cyber war against us."[44]

The system that eventually developed, however, was quite different from what was originally planned. Today's federal Critical Infrastructure Warning Information Network (CWIN) is still being developed, with plans to let government insiders share data on critical infrastructure sectors without risk of intrusion from outside sources.[45] In the words of the developers, "CWIN is DHS' only survivable, critical communications tool not dependent on the Public Switch Network (PSN) or the public internet that can communicate both data and voice information in a collaborative environment in support of infrastructure restoration." The CWIN provides a survivable, dependable method of communication allowing DHS to communicate with other federal agencies, state and local government, the private sector, and international organizations in the event that primary methods of communication are unavailable. **Library Extra 15–4** provides additional insight into the issue of cyberterrorism, and **Library Extra 15–5** is a Department of Homeland Security document describing the CWIN.

Terrorism and Technology

The technological sophistication of state-sponsored terrorist organizations is rapidly increasing.

The technological sophistication of state-sponsored terrorist organizations is rapidly increasing. Handguns and even larger weapons are now being manufactured out of plastic polymers and ceramics; they are capable of firing Teflon-coated, armor-piercing hardened ceramic bullets and are extremely powerful as well as impossible to discern with metal detectors. The black market makes available other sinister items, including liquid metal embrittlement (LME), a chemical that slowly weakens any metal it contacts, which some experts say could be applied with a felt-tipped marker to fuselage components in domestic aircraft, causing delayed structural failure.[46] Backpack-type electromagnetic pulse generators may be used by terrorists who would carry them into major cities, set them up next to important computer installations, and activate them to wipe out billions of items of financial, military, or other information now stored on magnetic media. International terrorists, along with the general public, have easy access to maps and other information that could be used to cripple the nation. The approximately 500 extremely high-voltage (EHV) transformers on which the nation's electric grid depends, for example, are largely undefended but have been specified with extreme geographic accuracy on easily available Web-based power-network maps.

It is clear that at least some terrorist organizations are seeking to obtain weapons of mass destruction (WMDs) for possible chemical, biological, radiological, and nuclear threats. A CIA report made public in 2003 warned that al-Qaeda's end goal is to use WMDs and noted that the group had "openly expressed its desire to produce nuclear weapons" and that sketches and documents recovered from an al-Qaeda facility in Afghanistan contained plans for a crude nuclear device.[47] A 2008 report by the federal Commission on the Prevention of Weapons of Mass Destruction Proliferation and Terrorism contained the frightening conclusion that "unless the world community acts decisively and with great urgency, it is more likely than not that a weapon of mass destruction will be used in a terrorist attack somewhere in the world by the end of 2013."[48]

Earlier in 2003, a study by Harvard University researchers found that the United States and other countries were moving too slowly in efforts to help Russia and other former Soviet-bloc nations destroy poorly protected nuclear material and warheads left over from the cold war; the study also warned that most civilian nuclear reactors in Eastern Europe are "dangerously insecure."[49] Experts said the amount of plutonium needed to make one bomb can be smuggled out of a supposedly secure area in a briefcase or even in the pocket of an overcoat. Although the Harvard study is now more than ten years old, no one really knows how much bomb-grade nuclear material is available on the black market today.

Biological weapons were banned by the 1975 international Biological Weapons Convention (BWC),[50] but a biocrime called *bioterrorism*—defined by the Centers for Disease Control and Prevention (CDC) as the "intentional or threatened use of viruses, bacteria, fungi, or toxins from living organisms to produce death or disease in humans, animals, or plants"[51]—is of considerable concern today. The infamous anthrax letters mailed to at least four people in the United States in 2001 (discussed earlier) provide an example of a bioterrorism incident intended to create widespread fear among Americans; five people (including mail handlers) died, and 23 others were infected.[52] Other possible bioterrorism agents include botulism toxin, brucellosis, cholera, glanders, plague, ricin, smallpox, and tularemia Q fever as well as a number of viral agents such as viral hemorrhagic fevers and severe acute respiratory syndrome (SARS). Experts fear that technologically savvy terrorists could create their own novel bioweapons through bioengineering, a process that uses snippets of made-to-order DNA, the molecular code on which life is based.[53] Learn more about biological agents via the CDC Web site at **Web Extra 15–4**, and visit the Center for the Study of Bioterrorism via **Web Extra 15–5**. An intriguing paper on the topic of bioterrorism from the CDC is available as **Library Extra 15–6**.

The War on Terrorism

The most infamous incident of international terrorism in the United States took place on September 11, 2001, when members of Osama Bin Laden's al-Qaeda Islamic terrorist organization attacked New York City's World Trade Center and the Pentagon. The attacks left more than 3,000 people dead[54] and resulted in

■ **USA PATRIOT Act** A federal law (Public Law 107–56) enacted in response to terrorist attacks on the World Trade Center and the Pentagon on September 11, 2001. The law, officially titled the Uniting and Strengthening America by Providing Appropriate Tools Required to Intercept and Obstruct Terrorism Act, substantially broadened the investigative authority of law enforcement agencies throughout America and is applicable to many crimes other than terrorism. The law was slightly revised and reauthorized by Congress in 2006. Also called *Antiterrorism Act*.

billions of dollars' worth of property damage. The United States declared a worldwide war on international terrorism.

During the first years of President George W. Bush's presidency, terrorist attacks and corporate scandals demanded the attention of federal legislators and the Oval Office. Three important legislative initiatives resulted: the USA PATRIOT Act,[55] the Sarbanes-Oxley Act, and the HSA. In establishing the new DHS, the executive branch of the federal government was restructured. A few years later, in 2003, the National Security Council released the *National Strategy for Combating Terrorism*, which has since been revised. The revised strategy, published in 2006, remains the latest version available and sets the following goals:[56]

- Advance effective democracies as the long-term antidote to the ideology of terrorism
- Prevent attacks by terrorist networks
- Deny weapons of mass destruction to rogue states and terrorist allies who seek to use them
- Deny terrorists the support and sanctuary of rogue states
- Deny terrorists control of any nation they would use as a base and launching pad for terror
- Lay the foundations and build the institutions and structures we need to carry the fight forward against terror and help ensure our ultimate success

The USA PATRIOT Act

The **USA PATRIOT Act**, which stands for Uniting and Strengthening America by Providing Appropriate Tools Required to Intercept and Obstruct Terrorism, was designed primarily to fight terrorism, but it contains provisions that apply to other forms of criminal activity as well. The act permits longer jail terms for certain suspects arrested without a warrant, broadens searches conducted without notice, and enhances the power of prosecutors. The law also increases the ability of federal authorities to tap phones (including wireless devices), share intelligence information, track Internet usage, crack down on money laundering, and protect the country's borders.

The USA PATRIOT Act led some to questions whether the government threatened powers at the expense of individual rights and civil liberties. Prior to passage, the legislation had been questioned by the American Civil Liberties Union (ACLU), which feared the act would substantially reduce the constitutional rights of individuals facing justice system processing. After the bill became law, the ACLU pledged to work with the president and law enforcement agencies across the country "to ensure that civil liberties in America are not eroded."[57]

Department of Homeland Security

The Homeland Security Act of 2002, enacted to protect America against terrorism, established the federal DHS, which is also charged with protecting the nation's critical infrastructure against a terrorist attack.[58] The director is a member of the president's cabinet.

Experts have said that the creation of DHS is the most significant transformation of the U.S. government since 1947, when President Harry S. Truman merged the various branches of the armed forces into the Department of Defense in an effort to better coordinate the nation's defense against military threats.[59] DHS coordinates the activities of 22 disparate domestic agencies, the largest of which are (1) U.S. Customs and Border Protection (CBP), (2) U.S. Citizenship and Immigration Services (CIS), (3) the U.S. Coast Guard (USCG), (4) the Federal Emergency Management Agency (FEMA), (5) U.S. Immigration and Customs Enforcement (ICE), (6) the U.S. Secret Service (USSS), and (7) the Transportation Security Administration (TSA).

The Bureau of Immigration and Customs Enforcement (ICE), also known as U.S. Immigration and Customs Enforcement, is the largest investigative arm of the Department of Homeland Security. ICE is responsible for identifying and eliminating vulnerabilities in the nation's border, economic, transportation, and infrastructure security. The *Bureau of Customs and Border Protection (CBP)* is the unified border control agency of the United States, and has as its mission the protection of our country's borders and the American people. The *Bureau of Citizenship and Immigration Services (CIS)*, also known as U.S. Citizenship and Immigration Services, or USCIS, dedicates its energies to providing efficient immigration services and easing the transition to American citizenship. Figure 15–10 shows the organizational chart for the DHS. You can reach DHS on the Web via **Web Extra 15–6**.

Terrorism Commissions and Reports

Numerous government and private groups have issued reports on terrorism.

Numerous government and private groups have issued reports on terrorism and America's preparedness to deal with threats of terrorism, one of the most important

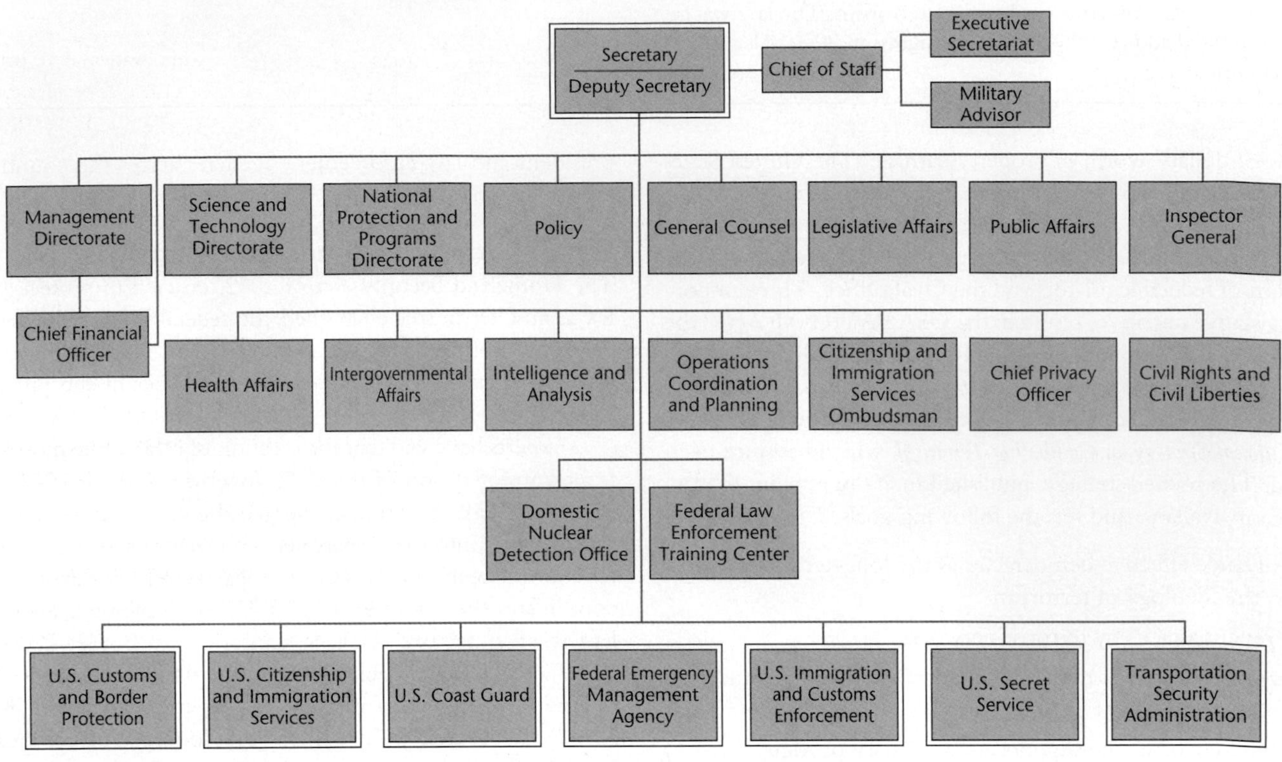

FIGURE 15-10 | **Department of Homeland Security, Organizational Chart**

being the Gilmore Commission (officially known as the Advisory Panel to Assess Domestic Response Capabilities for Terrorism Involving Weapons of Mass Destruction), established by Section 1405 of the National Defense Authorization Act for Fiscal Year 1999.[60] That act directed that a federally funded research and development center provide research, analytical, and other support to the advisory panel during the course of its activities and deliberations.

Under contract with the Department of Defense, RAND provided that support and was the corporate author of three annual Gilmore Commission reports to the president and Congress that have been issued. The first, published on December 15, 1999, provided an in-depth overview of terrorist threats facing the United States. The second report, on December 14, 2000, focused on the need for a national antiterrorism strategy encompassing the full spectrum of deterrence, prevention, preparedness, and response and called for coordination among state and local officials to address intelligence, law enforcement, fire services, public health, and emergency medical and emergency management issues involved in the fight against terrorism. The third Gilmore Commission report, published on December 15, 2001 (the first to be released after the events of September 11, 2001), emphasized the need for improvements in state and local response capabilities, enhanced immigration standards and better border control, improved security against cyberattacks, and an expanded role for the military in fighting terrorism. The three Gilmore Commission reports are available in their entirety as **Library Extras 15–7**, **15–8**, and **15–9**.

Another important group, the U.S. Commission on National Security in the 21st Century (also known as the Hart-Rudman Commission) has reported in three phases:

- **Phase I report—New World Coming: American Security in the 21st Century (September 15, 1999).** The Phase I report discussed relevant economic, technological, and intellectual influences throughout the global community and underscored the powerful forces of social and political fragmentation occurring in many places in the world. This new world order requires a new and comprehensive U.S. international strategy.
- **Phase II report—Seeking a National Strategy: A Concert for Preserving Security and Promoting Freedom (April 15, 2000).** The Phase II report suggested U.S. antiterrorism priorities for the future: defending the homeland; maintaining America's internal social cohesion, economic competitiveness, technological ingenuity, and military strength; assisting with the macroeconomic and political integration of key major

Brendan Smialowski/AFP/Getty Images/Newscom

Members of the National Commission on Terrorist Attacks upon the United States (aka the 9/11 Commission). The commission's report, released on July 22, 2004, called for a major overhaul of U.S. intelligence agencies and a realignment of federal expenditures on homeland security. Acts of terrorism generally involve a multitude of criminal law violations. What crimes were committed by the terrorists who attacked the World Trade Center and the Pentagon?

powers, such as China, Russia, and India; promoting growth of the global economy; establishing needed international laws and agreements; adapting existing alliances to meet new challenges; and helping sustain international stability.

- **Phase III report—Roadmap for National Security (January 31, 2001).** The Phase III report examined multiple potential threats to homeland security, emphasized the need to capitalize on America's strengths in the sciences and education, and suggested that the human requirements needed for adequate national security are not being met.

All three reports are available in their entirety as **Library Extras 15–10, 15–11**, and **15–12**.

After leaving Congress, former Senators Gary Hart and Warren Rudman collaborated on a follow-up antiterrorism report sponsored by the Washington, D.C.–based Council on Foreign Relations titled *America Still Unprepared—America Still in Danger.*[61] It concluded that the United States remained "dangerously unprepared" to prevent or respond to attacks by well-organized terrorist groups. "America's own ill-prepared response could hurt its people to a much greater extent than any single attack by a terrorist."

The National Commission on Terrorism (known as the Bremmer Commission) was established under the federal Omnibus Consolidated and Emergency Supplemental Appropriations Act of 1999 to review and assess the laws, regulations, policies, directives, and practices relating to combating international terrorism directed against the United States as well as to recommend changes needed to improve U.S. counterterrorism performance.[62] The commission's June 7, 2000, report, titled *Countering the Changing Threat of International Terrorism,* outlined the changing face of international terrorism and offered diplomatic, intelligence, and law enforcement options for addressing that threat; it is available in its entirety as **Library Extra 15–13**.

The 9/11 Commission said that the September 11 attacks should have come as no surprise.

On July 22, 2004, the National Commission on Terrorist Attacks upon the United States (the 9/11 Commission) released its highly anticipated 567-page report, which said that the September 11 attacks should have come as no surprise because the U.S. government had received clear warnings that Islamic terrorists were planning to strike at targets in the United States. The report stated that the United States was still not properly prepared to adequately deal with terrorist threats and called for the creation of a new federal intelligence-gathering center to unify more than a dozen federal agencies gathering terrorism-related intelligence at home and abroad. The report also commented that the United States and other economically advanced nations should create a global strategy of diplomacy and public relations to counter Islamic terror networks and to defeat their ideology. "To Muslim parents, terrorists like bin Laden have nothing to offer their children but visions of violence and death. America and its friends have the advantage—our vision can offer a better future." The entire 567-page report is available as **Library Extra 15–14**.

In December 2008, the Commission on the Prevention of Weapons of Mass Destruction Proliferation and Terrorism (mentioned earlier) reported to Congress on the threat from terrorists seeking to obtain and deploy biological and nuclear weapons; its report focused on weapons with the "greatest potential to kill in the most massive numbers."[63] It contained more than a dozen recommendations, including the following: "[The United States must] accelerate integration of effort among the counterproliferation, counterterrorism, and law enforcement communities to address WMD proliferation and terrorism issues; strengthen expertise in the nuclear and biological fields; prioritize pre-service and in-service training and retention of people with critical scientific, language, and foreign area skills; and ensure that the threat posed by biological weapons remains among the highest national intelligence priorities for collection and analysis." The commission went on to say, "The United States must build a national security workforce for the 21st century."[64] Read the commission's full 160-page report at **Library Extra 15–15**.

In 2010, the Bipartisan Policy Center's National Security Preparedness Group released a wide-ranging report on the evolving nature of terrorism. The report, *Assessing the Terrorist Threat,* made clear that the biggest threat to American national security may no longer come from large international terrorist organizations—but may come instead from small *decentralized* groups of homegrown terrorists, or even loners, who have bought into the ideology of terrorism. Although it is impossible to discuss each of the reports described in this chapter, they are available at **Library Extra 15–16**.

Countering the Terrorist Threat

The U.S. Department of State, in its publication *Patterns of Global Terrorism*, made a number of policy recommendations for use in the fight against international terrorism. One of the most significant was that "Money is like oxygen to terrorists, and it must be choked-off."[65] In September 2001, (then) President George W. Bush issued an executive order imposing stiff penalties on anyone providing financial support to terrorists or their organizations.[66] The order also blocked the assets of designated individuals and organizations linked to global terrorism; prohibited financial transactions with the terrorist groups, leaders, and corporate and charitable fronts listed in the order; and established America's ability to block the U.S. assets of (and deny access to U.S. markets to) any foreign banks refusing to freeze terrorists' assets.

In 2003, the White House released its official *National Strategy for Combating Terrorism*, which included a multipronged initiative aimed at reducing both the threat severity and international reach of international terrorist organizations.[67] The strategy had as goals: (1) defeating terrorists and their organizations by identifying, locating, and destroying them; (2) diminishing the underlying conditions that terrorists seek to exploit by resolving regional disputes; by fostering economic, social, and political development; by encouraging market-based economies; by supporting good governance and the rule of law; and by "winning the war of ideas" to ensure that ideologies that promote terrorism do not find fertile ground in any nation; and (3) defending U.S. citizens and interests at home and abroad by implementing strong and effective security measures and by enhancing measures intended to ensure the integrity, reliability, and availability of critical physical and information-based infrastructures (including transportation and information systems).

The July 2004 report of the 9/11 Commission proposed sweeping changes within the U.S. intelligence community, including the creation of the position of a national intelligence director (NID), and then the Intelligence Reform and Terrorism Prevention Act of 2004 (IRTPA) facilitated the creation of the NCTC under the newly created position of NID.[68] The NID would act as the principal adviser to the president, the National Security Council, and the Homeland Security Council for intelligence matters related to national security, and the NCTC would serve as the primary organization for integrating and analyzing all intelligence pertaining to terrorism and counterterrorism and for conducting strategic counterterrorism operational planning.[69]

Finally, in 2011, the Obama administration released its official National Strategy for Counterterrorism.[70] The strategy maintained a focus on deterring Islamic-inspired terrorism and promised to pressure "al-Qa'ida's core while emphasizing the need to build foreign partnerships and capacity . . . to strengthen our resilience." The authors of the strategy noted that it "augments our focus on confronting the al-Qa'ida-linked threats that continue to emerge from beyond its core safehaven in South Asia." The strategy makes it clear that "The preeminent security threat to the United States continues to be from *al-Qa'ida and its affiliate and adherents*." The avowed goals of the National Strategy are as follows:

- Protect the American People, Homeland, and American Interests.
- Disrupt, Degrade, Dismantle, and Defeat al-Qa'ida and Its Affiliates and Adherents.
- Prevent Terrorist Development, Acquisition, and Use of Weapons of Mass Destruction.
- Eliminate Safehavens.
- Build Enduring Counterterrorism Partnerships and Capabilities.
- Degrade Links between al-Qa'ida and Its Affiliates and Adherents.

Nasser Ishtayeh/Associated Press

Palestinian boys wearing green ribbons on their heads in support of Hamas and brandishing plastic rifles as they march through the streets of the West Bank town of Nablus in a protest rally against what their elders see as Israeli aggression. Some argue that terrorists already control the hearts and minds of young people in many parts of the world. What can be done to change that?

■ **foreign terrorist organization (FTO)** A foreign organization that engages in terrorist activity threatening the security of U.S. nationals or the national security of the United States and that is so designated by the U.S. secretary of state.

- Counter al-Qa'ida Ideology and Its Resonance and Diminish the Specific Drivers of Violence That al-Qa'ida Exploits.
- Deprive Terrorists of Their Enabling Means.

Learn more about countering terrorist threats at **Library Extra 15–17**, and the *National Strategy* is available in its entirety at **Library Extra 15–18**. Visit the NCTC at **Web Extra 15–7**.

Foreign Terrorist Organizations

From the late 1970s to the mid-1990s, U.S. antiterrorism policy focused largely on deterring and punishing state sponsors of terrorism as opposed to terrorist groups themselves.[71] In 1996, passage of the federal Anti-Terrorism and Effective Death Penalty Act signaled an important shift in policy:[72] It recognized the transnationalism of many terrorist organizations, created a legal category of **foreign terrorist organizations (FTOs)**, and banned funding, granting of visas, and other material support to such organizations and their members. The USA PATRIOT Act extended and strengthened the provisions of that legislation.[73]

Federal law has required that any organization considered for FTO designation must be *foreign* and engage in terrorist activity as defined in Section 212(a)(3)(B) of the Immigration and Nationality Act;[74] it must also threaten the security of U.S. nationals *or* the national security (national defense, foreign relations, *or* economic interests) of the United States. The U.S. Department of State has the authority to designate any group external to the United States as an FTO based on an exhaustive interagency review in which all evidence of a group's activity, from both classified and open sources, is scrutinized; the State Department, working closely with the Justice and Treasury Departments and the intelligence community, would prepare a detailed "administrative record" documenting the terrorist activity of the designated FTO. Under federal law, FTO designations are subject to judicial review, and in the event of a challenge to a group's FTO designation in federal court, the U.S. government would rely on the administrative records containing classified intelligence information to defend the designation decision. FTO designations expire in two years unless renewed.

Once an organization has been designated an FTO, a number of legal consequences ensue. It becomes unlawful for a person in the United States or subject to the jurisdiction of the United States to provide funds or other material support to a designated FTO, and representatives and certain members of a designated FTO can be denied visas or kept from entering the United States if they are aliens. Also, U.S. financial institutions must block funds of designated FTOs and their agents and report the blockage to the Office of Foreign Assets Control in the U.S. Department of the Treasury. Designated FTOs can be found in Table 15–5.

The State Department has the authority to designate foreign governments as *state sponsors of international terrorism.*

The State Department also has the authority to designate selected foreign governments as *state sponsors of international terrorism*, and four countries currently are so designated: Cuba, Iran, Sudan, and Syria. Cuba continues to be a safe haven for several terrorists and U.S. fugitives and maintains ties to state sponsors of terrorism and Latin American insurgents. Iran remains the most active state sponsor of terrorism in the world: Iran's Islamic Revolutionary Guard Corps (IRGC) and the Ministry of Intelligence and Security (MOIS) continue to be involved in the planning and support of terrorist acts and aid a variety of groups that use terrorism to pursue their goals, and the Iranian government continues to provide support to numerous terrorist groups, including the Lebanese Hezbollah, Hamas, and the Palestine Islamic Jihad (PIJ), all of which seek to undermine Middle East peace negotiations through the use of terrorism. Since 2007, Sudan has provided shelter for members of al-Qaeda, the Lebanese Hezbollah, al-Gama'a al-Islamiyya, Egyptian Islamic Jihad, the PIJ, and Hamas, in spite of being engaged in a counterterrorism dialogue with the United States since mid-2000. Syria offers safe haven and support to several terrorist groups, some of which oppose the Middle East peace negotiations. Learn more about terrorist activities in individual countries from the Department of State's Country Reports on Terrorism via **Library Extra 15–19**.

The 2001 USA PATRIOT Act created a Terrorist Exclusion List (TEL) with immigration consequences for groups on the list.[75] The federal government may deport aliens living in the United States who provide material assistance to organizations listed on the TEL and may refuse entry to the country to anyone who assists or solicits assistance from those organizations.

At the individual level, the U.S. government's Terrorist Identities Datamart Environment (TIDE) serves as a central repository of information on international terrorist identities.[76] TIDE supports the federal government's various terrorist screening systems or "watchlists" and the U.S. Intelligence Community's overall counterterrorism efforts. The Terrorist Identities Group (TIG), located in NCTC's Information Sharing and Knowledge Development Directorate (ISKD), is responsible for building and maintaining TIDE, whose database includes all information the U.S. government has on the identities of individuals who are known or lawfully suspected to be or who have been involved in terrorism-related activities. Federal agencies nominate individuals based on evaluations of available intelligence and law enforcement antiterrorism information; then

TABLE 15-5 Designated Foreign Terrorist Organizations as of Mid-2013

Abu Nidal Organization (ANO)	Kata'ib Hizballah (KH)
Abu Sayyaf Group (ASG)	Kurdistan Workers' Party (PKK)
Al-Aqsa Martyrs Brigade (AAMB)	Lashkar e-Tayyiba (LT)
Ansar al-Islam (AAI)	Lashkar i Jhangvi (LJ)
Ansar Dine (AD)	Liberation Tigers of Tamil Eelam (LTTE)
Army of Islam (AOI)	Libyan Islamic Fighting Group (LIFG)
Asbat al-Ansar (AAA)	Moroccan Islamic Combatant Group (GICM)
Aum Shinrikyo (AUM)	Mujahadin-e Khalq Organization (MEK)
Basque Fatherland and Liberty (ETA)	National Liberation Army (ELN)
Communist Party of Philippines/New People's Army (CPP/NPA)	Palestine Islamic Jihad - Shaqaqi Faction (PIJ)
	Palestine Liberation Front - Abu Abbas Faction (PLF)
Continuity Irish Republican Army (CIRA)	Popular Front for the Liberation of Palestine (PFLP)
Gama'a al-Islamiyya (IG)	Popular Front for the Liberation of Palestine-General Command (PFLP-GC)
Hamas	
Haqqani Network	Al-Qa'ida (AQ)
Harakat ul-Jihad-i-Islami (HUJI)	Al-Qa'ida in the Arabian Peninsula (AQAP)
Harakat ul-Jihad-i-Islami/Bangladesh (HUJI-B)	Al-Qa'ida in Iraq (AQI)
Harakat ul-Mujahideen (HUM)	Al-Qa'ida in the Islamic Maghreb (AQIM)
Hizballah	Real IRA (RIRA)
Indian Mujahideen (IM)	Revolutionary Armed Forces of Colombia (FARC)
Islamic Jihad Union (IJU)	Revolutionary Organization 17 November (17N)
Islamic Movement of Uzbekistan (IMU)	Revolutionary People's Liberation Party/Front (DHKP/C)
Jabhat al-Nusra	Revolutionary Struggle (RS)
Jaish-e-Mohammed (JEM)	Al-Shabaab (AS)
Jemaah Islamiya (JI)	Shining Path (SL)
Jundallah	Tehrik-e Taliban Pakistan (TTP)
Kahane Chai	United Self-Defense Forces of Colombia (AUC)

Source: U.S. Department of State, Office of the Coordinator for Counterterrorism. Current as of September 19, 2013.

federal data analysts create and enhance TIDE records based on their review of those nominations and daily transmit those data to the Terrorist Screening Center (TSC) for use in the government's consolidated watchlist. The watchlist supports screening processes to detect and interdict known and suspected terrorists at home and abroad and is used to create and maintain the Transportation Security Administration's "no-fly list," the Department of State's visa database, and other similar databases.

Present U.S. policy focuses largely on terrorist organizations like al-Qaeda and their affiliated networks and state supporters.[77] New brands of terrorists—individuals who are not affiliated with any established terrorist organization and are apparently not agents of any state sponsor—represent a significant new threat. For example, the terrorist Ramzi Ahmed Yousef, believed to have masterminded the 1993 World Trade Center bombing, apparently did not belong to any larger established terrorist group, although he may have had some ties to al-Qaeda operatives. The worldwide threat of individual or "lone wolf terrorism" (discussed in a box earlier in this chapter) is substantial and was recognized by outgoing FBI director Robert Mueller in 2013 when he told reporters affiliated with National Public Radio that "the core of al-Qaida has been decimated, and the accused Boston bombers and the Army psychiatrist who carried out a massacre at Fort Hood, Texas, to support the Taliban exemplify the new face of terrorism." Mueller continued, saying, "You have individuals that are not aligned with any particular group who can be radicalized and find a weapon of choice and then kill American innocent civilians. . . . and unfortunately, we have to be prepared for that. It's much more difficult to discern, but we could anticipate that there may be more in the future."[78]

Another problem that surfaced in the wake of incidents associated with Islamic fundamentalist groups was how to condemn and combat such terrorist activity—and the extreme and violent ideology of specific radical groups—without appearing to be anti-Islamic in general. A desire to punish a state for supporting international terrorism may also conflict with other foreign policy objectives involving that nation. Learn more about terrorism from the Terrorism Research Center via **Web Extra 15–8** and the Lawson Terrorism Information Center at **Web Extra 15–9**, or visit the NCTC via **Web Extra 15–10**.

The Future of Terrorism

The Congressional Research Service (CRS) identified three trends in modern terrorism.[79] The first trend—one that makes terrorism especially difficult to combat—is toward loosely organized, self-financed international terrorist networks. The second is toward terrorism that is religiously or ideologically motivated, and groups using religion as a pretext (such as radical Islamic fundamentalist groups) pose serious terrorist threats of varying kinds to U.S. interests and call upon other like-minded people throughout the world to join their causes. The third trend is the recent growth of cross-national links among different terrorist organizations, which may involve combinations of military training, funding, technology transfer, and political advice. The CRS cited intelligence reports showing, for example, that Chechen rebels have been trained in al-Qaeda terrorist camps in Afghanistan and even in Chechnya itself; al-Qaeda funding reputedly helped establish the Islamic separatist group Abu Sayyaf in the Philippines; and some intelligence reports have suggested the possibility of mid- and low-level cooperation between al-Qaeda and the Lebanese Hezbollah in weapons smuggling, money laundering, and training for terrorist operations.

> Looming over the issue of international terrorism is the proliferation of WMDs.

Looming over the entire issue of international terrorism is a trend toward proliferation of WMDs. Iran has been aggressively seeking nuclear arms capability; Iraq is thought to be stockpiling chemical and biological agents and rebuilding its nuclear weapons program. North Korea has admitted to having a clandestine program for uranium enrichment, and indications have also surfaced that al-Qaeda has attempted to acquire chemical, biological, radiological, and nuclear weapons. Stakes in the war against international terrorism are increasing, and margins for error in selecting appropriate policy instruments or combinations of them to prevent terrorist attacks are diminishing.

SUMMARY

- Comparative criminology is the study of crime on a cross-national level. By comparing crime patterns in one country with those in another, accepted local theories can be reevaluated in light of world experiences. *Globalization of knowledge*, a term describing the increased understanding due to sharing of information among cultures, plays a significant role in both criminological theory formation and American crime-control policies. Ethnocentrism, or culture-centeredness, can interfere with the work of comparative criminologists in gathering, analyzing, and presenting crime statistics by causing those statistics to only reflect the social and political arenas in which they were generated.
- Globalization refers to the increasing integration of previously isolated events in all areas of life and to its effects on people throughout the world. Globalization makes it impossible for U.S. policy makers to ignore criminal activity in other parts of the world. Transnational crime refers to unlawful activity undertaken and supported by organized criminal groups operating across national boundaries whose activities include fraudulent e-mail and phishing schemes, drug running, sex tourism, illegal trafficking in human beings and human organs, and international trade in weapons of mass destruction.
- The United Nations tells us that human smuggling and human trafficking are two of the fastest-growing areas of international criminal acidity today. Human smuggling involves illegal border crossings, either clandestinely or through deception, such as the use of fraudulent documents. Human trafficking, on the other hand, involves the exploitation of unwilling people through force, coercion, threat, or deception and includes human rights abuses such as debt bondage, deprivation of liberty, or lack of control over freedom and labor. Trafficking is often undertaken for purposes of sexual exploitation or labor exploitation, while smuggling usually involves direct payment to the smugglers by the people being smuggled.
- Terrorism is politically motivated violence planned and perpetrated against noncombatant targets by subnational groups or clandestine agents to bring about change in an existing social order, often with the threat of massive destruction and large numbers of casualties. Domestic and international terrorism are two main forms of terrorism; specific terrorist activities include cyberterrorism and attacks on information-management segments of our nation's critical infrastructure. The vigilance required to prevent both domestic and international terrorism has resulted in new laws restricting some freedoms that many Americans had previously taken for granted.
- Today's worldwide War on Terrorism, led by the U.S. government, followed the attacks of September 11, 2001, in which the World Trade Center site in New York City was destroyed, and the Pentagon was badly damaged. Soon after the attacks, the U.S. Congress enacted the USA PATRIOT Act, the Sarbanes-Oxley Act, and the Homeland Security Act. The Department of Homeland Security was established, and various federal agencies were organized under the homeland security umbrella. The federal government also developed a national strategy for combatting terrorism, and the strategy continues to evolve and inform our nation's antiterrorism efforts today.

KEY TERMS

comparative criminologist, 376
comparative criminology, 376
cyberterrorism, 388
domestic terrorism, 384
ethnocentrism, 377
foreign terrorist organization (FTO), 397
globalization, 376
human smuggling, 380
infrastructure, 388
international terrorism, 385
terrorism, 384
trafficking in persons (TIP), 380
USA PATRIOT Act, 393

QUESTIONS FOR REVIEW

1. What is comparative criminology? What are the advantages of a comparative approach in the study of criminology?
2. What is globalization? What role does globalization play in understanding criminal activities today?
3. What are the differences between human smuggling and human trafficking?
4. What is terrorism? What types of terrorism does this chapter discuss?
5. How is the War on Terrorism being fought, and what are some of its most important tools?

QUESTIONS FOR REFLECTION

1. What are the advantages of a comparative perspective in criminology? Are there any disadvantages? If so, what are they?
2. What types of terrorism has this chapter identified? Are there any that it might have missed? If so, what are they?
3. Has the "war against terror" affected you personally? If so, how?
4. Has the average American had to sacrifice any rights or freedoms in the fight against terrorism? If so, what rights or freedoms have been sacrificed?
5. Is it true that the only way to secure freedom is to curtail it during times of national crisis? Why or why not?

© AF archive/Alamy

EPILOGUE
FUTURE DIRECTIONS

LEARNING OUTCOMES

After reading this epilogue, you should be able to answer the following questions:

- What techniques are used in the field of futures research for assessing the future?
- What are some likely future crimes, and how will future criminal activity differ from criminal activity today?
- What can be predicted about the future of criminological theorizing?

■ **futurist** One who studies the future.
■ **future criminology** The study of likely futures as they impinge on crime and its control.

■ **Follow the author's tweets about the latest crime and justice news @schmalleger.**

Introduction

Canadian criminologist Gwynn Nettler once told a story of two people passing on a street in New York City.[1] One carried a pint of whiskey; the other had $100 in gold coins. In March 1933, near the end of the Prohibition era, the person with the alcohol would have been committing a crime, but the person carrying the gold would have been regarded as a law-abiding citizen. A year later, however, the same two people passing on the street would have occupied exactly the opposite legal positions: The repeal of Prohibition legalized carrying whiskey in most places, but gold hoarding became a federal crime in 1934 and remained so until 1974.

Future Studies Groups

It is easy to look back in time and assess the legal standing of people like those in Nettler's story, but predicting what crimes the future will bring is far more difficult. The future is an abstract concept through which human beings bring symbolic order to the present and meaning to past endeavors.[2] From our present point of view, multiple futures exist, each of which is more or less probable and may or may not come to pass. In other words, the future contains an almost limitless number of possibilities, any of which might unfold but only a few of which actually will. Those who study the future are called **futurists**, and their task is to effectively distinguish among these impending possibilities, assessing the likelihood of each and making more or less realistic forecasts based on such assessments. **Future criminology** is the study of likely futures as they relate to crime and its control, and futurists working in the area of criminology try to imagine how crime will appear in both the near and the distant future.

Some assumptions about the future, such as estimates of future world populations, can be based on existing and highly credible public or private statistics and mathematical analyses of trends, but others are more intuitive and result from the integration of a wide range of diverse materials derived from many different sources. As one futurist explained, "Before we can plan the future, we must make some assumptions about what that future will be like. Assumptions about the future are not like assumptions in a geometry exercise. They are not abstract statements from which consequences can be derived with mathematical precision. But we need to make some assumptions about the future in order to plan it, prepare for it, and prevent undesired events from happening."[3]

Best known among groups that study the future is the World Future Society, which publishes *The Futurist*, a journal of well-considered essays about probable futures. Individual futurists who have become well known to the general public include Alvin Toffler, author of the trilogy of futurist titles *Future Shock*,[4] *Powershift*,[5] and *The Third Wave*;[6] John Naisbitt, author of *Megatrends: Ten New Directions Transforming Our Lives*;[7] Peter F. Drucker, author of *Management Challenges for the 21st Century*[8] and *Post-Capitalist Society*;[9] and Francis Fukuyama, author of *Our Posthuman Future*[10] and *The End of History and the Last Man*.[11]

The Society of Police Futurists International represents the cutting edge of research into future crime-control policy.

Within criminology, the Society of Police Futurists International (PFI), representing the cutting edge of research into future crime-control policy, evolved from a conference of approximately 250 educators and practitioners representing most states and 20 different nations that was held at the National Academy of the Federal Bureau of Investigation (FBI) in Quantico, Virginia, in 1991; the society's Millennium Conference was held at the National Academy in July 2000. PFI members apply the principles of futures research to gain an understanding of the world as it is likely to be in the future.[12]

In 2002, the PFI joined with the FBI to create the Futures Working Group (FWG), whose aim is to "develop and encourage others to develop forecasts and strategies to ethically maximize the effectiveness of local, state, federal, and international law enforcement bodies as they strive to maintain peace and security in the 21st century."[13] A report by the FWG foresaw a future in which the increasing effects of globalization would lead to a world of new crimes, like energy smuggling, and produce conditions whereby what is good economically for oneself or one's company may not be good for one's country.[14] The FWG has regarded the Internet as highly influential in shaping the future of the social world: "The biggest change that the Information Age may bring about is the redefinition of boundaries. The boundaries between criminal syndicates, terrorist groups, and gangs will continue to disappear. Physical boundaries will be replaced by electronic and philosophical ones as individuals discover new virtual communities."[15] Learn more about the PFI at its Web site via **Web Extra EP–1**, and read the FWG's publication *Policing 2020: Exploring the Future of Crime, Communities, and Policing* at **Library Extra EP–1**. Also available on the PFI Web site is *The Joint Operational Environment: The World through 2030 and Beyond*, a publication of the U.S. Joint Forces Command, which can be viewed at **Library Extra EP–2**.

Dr. William Tafoya. Reprinted with permission

William L. Tafoya, founder of the Society of Police Futurists International (PFI). Regarded by many in the field as a visionary, Dr. Tafoya is a retired FBI special agent, teaching at the University of New Haven. What are the goals of the PFI?

Another group actively attempting to discern the future is the United Kingdom's government-led Foresight program, which "brings people, knowledge and ideas together to look ahead and prepare for the future."[16] Foresight's Crime Prevention Panel released a report in 2001 titled *Just around the Corner* that focused on the year 2020 and provided a summation of the views of 60 experts given three tasks: to describe crimes of the near future, to identify methods to reduce and detect those crimes, and to decide what role science and technology will play in future criminality and crime prevention.[17] According to Foresight's Crime Prevention Panel, a number of social characteristics will affect future crimes in Great Britain and throughout the world, including what the panel called "individuality and independence." The panel believed that greater individuality and personal independence will arise as traditional family forms decline over the next decade or two. Once traditional families no longer provide the "foundation" of society and more people find themselves living in single-person households, "there will be more self-centered, self-indulgent and hedonistic psychologies." Traditional limits on antisocial behavior will erode, the panel predicted, as individuals gravitate toward membership in like-minded groups, many of which "may reinforce rather than challenge anti-social views."

A second social characteristic that will affect crime in the future, according to the panel, is what it termed "Information Communication Technology (ICT) usage." The panel predicted that crimes like electronic theft and fraud will occur with increasing rapidity, reducing the likelihood that offenders will be caught, and Web sites will become highly targeted properties, with sites in English being the hardest hit. Such attacks will require that digital evidence in courts be increasingly accepted and that jurors, judges, and attorneys be educated in relevant technologies.

Technology is also leading to the growth of an impersonal society in which people meet and interact in virtual space rather than in physical society. As a consequence, physical space may become an increasingly hostile and dangerous place, what the panel termed "a dehumanized environment" in which "people may become less 'real' to one another leading to more extreme reactions, interactions and the reluctance to intervene in conflicts."

A third social characteristic, according to the panel, that is relevant to understanding and predicting future forms of criminality and that is having an impact on much of society—including technology, commerce, communication, and crime—is globalization, the increasingly international character of social life. "Already, crimes on the Internet, drug dealing, and smuggling show the power of global crime and the difficulties it poses for local level law enforcement." Local crimes and small-time perpetrators will be replaced or supplemented by crimes and criminal groups with global scope.

The panel noted that criminal organizations, like organizations everywhere, "are adapting to the opportunities offered by the flexibility of the Internet." Modern technology offers individuals new opportunities to commit crimes that may be virtually unsolvable: "The clear danger is being at the mercy of a small technologically knowledgeable elite." At the same time, the panel warned, large numbers of people either won't have the opportunity to acquire advanced technological skills or won't be able to learn them; the consequence will be a technologically disenfranchised underclass whose existence will "further fuel crime and reduce the opportunities for access to mainstream society." For more details about Foresight and for access to the complete report of Foresight's Crime Prevention Panel, visit **Web Extra EP–2**.

One of the newest groups to undertake the study of future crimes is the Future Crimes Institute, founded by Marc Goodman, an expert in cybercrime prevention. Goodman created the Future Crimes Institute to inspire and educate others on the security implications of disruptive technologies such as artificial intelligence, the social data revolution, synthetic biology, virtual worlds, robotics, ubiquitous computing, and location-based services.[18] The Institute has more than 1,000 associate members in 37 countries and brings together experts from around the world to discuss crime, security, and technology. Goodman also serves as the faculty advisor for security at Silicon Valley's Singularity University, which is a NASA- and Google-sponsored venture dedicated to using advanced science and technology to address humanity's grand challenges. The

■ **futures research** A type of multidisciplinary operations research that facilitates long-range planning based on (1) forecasting supported by mathematical models, (2) cross-disciplinary treatment of subject matter, (3) expert judgments, and (4) systems-analytical approach to problems.
■ **trend extrapolation** A technique of futures research that makes future predictions based on the projection of existing trends.
■ **cross-impact analysis** A technique of futures research that attempts to analyze one trend or event in light of the occurrence or nonoccurrence of a series of related events.
■ **Delphi Method** A technique of futures research that uses repetitive questioning of experts to refine predictions.
■ **environmental scanning** A technique of futures research that tries to identify future developments (trends or events) that could plausibly occur over a given period of time and that might affect one's area of concern.
■ **scenario writing** A technique of futures research intended to predict future outcomes that builds on environmental scanning by attempting to assess the likelihood of possible outcomes once important trends have been identified.

Future Crimes Institute can be reached on the Web at **Web Extra EP–3**, and a video of Goodman discussing the future of crime and global security can be viewed at **Web Extra EP–4**.

Techniques of Futures Research

Futures research has been described as "a multidisciplinary branch of operations research [whose principal aim] is to facilitate long-range planning based on (1) forecasting from the past supported by mathematical models, (2) cross-disciplinary treatment of its subject matter, (3) systematic use of expert judgment, and (4) a systems-analytical approach to its problems."[19] In the words of PFI founder **William L. Tafoya**, "Futures research offers both the philosophy and the methodological tools to analyze, forecast, and plan in ways rarely seen [in crime-control planning]. Guided by insight, imagination, and innovation, a new perspective awaits criminal justice professionals willing to attempt creative new approaches to dealing with crime and criminals."[20]

Central to futures research is a futurist perspective built around five principles:[21]

1. The future is determined by a combination of factors, not the least of which is human choice; what we decide today will have a significant effect tomorrow.
2. There are alternative futures, so a range of decisions and planning choices is always available in the present.
3. We operate in an interdependent, interrelated system, with any major decision, development, or force affecting one part of the system having the possibility of affecting the entire system.
4. Tomorrow's problems are developing today. Minor problems ignored today may have catastrophic consequences even a few years from now, so distinct trends and developments and even gradual changes cannot be ignored.
5. We should regularly develop possible responses to potential changes and monitor trends and developments, and we should not hesitate to use our collective creativity and judgment to develop forecasts, projections, and predictions—or to take action.

The techniques of futures research are many and varied. Perhaps the simplest is **trend extrapolation**, making future predictions based on the projection of existing trends. The technique of **cross-impact analysis** attempts to analyze one trend or event in light of the occurrence or nonoccurrence of a series of related events.[22] The social consequences of the aging baby-boomer population, for example, will be intimately affected by the future economic health of the U.S. economy, along with the availability of medical and social programs to care for geriatric segments of the population.

The Delphi Method elicits expert opinions until a general consensus is reached.

The **Delphi Method**, developed at RAND by Olaf Helmer and Norman Dalkey, involves four steps designed to elicit expert opinions until a general consensus is reached: (1) problem identification, (2) development of an expert panel, (3) questions directed at the panel, and (4) collection and synthesis of responses. The Delphi Method does not stop with one iteration of this sequence but provides feedback to the experts and allows them to refine their responses.

Simulations and models attempt to replicate the system under study by reproducing its conditions in a form that can be readily manipulated to assess possible outcomes. A wind tunnel, for example, provides an environment in which models of airplanes can be tested. Many of today's simulations are based on mathematical models and make use of computer technology in an effort to create simulated environments, and this is also true of demographic and economic models, which are sometimes used to predict future criminality.

Environmental scanning is a targeted effort to collect as much information as possible in "a systematic effort to identify in an elemental way future developments (trends or events) that could plausibly occur over the time horizon of interest" and that might affect one's area of concern because it is impossible to predict the future without having an informed sense of what is happening now, especially where important trends are concerned.[23] The technique of **scenario writing** builds on environmental scanning by attempting to assess the likelihood of a variety of possible outcomes once important trends have been identified, develops a list of possible futures, and assigns each

■ **strategic assessment** A technique of futures research that assesses the risks and opportunities facing those who plan for the future.

The ruins of the ancient Greek Temple of Apollo at Delphi, where the Oracle of Delphi prophesized. What is the Delphi Method used by futurists?

a degree of probability or likelihood; although not necessarily predicting a specific future, scenario writers tend to highlight a range of possible outcomes. **Strategic assessment** provides an appreciation of the risks and opportunities facing those who plan for the future. Whatever techniques a futurist employs, it is important to remember that techniques are no better than the data they use.

A comprehensive futures research approach might identify an important trend showing affluent middle- and upper-class citizens fleeing cities and suburbs for the safety of enclosed residential enclaves surrounded by secure perimeters and patrolled by paid private-security personnel. Many likely scenarios could then be envisioned: a further decline in America's cities as the moneyed classes abandon them, continued growth of street and property crimes in metropolitan areas, and rampant victimization of the urban working poor. Although crime-control strategies might be developed to counter the imagined threat to cities, many risks must be considered in any planning. A serious decline in the value of the dollar could cause gated communities to unravel and could create a shortfall of tax dollars needed to pay for enhanced policing in cities, or a new influx of large immigrant populations would likely add to the burgeoning number of inner-city dwellers, which would be another new dimension to overall crime-control planning. Futurists who have made their mark on criminology include Georgette Bennett; Bernard Levin; Richter H. Moore, Jr.; Allen Sapp; Gene Stephens; and William Tafoya. Their work, other emerging theoretical explanations for crime, and new suggestions for crime-control policy are discussed in this chapter. Learn more via **Web Extra EP–5**.

Future Crimes

Murder, rape, robbery, and the other types of "everyday" crime that have become mainstays of contemporary criminological analysis will continue to occur in the future, but other emergent forms of criminality will grow in frequency and number. Joseph F. Coates, president of the future-oriented think tank of Coates & Jarratt, predicted that by the year 2025, "socially significant crime—that is, the crimes that have the widest negative effects—in the advanced nations will be increasingly economic and computer based. Examples include disruption of business, theft, introduction of maliciously false information, and tampering with medical records, air traffic control, or national-security systems."[24] Another futurist predicted that "the top guns of twenty-first-century criminal organizations will be educated, highly sophisticated, computer-literate individuals who can wield state-of-the-art information technology to the best advantage—for themselves and for their organizations."[25]

In a wide-ranging overview of future crimes at the close of the twentieth century, **Richter H. Moore, Jr.** painted a picture of future criminality that included many dimensions: "Computer hackers are changing bank records, credit accounts and reports, criminal-history files, and educational, medical, and even military records."[26] Identity manipulation will be a nexus of future criminality. Genetic-based records," Moore wrote, "will include a birth-to-death dossier of a person and will be the method of criminal identification." The U.S. military is presently using genetic testing to assign unique identification codes to each of its soldiers; in the event of war, such codes enable the identification of human remains from as little as a single cell. DNA coding may form the basis for nearly foolproof identification technologies, taking the science of personal identification beyond fingerprinting, blood-type matching, or photography. The science of bioengineering, now undergoing clinical trials in the treatment of various diseases, could also be clandestinely employed for illegal modifications of human DNA, with the goal of effectively altering a person's identity, and the theft of computer-based genetic identification records could make it possible for one person to effectively imitate another in our future society.

Moore described many other crimes of the future. Soon, "criminal organizations will be able to afford their own satellites." Drug trafficking and money laundering could be coordinated via satellite communications, couriers and shipments could be tracked, and satellite surveillance could provide alerts of enforcement activity. Moore went on to say that "prostitution rings will use modern technology to coordinate global activities" and that children and fetuses may "become subject to unlawful trafficking." The illegal disposal of toxic materials, an activity already perpetrated by organized crime, may become even more profitable for criminal entrepreneurs as many more hazardous substances are produced in the face of ever-tighter controls. The supply of nuclear materials and military-quality armaments to "private armies, terrorists, hate groups, questionable regimes, independent crime groups, and individual criminals" will be a fact of life in the twenty-first century, as will the infiltration of governments and financial institutions by sophisticated criminals whose activities are supported by large illegally acquired fortunes.

Georgette Bennett, whose seminal book *Crimewarps* was published in 1987 and helped establish the study of criminal futures, predicted that American society will experience major changes (many of which have since happened) in both what society considers criminal and who future offenders will be:[27]

- Declines in street crimes, such as robbery and assault
- Increases in white-collar crimes, especially high-technology crimes
- Increased involvement of women in crime
- Increased crime commission among the elderly
- Shifts in high crime rates from the Frost Belt to the Sun Belt
- Safer cities but increased criminal activity in small towns and rural areas

The U.S. Joint Forces Command had this to say about future crimes in its publication *The Joint Operational Environment: The World through 2030 and Beyond*:

> Criminal organizations and elements will take advantage of information and communication technologies and the proliferation of weapons to develop very sophisticated capabilities. The destructive social, economic, and political impact of crime will increase in both its severity and sophistication. Transnational criminal activity, fueled by global connections to money and arms, will blur the lines between traditional military action and criminal activities. Criminal organizations will continue to form strategic alliances with states and nonstate actors, including terrorists. Terrorists and criminals will also be active in such an environment, ready to exploit the situation for their respective gains. United States joint forces, combined with law enforcement and intelligence activities in a collaborative information environment, will have to deal both with enemy military forces and [with] other nontraditional forces, such as criminal organizations, terrorists, or religious fanatics, who will seek to profit from instability.[28]

Learn more about the changing nature of crime in America via **Library Extra EP–3** and **Web Extra EP–6**.

New Criminologies

Along with futures research, emerging criminological theories provide a picture of what criminology will be like in the years and decades to come. In an intriguing article, Illinois State University criminal justice professor L. Edward Wells suggested that "when it comes to explaining crime, we seem to have an embarrassment of riches but a poverty of results."[29] In other words, although many explanations for criminal behavior have come and gone, "none has proven noticeably more effective in explaining, predicting, or controlling crime."[30] But that may be about to change, according to Wells. Contemporary criminological theorizing is interdisciplinary and conservative in its approach to crime causation, and major changes in the premises on which criminological theories are built are unlikely without significant ideological shifts or changes in basic components of the social structure, such as the economy, the political system, or the family, but significant social change creates the need for new theoretical formulations. "Legal events in the 1960s and 1970s changed abortion from a criminal act to a routine medical procedure."[31] An aversion to even minor physical force may require a redefinition of crimes like child abuse, spousal abuse, elder abuse, and sexual aggression. Both of these examples point to our basic understanding of criminal violence undergoing fundamental modifications that will result in a concomitant change in our attempts to theorize about its causes.

Wells saw similar possibilities for theoretical change due to advances in scientific knowledge. For example, if research on the human genome yields definitive evidence that some forms of aggression and violence are biologically grounded, that would provide the basis for an entirely new group of biological explanations for at least certain forms of criminal activity.

> Significant social change creates the need for new theoretical formulations.

Based on emerging explanations of crime, Wells made a number of specific predictions about new criminological theories:[32]

- They will be more eclectic and less tied to a single theoretical tradition or discipline.
- They will be more comparative and less confined to a single society or single dominant group within society.
- They will be predominantly individualistic, rather than collective, and voluntaristic, rather than deterministic.
- They will be more applied and more pragmatic in orientation.
- They will be more focused on explaining white-collar crime.
- They will reflect a renewed appreciation for the biological foundations of human behavior, assigning more theoretical substance to biological and medical factors.

From about 1960 to 1985, criminological theory building fell by the wayside as a generation of criminologists trained in quantitative analysis repeatedly tested existing ideas at the expense of developing new ones; but in the mid-1980s, a dynamic new era of theory building was unleashed. Frank P. Williams III and Marilyn D. McShane explained, "As if the restraints on theory building had created a pent-up demand, criminologists began exploring new theoretical constructs during the 1980s. Slowly at first, and then with great rapidity, theoretical efforts began to emerge."[33]

Many of these new approaches, including postmodernism, feminist criminology, and peacemaking criminology, were discussed in previous chapters. One more perspective that deserves special attention is what David P. Farrington termed the "risk factor prevention paradigm."[34] Farrington explained, "The basic idea of the paradigm is very simple: Identify the key risk factors for offending and implement prevention methods designed to counteract them." Farrington said that the risk factor prevention paradigm, which experienced "an enormous increase in influence in criminology" during the 1990s, is especially important because it holds the potential for guiding criminological research, crime-control policy, and theoretical development well into the twenty-first century. The main challenges for the paradigm "are to determine which risk factors are causes, to establish what are protective factors, to identify the active ingredients of multiple component interventions, to evaluate the effectiveness of area-based intervention programs, and to assess the monetary costs and benefits of interventions."

alphaspirit/Shutterstock

A futuristic security interface. What future technologies can you envision that might significantly impact criminal activity in the United States?

Crime-Control Policies of the Future

The well-known futurist **Gene Stephens** predicts a growth in crime worldwide.[35] Stephens explained that even though official measures show crime is currently on the decline in the United States, America was one of the first nations to experience a rapid rise in criminality because it was the most advanced nation on the globe. It was a highly diverse, multicultural, industrialized, and democratic society; it strongly supported individual freedoms; and it fostered a strong sense of personal independence among its citizens.

Multiculturalism and heterogeneity, according to Stephens, increase anomie, so previously isolated homogeneous societies like those of Japan, Denmark, China, Greece, and Middle Eastern countries face a growing cultural diversity due to international migration, expansion of new social ideals, and increases in foreign commerce. "Heterogeneity in societies will be the rule in the twenty-first century, and failure to recognize and plan for such diversity can lead to serious crime problems, especially in emerging multicultural societies." Stephens's thesis is best summarized in this passage from his work: "The connection between crime and culture cannot be overemphasized: There are high-crime and low-crime cultures around the world. In the years ahead, many low-crime cultures may become high-crime cultures because of changing world demographics and politicoeconomic systems. In general, heterogeneous populations in which people have lots of political freedom (democracy) and lots of economic choice (capitalism) are prime candidates for crime unless a good socialization system is created and maintained."

Homogeneous nations—in which citizens share backgrounds, life experiences, and values—produce citizens who are generally capable of complying with the wishes of the majority and who can legislate controls over behavior that are not difficult for most citizens to respect. In such societies, a tradition of discipline, a belief in the laws, and an acceptance of personal responsibility are typically the norm.

Diverse societies suffer from constant internal conflict.

Diverse societies suffer from constant internal conflict, much of it focusing on acceptable ways of living and working. Heterogeneous societies tend to place a strong emphasis on individualism, and disagreement about the law and social norms is rife. Characteristic of such cultures is the fact that lawbreakers tend to deny responsibility and go to great lengths to avoid capture and conviction. Stephens pointed out that in some highly homogeneous cultures, such as Japan, those who break norms will often punish themselves, even if their transgressions are not publicly discovered but that such self-punishing behavior would be almost unthinkable in an advanced heterogeneous society like that of the United States. "Some nations, such as the United States, face pervasive *anomie* due to their lack of restraints on human desires."

Heterogeneity can arise in numerous ways, in both heterogeneous and homogeneous societies. One source of increasingly important differences in American society is the growth of a technological culture with two distinct groups: those who are technologically capable and those who are incapable of utilizing modern technology. To these two groups, we could add a third: the technologically aware, those who realize the importance of technology but who—because of age, lack of education, poverty, or other life circumstances—have not yet acquired the skills necessary to participate fully in what our highly technological society has to offer. According to Stephens: "More people are turning to street crime and violence because they find themselves unprepared, educationally or emotionally, to cope with the requirements for success in the new era."

Another reason that crime rates are high in increasingly heterogeneous societies is that such societies often display a lack of consistent child-care philosophies and child-rearing methods. "In some societies," stated Stephens, "parents are seen as primarily responsible for their children, but all citizens share in that responsibility, since everyone's welfare is affected by the proper socialization of each child." In others, children are viewed as the parents' property, and little is expected of parents other than that they be biologically capable of reproducing; no requirements are set for parental knowledge, skills, income, education, and so on. Stephens described child-rearing practices in those societies as "helter-skelter, catch-as-catch-can child care." Lacking child-rearing standards in which the majority of members of society can meaningfully participate, heterogeneous societies tend to produce adults who are irresponsible and who do not adhere to legal or other standards of behavior.

Future crimes will be plentiful, with countries around the world experiencing explosive growth in their crime rates. Stephens commented, "The United States was the first industrialized, democratic, heterogeneous nation and thus the first to face the crime problems associated with *anomie*." Now other nations are undergoing increased modernization, with many entering the postmodern era previously occupied solely by the United States. "We can theorize that crime will be a growth industry in many countries as they find themselves gripped by the same social forces that have long affected the United States."

Other authors have also attempted to describe crime-control issues that may face future policymakers.[36] Moore identified the following seven issues that are likely to concern crime-control planners in the near future:[37]

1. **New criminal groups.** "Groups such as Colombian drug cartels, Jamaican posses, Vietnamese gangs, various Chinese groups, and Los Angeles black street gangs are now a much bigger concern than the Mafia," and the criminal activity and influence of these new groups are growing rapidly. Traditional law enforcement responses, such as those developed to deal with Italian American Mafia organizations, may be inappropriate in the face of the new challenges these groups represent.
2. **Language barriers.** "U.S. law-enforcement officials now find themselves hampered by a lack of understanding about the language and culture of some of the new criminal groups [operating in America.]" Cuban, Mexican, Colombian, Japanese, and Chinese criminals and criminal organizations are becoming commonplace, and such groups are increasingly involved in international communications and travel.
3. **Distrust by ethnic communities.** More recent immigrant groups have been slow to assimilate into American culture and society, strongly holding on to native identities and distancing themselves from formal agencies of social control, such as the police. "In many of their countries of origin, new immigrants see police as corrupt, self-serving individuals, a viewpoint often not without foundation." A distrust of police and government representatives is

■ ***Kriminalpolitik*** The political handling of crime; also a criminology-based social policy.

nearly instinctual for members of such groups, making the work of law enforcement within the context of immigrant communities challenging and difficult.

4. **Greater reliance on community involvement.** "[D]ue to the increasing costs of electronic surveillance, informant programs, undercover operations, and witness-protection programs, police are now encouraging community members to become more involved in their own security." The involvement of private citizens in the battle against crime may be the only realistic solution to the problem; neighborhood watch programs, community volunteers in criminal justice organizations, and other neighborhood self-help programs such as school- and church-based education all may have a part in the future of neighborhood-based crime-control policy.
5. **More marketplace regulation.** Decriminalization and legalization will be of increasingly greater concern to future legislators, who will focus on regulating the marketplace for criminal activities like gambling, drug trafficking, and prostitution.
6. **Reduced public demand.** Future crime-control policies will aim to reduce involvement in criminal activity by providing better education and mandating other policies that will lower the demand for drugs and other illegal services.
7. **Increased treatment.** In the future, a greater emphasis will be placed on the treatment of all forms of criminality, including drug abuse, gambling, and rape. This approach contrasts with today's "get tough" policies.

Learn more about possible crime-control policies of the future from **Library Extra EP–4**.

Can We Solve the Problem of Crime?

In 1956, European writer Hermanus Bianchi emphasized what he saw as the difference between criminology and what he termed ***Kriminalpolitik***, meaning the political handling of crime or a criminology-based social policy.[38] Criminology should be considered a "metascience" or "a science of wider scope [than that of criminal law, jurisprudence, criminal justice, or corrections] whose terminology can be used to clarify the conceptions of its subdisciplines. Far from being a mere auxiliary to the criminal law, it is therefore superior to it."[39] Bianchi believed that if criminology were to remain pure, it could not afford to "sully its hands" with political concerns.

Today, the image esteemed by criminologists and the expectations they hold for their discipline are quite different than in Bianchi's time. Many criminologists expect to work hand in hand with politicians and policy makers in forging crime-control agendas based on scientific knowledge and criminological theorizing and would say that this change in attitude represents a maturation of the discipline of criminology.

Whether effective crime-control policies can ever be implemented is a different matter. Some critics have argued that only drastic policy-level changes can address the real issues underlying high rates of crime and criminal activity; drug legalization, elimination of guns throughout America, nightly curfews, and closer control of media violence may be necessary before crime can be curbed. "Reforms that substantially will lower the crime rate are unlikely because of cultural taboos," commented Lawrence Friedman, a Stanford University law professor and author of the book *Crime and Punishment in American History*.[40] "If you add up all the taboos we have—against legalization of drugs, real gun control, paying taxes for social programs we might at least try—it's hard not to come to the conclusion that there isn't much we can do about crime." Many existing taboos are rooted in citizens' demands for individual freedoms. "At one time in South Korea," explained Friedman, "they had an absolute curfew between midnight and 5 A.M. The police kept everyone off the streets. It was as hard on burglars as other citizens and very effective at squelching crime. But most Americans would consider that an unacceptable inroad on their personal lives."[41]

Complicating the picture further are the numerous interest groups, each with its own agenda, that are clamoring to be heard by policy makers. Robert D. Pursley, professor of criminal justice at Buffalo State College, stated, "Our nation's efforts to deal with crime remind us that crime, among other things, is a highly political issue that has been transformed into a racially volatile subject. This issue provides an excellent window into political policymaking. Opposing ideological lines have divided our efforts to develop comprehensive anticrime programs. Deep fissures in our social fabric have contributed to conflicting attitudes about crime and its control."[42]

Racial divisiveness has created one of those fissures. According to Pursley, "Our anticrime programs and studies of traditional street crimes, especially those involving violence, show that such crimes are disproportionately the acts of young African-American males. So long as black men commit violent crimes at a rate that is six to eight times higher than that found among whites and three to four times higher than that among Latino males, race and crime will be threads of the same cloth. These facts have become unpopular and certainly not politically correct to discuss in certain circles, but they remain facts. No attempt to silence those who raise such issues by denouncing them as 'racists' can conceal these statistics."[43]

For some groups in some locales, violations of the criminal law are simply part of the landscape. Among certain segments of the American population, crime may be an accepted way of doing business, and criminal activity, even when discovered, might not necessarily be stigmatizing. Those who commit crimes could continue to hold positions of prestige or highly visible public offices if their constituencies fail to condemn their illicit behavior and may even serve as role models—albeit dubious role models—to youngsters. Although such a perspective is undoubtedly a minority point of view, it seriously impacts the ability of policy makers to establish consistent policies in the battle against crime.

KEY TERMS

cross-impact analysis, 404
Delphi Method, 404
environmental scanning, 404
future criminology, 402
futurist, 402
futures research, 404
***Kriminalpolitik*, 409**
scenario writing, 404
strategic assessment, 405
trend extrapolation, 404

KEY NAMES

Georgette Bennett, 406
Richter H. Moore, Jr., 405
Gene Stephens, 407
William L. Tafoya, 404

QUESTIONS FOR REVIEW

1. What techniques are used in the field of futures research for assessing the future?
2. What are some likely future crimes, and how will future criminal activity differ from criminal activity today?
3. What can be predicted about the future of criminological theorizing?

QUESTIONS FOR REFLECTION

1. This text emphasizes the theme of social problems versus social responsibility. Which perspective do you think will be more dominant in twenty-first-century crime-control planning? Why?
2. Do you believe it is possible to know the future? What techniques are identified in this chapter for assessing possible futures? Which one of these do you think holds the most promise? Why?
3. What kinds of crime-control policies do you think the future will bring? Will they be consistent with present understandings of civil liberties? Why or why not?

Glossary

acquaintance rape A rape characterized by a prior social, although not necessarily intimate or familial, relationship between the victim and the perpetrator.

addiction A chronic brain disease characterized by compulsive drug seeking and use despite harmful consequences.[1]

administrative law Law that regulates many daily business activities. Violations of these regulations generally result in warnings or fines, depending on their adjudged severity.

adolescence-limited offender A juvenile offender who abandons delinquency upon maturity.

Age of Reason *See* Enlightenment.

aggravated assault (UCR) An unlawful attack by one person upon another for the purpose of inflicting severe or aggravated bodily injury. *See also* simple assault.

allele Variation of a gene.

alloplastic adaptation A form of adjustment that results from changes in the environment surrounding an individual.

altruism Selfless, helping behavior.

androcentricity A male-dominated perspective, as in the case of criminologists who study only the criminality of males.

anomie A social condition in which norms are uncertain or lacking.

anomie theory *See* strain theory.

Anti-Drug Abuse Act A federal law (Public Law 99–570) enacted in 1986 that established new federal mandatory minimum sentences for drug offenses.

antisocial (asocial) personality An individual who is unsocialized and whose behavior pattern brings him or her into repeated conflict with society.

antisocial personality disorder (ASPD) A psychological condition exhibited by an individual who is unsocialized and whose behavior pattern brings him or her into conflict with society.[2]

applied research Any research based on scientific inquiry that is designed and carried out with practical applications in mind.

Arrestee Drug Abuse Monitoring (ADAM) Program A National Institute of Justice program that tracks trends in the prevalence and types of drug use among booked arrestees in urban areas.

arson The willful or malicious burning (or attempt to burn), with or without intent to defraud, of a house, public building, motor vehicle or aircraft, or personal property of another.

asocial personality *See* antisocial (asocial) personality.

assault *See* aggravated assault; simple assault.

asset forfeiture The authorized seizure of money, negotiable instruments, securities, or other things of value. In federal antidrug laws, it is the authorization of judicial representatives to seize all monies, negotiable instruments, securities, or other things of value furnished or intended to be furnished by any person in exchange for a controlled substance, as well as all proceeds traceable to such an exchange.

atavism A term used by Cesare Lombroso to suggest that criminals are physiological throwbacks to earlier stages of human evolution. The term is derived from the Latin term *atavus*, which means "ancestor."

attachment theory A social-psychological perspective on delinquent and criminal behavior holding that the successful development of secure attachment between a child and his or her primary caregiver provides the basic foundation for all future psychological development.

audit trail A record of computer activities that enables auditors to reconstruct and review the sequence of activities surrounding each event in one or more related transactions from inception to output of final results back to inception.

autoplastic adaptation A form of adjustment that results from changes within an individual.

Balanced and Restorative Justice (BARJ) Model A form of restorative justice which holds that the community, victim, and offender should receive balanced attention and all three should gain tangible benefits from their interactions with the justice system.

bank fraud Any fraud or embezzlement that occurs within or against financial institutions that are insured or regulated by the U.S. government. Fraud of financial institutions includes commercial-loan fraud, check fraud, counterfeit negotiable instruments, mortgage fraud, and false credit applications.

behavioral genetics The study of genetic and environmental contributions to individual variations in human behavior.

behaviorism A psychological perspective that stresses observable behavior and disregards unobservable events that occur in the mind.

behavior theory A psychological perspective positing that behavior that is rewarded will increase in frequency and behavior that is punished will decrease in frequency.

bias crime *See* hate crime.

biological theories Theories that maintain that the basic determinants of human behavior, including criminality, are constitutionally or physiologically based and often inherited.

biopsychology A field of study that combines the principles of psychology with those of neuroscience and biology. It examines how thoughts and behavior are mediated by interaction between the brain (especially neurotransmitters) and the environment; also known as *behavioral psychology* and *behavioral neuroscience*.

biosocial criminology A theoretical perspective that sees the interaction between biology and the environment as key to understanding human behavior, including criminality.

booster A frequent shoplifter.

born criminal An individual who is born with a genetic predilection toward criminality.

bourgeoisie The "haves," or the class of people who own the means of production in the Marxist theory.

Brady Handgun Violence Prevention Act A federal law (Public Law 103–159) enacted in 1993 that initiated a national background checking system for all potential gun purchasers.

Brawner rule A somewhat vague rule for determining insanity created in the 1972 federal court case of *United States* v. *Brawner*

(471 F.2d 969), since superseded by statute, that asks the jury to decide whether the defendant could be justly held responsible for the criminal act with which he or she stands charged in the face of any claims of insanity or mental incapacity.

broken windows theory A perspective on crime causation that holds that physical deterioration in an area leads to increased concerns for personal safety among area residents and to higher crime rates in that area.

Buck* v. *Bell A U.S. Supreme Court case decided in 1927 that upheld state statutes authorizing the sterilization of individuals who were determined to have "bad genes," and which supported the eugenics movement of the early twentieth century.

burglary The trespassory breaking and entering of the dwelling house of another in the nighttime with the intent to commit a felony; also the unlawful entry of a structure to commit a felony or a theft.

burglary (UCR) The unlawful entry of a structure to commit a felony or a theft.

Cambridge Study in Delinquent Development A longitudinal (life course) study of crime and delinquency tracking a cohort of 411 boys born in London in 1953.

capable guardian One who effectively discourages crime.

capital punishment The legal imposition of a sentence of death upon a convicted offender; also known as the *death penalty*.

carjacking The stealing of a car while it is occupied.

Chicago Area Project A program originating at the University of Chicago during the 1930s that focused on urban ecology and that attempted to reduce delinquency, crime, and social disorganization in transitional neighborhoods.

Chicago School of criminology An ecological approach to explaining crime that examines how social disorganization contributes to social pathology.

child pornography A visual representation of any kind that depicts a minor engaging in sexually explicit conduct that is obscene and that lacks serious literary, artistic, political, or scientific value.

child sexual abuse (CSA) A term encompassing a variety of criminal and civil offenses in which an adult engages in sexual activity with a minor, exploits a minor for purposes of sexual gratification, or exploits a minor sexually for purposes of profit.

chromosomes Bundles of genes.

civil law The body of law that regulates arrangements between individuals, such as contracts and claims to property.

Classical School A criminological perspective of the late 1700s and early 1800s that had its roots in the Enlightenment and that held that humans are rational beings, that crime is the result of the exercise of free will, and that punishment can be effective in reducing the incidence of crime to the degree it negates the pleasure to be derived from crime commission.

clearance rate The proportion of reported or discovered crimes within a given offense category that are solved.

Code of Hammurabi An early set of laws established by the Babylonian king Hammurabi, who ruled the ancient city from 1792 to 1750 B.C.

cognitive information-processing theory (CIP) A psychological perspective that involves the study of human perceptions, information processing, and decision making.

cohort A group of individuals having certain significant social characteristics in common, such as gender and date and place of birth.

cohort analysis A social scientific technique that studies a population with common characteristics over time. Cohort analysis usually begins at birth and traces the development of cohort members until they reach a certain age.

comfort serial killers Serial killers motivated by financial or material gain.

Commission on Law Observance and Enforcement *See* Wickersham Commission.

common law Law originating from usage and custom rather than from written statutes. The term refers to nonstatutory customs, traditions, and precedents that help guide judicial decision making.

Communications Decency Act (CDA) A 1996 federal statute labeled Title 5 of the federal Telecommunications Act of 1996 (Public Law 104–104, 110 Stat. 56) that seeks to protect minors from harmful material on the Internet and that criminalizes the knowing transmission of obscene or indecent messages to any recipient under 18 years of age. In 1997, in *Reno* v. *ACLU* (521 U.S. 844), the U.S. Supreme Court found the bulk of the CDA to be unconstitutional, ruling that it contravenes First Amendment free speech guarantees.

comparative criminologist A criminologist involved in the cross-national study of crime.

comparative criminology The cross-national study of crime.

Comprehensive Crime Control Act A far-reaching federal law (Public Law 98–473) enacted in 1984 that mandated new federal sentencing guidelines, eliminated parole at the federal level, limited the use of the insanity defense in federal criminal courts, and increased federal penalties associated with drug dealing.

Comprehensive Strategy for Serious, Violent, and Chronic Juvenile Offenders program A National Institute of Justice initiative that provides participating communities with a framework for preventing delinquency, intervening in early delinquent behavior, and responding to serious, violent, and chronic offending. The strategy is based on a social development model.

computer abuse An unlawful incident associated with computer technology in which a victim suffers loss or a perpetrator reaps benefit.[3]

computer crime Any violation of a federal or state computer crime statute. The term is now being replaced with *cybercrime*.

computer-related crime An illegal act using computer technology in its perpetration, investigation, or prosecution.

computer virus A program designed to invade computer systems and either modify the way they operate or alter the information they store.

conditioning A psychological principle that holds that the frequency of any behavior can be increased or decreased through reward, punishment, or association with other stimuli.

conduct norm A shared expectation of a social group relative to personal conduct.

confidentiality *See* data confidentiality.

conflict perspective An analytical perspective on social organization that holds that conflict is a fundamental aspect of social life and can never be fully resolved.

confounding effect A rival explanation or competing hypothesis that is a threat to the internal or external validity of a research design.

consensus perspective An analytical perspective on social organization that holds that most members of society agree about what is right and wrong and that the various elements of society work together toward a common vision of the greater good.

constitutional theories Theories that explain criminality by reference to offenders' body types, inheritance, genetics, or external observable physical characteristics.

constitutive criminology The study of the process by which human beings create an ideology of crime that sustains the notion of crime as a concrete reality.

containment An aspect of the social bond that acts as a stabilizing force to prevent individuals from committing crimes and that keeps them from engaging in deviance.

containment theory A form of control theory that suggests that a series of both internal and external factors contributes to law-abiding behavior.

control group A group of experimental subjects that, although the subject of measurement and observation, is not exposed to the experimental intervention.

controlled experiment An experiment that attempts to hold conditions (other than the intentionally introduced experimental intervention) constant.

control ratio The amount of control to which a person is subject versus the amount of control that person exerts over others.

control theory *See* social control theory.

controlled substances Chemical substances or drugs as defined under the 1970 federal Controlled Substances Act.

convict criminology A radical paradigm consisting of writings on criminology by convicted felons and ex-inmates who have acquired academic credentials or who are associated with credentialed others; also known as *alternative criminology*.

corporate crime A violation of a criminal statute by an organization or its executives, employees, or agents acting on its behalf and for its benefit.[4]

corporate fraud A type of organizational fraud, such as accounting schemes, self-dealing by corporate executives, obstruction of justice, insider trading, kickbacks, and misuse of corporate property for personal use.

correctional psychology The branch of forensic psychology concerned with the diagnosis and classification of offenders, the treatment of correctional populations, and the rehabilitation of inmates and other law violators.

correlation A causal, complementary, or reciprocal relationship between two measurable variables. *See also* statistical correlation.

Cosa Nostra *See* La Cosa Nostra.

crime Any human conduct in violation of the criminal laws of the federal government or a local jurisdiction with the power to make such laws.

crime typology A classification of crimes along a particular dimension, such as legal categories, offender motivation, victim behavior, or characteristics of individual offenders.

Crime Victims' Rights Act A 2004 federal law that establishes statutory rights for victims of federal crimes and gives victims the necessary legal authority to assert those rights in federal courts.

criminal anthropology The scientific study of the relationship between human physical characteristics and criminality.

criminal behavior Human activity, both intentional and negligent, that violates the criminal law. It may include a failure to act when there is a legal obligation to do so.

criminal career The longitudinal sequence of crimes committed by an individual offender.

criminal enterprise A group of individuals with an identified hierarchy engaged in significant criminal activities.

criminal homicide The illegal killing of one human being by another.

criminal homicide (UCR) The UCR category that includes and is limited to all offenses of causing the death of another person without justification or excuse.

criminalist A specialist in the collection and examination of the physical evidence of crime.

criminality A behavioral predisposition that disproportionately favors criminal activity.

criminality index The actual extent of the crime problem in a society. The criminality index is computed by adding the actual crime rate and the latent crime rate.

criminalize To make illegal.

criminal justice The scientific study of crime, the criminal law, and components of the criminal justice system, including the police, courts, and corrections.

criminal justice system The various agencies of justice, especially the police, courts, and corrections, whose goal it is to apprehend, convict, punish, and rehabilitate law violators.

criminal law The body of law that regulates actions that have the potential to harm the interests of the state or the federal government.

criminaloid A term used by Cesare Lombroso to describe the occasional criminal who is enticed into criminality primarily by environmental influences.

criminal psychology The application of the science and profession of psychology to questions and issues relating to law and the legal system; also known as *forensic psychology*.

criminal receiver *See* fence.

criminogenic needs Dynamic attributes (also known as *dynamic risk factors*) of offenders and their circumstances that are associated with rates of recidivism.

criminologist One who is trained in the field of criminology; also one who studies crime, criminals, and criminal behavior.

criminology An interdisciplinary profession built around the scientific study of crime and criminal behavior, including their forms, causes, legal aspects, and control.

criminology of place A perspective that emphasizes the importance of geographic location and architectural features as they are associated with the prevalence of criminal victimization; also known as *environmental criminology*.

critical criminology A perspective that holds that crime is the natural product of a capitalist system.

cross-impact analysis A technique of futures research that attempts to analyze one trend or event in light of the occurrence or nonoccurrence of a series of related events.

cultural transmission The idea that delinquency is transmitted through successive generations of people living in an area through the same process of social communication as languages, roles, and attitudes are transmitted.

culture conflict theory A sociological perspective on crime that suggests that the root cause of criminality can be found in a clash of values between variously socialized groups over what is acceptable or proper behavior; also known as *cultural deviance theory*.

cybercrime Any crime that involves the use of computers or the manipulation of digital data as well as any violation of a federal or state cybercrime statute.

Cyber Security Enhancement Act (CSEA) A federal law found in the Homeland Security Act of 2002 that directs the U.S. Sentencing Commission to take specific factors into account in creating new sentencing guidelines for cybercriminals.

cyberspace The computer-created matrix of virtual possibilities, including online services, in which human beings interact with one another and with the technology itself.

cyberstalking An array of high-technology options, including e-mail and the Internet, that an offender uses to harass or "follow" another individual.

cyberterrorism A form of terrorism that makes use of high technology, especially computer technology and the Internet, in planning and carrying out terrorist attacks

cycloid A term developed by Ernst Kretschmer to describe a particular relationship between body build and personality type. The cycloid personality, which was associated with a heavyset, soft type of body, was said to vacillate between normality and abnormality.

dangerous drug A controlled substance other than cocaine, opiates, and cannabis products. Amphetamines, LSD, methamphetamines, methcathinone, and phencyclidine (PCP), as well as designer drugs, are all considered dangerous drugs.

dangerousness The likelihood that a given individual will later harm society or others. Dangerousness is often measured in terms of recidivism, or the likelihood of new crime commission or rearrest for a new crime within a five-year period following arrest or release from confinement.

dark figure of crime The numerical total of unreported crimes not reflected in official crime statistics.

data confidentiality The ethical requirement of social scientific research to protect the confidentiality of individual research participants while preserving justified research access to the information participants provide.

data encryption The process by which information is encoded, making it unreadable to all but its intended recipients.

date rape The unlawful forced sexual intercourse with a woman against her will that occurs within the context of a dating relationship.

***Daubert* standard** A test of scientific acceptability applicable to the gathering of evidence in criminal cases.

DCS–3000 An FBI-developed network diagnostic tool that is capable of assisting in criminal investigations by monitoring and capturing large amounts of Internet traffic.

death penalty *See* capital punishment.

deconstructionist theory A postmodern perspective that challenges existing criminological theories in order to debunk them and that works toward replacing traditional ideas with concepts seen as more appropriate to the postmodern era.

decriminalization The redefinition of certain previously criminal behaviors as regulated activities that become "ticketable" instead of "arrestable."

defensible space The range of mechanisms that combine to bring an environment under the control of its residents.

delinquency Violations of the criminal law and other misbehavior committed by young people.

Delphi Method A technique of futures research that uses repetitive questioning of experts to refine predictions.

demographics The characteristics of population groups, usually expressed in statistical fashion.

demography The study of the characteristics of population groups.

descriptive statistics The statistics that describe, summarize, or highlight the relationships within data that have been gathered.

designer drug A new substance designed by slightly altering the chemical makeup of other illegal or tightly controlled drugs.[5]

desistance A person's cessation of criminal activity or termination of a period of involvement in offending behavior.

desistance phenomenon The observable decrease in crime rates that is invariably associated with age.

determinate sentencing A criminal punishment strategy that mandates a specified and fixed amount of time to be served for every offense category. Under the strategy, for example, all offenders convicted of the same degree of burglary would be sentenced to the same length of time behind bars. It is also known as *fixed sentencing*.

deterrence The prevention of crime. *See also* general deterrence; specific deterrence.

deterrence strategy A crime-control strategy whose goal is to lessen motivation for a crime by increasing the perceived sureness or severity of its penalty.[6]

deviant behavior Any human activity that violates social norms.

differential association The sociological thesis that criminality, like any other form of behavior, is learned through a process of association with others who communicate criminal values.

differential identification theory An explanation for crime and deviance that holds that people pursue criminal or deviant behavior to the extent that they identify themselves with real or imaginary people from whose perspective their criminal or deviant behavior seems acceptable.

Digital Theft Deterrence and Copyright Damages Improvement Act A 1999 federal law (Public Law 106–160) that amends Section 504(c) of the Copyright Act increasing the amount of damages that could be awarded in cases of copyright infringement.

disclosure (of research methods) The provision of information to potential subjects informing them of the nature of the research methods to be used by the social scientific study in which their involvement is planned.

discrediting information Any information that is inconsistent with the managed impressions being communicated in a given situation.

displacement A shift of criminal activity from one location to another.

distributive justice The rightful, equitable, and just distribution of rewards within a society.

dizygotic (DZ) twin A twin who develops from a separate ovum and who carries the genetic material shared by siblings.

DNA fingerprinting *See* DNA profiling.

DNA profiling The use of biological residue found at a crime scene for genetic comparisons in aiding the identification of criminal suspects.

domestic terrorism The unlawful use of force or violence by an individual or group based and operating entirely within the United States and its territories, without foreign influence, directed at the U.S. government, the civilian population, or any segment thereof for political or social objectives.[7]

dramaturgical perspective A theoretical point of view that depicts human behavior as centered around the purposeful management of interpersonal impressions; also known as *dramaturgy*.

dramaturgy *See* dramaturgical perspective.

drug-defined crime A violation of the laws prohibiting or regulating the possession, use, or distribution of illegal drugs.

drug-related crime A crime in which drugs contribute to the offense (excluding violations of drug laws).

drug trafficking The manufacturing, distributing, dispensing, importing, and/or exporting of a controlled substance or a counterfeit substance.[8]

Durham rule A standard for judging legal insanity that holds that an accused is not criminally responsible if his or her unlawful act was the product of mental disease or mental defect.

ecological theory A type of sociological approach that emphasizes demographics (the characteristics of population groups) and geographics (the mapped location of such groups relative to one another) and that sees the social disorganization that characterizes delinquency areas as a major cause of criminality and victimization.

ectomorph A body type originally described as thin and fragile, with long, slender, poorly muscled extremities and delicate bones.

ego The reality-testing part of the personality; also known as the *reality principle.* More formally, it is the personality component that is conscious, most immediately controls behavior, and is most in touch with external reality.[9]

electroencephalogram (EEG) The electrical measurement of brain wave activity.

Electronic Frontier Foundation (EFF) A nonprofit organization formed in July 1990 to help ensure that the principles embodied in the Constitution and the Bill of Rights are protected as new communications technologies emerge.

encryption *See* data encryption.

endomorph A body type originally described as soft and round or overweight.

Enlightenment A social movement that arose during the eighteenth century and that built upon ideas like empiricism, rationality, free will, humanism, and natural law; also known as *Age of Reason.*

environmental crime A violation of the criminal law committed by businesses, business officials, organizational entities, and/or individuals that damages some protected or otherwise significant aspect of the natural environment.

environmental criminology A perspective that emphasizes the importance of geographic location and architectural features as they are associated with the prevalence of criminal victimization; also known as *criminology of place.*

environmental scanning A technique of futures research. It is a "systematic effort to identify in an elemental way future developments (trends or events) that could plausibly occur over the time horizon of interest."[10]

epigenetics The study of the chemical reactions that occur within a genome, and that switch parts of the genome on or off at strategic times and locations.

ethnic succession The continuing process whereby one immigrant or ethnic group succeeds another by assuming its position in society.

ethnocentrism The phenomenon of "culture-centeredness" by which one uses one's own culture as a benchmark against which to judge all other patterns of behavior.

eugenic criminology A perspective that holds that the root causes of criminality are passed from generation to generation in the form of "bad genes."

eugenics The study of hereditary improvement by genetic control.

evidence based Any evidence built on scientific findings, especially practices and policies founded on the results of randomized, controlled experiments.

evidence-based criminology A form of contemporary criminology that makes use of rigorous social scientific techniques, especially randomized, controlled experiments and the systematic review of research results; also known as *knowledge-based criminology.*

evolutionary ecology An approach to understanding crime that draws attention to the ways people develop over the course of their lives.

evolutionary neuroandrogenic (ENA) theory A perspective that holds that (1) the propensity for crime commission evolved among humans beings as part of the male reproductive strategy, and (2) a particular neurochemistry, which is characteristic of males, increases the probability of criminality among males relative to females.

evolutionary perspective A theoretical approach that (1) seeks to explain behavior with reference to human evolutionary history and (2) recognizes the influence that genes have over human traits.

experiment *See* controlled experiment; quasi-experimental design.

experimental criminology *See* evidence-based criminology.

expert system A system of computer hardware and software that attempts to duplicate the decision-making processes used by skilled investigators in the analysis of evidence and in the recognition of patterns that such evidence might represent.

exposure-reduction theory A theory of intimate homicide that claims that a decline in domesticity, accompanied by an improvement in the economic status of women and a growth in domestic violence resources, explains observed decreases in intimate-partner homicide.

expressive crime A criminal offense that results from acts of interpersonal hostility, such as jealousy, revenge, romantic triangles, and quarrels.

external validity The ability to generalize research findings to other settings.

felony A serious criminal offense, specifically one punishable by death or by incarceration in a prison facility for a year or more.

felony murder An unlawful homicide that occurs during the commission or attempted commission of a felony or certain felonies specified by law.

feminist criminology A corrective model intended to redirect the thinking of mainstream criminologists to include gender awareness.

fence An individual or a group involved in the buying, selling, and distribution of stolen goods.

First and Fourth Amendments to the U.S. Constitution The amendments that guarantee each person freedom of speech and security in his or her "persons, houses, papers, and effects, against unreasonable searches and seizures."

first-degree murder A criminal homicide that is planned or involves premeditation.

Five Factor Model A psychological perspective that builds on the Big Five core traits of personality.

focal concern A key value of any culture, especially a delinquent subculture.

folkways A time-honored custom. Although folkways carry the force of tradition, their violation is unlikely to threaten the survival of the group. *See also* mores.

forcible rape (UCR) The carnal knowledge of a person forcibly and against his or her will.

foreign terrorist organization (FTO) A foreign organization that engages in terrorist activity threatening the security of U.S. nationals or the national security of the United States and that is so designated by the U.S. secretary of state.

forensic psychiatry A branch of psychiatry having to do with the study of crime and criminality.

forensic psychology The application of the science and profession of psychology to questions and issues relating to law and the legal system; also known as *criminal psychology.*

forfeiture *See* asset forfeiture.

frontal brain hypothesis A perspective that references physical changes in certain parts of the brain to explain criminality.

frustration-aggression theory A theory that holds that frustration, which is a natural consequence of living, is a root cause of crime. Criminal behavior can be a form of adaptation when it results in stress reduction.

future criminology The study of likely futures as they impinge on crime and its control.

futures research "A multidisciplinary branch of operations research [whose principal aim] is to facilitate long-range planning based on (1) forecasting from the past supported by mathematical models, (2) cross-disciplinary treatment of its subject matter, (3) systematic use of expert judgments, and (4) a systems-analytical approach to its problems."[11]

futurist One who studies the future.

gateway offense An offense, usually fairly minor in nature, that leads to more serious offenses.

gender gap The observed differences between male and female rates of criminal offending in a given society.

gender ratio problem The need for an explanation of the fact that the number of crimes committed by men far exceeds the number of crimes committed by women in almost all categories.

gene expression The process by which the coded information that is stored within a gene is used to create a biological product, usually a protein. Also, the manifestation of a trait in an individual carrying the gene or genes that determine that trait.

gene pool The total genetic information of all the individuals in a breeding population.

general deterrence A goal of criminal sentencing that seeks to prevent others from committing crimes similar to the one for which a particular offender is being sentenced.

general strain theory (GST) A perspective that suggests that law-breaking behavior is a coping mechanism enabling those who engage in it to deal with the socioemotional problems generated by negative social relations.

general theory A theory that attempts to explain all (or at least most) forms of criminal conduct through a single overarching approach.

general theory of crime (GTC) A perspective on crime, developed by Travis Hirschi and Michael Gottfredson, that asserts "that the operation of a single mechanism, low self-control, accounts for 'all crime, at all times,' [including] acts ranging from vandalism to homicide, from rape to white-collar crime."[12]

genes Parts of the human genome. They are made of DNA and carry coded instructions for making everything the body needs.

genetic determinism The belief that genes are the major determining factor in human behavior.

globalization A process of social homogenization that everyday experiences can foster by standardized cultural expressions through the diffusion of goods and ideas around the world.[13]

green criminology The study of environmental harm, crime, law, regulation, victimization, and justice.

guilty but mentally ill (GBMI) A finding that offenders are guilty of the criminal offense with which they are charged, but because of their prevailing mental condition, they are generally sent to psychiatric hospitals for treatment rather than to prison. Once they have been declared cured, such offenders can be transferred to correctional facilities to serve out their sentences.

habitual offender statute A law intended to keep repeat criminal offenders behind bars. These laws sometimes come under the rubric of "three strikes and you're out."

hacker A person who uses computers for exploration and exploitation.

hard determinism The belief that crime results from forces beyond the control of the individual.

hate crime A criminal offense in which the motive is hatred, bias, or prejudice based on the actual or perceived race, color, religion, national origin, ethnicity, gender, or sexual orientation of another individual or group of individuals.

Hate Crimes Sentencing Enhancement Act A federal law (28 U.S. Code, Section 994) enacted in 1994 as part of the Violent Crime Control and Law Enforcement Act that required the U.S. Sentencing Commission to increase penalties for crimes in which the victim was chosen due to actual or perceived color, ethnicity, religion, gender, disability, or sexual orientation.

hedonistic calculus The belief, first proposed by Jeremy Bentham, that behavior holds value to any individual undertaking it according to the amount of pleasure or pain it can be expected to produce for that person. *See also* utilitarianism.

hedonistic serial killers Serial killers who derive pleasure from killing.

heredity The passing of traits from parent to child.

heritability A statistical construct that estimates the amount of variation in the traits of a population that is attributable to genetic factors.

Heroin Signature Program (HSP) A Drug Enforcement Administration program that identifies the geographic source of a heroin sample through the detection of specific chemical characteristics in the sample peculiar to the source area.

homicide The killing of one human being by another.

hormone A chemical substance produced by the body that regulates and controls the activity of certain cells or organs.

household crime (NCVS) An attempted or completed crime that does not involve confrontation, such as burglary, motor vehicle theft, and household larceny.

human agency The active role that people take in their lives; the fact that people are not merely subject to social and structural constraints but actively make choices and decisions based on the alternatives they see before them.

human development The relationship between the maturing individual and his or her changing environment, as well as the social processes that the relationship entails.

human ecology The interrelationship between human beings and the physical and cultural environments in which they live.

human genome A complete copy of the entire set of human gene instructions.

human smuggling A type of illegal immigration in which an agent is paid to help a person cross a border clandestinely.[14]

human trafficking *See* trafficking in persons (TIP).

hypoglycemia A medical condition characterized by low blood sugar.

hypothesis An explanation accounting for a set of facts that can be tested by further investigation.[15]

id The aspect of the personality from which drives, wishes, urges, and desires emanate. More formally, this division of the psyche is associated with instinctual impulses and demands for immediate satisfaction of primitive needs.[16]

identity theft The unauthorized use of another individual's personal information to commit fraud.

Identity Theft and Assumption Deterrence Act The first federal law to make identity theft a crime. The 1998 statute makes it a crime whenever anyone "knowingly transfers or uses, without lawful authority, a means of identification of another person with the intent to commit, or to aid or abet, any unlawful activity that constitutes a violation of federal law, or that constitutes a felony under any applicable state or local law."

Identity Theft Penalty Enhancement Act A 2004 federal law that added two years to federal prison sentences for criminals convicted of using stolen credit card numbers and other personal data to commit crimes.

illegitimate opportunity structure A subcultural pathway to success that the wider society disapproves of.

impression management The intentional enactment of practiced behavior that is intended to convey to others one's desirable personal characteristics and social qualities.

incapacitation The use of imprisonment or other means to reduce the likelihood that an offender will be capable of committing future offenses.

individual-rights advocate One who seeks to protect personal freedoms in the face of criminal prosecution.

inferential statistics Any statistics that specify how likely findings are to be true for other populations or in other locales.

informed consent The ethical requirement of social scientific research that research subjects be informed about the nature of the research to be conducted, their anticipated role in it, and the uses to which the data they provide will be put.

infrastructure The basic facilities, services, and installations needed for the functioning of a community or society, such as its transportation and communications systems, water and power lines, and public institutions.[17]

insanity (legal) A legally established inability to understand right from wrong or to conform one's behavior to the requirements of the law.

insanity (psychological) A persistent mental disorder.[18]

insider trading A type of equity trading based on confidential information about important events that may affect the price of the issue being traded.

institutional robbery A robbery that occurs in a commercial setting, such as a convenience store, gas station, and bank.

instrumental crime A goal-directed offense that involves some degree of planning by the offender and little or no precipitation by the victim.

instrumental marxism A perspective that holds that those in power intentionally create laws and social institutions that serve their own interests and keep others from becoming powerful.

integrated theory An explanatory perspective that merges (or attempts to merge) concepts drawn from different sources.

interactional theory A theoretical approach to exploring crime and delinquency that blends social control and social learning perspectives.

interactionist perspective *See* social process theory.

interdiction An international drug-control policy whose goal is to stop drugs from entering the country illegally.

internal validity The certainty that experimental interventions did indeed cause the changes observed in the study group; also the control over confounding factors that tend to invalidate the results of an experiment.

international terrorism The unlawful use of force or violence by an individual or group with a connection to a foreign power or whose activities transcend national boundaries against people or property to intimidate or coerce a government, the civilian population, or any segment thereof for political or social objectives.[19]

Internet The world's largest computer network for moving data and making information accessible.

intersubjectivity A scientific principle that requires that independent observers see the same thing under the same circumstances for observations to be regarded as valid.

intimate-partner assault A gender-neutral term used to characterize assaultive behavior that takes place between individuals involved in an intimate relationship.

irresistible-impulse test A standard for judging legal insanity that holds that a defendant is not guilty of a criminal offense if the person, by virtue of his or her mental state or psychological condition, was not able to resist committing the crime.

Italian School of Criminology A perspective on criminology developed in the late 1800s that held that criminals can be identified by physical features and are throwbacks to earlier stages of human evolution. The Italian School was largely based on studies of criminal anthropology.

jockey A professional car thief involved in calculated steal-to-order car thefts.

joyriding An opportunistic car theft, often committed by a teenager, for fun or thrills.

Juke family A well-known "criminal family" studied by Richard L. Dugdale.

just deserts model The notion that criminal offenders deserve the punishment they receive at the hands of the law and that punishments should be appropriate to the type and severity of crime committed.

justice model A contemporary model of imprisonment in which the principle of just deserts forms the underlying social philosophy.

Kallikak family A well-known "criminal family" studied by Henry H. Goddard.

Kefauver Committee The popular name for the federal Special Committee to Investigate Organized Crime in Interstate Commerce, formed in 1951.

Kriminalpolitik The political handling of crime; also a criminology-based social policy.

labeling theory An interactionist perspective that sees continued crime as a consequence of limited opportunities for acceptable behavior that follow from the negative responses of society to those defined as offenders; also known as *social reaction theory*.

La Cosa Nostra A criminal organization of Sicilian origin; also known as *Mafia*. The term literally means "our thing."

larceny The unlawful taking or attempted taking of property (other than a motor vehicle) from the possession of another, by stealth, without force or deceit, with intent to permanently deprive the owner of the property.

larceny-theft (UCR) The unlawful taking, carrying, leading, or riding away of property (other than a motor vehicle) from the possession or constructive possession of another (attempts are included).

latent crime rate A rate of crime calculated on the basis of crimes that would likely be committed by those who are in prison or jail or who are otherwise incapacitated by the justice system.

law-and-order advocate One who suggests that under certain circumstances involving criminal threats to public safety, the interests of society should take precedence over individual rights.

Law Enforcement Assistance Administration (LEAA) A federal program, established under Title 1 of the Omnibus Crime Control and Safe Streets Act of 1967, designed to provide assistance to police agencies.

learning theory *See* social learning theory.

left realism A conflict perspective that insists on a pragmatic assessment of crime and its associated problems; also known as *radical realism* or *critical realism*.

left-realist criminology An approach to criminology based on ideas inherent in the perspective of left realism.

legalization The elimination of laws and criminal penalties associated with certain behaviors—usually the production, sale, distribution, and possession of a controlled substance.

liberal feminism A feminist perspective in criminology that sees gender-role socialization as the primary source of women's oppression.

life course The different pathways through the age-differentiated life span; also the course of a person's life over time.

life course–persistent offender An offender who, as a result of neuropsychological deficits combined with poverty and family dysfunction, displays patterns of misbehavior throughout life.

life course perspective A perspective that draws attention to the fact that criminal behavior tends to follow a distinct pattern across the life cycle; also known as *life course criminology*.

lifestyle theory Another term for the routine activities approach of Lawrence Cohen and Marcus Felson. *See also* routine activities theory.

Mafia A criminal organization of Sicilian origin; also known as *La Cosa Nostra*.

mala in se An act that is thought to be wrong in and of itself.

mala prohibita An act that is wrong only because it is prohibited.

Marxist criminology A perspective on crime and crime causation based on the writings of Karl Marx.

Marxist feminism A perspective in feminist criminology that sees the oppression of women as caused by their subordinate class status within capitalist societies.

masculinity hypothesis The belief that, over time, men and women will commit crimes that are increasingly similar in nature, seriousness, and frequency. Increasing similarity in crime commission was predicted to result from changes in the social status of women.

mass murder The illegal killing of three or more victims at one location within one event.

mesomorph A body type described as athletic and muscular.

meta-analysis A study that combines the results of other studies about a particular topic of interest; a comprehensive and systematic review of other studies.

metatheory A theory about theories and the theorizing process.

misdemeanor A criminal offense that is less serious than a felony and is punishable by incarceration, usually in a local confinement facility, typically for a year or less.

M'Naughten rule A standard for judging legal insanity that requires that offenders did not know what they were doing, or if they did, that they did not know it was wrong.

modeling A form of social learning in which people learn how to act by observing others.

money laundering The process of converting illegally earned assets from cash to one or more alternative forms to conceal factors such as illegal origin and true ownership.[20]

Monitoring the Future A national self-report survey on drug use that has been conducted since 1975.

monozygotic (MZ) twin One of two twins who develop from the same egg and who carry virtually the same genetic material.

moral development theory A perspective on crime causation holding that individuals become criminal when they have not successfully completed their intellectual development from child- to adulthood.

moral enterprise The efforts made by an interest group to have its sense of moral or ethical propriety enacted into law.

mores The behavioral proscriptions covering potentially serious violations of a group's values. Examples include strictures against murder, rape, and robbery. *See also* folkways.

motor vehicle theft (UCR) The theft or attempted theft of a motor vehicle. In the FBI's definition, this offense category includes the stealing of automobiles, trucks, buses, motorcycles, motor scooters, and snowmobiles.

murder An unlawful homicide.

narcoterrorism The distribution of a controlled substance in order to provide something of pecuniary value to a person or group that has engaged or is engaging in terrorist activity.

National Advisory Commission on Criminal Justice Standards and Goals A federal body commissioned in 1971 by President Richard Nixon to examine the nation's criminal justice system and to set standards and goals to direct the development of the nation's criminal justice agencies.

National Crime Victimization Survey (NCVS) A survey conducted annually by the Bureau of Justice Statistics that provides data on surveyed households reporting they were affected by crime.

National Incident-Based Reporting System (NIBRS) An enhanced statistical-reporting system to collect data on each incident and arrest within 22 crime categories.

National Survey on Drug Use and Health (NSDUH) A national survey of illicit drug use among people 12 years of age and older that is conducted annually by the Substance Abuse and Mental Health Services Administration.

National Violence against Women (NVAW) Survey A national survey of the extent and nature of violence against women conducted between November 1995 and May 1996 funded through grants from the National Institute of Justice and the U.S. Department of Health and Human Services National Center for Injury Prevention and Control.

National Youth Survey (NYS) A longitudinal panel study of a national sample of 1,725 individuals that measured self-reports of delinquency and other types of behavior.

natural law The philosophical perspective that certain immutable laws are fundamental to human nature and can be readily ascertained through reason. Human-made laws, in contrast, are said to derive from human experience and history—both of which are subject to continual change.

natural rights The rights that, according to natural law theorists, individuals retain in the face of government action and interests.

negative affective state An adverse emotion such as anger, fear, depression, and disappointment that derives from the experience of strain.

negligent homicide The act of causing the death of another person by recklessness or gross negligence.

neoclassical criminology A contemporary version of classical criminology that emphasizes deterrence and retribution, with reduced emphasis on rehabilitation.

neuroplasticity The ability of the brain to alter its structure and function in response to experience.

neurosis A functional disorder of the mind or of the emotions involving anxiety, phobia, or other abnormal behavior.

neurotransmitters Chemical substances that facilitate the flow of electrical impulses from one neuron to the next across nerve synapses.

No Electronic Theft Act (NETA) A 1997 federal law (Public Law 105–147) that criminalizes the willful infringement of copyrighted works, including by electronic means, even when the infringing party derives no direct financial benefit from the infringement (such as when pirated software is freely distributed online). In keeping with requirements of the NETA, the U.S. Sentencing Commission enacted amendments to its guidelines on April 6, 2000, to increase penalties associated with electronic theft.

nonprimary homicide A murder that involves victims and offenders who have no prior relationship and that usually occurs during the course of another crime such as robbery.

nothing-works doctrine The belief popularized by Robert Martinson in the 1970s that correctional treatment programs have little success in rehabilitating offenders.

nurturant strategy A crime-control strategy that attempts "to forestall development of criminality by improving early life experiences and channeling child and adolescent development" in desirable directions.[21]

occasional offender A criminal offender whose offending patterns are guided primarily by opportunity.

occupational crime Any act punishable by law that is committed in the course of an individual's legal occupation.[22]

offense A violation of the criminal law or, in some jurisdictions, a minor crime, such as jaywalking, sometimes described as "ticketable."

offense specialization A preference for engaging in a certain type of offense to the exclusion of others.

Office of Juvenile Justice and Delinquency Prevention (OJJDP) A national office that provides monetary assistance and direct victim-service programs for juvenile courts.

Office of National Drug Control Policy (ONDCP) A national office charged by Congress with establishing policies, priorities, and objectives for the nation's drug-control program. The ONDCP is responsible for developing and disseminating the *National Drug-Control Strategy*.

omertà The informal unwritten code of organized crime, which demands silence and loyalty, among other things, of family members.

Omnibus Anti-Drug Abuse Act A federal law (Public Law 100–690) enacted in 1988 that substantially increased federal penalties for recreational drug users and created a new cabinet-level position (known unofficially as the drug czar) to coordinate the drug-fighting efforts of the federal government.

Omnibus Crime Control and Safe Streets Act A federal law enacted in 1967 to eliminate the social conditions that create crime and to fund many anticrime initiatives nationwide.

operant behavior Any behavior that affects the environment in such a way as to produce responses or further behavioral cues.

operationalization The process by which concepts are made measurable.

opportunity structure A path to success. Opportunity structures may be of two types: legitimate and illegitimate.

organized crime The unlawful activities of the members of a highly organized, disciplined association engaged in supplying illegal goods and services, including gambling, prostitution, loan-sharking, narcotics, and labor racketeering.[23]

Panopticon A prison designed by Jeremy Bentham that was to be a circular building with cells along the circumference, each clearly visible from a central location staffed by guards.

paradigm An example, a model, or a theory.

paranoid schizophrenic A schizophrenic individual who suffers from delusions and hallucinations.

Part I offenses The crimes of murder, rape, robbery, aggravated assault, burglary, larceny, and motor vehicle theft, as defined under the FBI's Uniform Crime Reporting Program; also known as *major crimes*.

Part II offenses The less serious offenses as identified by the FBI for the purpose of reporting arrest data.

participant observation A strategy in data gathering in which the researcher observes a group by participating, to varying degrees, in the activities of the group.[24]

participatory justice A relatively informal type of criminal justice case processing that makes use of local community resources rather than requiring traditional forms of official intervention.

patriarchy The tradition of male dominance.

peacemaking criminology A perspective that holds that crime-control agencies and the citizens they serve should work together to alleviate social problems and human suffering and thus reduce crime.

peace model An approach to crime control that focuses on effective ways for developing a shared consensus on critical issues that could seriously affect the quality of life.

penal couple A term that describes the relationship between offender and victim; also the two individuals most involved in the criminal act: the offender and the victim.

persistence The act of continuing in crime; also continual involvement in offending.

persistent thief One who continues in common law types of property crimes despite no better than an ordinary level of success.

personality The characteristic patterns of thoughts, feelings, and behaviors that make a person unique, and that tend to remain stable over time. Personality influences an individual's thoughts, behavior, and emotions.

personal robbery A robbery that occurs on the highway or street or in a public place (also known as *mugging*) or that occurs in a residence.

pharmaceutical diversion The process by which legitimately manufactured controlled substances are diverted for illicit use.

phenomenological criminology The study of crime as a social phenomenon that is created through a process of social interaction.

phenomenology The study of the contents of human consciousness without regard to external conventions or prior assumptions.

phishing An Internet-based scam whose goal is to steal valuable personal information such as credit card or Social Security numbers, user IDs, and passwords.[25]

phone phreak A person who uses switched, dialed-access telephone services for exploration and exploitation.

phrenology The study of the shape of the head to determine anatomical correlates of human behavior.

piracy *See* software piracy.

pluralist perspective An analytical approach to social organization that holds that a multiplicity of values and beliefs exists in any complex society but that most social actors agree on the usefulness of law as a formal means of dispute resolution.

Ponzi scheme A form of high-yield-investment fraud that uses money collected from new investors, rather than profits from the purported underlying business venture, to pay high rates of return promised to earlier investors.

positivism The application of scientific techniques to the study of crime and criminals.

postcrime victimization Any problem that tends to follow from initial victimization; also known as *secondary victimization*.

postmodern criminology A brand of criminology that developed following World War II and that builds on the tenets inherent in postmodern social thought.

postmodern feminism A perspective within modern criminology that questions the social construction of concepts that are typically used in any discussion of crime and justice.

power-control theory A perspective that holds that the distribution of crime and delinquency within society is to some degree founded upon the consequences that power relationships within the wider society hold for domestic settings and for the everyday relationships among men, women, and children within the context of family life.

power seekers Serial killers who relish having power over another human being.

prenatal substance exposure Fetal exposure to maternal drug and alcohol use. Prenatal substance exposure can significantly increase a child's risk for developmental and neurological disorders.

primary deviance The initial deviance often undertaken to deal with transient problems in living.

primary homicide A murder involving a family member, friend, or acquaintance.

primary research Any research characterized by original and direct investigation.

professional criminal A criminal offender who makes a living from criminal pursuits, is recognized by other offenders as professional, and engages in offending that is planned and calculated.

Project on Human Development in Chicago Neighborhoods (PHDCN) An intensive study of Chicago neighborhoods employing longitudinal evaluations to examine the changing circumstances of people's lives in an effort to identify personal characteristics that may lead toward or away from antisocial behavior.

proletariat The "have-nots," or the working class, in Marxist theory.

property crime According to the FBI's Uniform Crime Reporting program, a crime category that includes burglary, larceny, motor vehicle theft, and arson.

prosocial bond A bond between the individual and the social group that strengthens the likelihood of conformity. Prosocial bonds are characterized by attachment to conventional social institutions, values, and beliefs.

prostitution The offering of one's self for hire for the purpose of engaging in sexual relations, or the act or practice of engaging in sexual activity for money or its equivalent.

protection/avoidance strategy A crime-control strategy whose goal is to reduce criminal opportunities by changing people's routine activities, increasing guardianship, or incapacitating convicted offenders.[26]

psychiatric criminology Any theory that is derived from the medical sciences, including neurology, and that, like other psychological theories, focuses on the individual as the unit of analysis. Psychiatric theories form the basis of psychiatric criminology. *See also* forensic psychiatry.

psychiatric theory A theory derived from the medical sciences, including neurology, and that, like other psychological theories, focuses on the individual as the unit of analysis.

psychoactive substance A substance that affects the mind, mental processes, or emotions.

psychoanalysis The theory of human psychology founded by Sigmund Freud on the concepts of the unconscious, resistance, repression, sexuality, and the Oedipus complex.[27]

psychoanalytic theory A psychiatric approach developed by Sigmund Freud that emphasizes the role of personality in human behavior and that sees deviant behavior as the result of dysfunctional personalities.

psychological profiling The attempt to categorize, understand, and predict the behavior of certain types of offenders based on behavioral clues they provide.

psychological theory A theory derived from the behavioral sciences that focuses on the individual as the unit of analysis. Psychological theories place the locus of crime causation within the personality of the individual offender.

psychopath An individual who has a personality disorder, especially one manifested in aggressively antisocial behavior, and who is lacking in empathy; also known as *sociopath*.

psychopathology A psychological disorder that causes distress for either the individual or someone in the individual's life.[28] It is also the study of pathological mental conditions (mental illness).

psychopathy A personality disorder characterized by antisocial behavior and lack of affect.

psychosis A form of mental illness in which sufferers are said to be out of touch with reality.

psychotherapy A form of psychiatric treatment based on psychoanalytical principles and techniques.

public policy A course of action that government takes in an effort to solve a problem or to achieve an end.

punishment An undesirable behavioral consequence likely to decrease the frequency of occurrence of that behavior.

pure research Any research undertaken simply for the sake of advancing scientific knowledge.

qualitative method A research technique that produces subjective results or results that are difficult to quantify.

quantitative method A research technique that produces measurable results.

quasi-experimental design An approach to research that, although less powerful than experimental designs, is deemed worthy of use when better designs are not feasible.

Racketeer Influenced and Corrupt Organizations (RICO) Act A statute that was part of the federal Organized Crime Control Act of 1970 and that is intended to combat criminal conspiracies.

radical criminology A perspective that holds that the causes of crime are rooted in social conditions that empower the wealthy and the politically well organized but disenfranchise the less fortunate; also known as *critical criminology* and *Marxist criminology*.

radical feminism A perspective that holds that any significant change in the social status of women can be accomplished only through substantial changes in social institutions such as the family, law, and medicine. Radical feminism argues, for example, that the structure of current legal thinking involves what is fundamentally a male perspective, which should be changed to incorporate women's social experiences and points of view.

randomization The process whereby individuals are assigned to study groups without biases or differences resulting from selection.

rape (NCVS) Carnal knowledge through the use of force or the threat of force, including attempts. Statutory rape (without force) is excluded. Both heterosexual and homosexual rape are included.

rape The penetration, no matter how slight, of the vagina or anus with any body part or object, or oral penetration by a sex organ of another person, without the consent of the victim. *See* also *forcible rape*.

rape myth A false assumption about rape, such as "When a woman says no, she really means yes." Rape myths characterize much of the discourse surrounding sexual violence.

rape-shield law A statute providing for the protection of rape victims by ensuring that defendants do not introduce irrelevant facts about the victim's sexual history into evidence.

rational choice theory A perspective that holds that criminality is the result of conscious choice and that predicts that individuals choose to commit crime when the benefits outweigh the costs of disobeying the law.

reaction formation The process by which a person openly rejects that which he or she wants or aspires to but cannot obtain or achieve.

realist criminology *See* left realism.

recidivism The repetition of criminal behavior.

recidivism rate The percentage of convicted offenders who have been released from prison and who are later rearrested for a new crime, generally within five years following release. *See also* dangerousness.

reintegrative shaming A form of shaming, imposed as a sanction by the criminal justice system, that is thought to strengthen the moral bond between the offender and the community.

relative deprivation A sense of social or economic inequality experienced by those who are unable, for whatever reason, to achieve legitimate success within the surrounding society.

replicability A scientific principle that holds that valid observations made at one time can be made again later if all other conditions are the same.

repression The psychological process through which a person rejects his or her own desires and impulses toward pleasurable instincts by excluding them from consciousness, thereby removing them from awareness and rendering them unconscious.

research The use of standardized, systematic procedures in the search for knowledge.[29]

research design The logic and structure inherent in an approach to data gathering.

resilience The psychological ability to successfully cope with severe stress and negative events.

restitution A criminal sanction, especially the payment of compensation by the offender to the victim.

restorative justice A postmodern perspective that stresses "remedies and restoration rather than prison, punishment and victim neglect."[30]

retribution The act of taking revenge on a criminal perpetrator.

reward A desirable behavioral consequence likely to increase the frequency of occurrence of that behavior.

risk analysis *See* threat analysis.

risk assessment The practice of using a structured instrument that combines information about individuals in order to classify them as being low, moderate, or high risk for violent behavior, reoffending, or continued criminal activity.

robbery (UCR) The taking of or attempting to take anything of value from the care, custody, or control of a person or persons by force or threat of force or violence or by putting the victim in fear.

routine activities theory A brand of rational choice theory that suggests that lifestyles contribute significantly to both the volume and the type of crime found in any society; also known as *lifestyle theory*.

Sarbanes-Oxley Act Officially known as the Public Company Accounting Reform and Investor Protection Act, requires chief executive officers and chief financial officers to personally vouch for the truth and fairness of their companies' financial disclosures and establishes an independent oversight board to regulate the accounting profession. The law also gives the federal Securities and Exchange Commission the authority to bar dishonest corporate directors and officers from ever again serving in positions of corporate responsibility, and increases the maximum federal prison term for common types of corporate fraud from 5 to 20 years.

scenario writing A technique intended to predict future outcomes that builds on environmental scanning by attempting to assess the likelihood of a variety of possible outcomes once important trends have been identified.

schizoid A person characterized by schizoid personality disorder. Such disordered personalities appear to be aloof, withdrawn, unresponsive, humorless, dull, and solitary to an abnormal degree.

schizophrenia A serious mental illness that distorts the way a person thinks, feels, and behaves. Primary features of schizophrenia include the inability to distinguish between real and imagined experiences and the inability to think logically.

script Generalized knowledge about specific types of situations that is stored in the mind.

secondary deviance Any deviant behavior that results from official labeling and from association with others who have been so labeled.

secondary research A new evaluation of existing information that had been collected by other researchers.

secondary victimization *See* postcrime victimization.

second-degree murder A criminal homicide that is unplanned and that is often described as a "crime of passion."

securities and commodities fraud A crime involving investments, such as stock-market manipulation, high-yield-investment fraud (Ponzi schemes, pyramid schemes, and prime bank schemes), advance fee fraud, hedge fund fraud, commodities fraud, foreign exchange fraud, and broker embezzlement.

securities fraud The theft of money resulting from intentional manipulation of the value of equities, including stocks and bonds. Securities fraud also includes theft from securities accounts and wire fraud.

selective disinhibition A loss of self-control due to the characteristics of the social setting, drugs or alcohol, or a combination of both.

selective incapacitation A social policy that seeks to protect society by incarcerating those individuals deemed to be the most dangerous.

self-control A person's ability to alter his or her own mental and emotional states and behavioral responses.

self-report survey A survey in which anonymous respondents, without fear of disclosure or arrest, are asked to confidentially report any violations of the criminal law that they have committed.

separation assault Any violence inflicted by partners on significant others who attempt to leave an intimate relationship.

serial murder A criminal homicide that involves the killing of several victims in three or more separate events.

serotonin A neurotransmitter that is commonly found in the pineal gland, the digestive tract, the central nervous system, and blood platelets.

sex trafficking The recruitment, harboring, transportation, provision, or obtaining of a person for the purpose of a commercial sex act.

sexual selection A form of natural selection that influences an individual's ability to find or choose a mate.

sibling offense An offense or incident that culminates in homicide. The offense or incident may be a crime, such as robbery, or an incident that meets a less stringent criminal definition, such as a lover's quarrel involving assault or battery.

simple assault (NCVS) An attack without a weapon, resulting either in minor injury or in undetermined injury requiring less than two days of hospitalization. *See also* aggravated assault.

situational action theory (SAT) A perspective on crime holding that criminal behavior is the result of human decision making based on personal morality when viewed within the context of the existing situation. SAT stresses the importance of moral interpretations over a person's ability to exercise self-control.

situational choice theory A brand of rational choice theory that views criminal behavior "as a function of choices and decisions made within a context of situational constraints and opportunities."[31]

situational crime prevention A social policy approach whose goal is to develop greater understanding of crime as well as more effective crime-prevention strategies by focusing on physical, organizational, and social environments that make crime possible.[32]

snitch An amateur shoplifter.

social bond The link, created through socialization, between individuals and the society of which they are a part.

social capital The degree of positive relationships with others and with social institutions that individuals build up over the course of their lives.

social class A distinction made between individuals on the basis of important defining social characteristics.

social cognition theory A perspective which holds that people learn how to act by observing others.

social contract The Enlightenment-era concept that human beings abandon their natural state of individual freedom to join together and form society. In the process of forming a social contract, individuals surrender some freedoms to society as a whole, and government, once formed, is obligated to assume responsibilities toward its citizens and to provide for their protection and welfare.

social control theory A perspective that predicts that when social constraints on antisocial behavior are weakened or absent, delinquent behavior emerges. Rather than stressing causative factors in criminal behavior, social control theory asks why people actually obey rules instead of breaking them.

social development perspective An integrated view of human development that examines multiple levels of maturation simultaneously, including the psychological, biological, familial, interpersonal, cultural, societal, and ecological levels. Also known as *social development theory*.

social disorganization A condition said to exist when a group is faced with social change, uneven development of culture, maladaptiveness, disharmony, conflict, and lack of consensus.

social disorganization theory A perspective on crime and deviance that sees society as a kind of organism and crime and deviance as a kind of disease or social pathology. Theories of social disorganization are often associated with the perspective of social ecology and with the Chicago School of criminology, which developed during the 1920s and 1930s.

social ecology An approach to criminological theorizing that attempts to link the structure and organization of a human community to interactions with its localized environment.

social epidemiology The study of social epidemics and diseases of the social order.

socialist feminism A perspective within modern criminology that sees gender oppression as a consequence of the interaction between the economic structure of society and gender-based roles.

socialization The lifelong process of social experience whereby individuals acquire the cultural patterns of their society.

social learning theory A perspective that places primary emphasis on the role of communication and socialization in the acquisition of learned patterns of criminal behavior and the values that support that behavior; also known as *learning theory*.

social life The ongoing and (typically) structured interaction that occurs between persons in a society, including socialization and social behavior in general.

social pathology A concept that compares society to a physical organism and that sees criminality as an illness.

social policy A government initiative, program, or plan intended to address problems in society. The "war on crime," for example, is a kind of generic (large-scale) social policy—one consisting of many smaller programs.

social problems perspective The belief that crime is a manifestation of underlying social problems, such as poverty, discrimination, pervasive family violence, inadequate socialization practices, and the breakdown of traditional social institutions.

social process The interaction between and among social institutions, individuals, and groups.

social process theory A theory that asserts that criminal behavior is learned in interaction with others and that socialization processes that occur as the result of group membership are the primary route through which learning occurs; also known as the *interactionist perspective*.

social relativity The notion that social events are differently interpreted according to the cultural experiences and personal interests of the initiator, the observer, or the recipient of that behavior.

social responsibility perspective The belief that individuals are fundamentally responsible for their own behavior and that they choose crime over other, more law-abiding courses of action.

social structure The pattern of social organization and the interrelationships among institutions characteristic of a society.

social structure theory A theory that explains crime by reference to some aspect of the social fabric. These theories emphasize relationships among social institutions and describe the types of behavior that tend to characterize groups of people rather than individuals.

sociobiology "The systematic study of the biological basis of all social behavior."[33]

sociological theory A perspective that focuses on the nature of the power relationships that exist between social groups and on the influences that various social phenomena bring to bear on the types of behaviors that tend to characterize groups of people.

sociopath *See* psychopath.

soft determinism The belief that human behavior is the result of choices and decisions made within a context of situational constraints and opportunities.

software piracy The unauthorized and illegal copying of software programs.

somatotyping The classification of human beings into types according to body build and other physical characteristics.

specific deterrence A goal of criminal sentencing that seeks to prevent a particular offender from engaging in repeat criminality.

spousal rape The rape of one spouse by the other. The term usually refers to the rape of a woman by her husband.

stalking A course of conduct directed at a specific person that involves repeated visual or physical proximity; nonconsensual communication; verbal, written, or implied threats; or a combination thereof that would cause a reasonable person fear as well as a constellation of behaviors involving repeated and persistent attempts to impose on another person unwanted communication and/or contact.

state-organized crime Any act defined by law as criminal that is committed by a state official during his or her work as a representative of the state.[34]

statistical correlation The simultaneous increase or decrease in value of two numerically valued random variables.[35]

statistical school A criminological perspective with roots in the early 1800s that seeks to uncover correlations between crime rates and other types of demographic data.

statute A formal written enactment by a legislative body.[36]

statutory law Law in the form of statutes or formal written strictures made by a legislature or governing body with the power to make law.

stigmatic shaming A form of shaming, imposed as a sanction by the criminal justice system, that is thought to destroy the moral bond between the offender and the community.

strain theory A sociological approach that posits a disjuncture between socially and subculturally sanctioned means and goals as the cause of criminal behavior; also known as *anomie theory*.

strategic assessment A technique that assesses the risks and opportunities facing those who plan for the future.

structural Marxism A perspective that holds that the structural institutions of society influence the behavior of individuals and groups by virtue of the type of relationships created. The criminal law, for example, reflects class relationships and serves to reinforce those relationships.

subcultural theory A sociological perspective that emphasizes the contribution made by variously socialized cultural groups to the phenomenon of crime.

subculture A collection of values and preferences that is communicated to subcultural participants through a process of socialization.

subculture of violence thesis The belief that certain groups or subcultures in society have values and attitudes that are conducive to crime and violence.

sublimation The psychological process whereby one aspect of consciousness comes to be symbolically substituted for another.

substantial-capacity test A standard for judging legal insanity that requires that a person lack the mental capacity needed to understand the wrongfulness of his or her act or to conform his or her behavior to the requirements of the law.

superego The moral aspect of the personality; much like the conscience. According to Freud, this part of the psyche develops by incorporating the community's (perceived) moral standards, is mainly unconscious, and includes the conscience.[37]

supermale A male individual displaying the XYY chromosome structure.

superpredator A member of a new generation of juveniles "who [is] coming of age in actual and 'moral poverty' without the benefits of parents, teachers, coaches and clergy to teach [him or her] right from wrong and show [him or her] 'unconditional love.'"[38] The term is often applied to inner-city youths.

survey research A social science data-gathering technique that involves the use of questionnaires.

tagging The process whereby an individual is negatively defined by agencies of justice; also known as *labeling*.

target hardening The reduction in criminal opportunity for a particular location, generally through the use of physical barriers, architectural design, and enhanced security measures.

technique of neutralization A culturally available justification that can provide criminal offenders with the means to disavow responsibility for their behavior.

TEMPEST A standard developed by the U.S. government that requires that electromagnetic emanations from computers designated as "secure" be below levels that would allow radio receiving equipment to read the data being computed.

terrorism Any premeditated, politically motivated violence perpetrated against noncombatant targets by subnational groups or clandestine agents, usually intended to influence an audience.[39]

test of significance A statistical technique intended to provide researchers with confidence that their results are, in fact, true and not the result of sampling error.

testosterone The primary male sex hormone produced in the testes. Its function is to control secondary sex characteristics and sexual drive.

Thanatos A death wish.

theoretical criminology A subfield of general criminology, it posits explanations for criminal behavior.

theory A series of interrelated propositions that attempt to describe, explain, predict, and ultimately control some class of events. A theory gains explanatory power from inherent logical consistency and is "tested" by how well it describes and predicts reality.

threat analysis A complete and thorough assessment of the kinds of perils facing an organization; also known as *risk analysis*.

three-strikes legislation A criminal statute that mandates life imprisonment for criminals convicted of three violent felonies or serious drug offenses.

total institution A facility from which individuals can rarely come and go and in which communal life is intense and circumscribed. Individuals in total institutions tend to eat, sleep, play, learn, and worship together.

trafficking in persons (TIP) The exploitation of unwilling or unwitting people through force, coercion, threat, or deception.

traits Notable features or qualities of a biological entity. Traits may be classified as physical, behavioral, or psychological. Traits are passed from generation to the next.

translational criminology A form of criminology whose purpose it is to translate the results of research into workable social policy.

transnational organized crime Any unlawful activity undertaken and supported by organized criminal groups operating across national boundaries.

trend extrapolation A technique of futures research that makes future predictions based on the projection of existing trends.

tribalism The attitudes and behavior that result from strong feelings of identification with one's own social group.

truth in sentencing A close correspondence between the incarceration sentence given the offender and the time actually served prior to prison release.[40]

Twelve Tables Early Roman laws written circa 450 B.C. that regulated family, religious, and economic life.

unicausal The characteristic of having one cause. Unicausal theories posit only one source for all that they attempt to explain.

Uniform Crime Reporting (UCR) Program A Federal Bureau of Investigation data-gathering initiative that provides an annual tally of statistics consisting primarily of information on crimes reported to the police and on arrests.

USA PATRIOT Act A federal law (Public Law 107–56) enacted in response to terrorist attacks on the World Trade Center and the Pentagon on September 11, 2001. The law, officially titled the Uniting and Strengthening America by Providing Appropriate Tools Required to Intercept and Obstruct Terrorism Act, substantially broadened the investigative authority of law enforcement agencies throughout America and is applicable to many crimes other than terrorism. The law was slightly revised and reauthorized by Congress in 2006. Also called *Antiterrorism Act*.

utilitarianism *See* hedonistic calculus.

variable A concept that can undergo measurable changes.

verstehen The kind of subjective understanding that can be achieved by criminologists who immerse themselves in the everyday world of the criminals they study.

victim-impact statement A written document that describes the losses, suffering, and trauma experienced by the crime victim or by the victim's survivors. In jurisdictions where victim-impact statements are used, judges are expected to consider them in arriving at an appropriate sentence for the offender.

victimization rate (NCVS) A measure of the occurrence of victimizations among a specified population group. For personal crimes, the rate is based on the number of victimizations per 1,000 residents age 12 or older. For household crimes, the victimization rates are calculated using the number of incidents per 1,000 households.

victimogenesis The contributory background of a victim as a result of which he or she becomes prone to victimization.

victimology The study of victims and their contributory role, if any, in crime causation.

victim-precipitated homicide A killing in which the victim was the first to commence the interaction or was the first to resort to physical violence.

victim precipitation Any contribution made by the victim to the criminal event, especially something that led to its initiation.

victim proneness An individual's likelihood of victimization.

Victims of Crime Act (VOCA) A federal law enacted in 1984 that established the federal Crime Victims Fund. The fund uses monies from fines and forfeitures collected from federal offenders to supplement state support of local victims' assistance programs and state victims' compensation programs.

victim-witness assistance program A program that counsels victims, orients them to the justice process, and provides a variety of other services, such as transportation to court, child care during court appearances, and referrals to social services agencies.

Violence against Women Act (VAWA) A federal law enacted as a component of the 1994 Violent Crime Control and Law Enforcement Act and intended to address concerns about violence against women. The law focused on improving the interstate enforcement of protection orders, providing effective training for court personnel involved with women's issues, improving the training and collaboration of police and prosecutors with victim service providers, strengthening law enforcement efforts to reduce violence against women, and increasing services to victims of violence. President Clinton signed the reauthorization of this legislation, known as the Violence against Women Act 2000, into law on October 28, 2000.

Violent Crime Control and Law Enforcement Act A federal law (Public Law 103–322) enacted in 1994 that authorized spending billions of dollars on crime prevention, law enforcement, and prison construction. It also outlawed the sale of certain types of assault weapons and enhanced federal death-penalty provisions.

Violent Criminal Apprehension Program (VICAP) The program of the Federal Bureau of Investigation focusing on serial murder investigations and the apprehension of serial killers.

virus *See* computer virus.

visionary serial killers Serial killers motivated by auditory or visual hallucinations.

white-collar crime Any violation of the criminal law committed by a person of respectability and high social status in the course of his or her occupation.

Wickersham Commission A commission (officially known as the Commission on Law Observance and Enforcement) created by President Herbert Hoover in 1931 whose mandate was to improve justice system practices and to reinstate law's role in civilized governance. The commission made recommendations concerning the nation's police forces and described how to improve policing throughout America.

workplace violence The crimes of murder, rape, robbery, and assault committed against persons who are at work or on duty.

Notes

CHAPTER 1: WHAT IS CRIMINOLOGY?

1. CTV Global Media, "CSI: Miami," http://www.ctv.ca/servlet/ArticleNews/show/CTVShows/1064338847511_59746366 (accessed March 10, 2007).
2. Gerard Gilbert, "CSI: The Cop Show That Conquered the World," (London) *Independent,* December 19, 2006, http://www.findarticles.com/p/articles/mi_qn4158/is_20061219/ai_n17081057 (accessed March 10, 2007).
3. Sara Bibel, "'CSI: Crime Scene Investigation' Is the Most-Watched Show in the World," TV by the Numbers, June 14, 2012, http://tvbythenumbers.zap2it.com/2012/06/14/csi-crime-scene-investigation-is-the-most-watched-show-in-the-world-2/138212/ (accessed July 26, 2012).
4. From the standpoint of the law, the proper word is *conduct* rather than *behavior* because the term *conduct* implies intentional and willful activity, whereas *behavior* refers to any human activity—even that which occurs while a person is unconscious as well as that which is unintended.
5. Paul W. Tappan, "Who Is the Criminal?" *American Sociological Review,* Vol. 12 (1947), pp. 96–102.
6. Edwin Sutherland, *Principles of Criminology,* 4th ed. (New York: Lippincott, 1947).
7. John F. Galliher, *Criminology: Human Rights, Criminal Law, and Crime* (Upper Saddle River, NJ: Prentice Hall, 1989), p. 2.
8. C. D. Shearing, "Criminologists Must Broaden Their Field of Study beyond Crime and Criminals," in R. Boostrom, ed., *Enduring Issues in Criminology* (San Diego, CA: Greenhaven, 1995).
9. Ezzat Fattah, *Introduction to Criminology* (Burnaby, British Columbia: School of Criminology, Simon Fraser University, 1989).
10. Hermann Mannheim, *Comparative Criminology* (Boston: Houghton Mifflin, 1965).
11. Ron Claassen, "Restorative Justice: Fundamental Principles," http://www.fresno.edu/pacs/rjprinc.htm (accessed May 5, 2007).
12. H. Schwendinger and J. Schwendinger, "Defenders of Order or Guardians of Human Rights?" in I. Taylor, P. Walton, and J. Young, eds., *Critical Criminology* (London: Routledge and Kegan Paul, 1975).
13. Ibid.
14. Jeffrey H. Reiman, *The Rich Get Richer and the Poor Get Prison,* 4th ed. (Boston: Allyn & Bacon, 1997).
15. Fattah, *Introduction to Criminology.*
16. Matthew Robinson, "Defining 'Crime,'" http://www.appstate.edu/~robinsnmb/smokeharms.htm (accessed November 4, 2006).
17. Piers Beirne and James W. Messerschmidt, *Criminology* (San Diego, CA: Harcourt Brace Jovanovich, 1991), p. 20.
18. Susan Spencer-Wendel, "Let 'Em Sag, Judge Rules on Riviera Beach's No-Baggy-Pants Law," *Palm Beach Post,* April 22, 2009, http://www.palmbeachpost.com/localnews/content/local_news/epaper/2009/04/22/0422saggy.html (accessed March 24, 2010).
19. Neal J. Riley, "S.F. Barely Passes Public-Nudity Ban," *San Francisco Chronicle,* November 21, 2012, http://www.chron.com/bayarea/article/S-F-barely-passes-public-nudity-ban-4055606.php#photo-3732744 (accessed February 1, 2013).
20. American Gaming Association, FAQ, http://www.americangaming.org/industry-resources/faq (accessed July 26, 2013).
21. "Girl, 12, Arrested in New York for Doodling on School Desk," *USA Today,* February 5, 2010, http://www.usatoday.com/news/nation/2010-02-05-girl-arrested-doodling_N.htm (accessed March 30, 2010).
22. Piers Beirne, *Inventing Criminology* (Albany: State University of New York Press, 1993).
23. See also Paul Topinard, *Anthropology* (London: Chapman and Hall, 1894).
24. Joseph F. Sheley, *Criminology: A Contemporary Handbook* (Belmont, CA: Wadsworth, 1991), p. xxiii.
25. Edwin H. Sutherland, *Criminology* (Philadelphia: Lippincott, 1924), p. 11.
26. Edwin H. Sutherland, *Principles of Criminology* (Chicago: University of Chicago Press, 1934).
27. "Sutherland, Edwin H.," *Encyclopedia of Criminology,* http://www.fitzroydearborn.com/chicago/criminology/sample-sutherland-edwin.asp (accessed November 15, 2007).
28. Edwin H. Sutherland and Donald R. Cressey, *Criminology,* 9th ed. (Philadelphia: Lippincott, 1974), p. 3.
29. Gennaro F. Vito and Ronald M. Holmes, *Criminology: Theory, Research, and Policy* (Belmont, CA: Wadsworth, 1994), p. 3.
30. Clemens Bartollas and Simon Dinitz, *Introduction to Criminology: Order and Disorder* (New York: Harper & Row, 1989), p. 548.
31. Marvin E. Wolfgang and Franco Ferracuti, *The Subculture of Violence: Towards an Integrated Theory in Criminology* (London: Tavistock, 1967).
32. European Society of Criminology, Constitution, Section 1 (d), http://www.esc-eurocrim.org/constitution.shtml (accessed July 10, 2007).
33. Jack P. Gibbs, "The State of Criminological Theory," *Criminology,* Vol. 25, No. 4 (November 1987), pp. 822–823.
34. Jim Short, "President's Message: On Communicating, Crossing Boundaries and Building Bridges," *The Criminologist,* Vol. 22, No. 5 (September/October 1997), p. 1.
35. Available through Sage Publications, Thousand Oaks, CA.
36. Piers Beirne and Colin Sumner, "Editorial Statement," *Theoretical Criminology,* Vol. 1, No. 1 (February 1997), pp. 5–11.
37. There are those who deny, however, that criminology deserves the name *discipline.* See, for example, Don C. Gibbons, *Talking about Crime and Criminals: Problems and Issues in Theory Development in Criminology* (Upper Saddle River, NJ: Prentice Hall, 1994), p. 3.
38. Charles F. Wellford, "Controlling Crime and Achieving Justice: The American Society of Criminology 1996 Presidential Address," *Criminology,* Vol. 35, No. 1 (1997), p. 1.
39. Gibbons, *Talking about Crime and Criminals,* p. 4.
40. *The American Heritage Dictionary* on CD-ROM (Boston: Houghton Mifflin, 1992).

41. *The American Heritage Dictionary of the English Language,* 3rd ed. (Boston: Houghton Mifflin, 1996).
42. This list is not meant to be exclusive. There are many other journals in the field, too many to list here.
43. Sutherland, *Principles of Criminology.*
44. Don M. Gottfredson, "Criminological Theories: The Truth as Told by Mark Twain," in William S. Laufer and Freda Adler, eds., *Advances in Criminological Theory,* Vol. 1 (New Brunswick, NJ: Transaction, 1989), p. 1.
45. Gregg Barak, *Integrating Criminologies* (Boston: Allyn & Bacon, 1998), p. 5.
46. Don C. Gibbons, "Talking about Crime: Observations on the Prospects for Causal Theory in Criminology," *Criminal Justice Research Bulletin* (Sam Houston State University), Vol. 7, No. 6 (1992).
47. Ibid.
48. National Institute of Justice, "What Is Translational Criminology?," *NIJ Journal,* No. 268 (November 3, 2011), http://www.nij.gov/nij/journals/268/criminology.htm (accessed May 1, 2012).
49. Editorial, "In Denial about On-Screen Violence," *New Scientist,* April 21, 2007, p. 5.
50. Congressional Public Health Summit, Joint Statement on the Impact of Entertainment Violence on Children, July 26, 2000.
51. Federal Trade Commission, *Marketing Violent Entertainment to Children* (Washington, DC: U.S. Government Printing Office, 2000).
52. Sue Pleming, "U.S. Report Says Hollywood Aims Violence at Kids," Reuters wire service, September 11, 2000.
53. "Editorial: In Denial about On-Screen Violence," *New Scientist,* April 21, 2007, http://www.newscientist.com/channel/opinion/mg19426003.600-editorial-in-denial-about-onscreen-violence.html (accessed August 1, 2007).
54. Lydia Saad, "Crime Tops List of Americans' Local Concerns," Gallup Organization, June 21, 2000, http://www.gallup.com/poll/releases/pr000621.asp (accessed February 20, 2004).
55. National Institute of Justice, "What Is Translational Criminology?," *NIJ Journal,* No. 268 (November 3, 2011), http://www.nij.gov/nij/journals/268/criminology.htm (accessed May 1, 2012).
56. Alfred Blumstein, "Making Rationality Relevant: The American Society of Criminology 1992 Presidential Address," *Criminology,* Vol. 31, No. 1 (February 1993), p. 1.
57. Ibid.
58. John P. Crank, *Understanding Police Culture* (Cincinnati, OH: Anderson, 1998), p. 15.
59. Public Law 103–322.
60. For a good overview of this issue, see Wesley G. Skogan, ed., *Reactions to Crime and Violence: The Annals of the American Academy of Political and Social Science* (Thousand Oaks, CA: Sage, 1995).
61. For an excellent discussion of crime as a social event, see Leslie W. Kennedy and Vincent F. Sacco, *Crime Counts: A Criminal Event Analysis* (Toronto: Nelson Canada, 1996).
62. For a good discussion of the social construction of crime, see Leslie T. Wilkins, "On Crime and Its Social Construction: Observations on the Social Construction of Crime," *Social Pathology,* Vol. 1, No. 1 (January 1995), pp. 1–11.
63. For a parallel approach, see Terance D. Miethe and Robert F. Meier, *Crime and Its Social Context: Toward an Integrated Theory of Offenders, Victims, and Situations* (Albany: State University of New York Press, 1995).
64. Joan McCord, "Family Relationships, Juvenile Delinquency, and Adult Criminality," *Criminology,* Vol. 29, No. 3 (August 1991), pp. 397–417.
65. Elizabeth Candle and Sarnoff A. Mednick, "Perinatal Complications Predict Violent Offending," *Criminology,* Vol. 29, No. 3 (August 1991), pp. 519–529.
66. Carol W. Kohfeld and John Sprague, "Demography, Police Behavior, and Deterrence," *Criminology,* Vol. 28, No. 1 (February 1990), pp. 111–136.
67. Leslie W. Kennedy and David R. Forde, "Routine Activities and Crime: An Analysis of Victimization in Canada," *Criminology,* Vol. 28, No. 1 (February 1990), p. 137.
68. William G. Doerner, "The Impact of Medical Resources on Criminally Induced Lethality: A Further Examination," *Criminology,* Vol. 26, No. 1 (February 1988), pp. 171–177.
69. Ibid., p. 177.
70. Jeff Ferrell, "Criminological Verstehen: Inside the Immediacy of Crime," *Justice Quarterly,* Vol. 14, No. 1 (1997), p. 11.
71. James F. Gilsinan, "They Is Clowning Tough: 911 and the Social Construction of Reality," *Criminology,* Vol. 27, No. 2 (May 1989), pp. 329–344.
72. See, for example, Miethe and Meier, *Crime and Its Social Context.*
73. For a good discussion of the historical development of criminology, see Leon Radzinowicz, *In Search of Criminology* (Cambridge: Harvard University Press, 1962).
74. As quoted in W. Wayt Gibbs, "Trends in Behavioral Science: Seeking the Criminal Element," *Scientific American,* Vol. 272, No. 3 (March 1995), pp. 100–107.
75. Wellford, "Controlling Crime and Achieving Justice," p. 4.

CHAPTER 2: WHERE DO THEORIES COME FROM?

1. Although witnesses agreed that Eugene gnawed on his victim's face, autopsy results showed no human remains in Eugene's stomach.
2. Some of the details for this story come from Seniboye Tienabeso, "Miami Cannibal Told Victim, 'I'm Going to Kill You,'" ABC News, August 9, 2012, http://abcnews.go.com/US/miami-cannibal-victim-attacker-ripped-ribbons/story?id=16967183 (accessed January 4, 2013).
3. "Medical Examiner: Causeway Cannibal Not High on Bath Salts," CBS Miami, June 27, 2012, http://miami.cbslocal.com/2012/06/27/medical-examiner-causeway-cannibal-not-high-on-bath-salts (accessed January 4, 2013).
4. "Girlfriend Recalls Rudy Eugene's Final Day," CBS Miami, May 31, 2012, http://miami.cbslocal.com/2012/05/31/girlfriend-recalls-rudy-eugenes-final-day (accessed January 3, 2013).
5. Lawrence W. Sherman, *Evidence-Based Policing* (Washington, DC: Police Foundation, 1998), p. 4.
6. David Weisburd, Lorraine Mazerolle, and Anthony Petrosino, "The Academy of Experimental Criminology: Advancing Randomized Trials in Crime and Justice," http://www.crim.upenn.edu/aec/AECCriminologist417.doc (accessed May 20, 2010).
7. David P. Farrington, Lloyd Ohlin, and James Q. Wilson, *Understanding and Controlling Crime* (New York: Springer-Verlag, 1986).
8. Lawrence W Sherman, *Policing Domestic Violence* (New York: Free Press, 1992).

9. Anthony Petrosino et al., "Toward Evidence-Based Criminology and Criminal Justice," *International Journal of Comparative Criminology*, Vol. 3 (2003), 191–213.
10. American Society of Criminology, "The ASC Announces a New Division: The Division of Experimental Criminology," https://www.asc41.com/DECannouncement.html (accessed April 7, 2010).
11. David Weisburd, "Editor's Introduction," *Journal of Experimental Criminology*, Vol. 1 (2005), p. 3.
12. John H. Laub, "The Life Course of Criminology in the United States: The American Society of Criminology 2003 Presidential Address," *Criminology*, Vol. 42, No. 1 (February 2004), pp. 1–26.
13. Ibid., p. 7.
14. Ibid.
15. As discussed by Piers Beirne and Colin Summer, "Editorial Statement," *Theoretical Criminology: An International Journal*, Vol. 1, No. 1 (February 1997), pp. 5–11.
16. Hermann Mannheim, *Comparative Criminology* (Boston, MA: Houghton Mifflin, 1967), p. 20.
17. Details for this story come from Paul Stokes, "Extra Police Put on the Beat for Full Moon," *The Telegraph*, June 7, 2006, http://www.telegraph.co.uk/news/main.jhtml?xml=/news/2007/06/06/nmoon106.xml (accessed July 12, 2007).
18. Don M. Gottfredson, "Criminology Theories: The Truth as Told by Mark Twain," in William S. Laufer and Freda Adler, eds., *Advances in Criminological Theory*, Vol. 1 (New Brunswick, NJ: Transaction, 1989), p. 3.
19. Kenneth R. Hoover, *The Elements of Social Scientific Thinking*, 5th ed. (New York: St. Martin's, 1992), p. 34.
20. Ibid., p. 35.
21. Todd Clear, "Policy and Evidence: The Challenge to the American Society of Criminology—2009 Presidential Address to the American Society of Criminology," *Criminology*, Vol. 48, No. 1 (2010), p. 6.
22. Ibid.
23. Susette M. Talarico, *Criminal Justice Research: Approaches, Problems and Policy* (Cincinnati, OH: Anderson, 1980), p. 3.
24. Ibid.
25. For a good review of secondary research, see J. H. Laub, R. J. Sampson, and K. Kiger, "Assessing the Potential of Secondary Data Analysis: A New Look at the Gluecks' Unraveling Juvenile Delinquency Data," in Kimberly L. Kempf, ed., *Measurement Issues in Criminology* (New York: Springer-Verlag, 1990), pp. 241–257; and Robert J. Sampson and John H. Laub, *Crime in the Making* (Cambridge, MA: Harvard University Press, 1993).
26. Sampson and Laub, *Crime in the Making*, p. 3.
27. Larry S. Miller and John T. Whitehead, *Introduction to Criminal Justice Research and Methods* (Cincinnati, OH: Anderson, 1996).
28. *The American Heritage Dictionary of the English Language*, 4th ed., (Chicago: Houghton Mifflin Harcourt Publishing Company, 2010), http://www.yourdictionary.com/hypothesis.
29. Donald T. Campbell and Julian C. Stanley, *Experimental and Quasi-Experimental Designs for Research* (Chicago: Rand-McNally, 1966), p. 35.
30. Ibid., p. 5, from which many of the descriptions that follow are adapted.
31. Ibid., p. 34.
32. According to Denise C. Gottfredson, "[M]idnight basketball programs are not likely to reduce crime." Gottfredson cites research (J. G. Ross et al., "The Effectiveness of an After-School Program for Primary Grade Latchkey Students on Precursors of Substance Abuse," *Journal of Community Psychology*, OSAP Special Issue [1992], pp. 22–38) showing that such programs may actually increase the risk for delinquency by increasing risk taking and impulsiveness. See Denise C. Gottfredson, "School-Based Crime Prevention," in Lawrence W. Sherman et al., *Preventing Crime: What Works, What Doesn't, What's Promising* (Washington, DC: National Institute of Justice, 1998), http://www.ncjrs.org/works/chapter5.htm (accessed June 15, 2004).
33. Shawn Bushway and David Weisburd, "Acknowledging the Centrality of Quantitative Criminology in Criminology and Criminal Justice," *The Criminologist*, Vol. 31, No. 4 (2006), p. 1.
34. Lawrence W. Sherman et al., *Evidence-Based Crime Prevention* (New York: Routledge, 2002).
35. Frank E. Hagan, *Research Methods in Criminal Justice and Criminology*, 6th ed. (New York: Allyn & Bacon, 2003).
36. Jeff Ferrell, "Criminological Verstehen: Inside the Immediacy of Crime," *Justice Quarterly*, Vol. 14, No. 1 (1997), p. 11.
37. William Foote Whyte, *Street Corner Society: The Social Structure of an Italian Slum* (Chicago: University of Chicago Press, 1943), pp. v–vii.
38. Ibid., p. vii.
39. Hagan, *Research Methods in Criminal Justice and Criminology*.
40. Nicole Vanden Heuvel, *Directory of Criminal Justice Information Sources*, 8th ed. (Washington, DC: National Institute of Justice, 1992), p. 145.
41. Hagan, *Research Methods in Criminal Justice and Criminology*.
42. Hoover, *The Elements of Social Scientific Thinking*, p. 34.
43. Abraham Kaplan, *The Conduct of Inquiry: Methodology for Behavioral Science* (San Francisco: Chandler, 1964), p. 134.
44. Ibid.
45. See American Society of Criminology, "Critical Criminal Justice Issues," 1994; available from the National Institute of Justice via http://www.ncjrs.gov/App/AbstractDB/AbstractDBDetails.aspx?id=158837.
46. Avshalom Caspim et al., "Are Some People Crime-Prone? Replications of the Personality-Crime Relationship across Countries, Genders, Races, and Methods," *Criminology*, Vol. 32, No. 2 (May 1994), pp. 162–195.
47. Kaplan, *The Conduct of Inquiry*, p. 172.
48. As with almost anything else, qualitative data can be assigned to categories, and the categories can be numbered. Hence, qualitative data can be quantified, although the worth of such effort is subject to debate.
49. Sanyika Shakur, *Monster: The Autobiography of an L.A. Gang Member* (New York: Penguin, 1993), pp. 45–46.
50. Ibid., p. xiv.
51. Ferrell, "Criminological Verstehen," p. 10.
52. Academy of Criminal Justice Sciences, *Code of Ethics*, Section 18.
53. Ibid., Section 19.
54. National Institute of Justice, *Human Subjects and Privacy Protection*, http://www.nij.gov/funding/humansubjects/welcome.htm (accessed June 1, 2013).
55. Ferrell, "Criminological Verstehen," p. 8.
56. Hagan, *Research Methods in Criminal Justice and Criminology*.
57. Ibid.

58. See Dennis Cauchon, "Study Critical of D.A.R.E. Rejected," *USA Today,* October 4, 1994, p. 2A.
59. See Susan T. Ennett et al., "How Effective Is Drug Abuse Resistance Education? A Meta-Analysis of Project DARE Outcome Evaluations," *American Journal of Public Health,* Vol. 84, No. 9 (September 1994), pp. 1394–1401.
60. Susan T. Ennett et al., "Long-Term Evaluation of Drug Abuse Resistance Education," *Addictive Behaviors,* Vol. 19, No. 2 (1994), pp. 112–125.
61. Donald R. Lynam and Richard Milich, "Project DARE: No Effects at 10-Year Follow-Up," *Journal of Consulting and Clinical Psychology,* Vol. 67, No. 4 (August 1999), pp. 590–593.
62. Kevin Helliker, "The Case for Alcoholics Anonymous: It Works Even If the Science Is Lacking," *Wall Street Journal,* October 17, 2006, p. D1.
63. American Society of Criminology, "Draft Code of Ethics," Section II, paragraph 7 (unpublished manuscript).
64. Faye S. Taxman, "Research and Relevance: Lessons from the Past, Thoughts for the Future," *Criminology and Public Policy,* Vol. 3, No. 2 (March 2004), p. 170.
65. Julian Leigh, "Mandatory Arrest Laws Can Reduce Domestic Violence," in Tamara L. Roleff, ed., *Domestic Violence: Opposing Viewpoints* (San Diego, CA: Greenhaven Press, 2000).
66. James Austin, "Why Criminology Is Irrelevant," *Criminology and Public Policy,* Vol. 2, No. 3 (July 2003), pp. 557–564.
67. The Campaign for an Effective Crime Policy, *The Impact of Three Strikes and You're Out Laws: What Have We Learned?* (Washington, DC: CECP, 1997).
68. Fox Butterfield, no headline, New York Times News Service Online, April 16, 1997.
69. Sherman et al., *Preventing Crime.*
70. Lawrence W. Sherman, "Evidence and Liberty: The Promise of Experimental Criminology," *Criminology & Criminal Justice,* Vol. 9, No. 1 (2009), pp. 5–28. Copyright © 2009, SAGE Publications. Reprinted by Permission of SAGE and the author.
71. Patricia Van Voorhis et al., "The Impact of Family Structure and Quality on Delinquency: A Comparative Assessment of Structural and Functional Factors," *Criminology,* Vol. 26, No. 2 (May 1988), pp. 235–261.
72. David F. Greenberg, "Comparing Criminal Career Models," *Criminology,* Vol. 30, No. 1 (February 1992), pp. 132–140.
73. This list of journals is representative at best. For a much more complete list, see Michael S. Vaughn et al., "Journals in Criminal Justice and Criminology: An Updated and Expanded Guide for Authors," *Journal of Criminal Justice Education,* Vol. 15, No. 1 (Spring 2004), pp. 61–192.
74. American Psychological Association, *Publication Manual of the American Psychological Association,* 5th ed. (Washington, DC: APA, 2001).
75. William Strunk, Jr., and E. B. White, *The Elements of Style,* 4th ed. (New York: Longman, 2000).
76. Mary-Claire van Leunen, *A Handbook for Scholars,* rev. ed. (Oxford: Oxford University Press, 1992).

CHAPTER 3: CLASSICAL AND NEOCLASSICAL THOUGHT

1. "About Listverse" (accessed February 10, 2012).
2. "Top 10 Tips to Commit the Perfect Crime," http://listverse.com/2007/08/16/top-10-tips-to-commit-the-perfect-crime/ (accessed February 10, 2012).
3. Ibid.
4. William Graham Sumner, *Folkways* (New York: Dover, 1906).
5. Marvin Wolfgang, "The Key Reporter," *Phi Beta Kappa,* Vol. 52, No. 1.
6. Roman influence in England had ended by A.D. 442, according to Crane Brinton, John B. Christopher, and Robert L. Wolff, *A History of Civilization,* 3rd ed., Vol. 1 (Upper Saddle River, NJ: Prentice Hall, 1967), p. 180.
7. Howard Abadinsky, *Law and Justice* (Chicago: Nelson-Hall, 1988), p. 6.
8. Edward McNall Burns, *Western Civilization,* 7th ed. (New York: W. W. Norton, 1969).
9. Ibid.
10. Brinton, Christopher, and Wolff, *A History of Civilization,* p. 274.
11. Harry V. Jaffa and Ernest van den Haag, "Of Men, Hogs, and Law: If Natural Law Does Not Permit Us to Distinguish between Men and Hogs, What Does?" *National Review,* February 3, 1992, p. 40.
12. Abraham Lincoln, Speech on the Kansas-Nebraska Act, October 16, 1854.
13. Referred to in official transcripts as Rudolf Franz Ferdinand Hoess.
14. International Military Tribunal, "One Hundred and Eighth Day, Monday, 4/15/1946, Part 03," in Trial of the Major War Criminals before the International Military Tribunal, Vol. XI. Proceedings: 4/8/1946–4/17/1946 (Nuremberg: International Military Tribunal, 1943), pp. 398–400.
15. The quotations attributed to Beccaria in this section are from Cesare Beccaria, *Essay on Crimes and Punishments* (Livorno, Italy: Tipografia Coltellini, 1764).
16. The quotations attributed to Bentham in this section are from Bentham, *An Introduction to the Principles of Morals and Legislation* (Oxford: Clarendon Press, 1907); reprint of the 1823 edition, first printed 1780.
17. R. Martinson, "What Works: Questions and Answers about Prison Reform," *Public Interest,* No. 35 (1974), pp. 22–54.
18. James Q. Wilson, *Thinking about Crime* (New York: Vintage, 1975).
19. David Fogel, *We Are the Living Proof: The Justice Model of Corrections* (Cincinnati, OH: Anderson, 1975).
20. Conrad P. Rutkowski, "Fogel's 'Justice Model': Stop Trying to Reform. Punish, but Treat All Alike," *Illinois Issues,* February 1976.
21. Felton M. Earls and Albert J. Reiss, *Breaking the Cycle: Predicting and Preventing Crime* (Washington, DC: National Institute of Justice, 1994), p. 49.
22. L. E. Cohen and Marcus Felson, "Social Change and Crime Rate Trends: A Routine Activity Approach," *American Sociological Review,* Vol. 44, No. 4 (August 1979), pp. 588–608. Also see Marcus Felson and L. E. Cohen, "Human Ecology and Crime: A Routine Activity Approach," *Human Ecology,* Vol. 8, No. 4 (1980), pp. 389–406; Marcus Felson, "Linking Criminal Choices, Routine Activities, Informal Control, and Criminal Outcomes," in Derek B. Cornish and Ronald V. Clarke, eds., *The Reasoning Criminal: Rational Choice Perspectives on Offending* (New York: Springer-Verlag, 1986), pp. 119–128; and Ronald V. Clarke and Marcus Felson, eds., *Advances in Criminological Theory: Routine Activity and Rational Choice* (New Brunswick, NJ: Transaction, 1993).

23. Cohen and Felson, "Social Change and Crime Rate Trends," p. 595.
24. For a test of routine activities theory as an explanation for victimization in the workplace, see John D. Wooldredge, Francis T. Cullen, and Edward J. Latessa, "Victimization in the Workplace: A Test of Routine Activities Theory," *Justice Quarterly*, Vol. 9, No. 2 (June 1992), pp. 325–335.
25. Marcus Felson, *Crime and Everyday Life: Insight and Implications for Society* (Thousand Oaks, CA: Pine Forge Press, 1994).
26. Gary LaFree and Christopher Birkbeck, "The Neglected Situation: A Cross-National Study of the Situational Characteristics of Crime," *Criminology*, Vol. 29, No. 1 (February 1991), p. 75.
27. Ronald V. Clarke and Derek B. Cornish, eds., *Crime Control in Britain: A Review of Police and Research* (Albany: State University of New York Press, 1985), p. 8.
28. Ronald V. Clarke, "Situational Crime Prevention—Everybody's Business," paper presented at the 1995 Australian Crime Prevention Council conference, http://barney.webace.com.au/~austcpc/conf95/clarke.htm (accessed December 2, 2000).
29. See Derek B. Cornish and Ronald V. Clarke, "Understanding Crime Displacement: An Application of Rational Choice Theory," *Criminology*, Vol. 25, No. 4 (November 1987), p. 933.
30. See Tomislav V. Kovandzic, Lynne M. Vieraitis, and Denise Paquette Boots, "Does the Death Penalty Save Lives? New Evidence from State Panel Data, 1977 to 2006," *Criminology and Public Policy*, Vol. 8, No. 4 (2009), pp. 803–843.
31. Werner Einstadter and Stuart Henry, *Criminological Theory: An Analysis of Its Underlying Assumptions* (Fort Worth, TX: Harcourt Brace, 1995), p. 70.
32. Daniel J. Curran and Claire M. Renzetti, *Theories of Crime* (Boston: Allyn & Bacon, 1994), p. 18.
33. Jack Katz, *Seductions of Crime: Moral and Sensual Attractions in Doing Evil* (New York: Basic Books, 1988), p. 8.
34. Ibid., p. 3.
35. Ibid., p. 76.
36. Ibid., p. 71.
37. Bill McCarthy, "Not Just 'for the Thrill of It': An Instrumentalist Elaboration of Katz's Explanation of Sneaky Thrill Property Crimes," *Criminology*, Vol. 33, No. 4 (1995), pp. 519–538.
38. The quotations attributed to Weisburd in this section are from David Weisburd, "Reorienting Crime Prevention Research and Policy: From the Causes of Criminality to the Context of Crime," *NIJ Research Report* (Washington, DC: National Institute of Justice, June 1997).
39. See P. Brantingham and P. Brantingham, "Situational Crime Prevention in Practice," *Canadian Journal of Criminology* (January 1990), pp. 17–40; and R. V. Clarke, "Situational Crime Prevention: Achievements and Challenges," in M. Tonry and D. Farrington, eds., *Building a Safer Society: Strategic Approaches to Crime Prevention, Crime and Justice: A Review of Research*, Vol. 19 (Chicago: University of Chicago Press, 1995).
40. Quotes in this paragraph and the next are taken from Weisburd, "Reorienting Crime Prevention Research and Policy."
41. See, for example, J. E. Eck and D. Weisburd, eds., *Crime and Place: Crime Prevention Studies*, Vol. 4 (Monsey, NY: Willow Tree Press, 1995).
42. Marcus Felson and Ronald V. Clarke, *Opportunity Makes the Thief: Practical Theory for Crime Prevention* (London: British Home Office, 1998), p. 33.
43. Ibid.
44. Laura J. Moriarty and James E. Williams, "Examining the Relationship between Routine Activities Theory and Social Disorganization: An Analysis of Property Crime Victimization," *American Journal of Criminal Justice*, Vol. 21, No. 1 (1996), pp. 43–59.
45. Ibid., p. 43.
46. Ibid., p. 46.
47. M. Lyn Exum, "The Application and Robustness of the Rational Choice Perspective in the Study of Angry Intentions to Aggress," *Criminology*, Vol. 40, No. 4 (2002), p. 933, citing Allen E. Liska and Stephen F. Messner, *Perspectives on Crime and Deviance*, 3rd ed. (Upper Saddle River, NJ: Prentice Hall, 1999).
48. Dolf Zillman, *Hostility and Aggression* (Hillsdale, NJ: Lawrence Erlbaum Associates, 1979), p. 279.
49. David Lee and Justin McCrary, "Crime, Punishment, and Myopia," NBER Working Paper No. W11491 (Cambridge, MA: National Bureau of Economic Research, 2005). Available at SSRN: http://ssrn.com/abstract=762770.
50. Ibid.
51. Francesco Drago, Roberto Galbiati, and Pietro Vertova, "The Deterrent Effects of Prison: Evidence from a Natural Experiment," *Journal of Political Economy*, Vol. 117 (2009), pp. 257–280.
52. Kenneth D. Tunnell, "Choosing Crime: Close Your Eyes and Take Your Chances," *Justice Quarterly*, Vol. 7 (1990), pp. 673–690.
53. See R. Barr and K. Pease, "Crime Placement, Displacement and Deflection," in M. Tonry and N. Morris, eds., *Crime and Justice: A Review of Research*, Vol. 12 (Chicago: University of Chicago Press, 1990).
54. For a good summation of target hardening, see Ronald V. Clarke, *Situational Crime Prevention* (New York: Harrow and Heston, 1992).
55. For a good summation of studies on displacement, see R. Hesseling, "Displacement: A Review of the Empirical Literature," in R. V. Clarke, ed., *Crime Prevention Studies*, Vol. 3 (Monsey, NY: Willow Tree Press, 1994).
56. C. S. Lewis, "The Humanitarian Theory of Punishment," *Res Judicatae*, Vol. 6 (1953), pp. 224–225.
57. Tracey L. Snell, *Capital Punishment, 1999* (Washington, DC: Bureau of Justice Statistics, 2000).
58. See, for example, W. C. Bailey, "Deterrence and the Death Penalty for Murders in Utah: A Time Series Analysis," *Journal of Contemporary Law*, Vol. 5, No. 1 (1978), pp. 1–20; and William Bailey, "An Analysis of the Deterrent Effects of the Death Penalty for Murder in California," *Southern California Law Review*, Vol. 52, No. 3 (1979), pp. 743–764.
59. See, for example, B. E. Forst, "The Deterrent Effect of Capital Punishment: A Cross-State Analysis of the 1960s," *Minnesota Law Review*, Vol. 61 (1977), pp. 743–764.
60. Scott H. Decker and Carol W. Kohfeld, "Capital Punishment and Executions in the Lone Star State: A Deterrence Study," *Criminal Justice Research Bulletin* (Criminal Justice Center, Sam Houston State University), Vol. 3, No. 12 (1988).
61. Tomislav V. Kovandzic, Lynne M. Vieraitis, and Denise Paquette Boots, "Does the Death Penalty Save Lives? New Evidence from State Panel Data, 1977 to 2006," *Crime and Public Policy*, Vol. 8, No. 4 (2009), p. 803.
62. Committee on Law and Justice, *Deterrence and the Death Penalty* (Washington, DC: National Academy of Sciences, 2012).

63. Information and quotes in this paragraph are from the Death Penalty Information Center's Web site, http://www.deathpenaltyinfo.org (accessed December 15, 2007).
64. As some of the evidence presented before the Supreme Court in *Furman* v. *Georgia,* 408 U.S. 238 (1972), suggested.
65. *McCleskey* v. *Kemp,* 481 U.S. 279 (1987).
66. Formerly known as the National Committee to Prevent Wrongful Executions.
67. The Constitution Project, *Mandatory Justice: Eighteen Reforms to the Death Penalty* (Washington, DC: The Constitution Project, 2001).
68. Bureau of Justice Statistics Press Release, "U.S. Prison Population Declined for Third Consecutive Year During 2012," July 25, 2013 (accessed July 27, 2013).
69. Marvin Wolfgang, Thorsten Sellin, and Robert Figlio, *Delinquency in a Birth Cohort* (Chicago: University of Chicago Press, 1972).
70. Randy Martin, Robert J. Mutchnick, and W. Timothy Austin, *Criminological Thought: Pioneers Past and Present* (New York: Macmillan, 1990), p. 17.
71. Ibid., p. 18.
72. Walter Moore, "An Alternative Take on the State of Los Angeles," *Press-Telegram,* April 26, 2012, http://www.presstelegram.com/opinions/ci_20461647/oped-an-alternate-take-state-los-angeles (accessed May 20, 2012).
73. Ibid.

CHAPTER 4: EARLY BIOLOGICAL PERSPECTIVES ON CRIMINAL BEHAVIOR

1. Megan Visscher, "How Food Can Cut Crime," *Ode Magazine,* February 9, 2010, http://www.care2.com/greenliving/how-food-can-cut-crime.html?page=4 (accessed March 11, 2012).
2. C. B. Gesch, S. M. Hammond, S. E. Hampson, A. Eves, and M. J. Crowder, "Influence of Supplementary Vitamins, Minerals and Essential Fatty Acids on the Antisocial Behavior of Young Adult Prisoners: Randomized, Placebo-Controlled Trial," *British Journal of Psychiatry,* Vol. 181 (July 2002), pp. 22–28.
3. Visscher, op. cit.
4. C. Ray Jeffery, "Biological Perspectives," *Journal of Criminal Justice Education,* Vol. 4, No. 2 (fall 1993), pp. 292–293.
5. Anthony Walsh and Craig Hemmens, eds., *Introduction to Criminology: A Text/Reader,* 2nd ed. (Thousand Oaks, CA: Sage, 2011), p. 272.
6. Auguste Comte, *A System of Positive Polity,* trans. John Henry Bridges (New York: Franklin, 1875; originally published in four volumes, 1851–1854).
7. See K. L. Henwood and N. F. Pidgeon, "Qualitative Research and Psychological Theorising," *British Journal of Psychology,* Vol. 83 (1992), pp. 97–111.
8. Cesare Lombroso, "Introduction," in Gina Lombroso-Ferrero, *Criminal Man According to the Classification of Cesare Lombroso* (1911; reprint, Montclair, NJ: Patterson Smith, 1972), p. xiv.
9. See Robert Fletcher, "The New School of Criminal Anthropology," *The American Anthropologist,* Vol. IV, No. 3 (July 1891), pp. 201–236.
10. Lombroso, "Introduction," in Lombroso-Ferrero, *Criminal Man According to the Classification of Cesare Lombroso,* p. xv.
11. Charles Darwin, *Descent of Man: And Selection in Relation to Sex,* rev. ed. (London: John Murray, 1874), p. 137.
12. The English-language version appeared in 1895 as Cesare Lombroso, *The Female Offender* (New York: D. Appleton, 1895).
13. Marvin Wolfgang, "Cesare Lombroso," in Hermann Mannheim, *Pioneers in Criminology,* 2nd ed. (Montclair, NJ: Patterson Smith, 1972), p. 254.
14. Charles Goring, *The English Convict: A Statistical Study* (London: His Majesty's Stationery Office, 1913; reprint, Montclair, NJ: Patterson Smith, 1972), p. 15.
15. Ibid.
16. Earnest A. Hooton, *Crime and the Man* (Cambridge, MA: Harvard University Press, 1939; reprint, Westport, CT: Greenwood Press, 1972).
17. Earnest A. Hooton, *The American Criminal: An Anthropological Study* (Cambridge, MA: Harvard University Press, 1939).
18. Nichole Hahn Rafter, "Criminal Anthropology in the United States," *Criminology,* Vol. 30, No. 4, 1992, p. 525.
19. L. Arseneault et al., "Minor Physical Anomalies and Family Adversity as Risk Factors for Violent Delinquency in Adolescence," *American Journal of Psychiatry,* Vol. 157, No. 6 (June 2000), pp. 917–923.
20. William H. Sheldon, *Varieties of Delinquent Youth* (New York: Harper & Brothers, 1949).
21. Ibid.
22. See Joseph D. McInerney, "Genes and Behavior: A Complex Relationship," *Judicature,* Vol. 83, No. 3 (November–December 1999).
23. Sir Francis Galton, *Inquiry into Human Faculty and Its Development,* 2nd ed. (London: J. M. Dent and Sons, 1907).
24. Richard Louis Dugdale, *The Jukes: A Study in Crime, Pauperism, Disease, and Heredity,* 3rd ed. (New York: G. P. Putnam's Sons, 1895).
25. Arthur H. Estabrook, *The Jukes in 1915* (Washington, DC: Carnegie Institute of Washington, 1916).
26. Henry Herbert Goddard, *The Kallikak Family: A Study in the Heredity of Feeblemindedness* (New York: Macmillan, 1912).
27. See Nicole Hahn Rafter, *Creating Born Criminals* (Urbana: University of Illinois Press, 1997).
28. See Nicole Hahn Rafter, ed., *White Trash: The Eugenics Family Studies, 1877–1919* (Boston: Northeastern University Press, 1988).
29. *Buck* v. *Bell,* 274 U.S. 200, 207 (1927).
30. P. A. Jacobs, M. Brunton, and M. Melville, "Aggressive Behavior, Mental Subnormality, and the XYY Male," *Nature,* Vol. 208 (1965), p. 1351.
31. Webster's defines *karyotype* as "a photomicrograph of metaphase chromosomes in a standard array" (*Webster's II New College Dictionary* [Chicago, IL: Houghton Mifflin Harcourt, 2005], p. 618).
32. Anthony Walsh, *Biology and Criminology: The Biosocial Synthesis* (New York: Routledge, 2009), p. 268.
33. See David A. Jones, *History of Criminology: A Philosophical Perspective* (Westport, CT: Greenwood Press, 1986), p. 124.
34. As reported by S. A. Mednick and J. Volavka, "Biology and Crime," in N. Morris and M. Tonry, *Crime and Justice: An Annual Review of Research,* Vol. 2 (Chicago: University of Chicago Press, 1980), pp. 85–158; and D. A. Andrews and James Bonta, *The Psychology of Criminal Conduct* (Cincinnati, OH: Anderson, 1994), pp. 126–127.
35. T. Sarbin and J. Miller, "Demonism Revisited: The XYY Chromosomal Anomaly," *Issues in Criminology,* Vol. 5 (1970), p. 199.
36. Johannes Lange, *Verbrechen als Schicksal* (Leipzig: Georg Thieme, 1929).

37. Karl O. Christiansen, "A Preliminary Study of Criminality among Twins," in Sarnoff Mednick and Karl Christiansen, eds., *Biosocial Bases of Criminal Behavior* (New York: Gardner Press, 1977).
38. The Minnesota Twin Family Study, http://www.psych.umn.edu/psylabs/mtfs (accessed August 10, 2007).
39. T. J. Bouchard et al., "Sources of Human Psychological Differences: The Minnesota Study of Twins Reared Apart," *Science*, Vol. 250, No. 4978 (1990), pp. 223–228.
40. Peter McGuffin and Anita Thapar, "Genetic Basis of Bad Behaviour in Adolescents," *Lancet*, Vol. 350 (August 9, 1997), pp. 411–412.
41. Wendy Slutske et al., "Modeling Genetic and Environmental Influences in the Etiology of Conduct Disorder: A Study of 2,682 Adult Twin Pairs," *Journal of Abnormal Psychology*, Vol. 106, No. 2 (1997), pp. 266–279.
42. Louise Arseneault et al., "Strong Genetic Effects on Cross-Situational Antisocial Behaviour among 5-Year-Old Children According to Mothers, Teachers, Examiner Observers, and Twins' Self-Reports," *Journal of Child Psychology and Psychiatry*, Vol. 44, No. 6 (September 2003), pp. 832–848.
43. Ibid.
44. Jeanette Taylor et al., "Genetic and Environmental Influences on Psychopathy Trait Dimensions in a Community Sample of Male Twins," *Journal of Abnormal Child Psychology*, Vol. 31, No. 6 (December 2003), pp. 633–645.
45. Konrad Lorenz, *On Aggression* (New York: Harcourt, Brace and World, 1966).
46. Ibid., p. 23.
47. Ibid., p. 38.
48. Ibid., p. 249.
49. Ibid.
50. Edward O. Wilson, *Sociobiology: The New Synthesis* (Cambridge, MA: Harvard Univ. Press, 1980).
51. Arthur Fisher, "Sociobiology: Science or Ideology?", *Society*, July/August 1992, pp. 67-79.
52. John H. Beckstrom, *Evolutionary Jurisprudence: Prospects and Limitations on the Use of Modern Darwinism Throughout the Legal Process* (Champaign, IL: Univ. of Illinois Press, 1989).
53. Michael Ruse, "Edward O. Wilson on Sociobiology," *The Chronicle of Higher Education*, March 31, 2010.
54. Taken from "Hope for the 'Hopeless,'" *Crime Times*, Vol. 10, No. 2 (2004), p. 2.

CHAPTER 5: BIOSOCIAL AND OTHER CONTEMPORARY PERSPECTIVES

1. Marc Lallianilla, "Genetics May Provide Clues to Newtown Shooting," *Livescience*, http://www.livescience.com/25853-newtown-shooter-dna.html December 28, 2012, (accessed January 2, 2013).
2. Rick Weiss, "Genome Project Completed," *Washington Post*, April 15, 2003, p. A6.
3. James Watson and Francis Crick, "Molecular Structure of Nucleic Acids: A Structure for Deoxyribose Nucleic Acid," *Nature*, Vol. 171 (April 1953), p. 737.
4. Mary Kugler, "What Are Genes, DNA and Chromosomes?" About.com, http://rarediseases.about.com/od/geneticdisorders/a/genesbasics.htm (accessed December 6, 2012).
5. Mary Kugler, "What Are Genes, DNA and Chromosomes?" About.com, http://rarediseases.about.com/od/geneticdisorders/a/genesbasics.htm (accessed December 6, 2012).
6. McKusick-Nathans Institute of Genetic Medicine, "The 1,000 Genomes Project," The Johns Hopkins University, 2010, http://www.hopkinsmedicine.org/geneticmedicine/news/Newsletter-Stories/2010_12/2010_12_1000_genomes.html (accessed January 3, 2013).
7. Much of the information and some of the wording in this section come from the National Human Genome Research Institute's Web page, http://www.nhgri.nih.gov/HGP (accessed November 16, 2007).
8. Geoffrey Cowley and Carol Hallin, "The Genetics of Bad Behavior: A Study Links Violence to Heredity," *Newsweek*, November 1, 1993, p. 57.
9. H. G. Brunner, M. Nelen, X. O. Breakefield, H. H. Ropers, B. A. van Oost, "Abnormal Behavior Associated with a Point Mutation in the Structural Gene for Monoamine Oxidase A," *Science*, Vol. 262, No. 5133 (Oct. 22, 1993), pp. 578–580.
10. Quoted in Tim Friend, "Violence Linked to Gene Defect: Pleasure Deficit May Be the Spark," *USA Today*, May 9, 1996. See the original research at Kenneth Blum et al., "Reward Deficiency Syndrome," *American Scientist*, Vol. 84 (March/April 1996), pp. 132–145, http://www.sigmaxi.org/amsci/Articles/96Articles/Blum-full.html (accessed January 5, 2005).
11. See, for example, M. Rutter, H. Giller, and A. Hagell, *Antisocial Behavior by Young People* (Cambridge: Cambridge University Press, 1998).
12. Avshalom Caspi et al., "Role of Genotype in the Cycle of Violence in Maltreated Children," *Science*, Vol. 298, No. 2 (August 2002), p. 851.
13. For more information on the Dunedin Multidisciplinary Health and Development Study, see T. E. Moffitt et al., *Sex Differences in Antisocial Behavior: Conduct Disorder, Delinquency and Violence in the Dunedin Longitudinal Study* (Cambridge: Cambridge University Press, 2001). Visit the Dunedin Multidisciplinary Health and Development Research Unit on the Web at http://healthsci.otago.ac.nz/dsm/dmhdru.
14. Ibid.
15. Nilsson Oreland et al., "Monoamine Oxidases: Activities, Genotypes and the Shaping of Behaviour," *Journal of Neural Transmission*, April 12, 2007; and Rickard L. Sjöberg et al., "Adolescent Girls and Criminal Activity: Role of MAOA-LPR Genotype and Psychosocial Factor," *American Journal of Medical Genetics Part B: Neuropsychiatric Genetics*, Vol. 144B, No. 2 (October 2006), pp. 159–164.
16. Kevin M. Beaver, Matt DeLisi, Michael G. Vaughn, and John Paul Wright, "The Intersection of Genes and Neuropsychological Deficits in the Prediction of Adolescent Delinquency and Low Self-Control," *International Journal of Offender Therapy and Comparative Criminology*, Vol. 20, No. 10, (2008), p. 17.
17. National Geographic Television, "Inside the Warrior Gene," http://natgeotv.com/ca/inside-the-warrior-gene/about (accessed January 2, 2013).
18. A. E. Baum et al., "A Genome-Wide Association Study Implicates Diacylglycerol Kinase Eta (DGKH) and Several Other Genes in the Etiology of Bipolar Disorder," *Molecular Psychiatry*, advance online publication, http://doi:10.1038/sj.mp.4002012 (accessed May 8, 2007).
19. National Institute on Drug Abuse, "Genetics of Addiction: A Research Update from the National Institute on Drug Abuse," http://www.drugabuse.gov/tib/genetics.html (accessed May 1, 2010).
20. Nathalie M. G. Fontaine, Eamon J. P. McCory et al., "Predictors and Outcomes of Joint Trajectories of Callous–Unemotional

Traits and Conduct Problems in Childhood," *Journal of Abnormal Psychology,* Vol. 123, No. 3 (August 2011), pp. 740–741.

21. Twins Early Development Study, "TEDS," http://www.teds.ac.uk/about.html (accessed January 27, 2012).
22. Danielle Boisvert, John Paul Wright, Valerie Knopik and Jamie Vaske, "A Twin Study of Sex Differences in Self-Control," *Justice Quarterly,* Vol. 30, No. 3 (2013), pp. 529–559.
23. Anthony Walsh, "Behavior Genetics and Anomic/Strain Theory," in Anthony Walsh and CaigCraig Hemmens, eds., *Introduction to Criminology: A Text/Reader* (Thousand Oaks, CA: Sage, 2010), p. 284.
24. The University of Utah, Genetic Science Learning Center, "Epigenetics," http://learn.genetics.utah.edu/content/epigenetics (accessed February 2, 2013).
25. J. D. McInerney, "Genes and Behavior: A Complex Relationship," *Judicature,* Vol. 80, No. 3 (1999), pp. 112–115.
26. See "The Genome Changes Everything: A Talk with Matt Ridley," http://www.edge.org/3rd_culture/ridley03/ridley_print.html (accessed February 10, 2007).
27. Matt Ridley, "What Makes You Who You Are?" *Time,* June 2, 2003, pp. 55–63.
28. Kevin M. Beaver and Anthony Walsh, "Biosocial Criminology," in Kevin M. Beaver and Anthony Walsh, eds., *The Ashgate Research Companion to Biosocial Theories of Crime* (Burlington, VT: Ashgate Publishing, 2011), p. 7.
29. See Adrian Raine et al., "Prefrontal Glucose Deficits in Murderers Lacking Psychosocial Deprivation," *Neuropsychiatry, Neuropsychology, and Behavioral Neurology,* Vol. 11, No. 1 (1998), pp. 1–7; and Adrian Raine et al., "Selective Reductions in Prefrontal Glucose Metabolism in Murderers," *Biological Psychiatry,* Vol. 36 (September 1, 1994), pp. 319–332.
30. "PET Study: Looking Inside the Minds of Murderers," *Crime Times,* Vol. 1, No. 1–2 (1995), http://www.crime-times.org/95a/w95ap1.htm (accessed November 15, 2006).
31. Ibid.
32. Raine et al., "Selective Reductions in Prefrontal Glucose Metabolism in Murderers."
33. Adrian Raine, Monte Buchsbaum, and Lori LaCasse, "Brain Abnormalities in Murderers Indicated by Positron Emission Tomography," in Kevin M. Beaver and Anthony Walsh, eds., *Biosocial Theories of Crime* (Burlington, VT: Ashgate, 2010), pp. 465–478.
34. Adrian Raine, J. Reid Meloy, Susan Bihrle, Jackie Stoddard, Lori LaCasse, and Monte S. Buchsbaum, "Reduced Prefrontal and Increased Subcortical Brain Functioning Assessed Using Positron Emission Tomography in Predatory and Affective Murderers," in Kevin M. Beaver and Anthony Walsh, eds., *Biosocial Theories of Crime* (Burlington, VT: Ashgate, 2010), pp. 479–492.
35. "Researchers Explore the Brain for Clues to the Causes of Anti-Social Behavior," AAAS 2011 Annual Meeting News, February 25, 2011, http://news.aaas.org/2011_annual_meeting/0225nature-nurture-in-antisocial-behavior.shtml (accessed January 27, 2011).
36. "Kids' Brains May Hold Clues to Future Criminals," CNN Health, February 21, 2011, http://thechart.blogs.cnn.com/2011/02/21/kids-brains-may-hold-clues-to-future-criminals (accessed January 27, 2012).
37. James H. Fallon, "Neuroanatomical Background to Understanding the Brain of the Young Psychopath," *Ohio State Journal of Criminal Law,* Vol. 3 (2006), pp. 340–367.
38. Daniel Strueber, Monika Lueck, and Gerhard Roth, "The Violent Brain," *Scientific American,* November 29, 2006, http://www.scientificamerican.com/article.cfm?id=the-violent-brain (accessed February 21, 2012).
39. Katie Moisse, "Communication Breakdown in Brain Caused by a Gene Defect May Contribute to Schizophrenia," *Scientific American,* April 1, 2010, http://www.scientificamerican.com/article.cfm?id=schizophrenia-gene-mechanism (accessed May 20, 2010). See also Torfi Sigurdsson et al., "Impaired Hippocampal-Prefrontal Synchrony in a Genetic Mouse Model of Schizophrenia," *Nature,* Vol. 464, No. 7289 (2010), pp. 763–667.
40. See, for example, A. R. Mawson and K. J. Jacobs, "Corn Consumption, Tryptophan, and Cross National Homicide Rates," *Journal of Orthomolecular Psychiatry,* Vol. 7 (1978), pp. 227–230; and A. Hoffer, "The Relation of Crime to Nutrition," *Humanist in Canada,* Vol. 8 (1975), p. 8.
41. "Flu in Pregnancy Changes Fetal Brain," *New Scientist,* January 30, 2010, p. 15.
42. Douglas S. Massey, "Segregation and Stratification: A Biosocial Perspective," in Kevin M. Beaver and Anthony Walsh, eds., *Biosocial Theories of Crime* (Burlington, VT: Ashgate, 2010), p. 62
43. "Childhood Abuse Hurts the Brain," *Harvard University Gazette,* May 22, 2003, http://www.news.harvard.edu/gazette/2003/05.22/01-brain.html (accessed June 4, 2010).
44. Ibid.
45. Violence Makes a Kid's Brain Like That of a Soldier," *New Scientist,* December 10, 2011, p. 12.
46. Christian Jarrett, "Predicting Reoffending?" *The Psychologist,* April 23, 2013.
47. See Proceedings of the National Academy of Sciences of the United States of America, *Biological Embedding of Early Social Adversity: From Fruit Flies to Kindergartners—the Sackler Colloquium,* October 16, 2012, http://www.pnas.org/content/109/suppl.2 (accessed February 2, 2013).
48. Marla B. Sokolowski, W. Thomas Boyce, and Bruce S. McEwen, "Scarred for Life?," *New Scientist,* January 26, 2013, p. 28.
49. Antoine Lutz et al., "Long-Term Meditators Self-Induce High-Amplitude Gamma Synchrony during Mental Practice," *Proceedings of the National Academy of Sciences,* Vol. 101, No. 46 (November 16, 2004), pp. 16369–16373.
50. Jeffrey M. Schwartz and Sharon Begley, *The Mind and the Brain: Neuroplasticity and the Power of Mental Force* (New York: Regan Books, 2002).
51. Anthony Walsh, *Biosocial Criminology: Introduction and Integration* (Cincinnati, OH: Anderson, 2002), p. ix.
52. Ibid.
53. D. Hill and W. Sargent, "A Case of Matricide," *Lancet,* Vol. 244 (1943), pp. 526–527.
54. William Dufty, *Sugar Blues* (Pandor, PA: Chilton, 1975).
55. See *Court TV*'s Crime Library, "Twinkies as a Defense," http://www.crimelibrary.com/criminal_mind/psychology/insanity/7.html (accessed August 8, 2007).
56. Nanci Hellmich, "Sweets May Not Be Culprit in Hyper Kids," *USA Today,* February 3, 1994, p. 1A (reporting on a study published in the *New England Journal of Medicine*).
57. Ibid., p. 1A.
58. See, for example, C. Hawley and R. E. Buckley, "Food Dyes and Hyperkinetic Children," *Academy Therapy,* Vol. 10 (1974), pp. 27–32; and Alexander Schauss, *Diet, Crime and Delinquency* (Berkeley, CA: Parker House, 1980).

59. "Special Report: Measuring Your Life with Coffee Spoons," *Tufts University Diet and Nutrition Letter,* Vol. 2, No. 2 (April 1984), pp. 3–6.

60. See, for example, "Special Report: Does What You Eat Affect Your Mood and Actions?," *Tufts University Diet and Nutrition Letter,* Vol. 2, No. 12 (February 1985), pp. 4–6.

61. See *Tufts University Diet and Nutrition Newsletter,* Vol. 2, No. 11 (January 1985), p. 2; and "Special Report: Why Sugar Continues to Concern Nutritionists," *Tufts University Diet and Nutrition Letter,* Vol. 3, No. 3 (May 1985), pp. 3–6.

62. "School Study: Supplementation Decreases Delinquent Behaviors, Raises IQ," *Crime Times,* Vol. 6, No. 2 (2000), p. 3, http://www.crimetimes.org/00b/w00bp3.htm (accessed March 10, 2012).

63. S. J. Schoenthaler and D. Bier, "The Effect of Vitamin-Mineral Supplementation on Juvenile Delinquency Among American Schoolchildren: A Randomized, Double-blind Placebo-controlled Trial," *Journal of Alternative Complementary Medicine,* Vol. 6, No. 1 (February 2000), pp. 31–35.

64. I. B. Helland et al., "Maternal Supplements with Very-Long-Chain Omega-3 Fatty Acids during Pregnancy and Lactation Augment Children's IQ at 4 Years of Age," *Pediatrics,* Vol. 111, No. 1 (January 2003), pp. 39–44.

65. Ĉ. Iribarren et al., "Dietary Intake of Omega-3, Omega-6 Fatty Acids and Fish: Relationship with Hostility in Young Adults—The CARDIA Study," *European Journal of Clinical Nutrition,* Vol. 50, No. 1 (January 2004), pp. 24–31.

66. David Benton, "The Impact of Diet on Anti-Social, Violent and Criminal Behaviour," *Neuroscience and Biobehavioral Reviews,* Vol. 31 (2007), pp. 752–774.

67. Avery Johnson, "Links Tighten Between IQ, Breast-Feeding," *The Wall Street Journal,* July 29, 2013, http://online.wsj.com/article/SB10001424127887324809004578635783141433600.html (accessed August 8, 2013).

68. Roger D. Masters, Brian Hone, and Anil Doshi, "Environmental Pollution, Neurotoxicity, and Criminal Violence," in J. Rose, ed., *Environmental Toxicology* (London and New York: Gordon and Breach, 1997).

69. Peter Montague, "Toxics and Violent Crime," *Rachel's Environment and Health Weekly,* No. 551 (June 19, 1997).

70. See, for example, Rick Nevin, "How Lead Exposure Relates to Temporal Changes in IQ, Violent Crime, and Unwed Pregnancy," *Environmental Research,* Vol. 83, No.1 (May 2000), pp. 1–22.

71. Quoted in Alison Motluck, "Pollution May Lead to a Life of Crime," *New Scientist,* Vol. 154, No. 2084 (May 31, 1997), p. 4.

72. L. Goldschmidt, N. L. Day, and G. A. Richardson, "Effects of Prenatal Marijuana Exposure on Child Behavior Problems at Age 10," *Neurotoxicology and Teratology,* Vol. 22, No. 3 (May/June 2000), pp. 325–336.

73. David Fergusson, Lianne Woodward, and L. John Horwood, "Maternal Smoking during Pregnancy and Psychiatric Adjustment in Late Adolescence," *Archives of General Psychiatry,* Vol. 55 (August 1998), pp. 721–727.

74. Jacob F. Orlebeke, Dirk L. Knol, and Frank C. Verhulst, "Increase in Child Behavior Problems Resulting from Maternal Smoking during Pregnancy," *Archives of Environmental Health,* Vol. 52, No. 4 (July/August 1997), pp. 317–321.

75. Travis C. Pratt, Jean Marie McGloin, and Noelle E. Fearn, "Maternal Cigarette Smoking during Pregnancy and Criminal/Deviant Behavior: A Meta-Analysis," *International Journal of Offender Therapy and Comparative Criminology,* Vol. 50, No. 6 (2006), pp. 672–690.

76. See, for example, Ann Pytkowicz Streissguth et al., "Fetal Alcohol Syndrome in Adolescents and Adults," *Journal of the American Medical Association,* Vol. 265, No. 15 (April 17, 1991).

77. Tresa M. Roebuck, Sarah N. Mattson, and Edward P. Riley, "Behavioral and Psychosocial Profiles of Alcohol-Exposed Children," *Alcoholism: Clinical and Experimental Research,* Vol. 23, No. 6 (June 1999), pp. 1070–1076.

78. See, for example, D. H. Fishbein, "The Psychobiology of Female Aggression," *Criminal Justice and Behavior,* Vol. 19 (1992), pp. 99–126.

79. T. I. Paus et al., "Sexual Dimorphism in the Adolescent Brain: Role of Testosterone and Androgen Receptor in Global and Local White Matter," *Hormones and Behavior,* Vol. 57 (2010), pp. 63–75.

80. See, for example, R. T. Rada, D. R. Laws, and R. Kellner, "Plasma Testosterone Levels in the Rapist," *Psychosomatic Medicine,* Vol. 38 (1976), pp. 257–268.

81. "The Insanity of Steroid Abuse," *Newsweek,* May 23, 1988, p. 75.

82. Dan Olweus et al., "Testosterone, Aggression, Physical and Personality Dimensions in Normal Adolescent Males," *Psychosomatic Medicine,* Vol. 42 (1980), pp. 253–269.

83. Richard Udry, "Biosocial Models of Adolescent Problem Behaviors," *Social Biology,* Vol. 37 (1990), pp. 1–10.

84. Dan Olweus, "Testosterone and Adrenaline: Aggressive Antisocial Behavior in Normal Adolescent Males," in Sarnoff A. Mednick, Terrie E. Moffitt, and Susan A. Stack, eds., *The Causes of Crime: New Biological Approaches* (Cambridge: Cambridge University Press, 1987), pp. 263–282.

85. Alan Booth and D. Wayne Osgood, "The Influence of Testosterone on Deviance in Adulthood: Assessing and Explaining the Relationship," *Criminology,* Vol. 31, No. 1 (1993), p. 93.

86. E. G. Stalenheim et al., "Testosterone as a Biological Marker in Psychopathy and Alcoholism," *Psychiatry Research,* Vol. 77, No. 2 (February 1998), pp. 79–88.

87. Michelle M. Wirth and Oliver C. Schultheiss, "Basal Testosterone Moderates Responses to Anger Faces in Humans," *Physiology and Behavior,* Vol. 90 (2007), pp. 496–505.

88. Ibid., p. 502.

89. Richard Udry, Luther Talbert, and Naomi Morris, "Biosocial Foundations for Adolescent Female Sexuality," *Demography,* Vol. 23 (1986), pp. 217–227.

90. James M. Dabbs, Jr., and Marian F. Hargrove, "Age, Testosterone, and Behavior among Female Prison Inmates," *Psychosomatic Medicine,* Vol. 59 (1997), pp. 447–480.

91. A. Maras et al., "Association of Testosterone and Dihydrotestosterone with Externalizing Behavior in Adolescent Boys and Girls, *Psychoneuroendocrinology,* Vol. 28, No. 7 (October 2003), pp. 932–940.

92. *Regina* v. *English,* unreported, Norwich Crown Court, November 10, 1981.

93. Paul C. Bernhardt, "Influences of Serotonin and Testosterone in Aggression and Dominance: Convergence with Social Psychology," *Current Directions in Psychological Science,* Vol. 6, No. 2 (April 1997), pp. 44–48.

94. Don Cherek and Scott Lane, "Effects of d,1-Fenfluramine on Aggressive and Impulsive Responding in Adult Males with a History of Conduct Disorder," *Psychopharmacology,* Vol. 146 (1999), pp. 473–481.

95. Ibid.
96. Anastasia Toufexis, "Seeking the Roots of Violence," *Time,* April 19, 1993.
97. See, for example, Jeffrey Halperin et al., "Serotonergic Function in Aggressive and Nonaggressive Boys with ADHD," *American Journal of Psychiatry,* Vol. 151, No. 2 (February 1994), pp. 243–248.
98. Roger D. Masters, Brian Hone, and Anil Doshi, "Environmental Pollution, Neurotoxicity, and Criminal Violence," in J. Rose, ed., *Environmental Toxicology* (London and New York: Gordon and Breach, 1997).
99. Terrie E. Moffitt et al., "Whole Blood Serotonin Relates to Violence in an Epidemiological Study," *Biological Psychiatry,* Vol. 43, No. 6 (March 15, 1998), pp. 446–457.
100. Ibid.
101. H. Soderstrom et al., "New Evidence for an Association between the CSF HVA:5–HIAA Ratio and Psychopathic Traits," *Journal of Neurology, Neurosurgery and Psychiatry,* Vol. 74 (2003), pp. 918–921.
102. Angela D. Crews, "Biological Theory," in J. Mitchell Miller, ed., *21st Century Criminology: A Reference Handbook* (Thousand Oaks, CA: Sage, 2009), p. 196.
103. Keith McBurnett et al., "Low Salivary Cortisol and Persistent Aggression in Boys Referred for Disruptive Behavior," *Archives of General Psychiatry,* Vol. 57, No. 1 (January 2000), pp. 38–43.
104. Ibid.
105. See E. G. Stalenheim, L. von Knorring, and L. Wide, "Serum Levels of Thyroid Hormones as Biological Markers in a Swedish Forensic Psychiatric Population," *Biological Psychiatry,* Vol. 43, No. 10 (May 15, 1998), pp. 755–761; and P. O. Alm et al., "Criminality and Psychopathy as Related to Thyroid Activity in Former Juvenile Delinquents," *Acta Psychiatrica Scandinavica,* Vol. 94, No. 2 (August 1996), pp. 112–117.
106. Paul J. Zak, "The Trust Molecule," WSJ.com, April 27, 2012, http://professional.wsj.com/article/SB1000142405270230481130457736578299532036 6.html?mod=WSJPRO_hps_MIDDLESecondNews#printMode (accessed August 2, 2012).
107. Leah E. Daigle, "Biochemical Theories of Criminal Behavior," in Richard A Wright and J. Mitchell Miler, eds., *Encyclopedia of Criminology,* Vol. 1 (London: Routledge, 2005), p. 103.
108. Joseph Goldstein, "It Has Been Frigid Outside, but Also a Lot Less Dangerous," *New York Times,* January 25, 2013, http://www.nytimes.com/2013/01/26/nyregion/cold-wave-cut-murders-in-new-york-city-significantly.html (accessed March 4, 2013).
109. J. Rotton and E. G. Cohn, "Weather, Climate, and Crime," in R. Bechtel and E. Churchman, eds., *The 2002 Handbook of Environmental Psychology* (New York: Wiley, 2002), pp. 461–498.
110. E. G. Cohn and J. Rotton, "Assault as a Function of Time and Temperature: A Moderator-Variable Time-Series Analysis," *Journal of Personality and Social Psychology,* Vol. 72 (1997), pp. 1322–1334.
111. J. Rotton and E. G. Cohn, "Violence as a Curvilinear Function of Temperature in Dallas: A Replication," *Journal of Personality and Social Psychology,* Vol. 78 (2000), pp. 1074–1081.
112. E. G. Cohn and J. Rotton, "Weather, Seasonal Trends, and Property Crimes in Minneapolis, 1987–1988: A Moderator-Variable Time-Series Analysis of Routine Activities," *Journal of Environmental Psychology,* Vol. 20 (2000), pp. 257–272.
113. J. Rotton and E. G. Cohn, "Temperature, Routine Activities, and Domestic Violence: A Reanalysis," *Victims and Violence,* Vol. 16 (2001), pp. 203–215.
114. J. Rotton and E. G. Cohn, "Weather, Disorderly Conduct, and Assaults: From Social Contact to Social Avoidance," *Environment and Behavior,* Vol. 32 (2000), pp. 649–671.
115. Thomas J. Schory et al., "Barometric Pressure, Emergency Psychiatric Visits, and Violent Acts," *Canadian Journal of Psychiatry,* Vol. 48 (October 2003), pp. 624–627.
116. Monte Morin, "Violence Will Rise as Climate Changes, Scientists Predict," *The Los Angeles Times,* August 1, 2013, http://www.latimes.com/news/science/la-sci-climate-change-conflict-20130802,0,3466600.story (accessed August 8, 2013).
117. James Q. Wilson and Richard J. Herrnstein, *Crime and Human Nature* (New York: Simon & Schuster, 1985).
118. Quoted in Karen J. Winkler, "Criminals Are Born as Well as Made, Authors of Controversial Book Assert," *Chronicle of Higher Education,* January 16, 1986, p. 5.
119. Wilson and Herrnstein, *Crime and Human Nature.*
120. Winkler, "Criminals Are Born as Well as Made," p. 8.
121. Anthony Walsh, *Biosocial Criminology: Introduction and Integration* (Cincinnati, OH: Anderson, 2002), p. vii.
122. Anthony Walsh, "Biological Theories of Criminal Behavior," in Richard A. Wright and J. Mitchell Miller, eds., *Encyclopedia of Criminology,* Vol. 1 (New York: Routledge, 2005), p. 106.
123. Ibid.
124. Ibid.
125. Diana Fishbein, *Biobehavioral Perspectives in Criminology* (Belmont, CA: Wadsworth, 2001), pp. 2–3.
126. C. Ray Jeffery, "Biological Perspectives," *Journal of Criminal Justice Education,* Vol. 4 (1993), p. 300.
127. Leanne Fiftal Alarid et al., "Women's Roles in Serious Offenses: A Study of Adult Felons," *Justice Quarterly,* Vol. 13, No. 3 (September 1996), pp. 432–454.
128. Kevin Beaver, "Foreword," in Anthony Walsh, ed., *Feminist Criminology through a Biosocial Lens* (Durham, NC: Carolina Academic Press, 2011), p. 11.
129. Federal Bureau of Investigation, *Crime in the United States, 2012* (Washington, DC: U.S. Department of Justice, 2013).
130. Freda Adler, *Sisters in Crime: The Rise of the New Female Criminal* (New York: McGraw-Hill, 1975).
131. Darrell J. Steffensmeier, "Sex Differences in Patterns of Adult Crime, 1965–1977: A Review and Assessment," *Social Forces,* Vol. 58 (1980), pp. 1098–1099.
132. T. Bernard, J. Snipes, and A. Gerould, *Vold's Theoretical Criminology* (New York: Oxford University Press, 2010), cited in Anthony Walsh, ed., *Feminist Criminology through a Biosocial Lens* (Durham, NC: Carolina Academic Press, 2011), p. xi.
133. Anthony Walsh, ed., *Feminist Criminology through a Biosocial Lens* (Durham, NC: Carolina Academic Press, 2011), p. 22.
134. Ibid.
135. Laura Klappenbach, "Sexual Selection," About.com, 2 (accessed January 10, 2012).
136. I. Silverman, J. Choi, and M. Peters, "The Hunter-Gatherer Theory of Sex Differences in Spatial Abilities: Data from 40 Countries," *Archives of Sexual Behavior,* Vol. 36 (2007), pp. 261–268.
137. A. Walsh and L. Ellis, *Criminology: An Interdisciplinary Approach* (Thousand Oaks, CA: Sage, 2007).
138. Walsh, ed., *Feminist Criminology,* p. 125.
139. Kevin M. Beaver, John Paul Wright, and Anthony Walsh, "A Gene-Based Evolutionary Explanation for the Association between Criminal Involvement and Number of Sex Partners," in

Kevin M. Beaver and Anthony Walsh, eds., *Biosocial Theories of Crime* (Burlington, VT: Ashgate, 2010), p. 351.

140. Anthony Walsh and Craig Hemmens, *Introduction to Criminology: A Text/Reader,* 2nd ed. (Thousand Oaks, CA: Sage, 2011), p. 269.

141. Lee Ellis, "A Theory Explaining Biological Correlates of Criminality," in Anthony Walsh and Craig Hemmens, eds., *Introduction to Criminology: A Text/Reader,* 2nd ed. (Thousand Oaks, CA: Sage, 2011), pp. 299–306.

142. Jerome H. Barkow, Leda Cosmides, and John Tooby, eds., *The Adapted Mind: Evolutionary Psychology and the Generation of Culture* (New York: Oxford University Press, 1992).

143. Steven Pinker, *The Blank Slate: The Modern Denial of Human Nature* (New York: Viking, 2002).

144. Lee Ellis and Anthony Walsh, "Gene-Based Evolutionary Theories in Criminology," *Criminology,* Vol. 35, No. 2 (1997), pp. 229–230.

145. Terrie E. Moffitt, "The New Look of Behavioral Genetics in Developmental Psychopathology: Gene-Environment Interplay in Antisocial Behaviors," in Kevin M. Beaver and Anthony Walsh, eds., *Biosocial Theories of Crime* (Burlington, VT: Ashgate, 2010), p. 185.

146. Elizabeth Englander, *Understanding Violence,* 3rd ed. (Mahwah, NJ: Lawrence Erlbaum Associates, 2007).

147. Lee Ellis, Lee. (2005). "Theory Explaining the Biological Correlates of Criminality," *European Journal of Criminology,* Vol. 2, No. 3, pp. 287–314.

148. Julian Roberts and T. Gabor, "Lombrosian Wine in a New Bottle: Research on Crime and Race," *Canadian Journal of Criminology,* Vol. 32, pp. 291–313.

CHAPTER 6: PSYCHOLOGICAL AND PSYCHIATRIC FOUNDATIONS OF CRIMINAL BEHAVIOR

1. "Giffords, Other Survivors to Observe 1-Year Mark of Shooting Rampage in Tucson," Associated Press, December 29, 2011, http://www.washingtonpost.com/national/giffords-other-survivors-to-observe-1-year-mark-of-shooting-rampage-in-tucson/2011/12/29/gIQAOgNsOP_story.html?hpid=z4 (accessed May 1, 2012).

2. "Jared Loughner Enters Guilty Plea after Being Found Competent to Stand Trial," *The Guardian*, http://www.guardian.co.uk/world/2012/aug/07/jaredloughner-pleads-guilty-arizona (accessed May 5, 2011).

3. Paul Farhi, "Publications Grapple with Jared Loughner Mug Shot," *Washington Post* (January 11, 2011). Retrieved July 17, 2013.

4. American Board of Forensic Psychology, http://www.abfp.com/brochure.html (accessed November 22, 2007).

5. See the American Academy of Psychiatry and the Law, http://www.aapl.org (accessed August 2, 2012).

6. Laurence Steinberg, "The Juvenile Psychopath: Fads, Fictions, and Facts," *National Institute of Justice Perspectives on Crime and Justice: 2001 Lecture Series,* Vol. V (Washington, DC: NIJ, 2002), pp. 35–64.

7. Ibid.

8. Nicole Hahn Rafter, "Psychopathy and the Evolution of Criminological Knowledge," *Theoretical Criminology,* Vol. 1, No. 2 (May 1997), p. 236.

9. Nolan D. C. Lewis, "Foreword," in David Abrahamsen, *Crime and the Human Mind* (New York: Columbia University Press, 1944; reprint, Montclair, NJ: Patterson Smith, 1969), p. vii.

10. As noted by Rafter, "Psychopathy and the Evolution of Criminological Knowledge." See Richard von Krafft-Ebing, *Psychopathia Sexualis* (1886; reprint, New York: Stein and Day, 1965); and Richard von Krafft-Ebing, *Textbook of Insanity* (Germany, 1879; reprint, Philadelphia: F. A. Davis, 1904).

11. Bernard H. Glueck, *Studies in Forensic Psychiatry* (Boston: Little, Brown, 1916).

12. William Healy, *The Individual Delinquent* (Boston: Little, Brown, 1915).

13. Early writings about the psychopathic personality focused almost exclusively on men, and most psychiatrists appeared to believe that very few women (if any) possessed such traits.

14. Hervey M. Cleckley, *The Mask of Sanity*, 4th ed. (St. Louis, MO: C. V. Mosby, 1964).

15. "Charles Manson," Research This Stuff, http://www.researchthisstuff.com/Charles_Manson_001.htm (accessed July 3, 2009).

16. Quoted in Joseph P. Newman and Chad A. Brinkley, "Psychopathy: Rediscovering Cleckley's Construct," *Psychopathology Research*, Vol. 9, No. 1 (March 1998).

17. Gwynn Nettler, *Killing One Another* (Cincinnati: Anderson, 1982), p. 179.

18. Ralph Serin, "Can Criminal Psychopaths Be Identified?" Correctional Service of Canada, October 22, 1999, http://www.csc-scc.gc.ca/text/pblct/forum/e012/e0121.shtml (accessed December 20, 2006).

19. David T. Lykken, *The Antisocial Personalities* (Hillsdale, NJ: Lawrence Erlbaum, 1995).

20. Robert D. Hare, "Checklist for the Assessment of Psychopathy in Criminal Populations," in M. H. Ben-Aron, S. J. Hucker, and C. D. Webster, eds., *Clinical Criminology* (Toronto: University of Toronto, Clarke Institute of Psychiatry, 1985), pp. 157–167. Hare developed this checklist on Cleckley's characteristics commonly found in psychopaths.

21. See Steinberg, "The Juvenile Psychopath," from which some of the wording in this paragraph is adapted.

22. Kent A. Kiehl et al., "Temporal Lobe Abnormalities in Semantic Processing by Criminal Psychopaths as Revealed by Functional Magnetic Resonance Imaging," *Psychiatry Research: Neuroimaging*, Vol. 130 (2004), pp. 27–42.

23. Ibid.

24. Julia C. Keller, "Aha! Study Finds Eureka Moments Light Up Brain," *Science and Theology News*, June 2004, http://www.stnews.org/feat_aha_0604.html (accessed December 12, 2006).

25. Bertine Lahuis, Chantal Kemmer, and Herman Van Engeland, "Magnetic Resonance Imaging Studies on Autism and Childhood-Onset Schizophrenia in Children and Adolescents," *Acta Neuropsychiatrica*, Vol. 15, No. 3 (June 2003), p. 140.

26. Ivan Semeniuk, "How We Tell Right from Wrong: An Interview with Marc Hauser," *New Scientist*, March 3, 2007, p. 44.

27. Michael Caldwell et al., "Treatment Response of Adolescent Offenders with Psychopathy Features: A 2-Year Follow-Up," *Criminal Justice and Behavior*, Vol. 33, No. 5 (2006), pp. 571–576.

28. Peter Aldhous, "Violent, Antisocial, Past Redemption?" *New Scientist*, April 14, 2007, pp. 8–9.

29. American Psychiatric Association, *Diagnostic and Statistical Manual of Mental Disorders*, 2nd ed. (Washington, DC: American Psychiatric Association, 1968).

30. Ibid., p. 43.

31. R. D. Hare, *Psychopathy: Theory and Research* (New York: John Wiley and Sons, 1970).

32. L. N. Robins, *Deviant Children Grow Up* (Baltimore: Williams and Wilkins, 1966).
33. S. B. Guze, *Criminality and Psychiatric Disorders* (New York: Oxford University Press, 1976).
34. Hans J. Eysenck, *Crime and Personality* (Boston: Houghton Mifflin, 1964).
35. Intelligence may also be seen as an ability. See, for example, Colin G. DeYoung, "Intelligence and Personality," in R. J. Sternberg and S. B. Kaufman, eds., *The Cambridge Handbook of Intelligence* (New York: Cambridge University Press, 2011), p. 2.
36. Some early personality theorists considered intelligence to be part of personality. See, for example, R. B. Cattell, *Personality* (New York: McGraw-Hill, 1950); and J. P. Guilford, *Personality* (New York: McGraw-Hill, 1959).
37. Ibid., p. 92.
38. Hans J. Eysenck, "Personality and Criminality: A Dispositional Analysis," in William S. Laufer and Freda Adler, eds., *Advances in Criminology Theory*, Vol. 1 (New Brunswick, NJ: Transaction, 1989), p. 90.
39. Eysenck, *Crime and Personality*, pp. 35–36.
40. Colin G. DeYoung, "Intelligence and Personality," in R. J. Sternberg and S. B. Kaufman, eds., *The Cambridge Handbook of Intelligence* (New York: Cambridge University Press, 2011), pp. 711–737.
41. Jean Piaget, *The Moral Judgment of the Child* (London: Kegan Paul, Trench, Triibner & Co., 1932). See also J. Piaget, *The Child's Construction of Reality* (London: Routledge and Kegan Paul, 1955).
42. Cited in Holly K. Craig and Tanya M. Gallagher, "The Structural Characteristics of Monologues in the Speech of Normal Children: Syntactic Nonconversational Aspects," *Journal of Speech, Language, and Hearing Research*, Vol. 22 (March 1979), pp. 46–62.
43. Lawrence Kohlberg, *Stages in the Development of Moral Thought and Action* (New York: Holt, Rinehart and Winston, 1969).
44. Sergio Herzog, "Moral Judgment, Crime Seriousness, and the Relations between Them: An Exploratory Study," *Crime and Delinquency*, December 27, 2012.
45. K. Dodge, "A Social Information Processing Model of Social Competence in Children," *Minnesota Symposium in Child Psychology*, Vol. 8 (1986), pp. 77–125.
46. J. Lochman, Self and Peer Perceptions of Attributional Biases of Aggressive and Non-aggressive Boys in Dyadic Interactions," *Journal of Consulting and Clinical Psychology*, Vol. 55 (1987), pp. 404–410.
47. Calvin Langton and W. Marshall. "Contagion in Rapists: Theoretical Patterns by Typological Breakdown," *Aggression and Violent Behaviour*, Vol. 6 (2001), pp. 499–518.
48. R. C. Schank and R. P. Abelson, *Scripts, Plans, Goals and Understanding, an Inquiry into Human Knowledge Structures* (Hillsdale, NJ: Lawrence Erlbaum, 1977).
49. Helen Gavin and David Hockey, "Criminal Careers and Cognitive Scripts: An Investigation into Criminal Versatility," *The Qualitative Report*, Vol. 15, No. 2 (March 2010), pp. 389–410.
50. Ibid.
51. Samuel Yochelson and Stanton E. Samenow, *The Criminal Personality*, Vols. I, II, and III (New York, Aronson, 1976 and 1977).
52. Ibid.
53. Stanton E. Samenow, *Inside the Criminal Mind*, 2nd ed. (New York: Crown Publishers, 2004), p. xxi.
54. Ibid., p. 212.
55. August Aichorn, *Wayward Youth* (New York: Viking Press (1935).
56. Marti Olsen Laney, *The Hidden Gifts of the Introverted Child* (New York: Workman Publishing, 2006).
57. Mark Solms, "Freud Returns," *Scientific American*, Vol. 290, No. 5 (May 2004), pp. 82–90.
58. Eric R. Kandel, "Biology and the Future of Psychoanalysis: A New Intellectual Framework for Psychiatry Revisited," *American Journal of Psychiatry*, Vol. 156 (April 1999), pp. 505–524.
59. Nettler, *Killing One Another*, p. 159.
60. Ibid., p. 155.
61. Runa Munkner, Soeren Haastrup, Torben Joergensen, and Peter Kramp, "The Temporal Relationship between Schizophrenia and Crime," *Social Psychiatry and Psychiatric Epidemiology*, Vol. 38, No. 7 (July 2003), pp. 347–353.
62. Elizabeth Walsh, Alec Buchanan, and Thomas Fahy, "Violence and Schizophrenia: Examining the Evidence," *The British Journal of Psychiatry*, Vol. 180 (2002), pp. 490–495.
63. Seena Fazel, Niklas Långström, Anders Hjern, Martin Grann, and Paul Lichtenstein, "Schizophrenia, Substance Abuse, and Violent Crime," *Journal of the American Medical Association*, Vol. 301, No. 19 (2009), pp. 2016–2023.
64. J. Dollard et al., *Frustration and Aggression* (New Haven, CT: Yale University Press, 1939).
65. Andrew F. Henry and James F. Short, Jr., *Suicide and Homicide: Economic, Sociological, and Psychological Aspects of Aggression* (Glencoe, IL: Free Press, 1954).
66. Stewart Palmer, *A Study of Murder* (New York: Crowell, 1960).
67. Seymour L. Halleck, *Psychiatry and the Dilemmas of Crime: A Study of Causes, Punishment and Treatment* (Berkeley: University of California Press, 1971).
68. Ibid., p. 78.
69. Ibid., p. 80.
70. Ibid.
71. Ibid.
72. Arnold S. Linsky, Ronet Bachman, and Murray A. Straus, *Stress, Culture, and Aggression* (New Haven, CT: Yale University Press, 1995).
73. Ibid., p. 7.
74. D. A. Andrews and J. Bonta, *The Psychology of Criminal Conduct*, 2nd ed. (Cincinnati, OH: Anderson Publishing Co., 1998).
75. D. A. Andrews and J. Bonta, "Rehabilitating Criminal Justice Policy and Practice," *Psychology, Public Policy, and Law*, Vol. 16, No. 1 (2010), pp. 39–55.
76. Adapted from Tony Ward and Claire Stewart, "Criminogenic Needs and Human Needs: A Theoretical Model," *Psychology, Crime and Law*, Vol. 9, No. 2 (2003), pp. 125–143.
77. Andrews and Bonta, "Rehabilitating Criminal Justice Policy and Practice," p. 46.
78. Ward and Stewart, p. 128.
79. Ibid.
80. Ward and Stewart, p. 131.
81. Ward and Stewart, p. 132.
82. See Mary D. Salter Ainsworth, "John Bowlby, 1907–1990," *American Psychologist*, Vol. 47 (1992), p. 668.
83. John Bowlby, "The Nature of the Child's Tie to Its Mother," *International Journal of Psycho-Analysis*, Vol. 39 (1958), pp. 350–373.
84. See John Bowlby, *Maternal Care and Mental Health*, World Health Organization Monograph (1951); and *John Bowlby, A Secure Base* (New York: Basic Books, 1988).

85. Bowlby, *A Secure Base*, p. 11.
86. David P. Farrington and Donald J. West, "Effects of Marriage, Separation, and Children on Offending by Adult Males," *Current Perspectives on Aging and the Life Cycle*, Vol. 4 (1995), pp. 249–281.
87. Stephen A. Cernkovich and Peggy C. Giordano, "Family Relationships and Delinquency," *Criminology*, Vol. 25 (1987), pp. 295–313.
88. Gabriel Tarde, *The Laws of Imitation*, trans. E. C. Parsons (1890; reprint, Gloucester, MA: Peter Smith, 1962).
89. Albert Bandura, "The Social Learning Perspective: Mechanisms of Aggression," in Hans Toch, ed., *Psychology of Crime and Criminal Justice* (Prospect Heights, IL: Waveland, 1979), p. 198.
90. Albert Bandura, *Social Learning Theory* (Englewood Cliffs, NJ: Prentice Hall, 1977).
91. Ibid., p. 199.
92. M. M. Lefkowitz et al., "Television Violence and Child Aggression: A Follow-up Study," in G. A. Comstock and E. A. Rubinstein, eds., *Television and Social Behavior*, Vol. 3 (Washington, DC: U.S. Government Printing Office, 1972), pp. 35–135.
93. John C. Norcross, Gerald P. Koocher, and Ariele Garofalo, "Discredited Psychological Treatments and Tests: A Delphi Poll," *Professional Psychology: Research and Practice*, Vol. 37, No. 5 (2006), pp. 515–522.
94. North Carolina Department of Public Safety, *Cognitive Behavioral Interventions (CBI): Standard Operating Procedures* (December 2001).
95. Friedrich Losel, "Treatment and Management of Psychopaths," *NATO ASI Series*, Vol. 88 (1998), pp. 303–354.
96. *Brown* v. *Entertainment Merchants Association*, U.S. Supreme Court, No. 08-1448 (decided June 27, 2011).
97. For one of the first and still definitive works in the area of selective incapacitation, see Peter Greenwood and Allan Abrahamsen, *Selective Incapacitation* (Santa Monica, CA: Rand, 1982).
98. M. A. Peterson, H. B. Braiker, and S. M. Polich, *Who Commits Crimes?* (Cambridge, MA: Oelgeschlager, Gunn & Hain, 1981).
99. Jeremy Travis, "But They All Come Back," papers from the Executive Session on Sentencing and Corrections, No. 7 (Washington, DC: National Institute of Justice, 2000).
100. James L. Johnson et al., "The Construction and Validation of the Federal Post Conviction Risk Assessment (PCRA)," *Federal Probation* (September 2011), http://www.uscourts.gov/uscourts/FederalCourts/PPS/Fedprob/2011-09/construction.html (accessed August 29, 2013).
101. Tracy L. Fass, "The LSI-R and the COMPAS: Validation Data on Two Risk-Needs Tools," *Criminal Justice and Behavior*, July 8, 2008, doi:10.1177/0093854808320497 (accessed August 10, 2013).
102. Christopher T. Lowenkamp and Kristin Bechtel, "Predictive Validity of the LSI-R on a Sample of Offenders Drawn from the Records of the Iowa Department of Corrections Data Management System," *Federal Probation*, Vol. 71, No. 3 (December 2007), pp. 25–29.
103. Ibid.
104. See, for example, A. M. Holsinger, C. T. Lowenkamp, and E. J. Latessa, "Ethnicity, Gender, and the Level of Service Inventory–Revised," *Journal of Criminal Justice*, Vol. 31 (2003), pp. 309–320; and D. G. Kroner and J. F. Mills, "The Accuracy of Five Risk Appraisal Instruments in Predicting Institutional Misconduct and New Convictions," *Criminal Justice and Behavior*, Vol. 28 (2001), pp. 471–489.
105. For further discussion of the risk-needs-responsivity model, see Andrews and Bonta, *The Psychology of Criminal Conduct*; for discussion of the Good Lives Model, see T. Ward and T. Gannon, "Rehabilitation, Etiology, and Self-Regulation: The Good Lives Model of Sexual Offender Treatment," *Aggression and Violent Behavior*, Vol. 11 (2006), pp. 77–94.
106. Robin J. Wilson and Pamela M. Yates, "Effective Interventions and the Good Lives Model: Maximizing Treatment Gains for Sexual Offenders," *Aggression and Violent Behavior*, Vol. 14 (2009), pp. 157–161.
107. Andrews and Bonta, "Rehabilitating Criminal Justice Policy and Practice," pp. 39–55.
108. Ibid., p. 157.
109. T. Gannon, "Rehabilitation, Etiology, and Self-Regulation," p. 159.
110. D. A. Andrews, James Bonta, and J. Stephen Wormith, "The Risk-Needs-Responsivity (RNR) Model: Does Adding the Good Lives Model Contribute to Effective Crime Prevention?" *Criminal Justice and Behavior*, Vol. 38, No. 7 (July, 2011), pp. 735–755.
111. The 1984 Amendment to § 200 of Title II (§ 200–2304) of Pub. L. 98–473 is popularly referred to as the "1984 Comprehensive Crime Control Act."
112. U.S. Sentencing Commission, *Federal Sentencing Guidelines Manual* (Washington, DC: U.S. Government Printing Office, 1987), p. 10.
113. Jill Peay, "Dangerousness—Ascription or Description," in M. P. Feldman, ed., *Developments in the Study of Criminal Behavior*, Vol. 2, *Violence* (New York: John Wiley and Sons, 1982), p. 211, citing N. Walker, "Dangerous People," *International Journal of Law and Psychiatry*, Vol. 1 (1978), pp. 37–50.
114. See, for example, Michael Gottfredson and Travis Hirschi, *A General Theory of Crime* (Stanford, CA: Stanford University Press, 1990); and Travis Hirschi and Michael Gottfredson, "Age and the Explanation of Crime," *American Journal of Sociology*, Vol. 89 (1983), pp. 552–584.
115. MacArthur Research Network on Mental Health and the Law, "The MacArthur Violence Risk Assessment Study," September 2005, p. 4, http://www.macarthur.virginia.edu/risk.html (accessed February 22, 2013).
116. Ibid.
117. Jennifer L. White et al., "How Early Can We Tell? Predictors of Childhood Conduct Disorder and Adolescent Delinquency," *Criminology*, Vol. 28, No. 4 (1990), pp. 507–528.
118. David P. Farrington et al., "Advancing Knowledge About the Onset of Delinquency and Crime," in B. B. Lahey and A. E. Kazdin, eds., *Advances in Clinical Child Psychology*, Vol. 13 (New York: Plenum, 1990), pp. 283–342.
119. Paul C. Vitz, "The Use and Abuse of Freud," a review of *Freudian Fraud: The Malignant Effect of Freud's Theory on American Thought and Culture* by E. Fuller Torrey (Leadership U., 1993), p. 52.
120. J. Bonta, M. Law, and R. K. Hanson, "The Prediction of Criminal and Violent Recidivism among Mentally Disordered Offenders: A Meta-analysis," *Psychological Bulletin*, Vol. 123 (1998), pp. 123–142.
121. Mark Solms, "Freud Returns," *Scientific American*, Vol. 290, No. 5 (May 2004), pp. 82–90.
122. Cathy Spatz Widom and Hans Toch, "The Contribution of Psychology to Criminal Justice Education," *Journal of Criminal Justice Education*, Vol. 4, No. 2 (Fall 1993), p. 253.
123. Interview by Amy Goldman, February 27, 1998, http://www.serialkillers.net/interviews/jdouglas2bak.html (accessed December 20, 2000).

124. See John Douglas and Alan Burgess, "Criminal Profiling: A Viable Investigative Tool against Violent Crime," *FBI Law Enforcement Bulletin,* December 1986.
125. Robert R. Hazelwood and John E. Douglas, "The Lust Murderer," *FBI Law Enforcement Bulletin,* April 1980.
126. Ibid.
127. Ibid.
128. Lea Winerman, "Criminal Profiling: The Reality behind the Myth," Monitor on Psychology, July/August 2004, http://www.apa.org/monitor/julaug04/criminal.aspx (accessed May 4, 2013).
129. University of Liverpool, School of Psychology, "Centre for Investigative Psychology," http://www.liv.ac.uk/psychology/centres/centre-for-investigative-psychology/about (accessed May 2, 2013).
130. Scott O. Lilienfeld, Steven Jay Lynn, John Ruscio, and Barry L. Beyerstein, *50 Great Myths of Popular Psychology* (Malden, MA: Wiley-Blackwell, 2010), p. 215.
131. B. Snook, J. Eastwood, P. Gendreau, C. Goggin, and R. M. Cullen, "Taking Stock of Criminal Profiling: A Narrative Review and Meta-analysis, *Criminal Justice and Behavior,* Vol. 34 (2007), pp. 437–453.
132. In civil proceedings, however, the state may confine a mentally ill person if it shows "by clear and convincing evidence that the individual is mentally ill and dangerous" (*Jones* v. *United States,* 463 U.S. 354 [1983]).
133. Seymour L. Halleck, *Psychiatry and the Dilemmas of Crime: A Study of Causes, Punishment and Treatment* (Berkeley: University of California Press, 1971), p. 213.
134. M. Phillips, A. Wolf, and D. Coons, "Psychiatry and the Criminal Justice System: Testing the Myths," *American Journal of Psychiatry,* Vol. 145 (1988), pp. 605–610.
135. Ibid.
136. E. Silver, C. Cirincoine, and H. J. Steadman, "Demythologizing Inaccurate Perceptions of the Insanity Defense," *Law and Human Behavior,* Vol. 18, pp. 63–70.
137. M. Kimberly MacLin, "Psychological Theories of Criminal Behavior," in Richard A. Wright and J. Mitchell Miller, eds., *Encyclopedia of Criminology,* Vol. 2 (New York: Routledge, 2005), p. 1337.

CHAPTER 7: SOCIAL STRUCTURE THEORIES

1. Charles R. Tittle, "Theoretical Developments in Criminology," *Criminal Justice 2000* (Washington, DC: National Institute of Justice, 2000), p. 70.
2. See Anthony Walsh, *Biosocial Criminology: Introduction and Integration* (Cincinnati: Anderson, 2002).
3. Emile Durkheim, *The Division of Labor in Society,* trans. George Simpson (1893; reprint, New York: Free Press, 1947).
4. Ferdinand Toennies, *Community and Society,* trans. Charles P. Loomis (1887; reprint, East Lansing: Michigan State University Press, 1957).
5. Georg Simmel, "The Metropolis and Mental Life," in Donald N. Levine, ed., *On Individuality and Social Forms* (Chicago: University of Chicago Press, 1903).
6. Durkheim, *The Division of Labor in Society,* p. 80.
7. W. I. Thomas and Florian Znaniecki, *The Polish Peasant in Europe and America* (Boston: Gorham, 1920).
8. Robert Park and Ernest Burgess, *The City* (Chicago: University of Chicago Press, 1925).
9. "Human Ecology," *Encyclopaedia Britannica* online, http://britannica.com (accessed March 7, 2007).
10. Peter Haggett, "Human Ecology," in Alan Bullock and Oliver Stallybrass, eds., *The Fontana Dictionary of Modern Social Thought* (London: Fontana, 1977), p. 187.
11. For an excellent contemporary review of measuring the extent of social disorganization, see Barbara D. Warner and Glenn L. Pierce, "Reexamining Social Disorganization Theory Using Calls to the Police as a Measure of Crime," *Criminology,* Vol. 31, No. 4 (November 1993), pp. 493–513.
12. Edwin M. Lemert, *Social Pathology* (New York: McGraw-Hill, 1951), p. 3.
13. Ibid., p. 7.
14. Clifford R. Shaw et al., *Delinquency Areas* (Chicago: University of Chicago Press, 1929).
15. David Matza, *Becoming Deviant* (Upper Saddle River, NJ: Prentice Hall, 1969).
16. Lawrence W. Sherman, Patrick R. Gartin, and Michael E. Buerger, "Hot Spots of Predatory Crime: Routine Activities and the Criminology of Place," *Criminology,* Vol. 27, No. 1 (1989), pp. 27–55.
17. See, for example, David Weisburd et al., *Putting Crime in Its Place: Units of Analysis in Geographic Criminology* (New York: Springer Science+Business Media, 2009); John E. Eck and David Weisburd, eds., *Crime and Place* (Monsey, NY: Criminal Justice Press, 1995); and Anthony A. Braga, "The Effects of Hot Spots Policing on Crime," *Annals of the American Academy of Political and Social Science,* Vol. 578 (2001), pp. 104–125.
18. National Research Council, Committee to Review Research on Police Policy and Practices, *Fairness and Effectiveness in Policing: The Evidence,* edited by Wesley Skogan and Kathleen Frydl (Washington, DC: The National Academies Press, 2004), p. 35.
19. Rodney Stark, "Deviant Places: A Theory of the Ecology of Crime," *Criminology,* Vol. 25, No. 4 (1987), p. 893.
20. Ibid.
21. James Q. Wilson and George Kelling, "Broken Windows," *Atlantic Monthly,* March 1982, pp. 1–11.
22. David Thacher, "Order Maintenance Reconsidered: Moving beyond Strong Causal Reasoning," *Journal of Criminal Law and Criminology,* Vol. 94, No. 2 (2004), pp. 381–414.
23. James Q. Wilson and George L. Kelling, "Broken Windows: The Police and Neighborhood Safety," *Atlantic Monthly,* March 1982, http://www.theatlantic.com/politics/crime/windows.htm (accessed January 10, 2005).
24. Oscar Newman, *Architectural Design for Crime Prevention* (Washington, DC: U.S. Department of Justice, 1973). See also Oscar Newman, *Creating Defensible Space* (Washington, DC: Office of Housing and Urban Development, 1996).
25. Oscar Newman, *Defensible Space: Crime Prevention through Urban Design* (New York: Macmillan, 1972), p. 3. See also Ralph B. Taylor and Adele V. Harrell, *Physical Environment and Crime* (Washington, DC: National Institute of Justice, May 1996).
26. Sherman, Gartin, and Buerger, "Hot Spots of Predatory Crime," p. 31.
27. Ibid., p. 49.
28. Peter Hermann, "District Police Embrace Concept of Preventing Crime through Design," *The Washington Post,* September 3, 2012, http://www.washingtonpost.com/local/crime/district-police-embrace-concept-of-preventing-crime-through-design/2012/09/

03/ebe49518-e621-11e1-8741-940e3f6dbf48_story.html?hpid=z6 (accessed May 1, 2013).

29. Bernard E. Harcourt, *Illusion of Order: The False Promise of Broken Windows Policing* (Cambridge: Harvard University Press, 2001).
30. Robert J. Sampson and Stephen W. Radenbush, "Systematic Social Observation of Public Spaces: A New Look at Disorder in Urban Neighborhoods," *American Journal of Sociology*, Vol. 105 (1999), p. 603.
31. Thacher, "Order Maintenance Reconsidered," p. 386.
32. Thomas M. Arvanites and Robert H. Defina, "Business Cycles and Street Crime," *Criminology*, Vol. 44, No. 1 (2006), p. 141.
33. Emile Durkheim, *Suicide: A Study in Sociology* (New York: Free Press, 1897).
34. Robert K. Merton, "Social Structure and Anomie," *American Sociological Review*, Vol. 3, No. 5 (October 1938), pp. 672–682; and Robert K. Merton, *Social Theory and Social Structure*, rev. ed. (New York: Free Press, 1957).
35. Merton, "Social Structure and Anomie," p. 681.
36. Thomas M. Arvanites and Robert H. Defina, "Business Cycles and Street Crime," *Criminology*, Vol. 44, No. 1 (2006), pp. 139–164.
37. Steven F. Messner and Richard Rosenfeld, *Crime and the American Dream* (Belmont, CA: Wadsworth, 1994), p. 68.
38. J. Blau and P. Blau, "The Cost of Inequality: Metropolitan Structure and Violent Crime," *American Sociological Review*, Vol. 147 (1982), pp. 114–129.
39. Masahiro Tsushima, "Economic Structure and Crime: The Case of Japan," *Journal of Socio-Economics*, Vol. 25, No. 4 (winter 1996), p. 497.
40. Thomas F. Pettigrew, "Applying Social Psychology to International Social Issues," *Journal of Social Issues* (winter 1998), pp. 663–676.
41. Robert Agnew, "Foundation for a General Strain Theory of Crime and Delinquency," *Criminology*, Vol. 30, No. 1 (February 1992), pp. 47–87.
42. Adapted from Robert Agnew, *Pressured into Crime: An Overview of General Strain Theory* (Los Angeles: Roxbury, 2006), pp. 193–196.
43. Ibid., p. 60.
44. Agnew, "Foundation for a General Strain Theory of Crime and Delinquency."
45. Ibid., p. 48.
46. Raymond Paternoster and Paul Mazerolle, "General Strain Theory and Delinquency: A Replication and Extension," *Journal of Research in Crime and Delinquency*, Vol. 31, No. 3 (1994), pp. 235–263.
47. Robert Agnew and Helene Raskin White, "An Empirical Test of General Strain Theory," *Criminology*, Vol. 30, No. 4 (1992), pp. 475–499.
48. Lisa M. Broidy, "A Test of General Strain Theory," *Criminology*, Vol. 39, No. 1 (2002), pp. 9–35.
49. Ibid., p. 29.
50. Ibid.
51. Robert Agnew et al., "Strain, Personality Traits, and Delinquency: Extending General Strain Theory," *Criminology*, Vol. 40, No. 1 (2002), pp. 43–71.
52. Ibid., p. 47.
53. Joan R. Hipp, "Spreading the Wealth: The Effect of the Distribution of Income and Race/Ethnicity across Households and Neighborhoods on City Crime Trajectories," National Institute of Justice unpublished research report, May 27, 2010.
54. Thorsten Sellin, *Culture Conflict and Crime* (New York: Social Science Research Council, 1938).
55. Sellin, *Culture Conflict and Crime*, p. 68.
56. Frederic M. Thrasher, *The Gang* (Chicago: University of Chicago Press, 1927).
57. William F. Whyte, *Street Corner Society: The Social Structure of an Italian Slum* (Chicago: University of Chicago Press, 1943).
58. The quotations attributed to Miller in these paragraphs are from Walter Miller, "Lower Class Culture as a Generating Milieu of Gang Delinquency," *Journal of Social Issues*, Vol. 14, No. 3 (1958), pp. 5–19.
59. Gresham Sykes and David Matza, "Techniques of Neutralization: A Theory of Delinquency," *American Sociological Review*, Vol. 22 (December 1957), pp. 664–670.
60. See Volkan Topalli, "When Being Good Is Bad: An Expansion of Neutralization Theory," *Criminology*, Vol. 43 (2005), p. 797.
61. As cited in Topalli, "When Being Good Is Bad," p. 797.
62. David Matza, *Delinquency and Drift* (Piscataway, New Jersey: Transaction, 1990), p. 28.
63. Robert Agnew, "The Techniques of Neutralization and Violence," *Criminology*, Vol. 32, No. 4 (1994), p. 555.
64. Ibid.
65. Topalli, "When Being Good Is Bad."
66. Ken Levi, "Becoming a Hit Man: Neutralization in a Very Deviant Career," *Urban Life*, Vol. 10 (1981), pp 47–63.
67. Lois Presser, "Remorse and Neutralization among Violent Male Offenders," *Justice Quarterly*, Vol. 20, No. 4 (2003), pp. 801–825.
68. Orly Turgeman-Goldschmidt, "The Rhetoric of Hackers' Neutralizations," in Frank Schmalleger and Michale Pittaro, eds., *Crimes of the Internet* (Upper Saddle River, NJ: Prentice Hall, 2008).
69. See, for example, Dorothy E. Denning, "Activism, Hacktivism, and Cyberterrorism: The Internet as a Tool for Influencing Foreign Policy," *Computer Security Journal*, Vol. 16 (2000), pp. 15–35; and Tim Jordan and Paul Taylor, *Hacktivism and Cyberwars: Rebels with a Cause?* (New York: Routledge, 2004).
70. Franco Ferracuti and Marvin Wolfgang, *The Subculture of Violence: Toward an Integrated Theory of Criminology* (London: Tavistock, 1967).
71. Ferracuti and Wolfgang, *The Subculture of Violence*.
72. Ibid., p. 151.
73. Ibid., pp. 159–160.
74. For an excellent review of the literature, see F. Frederick Hawley, "The Southern Violence Construct: A Skeleton in the Criminological Closet," paper presented at the annual meeting of the American Society of Criminology, 1988.
75. Bertram Wyatt-Brown, *Southern Honor: Ethics and Behavior in the Old South* (Oxford: Oxford University Press, 1983).
76. James W. Clarke, *The Lineaments of Wrath: Race, Violent Crime, and American Culture* (New Brunswick, NJ: Transaction, 1998), p. 4.
77. Ibid.
78. Franklin Zimring et al., "Punishing Homicide in Philadelphia: Perspectives on the Death Penalty," *University of Chicago Law Review*, Vol. 43 (1976), pp. 227–252.
79. Richard A. Cloward and Lloyd E. Ohlin, *Delinquency and Opportunity: A Theory of Delinquent Gangs* (Glencoe, IL: Free Press, 1960).

80. Ibid., p. 7.
81. Ibid., p. 13.
82. Ibid., p. 16.
83. Ibid., p. 19.
84. Ibid., p. 3.
85. Ibid., p. 37.
86. Ibid., pp. 12–13.
87. Albert Cohen, *Delinquent Boys: The Culture of the Gang* (New York: Free Press, 1955), p. 13.
88. Ibid.
89. Donald J. Shoemaker, *Theories of Delinquency: An Examination of Explanations of Delinquent Behavior* (New York: Oxford University Press, 1984), p. 102, citing Cohen.
90. Cohen, *Delinquent Boys*, p. 76.
91. Ibid., p. 121.
92. Shoemaker, *Theories of Delinquency*, p. 105.
93. Elijah Anderson, *The Code of the Street: Decency, Violence, and the Moral Life of the Inner City* (New York: W. W. Norton, 1990).
94. Arlen Egley, Jr., and James C. Howell, *Highlights of the 2010 National Youth Gang Survey* (Washington, DC: Office of Juvenile Justice and Delinquency Prevention, 2012).
95. National Gang Crime Research Center, *Achieving Justice and Reversing the Problem of Gang Crime and Gang Violence in America Today: Preliminary Results of the Project Gangfact Study* (Chicago: National Gang Crime Research Center, 1996).
96. Carl Rogers, "Children in Gangs," in *Criminal Justice, 1993–94* (Guilford, CT: Dushkin, 1993), pp. 197–199.
97. "Youths Match Power, Fear, Guns," *Fayetteville (NC) Observer-Times*, September 6, 1993, p. 2A.
98. The quotations attributed to Curry and Spergel in this section are from G. David Curry and Irving A. Spergel, "Gang Homicide, Delinquency, and Community," *Criminology*, Vol. 26, No. 3 (1988), pp. 381–405.
99. Ibid., p. 401.
100. Finn-Aage Esbensen, "A National Gang Strategy," in J. Mitchell Miller and Jeffrey P. Rush, eds., *Gangs: A Criminal Justice Approach* (Cincinnati: Anderson, 1996).
101. Cited in Mary H. Glazier, review of J. Mitchell Miller and Jeffrey P. Rush, eds., *Gangs: A Criminal Justice Approach*, in *Criminologist* (July/August 1996), p. 29.
102. Joan McCord and Kevin P. Conway, *Co-Offending and Patterns of Juvenile Crime* (Washington, DC: National Institute of Justice), p. 1.
103. Steven Schlossman et al., *Delinquency Prevention in South Chicago: A Fifty-Year Assessment of the Chicago Area Project* (Santa Monica, CA: RAND, 1984).
104. J. Robert Lilly, Francis T. Cullen, and Richard A. Ball, *Criminological Theory: Context and Consequences* (Newbury Park, CA: Sage, 1989), p. 80.
105. Lamar T. Empey, *American Delinquency: Its Meaning and Construction* (Homewood, IL: Dorsey, 1982), p. 243.
106. See James DeFronzo, "Welfare and Burglary," *Crime and Delinquency*, Vol. 42 (1996), pp. 223–230.
107. Because overall rates of crime rose throughout much of the 1970s and 1980s, the effectiveness of such programs remains very much in doubt.
108. Public Law 104–193 (August 22, 1996).
109. Section 103 of the Welfare Reform Act of 1996.
110. See, for example, George L. Kelling, "Crime Control, the Police, and Culture Wars: Broken Windows and Cultural Pluralism," in National Institute of Justice, *Perspectives on Crime and Justice: 1997–1998 Lecture Series* (Washington, DC: National Institute of Justice, 1998).
111. Robert J. Bursik, "Social Disorganization and Theories of Crime and Delinquency: Problems and Prospects," *Criminology*, Vol. 26, No. 4 (1988), p. 519.
112. Stephen J. Pfohl, *Images of Deviance and Social Control* (New York: McGraw-Hill, 1985), p. 167.
113. Travis Hirschi, in review of Delbert S. Elliott, David Huizinga, and Suzanne S. Ageton, *Explaining Delinquency and Drug Use*, in *Criminology*, Vol. 25, No. 1 (February 1987), p. 195.
114. John Hagan, "Defiance and Despair: Subcultural and Structural Linkages between Delinquency and Despair in Life Course," *Social Forces*, Vol. 76, No. 1 (September 1997), p. 119.
115. Ibid.
116. Gwynn Nettler, *Killing One Another* (Cincinnati: Anderson, 1982), p. 67.
117. Margaret Anderson, "Review Essay: Rape Theories, Myths, and Social Change," *Contemporary Crises*, Vol. 5 (1983), p. 237.
118. Bradley R. Entner Wright et al., "Reconsidering the Relationship between SES and Delinquency: Causation But Not Correlation," *Criminology*, Vol. 37, No. 1 (February 1999), pp. 175–194.
119. R. Larzelre and G. R. Patterson, "Parental Management: Mediator of the Effect of Socioeconomic Status on Early Delinquency," *Criminology*, Vol. 28 (1990), pp. 301–323.
120. Nettler, *Killing One Another*, p. 54.
121. James Q. Wilson, *The Moral Sense* (New York: Free Press, 1993).

CHAPTER 8: THEORIES OF SOCIAL PROCESS AND SOCIAL DEVELOPMENT

1. Chris Jansing, "Natalee Holloway Suspect Joran van der Sloot Admits Killing Woman in Peru," MSNBC TV, January 12, 2012, http://www.msnbc.msn.com/id/45954171/ns/world_news-americas/#.Tw-fJiO5dhE (accessed March 12, 2012).
2. Frank Bajak, "Peru Court Sentences Van der Sloot to 28 Years," Associated Press, January 13, 2012, http://www.google.com/hostednews/ap/article/ALeqM5jajjHkBVW2klSZb2fTAdyV1sRsOA?docId=b61a4dfc829e429a942854d33b86cde5 (accessed March 12, 2012).
3. Edwin Sutherland, *Principles of Criminology*, 3rd ed. (New York: Lippincott, 1939).
4. Edwin H. Sutherland and Donald R. Cressey, *Criminology* (New York: Lippincott, 1978).
5. Robert Burgess and Ronald L. Akers, "A Differential Association–Reinforcement Theory of Criminal Behavior," *Social Problems*, Vol. 14 (1966), pp. 363–383.
6. Ibid., p. 364.
7. Ronald L. Akers, *Deviant Behavior: A Social Learning Approach* (Belmont, CA: Wadsworth, 1973).
8. Ibid.
9. Ronald L. Akers, *Social Learning and Social Structure: A General Theory of Crime and Deviance* (Boston: Northeastern University Press, 1998).
10. Ronald L. Akers, *Deviant Behavior: A Social Learning Approach*, 3rd ed. (Belmont, CA: Wadsworth, 1985), pp. 40–41.
11. Gang Lee, Ronald L. Akers, and Marian J. Borg, "Social Learning and Structural Factors in Adolescent Substance Use," *Western Criminology Review*, Vol. 5, No. 1 (2004), p. 17.

12. Daniel Glaser, "Differential Association and Criminological Prediction," *Social Problems*, Vol. 8 (1960), pp. 6–14.
13. Daniel Glaser, "Differential Identification," in Henry N. Pontel, ed., *Social Deviance: Readings in Theory and Research*, 3rd ed. (Upper Saddle River, NJ: Prentice Hall 1999), p. 146.
14. Travis C. Pratt, Francis T. Cullen, Christine S. Sellers, L. Thomas Winfree, Jr., Tamara D. Madensen, Leah E. Daigle, Noelle E. Fearn and Jacinta M. Gau, "The Empirical Status of Social Learning Theory: A Meta-Analysis," *Justice Quarterly*, Vol. 27, No. 6 (December 2010), pp. 765–802.
15. Charles R. Tittle, "Theoretical Developments in Criminology," in National Institute of Justice, ed., *The Nature of Crime: Continuity and Change*, Vol. 1 of *Criminal Justice 2000* (Washington, DC: National Institute of Justice, 2000), p. 65.
16. For a good overview of social control approaches, see George S. Bridges and Martha Myers, eds., *Inequality, Crime, and Social Control* (Boulder, CO: Westview Press, 1994).
17. Walter C. Reckless, *The Crime Problem*, 4th ed. (New York: Appleton-Century-Crofts, 1967).
18. Ibid., p. 470.
19. Ibid.
20. Ibid., p. 475.
21. Ibid.
22. Howard B. Kaplan, "Self-Derogation and Violence," paper presented at the first meeting of the International Society for Research on Aggression, Toronto, 1974. See also Howard B. Kaplan and A. D. Pokorny, "Self-Derogation as an Antecedent of Suicidal Responses," paper presented at the Eighth International Congress on Suicide Prevention and Crisis Intervention, Jerusalem, October 19–22, 1975.
23. Howard B. Kaplan, *Deviant Behavior in Defense of Self* (New York: Academic Press, 1980).
24. M. Rosenberg, C. Schooler, and C. Schoenbach, "Self-Esteem and Adolescent Problems: Modeling Reciprocal Effects," *American Sociological Review*, Vol. 54 (1989), pp. 1004–1018.
25. L. E. Wells, "Self-Enhancement through Delinquency: A Conditional Test of Self-Derogation Theory," *Journal of Research in Crime and Delinquency*, Vol. 26, No. 3 (1989), pp. 226–252.
26. K. Leung and F. Drasgow, "Relation between Self-Esteem and Delinquent Behavior in Three Ethnic Groups: An Application of Item Response Theory," *Journal of Cross-Cultural Psychology*, Vol. 17, No. 2 (1986), pp. 151–167.
27. G. Calhoun, Jr., S. Connley, and J. A. Bolton, "Comparison of Delinquents and Non-Delinquents in Ethnicity, Ordinal Position and Self-Perception," *Journal of Clinical Psychology*, Vol. 40, No. 1 (1984), pp. 323–328.
28. D. Oyserman and H. R. Markus, "Possible Selves in Balance: Implications for Delinquency," *Journal of Social Issues*, Vol. 46, No. 2 (1990), pp. 141–157.
29. Daphna Oyserman and Hazel Markus, "The Sociocultural Self," in J. Suls, ed., *Psychological Perspectives on the Self*, Vol. 4 (Hillsdale, NJ: Erlbaum, 1993), pp. 187–220.
30. Travis Hirschi, *Causes of Delinquency* (Berkeley: University of California Press, 1969).
31. Tittle, "Theoretical Developments in Criminology," p. 65.
32. Ibid.
33. Ibid.
34. Ibid.
35. Ibid.
36. Ibid.
37. Ibid.
38. Ibid.
39. Michael Gottfredson and Travis Hirschi, *A General Theory of Crime* (Stanford, CA: Stanford University Press, 1990).
40. Teresa C. LaGrange and Robert A. Silverman, "Low Self-Control and Opportunity: Testing the General Theory of Crime as an Explanation for Gender Differences in Delinquency," *Criminology*, Vol. 37, No. 1 (1999), p. 41.
41. Gottfredson and Hirschi, *A General Theory of Crime*.
42. See also Michael R. Gottfredson and Travis Hirschi, "Criminality and Low Self-Control," in John E. Conklin, ed., *New Perspectives in Criminology* (Boston: Allyn & Bacon, 1996).
43. Werner Einstadter and Stuart Henry, *Criminological Theory: An Analysis of Its Underlying Assumptions* (Fort Worth, TX: Harcourt Brace, 1995), p. 189.
44. Kelli Phythian, Carl Keane, and Catherine Krull, "Family Structure and Parental Behavior: Identifying the Sources of Adolescent Self-Control," *Western Criminology Review*, Vol. 9, No. 2 (2008), pp. 73–87.
45. Ibid., p. 73.
46. Carter Hay and Walter Forrest, "The Development of Self-Control: Examining Self-Control Theory's Stability Thesis," *Criminology*, Vol. 44, No. 4 (November 2006), pp. 739–772.
47. Constance L. Chapple, "Self-Control, Peer Relations, and Delinquency," *Justice Quarterly*, Vol. 22, No. 1 (March 2005), pp. 89–106.
48. Ibid., p. 101.
49. Douglas Longshore, "Self-Control and Criminal Opportunity: A Prospective Test of the General Theory of Crime," *Social Problems*, Vol. 45, No. 1 (February 1998), pp. 102–114.
50. Gottfredson and Hirschi, *A General Theory of Crime*, p. 88.
51. Longshore, "Self-Control and Criminal Opportunity."
52. Travis C. Pratt and Francis T. Cullen, "The Empirical Status of Gottfredson and Hirschi's General Theory of Crime: A Meta-Analysis," *Criminology*, Vol. 38, No. 3 (2000), pp. 931–964.
53. Carter Hay, "Parenting, Self-Control, and Delinquency: A Test of Self-Control Theory," *Criminology*, Vol. 39, No. 3 (2001), pp. 707–736.
54. Ibid., p. 725.
55. Karen L. Hayslett-McCall and Thomas J. Bernard, "Attachment, Masculinity, and Self-Control: A Theory of Male Crime Rates," *Theoretical Criminology*, Vol. 6, No. 1 (February 2002), pp. 5–33.
56. Per-Olof H. Wikström and Kyle H. Treiber, "Violence as Situational Action," *International Journal of Conflict and Violence*, Vol. 3, No. 1 (2009), pp. 75–96.
57. Per-Olof H. Wikström and Kyle Treiber, "The Role of Self-Control in Crime Causation Beyond Gottfredson and Hirschi's General Theory of Crime," *European Journal of Criminology*, Vol. 4, No. 237 (2007), pp. 237–264.
58. Ibid., p. 77.
59. Steven F. Messner, "Morality, Markets, and the ASC: 2011 Presidential Address to the American Society of Criminology," *Criminology*, Vol. 50, No. 1 (2012), p. 8.
60. Christian Seipel and Stefanie Eifler, "Opportunities, Rational Choice, and Self-Control On the Interaction of Person and Situation in a General Theory of Crime," *Crime and Delinquency*, Vol. 56, No. 2 (April 2010), pp. 167–197. DOI 10.1177/0011128707312525.

61. Kevin M. Beaver et al., "The Relationship between Self-Control and Language: Evidence of a Shared Etiological Pathway," *Criminology*, Vol. 46, No. 4 (2008), pp. 939–970.
62. Gregory M. Zimmerman, Ekaterina V. Botchkovar, Olena Antonaccio, and Lorine A. Hughes, "Low Self-Control in 'Bad' Neighborhoods: Assessing the Role of Context on the Relationship between Self-Control and Crime," *Justice Quarterly*, 2012.
63. Charles R. Tittle, *Control Balance: Toward a General Theory of Deviance* (Boulder, CO: Westview Press, 1995).
64. For an excellent summation of control–balance theory, see Alex R. Piquero and Matthew Hickman, "An Empirical Test of Tittle's Control Balance Theory," *Criminology*, Vol. 37, No. 2 (1999), pp. 319–341.
65. Tittle, *Control Balance*, p. 181.
66. Piquero and Hickman, "An Empirical Test of Tittle's Control Balance Theory," p. 327.
67. Tittle, *Control Balance*, p. 95. For a good critique of control–balance theory, see Joachim J. Savelsberg, "Human Nature and Social Control in Complex Society: A Critique of Charles Tittle's Control Balance," *Theoretical Criminology*, Vol. 3, No. 3 (August 1999), pp. 331–338.
68. "Killer's Admission to Law School Criticized," *Fayetteville (NC) Observer-Times*, September 12, 1993, p. 14A.
69. See the biography of James Hamm at the Middle Ground Prison Reform, Inc., Web site, http://www.middlegroundprisonreform.org/hamm (accessed January 10, 2007).
70. Frank Tannenbaum, *Crime and the Community* (New York: Atheneum Press, 1938), pp. 17–18.
71. Ibid., p. 19.
72. Edwin M. Lemert, *Social Pathology: A Systematic Approach to the Theory of Sociopathic Behavior* (New York: McGraw-Hill, 1951), p. 76.
73. Ibid.
74. Howard Becker, *Outsiders: Studies in the Sociology of Deviance* (New York: Free Press, 1963).
75. Ibid., p. 1.
76. Ibid., p. 9.
77. Ibid., p. 147.
78. NORML, "About NORML," http://norml.org/about (accessed February 23, 2012).
79. Ibid., pp. 37–38.
80. Jon Gunnar Bernburg and Marvin D. Krohn, "Labeling, Life Chances, and Adult Crime: The Direct and Indirect Effects of Official Intervention in Adolescence on Crime in Early Adulthood," *Criminology*, Vol. 41, No. 4 (2003), pp. 1287–1318.
81. Robert J. Sampson and John H. Laub, "A Life-Course Theory of Cumulative Disadvantage and the Stability of Delinquency," in Terence P. Thornberry, ed., *Developmental Theories of Crime and Delinquency* (New Brunswick, NJ: Transaction, 1997).
82. Bernburg and Krohn, "Labeling, Life Chances, and Adult Crime."
83. Legal Action Center, "After Prison: Roadblocks to Reentry," 2008, http://lac.org/roadblocks-to-reentry.
84. Mike S. Adams, "Labeling and Differential Association: Towards a General Social Learning Theory of Crime and Deviance," *American Journal of Criminal Justice*, Vol. 20, No. 2 (1996), pp. 147–164.
85. Ibid., p. 160.
86. Emily Restivo and Mark M. Lanier, "Measuring the Contextual Effects and Mitigating Factors of Labeling Theory," *Justice Quarterly*, 2013, http://dx.doi.org/10.1080/07418825.2012.756115.
87. John Braithwaite and Heather Strang, *The Right Kind of Shame for Crime Prevention*, RISE Working Papers, Number 1 (Australian National University, 1997), http://www.aic.gov.au/rjustice/rise/working/risepap1.html (accessed March 11, 2005).
88. A number of papers have been released in the Reintegrative Shaming Experiments (RISE) series. They include Braithwaite and Strang, *The Right Kind of Shame for Crime Prevention*; Heather Strang and Lawrence W. Sherman, *The Victim's Perspective* (Canberra: Australian National University, 1997); Lawrence W. Sherman and Geoffrey C. Barnes, *Restorative Justice and Offenders' Respect for the Law* (Canberra: Australian National University, 1997); and Lawrence W. Sherman and Heather Strang, *Restorative Justice and Deterring Crime* (Canberra: Australian National University, 1997).
89. John Braithwaite and Heather Strang, *Restorative Justice and Offenders' Respect for the Law*, RISE Working Papers, Number 3 (Australian National University, 1997), http://www.aic.gov.au/rjustice/rise/working/risepap3.html (accessed March 11, 2005).
90. Ibid.
91. Erving Goffman, *The Presentation of Self in Everyday Life* (Garden City, NY: Doubleday, 1959).
92. Goffman, *The Presentation of Self in Everyday Life*, pp. 9–10.
93. Erving Goffman, *Stigma: Notes on the Management of Spoiled Identity* (Upper Saddle River, NJ: Prentice Hall, 1963).
94. Ibid., p. 5.
95. Ibid., p. 138.
96. Erving Goffman, *Asylums: Essays on the Social Situation of Mental Patients and Other Inmates* (Garden City, NY: Anchor, 1961).
97. P.L. 93–415; 42 U.S. Code Section 5667e.
98. See, for example, Information Technology International's initial report data at http://www.itiincorporated.com/showpage.asp?sect=proj&pid=6 (accessed June 8, 2007).
99. See Kevin Haggerty et al., *Preparing for the Drug Free Years* (Washington, DC: Office of Juvenile Justice and Delinquency Prevention, 1999), http://www.ncjrs.org/html/jjbulletin/9907/theo.html (accessed March 11, 2005).
100. Haggerty et al., *Preparing for the Drug Free Years.*
101. Material in this paragraph is adapted from Finn-Aage Esbensen, "Preventing Adolescent Gang Involvement," *OJJDP Juvenile Justice Bulletin* (Washington, DC: Office of Juvenile Justice and Delinquency Prevention, September 2000).
102. See R. E. Tremblay et al., "From Childhood Physical Aggression to Adolescent Maladjustment: The Montreal Prevention Experiment," in R. D. Peters and R. J. McMahon, eds., *Preventing Childhood Disorders, Substance Abuse, and Delinquency* (Thousand Oaks, CA: Sage, 1996), pp. 268–298.
103. Randy Martin, Robert J. Mutchnick, and W. Timothy Austin, *Criminological Thought: Pioneers Past and Present* (New York: Macmillan, 1990), p. 368.
104. Laurie Taylor, "Erving Goffman," *New Society*, December 1968, p. 836.
105. George Psathas, "Ethnomethods and Phenomenology," in Donald McQuarie, ed., *Readings in Contemporary Sociological Theory: From Modernity to Post-Modernity* (Toronto: Prentice Hall Canada, 1999).
106. For some influential writings of the period, see K. F. Riegel, "Toward a Dialectical Theory of Development," *Human Development*, Vol. 18 (1975), pp. 50–64; and U. Bronfenbrenner, *The Ecology of Human Development* (Cambridge: Harvard University Press, 1979).

107. R. M. Lerner, "Early Adolescence: Towards an Agenda for the Integration of Research, Policy and Intervention," in R. M. Lerner, ed., *Early Adolescence: Perspectives on Research, Policy, and Intervention* (Hillsdale, NJ: Erlbaum, 1993), pp. 1–13.

108. See T. P. Thornberry, *Developmental Theories of Crime and Delinquency* (Piscataway, NJ: Transaction, 1997).

109. Elaine Eggleston Doherty, "Self-Control, Social Bonds, and Desistance," *Criminology*, Vol. 44, No. 4 (November 2006), pp. 807–808.

110. A. Blumstein et al., eds., *Criminal Careers and Career Criminals* (Washington, DC: National Academy Press, 1986).

111. See Alfred Blumstein et al., "Introduction: Studying Criminal Careers," in Blumstein et al., eds., *Criminal Careers and Career Criminals*, p. 12.

112. Blumstein et al., *Criminal Careers and Career Criminals*, pp. 12–30.

113. Robert J. Sampson and John H. Laub, *Crime in the Making: Pathways and Turning Points through the Life Course* (Cambridge: Harvard University Press, 1993).

114. G. H. Elder, Jr., "Perspectives on the Life-Course," in G. H. Elder, Jr., ed., *Life-Course Dynamics* (Ithaca, NY: Cornell University Press, 1985).

115. Philip W. Harris, Wayne N. Welsh, and Frank Butler, "A Century of Juvenile Justice," in *Criminal Justice 2000*, Vol. 1 (Washington, DC: National Institute of Justice, 2000).

116. Elder, *Life-Course Dynamics*.

117. Robert J. Sampson and John H. Laub, "Understanding Variability in Lives through Time: Contributions of Life-Course Criminology," in Alex Piquero and Paul Mazerolle, eds., *Life-Course Criminology: Contemporary and Classic Readings* (Belmont, CA: Wadsworth, 2001), p. 243.

118. Marc LeBlanc and Rolf Loeber, "Developmental Criminology Updated," in Michael Tonry, ed., *Crime and Justice: A Review of Research*, Vol. 23 (Chicago: University of Chicago Press, 1998).

119. Adapted from Harris, Welsh, and Butler, "A Century of Juvenile Justice," p. 379.

120. Glen H. Elder, Jr., "Time, Human Agency, and Social Change: Perspectives on the Life Course," *Social Psychology Quarterly*, Vol. 57, No. 1 (1994), pp. 4–15.

121. Glen H. Elder, Jr. and Monica Kirkpatrick Johnson, "The Life Course and Aging: Challenges, Lessons, and New Directions," in Richard A. Settersten, Jr., ed., *Invitation to the Life Course: Toward New Understandings of Later Life* (Amityville, NY: Baywood Publishing, 2002), pp. 49–84.

122. See, for example, the collected papers of Sheldon Glueck, 1916–1972, which are part of the David L. Bazelon collection at Harvard University Law School (Cambridge, MA); Sheldon and Eleanor Glueck, *500 Delinquent Women* (New York: Alfred A. Knopf, 1934); and Sheldon and Eleanor Glueck, *500 Criminal Careers* (New York: Alfred A. Knopf, 1930). Results of the Gluecks' work were also reported in S. Glueck and E. Glueck, *Unraveling Juvenile Delinquency* (New York: The Commonwealth Fund, 1950).

123. Sheldon Glueck and Eleanor Glueck, *Delinquents and Nondelinquents in Perspective* (Cambridge: Harvard University Press, 1968).

124. David S. Kirk, "Residential Change as a Turning Point in the Life Course of Crime: Desistance or Temporary Cessation?" *Criminology*, Vol. 50, No. 2 (2012), p. 1.

125. John H. Laub and Robert J. Sampson, "Urban Poverty and the Family Context of Delinquency: A New Look at Structure and Process in a Classic Study," *Child Development*, Vol. 65 (1994), pp. 523–540. See also John H. Laub and Robert J. Sampson, "Turning Points in the Life Course: Why Change Matters to the Study of Crime," *Criminology*, Vol. 31, No. 3 (1993), pp. 301–325; and Robert J. Sampson and John H. Laub, "Crime and Deviance in the Life Course," *Annual Review of Sociology*, Vol. 18 (1992), pp. 63–84.

126. See John H. Laub and Leana C. Allen, "Life Course Criminology and Community Corrections," *Perspectives*, Vol. 24, No. 2 (spring 2000), pp. 20–29.

127. Sampson and Laub, "Crime and Deviance in the Life Course," pp. 63–84.

128. John H. Laub, "The Life Course of Criminology in the United States: The American Society of Criminology 2003 Presidential Address," *Criminology*, Vol. 42, No. 1 (2004), pp. 1–26.

129. G. B. Trasler, "Aspects of Causality, Culture, and Crime," paper presented at the Fourth International Seminar at the International Centre of Sociological, Penal and Penitentiary Research and Studies, Messina, Italy, 1980.

130. Laub and Sampson, "Turning Points in the Life Course."

131. Ibid.

132. Bradley R. Entner Wright et al., "The Effects of Social Ties on Crime Vary by Criminal Propensity: A Life-Course Model of Interdependence," *Criminology*, Vol. 39, No. 2 (2001), pp. 321–348.

133. See Laub and Allen, "Life Course Criminology and Community Corrections," pp. 20–29.

134. Sampson and Laub, *Crime in the Making*.

135. Matthew G. Yeager, "Life-Course Study of Released Prisoners Suggests Importance of Employment for Offender Reintegration and Community Safety," *Offender Programs Report*, Vol. 7, No. 2 (July–August 2003), pp. 1, 28–32.

136. Robert J. Sampson, John H. Laub, and Christopher Wimer, "Does Marriage Reduce Crime? A Counterfactual Approach to Within-Individual Causal Effects," *Criminology*, Vol. 44, No. 3 (2006), pp. 465–508.

137. Ronald L. Simons et al., "A Test of Life-Course Explanations for Stability and Change in Antisocial Behavior from Adolescence to Young Adulthood," *Criminology*, Vol. 40, No. 2 (2002), pp. 401–434.

138. Lisa M. Broidy and Elizabeth E. Cauffman, "Understanding the Female Offender," National Institute of Justice, unpublished report, 2006.

139. Terrie E. Moffitt, "Adolescence-Limited and Life-Course-Persistent Antisocial Behavior," *Psychological Review* (1993), Vol. 100, pp. 674–701.

140. Adapted from Tittle, "Theoretical Developments in Criminology."

141. Moffitt, "Adolescence-Limited and Life-Course Persistent Antisocial Behavior."

142. Family and Youth Services Bureau, *Understanding Youth Development: Promoting Positive Pathways of Growth* (Washington, DC: U.S. Department of Health and Human Services, 2000).

143. Marvin E. Wolfgang, "Crime in a Birth Cohort," Proceedings of the American Philosophical Society, Vol. 117, No. 5 (October 25, 1973), pp. 404-411.

144. A. Quetelet, *A Treatise on Man and the Development of His Facilities* (Gainesville, FL: Scholars Facsimiles and Reprints, 1969).

145. Sheldon Glueck and Eleanor Glueck, *Later Criminal Careers* (New York: The Commonwealth Fund, 1937), p. 105.

146. Walter R. Grove, "The Effect of Age and Gender on Deviant Behavior: A Biopsychosocial Perspective," in Alice S. Rossi, ed., *Gender and the Life Course* (New York: Aldine, 1985).

147. Ibid., p. 128.
148. See David P. Farrington, "The Twelfth Jack Tizard Memorial Lecture: The Development of Offending and Antisocial Behavior from Childhood—Key Findings from the Cambridge Study in Delinquent Development," *Journal of Child Psychology and Psychiatry*, Vol. 360 (1995), pp. 929–964; and Donald J. West and David P. Farrington, *The Delinquent Way of Life: Third Report of the Cambridge Study in Delinquent Development* (London: Heinemann, 1977).
149. David P. Farrington, "Explaining and Preventing Crime: The Globalization of Knowledge—The American Society of Criminology 1999 Presidential Address," *Criminology*, Vol. 38, No. 1 (February 2000), pp. 1–24.
150. Piquero and Mazerolle, *Life-Course Criminology*, p. xv.
151. Rolf Loeber and Marc LeBlanc, "Toward a Developmental Criminology," in M. Tonry and N. Morris, eds., *Crime and Justice: A Review of Research*, Vol. 12 (Chicago: University of Chicago Press, 1990).
152. Stephanie R. Hawkins et al., *Resilient Girls: Factors That Protect against Delinquency* (Washington, DC: Office of Justice Programs, 2009), p. 1.
153. Ibid., p. 9.
154. Marvin Wolfgang, Robert Figlio, and Thorsten Sellin, *Delinquency in a Birth Cohort* (Chicago: University of Chicago Press, 1972).
155. Marvin Wolfgang, Terence Thornberry, and Robert Figlio, *From Boy to Man, from Delinquency to Crime* (Chicago: University of Chicago Press, 1987).
156. Steven P. Lab, "Analyzing Change in Crime and Delinquency Rates: The Case for Cohort Analysis," *Criminal Justice Research Bulletin*, Vol. 3, No. 10 (Huntsville, TX: Sam Houston State University, 1988), p. 2.
157. Lawrence E. Cohen and Richard Machalek, "A General Theory of Expropriative Crime: An Evolutionary Ecological Approach," *American Journal of Sociology*, Vol. 94, No. 3 (1988), pp. 465–501; and Lawrence E. Cohen and Richard Machalek, "The Normalcy of Crime: From Durkheim to Evolutionary Ecology," *Rationality and Society*, Vol. 6 (1994), pp. 286–308.
158. Bryan Vila, "Human Nature and Crime Control: Improving the Feasibility of Nurturant Strategies," *Politics and the Life Sciences*, Vol. 16, No. 1 (March 1997), pp. 3–21.
159. Ibid.
160. Terence Thornberry, "Toward an Interactional Theory of Delinquency," *Criminology*, Vol. 25 (1987), pp. 863–891.
161. See Terence P. Thornberry et al., "Delinquent Peers, Beliefs, and Delinquent Behavior: A Longitudinal Test of Interactional Theory," *Criminology*, Vol. 32, No. 1 (1994), pp. 47–53.
162. Terence P. Thornberry et al., "Testing Interactional Theory: An Examination of Reciprocal Causal Relationships among Family, School and Delinquency," *Journal of Criminal Law and Criminology*, Vol. 82 (1991), pp. 3–35.
163. Carolyn Smith and Terence P. Thornberry, "The Relationship between Childhood Maltreatment and Adolescent Involvement in Delinquency," *Criminology*, Vol. 33, No. 4 (1995), pp. 451–477.
164. Suman Kakar, "Youth Gangs and Their Families: Effects of Gang Membership on Their Families' Subjective Well-Being," *Journal of Crime and Justice*, Vol. 21 (1998), pp. 157–171.
165. Barbara Tatem Kelley et al., *Developmental Pathways in Boys' Disruptive and Delinquent Behavior* (Washington, DC: Office of Juvenile Justice and Delinquency Prevention, December 1997).
166. R. Loeber and D. F. Hay, "Developmental Approaches to Aggression and Conduct Problems," in M. Rutter and D. F. Hay, eds., *Development through Life: A Handbook for Clinicians* (Oxford, England: Blackwell Scientific, 1994).
167. Ibid.
168. The Causes and Correlates of Delinquency study is being conducted by Terence P. Thornberry of the Rochester Youth Development Study at the State University of New York at Albany, New York; Rolf Loeber of the Pittsburgh Youth Study at the University of Pittsburgh; and David Huizinga of the Denver Youth Survey at the University of Colorado.
169. Adapted from Katharine Browning et al., "Causes and Correlates of Delinquency Program," OJJDP Fact Sheet (Washington, DC: U.S. Department of Justice, April 1999).
170. Compiled from Katharine Browning and Rolf Loeber, "Highlights of Findings from the Pittsburgh Youth Study," OJJDP Fact Sheet (Washington, DC: U.S. Department of Justice, February 1999); Katharine Browning, Terence P. Thornberry, and Pamela K. Porter, "Highlights of Findings from the Rochester Youth Development Study," OJJDP Fact Sheet (Washington, DC: U.S. Department of Justice, April 1999); and Katharine Browning and David Huizinga, "Highlights of Findings from the Denver Youth Survey," OJJDP Fact Sheet (Washington, DC: U.S. Department of Justice, April 1999).
171. Browning and Huizinga, "Highlights of Findings from the Denver Youth Survey."
172. Family and Youth Services Bureau, *Understanding Youth Development: Promoting Positive Pathways of Growth.*
173. Quotations in the following list are taken from Kelley et al., *Developmental Pathways in Boys' Disruptive and Delinquent Behavior.*
174. Ibid., p. 14.
175. See Felton J. Earls and Albert J. Reiss, *Breaking the Cycle: Predicting and Preventing Crime* (Washington, DC: National Institute of Justice, 1994), http://www.ncjrs.org/txtfiles/break.txt (accessed March 12, 2006).
176. Ibid.
177. Ibid.
178. Adapted from the MacArthur Foundation, "The Project on Human Development in Chicago Neighborhoods," http://www.macfound.org/research/hcd/hcd_5.htm (accessed January 5, 2006).
179. "Study of Chicago Finds Neighborhood Efficacy Explains Reductions in Violence," Project on Human Development in Chicago Neighborhoods press release, http://phdcn.harvard.edu/press/index.htm (accessed January 5, 2006).
180. Vila, "Human Nature and Crime Control," p. 10.
181. Robert W. Sweet, Jr., "Preserving Families to Prevent Delinquency," *Office of Juvenile Justice and Delinquency Prevention Model Programs, 1990* (Washington, DC: U.S. Department of Justice, April 1992).
182. Ibid.
183. Farrington, "The Twelfth Jack Tizard Memorial Lecture," p. 929.

CHAPTER 9: SOCIAL CONFLICT THEORIES

1. "Occupy Wall Street: About," http://occupywallst.org/about (accessed May 3, 2013).
2. "Communism," *Encyclopedia Britannica* online, http://britannica.com (accessed January 3, 2007).
3. Raymond J. Michalowski, "Perspectives and Paradigm: Structuring Criminological Thought," in Robert F. Meier, ed., *Theory in Criminology* (Beverly Hills, CA: Sage, 1977), pp. 17–39.

4. Roscoe Pound, *Social Control through the Law: The Powell Lectures* (Hamden, CT: Archon, 1968), pp. 113–114.
5. Although Pound's postulates originally referred only to men, we have here used the now-conventional phrase "men and women" throughout the postulates to indicate that Pound was speaking of everyone within the social group. No other changes to the original postulates have been made.
6. Adapted from Michalowski, "Perspectives and Paradigm."
7. William Bonger, *Criminality and Economic Conditions* (Bloomington: Indiana University Press, 1969). It was originally published in Amsterdam as *Criminalite et Conditions Economiques* (1905) and was translated into English in 1916.
8. Georg Simmel, *Conflict and the Web of Group Affiliations* (New York: Free Press, 1964). It was originally published in 1908.
9. Adapted from Michalowski, "Perspectives and Paradigm."
10. Richard Quinney, *Class, State, and Crime: On the Theory and Practice of Criminal Justice* (New York: David McKay, 1977).
11. Vance Packard, *The Status Seekers* (London: Harmondsworth, 1961).
12. George B. Vold, *Theoretical Criminology* (New York: Oxford University Press, 1958).
13. Ibid., p. 205.
14. Ibid., pp. 208–209.
15. Ralf Dahrendorf, *Class and Class Conflict in Industrial Society* (Stanford, CA: Stanford University Press, 1959).
16. Ralf Dahrendorf, "Out of Utopia: Toward a Reorientation of Sociological Analysis," *American Journal of Sociology*, Vol. 64 (1958), pp. 115–127.
17. Austin Turk, *Criminality and Legal Order* (Chicago: Rand McNally, 1969), p. vii.
18. Ibid.
19. William J. Chambliss, "Toward a Political Economy of Crime," in C. Reasons and R. Rich, eds., *The Sociology of Law* (Toronto: Butterworth, 1978), p. 193.
20. William Chambliss and Robert T. Seidman, *Law, Order, and Power* (Reading, MA: Addison-Wesley, 1971), p. 33.
21. Adapted from ibid., pp. 473–474.
22. William J. Chambliss, *Crime and the Legal Process* (New York: McGraw-Hill, 1969), p. 88.
23. Chambliss, "Toward a Political Economy of Crime."
24. Ibid.
25. Ibid.
26. Richard Quinney, *Critique of the Legal Order: Crime Control in Capitalist Society* (Boston: Little, Brown, 1974), p. 16.
27. Quinney, *Class, State, and Crime*, p. 58.
28. Ibid.
29. Ibid., p. 61.
30. Ibid., p. 65.
31. Jeffrey H. Reiman, *The Rich Get Richer and the Poor Get Prison: Ideology, Class and Criminal Justice*, 6th ed. (Boston: Allyn & Bacon, 2000).
32. Gresham M. Sykes, "Critical Criminology," *Journal of Criminal Law and Criminology*, Vol. 65 (1974), pp. 206–213.
33. The quotations attributed to Currie in this section are from Elliott Currie, "Market, Crime, and Community," *Theoretical Criminology*, Vol. 1, No. 2 (May 1997), pp. 147–172.
34. Michael J. Lynch and W. Byron Groves, *A Primer in Radical Criminology*, 2nd ed. (Albany, NY: Harrow & Heston, 1989), p. 126.
35. Ibid., p. 128.
36. Raymond J. Michalowski, *Order, Law, and Crime: An Introduction to Criminology* (New York: Random House, 1985), p. 410.
37. Lynch and Groves, *A Primer in Radical Criminology*, p. 130.
38. William V. Pelfrey, *The Evolution of Criminology* (Cincinnati: Anderson, 1980), p. 86.
39. For a good overview of critiques of radical criminology, see J. F. Galliher, "Life and Death of Liberal Criminology," *Contemporary Crisis*, Vol. 2, No. 3 (July 1978), pp. 245–263.
40. Jackson Toby, "The New Criminology Is the Old Sentimentality," *Criminology*, Vol. 16 (1979), pp. 516–526.
41. Ibid.
42. Hermann Mannheim, *Comparative Criminology* (Boston: Houghton Mifflin, 1965), p. 445.
43. Carl Klockars, "The Contemporary Crisis of Marxist Criminology," *Criminology*, Vol. 16 (1979), pp. 477–515.
44. Ibid.
45. Werner Einstadter and Stuart Henry, *Criminological Theory: An Analysis of Its Underlying Assumptions* (Toronto: Harcourt, 1995), p. 233.
46. For an excellent review of critical realism in a Canadian context, see John Lowman and Brian D. MacLean, eds., *Realist Criminology: Crime Control and Policing in the 1990s* (Toronto: University of Toronto Press, 1994).
47. Daniel J. Curran and Claire M. Renzetti, *Theories of Crime* (Boston: Allyn & Bacon, 1994), p. 283.
48. See M. D. Schwartz and W. S. DeKeseredy, "Left Realist Criminology: Strengths, Weaknesses, and the Feminist Critique," *Crime, Law, and Social Change*, Vol. 15, No. 1 (January 1991), pp. 51–72; W. S. DeKeseredy and B. D. MacLean, "Exploring the Gender, Race, and Class Dimensions of Victimization: A Left Realist Critique of the Canadian Urban Victimization Survey," *International Journal of Offender Therapy and Comparative Criminology*, Vol. 35, No. 2 (summer 1991), pp. 143–161; and W. S. DeKeseredy and M. D. Schwartz, "British and U.S. Left Realism: A Critical Comparison," *International Journal of Offender Therapy and Comparative Criminology*, Vol. 35, No. 3 (fall 1991), pp. 248–262.
49. See Jock Young, "The Failure of Criminology: The Need for a Radical Realism," in R. Matthews and J. Young, eds., *Confronting Crime* (Beverly Hills, CA: Sage, 1986), pp. 4–30; Jock Young, "The Tasks of a Realist Criminology," *Contemporary Crisis*, Vol. 11, No. 4 (1987), pp. 337–356; and Jock Young, "Radical Criminology in Britain: The Emergence of a Competing Paradigm," *British Journal of Criminology*, Vol. 28 (1988), pp. 159–183.
50. D. Brown and R. Hogg, "Essentialism, Racial Criminology, and Left Realism," *Australian and New Zealand Journal of Criminology*, Vol. 25 (1992), pp. 195–230.
51. Roger Matthews and Jock Young, "Reflections on Realism," in Jock Young and Roger Matthews, eds., *Rethinking Criminology: The Realist Debate* (Newbury Park, CA: Sage, 1992).
52. Don C. Gibbons, *Talking about Crime and Criminals: Problems and Issues in Theory Development in Criminology* (Upper Saddle River, NJ: Prentice Hall, 1994), p. 170.
53. Piers Beirne and James W. Messerschmidt, *Criminology* (New York: Harcourt Brace Jovanovich, 1991), p. 501.
54. Gibbons, *Talking about Crime and Criminals*, p. 165, citing Loraine Gelsthorpe and Alison Morris, "Feminism and Criminology in Britain," *British Journal of Criminology* (spring 1988), pp. 93–110.
55. Sally S. Simpson, "Feminist Theory, Crime and Justice," *Criminology*, Vol. 27, No. 4 (1989), p. 605.

56. Roslyn Muraskin and Ted Alleman, eds., *It's a Crime: Women and Justice* (Upper Saddle River, NJ: Prentice Hall, 1993), p. 1.
57. As stated in Amanda Burgess-Proctor, "Intersections of Race, Class, Gender, and Crime: Future Directions for Feminist Criminology," *Feminist Criminology*, Vol. 1, No. 27 (2006), p. 29.
58. Carol Pateman, "Feminist Critiques of the Public/Private Dichotomy," in Anne Phillips, ed., *Feminism and Equality* (Oxford, England: Blackwell, 1987).
59. F. P. Williams III and M. D. McShane, *Criminological Theory* (Upper Saddle River, NJ: Prentice Hall, 1994), p. 238.
60. Ibid.
61. Amanda Burgess-Proctor, "Intersections of Race, Class, Gender, and Crime," p. 29.
62. James W. Messerschmidt, *Capitalism, Patriarchy and Crime: Toward a Socialist Feminist Criminology* (Totowa, NJ: Rowman and Littlefield, 1986).
63. Freda Adler, *Sisters in Crime: The Rise of the New Female Criminal* (New York: McGraw-Hill, 1975).
64. Rita J. Simon, *Women and Crime* (Lexington, MA: Lexington Books, 1975).
65. Damien Cave, "Mexico's Drug War, Feminized," *New York Times*, August 13, 2011.
66. Carol Smart, *Women, Crime and Criminology: A Feminist Critique* (London: Routledge, 1977).
67. Kathleen Daly and Meda Chesney-Lind, "Feminism and Criminology," *Justice Quarterly*, Vol. 5, No. 5 (December 1988), p. 527.
68. The following list is adapted from ibid., pp. 497–535.
69. Susan Caulfield and Nancy Wonders, "Gender and Justice: Feminist Contributions to Criminology," in Gregg Barak, ed., *Varieties of Criminology: Readings from a Dynamic Discipline* (Westport, CT: Praeger, 1994), pp. 213–229.
70. John Hagan, *Structural Criminology* (New Brunswick, NJ: Rutgers University Press, 1989), p. 130.
71. Ibid.
72. Daly and Chesney-Lind, "Feminism and Criminology," p. 506.
73. Ibid.
74. Ibid., p. 514.
75. For an intriguing analysis of how existing laws tend to criminalize women and their reproductive activities, see Susan O. Reed, "The Criminalization of Pregnancy: Drugs, Alcohol, and AIDS," in Muraskin and Alleman, eds., *It's a Crime*, pp. 92–117; and Drew Humphries, "Mothers and Children, Drugs and Crack: Reactions to Maternal Drug Dependency," in Muraskin and Alleman, eds., *It's a Crime*, pp. 131–145.
76. Dawn H. Currie, "Feminist Encounters with Postmodernism: Exploring the Impasse of the Debates on Patriarchy and Law," *Canadian Journal of Women and Law*, Vol. 5, No. 1 (1992), p. 10.
77. For an excellent overview of feminist theory in criminology and for a comprehensive review of research regarding female offenders, see Joanne Belknap, *The Invisible Woman: Gender, Crime and Justice* (Belmont, CA: Wadsworth, 1996).
78. Such studies are still ongoing and continue to add to the descriptive literature of feminist criminology. See, for example, Deborah R. Baskin and Ira Sommers, "Female Initiation into Violent Street Crime," *Justice Quarterly*, Vol. 10, No. 4 (December 1993), pp. 559–583; Scott Decker et al., "A Woman's Place Is in the Home: Females and Residential Burglary," *Justice Quarterly*, Vol. 10, No. 1 (March 1993), pp. 143–162; and Jill L. Rosenbaum, "The Female Delinquent: Another Look at the Role of the Family," in Muraskin and Alleman, eds., *It's a Crime*, pp. 399–420.
79. Ronald L. Akers, *Criminological Theories: Introduction and Evaluation* (Los Angeles: Roxbury, 1994), p. 39.
80. Karen Heimer, "Changes in the Gender Gap in Crime and Women's Economic Marginalization," in *The Nature of Crime: Continuity and Change,* Vol. 1 of *Criminal Justice 2000* (Washington, DC: National Institute of Justice, 2000), p. 428.
81. Daly and Chesney-Lind, "Feminism and Criminology," p. 512.
82. Citing Allison Morris, *Women, Crime and Criminal Justice* (New York: Blackwell, 1987).
83. Gregg Barak, "Introduction: Criminological Theory in the 'Postmodernist' Era," in Gregg Barak, ed., *Varieties of Criminology*, pp. 1–11.
84. Joycelyn M. Pollock, *Criminal Women* (Cincinnati: Anderson, 1999), p. 146.
85. See, for example, Stuart Henry and Dragan Milovanovic, *Constitutive Criminology: Beyond Postmodernism* (London: Sage, 1995); and Milovanovic, *Postmodern Criminology* (New York: Routledge, 1997).
86. Milovanovic, *Postmodern Criminology*.
87. Henry and Milovanovic, *Constitutive Criminology*, p. 118.
88. Werner Einstadter and Stuart Henry, *Criminological Theory: An Analysis of Its Underlying Assumptions* (Fort Worth, TX: Harcourt Brace, 1995).
89. Ian Taylor, Paul Walton, and Jock Young, *The New Criminology: For a Social Theory of Deviance* (London: Routledge, 1973); and Ian Taylor, Paul Walton, and Jock Young, *Critical Criminology* (London: Routledge, 1975).
90. Ian Taylor, "Crime and Social Criticism," *Social Justice*, Vol. 26, No. 2 (1999), p. 150.
91. Ibid.
92. For examples of how this might be accomplished, see F. H. Knopp, "Community Solutions to Sexual Violence: Feminist/Abolitionist Perspectives," in Harold E. Pepinsky and Richard Quinney, eds., *Criminology as Peacemaking* (Bloomington: Indiana University Press, 1991), pp. 181–193; and S. Caringella-MacDonald and D. Humphries, "Sexual Assault, Women, and the Community: Organizing to Prevent Sexual Violence," in Pepinsky and Quinney, eds., *Criminology as Peacemaking*, pp. 98–113.
93. Richard Quinney, "Life of Crime: Criminology and Public Policy as Peacemaking," *Journal of Crime and Justice*, Vol. 16, No. 2 (1993), pp. 3–9.
94. See, for example, Harold E. Pepinsky, "This Can't Be Peace: A Pessimist Looks at Punishment," in W. B. Groves and G. Newman, eds., *Punishment and Privilege* (Albany, NY: Harrow and Heston, 1986); Harold E. Pepinsky, "Violence as Unresponsiveness: Toward a New Conception of Crime," *Justice Quarterly*, Vol. 5 (1988), pp. 539–563; and Pepinsky and Quinney, eds., *Criminology as Peacemaking*.
95. See, for example, Richard Quinney, "Crime, Suffering, Service: Toward a Criminology of Peacemaking," *Quest*, Vol. 1 (1988), pp. 66–75; Richard Quinney, "The Theory and Practice of Peacemaking in the Development of Radical Criminology," *Critical Criminologist*, Vol. 1, No. 5 (1989), p. 5; and Richard Quinney and John Wildeman, *The Problem of Crime: A Peace and Social Justice Perspective*, 3rd ed. (Mayfield, CA: Mountain View Press, 1991)—originally published as *The Problem of Crime: A Critical Introduction to Criminology* (New York: Bantam, 1977).
96. All of these themes are addressed, for example, in Pepinsky and Quinney, eds., *Criminology as Peacemaking*.

97. Quinney and Wildeman, *The Problem of Crime*, pp. vii–viii.
98. Bo Lozoff and Michael Braswell, *Inner Corrections: Finding Peace and Peace Making* (Cincinnati: Anderson, 1989).
99. Clemens Bartollas and Michael Braswell, "Correctional Treatment, Peacemaking, and the New Age Movement," *Journal of Crime and Justice*, Vol. 16, No. 2 (1993), pp. 43–58.
100. Ibid.
101. For a good overview of such programs, see Thomas E. Carbonneau, *Alternative Dispute Resolution: Melting the Lances and Dismounting the Steeds* (Chicago: University of Illinois Press, 1989).
102. Peter Finn and Andrea K. Newlyn, *Miami's "Drug Court": A Different Approach* (Washington, DC: National Institute of Justice, June 1993), p. 2.
103. Fay Honey Knopp, "Community Solutions to Sexual Violence: Feminist-Abolitionist Perspectives," in Pepinsky and Quinney, eds., *Criminology as Peacemaking*, p. 183.
104. Ibid.
105. Daniel Van Ness and Karen Heetderks Strong, *Restoring Justice* (Cincinnati: Anderson, 1997), p. 31.
106. Office of Juvenile Justice and Delinquency Prevention, *Balanced and Restorative Justice: Program Summary* (Washington, DC: OJJDP, no date), p. 2, from which some of the wording in this section is adapted.
107. Milwaukee County District Attorney's Office, "Community Conferencing Program," no date.
108. Ibid.
109. Donald Black, *Moral Time* (New York: Oxford University Press, 2011).
110. Stephen C. Richards, "Introducing the New School of Convict Criminology," *Social Justice*, Vol. 28, No. 1 (2001), p. 177.
111. J. I. Ross and S. C. Richards, *Convict Criminology* (Belmont, CA: Thomson Wadsworth, 2002).
112. Stephen C. Richards and Jeffrey Ian Ross, "Convict Criminology," in Richard A. Wright and J. Mitchell Miller, eds., *Encyclopedia of Criminology*, Vol. 1 (New York: Routledge, 2005), pp. 232–236.
113. Ibid.
114. John Irwin, *The Felon* (Upper Saddle River, NJ: Prentice Hall, 1970).
115. K. C. Carceral et al., *Behind a Convict's Eyes: Doing Time in a Modern Prison* (New York: Wadsworth, 2003).
116. K. C. Carceral and Thomas J. Bernard, *Prison, Inc.: A Convict Exposes Life inside a Private Prison* (New York: New York University Press, 2006).
117. The following list is adapted from Richards and Ross, "Convict Criminology"; and Matthew B. Robinson, *Justice Blind: Ideals and Realities of American Criminal Justice*, 2nd ed. (Upper Saddle River, NJ: Prentice Hall, 2005)

CHAPTER 10: CRIMES AGAINST PERSONS

1. "Police Union Warns Visitors about 'War-Like'" Detroit," *Police Magazine*, October 8, 2012, http://www.policemag.com/channel/patrol/news/2012/10/08/police-union-warns-visitors-about-war-like-detroit.aspx (accessed May 3, 2013).
2. FBI, *Crime in the United States, 2012—Preliminary Data* (Washington, DC: FBI 2013).
3. Access NCJRS on the Web at http://www.ncjrs.gov.
4. This and other UCR statistics in this chapter are taken from Federal Bureau of Investigation, *Crime in the United States, 2012* (Washington, DC: FBI, 2013).
5. Information in this paragraph come from: Samuel Weigley, Alexander E. M. Hess and Michael B. Sauter, "The Most Dangerous Cities in America," 247 Wall Street, June 11, 2012, http://247wallst.com/special-report/2012/06/11/the-most-dangerous-cities-in-america-2 (accessed August 23, 2013).
6. Ibid., citing John Roman, senior fellow at the Urban Institute.
7. Marvin Wolfgang and Franco Ferracuti, *The Subculture of Violence: Towards an Integrated Theory in Criminology* (1967; reprint, Beverly Hills, CA: Sage, 1982).
8. Marc Reidel and Margaret A. Zahn, *The Nature and Patterns of American Homicide* (Washington, DC: U.S. Government Printing Office, 1985). See also Margaret A. Zahn and P. C. Sagi, "Stranger Homicide in Nine American Cities," *Journal of Criminal Law and Criminology*, Vol. 78, No. 2 (1987), pp. 377–397.
9. Kirk R. Williams and Robert L. Flewelling, "The Social Production of Criminal Homicide: A Comparative Study of Disaggregated Rates in American Cities," *American Sociological Review*, Vol. 53, No. 3 (1988), pp. 421–431.
10. Lynne A. Curtis, *American Violence and Public Policy* (New Haven, CT: Yale University Press, 1985); and Lynne A. Curtis, *Violence, Race and Culture* (Lexington, MA: Lexington Books, 1975).
11. Claude S. Fisher, "Toward a Subcultural Theory of Urbanism," *American Journal of Sociology*, Vol. 80 (1975), p. 1335.
12. Steven Messner, "Poverty, Inequality and Urban Homicide Rate," *Criminology*, Vol. 20 (1982), pp. 103–114; and Steven Messner, "Regional and Racial Effects on the Urban Homicide Rate," *American Journal of Sociology*, Vol. 88 (1983), pp. 997–1007.
13. Robert Sampson, "Neighborhood Family Structure and the Risk of Personal Victimization," in James Byrne and Robert J. Sampson, eds., *The Social Ecology of Crime* (New York: Springer-Verlag, 1985); and Robert J. Sampson, "Structural Sources in Variation in Race-Age Specific Rates of Offending across Major U.S. Cities," *Criminology*, Vol. 23, No. 4 (1985), pp. 647–673.
14. Marvin E. Wolfgang, *Patterns in Criminal Homicide* (New York: Wiley, 1958).
15. Ibid.
16. Rosert Nash Parker and Dwayne M. Smith, "Deterrence, Poverty and Type of Homicide" *American Journal of Sociology*, Vol. 85 (1979), pp. 614–624; and M. Dwayne Smith and Robert Nash Parker, "Types of Homicide and Variation in Regional Rates," *Social Forces*, Vol. 59 (1980), pp. 136–147.
17. The distinction between expressive and instrumental crimes has been incorporated into much research on different crimes. This approach originated in the work of Richard Block and Franklin Zimring, "Homicide in Chicago, 1965–1970," *Journal of Research in Crime and Delinquency*, Vol. 10 (1973), pp. 1–12.
18. Williams and Flewelling, "The Social Production of Criminal Homicide."
19. Laura Dugan, Daniel S. Nagin, and Richard Rosenfeld, "Explaining the Decline in Intimate Partner Homicide," *Homicide Studies*, Vol. 3, No. 3 (1999), p. 189
20. Ibid., p. 208.
21. Terance D. Miethe and Kriss A. Drass, "Exploring the Social Context of Instrumental and Expressive Homicides: An Application of Qualitative Comparative Analysis," *Journal of Quantitative Criminology*, Vol. 15, No. 1 (1999), p. 3.

22. Carolyn Rebecca Block and Richard Block, "Beginning with Wolfgang: An Agenda for Homicide Research," *Journal of Crime and Justice*, Vol. 24, No. 2 (1991), p. 42.
23. Ibid., p. 54.
24. Wolfgang, *Patterns in Criminal Homicide*, p. 2.
25. Ibid., p. 9.
26. Ibid.
27. Philip J. Cook and Mark H. Moore, "Guns, Gun Control, and Homicide," in M. Dwayne Smith and Margaret A. Zahn, eds., *Studying and Preventing Homicide: Issues and Challenges* (Thousand Oaks, CA: Sage, 1999), p. 252.
28. Ibid., p. 254.
29. Ibid., p. 266.
30. Reprinted as Paul J. Goldstein, "The Drugs/Violence Nexus: A Tripartite Conceptual Framework," in James A. Inciardi and Karen McElrath, eds., *The American Drug Scene* (Los Angeles: Roxbury, 1995).
31. R. N. Parker and K. Auerhahn. "Drugs, Alcohol, and Homicide: Issues in Theory and Research," in M.D. Smith and M. Zahn, eds. *Homicide: A Sourcebook of Social Research* (Thousand Oaks, CA: Sage Publications, 1998), pp. 176–194.
32. Ibid.
33. Ibid., p. 108.
34. Ibid.
35. Robert Nash Parker, "Bringing 'Booze' Back In: The Relationship between Alcohol and Homicide," *Journal of Research in Crime and Delinquency*, Vol. 32, No. 1 (1995), pp. 3–38.
36. Ibid., p. 4.
37. Ibid., p. 25.
38. Bureau of Justice Statistics, *Report to the Nation on Crime and Justice*, 2nd ed. (Washington, DC: U.S. Government Printing Office, 1988), p. 4.
39. James Alan Fox and Jack Levin, "Serial Murder: Myths and Realities," in Smith and Zahn, eds., *Studying and Preventing Homicide: Issues and Challenges* (Thousand Oaks, CA: Sage, 1999), p. 84.
40. Ibid.
41. Ibid.
42. Ronald Holmes and J. DeBurger, "Profiles in Terror: The Serial Murderer," *Federal Probation*, Vol. 49, No. 3 (1985), pp. 29–34.
43. Fox and Levin, "Serial Murder."
44. Stephen T. Holmes, Eric Hickey, and Ronald M. Holmes, "Female Serial Murderesses: Constructing Different Typologies," *Journal of Contemporary Criminal Justice*, Vol. 7, No. 4 (1991), pp. 245–256.
45. Ibid.
46. Ibid.
47. Michael D. Kelleher and C. L. Kelleher, *Murder Most Rare: The Female Serial Killer* (Westport, CT: Praeger, 1998).
48. Ibid., p. 11.
49. Ibid., p. 7.
50. James Alan Fox and Jack Levin, "Multiple Homicide: Patterns of Serial and Mass Murder," *Crime and Justice*, Vol. 23 (1998), pp. 407–455.
51. Ibid., p. 428.
52. Ibid.
53. Thomas O'Reilly-Fleming, "The Evolution of Multiple Murder in Historical Perspective," in Thomas O'Reilly-Fleming, ed., *Serial and Mass Murder: Theory, Research, and Policy* (Toronto: Canadian Scholars' Press, 1996).
54. Stephanie Simon and Aaron Pressman, "Boston Marathon Bombing Investigation Turns to Motive," Reuters, April 20, 2013, http://www.reuters.com/article/2013/04/20/us-usa-explosions-boston-shooting-idUSBRE93I0GQ20130420 (accessed May 20, 2013).
55. Solomon Banda, "James Holmes, Alleged Aurora Shooter, Shows No Emotion to Court Discussion of Victims' Charity," *Huffington Post*, August 16, 2012, http://www.huffingtonpost.com/2012/08/17/james-holmes-court-appearance-victims_n_1795932.html (accessed August 17, 2012).
56. Joe Taschler, Security Experts Prepare Steps to Deal with 'Active Shooters,'" *Journal Sentinel*, August 13, 2012, http://www.jsonline.com/business/security-experts-prepare-steps-to-deal-with-active-shooters-9t6d08i-166029386.html (accessed August 17, 2012).
57. Jack Levin and James Alan Fox, "A Psycho-social Analysis of Mass Murder," in O'Reilly-Fleming, ed., *Serial and Mass Murder*, p. 65.
58. Ibid., p. 66.
59. Ibid., p. 69.
60. Ibid., p. 71.
61. Ibid., p. 69.
62. James Alan Fox and Jack Levin, *Overkill: Mass Murder and Serial Killing Exposed* (New York: Dell, 1996), p. 149.
63. U.S. Department of Justice, Office of Public Affairs, news release, "Attorney General Eric Holder Announces Revisions to the Uniform Crime Report's Definition of Rape," January 6, 2012, http://www.justice.gov/opa/pr/2012/January/12-ag-018.html (accessed March 12, 2012).
64. E-mail communication with the Criminal Justice Information Services Division of the FBI, January 6, 2012.
65. Centers for Disease Control, National Center for Injury Prevention and Control, *National Intimate Partner and Sexual Violence Survey Factsheet*, (Atlanta, GA: Centers for Disease Control, National Center for Injury Prevention and Control, November 2011).
66. Susan Brownmiller, *Against Our Will: Men, Women, and Rape* (New York: Simon & Schuster, 1975).
67. Dianne Herman, "The Rape Culture," in Jo Freeman, ed., *Women: A Feminist Perspective* (Palo Alto, CA: Mayfield, 1984).
68. Catherine MacKinnon, *Toward a Feminist Theory of the State* (Cambridge: Harvard University Press, 1989); and Catherine MacKinnon, *Only Words* (Cambridge: Harvard University Press, 1993).
69. See Andrea Dworkin, *Pornography: Men Possessing Women* (New York: Plenum, 1981); Andrea Dworkin, "Questions and Answers," in Diana E. H. Russell, ed., *Making Violence Sexy: Feminist Views on Pornography* (New York: Teachers College Press, 1993); and Andrea Dworkin, "Against the Male Flood: Censorship, Pornography, and Equality," in Patricia Smith, ed., *Feminist Jurisprudence* (New York: Oxford University Press, 1993).
70. Robin Morgan, *The Word of a Woman: Feminist Dispatches, 1968–1992* (New York: W. W. Norton, 1992), p. 88.
71. Brownmiller, *Against Our Will.*
72. James W. Messerschmidt, *Masculinities and Crime: Critique and Reconceptualization of Theory* (Lanham, MD: Rowman and Littlefield, 1993).
73. Ngaire Naffine, *Feminism and Criminology* (Philadelphia: Temple University Press, 1996), p. 101.
74. Diana Scully and Joseph Marolla, "Riding the Bull at Gilley's: Convicted Rapists Describe the Rewards of Rape," *Social Problems*, Vol. 32, No. 2 (1985), p. 252.

75. Nicholas Groth, *Men Who Rape: The Psychology of the Offender* (New York: Plenum, 1979).
76. Scully and Marolla, "Riding the Bull at Gilley's."
77. Scully and Marolla, "Riding the Bull at Gilley's."
78. Diana E. H. Russell, *Rape in Marriage* (Bloomington, Indiana: Indiana University Press, 1990).
79. Larry Baron and Murray A. Straus, *Four Theories of Rape in American Society: A State-Level Analysis* (New Haven, CT: Yale University Press, 1989).
80. For examples, see Peggy Reeves Sanday, "The Socio-Cultural Context of Rape: A Cross-Cultural Study," *Journal of Social Issues*, Vol. 37 (1981), pp. 5–27.
81. Baron and Straus, *Four Theories of Rape in American Society*.
82. Robert T. Sigler, Ida M. Johnson, and Etta F. Morgan, "Forced Sexual Intercourse: Contemporary Views," in Roslyn Muraskin, ed., *It's a Crime: Women and Justice* (Upper Saddle River, NJ: Prentice Hall, 2000), p. 352.
83. Randy Thornhill, "The Biology of Human Rape," *Jurimetrics*, Vol. 39, No. 2 (1999), p. 138.
84. Randy Thornhill and Craig T. Palmer, *A Natural History of Rape* (Cambridge: MIT Press, 2000), p. 53.
85. Martin Daly and Margo Wilson, *Homicide* (New York: Aldine De Gruyter, 1988), p. 140.
86. Thornhill and Palmer, *A Natural History of Rape*, p. 199. See also Katharine K. Baker, "What Rape Is and What It Ought Not to Be," *Jurimetrics*, Vol. 30, No. 3 (1999), p. 233.
87. R. R. Hazelwood and A. N. Burgess, eds., *Practical Aspects of Rape Investigation: A Multidisciplinary Approach* (New York: CRC Press, 1995).
88. Dennis J. Stevens, *Inside the Mind of a Serial Rapist* (San Francisco: Austin and Winfield, 1999), p. 39.
89. Diana Scully, *Understanding Sexual Violence: A Study of Convicted Rapists* (New York: Routledge, 1990).
90. Ibid., p. 59.
91. Ibid.
92. Ibid.
93. See Frances P. Bernat, "Rape Law Reform," in James F. Hodgson and Debra S. Kelley, eds., *Sexual Violence: Policies, Practices, and Challenges in the United States and Canada* (New Brunswick, CT: Praeger, 2001).
94. Pub. L. 102–325, section 486(c).
95. Carol Bohmer and Andrea Parrot, *Sexual Assault on Campus: The Problem and the Solution* (New York: Lexington Books, 1993), pp. 15–16.
96. Patricia Yancey Martin and Robert A. Hummer, "Fraternities and Rape on Campus," *Gender and Society*, Vol. 3, No. 4 (1989), p. 462.
97. Pub. L. 108–79.
98. Dee Halley, "The Prison Rape Elimination Act of 2003: Addressing Sexual Assault in Correctional Settings," *Corrections Today* (June 2005), pp. 30, 100.
99. Office of Justice Programs, *PREA Data Collection Activities, 2013* (Washington, DC: Bureau of Justice Statistics, June 2013).
100. Halley, "The Prison Rape Elimination Act of 2003," p. 2.
101. Ibid., p. 42.
102. Ibid., p. 1.
103. Hans Toch, *Living in Prison: The Ecology of Survival* (New York: Free Press, 1977), p. 151.
104. Robert A. Prentky, Raymond A. Knight, and Austin F. S. Lee, *Child Sexual Molestation: Research Issues* (Washington, DC: National Institute of Justice, 1997), p. 1.
105. G. G. Abel, J. V. Becker, M. S. Mittelman, J. Cunningham-Rathner, J. L. Rouleau, and W. D. Murphy, "Self-Reported Sex Crimes of Nonincarcerated Paraphiliacs," *Journal of Interpersonal Violence*, Vol. 2 (1987), pp. 3–25.
106. Child Molestation Research and Prevention Institute, "Some Facts," http://www.childmolestationprevention.org (accessed June 5, 2007).
107. Abel et al., "Self-Reported Sex Crimes of Nonincarcerated Paraphilics."
108. B. M. Maletzky, "Factors Associated with Success and Failure in the Behavioral and Cognitive Treatment of Sexual Offenders," *Annals of Sex Research*, Vol. 6 (1993), pp. 241–258.
109. Robert A. Prentky, Raymond A. Knight, and Austin F. S. Lee, *Child Sexual Molestation: Research Issues* (Washington, DC: National Institute of Justice, 1997), from which much of the information and some of the wording in this section is taken.
110. A. Nicholas Groth, W. F. Hobson, and T. S. Gary, "The Child Molester: Clinical Observations," *Journal of Social Work and Child Sexual Abuse*, Vol. 1, No. 2 (1982), pp. 129–144.
111. Prentky et al., *Child Sexual Molestation: Research Issues*.
112. Ibid., p. 3.
113. R. A. Prentky and R. A. Knight, "Age of Onset of Sexual Assault: Criminal and Life History Correlates," in G. C. N. Hall, R. Hirschman, J. R. Graham, and M. S. Zaragoza, eds., *Sexual Aggression: Issues in Etiology, Assessment, and Treatment* (Washington, DC: Taylor & Francis, 1993), pp. 43–62.
114. Prentky et al., *Child Sexual Molestation: Research Issues*.
115. Charlotte Bunch, "The Intolerable Status Quo: Violence against Women and Children," in UNICEF, *The Progress of Nations* (1997).
116. Details for this story come from "Robber Sentenced for Shooting Pregnant Teller," http://crime.about.com/b/2010/02/15/robber-sentenced-for-shooting-pregnant-teller.htm (accessed April 29, 2010).
117. Note that although purse snatching and pocket picking involve the express goal of taking someone's property, they are classified as property crimes because they do not involve the same type of direct contact with the victim as does robbery.
118. Terance D. Miethe and David McDowall, "Contextual Effects in Models of Criminal Victimization," *Social Forces*, Vol. 71, No. 3 (1993), pp. 741–760.
119. Terance D. Miethe and Richard C. McCorkle, *Crime Profiles: The Anatomy of Dangerous Persons, Places, and Situations* (Los Angeles: Roxbury, 1998).
120. Scott A. Hendricks et al., "A Matched Case-Control Study of Convenience Store Robbery Risk Factors," *Journal of Occupational and Environmental Medicine*, Vol. 41, No. 11 (1999), p. 995.
121. Richard T. Wright and Scott H. Decker, *Armed Robbers in Action: Stickups and Street Culture* (Boston: Northeastern University Press, 1997), p. 88.
122. Floyd Feeney, "Robbers as Decision Makers," in Derek B. Cornish and Ronald V. Clarke, eds., *The Reasoning Criminal* (New York: Springer Verlag, 2009).
123. Brian A. Reaves, *Using NIBRS Data to Analyze Violent Crime* (Washington, DC: U.S. Department of Justice, Office of Justice Programs, Bureau of Justice Statistics, 1993).

124. FBI, *Crime in the United States, 2012.*
125. Ibid.
126. Thomas Gabor et al., *Armed Robbery: Cops, Robbers, and Victims* (Springfield, IL: Charles C. Thomas, 1987).
127. Mark A. Peterson and Harriet B. Braiker, *Doing Crime: A Survey of California Prison Inmates* (Santa Monica, CA: RAND Corporation, 1980).
128. Mark A. Peterson and Harriet B. Braiker, *Who Commits Crimes: A Survey of Prison Inmates* (Boston: Oelgeschlager, Gunn, and Hain, 1981).
129. Martha J. Smith and Ronald V. Clarke, "Crime and Public Transport," in Michael Tonry, ed., *Crime and Justice: A Review of Research*, Vol. 27 (Chicago: University of Chicago Press, 2000), pp. 169–234.
130. Ibid.
131. Ibid.
132. Ibid., p. 181.
133. Ibid., p. 182.
134. Derek Cornish, "The Procedural Analysis of Offending and Its Relevance for Situational Prevention," in Ronald V. Clarke, ed., *Crime Prevention Studies*, Vol. 3 (Monsey, NY: Criminal Justice Press, 1994), cited in Smith and Clarke, "Crime and Public Transport," in Tonry, ed., *Crime and Justice*, p. 181.
135. Smith and Clarke, "Crime and Public Transport," p. 181.
136. "Supreme Court Lets Taxi-Stop Rulings Stand: NYC Searchers Too Intrusive, But Boston Sweeps Legal," APBnews.com, December 4, 2000, http://www.apbnews.com/newscenter/breakingnews/2000/12/04/taxi1204_01.html (accessed January 14, 2001).
137. Feeney, "Robbers as Decision Makers."
138. Ibid., p. 59.
139. Bruce A. Jacobs and Richard Wright, "Stick-Up, Street Culture, and Offender Motivation," *Criminology*, Vol. 37, No. 1 (1999), p. 150.
140. S. Morrison and I. O'Donnell, "An Analysis of the Decision Making Processes of Armed Robbers," in R. Homel, ed., *The Politics and Practice of Situational Crime Prevention,* Vol. 5 of *Crime Prevention Studies* (Monsey, NY: Criminal Justice Press, 1996). See also Gabor et al., *Armed Robbery.*
141. Jacobs and Wright, "Stick-Up, Street Culture, and Offender Motivation."
142. Ibid., pp. 167–168.
143. Trevor Bennett and Fiona Brookman, "A Qualitative Study of the Role of Violence in Street Crime," reported in Annika Howard, "Street Robbery Is Not Just about Money," *Medical News Today*, http://www.medicalnewstoday.com/printerfriendlynews.php?newsid=57730, December 1, 2006 (accessed August 24, 2007).
144. Richard T. Wright and Scott H. Decker, *Armed Robbers in Action: Stickups and Street Culture* (Boston: Northeastern University Press, 1997), p. 62.
145. Ibid., p. 63.
146. Ibid.
147. Ibid., p. 66.
148. Bruce A. Jacobs, Volkan Topalli, and Richard Wright, "Managing Retaliation: Drug Robbery and Informal Sanction Threats," *Criminology*, Vol. 38, No. 1 (2000), p. 173.
149. Ibid.
150. Ibid., p. 177.
151. Ibid.
152. Wright and Decker, *Armed Robbers in Action*, p. 67.
153. Jacobs, Topalli, and Wright, "Managing Retaliation," p. 180.
154. Ibid., p. 185.
155. Ibid.
156. Ibid., p. 172.
157. Ibid., p. 194.
158. Ibid.
159. J. Miller, "Up It Up: Gender and the Accomplishment of Street Robbery," *Criminology*, Vol. 36 (1998), p. 37.
160. FBI, *Crime in the United States, 2009*, based on arrests.
161. Miller, "Up It Up."
162. Ibid.
163. Bennett Loudon, "Woman Accused of Punching Walmart Greeter," *Rochester Democrat and Chronicle*, http://www.democratandchronicle.com/article/20111226/NEWS01/112260313/Jacquetta-Simmons-accused-hitting-elderly-Walmart-worker December 25, 2011.
164. Bureau of Justice Statistics, *Criminal Victimization 2006* (Washington, DC: U.S. Department of Justice, Office of Justice Programs, 2007), p. 172.
165. Miethe and McCorkle, *Crime Profiles*, p. 25.
166. Ibid., p. 27.
167. Callie Marie Rennison, *Criminal Victimization, 1999: Changes 1998–1999 with Trends 1993–1999* (Washington, DC: U.S. Department of Justice, Office of Justice Programs, 2000).
168. Robert J. Sampson, "Personal Violence by Strangers: An Extension and Test of Predatory Victimization," *Journal of Criminal Law and Criminology*, Vol. 78, No. 2 (1987), p. 342.
169. Richard J. Gelles, *The Violent Home: A Study of Physical Aggression between Husbands and Wives* (Beverly Hills, CA: Sage, 1974).
170. Michael Hindelang, *Criminal Victimization in Eight American Cities* (Cambridge, MA: Ballinger, 1976).
171. Evan Stark, A. Flitcraft, and W. Frazier, "Medicine and Patriarchal Violence: The Social Construction of a Private Event," *International Journal of Health Service*, Vol. 9, No. 3 (1979), pp. 461–493.
172. Murray A. Straus, "The National Family Violence Surveys," in Murray A. Straus and Richard J. Gelles, eds., *Physical Violence in American Families: Risk Factors and Adaptations to Violence in 8,145 Families* (New Brunswick, NJ: Transaction, 1990).
173. Murray A. Straus, "The Conflict Tactics Scales and Its Critics: An Evaluation and New Data on Validity and Reliability," in Straus and Gelles, eds., *Physical Violence in American Families.*
174. Murray A. Straus and Richard J. Gelles, "How Violent Are American Families? Estimates from the National Family Violence Research and Other Studies," in G. Hotaling, ed., *New Directions in Family Violence Research* (Newbury Park, CA: Sage, 1988).
175. FBI, *Crime in the United States, 2006.*
176. Ibid.
177. Ibid.
178. Neil Websdale, *Rural Woman Battering and the Justice System* (Thousand Oaks, CA: Sage, 1997).
179. Martha R. Mahoney, "Legal Issues of Battered Women: Redefining the Issue of Separation," *Michigan Law Review*, Vol. 90, No. 1 (1991), p. 6.

180. Websdale, *Rural Woman Battering and the Justice System.*
181. James Ptacek, *Battered Women in the Courtroom* (Boston: Northeastern University Press, 1999).
182. Ibid., p. 29.
183. Ibid., p. 82.
184. Ibid.
185. Federal Bureau of Investigation, *Workplace Violence: Issues in Response* (Quantico, VA: FBI, 2004), from which the quotes and information in this section are taken.
186. Erika Harrell, *Workplace Violence, 1993–2009* (Washington, DC: Bureau of Justice Statistics, 2011).
187. Some of the wording in this paragraph is adapted from ibid., p. 13.
188. Some of the wording in this paragraph is adapted from ibid., p. 14.
189. Harrell, *Workplace Violence, 1993–2009*; see also Detis T. Duhart, *Violence in the Workplace, 1993–99* (Washington, DC: Bureau of Justice Statistics, 2001).
190. National Institute for Occupational Safety and Health, "Violence in the Workplace: Risk Factors and Prevention Strategies," July 1996, http://www.cdc.gov/niosh/violcont.html (accessed July 21, 2006).
191. Ibid.
192. Kevin Johnson and David Jackson, "Holocaust Museum Killing Stuns Nation," *USA Today*, June 11, 2009.
193. 28 U.S.C.A., Section 534.
194. Public Law 103–322.
195. Bureau of Justice Assistance, *Addressing Hate Crimes: Six Initiatives That Are Enhancing the Efforts of Criminal Justice Practitioners* (Washington, DC: U.S. Department of Justice, 2000).
196. Matthew Shepard and James Byrd, Jr., Hate Crimes Prevention Act, H.R. 2647.
197. FBI, *Crime in the United States, 2011.*
198. James B. Jacobs and Kimberly A. Potter, "Hate Crimes: A Critical Perspective," in Michael Tonry, ed., *Crime and Justice: A Review of Research* (Chicago: University of Chicago Press, 1997), p. 19.
199. "FBI: Man Arrested in ESPN Reporter Nude Video Case Has Buffalo Connection," WKBW-TV News, http://www.msnbc.com/id/33152457 (accessed May 4, 2010).
200. "Sheriff: Accused Jewel Stalker Says God Led Him," Associated Press, September 22, 2009.
201. Violence against Women Grants Office, *Stalking and Domestic Violence: The Third Annual Report to Congress under the Violence against Women Act* (Washington, DC: Violence against Women Grants Office, 1998).
202. Ibid., p. 6.
203. Ibid.
204. Katrina Baum, Shannan Catalano, and Michael Rand, *Stalking Victimization in the United States* (Washington, DC: Bureau of Justice Statistics, 2009).
205. Ibid.
206. Patricia Tjaden and Nancy Thoennes, *Stalking in America: Findings from the National Violence against Women Survey* (Washington, DC: National Institute of Justice, 1998).
207. Paul E. Mullen et al., "Assessing and Managing the Risks in the Stalking Situation," *Journal of the American Academy of Psychiatry and Law*, Vol. 34 (2006), pp. 439–450; and Paul E. Mullen et al., "Study of Stalkers," *American Journal of Psychiatry*, Vol. 156 (August 1999), pp. 1244–1249.
208. Ibid.
209. Ibid., p. 8.
210. Ibid. See also P. Tjaden and N. Thoennes, *Extent, Nature, and Consequences of Intimate Partner Violence: Findings from the National Violence against Women Survey* (Washington, DC: U.S. Department of Justice, 2000).
211. Tjaden and Thoennes, *Stalking in America.*
212. Ibid., p. 8.
213. Ibid., p. 10.
214. Ibid.
215. Ibid.
216. T. Gregorie, *Cyberstalking: Dangers on the Information Highway* (Arlington, VA: National Center for Victims of Crime, 2000).
217. Janet Reno, *Cyberstalking: A New Challenge for Law Enforcement and Industry—A Report from the U.S. Attorney General to the Vice President* (Washington, DC: U.S. Department of Justice, 1999).

CHAPTER 11: CRIMES AGAINST PROPERTY

1. "Stolen Matisse Recovered in US," BBC, http://www.bbc.co.uk/news/entertainment-arts-18898804 (accessed March 5, 2013).
2. "Some of the Biggest Art Thefts in Recent Times," Associated Press, May 20, 2010, http://www.boston.com/news/world/europe/articles/2010/05/20/some_of_the_biggest_art_thefts_in_recent_times/ (accessed May 3, 2013).
3. William Spain, "Art Crime of the Century Still Frustrates: Empty Frames Still Hang in Boston Museum," APB News, June 16, 2000, http://apbnews.com/newscenter/breakingnews/2000/06/16/artcrime_gardner0161_01.html (accessed December 1, 2000).
4. William Spain, "Inside the World of Art Theft: Trade Ranks Third after Drugs, Arms Sales," APB News, June 16, 2000, http://apbnews.com/newscenter/breakingnews/2000/06/16/artcrime0616_01.html (accessed September 3, 2004).
5. Ibid.
6. Ibid.
7. Ibid.
8. Federal Bureau of Investigation, *Crime in the United States, 2012* (Washington, DC: FBI, 2013).
9. Herbert Koppel, *Lifetime Likelihood of Victimization* (Washington, DC: Bureau of Justice Statistics, 1987).
10. This is true even though the NCVS does not record burglaries of businesses or commercial properties.
11. FBI, *Crime in the United States, 2012.*
12. Neil Shover, "Burglary," in Michael Tonry, ed., *Crime and Justice: A Review of Research* (Chicago: University of Chicago Press, 1991).
13. For representative examples of this perspective, see Michael J. Hindelang, *Criminal Victimization in Eight American Cities* (Cambridge, MA: Ballinger, 1978); and Michael J. Hindelang, Michael R. Gottfredson, and James Garolfalo, *Victims of Personal Crime: An Empirical Foundation for a Theory of Personal Victimization* (Cambridge, MA: Ballinger, 1978).
14. For representative discussions of this perspective, see Lawrence E. Cohen and Marcus Felson, "Social Change and Crime Rate Trends: A Routine Activity Approach," *American Sociological Review*, Vol. 44 (1979), pp. 588–607; and Marcus Felson and Lawrence E. Cohen, "Human Ecology and Crime: A Routine Activity Approach," *Human Ecology*, Vol. 8 (1980), pp. 398–405.

15. Marcus Felson, "Linking Criminal Choices, Routine Activities, Informal Control, and Criminal Outcomes," in Derek B. Cornish and Ronald V. Clarke, eds., *The Reasoning Criminal: Rational Choice Perspectives on Offending* (New York: Springer-Verlag, 1986), p. 127.
16. Lawrence E. Cohen and David Cantor, "Residential Burglary in the United States: Life-Style and Demographic Factors Associated with the Probability of Victimization," *Journal of Research in Crime and Delinquency*, Vol. 18, No. 1 (1981), pp. 113–127.
17. Robert J. Sampson and John D. Wooldredge, "Linking the Micro- and Macro-Level Dimensions of Lifestyle-Routine Activity and Opportunity Models of Predatory Victimization," *Journal of Quantitative Criminology*, Vol. 3 (1987), pp. 371–393.
18. Ibid.
19. Mike Maguire, *Burglary in a Dwelling* (London: Heinemann, 1982), cited in Shover, "Burglary," p. 89.
20. Shover, "Burglary," p. 90.
21. Ibid., p. 91.
22. Terance D. Miethe and Richard C. McCorkle, *Crime Profiles: The Anatomy of Dangerous Persons, Places, and Situations* (Los Angeles: Roxbury, 1998).
23. Jennifer L. Truman and Michael Planty, *Criminal Victimization, 2011* (Washington, DC: BJS, 2012).
24. Kenneth D. Tunnell, *Choosing Crime: The Criminal Calculus of Property Offenders* (Beverly, MA: Wadsworth, 1992), p. 5.
25. See Paul F. Cromwell, James N. Olson, and D'Aunn Wester Avary, *Breaking and Entering: An Ethnographic Analysis of Burglary* (Newbury Park, CA: Sage, 1991); and Richard T. Wright and Scott H. Decker, *Burglars on the Job: Streetlife and Residential Break-Ins* (Boston: Northeastern University Press, 1994), p. 35.
26. Cromwell, Olson, and Avary, *Breaking and Entering*.
27. Wright and Decker, *Burglars on the Job*.
28. Ibid., p. 38.
29. Ibid., pp. 45–46.
30. Ibid., p. 47.
31. Wright and Decker, *Burglars on the Job*, p. 51.
32. Ibid.
33. Ibid., p. 56.
34. Ibid.
35. Jack Katz, *Seductions of Crime: Moral and Sensual Attractions in Doing Evil* (New York: Basic Books, 1990), p. 79.
36. Tunnell, *Choosing Crime*, p. 41.
37. Wright and Decker, *Burglars on the Job*, p. 63.
38. Ibid.
39. Ibid., p. 72.
40. Ibid., p. 73.
41. Shover, "Burglary," p. 83.
42. Ibid., p. 80.
43. Ibid., p. 110.
44. Ibid., p. 113.
45. Ibid., p. 86.
46. Bureau of Justice Statistics, *Criminal Victimization, 1999*, Tables 81 and 83.
47. Ibid., Tables 87 and 89.
48. Laura Dugan, "The Effect of Criminal Victimization on a Household's Moving Decision," *Criminology*, Vol. 37, No. 4 (1999), pp. 903–930.
49. Eric Baumer et al., "The Influence of Crack Cocaine on Robbery, Burglary, and Homicide Rates: A Cross-City, Longitudinal Analysis," *Journal of Research in Crime and Delinquency*, Vol. 35, No. 3 (1998), pp. 316–340.
50. Ibid., p. 317.
51. Ibid.
52. Ibid., p. 319.
53. Louis B. Schlesinger and Eugene Revitch, "Sexual Burglaries and Sexual Homicide: Clinical, Forensic, and Investigative Considerations," *Journal of the American Academy of Psychiatry and the Law*, Vol. 27, No. 2 (1999), p. 228.
54. Ibid., p. 232.
55. Mark Warr, "Rape, Burglary, and Opportunity," *Journal of Quantitative Criminology*, Vol. 4, No. 3 (1988), pp. 275–288.
56. Ibid., pp. 217–218.
57. Ibid., p. 287.
58. Ibid., p. 286.
59. Ramona R. Rantala and Thomas J. Edwards, *Effects of NIBRS on Crime Statistics* (Washington, DC: Office of Justice Programs, 2000), p. 12.
60. David Barry, "Thieves Peel Off with 1,200 Orange Trees: Culprits Strike California Groves at Night," APB News, November 27, 2000, http://www.apbnews.com/newscenter/breakingnews/2000/11/27/trees1127_01.html (accessed December 1, 2000).
61. Federal Bureau of Investigation, *Crime in the United States, 2006* (Washington, DC: FBI, 2007).
62. President's Commission on Law Enforcement and Administration of Justice, *The Challenge of Crime in a Free Society* (New York: Avon, 1968), p. 64.
63. Richard C. Hollinger and Lynn Langton, *2003 National Retail Security Survey: Final Report* (Tallahassee, FL: University of Florida, 2004).
64. Thomas Gabor, *Everybody Does It! Crime by the Public* (Toronto: University of Toronto Press), p. 80.
65. Dick Silverman, "Crime and Punishment," *Footwear News*, November 1999, http://www.allbusiness.com/crime-law/criminal-offenses-property/9030609-1.html (accessed July 28, 2009).
66. Sheila Marikar, "Caroline Giuliani, Daughter of Ex-NYC Mayor, Arrested for Shoplifting," ABC News, August 4, 2010, http://abcnews.go.com/Entertainment/TheLaw/caroline-giuliani-daughter-rudy-giuliani-arrested-shoplifting/story?id=11326577#.Ty7OkV2WZyo (accessed March 3, 2012).
67. "Caroline Giuliani Makes Deal in Shoplifting Case," Associated Press, August 31, 2010, http://abclocal.go.com/wabc/story?section=news/local&id=7641361 (accessed March 3, 2012).
68. Brandi Fowler, "Lindsay Lohan: Images of Missing Necklace Surveillance Video Surface on the Web," E! News, March 6, 2011, http://www.eonline.com/news/229566/lindsay-lohan-images-of-missing-necklace-surveillance-video-surface-on-the-web (accessed April 21, 2013).
69. Lloyd W. Klemke, *The Sociology of Shoplifting* (Westport, CT: Praeger, 1992).
70. Lloyd W. Klemke, "Exploring Juvenile Shoplifting," *Sociology and Social Research*, Vol. 67, No. 1 (1982), pp. 59–75.
71. Mary Owen Cameron, *The Booster and the Snitch: Department Store Shoplifting* (New York: Free Press of Glencoe, 1964).
72. Klemke, "Exploring Juvenile Shoplifting," p. 71.
73. Eric Tucker and Thomas Watkins, "For Flash Mobsters, Crowd Size a Tempting Cover," Associated Press, August 9, 2011 (accessed February 21, 2012).

74. Joe Larocca, "NRF Issues Guidelines for Retailers in Handling 'Criminal Flash Mobs,' " National Retail Federation, Retail's Big Blog, http://blog.nrf.com/2011/08/02/nrf-issues-guidelines-for-retailers-in-handling-criminal-flash-mobs/ (accessed February 21, 2012).

75. National Retail Federation, "Multiple Offender Crimes: Preparing for and Understanding the Impact of Their Tactics," http://www.nrf.com/modules.php?name=Documents&op=viewlive&sp_id=6788 (accessed February 21, 2012).

76. The President's Identity Theft Task Force, *Combating Identity Theft: A Strategic Plan* (Washington, DC: U.S. Department of Justice, 2007), from which much of the information comes and from which some of the wording is taken or adapted.

77. See Business Software Alliance, "Consumer Confidence in Online Shopping Buoyed by Security Software Protection, BSA Survey Suggests," January 12, 2006, http://www.bsacybersafety.com/news/2005-Online-Shopping-Confidence.cfm.

78. U.S. Code, Title 18, Section 1028.

79. H.R. 1731 (2004).

80. Lynn Langton, *Identity Theft Reported by Households, 2005–2010* (Washington, DC: Bureau of Justice Statistics, 2011).

81. Information in this paragraph comes from Katrina Baum, *Identity Theft, 2005* (Washington, DC: Bureau of Justice Statistics, 2007).

82. The information and some of the wording in this section is taken from The President's Identity Theft Task Force, *Combating Identity Theft: A Strategic Plan*.

83. See U.S. Attorney's Office, Southern District of Florida, press release, July 19, 2006, http://www.usdoj.gov/usao/fls/PressReleases/060719-01.html.

84. FBI, *Crime in the United States, 2011*.

85. BJS, *Criminal Victimization, 1999*, Tables 87 and 89.

86. Ibid., Table 61.

87. Ibid.

88. Shannan M. Catalano and Michael R. Rand, *Criminal Victimization, 2006* (Washington, DC: Bureau of Justice Statistics, 2007).

89. Ibid.

90. Caroline Wolf Harlow, *Motor Vehicle Theft* (Washington, DC: Bureau of Justice Statistics, 1988).

91. Ibid.

92. Kevin Blake, "What You Should Know about Car Theft," *Consumer's Research*, October 1995, cited in Miethe and McCorkle, eds., *Crime Profiles*, p. 156.

93. Miethe and McCorkle, *Crime Profiles*.

94. Pub. L. 98–547, 98 Stat. 2754 (1984).

95. Patricia M. Harris and Ronald V. Clarke, "Car Chopping, Parts Marking and the Motor Vehicle Theft Law Enforcement Act of 1984," *Sociology and Social Research*, Vol. 75 (1991).

96. Miethe and McCorkle, *Crime Profiles*, p. 156.

97. Michael Gottfredson and Travis Hirschi, *A General Theory of Crime* (Stanford, CA: Stanford University Press, 1990), p. 35.

98. Miethe and McCorkle, *Crime Profiles*; and Ronald V. Clarke and Patricia M. Harris, "Auto Theft and Its Prevention," in Tonry, ed., *Crime and Justice*.

99. Miethe and McCorkle, *Crime Profiles*.

100. For research reporting on effect of social class, see Charles H. McCaghy, Peggy C. Giordano, and Trudy Knicely Henson, "Auto Theft: Offender and Offense Characteristics," *Criminology*, Vol. 15 (1977), pp. 367–385.

101. FBI, *Crime in the United States*, 2012.

102. Ibid.

103. Federal Bureau of Investigation, *Crime in the United States, 2012* (Washington, DC: FBI, 2013).

104. Ken Brownlee, "Ignoring Juvenile Arson Is Like Playing with Fire," *Claims*, Vol. 48, No. 3 (March 2000), p. 106.

105. Eileen M. Garry, *Juvenile Firesetting and Arson*, Office of Juvenile Justice and Delinquency Prevention Fact Sheet 51 (Washington, DC: Office of Juvenile Justice and Delinquency Prevention, 1997).

106. Ibid., p. 1.

107. Cited in Gabor, *Everybody Does It!*, p. 11.

108. Edwin Sutherland, *The Professional Thief* (Chicago, IL: University of Chicago Press, 1937), p. 172.

109. Neal Shover, *Great Pretenders: Pursuits and Careers of Persistent Thieves* (Boulder, CO: Westview, 1996), p. xiii.

110. Ibid., pp. xii–xiii.

111. Ibid., p. 63.

112. Mark S. Fleisher, *Beggars and Thieves: Lives of Urban Street Criminals* (Madison: University of Wisconsin Press, 1995).

113. Malcolm W. Klein, "Offense Specialization and Versatility among Juveniles," *British Journal of Criminology*, Vol. 24 (1984), pp. 185–194.

114. Ibid., p. 186.

115. Shover, "Burglary," in Tonry, ed., *Crime and Justice*.

116. See Shover, *Great Pretenders*; and Shover, "Burglary," in Tonry, ed., *Crime and Justice*.

117. John R. Hepburn, "Occasional Property Crime," in Robert F. Meier, ed., *Major Forms of Crime* (Beverly Hills, CA: Sage, 1984).

118. Ibid., p. 76.

119. Richard T. Wright and Scott H. Decker, *Burglars on the Job: Streetlife and Residential Break-Ins* (Boston: Northeastern University Press, 1994), p. 35.

120. See Center for Problem-Oriented Policing, "Crime Analysis for Problem Solvers in 60 Small Steps," from which the wording for this definition is taken, http://www.popcenter.org/learning/60steps/index.cfm?stepNum=10 (accessed May 31, 2007).

121. Neil Alan Weiner, "Violent Criminal Careers and 'Violent Career Criminals': An Overview of the Research Literature," in Neil Alan Weiner and Marvin E. Wolfgang, eds., *Violent Crime, Violent Criminals* (Newbury Park, CA: Sage, 1989), p. 39.

122. A. Blumstein et al., eds., *Criminal Careers and "Career Criminals,"* 2 vols. (Washington, DC: National Academy Press, 1986).

123. D. S. Elliott, "Serious Violent Offenders: Onset, Developmental Course, and Termination: 1993 Presidential Address," *Criminology*, Vol. 32, No. 1 (1994), pp. 1–22. See also D. S. Elliott, D. Huizinga, and B. Morse, "Self-Reported Violent Offending: A Descriptive Analysis of Juvenile Violent Offenders and Their Offending Careers," *Journal of Interpersonal Violence*, Vol. 1, No. 4 (1987), pp. 472–514.

124. Michael R. Gottfredson and Travis Hirschi, "Science, Public Policy, and the Career Paradigm," *Criminology*, Vol. 26 (1988), pp. 37–55.

125. Fleisher, *Beggars and Thieves*, p. 11.

126. Ibid., p. 10.

127. Ibid., p. 11.

128. Dermot Walsh, "Victim Selection Procedures among Economic Criminals: The Rational Choice Perspective," in Derek B. Cornish and Ronald V. Clarke, eds., *The Reasoning Criminal:*

Rational Choice Perspectives on Offending (New York: Springer-Verlag, 1986), p. 40.

129. Ibid., p. 50.
130. Thomas Bennett and Richard Wright, *Burglars on Burglary* (Aldershot, Hants, England: Gower, 1984).
131. Walsh, "Victim Selection Procedures among Economic Criminals," p. 50.
132. Neil Shover and David Honaker, "The Socially Bounded Decision Making of Persistent Property Offenders," *Howard Journal*, Vol. 31, No. 4 (1992), p. 290.
133. Darrell J. Steffensmeier, *The Fence: In the Shadow of Two Worlds* (Savage, MD: Rowman and Littlefield, 1986), p. 10.
134. Ibid., p. 9.
135. Ibid. See also Wright and Decker, *Burglars on the Job*.
136. Steffensmeier, *The Fence*, p. 9.
137. Ibid.
138. Carl B. Klockars, *The Professional Fence* (New York: Free Press, 1974).
139. Steffensmeier, *The Fence*.
140. Ibid., p. 13.
141. Ibid.
142. Cromwell, Olson, and Avary, *Breaking and Entering*.
143. Wright and Decker, *Burglars on the Job*, p. 167.
144. Shover, "Burglary," in Tonry, ed., *Crime and Justice*, p. 103.
145. Wright and Decker, *Burglars on the Job*, p. 169.
146. Steffensmeier, *The Fence*, p. 25.
147. Ibid., p. 23.
148. Ibid., p. 21.
149. Wright and Decker, *Burglars on the Job*, p. 179.
150. Ibid., pp. 175–176.
151. Cromwell, Olson, and Avary, *Breaking and Entering*, p. 74.
152. Ibid., p. 75.
153. Cromwell, Olson, and Avary, *Breaking and Entering*, p. 76.
154. Ibid., p. 77.
155. Ibid.
156. Stuart Henry, *The Hidden Economy: The Context and Control of Borderline Crime* (Oxford, England: Martin Robertson, 1978).

CHAPTER 12: WHITE-COLLAR AND ORGANIZED CRIME

1. Details for this story come from: FBI, "Health Care Fraud Takedown," press release, September 7, 2011, http://www.fbi.gov/news/stories/2011/september/fraud_090711/fraud_090711 (accessed March 15, 2012).
2. Edwin H. Sutherland, "White-Collar Criminality," *American Sociological Review*, Vol. 5, No. 1 (February 1940), pp. 2–10.
3. Travis Hirschi and Michael Gottfredson, "Causes of White-Collar Crime," *Criminology*, Vol. 25, No. 4 (1987), p. 952.
4. Donald J. Newman, "White-Collar Crime: An Overview and Analysis," *Law and Contemporary Problems*, Vol. 23, No. 4 (Autumn 1958).
5. President's Commission on Law Enforcement and Administration of Justice, *The Challenge of Crime in a Free Society* (Washington, DC: U.S. Government Printing Office, 1967), p. 47.
6. For excellent reviews of the evolution of the concept of white-collar crime, see K. Schlegel and D. Weisburd, "White-Collar Crime: The Parallax View," in Kip Schlegel and David Weisburd, eds., *White-Collar Crime Reconsidered* (Boston: Northeastern University Press, 1992), pp. 3–27; and K. Schlegel and D. Weisburd, "Returning to the Mainstream: Reflections on Past and Future White-Collar Crime Study," in Schlegel and Weisburd, eds., *White-Collar Crime Reconsidered*, pp. 352–365.
7. Task Force on Organized Crime, *Organized Crime* (Washington, DC: U.S. Government Printing Office, 1976).
8. Ibid.
9. Michael L. Benson, Francis T. Cullen, and William J. Maakestad, *Local Prosecutors and Corporate Crime* (Washington, DC: National Institute of Justice, 1993).
10. *New York Central and Hudson River Railroad Co.* v. *United States*, 212 U.S. 481 (1909).
11. Jonathan D. Glater and Kurt Eichenwald, "Audit Lapse at WorldCom Puzzles Some," *New York Times*, June 28, 2002, p. 1C.
12. *Arthur Andersen LLP* v. *United States*, 544 U.S. 696 (2005).
13. "Epoxy Company Indicted for Manslaughter in Big Dig Death," *Tollroads News*, August 8, 2007, http://www.tollroadsnews.com/node/3063 (accessed April 10, 2010).
14. "Epoxy Company to Pay Millions in Big Dig Collapse," WBZ-TV, December 17, 2008, http://wbztv.com/bigdig/big.dig.agreement.2.889425.html (accessed April 9, 2010).
15. Charles Kennedy, "BP Pleads Guilty to Criminal Charges in Deepwater Horizon Case," Oil Price, November 15, 2012, http://oilprice.com/Latest-Energy-News/World-News/BP-Pleads-Guilty-to-Criminal-Charges-in-Deepwater-Horizon-Case.html (accessed August 29, 2013).
16. Brandon L. Garrett, "Globalized Corporate Prosecutions," Vol. 97 (December 2011), *Virginia Law Review*, p. 1775.
17. Federal Bureau of Investigation, "Financial Crimes Report to the Public, Fiscal Year 2007," http://www.fbi.gov/publications/financial/fcs_report2007/financial_crime_2007.htm#financial (accessed May 10, 2012), from which much of the material in this section is derived.
18. Ibid.
19. Ibid.
20. Ibid.
21. Ibid.
22. Ibid.
23. Ibid.
24. Clifford Karchmer and Douglas Ruch, "State and Local Money Laundering Control Strategies," *NIJ Research in Brief* (Washington, DC: National Institute of Justice, 1992), p. 1.
25. "Wachovia to Pay $160M Settlement," *Business Journal*, March 18, 2010, http://www.bizjournals.com/triad/stories/2010/03/15/daily30.html (accessed May 2, 2010).
26. U.S. Code, Title 18, Section 1956.
27. U.S. Drug Enforcement Administration, "Money Laundering," http://www.usdoj.gov/dea/programs/money.htm (accessed June 18, 2007).
28. See Bernie Becker, "U.S. Report Details Money Laundering," *New York Times*, February 4, 2010, http://dealbook.blogs.nytimes.com/2010/02/04/us-report-details-money-laundering (accessed August 24, 2010).
29. Of course, environmental damage inflicted by corporations can result in civil liability as well as violate criminal statutes.
30. "Alaska Hit by 'Massive' Oil Spill," BBC News, March 11, 2006, http://news.bbc.co.uk/2/hi/americas/4795866.stm (accessed May 2, 2010).

31. "BP Fined $60 Million for Alaska Oil Spill, Texas Air Toxics," Environment News Service, November 1, 2007, http://www.ens-newswire.com/ens/nov2007/2007-11-01-095.asp (accessed May 2, 2010).
32. "BP Could Pay U.S. $25 Billion for Gulf Oil Spill: Analyst," Google News, January 19, 2012, http://www.google.com/hostednews/afp/article/ALeqM5if9Va_XAcDMrIPE7x6ppzdy8YMSw?docId=CNG.cb899fe5256d3216e8a921771e991d78.301 (accessed May 10, 2013).
33. John Kane and April Wall, "Identifying the Links between White-Collar Crime and Terrorism," National White Collar Crime Center, September 2004.
34. Edwin H. Sutherland, "White-Collar Criminality."
35. Ibid.
36. Ibid.
37. Hirschi and Gottfredson, "Causes of White-Collar Crime," p. 949.
38. Ibid., p. 951.
39. Ibid., p. 956.
40. Ibid., p. 960.
41. Ibid.
42. Braithwaite began many of his studies of white-collar crime with investigations into the criminal activities of pharmaceutical company executives. See, for example, John Braithwaite, *Corporate Crime in the Pharmaceutical Industry* (London: Routledge and Kegan Paul, 1984).
43. For a test of this thesis, see Anne Jenkins and John Braithwaite, "Profits, Pressure and Corporate Lawbreaking," *Crime, Law, and Social Change*, Vol. 20, No. 3 (1993), pp. 221–232.
44. John Braithwaite, "Poverty, Power, White-Collar Crime and the Paradoxes of Criminological Theory," *Australian and New Zealand Journal of Criminology*, Vol. 24, No. 1 (1991), pp. 40–48.
45. Toni Makkai and John Braithwaite, "Criminological Theories and Regulatory Compliance," *Criminology*, Vol. 29, No. 2 (1991), pp. 191–217.
46. John Braithwaite and Gilbert Geis, "On Theory and Action for Corporate Crime Control," *Crime and Delinquency*, Vol. 28, No. 2 (1982), pp. 292–314. See also Brent Fisse and John Braithwaite, *The Impact of Publicity on Corporate Offenders* (Albany: State University of New York Press, 1983).
47. Brent Fisse and John Braithwaite, "Accountability and the Control of Corporate Crime: Making the Buck Stop," in Mark Findlay and Russell Hogg, eds., *Understanding Crime and Criminal Justice* (North Ryde, Australia: Law, 1988), pp. 93–127.
48. Brent Fisse and John Braithwaite, *Corporations, Crime and Accountability* (New York: Cambridge University Press, 1994).
49. John Braithwaite, "Criminological Theory and Organizational Crime," *Justice Quarterly*, Vol. 6, No. 3 (1989), pp. 333–358.
50. Joan Biskupic, "Why It's Tough to Indict CEOs," *USA Today*, July 24, 2002, p. 1A.
51. Ibid.
52. See "Executive Order Establishment of the Corporate Fraud Task Force," July 9, 2002, http://www.whitehouse.gov/news/releases/2002/07/20020709-2.html (accessed January 2, 2005).
53. John R. Wilke, *The Wall Street Journal Online*, July 17, 2007, http://online.wsj.com/article/SB118469845609569168.html (accessed September 1, 2007).
54. Ibid.
55. Joe Palazzolo, "DOJ Unveils Financial Crime Task Force," *Main Justice*, November 17, 2009 (accessed May 8, 2012).
56. Pub. L. 111–21.
57. Pub. L. 111–5.
58. Pub. L. 110–343.
59. "Financial Crimes, Trade Enforcement Targeted in State of the Union," The Blog of Legal Times, January 25, 2012, http://legaltimes.typepad.com/blt/2012/01/financial-crimestrade-enforcement-targeted-in-state-of-the-union-.html (accessed January 25, 2012).
60. 15 U.S.C. Section 1.
61. 15 U.S.C. Sections 12–27.
62. 15 U.S.C. Section 77.
63. 15 U.S.C. Section 78.
64. Much of the information in this section comes from Julian Symons, *A Pictorial History of Crime* (New York: Bonanza, 1966).
65. Ibid.
66. Howard Abadinsky, *Organized Crime*, 9th ed. (New York: Wadsworth, 2010), p. 132.
67. John Kilber, *Capone: The Life and World of Al Capone* (Greenwich, CT: Fawcett, 1971).
68. William R. Schroeder, "Money Laundering," *FBI Law Enforcement Bulletin*, May 2001, p. 1.
69. Abadinsky, *Organized Crime.*
70. Ibid., p. 5.
71. U.S. Code, Title 21, Section 848(c)(2).
72. New York Penal Law, Section 460.00.
73. New York Penal Law, Section 460.10(3).
74. Much of the information and the quotes in this section come from Federal Bureau of Investigation, "Organized Crime: Eurasian Organized Crime," http://www.fbi.gov/hq/cid/orgcrime/eocindex.htm (accessed May 20, 2013).
75. Ibid.
76. Ibid.
77. Much of the information and the quotes in this section come from Federal Bureau of Investigation, "Organized Crime: Asian Criminal Enterprises," http://www.fbi.gov/hq/cid/orgcrime/asiancrim.htm (accessed May 20, 2013).
78. Ibid.
79. Ibid.
80. Much of the information and the quotes in this section come from Federal Bureau of Investigation, "Organized Crime: African Criminal Enterprise," http://www.fbi.gov/hq/cid/orgcrime/africancrim.htm (accessed May 20, 2013).
81. Ibid.
82. Much of the information and the quotes in this section come from Federal Bureau of Investigation, "Organized Crime: Middle Eastern Criminal Enterprises," http://www.fbi.gov/hq/cid/orgcrime/middle_eastern.htm (accessed May 20, 2013).
83. Ibid.
84. John T. Picarelli, "Responding to Transnational Organized Crime: Supporting Research, Improving Practice," *NIJ Journal*, No. 268 (October 2011), pp. 4–9.
85. Gary T. Dempsey, "Is Russia Controlled by Organized Crime?" *USA Today* magazine, May 1999.
86. Richard Lindberg and Vesna Markovic, "Organized Crime Outlook in the New Russia: Russia Is Paying the Price of a Market Economy in Blood," Search International, http://www.searchinternational.com/Articles/crime/russiacrime.htm (accessed January 24, 2009).

87. Ibid.
88. Dempsey, "Is Russia Controlled by Organized Crime?"
89. Lindberg and Markovic, "Organized Crime Outlook in the New Russia."
90. Ibid.
91. The Organized Crime Control Act of 1970, Pub. L. 91–452, 84 Stat. 922 (October 15, 1970).
92. United States Code, Title 18, Chapter 96, Section 1961.
93. Gary W. Potter, *Criminal Organizations: Vice, Racketeering, and Politics in an American City* (Prospect Heights, IL: Waveland, 1994), p. 183.
94. Ibid.
95. Abadinsky, *Organized Crime*, p. 507.
96. Ibid., p. 508.
97. "'Junior' Gotti Gets Nearly 6 1/2 Years," Associated Press, September 3, 1999.
98. "5-Year Prison Term for Mafia Turncoat," *USA Today*, September 27, 1994, p. 3A.
99. Peter Maas, *Underboss: Sammy the Bull Gravano's Story of Life in the Mafia* (New York: HarperCollins, 1997). According to Ronald Kuby, an attorney suing Gravano to reclaim book royalties under New York's Son of Sam law, to avoid provisions of the law, a roundabout method had been used to pay Gravano. Kuby claimed that documents would show that author Peter Maas, Gravano, HarperCollins, and International Creative Management (the agent for the book) had conspired to hide payments made to Gravano. To learn more about the case, visit http://www.crimelibrary.com/gangsters2/gravano/24.htm.
100. "'Sammy the Bull' Faces More Drug Charges," Associated Press, December 21, 2000.
101. Shelley Murphy and Kevin Cullen, *Boston Globe*, "Stephen Rakes, who Accused Whitey Bulger of Stealing his South Boston Liquor Store, Found Dead in Lincoln," July 18, 2013, http://www.boston.com/metrodesk/2013/07/18/stephen-rakes-man-who-accused-whitey-bulger-stealing-his-south-boston-liquor-store-has-died-cause-death-under-investigation/A1zdIswfBrKiJEFH5GfntL/story.html (accessed August 29, 2013).
102. Alexandra Pournaras and Tracy Connor, "Whitey Bulger Convicted of Racketeering, Conspiracy," NBC News, http://usnews.nbcnews.com/_news/2013/08/12/19989231-whitey-bulger-convicted-of-racketeering-conspiracy?lite (accessed August 29, 2013).

CHAPTER 13: DRUG AND SEX CRIMES

1. Michael Winter, "14 Coast Guard Cadets Dismissed for Using Fake Pot 'Spice,' " *USA Today*, January 9, 2012, http://content.usatoday.com/communities/ondeadline/post/2012/01/14-coast-guard-cadets-dismissed-for-using-fake-pot-spice/1 (accessed May 5, 2012).
2. This quote is taken from http://librearts.com/wsn8439.html (accessed September 21, 2007).
3. Data in this section are derived from Substance Abuse and Mental Health Services Administration, *2011 National Survey on Drug Use and Health* (Rockville, MD: SAMHSA, 2012).
4. Numbers total more than 100% because of rounding.
5. Drug Enforcement Administration, "Overview of Drug Use in the United States," http://www.dea.gov/stats/overview.htm (accessed April 8, 2007).
6. Bureau of Justice Statistics, *Drug and Crime Facts, 1993* (Washington, DC: U.S. Department of Justice, August 1994).
7. Information in this section comes from National Institute on Drug Abuse, *Monitoring the Future: National Results on Adolescent Drug Use—Overview of Key Findings, 2012* (Bethesda, MD: National Institutes of Health, 2013), p. 10.
8. National Drug Intelligence Center, *The Economic Impact of Illicit Drug Use on American Society* (Washington, DC: U.S. Department of Justice, 2011).
9. Centers for Disease Control and Prevention, "Drug-Associated HIV Transmission Continues in the United States," http://www.cdc.gov/hiv/resources/factsheets/idu.htm, accessed March 12, 2013.
10. National Narcotics Intelligence Consumers Committee, *The NNICC Report, 1996: The Supply of Illicit Drugs to the United States* (Arlington, VA: Drug Enforcement Administration, 1997), p. 69.
11. Michael D. Lyman and Gary W. Potter, *Drugs in Society: Causes, Concepts and Control* (Cincinnati: Anderson, 1991), p. 45.
12. National Institute on Drug Abuse, *The Science of Addiction: Drugs, Brains, and Behavior* (Washington, DC: U.S. Department of Health and Human Services, 2007), p. 5.
13. National Institute on Drug Abuse, "NIDA InfoFacts: Understanding Drug Abuse and Addiction," http://www.drugabuse.gov/infofacts/understand.html (accessed May 10, 2010).
14. Ibid.
15. As defined by federal law and precedent.
16. Ibid., p. 35.
17. Ibid., p. 79.
18. Bureau of Justice Statistics, *Drugs, Crime and the Justice System* (Washington, DC: U.S. Government Printing Office, 1992), p. 2.
19. Ibid.
20. Ibid., p. 126.
21. Ibid., p. 2.
22. U.S. Department of Justice, "Member of Afghan Taliban Sentenced to Life in Prison in Nation's First Conviction on Narco-terror Charges," press release, December 22, 2008.
23. The federal narcoterrorism statute is found at 21 U.S.C. § 960a, which reads that anyone who "attempts or conspires to do so, knowing or intending to provide, directly or indirectly, anything of pecuniary value to any person or organization that has engaged or engages in terrorist activity."
24. Pub. L. 104–305.
25. " 'Rophies' Reported Spreading Quickly throughout the South," *Drug Enforcement Report*, June 23, 1995, pp. 1–5.
26. Mike O'Sullivan, "Washington State Gears Up for Marijuana Industry," Voice of America, April 22, 2013, http://www.voanews.com/content/washington_state_gears_up_for_marijuana_industry/1646461.html (accessed May 30, 2013).
27. Kristen Wyatt, "Legal Weed Draws Tourists to Colorado, Washington, for 4/20 Marijuana Holiday," *Huffington Post*, April 15, 2013, http://www.huffingtonpost.com/2013/04/15/legal-pot-draws-tourists-_0_n_3084301.html (accessed May 30, 2013).
28. U.S. Dept. of Justice, Memorandum for all United States Attorneys, "Guidance Regarding Marijuana Enforcement," August 29, 2013.
29. For an excellent overview of policy initiatives in the area of drug control, see Doris Layton MacKenzie and Craig D. Uchida, *Drugs and Crime: Evaluating Public Policy Initiatives* (Thousand Oaks, CA: Sage, 1994).
30. Drug Enforcement Administration, "2010 Domestic Cannabis Eradication/Suppression Program Statistical Report," http://www.justice.gov/dea/programs/marijuana_seizure_results.pdf (accessed March 5, 2012).

31. 21 U.S.C. Section 881(a)(6).
32. Jason McLure, "Maine Town is Shaken by Zumba Prostitution Scandal," Yahoo! News, October 17, 2012, http://en-maktoob.news.yahoo.com/maine-town-shaken-zumba-prostitution-scandal-222159193--sector.html (accessed May 20, 2013).
33. John Schriffen, "Zumba Sex Scandal: Alexis Wright Pleads Guilty to 20 Counts," ABC News, March 29, 2013, http://abcnews.go.com/US/zumba-sex-scandal-alexis-wright-pleads-guilty-20/story?id=18842770#.UXW3Xat4bYg (accessed May 20, 2013).
34. Federal Bureau of Investigation, *Crime in the United States, 2006* (Washington, DC: FBI, 2007).
35. John Stuart Mill, *On Liberty* (1859), chapter 1.
36. Much of the information in this section is derived from the Law Library: American Law and Legal Information, "Typology of Prostitution," *Crime and Justice*, Vol. 3, http://law.jrank.org/pages/1879/Prostitution-Typology prostitution.html (accessed July 10, 2007).
37. Marilyn C. Moses, "Understanding and Applying Research on Prostitution," *NIJ Journal*, No. 255 (November 2006), http://www.ojp.usdoj.gov/nij/journals/255/prostitution_research.html (accessed July 25, 2007).
38. Martin A. Monto, "Focusing on the Clients of Street Prostitutes: A Creative Approach to Reducing Violence against Women," final report submitted to the National Institute of Justice, Washington, DC: June 9, 2000, http://www.ncjrs.gov/pdffiles1/nij/grants/182860.pdf (accessed July 25, 2007).
39. Andrea Dworkin, *Intercourse* (New York: Free Press, 1987).
40. Ronald Weitzer, "The Growing Moral Panic over Prostitution and Sex Trafficking," *The Criminologist*, Vol. 30, No. 5 (September/October, 2005), pp. 1 and 3.
41. Ibid.
42. Janice G. Raymond, "10 Reasons for Not Legalizing Prostitution," Coalition against Trafficking in Women International, March 25, 2003, http://www.rapereliefshelter.bc.ca/issues/prostitution_legalizing.html (accessed July 25, 2007).

CHAPTER 14: TECHNOLOGY AND CRIME

1. Details for this story come from Mantik Kusjanto, "Kim Dotcom: Police Cut Way into Mansion to Arrest Megaupload Founder," *Huffington Post*, via Reuters, January 21, 2012, http://www.huffingtonpost.com/2012/01/21/kim-dotcom-megaupload-arrest_n_1220491.html (accessed January 21, 2012).
2. Patrik Jonsson, "If Feds Can Bust Megaupload, Why Bother with Anti-piracy Bills?" *Christian Science Monitor*, January 21, 2012, http://www.csmonitor.com/USA/2012/0121/If-feds-can-bust-Megaupload-why-bother-with-anti-piracy-bills (accessed January 21, 2012).
3. Verizon, "2013 Data Breach Investigations Report," http://www.verizonenterprise.com/DBIR/2013/ (accessed May 21, 2013).
4. Bill Gertz, "White House Hack Attack," September 30, 2012, http://freebeacon.com/white-house-hack-attack (accessed May 21, 2013).
5. "US Mulls Actions against China Cyberattacks," Associated Press, January 31, 2013, http://www.foxnews.com/tech/2013/01/31/us-mulls-action-against-china-cyberattacks/ (accessed May 31, 2013).
6. Catherine H. Conly and J. Thomas McEwen, "Computer Crime," *NIJ Reports*, January/February 1990, p. 3.
7. Ibid.
8. David McGuire, "Study: Online Crime Costs Rising," *Washington Post*, May 24, 2004, http://www.washingtonpost.com/wp-dyn/articles/A53042-2004May24.html (accessed July 30, 2005).
9. Sources from Deloitte & Touche, Center for Security & Privacy Solutions, "Cyber Crime: A Clear and Present Danger" (Deloitte & Touche, 2010), http://www.deloitte.com/assets/Dcom-UnitedStates/Local%20Assets/Documents/AERS/us_aers_Deloitte%20Cyber%20Crime%20POV%20Jan252010.pdf (accessed March 12, 2012), pp. 5, 7.
10. Computer Security Institute, "2010/2011 Computer Crime and Security Survey," http://gocsi.com/survey.
11. Business Software Alliance, "2010 Global Piracy Study," http://portal.bsa.org/globalpiracy2010/downloads/study_pdf/2010_BSA_Piracy_Study-Standard.pdf, May 2011 (accessed July 27, 2012).
12. The Anti-Phishing Working Group, "Phishing Activity Trends Report: 1st Half 2011," http://www.antiphishing.org/reports/apwg_trends_report_h1_2011.pdf (accessed July 27, 2012)
13. Gregg Keizer, "Gartner: Phishing Attacks Threaten E-Commerce," Security Pipeline.com, http://www.securitypipeline.com/news/20000036 (accessed July 30, 2007).
14. This and most other definitions related to computer crime in this chapter are taken from Donn B. Parker, *Computer Crime: Criminal Justice Resource Manual* (Washington, DC: National Institute of Justice, 1989).
15. Kevin Thompson, *Cyber Security* (Washington, DC: U.S. Department of Homeland Security, Command, Control and Interoperability Division, June 24, 2009), p. 6.
16. Pub. L. 104–104, 110 Stat. 56.
17. *Reno* v. *ACLU*, 521 U.S. 844 (1997).
18. Enacted as Section 225 of the Homeland Security Act of 2002, H.R. 5710.
19. Parker, *Computer Crime*.
20. J. Bloombecker, "A Security Manager's Guide to Hacking," *DATAPRO Reports on Information Security*, Report IS35–450–101, 1986.
21. Paul Keegan, "High Tech Pirates Collecting Phone Calls," *USA Today*, September 23, 1994, p. 4A.
22. Ibid.
23. Marc Robins, "Case of the Ticked-Off Teens," *Infosecurity News*, July/August 1993, p. 48.
24. For more information, see Ronald R. Thrasher, "Voice-Mail Fraud," *FBI Law Enforcement Bulletin*, July 1994, pp. 1–4.
25. FBI, "Gamer Charged with Hacking into and Disabling New Hampshire Gaming Company's Computer Servers," November 15, 2012, press release, http://www.fbi.gov/boston/press-releases/2012/gamer-charged-with-hacking-into-and-disabling-new-hampshire-gaming-companys-computer-servers (accessed May 3, 2013), from which much of the wording of this story is taken.
26. Paul Saffo, "Desperately Seeking Cyberspace," *Personal Computing*, May 1989, p. 247.
27. John Markoff, "Cyberpunks," *New York Times Upfront*, Vol. 132, No. 15 (March 27, 2000), pp. 10–14.
28. J. Maxfield, "Computer Bulletin Boards and the Hacker Problem," *EDPACS: The Electric Data Processing Audit, Control and Security Newsletter* (Arlington, VA: Automation Training Center, October 1985).

29. Percy Black, personal communication, 1991, as cited in M. E. Kabay, "Computer Crime: Hackers" (undated electronic manuscript).
30. John Perry Barlow, "Crime and Puzzlement: In Advance of the Law on the Electronic Frontier," *Whole Earth Review* (fall 1990), p. 44.
31. Ibid.
32. Parker, *Computer Crime*.
33. For insight into how security techniques often lag behind the abilities of criminal perpetrators in the high-technology arena, see James A. Fagin, "Computer Crime: A Technology Gap," *International Journal of Comparative and Applied Criminal Justice*, Vol. 15, Nos. 1 and 2 (spring/fall 1991), pp. 285–297.
34. Eureka Aerospace, "High-Power Compact Microwave Source for Vehicle Immobilization: Final Report," U.S. Department of Justice, National Institute of Justice, April 20, 2006, https://www.ncjrs.gov/pdffiles1/nij/grants/236756.pdf.
35. "DNA Frees Man Sentenced to Life," Associated Press, January 16, 2001, http://www.msnbc.com/news/517172.asp (accessed January 17, 2005).
36. Michael Schrage, "Today, It Takes a Scientist to Catch a Thief," *Washington Post*, March 18, 1994.
37. *Daubert* v. *Merrell Dow Pharmaceuticals, Inc.*, 509 U.S. 579 (1993).
38. *Frye* v. *United States*, 54 App. D.C. 46, 47, 293 F. 1013, 1014 (1923).
39. Federal Rules of Evidence, Article IV, Rule 402.
40. For the application of *Daubert* to DNA technology, see Barry Sheck, "DNA and *Daubert*," *Cardozo Law Review*, Vol. 15 (1994), p. 1959.
41. Schrage, "Today, It Takes a Scientist to Catch a Thief."
42. FBI press release, October 13, 1998, http://www.fbi.gov/pressrm/pressrel/pressrel98/dna.htm (accessed January 22, 2003).
43. U.S. Code, Title 42, Section 14132.
44. "British Police to Use DNA to Catch Burglars," Reuters, June 16, 1994.
45. Schrage, "Today, It Takes a Scientist to Catch a Thief."
46. Edward Connors et al., *Convicted by Juries, Exonerated by Science: Case Studies in the Use of DNA Evidence to Establish Innocence after Trial* (Washington, DC: National Institute of Justice, 1996).
47. Ibid.
48. *Maryland* v. *King*, U.S. Supreme Court, No. 12-207 (decided June 3, 2013).
49. Japan Electronics Industry Association, Industry Monitor: High-Tech Sector, "Security Software Demand to Show Strong Growth—Week Ended June 27, 2004," http://www.irstreet.com/top/im/im20040627.pdf (accessed July 30, 2006).
50. Kate Dostart, "Network Security, Content Security Markets to Grow in 2007," Networking.com, March 29, 2007, http://searchnetworking.techtarget.com/originalContent/0,289142,sid7_gci1249441,00.html (accessed June 27, 2007).
51. Parker, *Computer Crime*, p. xiii.
52. The FBI's contemporary cyberinvestigations Web page is available at http://www.fbi.gov/cyberinvest/cyberhome.htm.
53. As modified in 1986, 1988, and later years.
54. The Liberty Coalition, "Carnivore/DCS–1000," http://www.libertycoalition.net/backgrounders/carnivore-dcs-1000 (accessed June 17, 2007).
55. John Naisbitt, *Megatrends: Ten New Directions Transforming Our Lives* (New York: Warner, 1982), p. 36.
56. Ibid.
57. Gary H. Anthes, "White House Launches Cybershield," *Computerworld*, July 22, 1996, p. 29.
58. M. J. Zuckerman, "Clinton to Get Cyberterror Plan," *USA Today*, October 9, 1997, p. 1A.
59. The quotations attributed to the President's Working Group in this section are from President's Working Group on Unlawful Conduct on the Internet, *The Electronic Frontier: The Challenge of Unlawful Conduct Involving the Use of the Internet* (Washington, DC: White House, 2000), http://www.usdoj.gov/criminal/cybercrime/unlawful.htm (accessed April 16, 2007).
60. United States Computer Emergency Readiness Team, "About Us," http://www.us-cert.gov/aboutus.html (accessed August 1, 2007).
61. National Security Presidential Directive 54; Homeland Security Presidential Directive 23 (NSPD-54/HSPD-23).
62. "Introducing the New Cybersecurity Coordinator," White House Blog, December 22, 2009, http://www.whitehouse.gov/blog/2009/12/22/introducing-new-cybersecurity-coordinator (accessed May 12, 2010).
63. Original EFF "Statement of Purpose," from the EFF Web site, http://eff.org/abouteff.html (accessed April 20, 2001). For the EFF's most recent statement of purpose, see http://www.eff.org/about (accessed June 2, 2013).

CHAPTER 15: GLOBALIZATION AND TERRORISM

1. Mosi Secret, "Doofy? Casper? Scarface Would Cringe," *New York Times*, January 5, 2012, http://www.nytimes.com/2012/01/06/nyregion/ten-suspected-members-of-feared-gang-indicted.html?_r=1&ref=organizedcrime&gwh=097BB65522B2DEA0AA410CF6BBBB4578 (accessed January 15, 2012).
2. Kevin Johnson, "MS-13 Gang Growing Extremely Dangerous, FBI Says," *USA Today*, January 5, 2006, http://www.usatoday.com/news/nation/2006-01-05-gang-grows_x.htm (accessed January 25, 2012).
3. Gregory J. Howard, Graeme Newman, and William Alex Pridemore, "Theory, Method, and Data in Comparative Criminology," in David Duffee, ed., *Criminal Justice 2000: Volume IV—Measurement and Analysis of Criminal Justice* (Washington, DC: NIJ, 2000), p. 189.
4. Adapted from "Globalization," *Encyclopedia Britannica, 2007*, Encyclopedia Britannica Premium Service, http://www.britannica.com/eb/article?eu5369857 (accessed July 23, 2007).
5. Robert Lilly, "Forks and Chopsticks: Understanding Criminal Justice in the PRC," *Criminal Justice International* (March/April 1986), p. 15.
6. See United Nations Office on Drugs and Crime, "Compiling and Comparing International Crime Statistics," http://www.unodc.org/en/crime_cicp_surveys_3.html (accessed June 5, 2007).
7. For information about the latest survey, see *The Tenth United Nations Survey of Crime Trends and Operations of Criminal Justice Systems* (New York: United Nations, 2012), http://www.unodc.org/unodc/en/data-and-analysis/Tenth-United-Nations-Survey-on-Crime-Trends-and-the-Operations-of-Criminal-Justice-Systems.html (accessed July 10, 2013).
8. "Which Country Has the Fewest Cars," Big Site of Amazing Facts, http://www.bigsiteofamazingfacts.com/which-country-has-the-fewest-cars (accessed July 2, 2013).

9. United Nations Office on Drugs and Crime, "The 2012 United Nations Survey of Crime Trends and Operations of Criminal Justice Systems," http://www.unodc.org/unodc/en/data-and-analysis/statistics/crime/cts-data-collection.html (accessed April 25, 2013).
10. Human Smuggling and Trafficking Center, *Distinctions between Human Smuggling and Human Trafficking* (Washington, DC: January 2005).
11. Ibid., p. 2.
12. Raimo Väyrynen, "Illegal Immigration, Human Trafficking, and Organized Crime," United Nations University/World Institute for Development Economics Research, Discussion Paper No. 2003/72 (October 2003), p. 16.
13. Details for this story come from "Immigrant Smuggler Faulted in 19 Deaths Sentenced to Life in Prison," Associated Press, January 18, 2007, http://www.usatoday.com/news/nation/2007-01-18-smuggler_x.htm.
14. Pub. L. 108–458, December 17, 2004.
15. Global Fast, "Impact Areas: Freedom," http://www.globalfast.org/gfx/end_slavery.php (accessed August 1, 2009).
16. United Nations Office on Drugs and Crime, *Global Report on Trafficking in Persons* (New York: United Nations, 2009), p. 6.
17. International Labor Organization, "Fact Sheet: Trafficking of Children, a Worst Form of Child Labour," http://www.ilo.org/public/english/region/asro/bangkok/child/trafficking/downloads/fact_sheet_november_01_tdm.pdf (accessed August 1, 2009).
18. U.S. Code, Title 8, Section 1324.
19. Pub. L. 89–236.
20. Trafficking Victims Protection Act of 2000, Division A of Pub. L. 106–386, Section 108, as amended.
21. *Global Report on Trafficking in Persons*, p. 7.
22. Ibid.
23. U.S. Department of State, *Patterns of Global Terrorism, 2001* (Washington, DC: U.S. Government Printing Office, 2002), http://www.state.gov/s/ct/rls/pgtrpt/2001/ (accessed January 2, 2003). Note: Until 2004, the U.S. Department of State made *Patterns of Global Terrorism* available to the public annually. As of 2004, however, the report became unavailable after its methodology was challenged by the Bush administration.
24. TE-SAT. p. 9.
25. Paul R. Pillar, *Terrorism and U.S. Foreign Policy* (Washington, DC: The Brookings Institution, 2001).
26. See Michael J. Lynch and W. Byron Groves, *A Primer in Radical Criminology* (Monsey, NY: Willow Tree Press, 1990), p. 39; and Michael J. Lynch et al., *The New Primer in Radical Criminology: Critical Perspectives on Crime, Power & Identity* (Monsey, NY: Willow Tree Press, 2000).
27. Adapted from "FBI Policy and Guidelines: Counterterrorism," http://www.fbi.gov/contact/fo/jackson/cntrterr.htm (accessed March 4, 2008).
28. Ibid.
29. Brian Bennett, "'Sovereign Citizen' Movement Now on FBI's Radar," *Los Angeles Times*, February 23, 2012, http://www.latimes.com/news/nationworld/nation/la-na-terror-cop-killers-20120224,0,5474022.story (accessed February 25, 2012).
30. Ibid.
31. National Counterterrorism Center, *2010 Report on Terrorism* (Washington, DC: NCC, April 2011), http://www.nctc.gov/witsbanner/docs/2010_report_on_terrorism.pdf (accessed March 5, 2012).
32. Ibid., pp. 5–10.
33. See Barry Collin, "The Future of Cyberterrorism," *Crime and Justice International* (March 1997), pp. 15–18.
34. John Arquilla and David Ronfeldt, *The Advent of Netwar* (Santa Monica, CA: RAND, 1996).
35. Adapted from Dictionary.com, http://dictionary.reference.com/search?q=infrastructure (accessed January 10, 2007).
36. The PCCIP was established by Executive Order 13010.
37. Dorothy E. Denning, "Activism, Hactivism, and Cyberterrorism: The Internet as a Tool for Influencing Foreign Policy," paper presented at the Internet and International Systems: Information Technology and American Foreign Policy Decisionmaking Workshop, San Francisco, CA, December 10, 2001.
38. Critical Infrastructure Assurance Office, "Resource Library," http://www.ciao.gov/resource/index.html (accessed January 10, 2002).
39. Executive Order 13231 (Critical Infrastructure Protection in the Information Age), October 16, 2001.
40. President's Critical Infrastructure Protection Board, *The National Strategy to Secure Cyberspace* (Washington, DC: U.S. Government Printing Office, September 18, 2002), p. 3.
41. Ibid.
42. "Ridge Creates New Division to Combat Cyber Threats," Department of Homeland Security press release, June 6, 2003, http://www.dhs.gov/dhspublic/display?content=916 (accessed September 20, 2006).
43. U.S. General Services Administration, "GovNet Planned to Protect Critical Government IT Functions from Cyber Attacks," GSA news release number 9890, October 10, 2001, http://w3.gsa.gov/web/x/publicaffairs.nsf/dea168abbe828fe9852565c600519794/1c10e9ac670553b885256ae100668beb?OpenDocument (accessed January 21, 2005).
44. "U.S. Plans New Secure Government Internet," Associated Press, October 11, 2001.
45. "Government Creates Its Own Private Cyber Network," Fox News, http://www.foxnews.com/story/0,2933,82273,00.html March 26, 2003 (accessed May 2, 2013).
46. The technological devices described in this section are discussed in G. Gordon Liddy, "Rules of the Game," *Omni*, January 1989, pp. 43–47, 78–80.
47. CIA Directorate of Intelligence, *Terrorist CBRN: Materials and Effects* (Washington, DC: CIA, 2003).
48. Commission on the Prevention of Weapons of Mass Destruction Proliferation and Terrorism, *World at Risk: The Report of the Commission on the Prevention of WMD Proliferation and Terrorism* (Washington, DC: The Commission, 2008), p. xv.
49. Matthew Bunn, Anthony Wier, and John P. Holden, *Controlling Nuclear Warheads and Materials: A Report Card and Action Plan* (Cambridge: Nuclear Threat Initiative and Harvard University, 2003).
50. *Fact Sheet: The Biological Weapons Convention* (Washington, DC: Bureau of Arms Control, 2002), http://www.state.gov/t/ac/rls/fs/10401.htm (accessed August 8, 2006).
51. Ali S. Kahn et al., *Biological and Chemical Terrorism: Strategic Plan for Preparedness and Response* (Atlanta, GA: Centers for Disease Control, April 21, 2000), http://www.cdc.gov/mmwr/preview/mmwrhtml/rr4904a1.htm (accessed August 2, 2007).

52. Council on Foreign Relations, "Terrorism: Questions and Answers—The Anthrax Letters," http://www.terrorismanswers.com/weapons/anthraxletters.html (accessed August 3, 2006).
53. See Rick Weiss, "DNA by Mail: A Terror Risk," *Washington Post*, July 18, 2002.
54. The New York City Office of Emergency Management said that 2,795 people died in the attacks on the World Trade Center. Another 184 people died in the attack on the Pentagon (including those aboard the crashed airliner), and 44 people died aboard hijacked United Airlines Flight 93, which crashed in a Pennsylvania field.
55. Pub. L. 107–56.
56. National Security Council, *National Strategy for Combating Terrorism* (Washington, DC, NSC, 2006), p. 1.
57. Stefanie Olsen. "PATRIOT Act Draws Privacy Concerns," CNET News.com, October 26, 2001, http://news.cnet.com/news/0–1005–200–7671240.htm?tag=rltdnws (accessed November 3, 2002).
58. Pub. L. 107–296.
59. U.S. Department of Homeland Security, "DHS Organization: Building a Secure Homeland," http://www.dhs.gov/dhspublic/theme_home1.jsp (accessed August 2, 2004).
60. Pub. L. 105–261.
61. Gary Hart, Warren B. Rudman, and Stephen E. Flynn, *America Still Unprepared—America Still in Danger* (Washington, DC: Council on Foreign Relations, 2002).
62. Pub. L. 105–277.
63. Commission on the Prevention of Weapons of Mass Destruction Proliferation and Terrorism, *World at Risk*, pp. xv, xvi.
64. Ibid., p. xxvi.
65. U.S. Department of State, *Patterns of Global Terrorism 2001* (Washington, DC: U.S. Government Printing Office, 2002), http://www.state.gov/s/ct/rls/pgtrpt/2001 (accessed January 2, 2003). Previously available annually, *Patterns of Global Terrorism* has been superseded by the National Counterterrorism Center's yearly *Report on Terrorist Incidents*, http://www.terrorisminfo.mipt.org/pdf/Country-Reports-Terrorism-2006-NCTC-Annex.pdf.
66. Executive Order 13224.
67. National Security Council, *National Strategy for Combating Terrorism* (Washington, DC: The White House, 2006).
68. The NCTC was established by Executive Order in 2004, although Congress codified the NCTC in the Intelligence Reform and Terrorism Prevention Act of 2004 (IRTPA) and placed the NCTC within the Office of the Director of National Intelligence.
69. National Counterterrorism Center, *NCTC and Information Sharing* (Washington, DC: NCTC, 2006), p. I, from which some of the wording in this paragraph is taken.
70. *National Strategy for Counterterrorism* (Washington, DC: The White House, June 2011).
71. Congressional Research Service, *Terrorism, the Future, and U.S. Foreign Policy* (Washington, DC: Library of Congress, April 11, 2003), from which the material in this section is derived.
72. Pub. L. 104–132.
73. Pub. L. 107–56.
74. U.S. Code, Title 8, Section 1-1599.
75. Pub. L. 107–56.
76. Information in this paragraph is taken from National Counterterrorism Center, "Terrorist Identities Datamart Environment (TIDE)," May 20, 2007, http://www.nctc.gov/docs/Tide_Fact_Sheet.pdf (accessed June 11, 2007).
77. Information in this paragraph comes from Congressional Research Service, *Terrorism, the Future, and U.S. Foreign Policy*, p. 6.
78. Carrie Johnson, "Outgoing FBI Boss on His Legacy and What Kept Him up at Night," National Public Radio, August 22, 2013, http://www.npr.org/2013/08/23/214549458/outgoing-fbi-boss-on-his-legacy-and-what-kept-him-up-at-night (accessed September 21, 2013).
79. Congressional Research Service, *Terrorism, the Future, and U.S. Foreign Policy*, p. 5.

EPILOGUE: FUTURE DIRECTIONS

1. This story is adapted from Gary LaFree et al., "The Changing Nature of Crime in America," in Gary LaFree, ed., *The Nature of Crime—Continuity and Change,* Vol. 3 of *Criminal Justice 2000* (Washington, DC: National Institute of Justice, 2000).
2. Darlene E. Weingand, "Futures Research Methodologies: Linking Today's Decisions with Tomorrow's Possibilities," paper presented at the Sixty-First International Federation of Library Associations and Institutions annual conference, August 20, 1995, http://www.ifla.org/IV/ifla61/61-weid.htm (accessed June 16, 1998, and July 10, 2007).
3. Joseph F. Coates, "The Highly Probable Future: 83 Assumptions about the Year 2025," *Futurist,* Vol. 28, No. 4 (July/August 1994), p. 51.
4. Alvin Toffler, *Future Shock* (New York: Random House, 1970).
5. Alvin Toffler, *Powershift: Knowledge, Wealth and Violence at the Edge of the 21st Century* (New York: Bantam Books, 1990).
6. Alvin Toffler, *The Third Wave* (New York: Bantam, 1981).
7. John Naisbitt, *Megatrends: Ten New Directions Transforming Our Lives* (New York: Warner, 1982).
8. Peter F. Drucker, *Management Challenges for the 21st Century* (New York: Harper, 1999).
9. Peter F. Drucker, *Post-Capitalist Society* (New York: Harper, 1994).
10. Francis Fukuyama, *Our Posthuman Future: Consequences of the Biotechnology Revolution* (New York: Farrar, Straus and Giroux, 2002).
11. Francis Fukuyama, *The End of History and the Last Man* (New York: Avon Books, 1992).
12. Although this chapter cannot cover all future aspects of the criminal justice system, readers are referred to C. J. Swank, "Police in the Twenty-First Century: Hypotheses for the Future," *International Journal of Comparative and Applied Criminal Justice*, Vol. 17, Nos. 1 and 2 (spring/fall 1993), pp. 107–120, for an excellent analysis of policing in the future.
13. Joseph A. Schafer, ed., *Policing 2020: Exploring the Future of Crime, Communities, and Policing* (Quantico, VA: Futures Working Group, 2007).
14. Ibid.
15. Ibid., p. 32.
16. Foresight, http://www.foresight.gov.uk (accessed March 22, 2012).
17. The quotations attributed to the panel in this section are from Foresight Crime Prevention Panel, "Just around the Corner: A Consultation Document," http://www.foresight.gov.uk/servlet/DocViewer/docnoredirect=883 (accessed January 22, 2012).
18. The Future Crimes Institute, "About," http://www.futurecrimes.com/about, February 27, 2011 (accessed May 30, 2013), from which some of the wording in this paragraph is taken.
19. Society of Police Futurists International, *PFI: The Future of Policing*, no date.

20. William L. Tafoya, "Futures Research: Implications for Criminal Investigations," in James N. Gilbert, ed., *Criminal Investigation: Essays and Cases* (Columbus, OH: Charles E. Merrill, 1990), p. 214.
21. Frederick R. Brodzinski, "The Futurist Perspective and the Managerial Process," *Utilizing Futures Research*, No. 6 (1979), pp. 8–19.
22. Weingand, "Futures Research Methodologies."
23. George F. Cole, "Criminal Justice in the Twenty-First Century: The Role of Futures Research," in John Klofas and Stan Stojkovic, eds., *Crime and Justice in the Year 2010* (Belmont, CA: Wadsworth, 1995).
24. Joseph F. Coates et al., *2025: Scenarios of U.S. and Global Society Reshaped by Science and Technology* (Winchester, VA: Oakhill Press, 1997).
25. Richter H. Moore, Jr., "Wiseguys: Smarter Criminals and Smarter Crime in the Twenty-First Century," *Futurist*, Vol. 28, No. 5 (September/October 1994), p. 33.
26. The quotations attributed to Moore in this section are from ibid., pp. 33–37.
27. Georgette Bennett, *Crimewarps: The Future of Crime in America* (Garden City, NY: Anchor/Doubleday, 1987).
28. U.S. Joint Forces Command, *The Joint Operational Environment: The World through 2030 and Beyond* (CreateSpace, 2007).
29. L. Edward Wells, "Explaining Crime in the Year 2010," in Klofas and Stojkovic, eds., *Crime and Justice in the Year 2010*, pp. 36–61.
30. Ibid.
31. Ibid., pp. 48–49.
32. Ibid.
33. Frank P. Williams III and Marilyn D. McShane, *Criminological Theory*, 2nd ed. (Upper Saddle River, NJ: Prentice Hall, 1994), p. 257.
34. The quotations attributed to Farrington in this section are from David P. Farrington, "Explaining and Preventing Crime: The Globalization of Knowledge," *Criminology*, Vol. 38, No. 1 (February 2000), pp. 1–24.
35. The quotations attributed to Stephens in this section are from Gene Stephens, "The Global Crime Wave," *Futurist*, Vol. 28, No. 4 (July/August 1994), pp. 22–29.
36. For an interesting and alternative view of the future—one that evaluates what might happen if the insight provided by feminist perspectives on crime were implemented—see M. Kay Harris, "Moving into the New Millennium: Toward a Feminist Vision of Justice," in Barry W. Hancock and Paul M. Sharp, eds., *Public Policy, Crime, and Criminal Justice*, 2nd ed. (Upper Saddle River, NJ: Prentice Hall, 2000), pp. 407–419.
37. The quotations in the numbered list are taken from Moore, "Wiseguys," p. 33.
38. Hermanus Bianchi, *Position and Subject-Matter of Criminology* (Amsterdam: North-Holland, 1956).
39. Hermann Mannheim, *Comparative Criminology* (New York: Houghton Mifflin, 1965), p. 18.
40. Lawrence Friedman, *Crime and Punishment in American History* (New York: Basic Books, 1993).
41. "Can Anything Really Be Done?" *USA Today* magazine, Vol. 122, No. 2587 (April 1994), p. 6.
42. Robert D. Pursley, *Introduction to Criminal Justice*, 6th ed. (New York: Macmillan, 1991), p. 677.
43. Ibid.

Name Index

T

V

W

Y

Z

Subject Index

S

W

X

Y